GW01255252

The Virgin Alternative Guide to British Universities

The Virgin Alternative Guide to British Universities

Piers Dudgeon

This edition first published in 2006
by Virgin Books Ltd
Thames Wharf Studios
Rainville Road
London W6 9HA

First published in Great Britain in 1997 by Virgin Books Ltd

A catalogue record for this title is available from the British Library.

ISBN 0 7535 1150 3

Design & Technical Consultant
Jonathan Horner

Printed and bound by
Creative Print and Design (Wales),
Ebbw Vale

THE VIRGIN ALTERNATIVE GUIDE

'The best bar none... Most university guides tell you what grades are needed for entry, but fail to give any impression of what it's really like... *The Virgin Alternative Guide* bridges this gap. Amusing contributions from students already on their way to degrees detail the nitty gritty of student life at each institution, including accommodation, health, living on a shoestring, low- and high- workload courses, union life, societies, sports and – last but not least – watering holes and where to get a decent curry... The guide is based on thorough research [and] includes an official facts section, covering acceptance requirements to employment expectations.'
Times Educational Supplement

'Glistening with success – a worthy contender for the best all-purpose buy for the aspiring undergraduate.'
Yorkshire Post

'This is a very impressive piece of work... a serious and honest picture of student life at each major higher education establishment in the UK... VAG looks set to take over as the nation's favourite antidote to the occasional excesses of the higher education marketing professionals.'
Careers Adviser

'The guide offers racy but reliable profiles that focus as much on the way of life as academic considerations.'
Daily Telegraph

'The value of this book lies in the info-crammed pages on universities, starting with Aberdeen and ending with York.'
The London Evening Standard

'Lesson learned... Get studying this guide!'
Sun

'Welcome to VAG, an invaluable assessment... raw, earthy and direct.'
Wolverhampton Express & Star

'It's the warts and all approach to help students make their choices.'
Leicester Mercury

'Serious and honest'
Times Higher Educational Supplement

'Where you can believe what you read'
Cardiff Western Mail

'Just the thing to make a truly informed choice'
Dundee Sunday Post

CONTENTS

UK UNIVERSITIES

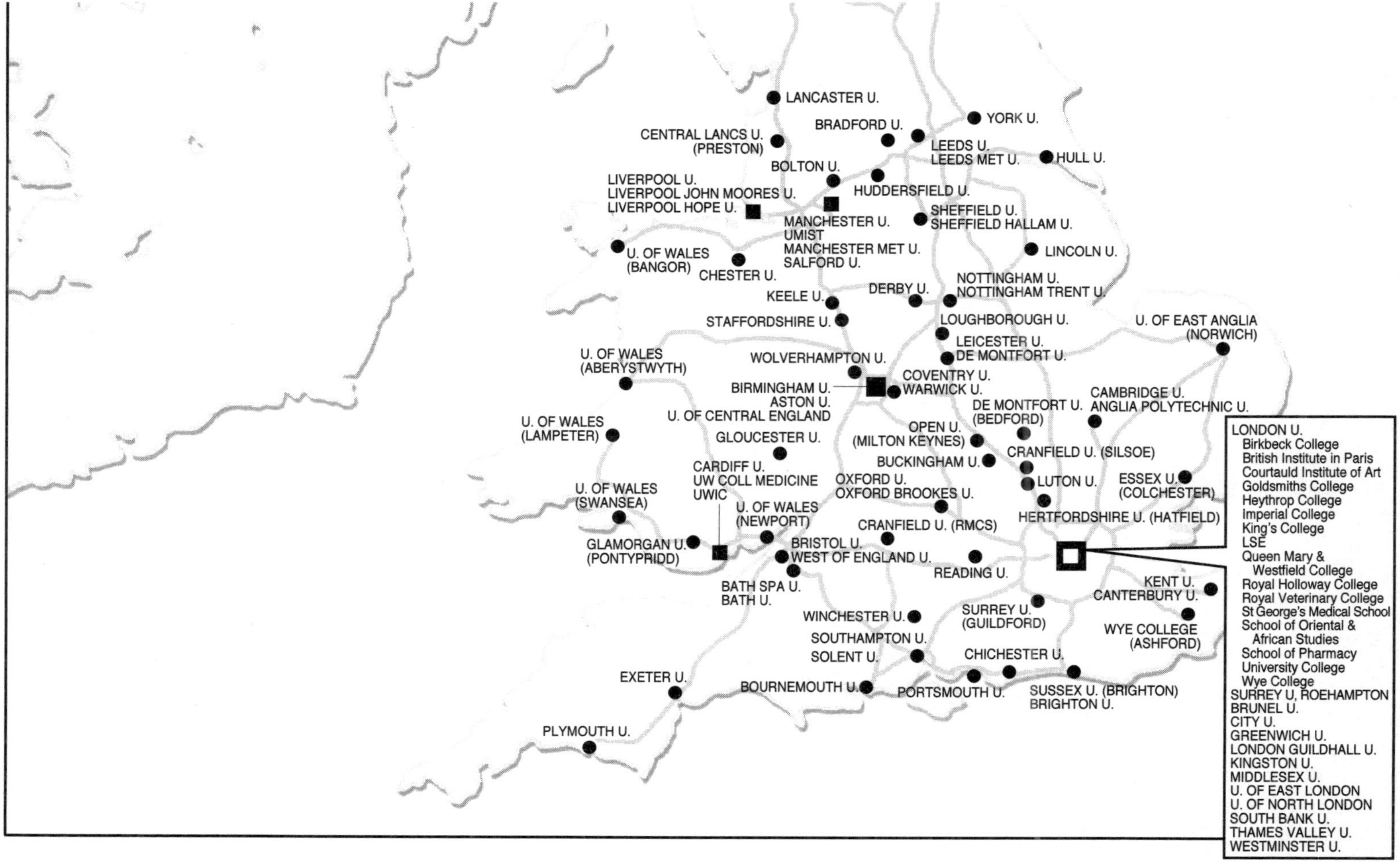
LANCASTER U.
YORK U.
BRADFORD U.
CENTRAL LANCS U. (PRESTON)
LEEDS U.
LEEDS MET U.
HULL U.
BOLTON U.
LIVERPOOL U.
LIVERPOOL JOHN MOORES U.
LIVERPOOL HOPE U.
HUDDERSFIELD U.
SHEFFIELD U.
SHEFFIELD HALLAM U.
MANCHESTER U.
UMIST
MANCHESTER MET U.
SALFORD U.
LINCOLN U.
U. OF WALES (BANGOR)
CHESTER U.
KEELE U.
DERBY U.
NOTTINGHAM U.
NOTTINGHAM TRENT U.
STAFFORDSHIRE U.
LOUGHBOROUGH U.
U. OF EAST ANGLIA (NORWICH)
LEICESTER U.
DE MONTFORT U.
U. OF WALES (ABERYSTWYTH)
WOLVERHAMPTON U.
COVENTRY U.
WARWICK U.
BIRMINGHAM U.
ASTON U.
U. OF CENTRAL ENGLAND
DE MONTFORT U. (BEDFORD)
CAMBRIDGE U.
ANGLIA POLYTECHNIC U.
U. OF WALES (LAMPETER)
GLOUCESTER U.
OPEN U. (MILTON KEYNES)
CRANFIELD U. (SILSOE)
BUCKINGHAM U.
CARDIFF U.
UW COLL MEDICINE
UWIC
OXFORD U.
OXFORD BROOKES U.
LUTON U.
ESSEX U. (COLCHESTER)
U. OF WALES (SWANSEA)
U. OF WALES (NEWPORT)
HERTFORDSHIRE U. (HATFIELD)
CRANFIELD U. (RMCS)
GLAMORGAN U. (PONTYPRIDD)
BRISTOL U.
WEST OF ENGLAND U.
READING U.
KENT U.
CANTERBURY U.
BATH SPA U.
BATH U.
SURREY U. (GUILDFORD)
WINCHESTER U.
WYE COLLEGE (ASHFORD)
SOUTHAMPTON U.
SOLENT U.
CHICHESTER U.
EXETER U.
BOURNEMOUTH U.
PORTSMOUTH U.
SUSSEX U. (BRIGHTON)
BRIGHTON U.
PLYMOUTH U.
LONDON U.
Birkbeck College
British Institute in Paris
Courtauld Institute of Art
Goldsmiths College
Heythrop College
Imperial College
King's College
LSE
Queen Mary & Westfield College
Royal Holloway College
Royal Veterinary College
St George's Medical School
School of Oriental & African Studies
School of Pharmacy
University College
Wye College
SURREY U, ROEHAMPTON
BRUNEL U.
CITY U.
GREENWICH U.
LONDON GUILDHALL U.
KINGSTON U.
MIDDLESEX U.
U. OF EAST LONDON
U. OF NORTH LONDON
SOUTH BANK U.
THAMES VALLEY U.
WESTMINSTER U.

INTRODUCTION

WHY ALTERNATIVE?

'Alternative' once spelled Revolution on the campuses of British universities, a revolt against capitalism and a Big Brother rather different to the comic-strip one we watch on our plasma screens today. The world has changed. Today's undergraduate students are part of a revolution of a very different sort.

The Virgin Alternative Guide is a response to the huge changes going on in Higher Education and the challenge that these changes represent to YOU, as you make what so many insist is 'the most important decision you will ever make in your life'. Whether that is true, or another symptom of the high pressure marketing from which this book is designed to release you, is debatable.

What *is* true is that the recent increase in the number of universities offering degree courses, the interference of the government in the matter of student selection, the sophistication of the marketing techniques being employed by universities to secure as large a share of the Government funding cake as they can, the influence of top employers on course design, and the increasingly outmoded advice of parents, all combine to justify an ALTERNATIVE approach that hands the choice back to you.

WHAT DO YOU NEED TO KNOW?

We begin our research by asking universities to respond in writing to questions designed to our purpose. We then gather statistics from Government agencies, the Quality Assurance Agency (QAA), the Higher Education Statistics Agency (HESA), UCAS, and so on. From this we construct statistical profiles of each university and their student bodies, and see how well, relative to each other, they are set up to serve their purpose – how they perform in teaching inspections and research assessments across a whole range of subjects, what their particular niche strengths are, what proportion of their students graduate with first class or upper-second class degrees, whether applications are going up or down and what percentage of applicants each university accepts, how many students drop-out before completing their courses, and where those who stay end up in employment as graduates.

Armed with these profiles, we talk to sixthformers at school and to their careers teachers, the best of whom have a clear sense of what each university is good for and where their strengths lie.

Then we approach the Student Unions at each university with questions about facilities and opportunity in extra-curricular activities, such as sport, politics, the arts, media, etc. And, to restore a sense of balance, we visit the unis ourselves and employ student moles to give their view from the ground. Contact with students comes via school careers teachers lively enough to keep tabs on past years' sixth-formers, via student newspaper editors, from people writing in who found the book useful (see *Editorial Team*, below), and from a network of friends, and friends of friends at university, who want to become involved.

CHOOSING A UNIVERSITY FOR STUDY

Government interference in student selection means that it is no longer as simple as saying that a particular course at a particular university has a points requirement, and that if you are not up to that requirement there is no point in applying.

Universities are now under serious pressure to take applicants without the points requirement. Each university has a benchmark to meet in this matter, if an applicant comes from what they refer to as a 'low participation neighbourhood', or from the three poorest socio-economic groups IIIM (skilled manual), IV (partly skilled) and V (unskilled). The idea is to give people who hitherto never had a chance of going to university the opportunity to do so. It is the biggest exercise in social engineering since University College London set up shop as 'the Cockney College' in 1826 to challenge Oxford and Cambridge's policy to take exclusively from the privileged classes.

I have met a sense of despair among some independent school children that this policy puts them at a disadvantage, victims to 'positive discrimination'. Why should applicants from these social groups have an edge, when many families of public school children make huge sacrifices to see their children through the best schools they can afford? It is a valid question. Where lies the sense in selecting for an academic process on the basis of class rather than academic excellence? If the state school system is not working, how can we expect our universities to sort it out when the child is 18?

A few years ago, we followed a boy who won a place at Durham University with the right background for the Government's widening participation policy. He had only one AS level and a GNVQ. We were really hopeful for him. He gave his views for the Guide and clearly enjoyed his time at Durham, despite on one occasion falling foul of the notorious Durham rah culture. He got his degree, applied to join the RAF and was turned down. Why? Because he didn't have any A levels.

Most cannot afford to ignore A level requirements. It is the first limiter on choice of university. And limiters we will need, given the number of universities now at our disposal.

Consider the course itself and how it is designed. Read the Academia sections of our profiles. Look at the statistics in the *Academic Excellence* and *At A Glance* boxes. Consider employment rates and particular strengths. Consider where you want the course to take you.

When you have an idea of ten or more unis, read our reviews and consider where you will be happy. City, town or countryside? Lively, impersonal, expensive London? Wild, exciting, affordable Newcastle? Laid-back, rural Lampeter? Streetwise metropolitan Manchester? Secluded, tight-knit Stirling? How would you respond?

Where there's big-city action, there needs to be Student Union support – late-night bussing, pay-later taxi arrangements, info about off-limits areas, etc. Get a feel of what's on offer. What kind of situation suits you? Will you thrive on a self-contained campus – Nottingham, Exeter, Bath, Sussex, or at a civic uni, where the buildings are dotted around the city – Bristol, Leeds, Central England, Sheffield? Do you favour strong, public-school-style college loyalties – Durham, Lancaster, Oxbridge, or the more diverse mix of Liverpool John Moores, Leeds Met? Which are the most happening university cities? Which campuses deliver a real buzz? Where's the best social life? Where are the best facilities? Which are good at sport (and how good)? Where does music, theatre, dance, film thrive? What's the student media like? London and some other cities are very expensive. What price survival? Our cost of survival estimate is a student view of cash in pocket for food, beer, local travel + two nights out a week. Accommodation costs are given separately.

Above all, consider what value a university will add to your life, not just in academic terms, but in cultural terms, not simply to enhance certain skills for employers to exploit, but for yourself. For it is time to do something for yourself.

WHICH UNIVERSITIES ARE THE BEST?

Universities have two functions, teaching and research. The latter earns vast sums for them. How well a uni is set up to teach is the first priority. Student-staff ratios (which vary from 8-to-1 to 26-to-1 across all universities) and views from students about the kind of teaching support and resources available are of interest. Especially significant are departments that show flair in curriculum design – either vocational flair, where a subject is given an application that converts directly into an inspired career prospect, or creative flair, where cross-faculty combinations remove blinkers, provoke original thought associations, and make articulate, innovative and adaptable students in any field. We advise you at all costs to avoid those unis that combine everything with everything else in the curriculum without any guiding principle other than timetable feasibility.

To point up teaching ability, we highlight departments that achieve Excellent ratings (18+ points out of 24) in the Quality Assurance Agency inspections. Consistent Excellence over the years suggests a teaching culture with deep-rooted character (York, for example). We have a Subject Entry Table, which carries teaching inspection results. Note especially those cases where there is a high rating for teaching of a course that demands lower points at A level. It's indicative of maximum value.

But, I hear you say, that's all very well. What happens when you opt for a uni with low entry requirements and a future employer is not impressed? In fact, employers these days are amazingly well informed. Increasingly they influence, even design courses, and they know better than anyone which universities are good for employability.

You will notice a lot in the book about where particular courses actually lead in terms of employment. Our info on graduate employability is no longer limited to how many graduates each uni manages to get in employment six months after graduation – fairly meaningless, as there's only a handful of percentage points between the worst and the best university records. Today, we tap in to the Government's Higher Statistics Agency database in Cheltenham, which records where almost everybody ends up and from which uni/subject/department they come. We now know, for example, that City University or Heriot-Watt are more focused on getting graduates jobs in the financial sector than Oxford, and which departments they come from. So, if you want a job in the financial sector, it should interest you to look at all these and, indeed, at London Metropolitan, York, Essex, Bournemouth, East Anglia and Imperial College. This year we have an interesting new line of information sourced in the statistics agency, HESA, and developed in the pages of the *Times Higher Education Supplement*. It pinpoints which unis get their student real 'graduate track' jobs, real jobs that students might expect to get only by going to university. Suddenly, Bradford, Bath, City, Newcastle, Surrey, Aston, and Queen Margaret University College in Edinburgh shine through. Bradford in fact comes second to Cambridge with 81.5% of their graduates getting graduate track jobs within six months after graduation. There is a huge gap between the top university, with 84.5% 'graduate track' employment, and the bottom uni, with a mere 49.3%.

A survey just published by the Association of Graduate Recruiters suggests that the Government's determination to get 50% of young people into university by 2010 has seen a deterioration of educational standards. More than half of companies canvassed confirmed that they are having problems finding sufficiently able graduates to fill their graduate vacancies. The problem is not a scarcity of graduates with first class or upper second class degrees. It is a problem of employability. The feeling is that there is a lack of graduates coming through with specialist training, that there are too many soft degrees that lead nowhere, but also that basic skills of thinking, decision-making, communication, leadership, are simply not there.

This wakes us up to the fact that *value* is about good teaching *plus*. Employers have understood this for ages. Research shows that graduate recruiters seek at least two qualities above degree classification: enthusiasm and oral communication, an ability not to be PC or pushy, but to speak clearly, to argue logically, persuasively, and to be interesting. Almost as highly rated is an ability to solve problems, to communicate effectively using the written word, to exercise so-called personal/transferable skills (presenting and marketing yourself), to work well as a team member, etc... Our core message to university applicants is that you will acquire these skills most effectively not in the lecture theatre or tutorial, but by becoming immersed in a vibrant student culture, which, in this guide it is our purpose to rate, uni by uni.

By 'culture', people understand 'theatre, classical music, art', but that is popular usage. Think of culture in the scientific sense as a nutrient substance in which micro-organisms appear and grow. For micro-organisms read 'skills graduate recruiters want'. For culture read 'the total range of activities and ideas of a group of students at a particular university'.

When you go to university the first thing you will have to survive is Freshers Week, a mad round of drinking and clubbing and getting to know other first-year undergraduates. Central to this first week will be the Freshers Fair, where the student societies set out their stalls and try and get you to become a member. These societies cover anything you care to imagine, from Islamic Soc to Cock Soc – that's generally something to do with cocktails. Consider how some of these could impart skills and broaden your perspective on life. Debating or Drama would obviously enhance oral communication; Rugby, teamwork; Role-play, problem-solving; the university magazine, your written communication skills... and Cock Soc possibly your stamina. Above all, *get involved*, and right now make your choice on this basis from among the cultural tapestries that unfurl before you.

PICK YOURSELF UP AND GO

The increasing cost of higher education is making it more difficult for students to uproot from their home environment. But a highly significant part of the value of going to university is to encourage independence. At the Guide, we want to encourage students to pick themselves up and go... Roots feed a plant, but they also tie it down. University is a place where you can work out your own thing, break free and grow to a position of autonomy and independence, a place where you can assess, use and not be used by, the values on which you were brought up.

LONDON UNIVERSITY ACCOMMODATION

These are very good reasons to get out of your home town or city altogether, and if you do find yourself at one of the colleges of London University, and must face the possibility of staying in their intercollegiate halls, it is as well that you have some basic contact information so that you sort out what's available sooner rather than later. There are entries for the colleges of LU in the Guide, but no entry for the University itself. Main contact details are as follows:

University of London, Senate House, Malet Street, London WC1E 7HU. Tel: +44 (0)20 7862 8000. WEB http://www.lon.ac.uk

Contact details for halls are as follows, rents are approximately £113-£128 for a single, around £100 for a twin.

Hughes Parry Hall, Cartwright Gardens, WC1 (Male and female). Canterbury Hall, Cartwright Gardens, WC1 (Male and female). Contact: Bursars Office, Hughes Parry Hall, 19-26 Cartwright Gardens, London WC1H 9EF. Tel: 00 44 (0)20 7685 4000. Fax: 00 44 (0)20 7121 7500. Email: hughesparry@hotmail.com

College Hall (Female only), Malet Street, London WC1E 7HZ. Tel: 00 44 (0)20 7685 2000. Fax: 00 44 (0)20 7636 6591. Email: info.college@lon.ac.uk

Commonwealth Hall, Cartwright Gardens, WC1 (Male and female), Bursars Office, 1-11 Cartwright Gardens, London WC1H 9EB. Tel: 00 44 (0)20 7685 3500. Fax: 00 44 (0)20 7121 7000. Email cwh@lon.ac.uk

Connaught Hall, Tavistock Square, WC1 (Male and female), Bursars Office, 36- 45 Tavistock Square, London WC1H 9EX. Tel: 00 44 (0)20 7756 8200. Fax: 00 44 (0)20 7383 4109. Email: Bursar.Connaught @ConnaughtHall.lon.ac.uk

International Hall (Male and female), Bursars Office, Lansdowne Terrace, London WC1N 1DJ. Tel: 00 44 (0)20 7822 3000. Fax: 00 44 (0)20 7278 9720. Email: info.ih@lon.ac.uk

Nutford House (Male and female), Bursars Office, Nutford House, Brown Street, London W1H 5UL. Tel: 00 44 (0)20 7569 0110. Fax: 00 44 (0)20 7258 1781. Email: info.nutford@lon.ac.uk

THE EDITORIAL TEAM

We would like to thank all those students who filled in questionnaires and/or agreed to be interviewed, and those students who actually wrote copy. If you are reading this and are about to go to university, drop us a line, join the editorial team for 2008. Financial and other rewards, and the chance to get yourself in print (looks great on the CV) are the lure, so tarry not. Contact me, Piers Dudgeon, at The Virgin

Alternative Guide, Grove Farm, Sawdon, North Yorkshire YO13 9DY.

Our thanks also to the university statistics departments and admin offices who have provided us with answers to our many questions, to the Quality Assurance Agency for England, and the Funding Councils for Scotland and Wales, who have helped provide us with the teaching assessments, to HESA, the Higher Education Statistics Agency, who supplied demographic facts and figures and amazingly detailed information about first degree qualifiers entering employment. This is copyright information which we have used with their permission and we are happy to print their disclaimer that HESA cannot accept responsibility for any inferences or conclusions which we have made or derived from their data. We are grateful, too, to BUSA - the British Universities Sports Association - who supplied overall team placings for both men and women last session; to the NSDF - National Student Drama Festival and everyone who supplied us with information about national awards won by students in the arts and media.

WHAT PRICE AN EDUCATION?

For the first time, we publish the cost to full-time UK/EU students of a university degree in England, Scotland and Wales, and information about the awards that universities and Government offer to defray costs.

Each uni has a different arrangement, and it is as well to take them on board. Maximum fee charges (2006) for English students are: £3000 at an English or Northern Irish uni; £1200 at a Welsh uni; £1700 at a Scottish establishment, except courses in Medicine in Scotland, when the maximum is £2700.

To defray these fees, from 2006 a Maintenance grant of £2700 p.a.is available to UK (not EU) students from the British Government where a person's 'household income' (your family's income) is £17500 p.a. or less. A partial grant will be available where family income is between £17501 and £37425. For PGCE students, a grant of £1700 is available to all, the remaining £1500 (of the £2700) is means tested. See www.dfes.gov.uk/studentsupport/students/200_2006_entry.shtml for the detail, and note that the payment of fees may be deferred until you are earning. There is a loan system to enable you to defer payment in this way.

In 2007/8, all 2006 fees are likely to rise in line with inflation and beyond those quoted in this book.

At Welsh universities, fees for 2006 for non-overseas students will remain at £1200 p.a. A variable fee (up to £3000 p.a.) will be charged from 2007/8. Students from Wales and non UK/EU countries (i.e. not English students) will be eligible for a £1800 grant from the Welsh Assembly.

The Scottish Executive, while not charging Scottish students fees, is charging English students, in order to discourage 'fee refugees' from overwhelming the country's universities. From 2006, English students will be charged £1700 a year for all but medical courses, for which they will be charged £2700. Ministers said the changes would dissuade English students from seeing Scotland as a 'cheap option'.

STATISTICS

The Joint Funding Council's Research Assessment gives an idea of a university's academic strength in depth. They rated subjects on an ascending points system of quality: 1, 2, 3a, 3b, 4, 5 and 5*. We have included those given 5, 5* and 6*, ignoring the lower levels. Grade 5 indicates International Excellence in some sub-areas and National Excellence in virtually all others; 5* indicates International Excellence in a majority of sub-areas and attainable levels of National Excellence in all others. Later, a number of university departments were awarded top-flight 6* status, the best you can get. As you read through the book, you will begin to notice the Academic Excellence box for each entry, which carries this important information. Heed it.

Throughout, we refer to teaching assessments and teaching inspections, and each uni carries an Academic Excellence box, which makes use of them. The ratings and scores are the result of inspections by the QAA and Higher Education Funding Councils for Scotland and Wales. Only

Government-funded institutions are subject to inspection (Buckingham University is not). England and Wales began their programme of inspections with three ratings, Excellent, Satisfactory, Unsatisfactory, while Scotland marked their assessments Excellent, Highly Satisfactory, Satisfactory, Unsatisfactory. Later England and Scotland scored universities with points (maximum 4) on each of six criteria:

4 points each: maximum score = 24 points

1. Curriculum Design, Content, Organisation
2. Teaching Learning and Assessment
3. Student Progression and Achievement
4. Student Support and Guidance
5. Learning Resources
6. Quality Assurance and Enhancement

So, when you come across these assessments, bear in mind that the top mark is 24 (or Excellent) and we don't regard a course worth recommending if it is not rated better than 17 (or Satisfactory).

Just to confuse us further, the QAA has in recent years adopted yet another way of assessing course teaching. Assessments are in two parts: *Academic Standards* and *Quality of Learning Opportunities*. Academic Standards (curriculum, student achievement, etc) are marked with a **C** for Confidence, or **NC** for No Confidence. Often there is then more detail. *Quality of Learning Opportunities* is defined under three headings: Teaching & Learning, Student Progression, and Learning Resources. Each section is marked **C** (Commendable) or **A** (Approved) or **F** (Failing). So, in the Subject Entry Table, which follows, if you read **C**, it means that there is Confidence in the provision; if **C/CAC,** that there is a mixed assessment of the teaching – two aspects are Commendable, but one (in this case, the second, Student Progression) is merely approved. The best a course can do is **C/CCC**; the worst is **NC/FFF**. The latter never shows. Today, the assessments are softer in the marking than they were, but if there is a recent assessment of a course you are considering, read the assessment in depth on www.qaa.ac.uk.

Piers Dudgeon, February 2006

WHICH SUBJECT? WHICH UNI FOR BEST VALUE?

Browse our Subject table on the following pages, use the UCAS course finder (www.ucas.com), then return to read the VAG profiles to find out which uni will suit you.

Column 1 shows the ball-park official offer level – always the lowest is shown, the base point level of entry; there are sometimes thousands of different courses for a subject with varying entry requirements. **Column 2** of the tables lists university or college. **Column 3** shows the teaching ratings by outside inspectors.

Column 2: A full account of the new points tarrif is given on the UCAS website. A level points: A = 120 points; B = 100 points; C = 80 points; D = 60 points; E = 40 points.

Column 3: See Introduction above for an explanation of how the ratings work: points out of 24, Excellent, Highly Satisfactory, Satisfactory, etc. The points system for entry requirements is as follows:

Look with a curious eye at these top-value universities that have scored well at inspection and ask less at A level. Equally, look with suspicion at the high-demanding unis which have not performed well on inspection.

ACCOUNTANCY/FINANCE

Specific Accounting teaching assessments undertaken: De Montfort, East London, Edinburgh, Leeds MetLondon South Bank, Napier, Paisley, Strathclyde. See www.qaa.ac.uk/reviews/reports/subjIndex.asp

ENTRY	UNI/COLLEGE	RATING
		Economics/Maths
High		
320 points +		
	Warwick	24/22
	Queen's Belfast	24/22
	Manchester	24/22
	Exeter	22/22
	Southampton	24/20
Medium-High		
280-320 points		
	Newcastle	23/23
	Glasgow	Highly Satis
	Cardiff	Excellent
	City	22/23
	UEA	23/23
	Lancaster	–/22
	Bristol	23/23
	Reading	22/21
	Aston	–/19
	Birmingham	23/24
	Sheffield	21/21
	Leeds	22/22
	Edinburgh	C/CCC
	LSE	23/22
	Nottingham	24/23
	Kent	23/21
	Hull	22/22
	Liverpool	22/23
	Royal Holloway	–/22
	Manchester	24/22
	Loughborough	23/22
	Strathclyde	C/CCC
	Northumbria	22/21
	Brunel	22/22
	Swansea	
	Ulster	22/22
	Westminster	–/20
	Essex	24/20
	Durham (Stockton)	
Medium		
220-260 points		
	Bradford	21/
	Abertay Dundee	Satisfactory
	Bangor	
	Queen's Belfast	24/22
	Gloucestershire	
	City	22/23
	Keele	23/22
	Durham (Stockton)	24/21
	Aberdeen	Highly Satis
	Stirling	Highly Satis
	Oxford Brookes	24/22
	Westminster	–/20

ENTRY	UNI/COLLEGE	RATING
Medium	Kingston	21/23
220-260 points	Robert Gordon	Highly Satis
	Aberystwyth	Excellent
	Bournemouth	22/–
	Brighton	–/22
	Nottingham Trent	22/21
	Westminster	20/20
	Manchester Met	20/20
	Buckingham	
	Leeds Met	24/–
	De Montfort	C/CAC
	Cardiff UWIC	
	Dundee	Excellent
	Liverpool JM	22/21
	Central England	21/–
	Sheffield Hallam	22/23
	Heriot-Watt	Highly Satis
	Salford	20/21
	Glamorgan	Excellent
	Coventry	23/23
Low-Medium		
80-200 points		
	Glasgow Cal	Highly Satis
	Paisley	C/CCC
	Bristol UWE	23/21
	London Met	24/21
	Wolverhampton	22/20
	Hertfordshire	23/21
	Huddersfield	–/21
	Portsmouth	21/22
	Plymouth	–/20
	Sunderland	
	East London	C/CAC
	London South Bank	C/ACC
	Teesside	
	Luton	
	Staffordshire	24/–
	Northampton	
	Anglia Ruskin	20/–
	Middlesex	21/20
	Southampton Solent	22/–
	Bolton	–/20
	Greenwich	20/19
	Gloucestershire	
	Bucks Chilterns	
	Thames Valley	19/–
	Newport	
	Central Lancs	22/19
	Northumbria	22/21
	Central England	21/
	Leeds Met	C/CAC
	Canterbury	–/22
	Hertfordshire	23/21
	Derby	–/21
	Lincoln	
	Napier	C/CCC
	Huddersfield	
	Northumbria	
	Plymouth	–/20
	Worcester	
	Portsmouth	21/22

AGRICULTURE, FORESTRY, AGRICULTURAL SCIENCES

Go to www.qaa.ac.uk/reviews/reports/subjIndex.asp for recent teaching inspections; www.qaa.ac.uk/reviews/reports/archive/oldSubjIndex.asp for reports prior to 2000.

ENTRY	UNI/COLLEGE	RATING
Medium-High 280-320 points		
	Edinburgh	
	Newcastle	22
	Stirling	
	Imperial	22
Low-Medium 220-260 points		
	Stirling	
	Aberdeen	
	Newcastle	22
	Bangor - Forestry	Excellent
	- Agriculture	Satisfactory
	Nottingham	23
	Queen's Belfast	21
	Reading	21
	Wye/Imperial	22
	Queen's Belfast	21
Low 100-200 points		
	Aberystwyth - Agric.	Satisfactory
	- Forestry	Excellent
	Nottingham Trent	C/CCC
	Plymouth	22
	Scot Agric Coll	C/CCC
	Sparsholt	20.C/CCC
	Harper Adams	23
	Bristol West England	20
	Derby	
	Wolverhampton	
	Central Lancs	18
	Salford	
	Quee'ns Blfast	21
	Greenwich	20
	Highlands & Islands	C/C-A/C
	Liverpool JM	
	Writtle	19
	Bishop Burton	C/CCA
	Royal College Agric	

BIOSCIENCES

Assessments have been made for both molecular and organismal biosciences; where the outcome was different in each case, the first of the two scores in column 3 relates to organismal biosciences.

ENTRY	UNI/COLLEGE	RATING
High 320 points +		
	Cambridge	24
	Cardiff	Excellent
	Durham	24
	East Anglia	22
	Exeter	22
	Imperial College	22
	Leicester	22
	Manchester	23
	Royal Holloway	24, 21
	Nottingham	23
	Oxford	24
	St Andrews	Excellent
	Sussex	22
	University College	24, 22
	Warwick	23
	York	24
Medium-High 280-300 points		
	Anglia Ruskin	21
	Aberdeen	Excellent
	Aston	23
	Birmingham	24, 23
	Bristol	22, 24
	Cardiff	Excellent
	Durham	24
	Dundee	Excellent
	Essex	23
	Glasgow	Excellent
	East Anglia	22
	Edinburgh	Excellent
	Hull	23
	King's College (KCL)	22
	Leeds	22, 23
Medium-High 280-300 points	St George's London	
	Leicester	22
	Liverpool	19
	Manchester	23
	University College	24, 22
	Queen Mary	22
	Manchester Met	22
	Southampton	23
	Swansea	Excellent
	Lancaster	21
	Newcastle	22, 24
	Reading	21
	Royal Holloway	24, 21
	St Andrews	Excellent
	Napier	Highly satis
	Sheffield	24
	Stirling	Higly satis
	Strathclyde	Highly satis
	Surrey	21, 22
	Sussex	22
Medium 200-260 points		
	Anglia Ruskin	21
	Kent	24
	Leeds	22, 23
	Brighton	22
	Bradford	20
	Bristol UWE 24	
	Central Lancashire	22
	Aberystwyth	Excellent
	Bangor	Excellent
	Chester College	21
	Coventry	16, 19
	Gloucestershire	
	Keele	22, 21
	Lancaster	21
	Plymouth	22
	St Andrews	Excellent
	Stirling	Higly satis
	Salford	24
	Queen's Belfast	21
	Ulster	21, 22

ENTRY	UNI/COLLEGE	RATING
Medium		
200-260 points		
	De Montfort	21
	Glasgow Caledonian	Highly satis
	Heriot-Watt	Highly satis
	Huddersfield	22
	Kingston	24
	London South Bank	20
	Leicester	22
	Northumbria	21
	Robert Gordon	
	Nottingham Trent	24
	Oxford Brookes	23
	Portsmouth	22
	Staffordshire	22
	Sunderland	24
	Sheffield Hallam	22
	Ulster	22
	Wolverhampton	23
Low		
80-180 points		
	Roehampton	23
	Bristol West England	24
	Abertay Dundee	Highly satis
	Anglia Ruskin	21
	Bolton	22
	Bradford	20
	Canterbury	21
	Cardiff (UWIC)	Excellent
	Essex	23
	Glasgow Caledonian	Highly satis
	Heriot-Watt	Highly satis

ENTRY	UNI/COLLEGE	RATING
Low	Huddersfield	22
80-180 points	Leeds Met	
	De Montfort	21
	Derby	22
	East London	19
	Portsmouth	22
	Sheffield Hallam	22
	Glamorgan	Satisfactory
	Greenwich	20
	Hertfordshire	21
	Northumbria	21
	Nottingham Trent	24
	Glasgow Caledonian	Highly satis
	Heriot-Watt	Highly satis
	Huddersfield	22
	Lincoln	
	Liverpool	19
	Liverpool J Moores	23, 22
	Luton	22
	Manchester Met	22
	Middlesex	
	London Met	18
	Northampton	
	Paisley	Highly satis
	Queen Margaret UC	Excellent
	Robert Gordon	
	London South Bank	20
	Teesside	
	Westminster	21
	Worcester	20
	Central Lancashire	22
	Wolverhampton	23

BUSINESS/MANAGEMENT

Go to www.qaa.ac.uk/reviews/reports/subjIndex.asp for recent teaching inspections; www.qaa.ac.uk/reviews/reports/archive/oldSubjIndex.asp for reports prior to 2000.

ENTRY	UNI/COLLEGE	RATING
High		
320 points +		
	Aston	24
	Bath	
	Birmingham	21
	City	23
	Exeter	22
	Imperial	
	Keele	21
	King's	
	Leeds	22
	Liverpool	23
	LSE	24
	Newcastle	
	Nottingham	Excellent
	Nottingham Trent	Excellent
	Queen Mary	
	St Andrews	C/CCC
	Sheffield	
	Southampton	23
	Sussex	
	Warwick	
	York	22
Medium-High		
260-300 points		
	Aberdeen	Brunel

ENTRY	UNI/COLLEGE	RATING
Medium-High	Cardiff	
260-300 points	Chester	21
	De Montfort	
	East Anglia	23
	Essex	
	Exeter	22
	Glasgow	
	Imperial	
	Reading	21
	SOAS	
	Gloucestershire	
	Kent	21
	Heriot-Watt	
	Hull	23
	Keele	21
	Lancaster	
	Leicester	
	Kingston	
	Liverpool	23
	Leeds	22
	LSE	24
	Loughborough	22
	Manchester	24
	Oxford Brookes	24
	Queen's Belfast	23
	Salford	
	Stirling	
	Swansea	
	Strathclyde	
	Northumbria	22. C
	Surrey	Excellent
	Ulster	24
	Westminster	20

ENTRY	UNI/COLLEGE	RATING
Medium		
200-240 points		
	Aberystwyth	
	Bangor	
	Bradford	
	Bristol West England	23
	Central England	21
	Durham	
	Edinburgh	C/CCC
	Coventry	22
	Gloucestershire	
	Huddersfield	
	Abertay Dundee	C/AAA
	Kent	21
	Kingston	
	Lampeter	
	Liverpool J Moores	22
	Manchester Met	23
	Napier	
	Newcastle	
	Nottingham Trent	
	Plymouth	
	Aberdeen	
	De Montfort	
	Hertfordshire	23
	Hull	23
	Salford	
	Sheffield Hallam	21
	Staffordshire	
	Roehampton	
	Bournemouth	22
	Brighton	
	Buckingham	
	Portsmouth	
	Robert Gordon	
	Westminster	20
	Winchester	22
Low		
60-180 points		
	Anglia Ruskin	20. C

ENTRY	UNI/COLLEGE	RATING
Low	Bath Spa	20
60-180 points	Bolton	
	Buckingham Chilts	22
	Canterbury	21
	Cardiff UWIC	
	Central Lancashire	22
	Chichester	19
	De Montfort	
	Derby	22
	Doncaster	22
	East London	
	Glamorgan	
	Glasgow Caledonian	
	Greenwich	20
	Highlands & Islands	C/CCA
	Leeds Metropolitan	24
	Lincoln	
	Liverpool Hope	24
	Liverpool J Moores	22
	Luton	
	Middlesex	22
	London Met	24
	Newport	
	Nescot	
	Northampton	
	Northumbria	22.C
	Paisley	
	Sunderland	C/CCC
	Queen Margaret	
	St Mary's College	17
	Salford	
	Scottish Agricultural	
	Sheffield Hallam	21
	Southampton Solent	22
	London South Bank	20
	Teesside	
	Thames Valley	19. C
	Wolverhampton	23
	Worcester	21
	York St John UC	21

COMPUTER

Go to www.qaa.ac.uk/reviews/reports/subjIndex.asp for recent teaching inspections; www.qaa.ac.uk/reviews/reports/archive/oldSubjIndex.asp for reports prior to 2000.

ENTRY	UNI/COLLEGE	RATING
High		
320 points +		
	Oxford	Excellent
	Birmingham	Satisfactory
	Cambridge	Excellent
	Imperial	Excellent
	Kent	Excellent
	Bristol	Satisfactory
	York	Excellent
	UCL	Satisfactory
	Manchester	Excellent
	Warwick	Excellent
	Southampton	Excellent
	St Andrews	Highly Satis. C/CCC
	King's Coll	Satisfactory
	Leeds	Satisfactory
	Durham	Satisfactory
	Nottingham	Satisfactory
	Bath	Satisfactory

ENTRY	UNI/COLLEGE	RATING
	Reading	Satisfactory
	Strathclyde	Highly Satis
	UEA	Satisfactory
	Aston	Satisfactory
	City	Satisfactory
Medium-High		
280-300 points		
	King's Coll	Satisfactory
	Heriot-Watt	Highly Satis
	Queen Mary	Satisfactory
	Manchester	Excellent
	Nottingham Trent	Satisfactory
	Royal Holloway	Satisfactory
	Sheffield	Satisfactory
	Sussex	Satisfactory
	Greenwich	Satisfactory
	Essex	Satis. C
	Kent	Excellent
	Liverpool	Satisfactory
	Abertay Dundee	Satisfactory
	Cardiff	Satisfactory
	Lancaster	Satisfactory
	Loughborough	Satisfactory
	Northumbria	Satisfactory
	Reading	Satisfactory
	Surrey	Satis. C

ENTRY	UNI/COLLEGE	RATING
Medium-High		
280-300 points		
	Dundee	Satisfactory
	Bournemouth	Satisfactory
	Exeter	Excellent
	UEA	Satisfactory
	Edinburgh	Excellent
	Glasgow	Excellent
	Queen's Belfast	Satisfactory
	Aberystwyth	Satisfactory
	St Andrews	Highly Satis
	Strathclyde	Highly Satis
	Swansea	Excellent
	Newcastle	Satisfactory
	Brunel	Satisfactory
	Leicester	Satisfactory
	Aston	Satisfactory
	Ulster	Satisfactory
	Westminster	Satisfactory
Low-Medium		
220-260 points		
	Aston	Satisfactory
	Abertay Dundee	Satisfactory
	Bradford	Satisfactory
	Brunel	Satisfactory
	Paisley	Satisfactory
	Sunderland	Satisfactory
	Portsmouth	Satisfactory
	Northumbria	Satisfactory
	Dundee	Satisfactory
	Reading	Satisfactory
	Strathclyde	Highly Satis
	Hull	Satisfactory
	Lancaster	Satisfactory
	Plymouth	Satisfactory
	Aberdeen	Satisfactory
	Brighton	Satisfactory
	Stirling	Satisfactory
	Keele	Satisfactory
	Oxford Brookes	Satisfactory
	Goldsmiths	
	Greenwich	Satisfactory
	Kent	Excellent
	Kingston	Satisfactory
	Aberystwyth	Satisfactory
	Salford	Satisfactory
	Bangor	
	Ulster	Satisfactory
	Hertfordshire	Satisfactory
	Liverpool	Satisfactory
	Heriot-Watt	Highly Satis
	Bristol UWE	Satisfactory
	Nottingham Trent	Satisfactory
	Manchester Met	Satisfactory
	Coventry	Satisfactory
	Buckingham	
	Chester	Satisfactory

ENTRY	UNI/COLLEGE	RATING
	Glamorgan	Satisfactory
	Westminster	Satisfactory
	Staffordshire	Satisfactory
Low		
80-200 points		
	Abertay Dundee	Satisfactory
	Bradford	Satisfactory
	Glasgow Cal	Satis. C/CAC
	Brunel	Satisfactory
	Coventry	Satisfactory
	City	Satisfactory
	Roehampton	Satisfactory
	London South Bank	Satis. C/CAC
	Huddersfield	Satisfactory
	Leeds Met	Satis. C/CCC
	Lincoln	Satisfactory
	Liverpool JM	Satisfactory
	Luton	Satisfactory
	Middlesex	Satisfactory
	Central England	Satisfactory
	Central Lancs	Satisfactory
	Teesside	Excellent
	Hull	Satisfactory
	Kent	Excellent
	Dundee	Satisfactory
	Bournemouth	Satisfactory
	Plymouth	Satisfactory
	Anglia Ruskin	Satis. C/CCC
	Northumbria	Satisfactory
	Cardiff UWIC	Satisfactory
	Sheffield Hallam	Satisfactory
	East London	Satisfactory
	Lampeter	
	Liverpool Hope	Satisfactory
	Bolton	Satisfactory
	Wolverhampton	Satisfactory
	Canterbury	Satisfactory
	Worcester	
	Bell	
	Napier	Satis. C/CCC
	Sunderland	Satisfactory
	Portsmouth	Satisfactory
	De Montfort	Satisfactory
	Derby	Satisfactory
	Greenwich	Satisfactory
	Gloucestershire	Satisfactory
	Northampton	Satisfactory
	Bucks Chilterns UC	Satisfactory
	Newport	Satisfactory
	Liverpool	Satisfactory
	London Met	Satis. C/CAC
	Southampton Solent	Satisfactory
	Thames Valley	Satisfactory
	Robert Gordon	
	Paisley	Satisfactory
	Highlands & Islands	
	Glamorgan	Satisfactory

DENTISTRY

ENTRY	UNI/COLLEGE	RATING
High		
320 points +		
	Queen's Belfast	24
	Bristol	19
	Liverpool	21
	Birmingham	22
	Dundee	Highly Satis
	Glasgow	Highly Satis
	King's College	24
	Leeds	23
	Manchester	24
	Newcastle	23
	Queen Mary	24
	Sheffield	23
	Cardiff	Excellent

ENTRY	UNI/COLLEGE	RATING
Low-Medium		
*120-240 points**		
	Cardiff UWIC	Excellent
	Manchester Met	21
	Dundee	Highly Satis
	Britol UWE	21

*These are Dental Technology or Oral Health degrees.

ECONOMICS

Go to www.qaa.ac.uk/reviews/reports/subjIndex.asp for recent teaching inspections; www.qaa.ac.uk/reviews/reports/archive/oldSubjIndex.asp for reports prior to 2000.

ENTRY	UNI/COLLEGE	RATING
High		
320 points +		
	Oxford	23
	Cambridge	24
	Exeter	23
	UEA	23
	Warwick	24
	LSE	23
	Nottingham	24
	Cardiff	Satisfactory
	Durham	24
	Newcastle	23
	Queen's Belfast	24
	UCL	24
	Aston	
	Bath	24
	Reading	21
	St Andrews	Exce. C/CCC
	Bristol	23
	Manchester	24
	Birmingham	23
	Leeds	22
	Southampton	24
	Lancaster	
	York	24
	Royal Holloway	22
Medium-High		
280-300 points		
	Dundee	Satisfactory
	Edinburgh	Satisfactory
	Essex	24
	Nottingham	24
	Cardiff	Satisfactory
	Leicester	24
	Surrey	23
	Sussex	21
	UEA	23
	Glasgow	Satis. C/CCA
	Hull	22
	Leeds	22
	Loughborough	23
	Queen Mary	21
	Queen's Belfast	24
	Sheffield	21
	Swansea	Satisfactory
	UCL	24
	Newcastle	23
	Brunel	22
	SOAS	21
	Kent	
	Liverpool	22
	Exeter	23
	Lancaster	
	Strathclyde	Satis. C/CCC
	Westminster	
Medium		
220-260 points		
	Aberdeen	Exc. C/CCC
	Bradford	21
	City	22
	Goldsmiths	22
	Keele	23
	Queen's Belfast	24
	Salford	20
	Swansea	Satisfactory
	Heriot-Watt	Satisfactory
	Stirling	Exc. C/CCC
	Aberystwyth	Excellent
	Nottingham Trent	22
	Buckingham	
	Dundee	Satisfactory
	Kingston	21
	Manchester Met	20
	Oxford Brookes	24
	Anglia Ruskin	
	Bangor	Satisfactory
	Robert Gordom	Ulster
	Staffordshire	24
Low		
80-200 points		
	Bolton	
	Abertay Dundee	Exc. C/CCC
	Bristol UWE	23
	Central England	21
	Central Lancs	
	Liverpool JMoores	
	Northumbria	22
	Glamorgan	Satisfactory
	Leeds Met	24
	Napier	Satisfactory
	Glasgow Cal	
	Greenwich	20
	East London	20
	Hertfordshire	22
	Kingston	21
	Portsmouth	21Teesside
	Middlesex	21
	Northampton	
	London Met	23
	Paisley	Satis. C/CCC
	Sunderland	
	Plymouth	
	Worcester	

ENGINEERING MECHANICAL, PRODUCTION

Go to www.qaa.ac.uk/reviews/reports/subjIndex.asp for recent teaching inspections; www.qaa.ac.uk/reviews/reports/archive/oldSubjIndex.asp for reports prior to 2000.

ENTRY	UNI/COLLEGE	RATING
High 320 points +		
	Bath	Excellent
	Cambridge	23
	City	Satisfactory, 19
	Glasgow	Highly Satis
	Imperial	Satisfactory, 22
	Oxford	23
	Queen's Belfast	Satisfactory, 21
	Bristol	Excellent
	Durham	22
	Newcastle	Satisfactory
	Liverpool	Satisfactory, 20
	Birmingham	Satisfactory, 20
	Queen Mary	Satisfactory
	Strathclyde	Excellent
	Swansea	Satisfactory
	UCL	Satisfactory
	Brunel	Satisfactory, 20
	Southampton	Satisfactory, 21
	Cardiff	Excellent
	Loughborough	Satisfactory, 23
	Manchester	Excellent
	Warwick	
	Sheffield	Excellent, 24
Medium-High 280-300 points		
	Aberdeen	Highly Satis
	Bradford	Satisfactory
	UCL	Satisfactory
	King's Coll	Satisfactory
	Liverpool	Satisfactory, 20
	Robert Gordon	Highly Satis
	Sheffield	Excellent, 24
	Strathclyde	Excellent
	Staffordshire	Satisfactory
	Sussex	Satisfactory
	Leeds	Satisfactory
	Portsmouth	Satis. C
	Queen's Belfast	Satisfactory, 21
	Lancaster	Satisfactory
	Newcastle	Satisfactory
	Nottingham	Excellent, 24
	Birmingham	Satisfactory, 20
	Brighton	Satisfactory
	Edinburgh	Satis. C/CCC
	Heriot-Watt	Highly Satis. C/CCC
	Hertfordshire	22
	Kingston	Satisfactory, 24
	Manchester	Excellent
	Warwick	
	Exeter	
	Brunel	Satisfactory, 20
	Cardiff	Excellent
	Loughborough	Satisfactory, 23
	Aston	Satisfactory
	Dundee	
	Leicester	
	Surrey	Satisfactory
	Reading	Excellent
	Oxford Brookes	Satisfactory

ENTRY	UNI/COLLEGE	RATING
Low-Medium 220-260 points		
	Plymouth	Satisfactory
	Leicester	
	Aston	Satisfactory
	Bradford	Satisfactory
	Brighton	Satisfactory
	Coventry	Excellent, 18
	Harper Adams	Satisfactory
	Glasgow	Highly Satis
	City	Satisfactory, 19
	Exeter	
	Hull	
	Reading	Excellent
	Oxford Brookes	Satisfactory
	Surrey	Satisfactory
	Sheffield	Excellent, 24
	Queen Mary	Satisfactory
	Central Lancs	Satisfactory
	Central England	Satisfactory, 19
	Hertfordshire	22
	Manchester Met	Excellent
	Northumbria	Satisfactory
	Brunel	Satisfactory, 20
	Aberdeen	Highly Satis
	Dundee	
	Bristol West England	Satisfactory
	Central Lancs	Satisfactory
	Heriot-Watt	Highly Satis
	Huddersfield	Satis. C/CCC
	Napier	Satisfactory
	Ulster	Satisfactory
	Abertay Dundee	Highly Satis C/CAC
	Kingston	Satisfactory, 24
	Greenwich	Satisfactory
	Derby	Satisfactory
	Glamorgan	Satisfactory
	Lancaster	Satisfactory
	Portsmouth	Satisfactory
	Robert Gordon	Highly Satis
	Sheffield Hallam	Satisfactory, 21
	Swansea	Satisfactory
Low 80-200 points		
	Central Lancs	Satisfactory
	Leicester	
	Liverpool	Satisfactory, 20
	London South Bank	18
	Glasgow Cal	Satis. C/CAC
	Hull	
	Sunderland	Satisfactory, 19
	Brighton	Satisfactory
	Teesside	Satis. C/CAC
	Coventry	Excellent, 18
	Huddersfield	Satisfactory
	Northumbria	Satisfactory
	Dundee	
	Brunel	Satisfactory, 20
	Aberdeen	Highly Satis
	Hertfordshire	22
	Oxford Brookes	Satisfactory
	Paisley	Highly Satis C/CAC
	Portsmouth	Satisfactory
	Sheffield Hallam	Satisfactory, 21
	Glamorgan	Satisfactory
	Wolverhampton	Satisfactory
	Abertay Dundee	Highly Satis
	Kingston	Satisfactory, 24

ENTRY	UNI/COLLEGE	RATING
Low		
80-200 points		
	Greenwich	Satisfactory
	Liverpool JM	Satisfactory
	Plymouth	Satisfactory
	Bolton	Satisfactory
	Highlands & Islands	
	Cardiff UWIC	Satisfactory

ENGLISH

Go to www.qaa.ac.uk/reviews/reports/subjIndex.asp for recent teaching inspections; www.qaa.ac.uk/reviews/reports/archive/oldSubjIndex.asp for reports prior to 2000.

ENTRY	UNI/COLLEGE	RATING
High		
320 points +		
	Oxford	Excellent
	Cambridge	Excellent
	UCL	Excellent
	King's College	Satisfactory
	Birmingham	Excellent
	UEA	Satisfactory
	Manchester	Satisfactory
	St Andrews	Highly Satis
	Southampton	Excellent
	Sussex	Excellent
	Newcastle	Excellent
	Durham	Excellent
	Exeter	Excellent
	Bristol	Excellent
	Leeds	Excellent
	Sheffield	Excellent
	Warwick	Excellent
	Cardiff	Excellent
	Liverpool	Excellent
	York	Excellent
	Nottingham	Excellent
	Royal Holloway	Satisfactory
	Lancaster	Excellent
	Leicester	Excellent
	Reading	Satisfactory
	Loughborough	23
	Kent	Satisfactory
Medium-High		
280-300 points		
	Birmingham	Excellent
	Bournemouth	
	Brighton	
	Brunel	Satisfactory
	Glasgow	Excellent
	Kingston	Satisfactory
	Lancaster	Excellent
	Oxford Brookes	Excellent
	Swansea	Satisfactory
	Kent	Satisfactory
	UEA	Satisfactory
	Edinburgh	Highly Satis C/CCC
	Queen Mary	Excellent
	Cardiff	Excellent
	Liverpool	Excellent
	Keele	Satisfactory
	King's College	Satisfactory
	Leicester	Excellent
	Manchester	Satisfactory
	Newcastle	Excellent
	Nottingham	Excellent
	Durham	Excellent
	Exeter	Excellent
	Bristol	Excellent

ENTRY	UNI/COLLEGE	RATING
Medium-High	Leeds	Excellent
280-300 points	Portsmouth	Satisfactory
	Sheffield	Excellent
	Reading	Satisfactory
	Loughborough	23
	Goldsmiths	Satisfactory
	Queen's Belfast	Excellent
	Dundee	Exc. C/CCC
	Essex	Satisfactory
	Hull	Satisfactory
	Sheffield Hallam	Excellent
	Strathclyde	Highly Satis C/CCC
	Bristol UWE	Excellent
Medium		
220-260 points		
	Birmingham	Excellent
	Bradford	
	Brighton	
	UEA	Satisfactory
	Lincoln	
	Oxford Brookes	Excellent
	Portsmouth	Satisfactory
	Sheffield Hallam	Excellent
	Manchester Met	Satisfactory
	Nottingham Trent	Satisfactory
	Huddersfield	Satisfactory
	Dundee	Exc. C/CCC
	Essex	Satisfactory
	Aberystwyth	Excellent
	Hull	Satisfactory
	Northumbria	Excellent
	Stirling	Excellent
	Ulster	Satisfactory
	Aberdeen	Highly Satis
	Bangor	Satisfactory
	Winchester	Satisfactory
	Bath Spa	Excellent
	Chester	Excellent
	Chichester	Satisfactory
	Kingston	Satisfactory
	Leeds	Excellent
	Liverpool	Excellent
	Liverpool JM	Satisfactory
	Plymouth	Satisfactory
	Gloucestershire	Satisfactory
	Glamorgan	
	Salford	Satisfactory
	Staffordshire	Satisfactory
	Swansea	Satisfactory
Low		
80-220 points		
	Derby	
	Paisley	
	Bolton	
	Leeds Met	C/CCC
	Lampeter	Satisfactory
	Wolverhampton	Satisfactory
	Teesside	Satisfactory
	York St John UC	Satisfactory
	Northampton	Satisfactory
	Westminster	Satisfactory

ENTRY	UNI/COLLEGE	RATING
Low		
80-220 points		
	Worcester	Satisfactory
	London Met	Excellent
	Central England	Satisfactory
	Kingston	Satisfactory
	London South Bank	C/CCA
	Luton	Satisfactory
	Middlesex	Satisfactory
	Portsmouth	Satisfactory
	Roehampton	Satisfactory
	Hertfordshire	Satis. C/CCA
	Northumbria	Excellent
	East London	Excellent
	Bangor	Satisfactory

ENTRY	UNI/COLLEGE	RATING
Low	Coventry*	
80-220 points	Liverpool Hope	Satisfactory
	Canterbury	Satisfactory
	Cumbria	
	Bristol UWE	Excellent
	Falmouth UC	
	De Montfort	Satisfactory
	Greenwich	Satisfactory
	Buckingham	
	Newport	
	Sunderland	Satisfactory
	Bucks Chilterns UC	C/CAC
	St Mary's	Satisfactory

*for non-native English speakers

HISTORY

ENTRY	UNI/COLLEGE	RATING
High		
320 points +		
	Oxford	Excellent
	Cambridge	Excellent
	LSE	Excellent
	Royal Holloway	Excellent
	York	Excellent
	St Andrews	Excellent
	Southampton	Satisfactory
	Warwick	Excellent
	Birmingham	Excellent
	Bristol	Satisfactory
	UEA	Satisfactory
	Cardiff	Satisfactory
	Durham	Excellent
	King's College	Excellent
	Leicester	Excellent
	Liverpool	Excellent
	Manchester	Satisfactory
	Newcastle	Satisfactory
	Nottingham	Satis. C/CCC
	Sheffield	Excellent
	SOAS	Satisfactory
	Leeds	Satisfactory
	UCL	Excellent
	Exeter	Satisfactory
	Sussex	Satisfactory
Medium-High		
280-300 points		
	Edinburgh	Excellent
	Southampton	Satisfactory
	Manchester	Satisfactory
	Glasgow	Highly Satis C/CCC
	Leeds	Satisfactory
	Kent	Satisfactory
	Nottingham	Satis. C/CCC
	Oxford Brookes	Satisfactory
	UEA	Satisfactory
	Lancaster	Excellent
	Liverpool	Excellent
	Cardiff	Satisfactory
	Hull	Excellent
	Reading	Satisfactory
	Dundee	Highly Satis
	Leicester	Excellent
	Essex	Satisfactory
	Queen Mary	Satisfactory

ENTRY	UNI/COLLEGE	RATING
Medium-High	UCL	Excellent
280-300 points	Keele	Satisfactory
	Brunel	Satisfactory
	Goldsmiths	Satisfactory
	Queen's Belfast	Excellent
	Aberdeen	Highly Satis
	Strathclyde	Highly Satis C/CCC
	Bristol UWE	Satisfactory
Medium		
220-260 points		
	Aberystwyth	Satisfactory
	Westminster	Satisfactory
	Bangor	Satisfactory
	Kent	Satisfactory
	Lincoln	
	Sheffield Hallam	Satisfactory
	Plymouth	Satisfactory
	Huddersfield	Satis. C/CCC
	Kingston	Satisfactory
	Brighton	
	Cardiff	Satisfactory
	Glasgow Caledonian	
	Gloucestershire	Satisfactory
	Northumbria	Satisfactory
	Nottingham	Satisfactory
	Nottingham Trent	Satisfactory
	Portsmouth	Satisfactory
	Swansea	Excellent
	Dundee	Highly Satis
	Leicester	Excellent
	SOAS	Satisfactory
	Brunel	Satisfactory
	Chester	Satisfactory
	Goldsmiths	Satisfactory
	Chichester	Satisfactory
	Bradford	Satisfactory
	Greenwich	Satisfactory
	Aberdeen	Highly Satis
	Glamorgan	Satisfactory
	Oxford Brookes	Satisfactory
	Stirling	Highly Satis C/CCC
	Winchester	Satisfactory
	Ulster	Satisfactory
Low		
80-200 points		
	Bournemouth	
	Central Lancs	Satisfactory
	Cardiff UWIC	

ENTRY	UNI/COLLEGE	RATING
Low		
80-200 points		
	Coventry	23
	Derby	Satisfactory
	East London	Satisfactory
	Glasgow Caledonian	
	Liverpool Hope	Satisfactory
	London Met	Satisfactory
	Liverpool JMoores	Satisfactory
	Middlesex	Satisfactory
	Hertfordshire	Satis. C/CCC
	Huddersfield	Satis. C/CCC
	Leeds Met	Satis. C/CCC
	Lincoln	
	Lampeter	Satisfactory
	Manchester Met	Satisfactory
	Winchester	Satisfactory

ENTRY	UNI/COLLEGE	RATING
Low	York St John UC	Satisfactory
80-200 points	Teesside	Satis. C/CCC
	Wolverhampton	Satisfactory
	Staffordshire	Satisfactory
	Cumbria	
	Roehampton	Satisfactory
	Salford	Satisfactory
	Northampton	Satisfactory
	Buckingham	
	Newport	Satis (Comb Sts)
	Worcester	Satisfactory
	Bolton	Satisfactory
	Canterbury	Excellent
	De Montfort	Satis. C/CCC
	Sunderland	Satis. C/CCC
	Bath Spa	Satisfactory
	St Mary's	Satisfactory

LANGUAGES

Go to www.qaa.ac.uk/reviews/reports/subjIndex.asp for recent teaching inspections; www.qaa.ac.uk/reviews/reports/archive/oldSubjIndex.asp for reports prior to 2000.

ENTRY	UNI/COLLEGE	RATING
High		
320 points +		
	Oxford	21
	Cambridge	22
	Cardiff	Satisfactory
	British Institute	18
	Manchester	19, Fr.; 21, Ger.
	Newcastle	22
	St Andrews	22
	Royal Holloway	21, Fr.; 19, Ger.
	Glasgow	22
	Bristol	20, Fr.; 21, Ger.
	Durham	22
	Leeds	22, Fr.; 22, Ger.
	Surrey	18
	York	22
	UCL	21, Fr.; 23, Ger.
	Southampton	18
Medium-High		
280-300 points		
	Manchester	19, Fr.; 21, Ger.
	Birmingham	18, Fr.; 19, Ger.
	Durham	22
	Edinburgh	21
	King's Coll	21, Fr.; 20, Ger.
	St Andrews	22
	Leeds	22, Fr.; 22, Ger.
	Sheffield	21, Fr.; 20, Ger.
	Heriot-Watt	21
	Essex	
	SOAS	23
	York	22
	Nottingham	16, Fr.; 22, Ger.
	Liverpool	22, Fr.; 19, Ger.
	Warwick	21, Fr.; 23, Ger.
	Cardiff	Satisfactory
	Reading	21, Fr.; 20, Ger.
	Swansea	Satis, Fr.; Ex,Ger.
	Bradford	18
	Queen's Belfast	20, Fr.; 19, Ger.
	Sussex	22, Fr.; 17, Ger.
	Bath	19

ENTRY	UNI/COLLEGE	RATING
Medium-High	Lancaster	20, Fr.; 19, Ger.
280-300 points	Kent	19
	Exeter	22, Fr.; 24, Ger.
	Surrey	18
	UEA	19
	Hull	21
	Aberdeen	22
	Strathclyde	22
	Aston	22
Low-Medium		
220-260 points		
	Aberdeen	22
	Keele	20, Fr.; 19, Ger.
	Bangor	Satisfactory
	Salford	20
	Ulster	20, Fr.; 19, Ger.
	Leicester	19, Fr.; 21, Ger.
	Goldsmiths	17
	Stirling	20
(Fr. only)	Brighton	20
	Oxford Brookes	22
	Queen Mary	23
	Aberystwyth	
	Chester	19
	Staffordshire	21
	London South Bank	22
	Anglia	21
	Nottingham Trent	17
	Portsmouth	23, Fr.; 21, Ger.
Low		
160-200 points		
(Fr. only)	Roehampton	19
	Strathclyde	22
	Bristol West England	21
	London Met	19
	Liverpool JM	19
	East London	18
	Manchester Met	21
	Wolverhampton	19, Fr.; 17, Ger.
	Westminster	23, Fr.; 20, Ger.
	Glamorgan	
	Coventry	21
	Northumbria	23
	Hertfordshire	
	Napier	19
	Plymouth	
	Sheffield Hallam	19
	York St John UC	

ENTRY	UNI/COLLEGE	RATING
Low		
160-200 points		
	Central Lancs	21
	Newport	
	Leeds Met	19

LAW

*All candidates for unis asterisked are required to sit the National Admissions Test for Law (LNAT).

Go to www.qaa.ac.uk/reviews/reports/subjIndex.asp for recent teaching inspections.

ENTRY	UNI/COLLEGE	RATING
High		
320 points +		
	Bristol*	Excellent
	Cambridge*	Excellent
	Birmingham*	Satisfactory
	Leeds	Satisfactory
	Oxford*	Excellent
	UCL*	Excellent
	Durham*	Excellent
	King's Coll	Excellent
	Manchester	Excellent
	Nottingham*	Excellent
	Queen's Belfast	Excellent
	Sheffield	Excellent
	Warwick	Excellent
	Reading	Satisfactory
	Glasgow	Highly Satis C/CCC
	LSE	Excellent
	Southampton	Satisfactory
	Leicester	Excellent
	Cardiff	Satisfactory
	Essex	Excellent
	Exeter	Satisfactory
	Lancaster	Satisfactory
	Newcastle	Satisfactory
	Oxford Brookes	Excellent
	Queen Mary	Satisfactory
	City	Satisfactory
	UEA*	Excellent
	Sussex	Satisfactory
	SOAS	Excellent
	Liverpool	Excellent
	Kingston	Satisfactory
	Kent	Satisfactory
	Stirling	
	Surrey	
	Strathclyde	Highly Satis C/CCC
Medium-High		
260-300 points		
	Dundee	Highly Satis C/CCC
	Liverpool	Excellent
	Surrey	
	Swansea	Satisfactory
	Cardiff	Satisfactory
	Derby	Satisfactory
	Oxford Brookes	Excellent
	Kingston	Satisfactory
	Edinburgh	Highly Satis
	Glamorgan	Satisfactory
	LSE	Excellent
	Central England	Satisfactory
	Brunel	Satisfactory

ENTRY	UNI/COLLEGE	RATING
Medium-High	De Montfort	Satisfactory
260-300 points	Manchester Met	Satisfactory
	Nottingham Trent	Satisfactory
	Strathclyde	Highly Satis C/CCC
	Ulster	Satisfactory
	Hull	Satisfactory
	Keele	Satisfactory
	Stirling	
	Staffordshire	Satis. C/CCC
	Westminster	Satisfactory
	Aberdeen	Highly Satis
Medium		
220-260 points		
	Aston	
	Liverpool JM	Satis. C
	Westminster	Satisfactory
	Huddersfield	Satis. C/CAC
	Gloucestershire	
	Greenwich	Satisfactory
	Heriot-Watt	
	Lincoln	Satisfactory
	De Montfort	Satisfactory
	Plymouth	Satis. C
	Central Lancs	Satisfactory
	Glasgow Cal	Satisfactory
	Portsmouth	
	Buckingham	
	London South Bank	Satisfactory
	Manchestere Met	Satisfactory
	Robert Gordon	
	Bournemouth	Satisfactory
	Hertfordshire	Satisfactory
	Aberdeen	Highly Satis
	Brunel	Satisfactory
	Bristol UWE	Excellent
	Brighton	
	Northumbria	Excellent
	Coventry	Satisfactory
	Sheffield Hallam	Satisfactory
	Kingston	Satisfactory
	Napier	C/CCA
	Abertay Dundee	Satisfactory
	Bangor	
	Aberystwyth	Satisfactory
	Glamorgan	Satisfactory
	Stirling	
	Sunderland	
	Thames Valley	Satisfactory
	Swansea	Satisfactory
	Chester	
Low		
80-200 points		
	Luton	Satisfactory
	East London	Satis. C/CAC
	Bolton	
	Derby	Satisfactory
	London Met	Satis. C/CAC
	Glasgow Cal	Satisfactory
	Plymouth	Satisfactory
	Wolverhampton	Satisfactory
	Northampton	Satisfactory
	Glamorgan	Satisfactory

ENTRY	UNI/COLLEGE	RATING
Low		
80-200 points		
	Bucks Chilterns	C/CAA
	Thames Valley	Satisfactory
	Middlesex	Satisfactory
	Paisley	
	Southampton Solent	Satisfactory
	Teesside	Satis. C/CAA
	Leeds Met	C/CCA
	Salford	
	Canterbury	
	Liverpool Hope	
	Newport	

MEDIA

Go to www.qaa.ac.uk/reviews/reports/subjIndex.asp for recent teaching inspections.

ENTRY	UNI/COLLEGE	RATING
High		
320 points +	Sussex	21
	Goldsmiths	22
	Cardiff	Satisfactory
	Manchester	
Medium-High		
260-300 points		
	Bournemouth	22
	Sheffield	
	Birmingham	
	Newcastle	
	Goldsmiths	22
	Royal Holloway	
	Stirling	Highly Satis
	Essex	
	Nottingham Trent	21
	City	19
	Lancaster	
	Lincoln	17
	Southampton Solent	18
	Liverpool JM	22
	UEA	23
	Central Lancs	22
	Central England	21
	Leeds	22
	Sheffield Hallam	19
	Bradford	
	Sunderland	22
	Strathclyde	
	Aston	
	Keele	
	Salford	
	Brunel	20
	Ulster	21
	Aberystwyth	
	Surrey	
	Loughborough	
	Brighton	
	Dundee	
	Queen Mary	
	De Montfort	20
	Wolverhampton	19
	Staffordshire	20
Low-Medium		
200-240 points		
	Westminster	23
	Napier	Highly Satis
	Brighton	
	Staffordshire	20
	Falmouth UC	18
	Salford	
	Kingston	
	Bath Spa	
	Chester	

ENTRY	UNI/COLLEGE	RATING
Medium-High	Swansea	
200-240 points	Bangor	
	City	19
	Queen Margaret	
	Central Lancs	22
	Winchester	18
	Hertfordshire	
	Manchester Met	
	Gloucestershire	20
	Glamorgan	
	Lampeter	
	Liverpool JM	22
	Robert Gordon	
	De Montfort	20
	Lincoln	17
	Central England	21
	Wolverhampton	19
	Middlesex	
	Plymouth	21
	Southampton Solent	18
	Ulster	21
	Portsmouth	
	Coventry	18
Low		
80-180 points		
	Bolton	20
	Abertay Dundee	
	Cardiff UWIC	
	Central Lancashire	
	Derby	
	Liberpool Hope	
	Glasgow Cal	Highly Satis
	Canterbury	20
	York St John UC	20
	UEA	23
	Cardiff	Satisfactory
	Worcester	
	Southampton Solent	18
	Bucks Chilterns UC	18
	St Mary's	
	Lincoln	17
	Liverpool JM	22
	Portsmouth	
	Thames Valley	
	Huddersfield	18
	London South Bank	20
	Paisley	
	University of the Arts	20
	Central England	21
	Lampeter	
	Northampton	21
	Northumbria	
	Swansea	
	Cumbria	19
	Wolverhampton	19
	Luton	22
	Leeds Met	19
	Middlesex	
	Teesside	

ENTRY	UNI/COLLEGE	RATING
Low 80-180 points		
	Queen's Belfast	
	Greenwich	19
	East London	16
	Chichester	24
	Ravensbourne	

MEDICINE

All candidates applying to read Medicine at universities marked with an asterisks are required to take a written test to assess scientific aptitude: the Biomedical Admissions Test (BMAT).

ENTRY	UNI/COLLEGE	RATING
Above 340 points		
	*Cambridge	21
	*Oxford	21
	Queen's Belfast	22
	Cardiff	
	*UCL	21
	Imperial	21
	Peninsula Med School	
	Edinburgh	Highly satis.
340 points		
	Birmingham	20
	Bristol	20
	Durham	
	UEA	
	Keele	
	Brighton & Sussex	
	Hull-York	
340 points	Leicester	23
	Manchester	24
	Newcastle	24
	Nottingham	
	Uni Wales Coll Med	Excellent
	London St George's	23
	Dundee	Excellent
	King's College	22
	Liverpool	24
	Queen Mary	21
	Southampton	24
	St Andrews	Highly satis.
	Leeds	18
320 points		
	Aberdeen	Excellent
	Glasgow	Excellent
	Dundee	Excellent
	Sheffield	19
200-220 points		
	Thames Valley	
	Southampton	24
	London St George's	23

These last 3 are foundation courses.

PSYCHOLOGY

ENTRY	UNI/COLLEGE	RATING
High 320 points +		
	Cambridge	24
	Oxford	24
	Durham	23
	Lancaster	24
	Leeds	23
	Sheffield	22
	UCL	22
	St Andrews	Excellent
	Bath	
	Nottingham	24
	Birmingham	23
	Liverpool	22
	Warwick	21
	York	24
	Bristol	23
	Cardiff	Excellent
	LSE	23
	Oxford Brookes	23
	Royal Holloway	24
	Sussex	21
	Kent	22
	Newcastle	24
	Manchester	22
	Reading	24
	Surrey	22
	Leicester	24
	Southampton	21
	Exeter	23
	Queen's Belfast	24
Medium-High 260-300 points		
	UEA	
	Edinburgh	Highly Satis
	Bath	
	Durham	23
	Kent	22
	City	21
	Nottingham Trent	22
	Goldsmiths	22
	Brunel	22
	Oxford Brookes	23
	Kingston	
	Northumbria	22
	Dundee	Excellent
	Leeds	23
	Sheffield	22
	Surrey	22
	Bournemouth	
	Central Lancs	24
	Loughborough	24
	Manchester Met	22
	Essex	22
	Hull	23
	Swansea	Excellent
	Keele	23
	Leicester	24
	Southampton	21
	Stirling	Excellent
	Portsmouth	23
	Exeter	23
	Aston	22
	Hertfordshire	23

ENTRY	UNI/COLLEGE	RATING
Medium-High		
260-300 points		
	Bangor	Excellent
	Glasgow	Excellent
	Bradford	
	Strathclyde	Highly Satis
	Sheffield Hallam	24
	Bristol UWE	22
	Lincoln	21
Medium		
220-240 points		
	Aberdeen	Highly Satis
	Coventry	21
	Glasgow Cal	Highly Satis
	Wolverhampton	21
	Glamorgan	Satisfactory
	Greenwich	22
	Queen Margaret	
	Dundee	Excellent
	Huddersfield	20
	Plymouth	23
	Central Lancs	24
	Kingston	
	Winchester	21
	Manchester Met	22
	Westminster	24
	York St John UC	20
	Liverpool JMoores	19
	Nottingham Trent	22
	Hertfordshire	23
	Stirling	Excellent
	Swansea	Excellent
	Derby	20
	Bristol UWE	22
	Gloucestershire	21
	Heriot-Watt	
	Bolton	24
	Chester	20
	Southampton Solent	19
	Ulster	23

ENTRY	UNI/COLLEGE	RATING
	Thames Valley	20
Low		
100-200 points		
	Sunderland	20
	Abertay Dundee	Highly Satis
	Bath Spa	21
	East London	**23**
	Cardiff UWIC	Excellent
	Exeter	23
	Dundee	Excellent
	Luton	22
	Roehampton	23
	Northampton	20
	Northumbria	22
	Nottingham Trent	22
	London Met	22
	Huddersfield	20
	London South Bank	20
	De Montfort	22
	Teesside	20
	Buckingham	
	Central England	
	Greenwich	22
	Westminster	24
	Worcester	20
	Portsmouth	23
	Heriot-Watt	
	Manchester Met	22
	Bournemouth	
	Middlesex	21
	Liverpool Hope	22
	Canterbury	20
	Paisley	Highly Satis
	Bristol UWE	22
	Wolverhampton	21
	Glamorgan	Satisfactory
	Bucks Chilterns	21
	Leeds Met	20
	Staffordshire	23

SOCIOLOGY

ENTRY	UNI/COLLEGE	RATING
High		
320 points +		
	Cambridge	
	Durham	21
	Manchester	21
	Cardiff	Satisfactory
	Warwick	24
	Exeter	21
	Sheffield	Excellent
Medium-High		
280-300 points		
	Sussex	24
	Essex	22
	Durham	21
	Newcastle	
	UEA	16
	Glasgow	Excellent
	Nottingham	21
	Leeds	20
	Sheffield	Excellent
	Birmingham	24
	Edinburgh	Excellent
	Bristol	21
	Goldsmiths	21

ENTRY	UNI/COLLEGE	RATING
Medium-High	Royal Holloway	21
280-300 points	Brighton	
	Aston	
	LSE	20
	Salford	20
	Cardiff	Satisfactory
	Liverpool	21
	York	23
	Leicester	19
	Queen's Belfast	19
	Reading	22
	Bath	19
	Loughborough	23
	Strathclyde	Highly Satis
	Southampton	21
Medium		
220-260 points		
	Keele	22
	Bradford	17
	Brighton	
	Bangor	Satisfactory
	Nottingham Trent	19
	Kent	21
	Lancaster	21
	De Montfort	17
	Derby	18

ENTRY	UNI/COLLEGE	RATING
Medium 220-260 points		
	East London	19
	Hull	20
	Westminster	18
	Huddersfield	
	City	19
	Leicester	19
	Goldsmiths	21
	Salford	20
	Aberdeen	Excellent
	Sheffield Hallam	22
	Oxford Brookes	21
	Queen Margaret UC	
	Kingston	21
	Coventry	21
	Central England	18
	Portsmouth	20
	Liverpool JM	18
	Stirling	Excellent
	Swansea	Satisfactory
	Brunel	22
	Ulster	17
	Liverpool Hope	22
Low 100-200 points		
	Manchester Met	21
	Plymouth	20

ENTRY	UNI/COLLEGE	RATING
Low 100-200 points	Bristol UWE	23
	Coventry	21
	Greenwich	23
	London South Bank	19
	Roehampton	20
	Northumbria	20
	Staffordshire	17
	Central Lancs	18
	Gloucestershire	20
	Middlesex	19
	Abertay Dundee	
	Northampton	20
	Teesside	19
	Worcester	21
	Bath Spa	22
	Sunderland	21
	Glamorgan	Satisfactory
	Bucks Chilterns	16
	Thames Valley	22
	London Met	17
	Abertay Dundee	
	St Mary's	20
	Napier	
	Cardiff UWIC	
	Glasgow Caledonian	Highly Satis.
	Wolverhampton	20
	Paisley	Highly Satis.
	Leeds Metropolitan	

SPORT/SPORT SCIENCE

Go to www.qaa.ac.uk/reviews/reports/subjIndex.asp for recent teaching inspections; www.qaa.ac.uk/reviews/reports/archive/oldSubjIndex.asp for reports prior to 2000.

ENTRY	UNI/COLLEGE	RATING
High 300 points +		
	Loughborough	23
	Bath	23
	Birmingham	22
	Exeter	21
	Durham	23
	Glasgow	
	Hertfordshire	23
	Leeds	
Medium-High 260-280 points		
	Leeds	
	Liverpool JM	24
	Stirling	
	Ulster	23
	Swansea	
	Aberdeen	
	Edinburgh	
	Loughborough	23
	Queen Mary	
	Glamorgan	
	Bangor	
	Brunel	23
	Durham	23
	Northumbria	21
	Hertfordshire	23
	Sheffield Hallam	24
	Brighton	22
	Essex	
	Central Lancs	24

ENTRY	UNI/COLLEGE	RATING
Medium-High 260-280 points	Kingston	22
	Bolton	21
	Staffordshire	22
	Gloucestershire	21
	Middlesex	22
	Portsmouth	21
Low-Medium 220-240 points		
	Liverpool JM	24
	Sunderland	20
	Oxford Brookes	22
	Manchester Met	22
	Hull	20
	Sheffield Hallam	24
	Abertay Dundee	
	Bournemouth	
	Salford	19
	Nottingham Trent	22
	Staffordshire	22
	Winchester	21
	York St John UC	21
	Kent	
	Robert Gordon	
	Bradford	
	Napier	
	Strathclyde	
	Gloucestershire	21
	Chester	23
Low 80-200 points		
	Liverpool Hope	19
	Cardiff UWIC	
	Swansea	
	Abertay Dundee	
	Loughborough	23
	Bournemouth	
	Birmingham	22

ENTRY	UNI/COLLEGE	RATING
Low		
80-200 points		
	Salford	19
	Nottingham Trent	22
	Aberdeen	
	Liverpool JM	24
	Leeds Met	22
	York St John UC	21
	De Montfort	23
	Plymouth	23
	Bolton	21
	Sheffield Hallam	24
	Newport	
	Canterbury	21
	Glamorgan	
	Bucks Chilterns	21
	St Mary's	21
	Thames Valley	22
	Coventry	21
	Wolverhampton	22

ENTRY	UNI/COLLEGE	RATING
Low	Strathclyde	
80-200 points	Northampton	19
	East London	
	Westminster	24
	Gloucestershire	21
	London South Bank	22
	Greenwich	20
	Chichester	21
	Huddersfield	22
	Luton	22
	Middlesex	22
	London Met	21
	Roehampton	21
	Teesside	21
	Worcester	22
	Southampton Solent	21
	Lincoln	
	Derby	
	Glasgow Caledonian	
	Bristol UWE	

VETERINARY SCIENCE

*Candidates applying to read Veterinary Surgery at Bristol are required to take a written test to assess scientific aptitude: the Biomedical Admissions Test (BMAT).

Go to www.qaa.ac.uk/reviews/reports/subjIndex.asp for recent teaching inspections; www.qaa.ac.uk/reviews/reports/archive/oldSubjIndex.asp for reports prior to 2000.

ENTRY	UNI/COLLEGE	RATING
High		
300 points +		
	*Bristol	24
	Cambridge	23
	Royal Vet College	24
	Edinburgh	Excellent
	Glasgow	Excellent

ENTRY	UNI/COLLEGE	RATING
	Liverpool	24
300 points		
	*Bristol	24
	Liverpool	24
	Royal Vet College	24
	Nottingham	
160-200 points		
	Middlesex	
	Central Lancashire	
	Napier	
	Anglia Ruskin	
	Bristol UWE	
	*Bristol	24
	Harper Adams	

These last are Veterinary Nursing degrees.

UNIVERSITY OF ABERDEEN

The University of Aberdeen
Regent Walk
Aberdeen AB24 3FX

TEL 01224 272090/91
FAX 01224 272576
EMAIL sras@abdn.ac.uk
WEB www.abdn.ac.uk

Aberdeen University Students' Association
50-52 College Bounds
Aberdeen AB24 3TU

TEL 01224 272965
FAX 01224 272977
EMAIL office@ausa.org.uk
WEB www.ausa.org.uk

VAG VIEW

Aberdeen is the oldest university outside Oxbridge, its Chair of Medicine was the first established in the English-speaking world, and King's College Aberdeen was founded in 1495.

As one of four ancient universities in Scotland, the teaching is traditional, seminars, tutorials, etc, and some of the lecture rooms full of traditional character (and draughts). But there is a £198 million spend on lecture theatres in process, and following the closure of the Gallowgate student union, a new student centre opened in 2006.

Aberdeen has a good reputation without the stigma of being an Oxbridge wannabe, like St Andrews or Edinburgh. It, like the city, prides itself on a lack of pretension, and has had good showings in the university league tables. Whether that means anything is up for debate, but there are those who think that it does.

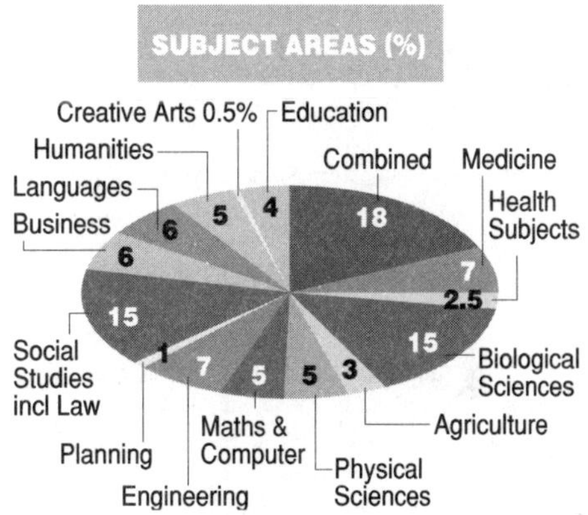

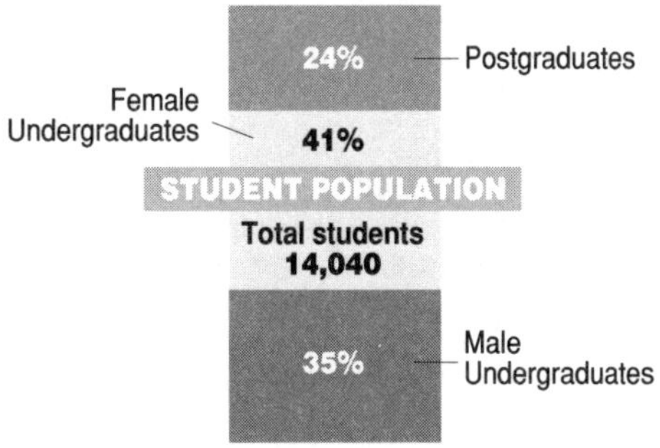

FEES, BURSARIES

In a bid to discourage 'fee refugees' from overwhelming the country's universities, from 2006 English students will be charged £1700 p.a. for all courses at Scottish universities, except Medicine, for which they will be charged £2700 p.a. These will rise with inflation. 31 Entrance Bursaries available for 2006 entry worth £1000 p.a. 10 + sports bursaries. 20 Merit Bursaries (£1000 p.a.) for students resident in UK with outstanding academic qualifications; last year there was a one in four chance of success.

Several awards made each year to outstanding musicians, including organ, choral or instrumental scholarships. Elizabeth Wilson Scholarship for Agriculture students resident in the North East of Scotland for five years. Charles Sutherland Scholarship for Agriculture, Engineering and Economics.

UNIVERSITY/STUDENT PROFILE

University since	**1495**
Situation/style	**Civic**
Student population	**14040**
Undergraduates	**10730**
- mature	**10%**
- non EU undergraduates	**19%**
- male/female	**46:54**
- non-traditional student intake	**25%**
- state school intake	**84%**
- drop-out rate	**9.4%, high**
- undergraduate applications	**Consistent**

CAMPUS

Aberdeen is on the North East coast of Scotland,

ACADEMIC EXCELLENCE

TEACHING:	
(Rated Excellent, Highly Satis. or 17+ out of 24)	
Economics, Geography, Sociology, Medicine, Cellular & Molecular Biology, Organismal Biology, French Studies.	**Excellent**
Chemistry, Geology, Maths & Statistics, Civil Engineering, Mechanical +Manufacturing Engineering, Theol., Finance & Accounting, History of Art, History, Law, Philosophy, Politics, English, Psychology.	**Highly Satis.**
Euro langs. other than French	**22**
Planning & Landscape	**19**
RESEARCH:	
*Top grades 5/5**	
French	**Grade 5***
Community-based Clinical Subjects, Physiology, Biological Sciences, Plant & Soil Science, Pure Maths, Town and Country Planning, Law, Sociology, Theology	**Grade 5**

pretty much final step on the way to the Arctic (a couple of farms and the odd island notwithstanding). Easily reachable, if you've a bit of time on your hands, Aberdeen provides a safe haven for those trying to get as far away as possible from parents, and the rest of civilisation.

The Granite City, as it is accurately called, harbours a bit of a cosmopolitan atmosphere (there's some docks) and a very long beach. The climate is raw, as are the people, but when the sun shines, everything warms up and it's actually a beautiful city.

The city itself is framed around Union Street (surely the only street in the world to have two McDonald's on it), with the main university campus about a mile (and a lung-busting hill) north of the main centre. This is King's College campus, the oldest part of the university, located in the imaginatively entitled Old Aberdeen. There are other campuses (or should that be campii?), one in town which is not used anymore, except to keep dead bodies for first year medics to play about with, the hospital, where they keep the live bodies for the rest of the medics to play about with, and the Hilton campus for Education, complete with its own halls of residence, established at the end of 2001 after the uni's merger with the Aberdeen arm of the Northern College of Education.

The university loves the fact that King's is around 500 years old and makes a point of telling you this at every opportunity. Look out for marketing-gone-mad photos of King's College all over the shop (the King's College Visitors' Centre Shop, to be precise) and on postcards, T-shirts, mugs, biros, novelty condoms (if only) and other useful items.

A traditional uni without the stigma of being an Oxbridge wannabe like St Andrews or Edinburgh. Excellent reputation in subjects for the professions - Law, Medicine, etc. Big spend in process on modernisation and great new student complex opened in 2006.

STUDENT PROFILE

They have a fair intake of non-traditional applicants. The successful completion of the Summer School for Access guarantees a place on most of the uni's degree courses. Success in this has been achieved without the usual flip side of a high drop-out rate.

Writes Rob Littlejohn, 'The students come in eight distinct groups: **Aberdonians,** who talk smugly about pubs in other parts of town and watch quietly as we get lost; **Country Teuchters** (pronounced *'choochters'* – there you know some local dialect already), very similar to Aberdonians, but without the urban sophistication; **Edinburgh Public Schoolers,** a feature of most Scottish unis with better English accents than most of those south of the border and more money than sense; **Other Scots** – Scotland has a greater tradition of staying at home to study and we do get some Edinburghers keen to distance themselves from a public school education, Glaswegians pining for home, sectarianism and annoying accents, and Dundonians just happy to be somewhere else. There's also the **Huge Bands of Others** – Northern Irish, random English, foreign students and Greeks, the final lot warranting their own category for sheer number!'

ACADEMIA & JOBS

89% of Aberdeen's teaching is either Excellent or Highly Satisfactory, and they achieved a whole host of world-class Grade 5* and Grade 5s for research (see *Academic Excellence* box). The French department achieved the only 5* rating for the subject in the UK.

AT A GLANCE

ACADEMIC FILE:	
Subjects assessed	**26**
Excellent/Highly Satisfactory	**89%**
Typical entry requirements	**340 points**
Application acceptance rate	**19%**
AAR in Medicine	**14%**
Students-staff ratio	**15:1**
First/2:1 degree pass rate	**67%**
ACCOMMODATION FILE:	
Guarantee to freshers	**100%**
Style	**Halls, flats**
Catered	**41%**
En suite	**3%**
Approx price range pw	**£53.50-£105**
City rent pw	**£60**

WHAT IT'S REALLY LIKE

UNIVERSITY:	
Social Life	★★★★
Campus scene	**Small & friendly**
Student Union services	**Good**
Politics	**Student issues**
Sport	**Competitive**
National team position	**29th**
Sport facilities	**Improving**
Arts opportunities	**Drama, music exc.; film good; dance, art poor**
Student newspaper	**Gaudie**
Nightclub	**Chalkies, G-Spot**
Bars	**New student centre**
Union ents	**Guarded promise**
Union clubs/societies	**100**
Most popular society	**Cinema Club**
Parking	**Adequate**
CITY:	
Entertainment	★★★★
Scene	**Intoxicating**
Town/gown relations	**Good**
Risk of violence	**Low**
Cost of living	**Above average**
Student concessions	**Average**
Survival + 2 nights out	**£75 pw**
Part-time work campus/town	**Average/excellent**

There are three 'Colleges': Arts and Social Sciences, Life Sciences and Medicine, and Physical Sciences, which administer 590+ programmes across arts and social sciences, education, engineering, law, medicine and science.

The uni's reputation lies in its traditional founding disciplines – Medicine, Law, Divinity and Engineering. Research-wise, there's innovation in the medical sciences in particular. Four Nobel prizes have been awarded for work carried out or begun at the University, including the invention of the life-saver insulin. A key role was played in the invention of Magnetic Resonance Imaging (MRI) and the discovery of enkephalins.

There's a 14% application acceptance rate into Medicine, far better than the 11% average. Good mix of lectures, problem-based learning, clinical experience: emphasis on clinical aspect and patient contact straight away. Entry GCSE English Lang, Maths, Chemistry. ABB at A level or AAAAAB at Highers including Chemistry plus 2 from Biology, Maths and Physics.

Elsewhere in the sciences, Marine Resource Management and Tropical Environmental Science are unique to Aberdeen, while unique in Scotland are Gender Studies, Cultural History, Rural Land & Business Management, Rural Planning & Economic Development, and Politics & International Relations.

Recently introduced programmes include BMus (Music), a combo of music and education, and a Physical Sciences programme with practical aspects of computer science.

Every student gets their own personal Adviser of Studies to help shape the programme and offer support. The University library, spread over 5 sites, is one of the largest in Scotland, with over one million volumes in stock. They have 1000+ computers (up-dated on a four-year cycle), many of which are available to students 24/7.

Many graduates go on to research in Medicine and Medical Sciences, Environmental and Life Sciences and Arts and Social Sciences. There are strong relationships with industry as well as with major research centres and international universities.

Other particular employment strengths include education (they major on Primary Teaching) and their wide-ranging cross-faculty combined honours courses yield a large number of jobs in areas such as accountancy-finance, property and agriculture.

Also, large numbers of graduates find their way into estate agency and management through single subject degrees, such as Property, Planning & Development, Rural Development or Rural Land & Business Management. Town & Country Planning earned a 19 point score at the teaching assessments and international Grade 5 for research.

Would-be solicitors should note Aberdeen's speciality in European, particularly Belgian Law. Quite a few graduates find employment in the police force.

WHERE ABERDEEN GRADUATES END UP

Health & Social Work: 24%; Education: 8%; Wholesale/Retail: 8%; Manufacturing: 4%; Financial Activities: 5%; Public Administration, Civil Service & Defence: 7%; Hotel/ Restaurant: 6%; Transport & Communications (including Telecommunications): 2%; Construction:1%; Agriculture: 2%; Mining/Oil Extracting: 9%; Personnel: 0.5%; Computer: 1.5%; Business & Management: 1%; Accountancy: 3%; Media (including Film): 1%; Legal 1%; Architecture: 0.5%; Publishing: 1%; Advertising: 0.5%.

Approximate 'graduate track' employed **72%**

Close ties with the North Sea oil industry bring engineering and geology io prominence. Degrees include Offshore Eng, Engineering with Safety & Reliability, etc, Petroleum Geology, Geology, etc. All Engineers follow a general course for the first two years. In oil extraction/mining consultancy, they capture around 13% of the job market.

SOCIAL SCENE

STUDENTS' ASSOCIATION Following the closure of the Gallowgate Student Union a few years ago, students were resigned to using a bar **(Chalkies)** at the Education faculty Hilton campus and a nightclub **(The G-Spot)**, but from this years there's to be a new student centre, housing catering and retail outlets, an internet café and a bar.

SPORT Plans for a new £23 million Regional Sports centre are also about to come to fruition. The centre will be constructed in partnership with the Local Council and Sportscotland and will offer a wide range of sporting facilities, including a full size indoor football pitch, indoor and outdoor athletics facilities, squash courts, full size hockey pitch and performance gym.

The new centre will be the base for the Sports Union's 54 affiliated clubs and Intra Mural sports programme.

TOWN Aberdeen can infuriate anyone not just wanting cheesy tunes and cheap drinks; most students love it. The pubs are numerous and range from the swanky to the wanky, with a number of solidly down to earth ones in between. There are only a few pubs near the campus, but town is overflowing. The clubs are either shiny and annoying or a dive with very sticky floors and, as long as you rotate your evenings out, there should be enough to keep you interested throughout your four years.

For the more discerning arts lovers, besides the bus to Glasgow or Edinburgh, there's the renowned **Lemon Tree** which gets decent bands and alternative theatre and, for a city its size, all the venues do well, perhaps too well for the Union.

PILLOW TALK

Halls of Residence, either on-campus or nearby, offer traditional single study bedrooms or self-catering flats. These and university-administered property in the city have trained wardens in residence. A student survey organised by accommodationforstudents.com, the UK's No 1 student accommodation website, recently rated Aberdeen top with a score of 62%.

GETTING THERE

☛ By road: from south, A92 and ring road where you'll pick up signs; from north, A96 or the A92.
☛ By rail: Edinburgh, 2:30; Dundee, 1:15; Newcastle, 4:50; London King's Cross, 7:00.
☛ By air: Aberdeen International Airport.
☛ By coach: London, 11.30; Birmingham, 12.35.

UNIVERSITY OF ABERTAY DUNDEE

The University of Abertay Dundee
Bell Street
Dundee DD1 1HG

TEL 01382 308080
FAX 01382 308081
EMAIL sro@abertay.ac.uk
WEB www.abertay.ac.uk

Abertay Dundee Students' Association
158 Marketgait
Dundee DD1 1NJ

TEL 01382 308950
FAX 01382 206569
EMAIL enquiries@abertayunion.com
WEB www.abertayunion.com

VAG VIEW

Located on a modern campus in the city centre, Abertay has four academic schools: School of Computing, the Dundee Business School, School of Science & Engineering and the School of Social & Health Sciences. Formerly, it was the Dundee Institute of Technology.

Among its research centres is the International Centre for Computing and Virtual Entertainment (IC-CAVE), the country's first dedicated research and development facility for computer games and virtual entertainment. A defining mark is that Abertay was the first university to offer Computer Games Technology as a degree, a course designed in conjunction with ex-Abertay student David Jones, the creator of Lemmings and Grand Theft Auto.

Now, too, it is a force in sport (see Academia *and* Sport *below), even though it has virtually no facilities of its own. Its own success looks like pushing it faster, and with more commitment than commentators might have supposed likely, out of its localised self-image into a more rounded extra-curricular experience that is the real bonus of a university education, and which up to now it has lacked. Drop-out rate is very high.*

FEES, BURSARIES

Fees for English: from 2006 English students will be charged £1700 p.a. for all courses at Scottish universities, except Medicine, for which they will be charged £2700 p.a. Bursaries derive from The Hardship Fund - £1000, means tested; Mature Student Bursary Fund - £1000, targeted at childcare, accommodation and travel costs; The Nine Incorporated Trades of Dundee: £4500 to fund seven scholarships for students in financial need to follow part-time masters courses in business (beneficiaries must be part-time, studying management-related degree); The Robert Reid Trust: £1000 for students from wider access background suffering financial hardship; Centenary Scholarships: £1000 applicantts must submit an essay of 1500 words; Abertay Sporting Excellence Fund - grants to students in support of approved travel and association costs for those who have achieved sporting excellence at national level.

UNIVERSITY/STUDENT PROFILE	
University since	**1994**
Situation/style	**Civic**
Student population	**4500**
Undergraduates	**4050**
- mature	**33%**
- non EU undergraduates	**5%**
- male/female	**49/51**
- non-traditional student intake	**31%**
- state school intake	**98%**
- drop-out rate	**21%, v. high**
- undergraduate applications	**Down 12%**

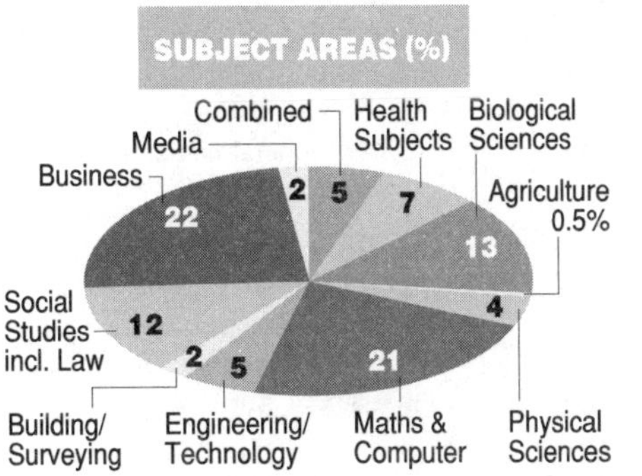

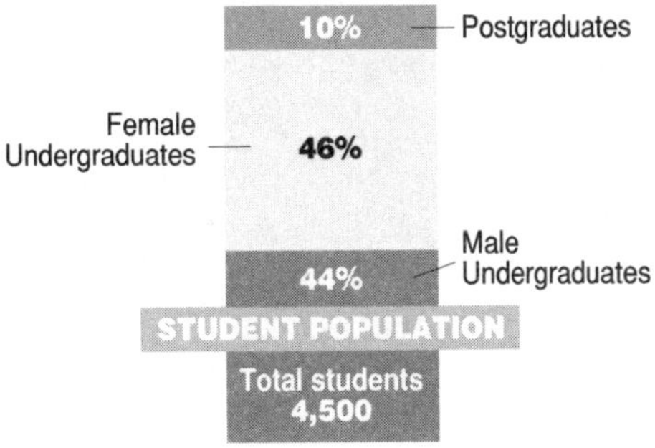

STUDENT PROFILE

There is a huge student community in Dundee, with two universities and three colleges. Abertay accounts for a high local intake and sizeable mature and overseas student populations. The uni gained the largest access partnership grant from the Scottish Funding Council last year for coming third in a British league table measuring intake of students from disadvantaged neighbourhoods. Sadly they have not managed to peg the concomitant drop-out rate, which is computed to be a depressing 21%, but maybe this is a necessary settling down period, as they look for a more diverse mix and build an extracurricular scene.

ACADEMIA & JOBS

Sports Trainers and Coaches flow strongest out of

WHERE ABERTAY GRADUATES END UP

Health & Social Work: 13%; Education: 8%; Wholesale/Retail: 15%; Manufacturing: 5%; Financial Activities: 9%; Public Administration, Civil Service & Defence: 12%; Hotel/Restaurant: 3%; Transport & Communications (incl. Telecommunications): 3%; Construction: 4%; Personnel: 1%; Computer: 5%; Business & Management: 1%; Accountancy: 2%; Media (including Film): 1%; Legal 1.5%; Architecture: 1%; Publishing: 0.5%; Sport: 7%.

Approximate 'graduate track' employed **58%**

Abertay Dundee and Leeds Met. More than 7% of graduates of Abertay are so placed. There's a new sports science laboratory for their BSc Sport Coaching & Development and Sport, Health & Exercise. And there's a canny nose for Management Science too.

Computer programmers are also rife at Abertay, and they are well set to exploit the global computer games job sector, specialist degrees finding graduates careers in companies such as Hasbro, Waddingtons, Disney and Warner Brothers. Along with an MSc in software engineering and a degree course in computer games writing, there is a BSc in computer games with Japanese, and a BA in Interactive Entertainment Design, which focuses on the new media and creative industries.

This is a specialist field and there are good resources, including a computer arts design studio, and one networked PC for every four students. They were the first uni to offer a degree in Computer Games Technology. See, too, Computing (Games Development). Specialist pathway (option) in Information Systems, open to most degrees

Nurses (SEN, SRN, RGN, etc) pour out of Abertay in similar quantity. New teaching and research facilities in the School of Social & Health Science were officially opened this August.

Consider, too, their BSc Forensic Sciences degree and BSc Forensic Psychobiology. Bestselling crime writer Ian Rankin has just opened a gruesome scene-of-the-crime-house there, and employment figures show that the department is highly productive.

Abertay is Scotland's top university for environmental research according to the national research assessment exercise. The Abertay Centre for the Environment, a £4 million research and knowledge transfer centre part-funded by the European Union, designed to provide small and medium-sized companies in Eastern Scotland with expert help in devising more environmentally-friendly products, services and processes.

There's a good reputation, too, for placing graduates from their BSc Civil Engineering and Dip HE Civil Engineering Studies, and although there's no dedicated BSc degrees in Quantity Surveying there's a strong current of graduates finding employment in this area, too. 180 points will get you in

Finally, Abertay are European Law Specialists, and have a dedicated BA European Business Law.

AT A GLANCE

ACADEMIC FILE:	
Subjects assessed	**14**
Excellent/Highly Satisfactory	**50%**
Typical entry requirements	**218 points**
Application acceptance rate	**20%**
Students-staff ratio	**17:1**
First/2:1 degree pass rate	**50%**
ACCOMMODATION GUARANTEE:	
If freshers apply by Sept. 1	**100%**
Style	**Halls, flats, houses**
En-suite	**20%**
Price range pw	**£39-£65**
City rent pw	**£38-£60**

ACADEMIC EXCELLENCE

TEACHING:	
Economics.	**Excellent**
Chemistry, Maths & Statistics, Mechanical + Manufacturing Engineering, Civil Engineering, Cellular & Molecular Biology, Psychology.	**Highly Satis.**
RESEARCH EXCELLENCE:	
*Top grades 5/5**	**None**

SOCIAL SCENE

STUDENTS' ASSOCIATION As a result of the local intake, weekends didn't used to figure much in the Students' Association ents calendar, and the extra-curricular life was fairly lame. But now they have a £6 million Student Centre, which opened its doors to students for the first time in Spring 2005, and was officially opened in October by Midge Ure. The building includes bars, a bistro, shop,

WHAT IT'S REALLY LIKE	
UNIVERSITY:	
Social Life	★★★
Campus scene	**Local, friendly**
Student Union services	**Developing**
Politics	**Activity low**
Sport	**25 clubs**
National teamposition	**73rd**
Sport facilities	**Building fast**
Arts	**Dance, music, film average; art, drama poor**
Student magazine	**None**
Nightclub	**Basement**
Bars	**Lounge/Bistro, Sports Bar, Rooftop garden**
Union ents	**Wednesdays, Playground; Fridays, Slinky**
Union clubs/societies	**35**
Most popular society	**Role-Playing**
Parking	**Adequate**
CITY:	
Entertainment	★★★★
Scene	**Pubs, good live**
Town/gown relations	**Average**
Risk of violence	**Low**
Cost of living	**Average**
Student concessions	**Good**
Survival + 2 nights out	**£60 pw**
Part-time work campus/town	**Excellent/average**

nightclub, theatre and exhibition space, as well as offices for the Students' Association and Welfare.

Daytime obsessions are satisfied this year by thirty-five clubs and societies, mainly sport.

Sport Underway is an Elite Athletes Development Programme, which supports staff and students competing at national and international level. Good variety of sports/pursuits available at the recreational level, with intra-mural activities, club sports and institutional competitions available to the progressively more serious competitor.. Besides their own gym facilities and £500,000 sports science laboratory (one of the best medicine facilities in the country), students must make do with free access to local facilities, walking distance or under 10 minutes by bus. These include Astroturf pitches and good swimming pools as well as the Caird Park Athletics Stadium, an International Sports Complex, and the Olympia, Lynch, Lochee and Douglas Sports Centres. Thera are also two premier league football clubs, the Scottish National Golf Centre, and championship courses at St Andrew and Carnoustie all within minutes of Dundee plus, in the nearby mountains, the Glenshee Ski Slopes.

With the success of their coaching degree and now the uni teams, there is an awareness of sport which will attract big investment in the future.

Town Pubs are the focus and the cost of living is low compared to Aberdeen, Glasgow and Edinburgh. See *Dundee Uni* entry.

PILLOW TALK

All freshers who return their accommodation application forms by September 1 in their year of entry are guaranteed places in self-catering halls/flats/houses, some of which are en suite.

Currently planning the construction of a 500-bed-space student village, provisionally scheduled for completion in time for the 2007/08 academic year.

GETTING THERE

- ☛ By road: M90, M85, A85, A972.
- ☛ By rail: Newcastle, 3:00; London Euston, 6:00.
- ☛ By air: Dundee Airport for internal flights; Edinburgh International Airport is an hour away.
- ☛ By coach: London, 10:05; Birmingham, 10:05; Newcastle, 6:05

UNIVERSITY OF WALES, ABERYSTWYTH

The University of Wales, Aberystwyth
Old College
King Street
Aberystwyth
Ceredigion SY23 2AX

TEL 01970 622021
FAX 01970 627410
EMAIL university-admissions@aber.ac.uk
WEB www.aber.ac.uk

Aberystwyth Guild of Students
The Union,
Penglais,
Aberystwyth
Ceredigion SY23 3DX

TEL 01970 621700
FAX 01970 621701
EMAIL sss@aber.ac.uk
WEB www.union.aber.ac.uk

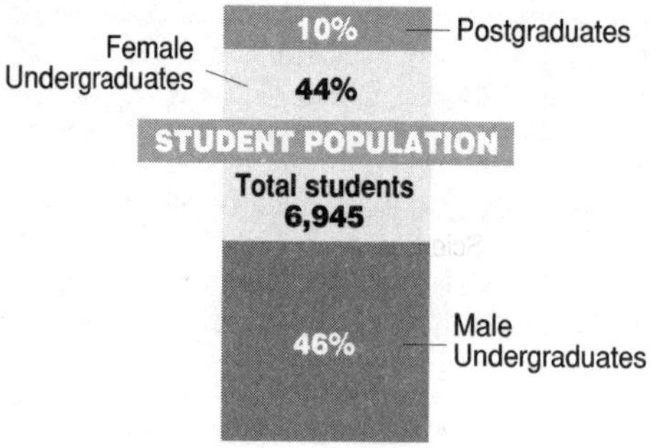

UNIVERSITY/STUDENT PROFILE	
University College since	**1872**
Situation/style	**Campus-by-the-sea**
Student population	**6945**
Undergraduates	**6263**
- mature	**12%**
- non EU undergraduates	**4%**
- male/female	**51/49**
- non-traditional student intake	**30%**
- state school intake	**93%**
- drop-out rate	**5% low**
- undergraduate applications	**Constant**

VAG VIEW

The value of the Aber experience can be measured on a number of fronts, though it may seem, at first, that it makes its appeal by satisfying a host of minority interests.

Aber's location, for example, might make it a top choice for many applicants, while others might find this small seaside town limiting. Its academic strengths are in niche areas and will, inevitably, again appeal to some and not others: countryside management, tourism, international politics, Welsh/Celtic studies, Irish, geography and earth sciences, equine science, marine & freshwater biology, information & library studies, theatre, film and TV (there's a £3.5-million centre for these).

The uni certainly has its specialisms, its very Welshness can seem daunting to some, but it isn't long before you realise that what makes Aber a good bet is the way it delivers every aspect of student services right through academia and into the social side of the Students' Guild, to meet the needs of students, whatever their expectations.

The statistics speak for themselves – a high intake of students for whose families 'going to university' is not traditional, and a low drop-out rate, which indicates that once here, they want to stay.

The statistics speak for themselves – a high intake of students for whose families 'going to university' is not traditional (30%), and a tiny drop-out rate (5%), which indicates that once here, they want to stay.

AT A GLANCE	
ACADEMIC FILE:	
Subjects assessed	**19**
Excellent	**42%**
Typical entry requirements	**290 points**
Application acceptance rate	**25%**
Student-staff ratio	**22:1**
First/2:1 degree pass rate	**63%**
ACCOMMODATION FILE:	
Guarantee to freshers	**100%**
Style	**Halls, flats, houses**
Catered	**25%**
En-suite	**10%**
Price range pw	**£42-£86**
Town rent pw	**£50-£60**

FEES, BURSARIES

UK & EU Fees for 2006 are £1200; for 2007, £3000. Entrance scholarships worth up to £3600 are available for all subjects, plus bursaries worth £2000 for selected subjects. Also other awards are available for sporty, disabled, ethnic and musical applicants, and there are special bursaries of up to £2,000 for students from low income families.

CAMPUS

'Think Wales; think west; think coast,' write Pete Liggins and Kate Glanville. 'It is then slap bang in the middle, a lovely seaside town whose two main industries are tourists in the summer and students in the closed season.'

Most of the university, including the main

Students' Guild building, is contained within the Penglais campus, set on a hill above beautiful Cardigan Bay. But there is another campus at Llanbadarn, less than a mile away and home to the Department of Information and Library Studies, the College of Further Education and the Institute of Rural Studies (a key element in Aber, they are, relative to size, the second largest graduate provider to land-based industries).

The sites are linked by a common telephone system, and there's a good bus service (if you're too lazy to walk).

STUDENT PROFILE

The student body is diverse. There are plenty of English here, though homage is paid to the Welsh hosts by their own countrymen, and the Students' Guild, or *Yr Undeb* as it translates in Welsh, plays a key role in supporting the native lingo: 'The unwritten rule is that you should accept anyone's right to speak in Welsh and not get paranoid that they are talking about you if you can't understand.'

SUBJECT AREAS (%)

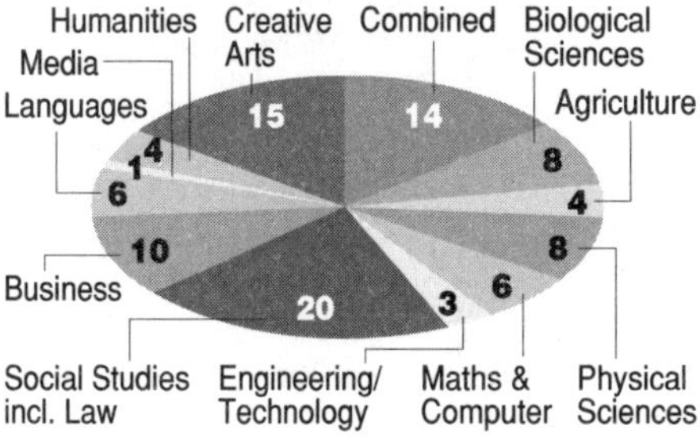

ACADEMIA & JOBS

Based at the Llanbadarn campus, less than a mile away from main Penglais, the Agriculture Institute offers the 4-year Agriculture with Animal Science cheap; there's also a 3-year option, Animal Science degree – health, nutrition, physiology, welfare of animals – but more searching at entry Animal degrees share Year One with other agric degrees.

You can also do Agriculture with Business, Marketing, or Equine Studies/Science (there's a fine Equine Centre and a new BSc Equine & Human Sport Science this year). Look, too, at the 4-year Organic Agriculture. Teaching Inspection Satisfactory, Forestry Excellent, but no Grades 5*/5 for research.

A core strength is Countryside Management (see also Agriculture & Countryside Conservation and Sustainable Rural Development). From the Institute of Rural Studies come BSc Hons Countryside Conservation/ Management or Rural Resources Mgt (HNDs are also available).

In the Institute of Geography & Earth Sciences, there's Earth Planetary & Space Science, Environmental Earth Science (and with Education), Geography (there's a well-trod pathway for cartographers), and Water Sciences (see also the Marine Biology degrees). They took 'Excellent' in the assessments.

For years Aber has had a sound reputation for research in Politics (Grade 5*/world class), and there's something of a track record for vociferous politicking among the students, albeit quite far back in the uni's history. There's a new £5 million HQ for the world-renowned Department of International Politics. For graduates today, all this opens up a sound route into the Defence industry. There is an Excellent teaching assessment and top grade for research.

Another strong research area is Drama/ Dance/Performing Arts, and this strength also comes out in the uni's employment figures. Arts

ACADEMIC EXCELLENCE

TEACHING:	
English, Info/Library Studies, Welsh, Earth Studies (incl. Enviro Science, Geography & Geology), Politics, Biological Sciences, Accounting & Finance, Economics	**Excellent**
RESEARCH:	
*Top grades 5/5**	
Celtic Studies, Politics	**Grade 5***
Drama/Dance/Performing Arts	**Grade 5**

WHERE ABERYSTWYTH GRADUATES END UP

Health & Social Work: 6%; Education: 8%; Wholesale/Retail: 15%; Manufacturing: 7%; Financial Activities: 6%; Public Administration, Civil Service & Defence: 13%; Hotel/Restaurant: 6%; Transport & Communications (including Telecommunications): 5%; Construction:1%; Agriculture: 2%; Personnel: 4%; Computer: 6%; Business & Management: 3%; Accountancy: 4%; Media (including Film): 2%; Legal 2%; Publishing: 2%; Sport: 2%.

Approximate 'graduate track' employed **56%**

WHAT IT'S REALLY LIKE

UNIVERSITY:	
Social Life	★★★★
Campus scene	**Contained, safe tight-knit & fun**
Student Union services	**Good**
Politics	**Top-up fees, Welsh education**
Sport	**44 clubs**
National team position	**79th**
Sport facilities	**Good**
Arts opportunities	**Good Arts Centre**
Student magazine	**The Courier Yr Utgom**
Student radio	**Bay Radio**
Nightclub	**The Joint**
Bars	**Bar 9, Cwrt Mawr, Outback**
Union ents	**Comedy, cheese, clubnights beach parties**
Union clubs/societies	**40**
Parking	**Good**
TOWN:	
Entertainment	★★
Scene	**Scenic seaside**
Town/gown relations	**Good**
Risk of violence	**Low**
Cost of living	**Average**
Student concessions	**Poor**
Survival + 2 nights out	**£55 pw**
Part-time work campus/town	**Good**

administrators, managers, and stage managers come out of here in number.

There is a good administrative reputation all round, it seems, with managers and administrators of one sort or another heading Aber's graduate employment list. Would-be museum archivists, curators, librarians should look with respect at their BA Museum & Gallery Studies and BA Information & Library Studies. There is a host of possible combinations. The latter, which asks only 180 points at entry, can be combined with American Studies, Art History, Drama, Fine Art, languages, Film & TV, etc, and their Museum & Gallery Studies joins the same joint honours scheme. The whole mind set in this area also favours research jobs in media and government.

But look, too, at the computer provision – software engineers dominate the employment figures. New courses include Artificial Intelligence and Robotics, Computer Graphics Vision and Games, Mobile and Wearable Computing.

Accountancy & Finance degrees are another strong employment niche. Finally, note, too, Aberystwyth's specialist LLB Human Rights and specialist European Law and Business & Commercial Law degrees. In 2005 they introduced a new degree scheme in Criminology and new Legal Practice scheme. Law students can qualify now in Aber without need to proceed to Law College, and the fact that the Law Dept allows non-Law graduates to take a 2-year full-time or 3-year part-time Senior Status law degree.

The university's library has over 700,000 volumes and 4000 current periodicals in stock, as well as CD Roms, networked databases and other electronic sources, and a campus-wide, on-line teaching and learning initiative available to all students. You will also have access to the National Library of Wales (over six million books, maps and prints).

SOCIAL SCENE

Aberystwyth is a small town but with students making up half the town's population if you are out for the night then you are bound to bump into someone you know or some one you would sooner forget. The best time in Aber is those sun shimmering days when there are half a dozen beach fire parties to chill out at.

STUDENTS' GUILD Llanbadarn has a shop and **Y Gwyllt - The Outback** (bar), entertainment facilities, discos and pool room. Back at base camp, in the Guild building (opened 2001), there's **Bar 9** and a nightclub, the **Joint**. **Cwrt Mawr Bar** is the halls pub on Penglais campus.

Unsurprisingly, this coastal resort is not a draw for big name bands, but 'live' is definitely part of the ents menu, which includes Monday comedy, karaoke; Wednesday night *Reload* and *Clasic hits*; Thursday night *Double Vision* and *£1 party*; Friday night *Flirt* and *Chart*; Saturday has a rolling program: *Beer Keller*, *School night*, and bands e.g. GLC. See www.aberguild.co.uk/ents/

Besides all this there are dance, art and drama workshop spaces, an art cinema, studio theatre and art gallery. Student media is pre-eminent with *The Courier* (*Yr Utgorn - www.thecourier.org.uk/*), *Ur Ytgorn* - Welsh language magazine, and Bay Radio. Oh, and the most active student society (one of about 50) is Indie Soc.

Political activity is high compared to many. Active Welsh Language Campaign. International Human rights and Peace and Justice issues are to the fore. The Guild offers a range of NSLP skills courses, some to help develop skills through running clubs and societies, being a course-rep, getting involved in the student media or community projects. Others are straight 'key skills' courses of the kind that employers like to see developed alongside academic achievement. Doing these add credits and commands cash prizes.

Sport It's a big thing at Aber, American Football being the current area of excellence. There are fifty acres of pitches and specialist facilities for water sports, including a boat house, an indoor swimming pool, two sports halls, an all-weather floodlit sports pitch, squash courts and indoor facilities for football, badminton, basketball, hockey and tennis. Cardigan Bay and nearby Snowdonia offer windsurfing and skiing opportunities, respectively, and there is orienteering, mountain-biking, rambling, sub-aqua and hang-gliding too.

Town On the entertainments front in town, there's a one-screen cinema, where films tend to be shown around two to three weeks after their actual release date. The flick makes up for this by being cheap, friendly and licensed – so you can have a pint while watching the film – and the programme sports some of the cheapest and best local advertising you will ever have the pleasure to view. The cinema's ethos seems to sum up the whole town; everything is more laid back here: the sun shines and things slow down; it's life without the big city stresses.

Aber is also blessed with a number of pubs – 'beyond definition; every taste should be catered for somewhere. There is something of a worrying trend, however, towards refitting and furbishing with an emphasis on American *tack*, for each of these is a true local – one in particular won't serve a pint of Guinness in less than five minutes.'

Safety is not an issue in Aberystwyth.

PILLOW TALK

Accommodation prices range from £42.20 for a twin room space (self-catering) to £86.48 for a single room in a catered residence, whereas in town, it's £50 to £60 per week energy exclusive for a single room (self-catering) with 50% retainer charged during the summer vacation. Plans are afoot for a new residence (self-catered) on the seafront in partnership with a private sector provider; the uni will manage the accommodation. All students' bedrooms linked to the internet.

GETTING THERE

☛ By road: A484 from north or south; A44 from the east.

☛ By rail: London Euston, 5 hours. Chart your route carefully or you'll end up on a slow local line through the mid-Wales countryside.

☛ By coach: London, 7:00; Newcastle, 11:00

ANGLIA RUSKIN UNIVERSITY

Anglia Ruskin University
East Road
Cambridge CB1 1PT

TEL 0845 271 3333
FAX 01245 251789
EMAIL answers@apu.ac.uk
WEB www.apu.ac.uk

Anglia Students' Union
East Road
Cambridge CB1 1PT

TEL 01223 460008
FAX 01223 417718
EMAIL r.tuckly@apsu.ac.uk
WEB www.apsu.com

VAG VIEW

The university comes out of Cambridgeshire College of Arts and Technology and the Essex Institute of Higher Education, which merged in 1989 to form Anglia Higher Education College. In 1991, this became Anglia Polytechnic, and Anglia Polytechnic University in 1992. Its recent renaming as Anglia Ruskin University dispenses with its poly status for good.

It was a very swift rise. The student population increased from 7,000 in 1992 to the current level of 28,140, making it one of the fastest growing universities in the UK.

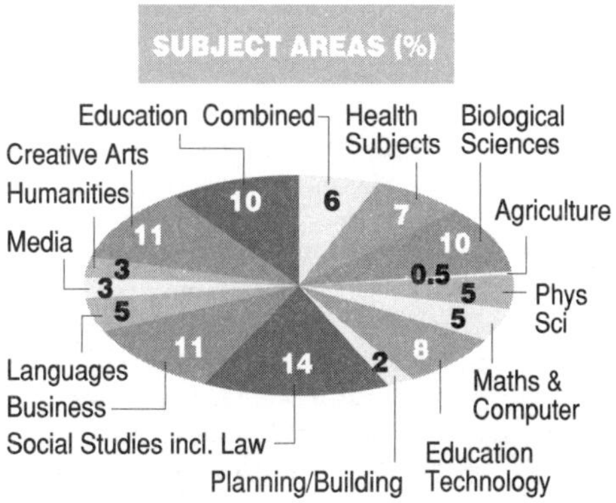

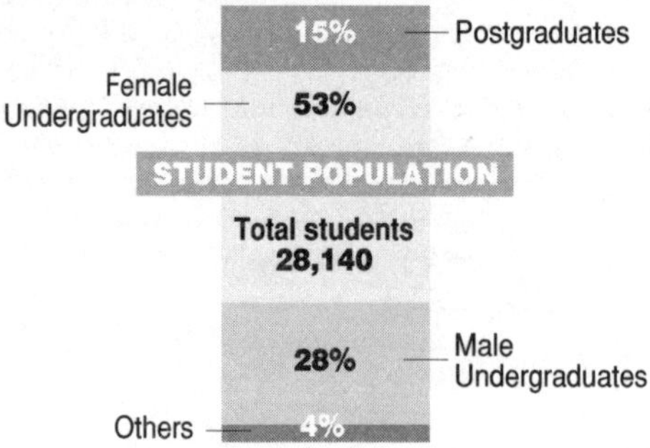

UNIVERSITY/STUDENT PROFILE	
University since	**1992**
Situation/style	**City/town campuses**
Student population	**28140**
Undergraduates	**22713**
- mature	**71%, v. high**
- non EU undergraduates	**5%**
- male/female	**34/66**
- non-traditional student intake	**36%, high**
- state school intake	**96%**
- drop-out rate	**9%**
- undergraduate applications	**Constant**

Perhaps this, together with its large non-traditional student intake (36%) and relatively under-developed student culture, led to the high drop-out rate with which we associate it, but now they have that under control (9% only), and new sports and student centres at the Chelmsford campus have further stabilised the situation.

CAMPUSES

Anglia Ruskin is based in Cambridge city centre and in Chelmsford, Essex, home since Spring 2000 to the School of Education and, since September 2002, to the Ashcroft International Business School, part-funded by the entrepreneur Lord Ashcroft KCMG, who was appointed chancellor of the university in November 2001. A new sports hall and student centre was also opened here in September 2004. This and further construction in process at Cambridge is part of a huge project to concentrate and enhance resources at the two campuses, and simplify and rationalise Anglia's once more scattered base.

FEES, BURSARIES

UK & EU Fees £3000 p.a. Bursary for students in receipt of full HE Maintenance Grant £300 p.a. Also twelve foundation scholarships, usually between £250 and £750, selective sports scholarships and bursaries in cricket, rowing, athletics and swimming.

STUDENT PROFILE

There's an eclectic mix of arty types, nurses, laddish engineers and teachers. This is not a traditional university; there are many local and mature students who come here more for Anglia's tickets into industry than anything else. Many are part-time, sponsored by employers, on employment related under-graduate and post-graduate courses.

Writes Jill Walker. 'We have lots of mature students (71%) who work hard and make everyone work harder 'cos they are the only ones to do the reading. Lots of students are local. Cambridge is far more international than Chelmsford.'

ACADEMIA & JOBS

The whole point about degree work at Anglia is that it is vocationally orientated, degrees translate into jobs. Anglia have enjoyed a tradition of working with industry for many years. Programmes are designed in collaboration with employers in the health sector, in local government, in the legal sector, in engineering, in science-based industries, in the ICT sector, in media. There are work placements available with over 100 companies, and in-company award-bearing courses for such as Marconi, Ford, and Suffolk County Council.

There are eight Schools of study: Arts &Letters, Applied Sciences, Law, Languages and Social Sciences, Ashcroft International Business School, Education, Design and Communication Systems, Healthcare Practice and Community Health and Social Studies.

Training teachers was and is one of Anglia's core commitments, but health is now just as much a defining strength. Look closely at their Pharmacy, Genetics, Health & Social Care degrees.

Well over 2500 graduate nurses pour out of our universities each year. Anglia offer Adult, Child, Learning Disabilities and Mental Health degrees. Note especially their BSc Midwifery, which dropped only one point at the assessments and has a low entry requirement

Again, Anglia is one of very few universities to offer optometry and ophthalmic .dispensing, the science of testing eyesight and prescribing corrective lenses. They have some 5% of the graduate employment market. They are also a big player in natural health therapy, which means work for some in traditional practices as well as in health promotion and natural health retail outlets. Undergraduates study acupuncture, reflexology

WHERE ANGLIA GRADUATES END UP

Health & Social Work: 15%; Education: 15%; Wholesale/Retail: 16%; Manufacturing: 8%; Financial Activities: 6%; Public Administration, Civil Service & Defence: 7%; Hotel/Restaurant: 6%; Transport & Communications (including Telecommunications): 4%; Construction:1%; Personnel: 3%; Computer: 3%; Business & Management: 3%; Accountancy: 2%; Legal 2%; Architecture: 1%; Publishing: 2%; Artistic/Literary: 1%; Sport: 1%.

Approximate 'graduate track' employed **63%**

ACADEMIC EXCELLENCE

TEACHING:	
(Rated Excellent or 17+ out of 24)	
Social Work, Music, English.	**Excellent**
Philosophy	**24**
Nursing, Theology	**23**
Psychology	**22**
Modern Languages, Molecular & Organismal Biosciences, Art & Design	**21**
Sociology, Building & Civil Eng, Politics, Health, Management/ Business/Accounting	**20**
Land/Property Mgt, Town/ Country Planning, Electron & Electrical Eng, Mechanical/ Aeronautical & Manuf Eng, Education	**19**
Communication/Media Studies, Tourism/Hospitality Mgt, History of Art	**18**
RESEARCH:	
*Top grades 5/5**	
English Language & Literature	**Grade 5**

and aromatherapy. Interesting, too, is Anglia's Vet Nursing degree at the College of West Anglia (Kings Lynn: www.col.westanglia.ac.uk).

For Law there was recently a fillip. The Legal Practice Course, which you will need to become a solicitor whether or not you undertake a law degree was adjudged Good.

21% of graduates who go into the police force come via Social Studies departments (which include Policing and many Criminology and Criminal Justice degrees as well as Law). But around 13% come via Biological Sciences (which include Psychology and Forensic Science). Anglia is one of the nation's leaders in this area, and this year sees two new degrees: Forensic Biology and Forensic Computing & Digital Investigation.

More traditional is their reputation for art and design. They offer Illustration as an integral part of the graphics course. A new Fine Art course was launched in 2004.

Look, also, at their large programme of drama degrees, which sets the scene at the **Mumford Theatre** on Cambridge Campus, and at a range of new degrees in the area of performing arts launched in 2004.

Would-be sound recordists should be aware of the HND and BSc Audio & Music Technology and various other courses combining with Music or Computer Science or Electronics or Internet Technology. There's also a new Broadcasting degree, and interesting developments in Electronics Engineering and Popular Music. This is a productive employment niche area for the uni.

Another significant graduate employment area is opened up by the Sports Science degree, which has links with the English Cricket Board's local Centre of Excellence. Anglia is among the Top 10 producers of physical training instructors in Education.

SOCIAL SCENE

STUDENTS' UNION Cambridge campus: new Helmore Building, complete with new Student Union office, music, arts and language laboratory facilities, new

AT A GLANCE

ACADEMIC FILE:	
Subjects assessed	**33**
Excellent	**73%**
Typical entry requirements	**229 points**
Application acceptance rate	**23%**
Students-staff ratio	**21:1**
First/2:1 degree pass rate	**55%**
ACCOMMODATION FILE:	
Guarantee to freshers	**100% if Anglia 1st choice**
Style	**Houses, flats**
Catered	**None**
En-suite	**Chelms,95%; Camb, 35%**
Price range pw	**£54-£93.50, Camb; £71-£74.73, Chelm**
City rent pw	**£70-£90 Camb; £60-£80 Chelm**

bar (**Kudos**) and nightclub/venue (**Academy**). Chelmsford: New Tindal building with Student Union office and new bar/venue (**Kudos**) and restaurant.

Ents - Cambridge: '*Touch*' club night on a Friday (cheesey tunes/disco); on Wednesday the union becomes pre-club venue for night out in the city's **Twenty Two - The Nightclub**; then there are open mic nights/comedy on a Tuesday. Sunday night has a quiz. They also showcase up and coming bands.

Chelmsford: *Spanked* on Tuesdays - fun and games; *Funkin' Marvellous* - Friday Night clubnight; *Rock It* - rock night on a Saturday.

Sport There are tennis courts and a multigym on the Cambridge campus, and 100 metres away the Kelsey Kerridge Sports Centre with gym and nearby swimming pool. Half a mile north of the campus there are three football pitches, a rugby pitch and a cricket square. Ex-England Cricketers Mike Gatting and Peter Such helped to launch Anglia's new sports scholarships and bursaries. Rowing crews rack their eights at Cambridge Uni's Emmanuel College Boat House. At Chelmsford Campus, there's a new sports centre.

PILLOW TALK

100% of applicants applying before release oif A level results can be guranteed uni accommodation. Chelmsford has en-suite rooms in a student village and 1 house, normally female only. Cambridge campus has halls, flats and houses, and from 2006 Sedley Court, not managed by the university.

GETTING THERE - Cambridge

☛ By road (from London): M25/J27, M11/J11, A10. From west or east: A45. From northwest: A604. From Stansted Airport: M11.

WHAT IT'S REALLY LIKE

UNIVERSITY:	
Social Life	★★★-★★★★
Campus scene:	**Diverse**
Student Union services	**Improving**
Politics	**Cambridge: interest high; Chelmsford low**
Most popular societies	**Camb: RAG; Chelm: Mission Croatia**
Sport	**55 clubs**
National team position	**109th**
Sport facilities	**Big changes**
Arts opportunities	**Drama, music exc; dance good; film, art average**
Student newspaper	**The Apex**
Radio station	**Being set up**
Bars	**Kudos**
Union ents	**New nightclubs + tie-up with town**
Union clubs/societies	**32**
Parking	**Poor. Student issue at Chelmsford**

☛ By train: London's Liverpool Street, under the hour; Nottingham, 2:30; Sheffield, Birmingham New Street, 3:00.

☛ By coach: London, 1:50; Birmingham, 2:45; Leeds, 5:00; Bristol, 5:30.

GETTING THERE - Chelmsford

☛ By road: A12, A130 or A414.

☛ By rail: London Liverpool Street, 35 mins.

☛ By air: 10 miles from the M25 and access to Stansted Airport and Heathrow.

☛ By coach: London, 1:40; Norwich, 5:00.

ASTON UNIVERSITY, BIRMINGHAM

Aston University, Birmingham
Aston Triangle
Birmingham B4 7ET

TEL 0121 359 6313
FAX 0121 333 6350
EMAIL j.r.seymour@aston.ac.uk
WEB www.aston.ac.uk

Aston Students' Guild
The Triangle
Birmingham B4 7ES

TEL 0121 359 6531
FAX 0121 333 4218
EMAIL president@aston.ac.uk
WEB www.astonguild.org.uk

VAG VIEW

Aston University, Birmingham, is a small university, independent, and slap bang in the eye of the urban vortex, yet sheltered from its sometimes violent excesses in an attractive, green-field campus bowl – a tasty morsel in Birmingham's tangled spaghetti junction. As a student said, looking out, 'The dual carriageway acts as a kind of natural barrier. You go under the flyover and suddenly, wow! It's Birmingham.'

Aston stands for science, engineering and business, the strength of particular areas of science highlighted by teaching assessments – Pharmacy (full marks), Biological Sciences and Optometry (23/24), and the teaching of the BSc Human Psychology courses scored 22/24 ahead of the uni's traditionally strong engineering departments (19, 20 and 21).

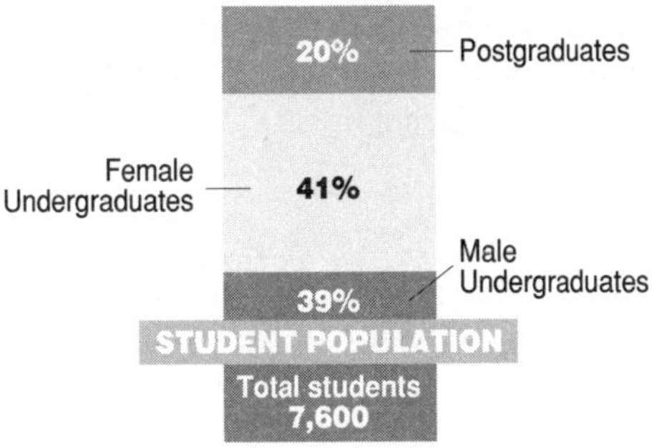

UNIVERSITY/STUDENT PROFILE	
University since	**1966**
Situation/style	**City campus**
Student population	**7600**
Undergraduates	**6100**
- mature	**8%**
- non EU undergraduates	**10%**
- male/female	**49/51**
- non-traditional student intake	**40%**
- state school intake	**92%**
- drop-out rate	**4.5%, low**
- undergraduate applications	**Constant**

Then all its business and management courses scored full marks – 24/24, and you see why they say the Business School is one of the best in Europe.

Aston is heavy on workload, extremely well resourced and geared to top-class employment by means of industry contact, study-abroad programmes, language combinations (the QAA rate German and French at 22/24) and sandwich courses. Most Aston undergraduates are on sandwich courses, and one advantage of coming here is that your friends, like you, are up for four years. Successful applicants score around 300+ points at A level, and yet the uni also manages to be ranked very high (39.5%) for widening access to those groups historically less likely to enter higher education, and the drop-out rate is low (4.5%).

Their marketing is keen. For Open Day there is a student ambassador scheme. Twenty to thirty student guides take prospective students (and often their parents) on campus tours.

FEES, BURSARIES

UK & EU Fees: £3000. Bursary for students in receipt of full HE Maintenance Grant is £750 per year for students receiving full maintenance grant, but on sliding scale - visit www.aston.ac.uk/fees. Other awards include Talented Athletes Scholarship Scheme - training, coaching and travel expenses support. Students studying engineering, modern languages and pure sciences qualify for an automatic £750 award per year. Further support is available through the Disabled Students' Allowance Scheme. There are also placement allowances and placement bursaries - £1000 to every student who undertakes a sandwich placement year. Students on their Year Abroad qualify for a £1500 award for that year. Many Aston students are also paid a salary on their placement year. The Tuition Fee for the Placement year or year abroad is £1500 for that year, so effectively there is only a small or no fee to pay for that year.

70% of students take sandwich placements as part of their degrees. 95% are paid, with average salary of £13000 per year. 10% take year abroad programmes, either working or studying. Aston have links with companies and universities in over 25 countries for year abroad placements.

CAMPUS

Aston is very defined, very straightforward, very scientific. You get what you see at The Triangle. The clean lines of this modern, high-rise, plate-glass, green-field Birmingham city campus (complete with artificial lake) brook no idle intent. And the no-nonsense efficiency far from cripples any desire for after-work pleasure, either at the

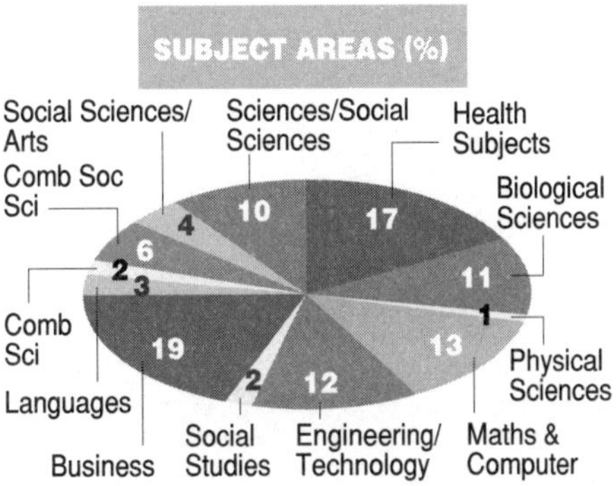

AT A GLANCE

ACADEMIC FILE:	
Subjects assessed	**17**
Excellent	**71%**
Typical entry requirements	**300 points**
Application acceptance rate	**16%**
Students-staff ratio	**16:1**
First/2:1 degree pass rate	**65%**
ACCOMMODATION FILE:	
Guarantee to freshers	**100%**
Style	**Flats**
En-suite	**35%**
Price range pw	**£57-£89**
City rent pw	**£45-£65**

Students' Guild or a walk away in the centre of Brum itself. Do not, however, be over-sensitive to the attentions that will be heaped upon you the moment you walk through the doors, for this is a determinedly close-knit community.

STUDENT PROFILE

You pick up serious suits in the business section, earnest, professional techies behind the superb lighting and sound systems in the **Guild Hall**, as they prepare for some serious Aston student live music evening (they know how to put a party together: Fusion – dance music – is the most popular society), and then there's the fresh-faced authenticity that binds it all together. Aston is the only university where someone like me will be met by union and university executives around the same table. There are no divides and there is an exuberance about their open, genuinely caring attitude, which some might find intrusive or a contra-current to the existential flow of undergraduate life, but it is in fact quite disarming. See what you think, sign up for Open Day.

Each year 150 volunteers elect to become Aston aunties and welcome freshers, on the basis that Auntie knows best. Every year they have different slogans, like 'We are family!' or 'The cream of Brum.'

For Fresher's Week they do city tours, campus tours, supermarket trips (?!), cultural crawls, canal cruises, fun things like go-karting and paintballing, an Alton Towers trip, and the departments all have other things organised, library visits and so on.

'We've all been out manning the car parks in the pouring rain, and the arrivals this year have been fantastic. I have been watching with admiration this year, as aunties go up to cars with a "Welcome, my name's so-and-so, I'm an auntie!" That's your first impression of Aston. We had a classic quote yesterday from a student whose parents had just left: "Oh, I haven't even been here for twelve hours yet and I feel at home already!"'

If any other union bod had said this I wouldn't have believed it. It's the sort of unlikely... but at Aston what you see really *is* what you get. You can thrust, you can parry, but 'you won't hear a thing against Aston from us,' admitted one of the Guild sabbaticals. The attitude ensures one of the friendliest student environments in the UK.

ACADEMIA & JOBS

Broadly, Aston consists of three faculties: Life & Health Sciences; Engineering & Applied Science (Civil Engineering, Chemical Eng. and Applied Chemistry, Mechanical & Electrical Eng., Electronic and Applied Physics, Computer Science and Applied Maths); and Management Languages & European Studies. The latter includes the Aston Business School and School of Languages and European Studies. Note that Spanish is now offered in addition to French and German, and English Language is now also an option.

There are very good degrees dedicated to Optometry, the science of testing eyesight and prescribing corrective lenses. Nationally, more than 450 graduates become opticians each year. The leader in the field is Aston with around 27% of the graduate market. If you have your eyes tested in England there's a good chance that it will be an Aston graduate doing it. Teaching inspection 23. Grade 5 for research, that's international standing. See also the NHS-funded, 4-year professional health care degree in Audiology.

Aston also shines jobs-wise in the Pharmacy department, turning around 12% of its graduates into fully fledged pharmacists. The MPharm will take 5 not the usual 4 years if you elect to come in on a Foundation course rather than make the 300-point requirement at A level. They got full marks in the teaching assessments, one better than The School of Pharmacy in London.

Psychologists are another breed made by Aston better than by most. The programmes are various: BSc Human Psychology has a 4-year sandwich version and a Foundation course 'Year Zero' option. Look, too at Psychology with Management.

The Business School is one of the largest in Europe and one of only a handful in the world to have triple accreditation from the major European (EQUIS), American (AACSB) and MBA benchmarks of quality for business education. Related courses tackle the behavioural side of enterprise, such as Organisational Studies, Human Psychology and Psychology with Management.

The Aston Business School is a vital part of what this uni is all about. There's a Grade 5 for

ACADEMIC EXCELLENCE

TEACHING:	
(Rated Excellent or 17+ out of 24)	
Pharmacy, Businesss & Management	**24**
Biological Biosciences, Optometry	**23**
German, French, Psychology	**22**
Electronic Engineering	**21**
Civil Engineering	**20**
Chemical Eng, Maths	**19**
RESEARCH:	
*Top grades 5/5**	
Optometry, General Engineering, Business & Management, European Studies	**Grade 5**

research and full marks (24 points) at assessment. Note the 4-year sandwich BSc International Business & Economics (could add on French, Spanish or German), the International Business & Management degree, which offers the possibility of placement across the world. Look too at the 5-year sandwich Int. Foundation in Business/Business BScs. There are also Business Computing options, and a whole raft of Business Administration combinations, with European Studies for instance.

Around 5% of Aston's graduates are among the 4,500-odd graduates going into Banking each year, and the uni figures impressively in management consultancy, too. Another 5%+ go into the Transport business. Three BSc degrees are relevant here: Transport Management, Transport Planning, Transport & Environmental Planning.

Aston's Business School also dominate graduate employment in the areas of marketing and market research. The BSc Marketing (300 points), which comes also in a Joint Hons programme with Languages and Biochemistry – nice niche area).

And a word in favour of their electronic engineering and computer provision. For would-be software engineers on the smaller-uni ticket there are three key unis, Essex, UMIST and Aston.

They had the 4th highest percentage of graduates entering graduate level employment or further study in 2005, and consistently (over 20 years) the highest or 2nd highest percentage of graduates entering employment 6 months after graduating.

WHAT IT'S REALLY LIKE

UNIVERSITY:	
Social Life	★★★★
Campus scene	**Lively, caring suits & techies**
Student Union services	**Good**
Politics	**Interest low**
Sport	**40 clubs**
National team position	**97th**
Sport facilities	**40 clubs**
Arts opportunities	**Dance, music excellent; drama good**
Student newspaper	**The Aston Times**
Nightclub	**Guild Hall**
Bars	**Einstein's, Blue Room, The Loft**
Union ents	**Flux, Insomnia, Revive, Fondue, School Daze, Ukg**
Union clubs/societies	**82**
Most popular societiy	**Fusion (dance music), Islamic**
Parking	**No**
CITY:	
Entertainment	★★★★★
Scene	**Excellent**
Town/gown relations	**Average**
Risk of violence	**Off-campus high**
Cost of living	**High**
Student concessions	**Excellent**
Survival + 2 nights out	**£75 pw**
Part-time work campus/town	**Average/excellent**

SOCIAL SCENE

Students' Guild The Guild offers 3 bars, **Einstein's** (basement with big screen and two man-size pool tables), the **Blue Room** (a café by day) and **The Loft**. Then there's the **Guild Hall**, which, together with the Blue Room, gives a max building capacity of 1150. There are five events a week: house, trance; 70s, '80s funk & disco; '80s, early '90s; garage, R&B; cheese & commercial dance. They get their uni tour live acts too.

> ***Aston is mainly for science, engineering and business. It is very defined, very straightforward, very scientific. You get what you see at The Triangle, and students do seem to enjoy themselves.***

Ents is not the only extra-curricular focus. There are masses of sports clubs and societies on offer, with Islamic gaining ground this last year.

WHERE ASTON GRADUATES END UP

Health & Social Work: 17%; Education: 3%; Wholesale/Retail: 19%; Manufacturing: 11%; Financial Activities: 9%; Public Administration, Civil Service & Defence: 4%; Hotel/Restaurant: 1%; Transport & Communications (including Telecommunications): 6%; Construction: 2%; Personnel: 2%; Computer: 5%; Business & Management: 4%; Accountancy: 2%; Legal 1%; Advertising, 1%; Architecture: 1%; Publishing: 2%; Media, 0.5%.

Approximate 'graduate track' employed **72%**

Media-wise there's the student magazine, *Helios*; there was a Radio Society which, for whatever reason, disbanded. 'We are a small uni and the same people are involved in putting on events and entertainments would be doing the radio or TV. The Drama Club is very active; we have eighty clubs and societies altogether.'

Sport New University sports facilities include £300,000 all-weather floodlit pitch (off campus) and extension to Fitness Centre. On campus there are two sports centres – Woodcock (with swimming pool) and Gem Sports Hall (with a synthetic floodlit pitch), while out of the city the Recreation Centre spans 95 acres. There is slim evidence of national standards, it is sport for everyone; 'relaxed' is the word used, although the options are varied enough to include American Football.

Town See, page 62, below: *Student Birmingham* .

PILLOW TALK

Self catering flats and houses, all on campus, all within 2 mins walk of each other and 5 mins walk of all other campus facilities (Students' Union/Guild, Departments, Sports Centres, Library etc). Flats vary in size from 4-12 students sharing. Freshers tend to be in larger flats. Convenient, friendly, safe. Internet Access in all accommodation. All prices include bills. Telephones in all flats.

Price range pw is £57 for standard, £89 en suite for forty weeks, including all bills and cleaning. Plans are afoot for additional on-campus, en-suite accommodation for 2007-8.

GETTING THERE

☛ By road: M6/J6, A38M 3rd exit, then first exit at Lancaster Circus roundabout.
☛ By rail: Bristol Parkway, Sheffield, 1:30; London Euston, 1:40; Liverpool, Manchester, 2:00; Leeds, 3:00. New Street 12 mins' walk from campus.
☛ By air: Birmingham International Airport.
☛ By coach: London, 2:40; Bristol, 2:00.

UNIVERSITY OF WALES, BANGOR

University of Wales, Bangor
Gwynedd LL57 2DG

TEL 01248 382017
FAX 01248 370451
EMAIL admissions@bangor.ac.uk
WEB www.bangor.ac.uk

Bangor Students' Union
Gwynedd LL57 2TH

TEL 01248 388031
FAX 01248 388020
EMAIL undeb@undeb.bangor.ac.uk
WEB www.undeb.bangor.ac.uk

VAG VIEW

Bangor started life on 18 October, 1884, in an old coaching inn – a promising beginning, particularly as half the student intake was female, which was swimming against the tide in 1884.

Today Bangor is almost two-thirds female and, while no overly demanding at entry (avg 270 points), has risen to become one of the best unis in the UK.

Don't take it just from me, look at the rigorous standards of teaching (see our Academic Excellence box), and the high level of non-traditional student intake (31%) matched by a low level of drop-outs (6%). Clearly, value added is high, and the word is out – applications are again up this year.

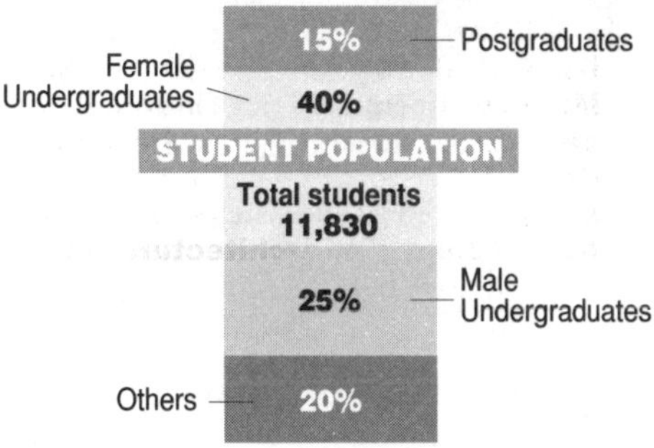

FEES, BURSARIES

In 2006, home students will pay up to £1200; from 2007/8 up to £3000 p.a. Permanent Welsh residents may then be eligible for an annual £1800 fee grant. There'll be bursaries for students in receipt of full HE Maintenance Grant, amounts to be confirmed. There are also sport and academic scholarships, most around £500 p.a. – £30000-worth of the latter with geographical or subject criteria. They'll also be introducing a number of bursary awards for 2006 and 2007 entry. See www.bangor.ac.uk

CAMPUS

Setting the whole deal in context for the semi-final of University Challenge, Jeremy Paxman described the natural environs of Bangor – just across the Menai Strait from the Isle of Anglesey – as 'one of the most beautiful locations of any British university, between the beaches of Anglesey and the mountains of Snowdonia.'

North Wales is different from the rest of Wales: they're the real Welsh up here and Welsh is still the natural language over much of Gwynedd. It is a small, town-size 'city' community that manages not to protest at the regular incursion of a student population which now totals, in all, some 11,000 students, and more than doubles the local population at the start of each term. Relations with the natives couldn't be better, however. Perhaps it has something to do with living between spectacular, inspirational Snowdonia and the sea. While not exactly a campus university, all the buildings, with the exception of the School of Ocean Sciences, which is a few miles from the Menai Bridge, are within walking distance of one another.

It is also cheap and safe.

STUDENT PROFILE

This is a large Welsh population, large and largely female, and a sizeable mature population. They have a vibrant volunteer community and one of the UK's largest and most established peer guide/'student mentoring' programme, ensuring a fine welcome and continuing student care.

Cutting-edge cool it is not. However, if you come to Bangor, you'll fall in love with the surroundings. You may be sporty, interested in outward bound perhaps, maybe a classical music lover (there is an international reputation for music here), but, as one student put it, 'you'll probably find more night life in a tramp's vest.' Fortunately for those interested in the tramp's vest department, the Students' Union is currently more active than it has ever been.

There's a healthy overseas contingent, too, and the uni goes out of its way to help them settle. The International Welfare Unit assists and advises, and orientation days are arranged to help international students get acclimatised to the country. The ELCOS (English Language Courses for Overseas Students) Unit provides instruction for those whose language skills need polishing. There's also an organisation (called 'Shekina') which offers help to wives and husbands of students and organises a range of activities, including English language courses.

For all freshers, Bangor has one of the largest welcoming schemes of any university, with second and third year students involved in a mentoring scheme to help new students settle in during their first weeks at University.

ACADEMIA & JOBS

First, note the very high level of inspection results and research garlands in our *Academic Excellence* box (page 52). It stands to reason that all those subjects are worth studying here.

Some 14% of graduates become primary school teachers, a vital percentage of the overall graduate output destined for Education, which also includes secondary teachers and higher education lecturers. But Education is not the largest subject area out of which degree qualifiers emerge from this uni.

That is given to Biological Science – roughly a fifth of graduate output, which produces an array of employment from lecturers to laboratory

UNIVERSITY/STUDENT PROFILE

University College since	**1884**
Situation/style	**Rural bliss**
Student population	**11830**
Undergraduates	**7691**
- mature	**30%**
- non EU undergraduates	**5%**
- male/female	**39/61**
- non-traditional student intake	**31%**
- state school intake	**93%**
- drop-out rate	**6%**
- undergraduate applications	**Up 9%**

SUBJECT AREAS (%)

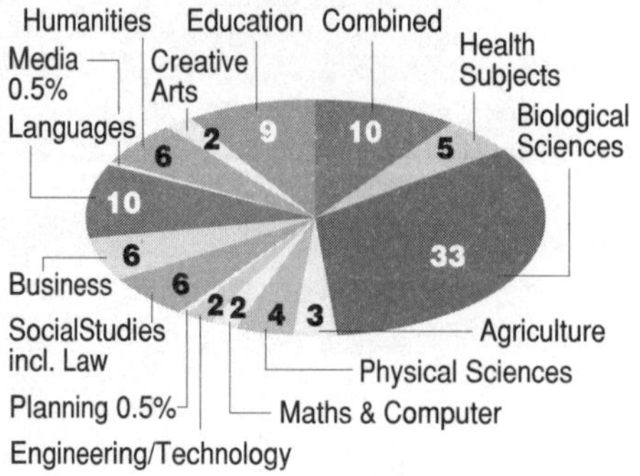

technicians, biologists to clinical and educational psychologists, chemists to animal health nurses and RSPCA inspectors, market research and business analysts to army officers, and physical training instructors to zoologists. Bangor are graduate employment leaders in zoology.

Biological Science courses range through Biology, Biomedical and Biomolecular Sciences, a series of Marine and Ocean Sciences (note the popular joint honours option of Marine Biology and Zoology, and unusual courses such as Marine Chemistry). New is a BSc Chemistry with Biomolecular Sciences.

A major new £3.5 million cancer research centre has just opened at the University. The North West Cancer Research Fund Institute at the University's School of Biological Sciences will conduct fundamental research into the causes of cancer.

Then come the Zoology degrees (since 2004, with Conservation; also Marine Zoology; and a new BSc Marine Vertebrate Zoology is currently up for approval), and the BSc Psychology degrees (with such as Computing, Sport Science – rated 2nd in the UK, Neuropsychology, Clinical and Child Language elements). They have a world-class Grade 5* research rating for Psychology.

The uni is also successful in finding graduates employment in the areas of community and youth work and social work. A new BA Honours Social Work course is planned for 2005 entry. In a similar area, look at a new postgraduate diploma in Occupational Therapy. See, too, the BA Health and Social Care degrees, BA Psychology (also with Community Development) and Sociology. Also, Bangor is a big producer of hospital staff nurses (SEN) and, through the BSc Diagnostic Radiography and Imaging, medical radiographers. A £3.5M Cancer Research Institute is in the making here, too.

Another defining element is the Agriculture & Forestry Department, rated international Grade 5 for research. Although forestry is fairly limited employment-wise, Bangor is the most productive nationally. They have some interesting specialities, including Conservation & Forest Ecosystems, but also the traditional degree or Agroforestry or Forestry. There's an 'Excellent' for teaching and an international Grade 5 for research.

Environmental degrees (Chemistry, Conservation, Forensics, Science: the uni is ideally situated for the study of all things environmental, and there is a new £5 million building dedicated to that) draw the picture ever more clearly, and environmental officers are a definitive part of Bangor's graduate employment profile.

The development in 2004 of Law combination degrees - with Accounting & Finance, Business Studies, Criminal Justice, and Law with Social Policy and a unique Law with Environmental Conservation - continues this year with French, German, Italian, Spanish and Welsh.

ACADEMIC EXCELLENCE

TEACHING:	
Chemistry, Welsh, Music, Ocean Sciences, Theology, Psychology, Forest Sciences, Biological Sciences.	**Excellent**
RESEARCH:	
*Top grades 5/5**	
Psychology, Welsh	**Grade 5***
Agric & Forest Sciences, Accountancy & Finance, Sport/Health/Exercise Sciences, Music	**Grade 5**

A new £10 million Business and Management Centre is currently underway to house Bangor's School for Business and Regional Development, to be equipped with state-of-the-art facilities for over 500 students.

There's also a reputation for training museum archivists, curators, librarians. They come from across the board – humanities, languages, biological sciences and Law. There's also a preponderance of translators sufficient to put the Language Department among the Top 10 nationally. Note the new BA Music and Modern Languages (Joint Honours).

Unique is the three languages degree (choose from combinations of French, German, Italian, and Spanish). Their Multi-Media Language Centre is a pioneer of digital language-laboratory technology. True to the uni's roots in North Wales, they offer degrees in a number of subjects through the medium of Welsh, as well as informal tuition in Welsh in various subjects. Naturally, too, they scored a Grade 5* for research into the mother tongue.

A notable feature is the special provision for students with disabilities – study support centres which house CCTVs, scanners and braille embossers. They also have induction loops and infra-red transmission equipment to help those with hearing difficulties, and ramps and lifts in the main buildings to help those with mobility problems. Their Dyslexia Unit is internationally renowned.

AT A GLANCE

ACADEMIC FILE:	
Subjects assessed	**20**
Excellent	**45%**
Typical entry requirements	**270 points**
Application acceptance rate	**22%**
Student-staff ration	**17:1**
First/2:1 degree pass rate	**56%**
ACCOMMODATION FILE:	
Guarantee to freshers	**100%**
Style	**Halls**
Catered	**15%**
En-suite	**40%**
Price range pw	**£48-£72**
Town rent pw	**£40**

SOCIAL SCENE

STUDENTS' UNION The uni has made a £1-million investment in the Students' Union. There's a 1,000-capacity, award-winning **Amser/Time** nightclub (open to the public and students at a discount) and two bars: the 390-capacity **Main** (**Prif Far**) and the 100-capacity basement bar, **Jock's**. Prices are very low.

Wednesday is *Trash @* Main (rock, metal, indie), Friday is Racubah, Saturday Elevate (hard house & hard trance); Friday is *Sugar & Spice @* Amser/Time (chart hits). Otherwise, national tours – Cream, NME, orange, DJs: Rob Tissera, Mr Scruff, Scratch Perverts, Stanton Warriors, Norman J. Live music has brought Robert Plant, Toploader, Weetus, hundred Reasons, Funeral for a Friend, Lamarr, Dreamteam, etc.

It has risen to become one of the best universities academically... and, even if you accept a student's claim that you'd find more night life in a tramp's vest, Bangor, because of its geographical position, makes a plausible case.

There are twenty-five student societies – Community Action (student volunteers) is probably the most popular, mountain walking and football close behind. There's a Welsh-language student magazine called *Y ddraenen* and an English newspaper, *Seren*. Note also the new BA Journalism & Media Studies this year.

Political activity is high, but centred on...Welsh language recognition. The drama soc, Rostra, is very popular. The uni has its own professional chamber ensemble and student symphony orchestra, chamber choir, opera group, chamber ensembles and concert band.

SPORT Rock climbing, paragliding, mountain biking, canoeing, sailing, and surfing are available as well as the usual team sports – rugby, hockey and football. Women's Rugby is traditionally strong. 1500+ participate weekly in sporting activities. You will benefit from a Lottery-sourced, £4.5 million extension to the sports hall. There's great emphasis on sport, thanks to the Sports Science and PE courses. Outward-bound activities, such as mountaineering, are especially popular, as are rowing, sailing and canoeing. Sports scholarships are worth £1500 p.a.

TOWN 'As far as towns go, we ain't no Liverpool or Birmingham,' writes Becki Thurston, 'but that doesn't mean we're pants and boring. Although it's designated a city, it's diddy. The bonus is that we

WHERE BANGOR GRADUATES END UP

Health & Social Work: 14%; Education: 23%; Wholesale/Retail: 9%; Manufacturing: 7%; Financial Activities: 6%; Public Administration, Civil Service & Defence: 10%; Hotel/Restaurant: 4%; Transport & Communications (including Telecommunications): 3%; Construction:1%; Agriculture: 2%; Personnel: 3%; Business & Management: 2%; Accountancy: 0.5%; Media (including Film): 1.5%; Legal 0.5%; Publishing: 1%; Sport: 2%.

take over. There's nowhere doesn't feel like home. Wherever you go, wherever you are, you'll bump into someone you know. Trouble is, people know who you snogged last night, even before you've sobered up enough to realise!'

A positive advantage of Bangor's size is that competition between pubs etc. is strong. So prices are low. Besides pubs - Irish, Wetherspoons, **Fat Cat** and late-night pub/clubs **Joot** and **Joop**, you'll find café bars, restaurants (Spanish, Italian, Greek, Chinese, Indian), and two more nightclubs - **Octagon** and **Bliss**.

For arts lovers the city offers a varied mix of classical concerts; there are regular visits from such as the BBC National Orchestra for Wales and foreign orchestras, and the **Centre for Creative & Performing Arts**.

PILLOW TALK

A major re-development includes a large-scale building project on the Ffriddoedd accommodation site, which will see more en-suite accommodation being built. Nice, confident touch in offering summer-vacation halls accommodation to prospective undergraduates - with or without parents - to get a taste of the place. One hall exclusively for Welsh speakers.

GETTING THERE

☛ By road: A5, A55, A487; 90 minutes from M56.
☛ By rail: London Euston, 4:00; Birmingham New Street, 3:00; Manchester Oxford Road, 2:30; Liverpool Lime Street, 2:15.
☛ By coach: London, 8:00; Leeds, 6:15.

WHAT IT'S REALLY LIKE

UNIVERSITY:	
Social Life	★★★★
Campus scene	**Outdoor, cheap, close-knit, Welsh, and full of life**
Student Union services	**Good**
Politics	**Internal**
Sport	**40 clubs**
National team position	**74th**
Sport facilities	**Good**
Arts opportunities	**OK**
Student newspaper	**Seren, Y ddraenen**
Student radio	**Storm FM**
Nightclub	**Amser/Time**
Bars	**Main/Prif Far, Jock's Bar**
Union ents	**Live acts, DJs, comedy**
Union clubs/societies	**25**
Most active societies	**Mountain walking, Football, Community Action**
Parking	**Good**
CITY:	
Entertainment	★★
Scene	**Scenic, fun**
Town/gown relations	**Average-poor**
Risk of violence	**Low**
Cost of living	**Low**
Student concessions	**OK**
Survival + 2 nights out	**£30-£50 pw**
Part-time work campus/town	**Good**

UNIVERSITY OF BATH

The University of Bath
Claverton Down
Bath BA2 7AY

TEL 01225 384220
FAX 01225 386675
EMAIL t.trueman@bath.ac.uk
WEB www.bath.ac.uk

Bath Students' Union
Claverton Down
Bath BA2 7AY

TEL 01225 826612
FAX 01225 444061
EMAIL union@bath.co.uk
WEB www.bathstudent.com

VAG VIEW

Bath is a small science and business-based university with a huge, world-wide reputation. There's no arts provision, yet it's first choice for many capable of Oxbridge, and as there are no arts undergraduates, the techies like it because they get to tread the boards rather than be banished backstage merely to fiddle with the wires.

Value is most obviously visible in the high teaching and research assessments, in its sports record, facilities and coaching expertise, and in its highly focused graduate employment record, bolstered by its language

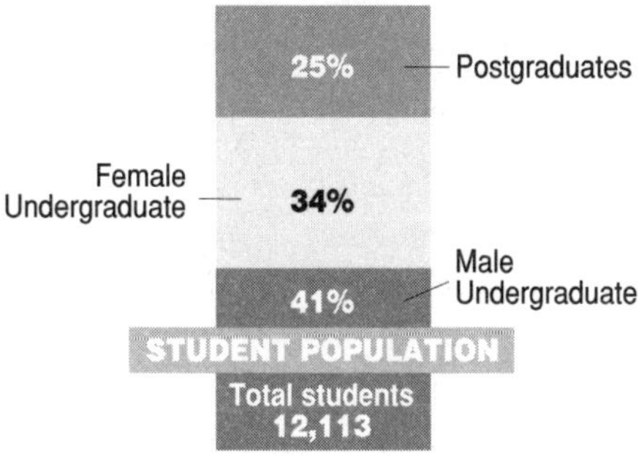

courses, IT facility and a very good sandwich-course provision.

CAMPUS

The self-contained campus is situated 2 miles south-east of the city, up Bathwick hill. City and uni are linked by a special bus service – 'not always reliable, but quick, cheap and easy, and, like some people I know, it runs till 3 am most nights,' I was told.

Reports Ally Bradshaw: 'You would not be alone in assuming that the University of Bath would reflect some of the city's elegance in appearance. A trip to the main campus therefore would leave you feeling disappointed, with teaching taking place around a central parade of purely functional, concrete buildings dating from the 1960s.'

A central building houses the Library and Learning Centre (with 24-hour access), the Careers Office and Students' Union, all set around The Parade, a walkway not unlike a shopping precinct. The concrete and golden Bath stone buildings are unique, but, as I discovered, on a wet, wintry, foggy day they do not look their best.

Writes Ally, 'The only redeeming feature is the lake, located next to the Parade Bar so that you can enjoy an idyllic view whilst having lunch or getting drunk.

'Campus can feel somewhat remote from the city,' admits Ally, 'and by the end of the first year I think it will come as a welcome relief to move out of halls and into town. Weekends are very quiet, but the uni is going some way to atone for this by loaning out board games free of charge (Scrabble tonight – yes!).'

Bath is also constructing £200-million campus in Swindon to accommodate 8000 students. It is a natural development from the college they opened there in 2000, designed to respond to local needs. The new uni, the only one for 30 miles, will nuzzle up to Queen Margaret Hospital in the town and specialise in healthcare subjects, as well as traditional strengths – engineering, biotechnology and management.

FEES, BURSARIES

UK & EU Fees, 2006/7: £3000 p.a. Bursary for students in receipt of full HE Maintenance Grant, £1500. If in receipt of a partial HE Maintenance Grant, there's a bursary of between £300 and £1200. For the past 25 years, Bath has offered sports scholarships. Also on offer are scholarships for students of chemistry, chemical engineering, modern languages and European studies.

STUDENT PROFILE

Bath students are highly focused. 'Students are generally dedicated to their work,' accepts Ally Bradshaw, 'especially the mathematicians and architects, reflecting to some extent the competition for places on all courses.'

Writes Anna Kennedy: 'Although the uni is small and not as socially diverse as some larger universities, it is not claustrophobic and it feels like a community. You get to know everyone really quickly and don't feel anonymous like you might in a bigger university.' First-year student Ally agrees it is a welcoming place 'The university is small, friendly and "bonded". There is a definite community feel around campus and everyone looks out for each other.'

ACADEMIA & JOBS

Bath concentrate on seven areas – Sciences, Social Sciences (Economics, Politics, Psychology, Social Policy, Social Work, Sociology), Engineering, Pharmacy & Pharmacology, Business, Languages, and Sport. There's a top-notch record from inspections, see *Academic Excellence* box (page 57). A Department of Computer Science opened in October 2001.

Bath's impact on the employment market for engineers is impressive to say the least. Year on year they come high up in the Top 10,

UNIVERSITY/STUDENT PROFILE

University since	**1966**
Situation/style	**City campus**
Student population	**12113**
Undergraduates	**9052**
- mature	**13%**
- non EU undergraduates	**9%**
- male/female	**55/45**
- non-traditional student intake	**18.5% low**
- state school intake	**77%**
- drop-out rate	**3%, low**
- undergraduate applications	**Constant**

SUBJECT AREAS (%)

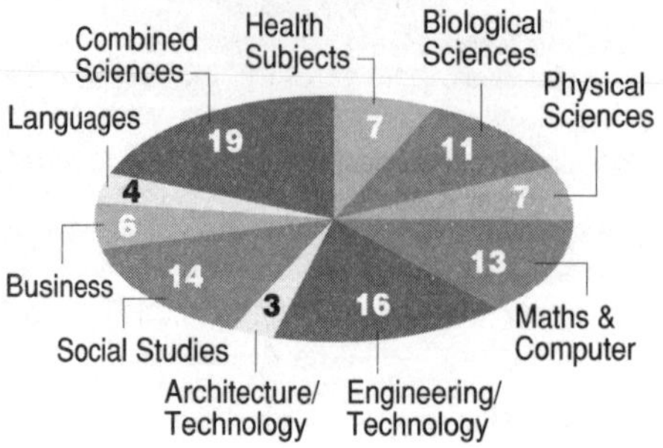

offering 4/5-year MEng Aerospace, Automotive, Mechanical, Manufacturing and Innovation/ Engineering Design degrees, with French or German, and useful sandwich possibilities. Teaching assessments range from 20 to Excellent in Engineering. Mechanical, Aeronautical and Manufacturing Engineering took world-class Grade 6* ratings at the research assessments. Now, they have won a £1 million grant to establish the Bath Institute for Complex Systems, which brings together scientists from maths, statistics, engineering, physics and biology to consider issues that will benefit areas such as aviation, communications technology and the oil industry.

Their language facility in the Humanities & Social Sciences faculty, which spills into other areas (Management included – see their excellent International management degrees), assures them a strong line in graduate translators and interpreters, even if it scored only 19 at assessment.

They lead the way, too, in guiding Electrical Engineering graduates into Telecommunications. Assessments again scored only 20 points out of 24, but the acid test is employment and employers love their graduates. Three new research laboratories costing over £1 million place the uni at the forefront of telecommunications, space and radio engineering research.

Defence, in particular the Royal Air Force, pick up graduates from this key area of Bath's academic programme. The Psychology & Communications Engineering tie-up holds intriguing possibilities.

Again, more than 4% of their graduates (engineering, science and computer science) become software engineers. They are strong, too, in placing computer programmers and systems analysts. Look at their BSc Computer Science, Computer Info Systems and Computer Software Theory – all 3/4 years depending on whether you opt for an industrial placement. Look, too, at the Physics with Computing 4-year sandwich.

Another key area is Architecture. Becoming an architect is a 6-year commitment, a 3-year BA Hons, a year practice placement followed by a 2-year BArch. See their 4-year sandwich BSc/Arch in the Faculty of Engineering & Design. There's an international Grade 5 award for research.

In science, Bath regularly find more physicists jobs than most other unis, and full marks at the teaching assessments give confidence. Entry for around BBC. They are among the top providers, too, for would-be biologists, and there's a Grade 5 for research here. Look also at the Chemistry degrees with Management or Drug Discovery add-ons. For pharmaceutical manufacture and pharmacy, Bath also leads, this time with a world-class Grade 5* for research. Pharmacology comes as BSc in 3 years or as a MPharmacol in a 4-year sandwich.

Accountants and stockbrokers stream from the mathematical sciences and management areas. Finance, accountancy and business management are key strengths – around a quarter of the graduate employment picture. Meanwhile, the BSc Sociology with Human Resource Management gives them a certain dominance in personnel.

Strangely, Bath have among the best sports facilities in the country, but deliver small numbers into the sector. I was told. 'The sports science course we now offer is really competitive; there are literally thousands of applicants,' but employment leaders are Loughborough, Leeds Met, Bucks Chilterns (half the size of Loughborough), St Martin's (smaller again), St Mary's (smaller even than St Martin's), Liverpool John Moores, Surrey Roehampton, Southampton Solent, Brunel and Brighton.

Foundation Degrees are now offered in Addictions Counselling, Computing, Digital Media Arts (Multimedia), Digital Media Arts (Moving Image Production), Youth Work and Sport - Sports Performance or Coaching or Sports Therapy) or Health and Fitness Training.

Students with disabilities and learning difficulties now have free access to state-of-the-art laptops that cater specifically for their learning needs. The Assistive Technologies Initiative (ATI) will enable students at the University to borrow from a pool of 64 laptops containing software that can do everything from translating speech into written text, to helping people 'map' their thoughts and ideas. The University currently has 376 students who are registered as having a disability or learning difficulty - 224 with dyslexia - all of whom will be eligible for ATI support.

The proportion of employed Bath graduates in

professional jobs is particularly impressive: 46% compared with the national average of 25%. Graduate employers target the uni, with 320 visiting in 2004-5 for recruitment purposes.

Many students do a work placement (either one year or two periods of six months) as part of their degree programme, and help getting good vacation experience is provided by the Careers Advisory Service.

Vectura, a company established by academics at the uni, is among the top four university spin-off companies in the UK. Now, a new Student Enterprise Centre gives students free access to the training, support and resources they need to turn their business ideas into reality. Based in the Students' Union, the Centre facilities include a suite of five computers, meeting rooms and two dedicated business support professionals as part of the Student Enterprise Team.

ACADEMIC EXCELLENCE

TEACHING:

(Rated Excellent or 17+ out of 24)

Mechanical Engineering.	**Excellent**
Architecture, Business & Management Studies, Social Policy & Administration	
Physics, Maths, Biosciences	**24**
Politics, Economics Pharmacology.	
Education, Sport	**23**
Civil Engineering	**22**
Materials Technology	**21**
Chemical Engineering, Electric & Electron Eng	**20**
Modern Languages, Sociology	**19**

RESEARCH:

Special 6 status:*	
Applied Maths, Mech, Aero, Manuf Engineering	**Grade 6***
*Top grades 5/5**	
Pharmacy, Applied Maths, Mechanical/Aeronautical/ Manufacturing Eng,	**Grade 5***
Biological Sciences, Pure Maths, Statistics, Built Environment, Social Policy, Business/Management, European Studies, Education	**Grade 5**

STUDENT SCENE

Students' Union 'Freshers' Week is amazing,' reports Anna, 'and really helps you meet people. There's a different theme every night culminating with the infamous Toga Party, a rare opportunity to go out in public wearing just a bed sheet! The Pub Crawl is another highlight – the mission: to visit twenty of Bath's finest drinking establishments and well, get drunk!

'Following Freshers Week, first years have the option of socialising at the **Parade Bar**, **Plug** or **Element**, all on campus. The **Parade Bar** is the most upmarket of the three where you can go for a coffee or a cocktail, whichever takes your fancy. The Plug is a small pub style area with pool tables and a big TV for all the sports matches (beware of the Welsh contingent out in full force whenever the rugby's on)! **Element** is the university's nightclub which plays host on Wednesday nights to *Score*, Friday nights to *Funky Guppy*. Other regular ents include Karoke on Thursday and Comedy or live bands on Tuesday at **Plug**. If you're after cheesy music and cheap drinks then **Element** is the place to go.

'On a Monday night most venture into town to take advantage of the student offers at various pubs and bars. Like the campus, the city feels very safe and there's a regular bus service running until late. For those looking for the bigger club scene, Bristol is not far away and the uni organises regular socials.

'There are 85 societies on offer (including bee keeping) so it is really easy to get involved. Resist the temptation to join all of the societies at the Fresher Fair. They all put their best looking members on the stands and offer incentives like honey sandwiches and vodka to join them. Believe me, it's hard but it will be a very expensive mistake to give in to them!'

'We may not have the sort of student

WHERE BATH GRADUATES END UP

Health & Social Work: 8%; Education: 4%; Wholesale/Retail: 10%; Manufacturing: 18%; Financial Activities: 10%; Public Administration, Civil Service & Defence: 8%; Hotel/Restaurant: 2%; Transport & Communications (including Telecommunications): 4%; Construction:2%; Personnel: 3%; Computer: 4%; Business & Management: 6%; Accountancy: 7%; Media (including Film): 0.5%; Architecture: 2%; Publishing: 2%; Advertising: 0.5%; Sport: 1%.

Approximate 'graduate track' employed **77%**

WHAT IT'S REALLY LIKE

UNIVERSITY:	
Social Life	★★★★
Campus scene	**Busy, friendly**
Student Union services	**Professional**
Politics	**Union active**
Sport	**48 clubs**
National team position	**2nd**
Sport facilities	**Excellent**
Arts opportunities	**Good**
Student newspaper	**Impact**
Student radio	**URB**
Student Radio Awards	**3 awards 2005**
Student TV	**CTV**
Nightclub	**Elements**
Bars	**Plug, Parade, Claverton Rooms**
Union ents	**Score, Funky Guppy, etc**
Union clubs/societies	**85**
Parking	**No 1st years**
CITY:	
Entertainment	★★★
Scene	**Average clubs, good pubs**
Town/gown relations	**Good**
Risk of violence	**Low**
Cost of living	**High**
Student concessions	**Good**
Survival + 2 nights out	**£70 pw**
Part-time work campus/town	**Excellent/good**

traditionally likely to be involved in the arts,' another student told me, 'but that is what actually attracts students here. If we offered a drama course it would be the drama students who would be in all the plays, whereas, here, students have a lot better chance to be involved because there isn't a specific drama course, a specific music course and so on.'

The centre for arts is **The Arts Barn** – drama, dance, music, studio workshop space for visual arts and crafts. BUST is the provocatively named drama society. There's a musicals society, opera, a choral society – 'not quite so elitist as the chamber choir'. They also have student bands and orchestras.

Media-wise, there's a weekly newspaper, *Impact*, a radio station, URB, and a TV station, CTV, with monitors installed in the Plug Bar. Politics brings societies for the three main parties into action, and the popular Debating Soc.

'Sorted' is a Students Union employee scheme, the programme aims to train, educate and develop students in key skills and aid Students Union officers and representatives to fulfil their roles more effectively. Why get involved? 'Despite having top qualifications, employers have suggested that many graduates of today lack the important skills needed for the world of work. "Sorted" is designed specifically to develop both you and your career prospects. It provides CV filling, life-enhancing opportunities from experts and professionals as well as experienced student trainers.'

Tamara Johnson reckons minimum amount a new student needs to live on to cover all living expenses: rent, books, food, telephones, fun, if living in, is around £5750 p.a. If living out, £6750.

Sport There are fantastic sports facilities on campus, ranging from an Olympic size swimming pool, 8-lane athletics track, squash, badminton and tennis courts. They attract the sporting elite, but unlike practically any other university, all the sports facilities are free to students. Right on campus there's a generous range of team pitches and no facility is more than a stroll away. The sports village complex, partly built with Lottery money, offers the floodlit running track; 50-metre and 25-metre pools; a 4-court tennis hall; 16 hard tennis courts; 2 synthetic grass pitches; a shooting range; sports hall; squash courts; a performance testing lab; weight training rooms; a physio centre, etc.

Nor does all this professionalism keep the keen amateur away – a statistic, much bandied, is that 80% of students make use of what's on offer (in all, fifty-two sporting clubs, including American Football). 'The frequent socials and notorious initiations for many of the clubs are an added bonus,' observes Ally. 'Look out for pink fairies, emergency service men and women and some that look like they've escaped from Rocky Horror all roaming around campus on a Wednesday night!'

AT A GLANCE

ACADEMIC FILE:	
Subjects assessed	**21**
Excellent	**86%**
Typical entry requirements	**375 points**
Application acceptance rate	**12%**
Students-staff ratio	**15:1**
First/2:1 degree pass rate	**75%**
ACCOMMODATION FILE:	
Guarantee to freshers	**Apply by 31.7**
Style	**Halls**
Catered	**None**
En-suite	**55%**
Approx price range pw	**£60-£98.50**
City rent pw	**£58-£75**

PILLOW TALK

'Accommodation on campus varies greatly in style and character,' continues Ally. 'The Eastwood "ghetto" terraces are known for being the lowest standard of the main halls, yet what they lack in polish, its residences make up for in spirit, defending their notorious party reputation to the end. The Norwood residents occupy five floors above the nightclub, allowing some of them to enjoy the music from it every night of the week without having to leave their rooms. Westwood terraces feature the famous 'pod', a unique concept of fitting an entire bathroom into a shower, which prior to this year had meant that demand for these rooms was the highest.

However, full en-suite bathrooms and fitted kitchens have ensured that the newly built Solsbury and Marlborough Courts have taken over the title of the 'posh' digs. Huge floor to ceiling windows in every kitchen makes 'Molsbury' feel spacious and also invites comparisons to an art farm, with movements on every floor being visible to an outside observer.'

GETTING THERE

- By road: M4/J18, A46.
- By rail: London Paddington or Southampton, 1:30; Birmingham, 2:15; Cardiff, 1:50.
- By air: Bristol Airport.
- By coach: London, Birmingham, 3:15

BATH SPA UNIVERSITY

Bath Spa University
Newton St Loe
Bath BA2 9BN

TEL 01225 875875
FAX 01225 875444
EMAIL enquiries@bathspa.ac.uk
WEB www.bathsap.ac.uk

VAG VIEW

Bath Spa, a University College since 1999 and a uni since 2005, came out of Bath Academy of Art, Bath College of Education and Newton Park College, the last two being originally teacher training colleges. There are now 4 faculties – Applied Sciences, Art and Music, Education and Human Sciences, and Humanities – on 2 campuses: Sion Hill and Newton Park.

The most extensive building programme in Bath Spa's history, amounting to £11 million, is in progress and includes a Students' Union social facility, library and ICT suites, a new Performing Arts arena with a 214 seat theatre, rehearsal spaces, associated technical accommodation and changing facilities; a new refectory; and a Creative Writing Centre housed in a campus-based, 14th-century Gatehouse renovated in collaboration with English Heritage and equipped with the very latest computers and audio-visual equipment.

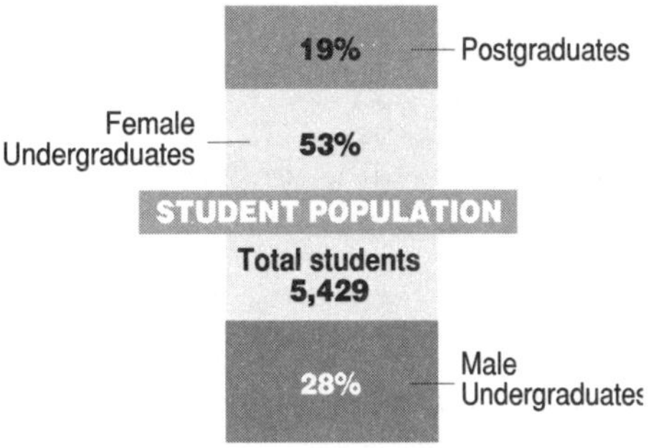

UNIVERSITY/STUDENT PROFILE	
University since	**2005**
Situation/style	**City campus**
Student population	**5429**
Undergraduates	**4380**
- mature	**32%**
- non EU undergraduates	**3%**
- male/female	**33/66**
- non-traditional student intake	**30%**
- state school intake	**92%**
- drop-out rate	**8%**
- undergraduate applications	**Up 6%**

FEES, BURSARIES

UK & EU Fees p.a. £3000. Max bursary for students in receipt of HE Maintenance grant, £1150. Scholarships of £1000 for eligible students on some science-based courses (Biology, Diet and Health, Environmental Science, Food Nutrition and Consumer Protection, Geographic Information Systems, Development Geography).

CAMPUSES

Newton Park is 4 miles west of the city in a landscaped saucer of Duchy of Cornwall countryside, an original Capability Brown design, with a Georgian manor house at its administrative hub and a cash dispenser, recently installed by the Students' Union. There are half hourly and late-night buses to and from town.

Sion Hill is within walking distance of the city centre on the north side and is reserved for Art and Design. It comprises a large modern building and the Georgian crescent Somerset Place, set in attractive grounds.

SUBJECT AREAS (%)

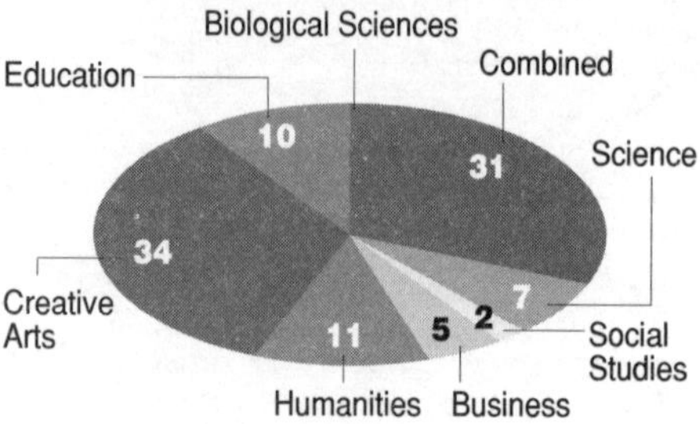

STUDENT PROFILE

It is a small, quiet, supportive community, appealing particularly to females (66% of undergrads, 53% of total) and mature undergraduates (32%) One student told of its 'friendly, warming atmosphere.' She admitted, 'I arrived a timid, not-sure-why-I-was-leaving-home type of person ... if you have a shell to come out of, you'll discard it within weeks of coming here.'

It is far from being some sort of specialist dumping ground for sensitive souls, however. Bath Spa comes out high in any league table of new unis and university colleges.

ACADEMIA & JOBS

Course design displays individuality and flair. By far the majority of the 30-odd per cent of Bath Spa graduates who find employment in Education do so as primary school teachers, some specialist music teachers among them, for music is another vital string to their bow.

Music technology is one of the fastest growing career opportunities. Graduates are entering the recording industry, new media (web audio, sound design, game audio, VR), the broadcasting industry (composing for TV, film, radio, etc) and the music technology industry (product development, software design). Bath Spa's relevant degree is the BA Creative Music Technology. There are excellent facilities and well-used industry links. The degree is part of an impressive department, which includes a Foundation and BA degree in Commercial Music – performance and songwriting are key elements (students played their first live gig in January 2002) – a BA (Hons) Music and a BA Performing Arts. It's a very creative scene at Bath Spa. At Newton Park, an academic interest in music is given a performance dimension at the **Michael Tippett Centre**, recently refurbished and extended to make a 250-seater auditorium.

ACADEMIC EXCELLENCE

TEACHING:	
(Rated Excellent or 17+ out of 24)	
English, Environmental Studies	**Excellent**
Theology	**23**
Sociology, Art & Design Education	**22**
Environmental Biology, Psychology	**21**
Business/Management	**20**
RESEARCH:	
*Top grades 5/5**	**None**

More than 5% of Bath Spa graduates find their way into jobs as graphic designers, and there's a strong pathway among fine artists, too (painting, sculpture and media).

Again, the excellent BA Creative Studies in English, backed by an MA and taught by

WHERE BATH SPA GRADUATES END UP

Health & Social Work: 4%; Education: 29%; Wholesale/Retail: 15%; Manufacturing: 5%; Financial Activities: 4%; Public Administration, Civil Service & Defence: 8%; Hotel/Restaurant: 7%; Transport & Communications (including Telecommunications): 2%; Personnel: 3%; Media (including Film): 1%; Legal 1%; Architecture: 1%; Publishing: 3%; Advertising: 1%; Artistic/Literary: 4%; Sport: 0.5%

Approximate 'graduate track' employed **52%**

practising writers essentially in workshop context, launches many a Bath Spa graduate into print as journalist, editor or author.

See also Environmental Science, Food Management (this is another strong employment pathway), Human Ecology, Remote Sensing & Geographic Information Systems, and Social Science.

Then there are the regular BA and BSc single awards, for which a second subject must be selected in the first year: arts, humanities, social science, business, religion, health, etc. Finally combined BA/BSc awards give subjects equal weight.

On the teacher education front, there's a three-year BA/BSc Hons degree with a guaranteed PGCE place (primary).

New Foundation Degrees are Development Geography, Applied Art and Design. Management and Management Systems.

SOCIAL SCENE

New student facilities on campus include a refectory, delicatessan, SU bar, lounge, shop and offices, as Bath Spa tools up for life as a university. Say the SU: 'The campus estate is absolutely beautiful and provides a perfect study environment. Bath and Bristol are just a bus ride away. Small numbers creates a real community aspect and a sense of belonging. The new SU is amazing – chill out in the afternoon over coffee and bacon sandwiches or get your groove on in the evening on one of the biggest dance floors and largest capacity clubs in Bath.'

Ents are Monday: Open Mic or Race Night, karaoke or bingo; Tuesday pool or salsa; Wednesday is *Flirt* ('No. 1 National Student Club Night'); Thursday, Band Nite; Friday: *Friday Flux* ('Biggest Night of the Week'); Sunday is Quiz or Film Night.

AT A GLANCE

ACADEMIC FILE:	
Subjects assessed	**12**
Excellent	**75%**
Typical entry requirements	**235 points**
Application acceptance rate	**19%**
Students-staff ratio	**18:1**
First/2:1 degree pass rate	**63%**
ACCOMMODATION FILE:	
Guarantee to freshers	**90%**
Style	**Flats in hall**
Catered	**None**
En suite	**46%**
Approx price range pw	**£65-£89**
City rent pw	**£58-£75**

WHAT IT'S REALLY LIKE

UNIVERSITY:	
Social Life	★★★
Campus scene	**Quiet/mature teachers, funky artists**
Politics	**Relaxed**
Sport	**10 clubs**
Arts opportunities	**Excellent**
Student news & mag	**H20**
Radio station	**In progress**
Bar/venue	**SU bar and lounge**
Union ents	**Flirt, Friday Flux + live bands, karaoke, etc**
Union Clubs/Societies	**25**
Most active society	**Rugby**
Parking	**None**
CITY:	
Entertainment	★★★
Scene	**Average clubs, good pubs**
Town/gown relations	**Good**
Risk of violence	**Low**
Cost of living	**Average**
Student concessions	**Good**
Survival + 2 nights out	**£60 pw**
Part-time work campus/town	**Average/good**

PILLOW TALK

All self-catering halls, divided into flats. Most on campus, with one new off-site block (located between the university and the town centre).

GETTING THERE

☛ By road Newton Park: from London and east: M4/J18, A46, A4, A39 to Wells, turn left after 200 yards into Newton Park Estate. By road Sion Hill: M4/J18, A46, A420, first left to Hamswell, at second give-way take a right and second right into Landsdown Crescent, over crossroads, first right to Sion Hill on your right.

☛ By rail: London Paddington or Southampton, 1:30; Birmingham, 2:15; Cardiff, 1:50.

☛ By air: Bristol Airport.

BIRKBECK COLLEGE

Birkbeck College
University of London
Malet Street
London WC1E 7HX
TEL 020 7631 6000
FAX 020 7631 6351
EMAIL admissions@admin.bbk.ac.uk
WEB www.bbk.ac.uk

Learn as you earn – Birkbeck College, founded in 1823 as the London Mechanics' Institution, became a school of London University in 1920. It provides part-time degrees for adults engaged otherwise during the day.

COLLEGE PROFILE

College of London Uni since	**1920**
Situation/style	**City site**
Student population	**16645**
Undergraduates: part-time	**12085**
full-time	**5**
Accommodation	**None**

FACULTIES/SCHOOLS:
English & Humanities; History, Classics & Archaeology; History of Art, Film & Visual Media; Languages, Linguistics & Culture, Law, Philosophy, Politics & Sociology

STUDENT BIRMINGHAM - THE CITY

Birmingham has shaken off its grey image to incredible effect in the last decade. Developments right across Britain's second city total hundreds of millions of pounds. Improved social and shopping facilities carry the bonus of better graduate job prospects and mean that whatever you're after from your student career, Birmingham can probably supply.

The most dramatic recent development has to have been Birmingham's **Bull Ring Centre**. There's been a market here at least since 1154, when Peter de Birmingham, a local landowner, obtained a Royal Charter for a cattle and food market. In 1964 a new concrete-smothered mixed market of indoor shops and outdoor stalls was built, a design unintegrated with the city that proved to be locked into its time and of questionable practical form. In 2000 it was reduced to a hole in the ground, and then recently it opened anew in spectacular form to public applause. The big name designers and retailers, like **Selfridges**, have flocked their in droves, and Birmingham Retail has been resurrected, the time the whole operation took to complete giving the rest of Brum's shopping world a chance to flourish, with such as **Mailbox** offering us a chance to drool at **Harvey Nichs**, Armani, DKNY, etc, even if many students will stick to the pedestrianised areas around New Street and the Pallasades, where every high street store you could want is juxtaposed with designer off-cut stores and street markets.

CAFES, PUBS, CLUBS

Aston students report, 'There are so many places to go, and so much to do that you will always be spoilt for choice... Spend an evening in a canalside café, pub or restaurant, take a trip to the cinema, theatre or ballet or laugh the night away at the **Glee Comedy Club**. The Broad Street, Brindley Place/Mailbox area is particularly popular with our students and has lots of places to eat and drink beside the canals, for example **The Works**, **Flares** (2 floors of cheese), **Hard Rock Café**, **Bar Epernay** (rotating piano), **Fifty Two Degrees North**, the pricier **Zinc** and Aussie-themes **Walkabout** (amongst many others). Rumour has it that there are 100 pubs and bars within a one-mile radius of the Aston University Campus – **The Square Peg** (Wetherspoons), **Bar Med**, **Chambers**, **Sack of Potatoes** (facing Aston Uni), **Gosta Green** (It's A Scream), the stylish **RSVP Bar**...the list is endless. Numerous pre-clubbars like **Poppy Red**, **Ipanema**, **The Living Room**, and **SoBar** are also open late, as you would expect from a real entertainment city like Birmingham. The bars, cafés and clubs at **The Arcadian Centre** (near the Chinese Quarter) are also popular with students.

Birmingham is bursting with clubs playing anything from dance, house, drum 'n' bass and jungle, to hard rock, 70s, 80s, lounge, soul, jazz and garage. **The Que Club** (one of the largest clubs in the UK) alas is no more, but clubs like **The Sanctuary**, **The Medicine Bar**, **Bakers**, new club **Air** (home to Godskitchen), **The Works** and **Bobby Brown's** play host to top DJs and attract clubbing aficionados from across the UK in their coachloads.

LIVE

The recently opened **Birmingham Academy** is the best local venue – it's one of the essential stops on any band's UK tour, its reputation boosted far and wide in 2001 by Radio 1's hosting most of its One Live in Birmingham events there.

The **Wolverhampton Civic**, just a short train ride away, is still seen as a main Midland live venue, and the **NEC** is equally popular with bands of U2 or S Club proportions. In the smaller venues expect massively varying music styles and quality. **Ronnie Scott's** offers more than just jazz, whilst the **Fiddle and Bone** is a pub with a plethora of acts for free – from tribute bands to student musos through to Beethoven. Further into the backstreets you'll find a glut of pubs with fascinating (but sometimes frightening) live acts.

COMEDY, THEATRE, ARTS

Judging by the success of venues like the **Glee Club**, the new rock 'n' roll this may be. The venue attracts the best comic newcomers and the established talents of Eddie Izzard and Harry Hill – all for under a fiver if you go on a student night.

At the newly-revamped **Hippodrome** or **Alexandra Theatre** can be seen an array of Lloydesque and other West End shows, as well as the magnificent Welsh National Opera.

In the **Symphony Hall**, the renowned City of Birmingham Symphony Orchestra resides, playing host also to hundreds of international performers and offering a huge variety of classical music all year round.

For smaller fry the **Midlands Arts Centre**, or **MAC** as it is known, nestles comfortably on the edge of Cannon Hill Park near the University of Birmingham. With its combination of theatre, exhibitions, cinema and a damn fine bar it offers excellent choice and value. **The Electric Cinema**, showing arthouse, world and classic cinema in a charming setting, is the place to go if you want to see something different, although if it's Hollywood blockbusters you're after the **Odeon**, **UGC** and **Starcity** complexes offer about six billion different films, allegedly on twice as many screens.

For theatre **The Rep** in town has come in for a great deal of well-deserved praise lately with their showcase for new work, **The Door**, and also show fantastic productions in their main theatre. Stratford-upon-Avon is but a short train ride away, but watch out for the RSC's value for money student trips to productions there. For community productions (usually) as good as the professionals, check out the **Crescent Theatre**, offering Shakespeare and other productions.

For art you are spoilt in Brum, **The Barber Institute** on the University of Birmingham's campus is astounding. For more modern exhibitions head for **Ikon** or **The Angle** galleries.

Crucially all these places offer heavy discounts for students. Life with a 10% discount is what being a student is all about.

UNIVERSITY OF BIRMINGHAM

The University of Birmingham
Edgbaston
Birmingham B15 2TT

TEL 0121 414 3344
FAX 0121 414 3984
EMAIL admissions@bham.ac.uk
WEB www.bham.ac.uk

Birmingham Guild of Students
Edgbaston Park Road
Birmingham B15 2TU

TEL 0121 251 2300
FAX 0121 251 2301
EMAIL enquiries@guild.bham.ac.uk
WEB www.bugs.bham.co.uk

VAG VIEW

Birmingham is the original redbrick uni, with all that that entails beyond its masonry – none of the snobbery attached to Oxbridge and for many a reputation second only to it. The teaching is among the very best in the country and Brum's research record and graduate employment record, particularly in the areas of health, engineering, finance, accountancy and business are equally good. Together with the city and campus scenes, they serve to make this uni an exciting choice.

SUBJECT AREAS (%)

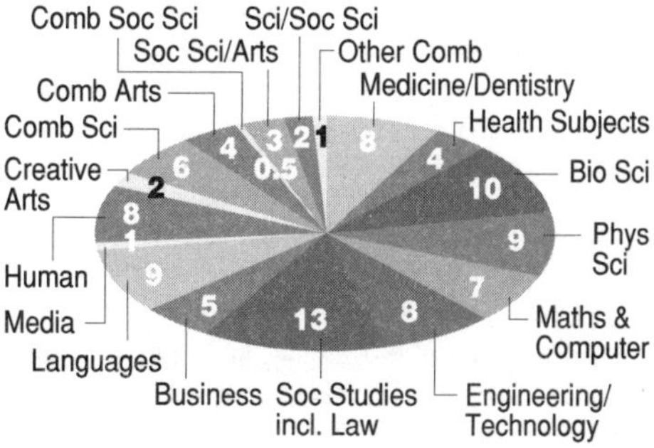

CAMPUS

The self-contained University of Birmingham campus lies a couple of miles south of the city in leafy Edgbaston. Parking is not encouraged.

FEES, BURSARIES

UK & EU Fees £3000 p.a. for first degrees. Bursaries of £800 pa for all students whose family income is £32k or less. University scholarships of £1200 p.a. for those who qualify for bursaries and who have approximately 340 tariff points (10% of students expected to qualify); also subject scholarships in e.g. physics, engineering, computer science.

STUDENT PROFILE

There's a relatively high public school intake, though nothing as large as Oxbridge, Bristol, Durham. Birmingham students come from all over. Southerners think that Brum is north enough for them. Northerners, already bored of Manchester, see it as the next best city without London's expense. Thanks to strong overseas links there's also a large international community. In fact, be it fashion, music or religion, anything goes. The gist is that there are loads of people with interests sympathetic to yours, and you'll meet them through lectures, accommodation or socialising.

UNIVERSITY/STUDENT PROFILE	
University since	**1900**
Situation/style	**Campus**
Student population	**26292**
Undergraduates	**17345**
- mature	**16%**
- non EU undergraduates	**7%**
- male/female	**44/56**
- non-traditional student intake	**23%**
- state school intake	**81%**
- drop-out rate	**8%**
- undergraduate applications	**Up 2%**

In an effort to ease the plight of disabled students, the uni has recently instigated a five-year action plan to adapt and re-design facilities and access points. The policy continues with increased disability staffing, expanded equipment pool, better assistive technology in libraries, more specialist software available across computer clusters, more support workers, etc.

For international students, there's now a 'Welcome Week' induction programme before the start of term, and three full-time Student Advisers and free lessons in English during term time.

ACADEMIA & JOBS

Involvement with the world beyond campus is an aspect of a number of courses, and the proximity of important industries and businesses, as well as artistic nuclei, is key. The Arts School non-vocational courses give special attention not just to *what* is studied, but *how* a subject is studied. Skills such as organisation, analysis, presentation, communication and problem-solving are to the fore.

Almost a fifth of Birmingham graduates go to work in the health sector. The degree in Medicine is the 4/5-year MBCgB. There's a 13.6% application acceptance rate (better than the 11% average), and a Black Country strategy in partnership with hospital trusts in Wolverhampton, Dudley, Sandwell and Walsall. Entry AAB, including Chemistry and another science (Biology, Physics or Maths). Biology must come at AS level if not at A; General Studies is not normally accepted. For dentists, it's the 5-year BDS; entry ABB.

Birmingham is one of the few unis offering non-Law graduates a 2-year full-time or 3-year part-time Senior Status Law Degree. They scored an Excellent in a recent inspection, and a Grade 5 in the research assessment. All candidates must sit the National Admissions Test for Law (LNAT).

It is not necessary to take a degree to become a qualified accountant any more than it is to become a solicitor, but at the last annual count nearly 3000 did and more than 850 degree courses are there to ensure the flow continues. Birmingham is the big graduate provider in this sector, with Warwick and Durham not far behind. Dedicated courses at the Birmingham Business School include a 3-year BSc Accounting & Finance and a 4-year Accounting & Finance with French/German (French/German required at A level). A level requirements are high. Maths or Statistics at A level are not required, but A/B Maths at GCSE is essential. Conceptual, analytical, ICT and problem-solving skill requirements are to the fore, but also communication/discursive skills and the ability to

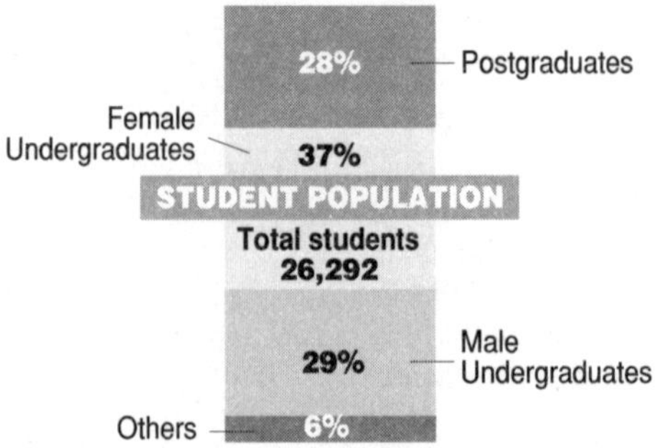

work on one's own (much coursework is outside the lecture hall). Work experience useful, but not essential.

The more accessible route is via the Economics Department - Single, Joint and Combined BSc Hons, including various Language mixes (Japanese among them), Money/Banking/ Finance, Economics and Modern Economic History, and Mathematical Economics and Statistics. Economics dropped only one point at the assessments.

Birmingham also lead in getting graduates jobs as tax experts and consultants, and for a job in banking, look at the BSc Money, Banking & Finance plus one year (well spent) to combine with French, German, Italian, Portuguese or Spanish.

Note the language interest; it's characteristic of all kinds of courses at Birmingham. The department (23 points for Russian at the assessments) keeps it high in the pecking order for graduates wanting jobs as interpreters and leads many into the area of human resource management. Social Sciences contribute 7% of graduates to this last sector:. See also a whole raft of new Public Policy degrees this year.

New Business School degrees include MBA Euro Banking and Finance, MBA Strategy and Procurement Management, MBA Strategy and Procurement Management (Hong Kong), MScCorporate Governance and Corporate Social Responsibility, MSc Human Resource Mgt, MSc Economic Competitiveness and International Business, MSc Economic Policy and International Business.

Would-be electrical, electronic and telecom. engineers note that full marks (24 points at the assessments) and a Grade 5 (international) accolade for research put this uni high on any discerning applicant's list. There are 3/4-year B/MEng options in Electronic & Electrical Eng, and a 4-year MEng option with international study.

There's a Business Management orientation available for most of what's on offer.

Look, too, at B/MEng degrees in Communication Sys-tems (also with possible Computer orientation), Computer Interactive Systems, Computer Science/Software Engineering, Electronic & Computer Eng. Finally, look over the Joint Hons BEng/MEng Electronic & Software Engineering. Again, it's full marks for teaching and a Grade 5 (international) level at research.

Nationwide, some 500 mechanical engineers find employment annually. Birmingham makes a valuable contribution to that figure. There are B/MEng Mechanical Eng or with Business Management or Automotive possibilities; there's also a Foundation course. See also the joint hons Mechanical & Material Engineering. 20 points at assessment.

In producing working physicists, Birmingham are top of the tree, finding more of them jobs than any other uni last time out. They scored 23 points at the assessments and an international Grade 5 for research (as did UCL, Leicester and Nottingham). Physical sciences is also a good route into Defence from here.

ACADEMIC EXCELLENCE

TEACHING:	
(Rated Excellent or 17+ out of 24)	
History, Music, Geography, English, Geology	**Excellent**
Sociology, Elect/Electron Eng Organismal Biosciences, Maths. Physiotherapy, Classics, Politics/International Studies.	**24**
Russian, Middle Eastern/ African Studies, Biochemistry, Physics, Molecular Biosciences, Psychology, Economics, Theol.	**23**
Dentistry, Italian, Iberian Studies, American Studies, HistoryArt, Dentistry, Nursing, Sport,Tourism Archaeology.	**22**
Chemical Engineering, Civil Engineering, Drama, Business, Education, Philosophy.	**21**
Manufac & Mechanical Eng Materials Technology, Medicine	**20**
German	**19**
French	**18**
RESEARCH:	
Special 6 status:*	
Clinical Lab Science, Anatomy, Chem. Eng, Metallurgy, Middle East/African Studies, Russian/ Eastern Euro, Sport	**Grade 6***
*Top grades 5/5**	
Clinical Lab. Sciences, Anatomy, Psychology, Chemical Eng, Metallurgy & Materials, Middle East/African Studies, Russian/E. European Studies, French, German/Dutch/Scand, Italian, Music, Sport.	**Grade 5***
Hospital-based Clinical, Pre-Clinical, Bio-Sciences, Chemistry, Physics, Pure Maths, Applied Maths, Computer, Civil Eng, Elec & Electron Eng, Law, Politics, German, English, Iberian & Latin American, Greek, History, History of Art, Theology, Educ.	**Grade 5**

WHAT IT'S REALLY LIKE

UNIVERSITY:	
Social Life	★★★★★
Campus scene	**Traditional, busy, cosmopolitan**
Student Union services	**Good**
Politics	**Activity high:**
Sport	**Key; 43 clubs**
National team position	**3rd**
Sport facilities	**Very good**
Arts opportunities	**Film excellent; drama, dance, music, art good**
Student newspaper	**Redbrick**
Student magazine	**Bugged**
Student radio	**Burn FM**
Radio Awards 2005	**1 nomination**
Student TV	**Guild Television**
Nightclub	**The Underground, Deb Hall**
Bars	**Joe's, Beorma**
Union ents	**Theme nights, comedy, drum 'n' bass, old skool, live bands**
Union clubs/societies	**150+**
Most active society	**Rock Soc**
Parking	**Poor**
CITY:	
Entertainment	★★★★★
Scene	**Excellent**
Town/gown relations	**Average**
Risk of violence	**High**
Cost of living	**High**
Student concessions	**Excellent**
Survival + 2 nights out	**£75 pw**
Part-time work campus/town	**Average/excellent**

Note, too, the Business Studies and Business Management/Management Sciences elements in their Physical and Biological Sciences programmes. Would-be zoologists should also be aware of BSc Biological Sciences: Animal Biology.

For media and government research jobs, Birmingham again leads the field. A third come from Social Sciences & Public Policy and Physical Sciences departments. See Media, Culture & Society or Public Policy, Government & Management. Look also at the International Studies combinations (Economics, Greek, German, French, Italian, Japanese, Portuguese, Spanish, Political Science) – same for Economics, Finance, etc. Also Political Science as single hons, Asian Studies with highly relevant combinations, BSc Public Policy, Government & Management, Russian Studies, Social Policy, etc. Also joint hons, such as Economics & Political Science, Planning & Public Policy, Government & Management, etc. It's all here.

> ***Birmingham is a big, bustling, happening place and there is that self-same disinterested, confident air that you notice at all our best universities. If you don't enjoy a three-year spell here, it is unlikely to be Birmingham's fault.***

Further employment strengths are evident in archaeology, in education (particularly for higher education lecturers), in psychology – BSc Psychology and the BSc Joint Hons Psychology with Artificial Intelligence explain why they are making waves in this sector. That and a world-class Grade 5* for research.

Music is another niche area. There's a world-renowned – Grade 5* – research rating, a Centre for Early Music Performance & Research, excellent rehearsal facilities and a brilliant Electro-Acoustic Music Studio, which is worth exploring in detail on the web. Five different degree routes are offered.

They are one of only three unis with a special Grade 6* research rating in Sport – the others are Liberpool John Moores and Manchester Met. See their Sport & Exercises Sciences and joint honours degrees. There's also an interesting civil engineering degree in Sports & Leisure Facilities Design.

The specialist BA Applied Golf Management Studies assumes a handicap on entry of 4.4 or less (this is a PGA requirement). Coaching is a key element and you'll be expected to take up a summer placement in the community. They also have a golf degree. – not a bad way to spend three years. You might consider their very strong student media as compatible in career terms.

SOCIAL SCENE

Guild of Students The main source of non-academic entertainment on campus is the union, called Birmingham Uni Guild of Students or BUGS for short. This isn't purely to baffle your non-Brummy friends – the Guild was the first union in the country and earned the right to a sophisticated name. By day they offer numerous eateries and bars, from **Joe's**, the typical trendy student bar, to the delicious hot food of **Café Connections**.

There's the chance to join one of over 150 societies, and a huge range of student services (legal advice, local info from the ARC (Advice &

WHERE BIRMINGHAM GRADUATES END UP

Health & Social Work: 19%; Education: 8%; Wholesale/Retail: 6%; Manufacturing: 10%; Financial Activities: 7%; Public Administration, Civil Service & Defence: 9%; Hotel/Restaurant: 2%; Transport & Communications (including Telecommunications): 3%; Construction: 1%; Personnel: 7%; Computer: 3%; Business & Management: 5%; Accountancy: 7%; Media (including Film): 1%; Legal 1%; Architecture: 1%; Publishing: 1%.

Approximate 'graduate track' employed **67%**

Representation Centre – currently in refurb.), part-time job info at the Job Zone, etc).

Media-wise Birmingham is top notch, everything together in the same spot – magazine, newspaper, radio and TV (see *What's It's Really Like* box). You can't do better if this is your interest. Radio & TV broadcasting and broadcast journalism are, like paper journalism, intensely competitive areas. Birmingham does well employment-wise for students, it has a good Media, Culture & Society degree in its Social Sciences faculty (which features, too, in Joint Hons) but the very fine student media set-up is also instrumental.

If there's a catch, it is that these Guild services are part-paid for by bar profits, so, whilst the Guild still costs less than non-student bars, it's often cheaper to go to student nights in the city centre than to stay on campus. As a result, freshers often go to hall bars before moving on to one of the city-centre clubs and bars. Students living in neighbouring Selly Oak or Harbourne frequent the many local student pubs and balti houses in those areas, as well as the most popular city club nights.

Guild nights are OK, however, and the nightclub, **The Underground** has recently been extended. There's also **Deb Hall**, used for full-building nightclub events, plays, dance shows and formal events, and the bars – **Joes** and **Beorma**, and **Cybercity** – games room, pool, etc.

Typically, there's *Curryoke Thursdays* (karaoke for free curry for 2), theme party nights at Joes on Friday – *Joes Presents...* (*Bad Taste, Tequila Night, 999 Emergency Services*, etc), and *Fab 'n' Fresh* at Joes and The Underground on Saturday.

On campus, artistic input is high. Across drama, dance, music and art, extra-curricular societies are very active. The Film Society is excellent. Musically, there's a chamber orchestra, an orchestra of 100 and a choir of 220. For art there's **The Barber Institute** – founded in 1932 it incorporates both Fine Art and Music departments and has been described as 'one of the finest small picture galleries in the world'. There's also a musical theatre group which nurtures, milks and dispenses talent that abounds among students. If you're into theatre, Birmingham is one of the places to be. There's a Guild group and a Drama Dept group in the uni's **Studio Theatre**; students perform all over the city (often before taking their productions to the Edinburgh Fringe), and there's a student humour night at the **Glee Club** in town.

If you do find yourself dipping into the overdraft it's easy to find a job at the Guild, where students are given decent wages for bar work, security, marketing, and other jobs. Alternatively, businesses around the city always want flexible, enthusiastic part-timers. Most of them advertise in the Guild's Job Zone.

Finally, sports-wise, Birmingham's teams were the third best in the country last year. Only Loughborough and Bath beat them overall.

AT A GLANCE

ACADEMIC FILE:	
Subjects assessed	**48**
Excellent	**85%**
Typical entry requirements	**380 points**
Application acceptance rate	**14%**
Student-staff ratio	**17:1**
First/2:1 degree pass rate	**67%**
ACCOMMODATION FILE:	
Fresher guarantee only to	**100%**
Style	**Halls, flats**
Catered	**28%**
En-suite	**37%**
Price range pw	**£68-£95**
Town rent pw	**£55**

SPORT The Munrow Sports Centre's mission statement 'to enhance the sporting experience of the university by providing opportunities at all levels' sums up the sporting situation. For the casual athlete the *Active Lifestyles Programme* offers weekly courses in martial arts, swimming, aerobics and team games.

The Athletic Union is made up of 40+ sports

clubs, each with a qualified coach. Last year they had the top one or two national places in athletics and cross country, badminton, gymnastics, hockey, mountainbike and cycling, netball, rowing, squash and triathlon.

Clubs exist also at inter-departmental and inter-hall levels. Interests are more than catered for by the 25m pool, two gyms, a climbing wall and full-size running track, as well as two floodlit, synthetic pitches, physiotherapy and sports science support, and a Fitness Services Unit for all levels.

In addition, there are coaching courses in a variety of sports and activities. And there's a degree in golf.

Off-campus, five miles from home, there are seventy acres of pitches served by coaches and minibuses, and by Lake Coniston in Cumbria, 170 miles away, they have a Centre for Outdoor Pursuits (watersports, mountaineering, mountain biking, etc).

The university supports 30 sports scholarships at international level. This year's scholars compete in skeleton bobsleigh, lacrosse, equestrianism, badminton, hockey, rugby union, cycling, gymnastics,triathlon, netball, athletics, golf and squash.

TOWN See *Birmingham Student City*, page 62. The city does have less desirable areas (name a city that doesn't) but the average student has little contact with them, and if you're sensible about sticking in groups after dark and not flashing your cash around you shouldn't have any problems. As in all student areas there are complaints from disgruntled locals about kick-out time noise and student mess, but the Guild liaises with residents and police to keep the peace.

PILLOW TALK

Most freshers live in university accommodation. The main area is the Vale, a beautiful grassy bit set around a lake which houses catered and self-catered halls, and the Hub Centre (new in 2004) with two bars, eating areas, welfare and committee rooms. It is just fifteen mins from the main area of campus. Other self-catered halls are either adjacent to the main campus (the ultra posh Jarratt Hall), boasting 620 en-suite bedrooms) or a bus journey away (The Beeches and Hunter Court). University House, the Oxbridge-style original residence, is ideally situated next to the Guild.

Elgar Court is a newish development – 236 single en-suite study bedrooms in flats for six. Shackleton Hall was refurbished in 2004, Maple Bank in 2005. A new development is planned to open Sept 2008.

Housing quality varies – new developments are modern, with Internet access and mod cons in kitchens, but are more pricey. As for the rest, the less you pay, the less you get.

The older, catered residences may seem old-fashioned in decor and organisation (set meal times, hall tutors) but offer a stress-free introduction to university life with plenty of people to meet and no cooking hassles.

GETTING THERE

☛ By road: A38. Avoid entry through suburbia from the M40; instead use M42/J1, A38.
☛ By rail: London Euston, 1:40; Bristol Parkway or Sheffield, 1:30; Liverpool Lime Street, Manchester Piccadilly,1:40; Leeds, 2:15. Frequent trains from New Street to University Station.
☛ By air: Birmingham Airport.
☛ By coach: London, 2:40; Bristol, 2:00; Manchester, 2:30.

UNIVERSITY OF BOLTON

The University of Bolton
Deane Road
Bolton BL3 5AB

TEL 01204 903903
FAX 01204 903809
EMAIL enquiries@bolton.ac.uk
WEB www.bolton.ac.uk

The old Bolton Institute was formed out of the Bolton Institute of Technology and Bolton College of Education (Technical). Subsequently, Bolton College of Art was incorporated. They have had the distinction

SUBJECT AREAS (%)

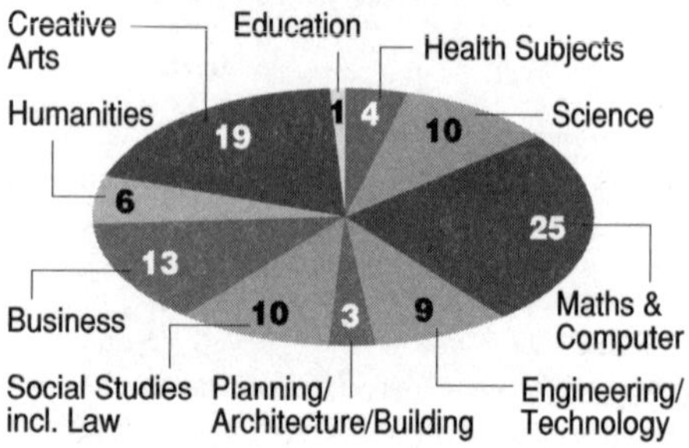

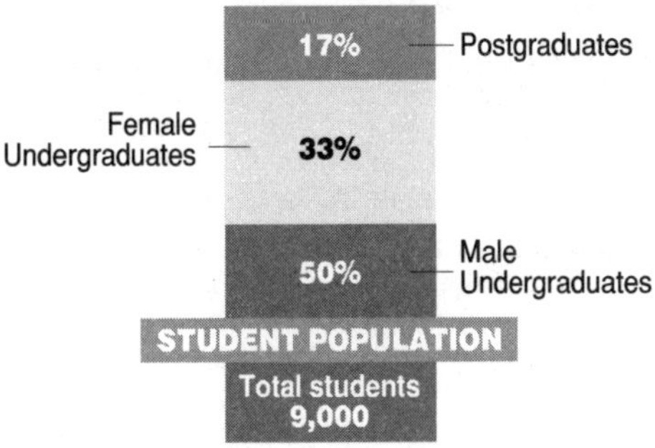

of being able to award their own degrees for some time, but in January 2005 they gained university status, and we can now expect the whole picture to begin changing rapidly.

CAMPUS

The uni operates out of two campuses, Deane Campus on the west side of town and Chadwick Campus on the east side. In June 2005 they opened The Design Studio on Deane Campus, a £6million remodelling of Deane Tower that has completely transformed the face of the uni's main campus. Accommodating all design disciplines, the studio provides an environment where students, researchers, academics and businesses can work together. New corporate hospitality facilities adjoin it, including lecture theatre, boardroom and breakout rooms - The Deane Suite. This is part of an extensive, phased landscaping and refurbishment programme which recently completed a one-stop-shop student centre and new laboratories for the uni's advanced materials research team, an area in which the uni is a leader.

FEES, BURSARIES

UK & EU Fees £3000 p.a. Bursary for students on full HE Maintenance Grant: £300 and on sliding scale if on partial grant up to £300. The Bolton Scholarship is also available from September 2006 for those who are progressing from a partner institution or one of our recognised courses – £700 p.a. to eligible students.

STUDENT PROFILE

Among undergraduates there is a large mature population (52%) and a third of undergrads are part-timers. It is a local intake, but also with quite a large take from overseas, so they are spreading their net wide. A fifth come from families new to the idea of university. Further education students account for around 6%. The diversity is impressive, but perhaps not surprisingly there is, at this stage, a very high drop-out rate (18%).

UNIVERSITY/STUDENT PROFILE

University since	**1902**
Situation/style	**Campus**
Student population	**9000**
Undergraduates	**7500**
- mature	**52%**
- non EU undergraduates	**11%**
- male/female	**52/48**
- non-traditional student intake	**42%, high**
- state school intake	**97%**
drop-out rate	**18%, high**
- undergraduate applications	**Up 20%**

ACADEMIA & JOBS

Departments are Art & Design, Built Environment, Business Studies, Business Logistics & Info Systems, Computing, Cultural & Creative Studies (from English to Media, from Arts in the Community to stage and screen - based at Chadwick), Education (Chadwick), Engineering & Design, Health & Social Studies, Management, Product Design & Development, Psychology & Life Sciences, Sport, Leisure & Tourism Management.

Bolton has strong links with business and professions with 79% of students on courses which lead to a vocational or professional qualification as well as an academic award.

Teaching assessments since the mid-1990s have been good and most recently very good, with Art & Design and Leisure, Tourism & Sport dropping only 3 points out of 24 on assessment, and Education and Health subjects (including nursing) scoring full marks, the latter getting a further boost from another expression of confidence in the provision this very year.

ACADEMIC EXCELLENCE

TEACHING: *(Rated Excellent or 17+ out of 24)*	
Education, Nursing, Health	**24**
Materials Technology	**23**
Organismal Biosciences	**22**
Art & Design, Leisure, Tourism, Sport	**21**
Civil Eng, Electro & Electronic Eng, Theatre, Film & TV Studies, Communications & Media, Maths	**20**
Modern Langs (French, German, Spanish), Building	**19**
RESEARCH:	
*Top grades 5/5**	**None**

WHAT IT'S REALLY LIKE	
UNIVERSITY:	
Social Life	★★★
Campus scene	**Largely local, very loyal**
Student Union services	**Galvanising itself**
Politics	**Little interest**
Sport	**13 clubs**
National team position	**96th**
Sport facilities	**Promising**
Arts opportunities	**Few**
Student newspaper	**Student Direct**
Nightclub/bar	**The Venue**
Union ents	**Live, and light ents progr. + tie-ups outside**
Union clubs/societies	**5**
Parking	**Available**
TOWN:	
Entertainment	★★
Scene	**Student club + pubs, etc**
Town/gown relations	**Good**
Risk of violence	**Average**
Cost of living	**Low**
Student concessions	**Good**
Survival + 2 nights out	**£50 pw**
Part-time work campus/town	**Average**

It's all a long way from the failures (Mechanical Engineering and Film & TV) in 1993 and 1996 respectively. Both were subsequently approved.

Built Environment is a particular strength, with a 23 -point assessment in Material Technology and a Grade 4 (national significance) for research. Computing is also an exciting area, with everything available to the student, from games design, through business computing to computer-aided product design and engineering.

Law (LLB) was introduced this year.

There has been a flexible approach to entry. 'It is what you are capable of doing, rather than what you have already done which interests us,' they used to say in their prospectus. From the start, applications from groups under-represented in higher education were encouraged. So, Bolton is deserving of its status as university because it has always been deliberately reaching out to non-traditional student types with sound teaching, and that is what the government wants of its universities.

If its drop-out rate is a high 18%, there is no reason not to expect their getting it under control, as so many others have managed Perhaps that will come when it gets its extra-curricular scene together

SOCIAL SCENE

STUDENT UNION The Union has shops at both campuses, a café, catering facilities and the **Venue** bar and, well, venue at Deane, with giant TV Screen, pool tables, jukebox and gaming machines. It's safe and grand for all it's meant to be, but it's early days, with little more to shout about than the **Venue Café's**, lighter bites (chip bun, spicy wedges etc), toasties, burgers (beef, chicken or vegetarian), pizza (you can even create your own), hot panini, jacket potatoes, and, wait for it, the Daily Special, 'details of which are written on the board'.

Ents-wise it's quiz on Monday, pool and big screen footie on Tuesday. Mid-week Wednesday is Student Night at **McCauleys** ('Bolton's student friendly nightclub') after drinks warm-up at the **Venue Café Bar**. Thursday is open mic night and Friday live local bands at the **Venue**.

Societies-wise it is again fairly undeveloped as yet, with only five catching the eye of freshers this year: Christian Union, Students with Disabilities, Islamic Soc, Afro Caribbean Soc and Motorsports (Bolton are strong in automobile engineering and product design and offer degrees in Motor Vehicle & Transport.) There's a newspaper, *Student Direct*, and a really quite good student union web site.

SPORT They are BUSA competitive and, positioned 96 for team sports this year, are already some way ahead of unis with longer histories. There are some interesting sport rehab., coaching, development and management degrees that will benefit their results in the future. Some interesting niche success stories already are badminton, basketball, hung kuen shoalin, king fu. Annual sports ball and award ceremony a high point of the social calendar.

TOWN Bolton's proximity to Manchester and to the

AT A GLANCE	
ACADEMIC FILE:	
Typical entry requirements	**150 points**
Application acceptance rate	**14%**
Students-staff ratio	**20:1**
First/2:1 degree pass rate	**57%**
ACCOMMODATION FILE:	
Guarantee to freshers	**100%**
Style	**Halls, flats**
Catered	**Some**
En-suite	**Limited**
Price range pw	**£55**
City rent pw	**£35-£45**

Pennine Moors makes for a nice balance. A couple of nights of Mancunian debauchery followed by a soul-searching chill-out on the wilderness of Tufton moor might be just the thing if you ever manage to tear yourself away from the campus scene. Bolton itself offers a handful of clubs, but McCauley's is fave.

There's a cinema complex, the ground-breaking Octagon Theatre (modern interpretations of Shakespeare and equally at home with Alan Bennett) and live music venue Albert Halls, which includes comedy, jazz, classical music. Buit it's nearby Manchester for the high life.

PILLOW TALK

Two modern purpose-built halls of residence provide 700 single study bedrooms on a self-catering basis. The Hollins (two blocks with flats of six to nine single study bedrooms) is adjacent to the Chadwick teaching site; the Orlando Village (eight blocks, each with eight six-bedroom flats, plus a common room) is 10 minutes walk from Deane. Both are close to the town centre. Freshers are the priority - 100% can be accommodated.

Cost for the 2005/2006 academic year was £2200 for 40 weeks, including Easter and Christmas vacations.

GETTING THERE

☛ By road: M61/J3, A666 for Chadwick; M61/J5, A58 for Deane. Good map on web site.
☛ By coach: London, 5-7:00; Liverpool 2:00.
☛ By rail: Manchester frequent.
☛ By air: Manchester Airport 30 mins.

BOURNEMOUTH UNIVERSITY

Bournemouth University
Talbot Campus
Fern Barrow
Poole
Dorset BH12 5BB

TEL 01202 524111
EMAIL enquiries@bournemouth.ac.uk
WEB www.bournemouth.ac.uk

Bournemouth Students' Union
Talbot Campus
Fern Barrow
Poole
Dorset BH12 5BB

TEL 01202 965774
FAX 01202 535990
EMAIL suvpcomms@bournemouth.ac.uk
WEB www.subu.org.uk

VAG VIEW

One point about Bournemouth is that it has found a way in to some seriously good employment niches. The other point is that this premier seaside resort university has some great extra-curricular opportunities.

CAMPUSES

Talbot (2 miles from the town centre) is the main campus; the other, Bournemouth, or Town Campus, is more of a collection of town sites, with teaching facilities for Business, Health, Design, Engineering, Computing, Conservation. There's a no-parking rule within a mile. Students are also discouraged from bringing cars on to Talbot, though many do. There's a free bus service between campuses and halls.

FEES, BURSARIES

UK & EU Fees, £3000 p.a. with £1000 bursary to applicants receiving full HE Maintenance grant and a sliding scale for those receiving partial maintenance grants. Also sporting and academic scholarships. Contact Student Financial support Adviser on 01202 965596.

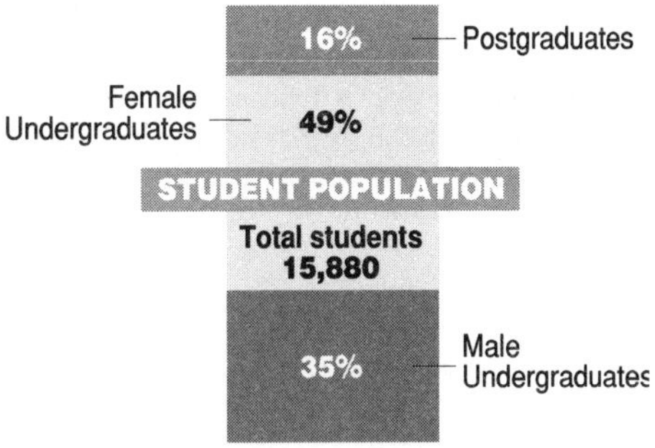

STUDENT PROFILE

'On first entry to the place you may think you've entered a photo shoot for a *Next* catalogue, owing to arrivistes trying to impress anyone who may be watching,' writes Aidan Goatley. 'Look more closely and you can spot those who've been there longer than a year and for whom ironing is not the most important thing in the world.'

In fact, the main campus is very studenty and unpretentious. This may be a career-orientated

UNIVERSITY/STUDENT PROFILE

University since	**1992**
Situation/style	**Campus**
Student population	**15880**
Undergraduates	**13375**
- mature	**25%**
- non EU undergraduates	**3%**
- male/female	**42/58**
- non-traditional student intake	**23%**
- state school intake	**99%**
drop-out rate	**8%**
- undergraduate applications	**Constant**

student body, but there's an excellent scene both in union and in town, and a relaxed feel.

ACADEMIA & JOBS

A £7.5 million Library & Learning Centre opened in January, 2003, and since last year there's a part-time entrepreneurial course – START – aimed at providing skills and professional support for anyone who wants to turn their ideas into commercial realities.

Around 4% of Bournemouth graduates become advertising account executives with major agencies like TBWA, JWT, WCRS, CIA Medianetwork, New PHD, Mediacom, and Mediapolis, or execs in publishing companies, public relations consultancies, research consultancies or in the marketing departments of other large companies. Bournemouth's Advertising and Marketing Communications needs 300 points (General Studies excluded). The course is 'twinned' with an agency through the Institute of Practitioners in Advertising. Six months work experience is part of it. Some move on to the MA in Marketing Communications. Lecturers here tend to be drawn from the world of work. It's all very practical, job-focused, and the uni overall is very media and business orientated.

They recently merged the Business School and School of Finance and Law. They are specialists in commercial & business law, and the uni has LLB Law & Taxation and BA Accounting & Taxation. You can also take the Common Professional Examination (CPE) here, which you'll need if you want to become a solicitor and don't have a law degree.

Managers and administrators, accountancy staff, marketing and sales managers, advisers, consultants, office and large company general managers proliferate on their graduate employment score card. Their degrees in business, sales and marketing are a main focus. Look at Business Management, a 2-year Foundation followed by 1-year top-up to BA, or the 3-year BA Business Studies (full or part-time, it also comes with Languages). For the more techno-minded, there's a 4-year sandwich BSc Business Information Systems Management – all for just 200 points. Later, there's a Doctorate in Business Administration and MAs in Human Resource Management, Information Systems Mgt and International Business Administration.

Note, too, the Media School Management courses, such as BA International Marketing Management, MAs in Corporate Communication, Marketing Communications and Services Marketing. You can also get as specific management-wise in Retail or Sports or Tourism, etc. Look at the 4-year sandwich International Marketing (Int. Retail Mkting HND top-up available too), 4-year sandwich Marketing or Leisure Marketing. Teaching inspection, 22.

They also have a ground-breaking 3-year, part-time, on-line Foundation Degree in Business and Management, launched by Bournemouth with Leeds Metropolitan and UK eUniversities (UkeU). The Army was the first major corporate client.

Of the many art colleges and universities with Animation degrees, few have as fruitful a line into the film and video world as Bournemouth, hosts to the National Centre for Computer Animation. The recent Grade 5 in research (Art & Design) suggests strength in depth in the area of visual image.

Recently the Media School unveiled a state-of-the-art Motion Capture facility. 'MoCap' tracks and records the movement of a human subject or object as computerised motion data so that three-

ACADEMIC EXCELLENCE

TEACHING:
(Rated Excellent or 17+ out of 24)

Media Production & Scriptwriting, Communication & Journalism & PR, Nursing & Midwifery, Archaeology, Business/Finance, Tourism	**22**
Land-based Enterprise (Agric), Subjects Allied to Medicine, Art & Design	**20**
Electrical & Electronic Eng. Food Qual/Service Industries	**19**
Product Design/Design Visualisation/Eng. Business Development, Modern Langs (Bus: French, Germ, Spanish)	**18**

RESEARCH:
*Top grades 5/5**

Art & Design	**Grade 5**

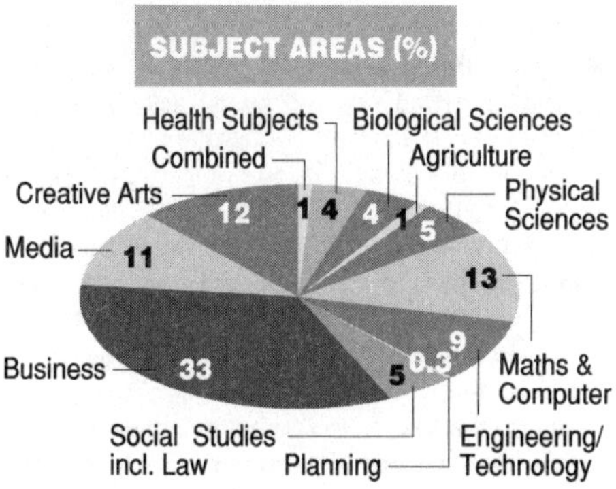

dimensional images can be animated with realistic motion in real time – animating characters in computer games, film or TV. Look at their animation degrres. There's a range of postgrad courses in Animation, Special Effects and Computer Games Technology & Design, too. The Wallisdown Campus of The Arts Institute at Bournemouth (www.arts-inst-bournemouth.ac.uk) is adjacent, and they have BA (Hons) Film & Animation Production. Students enrolling should have prior film or video experience.

Meanwhile, Bournemouth's BA Hons Television Production (Art & Design Faculty) offers practising TV producers, writers and technicians as your teachers. Great resources and top employment track record. Look also at their BA Hons Multimedia Journalism, Interactive Media Production degrees and Photomedia (Photography, Film & TV) degrees and MA Radio Production (there are also good PG Diplomas).

Activities are backed by good student media. *Nerve Magazine* was among the student awards in 2004, as was *Student Press* this year. Birst Radio scooped an award in 2005. You can contact the head of student media at suvpcomms@bournemouth.ac.uk

The student-run television station, also Nerve, won top honours as station of the year at the 2003 National Student Television Awards and was evident among the award winners again this year. The tie-up between extra-curricular and academic activities doesn't stop there. In 2004 student scriptwriter Howard Hunt became the first Briton to receive the Sir Peter Ustinov prize at the International Emmy Awards Ceremony in New York. The relevant degree is Scriptwriting for Film & TV. Media Production and Scriptwriting dropped only 2 points at the assessments. Those not making it straight into scriptwriting find work as script readers, editors, agents, production assistants, researchers, etc, or write for for radio, magazines, corporate videos, even computer games. Recent figures showed that 18 out of 23 traceable graduates were in permanent employ- ment, one was in temporary employment, two were in further study and one had opted for time out from a career to become a mother. There is also a strong Creative Writing degree.

Computer Science is another strong employment niche. Some 7% + graduates become software engineers or consultants or systems analysts. Look at BSc Software Engineering Management which makes full use of two of their curricular strengths, also BEng Electronic Systems Design, Computer Communications and Applied Computing & Electronics.

Other graduate employment strengths include BSc Archaeology Recently, renowned forensic archaeologist Prof Margaret Cox established the world's first International Forensic Centre of Excellence here.

In sport, golf is a speciality. The third year of their Sport Management (Golf) is spent in industry. The uni's expertise in Business Management and Communications, rather than sport per se, suggests an essentially different approach to the golf course at Birmingham, but no less hopeful employment wise. They're looking to get you employed in golf or health clubs, sports complexes, event management, tourism, local authorities, etc.

Finally, the 22-point teaching assessment scores in nursing and midwifery ensure a steady flow of students into the health sector. Out at Kingston Mauward College, there are also degrees in Animal Management/Health & Nursing Studies.

SOCIAL SCENE

STUDENTS' UNION SU night club, **The Old Fire Station** (**TOFS** for short) is the envy of many a Student Union up and down the country. It's very

AT A GLANCE

ACADEMIC FILE:	
Subjects assessed	**20**
Excellent	**70%**
Typical entry requirements	**280 points**
Application acceptance rate	**21%**
Students-staff ratio	**16:1**
First/2:1 degree pass rate	**57%**
ACCOMMODATION FILE:	
Guarantee to freshers	**Apply early**
Style	**Halls, flats, houses**
Catered	**None**
En-suite	**1,000+ rooms**
Price range pw	**£65-£88**
City rent pw	**£60-£100**

WHAT IT'S REALLY LIKE

UNIVERSITY:	
Social Life	★★★★
Campus scene	**Spin doctors & suits/up-beat ents**
Student Union services	**Good**
Politics	**Little interest**
Sport	**Relaxed**
National team position	**42nd**
Sport facilities	**Good**
Arts opportunities	**Available**
Student magazine	**Nerve**
Student newspaper	**Student Press**
Journalism Awards	**2005 winner**
Student radio	**Nerve FM, also Birst FM**
Student TV	**Nerve TV**
TV awards	**2005, 2 awards**
Nightclub	**The Old Fire Station**
Bars	**Dylans, D2**
Union ents	**Fancy Dress Mondays, Lollipop, Comedy Factory, RAG, one-off gigs**
Union clubs/societies	**40**
Parking	**Poor despite many with cars**
TOWN:	
Entertainment	★★★★
Scene	**Beach, shopping, night life vibrant**
Town/gown relations	**Good**
Risk of violence	**Average**
Cost of living	**High**
Student concessions	**Good**
Survival + 2 nights out	**£75 pw**
Part-time work campus/town	**Good**

cool and has three rooms to play in! The student special is a legendary Friday night out *Lollipop*, with more r'n'b and cheese than you can shake a stick at. Popular too are the funky fancy dress parties where themes include: *Back to Skool, Greece, Dr's and Nurses, Chav Party* and *Pyjama Party*. Wednesday's is live band night, Monday nights is also home to *Comedy Factory* where doors open at 8 and Saturday nights sees *Maison* on monthly rotation. The crowning success of the club this year has been the one-off events and the club has been at capacity with artists like Hard Fi, Soulwax and Alan Fletcher aka. Karl Kennedy.

Balls are frequent and memorable. There are plenty to chose from - Freshers, Christmas, Valentine's, Sport - and the Summer ball, the crème de le crème of the entertainment calendar. It is held in a large field just outside Bournemouth and is more like a festival than a ball. With three or four tents, thousands of students dressed in the craziest costumes you can imagine, dancing till the early hours of the morning. The survivors photograph is the *piece de resistance*, where all the remaining party people go down to the beach and have their photo taken as the sun comes up to prove their hardcore, all night status!

Talbot Campus is home to **Dylan's Bar**, with very cheap menu - pizza, burgers and healthier options like baked potatoes and omelettes. Evening entertainment includes quizzes, DJ's and live gigs. **D2** is a more relaxed sports bar where football is screened on the large projector screen. Both on campus bars are open seven days a week during term time.

What else is it good for? Well, media of course! *Nerve Magazine*, Radio, TV. These and Nerve Online and Nerve Events are fantastic opportunities to get involved. Nerve TV won two awards at the NaSTA Awards this year. Check out www.nervemedia.net. Also, Birst FM is the media department's MA station and *Student Press*, a paper run independently of the Student's Union won an award at the national Journalism Awards this year..

There's a vast array of clubs and societies to choose from from diving, computer gaming, poetry to horse riding and music, which is worth a mention: there's a good orchestra and choir.

There are also numerous volunteering opportunities to get involved in throughout the year with MAD days, Community Champions, etc. For more information log on to www.the-hub.org.uk. The Students' Union also provides a free confidential advice service on issues relating to accommodation, course and finances.

Serious, specialist graduate employment opportunities are on offer, and it all goes on in a Brighton-style seaside resort, bursting with hedonistic opportunity, yet it doesn't quite cut the mustard for student involvement.

Yet, for all this, Bournemouth still doesn't quite have the intense student culture of some other universities. It's not easy to pinpoint why although it may be to do with lack of participation.

SPORT With the arrival of the course in sports

WHERE BOURNEMOUTH GRADUATES END UP

Health & Social Work: 5%; Education: 4%; Wholesale/Retail: 11%; Manufacturing: 9%; Financial Activities: 11%; Public Administration, Civil Service & Defence: 5%; Hotel/Restaurant: 6%; Transport & Communications (including Telecommunications): 6%; Construction: 1%; Personnel: 5%; Computer: 10%; Business & Management: 6%; Accountancy: 1%; Media (including Film): 6%; Legal 1%; Architecture: 2%; Publishing: 2%; Advertising: 2%; Sport: 0.5%.

Approximate 'graduate track' employed **62%**

management (see *Academia*, page 72), a brand new golf simulator has been installed in the Department of Sport and Recreation. This joins the south coast's premier climbing facility, the Hot Rocks climbing wall. Proximity to the sea encourages windsurfing, sailing, paragliding, jet skiing, etc. The uni provides full-time instructors and facilities for a wide range of other sports, and there has been a huge improvement in their national placings recently (42nd). A sports hall includes squash courts and multigym. Cricketers play at the county-standard ground, Dean Park.

TOWN Dropped in the middle, where four roads meet, we found wall-to-wall pleasure, whatever your bent. There's no shortage of things to spend money on, and part-time opportunities for work are legion. It is an extraordinary place, a born-again English seaside resort, and if bar and club life proves too much, there's always the beach, and the New Forest is but a short drive away.

PILLOW TALK

Accommodation is guaranteed for first years, but the guarantee includes hotels and guest houses, so get in quick. Places in the student village on Talbot (3 to 7-bed houses; free internet access), and in Hurn House (single study bedroom with sink in central Bournemouth; free internet access), Cranborne House (single en-suite study bedroom 5 mins from Hurn House; no parking; internet access; subsidised uni bus) and brand new Purbeck House (single, en-suite study bedrooms close to Cranborne House; internet with one-off connection charge) are limited to 250, 152, 497 and 518 respectively. Rooms in Talbot are en suite. Abbotsbury House in Pokesdown, close to Bournemouth Hospital is the new residence (4-6 bed flats) for nurses.

As in most seaside resorts, town accommodation is plentiful and good.

GETTING THERE

☛ By road: M3/M27/A31/ A338, The Wessex Way; at second r/about follow uni signs to Talbot. From west A35 then A3049 (Wallisdown Road). For Bournemouth campus, leave A338 at St Paul's r/about (Travel Interchange junction) on to St Paul's road and find a car park.

☛ By rail: London Waterloo, 1:45; Bristol, 2:30; Manchester, 5:37.

☛ By coach: London, 2:15; Bristol, 3:10.

UNIVERSITY OF BRADFORD

The University of Bradford
Richmond Road
Bradford BD7 1DP

TEL 0800 073 1225
FAX 01274 236260
EMAIL course-enquiries@bradford.ac.uk
WEB www.bradford.ac.uk

Bradford University Union
Richmond Road
Bradford BD7 1DP

TEL 01274 233300
FAX 01274 235530
EMAIL ubu-communications@bradford.ac.uk
WEB www.ubui.co.uk

VAG VIEW

A university since 1966, it came out of Bradford Technical College, which itself grew out of the textile industry in the 1860s. Today the connection between higher education and the workplace remains key. Their slogan is 'Making Knowledge Work' and they have erected a 5-metre high, bronze sculpture to celebrate it. There's a first-class Modern Languages Department, which facilitates an international dimension to

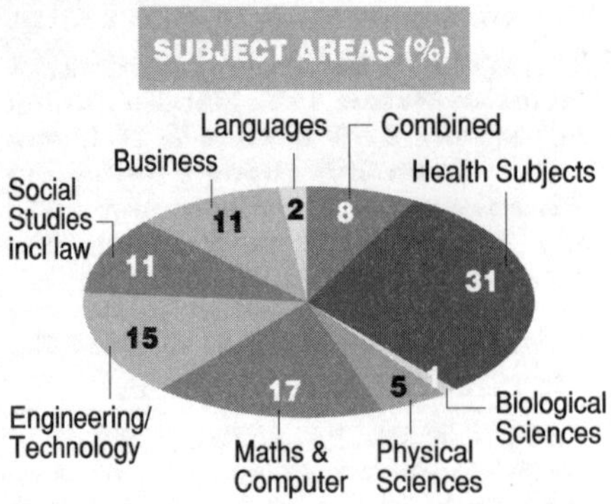

much else of what's on offer academically, and they ride high in the tables for graduate provision in the health industries, electronic & electrical manufacturing and in the pharmaceutical industry. More than a quarter of intake is now in health/medical sciences and Bradford has the country's largest Optometry Department.

What's more, students do actually like it here. Bradford is not London, nor is it Milton Keynes (thank God!), nor yet is it Leeds. Bradford may challenge the southern picture of where England is/should be, but what it offers undergraduates is a very studenty, close-knit, pub-based, curry-central experience, uninhibited by issues of wealth and class. To many a Bradford student, the southerner's picture of the acceptable face of the North, namely Leeds, because of its premier-league nightclubs and Harvey Nichs, appears rather expensive and, well, just a tad outré. *Bradford students can easily partake of Leeds, as the city is just a few moments down the road, but few do.*

This year, after much consultation with staff and students, the uni has earmarked £130 million to enhance existing buildings and create more social space for students, bringing facilities onto one campus.

UNIVERSITY/STUDENT PROFILE	
University since	**1966**
Situation/style	**City campus**
Student population	**10143**
Undergraduates	**7855**
- mature	**33%**
- non EU undergraduates	**20%**
- male/female	**48/52**
- non-traditional student intake	**49%, high**
- state school intake	**94%**
- drop-out rate	**11%**
- undergraduate applications	**Up 6%**

CAMPUS

The main campus, a ten-minute stroll from town, is compact and bounded by roads on all four sides. All teaching, except for Business Studies, is carried out on site, and there are many halls of residence.

It is a relatively small uni and has a reputation for being a particularly close-knit community. There's crime in the city, as in any city, but there's a safety bus at night to truck you anywhere from campus within a seven-mile radius. The union makes student safety an absolute priority.

FEES, BURSARIES

UK & EU Fees, £3000 plus £600 for sandwich year in 4-year course. Full Foundation Degrees also £3000, but £1200 for Foundation Year (£3,000 if in Clinical Sciences). If you are in receipt of a Maintenance grant, regardless of whether you receive a partial or full grant, you will be eligible for £500 bursary from the uni in your first year, £700 in your second, and £900 in your final year of full-time study.

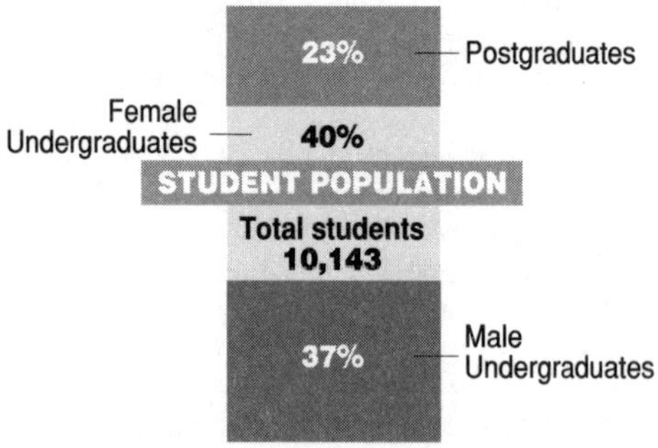

STUDENT PROFILE

They have an open access policy, a diverse student population and the kind of drop-out rate that suggests everyone's happy with that.

There is a particular welcome for overseas students and careful monitoring of all processes of integration. Most undergrads are scientists and techies, but life doesn't get too predictable.

ACADEMIA & JOBS

Broad study areas at Bradford are Archaeological Sciences, Chemical and Forensic Sciences, Computing & Informatics, Design & Technology, Engineering, Geography & Environmental Sciences, Health Studies, Humanities, ICT, Law, Life Sciences,

WHERE BRADFORD GRADUATES END UP

Health & Social Work: 5%; Education: 4%; Wholesale/Retail: 11%; Manufacturing: 9%; Financial Activities: 11%; Public Administration, Civil Service & Defence: 5%; Hotel/Restaurant: 6%; Transport & Communications (including Telecommunications): 6%; Construction: 1%; Personnel: 4%; Computer: 4%; Business & Management: 3%; Accountancy: 1%; Media (including Film): 2%; Legal 3%; Publishing: 1%; Advertising: 0.5%.

Approximate 'graduate track' employed **82%**

Management and Business, Media Studies, Psychology, Social Sciences.

Note the very good graduate track employment record (82% – only Cambridge Uni did better) against the relatively light average entry requirement (260 points).

There's a good ratio of PCs to students, and excellent facilities to log into library electronic sources via laptop. A wireless network has been established across the campus so that students can log in free from anywhere. Discounted 'Bradford-ready' student laptops are available

A Disability Office follows a proudly proactive strategy. An organisation called Impact targets ethnic students with a view to enhancing their employment chances.

Bacteriologists and microbiologists work with living organisms, an awareness of human health and environmental issues, food poisoning, drugs, viruses, bacteria and other bugs. It's an important field, and Bradford is a leader, one aspect of the health industry dimension which is indeed their single biggest area of graduate employment, and which includes a pioneering Clinical Science pathway into medicine. Some 30% of graduates do something connected with health, and a quarter of intake is now in health/medical sciences. BSc Hons Biomedical Sciences comes in at 260 points, Medical Microbiology the same. But the uni's expertise is ever wider – biochemists, pharmacists, medical scientists (see their BSc Applied Biomedical Sciences, new this year), physiotherapists (5% of all Bradford graduates), medical radiographers and midwives all look carefully at what is on offer here. A £6-million Institute of Pharmaceutical Innovation has recently been completed.

See their 3-4-tear (sandwich) BSc Chemistry with Pharmaceutical & Forensic Science and a 4-year MChem in this, also the 4-year MSci Forensic and Medical Sciences. Also their pharmaceutical management, pharmacy and pharmacology degrees

Bradford are among the leaders, too, in producing graduate ophthalmic opticians, almost a fifth of them in fact from the country's largest Optometry department. However, they're not giving away places for BSc Hons Optometry. Teaching inspection 23 out of 24 points.

Another fruitful avenue is BSc Archaeology. They earned 22 out of 24 points at the assessments and Grade 5 for research. At least one science will be required. New this year is a BA in it too

The uni's employment map is studded with systems analysts, software engineers, computer/IT consultants and programmers. Look at the Computing and Cybernetics faculties. There is a fine track record in film through its BSc Computer Animation & Special Effects degree, and the BSc Animatronics is especially interesting in that it teaches technology and skills to create, sculpt and animate motorised puppets – the 'live' monster that you see in movies. New to this field this year are Design for Computer Games and a BA in Computer Animation.

ACADEMIC EXCELLENCE

TEACHING:
(Rated Excellent or 17+ out of 24)

Philosophy, Politics	**24**
Pharmacology, Other Subjects Allied to Medicine, Nursing	**23**
Archaeology	**22**
Electric & Electronic Eng, Economics	**21**
Chemical Engineering, Civil Eng, General Eng, Molecular Biosci	**20**
Modern Langs (incl Russian)	**18**

RESEARCH:
*Top grades 5/5**

European Studies	**Grade 5***
Biomedical Sciences, Mechanical/Aeronautical/ Manufacturing Eng, Politics, Archaeology, Philosophy	**Grade 5**

Among their ICT & Computer Applications degrees is the new ICT with Media, and joining the BSc Media Technbology & Production is a raft of six BA Media Studies degrees (cinematics, animation, digital imaging, music techno, TV, web design).

AT A GLANCE

ACADEMIC FILE:	
Subjects assessed	**21**
Excellent	**62%**
Typical entry requirements	**260 points**
Application acceptance rate	**23%**
Students-staff ratio	**17:1**
First/2:1 degree pass rate	**54%**
ACCOMMODATION FILE:	
Guarantee to freshers	**100%**
Style	**Halls**
Catered	**None**
En suite	**5%**
Approx price range pw	**£46-£72**
City rent pw	**£35-£50**

Look, too, at another niche area – their Electrical and Electronic Engineering, Mobile Communications and Telecommunications degrees. Again, the Automotive Design Technology and Integrated Industrial Design (Eco Design, Sports Technology, etc) degrees make them leaders in starting careers for design and development engineers.

Would-be social workers and counsellors should also consider Bradford. The Social Work degree is accredited by the General Social Care Council. There's also BA Applied Criminal Justice Studies. New BA and BSc degrees in Psychology are on the brink of being approved.

Since September 2005, there is a fully fledged School of Law with an LlB, and you'll also find BSc Internet, Law & Society.

Other key strands take us further into the ethos of the place, Bradford's famed Department of Peace Studies (studied from the standpoints of ethics, psychology, sociology, history) and such as International Relations & Security Studies and Conflict Resolution.

SOCIAL SCENE

Principal gathering place at the **Richmond** (the uni building) is the **Steve Biko** bar (serves food as well), famous for its appearance in the *CAMRA Good Beer Guide* and distinguished, too, by an L-shaped pool table and jukebox. At the Communal Building there's a small nightclub, **Escape** (100), both with big screen TVs. Also in the Commie are the main venue, **The Basement** (1,300 capacity), home to cheesy/dance Friday night disco, *FND*, and now **Colours** (450), actually part of the Basement, though you can't see the joins, for late-night licence, smaller gigs and club-nights. Other clubnights are currently *Rock Sox* (rock/indie) and *Pop Sox* (cheese/retro), FND (Friday Night Disco) and Allsorts (LGBT night). Live acts too.

There's no arts faculty at Bradford but they have three of the most pulsating arts venues to be found anywhere. **Theatre in the Mill** is home to BUTG (Bradford Uni Theatre Group), which puts on a show (student or pro) every week and has the cheapest bar (**Scaff Bar**) in the uni. **The Tasmin Little Music Centre** does similar stuff for a student jazz ensemble, choral society, chamber choir and three orchestras, and an amazing series of *Music for Lunch* at the **Alhambra Studio** in Great Horton Road. Then there's **Gallery II** for art.

Student cinema, **BSC**, happens three times a week – art movies and the latest blockbusters, many only a few months after general release, all for a couple of quid. Showings are in **Great Hall** (capacity, 1300).

> ***Bradford may challenge the southern picture of where England is/should be, but what it offers is a very studenty, close-knit scene, uninhibited by issues of wealth or class, and a graduate track employment record second only to Cambridge.***

Media-wise there's *Scrapie*, the award-winning, fortnightly magazine, RamAir fm for student radio. Among some fifty societies, Twirl Soc and Amnesty are the most popular. Amnesty International is of course the foremost organisation in defence of human rights. Twirl Soc, you may be intrigued to discover is about twirling, throwing, juggling anything that spins in a circle of motion. Politics spins left, activity average – war, racism, recycling.

SPORT There are thirty-five sports clubs – women's volleyball is a particular strength. There's an on-campus sports centre (25m swimming pool, sauna suite, solarium, brand new Nautilus fitness suite, etc.), squash courts and two sets of playing fields, a dozen or so in all for cricket, football and rugby, plus 9000 square metres of artificial turf sand-grass for five-a-sides, netball and including a full-size hockey pitch. One site is behind the halls of residence, the other 4 miles from campus, where the pavilion has a bar.

TOWN Bradford is curry central and the cheapest

WHAT IT'S REALLY LIKE	
UNIVERSITY:	
Social Life	★★★★
Campus scene	**Close-knit, active, studenty**
Student Union services	**Good**
Politics	**Left - funding, war, racism, recycling**
Sport	**35 clubs**
National team position	**122nd**
Sport facilities	**Good**
Arts opportunities	**Excellent drama dance, film, music; art avg**
Student magazine	**Scrapie**
Student radio	**RamAir**
Nightclub	**Basement,**
Small venue	**Escape**
Bars	**Steve Biko, Courtyard**
Union ents	**Live plus club-nights Rock Sox, Pop Sox, disco - FND, Allsorts (LGBT)**
Union clubs/societies	**85**
Most popular societies	**Twirl Soc/Amnesty**
Parking	**Good**
CITY:	
Entertainment	★★★
Scene	**Curry central/ rough in parts**
Town/gown relations	**OK**
Risk of violence	**Average**
Cost of living	**Low**
Student concessions	**Excellent**
Survival + 2 nights out	**£40 pw**
Part-time work campus/town	**Good**

university city in the country. You'll be amazed by the cost, the quality and the sheer number of eateries. You eat it with chapatis here, not rice, and a three-year degree is barely enough time to be sure that you have found the best. Prices hover around £3 for a basic chicken dish with chapatis. At **Mumtaz Paan House** on Great Horton Road they charge by weight. Students have curry locals; staff and dishes become firm friends.

Bradford, a city of traditional pubs was shaken a few years ago with the advent of **Hogshead** (aka Bar Ikea), **Varsity**, the **Freestyle & Firkin** - not pubs, but bars where food is part of the deal. **Chicago Rock Café** also came to town - all on Great Horton Road, right by the uni. Still, there's atmosphere in older student haunts, however often they refurbish them - **The Peel** (Richmond Road), **Delius Lived Next Door** (Claremont) and the **Queens Hall**, though this is a bit *ex*-student: replete with MTV during the day, but suits and towny vibes at night.

Gaudi's (was **Tumbler's**) and **Club Rio** - Wednesday night (indie/'80s) are enjoyable venues almost on campus, the first tucked behind the Richmond, Club Rio practically next door to Longside halls. City clubs **Nexus** (was **Underworld**: late night cellar drinking), and **Pickwicks** (now **Bar Margaloof** but still known as Pickwicks: student DJs: pop, dance and indie) are a student institution.

PILLOW TALK

New in 2003 was Wardley House in the city centre - all bedrooms en suite and organised into flats. Trinity Hall, at the Laisteridge Lane site (5 mins from campus), offers en suite. It is overshadowed by the two tower blocks, Revis Barber Hall and Dennis Bellamy Hall. Also here is Charles Morris Hall for health students. The halls on the main campus are cheaper and uncatered, and there is little to choose between Shearbridge Green, Longside and Kirkstone , but Bradford and University halls get the thumbs down.

Planned for summer 2007 are new residential blocks with a mixture of en-suite and standard rooms, eventually with 1,000 bed spaces, the new facility to form Europe's first 'Sustainable Student Village', presenting students with the issues of living a sustainable lifestyle by experiencing it first hand.

GETTING THERE

☛ By road: M62 and M606 connect with national motorway network; from north, A629/A650; from northeast, A1 or A19, then A59, A658.
☛ By rail: London King's Cross, Birmingham, 3:00; Edinburgh, 4:00; Manchester, 1:00.
☛ By air: Leeds/Bradford Airport.
☛ By coach: London, 4:30; Manchester, 1-2:30.

STUDENT BRIGHTON - THE CITY

It's often been said there is something a little bit cheeky about Brighton & Hove. Made popular by the flamboyant Prince Regent, Brighton has a reputation for naughtiness and frivolity. What you will find is a welcoming city full of diversity and tolerance, perhaps the most cosmopolitan place in the UK. It's multitude of clubs, shops, restaurants and vast range of entertainment make Brighton and Hove the 'city by the sea' that really does have everything for everyone, so it's no wonder so many students never leave and settle for good.

NIGHTLIFE

The town has a huge array of clubs and pubs. The place to be for students on a Wednesday is *Ave It!* at **Creation**, where Brighton and Sussex Uni students dance the night away fuelled by the cut price drinks.

Students head for the seafront clubs, including **The Beach** and **Concorde2**, home of the famous *Big Beat Boutique*. If it's drum and bass you're after, lesbian and gay clubs, reggae or salsa, you won't be disappointed; check local listings for info. If trash is your thing go to **Dynamite Boogaloo** and revel in cheesy and camp disco 'toons' and be astounded by the almighty Dolly Rocket and Boogaloo Stu's outrageous live cabaret.

Midweek madness continues with the Latino feel and many participate in the carnival-style nights. You could be forgiven for thinking that no one works in Brighton, as week-night events are often as packed as the big weekend events.

EATS

Brighton boasts cuisine from almost every country in the world. Entire streets, like Preston Street on the Brighton/Hove border are devoted to gastronomic indulgence, there are late-night and 24-hour restaurants, shops and supermarkets for the night owls. There are over 400 restaurants including Cordon Bleu, English, French, Indian, Mexican, freshly caught fish (and chips), Japanese, Thai, tapas, Greek, Spanish, Lebanese, Egyptian, American, Cajun, greasy spoon, vegetarian, places with beautiful views of the sea, sushi and take-away. The numerous Italian eateries situated in the **Lanes** are locked in a price war, each bending over backwards to offer pizzas and pastas at amazingly cheap prices, making it possible to have a filling meal and a pint for under a fiver in a decent restaurant.

It is said that there are nearly as many pubs in Brighton & Hove as there are days in the year, they range from sophisticated late-night-cocktail-bars, high street pub chains to small independent owned drinking dens.

Do head for the student friendly **Ali-Cats** which is good for cocktails and shows free early evening movies. **Mrs Fitzherbert's** offers a cosy drink regular and acoustic nights. For THE student pub experience seek out **The Druid's** where the insatiable landlord Chippy offers students a warm welcome, great food and regular drinks promotions to make everyone feel at home.

SHOPS

With the best shopping south of the capital, there are more than 700 independently owned shops to browse. For designer clobber and antiques The **Laines** will suit any wannabe David Dickinson, but the prices will not be 'cheap as chips'. The North Laine is the bohemian centre of the town: with feel-good veggie cafés, bars, great second hand emporiums and a mishmash of fabric and clothes shops there is not much you can't get your mitts on in this district. Kemp Town boasts a fleamarket, a second hand book shop and is home to Brighton's own Lesbian and Gay quarter, with bars, clubs and shops to attract the Pink Pound. Big name stores can be found under one roof at **Churchill Square**, and the **Marina** has designer outlet stores in addition to a gigantic Asda, bowling alley,cinema, casino and other attractions.

STREET/BEACH LIFE

Whether it is the middle of winter and you want to blow away the cobwebs, or top up the tan in the summer you will find the beach is a welcome respite from the hub bub of city life. Boasting two piers, but only one you can walk on thanks to the huge fire a couple of years ago, you can visit fortune tellers, play the penny falls, buy more rock than you can shake a stick at and kiss me quick, squeeze me slow to your heart's content.

Highlights of the many events include the month-long **Brighton Festival** held in May, both ravellers and locals flock to the beach and streets to enjoy the food, drink, juggling, samba band processions, free film shows on huge screens, firework displays and annual events like the **Pride Parade** and the **Winter Solstice** 'Burning of the Clocks' extravaganzas mean you are never short of something to do. There is also talk of **Fatboy Slim** holding another of his legendary beach parties.

ARTS

All over the city, self-expression is the way. Brighton Uni's **Grand Parade Gallery** and the **Brighton Art Gallery** in Pavilion Gardens feature regular innovative ever changing exhibitions.

Innovative, contemporary art is also displayed in a multitude of cafés, bars and often in the street. There are many live venues, which again cater to all tastes. The **Dome** concert hall has hosted diverse artists including the London Philharmonic, Beverly Knight and Air.

In terms of comedy, theatre and film, Brighton is incredibly spoilt. **The Paramount Comedy Festival** comes to town in October bringing big name talent like Jo Brand, Bill Bailey and Johnny Vegas. The **Komedia Cabaret** bar has two different productions simultaneously each night with dealsfor students. **The Dome**, **Theatre Royal** and the **Brighton Centre** get the big-name touring artists in addition to the snooker championships. **The Gardner Arts Centre** on the University of Sussex campus plays host to art, film, theatre, comedy and music, and is nationally acclaimed. If it all gets too much you can always nip to the flicks, The **Odeon** is the most student-friendly offering discounts; the **UGC** is part of the **Marina** multiplex, and the **Duke of York's** the only cinema with legs (no it's true they are hanging off the roof!), a Brighton treasure and the oldest purpose-built cinema in Britain shows art-house and classic films.

It is almost as if Brighton was made for students; you cannot ask for a much better place to study.

Harvey Atkinson

UNIVERSITY OF BRIGHTON

The University of Brighton
Mithras House
Lewes Road
Brighton BN2 4AT

TEL 01273 644644
FAX 01273 642825
EMAIL admissions@brighton.ac.uk
WEB www.brighton.ac.uk

Brighton Students' Union
Cockcroft Building
Lewes Road
Brighton BN2 4GJ,

TEL 01273 642870
FAX 01273 600694
EMAIL ubsu@brighton.ac.uk
WEB www.ubsu.net

VAG VIEW

Brighton town has been re-born as a city, a seemingly inevitable consequence of our long-time perception of it as London-by-the-sea. Brighton city is an energetic, laid-back, imaginative, vibrant, artistic, commercial, alternative, innovative, refreshing coastal cocktail, and its very own uni evinces some of these elements too.

The creativity of Brighton students fits them perfectly into the picture. The uni traces its roots back to 1877, when the School of Art opened on Grand Parade, opposite the Royal Pavilion. The Faculty of Arts & Architecture, as it is today, is very much part of the city. The cream of the art world strut their funky stuff around Brighton, while the commercial, innovative and energetic bits find expression beyond its bounds in the Brighton Business School, the School of IT and the Chelsea School of Sport.

All is brought together through CPD, a Continuing Professional Development initiative – the uni works with local councils, health authorities and industry throughout the whole region to educate and re-educate 'the workforce', as they put it like something out of Soylent Green.

And now, in partnership with Sussex University up the road, they have launched

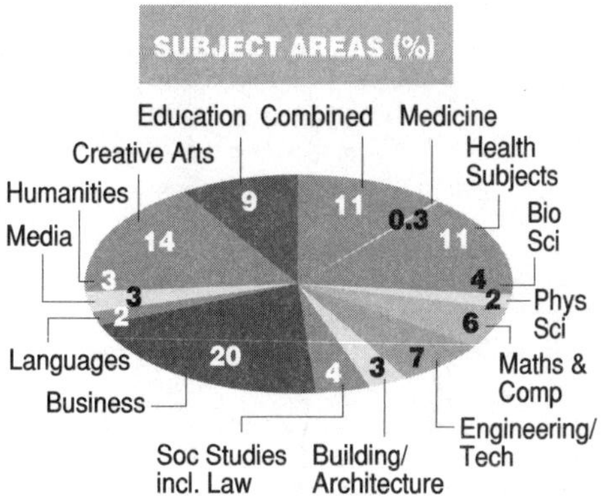

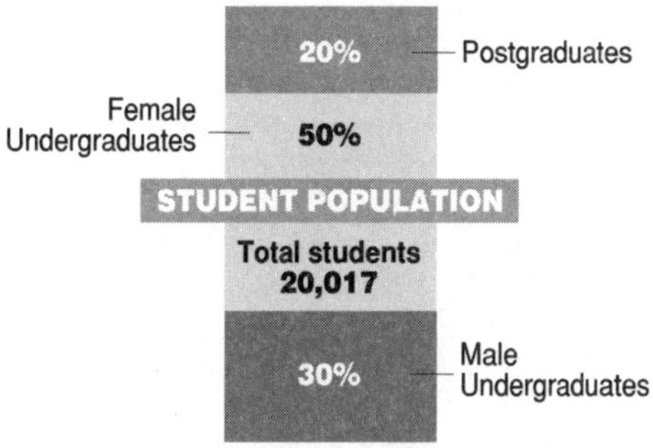

the Brighton & Sussex Medical School (see Academia, *page 83), and there'll be a training facility at the Royal Sussex County Hospital, the whole project ensuring ever closer links between the people's University of Brighton and the local community.*

Worth special mention, in line with its policy to facilitate access beyond the traditional uni-goer, their provision for student support has been consistently commended by the Quality Assurance Agency. Bursaries and loans are administered, with some 68% of students receiving advice and assistance on financial issues.

CAMPUS

Brighton University spreads through central Brighton and into the surrounding areas of Moulsecoomb, Falmer and Eastbourne. North up the Lewes Road from the self-conscious arts campus on **Grand Parade** – (rail and bus links are good, parking is not) – you get to the **Moulsecoomb Campus**, which houses the Business School, the Faculty of Science & Engineering, which includes pharmacy, maths, engineering, and the Faculty of IT. Further on you find the **Falmer Campus**, actually bang opposite the University of Sussex campus. While Grand Parade is the old art college and Moulsecoomb is the old technical college, the Falmer site was once Brighton's teacher training college and still offers teacher training today, along with health subjects.

Off to the east along the coast from Brighton, is the **Eastbourne Campus**, the uni's nationally renowned Chelsea School of Sports Science. They opened a £3-million sports centre there in November 2000. Outdoor pitches and indoor facilities are open to the public – widening access, integrating with the community. It's what this uni is all about, in case you hadn't heard.

Along the coast to the west, the Brighton-backed **University Centre Hastings** is delivering courses in information technology management and business, education, health and social care.

Find out which campus you're bound for and visit it - they are all very different.

UNIVERSITY/STUDENT PROFILE

University since	**1992**
Situation/style	**Seaside campuses**
Student population	**20017**
Undergraduates	**15937**
- mature	**39%**
- non EU undergraduates	**5%**
- male/female	**37/63**
- non-traditional student intake	**26%**
-state school intake	**93%**
- drop-out rate	**9%**
- undergraduate applications	**Up 10%**

FEES, BURSARIES

Fees £3000. Related bursaries, scale slides between £500 and £1000 depending on income: e.g. £30001 - £37425 - £500 per year; £17500 or less - £1000 per year. A hundred scholarships of £1000 each per year will be awarded on the basis of student achievement. There are various sports scholarships too, such as the elite athlete's squad and disabled athletes scholarships. They range from £300 to £1000.

STUDENT PROFILE

There is no typical Brighton student. It is all very disparate. The cutting-edge artistes may be the most visible in town, but creative arts is not representative of the whole student body.

Most notably, perhaps, students here are mature (34% of undergraduates), which means, not that they are all wrinklies but that they come here after their 21st birthday and may well be more work-orientated than your traditional undergrad freeloader. They are here for a clear-cut purpose.

There is also a big international intake. The 5% figure we give in the *Profile* box above refers only to the full-time first degree undergraduates. Many more from abroad come among the other half of HND undergrads, etc, in the 20000 total.

WHERE BRIGHTON GRADUATES END UP

Health & Social Work: 15%; Education: 16%; Wholesale/Retail: 11%; Manufacturing: 6%; Financial Activities: 8%; Public Administration, Civil Service & Defence: 4%; Hotel/Restaurant: 5%; Transport & Communications (including Telecommunications): 4%; Construction: 3%; Personnel: 3%; Computer: 2%; Business & Management: 3%; Accountancy: 1%; Media (including Film): 1%; Architecture: 2%; Publishing: 1%; Artistic/Literary: 5%; Sport: 3%.

Approximate 'graduate track' employed **61%**

Brighton has long been known internationally for its language-school history, so those same folk now flock across the Channel to the uni. 'We have a big language school here, do a lot of language work with all kinds of undergraduates.'

ACADEMIA & JOBS

The uni traces its roots back to 1877 when the School of Art opened on Grand Parade, opposite the Royal Pavilion. Today they have, besides the Fine Art (Painting, Printmaking, Sculpture), BA Fashion with Business. Successes in fashion and textiles have been both local and international and include employment with DKNY, Calvin Klein, Versace, Dolce & Gabbana, Valentino, Givenchy, Alexander McQueen, Hussein Chalayan and Julien MacDonald.

The cream of the art world strut their funky stuff around Brighton, while the commercial, innovative and energetic bits find expression beyond its bounds in the Brighton Business School, the School of IT and the Chelsea School of Sport.

Graphic artists, designers, illustrators, sculptors, ceramists and set designers also fare well, and the faculty leads graduates via Editorial Photography into the print industry via pre-production processes (origination/colour separation work). There's a Grade 5 rating for research, which indicates international status. Teaching inspection 22 out of 24. Clearly a talent and interest in art is essential and generally your portfolio will be crucial.

From Interior Architecture, Product Design (BSc), 3D Design, Music & Visual Art in the Art & Design Faculty to Civil Engineering, Design Engineering, Design Sports Technology in the Engineering Department, and BSc Architectural Technology in Science & Engineering, there is a strand which identifies the symbiotic nature of the uni's academic profile and weaves a colourful thread through the fabric of graduate employment nationally. What's more, entry is not demanding. Further design suggestions are made by BEng Hons Automotive Engineering, a big strength, where would-be racing car designers will be pitted at the Moulsecoomb campus, the old techno college just north of the city. Easy ride by train.

The creeping of skills out of one faculty into another has led to a rationalisation this year. They now have five faculties: Arts and Architecture; Education and Sport; Health; Management & Information Sciences; Science & Engineering.

In the vital health provision, there's a great reputation in Pharmacy, Biomedical Sciences, Biosciences, Nursing and even Acupuncture (BSc Oriental Medicine), and now they've teamed up with Sussex Uni in a new medical school.

The degree is a 5-year BMBS (Bachelor of Medicine, Bachelor of Surgery). A small, personal school, they are looking for commitment and compassion in their applicants, but it's not easy to get in - the application acceoptance rate was 10% in 2004 (11% is avg. across med. schools). You'll be based with the teacher trainees and other Health undergrads at Brighton Uni's Falmer Campus, readily accessible by road/train and bang opposite the Sussex University campus. Applications doubled in 2004.

Meanwhile, a joint bid from the universities of Brighton and Sussex to establish the first dental school in the South East outside London has been referred to Stage Two of the bidding process by the Department of Health and the Higher Education Funding Council for England. Note also the new Health & Social Care Foundation degree.

For pharmacists, there's BSc Pharmaceutical & Chemical Sciences (sandwich available) and MPharm. The School has been designated a 'preferred provider' by Boots plc. The new medical school can only raise its profile further. You'll be on the accessible Moulsecoomb Campus. Teaching Inspection 23.

Nationally, over 1000 graduates become physiotherapists each year. At Brighton, BSc

ACADEMIC EXCELLENCE

TEACHING
(Rated Excellent or 17+ out of 24)

Philosophy	**24**
Pharmacology & Pharmacy	**23**
Nursing, Maths, Art & Design, Subjects Allied to Medicine, Organismal, Molecular Biosciences, Library/Info Mgt, Tourism/Hospitality Mgt	**22**
History of Art, Civil Eng, Educ	**21**
Modern Languages (Dutch, French, German, Iberian Studies, Italian), Elec/Electron Engineering, Building.	**20**

RESEARCH:
*Top grades 5/5**

Biomedical Sciences, European Studies, Art & Design	**Grade 5**

Physiotherapy cuts the mustard in the jobs market, and there's a split tariff – entry is negotiable for mature students. Teaching inspection, 22 points. See, too, the new Occupational Therapy - BSc.

Bacteriologist and microbiologist graduates are similarly popular with employers. The uni is also up there in the Top 10 with its podiatry degrees.

Education is, of course, a major provision here – some 15% of Brighton's graduates will become teachers. Brighton is one of the new unis that outstrips traditionally strong, premier-league secondary school producers, Durham, Glasgow by sheer weight of number. Output: 50% secondary, 31% primary. You'll be at the Falmer site, opposite Sussex Uni. They gained top marks from Ofsted for Initial Teacher Education in 2002. Primary and Secondary Design and Technology made the highest category. English with QTS (7-14) asks 240 points at entry. Teaching inspection, 21.

For would-be physical training instructors (Education) Brighton leads the way nationally, the self-contained sporting campus is along the coast at Eastbourne, where this year state of the art facilities enabled a simulation by students of the first successful ascent of Mount Everest. Starting at the height of Everest Base Camp (17,600 ft), a relay of students climbed on a Stairmaster to the equivalent height of Everest (29,035ft) while carrying a rucksack and experiencing freezing weather conditions.

See also the new BA (Hons) Sport Journalism degree, which includes teaching for the National Council for the Training of Journalists certificate in magazine journalism. The BBC's director of sport, Peter Salmon, will be helping develop the broadcast aspect. See also the Foundation degree in Broadcasting.

The Faculty of Management and Information Sciences, new in 2003, combines the Business School, School of Service Management and the new school of Computing, Mathematics and Information Sciences, together with the research group CENTRIM. It was created to adapt to changes in the business and management world where the integration of IT and business is key to success.

In computing they offer a B/MEng Digital Electronics, Computing & Communications, BSc Computer Sciences or Computing, Digital Media Development, Informatique, Interactive Computing, Internet Computing or Internet Business Computing, Maths & Computing, Software Engineering, which produce a wealth of IT consultants. Sandwich modes are available. You'll be based at Moulsecoomb.

An interesting niche in the business provision holds a dedicated series of International Travel/Tourism Management degrees, which score well for employment. New this years are Entreprenuership in Hospitality/Ttravel & Tourism, and foundation degrees - Travel & Tourism Marketing and Tourism Enterprise Management.

Note, too, the language provision at this uni, which internationalises the business provision. Brighton has an international Grade 5 for research in European Studies, and a decent 20 points for undergraduate teaching in Modern Languages.

Other new degrees are Management in the Service Industries, Marketing Food & Drink, and Retail Management.

WHAT IT'S REALLY LIKE

UNIVERSITY:	
Social Life	★★
Campus scene	**Individual**
Student Union	**Aimless**
Politics	**Average; student issues, anti-war**
Sport	**70 clubs, very competitive out at Eastbourne**
National team position	**25th**
Sport facilities	**Good**
Arts opportunities	**Drama/Dance OK**
Student magzine	**Jon Doe**
Nightclub	**None**
Bars	**Falmer Bar**
Union ents	**Ave It! @ Creation**
Union societies	**50+**
Parking	**Not good**
TOWN:	
Entertainment	★★★★★
Scene	**Exceptional**
Town/gown relations	**OK**
Risk of violence	**Low**
Cost of living	**High**
Student concessions	**Good**
Survival + 2 nights out	**£100 pw**
Part-time work campus/town	**Average/excellent**

SOCIAL SCENE

STUDENTS' UNION The sad truth is that ents at Brighton have been flattened by a series of mishaps. First they had the **Basement**, a seriously good club/venue that was commandeered by the uni administration. Then they took over **Akademia,** a café bar and theatre on Manchester Street, which again was prised from them. Now all they have is **Falmer Bar, which has been under renovation**. Students make use of Sussex campus, and eat their heart out at The Retreat Café (Falmer) or Cockcroft Café (Moulescoomb), or go into Brighton, which is an amazing scene (see Student Brighton). The Union promotes the *Ave It!* clubnight on Wednesday nights at **Creation** on West Street. Out on the town can get expensive. Many of the jobs in Brighton are service sector based, so the wages reflect this, but there are opportunities for students to work in call centres and for local businesses where the rates of pay can be well above the minimum wage.

There are 50+ societies and 70+ sports clubs, and a student magazine called *Jon Doe*. They used to meddle with Sussex's radio station, but no longer apparently. There seems an aimlessness about the Students' Union, which is not matched by the uni admin, and which the students don't deserve. Perhaps the students couldn't care less what the Union puts on. Perhaps it has become superfluous because there is so much happening in town. See *Student Brighton*, above.

Sport Out at the sporty Eastbourne campus there's the new £3 million facility (see *Academia* above). Women's sport is particularly strong, though both sets of teams do well at inter-university level.

PILLOW TALK

Accommodation is all self-catered, mainly halls but also uni-leased houses/flats. They claim to be the cheapest in the south of England. New halls of residence on the university's Falmer campus opened in November 2003 providing an additional 162 en-suite rooms for students. This year there are new halls in Eastbourne - Welkins Halls. The multi-million pound complex will accommodate 354 students, all bedrooms have en-suite facilities with groups of six rooms sharing dining and kitchen areas.

AT A GLANCE

ACADEMIC FILE:	
Subjects assessed	**22**
Excellent	**73%**
Typical entry requirements	**250 points**
Application acceptance rate	**18%**
Students-staff ratio	**19:1**
First/2:1 degree pass rate	**54%**
ACCOMMODATION FILE:	
Guarantee to freshers	**58% live in**
Style	**Halls**
Catered	**None**
En suite	**66%**
Approx price range pw	**£60-£90**
City rent pw	**£70-£75**

GETTING THERE

- By air: Gatwick and Heathrow Airports.
- By road: M23 (past Gatwick), A23 to Brighton, on to A27 eastbound for Falmer, taking right turn (south on B2123) for Moulsecoomb. From east or west, A27, etc. For Eastbourne, A27 and signs south on to A22.
- By rail: London Victoria, 1:10. Change at Brighton for Moulscoomb and Falmer (8 mins).
- By coach: London, 1:50.

STUDENT BRISTOL - THE CITY

Billed by many as the London of the South West, Bristol has a distinctly West Country feel and the moment you hear the regional accents you'll know you're a long way from the gold-paved streets of London. Despite this regional feel Bristol itself is a buzzing multicultural city with loads going on and so much to offer that you'll feel as though you're reaping all the benefits of living in a capital city.

ROCK ON

Hills, churches and water are abundant in Bristol and the city has many lush green parks to stroll in. The tastefully-developed Harbourside houses many restaurants and galleries/art centres and is home to much of Bristol's social scene, especially in the summer when the Grolsch musical festivals come to the city (Massive Attack, Basement Jaxx and Kosheen have performed in previous years). In fact Bristol has a great music scene, born of the days when bands such as Massive Attack and Portishead made their name here. Centres such as **Colston Hall** and the **Carling Academy** host an array of local, national and International bands. Recent acts in the city are Hard-Fi, James Blunt, Babyshambles, The Magic Numbers and K T. Tunstall. The Junction and The Croft at Stokes Croft showcase more alternative or folk music.

The Student Union's **Anson Rooms** have also hosted their own share of great acts; last year saw the Kaiser Chiefs and Franz Ferdinand, while The Rakes are scheduled for the forthcoming term.

Clubs and pubs fill the city, though some are rather expensive. There are plenty of studentier hang-outs though. **Evolution** on the waterfront hosts great nights such as *Wedgies* on Wednesday and

Friday. **Bierkeller** and the **Carling Academy** have good student concessions and put on live alternative/rock music. A fledgling gay scene is to be found at the **Queen's Shilling** or **Vibes** at the bottom of Park Street.

Ninety percent of Bristol's off-licenses and many pubs are located on Whiteladies Road, near the University halls of residence. Ones worth a visit are Bohemia, **The Black Boy Inn** and the **Penny Farthing**. However, if you're looking for a more stylish joint you should head for **Sloanes** or **Henry J Beans**. And if your parents are in town then a trip to the lovely **Avon Gorge Hotel** is recommended - for a good view of the famous Clifton suspension bridge.

ART

The revamped **Arnolfini** on the Habourside offers a wide range of arty events - from performance poetry to contemporary art. The city of Bristol **Museum** is free entry and currently houses the throne of weapons (installed by artists using de-commissioned weapons from Mozambique) and a rather random collection of pianos and pottery.

Hours can be spent sipping bottomless coffee in cafés around the University areas though particularly good are the **Boston Tea Party** on Park Street and **Toby's Deli Diner** just off Tyndall Avenue. **The York café** in Clifton should also be road-tested for its great fry-up.

THEATRE, FILM

Theatres such as the Old Vic run great deals once a week when students pay a minimum contribution of £3.50 for a ticket. Bristol's **Old Vic** is on a par with London theatres with both the variety and standard of drama on offer. Recent plays such as Christopher Marlowe's Tamburlaine, starring Greg Hicks, got great reviews from the national press.

For musicals and flashy shows the **Hippodrome** is the place to go though you won't get such cheap tickets. More avant-garde or obscure plays/ performances can be found at **The Cube Microplex** (at Dove St South just off King Square). The art centre shows films and art exhibitions but also puts on all sorts of weird and wonderful events such as October's 'Ich bin ein Berliner' festival: a three day celebration of the said city showcasing electronic tunes, films and art.

If film's your thing then the city has a cinema to suit your every taste. **Cineworld**, **Vue**, **Showcase** and **Odeon** cinemas around Bristol show most Blockbusters and mainstream films while the **Watershed** and the Arnolfini on the Harbourside put on art house or International cinema. The **Imax** centre, also on the Harbourside, is worth a visit to see some incredible 3D and special effects. There are also several film festivals on throughout the year, the best being the 'Brief Encounters' short film fest and the self-explanatory 'Animated Encounters'.

OTHER ENTERTAINMENT

Sport is important in Bristol, even though the city lacks a top-flight football club. Bristol City have a large following and have enjoyed success in recent years, unlike local rivals Bristol Rovers.

For rugby, however, though relegated in 2003 from the Zurich Premiership, they are setting new records, finding their way back (and safely so) with extraordinary ease. They can rely too on Gloucestershire County Cricket Club to put a smile on their faces. A visit to all these clubs is well worthwhile.

Laura Cattell

UNIVERSITY OF BRISTOL

The University of Bristol
Senate House
Tyndall Avenue
Bristol BS8 1TH

TEL 0117 928 9000
0117 925 0177 (prospectus)
FAX 0117 925 1424
EMAIL admissions@bristol.ac.uk
WEB www.bris.ac.uk

Bristol Students' Union
Queens Road
Clifton
Bristol BS8 1LN

TEL 0117 954 5800
FAX 0117 954 5817
EMAIL president-ubu@bristol.ac.uk
WEB www.ubu.org.uk/

VAG VIEW

Still considered by many as the 'parent's choice' or the 'home for the Oxbridge rejects', Bristol is managing to break out of this restrictive mould and become a top-class and Internationally-renowned academic institution. Although the Independent School intake is consistently high, a widening participation scheme is gradually persuading applicants from previously under-represented groups. With the University focusing on the academic potential of a wider range of students, there is a growing proportion of mature and local students. Bristol's bid to become a world-status University is also reflected in the high percentage of overseas students - over 21% at the last count.

CAMPUS

Set a stone's throw from the city centre and near the trendy Clifton area, Bristol University is a great example of a city campus. It presents a safe but lively environment within a beautiful and vibrant city. University buildings such as the Gothic Wills Memorial Building and the 18th century Royal Fort House fit in well with the historic past of the city. The row of Victorian houses which form the Arts department is also a pretty place to spend your undergraduate days. This is all rather let down by the architectural eyesore that is the Student Union, a place which, luckily, is in line for demolition.

UNIVERSITY/STUDENT PROFILE

University since	**1909**
Situation/style	**Civic**
Student population	**22705**
Full-time undergraduates	**14860**
- mature	**12%**
- non-EU undergraduates	**6%**
- male/female	**44/56**
- non-traditional student intake	**14%**
-state school intake	**65%**
- drop-out rate	**8%**
- undergraduate applications	**Down 5%**

**see Introduction for key to tables*

FEES, BURSARIES

Fees £3000 p.a. Bursaries for those in receipt of full HR Maintenance Grant = £1,100, down to £500 min. if in receipt of partial HE Grant. Also bursaries for those in need living in the region, and sport and academic scholarships.

STUDENT PROFILE

What puts off state school kids that we talk to from the North was summarised in 1997 in the first edition of *The Virgin Guide* by a student called Tony Dunkels: 'Bristol University has the reputation, especially among some of its more northerly competitors, as being a bit of a shandy-drinkin', southern poof's university, comprising mostly ex-Oxbridge wannabes and the like.'

Today, if you provoke union bods along these lines they are genuinely hurt: 'The change has already occurred. It really isn't actively snooty any more.'

The truth is that the Sloanish element is a minority, it barely impinges on life here - less so than at Exeter, because it is all gathered together on a self-contained campus there - and if Bristol is exclusive, it is due to the high entry requirements that admit confident, ambitious and able students.

SUBJECT AREAS (%)

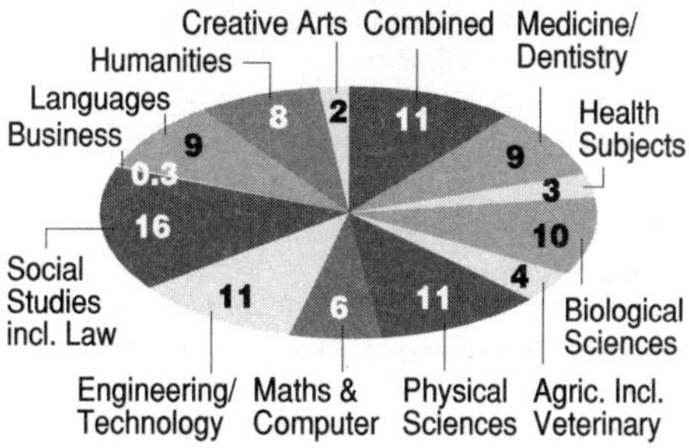

ACADEMIA & JOBS

Says Laura: 'Rated most recently in the Top 15 for both teaching and research Bristol University is more than a safe "parent's choice". Cutting edge for Medicine and Veterinary Science the uni is a mecca for the Science and Technology subjects. However, there are over 34 subjects on offer, and over 20% study Humanities or Languages. The Arts and Social Sciences library is a bit dark and dingy, but there are plenty of good faculty libraries if you need a quiet place to get some work done. There is excellent access to online journals and resources, and the IT provision is good. Staff are very helpful and range from the old-fashioned tweedy types to more dynamic younger ones.'

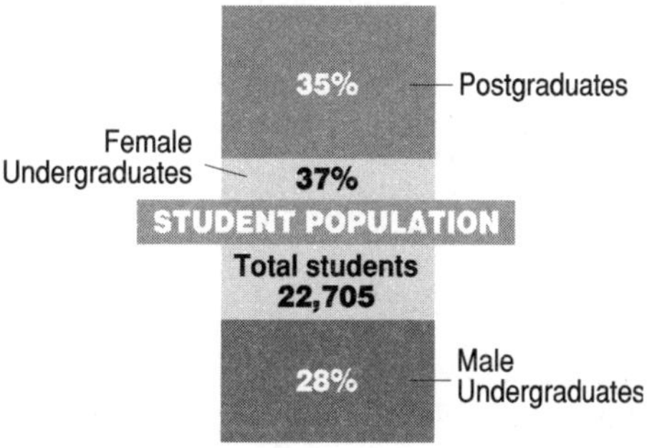

There's also a good careers service. A large number of Bristol graduates go either into the health industry or into commerce (finance, accounting, business management), but there are alternatives.

Would-be publishers and editors stream out of language, social and physical science, as well as health, and a strong tradition of student media has helped Employment figures are for similar reasons sound, too, in the realm of music, backed as that department is by an active student scene.

Into the Civil Service, popular routes are social studies, business and language departments, as well as biological and physical sciences. Strong extra-curricular activities support careers for many from Bristol in the army, the RAF and Royal Navy, and if it's a job in Defence you're after, consider the Engineering route. It's a 3/4/5-year B/MEng programme – the 5-year degree is Engineering Design, which ranks them high in the employment league for engineering design consultants. Aeronautical Eng comes with study in Europe, as does Computer Systems Eng and Mech Eng. There's also Avionic Systems, Electronic & Communications and such as Mathematics Modelling or Mathematics for Intelligent Systems.

Electrical & Electronic took full marks at the assessments and an international Grade 5 for research (as did Mechanical Eng) – many go into telecommunications from here. In Physical Sciences there's a rich BSc/MSci programme including such as Maths & Computer Sciences/Physics/Statistics/Study in Continental Europe, Physics with Astrophysics/Industrial Experience/again, European study. Entry requirements are high.

Social Studies also has a strong line into employment, producing charity and social workers and counsellors in number. They are world leaders in research, with a 6* rating. In the same faculty, Law comes with French or German (both 4 years), and non-Law graduates may opt for a 2-year full-time or 3-year part-time Senior Status Law degree here. All candidates must sit the National Admissions Test for Law (LNAT).

There is also a good record in producing tax experts and consultants at Bristol, the Faculty of Social Sciences & Law carrying a range of degrees involving economics, finance, mathematics, and of course accounting. Accounting & Finance, Accounting with Management, Accounting with Economics & Study in Continental Europe (4 years) bring us back to the core employment areas. Bristol is highly productive in accountancy, though not up with the giants (Birmingham, Warwick, Durham).

Where they really succeed in this sector is in investment and merchant banking – it's an area in which they take the lead nationally by quite a margin. Nearly half come through Economics, which scored 23 out of 24 at the assessments. Look at BSc Economics & Econometrics with Study in Continental Europe, Economics & Finance, etc.

Health is the strongest area, with dentists and doctors, veterinary surgeons and vet nurses finding certain employment. For the 5/6-year MB, ChB, you'll need to be able to tell them what you expect from a career as a doctor, that you are aware of the levels of commitment and challenge, and what you in particular have to offer. It's a 10% acceptance rate, with 344 undergrads joinging the course in 2004. Links are strong with special clinical academies in Bristol, Bath, Cheltenham,

ACADEMIC EXCELLENCE

TEACHING: *(Rated Excellent or 17+ out of 24)*	
Law, Mechanical Engineering, Chemistry, Geography, Applied Social Work, English.	**Excellent**
Electrical & Electronic Eng, Anatomy, Education, Molecular Biosciences, Veterinary	**24**
Drama: Theatre, Film, TV, Maths, Physics, Economics, Pharmacology, Philosophy, Politics, Psychology	**23**
Iberian Studies, Civil Eng, Aerospace Engineering, Organismal Biosciences	**22**
Sociology, Italian, German Classics/Ancient History	**21**
Russian, French, History of Art, Medicine, Theology	**20**
Dentistry	**19**

RESEARCH: *Top grades 5/5*/6**	
Clinical Lab Sci, Anatomy, Psychology, Biochemistry, Applied Maths, Statistics, Geography, Social Work, Russian, Drama	**Grade 6***
Community-based Clinical, Clinical Dentistry, Chemistry, Earth Sci, Civil Eng, Education	**Grade 5***
Clinical Laboratory Sciences, Biological Sciences, Veterinary, Physics, Pure Maths, Computer, Electrical/Electronic Eng, Mechanical Eng, Law, Politics, Social Policy, Sociology, Accounting, English, French, German/Dutch/Scandinavian, Italian, Classics, Philosophy, Theology, Music	**Grade 5**

Gloucester, Taunton, Swindon, where in years 3-5 you'll spend half your time. Entry typically AAB. 6-year prog: 3 un-related A-levels, usually non-science subjects; 5-year prog: A level Chemistry + two others (Biology good and can do one 'approved' non-science). Plus 6 Grade A GCSEs. The teaching assessment came in quite low at 20 points, but there's a world-class Grade 5*/6* for research into Community-based Clinical, Anatomy, Psychology, Biochemistry; Grade 5 Clinical Lab Sciences, Biological Sciences.

For dentists, it's the 5/6-year BDS. Entry AAB including Chemistry – the 6-year course allows entry with 2 non-science subjects. Teaching inspection again low at 19. Grade 5* for research..

For vets, there's the 5-year BVSc. Candidates must sit the Biomedical Admissions Test (BMAT). Also a 3-year Veterinary Pathogenesis and a 4-year Vet Nursing & Practice Administration. Teaching inspection 24 – better than for humans.

AT A GLANCE

ACADEMIC FILE:	
Subjects assessed	**37**
Excellent	**89%**
Typical entry requirements	**420 points**
Application acceptance rate	**10%**
Studentstaff ratio	**14:1**
First/2:1 degree pass rate	**81%, high**
ACCOMMODATION FILE:	
Guarantee to freshers	**90%**
Style	**Halls, houses**
Catered	**40%**
Approx price range pw	**£45-£110**
City rent pw	**£70**

SOCIAL SCENE

Students' Union Despite persistent rumours developing into definite plans this year to relocate the Union building closer to the Precinct in five years time, this year sees a brand new **Epi** bar, along with newly refurbished Union foyer., and continuing improvements eslewhere, including a renovation of the **AR2** small gig venue.

Three Union bars: **The Epi** (main student bar), **AR2** (for small gigs and as a bar for larger gigs in the adjacent **Anson Rooms**) and the Avon Gorge room (for large society events and awards ceremonies). **Café Zuma** serves hot and cold meals throughout the day. Main gig venue is the Anson Rooms, with 900 standing capacity, it plays host to up-and-coming bands. This year they've hosted the Magic Numbers, Kano, an official John Peel Day gig. Previously have hosted Prodigy, Coldplay and Chemical Brothers. Impressive gig listing can be found at www.ansonrooms.co.uk (new acts constantly added). The Epi has a weekly rota of events including karaoke evenings (Thurs), *Vodka* night (Mon); Wed - '*Propaganda*' night (new & classic indie/alternative music); Friday is a societies night; Saturday is *Fundraiser* night, live bands and . Various live music societies perform regularly in AR2, bringing undiscovered student talent to the Union.

Says Laura Cattell: 'The student attitude at Bristol is very much 'Work hard, play harder!' and so even if most of the student population do like the Monday 'Vodka' nights they'll still be at lectures on Tuesday morning.

Also the Union has two theatres: **The Winston Theatre** seats close to 200, while the **Lady Windsor Studio Theatre** is used for smaller productions.

Union societies are prodigious, 170 at the last count. Said a union bod: 'At Bristol we have massive diversity and truly cater for everyone's needs. For example our Debating Society is one of the best in the world, and Ballroom Dancing one of the best in the country. We also have ten performing arts societies that take four arts shows to the Edinburgh Fringe every year.'

Currently, most members are in the Music Society (BUMS) and Bristol Real Ale, though Bristol boasts an extremely active 'Student Community Action' office, which gives an average of 90,000 volunteer hours to the local community each year, and a leading RAG department, which raises over £100,000 every year. Recent additions include the Bristol Tea Society (complete with Decaf Rep!) and

WHERE BRISTOL GRADUATES END UP

Health & Social Work: 20%; Education: 6%; Wholesale/Retail: 5%; Manufacturing: 10%; Financial Activities: 12%; Public Administration, Civil Service & Defence: 6%; Hotel/Restaurant: 2%; Transport & Communications (including Telecommunications): 3%; Construction: 1%; Personnel: 5%; Computer: 3%; Business & Management: 4%; Accountancy: 6%; Media (including Film): 2%; Legal 2%; Architecture: 2%; Publishing: 2%; Advertising: 1%.

Approximate 'graduate track' employed **77%**

the aptly named BAPS (Bristol Anatomy and Physiology Society). They are also set to launch a new Union website at www.ubu.org.uk on 15th August 2006.

The Drama Society collects awards regularly, as does *Epigram*, the student newspaper (shortlisted for both best feature writer and best sports writer in 2005). Student radio is BURST, the new creative arts magazine: *Helicon*. They host the annual Screentest National Student Film Festival.

SPORT Says Laura: 'Sports-wise the University really does have something for everyone, from tennis to hang-gliding there are just so many societies. The flashy University sports centre on Tyndall Avenue has a large gym and daily fitness classes. And though it's a bit hard to find there is also a swimming pool on the ground floor of the Union building.'

The teams came 11th nationally last year. There are 54 sports clubs and a state of the art Sports Centre.

TOWN See *Bristol Student City* (page 85).

PILLOW TALK

Says Laura Cattell: 'Most first year students get allocated a place in halls which means a choice of two locations: Stoke Bishop and Clifton. There are nine halls of residence, but what is key here is the location. Stoke Bishop is about forty minutes from the University area with regular and cheap bus connections while halls based in Clifton are in one of the nicest parts of the city and just a fifteen minute walk from the University precinct. The best choice may seem obvious, but actually Stoke Bishop houses a larger number of students and therefore possesses a vibrant campus atmosphere which halls in Clifton really lack.

'That said you will learn to hate Black Boy hill as you traipse up and down it, to and from Stoke Bishop!'

WHAT IT'S REALLY LIKE	
UNIVERSITY:	
Social Life	★★★★★
Campus scene	**Lively, rich student culture**
Student Union services	**Good**
Politics	**Activity high, mainly student issues**
Sport	**54 clubs**
National team position	**11th**
Sport facilities	**Sports Centre**
Arts opportunities	**Cinema, theatre excellent**
Student newspaper	**Epigram**
Student magazine	**Helicon**
Student radio	**BURST**
Student TV	**UBFS**
Gig venues	**Anson Rooms, AR2**
Bars	**Epi, Avon Gorge**
Union ents	**Live, disco, etc**
Union clubs/societies	**170**
Most active societies	**Music, Real Ale**
Parking	**Poor**
CITY:	
Entertainment	★★★★★
Scene	**Full on waterfront and fringe**
Town/gown relations	**Clear differences**
Risk of violence	**Average-high**
Cost of living	**High**
Student concessions	**Good**
Survival + 2 nights out	**£80 pw**
Part-time work campus/town	**Good/excellent**

GETTING THERE

☛ By road: M4/J19, M32 or M5/J17 and follow signs to the zoo (an elephant).

☛ By rail: London Paddington or Birmingham New Street, 1:30; Nottingham, 3:00.

☛ By air: Bristol Airport.

☛ By coach: Birminghan, 2:00; London, 2:20

BRISTOL, UNIVERSITY OF THE WEST OF ENGLAND

Bristol, University of the West of England
Frenchay Campus
Coldharbour Lane
Bristol BS16 1QY

TEL 0117 32 83333
FAX 0117 32 82810
EMAIL admissions@uwe.ac.uk
WEB www.uwe.ac.uk

UWE Students' Union
Frenchay Campus
Coldharbour Lane
Bristol BS16 1QY

TEL 0117 32 82577
FAX 0117 32 82986
EMAIL union@uwe.ac.uk
WEB www.uwesu.net

VAG VIEW

Academically and in terms of graduate employment, there is much to convince students that UWE no longer deserves to be tarnished with the new-uni brush.

The problem has been rather that they have been short-dealed on campus. That is due to be sorted with a £150-million spend on facilities at Frenchay. First step was the Faculty of Education's move to this site and now, this year, a 'high-spec. student village, £80m student village with sports hall, all with good disability access. Most important: 'Following the implementation of a new constitution this academic year, UWESU have introduced a high participation, student representation system.' Long overdue.

FEES, BURSARIES

UK & EU Fees £3000 p.a. Bursary for students in receipt of full HE Maintenance grant: £1250; £750 if partial grant. See www.uwe.ac.uk/money. No top-up fees for placements. Guaranteed bursaries for students on Access courses. Several sports scholarships, to a maximum of £1000. Aardman Bursary for art, media and design courses; 5 Music bursaries up to £600 per year.

STUDENT PROFILE

Unlike most other unis established in 1992, there's a high intake from independent schools. Says Roy Delaney: 'I came from a Council House background, no pretensions me. When I signed up I was sitting next to a kid from Eton. We have a whole range, a real people mix.'

Another student said, 'West is the cool uni; we're more streetwise than Bristol students. A lot of UWE students congregate round the Arches to the west of Montpellier, Gloucester Road, Stokes Croft, Cheltenham Road. It's more Bohemian. Bristol students live in Clifton, Redland, more polished.'

UNIVERSITY/STUDENT PROFILE

University since	**1992**
Situation/style	**Campus/ city sites**
Student population	**27403**
Undergraduates	**22060**
- mature	**43%**
- non EU undergraduates	**3.6%**
- male/female	**40/60**
- non-traditional student intake	**28%**
- state school intake	**87%**
- drop-out rate	**8%**
- undergraduate applications	**Constant**

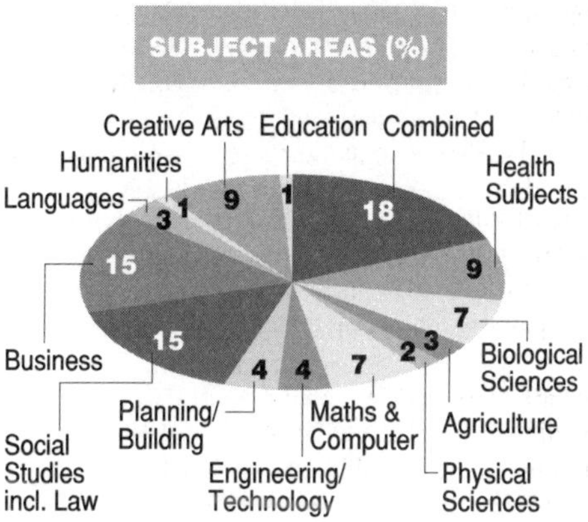

CAMPUS

Frenchay (address above) **Location:** north of the city, near Bristol Parkway Station. **Faculties:** Applied Sciences, Business, Built Environment, Computer, Engineering & Maths; Education; Humanities, Languages & Social Sciences; Law. Library has recent £6.5 million extension.

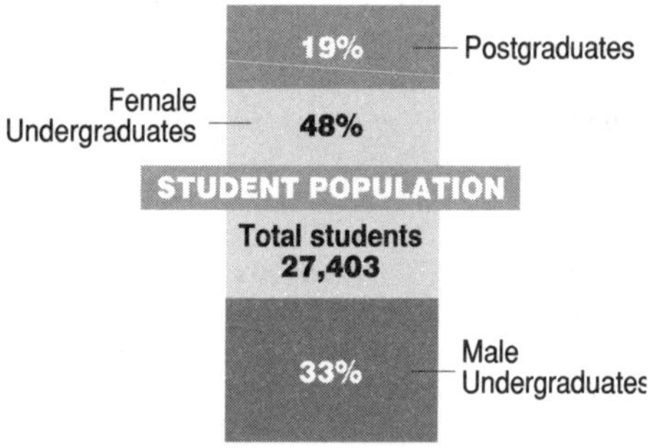

Bower Ashton Kennel Lodge Road, off Clanage Road, Bower Ashton, Bristol BS3 2JU; Tel: 0117 966 0222. **Location:** south of river, west but in easy reach of city centre. **Faculties:** Art, Media & Design. **Learning resources:** specialist library, well-equipped studios and workshops. **Sport facilities:** five-a-side football pitch; eighteen-hole pitch & putt close to hand. **Ents facilities:** opening hours short in **Bower's Bar**, but good, buzzy atmosphere.

St Matthias Oldbury Court Road, Fishponds, Bristol BS16 2JP; Tel: 0117 965 5384. **Location:**

sometime monastery, northeast of city centre, near Glenside (see below), good bus service to city action. **Faculty:** Humanities, Languages & Social Science; Applied Science; Psychology. **Accommodation:** two halls. **Learning resources:** library. **Sport facilities:** cricket square, two soccer pitches, gym. **Ents facilities:** **St Matt's** bar.

GLENSIDE Blackberry Hill, Stapleton, Bristol BS16 1DD. Tel: 0117 958 5655. **Location:** northeast of city centre, nearest to St Matthias, good bus service to city action. **Faculty:** Health & Social Care. **Accommodation:** purpose-built, self-catering. **Learning resources:** library. **Sport facilities:** space for aerobics, etc. **Ents facilities:** student/staff social club, good restaurant, not far from Frenchay.

THE HARTPURY CAMPUS Hartpury House, Gloucester GL19 3BE. Tel: 01452 702132. www.hartpury.ac.uk/. An Associate Faculty since 1997, the college comprises 200 hectares of countryside, with woodlands, farm, lake and equine centre. Animal Science, etc.

ACADEMIC EXCELLENCE

TEACHING :
(Rated Excellent or 17+ out of 24)

Law, Business & Management, English	**Excellent**
Organismal Biosciences, Pharmacology & Pharmacy, Molecular Biosciences, Education	**24**
Sociology, Town/Country Planning, Business, Economics	**23**
Communication & Media Studies, Land & Property Management., Art/Design, Psychology, Nursing	**22**
Modern Languages (French, German, Spanish, Linguistics), Building, Elec/Electron Eng, Politics, Maths, Subjects Allied to Medicine	**21**
Agriculture	**20**

RESEARCH:
*Top grades 5/5**

Accounting and Finance	**Grade 5**

ACADEMIA & JOBS

The nine subjects most recently assessed scored between 21 points out of 24 and full marks (for Education), which is exceptional.

In business and finance they do well, and their degrees represent good value, for entry requirements tend not to be high. Accountancy is at the top of the list employment-wise. There's a range of dedicated degrees with interesting add-ons – from business, finance, economics, law, tourism and maths to drama and early childhood studies (some connections looser than others). There's a Grade 5 rating for research; that's international standing.

More than 2500 graduates find work in the insurance/pension sector nationally, and UWE is a leading force, as they are for would-be investment analysts. It's worth noting that they dropped only one point at the teaching assessments for Business and Economics.

In the field of engineering, their record for employment in aeronautical engineering is second only to Loughborough, and they make it almost impossible not to get on their B/MEng Aerospace Manufacturing/Aerospace Systems programme, with 4- and 5-year extended courses incorporating Foundation years. In electrical/electronic engineering – another successful graduate employment area – there's a healthy 21 points out of 24 inspection result.

They also make an impact through Architectural Technology & Design and Architecture & Planning, and for jobs in town planning. See the BA Town & Country Planning (also a 1-year HND top-up), Planning with Leisure/Tourism/Transport, and Housing Policy with Management. Also, BSc Built & Natural Environments (+ Foundation). Teaching scored 23 out of 24 points.

There's also a steady stream into local/regional/central government administration, via Social, Economic & Political Studies departments, Business Administration, and such as BSc Public Health, a one-year top-up programme.

Strong recruitment, too, for the army, defence operatives and equipment engineers. Students often take the biological sciences route. They got full marks at the teaching assessments; as usual there's a realistic entry policy.

For environmental health and environmental officers there's a host of dedicated courses, such as BSc Environmental Health and Health, Safety & the Environment, and interesting modulations with statistics, management & sustainability, environmental protection, etc. They scored 21 points at the assessments. There's a science foundation year in a whole range of disciplines, including Environmental Health. For environmental officers, BA Environmental Management & Sustainability might interest non-scientists. Look, too, at BSc Geography &

Environmental Mgt or with Environmental Science.

Would-be property developers, note the 22-point assessment in Land & Property Management (see BA Property Mgt & Investment), and another employment strength, the curriculum mining rich seams in their planning, built environment and business provision – Construction & Property Management or Commercial Management, and, in particular, Property Development and Planning. Nationally, a third of the 200-odd graduates into property development come out of Built Environment and Building & Planning departments, while 20% graduate from Business departments. UWE accounts for a lot of them.

Nine per cent of UWE graduates go into education. They are leaders among the new unis in primary school teacher training, and scored full marks at the assessments

Law is another strength among the professions. They are specialists in European law and commercial & business law, and one of the unis to offer a Legal Practice Course (LPC), essential if you want to be a solicitor. A reporting assessor for the LPC Board has been out looking at Law degree teaching in institutions validated to run LPCs. UWE scored Excellent. They are also one of eight institutions where the BVC (Bar Vocational Course, essential to becoming a barrister) may be undertaken. See also their forensic science degrees. New this year is a 'crime scenes' lab; also degrees in Forensic Biology, Forensic Computing, Environmental Forensics; also Criminology.

Among management courses, employment is strong out of BA Business Studies with Human Resource Management. UWE's top-rated Business School dropped only one point at inspection. They are up there with the leaders among unis producing graduates to the transport industry.

Computer Science is another important feed. Principal employment strengths in computing include the computer games sector, and systems analysts. Look at the BSc Computer Systems Engineering, Computer Science, Computing & Information Systems and computing for Real Time Systems (with which there's an option to take time out in Europe or North America). Also the Internet Computing, AI and Robotics degrees.

AT A GLANCE

ACADEMIC FILE:	
Subjects assessed	**31**
Excellent	**77%**
Typical entry requirements	**260 points**
Application acceptance rate	**22%**
Students-staff ratio	**19:1**
First/2:1 degree pass rate	**56%**
ACCOMMODATION FILE:	
Guarantee to freshers	**100%**
Style	**Flats, halls, houses**
Catered	**None**
En-suite	**17%**
Price range pw	**£53-£60**
City rent pw	**£70**

Social Sciences are another important employment. Sociology scored 23 points out of 24 at assessment. Look also at BSc Hons Psychology (22 points; also comes with Sociology), BA Economics & Studies in Social Psychology, also BA Social Sciences (Social Policy).

Health-wise, nursing is a big feature and the range of degrees is wide – Health & Community Practice, Learning Disabilities, Adult Nursing, Care of the Older Person, Cancer Care, Emergency Care, Critical Care, Palliative Care, Mental Health, Children's, etc. Check campus situation, many are at Glenside in Bristol, but Adult and Mental are also available at the Gloucestershire site, where there are also Learning Disabilities and Children's Nursing degrees. Teaching inspection, 22

Also in Health, UWE's BSc in Physiotherapy accounts for roughly 6% of total graduate employment in this sector.

They also have a wide range of animal science degrees (even Equine Dental Science). A popular development has been Veterinary Nursing Science. and this year, Animal Science (Aquatic/Avian), Bioveterinary Science, and Veterinary Practice

WHERE UWE GRADUATES END UP

Health & Social Work: 14%; Education: 9%; Wholesale/Retail: 8%; Manufacturing: 11%; Financial Activities: 11%; Public Administration, Civil Service & Defence: 7%; Hotel/Restaurant: 3%; Transport & Communications (including Telecommunications): 5%; Construction: 2%; Personnel: 5%; Computer: 4%; Business & Management: 5%; Accountancy: 2%; Media (including Film): 2%; Legal 2%; Architecture: 3%; Publishing: 2%; Artistic/Literary: 1%; Sport: 1%.

Approximate 'graduate track' employed **54%**

Management. Note, you may be ensconced miles away at their Gloucestershire-based campus, Hartpury College.

Finally, media and art are important strengths. New this year is BA Film Studies, and there's a series of joint subject courses. Would-be directors, producers and theatre managers, see the drama degrees (it's a strong extra-curricular area too, and there's a new drama studio).

At last, there is a high participation, student representation system, and investment to increase student participation. The new sports facility includes a sports hall with eight badminton courts, aerobics studio, large fitness room and two glass back squash courts.

There are three linked practice-based art degrees, Fine Art in Studio, Fine Art in Context, Art & Visual Culture. Also Fashion/Textile Design. They scored 22 at assessment. Strong employment record for graphic artists, designers and illustrators.

SOCIAL SCENE

Students' Union 'Student reps ensure that the student voice is heard and that changes are made,' UWESU tell us. 'Reps across different faculties have ranked up many successes in 2004/5. There are many issues that have been brought up and debated by repsacross all faculties which has served to enhance the student experience.'

Escape Bar (traditional pub feel) is the main bar on the biggest campus, Frenchay. There's also **Venue Bar** (café culture by day, club by night), the main venue for club nights, bands, etc. Refurbishment is due Summer 2006. There are other bars at St Matthias (friendliest bar at Uni, where everybody knows your name), Glenside (perfect place for a pint before a big night out) and Bower (unique bar that students make their own) campuses.

Capacity at Frenchay's **Escape** and the **Venue** bar together is about 720. It's *Crunchie* every Friday night in Escape and Venue; *The Great Escape* on Saturday at Escape, and there are regular Friday nights in the campus bars. *Result* is the big Wednesday sports night. Tuesday: *Tiny African Badger* (Indie/live bands night) or Comedy Club. Recent live acts include Lemar, the Bodyrockers, DJ Spoony and Scott Mills.

Criticism of an uninvolved student union at UWE is being met by a new constitution which should be approved next year. 'There'll be a bigger voice on a national scale, and this should also mean that we have more entertainments on offer, a better quality of student media, and a better university all round,' they tell us.

In fact the media set-up has been good for a long time. There's *Westworld* (magazine), *Western Eye* (newspaper) and Hub (radio station). This year they walked away with three awards: Best Design, runner-up Best Magazine, Runner-up Best Travel Writer. 'We also have a very active Drama society, linked with the centre of Performing Arts which the university run, and the standard of our shows is very high. Among societies the Poly Players are a surprise – an 'English drawing room group, comedy': students write and perform their own plays around the sites.

Sport The **Recreation Centre** has been refurbished and contains two squash courts, a conditioning room, a C V Equipment room and a resistance machine room, plus the new LifeFitness

WHAT IT'S REALLY LIKE	
UNIVERSITY:	
Social Life	★★★★
Campus scene	**Diverse mix**
Politics	**Growing say**
Sport	**43 clubs, new sports hall 2007**
National team position	**65th**
Arts	**Drama very good**
Student magazine	**Westworld**
Student newspaper	**Western Eye**
Student Radio	**Hub**
Nightclub/venue	**Venue**
Central campus bar	**Escape**
Other campus bars	**St Matthias, Glenside, Bower**
Union ents	**Clubnights, good live bands**
Union clubs/societies	**40**
Most active societies	**Comets Cheerleaders**
Parking	**Poor**
CITY:	
Entertainment	★★★★★
Scene	**Full on waterfront and fringe**
Town/gown relations	**Good**
Risk of violence	**Average-high**
Cost of living	**High**
Student concessions	**Good**
Survival + 2 nights out	**£70-£100 pw**
Part-time work campus/town	**Good/Excellent**

Signature range of equipment. The uni's new sports facility is due for completion in August 2006 and contains an eight badminton court sports hall, aerobics studio, large fitness room including free weights and two glass back squash courts.

There are 43 clubs and they came 65th last year (not bad). They came 4th in the BUSA Rowing Championships, winning 1 gold, 5 silver & 4 bronze medals. Six UWE Women became the GB polo champions for the third year. They had 3 Gold Medals at successive BUSA Judo Championships. Another little gem is American Football – UWE entices deprived Bristol Uni students to join up.

PILLOW TALK

All 1st year undergraduate students who require accommodation are guaranteed a place in university-approved accommodation. Very wide range of flats and houses from harbourside city centre accommodation to en-suite on campus, new Frenchay Student Village, new en-suite accommodation with broadband access.

GETTING THERE

☛ By road to Frenchay, Glenside, St Matthias: M4/J19, M32 or M5/J16, A38; Bower Ashton, M5/J19, A369.
☛ By rail: London Paddington, Birmingham New Street, 1:30; Nottingham, 3:00.
☛ By air: Bristol Airport.
☛ By coach: Birmingham, 2:00; London, 2:20.

BRUNEL UNIVERSITY

Brunel University
Uxbridge
Middlesex UB8 3PH

TEL 01895 274000
FAX 01895 232806
EMAIL admissions@brunel.ac.uk
WEB www.brunel.ac.uk

Union of Brunel Students
Uxbridge
Middlesex UB8 3PH

TEL 01895 462200
FAX 01895 462300
EMAIL su.president@brunel.ac.uk
WEB www.ubsonline.net

VAG VIEW

Out of a 19th-century, technical background, Brunel established itself in the late 1960s as a science/technology/ engineering uni, which was 'all well and good if you had long oily hair, wore AC/DC T-shirts and had the personality of a walnut,' recalls Satiyesh Manoharajah. 'But, dammit, it just wasn't sexy. However, things have been a-changing these past few years. The Social Sciences, Arts and Media faculties have greatly expanded, bringing an influx of generally more exciting students and, indeed, women!'

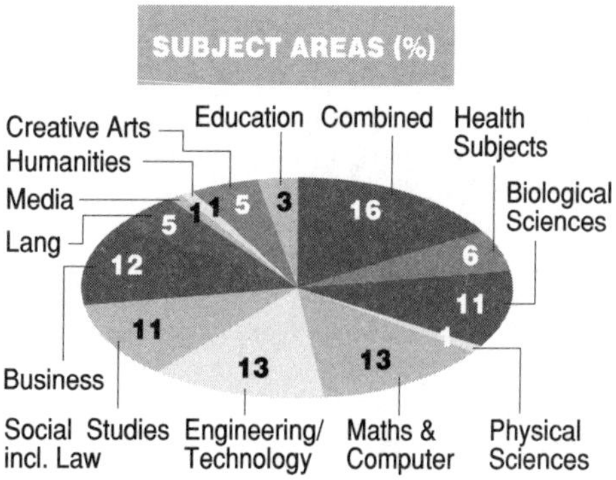

CAMPUSES

Brunel, the University of West London, is based northwest of the city, close to the M25, M40 and M4, Heathrow Airport is also just round the corner – fifty minutes by tube and thirty minutes by overland train to central London.

Uxbridge, always by far the biggest campus in this sometime university of satellite campuses, is this year the uni's *only* campus. Packed with bizarre, grey, concrete buildings, but well laid out, with all the main facilities (bars, small shop, HSBC bank and cash points, a **Waterstones** and travel agents), it has undergone a huge facelifet, the main excitements being a £6.5 million outdoor sports complex, a £7 million indoor athletics facility and a new £9 million Health Services and Social Care Building.

Says undergrad. Olly Wright: 'The library building, called the Bannerman Centre, the refurbished pubs and club, Indoor Athletics Centre and four new halls have made big changes to the landscape.'

FEES, BURSARIES

UK & EU Fees £3000 p.a. Bursaries: £200 - £300 for anyone in receipt of a HE Maintenance grant between £750 and £2700. 390 scholarships, mostly worth £2000-£3000 p.a. 150 will be awarded to students with exceptional tariff points/entry qualifications, another 150 to students from under-represented groups and who have exceptional tariff points/entry qualifications. The remainder will be awarded to students entering through clearing as late applicants, students who do not enter through the UCAS system, or students studying within one of the six West London Boroughs with which Brunel operates its widening participation scheme.

UNIVERSITY/STUDENT PROFILE	
University since	**1966**
Situation/style	**Suburban campuses**
Student population	**12910**
Undergraduates	**9781**
- mature	**20%**
- non EU undergraduates	**5%**
- male/female	**50/50**
- non-traditional student intake	**38%**
- state school intake	**92**
- drop-out rate	**6%**
- undergraduate applications	**Down 2%**

STUDENT PROFILE

Has Brunel also changed from being a uni for techies and geeks? 'There is more a mix of students doing a whole mix of courses,' writes Olly, 'but there is still the techie element doing the engineering courses. There are a few arty types, but nowhere near as many as at some unis. The general mix is of engineering, computing and sporty types. I was also not surprised to read in the *Guardian* online that there are Islamist groups active at Brunel. Some of them used to meet in a room 3 doors away from mine, although I have no idea what they were discussing. On the other hand the *Guardian* also claims that the BNP is operating in Brunel. I am yet to see any evidence of this.

SOCIAL SCENE

'The nightclub is still the **Academy** and has just been refurbished this summer. No extra space has been gained, which would have been useful as some nights it does fill up and some people are turned away. The new design is better than before, it is a space-age design with lots of stainless steel creating a more light and spacey feel. It is open seven days a week from 9pm or 10 till 2am, apart from Sunday when it shuts at 12.30am. But not to townies, as all entrants are checked against Brunel photographic identification on the door. Students may bring guests as long as they are students and have signed in at the student union reception.

'The best thing I have been to recently is Wednesday night, *Flirt*, who do club nights at other university campuses as well (www.flirt.co.uk). This is the regular night every Wednesday. Most other days are themed nights, with Monday open to societies to put on a night. Tuesdays are sport teams' night. Thursday is generally when any famous names would appear, for example Coolio, The Heartless Crew. Friday is *Elements*, a regular DJ who plays r&b, hip-hop, house, garage, dancehall, trance and drum and bass. Saturday starts off with comedy then moves to a retro disco, and Sunday is rock night. Some examples of themed nights I went to last year are *Pimps & Prostitutes*, *James Bond Night*, *Doctors & Nurses*, and the traditional 1st night for all freshers, *Pyjama Party*. One night the Union hired out a couple of poker tables, a blackjack table, a roulette wheel and some croupiers and put on a Casino night which was free and no real money was gambled, but still fun nonetheless.

'The bar is still **Loco's** and has also been refurbished, like something out of Star Trek, with all new leather sofas, chairs and tables, a no-smoking section, many plasma's covering the walls, three pool tables, a table football table, 2 fruit machines and a couple of monopoly machines. For a uni bar, the drinks are expensive, but compared to London prices they are cheap. At the top end of the scale, a pint of Stella is £2.30, while at the other end a pint of Carling is £1.75. These prices rise about 5% in the **Academy**! Again, this is not open to townies and there is security on the doors from 7pm. They also have a typical pub menu and serve food until 7pm.

'There is another pub on campus - **Bishops Bar,** not run by the Union, and generally the drink prices are lower, a pint of Carlsberg Export is £2. This is also the place to go to watch football, while **Loco's** generally shows rugby. **Bishops** has also

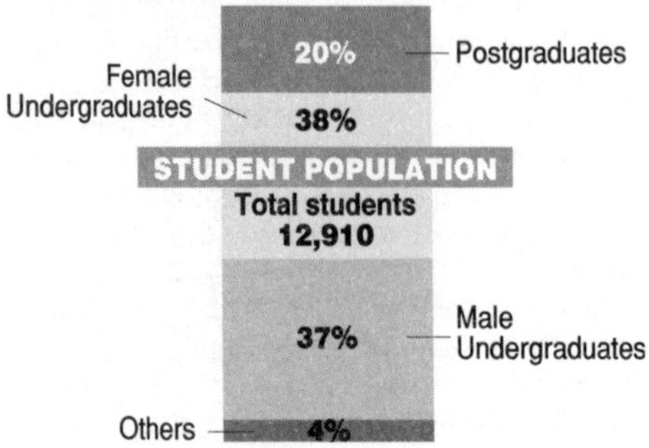

been newly refurbished and they are still in the process of finishing the balcony. Then there's the **Zest Bar**, located above the gym, a nice place to go to after a workout, smaller and generally quieter than the other two pubs, but still worth checking out if only for the San Miguel bottles. There is also a café which opened recently on the ground floor of the new library, always full of students and lecturers getting their caffeine hit, or a croissant.

'The local London students certainly do desert the uni at weekends, and their exit is noticeable by Friday afternoon when all the car parks empty, apart from one or two lonely cars. But there is still a good amount of students around and the **Academy** is certainly never lacking people on a Friday night.'

The Arts Centre is the platform for musical concerts throughout the year. Student groups include The Brunel Singers, an orchestra, guitar, brass, wind and string groups; all are professionally trained and music bursaries are awarded annually. Classes in photography and various visual art forms are given on a weekly basis by visiting professionals. There are several student drama groups.

ACADEMIC EXCELLENCE

TEACHING:	
(Rated Excellent or 17+ out of 24)	
Anthropology, Social Policy, Social Work	**Excellent**
Drama, Education, Government, Sport Sciences	**23**
Sociology, General Engineering, Economics, Maths, Molecular Biosciences, Nursing, Subjects Allied to Medicine, Psychology	**22**
Electrical & Electronic Eng American Studies	**21**
Mech, Aero & Manufacturing Eng (Design), Materials Technology, Film & TV Studies	**20**
RESEARCH:	
*Top grades 5/5**	
Applied Maths, General Eng, Mechanical/Aeronautical/ Manufacturing Eng, Law, Sociology, Library and Info Management	**Grade 5**

SPORT Brunel have just completed a £6.5 million outdoor sports complex and a new £7 million indoor athletics facility. 'Many of the students are doing sport science and related subjects,' says Olly. They are indeed one of the top unis for sport, coming 26th overall last year and with many championship finals to their credit. You can dabble, satisfy curiosity or take up fanatically more or less what you want to, even become part of a university team.

TOWN 'Mmm...the lovely town of Uxbridge... There are two shopping centres, **The Chimes** and **The Pavilions**, containing all the shops one could ever need. There is even an **Odeon** on the top floor of **Chimes**. Uxbridge also has a few nice student-happy pubs, like **The Hog's Head**, **The Zanzi Bar**, **The Metropolitan**. There's also a nightclub, **Royale's**, not recommended, plays cheesy pop and there is a guaranteed fight at 3am when everyone leaves, the only positive being the cheap drinks.

'Generally, the locals must be used to living with students as there is peace between us. There are many takeaways – if you go a day without a menu coming under your room door in halls then there is something wrong – four pizza houses, a few Indians and Chinese, all of very bad quality. Going out to eat is not much better. I did notice a newly opened restaurant next to the station last time I was there, which looked quite nice. There is also a good Chinese towards West Drayton.

ACADEMIA & JOBS

The new Health Services and Social Care Building, the greatly enhanced Library and recently opened state-of-the-art Information Technology Laboratory all point to a rosy future for Brunel.

The uni continues to introduce cutting-edge

WHERE BRUNEL GRADUATES END UP

Health & Social Work: 16%; Education: 10%; Wholesale/Retail: 10%; Manufacturing: 9%; Financial Activities: 8%; Public Administration, Civil Service & Defence: 8%; Hotel/Restaurant: 2%; Transport & Communications (including Telecommunications): 4%; Construction: 1%; Personnel: 6%; Computer: 7%; Business & Management: 7%; Accountancy: 1%; Media (including Film): 2%; Legal 2%; Publishing: 2%; Artistic/Literary: 2%; Sport: 1%.

Approximate 'graduate track' employed **55%**

WHAT IT'S REALLY LIKE	
UNIVERSITY:	
Social Life	★★★★
Campus scene	**Lively, trecky, sporty**
Student Union services	**Good**
Politics	**Average Student issues**
Sport	**Good**
National team position	**26th**
Sport facilities	**Good**
Arts opportunities	**Excellent drama, film; good art, dance, music**
Student magazine	**Route 66**
Student radio	**B-1000**
Nightclub	**Academy**
Bars	**Loco's Bar**
Union ents	**Good clubnites & live bands**
Union Clubs/Societies	**120**
Parking	**Good**
CITY:	
Entertainment	**★★★★★ (London)**
Scene	**Cheesy local club, good pubs, cinema. Mainly London beckons**
Town/gown relations	**Good**
Risk of violence	**Average**
Cost of living	**High**
Student concessions	**Good**
Survival + 2 nights out	**£100 pw**
Part-time work campus/town	**Average/Excellnt**

techno courses such as the BSc in Multimedia Technology & Design, but a few years ago it spread its wings, quadrupled in size and took on a broader academic brief – social work, sociology, politics, law, psychology, health (with a new course in Medical Genetics), sports studies, sciences and arts (from English to Film/TV Studies, from Drama to Creative Writing). Overall, teaching assessments have not been as good as some universities that demand less points at A level, but in some of these newer courses (Drama, Film & TV, Sport Sciences), it has performed especially well, as indeed it did in Education (23 points out of 24, see our *Academic Excellence* box, page 97).

> ***Out of a 19th-century, technical background, Brunel has become seriously good at Social Sciences and the Arts, bringing an influx of generally more exciting students and, indeed, women!***

Writes Naveed Mohammed, 'Pressure of work builds gradually in your first year, not too bad unless you go totally wild. It gets more intense after that. Computers are available freely as is the Internet and you can get network access in quite a few rooms in halls – the university is looking to have this in all rooms.'

Brunel welcomes applications from disabled students and those with special needs. They currently have three disability officers, one of whom is a Dyslexia Co-ordinator, who are available to help and advise students and potential applicants with special needs.

Distance Learning is now an established route to degrees at undergraduate and postgraduate level. In many cases the qualification can be earned without attending the university. In other cases, short periods of attendance may be required. Distance Learning awards are considered equivalent to those earned by full-time study. Contact the Admissions Office for information.

Brunel is up among the best for turning out actors, rivalling specialist colleges like The Royal Scottish Academy, The Liverpool Institute (LIPA), The East 15 Acting School, The Central School of Speech & Drama, Rose Bruford College, and The University of Arts, London. Stage Managers come most from RSAMD and then Central and Rose Bruford, followed in a pack by the WCMD, Brunel... Their Performing Arts Department, which includes the **Rambert School of Ballet & Contemporary Dance**, is a centre for Film & Television Studies (BA as single Hons, or feature of Joint or Major/Minor degrees) as well as drama and music (the latter with a strong practical emphasis and very good employment record).

There's also an interesting media dimension, with Film & TV Studies coupling with Drama or English or Music History - 20 points at the assessments for this.

In the Law Department (Grade 5 for research), they are specialists in Business & Commercial Law. Other social sciences show strong emphasis on politics, sociology (22 points for teaching; Grade 5 for research), psychology (also 22 points) and social anthropology. The American Studies connection that had been prevalent is now out of the window, and the Social Work degree is postgrad entry only, but comes strongly recommended.

In Education, which has a 23-point score at the teaching assessment, there is serious precedent:

51% go to primary, 37% to secondary. There's a long history, too, of producing graduate nurses and health-care professionals, following mergers with the London School of Occupational Therapy, the West Middlesex Hospital School of Physiotherapy and St Mary's Hospital School of Physiotherapy. Look especially at their BSc Occupational Therapy, which accounts for more than 7% of the graduate market Teaching inspection, 22.

They are leaders in finding jobs for graduates in Sport, as well. Players and would-be officials should look closely at the series of Sports Science degrees - coaching, admin. and development, fitness, PE, technology.

In Engineering there's a strong bent for design, for instance Mechanical Eng with B/MEng Automotive Design (4/5-year sandwich).

See also their BA and BSc Industrial Design and Technology degrees, and there's a whole raft of E&E Systems Engineering degrees, including 'Power Systems', 'Control Systems' and 'Communications Systems' degrees. The E & E engineering teaching has a 21-point teaching assessment and there are impressive Grade 5 (international quality) research ratings.

See, too, the 3/4-year (thick/thin sandwich) BEng Computer Systems/Systems Engineering courses.

Also, they offer the more tailored Motorsport Engineering with similar promise of work experience. All engineering scored between 20 and 22 points out of 24 at the teaching assessments.

No dedicated Software Eng degree, but Brunel is big in finding graduates work as software engineers and consultants.

AT A GLANCE

ACADEMIC FILE:	
Subjects assessed	**29**
Excellent	**69%**
Typical entry requirements	**285 points**
Application acceptance rate	**15%**
Student-staff ratio	**19:1**
First/2:1 degree pass rate	**66%**
ACCOMMODATION FILE:	
Guarantee to freshers:	**100%**
Style	**Halls, flats**
Catered	**3370 places**
En-suite	**1685**
Approx price range pw	**£70-105**
Local rent pw	**£70-£75**

PILLOW TALK

All freshers are guaranteed accommodation on campus, though there could be a delay for late candidates coming through clearing. We're talking halls and flats, many en-suite. Around 560 further en-suite rooms are being constructed in 2005/06.

Says Olly: 'The accommodation is all of good quality, with every room including a connection to the internet, all the most recently built halls all have en-suites, and the four brand new halls - : Bishop Hall, Kilmorey Hall, Lacy Hall and St Margarets Hall - are the largest rooms on site so far. The best halls would have to be these four, due to the size of rooms.'

GETTING THERE

☛ By Underground: **Uxbridge** – Metropolitan line and Piccadilly during peak hours. Then bus, U3 or U5.

UNIVERSITY OF BUCKINGHAM

The University of Buckingham
Hunter Street
Buckingham MK18 1EG

TEL 01280 820313
FAX 01280 824081
EMAIL admissions@buckingham.ac.uk
WEB www.buckingham.ac.uk

Students' Union
The University of Buckingham
Hunter Street
Buckingham MK18 1EG

TEL 01280 822522
FAX 01280 812791
EMAIL student.union@buckingham.ac.uk
WEB www.buckingham.ac.uk/life/social/su/

VAG VIEW

This is Britain's only independent university. Tuition fees are steep, but most degrees are completed within two years (note, however, that there are four terms in the Buckingham year). In line with its reputation for breaking new ground, a medical school is planned for 2008 - the first private UK medical school in over 200 years. It will specialise in offering fast-track training for prospective doctors.

CAMPUS

The three sites – Hunter Street, 8-acre Verney Park and the recently developed Chandos Road complex, are walking distance apart and within the town boundaries.

FEES, BURSARIES

From September 2006, the fees for UK/EU students will be £7500 p.a., for non-UK/EU students fees, £12500 (rising to £13000 in 2007) . The home-counties bursaries have been scrapped, but there are a number of scholarships available, for example the Sir Ray Tindle scholarship for journalism students, Desborough Scholarship for Business Studies and Marketing students.

STUDENT PROFILE

A popular picture of Buckingham is of a place for rich also-rans, but that isn't a view shared by all school sixthform advisers to whom we spoke. Many undergrads are mature and hie from overseas; as elsewhere, there are a few more women than men , though not apparently among undergraduates. 'Each student mixes with 79 other different nationalities,' they say, and since there are only 730-odd students there, that is quite a mix.

ACADEMIA & JOBS

There is much to be said for Buckingham's quiet, Oxbridge-style tutorial system, small-class tuition and 1:10 staff-student ratio. Departments include Accounting, Business, Economics, English Language Studies (EFL), English Literature,

UNIVERSITY/STUDENT PROFILE	
University since	**1976**
Situation/style	**Town campus**
Student population	**731**
Undergraduate population	**486**
- mature	**30%**
- non EU undergraduates	**65%**
- male/female	**55/45**

Financial Services, History, History of Art, Information Systems, International Hotel Management, International Studies, Law, Marketing, Politics and Psychology. Also available, and paired with English are degrees in multimedia journalism and media communications. They say that for A level candidates they ask for three passes, but combinations of A and/or AS levels are also considered.

As this is an independent institution, it is not obliged to be assessed by the Quality Assurance Agency for Higher Education (QAA). However, in November 2003, it submitted itself voluntarily for an Institutional Audit by the QAA and was awarded a judgement of Broad Confidence in the quality of its programmes and the academic standards of its awards. The new-style QAA Institutional Audit process introduced in 2002, does not award scores at subject level but departmental audits (Discipline Audit Trails) undertaken by the QAA during the Institutional Audit confirmed that the standard of student achievement was appropriate to the titles of the relevant awards in the subjects scrutinised.

Areas of particular strength - Buckingham's Law and Business Schools are very popular and highly regarded. The international nature of the university

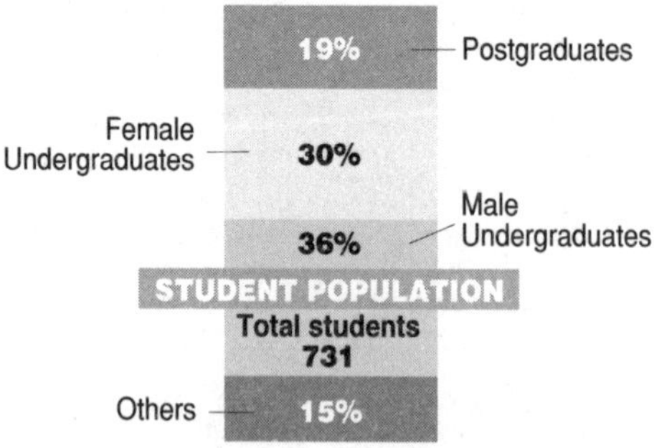

(the opportunity to study with students from over 80 different countries) also sets students up well to work abroad after they graduate. The uni is home to the new Aylesbury Vale Enterprise Hub - launched in November 2005, the hub will help support local entrepreneurs and new businesses. The Enterprise Hub network has been established to deliver a development programme, support and advice for entrepreneurs, start-up and early stage companies seeking to bring a technology or knowledge-based idea to market. Recent statistical evidence of Buckingham graduates in employment or further study (year/percent): 89% 2004.

There are libraries at each site, a language centre and a networked IT set-up (a computer suite at Verney Park is accessible 24/7). There's a trained teacher of the dyslexic, who works with students from the minute they arrive. Degree courses are very concentrated, however. The intensity of the academic experience leaves little time or desire for the worst excesses of student fun and games.

SOCIAL SCENE

Students' Union At one-tenth of the average size

of a British university, Buckingham provides a cosy enough environment. The union, located in the **Tanlaw Mill** on the Hunter Street site (refectory and **George's Bar**, pool tables, video games, lounge with Satellite TV), organises discos on Fridays and a Graduation Ball. Then there's the **Franciscan Building** (Verney Park) for private-hire cellar parties. There are currently eleven societies, mainly cultural or departmental, quite a few organised trips and a series of concerts and lectures. The most active student society is Bahamian. There's a magazine called *Cygnet*. For escape, there are various restaurants and traditional country pubs in Buckingham, or Milton Keynes (14 miles), Oxford (23 miles), London (58 miles). Bring a car.

SPORT Four all-weather tennis courts, one all-weather five-a-side pitch, a swimming pool, gym complex and sports field; other playing fields a mile away. There are riding schools in the vicinity. The uni teams are mainly locally competitive. Matches played against alumni and staff are also regular features. There is a campus fitness programme – aerobics classes, martial arts – and a well-equipped fitness centre.

PILLOW TALK

Guaranteed first-year, self-catered accommodation in mixed halls of residence at Hunter Street and Verney Park, or shared flats at Hunter Street. The past few months have seen the introduction of internet access.

GETTING THERE

☛ By road: make for Buckingham by-pass. M40/J9 from the south, then A41, A421. Also A422, A421, as well as A413 from the north.
☛ By rail: Buckingham has no station, the nearest are at Bicester and Milton Keynes. London Euston, 1:00; Birmingham New Street, 1:20.
☛ By air: Heathrow or Gatwick.
☛ By coach: London, 1:20.

WHAT IT'S REALLY LIKE

UNIVERSITY:	
Social Life	★★
Campus scene	**Small, friendly, multi-cultured, mature**
Politics	**Internal**
Sport	**Local & BUSA**
Arts opportunities	**Few**
Student magazine	**Cygnet**
Union ents	**Functions, films, discos, balls**
Union venue	**Tanlaw Mill**
Union Societies	**11, mainly cultural**
Parking	**Permit required**
TOWN:	
Entertainment	★★
Scene	**Trad pubs**
Risk of violence	**Low**
Student concessions	**Some**
Cost of living	**Average**
Survival + 2 nights out	**£50-£80 pw**
Part-time work campus/town	**Poor/Excellent**

AT A GLANCE

ACADEMIC FILE:	
Approx. points required	**200**
Student:staff ratio	**10:1**
ACCOMMODATION FILE:	
Guarantee to freshers	**100%**
Style	**Halls**
Catered	**None**
En suite	**20%**
Approx price range pw	**£75-£108**
Town rent pw	**£112**

BUCKINGHAMSHIRE CHILTERNS UNIVERSITY COLLEGE

Buckinghamshire Chilterns University College
Queen Alexandra Road
High Wycombe HP11 2JZ

TEL 01494 522141
FAX 01494 465432
EMAIL (see website)
WEB www.bcuc.ac.uk

VAG VIEW

BCUC can trace their history back to a School of Science and Art founded in 1893 and into Buckinghamshire College of Higher Education, formed in 1975 out of High Wycombe College of Technology and Art and Newland Park College of Education.

From 1992 Brunel University validated its degrees. Then, in 1999, four years after it had been given powers to award its own degrees, the college was confirmed by the Privy Council as a University College, so now it awards its own

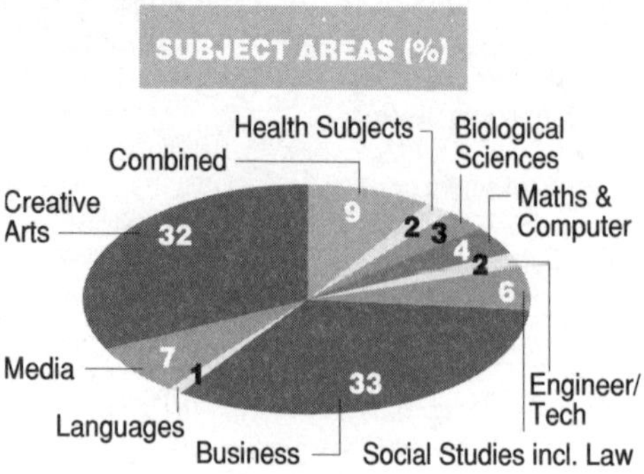

LOCATION

The college is sited at three locations within a short distance from London. Two – High Wycombe and Wellesbourne campuses – are within the market town of High Wycombe itself, and one – Chalfont Campus – is some ten miles to the east, centred on an eighteenth-century mansion and set in 200 acres close to the village of Chalfont St Giles. All faculties are located in High Wycombe other than Business (the largest) and Health (nursing), which are on Chalfont Campus.

STUDENT PROFILE

There is a large mature population and many undergraduates are reading for HNDs and the like. The state sector and non-traditional student intake is high.

ACADEMIA & JOBS

BCUC offer a major portfolio of degrees through six faculties: Applied Social Sciences & Humanities, Business, Art & Design, Health, Leisure & Tourism and Technology.

Advertising degree graduates from Bucks Chilterns are the most popular in the industry. The BA Advertising & Promotions Management and Business Studies and Advertising Strategy degrees have recently been joined by Advertising with Psychology and Business Management with Psychology.

In Art & Design there's a whole raft of excellent BA Graphic Design & Advertising options with specialist illustrative focuses. Other graduates in the faculty find work as graphic artists, designers and illustrators, in media & government research, in textiles (see their BA degrees in Textiles – 3 specialist pathways are available); there is also a Jewellery degree, which brings graduates into the Fashion industry. HND top-ups are possible. Entry is not too demanding. Teaching inspection, 20.

They are sector leaders, too, by a wide margin, in furniture design. High Wycombe has been associated with the craft for more than a century and BCUC delivers the largest range of furniture design programmes in the world. The sector supports around 400 graduates a year. There is everything here from BA Hons Conservation & Restoration, through Design & Craftsmanship to the HND top-up (2nd/3rd-year entry) Applied Furniture Studies. Then there's the BSc Furniture Manufacture & Design.

Communications & Media earned only 18 points on assessment, but this was some time ago and their media degrees are now difficult to ignore with masses of film studies, journalism, video production and the like combining with such as drama, english or creative writing.

The Technology faculty gets national prominence for its Centre for Rapid Design & Manufacture, while the Business faculty picks up on a college-wide emphasis on language acquisition, featuring European and international courses in collaboration with partners abroad. Jobs come thick and fast in retail, marketing and sales, and there's a niche area in transport planning and distribution. See the range of international, e-commerce, marketing and management degrees – teaching inspection 22 points. There's also a good record in personnel/human resource management, and 5% + of their graduates go into the hotel and restaurant industry annually, which puts them among the leaders among small unis. When it comes to managment there's a specialist line via Music Industry Management, as single subject or applied to Live Production, Marketing, Popular

COLLEGE/STUDENT PROFILE

University College since	**1999**
Situation/style	**Campus sites**
Student population	**9470**
Undergraduates	**8710**
- mature	**30%**
- non EU undergraduates	**7%**
- male/female	**42/58**
- non-traditional student intake	**36%**
- state school intake	**97%**
- drop-out rate	**8%**
- undergraduate applications	**Down 23%**

ACADEMIC EXCELLENCE

TEACHING:	
(Rated Excellent or 17+ out of 24)	
Nursing	**23**
Marketing/Human Resources	**22**
Psychology Tourism/Sport	**21**
Agriculture, Art & Design	**20**
Communications & Media	**18**
RESEARCH:	
*Top grades 5/5**	**None**

Music or Studio Production.

They are high among the country's suppliers of graduates into sport, too, offering BSc Sports Psychology and BA Sports Stadia Design & Management. Now, up for approval are Sport & Leisure Management and Sports Coaching Management. Teaching inspection, 21.

In the Health faculty, Nursing scored 23 points out of 24 in the teaching assessments. Their two BSc degrees: Nursing (with UKCC Registration) and Nursing Studies put them second to Oxford Brookes in supplying SEN, and they only lost 1 point at the assessments.

Finally, they are specialists in commercial and business law, and have a strong employment track record with BSc Policing See, too, BSc Criminology degrees, Psychology again playing its part.

SOCIAL SCENE

An active ents scene, profiled in monthly magazine, *The Noise*, is offered at both Chalfont and the main High Wycombe campus, where the bar is **The Lounge** and the nightclub is **The White Room**. '**Bar 1: Bar 2** at Chalfont has recently been refurbished with a fantastic new lighting and sound system. Both have regular club nights and live acts. Event of the year is the May Ball, 'a black-tie, 12-hour blinding party with over 2,000 members of BCSU (the union) attending.

High Wycombe itself has various pubs and nightclubs, a cinema, a theatre and a sports centre. A free minibus to the cinema is available to students, as are lifts home after ents nights.

There is an active sports scene at BUSA and loca; level. They came 94th nationally last year.

PILLOW TALK

There are two halls at High Wycombe – Brook Street and John North Halls, with self-catering accommodation for 500. At Chalfont a recent development brings the total rooms to 700 (some en suite); there's a choice of self-catering or catered accommodation here.

AT A GLANCE

ACADEMIC FILE:	
Subjects assessed	**13**
Excellent	**54%**
Typical entry requirements	**180 points**
Application acceptance rate	**20%**
Students-staff ratio	**20:1**
First/2:1 degree pass rate	**44%**
ACCOMMODATION FILE:	
Guarantee to freshers	**90%**
Style	**Self-catered Halls**
Approx cost pw (no food/food)	**£46/£76**
Town rent pw	**£60**

GETTING THERE

☛ By road to High Wycombe: M40/J4, A4010; to Newland Park, M40/J2, A355, right on to A40, left on to Potkiln Lane.

☛ By rail to High Wycombe: London Marylebone, 35 mins.

☛ By Underground to Chalfont: Chorley Wood (Metropolitan line).

WHERE BUCKS CHILTERNS GRADUATES END UP

Health & Social Work: 11%; Education: 3%; Wholesale/Retail: 19%; Manufacturing: 14%; Financial Activities: 6%; Public Administration, Civil Service & Defence: 5%; Hotel/Restaurant: 5%; Transport & Communications (including Telecommunications): 5%; Construction: 1%; Agriculture: 1%; Personnel: 3%; Computer: 2%; Business & Management: 2%; Media (including Film): 2%; Legal 2%; Architecture: 1%; Publishing: 3%; Advertising: 4%; Artistic/Literary: 3%; Sport: 4%.

Approximate 'graduate track' employed **44%**

THE UNIVERSITY OF CAMBRIDGE

Cambridge Admissions Office
The University of Cambridge
Kellet Lodge
Tennis Court Road
Cambridge CB2 1QJ

TEL 01223 333308
FAX 01223 366383
Email admissions@cam.ac.uk
WEB www.cam.ac.uk/admissions

Cambridge University Students' Union
11/12 Trumpington Street
Cambridge CB2 1QA

TEL 01223 356454/333313
FAX 01223 323244
EMAIL info@cusu.cam.ac.uk
WEB cusu.cam.ac.uk

VAG VIEW

Cambridge University began life early in the 13th century, more than 100 years later than Oxford. Its colleges have always been self-governing, with their own property and income, but the university itself is no slouch as investor: currently it has over £500 million of capital projects in development.

STUDENT PROFILE

First, Cambridge students are bright: 'If you're thinking of applying to Cambridge: congratulations!' writes Caroline Muspratt, who is studying Modern & Medieval Languages at Christ's. 'Why do I say that? Because even to consider applying, you must be a straight-A student, from a private school, with a white, middle-class background and parents who earn nearly £100K a year. Right?

'Wrong!. It's a common misconception that state school students, ethnic minorities, poor people, etc, don't get in. None of this matters. It won't affect your application, it won't change the friends you make, the societies you join, or the grades you get. I'm from a state school, I have working-class parents, and I'm the first person in my family ever to go to university. And yes, there are people here who went to Eton and have spent their whole lives being groomed for Cambridge: but students are students and the public-state divide is little more than a media fabrication. The university is extremely welcoming to overseas students and ethnic minorities: CUSU (the students' union) recently won a national award for ethnic diversity and its publication, *The Little Black Book*.'

Second, we must conclude from the foregoing that Cambridge students are intensely loyal, for the fact is that the uni *doesn't* meet its generously low application benchmarks either for state school applicants or for social class IIIM, IV or V applicants, or for applicants from so-called 'low participation neighbourhoods'.

It seems that the exclusive nature of the place rubs off pretty quickly on its students from whatever background they come. Asked what kind of relationship students have with townies and with neighbouring Anglia Polytechnbic Uni (which has a 95% state school intake as against Cambridge's 52%), working-class Caroline wrote: 'The two institutions rarely mix, though certain societies are open to students from both universities; for instance, an Anglia student was recently Production Manager on the Cambridge University student newspaper. The town and gown divide is more marked, and some city pubs tend to be students-only, or locals-only. There are places where town and gown happily mix – go into almost

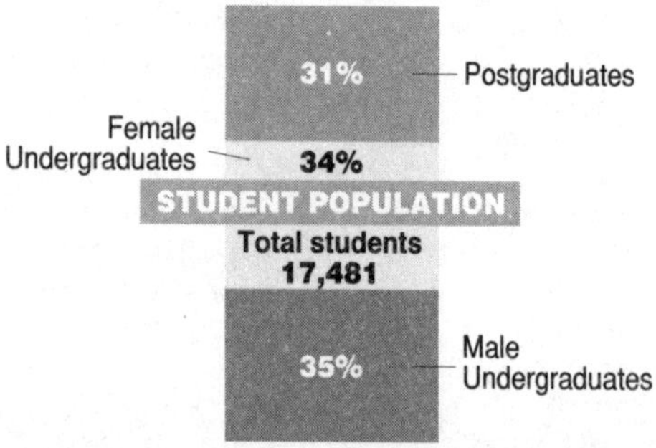

UNIVERSITY/STUDENT PROFILE	
University since	**1209**
Situation/style	**City collegiate**
Student population	**17481**
Undergraduates	**11982**
- mature	**7%**
- non EU undergraduates	**8%**
- male/female	**51/49**
- non-traditional student intake	**11%, low**
- state school intake	**57%, low**
- drop-out rate	**1%, low**
- undergraduate applications	**Up 7%**

any of the pubs on King Street, for example, and you'll meet some really friendly people.'

The reason that Caroline tends not to mix with these 'really friendly people' is that she is all bound up with the exclusive Cambridge experience, and this very exclusivity is what going to Cambridge is about. Nor can it be a bad thing if exclusivity only means, as Caroline writes, that 'Cambridge [is] one of the best universities in the world – the teaching quality is unsurpassed.' Can it?

Cambridge impresses and forms its students, it is a strong and ancient culture that few undergraduates would resist. It is exclusive not because it excludes applicants from state schools or working-class families, but because it is an exclusive environment in the sense of unique, and picks students at interview that will not be cowed by its strength, but will meet it with their own.

Now a third-year student, Katie Lydon went to school at Bolton Comprehensive. and is 'more than fulfilled,' and quite unable to identify the typical Cambridge student or dominant group, only the caricature: 'Cliques grow up around sports, drama and other activities, as well as drinking societies and simple friendship groups. Although there is the odd example of the elitist stereotype, they are in the minority. Some groups, like sports teams and drinking societies, can dominate bar areas and seem intimidating, but this only tends to happen a few times a term, or after sporting victories.'

FEES, BURSARIES

UK & EU Fees £3000 p.a. Bursary for students in receipt of full HE Maintenance grant: £3000 per year. If in receipt of partial HE Maintenance Grant, bursaries exist on a sliding scale, min. £250, max £2850 p.a: www.newtontrust.cam.ac.uk/cam/bursaries 2006/e.htm. For sports and music scholarships, see: www. sport.cam.ac.uk/bursaries/ and www.cam..ac.uk/a dmissions/undergraduate/musicawards/. Colleges also offer their own financial support, scholarships and prizes for academic achievement. Disabled applicants, see also www.cam.ac.uk/cambuniv/ disability/ support/ financial.html.

ACADEMIA & JOBS

Note that all Cambridge undergraduates study for the BA degree, whether they are reading an arts or science subject. Note, too, there are three graduate colleges not profiled below, which do take the odd bod for undergraduate studies if they have already done a degree elsewhere or are over 21 at entry. These are: Hughes Hall, CB1 2EW. Tel 01223 334 897. WEB www.hughes.cam.ac.uk. St Edmund's CB3 0BN. Tel 01223 336 086. WEB www.st-edmunds.cam.ac.uk. Wolfson CB3 9BB. Tel 01223 335 918. WEB www.wolfson.cam.ac.uk.

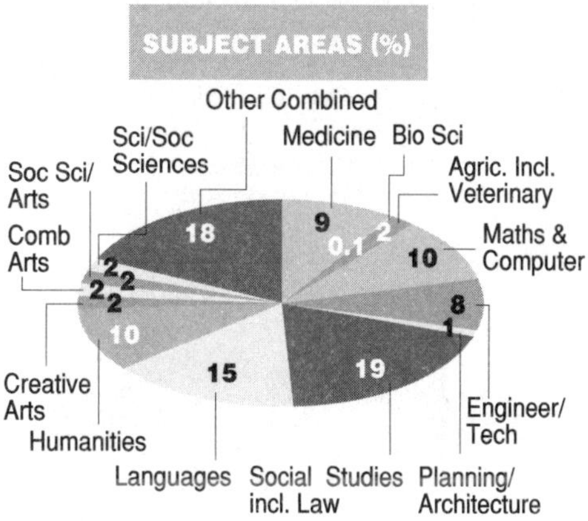

'The work ethic is very strong throughout the university,' warns Caroline. 'You'll be expected to study hard, and to achieve a lot in a short time... It can initially be intimidating, and I wasn't the only one who spent the first few weeks convinced that the interviewers had made a mistake. After a few alcohol-aided evenings out with other freshers, you realise that you are on a level pegging with most of them.

'Teaching is done through supervisions and lectures. Supervisions are given by fellows or research students to one or two students. It's a very intensive way of learning, and the short teaching term (eight weeks) means that there isn't much let up. This can take its toll, especially in the stressful summer exam term. Libraries are excellent, but...it can be difficult to get hold of books when the entire year is doing the same paper.'

The most popular sector for Cambridge graduates is health. The leading Medicine degree is the 5/6-year MB, BChir. Besides scoring AAA, including Chemistry, all candidates applying to read Medicine will in future sit a written test called the Biomedical Admissions Test (BMAT). The test is being used to assess scientific aptitude, not fitness to practise medicine (which will continue to be assessed in nterview) and focuses on scientific abilities relevant to the study of medicine.

The MB, BChir involves heavy science-based pre-clinical in first two years, core subject study (Anatomy through to Psychology) the speciality. A number of graduates go into full-time laboratory research. For those who don't there's the chance to do the PRHO at top Addenbrooke's Hospital. Teaching inspection, 21. Research, Grade 5*/6* for Clinical Lab Sciences, Community-based Clinical, Hospital-based Clinical, Psychol, Biochem; Grade 5 for Anatomy. The veterinary degree is a 6-year MB and not available at Peterhouse or King's colleges.

Teaching inspection, 23. Research grade 5.

Law is another key Cambridge profession. All candidates must sit the National Admissions Test for Law (LNAT). Non-Law graduates may apply for a 2-year Senior Status Law degree here.

Finance is, though, after health the most popular job sector for graduates from Cambridge. Among routes into investment analysis, banking, merchant banking and share dealing, Economics leads, engineering comes next. In that faculty specialisms such as Information & Computer Engineering and Management Studies are available. Languages are also a well-trammelled route. From Occitan to Hebrew-Biblical, the choice is wide. Then again, the mind-train of Classics is much sought after in the City of London, and interestingly Cambridge are levelling the playing field socially by introducing a four-year classics degree for students with little knowledge of Latin or Greek from school. Teaching inspection (Economics), 24. Classics scored full marks, too, and took a world-class 5*/6* rating for research.

Software consultants and engineers are popular areas for employment, too. Graduates come to them from Computer Science and Engineering in almost equal proportion, significant numbers (though less) through Mathematics. Specialisms in the 4-year Engineering degree include Information & Computer Engineering, Instrumentation & Control, amongst other subjects sympathetic to this career area. You can opt to study Mathematics with Computer Science.

The Publishing industry takes a shine to Cambridge language graduates in particular. Interestingly, BBC Worldwide is working with Cambridge on a range of new-generation foreign language courses. The agreement will result in the launch of a series of multi-media language courses over the next five years.

Humanities is another route to publishing; and journalists and editors come out of Engineering and Social Sciences, and of course student media – the magazines are *Inprint, May Anthologies,* etc; the newspapers *Varsity* and *Cambridge Student* – are regularly award winning, as is *CUR* and *CUTE* (radio and TV). Teaching inspection, 22.

AT A GLANCE

ACADEMIC FILE:	
Subjects assessed	**35**
Excellent	**97%**
Typical entry points	**510 v. high**
Application acceptance rate	**22%**
Student-staff ratio	**12:1**
First/2:1 degree pass rate	**90%**
ACCOMMODATION FILE	
Guarantee to freshers	**100%**
Style	**College rooms**
Catered	**Majority**
En suite	**Not known**
Price range pw	**£55-£90**
Town rent pw	**£80**

ACADEMIC EXCELLENCE

TEACHING: *(Rated Excellent or 17+ out of 24)*	
Chemistry, History, Law, Computer Science, Architecture, Music, English, Geography, Geology, Anthropology	**Excellent**
Psychology, Molecular Biosci, Organismal Biosci, Pharmacol, Economics, Classics, Philosophy	**24**
Archaeology, Educ, Celtic, Social/Pol Sciences, Theology, Anatomy, Maths, Chem Eng, Materials Science, General Eng, Oriental Studies, Physics & Astronomy, Vet Science	**23**
Modern Langs, Land Economy, History of Art	**22**
Medicine	**21**
RESEARCH: *Special grade 5/5*6**	
Clinical Laboratory Sciences, Community-based Clinical, Hospital-based Clinical, Psychol, Biochem, Zoology, Chemistry, Physics, Earth Sci, Pure Maths, Applied Maths, Statistics, Computer, General Eng, Metallurgy, Law, Celtic, English, French, German/Dutch/Scandinavian, Italian, Iberian, Linguistics, Classics, Archaeol, History, Hist & Philosophy of Science, Philosophy, Music	**Grade 6***
Asian Studies	**Grade 5***
Education, Theology, History of Art, Russian, Middle East & African, Business, Sociol, Economics, Anthropology, Geography, Town & Country Planning, Chemical Eng, Veterinary, Biotechnol, Plant Sciences, Genetics, Pharmacology, Anatomy	**Grade 5**

Another effect of cutting-edge student activity is in drama, whence graduate directors, producers and theatre managers proliferate (there being no vocational drama degree here). Arts administrators and managers are also legion.

The Music Tripos involves history, analysis and compositional technique – intellectual and practical skills with an increasing amount of freedom to develop. There is a world-class Grade 5*/6* research reputation, and a good track record in employment for musicians, conductors and composers.

Humanities graduates also become charity officers in quantity. Languages are again to the fore as preparation for lecturers in Adult Education, and in social work. Languages and Social & Political Sciences graduates find ready access to research jobs in media and government.

There are two Education routes, one where Education Studies is a complementary but subsidiary focus of Biosciences, English & Drama, English, Geography, History, Maths, Music or Religion; and the other available only at Homerton College, where the emphasis is on Education Studies and the other subjects are add-ons.

SOCIAL SCENE

Students' Union 'Fresher's Week is organised by college JCRs (Junior Common Rooms), involving pub crawls and ents,' writes Katie. 'What I found especially encouraging was the willingness of the different year groups to mingle, and the fact that you are assigned "college parents" in different years to help you settle in.'

Societies occupy the free time of a large number, and are a way to create a sympathetic circle of friends, wider than your college might allow. The Cambridge Union boasts more than 400 societies. The most active is LesBiGay. Drama Society is big on tours to America and Europe every year, and a high number of productions go to the Edinburgh Festival. Media-wise, the student papers, Varisty and Cambridge Student, and radio station CUR are award-winning, and positions like May Ball President, Union President and those on the JCRs are awarded after strenuous public hustings, since they develop the communication, teamwork and leadership skills sought by employers.'

WHAT IT'S REALLY LIKE

UNIVERSITY:	
Social Life	★★★★
Campus scene	**Bright, exclusive, focused, fun**
Student Union services	**Well organised, but no venue**
Politics	**Active, diverse campaigns**
Sport	**Huge.**
National team position	**6th**
Sport facilities	**Good**
Arts opportunities	**Drama/dance excellent, rest good**
Student magazine	**Inprint, May Anthologies, etc**
Student newspaper	**Varsity, Cambridge Student**
Journalism awards 2004	**1 win; 1 runner-up**
Student radio	**CUR**
Radio awards 2005	**5 nominations**
Student TV	**CUTE**
Nightclub	**None**
Union ents	**Town clubs + College JCRs**
Bars	**All colleges**
Union clubs/societies	**400+**
Parking	**Buy a bike**
CITY:	
Entertainment	★★★
Scene	**Cheesy clubs, great pubs**
Town/gown relations	**Average-poor**
Risk of violence	**Low**
Cost of living	**Average**
Student concessions	**Good**
Survival + 2 nights out	**£60 pw**
Part-time work campus/town	**Expellable offence**

WHERE CAMBRIDGE GRADUATES END UP

Health & Social Work: 16%; Education: 9%; Wholesale/Retail: 4%; Manufacturing: 10%; Financial Activities: 12%; Public Administration, Civil Service & Defence: 6%; Hotel/Restaurant: 1%; Transport & Communications (including Telecommunications): 3%; Personnel: 4%; Computer: 6%; Business & Management: 8%; Accountancy: 5%; Media (including Film): 2%; Legal 2%; Architecture: 2%; Publishing: 4%; Advertising: 1%; Artistic/Literary: 2%.

Approximate 'graduate track' employed **85%**

There is no central nightclub, but CUSU run popular student nights at local clubs and live acts or many and various.

Sport 'Sports facilities are abundant,' writes Katie, 'but vary between colleges. If sport is your thing, check out the college facilities, where exactly the playing fields and so on are before you apply. All have or share a boathouse and operate a novice rower training programme, which can be a really good way of getting to know people if you can hack the early mornings.

Town 'If you're looking for somewhere with 24-hour opportunity, forget Cambridge; take a 45-minute train ride to London.

'Club fare in town ranges from cheesy, sweaty through the slightly nicer smaller, more chilled and alternative. There is a student night every weeknight.

'What the city lacks in clubs, it makes up for in pubs. There are dozens in the town centre, ranging from cosy locals to trendy wine bars. New restaurants are springing up all the time, and Cambridge is,' says Katie, 'a very safe place to live,' but what does it all cost?

'Cambridge is a relatively cheap city,' writes Caroline. 'If you're trying to work out a budget, allow about £60 per week for food, going out two nights a week, and all the other bits and pieces you'll need. I tend to get through about £600 per eight-week term, not including room rent. Books and equipment usually come free of charge: for scientists, all the scary chemicals are provided, and for arts students, the libraries are amazingly well-stocked. Travel costs should be zero: you'll soon find that everything in Cambridge is within walking distance (unless you're at Girton).

PILLOW TALK

'Room rents are subsidised by the colleges and they are increasing, but you can currently expect to pay about £70 a week on average. Every college has a normal canteen and a Formal Hall. You'll pay about £2 per meal. In Formal Hall, you'll pay about £5, but for this you get a three-course meal with coffee, served by waiting staff as you sit on long, candlelit tables. Grace is said in Latin and vast quantities of wine and port are consumed.'

GETTING THERE

☛ By road: M25/J27, M11/J11, A10. From west or east, A45. From northwest, A604.

☛ By rail: London's Liverpool Street, under the hour; Nottingham, 2:30; Birmingham, 3:00.

☛ By air: Stansted Airport, M11.

☛ By coach: London, 1:50; Birmingham, 2:45; Leeds, 5:00; Bristol, 5:30.

COLLEGE CAMEOS
by Katie Lydon

CHRIST'S
Cambridge CB2 3BU
Tel 01223 334 953
WEB www.christs.cam.ac.uk

Founded in 1448, Christ's is a beautiful college situated in its own extensive grounds in the centre of town. It has a strong academic reputation, regularly tops the Tompkins Table, and there's a strong atmosphere of study. Library access is 24-hour access and computer facilities, including room connections, are available. Christ's also makes 'easy offers' to around a third of its intake.

The balance of north/south and state/independent school students is relatively good, with 49% of the 2000/01 intake coming from the state sector. Women are under represented, but not drastically.

Uniquely, there are two bars, though one closes at 8.30pm. The ents committee puts on around four themed nights a term, and there is a formidable biennial May Ball. The JCR publish an alternative prospectus (see web site).

The college sporting reputation has become good and the drama society, CADS, is well known and respected across the university. The college has a squash court and boathouse – sports pitches are twenty minutes away – and use of its own theatre; there is a cinema that puts on both recent releases and classic films.

Writes Christ's Caroline Muspratt of the accommodation: 'The rooms are generally very good apart from the "typewriter", a horrible building at the back of Christ's. You may be lucky enough to get an en-suite bathroom; otherwise you can be sharing with anything from three to twelve people. The kitchens are usually very small and ill-equipped: the college wants to encourage everyone to eat in Hall. Upper Hall opens for breakfast, lunch and dinner, and the food ranges from excellent to mediocre. Formal Hall, which starts later in the evening, is particularly good: you can book in guests, and the three-course meal is served in a medieval dining hall.'

CHURCHILL
Cambridge CB3 ODS
TEL 01223 336 202
WEB www.chu.cam.ac.uk

Churchill was founded in 1960. The distance (five-minute cycle) from town is more than compensated for by the extensive grounds, proximity to sports facilities and the relaxation of being off the tourist trail. Academically it is strong and improving – up six places to ninth in the *Tompkins Table* this year, dominant subjects are computing, natural sciences and engineering

The state school presence is high (around 70%), and men are the dominant sex (around 77%), though Churchill was the first all-male college to admit women (1972). While very different from and less photographed than its older, town centre counterparts, Churchill's modern architecture is Grade I listed and popular for its functionality.

College ents are regular and popular with students throughout the university, as is its huge bar. All rooms have network and phone connections, and there are extensive sports facilities on site.

CLARE
Cambridge CB2 1TL
Tel 01223 333 246
WEB www.clare.cam.ac.uk
Founded in 1326, Clare is the second oldest college. It occupies extensive grounds that begin in a town-centre huddle of other colleges, and stretch to straddle the River Cam across to the University Library and arts faculties. It is friendly and academically successful – rated in the top six of this year's *Tompkins Table* – and is continually over-subscribed. Students are quite evenly divided between the arts and sciences. English and engineering applicants are encouraged to take a gap year.

Clare choir is famed in Cambridge and throughout the country, and Clare is also home to some of the best alternative ents in the university. Its hugely popular cellar based venue hosts regular live band sessions ranging from jazz to drum 'n' bass, attracting names such as the James Taylor Quartet. Its May Ball is renowned and tickets sought after.

The drama and art societies are particularly good, and Clare sports teams, especially rugby and hockey (men's and women's) and boat club are strong.

Accommodation is usually very good, with most first years living together in the same court, many in en-suite bathrooms. In later years there is the opportunity to move out to the large houses that constitute Clare Colony, a short walk along the river.

CORPUS CHRISTI
Cambridge CB2 1RH
Tel 01223 338 056
WEB www.corpus.cam.ac.uk
Founded in 1352, Corpus is situated right in the centre of Cambridge, opposite Kings (popular myth claims that Corpus actually owns Kings' land and that the lease is soon to expire, to the amusement of the inhabitants of the smaller college). Small but friendly, Corpus' architecture is as pretty as that of its bigger neighbours, but the college is better than most at protecting its students from the constant tourist invasion that can be a liability of a central college.

Corpus places a strong emphasis on academic pursuits, and presents an incentive to achievement in the form of its controversial academic room ballot. Strengths are mainly in the arts, especially history and English, but it is also strong in engineering.

Traditionally enthusiasm is the only pre-requisite here for sport, and the college offers a wide range of facilities, including on-site squash and a strong boat club. There's an annual sports 'Challenge' with Corpus Christi, Oxford.

The JCR is active and the bar a central feature, though its opening hours are variable. The film society puts on a regular mix of classic and new titles, and the drama society (*The Fletcher Players*) is well known and has links with the intimate, adjacent venue, **The Playroom**.

DOWNING
Cambridge CB2 1DQ
Tel 01223 334 826
WEB www.dow.cam.ac.uk
Downing is one of the newer town centre colleges, founded in 1800 just off Cambridge's main shopping street, close to the science, architecture and engineering faculties (the Sidgwick arts site is a little further). Once through the gates one finds an array of unusual neo-classical architecture and large, open, green spaces. It's a peaceful retreat, brilliant in summer. The atmosphere is friendly and lively, politically neutral and relaxed.

Academically, Downing is always in the Top 10; all subjects are well represented; law and medicine are particular strengths. The library is well stocked and pleasant, with an especially good law section. The JCR organises a good Freshers' Week; bar, common room and TV room are excellent. Termly events usually attract big name DJs and are popular across the university. They are perennially successful in sports; particular strengths are rowing, rugby and athletics. There are network connections in all rooms.

EMMANUEL (EMMA)
Cambridge CB2 3AP
TEL 01223 334 290
WEB www.emma.cam.ac.uk

Emma is a relaxed, open college founded in 1584 in the centre of town, opposite the arts cinema and the largest pub in the country. Emma students come from a wide range of backgrounds. It offers scholarships and hardship funds; financial status should never be a barrier to entry.

Emma is also outstanding academically, consistently featuring among the top five colleges. Arts are a particular strength, and it is often the most popular choice for English applicants.

The bar runs weekly funk and cheese events and is the best and most popular in Cambridge. Sport is strong, especially women's rowing and football. There's a squash court and an outdoor swimming pool. The municipal (and indoor) pool is close by, as are most of the shops and both cinemas. Drama and film societies are prominent, and a May Ball happens every other year.

Most rooms have network connections; unusually, Emma offers a free, weekly laundry service.

FITZWILLIAM (FITZ)
Cambridge CB3 0DG
TEL 01223 332 057
WEB www.fitz.cam.ac.uk
Founded in 1969, Fitz is one of the newest colleges in the university, occupying modern, spacious, award-winning buildings – the oldest date from 1963, very different from the classical architecture elsewhere but regarded as functional and user-oriented in a way older colleges often aren't.

Being set a five-minute bike ride away from the town centre in open, generally quiet grounds, students have a reputation for being relaxed and sociable. The college is good academically, comes about mid-*Tompkins Table*, but is not as frenzied as some. A high proportion of its intake comes from state schools.

Tradition isn't as prominent as in other colleges, though there is just enough to remind you that you are at Cambridge. The bar is well-loved and is the centre of social activity, and what are widely thought of as some of the best ents in Cambridge are put on twice termly.

Sport, especially football, is strong, and the college has its own squash court and gym.

GIRTON
Cambridge CB3 0JG
TEL 01223 338 972
WEB www.girton.cam.ac.uk
Girton was founded as a women's college in 1869, began to admit men in 1979 and now the latter slightly outnumber the former. It sits on a beautiful 50-acre site a couple of miles out of the city centre and, uniquely, has its own student car park. Architecturally impressive and undisturbed by tourist invasion, the distance encourages a close-knit community and strong collegiate atmosphere; there's a 24-hour garage across the road for bits and pieces, and Girton village isn't far.

Girton isn't the most academic of colleges, the atmosphere is unpressured and relaxed. The **Cellar Bar** is the social focus and ents venue. Girton formal hall food is famed across the university for its quality, so much that the boat clubs and drinking societies of other colleges strive to get themselves invited for dinner. Sport is popular at Girton, and facilities include an on-site indoor heated swimming pool. The boat club is popular and does well.

Students initially live in college, then move out to nearby houses or Wolfson Court – much more central, near the University Library and Sidgwick site.

GONVILLE & CAIUS
Cambridge CB2 1TA
TEL 01223 332 447
WEB www.cai.cam.ac.uk
Founded as Gonville in 1348, 'Caius' (pronounced 'Keys') was added to the name in 1558. It occupies a convenient city centre site, but tourist traffic is less than might be expected as it sits between Trinity's famous Great court and King's Chapel.

Caius is academically strong, always in the top half of the *Tompkins Table*, and its particular strengths are in economics, law, history and medicine. The always accessible library is excellent, as are the computer rooms, and most student rooms are connected. Drama and music are popular, and *Caius Films* has become a prominent presenter of varied movies, drawing a cross-collegiate audience.

Sport is taken fairly seriously, with the boat club very successful. Squash, netball, football, hockey and racquet facilities are within a few minutes walk of college and served by a licensed pavilion.

Uniquely its students are compelled to buy forty-five dinner tickets per term at around £4 each. While this may seem a little expensive, the result *is* a stronger college atmosphere.

The college can accommodate all undergraduates well, though again, quite expensively.

HOMERTON
Hills Rd, Cambridge CB2 2PH
TEL 01223 507 252
WEB www.homerton.cam.ac.uk
Homerton was founded in 1695 as a college of education and moved to its present site in 1894. It

stills specialises in education, in education, Homerton College now other subjects, including Archaeology and Anthropology, Computing Science, Economics, Engineering, English, Geography, History, History of Art, Land Economy, Music, Natural Sciences, Oriental Studies, Philosophy, Social & Political Sciences, and Theology & Religious Studies.

Situated a bit out of the town centre, close to the railway station, Homerton tends to cultivate a fairly close community. There is a relatively high proportion of mature students, and women outnumber men. They recruit mainly from state schools, though students are drawn from all backgrounds.

Participation in university activities, such as journalism, drama and politics, is strong. Facilities are excellent – Homerton's on-site sound and dance studios are the rehearsal venue for many university productions. It also boasts its own gym, squash court and sports field. Men's rugby and women's rowing are both strong.

Students initially live in college, but there is the opportunity to move out into houses scattered around the town in later years.

JESUS

Cambridge CB5 8BL
TEL 01223 339 495
WEB www.jesus.cam.ac.uk

Jesus was founded in 1496 and, 'greener' and more open than some of its neighbours, overlooks the common and river from its spacious grounds, five minutes from the city centre.

Academically Jesus is relatively strong, and takes its students from a variety of backgrounds. The JCR bar is a popular social hub, but ents are few because of lack of room. Music and drama are strong, and the college offers exhibitions to organ and choral scholars.

Sport is very strong, and the college's location means that all of its facilities, which include pitches for soccer, American football, cricket, rugby and hockey, and squash and tennis courts, are on site. The boat club is a short walk across the common.

Accommodation for all undergraduates is in college or houses across the street – some of the latter have been recently refurbished and a new on-site block of en-suite accommodation opened.

KING'S

Cambridge CB2 1ST
TEL 01223 331 417
WEB www.kings.cam.ac.uk

Founded in 1441, King's and its famous chapel are most popularly representative of Cambridge. Its public perception, however, as the epitome of prestige and tradition in Cambridge, contrasts sharply with the reality. It takes over 80% of its students from the state sector and is reputedly obsessed with being politically correct. Its students aren't required to wear gowns at formal dinners or elsewhere – in fact, there are *no* formal arrangements for meals.

King's fame attracts more tourists than any other college, but most come only to visit the chapel, and careful controls ensure that this doesn't impinge on study too much.

Academically King's is average, but its students are the most diverse bunch in the university. The atmosphere is relaxed and while students work hard, they make time for other activities – university drama, politics and journalism all feature high numbers of King's students.

Ents, based in their **Cellar**, are among the best in Cambridge, with queues forming long before the tickets for their famous termly *Mingle* events go on sale. The choir is of course world famous, making several recordings a year, and choral and organ scholarships are offered. Sport isn't a King's strength, perhaps something to do with the fact that its rowers wear purple lycra?

LUCY CAVENDISH

Cambridge CB3 0BU
TEL 01223 330 280
WEB www.lucy-cav.cam.ac.uk

Lucy Cavendish was founded in 1965 as a college for mature women. It is placed in a pretty *cul-de-sac* behind St John's, five minutes from the city centre.

Academically, medicine, law and veterinary science are strong. Sport isn't a particular strength, although the first Lucy Cavendish rowing crew hit the river a couple of years ago. Having had to start at the bottom, its reputation has yet to rise to the surface. The college has its own gym and access to squash and badminton courts. There's a summer ball after the festivities of May Week have died down and its own students are still around.

A recently built block of rooms with en-suite facilities has increased the on-site accommodation available to students.

MAGDALENE

Cambridge CB3 0AG
TEL 01223 332 135
WEB www.magd.cam.ac.uk

Magdalene (pronounced 'Maudlin'), founded in 1542, straddles Bridge Street, alongside the river on the north side of the city. Its grounds meet those of St John's and allegedly trespass on its land, which why students of the former refer to Magdalene students as their 'villagers'.

You'll hear that there is an overwhelming public school presence, and that tradition is paramount, with a nightly, formal candlelit dinner. But Magdalene students claim no atmosphere of elitism or arrogance. Most regard the dinner (non-compulsory) as a pleasant social occasion rather than an imposed tradition.

Academically not outstanding, but its students participate widely in university sport, drama and journalism, and have recently had a heavy involvement with the Cambridge Union.

Facilities are good – the college shares playing fields with St John's – and it has its own Eton Fives court. Most impressive facility is its music room, with grand piano, two harpsichords and an organ. The bar and other social facilities are good, and well complemented by the adjacent **Pickerel Inn**.

NEW HALL
Huntingdon Rd, CB3 0DF
TEL 01223 762 229
WEB www.newhall.cam.ac.uk
Ten minutes walk from the city centre, New Hall was founded in the 1950s to increase access to Cambridge for women. It is still a women-only college, but contrary to popular myth is not an introverted, convent-like place.

Indisputably, many New Hall students are pooled here as second choice, but many others chose to be there, and the two 'groups' cohere to form a pleasant and sociable community. In a recent referendum held to decide whether to go co-ed, students voted in favour of remaining single-sex.

Academically New Hall is continually close to the bottom of the *Tompkins Table*. Particular strengths are medicine, physics and economics. The college hosts the largest contemporary exhibition of women's art in permanent residence.

Its futuristic **Dome** houses a famed rising kitchen, applauded when it appears at meal times, and is generally thought of as one of the best ent venues in the university, hosting large events with big-name DJs – including the respected termly *Vibrate* – and yes, men *are* allowed in. No May ball, but a garden party is held.

Sports facilities are good, including tennis, squash and netball courts, and the college is close to playing fields. New Hall rowers are feared by other colleges' women crews.

College accommodation is available to all undergraduates.

NEWNHAM
Cambridge CB3 9DF
TEL 01223 335 783
WEB www.newn.cam.ac.uk
Newnham was founded in 1871 as an all-women college, continues to admit female students only, and, like New Hall, is anything but insular – guests of both sexes are welcome around the clock...as long as they are accompanied.

The college is situated close to the river and Sidgwick arts site, in attractive grounds with extensive gardens (where, uniquely, you may walk on the grass). Students are from a mix of backgrounds, though predominantly state school. Unspectacular academically, Newnham's strengths are in the arts.

Sport facilities include cricket, hockey, lacrosse, football and rugby pitches, a croquet lawn and tennis courts. Newnham's is the oldest women's boat club in England. Newnham students are also heavily involved in life outside college, particularly in drama and journalism.

PEMBROKE
Cambridge CB2 1RF
TEL 01223 338 154
WEB www.pem.cam.ac.uk
Pembroke was founded in 1347 and enjoys the benefits of a central location without the hassles of being on the tourist trail. It has pretty gardens, hidden from the roads by high walls.

Academically strong, computer facilities are good, and student rooms are mostly connected to the network. Pembroke also has busy dramatic, musical and journalistic interests. *The Pembroke Players* and the musical society are known across the university, and the college has its own newspaper, *Pembroke Street*. They also have a popular bar and regular ents, a sports ground and boat club, and enjoy high-level participation and reasonable success in rowing, rugby, football, netball and hockey.

Accommodation is good and either in college or nearby houses; a new block has just been completed.

PETERHOUSE
Cambridge CB2 1RD
TEL 01223 338 223
WEB www.pet.cam.ac.uk
Peterhouse is the oldest and smallest college in Cambridge. Founded in 1284, the buildings are attractive and close to Pembroke and the engineering and science faculties.

Reputed to be more stringent than most in its interviewing and admissions procedures, Peterhouse has particular strengths in classics, English, history, law, engineering, maths, medicine and natural sciences. Its stereotype – oft denied – is that of a staunchly right-wing, public-school environment. Men outnumber women significantly, but allegations of a sexist culture appear unfounded as girls from other colleges choose to join Peterhouse choir and other activities. (the college has its own theatre). Sports are actively pursued, particularly rugby, football and rowing. The college also has its own magazine and many of its students are involved in university newspaper journalism.

QUEENS'

Cambridge CB3 9ET
TEL 01223 335 540
WEB www.quns.cam.ac.uk

Founded in 1448, in pleasant grounds straddling the river, and close to most faculties, Queens' is open, pleasant, and students say the most people-based college in Cambridge. Certainly its students come from staggeringly different backgrounds. Around the top of the academic league tables, strengths are in natural sciences, medicine, engineering, languages and law.

Facilities are fantastic, including a hall that hosts some of the biggest ents in Cambridge (such as the famed cheesy *Jingles*); it doubles as theatre or sporting venue. The entertainment schedule is the envy of the university, and there is a huge May Ball every other year. The drama society puts on some of the most innovative and controversial plays in Cambridge, there's a thriving gossip magazine, the film society provides a college cinema two nights a week, and the sporting ethos, while placing emphasis on enjoyment, embraces success at university level (there are squash courts and playing fields). Yet, Queen's still manages to remain a genuinely friendly, relaxing, unpretentious, but inspiring place to be.

College can accommodate all students, and all rooms are connected to the internet.

ROBINSON

Cambridge CB3 9AN
TEL 01223 339 143
WEB www.robinson.cam.ac.uk

Robinson is the newest Cambridge college, founded in 1979 and based in red-brick buildings behind the University Library and arts faculties, next to the uni rugby ground – slightly out of town (five-minute cycle), but close to sports facilities. Its 'new' status means tradition is kept to a minimum. Here, Cambridge stereotypes are despised and disproved.

Academically average, the emphasis is on personal freedoms and development. Robinson draws the majority of its intake from state schools; the atmosphere between staff and students is very open and respectful, with meetings open to everyone.

Ents are well attended and include karaoke and music nights featuring anything from cheese to jazz. The JCR publishes its own alternative prospectus – check the web site.

Accommodation is comfortable, functional and available to all undergraduates.

ST CATHERINE'S (CATZ)

Cambridge CB2 1RL
TEL 01223 338 319
WEB www.caths.cam.ac.uk

Catz is a small college on the main street, along from King's, almost opposite Corpus Christi, and within ten minutes' walk of the main arts, science and engineering faculties. Founded in 1473, its relatively small size makes for an inclusive community. There's a good social mix, though women are a minority (usually around 40%).

It has a tradition of academic excellence, though it has recently dropped in the *Tompkins Table*. Strengths are in natural sciences, geography and medicine. The library is new and well stocked.

Even though its ents are generally poor, Catz has a good social tradition: Freshers' Week is legendary, recently the bar and common room have been refurbished, and its formal dinners are popular and over-subscribed.

Music and drama are strong, and Catz has its own 150-capacity theatre in the **Octagon** buildings. The literary Shirley society is the best known in Cambridge. Sport is strong, notably rugby and athletics.

The boathouse is a short cycle away, and facilities are generally good – there's an Astroturf pitch, courts for racquet sports, and pitches for field sports. Swimming is a Catz strength, and though it doesn't have its own pool, the excellent, new town facility is close.

Students live initially in college, moving out to the Octagon colony of flats near the Sidgwick site in the second year.

ST JOHN'S

Cambridge CB2 1TP
TEL 01223 338 703
WEB www.joh.cam.ac.uk

St John's was founded in 1511 in the centre of Cambridge, next to its long-standing rival, Trinity. It is the second largest college in Cambridge and so is able to house all its undergraduates. Architecturally impressive, its buildings chart varied and increasingly modern styles, culminating in the listed Cripps Building, seen as ugly by some, but functional and popular accommodation for first years.

Academically, John's is very strong (fourth in the tables for the last couple of years, and generally in the top five) and boasts an impressive and very well-stocked new library. Its beautiful Old Library houses many ancient manuscripts. Computing facilities are excellent, with two main computer rooms and terminals scattered around the library and in the JCR. All student rooms in college have Internet connections. Book grants are automatic; travel grants and hardship loans are generous.

St John's choir is respected globally, the college chapel providing a beautiful setting, and the Jazz Society is famed across the university. Drama – the *Lady Margaret Players* – is a great tradition, the freshers' play a big draw, and they have their own venue in the **School of Pythagoras**, apparently the oldest university building in the country. The film society operates twice a week, and there are disco clubnights three times a term in the underground **Boiler Room**, noted for its drum 'n' bass, hip hop and cabaret. Sport is strong, especially rugby, football and the famous Lady Margaret Boat Club. There are extensive pitches at the back of college and a new boathouse just down the river. There are also squash, badminton, tennis and netball facilities. Finally, John's formal hall is arguably the best (and best value for money), and tickets for their May Ball are among the most sought after.

SELWYN
Cambridge CB3 9DQ
TEL 01223 335 896
WEB www.sel.cam.ac.uk
Selwyn was founded in 1882 and sits in pleasant grounds close to the Sidgwick site of arts faculties. The college's proximity to green fields and 15 mins distance from the bustle of the city centre gives it an atmosphere less claustrophobic than most.

Not noted for its academic reputation, though usually in the top half of the *Tompkins Table*, Selwyn's strengths include engineering, history and natural sciences.

There is an even mix between arts and science students and between men and women, and students come from a wide variety of backgrounds.

Facilities are good – the library is satisfactory. For arts students, faculty libraries are on the doorstep and can be equally accessible. Most student rooms are connected to the internet, and communal computer facilities are good.

Drama (*The Mitre Players*) have their own venue in the **Diamond**, and the music and film societies are also active.

Sport is not a major strength, except rowing, where in recent years Selwyn has become a force. The bar is popular, and there are several student run ents. The impressive May Ball is biennial.

All undergraduates can be accommodated either in college or in nearby houses.

SIDNEY SUSSEX
Cambridge CB2 3HU
TEL 01223 338 872
WEB www.sid.cam.ac.uk
Sidney was founded in 1596 on what is known to today's students as 'Sainsbury's Street'. The modern world beyond the gates may be extremely busy, but once inside you'll find architecture dating back 400 years and a relaxed and unpressured atmosphere.

Accommodating a balance of arts and science students, with an even ratio of women to men, Sidney isn't the most academic of colleges, although it is currently pushing its way up the *Tompkins Table*.

The bar is good and run by students, with a sound system better than that of most other college bars, pool table and table football. The frequent ents are well attended

College food has allegedly improved since it was voted second worst in Cambridge in 1993. Sport isn't strong. A sports ground, a short cycle away, is shared with Christ's; the boathouse is close.

Students are accommodated either in college or in nearby houses.

TRINITY
Cambridge CB2 1TQ
TEL 01223 338 422
WEB www.trin.cam.ac.uk
Founded in 1546, Trinity is the largest college in Cambridge. Situated centrally with beautiful views onto the river and the Backs and next to St John's, Trinity is its (friendly) rival in almost everything.

The college architecture is much admired, notably the Wren Library and Great Court, whose '*run*' was made famous in *Chariots of Fire* (though actually filmed at Eton).

There is an impressive academic record – they are rarely out of the top four or five in the *Tompkins Table* (No. 3 this year) – particularly in sciences. Contrary to popular belief, it recruits a significant majority from the state sector; women are, however, poorly represented (around 40%).

As befits the richest college in Cambridge, facilities are excellent, the library well stocked and computer facilities first class. Book grants are available to all students, room rents are among the lowest in the uni (although rooms have varying facilities, due to the age of the buildings, all are comfortable).

Ents aren't particularly notable, but the bar is well used, if a bit small. Extra-curricular activities are fervently pursued, and sport is strong. The boat club has recently listed several impressive victories, facilities are superb and nearby.

TRINITY HALL (Tit Hall)
Cambridge CB2 1TJ
TEL 01223 332 535
WEB www.trinhall.cam.ac.uk
Trinity Hall was founded in 1350 and nestles in pretty riverside grounds next to Trinity, its bigger and richer rival.

There is a popular myth about Trinity porters phoning their Tit Hall counterparts to ask them to turn the music down at some gig – the reply came that Trinity Hall was 'there first' and so would do as it pleased. This anecdote sums up the atmosphere – it's a close, strong community that refuses to be overshadowed by its neighbours simply because of its size. There's a good mix of students and of men and women.

Tit Hall is, according to the *Tompkins Table*, academically average, but its traditional strength is law. The new library, overhanging the river, is well stocked, if a little noisy in the summer, when it's a feature on guided punt tours.

Bar and JCR are lively and ents often referred to as the best. They face tough competition from King's, but are enjoyed for their individual style, the quality that best represents Tit Hall's students.

Sport and sporting facilities are good, and drama and music societies active.

CANTERBURY CHRIST CHURCH UNIVERSITY

Canterbury Christ Church
University
North Holmes Road
Canterbury
Kent CT1 1QU

TEL 01227 767700
FAX 01227 470442
EMAIL admissions@cant.ac.uk
WEB www.canterbury.ac.uk

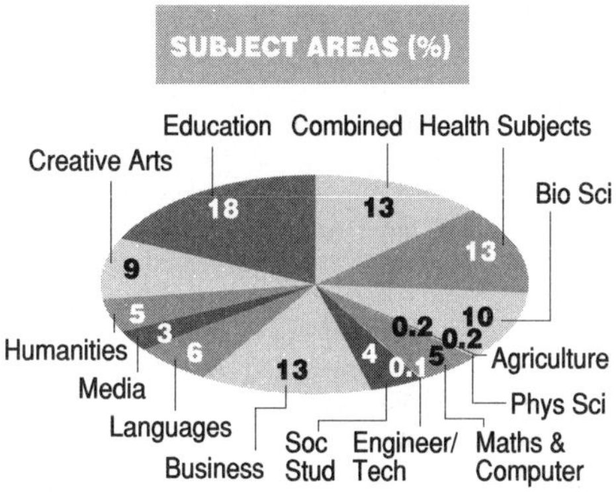

VAG VIEW

Canterbury Christ Church University, founded by the Church of England in 1962 (and currently boasting the Archbishop as Chancellor) just received full university status, having excelled as a university college awarding its own degrees since 1995. Located in modern buildings on an historic site (part of St Augustine's Abbey built in AD597), they began as a teacher training college.

CAMPUS

Canterbury is a good place to be, small and friendly, if not exactly jumping with action. It is just big enough to hold a cathedral, some run of the mill shops and a fair range of pubs – and on first visit you might wonder that there's room for two degree-awarding institutions. The more widely known of these is the University of Kent (UKC), a traditional campus university situated up what has become known to the thousands of UKC students who trundle up and down it daily as Mount Everest. C4's campus is situated around the other (east) side of the city.

There are also three other campuses: nearby **Broadstairs Campus** (Northwood Road, Broadstairs, Kent CT10 2WA; 01843 609120 - business, computing, digital media, education, health, commercial music, performing arts, policing), **Chatham Campus** (30 Pembroke Copurt, Chatham Maritime, Kent ME4 4UF; 01634 890800 - education, health and policing) and **Salomans Campus** - (David Salomans Estate, Broomhill Road, Southborough, Tunbridge Wells, Kent TN3 OTG; 01892 515152 - postgraduate study).

FEES, BURSARIES

UK & EU Fees £3000 p.a., with sliding scale bursaries to £800 max. according to parental income.

ACADEMIA & JOBS

There are four faculties, Arts & Humanities, Business & Sciences, Education, and Health.

Education is highly rated and more than a third of C4 graduates find work in this sector, but now the curriculum has expanded to include degrees in English, History, American Studies, International Business, Computing (including Animation), Art, Music, Radio, Film & TV (where there are links with Sky), Religion, Sport Science and social sciences, and since 1987 there has been a major expansion in courses for the paramedical and nursing professions.

They claim links with 'some 8,000 businesses managed through academic departments and the Centre for Enterprise and Business Development (CEBD)'. Recent teaching assessments have been uniformly good, but the real acid test was passed when subjects such as music (degrees include Popular Music & Technology), radio/film/TV, art (including Fine Art and Ceramics) and sport began to find popular expression in the extra-curricular life of the university, which is growing fast.

Nationally they are among the top suppliers of TV and film camera operators. See the uni's Film/Radio & TV Studies BA/BSc and the MA Media Production.

In the Health field, degrees include Midwifery, Nursing (Adult, Child, Mental Health), Occupational Therapy and Radiography - they account for 5% of the graduate job market with their BSc Medical Imaging (Radiography) - low entry requirements, good assessment results (22 points).

Worth noting, too, is a strong, traditional link with the police - the DIpHE and BSc in Policing, large number of combos with Applied Criminology and Forensic Investigation degrees translate with efficiency into jobs

Business finds sales managers jobs in quantity, and puts 5% or more of their graduates into work in the transport business. Traditionally they are strong, too, in travel - travel and tour agency managers.

Finally, some two dozen Sport & Exercise Science degrees ensures that they are making a mark nationally in this area of graduate employment, too.

There's a good deal of talk about disability support - 'from providing note-takers to sorting out car parking for students with Orange/Blue Badges.'

STUDENT SCENE

On a Monday the Students' Union take over one of the local nightclubs, a favourite for all-coming students, given C4's 28/72 male/female ratio Tuesday nights are either karaoke, live comedy or quiz nights at the C4 union, except that every other week students hike up Mount Everest to Kent Uni's nightclub **The Venue**. Wednesday, as at every uni in the UK, is Sports Fed night, where all the teams get horrifically drunk in the SU. Thursday sees the opening of **Frame 25**, the student cinema, which shows recent movies on a weekly basis. Friday night is *Funky Friday at C4* - could be disco or live, and currently running a Pop Factor competition with real-live special guest judge Mark Cowan, agent to X-Factor contestants, in the SU bar. There are balls all year round - Freshers', Halloween, Graduation, Christmas - the climax being the huge Summer Ball with fairground and bands.

Student media is big: C4 Online, C4 Radio, C4 TV, C4 *Bluebeard*, the official student mag., which began life as a joke magazine, but quickly developed. Also under C4 Media comes a new society - the tech crew that looks after all the technical equipment C4 Media use.

C4 Radio was the first British student radio station to broadcast all over the world via the Internet; C4 TV is highly successful and all-student run. Commended at the TV Student Awards in 2004 for 'C4 Digs' (an MTV-style Cribs show) and as producers of 'I'm A Student, Get Me Outta Here!', they went on to be highly commended at the 2005 awards in the Light Entertainment catgory.

There are 15 other societies, from Raise & Give to Trampolining, fromPagan to Asian, and there are lots of music groups and student bands, which, unfortunately, have been banned by the Council

STUDENT POPULATION

Total students 14,015

- Female Undergraduates: 57%
- Male Undergraduates: 22%
- Postgraduates: 20%
- Others: 1%

UNIVERSITY/STUDENT PROFILE

University since	2005
Situation/style	City campus
Student population	14015
Undergraduates	11080
- mature	42%, high
- non EU undergraduates	2%
- male/female	28/72
- non-traditional student intake	34%
- state school intake	96%
- drop-out rate	13%
- undergraduate applications	Up 15%

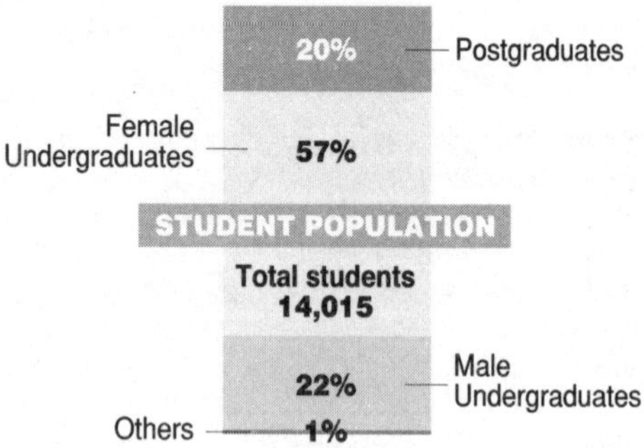

from playing in the union due to excessive noise levels.

TOWN Writes Dominic Conway: 'Nice big cathedral, old cobbled streets, strong whiff of history in the air and a two hour walk to the beach. That is Canterbury. To accommodate the evident wealth of students there are two clubs (plus some secret ones) and plenty good bars both on and off campus making it easy to party somewhere different every night for at least a fortnight. If you keep your ear to the ground local groups will put on authentic unpretentious rock shows and Whitstable hides a number of world class musicians playing jazz, blues, and Turkish folk music that even the most selective muso will be content with. Although it is quite a quaint place it is very lively and friendly ˆ the locals never seem to mind or complain about the amount of students!! There is also a wide variety of shops and supermarkets to take your pick from! The toughest thing about town is avoiding the temptation of spending all your money on a meal in one of the many restaurants and café bars that line the streets. Apart from that everything is very simple and easy to find. If you come to this Uni you will have everything really, countryside and seaside but still near to London, entertainment and nightlife but still a calm working environment.'

WHAT IT'S REALLY LIKE

COLLEGE:	
Social Life	★★★
Campus scene	**Lively, local**
Politics	**Left of Centre**
Sport	**Competitive + sport-for-all**
National team position	**86th**
Arts opportunities	**Excellent**
Student magazine	**Bluebeard**
Student radio	**C4 Radio**
Student TV	**C4 TV**
TV Awards, 2005	**Commendation**
Union ents	**Friday nights**
Live venue capacity	**450**
Union Clubs/Societies	**40**
Parking	**Very poor**
CITY:	
Entertainment	★★★
Scene	**Touristy, historic, very studenty; pubs OK**
Town/gown relations	**Good**
Risk of violence	**Low**
Cost of living	**Average**
Student concessions	**Adequate**
Survival + 2 nights out	**£80 pw**
Part-time work campus/town	**OK**

ACADEMIC EXCELLENCE

TEACHING:	
(Rated Excellent or 17+ out of 24)	
Geography, History	**Excellent**
Maths, Radio/Film/TV Studies, Nursing, Other Subjects Allied to Medicine, Theology	**22**
American Studies, Physics, Chemistry, Leisure/Sport, Business/ Managment, Biosciences	**21**
Psychology, Social Science, Media & Cultural Studies	**20**
Art & Design	**19**
RESEARCH:	
*Top grades 5/5**	**None**

SPORT is taken seriously, particularly with local rivals UKC. More than twenty teams, including American Football. Facilities could be a lot better: the uni's **St George's Fitness Centre** includes the usual weights and resistance equipment; a swimming pool lies a few minutes from campus; and strong links with UKC and the local public school, King's, help.

AT A GLANCE

ACADEMIC FILE:	
Subjects assessed	**23**
Excellent	**74%**
Typical entry requirements	**200 points**
Application acceptance rate	**23%**
Students-staff ratio	**21:1**
First/2:1 degree pass rate	**45%**
ACCOMMODATION FILE:	
Guarantee to freshers	**For those 20 miles away**
Style	**Halls, flats houses**
Approx price range pw	**£67-£82**
City rent pw	**£60-£70**

PILLOW TALK

First years are prioritised for halls. On the Canterbury Campus main site, Davidson, Lang and Temple halls are en suite, Fynden and Thorne are single rooms with washbasins. These are catered, but rent quoted does not include meals. Canterbury-based self-catered residences at College Court and Holmes Court are 2 mins from campusLanfranc and Oaten Hill are farther, but the latter is a refurbshed oates house and much in demand. Newest is the Parkham Road Student Village (2005), a 10-min walk from campus, with houses and flats for 3 to 7 students. Finally, there's Pin Hill, 15 mins away from campus, a development of 5 halls, Ramsey, Coggan, Runcie and Carey (all very episcopal) and Benson House (which has 40 en-suite rooms). Broadstairs and Chatham cmpuses both have self-catered residences.

GETTING THERE

☛ By road: M2 and A2 connect Canterbury to London and beyond.

☛ By coach: London Victoria, 1 hour 45 mins.

☛ By rail: two or three times an hour from London Victoria, Charing Cross and Waterloo East stations. The fast service takes 1 hour 20 mins.

STUDENT CARDIFF - THE CITY

You've perfected the dialect, stocked up on laverbread and exhausted your considerable repertoire of sheep jokes. Now it's time to face reality, you're going to Cardiff. Yes, it is in Wales, but yes, it is also the up-and-coming cosmopolitan British city and a place jam-packed per square yard with the best drinking, dancing and shopping outside of London. Note also that the Welsh know how to have a good time far better than any of us tight-arsed English and rarely worry about the results of such over-indulgence. Note also that, no matter how funny you think it may be, locals will soon tire of your comedy Welsh accent.

SHOPPING

The student loan in your back pocket is going to be burning a hole right about now. Interest free overdrafts and credit cards aren't much help either and the Welsh capital is a fine place to utilise the government's personal little gift to you. The **Capitol** shopping centre offers an array of stores from **H&M** (great for cheap clothes for a night out) to **Oasis**, the Gadget shop and **Virgin** mega store. All the usual High Street names are in the city (many with student discounts), but you're going to have to head a little off the beaten track if you really want to stand out from the crowd.

First stop, before you're over you're credit limit, is the **High Street Arcade**. And that had better be a very high credit limit because with shops selling **French Connection**, **Red or Dead**, **Versace** and other designer labels therein you're going to have to cut down on such extravagances as food and drink for a few weeks. Back out on Queen's Street you'll find **Top Shop** and **Dorothy Perkins** within a 100 metres of each other, with NUS discount and generally reasonable prices, you'll soon find yourself gravitating towards the entrances.

Also worth checking out is the **Castle Arcade**, with shops selling fashionable alternatives to what everybody else is wearing. For those of you of a baggy disposition, **Westworld** is situated just across the road, and with it a healthy selection of Carhartt and Box Fresh urbanwear.

FILM

With developments around the city centre, two new cinemas have popped up in the last couple of years, both with multiple screens. There's **Star Century** in the **Millennium Plaza** and the **UGC** opposite **Cardiff International Arena**, the former with enormous screens, comfy chairs, and student discounts! For those of you with Daddy's car, or at least a decent grasp of the bus timetable, the **UCI** on the Bay will surely have something for you on one of its twelve screens. Looking a little further afield than Hollywood is the **Chapter Arts Centre**. Critically acclaimed left-field productions and a gallery displaying high-calibre exhibits are all there to fire the cells that lectures couldn't.

ARTS

For the more culturally aware among you, Cardiff has a lot to offer. Besides the afore-mentioned Chapter Arts Centre, there is the beautifully located **National Museum & Gallery** everything from the pop-art of David Hockney's Photoworks to more traditional classical viewing. **The Centre for Visual Arts** also deserves a mention.

Stage-wise, the Welsh capital is blessed with both the **New Theatre** and **The Sherman**, the latter proving student friendly with its NUS concessions and reputation as a prime comedy venue (Craig Charles, Simon Fast Show Day, etc). The venue is also good for Wales' own new breed of playwrights.

EATING OUT

Whilst most bars south of Cathays are not going to suit your fragile student budget, there are a few gems to be uncovered. **UWIC's Union, Cardiff** has everything you would expect from a pub lunch – and more! With a menu ranging from your simple Jacket Potato or tasty Nacho's to 'Bush Ozzie Steak' and Pasanda Curry, not to mention the variety of specials all priced under a fiver!

Unfortunately for every Union Bar there are another five deco-influenced yuppie hangouts just waiting to sneer at your Oxfam-designer chic and intimidate you with a £3 warm frothy pint and undernourished nouvelle cuisine. If, as a result, you never stray further than the student ghettos of Cathays and Roath and their reassuring array of not-too-fancy pubs, takeaways and greasy spoons, then (and particularly if a post-tiles stomach-settler is what you're after) I would have to remind you of Ramon's and its hangover-easing array of fine fried food. Any student who claims not to have sampled one of Senor Ramon's infamous breakfasts is a liar.

If it's Italian you desire then the choice is varied. **Topo Gigio**, **Giovanni's** or **Waldos** all send a diner home happy. Likewise with **Old Orleans** and **The New York Deli** if ribs and fries is your choice. Indian and Chinese are too numerous to mention, no doubt you'll soon find a favourite of your own, a post-club hangout where, in your inebriated state, the kindly patron will serve you chips with curry sauce and gently mock your state of mind.

Vegetarians must visit Woodville Road. Never too far from most student lodgings **The Peppermint Lounge** and **Greenhouse** both offer excellent value specialist dishes.

PUBS

Besides the (UWIC) Union bars, **see UWIC entry**, with all the up to date student deals and freebie giveaways, **The George** is a student haven, running the usual scream pub offers, decent cheap food and a buoyant atmosphere. There are numerous others, **The End**, **Social**, **Gassy Jacks**, **Mackintosh**, **Pen & Wig** to name a few. The city centre is also awash with bars whose expensive drink prices succumb (as do nightclubs) to a student night, the conventional £1 a bottle or the more frivolous happy hour.

CLUBS & LIVE VENUES

Clubbing is an area in which Cardiff comes into its own. What has always been a healthy and vibrant scene is now growing still further into something rivalling the likes of Bristol, Liverpool and Manchester.

Through a combination of refurbishment, rethinking, new promoters and considerable cash, the city is now drawing in visitors for the club culture alone. The new breed of clubs such as **Jumping Jaks** and **Bar Risa** are particularly student friendly, with cheap entry fees and great offers. Then there's UWIC's own **Union, Cardiff** (was **Reds** long ago), currently the weekend showcase for the best of Wales's up and coming DJs (funky house with nights called *Shake* and *Right Here Right Now*). In addition there are places such as **Walkabout**, the **Great Western** (a Lloyds No. 1 bar, formerly **The Old Monk** and then **The Bush Pig**now), **The Square** and many more all on the same street!

On any given day there's a cheap night out in all of the big clubs. For chart and cheese play lists with cheap bottled lager most popular in the category has to be **Creation**. For acts as diverse as Super Furry Animals, The Beta Band, Barry Manilow and Courteney Pine in recent times, seek out venues like **The CIA**, **Millennium Stadium**, **Coal Exchange**, **St David's Hall**, and **The Great Hall**. Traditionalists will want to visit **Café Jazz** or **The Toucan Club**, where those of a jazz-funk-salsa-samba persuasion can strut their polyester-clad selves to some seriously groove-ridden DJs and live bands. They even offer samba lessons in-between.

Maybe it's devolution, maybe it's the untapped potential, hell, it may even be the Manics, Stereophonics and Catatonia whatever, Cardiff is living up to its remit as a capital city.

Lucy Walters

CARDIFF UNIVERSITY

Cardiff University
Cardiff CF10 3AT

TEL 029 2087 4839
FAX 029 2087 4457
EMAIL prospectus@cardiff.ac.uk
WEB www.cardiff.ac.uk

Cardiff Students' Union
Cardiff CF1 3QN

TEL 029 2078 1400
FAX 029 2078 1407
EMAIL studentsunion@cardiff.ac.uk
WEB cardiffstudents.com

VAG VIEW

August 2004 saw the merger of Cardiff University and the University of Wales College of Medicine, a step supported by £60 million. All of which helps make Cardiff one of the best deals going.

Tip-top uni academically, and yet with an acceptable, 17% application acceptance rate and a fantastic social scene. Yet there are many among English sixthformers who still quibble, which may be what keeps the acceptance rate at its promising level.

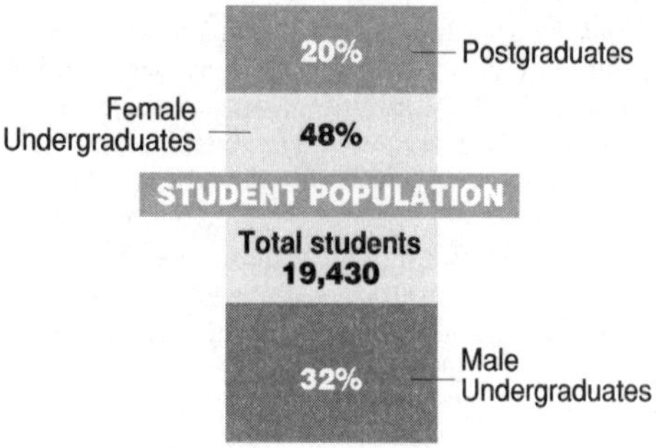

CAMPUS

Cardiff is a campus in the city, a kind of academic precinct, separate and yet part of the city. A short walk from the reassuringly classical lines of the main university buildings brings you to the fastest growing capital in Europe. Yet, when you go there what you notice is its compactness and accessibility, its clean lines and the way they have maintained the airiness of a wide open space. The city is also still a cheap place to live and the Students Union conspire to make it more affordable by employing 300 students to service their facilities. Moreover, the crime rate is livable with and decreasing on campus since the introduction of CCTV.

FEES, BURSARIES

UK & EU Fees p.a. 2006 are: Year 1, £1200; following years: £3000 p.a., although students from Wales and non UK EU countries will be eligible for a £1800 fee grant from the Welsh Assembly. See also Student Finance Wales website - www.studentfinancewales.co.uk.

Cardiff has more than 150 scholarships available in Chemistry, Computer Science, Earth Sciences, Engineering, Mathematics, Physics, Archaeology, German, Italian, Music and Welsh, most worth £1000 p.a.. More details at www.cardiff.ac.uk/2614

The Welsh Assembly Financial Contingency Fund (FCF), which cannot be used to pay tuition fees, makes up to £3500 available per student based on a needs assessment conducted by the university according to a formula to ensure fairness to all, but especially helping people from backgrounds that might not traditionally have progressed to HE. Any student at Cardiff studying more than 50% full time may apply.

STUDENT PROFILE

Writes Lisa Andrews: 'It's all rain, rugby and sheep, right? Wrong. Okay, so if you opt to study at Cardiff, chances are that nine times out of ten you'll get soaked on the way to lectures and spend the next hour dripping puddles in your pew. And on match days, it's hard to avoid the Welsh rugby spirit, if only because your quiet local is heaving with red-shirted fans. But with 12,000 students of 100 nationalities, Cardiff is nothing if not culturally diverse.'

The statistics support Lisa's case: 12% of degree undergraduates come from beyond Europe, and a highish independent school intake is balanced by a 22% recruitment from the lower socio-economic groups. It's a well-balanced picture, and there is no surprise that the drop-out rate is as low as 4%.

ACADEMIA & JOBS

Twenty-one subject areas have been assessed as Excellent, one of the best scores in the UK, and even if you may sometimes feel, like Lisa, that 'the research programmes in which many Cardiff lecturers are involved take a toll on their availability to students outside of lecture times,' you have to derive some confidence from the result.

UNIVERSITY/STUDENT PROFILE	
University since	**1883**
Situation/style	**Civic**
Student population	**19430**
Undergraduates	**15548**
- mature	**15%**
- non EU undergraduates	**12%**
- male/female	**40/60**
- non-traditional student intake	**22%**
- state sector intake	**85%**
- drop-out rate	**4%, low**
- undergraduate applications	**Up 2%**

The international calibre of research can be

gauged by the grades 5 and 5* listed in our *Academic Excellence* box. Agreements with Peking University and Tsinghua University will facilitate exchanges of senior academic staff. Meanwhile, Cardiff has become home to the UK's first Centre for Astrobiology – it will link the study of biology with astronomy. Recently, millions have been spent on the Chemistry Department, creating a new laboratory and other facilities, a 500-seater lecture theatre and resource centre, while £12 million is set aside for a new Life Sciences building.

Taking financial activities with accountancy and business, you could say that commerce outdoes health and public administration as Cardiff's top avenue for graduates to employment (see *Where Cardiff Graduates End Up* box), though the latter achieves second highest concentration country-wide, and health has just been boosted by the inclusion of The University of Wales College of Medicine. There is a whole host of international courses in accounting, economics and business administration (human resource managers do well too – see their BScEcon Sociology & Industrial Relations for something that aims true), and the

ACADEMIC EXCELLENCE

TEACHING:	
Mechanical Engineering, Chemistry, Architecture, Environmental Engineering, Maritime Studies, English Language, Optometry, Philosophy, Psychology, Town & Country Planning, Pharmacy, Electrical & Electronic Engineering, Archaeology & Ancient History, Biosciences, Accounting & Finance, Anatomy & Physiology, Biochemistry, Civil Eng, Dentistry, Medicine, Education.	**Excellent**
RESEARCH: *Top grades 5/5**	
Subjects Allied to Medicine, Psychology, Civil Eng, English, Theology, Education	**Grade 5***
Pharmacy, Mammalian & Medical Biology, Physics, Earth Sciences, Pure Maths, Computer, Electrical & Electronic Eng, Built Environment, Town/Country Planning, Law, Sociology, Business, European Studies, Celtic, Archaeology, History, Media Studies, Music, Clinical Laboratory Science	**Grade 5**

SUBJECT AREAS (%)

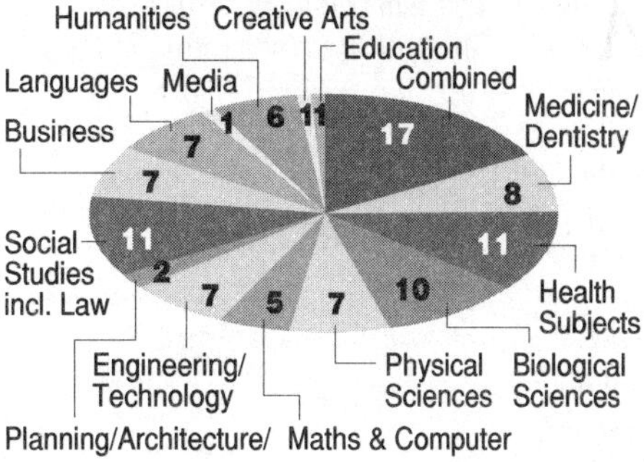

curriculum makes more than a few tax experts and consultants, too.

Meanwhile, the old University of Wales College of Medicine campus has a 920-bed hospital, and the 5/6-year MB BCh degree combines academic study well with clinical and communication skills. There's even a pre-med Foundation for Arts A level candidates or those with one Science and Arts. Entry demands two from Chemistry, Biology, Physics, Maths, Statistics (one being Chemistry or Biology) + Chemistry and Biology at AS, if not at A level. Teaching inspection, Excellent. Research grade 5. For dentistry, it's the 5/6-year BDS (Foundation year available).

Psychology is strong, too, with an Excellent in the assessments and a world-class Grade 5* for research. With Aston, Cardiff leads nationally for placing psychologists in employment. In the Faculty of Health & Life Sciences, it's BA Applied Psychology and BA Psychology. Then there's a 4-year integrated BSc sandwich, Applied Psychology, and simply BSc Hons Psychology.

Also in the Faculty of Health & Life Sciences, full marks at the assessments and a Grade 5 for research recommend Cardiff's biologists, and BSc Pharmacology, which leads large numbers into employment in pharmaceutical manufacturing and as chemists. There's a Foundation year leading to this and to MPharm (Pharmacy).

There's job certainty too in the Department of Occupational Therapy. Again Cardiff place more ophthalmic opticians than any uni other than Aston and Bradford. A new £16m development is underway to create a new state-of-the-art home for the School of Optometry and Vision Sciences. This will open in 2007. The space formerly occupied by the School of Optometry will provide improved facilities for the expanding School of Pharmacy.

Cardiff graduates find jobs in Defence via their 3/4/5-year B/MEng degrees – Computer Systems, Integrated Engineering, Manufacturing, etc, many

AT A GLANCE

ACADEMIC FILE:	
Subjects assessed	**40**
Excellent	**53%**
Typical entry requirements	**360 points**
Application acceptance rate	**17%**
Students-staff ratio	**15:1**
First/2:1 degree pass rate	**70%**
ACCOMMODATION FILE:	
Guarantee to freshers	**100%**
Style	**Halls, flats, houses**
Catered	**5%**
En-suite	**65%**
Price range pw	**£47-£71**
City rent pw	**£50+**

with a year in Spain, Germany, France or industry. Physical sciences, which took an international Grade 5 rating in the research assessments, is also a well-trod path to the same end. In physical sciences they have a BSc in Theoretical & Computational Physics; Astrophysics; Chemistry with Bioscience; Maths, Operational Research & Statistics; Maths & its Applications – the Maths degrees are an unusually strong route into Defence at Cardiff. Of course, Politics too makes some good connections.

Becoming an architect is a 6-year commitment, a 3-year BA Hons, a year's practice placement, followed by a 2-year BArch. Cardiff comes out top employment-wise. With its international research rating of Grade 5, and Excellent teaching assessment, as well as a clear lead in the employment table, the Welsh School of Architecture, which is housed as a department within the university, must be first choice for many. A 5-year sandwich BSc in Architectural Studies, including a 2-year postgrad BArch, looks after Parts 1 & 2 of the Royal Institute of British Architects (RIBA) exams. There's also facility to take Part 3 for final RIBA recognition. There are 3/4/5-year courses in Architectural Engineering for budding engineering design consultants (many are placed out of Cardiff), some offering a year in France, Germany or Spain.

> ***Cardiff is surely one of the best deals going: tip-top academically, still not the hardest to get into and a fantastic extra-curricular scene. There's no excuse to leave with just a degree listed on your CV.***

A BSc degree in City & Regional Planningleads many to find employment in government administration (local, regional, central). Besides the planning degree, look at Architecture and Engineering courses with a civil and environmental orientation.

Particularly fast-track employment comes for electronic and telecommunications engineers. The 4-year integrated sandwich Electronic BEng (or Electrical & Electronic) sits alongside a 5-year extended MEng sandwich course. There's also a Foundation option.

Cardiff is one of only three unis to be adjudged Excellent for Law by the Legal Practice Association (West of England and Nottingham Trent were the other two). They are also one of eight institutions where the Bar Vocational Course (BVC) may be undertaken (essential for barristers). Non-Law graduates may opt for a 2-year full-time or 3-year part-time Senior Status Law degree here. There's also a strong line into the Police. See their LLB Law & Criminology/Sociology/Welsh, etc.

For jobs in publishing, Cardiff are again among the big players, and for journalism they have one of the handful of industry-respected postgrad degrees that many careers advisers will recommend you take before you begin the search for full-time employment. The others are to be found at City, Falmouth College and Central Lancashire. To get on any of these you will have to be able to show experience of, and commitment to, journalism, as well as having a degree. Postgrad students must choose between three journalism options: newspaper, broadcast or magazine. Alternatively, you may choose to study public and media relations. As at City, you get visiting speakers from the media, but there's a 20,000-word dissertation to write.

Meanwhile, Cardiff's three BA Journalism, Film & Broadcasting degrees (also with Social Policy or Sociology) are good enough to get them into the Top 10 for employing journalists. Student media helps, it's often award-winning, controversial even. Newspaper is *Gair Rhydd* (which means Free Word and pulls 14,500 purchasers each week); radio station is Xpress.

The Department of Languages make translators and interpreters, but it's a limited field. The department is also a popular route into Adult Education, as are Biological and Physical Sciences.

Archaeology is another which shows excellent results employment-wise, the dedicated degrees scored an Excellent teaching rating.

Cardiff works with Student Click to run a scheme whereby students can hire top of the range

WHERE CARDIFF GRADUATES END UP

Health & Social Work: 14%; Education: 5%; Wholesale/Retail: 9%; Manufacturing: 7%; Financial Activities: 9%; Public Administration, Civil Service & Defence: 14%; Hotel/Restaurant: 4%; Transport & Communications (including Telecommunications): 4%; Construction: 1%; Personnel: 4%; Computer: 1%; Business & Management: 4%; Accountancy: 5%; Media (including Film): 2%; Legal 3%; Architecture: 4%; Publishing: 1%; Artistic/Literary: 1%; Sport: 1%.

Approximate 'graduate track' employed **70%**

lap top computers at very reasonable rates.

SOCIAL SCENE

STUDENTS' UNION 'Your NUS card is your passport to the best years of your life. Why? Because it gives you access to Cardiff Students' Union, independently recognised by, er, the *Independent* as the biggest and best equipped in Britain.

'The union is a top-class venue under continual enhancement. The **Tafarn** bar has recently been extended and refurbished and changed from 'olde worlde' style to a stylish modern design. Evenings in the Taf inevitably lead to nights in **Solus**, the union's 1,600-capacity, custom-built nightclub with an immense dance floor and state-of-the-art sound and lighting systems. With an eclectic music policy crossing the spectrum from big beat to cheese, few would dispute that **Solus** offers some of Cardiff's best nights out.'

For the more discerning, the union has a major concert hall which regularly hosts top bands. The adjoining **Seren Las**, a lunchtime café-bar and intimate club by night, acts as a chill-out room for top-name gigs and is also establishing itself as an underground hotspot for cutting edge drum 'n' bass and dance acts.

The union is not just popular for its bargain booze and carefree clubbing, either. You feel at Cardiff that the union actually looks after your interests. A disastrous undergraduate semester timetable, introduced a few years ago to allow staff more time for research has been abandoned following a successful campaign by the excellent student newspaper, *Gair Rhydd*. Xpress Radio won Bronze for Best Student Radio Station at the student awards this year. You can now view their popular *What's On?* Guide through cardiffstudents.com. It's updated weekly with all the latest news and events.

'Cardiff has one of the best Students' Unions in Britain,' writes Lisa. 'Besides the regular six-night ents programme, it is home to 60 sports clubs and 50 societies. High on the list are the Film Society, Act One, for drama, LGB, the lesbian/gay group, SHAG, sexual health awareness group, etc. Besides the campaigning *Gair Rhydd*, XPress Radio has teamed up with local station Galaxy 101 to ensure round the clock broadcasting on 106.2 FM. There's no excuse to leave with just a degree on your CV.'

SPORT All traditional sports are catered for and the uni is a major contender in the BUSA leagues, as well as a consistent producer at international level. The Talybont Sports Centre has a £2 million multi-purpose sports hall and there are 33 acres of pitches. Sports bursaries are available.

The uni forms part of the English Cricket

WHAT IT'S REALLY LIKE

UNIVERSITY:	
Social Life	★★★★★
Campus scene	**Vibrant premier scene**
Student Union services	**Good**
Politics	**Activity high**
Sport	**60 clubs**
National team position	**22nd**
Sport facilities	**Good**
Arts opportunities	**Excellent**
Student magazine	**Quench**
Student newspaper	**Gair Rhydd**
Journalism awards 2004	**Newspaper of Year**
Journalism awards 2005	**8 shortlistings, 3 runner-up awards**
Student radio	**XPress Radio**
Radio awards	**3 shortlistings**
Nightclub	**Solus**
Bars	**Tafarn, Seren Las**
Union ents	**6 nights a week**
Union clubs/societies	**110**
Parking	**Adequate**
CITY:	
Entertainment	★★★★
Scene	**Buzzing**
Town/gown relations	**OK**
Risk of violence	**Low**
Cost of living	**Low**
Student concessions	**Excellent**
Survival + 2 nights out	**£80 pw**
Part-time work campus/town	**Excellent**

Board's £300,000 Centres of Excellence scheme, which enables young cricketers to combine their talents with a higher education.

PILLOW TALK

University-owned accommodation in Cardiff has all home comforts with the added benefit of freedom from parental control.

All freshers are guaranteed a place in halls of residence, which are of a universally high standard. The bigger residences are over-subscribed, so consider one of the smaller halls – just as modern, but often with larger rooms and a more intimate atmosphere.

However, the university's biggest hall, Talybont, is student paradise, with its own bar and comprehensive sports facilities. It's also next to a 24-hour Tesco: perfect for those midnight munchies and obligatory trolley snatches! The lazy should avoid University Hall. Although recently subject to a £4-million refurbishment, it's a good half-hour away from the main college: the free bus service isn't so free – Uni Hall rent is a few hundred pounds extra per year to subsidise it – and all other halls are within easy walking distance.

New to their portfolio besides Talybont Court, which opened in Sept 2005 providing en-suite accommodation for 511 students, is Allensbank, which likewise provides its 191 students with en-suite accommodation and computer network connection points. A massive extension of the uni's computer network to the student residences has proved to be a huge success. Already more than 2000 network connection points have been installed in study/bedrooms and there are plans to install a further 3000.

GETTING THERE

- ☛ By road: M4/J32, A470 signposted Cardiff or M4/J29, A48(M)/A48 and A470 signposted City Centre. Make for the Cathays area of the city.
- ☛ By rail: London Paddington, 2:30.
- ☛ By air: Cardiff airport for USA and inland.
- ☛ By coach: London, 3:00; Manchester, 5:40.

UNIVERSITY OF WALES INSTITUTE, CARDIFF

University of Wales Institute, Cardiff
PO Box 377 Western Avenue
Cardiff CF5 2SG

TEL 029 2041 6070
FAX 029 2041 6286
EMAIL uwicinfo@uwic.ac.uk
WEB www.uwic.ac.uk

UWIC Students' Union
Cyncoed Road
Cardiff CF2 6XD

TEL 029 2041 6190
FAX 029 2076 5569
EMAIL studentunion@uwic.ac.uk
WEB www.uwicsu.co.uk

VAG VIEW

UWIC is where it's at for sport. They came in 4th place overall among BUSA teams last year. This is a small uni compared to Loughborough and Birmingham, two of those who pipped it, but the college's commitment, demonstrated in its first-class facilities and National Indoor Athletics Centre, is as complete as the students' commitment to the culture that goes with it, 'When a Cyncoed student hits the bar, anything goes,' recalls Rob Blunt, musing on 'one of life's unanswered questions: why the essay that was researched, drafted, redrafted and put in a week early always got a lower mark than the one scribbled at four in the morning, assisted by six pints of Caffreys?'

Academically, UWIC's assessment results are hardly much to shout about, and 230 points or less will see you in, but they are a unique force in many ways and their survival outside the union, proposed a few years ago with nearby Glamorgan Uni. is to be applauded.

CAMPUS LIFE

An achievement by the union is the purchase of two established venues in Cardiff city centre – **Reds** nightclub and **Stamps Bar** – a deal that makes Wednesday and Thursday student nights at **Union Cardiff**, as it is now known, on weekends showcases the best of Wales's up-and-coming DJs and plays funky house with nights called *Shake* and *Right Here Right Now*. Wednesdays is the official UWIC sports night, always sold out in advance.

Keeping the cost down for student living is the Stashcard, a debit card that can be used at all union outlets and at various retailers in the city.

CYNCOED CAMPUS Cyncoed Road, Cardiff CF2 6XD. **Faculties:** Education and Sport. **Ents & Ambience:** Teachers and wannabe sports stars, and the highest concentration of first years. What was once **Taffy's Bar** (capacity raised to 500 since recent refurb) is now **The Union, Cyncoed**, and is the main campus ents venue. It has a £15,000 sound and light system. Wednesday and Friday are the big nights.

4play on Wednesdays is the UWIC official sports night with DJ at **Union Cyncoed** and Club night at **Union Cardiff**. *Flirt* on Fridays at **Union Cyncoed** is the NUS branded night, with weekly themes such as school disco, traffic lights and Halloween. There are many other smaller weekly activities such as pool competitions, speed dating, playstation network held at **Union Cyncoed** and **Union Llandaff** (see below) and many live bands perform at Union HG

INSTITUTE/STUDENT PROFILE

University College since	**1996**
Situation/style	**Civic**
Student population	**9200**
Undergraduates	**7500**
- mature	**23%**
- non EU undergraduates	**2%**
- male/female	**47/53**
- non-traditional student intake	**27%**
- state school intake	**95%**
- drop-out rate	**10%**
- undergraduate applications	**Down 4%**

SPORT **Cyncoed** is where the multi-million pound athletics track and Sportlot-funded **National Indoor Athletic Stadium** are to be found alongside rugby, football and cricket pitches, indoor and outdoor tennis courts, gym, indoor cricket nets, swimming pool, volleyball, netball, basketball, badminton and squash courts, and a dance studio. As the **Wales Sports Centre for the Disabled** is also here, they've got some of the best resistance-training equipment available anywhere.

ACADEMIC EXCELLENCE

TEACHING:	
Psychology, Art & Design (Ceramics/Fine Art/Internal Architecture), Biomedical Sciences, Environmental Health, Speech Therapy, Podiatry, Applied Human Nutrition.	**Excellent**

COLCHESTER AVENUE CAMPUS Colchester Avenue, Cardiff CF3 7XR. **Faculties:** Business, Leisure and Food. **Ents & Ambience:** Workaday, daytime scene – Sky TV, darts and PlayStation, but no evening ents or bar at Colly Ave, as it's known. So it's off up the hill at Cyncoed, where you're likely to be housed, too, or across the road to the **Three Brewers**.

HOWARD GARDENS Howard Gardens, Cardiff CF2 1SP. **Faculty:** Fine Art. **Ents & Ambience:** Couldn't be more different from, more alternative to, the sporting scene that dominates the personality of UWIC. Once **Tommy's Bar** was the focus, now it's **Union Howard Gardens** (get the picture?). Eclectic ents on Tuesdays and Fridays.

LLANDAFF CAMPUS Western Avenue, Cardiff CF5 2YB. **Faculties:** Art, Design & Engineering and Community Health Sciences. **Ents & Ambience:** Complete makeover gives us **Union Llandaff** bar. Also – a first for UWIC – an Advice & Representation Centre (**ARC**) with an educational & welfare officer and full-time welfare adviser. Thursday and Saturday are disco nights here.

TOWN See *Cardiff Student City*, page 118.

FEES, BURSARIES

UK & EU Fees p.a. 2006 are: Year 1, £1200; following years: £3000 p.a., although students from Wales and non UK EU countries will be eligible for a £1800 fee grant from the Welsh Assembly.

WHERE UWIC GRADUATES END UP

Health & Social Work: 10%; Education: 22%; Wholesale/Retail: 11%; Manufacturing: 8%; Financial Activities: 7%; Public Administration, Civil Service & Defence: 12%; Hotel/Restaurant: 6%; Transport & Communications (including Telecommunications): 5%; Construction: 1%; Personnel: 6%; Legal 1%; Architecture: 1%; Publishing: 1%; Artistic/Literary: 1%; Sport: 5%.

Approximate 'graduate track' employed **65%**

WHAT IT'S REALLY LIKE

COLLEGE:	
Social Life	★★★★
Campus scene	**From sports crazy to arts cool**
Politics	**Student issues, interest low**
Sport	**Key**
National team position	**4th**
Sport facilities	**Excellent**
Arts	**Art, dance excellent; drama, music, film good**
Student newspaper	**Retro**
Nightclub	**Union Cardiff**
Bars	**The Union campus bars**
Union ents	**Cheesy, boozy**
Union clubs/societies	**7**
Most active society	**Chinese Soc**
Parking	**Just adequate**
CITY:	
Entertainment	★★★★★
Scene	**Brilliant**
Town/gown relations	**OK**
Risk of violence	**Average**
Cost of living	**Low**
Student concessions	**Excellent**
Survival + 2 nights out	**£70 pw**
Part-time work campus/town	**Average/excellent**

ACADEMIA & JOBS

New IT suites at Llandaff and Cyncoed campuses, with hundreds of additional work stations, are now available 24 hours a day.

UWIC puts some 62% of its Education graduates into primary school teaching, Education accounting for more than a fifth of all graduate jobs. Nevertheless more graduates come off the production line into the job market from Business and Administrative studies than from Education, and Creative Design and Health degrees are also popular springboards into employment.

Business degrees aim at jobs in accountancy, the restaurant and hotel industry, tourism and retail (see appropriate degree courses among the single subject BA Hons), and there's a new BA Marketing. UWIC managers and administrators proliferate in these areas and in leisure and sport, which is a defining mark of the institute. More than 4% of graduates go into sport, nearly half as coaches and trainers.

There are, too, some significant career niches. Would-be bacteriologists and microbiologists are especially well served at UWIC – second to none in the country. The Biomedical Sciences degrees find graduates jobs in the NHS, public health laboratory service, research institutes and the pharmaceutical, beverage and food industries, and you can come in on it via HND. There's also further study via an MSc in a specialist part of Toxicology of an MSc in Biomedical Sciences.

Again, UWIC turns out more environmental health officers than most. Environmental Science, Nutrition and Health degrees are to the fore here, and there's a strong HND health course route to this sector with such as Environmental Studies, Food & Consumer Science, Food Science & Technology, etc. The BSc Hons will take you further: 3/4-year Environmental Health, Environmental Risk Management, Applied Nutrition, Human Nutrition & Dietetics, Biomedical Sciences with Toxology. They have an 'Excellent' rating for teaching Biomedical Sciences, Environmental Health and Applied Human Nutrition.

BA Social Work and BA Sociology & Popular Culture, Community Education/Studies ensure some 4% of graduates jobs in social work or community and youth work.

Top flight employment-wise among their health provision are degrees in Podiatry (a new centre – E81OK – opened in 2003) and Speech Therapist/Clinical Language Science and Communication Studies.

They also have a productive BSc Dental Technology – Cardiff and Bristol dental schools recruit graduates from here. The 3-year BSc Hons Dental Technology teaches you how to fabricate restorations, prostheses, appliances – bespoke crowns, bridges and orthodontic appliances. Employment in NHS, private practices, dental schools, commercial laboratories, and nearby Cardiff and Bristol dental schools offer

AT A GLANCE

ACADEMIC FILE:	
Subjects assessed	**18**
Excellent	**39%**
Typical entry requirements	**230 points**
Application acceptance rate	**22%**
Students-staff ratio	**19:1**
First/2:1 degree pass rate	**49%**
ACCOMMODATION FILE:	
Guarantee to freshers	**55%**
Style	**Halls**
Catered	**50-60%**
En suite	**50%**
Approx price range pw	**£56-£79**
City rent pw	**£50+**

employment to one third before they even graduate.

Now there's also BSc Complementary Therapies.

Finally, Product Design and Graphic Communication degrees in the Art & Design faculty ensure a job. The faculty also carries Ceramics, Fine Art and Textile degrees that figure in the graduate employment picture too.

PILLOW TALK

They have 527 single study-bedrooms on Cyncoed, of which 165 are self-catered and en suite, and 50 are self-catered with shared bathroom facilities. The remaining 312 rooms are catered (meals provided centrally). At Plas Gwyn there are 391 rooms – all self-catered, en suite. The Fairwater Halls consist of 100 rooms – all catered for centrally. Recently, UWIC have acquired private sector Evelian Court – 250 self-catered, en-suite hall-style rooms, a few are doubles, a few are self-contained flats.

GETTING THERE

- By road: M4/J29, A48(M)/A48.
- By rail: London Paddington, 2:30.
- By air: USA and inland destinations.
- By coach: London, 3:00; Manchester, 5:40.

UNIVERSITY OF CENTRAL ENGLAND

University of Central England in Birmingham
Franchise Street
Perry Barr
Birmingham B42 2SU

TEL 0121 3315595
FAX 0121 3317994
EMAIL info@ucechoices.com
WEB www.uce.ac.uk

UCE Students' Union
Franchise Street
Perry Barr
Birmingham B42 2SU

TEL 0121 331 6801
FAX 0121 331 6802
EMAIL union.president@uce.ac.uk
WEB www.unionofstudents.com

VAG VIEW

The University of Central England is a huge, urban conglomeration of sites, incorporating business, engineering & technology, built environment, law & social sciences, computing, health, the Birmingham Institute of Art & Design, a theatre school, and two little gems – the Jewellery School, set in the old Jewellery Quarter, and the Birmingham Conservatoire.

Incredibly, the uni and the Students Union have managed to bring this apparently disparate thing together into what one student described as 'a really friendly university, whichever campus you study on and wherever you live.'

They have done this by means of a big spend, but also with a keen eye as to their essential ethos, which encompasses art and science and celebrates the real bonuses of our multicultural society. Suddenly, UCE is developing an exciting and vibrant social scene, and there's unprecedented energy in the Student Activities department. 'We are now actively building sports clubs, societies and volunteering opportunities,' we are told. 'SCRatch Radio has taken off, and for the first time there's a lively ents programme at the union bars.'

CAMPUS SITES

A CCTV system covers each site. 150 cameras are constantly monitored and the system is key to supporting the work of a 70-strong security team to ensure a safe environment in which to study.

Perry Barr Main UCE campus. **Location:** north of

SUBJECT AREAS (%)

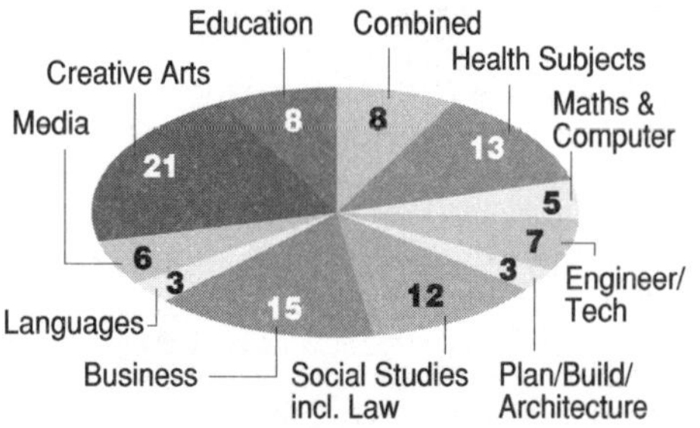

city; approach via M6/M5 Junction 7 and A34 Walsall Road. **Access to city:** 15 minutes by bus plus rail link to Birmingham New Street. **Accommodation:** two halls for 850 students – the Coppice and Oscott Gardens (en suite); both self-catering. **Bars: Bar 42**, pub/food in daytime, nightclub/venue in the evening.

WESTBOURNE CAMPUS Westbourne Road, Edgbaston. **Location:** south city suburb of Edgbaston, accessed via M5/J3, A456 or M5/J4, AA38. **Access to city:** regular, cheap and late-night bus service. **Accommodation:** one hall – 245 single study-bedrooms and 34 shared (two bedrooms and joint study); self-catering. **Bars:** Brand new Union facilities at this, the campus for the Faculty of Health, including a new shop, bar and Student Activities centre.

> ***From being scattered and diverse, suddenly UCE is developing an exciting and vibrant social scene. There's a strongly developing list of student activities, and for the first time a lively ents programme.***

UNIVERSITY/STUDENT PROFILE

University since	**1992**
Situation/style	**Civic**
Student population	**24492**
Undergraduates	**18823**
- mature	**61%**
- non EU undergraduates	**6%**
- male/female	**39/61**
- non-traditional student intake	**39%, high**
- state school intake	**97%**
- drop-out rate	**8%**
- undergraduate applications	**Up 7%**

GOSTA GREEN Big bonus - access to Aston Union facilities. **Location:** adjacent to Aston Uni campus, edge of city centre; accessed via M6/J6, A38M. Ignoring the signs to Aston, leave the A38M at third exit and take the first exit at Lancaster Circus r/about.

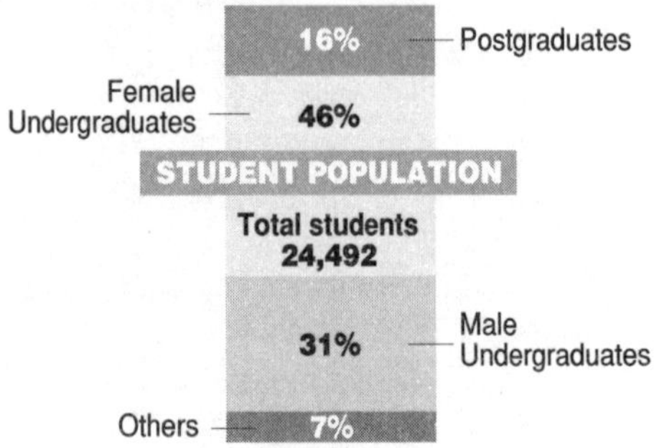

HAMSTEAD CAMPUS is a 16-acre residential campus 2 miles from the Perry Barr Campus, with good bus services between the two and to city centre. Both self-catering and catered rooms are available, and there's a bar operated by the Students Union.

FEES, BURSARIES

Fees: 'in 2006, for first degree UK and EU students are £3000. Students from lower income backgrounds will be eligible for grants for living costs. In addition, we will offer a bursary of £500 to anyone receiving a full or partial Maintenance grant.'

STUDENT PROFILE

As diverse as its campus sites, but with the emphasis clearly on work-purpose and real-world living. Many are mature, many local and many from overseas. It's an eclectic mix, but it's all

WHAT IT'S REALLY LIKE

UNIVERSITY:	
Social Life	★★★★
Campus scene	**Diverse but friendly & focused**
Student Union services	**Excellent**
Politics	**Practise bent**
Sport	**24 clubs**
National team position	**112th**
Sport facilities	**Extensive**
Arts opportunities	**Good**
Student magazine	**Spaghetti Junction**
Student radio	**SCRatch**
Student TV	**SUB TV**
Venue	**Bar 42**
Bars	**Bar 42, ibar, Village Inn, Theatre Bar, Pavilion**
Union ents	**Very popular**
Union clubs/societies	**33**
Parking	**OK**
CITY:	
Entertainment	★★★★★
Scene	**Excellent**
Town/gown relations	**Average**
Risk of violence	**Average-High**
Cost of living	**Average**
Student concessions	**Excellent**
Survival + 2 nights out	**£75 pw**
Part-time work campus/town	**Good**

WHERE CENTRAL ENGLAND GRADUATES END UP

Health & Social Work: 23%; Education: 13%; Wholesale/Retail: 11%; Manufacturing: 7%; Financial Activities: 7%; Public Administration, Civil Service & Defence: 6%; Hotel/Restaurant: 3%; Transport & Communications (including Telecommunications): 3%; Construction: 1%; Mining/Oil Extracting: 1%; Personnel: 5%; Computer: 2%; Business & Management: 5%; Accountancy: 2%; Media (including Film): 2%; Legal 3%; Architecture: 2%; Publishing: 2%; Advertising: 1%; Artistic/Literary: 2%; Sport: 0.5%.

Approximate 'graduate track' employed **60%**

beginning to come together in a recognisable ethos.

STUDENT SCENE

Student Community Action (SCA) is the Union volunteering project. It offers you the opportunity to get involved and gain some of the illusive key skills that employers are always asking for, as well as making a real different to the local community. They run schemes for young children and teenagers and worked with local prisons to allow offenders to learn new skills. A so-called LEAP campaign currently promotes sport for local school children and helps students develop skills to work alongside children in the future.

Ents-wise, **Bar 42** at Perry Barr Campus has Friday night cheese, *Toons;* Wednesday commercial dance and R&B, *Flirt*; Tuesday *Mish Mash* (live bands and Indie); sports & society events on Saturday; and quizzes on Sunday.

ibar is the brand new student bar, located at the prestigious **Millennium Point,** a £114 million complex, unveiled in 2001 beneath the IMAX cinema, open also to the public. Then there's The Conservatoire's **Theatre Bar** (see *Academia/ Faculties*, page 130), the **Village Inn** (friendly, local halls of residence bar at Hamstead halls), and **The Pavilion** out at Moor Lane Sports Centre. Parties and events are held every term in the **Village Inn** and **ibar**.

Societies: 33 societies are now up and running. Student magazine is *Spaghetti Junction.* SCRatch Radio is the student and community radio station, and there's a TV station too - SUB TV. There's a feeling that the extra-curricular side at UCE is on its feet and running. Drama, cheerleading, RAG (Raising and Giving) and ACS (Afro Caribbean Society) are the most active socs. 'The Union supports students getting involved in a host of different ways,' they say, 'whether you want to volunteer in the community or just try something new, we can find you something.'

SPORT Last year, Men's Hockey were BUSA league winners and Cricket reached the semi final in the BUSA knockouts. In Calella (UK Universities' annual sports tour to Spain) they won the mixed hockey and the men's football 7's tournaments. The Union runs the massive Moor Lane Sports Centre, with extensive conference and banqueting and partying facilities attached, playing host, too, to the annual Frisbee tournaments.

ACADEMIC EXCELLENCE

TEACHING:
(Rated Excellent or 17+ out of 24)

Music	**Excellent**
Art & Design, Education, Radiog/ Podiatry/Health Studies	**22**
Communication & Media Studies, Economics, Politics, Finance/Marketing	**21**
Town & Country Planning, History of Art, Nursing, Information Studies	**20**
Electrical & Electronic Eng, General Engineering, Automative & Manufacturing Engineering	**19**
Sociology, Building & Land & Property Mgt	**18**

ACADEMIA & JOBS

Multi-faceted UCE is proud to maintain its links with its past through the vocational nature of its courses, work placement ideology, strong links with industry, enlightened entry arrangements (GNVQ and Access courses – largely through its network of eighteen associated colleges) and part-timer education.

Facilities are good and UCE are hot on academic support – investment in fixed workstations, loan laptops and wireless network access is high; they have a mentoring and work experience scheme for minority ethic students; and there is a range of business support services for anyone with a commercially viable technology-based idea, and business idea competitions, with start-up prizes of £5000.

There are seven faculties:

UCE Birmingham Conservatoire
www.conservatoire.uce.ac.uk
Paradise Circus, Birmingham city centre
A little gem, a lively, creative environment, one of our best music colleges, it has been going in one form or another since 1859. Based in the heart of the city centre only a few minutes' walk from Symphony Hall, the Conservatoire has some of the finest performing and teaching facilities of its kind in the country, including the 520-seat Adrian Boult Hall, 150-seat Recital Hall customised for performance with live electronics, three recording studios and a specialised music library with around 95,000 individual scores and parts and 10,000 sound recordings. There's both a BMus (Hons) and a specialised BMus (Hons) Jazz. The Conservatoire also works in collaboration with the Technology Innovation Centre (tic) to provide a BSc (Hons) course in Music Technology.

UCE Birmingham Institute of Art & Design (BIAD)
www.biad.uce.ac.uk
Gosta Green
BIAD dates back to the Birmingham School of Design, founded in 1843. The Faculty is spread across five recently renovated and modernised sites. The main Gosta Green site, close to the city centre, is home to Fashion, Textiles and 3D Design, the School of Architecture, Dept of Visual Communication and School of Theoretical and Historical Studies. Students have access to adjacent Aston Uni union facilities. 'UCE is a friendly rival,' say the Aston Students Guild. 'They use our facilities. It's a nice balance to our scientists and business students; about half the people who use our coffee shop are the UCE Arts lot.'

BIAD's Dept of Media and Communication is based at Perry Barr, and the School of Jewellery has its own address in Victoria Street, Birmingham's historic Jewellery Quarter. The Department of Art has no less a magnificent home in a Grade I listed Venetian Gothic building in Margaret Street, in the city's museum and gallery district, while the historic Bournville Village Trust is home to the Bournville Centre for Visual Arts.

Birmingham School of Acting
www.bssd.ac.uk
The Link Building, Paradise Place
In May 2005 Birmingham School of Acting merged with UCE. Formerly Birmingham School of Speech and Drama, it was founded in 1936. The main focus is acting. Both of the School's courses are accredited by the National Council for Drama Training.

UCE Business School
www.business.uce.ac.uk
Galton Building, Perry Barr Campus

AT A GLANCE

ACADEMIC FILE:	
Subjects assessed	**23**
Excellent	**74%**
Typical entry requirements	**235 points**
Application acceptance rate	**18%**
Student-staff ratio	**16:1**
First/2:1 degree pass rate	**58%**
ACCOMMODATION FILE	
Guarantee to freshers	**If non-local & apply by 31.5**
Style	**Halls, flats**
Catered	**7%**
En-suite	**21%**
Price range pw	**£50-£85**
Town rent pw	**£60-£65**

Provision to 4,500 students is in Accountancy, Advertising, Business, Computing, Economics, Finance, Internet Systems, Human Resources, Management, Marketing, Multimedia, Software Engineering and Public Relations.

Faculty of Education
www.ed.uce.ac.uk
Attwood Building, Perry Barr Campus
The Faculty, both primary and secondary and based at Perry Barr, operates in the multi-ethnic context of the West Midlands. The students who join its initial teacher training courses are also from diverse backgrounds. Teaching inspection 22, special encouragement to mature students.

Faculty of Health
www.health.uce.ac.uk
Westbourne and Perry Barr Campuses
The Mary Seacole Library opened its doors to Health faculty students at Westbourne Campus this year, first phase of a £22m development to include a suite of clinical skills facilities, lecture theatres, students' union complex and a coffee bar. With nearly 7000 students enrolled on full and part-time courses, the Faculty of Health is one of the largest Higher Education centres of its kind in the UK. All undergraduate courses include practice placements.

Both the Perry Barr and Westbourne Campuses are equipped with the latest teaching resources. UCE accounts for a large number of non-hospital nurses (adult, child, disabilities and mental health) and senior hospital nurses (SRN, RGN), also for 12% of graduate midwives with their 3-year BSc (Hons) Midwifery. Other certainties in this sector are BSc (Hons) Diagnostic Radiography and BSc (Hons)

Radiotherapy. Then there's a particular niche – BSc (Hons) Speech & Language Therapy. Note also BSc (Hons) Social Work. Entry 160 points. BSc (Hons) Health Studies.

Faculty of Law, Humanities, Development & Society
www.lhds.uce.ac.uk
Perry Barr Campus
The Faculty delivers Law and Legal Studies, Criminal Justice and Criminology, Social and Policy Studies, Housing, English (including Literature, Linguistics and Drama), Property, Construction and Planning.

Thirty students spent the summer in the USA, working with American attorneys on death row cases. Interns took on a range of legal work, including preparing cross-examinations, direct client representation and dealing with expert witnesses. Commercial & business law is a speciality.

There's a well-trod pathway into the police force through the HND in Criminal Justice, BA Criminal Justice & Criminology or Policing, and Criminal Justice with Psychology.

There's a mock courtroom equipped with audio-visual facilities, a dedicated learning resource centre, a newly refurbished drama studio and high quality teaching and computer rooms.

Technology Innovation Centre
www.tic.ac.uk
Millennium Point
The Technology Innovation Centre (tic) is a key faculty of the University, offering a wide range of interactive media, ICT, design technology and advanced engineering courses. Its home, the Millennium Point building, a £114 million complex opened in 2001, provides state of the art facilities and encourages good links with industry.

PILLOW TALK

They guarantee a place in halls (see **Campus** above) for full-time students who hold an unconditional firm or conditional firm offer by 31 May, and live a distance from UCE 'that precludes commuting'. Every student room is equipped with a telephone line, and all halls have an Ethernet connection to the UCE Birmingham data network.

GETTING THERE

☛ By road: M1, M5, M6 and M40 all give ready access to the city. See also campus notes.
☛ By rail: Bristol Parkway or Sheffield, 1:30; London Euston, 1:40; Liverpool, 2:00; Leeds, 3:00.
☛ By air: regular internal and international flights to Birmingham International Airport, 15 mins' journey time by train to New Street.
☛ By coach: London, 2:40; Bristol, 2:00.

UNIVERSITY OF CENTRAL LANCASHIRE

University of Central Lancashire
Preston
Lancs PR1 2HE

TEL 01772 892400
FAX 01772 894539
EMAIL cenquiries@uclan.ac.uk
WEB www.uclan.ac.uk

Central Lancashire Students' Union
Fylde Road
Preston PR1 2TQ

TEL 01772 893000
FAX 01772 894970
EMAIL supresident@uclan.ac.uk
WEB www.yourunion.co.uk

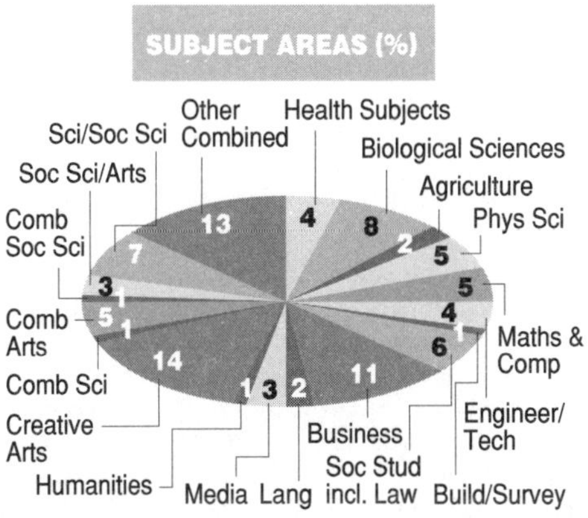

VAG VIEW

Central Lancashire traces its origins back to 1828, when Preston Institution for the Diffusion of Knowledge was founded. Thousands attend partner colleges in the north-west of England, and there are around 2,500 postgraduate students. Growth in student numbers makes them one of the largest universities in the country and the graph is set to continue over the next ten years with the development of electronic and distance learning.

Theirs was the first city-wide wireless network in the UK and third in the world.

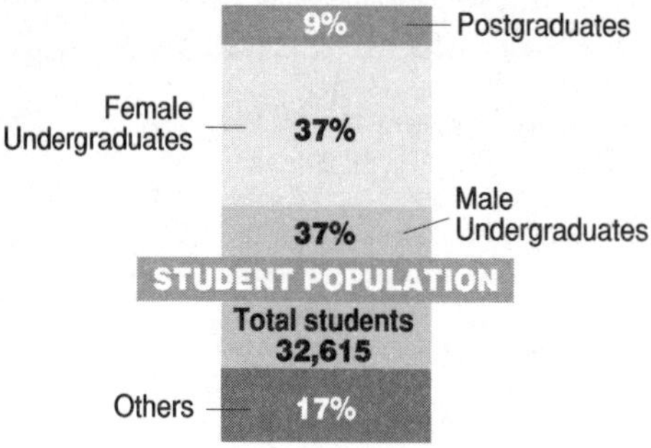

They are the leading advisors to the Home Office on cyberspace, the technology and user behaviour of the internet.

And the bricks and mortar are far from being ignored: £50 million is being invested in new buildings and facilities, including the new award-winning £6.5 million Student Union building.

Central Lancs is also known as a caring university. 'The i' is a one-stop-shop (info centre), a first point of contact for such as financial support, council tax enquires, international student guidance, to NUS card distribution, accommodation and disabled student advice. A fourth-year health student, confined in a wheelchair since infancy, went out of her way to praise its accessibility to the disabled, the helpfulness of staff, and for the chance they gave her of the 'few wild years' she had enjoyed there.

Wild indeed, and not only on its beautiful Cumbria Campus at Newton Rigg, Penrith, but also in its approach to entertainment in Preston, for which it has an ents-industry reputation.

UNIVERSITY/STUDENT PROFILE	
University since	**1992**
Situation/style	**Civic**
Student population	**32615**
Undergraduates	**24380**
- mature	**16%**
- non EU undergraduates	**9%**
- male/female	**50/50**
- non-traditional student intake	**36%**
- state sector intake	**96%**
drop-out rate	**10%**
- undergraduate applications	**Up 3%**

Central Lancs is ultimately about getting its graduates jobs, however, and it hunts high and low in recruitment. One unfortunate, if perhaps inevitable, result of its open access and expansionist policy has been a wild drop-out rate, but that is being tamed.

CAMPUSES

Besides Preston, they have the aforesaid **Penrith Campus** at the head of the Eden Valley, where the Faculty of Land-based Studies is based. Also **Carlisle Campus** for some of the business, computing, travel and tourism degrees.

FEES, BURSARIES

UK & EU Fees £3000 p.a. £1000 bursaries available for all full-time undergraduate students who come from homes where the principal earner's salary is less that £60,000 per year. 100 Excellence scholarships, valued in the region of £2000, will be offered in some specialist subject areas.

STUDENT PROFILE

Central Lancashire is recruiting a large number of undergraduates from the state sector and students from social groups who haven't traditionally benefited from a university education. The 16% mature student figure they quote is for undergraduates over 30 years. Those starting at over 21 make up almost half of undergraduates and a large number of exchange students mingle with an otherwise broadly local student population.

ACADEMIA & JOBS

Faculties are: Lancashire Business School, Health, Science, Cultural Legal and Social Studies and Design and Technology. Maximum QAA scores of 24 out of 24 in areas of American Studies, Psychology, Nursing and Midwifery, Education. Besides the 4-year BSc Midwifery, there's an 18-month pre-registration course. Look also at their Herbal Medicine and Homeopathy degrees.

They offer a hot executive route into the Civil Service via biological sciences and health (everything from Forensic Science an HND in Public Health and now a BA Public Health). Meanwhile, Civil Service administration takes from Business (good mixes with Psychology, Economics, Info Systems, Management) and creative arts (Design, etc) and the BSc/BA Combined hons programme, which is itself designed with flair.

Agriculture is another strong area. The Faculty of Land-based Studies incorporates the academic work of the Cumbria Campus and associate Myerscough College. They cover forestry, horticulture, equine studies, countryside subjects, animal science, farm management, tourism and leisure. The campus estate comprises 245 hectares and is made up of the Newton Rigg and Sewborwens farms. They ask 120 points for the 3/4-year BSc sandwich in Arboriculture, Forest & Woodland Management, Forestry & Environmental Mgt, Social & Community Forestry, Tropical forestry, Urban Forestry (with a Management possibility, and a 1-year BSc Forestry top-up from Forestry HND. Teaching inspection, 18. Recently, a popular development is the Veterinary Nursing degree. They ask 80 points.

There is an interesting employment niche in journalism, many of the excellent Journalism courses making a healthy mix with communications and design, and all backed to the hilt by an award-winning student media.

They feature in the Top 10 in various areas. Besides the BA Journalism (also offered with Eng Lit), there's Photography & Journalism; Fashion, Brand Promotion & Journalism; Audio Visual Media Studies & Journalism; Web & Multimedia with Journalism (the only BSc in the bunch); Film & Media degrees, and a TV production degree. Teaching inspection, 22.

Note, too, their industry-recommended postgraduate degrees – PGDip Newspaper Journalism, MA/PGDip Online Journalism, MA Strategic Communication and PGDip Broadcast Journalism. You will have to be able to show experience of, and commitment to, Journalism, and provide an audio tape for the PGDip.

Another sound area for graduate jobs is the art and design provision. Graduates become graphic artists, designers, illustrators, sculptors. You'll be interviewed with your portfolio to get on the BA Fine Arts, a broad-based introduction, followed by specialist studio work. There's an on-campus **Arts Centre** and a **Centre for Contemporary Art**, as well as a separate **Gallery**. The course has strong links with the **Harris Museum & Art Gallery** in Preston. Teaching inspection, 22.

The 4-year sandwich Fashion Promotion and Design asks 180-200 points (teaching inspection, 21) making it second most demanding at A level nationally, but they do get graduates jobs, and are especially strong on business/creative arts routes into retail management and buying: Retail Management with Fashion/Logistics/Marketing, dovetails with the Art & Design Faculty on Promotion and Marketing – across Fashion, Furniture, Jewellery, etc.

PR and publicity in general are strong graduate destinations. See BA Communication Studies, also BA Marketing & Public Relations, besides the BA Fashion Promotion. Teaching inspection, 22.

A not so dusty niche may be explored in their Antique & Design Studies. It is the only degree to bring a design perspective to theory and practice, ideal for the would-be antique dealer/restorer. You'll need around 180 points to get on it.

Central is home to the Cyberspace Research Unit, too, which has a national reputation for its research on children's use of the internet and the dangers therein. It acts as a policy advisor, trainer, teacher, and media spokesperson. Findings often contribute to policy-making at government level.

Recently an assessor for the LPC Board looked at their Law provision and, on a scale of Excellent, Very Good, Good, Satisfactory or Unsatisfactory, Central Lancs copped a Very Good. There's a strong employment track record for BA

ACADEMIC EXCELLENCE

TEACHING:
(Rated Excellent or 17+ out of 24)

American Studies, Psychology, Education, Nursing	**24**
Linguistics, Journalism & PR, Subjects Allied to Medicine, Art/Design Biological Sciences, Business/Accounting, Politics, Leisure/Tourism	**22**
Modern Languages	**21**
Building, General Engineering	**20**
History of Art/Architec/Design, Physics, Astronomy & Maths	**19**
Sociology, Agric & Forestry	**18**

WHERE CENTRAL LANCASHIRE GRADUATES END UP

Health & Social Work: 17%; Education: 6%; Wholesale/Retail: 16%; Manufacturing: 9%; Financial Activities: 9%; Public Administration, Civil Service & Defence: 8%; Hotel/Restaurant: 5%; Transport & Communications (including Telecommunications): 4%; Construction: 1%; Agriculture: 1%; Personnel: 4%; Computer: 2%; Business & Management: 5%; Accountancy: 1%; Media (including Film): 2%; Legal 2%; Architecture: 1%; Publishing: 2%; Artistic/Literary: 2%; Sport: 2%.

Approximate 'graduate track' employed **57%**

Criminology & Criminal Justice and Law & Criminology. Look, too, at the new BSc Police & Criminal Investigation, which breaks new ground by teaching practical as well as academic investigation skills. It is delivered from within the Centre for Forensic Science. On the Newton Rigg campus in Cumbria they have set up Cow Pasture Cottage, a reality crime scene where a catalogue of crimes are recreated to test students of one of Britain's leading forensic science centres.

Note also their Fire Safety and Fire Engineering degrees.

Their sporting provision finds top places in the employment league tables for physical training instructors. There are Sport Science/Psychology/Technology degrees, BA Golf Course Management and now BSc Sports Technology (Golf Operations) for those interested in refining player performance by means of coaching, materials, equipment, ergonomics. Take-up is partly at Myerscough College in Preston, where there's a golf course and indeed a Grand Prix track, of interest to putative racing car designers or team managers - see their Motor Sports Eng, BSc Motor Sport and BSc Motor Sport Operations. As at Coventry, they have their own uni racing team. The degrees cover Engineering and Team & Event Management. There's also a separate Event Management degree.

Thanks partly to the international dimension of so many courses, the uni leads the job field in providing lecturers to Further Education. Exchange programmes with Europe and America (American Studies scored full marks at the assessments) are legion and the International Society is very popular among students.

WHAT IT'S REALLY LIKE	
UNIVERSITY:	
Social Life	★★★★
Campus scene	**Local, diffuse, mature but lively**
Student Union services	**Average**
Politics	**Interest low**
Sport	**Competitive**
National team position	**66th**
Sport facilities	**Good**
Arts	**Drama, dance, film, music excellent; art good**
Student newspaper	**Pluto**
Student radio station	**Frequency 1350**
Nightclub	**The Venue**
Bars	**Polygon, Union Square**
Union ents	**Tokyo Jo (dance), Warehouse (alt), Mood (pop), Base (dance), Browns (blues), Squires (cheese)**
Union clubs/societies	**100**
Parking	**Adequate**
CITY:	
Entertainment	★★★
Scene	**Good clubs, excellent pubs**
Town/gown relations	**Good**
Risk of violence	**Low**
Cost of living	**Average**
Student concessions	**Good**
Survival + 2 nights out	**£50 pw**
Part-time work campus/town	**Good/average**

SOCIAL SCENE

STUDENTS' UNION **53Degrees**, the new venue and club, Brook Street, Preston 01772 893000, was winner of BEDA 'Best Venue" 2005. Combined capacity: 1600; Venue standing: 1200; Club standing: 400. Also, the **Main Room Mezzanine** can be separated as a 600-capacity club. Til 2 a.m. Thurs-Sat and Mon-Tues. All events open to the public. Live gigs currently The Paddingtons, The Research, Hundred Reasons, The Delays, The Levellers, Elavi (hip hop and r&b), The Jam Restart, Fun Lovin Criminals, We Are Scientists. Thursday night is *Promo*: DJ Darren Lee with chart hits, but also live acts, The Motorettes, Lady Fuzz, etc. Friday is *Stand & Deliver*, Carey Marx with support. Saturday is *So Effective* presents Gin n Juice. Others include *Sublime* (party), *Drink the Bar Dry* (drinks promos every Thurs), and special 3 a.m. licence for *Goodgreef* (Manchester Club of the Year, 2004; Best Club in the North - *Mixmag*, 2005). Also Comedy with candle-lit cabaret style seating.

Talking about performance, it is often forgotten that they have a serious crack at the arts too. For the last decade they've taken productions to the Edinburgh Fringe, and this year they've got a performing-arts degree module on offer.

Theatre, music, dance and art all go on in **St Peter's Church** and the **Grenfell Baines Gallery**, the uni's arts centre in town.

Student newspaper *Pluto* regularly picks up student journalism awards (though not this year), while the student website has won the *Guardian* award.

SPORT A £12-million outdoor multisport complex two miles from campus is now open. **The Preston Sports Arena** has 8-lane athletics track, 5 grass pitches, 2 floodlit all-weather, 4 floodlit netball and tennis courts, 1.5 km cycling circuit, 7 floodlit

AT A GLANCE

ACADEMIC FILE:	
Subjects assessed	**31**
Excellent	**65%**
Typical entry requirements	**250 points**
Application acceptance rate	**24%**
Students-staff ratio	**23:1**
First/2:1 degree pass rate	**53%**
ACCOMMODATION FILE:	
Guarantee to freshers	**66%**
Style	**Halls, flats, houses**
Catered	**None**
En-suite	**30%**
Price range pw	**£47-£70**
City rent pw	**£45-£72**

training grids, plus 18-station fitness suite. There's also the on-campus, recently refurbished **Foster Sports Centre** for badminton, tennis, basketball, volleyball, soccer, fencing, martial arts, etc. Nationally, they are about mid-table in the uni leagues. Good facilities are available at Newton Rigg for rugby, football, hockey, netball, basketball, tennis, badminton, and there's a purpose-built weights room. Cumbrian clubs include Climbing Club, Conservation Volunteers and Clay Pigeon. This year the indoor facilities have been upgraded.

TOWN And Preston? 'With something like 40–50 pubs within 5 minutes' walk of the university,' writes Neil Doughty, 'there's always somewhere to hide away out of the rain. Some might contest that with so many pubs you'd need to be careful to avoid the "locals only" places where the only use for sawdust is mopping up the blood after a fight. Not so! With 20,000 students making up a sixth of the in-term residents of Preston, the locals are well aware of the benefit of students to the local economy, and are very accommodating - loads of student discounts, tons of shops, a range of restaurants and two large-screen cinemas mean that there's always something to do when the workload lessens. Staff in venues all over town are always friendly. Even the nightclubs are relaxed both in terms of atmosphere and prices. With no dress code in the week, and drinks prices fair, the town is ideally suited to students.'

PILLOW TALK

They don't guarantee all freshers accommodation. There are self-catered halls, cluster flats (some en suite), houses and some all-female accommodation. There are new private-sector student flats close to campus. Get on to these quick.

GETTING THERE

☛ By road: travelling south, M6 (J32/M55), exit 1 (A6); travelling north, M6/J31, A59.
☛ By rail: London, 3:00; Manchester OxfordRoad, 50 mins; Lancaster, 23 mins.
☛ By coach: London, 5:15; Liverpool, 1:00.

UNIVERSITY OF CHESTER

The University of Chester
Parkgate Road
Chester CH1 4BJ

TEL 01244 511000
FAX 01244 511302
EMAIL enquiries@chester.ac.uk
WEB www.chester.ac.uk

VAG VIEW

Established by William Gladstone in 1839 as the first teacher-training college in the country with a Church of England foundation, it has just been granted full university status.

Chester is a Roman town with a picturesque centre, a thriving tourism industry and a lowish cost of living.

The university's curriculum has expanded beyond teaching education in recent years into health care, the applied sciences, humanities, social sciences, creative arts &

SUBJECT AREAS (%)

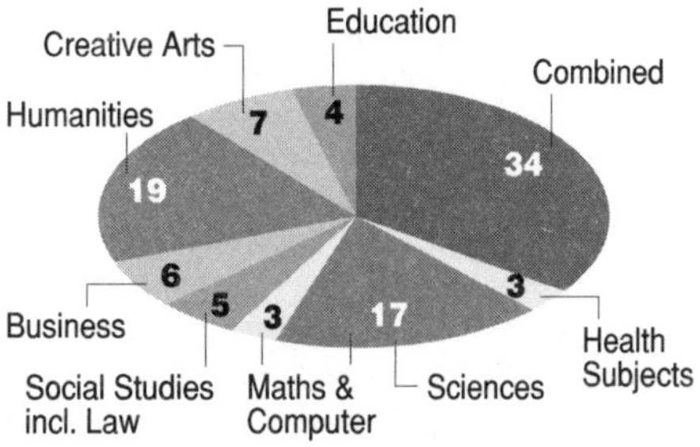

UNIVERSITY/STUDENT PROFILE

University since	**2005**
Situation/style	**City campus**
Student population	**10174**
Undergraduates	**8769**
- mature	**51%**
- non EU undergraduates	**1%**
- male/female	**25/75**
- non-traditional student intake	**36%**
- state sector intake	**97%**
drop-out rate	**15%**
- undergraduate applications	**Up 49%**

media, and business and management.

They have just announced that student applications for the 2005 intake increased by 49% – larger than at any other uni.

CAMPUS

The uni's Chester campus is a 32-acre site, 5 minutes' walk from the city centre, and has undergone a variety of developments over the last 18 months. New facilities include a high-tech fitness suite, a modern School of Health and Social Care building, a large state-of-the art multi-purpose building featuring a brasserie, computer suite, conference facilities and high specification teaching areas. Next to campus is a newly built block of self-catered apartments, offering en-suite rooms.

The Warrington campus is set on a 35-acre site a short bus ride away and has benefited from general improvements and refurbishments, including a modern dining area, new facilities within the Department of Media and a brand new Students' Union building, completed January 2006.

FEES, BURSARIES

UK & EU Fees: £3000 p.a. Bursary for students in receipt of full HE Maintenance grant: £1350. If partial grant, then min. £450 bursary. Two-thirds of students expected to receive a University of Chester bursary. There's also the Chester Sports Scholarship Scheme: £500 p.a., sport being a defining element of student life at Chester. For further information about the Chester Sports Scholarship Scheme please contact Dr Stewart Bruce-Low on (01244) 513437. Email: s.brucelow@chester.ac.uk.

Chester also offers an organ scholarship, currently worth £750, two music scholarships/ 'Director's Assistant' posts based around the choir, worth £250 each, and two similar positions based around the orchestra, currently worth £150 each. Alto, tenor and bass choral scholarships are available for positions in the Chester Cathedral Choir, worth £1750 p.a. and tenable for one year in the first instance. Further details from the Cathedral Organist, 12 Abbey Square, Chester CH1 2HU.

STUDENT PROFILE

There is a high number of undergraduates (36%) from backgrounds not traditionally associated with going to university, and many (51%) who are over 21 at inception. Very few, only 3%, hie from the independent school sector, and a whopping 14.5% at the last count don't make it through to the end.

It is also a largely (75%) female undergraduate population, once described by the uni as an 'overwhelming majority', but if you're a bloke you may find you'll be able to cope.

The lean is down to the numbers studying nursing, midwifery and education courses. Finally, very few of Chester's undergraduates come from outside the EU (0.7%). It is a notably local scene.

When it was a mere college of higher education, this was just as true, and noticeably it was a tight, compact unit, with an overwhelming, friendly and relaxed atmosphere. This is unlikely to change.

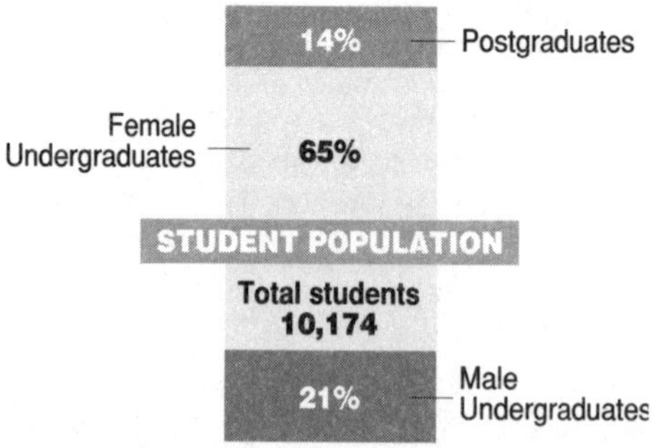

ACADEMIA

The uni has been re-organised into 7 schools of study: Applied & Health Sciences; Business, Management & Law, Arts & Media, Education, Health & Social Care, and Social Sciences.

Departments are Biological Sciences, Business, Computer Science, Education, English, Fine Art, Geography and Development Studies, Health & Social Care, History and Archaeology, Law, Leadership & Management, Maths, Media, Modern Languages, Performing Arts, Psychology, Social & Communication Studies, Sport and Exercise Sciences, Theology & Religious Studies, Work Related Studies.

Law is new, offered as an LLB and as combined honours. The department has close links with the Chester Centre of the College of Law where LPC and Graduate Diplomas can be studied for - the College of Law is the largest legal training and education establishment in Europe. Chester boasts

ACADEMIC EXCELLENCE

TEACHING:	
(Rated Excellent or 17+ out of 24)	
English	**Excellent**
Maths, Sport	**23**
Theology/Religious Studies, Health & Community	**22**
Business & Tourism, Nursing	**21**
Health Science/Studies, Psychology	**20**
Modern Languages (French, German, Spanish)	**19**

both Magistrates and Crown Courts, and hundreds of solicitors/barristers firms in the region.

Other new or recently added undergraduate courses include Creative Writing, Graphic Design, Photography, Advertising, Marketing, Film Studies, Popular Music and single honours Archaeology.

There are good teaching assessment results, particularly in the most prominent of all its departments, Physical Education/Sports Science, which daily colours the Chester campus lary green with sportswear, and scored 23 points out of 24 at inspection, pipping Theology, the subject truest to its foundation, which managed 22. Also popular are Drama, English and Psychology, which scored 20. Amongst students of science, maths (also 22) and computer, there's a particular attraction in a partnership with some 400 employers involved in course design, work placement, etc – all part of a career-based learning recipe evident in their cross-faculty BA/BSc degree programme and a solid graduate employment rate.

They were rated 'Good' by Ofsted for primary teacher-training and, for secondary – 'Good' in maths and MFL, 'Good to Very Good' in PE and 'Very Good' in Drama, Art and RE.

There are media facilities at Warrington, where an impressive reputation has been built with production courses and links to a range of media organisations including the BBC and Granada Television.

Business, Computer Science, Media, and Sport & Exercise Sciences are all at least part-based at Warrington.

The School of Health and Social Care is the major provider of pre-registration nursing and midwifery education across Cheshire and the Wirral. It also offers a wide range of undergraduate and postgraduate programmes for nurses, midwives and other health care professionals.

They offer nursing courses in Adult/Child Health, Learning Disability, Mental Health, and Midwifery. For DipHE students there are three intakes a year – February, June and September. For degree students, there is an annual intake in September. There is an annual midwifery intake in September (DipHE and BSc). Social work programmes at undergraduate level are offered at the Warrington campus.

SOCIAL SCENE

STUDENTSí UNION There are two headquarters, one on each of the campuses. The new bar on Warrington Campus (Wazza) is **Fu Bar** (was **Scholars**). It hosts live bands and, new for 2006, *T.P.I. Wednesday* (beach party time, grass skirts at the ready, with DJ Paul Webber, 8pm-1am); also games and quiz nights, and there's a re-launch of classic alternative night, *Deckheadz*. There's also *Padgates* club night on Saturday.

At the Chester campus there is a fractious history attached to the fun and games. Some years ago the so-called **Small Hall** venue had to be closed down. It was so popular that massive queues would form outside, and it fell victim to noise-pollution protestors. These problems still characterise student life on campus, judging by the SU's *Shhh* campaign to highlight problems caused to neighbours: 'We hope to alleviate tension with the local residents

WHAT IT'S REALLY LIKE

UNIVERSITY:	
Social Life	★★★
Campus scene	**Active**
Student Union services	**Average**
Politics	**Little interest**
Sport	**Key**
National team position	**80th (Chester) 122nd (Warrington)**
Sport facilities	**Good**
Arts opportunities	**Music, drama excellent**
Student newspaper	**Collegian**
Student Radio	**The Source**
Nightclub	**Max250, Fu-Bar**
Bars	**As above**
Union ents	**Cheesy**
Union clubs/societies	**Mainly sport**
Parking	**Adequate**
CITY:	
Entertainment	★★★
Scene	**Pubs cheesy, clubs OK**
Town/gown relations	**Complaining**
Risk of violence	**No**
Cost of living	**Average to low**
Student concessions	**Good**
Survival + 2 nights out	**£90 pw**
Part-time work campus/town	**Good/excellent**

AT A GLANCE

ACADEMIC FILE:	
Typical entry requirements	**145 points**
Application acceptance rate	**20%**
Students-staff ratio	**25:1**
First/2:1 degree pass rate	**44%**
ACCOMMODATION FILE:	
Availability to freshers	**85%**
Style	**Halls, flats, houses**
Catered	**45%**
En suite	**27%**
Approx price range pw	**£72-£107**
Town rent pw	**£40-£55**

and fellow students,' they say.

Still, **Max250**, the Chester student bar, will not be downed. *Freeky Fridays* is the big Friday Night out. You get to choose what you want to hear on the SU web site – from Chart to r&b to rap to dance. Fancy dress events occur every few weeks.

Society activity is as busy as you want to make it, though don't expect radical politics. Arts are well provided for, especially music and drama, with both the Drama Dept and Society putting on frequent productions. Consistent with its C of E foundation, there's an active Christian Union.

Sport Sport is of obsessive extra-curricular interest on the Chester campus, and there are constantly evolving facilities to support it, including a refurbished all-weather hockey pitch, a 25m pool, a fitness suite and sports hall – all part of a £5-million development. Chester is one of 90 educational establishments across the country delivering sporting services to a variety of Talented Athlete Scholarship Scheme (TASS) athletes.

Town Moving away from the campus into Chester itself, you'll find one of the most picturesque city centres in the country. If you have an urge to rush out and see something of extreme historical importance during a break from lectures, you won't be let down by the architectural minefield dating back to Roman times. You can get to almost anywhere in about 20 minutes. The big plus is that in comparison to most, Chester is relatively cheap and definitely a cheerful place in which to live.

Popular student haunts are the **Odeon** cinema and **Gateway Theatre**. And once you get bored of squeezing through the throngs of over-enthusiastic party goers in **Max250**, with over 60 pubs in Chester, most in walking distance, you really can't go wrong. There are various students nights at bars and clubs in town. Student-popular further afield are the **Carling Academy**, Liverpool, and **Royal Exchange Theatre**, Manchester.

PILLOW TALK

There's a wide range of accommodation available to first years – , shared flats, shared houses, quiet halls, on campus, off campus, fully catered, semi catered, self catered and meal deals. Top tip: Hollybank opened April 2005, brand new, self-catered, en-suite apartments, 20 yards from main entrance to Chester campus.

GETTING THERE

☛ By road: the uni is situated at the junction of the A540 and Cheyney Road.
☛ By rail: London Euston, 2:45; Sheffield, 2:25; Birmingham New Street, 1:45; Liverpool Lime Street, 40 mins; Manchester Oxford Road, 1:00.
☛ By coach: London, 6:00; Sheffield, 3:00.

UNIVERSITY OF CHICHESTER

The University of Chichester
Bishop Otter Campus
College Lane
Chichester PO19 4PE

TEL 01243 816002
FAX 01243 816078
EMAIL admissions@chi.ac.uk
WEB www.chi.ac.uk

Chichester University Students' Union
Bishop Otter Campus
College Lane
Chichester PO19 6PE

TEL 01243 816390
FAX 01243 816391
EMAIL student_union@ucc.ac.uk
WEB www.chisu.org

VAG VIEW

Situated between the South Downs and the sea at Chichester and at nearby Bognor Regis, Chichester University was once known as the West Sussex Institute of Higher Education, then as Chichester College of Higher Education, until 1999 when it became University College Chichester and gained the power to award its own degrees. Forty-nine per cent of its graduates go into Education, and Sports Science is the popular specialism, but more recently they have built a reputation in the schools of Visual and Performing Arts and Cultural Studies.

CAMPUSES

The Bishop Otter Campus, in name at least, takes us back to 1839 when Bishop Otter College was founded by the Church of England as a teacher training establishment; there is, today, a striking modern chapel in the grounds of campus, which itself lies within this walled cathedral city, widely known for its annual Festival of Music and Arts.

The less imaginatively named Bognor Regis Campus lies five miles hence. Bognor is, as it sounds, a rather passé seaside resort.

Bishop Otter is the bigger of the two, though Bognor has most of the teacher training. The campuses are far enough apart to cause something of a psychological split, so currently the Students' Union is preoccupied with getting the bus service between the two improved.

FEES, BURSARIES

UK & EU Fees: £3000 p.a. Bursary of £1000 for students receiving the full £2700 maintenance grant, and with a family income of £17500 or less. Sliding scale bursary if in receipt of partial grant, down to £250 min. There's also the 'Talented Sports Performer' Bursary Scheme: they offer up to £500 p.a. to outstanding sports persons.

STUDENT PROFILE

Lots of students are local and mature. There is a strong female presence and great sporting prowess.

UNIVERSITY/STUDENT PROFILE

University College since	**1999**
Situation/style	**Coastal sites**
Student population	**5473**
Undergraduates	**4700**
- mature	**32%**
- non EU undergraduates	**4%**
- male/female	**32/68**
- non-traditional student intake	**29%**
- state school intake	**97%**
- drop-out rate	**6%**
- undergraduate applications	**Constant**

ACADEMIA & JOBS

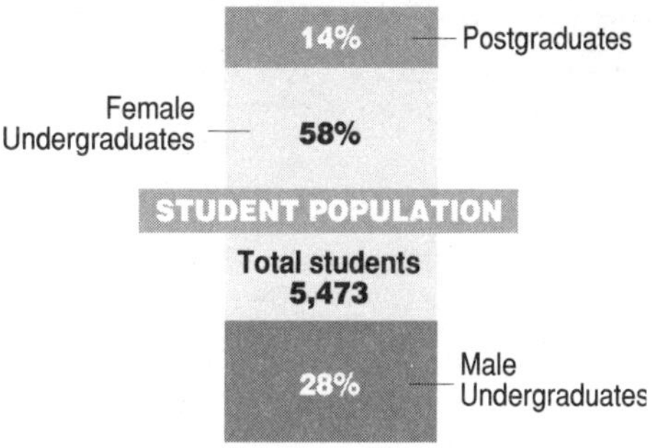

The college delivers a well-balanced modular course programme with a focus on sport, religion and the arts (look also at Adventure Education). Undergraduates may study for single honours, joint or major/minor programmes, or BA (QTS).

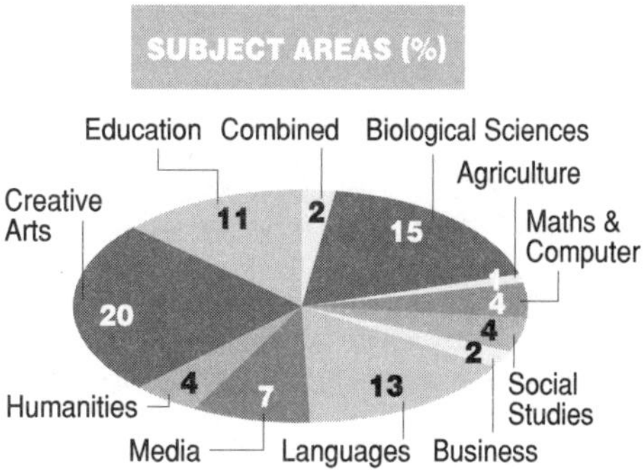

Almost half of graduates become teachers. Of those, 65% go into primary/32% secondary. Physical education with QTS is key.

The religious degrees reflect the college's past, of course, while Sport Science brings to mind the more pervasive modern interest of staff and students, and sustains a well-equipped Sports Centre. The School of Arts offers modules in Music, Dance, Art, and offers a unique course in Related Arts, which allows specialism in either of the three disciplines, but also looks for useful relationships

ACADEMIC EXCELLENCE

TEACHING:
(Rated Excellent or 17+ out of 24)

Media	**24**
Theology/Religious Studies	**23**
Art & Design	**22**
Drama/Dance/Cinematics, Sport	**21**
Health Science/Studies	**20**
Business	**19**

between them. There is a strong tradition in jazz and classical music and regular student music society performances and workshops (college and cathedral are regular venues). Dance (ballet, jazz and tap) is supported by a Studio, and, like music and art, involves public performance/exhibition at both student and professional level.

There's a Learning Resources Centre at Bishop Otter – a library (200,000 items), a media and computer facility, and art gallery. A similar centre at Bognor Regis has recently been refurbished.

SOCIAL SCENE

STUDENT UNION There's a new Union building at Chichester campus this year, with a 650 capacity **ZeeBar**. At Bognor, it's **The Mack**. The majority of students are local, so weekends are not that big, but ents are impressive for so small a clientele. A typical week sees *Flirt* on Monday, *Shagadelic* in Bognor on Tuesday. *Big Wednesday* is Sports Night in Chichester, while down in Bognor it's *The Alternative* (live music and DJ's). Thursday brings *Pre-Club Party* to Bognor, and *The Alternative* to Chichester. Friday is live music in Chichester. Sunday is Quiz Night on both camupuses. There were also 10 Paramount Comedy Nights this year (headline acts have included Alan Carr and Brendon Burns), and 4 balls every year – Freshers, Graduation, Christmas and Summer. Recent acts include Brandon Block, EZ Rollers, Jo O'Meara, DJ Spoony, Tim Westwood, El Presidente.

There are alternative music societies, arts societies, a role-playing games, society even an English Literature Appreciation Society. Oh, and an LGB (gay) Society flourishes, regularly holding events on campus and in a gay pub in the town. 'There's been a big growth,' says a bod at the union, which, for a moment, sounded a tad alarming.

Level of political activity has recently been impressively high, with a focus on Drink Awareness, Anti-Bullying, Mental Health Awreness, and a campaign for better inter-site transport and washing facilities.

SPORT Sport is key. Last year 6 teams won their BUSA leagues, and the uni moved to 49th overall in the national rankings. They also had 7 students representing their country as well as university. There are 13 different sports clubs, all, except netball, having both men's and women's teams.

PILLOW TALK

There is catered accommodation in halls at both sites, and higher capacity and en suite at Bognor. New self-catering halls of residence open at the Chichester Campus in September 2006, with 124 en-suite rooms with communal kitchens and lounges. They have also acquired 93 extra shared facility rooms close to the university, bringing total accommodation provided to 675 students. Still, accommodation is only guaranteed to International and Channel Island students. Remaining accommodation is allocated on a 'first

WHAT IT'S REALLY LIKE

UNIVERSITY:	
Social Life	★★★
Campus scene	**Female, sporty, closed weekends**
Student Union services	**Average-high**
Politics	**Active**
Sport	**Key**
National team position	**49th**
Sport facilities	**Good**
Arts opportunities	**Music, dance, drama excellent**
Student newspaper	**The Clash**
Nightclub	**ZeeBar**
Bars	**ZeeBar, The Mack**
Union ents	**Cheesy. 6 nights, not Saturday**
Union clubs/societies	**7**
Most popular society	**Business & Management Soc**
Parking	**Poor**
CITY:	
Entertainment	★★
Scene	**Arts good**
Town/gown relations	**Good**
Risk of violence	**Average**
Cost of living	**Low**
Student concessions	**Average**
Survival + 2 nights out	**£70 pw**
Part-time work campus/town	**Good/**

AT A GLANCE

ACADEMIC FILE:	
Subjects assessed	**12**
Excellent	**67%**
Typical entry requirements	**220 points**
Application acceptance rate	**19%**
Students-staff ratio	**22:1**
First/2:1 degree pass rate	**45%**
ACCOMMODATION FILE:	
Availability to UK freshers	**No guarantee**
Style	**Halls, hostels**
Catered	**80%**
En suite	**57%**
Approx price range pw	**£95-£116**
Town rent pw	**£55-£65**

come, first served' basis. So, get in wuick!

GETTING THERE

☛ By road: to Bishop Otter campus, A286 from the north. From east and west it's the A27. The road between Chichester Campus and Bognor is the A259.

☛ By rail: London Victoria, 0:45; Birmingham, 4:00.

☛ Frequent trains from Gatwick Airport.

☛ By coach: London, 4:40; Birmingham, 6:00.

CITY UNIVERSITY

City University
Northampton Square
London EC1V OHB

TEL 020 7040 5060
FAX 020 7040 8995
EMAIL registry@city.ac.uk
WEB www.city.ac.uk

City University Students' Union
Northampton Square
London EC1V 0HB

TEL 020 7040 5600
FAX 020 7040 5601
EMAIL president@city.ac.uk
WEB www.cusuonline.org

VAG VIEW

City University received its Royal Charter granting it full university status in 1966. The university is, as its name suggests, very much at the hub of City life and occupies a singular place in the world of higher education. They have a fine reputation in professional education and pride themselves on close contact with professional institutions, business and industry. Many of the programmes are accredited by professional bodies, and there is a very healthy graduate employment track record.

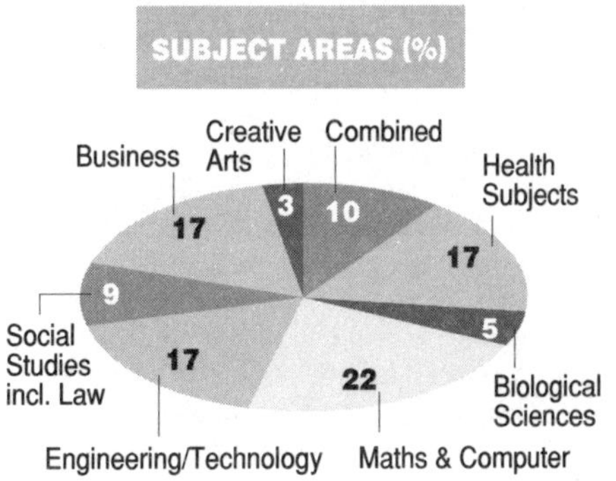

UNIVERSITY/STUDENT PROFILE	
University since	**1966**
Situation/style	**City sites**
Student population	**26172**
Undergraduates	**16750**
- mature	**30%**
- non EU undergraduates	**21%**
- male/female	**43/57**
- non-traditional student intake	**40%, High**
- state school intake	**85%, Low**
- drop-out rate	**7%**
- undergraduate applications	**Constant**

CAMPUS

City Uni inhabits the famed City of London, but is only fifteen minutes from the West End, a dawdle from Islington, with its theatres, cinemas, fashionable restaurants, trendy bars, clubs and traditional pubs, and a short way (in the opposite direction) from Clerkenwell, once-artisan London and now a fashionable area for cool, young, City-mile workers.

The main university buildings form part of Northampton Square. Main library, lecture theatres and Students' Union are here. The Department of Arts Policy and Management are nearby in the Barbican Centre. The Dept. of Radiography and halls of residence are also within walking distance. The St Bartholomew School of Nursing is some way

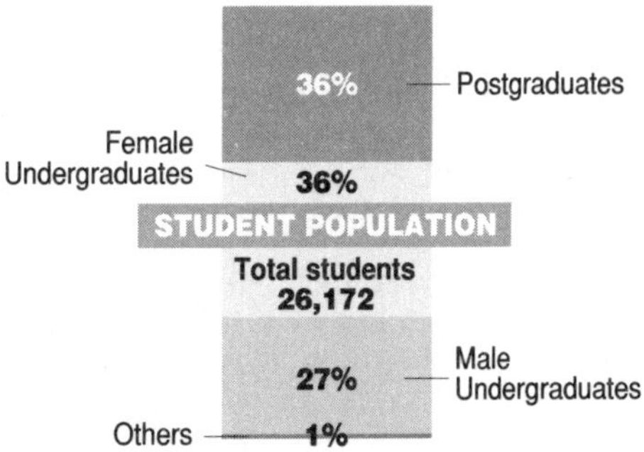

away in West Smithfield and Whitechapel in the East End. The Business School now occupies new premises in the heart of the city (see *Academia* below).

'City University is located within walking distance of no less than four tube stations (Barbican, Angel, Farringdon, Old Street), but strangely very few people can ever find it!' writes Catherine Teare. 'Tasteful, grassy Northampton Square, which supports a sizeable bandstand and water trough, has been the site for many an adventure for students – a place to chill in summer and the bandstand a place to shelter when raining. The men's rugby team used to use it for their initiation ceremonies – something about running round it in the buff!'

FEES, BURSARIES

UK & EU Fees: £3000 p.a. Bursaries awarded in shortage subjects. Contact the relevant school directly. Contact details on www.city.ac.uk.

STUDENT PROFILE

Full-time, first-degree undergraduates, many of whom are mature and from overseas, make up an unusually small percentage of the student body. Many more students are part-timers and there is a large number of postgraduate students. Says Catherine Teare: 'City University is like nowhere else. The mixture of cultures and personalities makes it one of the most diverse university communities in London.'

ACADEMIA & JOBS

Formerly the Northampton Institute, the uni places great emphasis on links with industry and with the professions – journalism, law, banking. A quarter of graduates go into commerce (financial activities, business, etc) and the Business School is now based in the heart of the City, providing, so they say, 'a state-of-the-art resource for management education in the 21st Century'. And then there's the health provision – 15% go into the sector. They have a School of Nursing and Midwifery, and there is a strategic link with University of London Queen Mary's School of Medicine & Dentistry, boosted by a recent £10-million investment. Now there's a new School of Allied Health Professions, which brings together Optometry & Visual Science, Language & Communication Science (speech therapy), Radiography, Health Management and Food Policy (postgrad only).

They produce masses of ophthalmic opticians. The leader in the field is Aston with around 27% of the graduate market. Bradford Uni and City follow. City does a 2-year Foundation in Dispensing Optics, which gives you a Diploma at the end and then the BSc Optometry, if you can hack the high entry requirements. Teaching inspection, 23. Research Grade 5. Two BSc Radiography degrees, Diagnostic and Therapeutic are also well-trod pathways into employment. See, too, the dedicated BSc route into speech therapy, another cert.

City sends around 10% of its graduates into banking, largely through the Cass Business School. A £50-million building was opened in 2003. The one dedicated course, BSc Banking & International Finance, is what attracts, but doesn't come cheap. Teaching inspection, 23. Research Grade 5. Merchant bankers, sharedealers and investment adviser/analysts also like City. Look at BSc Investment & Financial Risk Management (3 or 4-year sandwich).

ACADEMIC EXCELLENCE

TEACHING:
(Rated Excellent or 17+ out of 24)

Music	**Excellent**
Art & Design, Maths, Business & Management, Subjects Allied to Medicine	**23**
Economics	**22**
Electrical & Electronic Eng, Psychology, Library/Info Mgt	**21**
Nursing	**20**
Sociology, Land & Property Mgt, Mechanical & Aeronautical Engineering, Communication & Media Studies, Civil Eng.	**19**

RESEARCH:
*Top grades 5/5**

Music	**Grade 5***
Optometry, Law, Business/ Management, Library/Info Management, Art &Design	**Grade 5**

60% of 300+ graduates employed nationally as actuaries come via Mathematical Sciences faculties, then it's Business and Economics. City has very big muscle in this area. Half the staff in the Actuarial Science & Statistics Department are Fellows of the Institute of Actuaries. Again there's a high 'ask', but there's also a 4-year version with a first-year Foundation course. There's an appealing study abroad option, too.

City law graduates (who tend to be particularly well schooled in performance skills) have, in City's Inns of Court School of Law, one of a few institutions validated to run LPCs (Legal Practice Course, essential for solicitors) and came out of a recent LPC assessment with an Excellent rating.

Again, the passage from graduate to barrister is immensely smooth as The Inns of Court School of

WHERE CITY GRADUATES END UP

Health & Social Work: 19%; Education: 5%; Wholesale/Retail: 20%; Manufacturing: 5%; Financial Activities: 16%; Public Administration, Civil Service & Defence: 4%; Hotel/Restaurant: 1%; Transport & Communications (including Telecommunications): 3%; Construction: 1%; Personnel: 1%; Computer: 4%; Business & Management: 3%; Accountancy: 5%; Media (including Film): 5%; Legal 1%; Publishing: 2%; Sport: 0.5%.

Approximate 'graduate track' employed **80%**

Law is one of the few places you can study for the Bar Vocational Course (BVC). There's also a LLB Law & Property Valuation, and this year a new English & French Laws LlB.

Location favours City for journalism, too – you are in the very heart of British media, and you will be lectured by practitioners. The portfolio of degrees espouses the idea of combining journalistic skills with knowledge in a particular subject area – in Economics, Psychology, Sociology.

Note, too, City's renowned postgrad journo degrees: International Journalism Diploma/MA is practically orientated with a focus on both print and broadcast – very hands on, very productive. There is also a PhD for mid-career practitioners, who will submit a piece of work and undertake supervised research to produce a thesis.

They are also traditionally strong in engineering, though teaching inspections were disappointing (variously 19 and 21 points). Racing car enthusiasts should note an interesting niche, the 3-year BEng and BSc Automotive & Motorsport Engineering (4/5-year B/MEng degrees as well).

The BSc Computing Science degrees with AI/Distributed Systems/Games Technology/Music Informatics are gaining a fine reputation. There's also Business Computing Systems, Information Systems or Software Eng. Four-year sandwich courses, all of them, including integrated practical and professional training.

SOCIAL SCENE

Students' Union The renowned Journalism course (famed for launching our First Lady of Conflict, Kate Adie) provides welcome support to the extra-mural media side of life. The monthly glossy *Massive* keeps students well informed of forthcoming events and current hot topics, but rather worryingly the radio station (Divercity) and TV station (SUBtv) have gone!

The Students' Union has done well to try to give a stable base for the disparate and scattered student body, but frankly, other than the sound community life in one of the halls, student life at City is London-rather than university-central. Not all do warm to this, and you must be aware that you are not joining a student scene that you'd find at some other London unis.

'Does City have a campus life? Yes and No,' writes Catherine. 'Students use a number of sites dotted around London, which makes it hard for us to feel like we belong.

'Meeting places include the **University Refectory** (*interesting* food!), the Square and the Students' Union. There is a bar, a shop and an eaterie as well as a Student Advice Centre and clubs and societies.

'**Saddler's Bar** is open five days a week from 9am, but closes at 11pm. It has a Western theme (check out the saddles!) and offers a few more extras than the usual pub – pool tables, latest arcade titles, quizzes and a chill-out room on major party nights.'

There is, however, no longer a nightclub. The

WHAT IT'S REALLY LIKE

UNIVERSITY:	
Social Life	★★ - ★★★
Campus scene	**Closed weekends**
Student Union services	**Average**
Politics	**Avoided**
Sport	**24 clubs. Striving**
National team position	**116th**
Sport facilities	**Average**
Arts opportunities	**Some**
Student magazine	**Massive**
Nightclub	**Now a study area!**
Bars	**Saddlers**
Union ents	**With London clubs**
Union clubs/societies	**50+**
Most popular society	**Law, Islamic**
Parking	**Non-existent**
CITY:	
Entertainment	★★★★★
Scene	**Excellent local pubs, clubs, arts**
Town/gown relations	**Good**
Risk of violence	**High**
Cost of living	**High**
Student concessions	**Good**
Survival + 2 nights out	**£100 pw**
Part-time work campus/town	**Excellent**

Wonderbar venue, which once masqueraded during the day as **Poncho's**, a popular Tex Mex-style eaterie, MTV playing in the background to encourage rhythmic chewing., is no more! Instead they have a new study area/common room with widescreen TVs, Internet access and sofas where students can work in groups or just relax.

With the Union now more or less closed to ents, they organise things with outsiders, like *Quids In* with DJ Tommy A, leading on to Islington's **Elbow Room**. Monday nights is *Candyfloss* at **Islington Carling Academy,** with top r&b DJs, like Nicky Smood, Masterstepz and Rampage. They also hold events at **Ministry of Sound**, **Fabric** and **Turnmills**.

Strong lines into the professions – business, finance, law, health – and very much a London experience. But what have they done to the fun and games?

As for societies, there is little to shout about, other than that the diverse student population means a huge range of International Societies – from Cypriot to Afro-Caribbean – on offer. There have also been some effective student campaigns on Racism, Women's Safety and Islamophobia.

Town Location is all, as far as City is concerned - 5 mins walk from the attractions of Angel, Old Street, Shoreditch, Hoxton and Farringdon, and just a short bus ride form the West End.

If you walk north towards Angel you come to Upper Street, which must have the most bars and restaurants in one area after the West End. There is something for everyone, cheap and expensive. It has a friendly, safe atmosphere and a 24-hour Sainsbury's on Thursday to Saturday, so you can food-shop at 3am in the morning!

If you walk west down Roseberry Avenue, you come to **Exmouth Market** and its surrounding area. This offers pretty much the same as Upper Street, but on a smaller scale. Exmouth Market has some of the best sandwich shops in London and, especially in the summer, a really welcoming atmosphere.

Camden is a mere ten-minute tube ride away, while the West End is twenty minutes on the bus. Many clubs offer discounts to students with an NUS card, but you must make sure you go on the right night. The nearest places to shop are Holloway Road, Oxford Street and Camden.'

See also *London Student City*, page 292.

Sport Interest may be high but levels and facilities are not impressive, and now they no longer have Sports Night at the Wonderbar. There are pitches in Walthamstow; a small rowing club is based, of course, on the Thames; the Saddler's Sports Centre, with badminton, football, netball, tennis, aerobics and yoga and a good martial arts programme, a couple of squash courts; and some Islington facilities are popular nearby.

PILLOW TALK

All applicants over 18 living outside Greater London who firmly accept an offer of a place at City and submit an accommodation application form by 15 May are guaranteed a place in University accommodation. There are two halls of residence, both within walking distance of the main site. The first, Finsbury & Heyworth Halls, are linked by a bar/common room; fees include an evening meal and late breakfast on Saturdays and Sundays. Walter Sickert Hall, which overlooks the Regents Canal, is more plush, with en-suite, single study-bedrooms. Next to Finsbury/Heyworth is a block of purpose-built self-catering flats, which comprise three to six single study-bedrooms, living room/kitchen and showers. Newly available to first years are self-contained flats (single study-bedrooms with shared facilities) at Francis Rowley Court, about ten minutes' walk from the uni.

'City University has a number of rooms in halls,' Catherine reports, 'but not enough to accommodate every first year who needs one. I cannot lie, living

AT A GLANCE

ACADEMIC FILE:	
Subjects assessed	**19**
Excellent	**84%**
Typical entry requirements	**300 points**
Application acceptance rate	**13%, low**
Students-staff ratio	**17:1**
First/2:1 degree pass rate	**59%**
ACCOMMODATION FILE:	
Guarantee to freshers	**Non-Londoners who apply before May 15**
Style	**Halls**
Catered	**None**
En suite	**23%**
Approx price range pw	**£89-£100**
City rent pw	**£85**

in London *is* expensive. You can end up paying £90 for a hovel with no heating, if you're not careful.

'The halls are a mixture of flats and single study-bedrooms. Some are en suite and some require you to share facilities with ten other people. Finsbury & Heyworth Halls have a bar, which creates more of a community than is present in other halls. It is run by the Students' Union and, unlike the union, is open at weekends.

'Popular private housing student areas include Hackney, Stoke Newington and Shoreditch.'

GETTING THERE

- All sites are well served by buses.
- Parking is difficult and expensive.
- Nearest Underground stations to main sites: Angel (Northern line), Farringdon and Barbican (Hammersmith & City, Metropolitan and Circle).
- For the School of Nursing, it's either Whitechapel (District and Metropolitan), Aldgate (Metropolitan), Aldgate East (Metropolitan and District), or Tower Hill (District).

COURTAULD INSTITUTE OF ART

The Courtauld Institute of Art
Somerset House
The Strand
London WC2R ORN

TEL 020 7848 2645
FAX 020 7848 2410
EMAIL ugadmissions@courtauld.ac.uk
WEB www.courtauld.ac.uk

The Courtauld, part of London University, is the international centre for the study of Art History, for which it scored 23 out of 24 points in the teaching assessments. Its library, galleries, quality of its scholarship, and proximity to centres of artistic interest, such as The Nationa and National Portrait galleries, The Royal Academy and The Hayward, make it a magnet for students all over the world.

INSTITUTE PROFILE	
Institute of London Uni since	**1932**
Status	**Uni College**
Degree awarding university	**London**
Situation/style	**City site**
Full-time undergraduates	**125**
ACCOMMODATION:	
Availability to freshers	**60%**
Style	**Intercollegiate Halls, see intro**
Approx cost pw	**£100-£118**
City rent pw	**£100+**
DEGREE COURSE:	**History of Art**

COVENTRY UNIVERSITY

Coventry University
Priory Street
Coventry CV1 5FB

TEL 024 7679 0790
FAX 024 7688 7845
EMAIL rao.cor@coventry.ac.uk
WEB www.coventry.ac.uk

Coventry University Students' Union
Priory Street
Coventry CV1 5FJ

TEL 024 7657 5200
FAX 024 7655 5239
EMAIL suexec@coventry.ac.uk
WEB www.coventry.ac.uk

VAG VIEW

After devastating bombing during the Second World War, Coventry rose from the ashes to become a major industrial force. Elements of what later became the university evolved during this time, and in 1970 the Coventry College of Art merged with Lanchester College of Technology and Rugby College of Engineering Technology to form Lanchester Polytechnic, named after a leading industrialist. In 1987 the name was changed to Coventry Polytechnic. Then, in 1992, the poly became Coventry University.

CAMPUS

The modern precinct campus is directly opposite the bombed-out ruins of the original cathedral. Looking around the ecclesiastical shell is a thought-provoking experience. Students from Cov were sketching it at the time I visited. Especially memorable is a sculpture of reconciliation (two figures embrace to express forgiveness for the

Luftwaffe's devastation of Coventry) created by Josefina de Vasconcellos and, as it happens, given by Richard Branson. An identical sculpture stands in the Peace Garden at Hiroshima, Japan.

FEES, BURSARIES

UK & EU fees: £3000 p.a. From 2006/07 the University will make available bursaries of £500 pa for students whose family income is up to £37425, £750 p.a., where family income is between £37425 and £47425. Also scholarships of £2000 p.a. for students with high entry qualifications or higher performance in sport, enterprise, creative or artistic endeavour; £1000 p.a. for certain students from partner institutions.

STUDENT PROFILE

There is a large mature student population, bent on vocational training. Many undergrads come via the state sector from the locality, but also a lot from overseas. A sizeable section of first degree undergrads are part-timers. You will not find it difficult to get in. The uni has been diligent in its open access policy, giving many families their first taste of a university education. Perhaps inevitably, there is a big drop-out rate of 18%.

UNIVERSITY/STUDENT PROFILE	
University since	**1992**
Situation/style	**City campus**
Student population	**18072**
Undergraduates	**9635**
- mature	**30%**
- non-EU undergratuates	**15%**
- male/female	**47/53**
- non-traditional student intake	**41%, high**
state school intake	**94%**
- drop-out rate	**10%**
- undergraduate applications	**Constant**

ACADEMIA & JOBS

The uni portfolio has this year undergone a complete restructure. There are 2 schools: Lifelong Learning and Art & Design, and 3 faculties: Health & Life Sciences; Business, Environment & Society; Engineering & Computing.

A school's careers master told us, 'They have deliberately gone for the vocational – that was their background. We have students for whom Coventry is exactly right.' Now, Cov tells us: 'STAR courses have been specifically designed for 2006 entrants and provide completely new, multidisciplinary teaching in various exciting, emerging fields. STAR Scholarships are available to attract students that not only have the potential to achieve high entry qualifications but also, thorough interview or presentation of portfolio, can demonstrate they have the drive and ambition to succeed throughout their studies.'

The continuing connection with industry helps mould its courses and keeps its employment record good and inward investment healthy, while a programme of expansion continues. Recently, they acquired the Odeon cinema on Jordan Well as home to the Performing Arts and Communications Culture & Media departments (courses in dance, theatre, music and arts practice lend a distinctly different timbre to academic life here), a new £20-million library opened, major investment was made in WebCT (electronic learning environment), and there's a £1.5-million spend for an Advanced Digitisation and Modelling Laboratory to enhance their research into automotive design.

For cars, boats planes, Coventry is still among the leaders. Would-be aeronautical engineers and manufacturers come bounding out of here, enough to ensure a place in the Top 10 graduate employment listings annually. Entry requirements may seem demanding, but time and again in Engineering you'll find a Foundation bridge if you can spare the extra year. Less well known are low-cost offers for Boat Design (indeed, all sorts of vehicle design) in the developing Art & Design faculty.

For automobile engineers, it's Loughborough, Oxford Brookes, Bath, Swansea Institute, Oxford and Coventry. It is mainstream fare for this city. The uni is nothing if not vocational and the car industry is central to its calling. There are BA hons degrees in 3D Design Representation, Automotive Design, and Automotive Design & Illustration, as well as the range of BEng hons. Engineering teaching assessments tend to be in the 18 point area, which is low considering some entry requirements; while Design is rated 22. Racing car

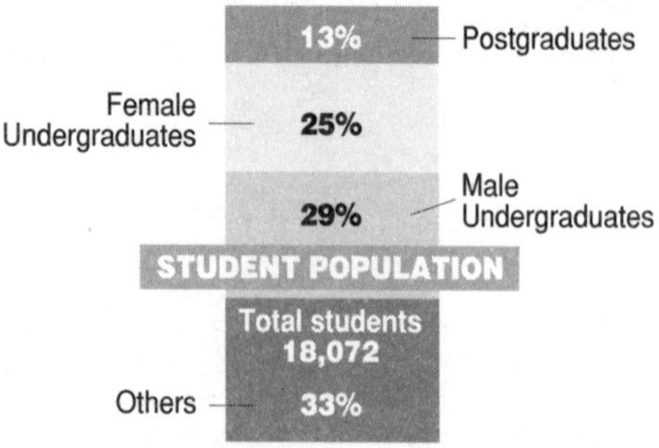

designers and team managers note: the 3-year degree in Motorsports asks is not demanding at entry. There are also Design and Management courses available that may take you into this far from secure job sector, though it must be said that 6 former Coventry Uni design students and a member of staff were identified by an *Autocar* survey as being among the 100 most influential Britons in the automotive industry. Note also their Advanced Digitising and Modelling Laboratory, opened in December 2002, formally known as the Bugatti Building. It provides full-sized vehicle design and styling facilities and is the only resource of its kind in the world attached to a university.

An exciting development has been the creation of the 20-acre Coventry University Technology Park, home to the TechnoCentre offering a focus for training, conferences and business opportunities), to the Enterprise Centre (a £3m development accommodating new small and medium-sized enterprises), and, at the creative core, the Innovation Village and Design Hub.

SUBJECT AREAS (%)

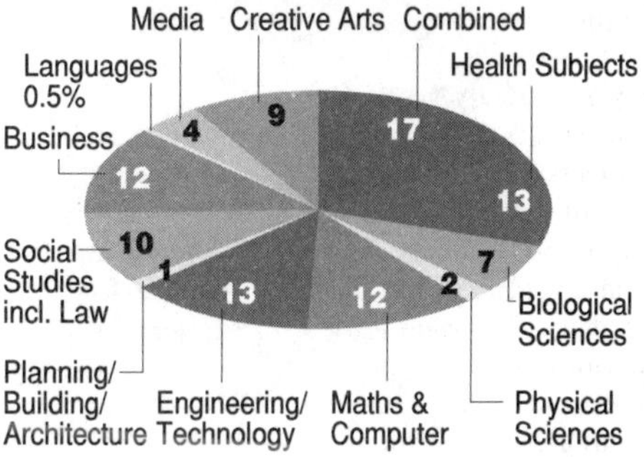

ACADEMIC EXCELLENCE

TEACHING:
(Rated Excellent or 17+ out of 24)

Mechanical Engineering, Geography.	**Excellent**
Subjects Allied to Medicine, Economics, History, Maths Politics	**23**
Building, Art/Design, Business & Management, Nursing	**22**
Sociology, Modern Languages, Psychology, Tourism/Leisure/ Sport	**21**
Town & Country Planning, Civil Eng, Biosciences	**19**
Communication & Media Studies, General Engineering, Mech/ Aero/Manuf Eng, Electric & Electronic Engineering	**18**

RESEARCH:
*Top grades 5/5** **None**

Design also favours graphic artists, designers and illustrators (often the advertising industry or journalism as destination). BSc Architectural Design Technology favours the would-be town planner, while jobs in the construction industry are very much available to Cov's Built Environment graduates – see Building Surveying, and Construction Management in particular. Teaching inspection, 19.

In the health arena, BSc Physiotherapy is in a cluster of employer-friendly health science degrees, which includes Nursing, Dietetics, Midwifery and Occupational Therapy, and dropped only one point at the teaching assessments. Coventry have 6% of the career quota for graduate physiotherapists nationally, and dropped only one point at the assessments.

Meanwhile, BSc Occupational Therapy turns out around 11% of graduate occupational therapists in work. In a less busy employment scene, among psychotherapists, Coventry has a good track record, too.

Look also at Biological Sciences (BSc Psychology, Applied Psychology, etc – 21 points at inspection).

Would-be solicitors note that Cov are European, commercial and business law specialists, and non-Law graduates may opt for a 2-year full-time or 3-year part-time Senior Status Law degree here.

Finally, if you have an adventurous streak and

WHERE COVENTRY GRADUATES END UP

Health & Social Work: 20%; Education: 8%; Wholesale/Retail: 11%; Manufacturing: 13%; Financial Activities: 7%; Public Administration, Civil Service & Defence: 7%; Hotel/Restaurant: 3%; Transport & Communications (including Telecommunications): 6%; Construction: 2%; Personnel: 7%; Computer: 2%; Business & Management: 2%; Media (including Film): 1%; Legal 2%; Architecture: 1%; Publishing: 1%; Advertising: 1%; Sport: 2%.

Approximate 'graduate track' employed **60%**

purposeful outlook, rifle through their Disaster Management courses. This is a genuine niiche. Coventry has 10 years experience teaching them.

SOCIAL SCENE

Student Union The most recent addition to the campus is a new student centre which offers a 'one-stop' service and features all the services students require on enrolment and throughout their time at the University. Students can get help on a range of issues including finance, registry, accommodation, international office, recruitment and admissions and student services.

> ***The continuing connection with industry helps mould its courses and keeps its employment record good and inward investment healthy, but it's no longer all science and engineering at Cov.***

The campus is a hive of activity revolving around the café/bar **ReUnion** on the top floor of the union building. It serves food from breakfast through to late-night munchies and screens all the top sporting fixtures.

Artie and indie types will be found in the **Golden Cross** and **Fads** cafeteria in the art block. Language and engineering students will be found in the library. Sporting people will be found at the union bar or slumped in the corner somewhere. Overseas students spring up everywhere.

Much of uni social life is dominated by societies, particularly sports, though the sometime award-winning media, currently *Source* (newspaper) and Source FM, do well too. Of more unusual societies, many different self-defence clubs and the Friends of Palestine group might be of interest. Most have their own local haunts: for example, the **Hope and Anchor** is frequented by 'The Lanch' Rugby Union team. Sporting societies often organise fund-raising events – Man 'O' Man, The Full Monty, the Slave Trade, etc. – and such events are high on the social calendar (and have to be seen to be believed!).

What was **The Planet** on the corner of Cox Street – a revolution in its day, is now the **Casbar**, **Studio** and **Chiller**. *Phase the Legend* is Friday's cheese in the Studio, there's funk in the chiller and 'just great music in the Casbar,' they tell me – *Trollied* is on Monday: drink promo and all rooms open. It's but a short walk from campus.

Sport The uni muscled in at 62nd in the overall BUSA ratings for team sports last year. Generally they do better. It's had its Olympic swimmers and pumped up a few boxing champions.

There are sports scholarships and central to campus a brand new Sports Centre with fitness suite, injury clinic, 4-court and 2-court halls and dance studio.

Thirty-seven acres of uni playing fields are at Westward Heath, 4 miles from the city centre, cater for rugby, soccer, hockey and cricket, and there's a 9-hole golf course.

Town Much-abused and deeply sensitive Coventry is about to be refurbished with new City squares and gardens (the first already built between the uni and the Cathedral), a huge open plaza for outdoor events and the restoration of medieval walls, with lighting schema, but already it has one of the most compact city centres in the country, and a much-loved traditional indoor market. The £33m **Sky Dome** complex houses a multi-screen cinema; bars

WHAT IT'S REALLY LIKE

UNIVERSITY:	
Social Life	★★★★
Campus scene	**Culturally mixed, good ents scene**
Student Union services	**Activity high**
Politics	**Internal**
Sport	**Average**
National team position	**62nd**
Sport facilities	**Average**
Arts opportunities	**Film, art exc.; dance, music popular; drama improving**
Student newspaper	**Source**
Student radio	**Source FM**
Cox Street Venue	**Casbar, Studio and Chiller**
Priory Street Venue	**ReUnion**
Union ents	**Eclectic**
Union clubs/societies	**50**
Parking	**Poor**
CITY:	
Entertainment	★★★
Scene	**A few choice clubs 'n pubs**
Town/gown relations	**Nothing special**
Risk of violence	**Variable**
Cost of living	**Low**
Student concessions	**OK**
Survival + 2 nights out	**£60 pw**
Part-time work campus/town	**Average/Good**

AT A GLANCE

ACADEMIC FILE:	
Subjects assessed	**28**
Excellent	**79%**
Typical entry requirements	**225 points**
Application acceptance rate	**21%**
Students-staff ratio	**20:1**
First/2:1 degree pass rate	**43%**
ACCOMMODATION FILE:	
Guarantee to freshers	**100%**
Style	**Halls, houses, flats, village**
Catered	**25%**
En suite	**15%**
Approx price range pw	**£50-£86**
City rent pw	**£50-£80**

and café bars, two nightclubs, and restaurants. There is also a 4,000-seat arena a popular concert venue that doubles up as an ice rink.

The **Herbert Art Gallery and Museum** and **Belgrade Theatre** provide the cultural dimension. Sport is, however, the coming thing, with the £60m **Coventry Arena** no longer a dream and a £20m project to include a rugby stadium and a football Academy of Excellence. The **City Sports Centre** has an Olympic-sized swimming pool.

Cost of living is quite low, and there are lots of student discounts. 'Most pubs in Cov are of the Rat, Parrot and Firkin ilk,' says Andrew Losowsky, 'but **The Golden Cross** and **The Hand and Heart** are worth a look for something different.'

PILLOW TALK

'Priory Hall is the largest of the student residences over 600 rooms,' writes Jennifer Johnston. 'It is dominated by lads who haven't yet discovered how to open a tin of beans – yes, you've guessed it – Priory is catered accommodation. Singer Hall is organised into flats and is self-catered. Caradoc Hall is a tower block of self-contained flats and is just out of the city centre. There are lots of suitable student houses in the Stoke, Earlsdon and Radford areas of the city, with good low rents.'

New accommodation includes university-owned Sherbourne House and Lynden House and non-university Liberty Park and Trinity Point.

GETTING THERE

☛ By road: from London M1/J17, M45, A45, signs for City Centre. From the south, M40/J15, A46, signs for City Centre. From the southwest, M5, M42/J6, A45. From Northwest, M6/J2, City Centre signs. From the north, M1/J21, end of M69, signs to City Centre.

☛ By rail: London Euston, 80 mins; Manchester Piccadilly, 2:30; Nottingham, 1:45; Bristol, 2:30.

☛ By air: Birmingham Airport.

☛ By coach: London, 1:20; Leeds, 4:00.

CUMBRIA INSTITUTE OF THE ARTS

Cumbria Institute of Art & Design
Brampton Road
Carlisle
Cumbria CA3 9AY

TEL 01228 400300
FAX 01228 514491
EMAIL admissions@cumbriacad.ac.uk
WEB www.cumbria.ac.uk

Located on three sites in Carlisle, the main green-field campus overlooking Rickerby Park and the River Eden – paradise indeed – Cumbria is also a cracking college academically, with teaching assessment scores of 21 out of 24 for Art & Design and 19 for Communication & Media. It is also exceptionally well resourced with electronic and media production facilities and a £4.5-million development incorporating a new library, theatre and dance studio, and improved teaching accommodation.

INSTITUTE PROFILE

Founded	**1822**
Status	**Art College**
Degree awarding university	**Central Lancashire**
Student population	**935**
Undergraduates	**905**
ACCOMMODATION:	
Availability to freshers	**25%**
Style	**Halls**
Cost pw (no food)	**£52-£55**
Town rent pw	**£45**

DEGREES:
Contemporary Culture, Creative Writing, Film Studies, Journalism, Dance, Drama, Music Theatre, Performing Arts, and various Art & Design faculty courses.

DARTINGTON COLLEGE OF ARTS

Dartington College of Arts
Totnes
Devon TQ9 6EJ

TEL 01803 861620
FAX 01803 861666
EMAIL registry@dartington.ac.uk
WEB www.dartington.ac.uk

Dartington – a village in the shadow of Dartmoor, nestling in the valley of the River Dart, lies just southeast of Buckfast Abbey and a couple of miles northwest of alternative lifestyle haven Totnes. It is an ideal setting to enjoy the intense, artistic Dartington experience and what the QAA inspectorate once described as their 'charismatic and innovative teaching'.

Good performance technology and recently overhauled Library and Resources Centre. Links with professional companies and projects with clients, both local and European, are part of the deal. They are not hung up on academic qualifications. They'll want to meet you and see what you have to offer personally and artistically.

The student bar is the hub. There's a pool table, games arcade and juke box, and hot food is served from 2-5pm. Ents include poetry slams, bands, jazz nights, competitions, quizzes and theme nights. Much entertainment is made by the students themselves, and at nearby Dartington Arts, an organisation that puts on all kinds of concerts, exhibitions, films and theatre. Freshers get priority for on-site accommodation.

COLLEGE PROFILE

Founded	**1961**
Status	**HE College**
Degree awarding university	**Plymouth**
Situation/style	**Rural campus**
Full-time undergraduates	**440**
ACCOMMODATION:	
Availability to freshers	**98%**
Style	**Halls**
Cost pw (no food)	**£53-£59**
Town rent pw	**£50**

DEGREE SUBJECT AREAS:
Writing, Arts Management, Theatre, Choreography, Music, Fine Art

DE MONTFORT UNIVERSITY

De Montfort University
The Gateway
Leicester LE1 9BH

TEL 08459 45 46 47
FAX 0116 255 0307
EMAIL enquiry@dmu.ac.uk
WEB www.dmu.ac.uk

De Montfort Students' Union
Mill Lane
Leicester LE2 7DR

TEL 0116 255 5576
FAX 0116 257 6309
EMAIL kbutler@dmu.ac.uk
WEB www.mydsu.com

VAG VIEW

From 2006, De Montfort will have one centre of education only – Leicester. DMU Bedford is to become part of a new university for Bedfordshire due to be created with Luton University in August 2006.

First smile on the inherently sad face of a restructuring strategy that disposed of six campuses in a few years (Scraptoft, Caythorpe, Riseholme, Holbeach and Lincoln City, and Kents Hill, Milton Keynes) and lost students one of the best prime live music venues in the country, **The Arena***, was a*

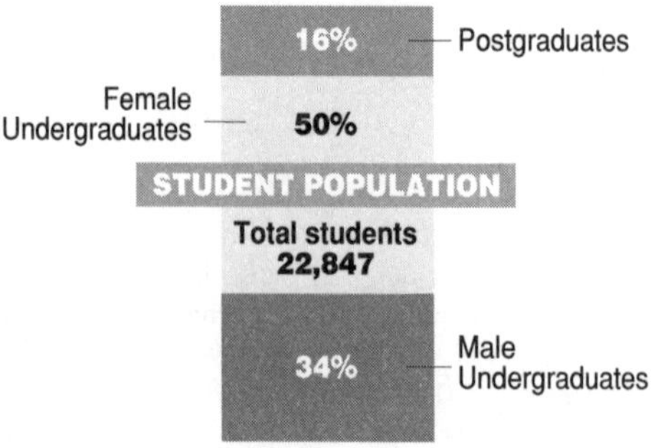

£9-million Campus Centre *building, which opened at Leicester in September 2003. With restaurants and bar, a Students' Union, a dance theatre and performing arts studios, it was an important pointer to the future.*

This and new student accommodation, which gives all first years a place in a hall at the centre of operations rather than 8 miles away at Scraptoft, are part of a £105-million development.

Among the partnerships that will enable this to happen, and in the long term possibly the most significant for all sorts of reasons, is one with the NHS, which is working to create a new professional/education/training centre on the Leicester General Hospital site, to link the Leicester and Warwick Medical School with DMU's health provision – nursing, midwifery, etc – and the NHS staff's own continuous professional development programme.

FEES, BURSARIES

UK & EU Fees: £3000 p.a. Bursary for students in receipt of full HE Maintenance grant: £300; if in receipt of partial HE Maintenance Grant: £500. DMU sports scholarships offer up to £1000 p.a. for 25 students representing England or Great Britain in their chosen sport. Academic Scholarships of £1000 are awarded to students who receive over 280 UCAS tariff points on entry to DMU. This is an automatic award to any student who achieves the required number of tariff points, irrespective of household income.

STUDENT PROFILE

There's a large mature undergraduate population and an open-access policy that brings in many who might not have gone to uni a few years ago. But they're such a fun-loving crew that neighbouring Leicester Uni students have been known to crash in on their excellent ents.

ACADEMIA & JOBS

Leicester faculties are: Art and Design; Business and Law; Computing Sciences and Engineering; Health and Life Sciences; and Humanities.

A feature of many of DMU's programmes is paid work placement. All sandwich courses have placement tutors with extensive employer contacts. The uni runs joint research projects with industry and business, in which students are involved. Employers help plan relevant student projects as well as providing our students with work experience and graduate jobs.

UNIVERSITY/STUDENT PROFILE	
University since	**1992**
Situation/style	**City campus**
Student population	**22847**
Undergrads	**19096**
- mature	**26%**
- non EU undergraduates	**3%**
- male/female	**40/60**
- non-traditional student intake	**41%, high**
state sector intake	**97%**
- drop-out rate	**10%**
- undergraduate applications	**Up 4%**

The Business Faculty leads the field for jobs in sales management. Personnel managers also prosper through the Human Resource Management degree. The Marketing degrees have strong relationships with Chartered Institute of Marketing: www.cim.co.uk and IDM: www. theidm.com. Students get exemptions from professional qualifications of both these bodies through study of certain marketing modules.

The BA Accounting and Finance course also offers the maximum exemptions from Association of Chartered Certified Accountants and CIMA qualifications – you can't get more exemptions from an undergraduate degree in the UK.

DMU is also a leader in Public Policy research. Look at the BA Public Policy, Government & Managment. The Local Governance Research Centre is internationally recognised.

In Computing Sciences & Engineering, look at BSc Audio & Recording Technology, run in conjunction with Confetti Studios and providing real world industry experience. Also, BSc Forensic Computing, developed in conjunction with electronic crime law enforcement specialists. BSc Broadcast Technology is run in conjunction with BBC Training and Development, and comes with an optional placement year. There's a strong tradition of student radio at DMU. BSc Media Production includes a practical component with the BBC Training and Development unit in Wood Norton. BSc Radio Productiongoves experience of producing programme material.

Another strong employment destination here is Further Education, via Creative Arts (22 at the assessments, everything from Textiles to Fine Art, Graphics to Photography), Engineering (19 points on assessment), Computer Science (Satisfactory), Social Science and Business (Excellent).

The art and design provision finds all sorts of avenues into employment. BA Contour Fashion is the only degree in the world to specialise in lingerie, bodywear, swimwear, performance

WHERE DE MONTFORT GRADUATES END UP

Health & Social Work: 11%; Education: 18%; Wholesale/Retail: 14%; Manufacturing: 10%; Financial Activities: 7%; Public Administration, Civil Service & Defence: 6%; Hotel/Restaurant: 3%; Transport & Communications (including Telecommunications): 4%; Construction: 1%; Personnel: 5%; Computer: 5%; Business & Management: 1%; Accountancy: 1%; Media (including Film): 1%; Legal 1%; Architecture: 1%; Publishing: 1%; Advertising: 1%; Artistic/Literary: 2%; Sport: 2%.

Approximate 'graduate track' employed **58%**

sportswear, 'structured' eveningwear and bridalwear, established apparently in 1947 at the request of the corset industry. Students visit underwear manufacturers throughout Europe and Asia, after Hong Kong businessman Andrew Sia set up the Ace Style Institute at the university. Look also at BSc Fashion Technology, as well as all the fashion and textile design and Retail Buying degrees. There is also the expected outpouring of graphic artists, designers and illustrators, and a prized degree in Furniture Design.

In the arts, through BA Arts Management in the Humanities Faculty, DMU turn out as many administrators as Cambridge. There are joint hons courses, too, with Dance, Drama Studies, Film Studies, Journalism, and Media Studies.

Dance is an area of growth for DMU. Dance, Drama and Cinematics are rated 22 out of 24. An MA Dance is available and the Bachelor degrees are offered as single and joint honours.

Nurses (adult, children's, mental health and learning disabilities nursing, also Dental Technology) and midwives dominate the health provision, but there are 50 places available on the BSc Speech & Language Therapy, and a very good chance of a job. Teaching inspection, 20. Note, there is a new Public Health degree.

There is also BSc Honours Audiology - all course fees are paid by the NHS. Annual bursaries of £2500 are available, and a year-long work placement commands a salary. 'Graduates of the course can expect a starting salary in the region of £21000 per annum,' says the university. Finally, Biomedical Sciences/Studies, Cell Biology &

ACADEMIC EXCELLENCE

TEACHING:	
(Rated Excellent or 17+ out of 24)	
Business & Management	**Excellent**
Politics	**24**
Land & Property Management, Leisure Industry & Sport	**23**
Drama/Dance/Cinematics, Art & Design, Nursing, Psychol	**22**
History of Art, Archit & Design, Molecular Biosciences, Pharmacology	**21**
Communication & Media Studies Speech & Language Therapy, Maths, Building, Education	**20**
Electric/Electron Engineering, Materials Technology,	**19**
RESEARCH:	
*Top grades 5/5**	
Politics, English	**Grade 5**

Genome Studies attract researchers and aspiring pathologists (21 ooints at assessment). There is a sound employment record for chemists from DMU, with two degrees feeding the habit: the 4-year Pharmacy and the Pharmaceutical & Cosmetic Science (Drug Delivery or Cosmetic Products) programme.

See also the BSc Human Psychology – there is a history of strong employment in psychotherapy at DMU, and this degree is accredited by the British Psychological Society as first step towards becoming a chartered psychologist. There's also a BA Social Work.

SUBJECT AREAS (%)

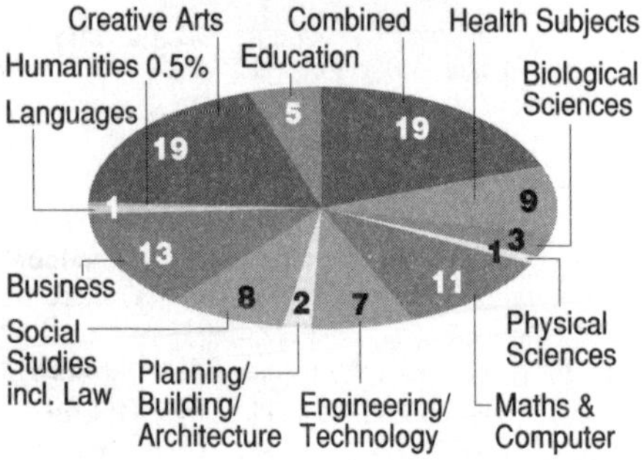

SOCIAL SCENE

Students' Union The Students' Union has moved

into 'a brand spanking new building in the centre of campus, offering the radio station a new studio and a venue called **Level 1** – DJ booth, laser lighting, amazing effects. We now have comfy leather sofas and funky chairs, a quadrant of bars – more drinking stations on your nights out.'

DMU are pulling in, centring their resources on the Leicester campus in a 10-year £105-million programme, part funded by a sell-off of the old campuses.

Regular ents nights are *Sun Random*, an eclectic mix of activity varying from comedy, to film previews, to karaoke to live gigs, anything Random goes! Monday os *Happy Mondays*, Students and Societies Night, where any club or society puts on ents and enhances their resources. Tuesday is Quiz Night. Wednesday is *Univibe*, a yea-old night of r&b flava musik, ranging from desi beats, ragga, bangra to hip hop. Thursday is *Kinky*, ar 21st-century disco night. Friday is *Toothpaste*, indie/rock night, with occasional live bands, like so far El Presidente & Imperial Vipers. Saturday is *Flirt*, cheese pop music with promotional acts, entertainment and fancy dress or themed nights. DJ sets that have featured thus far : Kate Lawler, Scott Mills, Fran Cosgrove, Chappers & Dave & more.

There is a real tradition for media. Radio station Demon Fm has won awards for many years and built up a huge reputation within the industry. In 2001 they were named Best Student Station in the UK by the SRA awards, in association with Radio 1. In 2003 they were nominated for a record five awards and won gold for Best Specialist Music and bronze for Best Female Presenter and Best Off-Air Branding. In 2004, Demon FM received the Best Female Presenter and Best Specialist Music Show awards. The station also received a bronze award in the Best Marketing category.

In 2005, a DMU student received the Diversity Award at the National Union of Students/Daily Mirror National Student Journalism Awards. The award was in recognition of his work on DMU student paper *The Demon*.

Town See *Leicester Student City*, page 269.

Sport At Leicester there's an emphasis on fun rather than serious competition. There's the John Sandford Sports Centre, a fitness studio, solarium, weight training and gym. Basketball team, the Leicester Riders, have strengthened their ties with

WHAT IT'S REALLY LIKE

UNIVERSITY:	
Social Life	★★★★
Campus scene	**Unpretentious, fun-loving, studenty**
Student Union services	**Good**
Politics	**Active**
Sport	**30 clubs**
National team position	**86th**
Sport facilities	**Good**
Arts opportunities	**Theatre, music & film good**
Student newspaper	**Demon**
Journalism Awards	**Winner 2005**
Student radio	**Demon FM**
Radio Awards	**Nominated 2005**
Student TV	**Demon TV**
TV Awards	**Highly comm. 2005**
Nightclub	**Level 1**
Bars	**Bars 1 to 4**
Union ents	**7 days a week**
Union clubs/societies	**30**
Most popular society	**Chinese Soc, Hindu Soc**
Parking	**Poor-adequate**
CITY/TOWN:	
Leicester Nightlife	★★★★★
City scene	**Top town - clubs, pubs, curries**
Town/gown relations	**OK**
Risk of violence	**Average**
Cost of living	**Average**
Student concessions	**Good**
Survival + 2 nights out	**£50-£80 pw**
Part-time work campus/town	**Good/Excellent**

AT A GLANCE

ACADEMIC FILE:	
Subject assessments	**27**
Excellent	**70%**
Typical entry requirements	**225 points**
Application acceptance rate	**22%**
Students-staff ratio	**19:1**
First Class/2:1 degree pass rate	**40%**
ACCOMMODATION FILE:	
Guarantee to freshers	**100% non-local**
Style	**Halls, flats**
Catered	**None**
En suite	**75% Leicester;**
Approx price range pw	**£59-£80.50**
Average city rent pw	**£60-£85**

DMU and are now known as the De Montfort University Leicester Riders. There are swimming, athletics and cycling facilities close to campus.

PILLOW TALK

All accommodation is in Leicester, is en suite and has internet access. Within the last two years 2000 new bed spaces have been built.

GETTING THERE

- ☛ Leicester by road: M1/J21 or M6 then M69.
- ☛ By rail: London St Pancras, 75 mins.
- ☛ By air: Birmingham International Airport or East Midlands International Airport.

UNIVERSITY OF DERBY

University of Derby
Kedleston Road
Derby DE22 1GB

TEL 01332 591167
EMAIL enquiries-admissions@derby.ac.uk
WEB www.derby.ac.uk

Derby University Students' Union
Derby DE22 1GB

TEL 01332 591507
FAX 01332 348846
EMAIL udsu@derby.ac.uk
WEB www.udsu-online.co.uk/

VAG VIEW

Since it became a university in 1992 Derby has expanded fast and operates now from seven sites. Committed to the ideal of higher education for all, it keeps its entry requirements low to that end and has weathered a rather high drop-out rate.

Now, despite disappointing application numbers in 2004, they are moving forward impressively. Last year they opened the £20m Buxton Campus, an historic Grade II listed building with one of the world's largest unsupported domes. The creation of a University Quarter in Derby is underway with additions to the main Kedleston Road Campus – a Clinical Skills Suite with up-to-the-minute digital diagnostic equipment and NHS-specification training wards. This year there's a brand new Students' Union bar based on award-winning design concepts by their own Architectural Venue Design students. Close by, a new Arts, Design and Technology Campus is taking shape – performance spaces, workshops and studios, as well as facilities for graphic design, film and photography, new media and sound production.*

UNIVERSITY/STUDENT PROFILE

University since	**1992**
Situation/style	**City campus**
Student population	**24690**
Undergraduates	**14461**
- mature	**66%**
- non EU undergraduates	**5%**
- male/female	**42/58**
- non-traditional student intake	**41%, high**
state school intake	**97%**
- drop-out rate	**11%**
- undergraduate applications	**Down 12%**

**see Introduction for key to tables*

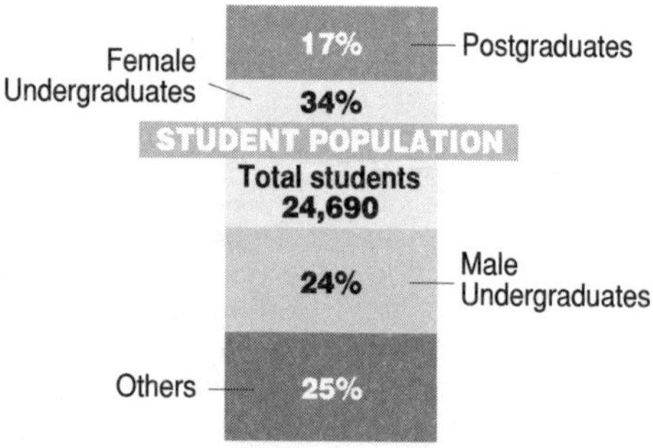

CAMPUS

Derby's campus sites range in size and facilities from the Ritz to B&B. The main site is **Kedleston Road**, 10 minutes walk from the city centre, where all the heavy stuff like law, business and science go on. There are many regular buses to it, it's the home of the Students Union, and the place where most things happen.

The other sites are scattered around, but are also generally well served in terms of transport.

Writes Mario Cacciottolo: **'Green Lane Campus** is a beautiful old Gothic structure near the town centre that is good to look at, but as it's listed there is absolutely no chance of having that much-needed extension.

'**Mickleover Campus** is allegedly made of cardboard, so a dry winter is crucial. It has two drama studios where regular student productions are held. The quality of performance is often high, so a visit is recommended, but the heating is pre-Noah, so bring a coat.

'**Cedars** is where stuff like occupational therapy gets done, though eventually all courses based here will move to the Kingsway Hospital site. Some of the facilities are in need of updating, especially the canteen.

'**Britannia Mill** is another attractive but larger building where art and design students glue and scribble. Not far from Kedleston Road, easily accessible, it's even next to a football pitch. What more do you want?

'**Jackson's Mill** is where the textile people get together to weave, and **High Peak** is the uni's latest site, situated in the north of the county and catering for courses like, well, catering and health and beauty.'

Then there's the new **Devonshire Royal Campus**, Buxton. Grade II listed, it has a dome bigger than St Paul's Cathedral's. Beneath it are an electronic library facility with Internet cafés and coffee bars.

> ***Derby's operation is about open access and the kind of educational intervention that will translate degrees into careers. The union, meanwhile, provides the anaesthetic. It's a workable collaboration.***

FEES, BURSARIES

UK & EU Fees: £3000. A high proportion of Derby students are eligible for bursaries. If in receipt of the full Maintence grant of £2700 you'll be awarded a uni bursary of £800; then, on a sliding scale down to £200 if you receive less than £1000 as grant. Also, if you're from Derby, or your immediate family has a DE postcode you'll get an extra bursary of £300. Again, if you come from one of the 53 local schools and colleges in Derby's Compact Scheme, there's another £400.

SUBJECT AREAS (%)

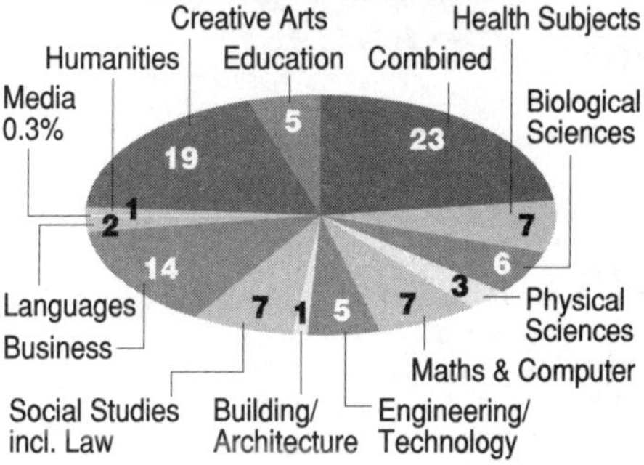

STUDENT PROFILE

Their open access policy has attracted a large mature and part-time student population and many from so-called 'low-participation neighbourhoods', students from families to whom university is a new experience. Though this has also resulted in a high drop-out rate, it's now apparently under control: many who come here are focused on what they are about. Theirs is a friendly educational community to which mature applicants are particularly welcome. 66% of undergraduates are over 21 at inception.

ACADEMIA & JOBS

Derby's schools are Art, Design & Technology; Business, Computing & Law; Education, Health & Sciences; and Universty of Derby, Buxton.

The academic bedrock is Education. Education and Health together find nearly a quarter of their graduates jobs. Education-wise, we're talking primary school teachers (around 4% of the total output of Derby graduates) and educational

WHERE DERBY GRADUATES END UP

Health & Social Work: 15%; Education: 9%; Wholesale/Retail: 13%; Manufacturing: 11%; Financial Activities: 8%; Public Administration, Civil Service & Defence: 9%; Hotel/Restaurant: 5%; Transport & Communications (including Telecommunications): 5%; Construction: 2%; Personnel: 4%; Computer: 4%; Business & Management: 2%; Accountancy: 0.5%; Media (including Film): 1%; Legal 1%; Publishing: 2%; Advertising: 1%; Artistic/Literary: 1%.

Approximate 'graduate track' employed **60%**

ACADEMIC EXCELLENCE

TEACHING: (Rated Excellent or 17+ out of 24)	
Geology	**Excellent**
Pharmacy	**24**
Educ, Biology, Subjects Allied to Medicine, Business, Theology	**22**
American Studies, Tourism, Maths/Computing	**21**
Art & Design, Psychology	**20**
Constr Mgt/Architec Tech, History of Art, Electrical & Electronic Eng, Nursing	**19**
Modern Languages, Sociology, Drama, Dance & Cinematics.	**18**
RESEARCH: *Top grades 5/5**	**None**

assistants, a handful of higher education lecturers and secondary school teachers.

The single largest sector within Health is Derby's BSc in Occupational Therapy, recognised by the College of Occupational Health and the Health Professions Council, which accounts for 4% of the uni's graduate output into employment, and around 7% of the national market. It scored 22 points at assessment.

Nurses – mainly non-hospital – account for around 3% of the health provision. Then there's a Diagnostic Radiography degree, also a cert for employment, and many a pathologist comes off their biological/forensic science provision. Note, too, they scored full marks (24 points) for Pharmacy at the teaching assessments.

Derby also do their bit in the natural health department. It's is a big growth area, seeding careers in complementary therapy practices, acupuncture, reflexology, aromatherapy, health promotion and jobs in natural health retail outlets with their BA Complementary Therapies and Healing Arts degrees. They also have BA Acupuncture.

Pointing up an approach which is quite Derby's own, an attitude or philosophy that finds expression in the pastoral and mediation aspects of other courses, are Applied Community & Youth Studies, Applied Social Care, Health & Community Studies, and Applied Social Work. The number of graduates into youth welfare, community and social work from Derby suggests the sense of this.

They do well, too, in arts management, with good combinations, such as Business Management & Theatre Studies. Also BA Theatre Arts and a host of other media degrees, Broadcast Media, Film & TV, etc. Figures indicate that their degrees in sound production – BSc Music Technology & Audio Systems Design and BSc Multimedia Technology and Music Production (entry 160-180 points, teaching inspection 19) – are sound value for employment.

The Business Psychology and Creative Writing combinations (the former with such as TV, Marketing, Sociology, etc) score in areas such as advertising. Graphic artists, designers and illustrators proliferate (see also the Architectural Design degrees), and Derby's BA Textile Design and Fashion Studies degrees – yours for 160 points (teaching Inspection 20) – also lead to jobs.

Systems analysts find work out of the computer side. There are new degrees, BSc Computing and BSc Computer Games Programming, and a whole host of Computer Information Systems combinations..

On the business side, employment-wise, sales managers and personnel officers seem to proliferate, the latter recommending the vocational validity of BA Human Resource Management. There are also well-trod pathways into catering and tourism, and transport planning and distribution, retail management and accommodation management.

SOCIAL SCENE

STUDENTS' UNION There's a move afoot for the Union, which once managed their own **Arms Bar** in town, to new premises at the Kedleston Road HQ. Now that they're opting for a more traditional campus base, with a wholly new bar being built and as yet un-named, they are engaged in a process of canvasing students for a name.

They'll use the new bar for 'niche-focus' ents, comedy nights, etc, and have fixed up deals with some interesting venues in town for the bigger stuff. derby is not short of clubs and bars. There's a UDSU weekly night at **Zanzibar**. They've linked up, too, with new club **Blue Bamboo**, and **First Floor** for indie rock nights. Meanwhile, they promise chart nights at **Revolution** and house music at **Susima**. In the past, the SU have attracted acts such as The Prodigy, Atomic Kitten, Jools Holland, and Girls Aloud.

Dusted is the student magazine, a 64-page monthly, largely put together by students from the Creative Writing Society. There's also D:One, the radio station, and they're in the process of launching their first TV station, UDSU TV. Societies range from African-Caribbean to Urban Music.

SPORT Not a serious contender in the national uni league – they came 114th in the BUSA team sports last year. On-site facilities, a gymnasium and pitches. American Football and martial arts, as well as rugby and cricket, are at the forefront, while support is growing for Ultimate Frisbee.

WHAT IT'S REALLY LIKE

UNIVERSITY:	
Social Life	★★★
Campus scene	**Friendly mix, good ents**
Student Union services	**Good**
Politics	**Not much**
Sport	**20 clubs.**
National team position	**114th**
Sport facilities	**Poor**
Arts opportunities	**OK drama**
Student magazine	**DUSTED**
Student radio	**D:One**
Nightclub	**None: town nights**
Bars	**UDSU Bar, The Lonsdale**
Union ents	**Rock, hiphop, cheese & big balls**
Union clubs/societies	**33**
Parking	**Poor**
CITY:	
Entertainment	★★★
Scene	**Small, friendly, pub rock/indie**
Town/gown relations	**Good**
Risk of violence	**Low**
Cost of living	**Low**
Student concessions	**Good**
Survival + 2 nights out	**£70 pw**
Part-time work campus/town	**Good/average**

Town Derby is nicely poised between 'friendly town' and 'sprawling metropolis'. There are plenty of shops that sell all necessities for the modern undergraduate (HMV, Sainsbury's, Waterstone's, Next, McDonald's), all within a neat and tidy shopping precinct. An increasing number offer student discounts. There is very little litter on the streets, as teams of council workers with picky-up-sticks regularly snap at your heels while you walk. The architecture is pleasant without being spectacular.

Asam Rashid Ali says: "There are many student-friendly bars in Derby that are safe, fun and not so expensive.' There's also a large variety of pubs, all of which are worth at least one visit, plus the **Derby Playhouse** (with which the SU secure good discounts) three cinemas, two of which are multiplexes and require a short trip by taxi. The third is at the Green Lane campus (the **Metro**) and dispenses arthouse fare.

PILLOW TALK

Halls with flats, lodges, and houses are of a good standard at various locations around the city; none is catered; 50% are en suite (all rooms at Peak Court are en suite). All the halls are wired up so you can subscribe to telephone and free internet use. Freshers are guaranteed accommodation if their applications are received by August 31.

AT A GLANCE

ACADEMIC FILE:	
Subjects assessed	**31**
Excellent	**61%**
Typical entry requirements	**200 points**
Application acceptance rate	**18%**
Student-staff ratio	**20:1**
First/2:1 degree pass rate	**50%**
ACCOMMODATION FILE:	
Guarantee to freshers	**100% in Derby**
Style	**Halls & houses**
Catered	**None**
En-suite	**50%**
Approx price pw	**£55-£74**
Town rent pw	**£42.50**

GETTING THERE

☛ By road: Kedleston Road campus is just off the A38, the main southwest/northeast thoroughfare which goes south to Exeter and meets the M1 at Junction 28. M1/J25 for access from the east, A6 from the southeast (Loughborough way).

☛ By rail: rail links with Derby are easy. London is two hours away.

UNIVERSITY OF DUNDEE

The University of Dundee
2 Airlie Place
Dundee DD1 4HN

TEL 01382 344160
FAX 01382 348150
EMAIL srs@dundee.ac.uk
WEB www.dundee.ac.uk

Dundee Students' Association
Airlie Place
Dundee DD1 4HP

TEL 01382 221841
FAX 01382 227124
EMAIL dusa@dundee.ac.uk
WEB www.dusa.dundee.ac.uk

VAG VIEW

Founded in 1883 as University College Dundee, seven years later it became part of the St Andrews Uni and remained so until it gained independence in 1967. Today, Dundee is a traditional, premier-league university, but unusually relaxed and friendly. It has a history, but isn't steeped in it. Nor does it feel bound by tradition to repeat tself.

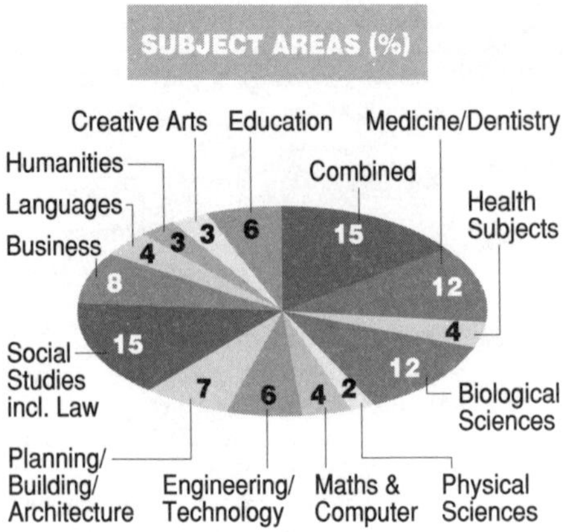

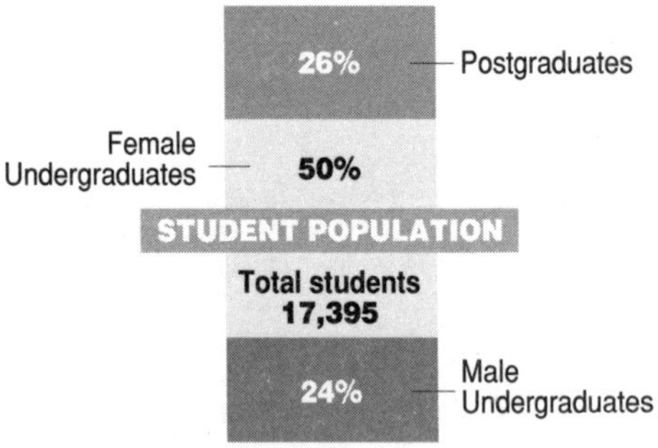

CAMPUS

'Dundee lies on the East Coast of Northern Scotland, a couple of hours away from Glasgow, Edinburgh and Aberdeen,' writes Sameen Farouk. 'Next door is St. Andrews. Dundee is one of a handful of genuine get-away-from-it-all universities. The scenery up here is breathtaking, a relief from the concrete jungles of other city universities. Weather-wise, Dundee isn't the Med but it's warm and mild for most of the year, just windy, and not much colder than the rest of the UK, even during the winter months.

'The main campus, with compact teaching facilities, IT centre, the main libraries, the art college, sports facilities, the union, the dental hospital, John Smith Bookshop, Bonar Hall, the famous Wellcome Trust building (all within five minutes walk of each other), is located on the edge of the town centre. It is safe, clean and increasingly accessible to the disabled community.

'The medical campus is located in the town's main hospital, Ninewells. Other sites, the nursing college (Kirkaldy in Fife, 35 miles from Dundee) and Northern College – the Faculty of Education & Social Work (Gardyne Road) are a little further out.'

FEES, BURSARIES

Fees for English students: £1700 (Medicine: £2700). See *Introduction*. The Leverhulme Trade Charities Trust provides bursaries for undergraduates. Approach the uni direct.

UNIVERSITY/STUDENT PROFILE	
University since	**1967**
Situation/style	**City campus**
Student population	**17395**
Undergraduates	**12885**
- mature	**3%**
- non EU undergraduates	**7%**
- male/female	**32/68**
- non-traditional student intake	**25%**
-state sector intake	**93%**
- drop-out rate	**10%**
- undergraduate applications	**Up 8%**

STUDENT PROFILE

'Without being steeped in outmoded tradition,' writes Hannah Hamilton, 'the university retains a strong self-image, and the students form a very real community around the central core of campus.'

Dundee attracts students from all walks of life and from all areas. The inevitable scattering of public school types joins a healthy dose of students from Ireland and a very strong international community.

'Dundee could never be criticised for being a quaint English retreat,' agrees Sameen. 'The university recruits internationally and has strong Arab, Chinese, Malaysian, Korean and Hispanic communities. There is also a substantial South-Asian population. The local communities are also targeted keenly, and there is a growing population of mature students.'

The 25% intake from poor areas last year together with its top-rated teaching assessments and research record (see *Academic Excellence* box) and its average drop-out rate (10%), makes Dundee one of the elite in the context of our Government's aspirations in higher education. What's more, its teacher-to-student ratio of 13.7 fares well relatively with other unis, and the academic ask is not too daunting.

ACADEMIA & JOBS

Characteristically, Dundee is a university for the professions, for medicine, for architecture, for finance (there's a stream of Economics and Business Economics degrees), and for law.

'I suppose, if you are a Scot, and you want to study medicine,' said a sixth-form careers mistress, 'Edinburgh would have to be high on the list, but people have had very good experiences of Dundee.'

In fact, in the assessments, Dundee achieved an Excellent rating in Medicine, where Edinburgh achieved only a Highly Satisfactory, and in 1998 they won the prestigious Queen's Anniversary Prize for their pioneering use of keyhole surgery, a success which directs interest to the extraordinary levels of research going on here. Known the world over for cancer research, a radical new approach to cancer treatment has resulted from the merger of the research teams of pioneering keyhole surgeon Professor Sir Alfred Cuschieri and Professor David Lane, who discovered 'the guardian angel of the cell', the p53 gene. The idea is to deliver gene therapy direct to tumours via keyhole surgery, using a specially developed 'poison umbrella' needle.

The degree in Medicine is 5/6-year MBChB. Integrated med school and hospital. Course problem/community-based, i.e. clinical experience from Year 1. Entry ABB at A level; AAABB at Highers, including Chemistry + another science, plus GCSE (or Standard Grade) Biology. Teaching inspection, Excellent. Research Grade 5*. For dentists it's the 5/6-year BDS. Entry AAB. Teaching inspection, Highly Satisfactory. Research Grade 5.

Dundee also produces psychologists in number (BBB, BBCC Highers). They have BSc Psychology and two other degrees – with Applied Computing or Statistics. Psychology is also part of the MA joint hons courses. They can be taken as 3 or 4 years. Teaching inspection, Excellent.

What grabs the visitor is the real sense of excitement around here – they leapt eleven places nationally in the research assessments, with medical and biological research achieving the highest accolades. A recent international survey by *The Scientist* named Dundee as the best UK scientific institution in which to work. Dario Alessi, Professor of the School of Life Sciences, said: 'The advantage of Dundee is that it's very small. Communication in science is so important.' He has access to 500 scientists within two minutes of his lab. 'You can't do these sort of things in London or Oxford.' Said Roland Wolf, director of biomedical research: 'You have this underlying feeling that important things are going to happen,' and the feeling is not confined to Medicine.

The Art & Design faculty demands attention: Textile Design took an Excellent in the undergraduate assessments; companies like Nike and Calvin Kline die for Dundee graduates; the uni is among the leaders for supplying graduates to architecture; and although the faculty fell from Grade 5 to 4 in the research assessments, there is a sense, day-to-day, that the art/design students add vigour and momentum to what is going on in the city.

Besides the reputation of BArch (Architecture, 260 points), they're in the Top 10 for town planning. Doing the business are a 4-year BSc Town & Regional Planning degree, also Environmental Management; MA Economics/Geography & Planning. Teaching inspection, 21.

On theme, the city of Dundee has reinvented itself, and the uni is, geographically and culturally, at the very heart of its new identity. Bang in the middle of the city's new cultural quarter with its

Traditionally a uni for the professions. And now, Dundee-chic! Are we to believe it? From Medicine to Art to pure hedonism, it seems that Dundee has it all.

ACADEMIC EXCELLENCE

TEACHING:

(Rated Excellent, Highly Satis. or 17+ out of 24)

Graphic & Textile Design, Finance & Accounting, Medicine, Cellular & Molecular Biology, Organismal Biology, English, Psychology.	**Excellent**
Civil Engineering, Physics, Environmental Science, Hospitality Studies, Maths & Statistics, History, Law, Politics, Social Work, Fine Art, Dentistry.	**Highly Satis.**
Planning & Landscape	**21**

RESEARCH:

Clinical Laboratory Sciences, Biological Sciences	**Grade 5***
Hospital-based Clinical Subjects, Clinical Dentistry, Applied Maths, Civil Eng, Law, History	**Grade 5**

WHERE DUNDEE GRADUATES END UP

Health & Social Work: 28%; Education: 7%; Wholesale/Retail: 9%; Manufacturing: 7%; Financial Activities: 6%; Public Administration, Civil Service & Defence: 8%; Hotel/Restaurant: 5%; Transport & Communications (including Telecommunications): 3%; Construction: 3%; Agriculture: 1%; Personnel: 2%; Computer: 1%; Accountancy: 4%; Media (including Film): 1%; Legal 2%; Architecture: 5%; Artistic/Literary: 3%.

Approximate 'graduate track' employed **69%**

pubs, clubs and gallery shops, the Art/Design Faculty, through its reputation in the fashion and design industries, provides a global dimension to 'Dundee-chic'.

A £9-million, Lottery-funded collaboration between uni and city has resulted in **Dundee Contemporary Arts**, a centre for visual arts with the university's **Visual Research Centre** at its hub, an art laboratory equipped with cutting edge facilities for producing design prototypes, videos, prints, artists' books, etc.

Artists, designers and media types should look closely at the faculty with its inventive Product & Media Design Department. Jobs for graduates are diverse, from graphic designers and illustrators to printers, publishing production managers, set designers and jewellery designer-makers. Entry to the BDes Jewellery & Metalwork is by means of a Foundation course in Art & Design. Teaching inspection, Highly Satisfactory.

In Law, they're internationally rated for research, European law specialists and the only uni to offer both Scots and English Law. Non-Law graduates may take a 2-year full-time or 3-year part-time Senior Status Law degree here. Now a new International Water Law Research Institute is to open, it's the first of its kind in the world, and is set to train future leaders to arbitrate water conflicts.

Then there's the Faculty of Education – 100% of their graduates go into primary teaching.

Says Sameen, 'The departments with particularly good reputations usually deserve them. However, much of it is up to you. Self-study is usually held to account through tutorial systems, but the personal tutor system seems still to be "in development". The campus IT facilities have been upgraded but there is still no general 24-hour access unlike all Dundee's neighbouring universities.'

WHAT IT'S REALLY LIKE

UNIVERSITY:	
Social Life	★★★★★
Campus scene	**Diverse**
Student Union services	**Average**
Politics	**Self-serving**
Sport	**Sport-for-all**
National team position	**53rd**
Sport facilities	**Good**
Arts opportunities	**Music, film, art excellent; drama good; dance avg**
Student newspaper	**Student Times**
Nightclub	**Mono**
Bars	**Liar, Pete's, Tav**
Union ents	**Eclectic: Pop Tart, Taste, Big, Club Tropicana**
Union clubs/societies	**60**
Most popular	**Faculty based**
Smoking policy	**Bars, halls OK**
Parking	**Poor**
CITY:	
Entertainment	★★★
Scene	**Pubs, good live**
Town/gown relations	**Average**
Risk of violence	**Low**
Cost of living	**Low**
Student concessions	**Good**
Survival + 2 nights out	**£60 pw**
Part-time work campus/town	**Excellent/ poor**

SOCIAL SCENE

STUDENTS' ASSOCIATION Décor ranges from the scruffy intimacy of **Pete's Bar**, to the pseudo-swank of **Mono**, with the **Liar** and **Tav** bars affording comfortable, if not exactly spectacular, drinking surroundings. Regular club nights cover most styles of music, with the four bars serving some of the cheapest drinks in Dundee.

The SA, which is disassociated from the NUS, the national body, is frequently rated as one of the best in the country, on account of such ents being provided seven nights a week through term time.

'Socially, it would appear that the mainstream Dundee student is a clubber,' writes Sameen Farouk, '– nightclubs are, after all, saturated with them and the Students' Union seems to do all in its power to satisfy them – but there are substantial sections of the student body, especially within the international community, for which this is not true.

'The campus union is the hub of most

activities. The **Liar Bar** helps students who need to get plastered on the cheap (some by afternoon!). The union holds many events, and the success of the well-attended *DoThisDoThat* is surely a testament to the hard work of the ents staff. Everyone seems to have a tale to tell from the **Mono** (particularly after *Skool Daze* nights). The secondary union venue is (grotty) **Pete's Bar**, which tends to hold less mainstream stuff, like the odd Bhangra night, salsa night, even a *Vietnam War* night! Much socialising is also organised by societies.

'Those wanting quieter breaks retreat to the **Chaplaincy Café**. Although religion can hardly be said to dominate campus life, Dundee has a growing religious diversity and the chaplaincy has become a popular venue, the hub of the Christian Students Society. The Islamic Society is also re-establishing itself, with support from the local community and the opening of prayer facilities. A new temple has also opened up here.

'The uni has one of the best arts colleges in the UK, and also the excellent **Dundee Contemporary Arts** venue (mentioned above), but Dundee can't really compete with big city arts. The two classy theatres feature good touring acts, particularly the **Rep**. There's a bit of a live comedy resurgence, too. Music-wise, the **Caird Hall** does occasionally attract big/rising names (like Travis, Gabrielle and Ocean Colour Scene recently), but its real strength is its jazz tradition: there is a strong following here, frequent shows and an annual festival.

'The main cinemas are a bit out of the way for most students, but the DCA does show excellent indy films and holds foreign film events.

'Budding fresher journalists are going to be hugely disappointed with what the *Student Times* has become. It's fall from the starry heights attained by the past editor led one regular journalist to comment that it had become an 'inside joke', as DUSA acted quickly to prevent it from touching radicalism again. Its only real strength seems to be that it's free and literally littered all over the campus.

SPORT 'The particularly popular activities are mainstream team sports like hockey, rugby, football (not cricket), boxing and the watersports, but most sports have strong societies. Around Dundee there is also a well-established martial arts scene. The uni sporting facilities are excellent and well managed, as is the on-campus swimming pool.

TOWN '**The Contemporary Arts Theatre** (DCA, see above) and the **Overgate Shopping Centre**; are both close to campus. Most major retailers have branches in the city centre and main high streets, but shopaholics would probably prefer to tackle the surrounding cities.

There's a competitive clubbing scene, and loads of bars. Dundee isn't vulnerable to big city problems, aside from homelessness. There are low crime rates, clean environments and decent public transport. Ethnic minorities will find very close-knit communities. Tayside police take a hard-line stance towards reported crime, notably assaults on students. However, some student areas are vulnerable to burglaries, and hall residents should beware of children with kleptomaniac tendencies. Dundee is also one of the cheapest cities in the UK.'

AT A GLANCE

ACADEMIC FILE:	
Subjects assessed	**27**
Excellent/Highly Satisfactory	**70%**
Typical entry requirements	**325 points**
Application acceptance rate	**18%**
Students-staff ratio	**14:1**
First/2:1 degree pass rate	**63%**
ACCOMMODATION FILE:	
Guarantee to freshers	**100%**
Style	**Halls, houses, flats**
Approx price range pw	**£48-£95**
City rent pw	**£38-£60**

PILLOW TALK

Not all would agree that the old halls were the best option: 'Personally, I found hall a bit of an expensive option.,' says Sameen. 'Landlords have good reputations. Private housing near the campus or in the town centre is usually spacious, of very good quality and shouldn't cost much more than £160 per month. Insurance rates are also low and students are exempt from paying for water, perhaps because they are not generally known to use much.'

However, a major building programme is about to reach completion – with new residences Belmont, Heathfield, Seabraes and West Park becoming available and all accommodation finally being en suite with full online and kitchen facilities.

GETTING THERE

☛ By road: M90, M85, A85, A972.
☛ By rail: Newcastle, 3:00; London Euston, 6:00.
☛ By air: Dundee Airport for internal flights; Edinburgh International Airport is an hour away.
☛ By coach: London, 10:05; Birmingham, 10:05; Newcastle, 6:05.

UNIVERSITY OF DURHAM

The University of Durham
Old Shire Hall
Old Elvet
Durham DH1 3HP

TEL 0191 374 2000
FAX 0191 374 7520
EMAIL admissions@durham.ac.uk
WEB www.dur.ac.uk

Durham Students' Union
Dunelm House
New Elvet
Durham DH1 3AN

TEL 0191 374 1777
FAX 0191 374 1778
EMAIL student.uniont@durham.ac.uk
WEB www.durham21.co.uk

VAG VIEW

Founded in 1832, Durham is, like Oxford and Cambridge, a collegiate university, although unlike the Oxbridge colleges, Durham's are purely residential; academically, it is faculty based. From October, 2006, applicants to Durham may opt for a new Durham-based college, the first for more than 30 years, named after the Northumberland-born writer, pioneer of women's education and social reformer Josephine Butler (see Durham Colleges *below).*

Durham offers all the advantages of the best of British universities and is demanding at entry, shamelessly going after Oxbridge rejects, delaying its selection until after those two more ancient universities have taken their pick. But they combine this policy with another, designed to net applicants from the region, particularly from among what the sector euphemistically calls non-traditional *higher education heartlands, 'low participation' neighbourhoods and social classes.*

Further south, in an urban regeneration area on Teesside, lies the Stockton campus, with generally lower entry requirements (though not always) to attract the 'new' university population. But the policy extends to the main Durham HQ too, so that sixthformers have got in to Durham with an AS level and a GNVQ, taken at a state school or sixthform college, with the result that the percentage of undergraduates at Durham from these non-traditional backgrounds is far greater than at Oxford or Cambridge, or indeed Bristol, and closer to Nottingham, Bath and Leeds.

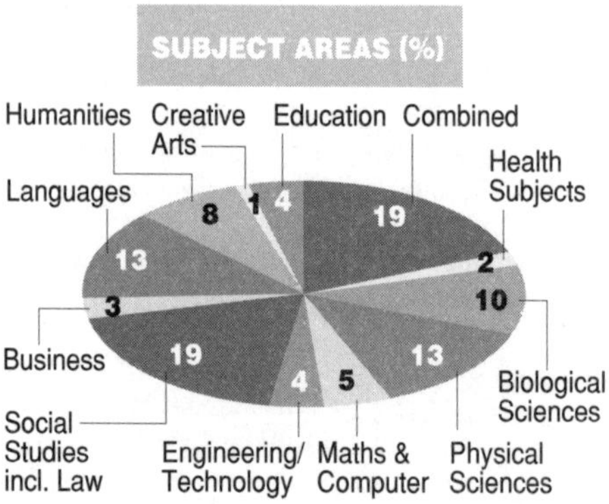

CAMPUS

Durham is a small, stunningly beautiful city, 16 miles south of Newcastle. The nucleus of the medieval city, where the five Bailey colleges and the Arts and Social Sciences Departments are located, is formed by a bend of the River Wear around a rocky peninsular, dominated by the 11th-century cathedral and castle.

The other campus, officially known as The University of Durham Queen's Campus, Stockton, lies south down the A1(M), on the outskirts of Middlesbrough. There are two colleges, John Snow and George Stephenson. Infrastructure and resources are good, from en-suite accommodation to library and IT resource centre, lecture rooms, laboratories and student recreational facilities.

FEES, BURSARIES

UK & EU Fees: £3000 p.a. Bursaries: £3000 if in receipt of full HE Maintence Grant; on a sliding scale £1500 to £600 if in receipt of partial grant.

STUDENT PROFILE

'Hi, I'm Alex Pharaoh and I came to Durham from a grammar school in North Yorkshire, aware that it had a reputation of being a haven for public schoolers and Oxbridge rejects, and, yes, a lot of people here do fall into one of these categories.'

'Hi, my name's Robin Siddle and I come from sixthform college in Scarborough. I thought there'd be a lot of yuppy people there, but there are only two colleges like that - Hatfield and Castle - the other ones are, like, normal...'

Times are changing. 'In what is almost a knee-jerk against Rah-culture,' writes Rik Fisher, 'there is more of an effort made to express personal style and individuality.'

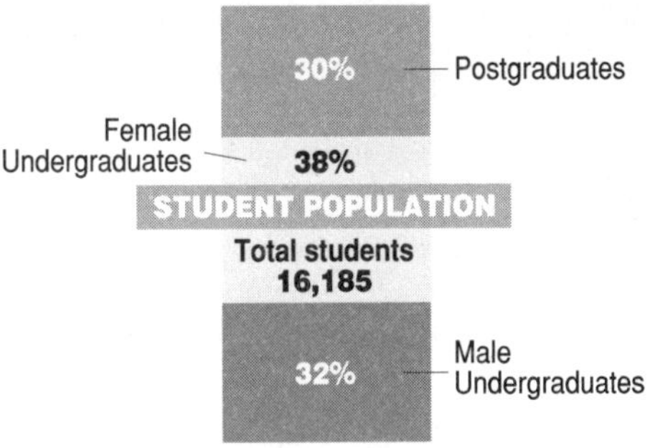

ACADEMIA & JOBS

Physics, psychology, biosciences, maths, philosophy, archaeology, theology, English, history, chemistry, law (candidates must sit the National Admissions Test for Law) - these topped the teaching and research assessments. Up there with the best, 86% of its assessments are Excellent, and in the last research exercise, they leapt from 18th to 12th place nationwide. Languages are an integral part of their graduate profile.

The medical faculty with neighbours Newcastle is primarily aimed at mature students, with a special Pre-medical programme for applicants without the necessary scientific background for Stage 1 entry. The actual medical course (MBBS) has two years at Stockton before transfer to Newcastle, where in years 3, 4 and 5, students will be assigned a regional clinical unit. Requirements for the degree are AAB, including 2 A levels, and to include chemistry or biology at A level or AS level. They also like one non-science subject at A or AS. 27:1 chance to get on the Pre-Med; 10:1 on the degree.

> ***'Hi, I am a state-school educated, second-year history student from the Midlands. I arrived at Durham with apprehension. I had heard the rumours that it was populated with snobby, southern Rahs, and was hoping they would be false.'***

Education is currently the single largest area of graduate employment, primary and secondary - 23 points at the teaching assessments, research assessment Grade 5.

This is a uni with great contacts in the City. In Accountancy, they are one of the three big graduate providers, along with Birmingham and Warwick. They have first-class links with the major firms. Nine per cent of their graduates go into the sector, and overall Durham supplies around 4% of the national quota to it. The dedicated Accountancy degree is Accounting & Finance at Stockton, with a relatively soft entry requirement of around 280 points. But at Durham, Economics is the most popular route in. There are all kinds of ways you can take it - as BA Hons, as major/minor, as BA Combined Hons or as a component of the BSc Natural Sciences degree. Among the language combinations is Economics with Arabic.

Natural Sciences, with subject combinations (Business, Economics, Maths, etc), is the second most popular way in. Again, there is a whole range of language possibilities which, together with the high-flyer, employer friendly Durham graduate profile, will warm Accountancy firms to the potential in their overseas business. Teaching inspection: Economics 24 points, Maths 21. Research: Applied Maths Grade 5*, Pure Maths Grade 5. They are big, too, in tax consultancy, banking and merchant banking. Of the 250 graduates who become investment/merchant bankers nationally each year, 24% come into the sector via Economics, 22% via Business courses, and 15% combining these subjects with other subjects. One third of graduates going into merchant banking from Durham carry a language with them. So you can begin to see the importance of this part of the Durham curriculum.

Defence is another employment strength,

UNIVERSITY/STUDENT PROFILE

University since	**1832**
Situation/style	**City collegiate**
Student population	**16185**
Undergraduates	**11310**
- mature	**7%**
- non-EU undergraduates	**3%**
- male/female	**47/53**
- non-traditional student intake	**16%, low**
- state school intake	**64%, low**
- drop-out rate	**2.5%, v. low**
- undergraduate applications	**Constant**

ACADEMIC EXCELLENCE

TEACHING:
(Rated Excellent or 17+ out of 24)

Chemistry, History, Law, Anthropology, Applied Social Work, English, Geography, Geology.	**Excellent**
Physics, Philosophy, Biosciences, Economics	**24**
Psychology, Archaeology, Theology, Subjects Allied to Medicine, Education, Sport	**23**
German, Linguistics, French, General Engineering	**22**
Sociology, Asian Studies, Middle Eastern/African Studies, Politics, Classics, Maths	**21**
Italian, Russian	**20**

RESEARCH:
*Special grade 6**

Chemistry, Geog, Law, English, History	**Grade 6***

*Top grades 5/5**

Applied Maths, Geography	**Grade 5***
Psychology, Physics, Biological Sciences, Pure Maths, General Eng, Anthropology, Accounting, French, Linguistics, Classics, Archaeology, Philosophy, Theology, Education	**Grade 5**

through Engineering & Technology, Physical Sciences, Social Sciences, Biological Sciences and Languages again. In engineering, there's BEng General Engineering, the variety coming for some after a 2-year general course in the MEng degrees: Aeronautics, Civil, Electronic (+ Systems Eng), Manufacturing, Mechanical, etc.

Physics, Physics with Astronomy, etc, are very strong. They took full marks in the assessments and an international Grade 5 for research. In the Institute of Computational Cosmology there's now a £1.4-million supercomputer, capable of making ten billion calculations a second and 'recreating the entire evolution of the universe'. Biosciences did similarly well – look at the 4-year BSc Biomedical Sciences at Stockton Campus, too.

With the passing out of Cranfield Uni from the undergraduate scene, Durham look set to have the single largest output of graduates into the British army. Contacts with the military are clearly good, for graduates come from a range of disciplines. Possibly it isn't a particular course so much as the Durham character that the forces are after.

Politics has an interesting Middle East bias in three degrees, and perhaps we should not be surprised to find the uni in the business of supplying to the British Intelligence Services.

Other social studies and languages (full marks and 22 points at the assessments respectively) find Durham graduates jobs in travel and tourism, as charity officers, market researchers, media and government researchers.

Future environmental officers graduate in physical sciences, biological sciences and in Agriculture. In Durham a steady flow of graduates go into the sector, which suggests a close look, among other courses, at MSci or BSc Geological and Geophysical Sciences, Ecology (optional placement), Environmental Geoscience, Earth Sciences, Geography (optional European Studies). Again, the Natural Sciences BSc combo features Earth Sciences and is very popular. Durham farmers come out of biological sciences, their degrees in Plant Science, Zoology, Ecology, etc.

Editors and other media appointments come out of languages, social sciences (which includes Psychology), physical sciences, maths and humanities. Student media (newspaper and radio) are part of the mix.

Said Alex Pharaoh. 'From what I've heard, and from what I've seen when my friends have left, graduating from this university gives a big head start in the fight for a career.'

DURHAM COLLEGES

The smaller collegiate system promotes involvement, sporting rivalries and the like. Each college has its own distinct identity.

The Durham college stereotype is described in the rivalry between the so-called **Bailey** colleges (John's, Chad's, Cuth's, University and Hatfield), situated in the Bailey area of the medieval city, and the **Hill** colleges (Trev's, Van Mildert, Mary's, Collingwood, Grey's and Aiden's), situated southwest of the Bailey. Sophie Vokes-Dudgeon reports: 'Pick your college carefully. Within a couple of days you'll have learned your college songs and rituals, and feel a strange affiliation with this set of buildings, which will manifest itself loudly on many a river bank or touch line throughout your life as a Durham student. The stereotypical image we have is of Rahs on the Bailey and Plebs on the Hill. And then there's St Hild & St Bede, the biggest college, a minute or two further out, perhaps with a more diverse mix than some of the others. Don't go entirely by the stereotypes though; be sure to visit

'The Hill colleges are more like a campus, all a drunken stagger from one another. Next to the Science site, computers and library too, but what you gain in convenience you lack in history and surroundings. The Bailey colleges are also near enough for a bar crawl, and the cobbled streets and cathedral backdrop make it far more aesthetically pleasing. Chad's and John's bars are barely big enough to swing a cat, however, and you may be more likely to stumble upon Evensong than a pint of lager in St John's. Hild Bede bar resembles an airport lounge, but the tow path leads to nightclub **Klute**?

'Colleges also differ in facilities. Hild Bede has a newish multigym, an abundance of tennis courts, squash courts, gyms, and beautiful if basic accommodation. Castle, on the other hand, offers third years the chance to live in a castle, while Collingwood gives you en-suite shower rooms and kettles. The choice is yours!'

'Trevs is very representative of the whole student body,' writes Eleanor. 'It is also friendly and has strong college spirit. There are loads of social events, two balls a year and one of the larger, and more tasteful bars. We are fairly standard when compared to other colleges. Our accommodation is decent, not as nice as Collingwood, however. Bailey accommodation tends to be the worst, as it is the oldest and they also room some students far from the main building, Cuth's is worst for this. Hill Colleges have purpose built accommodation blocks. John's is very religious, Van Mildert is good for music opportunities, Cuth's is famed for having a bar with proper opening hours!'

Says Alex: 'My college, Collingwood, is known as one of the best. We have the most modern accommodation, more en-suite rooms, more IT networked rooms, less room sharing, better central facilities, such as bar and gym, and allegedly, better food than others. We are the newest college, and have less tradition than those on the Bailey, which can be seen as a good or bad thing. We have a great social calendar – bar theme nights, "megaformal" dinners, bops, trips, sporting events and the legendary Summer Ball.'

Josephine Butler College opens in October 2006, the first new Durham-based college in 30+ years. Rooms are en suite and self-catering - 6 to a flat - on the southern edge of the city, close to the Science Site and main University Library. Special student rate buses are frequent. There'll also be a bar, a launderette, an IT Suite, a music practice room, a large hall, a variety of smaller rooms available for events, and special provision for the disabled, especially students with special dietary requirements. Flats are available from October to June, including the Christmas and Easter vacations.

'As well as first year students ("freshers"),' the uni says, 'members of other colleges are being invited to transfer Colleges to help create a vibrant, busy atmosphere right from the start. Sounds worth a punt if you're not at Durham for tradition.

SOCIAL SCENE

STUDENTS' UNION No raves, relatively few drugs; booze is the thing, college bops and black-tie formal dinners. Less formal are the discos and gigs at **Dunelm House**, the Students' Union building. 'The union puts on a range of ents with big name DJs common, but there is a noticeable lack of big bands,' writes Alex. 'Durham can't seem to attract them, but we can see many at Newcastle and Northumbria unions.'

The SU building and main bar, Kingsgate, have had a facelift this year and Pitstop, a new shop, has opened at the entrance to the building. **Kingsgate** is the union bar with balcony overlooking the river; it's open every day, and there are snacks. Food is served in the nearby **Riverside Café** until 11 pm and there's waitress service. Venues remain **Vane Tempest Hall** and the **Margot Fonteyn Ballroom**, where they host *Planet of Sound*, the regular Friday club night - a capacity sell-out. Wednesday Night one-offs also highly popular, such as Indie night *I Can't Believe It's Not Cheese* and *Back2School*.

Student media is first class, with *Palatinate* and Purple FM proving to be a worthy claw sharpener for the real thing. The union is active on welfare (Advice Centre, Nightline, etc) and politics extend into high profile – national media – fees campaign.

In student politics, Labour, Conservative and LibDem socs are all active, as well as People &

WHERE DURHAM GRADUATES END UP

Health & Social Work: 6%; Education: 16%; Wholesale/Retail: 6%; Manufacturing: 7%; Financial Activities: 12%; Public Administration, Civil Service & Defence: 11%; Hotel/Restaurant: 3%; Transport & Communications (including Telecommunications): 3%; Construction: 1%; Personnel: 1%; Computer: 4%; Business & Management: 4%; Accountancy: 9%; Media (including Film): 1.5%; Legal 2%; Publishing: 2%; Advertising: 1%; Sport: 1%.

Approximate 'graduate track' employed **69%**

WHAT IT'S REALLY LIKE

UNIVERSITY:	
Social Life	★★★★
Campus scene	**Collegiate fun 'n' games; opportunity to do more**
Student Union services	**Good**
Politics	**Active**
Sport	**Key; 46 clubs**
National team position	**5th**
Sport facilities	**Good**
Arts opportunities	**Good**
Student newspaper	**Palatinate**
Student radio	**Purple Radio**
Nightclub	**Fonteyn Ballroom**
Bars	**Kingsgate, Vane Tempest, Riverside Café**
Union ents	**Planet of Sound + dance & cheese**
Union societies	**124**
Most prominent socs.	**Big Band, Durham Revue, Ballads**
Parking	**Poor**
CITY:	
Entertainment	★★★
Scene	**Historic city, cheesy clubs, good pubs**
Town/gown relations	**Poor**
Risk of violence	**Low-avg.**
Cost of living	**High**
Student concessions	**Good**
Survival + 2 nights out	**£50-£150 pw**
Part-time work campus/town	**Average**

Planet and Fight Racism, Fight Imperialism. The Union has an active policy of independence from all political parties. Most debate sadly restricted to issues directly affecting Durham students.

Others of their 124 socieites include Pagan witches, Bellydancers, Medieval warmongerers and the Chemistry society.

Town When term begins, students herd in and outnumber locals. In the past it has proved to be a recipe for disaster. 'You don't go out on a weekend,' says Robin Siddell, 'because that's when all the locals are out. We haven't had any trouble really, it's just that the Londoners feel a bit nervous on a Friday and Saturday. They think they are going to get picked on because of the way they talk."

Writes Eleanor: 'Locals are generally friendly, and students are normally safe. Weekends are more dangerous, however, as county locals invade and they are more inclined to indulge in the favourite sport of student bashing."

Says Alex, 'There is some tension. The students who float into town for six months a year living off a combination of their student loan, large overdraft, or mummy and daddy, do cause irritation. Trouble is easily avoidable if you shun the pink shirt/bodywarmer/scarf, and don't talk in a loud southern accent on your mobile phone at 3 am, drunk, in the middle of the road, wearing a DJ.'

They have a university security patrol that goes round the city every night. They also have a night-bus which picks up all around town and drops off at all the colleges.

If clubbing is your thing, don't come to Durham. Writes Rick Fisher: 'Some just can't get enough of the dated eighties at **Klute** or the poppy pap at **DH1**, but as my mother is fond of telling me: consuming a generous helping of cheese before bedtime can be the stuff of nightmares.' But as Robin Siddell explains, there are alternatives: 'City nightlife has improved dramatically with the opening of many new bars and bar/clubs. Upstairs at *Cathedrals* (**the Loft**) on a Tuesday a live band plays till late. The beer is cheap and the atmosphere good, not hot and sweaty like other club venues. There's also a new, modern bar/nightclub overlooking the river, called **Chase**, which opened just 2 or 3 months ago. But take your cheque book with you – it's £2.55 for Carling (at College, a pint's around £1.30).

'Now, too, there's the late licensed bar/club **Walkabout**, one of the Australian sports-bar chain, probably the best thing to hit Durham in my three years here. It's open during the day, serves food such as crocodile and kangaroo, and has hundreds of TVs for worldwide sport. In the evening a dance

AT A GLANCE

ACADEMIC FILE:	
Subjects assessed	**36**
Excellent	**86%**
Typical entry points	**425, v. high**
Application acceptance rate	**14%, low**
Students-staff ratio	**14:1**
First/2:1 degree pass rate	**72%, high**
ACCOMMODATION FILE:	
Guarantee to freshers	**100%**
Style	**Halls, Durham; flats, Stockton**
Catered	**88%**
En suite	**32%**
Full board pw: Durham	**£127**
Self-catered pa: Stockton	**£87**
City rent pw	**£50-£100**

floor and DJ appear; the beer again is cheap. The only downside is that **Walkabout** replaced an old cinema, leaving us only one very small and busy Imax screen at the **Gala Theatre**.

'The old **DH1** nightclub has been revamped recently and is a little less sweaty, but, as a result, the prices have shot up and seem never to stop shooting up, so fewer students are willing to queue and the feeling is that it's not as good as it once was.

'**Klute** is where all the rugby boys go with there rah pink pashmina-wearing girlfriends, and it's like sardines in a can, though you can get a pass to a VIP lounge downstairs and drink cocktails in fish bowls.

'A Wetherspoons also just opened. **Varsity**, again fairly new, is possibly the best bar in town – high up on the river bank with a large balcony Then there's the boat, a buoyant after-club venue, small dance floor and an even smaller bar, but it's a good laugh.'

Sport Durham is very sporty, they came 5th last year, and the beautiful river is a temptress to hundreds of novice rowers. Durham finished 5th in the BUSA rankings last year, and has some nationally recognised student societies (for example, Durham University Caving Association). Academic concessions for sporty types are apparent, though not admitted. High standards are encouraged by inter-college rivalry, Castle vrs Hatfield (rugby), Castle vrs Hild Bede (rowing). College rowing crews are often better than other university crews. Sixty acres of playing fields are maintained to first-class standard.

GETTING THERE

- By road: A1/J6. Well served by coaches.
- By rail: King's Cross, 3:00; Edinburgh, 1:00.
- By air: Newcastle, Teesside Airports (25m).
- By coach: London, 5:30; Birmingham, 4:00.

UNIVERSITY OF EAST ANGLIA

The University of East Anglia
Earlham Road
Norwich NR4 7TJ

TEL 01603 591515
FAX 01603 591523
EMAIL admissions@uea.ac.uk
WEB www.uea.ac.uk

Union of University of East Anglia Students
Union House
Norwich
Norfolk NR4 7TJ

TEL 01603 593272
FAX 01603 250144
EMAIL su.comms@stu.uea.ac.uk
WEB www.stu.uea.ac.uk

VAG VIEW

Set apart in rural Norfolk, this excellent university was founded in the 1960s and reaches out to the world with innovation and flair. It is among the best on virtually any grounds you care to mention, and perhaps because they are so cut off from the world, the student body seems more aware, even wise, than most.

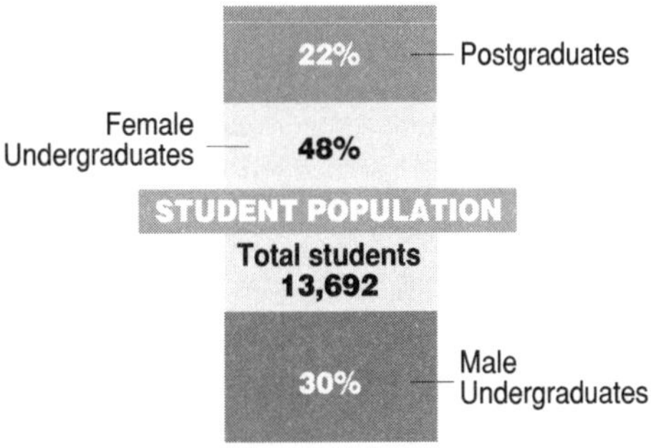

CAMPUS

UEA campus is 15 minutes by road from the centre of Norwich, a city less than fifteen miles away from the Norfolk Broads, an area of outstanding beauty and tranquillity. The campus, built on a 320-acre, sometime golf course, has won awards for its architecture – Denys Lasdun's ziggurats (glass-fronted buildings, tiered upwards like garden terraces after the ancient tiered mounds of Babylonia) continue to amaze, but, as student Daniel Trelfer declares, self-containment isn't to everyone's taste: 'Everything you need is on campus, but while some people are happy to live for twelve weeks inside a square quarter mile, others go insane and have to run to town to feel free again.'

FEES, BURSARIES

UK & EU Fees: £3000 p.a. Bursary of up to £540 for students in receipt of maximum State award of £2700; and on sliding scale down, if in receipt of partial grant. Also £500 scholarships for students entering with 3 A grades (or, if in receipt of state

UNIVERSITY/STUDENT PROFILE	
University since	**1964**
Situation/style	**Edge of city campus**
Student population	**13692**
Undergraduates	**10689**
- mature	**39%**
- non EU undergraduates	**5%**
- male/female	**40/60**
- non-traditional student intake	**21%**
- state school intake	**88%**
- drop-out rate	**7%**
- undergraduate applications	**Constant**

bursary, with ABB). There are also up to 12 £1000 Faculty Awards and up to eight £4000 Vice-Chancellor's Awards, both for outstanding merit.

STUDENT PROFILE

UEA has a well-balanced student population for a pukka uni, with close on 90% from state schools and a 21% take from non-traditional uni backgrounds. There is a large mature intake (39%) and a preponderance of females (60%, owing to the nursing degrees). The uni is constantly beset with criticisms about campus isolation and the dire effects of this upon its student clientele, but we see a pretty sharp focus on the business in hand, whether it's academic or extra-curricular, and a happy and fulfilled student body. Its drop-out rate of 7% is OK.

ACADEMIA & JOBS

UEA is made up of 23 academic departments known as Schools of Study, these are grouped into the Faculties of Arts & Humanities, Social Sciences, Science and the Institute of Health. New courses introduced this year include a BA Social Work, an academic and professional qualification that will enable graduates to become registered social workers.

Work-wise there are a few question marks. It's difficult for unis that specialise in humanities and languages to find the ideal job quickly for their graduates. Graduates have to start somewhere, and many who start as clerks no doubt find success in the end, but it has to be said that UEA does turn out a lot of them – not far off a fifth of their graduates launch themselves upon the world as clerks.

What are clerks and where do they come from? There are legal clerks, sales clerks, accounts clerks, admin clerks. But when we look at UEA, clerkdom might begin to look suspiciously like a hole in the ground for graduates who have not been looking where they're going, or that some of the areas of study don't translate so easily into jobs.

However, a recent survey of UEA's graduates showed that after 3 years (as opposed to 6 months), 81% had not experienced unemployment and 78% were in full-time employment, which must say something.

In point of fact, UEA looks after its humanities graduates well with jobs such as charity officer, museum archivist/curator, and there is a clear, if relatively limited, vocational springboard for Languages graduates via their BA Interpreting & Translating with Double Hons Languages – a 4-year degree. Also, the spread of graduate interest in the publishing industry is wide – it's a regular UEA niche, and a preponderance of those who get into the industry do come from the Languages dept.

ACADEMIC EXCELLENCE	
TEACHING: *(Rated Excellent or 17+ out of 24)*	
Law, Applied Social Work, Environmental Sciences, Developmental Studies.	**Excellent**
Politics, American Studies Philosophy	**24**
Economics, Media Studies Maths, Business, Subjects Allied to Medicine	**23**
History of Art, Architecture & Design, Molecular Biosciences, Organismal Biosciences	**22**
Drama, Dance & Cinematics	**21**
Sociology	**20**
Modern Langs & Linguistics, Electric & Electronic Engineering	**19**
Nursing	**18**
RESEARCH: *Top grades 5/5*/6**	
Environmental Sciences, Media Studies	**Grade 6***
History	**Grade 5***
Biol. Sciences, Chemistry, Pure Maths, Law, Social Work, English, History of Art, Philosophy	**Grade 5**

Of 36 graduate authors that emerged nationally, 28% came from Language departments, while 35% studied in Creative Arts or Humanities departments. UEA enjoys particular success in the literary firmament. There are twice-yearly literary festivals, a writer in residence, and it is here that Sir Malcolm Bradbury set the literary firmament alight with his creative writing school, out of which came Ian McEwan and Kazuo Ishiguro, among others.

Look at English or American Literature with Creative Writing (also Scriptwriting & Performance). There is also a fine reputation for the 4-year American Studies, which scored full marks in the assessments. Campus is home to the Arthur Miller Centre for American Studies.

Employment figures are given a fillip by the health provision, particularly Physiotherapy. Some 4% of UEA graduates become physiotherapists, the BSc degree rightly directing our attention to an expanding aspect in UEA's curriculum – see Midwifery, Nursing (Adult, Children, Learning Disability, Mental Health), Occupational Therapy, and the new programme in Medicine.

Theory and practice is integrated throughout in the 5-year MB BS, and clinical experience is yours from the outset, thanks to extensive collaboration with close-to-campus Norfolk & Norwich University Hospital. Entry AAB, including Grade A in Biology. 5 A/Bs in GCSE including Maths and English. Entry from 'approved access courses' is also encouraged, so consult the university.

UEA is also, as it happens, home to the Wellcome Unit for the History of Medicine.

Community youth workers and social workers also come out of this uni in abundance, and UEA are world leaders in research in this area. Naturally they come through social studies (and will come from the new Social Work degree), but also via languages and biological sciences; BSc Psychosocial Studies looks interesting.

They are European and American law specialists. All candidates must sit the National Admissions Test for Law (LNAT).

Key to the uni's identity is its concern for the environment. They are among the top suppliers of graduates to this sector. The feed is mainly through physical sciences. There's a sheaf of Ecology and Environmental Sciences BSc degrees, with options for European and North American experience (the same for Geophysical Sciences). There's also a BA and a BSc Development Studies (one with Overseas Experience). There was an 'Excellent' at the assessments and a world-class Grade 6* for research. The climatic research unit is a world authority, and the uni is home to the Tyndall Centre for Climate Change Research. For undergraduates, UEA marries Meteorology to Maths and Oceanography and offers a honeymoon in North America, Europe or ...industry. The Jackson Institute, with the largest environmental research programme in the UK, has also set up here, and there's a new Institute for Connective Environmental Research – an attempt to bring together science, industry, politics, business to make real steps forward in the area of environmentalism.

UEA is a top uni with an independent streak and a host of interesting specialisms. Self-containment on the old golf course is choice for some, others feel driven to to run to town to feel free again.

Eleven per cent of graduates go into finance, more than 6% into accounts and accountancy. BSc Accounting is available with Finance, Law and Management. Economics and Business both scored 23 out of 24 at the assessments.

Computing is another big area for jobs: graduate IT consultants, software engineers and systems analysts abound. There's a year in North

SUBJECT AREAS (%)

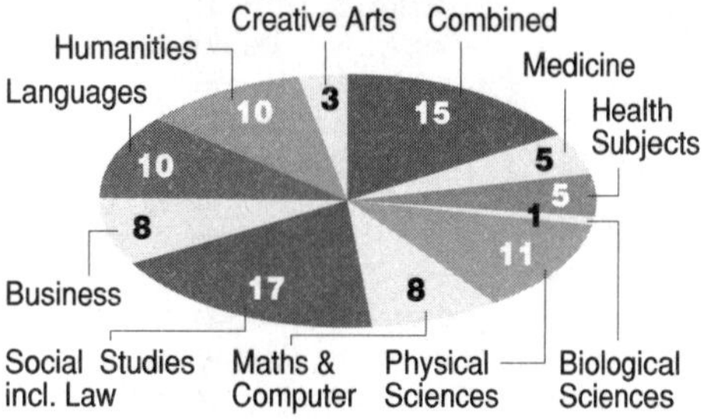

WHERE EAST ANGLIA GRADUATES END UP

Health & Social Work: 13%; Education: 7%; Wholesale/Retail: 10%; Manufacturing: 8%; Financial Activities: 11%; Public Administration, Civil Service & Defence: 8%; Hotel/Restaurant: 4%; Transport & Communications (including Telecommunications): 2%; Construction: 1%; Personnel: 9%; Computer: 3%; Business & Management: 4%; Accountancy: 3%; Media (including Film): 3%; Legal 3%; Architecture: 2%; Publishing: 4%; Advertising: 1%; Artistic/Literary: 1%.

Approximate 'graduate track' employed **54%**

WHAT IT'S REALLY LIKE

UNIVERSITY:	
Social Life	★★★★★
Campus scene	**Lively**
Student Union services	**Good**
Politics	**Active**
Sport	**48 clubs, but not obsessional**
National team position	**56th**
Sport facilities	**Good**
Arts opportunities	**Excellent**
Student magazine	**The Event**
Student newspaper	**Concrete**
Student radio	**Livewire**
Student Radio Awards	**2 noms 2005**
Student TV	**Nexus**
Student TV Awards	**2 wins 2005**
Nightclub	**The Waterfront**
Bars	**LCR, The Pub,**
Union ents	**Massive. Good live rock**
Union clubs/societies	**96**
Most popular society	**Livewire**
Parking	**Poor**
CITY:	
Entertainment	★★★
Scene	**OK pubs, clubs**
Town/gown relations	**Average**
Risk of violence	**Low**
Cost of living	**Average**
Student concessions	**Abundant**
Survival + 2 nights out	**£70 pw**
Part-time work campus/town	**Good/excellent**

AT A GLANCE

ACADEMIC FILE:	
Assessments	**24**
Excellent	**83%**
Typical entry requirements	**350 points**
Application acceptance rate	**18%**
Students-staff ratio	**16:1**
First/2:1 degree pass rate	**66%**
ACCOMMODATION FILE:	
Guarantee to freshers	**100% if from 12 miles away**
Style	**Houses, flats**
Catered	**None**
En-suite	**60-70%**
Price range pw	**£50-£82**
City rent pw	**£45-£52**

America with BSc Computing Science and Computer Systems Engineering.

SOCIAL SCENE

STUDENTS' UNION The SU is active on the Internet as a meeting place for websites from unions throughout the country (see www.stu.uea.ac.uk /info.uksu.html). They also have a lively reputation for journalism – their TV station is Nexus TV, their radio station, Livewire. *Concrete* is the newspaper, which incorporates *The Event* entertainment magazine and often wins national awards. Livewire was nominated twice in 2005 and Nexus won twice in its national award category. There is a track record for graduate careers in radio/TV and publishing, and top ratings for teaching and research in media/communications.

They boast around 100 societies and sports clubs. It is a highly developed student culture and has to be because campus is so cut off. Politics is a particularly interestng scene. Very active LibDem, Green Party and Anarchist societies. The three-weekly Union Council meeting is an active and passionate event. Current issues include ID cards, and at the top of the agenda are environmental and ethical issues. There's a Union boycott of Nestlé and student pressure on the uni authorities to become more environmentally friendly.

Gays get a good deal: LBG is among the most active societies, along with *Concrete* and Livewire. **The Studio** is the UEA theatre; drama is another top-scoring course rating. The union also has a reputation for being the biggest ents performer around, but it is a sad fact that for the past 4 years there has been no Freshers Week.

LCR (Lower Common Room) has been voted the best student venue in the country by the music industry's *Live!* magazine. Each year more than 50 live bands grace its stage; gigs are sold out months in advance. Travis, Supergrass, Athlete, Bloc Party, Magic Numbers, KT Tunstall, Mylo, Blondie, Motorhead, Goldfrapp and Zane Lowe are all part of the legend. Classic student nights like *Skool Daze* and *Club Retro* are also highly popular, as are comedy, poetry and an eclectic list of live acts.

Union Bars feature **The Pub** – all-day opening, pool tables, table footie, arcade machines, jukebox and large screen TV. A quieter, non-smoking alternative is **The Back Bar** – music-free and comfortable. Then there's the **Lunchbox** and **The Hive**, daytime coffee bar and late licence on Tuesdays and Thursdays for private parties. *Live in the Hive* includes (free) local bands, as well as karaoke, quizzes, games and comedy shows.

Besides the **LCR,** the uni has its own venue in Norwich – **The Waterfront**. There are three bars and two rooms of music. Every last Friday of the month it's *Rock Club* – bands and rock DJs. Otherwise it's live gigs and clubnights, like

Meltdown (indie, pop, rock & alternative), *Roobarb* (hard dance all-nighter), *Bounce* (drum 'n' bass).

Sport Good, though not top notch (halfway up/down the national team table); good facilities. The purpose-built Sportspark continues to attract students to UEA – a £17.6-million, integrated indoor and outdoor facility, including an Olympic-size swimming pool and a human performance laboratory opened recently. Women's hockey is very strong. Other big deals are football, tennis, trampolining, rugby, athletics, kerfball and American footie.

Town Apparently, Norwich has a pub for every day of the year. It also has the **Theatre Royal** (touring companies, RSC, National), **The Maddermarket**, a smaller, amateur but vibrant venue. The bohemian **King of Hearts** rules for music, art, jazz, literature readings, and **The Norwich Arts Centre** for live music, from rock and jazz to chamber music, exhibitions, dance workshops and comedy – David Baddiel, Frank Skinner, Lee & Herring and The Fast Show's Simon Day all played here. There are three cinemas – the **ABC** and the **Odeon** (in the heart of the excellent Magdalen Street curry scene – and **Cinema City** for arthouse.

PILLOW TALK

All first years who normally live outside a 12-mile radius of UEA are guaranteed study bedrooms in halls and flats, provided they meet a given deadline. The 1960s, 'architecturally unique ziggurats' of Norfolk Terrace and Suffolk Walk (families only) are next on the list for refurbishment. All accommodation is self-catering, Waveney Terraces, Orwell Close and Wolfson Close in groups of up to 15 study-bedrooms; Nelson Court and Constable Terrace are 'the closest thing to the Ritz', expensive and have architect-designed, en-suite rooms in slightly smaller groups. Since 1994 accommodation has also been offered in a student village across the road from the main uni entrance: 10 buildings with apartments for 6 to 8 students. If campus gets too much, you can opt for 5-person Mary Chapman Court flats beside the river in town.

GETTING THERE

☛ By road: A11(M), A47.
☛ By rail: London Liverpool Street, 2:00; Birmingham New Street, 4:00; Sheffield, 3:50.
☛ By air: Norwich Airport.
☛ By coach: London, 2:50; Birmingham, 6:00; Sheffield, 7:00.

UNIVERSITY OF EAST LONDON

The University of East London
Romford Road
London E15 4LZ

TEL 020 8223 3333
FAX 020 8590 7799
Email admiss@uel.ac.uk
WEB www.uel.ac.uk

UEL Students' Union
Block C
Longbridge Road
Dagenham RM8 2AS

TEL 020 8223 2420
FAX 020 8597 6987
EMAIL uelsu@hotmail.com
WEB www.uelsu.net

VAG VIEW

In UEL we have the former East London Poly. Its stated mission is 'to provide the highest possible quality of education in order to meet' – not the needs of the country or Europe or the world, but – 'the needs of individuals and of the communities and enterprises in our region.' The mission is no less ambitious for its narrower geographical focus, for in many ways UEL has its doors more widely open to the real world than most of its competitors, what with its high intake from beleaguered areas, its Refugee Bursaries, its low entry requirements

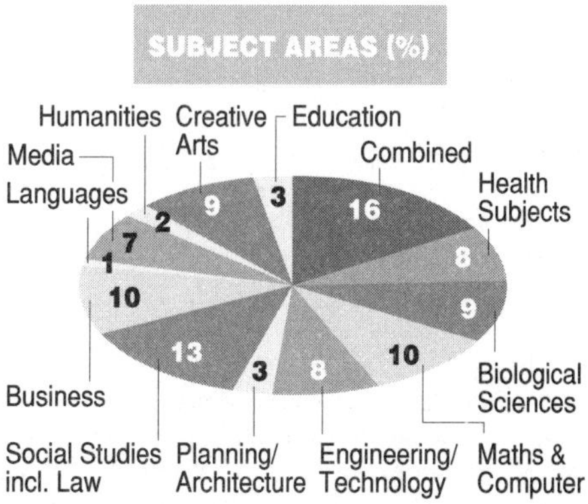

UNIVERSITY/STUDENT PROFILE	
University since	**1992**
Situation/style	**City sites**
Student population	**18200**
Undergraduates	**12500**
- mature	**66%, v. high**
- non EU undergraduates	**21%, v. high**
- male/female	**44/56**
- non-traditional student intake	**42%, high**
- state school intake	**97%**
drop-out rate	**13%**
- undergraduate applications	**Up 4%**

and determination to hang on to its students for the full term and equip them for a world that many off to Bristol and Durham can barely imagine.

Following a full-scale institutional audit by the Quality Assurance Agency in 2005, UEL was praised for its culture of equality and diversity, its equitable approach and support for its part-time staff and students, the effectiveness of its staff development, and the integration into the curriculum of skills development for students, particularly through the Skillzone, UEL's skills, pre-entry advice and guidance service.

Clearly they are doing something right. There is confidence aplenty, as they prepare to move out of the old Barking campus and concentrate their efforts on Docklands and Stratford.

They are embarked on a £110 million programme of expansion and renewal, to provide new facilities to come on stream in summer 2006.

CAMPUSES

Docklands Campus 4-6 University Way, London E16 2RD. Tel 020 8223 3000. Located on the waterfront of the Royal Albert Dock and opened in 2000, it is now expanding to serve 7000 students focused on the new economy, cultural and creative industries. The new Architecture and Visual Arts facility was completed in 2003, and a new Business School and Enterprise Centre will be in place this year. Two new buildings on the waterfront of Royal Albert Dock will house the Business School, Centre for Entrepreneurship, School of Computing and Technology, Learning Resource Centre and Knowledge Dock. The Business School includes a 650-seat trading floor, and a 400-seat lecture theatre. The design features a dynamic curved roof which forms a wing-shaped protective canopy and a winter garden overlooking the dock and London skyline. There's a restaurant, bar and cafés, and a Student Union development under construction. Also accommodation of course; see *Pillow Talk*.

Stratford Campus Romford Road, London E15 4LZ. Tel 020 8223 3000. A similar transformation is underway at Stratford campus, the historic heart of UEL and a centre for health, psychology, biosciences, law, and management in business and the public sector. With the completion of the **Great Hall** lecture theatre and **Café on the Green**, work is underway on a new Centre for Podiatry and Physiotherapy to provide clinical training facilities as part of UEL's expanding School of Health and Bioscience. Other facilities include **Fitness on the Green** (fitness and training centre), restaurant and **Students' Union Bar** (Maryland House). Again, for accommodation, see Pillow Talk.

FEES, BURSARIES

UK & EU Fees: £3000. Bursary for students in receipt of full HE Maintenance grant: £300. There are 200 Achievement scholarships of £1000 each to first-year students for sport, creativity or citizenship, and 50 refugee bursaries. UEL Progress bursaries of at least £500 go to all students who successfully complete their first semester.

STUDENT PROFILE

UEL have large ethnic and overseas populations, a very large mature student population (66%), and a

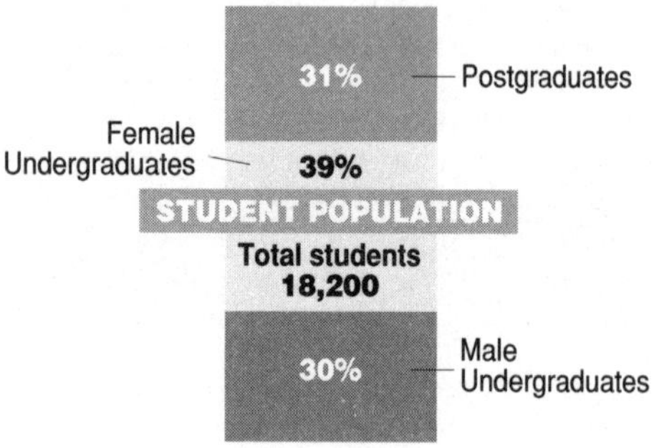

drop-out rate that they have battled to get under control and will conquer when they get their facilities together and teaching as good in every area as it is in some. There is a friendly, laid-back feel to the place. Students are getting on, and will do provided they're not bound fast by politically correct red tape.

WHERE EAST LONDON GRADUATES END UP

Health & Social Work: 23%; Education: 7%; Wholesale/Retail: 16%; Manufacturing: 7%; Financial Activities: 4%; Public Administration, Civil Service & Defence: 12%; Hotel/Restaurant: 2%; Transport & Communications (including Telecommunications): 3%; Construction: 2%; Personnel: 3%; Computer: 2%; Business & Management: 3%; Accountancy: 1%; Media (including Film): 2%; Legal 4%; Architecture: 2%; Publishing: 2%; Artistic/Literary: 1%; Sport: 3%.

Approximate 'graduate track' employed **53%**

ACADEMIA & JOBS

The uni's Skillzone is a learning support and employment service. They are good at raising money for this sort of thing; their mission is in line with Government policy; they are good at speaking the language of the times in which we live, and they know their way around the forms. In 2004, they successfully bid for a total of £15 million funding from the Office of the Deputy Prime Minister, the Higher Education Innovation Fund (HEIF), London Development Agency and European Regional Development Fund to develop 'the new Knowledge Dock Centre (KDC - everything must have initials), to be completed in spring 2006. The Knowledge Dock, formerly the Thames Gateway Technology Centre, now works with over 2,000 companies and entrepreneurs across the region. It provides a range of business services, training, consultancy, and funded programmes including the DTI flagship Knowledge Transfer Partnerships and the Shell Technology Enterprise Programme (STEP), for which it was named best new agency.'

UEL invests among the highest per student for library and learning resources. It is also a leader in disability and dyslexia support. Facilities include a regional ACCESS centre offering dyslexia screening and tutoring, technology training, exam support and an RNIB Resource Centre for blind and visually impaired students on Physiotherapy programmes.

At UEL, look for degrees in health, psychology, culture, social studies, art, computer and sport, and you will find jobs. In these areas, the uni fulfils its mission to meet 'the needs of individuals and of the communities and enterprises in our region.'

Over 7% of graduates finding employment out of East London Uni do so as social workers, probation officers or community youth workers, and this year there's a new degree in Youth Work. Single honours degrees offer such as Psychosocial Studies, Social Policy, Social Work Studies, Social Work, Third World Development, etc. This year there's a new BA (Hons) Youth and Community Work. Consider the ground carefully, for this is mainstream UEL territory. Their psychologists deal with real issues of the community in which they live and work. UEL's School of Psychology is rated excellent (23/24) for teaching and is now one of the leading schools in Britain for undergraduate and professional diploma programmes. They run a range of postgraduate programmes in partnership with RELATE, the Psychosynthesis and Education Trust, and the Tavistock Clinic, the UK's leading centre for post-graduate training in mental health.

Physiotherapy is a major career field for UEL – some 13% of its graduates become physiotherapists, and they boast a 100% employment record (as they do in teacher training). The route is straightforward – BSc Physiotherapy provides the single most popular route out of UEL into a job and the lowest entry requirement available anywhere. It is, however, available to mature students only. Teaching Inspection 20. See also the new BSc Podiatric Medicine.

There's also strength in sport academically – coaching, exercise science, etc – and new sports science laboratories, which shows up in the employment figures. Some 3% of graduates from UEL become sports trainers or coaches.

ACADEMIC EXCELLENCE

TEACHING:
(Rated Excellent or 17+ out of 24)

Architecture, English	**Excellent**
Psychology	**23**
Art & Design, Civil Eng,	**21**
Economics, Subjects Allied to Medicine	**20**
Sociology, Pharmacology, Education, Biosciences	**19**
Linguistics & Modern Languages, Mechanical, Manufacturing Eng.	**18**

RESEARCH:
*Top grades 5/5**

Communication/Cultural/Media	**Grade 5**

WHAT IT'S REALLY LIKE	
UNIVERSITY:	
Social Life	★★★★
Campus scene	**Authentic, urban culture**
Student Union services	**Average**
Politics	**Anti-racism & free education**
Sport	**Relaxed/20 teams**
National team position	**None**
Sport facilities	**Average**
Arts opportunities	**Some**
Student mag/news	**FUEL**
Student radio	**Hubbub**
Nightclub/Bars	**Duel 1, 2 and 3 - each campus**
Union ents	**Reggae, Smooth Grooves, Club Commercial, Frolic, Melting Pot**
Union clubs/societies	**40**
Most popular society	**Islamic**
Smoking policy	**NS except bars**
Parking	**Poor**
CITY:	
Entertainment	★★★★★
Scene	**Local clubs 'n uptown flavours**
Town/gown relations	**Poor**
Risk of violence	**Random**
Cost of living	**High**
Student concessions	**OK**
Survival + 2 nights out	**£60 pw**
Part-time work campus/town	**Good, must travel**

Also, respect their media degrees. They have a research grade which marks their work out as of national significance. Grade 5 does not come easy.

Computer technology is also strong, with IT consultants, computer operators and software engineers making a good show from degrees that include Computer Games Technology, Internet Technologies, Computer Networks with E-Commerce, etc.

Finally, graphic artists and designers and clothing designers proliferate from Fashion Design degrees, some with Marketing, Fine Art (sculpting has been a particular success) and Graphic Design. In 2003, they brought together the Schools of Architecture and Art and Design to form the School of Architecture and the Visual Arts, located in a new 6,000 sq m purpose-designed studio building at Docklands. UEL is rated Excellent for the teaching of architecture, and there's a strong pathway into the profession. They were one of a few Schools to be awarded unconditional validation by the Royal Institute of British Architects (RIBA) and the Architects Registration Board (ARB) in 2003.

SOCIAL SCENE

Political awareness is the most notable aspect at student level, and a culturally rich ents programme, including dedicated and *Mixed Flavour* discos – indie, soul, swing, '70s/'80s, jungle, hip hop, ragga – comedy nights, cabaret, live bands, video nights and the odd society 'do' (including plays on the **Venue** stage). One-offs include Spring Ball, Valentine Bash, Diwali Rave, Hallowe'en Night, Christmas Rave.

A lot of bar activity/events are laid on by students through cultural societies. Recently, there's been an attempt to simplify the basics by calling the bars at the three campuses **DUEL 1**, **DUEL 2**, **DUEL 3**, but now Barking is about to go, and there are new facilities in the offing at both Docklands and Stratford, which we must wait to see.

About thirty societies are up and running. Hard to tell which is the most active, but the Islamic society generally has the largest membership.

Student media includes a magazine, *Fuel*, and radio station (new venture), Hubbub. Natch, *Fuel* won the Commission for Racial Equality award for best student publication dealing with issues of race.

In the political arena, they are one of a handful of universities capable of organising a decent sit-in, getting together with Goldsmiths to do a *Rough Guide to Occupation*. Currently, they describe the level of activity as 'average, meaning less people compensate with great awareness and enthusiasm!'

Sport Relaxed attitude, twenty teams, not nationally competitive. Teams make use mainly of council pitches and halls that offer student discounts. A swimming pool is used for water polo, sub-aqua and canoeing; there are two gyms, facilities for aerobics, dance, badminton, table tennis, karate, circuit training, volleyball, basketball, indoor football, a squash court, four tennis courts, a fitness centre. Playing fields are a few miles away, at Little Heath. Badminton is available near the Stratford campus and there are other recreational activities on offer – golf, sailing, windsurfing, skiing, sub-aqua, riding, and weekend and vacation courses are arranged.

With the Olympics setting up stall around the corner, it's a good bet sport is going to be a major focus in the future, and they agree that there are plans to develop sports coaching, working with local authority partners to deliver sports programmes for young people, facilities and event management training, engaging and empowering local communities through voluntary action, disability sport in partnership with the National Paralympic Association, and support for elite performers at their new sports science laboratories.

Town 'Well it's London, so all bets are off,' said my informant. 'Cost of living is high, general things (food etc) are fairly priced compared to other places. It's the social side of things that costs so much. Start saving now. Risk of violence is, surprisingly random. Arguably, people would say London is prone to greater violence. But really it's all quite random. You'll need about £60 to live on if you want to go out at least two nights. Chance of employment is high. Both within the Students' Union and wider a-field.' See *London Student City*, page 292.

PILLOW TALK
Allocation priority is given to students with special needs, and then to students entering their first year at the university from outside the local area. A number of rooms are reserved for applicants whose normal place of residence is outside the UK. What can you expect? At Stratford, university house or flat-share at landscaped Park Village nearby. New accomm. at Cedars Road for this year. At Docklands, self-catering study-bedrooms and flats. A new 800-room student residence is under construction on the waterfront of the Royal Albert Dock. Featuring attractive courtyards and south-facing gardens, they'll open in 2007.

AT A GLANCE

ACADEMIC FILE:	
Subjects assessed	**23**
Excellent	**61%**
Typical entry requirements	**180 points**
Application acceptance rate	**26%, high**
Students-staff ratio	**21:1**
First/2:1 degree pass rate	**42%**
ACCOMMODATION FILE:	
Guarantee to freshers	**Generally all 1st years**
Style	**Halls**
Catering	**None**
En suite	**None**
Approx price range pw	**£76-£86**
City rent pw	**£65-£100**

GETTING THERE
☛ **Stratford** by Underground, Central Line; closest overland rail station is Maryland (connect London Liverpool Street).
☛ **Barking** by Underground, City & Hammersmith and District lines; Goodmayes overland station.
☛ **Docklands** via the Docklands Light Railway.

STUDENT EDINBURGH - THE CITY

Edinburgh has a worldwide reputation for being one of the most interesting and exciting places to live and study. It is a city of contradictions. On the one hand it is an ancient city, with dramatic architecture and a rich cultural history. On the other hand it is a cosmopolitan capital and a critical financial and political centre. It is also a 24-hour city with an eclectic range of bars and clubs to suit any taste. Edinburgh, with consummate ease, combines ancient with modern, and work with play, making it one of the most vibrant and exciting cities in Europe.

CITY SCAPE
Edinburgh is centred round the beautiful castle that heads up the tourist filled Royal Mile complete with ancient cobbled streets and historical landmarks aplenty. The city is compact making it easy to get around simply by walking, although if you do get tired feet, the extensive bus network is ready and waiting. The town is essentially split into two with the ancient splendour of Old town, which houses the University, and the Georgian New Town separated by the stunning Princes Street gardens. Pay a visit in the festive season and you will find an outdoor ice rink and huge Christmas market. This is also the site of the famed Edinburgh Hogmanay party that leads the world in celebrating the New Year.

COFFEE CULTURE
Edinburgh is typified by its coffee culture. You are never more than 5 minutes away from a good coffee and a comfy seat. Many of the best can be found around George Square, conveniently close to Edinburgh's central campus. **Assembly** and **Negociants** on Teviot place provide good lunches and tasty cocktails. The **Human Be-In** offers chic upmarket surroundings whilst the American style diner, **Favorit**, offers good food at good prices until early in the morning. **Bean Scene** on South Clerk Street offers a comfy haven away from the hustle and bustle. It also boasts its own record label of up and coming talent, and regular live performances

from its artists. For those who are star struck, the **Elephant House** is famed as J.K.Rowling's favourite coffee spot. It is where she wrote some of *Harry Potter*. It, and its smaller cousin, **Elephant and Bagels**, offer excellent food and friendly original decor. Those of you with a serious addiction to chocolate won't be disappointed with the range available in Edinburgh. **Plaisir du Chocolat** on the Royal Mile offers the best hot chocolate money can buy, but it will cost you a small fortune. **Chocolate Soup** in Hanover Square offers fabulous hot chocolates in a huge variety of flavours, served in the biggest cups known to man.

SILVER SCREEN

The city excels in cinemas. At the **Cameo** in Tollcross there's thematic music before the credits roll and the pleasure of enjoying a pint in its enticingly comfortable seats. **The Cameo** features a range of unusual films that you won't find at the big chain cinemas. It isn't arthouse cinema, but it is a break from the one-dimensional Hollywood blockbusters. **The Filmhouse** serves the more arty audience, excelling at foreign films. For Hollywood, head to the **UGC Multiplex** at Fountainpark or **Vue** cinema at the top of Leith Walk.

The city also holds an annual International Film Festival in August. The uni's Film Society offers membership at a bargain price of £15 and gets you entry to a massive range of great films throughout the academic year.

SPOTLIGHTS

Due mainly to the Edinburgh festival, the city has an excess of theatres. **The Playhouse** at the top of Leith Walk hosts all the major touring musicals. There are often generous student discounts. **The Lyceum** offers Shakespeare or post-modern avant-garde. The world famous **Traverse**, nestling nearby amongst high-class eateries, dishes up excellent experimental Scottish drama as well as having one of the hippest bars in Edinburgh. If you're into more mainstream theatre or opera, head to the **King's Theatre** or **Festival Theatre**. Then there's the only student-run pro theatre in the UK, **Bedlam** on Bristo Place. Regular favourites are the Improverts, who run a 'whose line it is anyway' style show, and perform every Friday in term time.

Edinburgh is also steeped in comedy grandeur due to the famed festival, but the laughs don't stop there: comedy continues all year round. Edinburgh University Students' Association hold one of the most famous venues, the **Pleasance**, which plays hosts to the Comedy Network every fortnight. Everyone, from Harry Hill to Frank Skinner, has played here on their way to fame. So, there is plenty of, 'I saw them before they were famous' boasting potential. **The Stand**, in York Place, is the city's only purpose-built comedy venue. It serves up good food and a great ambience in a cosy basement. **Jongleurs** comedy club in the **Omni Centre** is another venue. Although the comedy is average, there are usually good deals on the door.

RETAIL RELIEF

If you fancy some retail therapy, head down to Princes Street, which houses nearly all the major high street brands. If you fancy really splashing out, then George Street has all the fine boutiques, stuffed with luxury goods aplenty.

If retro is the requirement, **Armstrongs** and **The Rusty Zip** deliver the goods, while **Flip** on South Bridge is good for flares, cords and comedy seventies gear. For the ultimate in budget retailing, check out the numerous charity shops on Nicholson Street. Skaterkids are well-serviced in Edinburgh, with both **Cult Clothing** and **Odd One Out** especially popular with the baggy-trousered contingent.

For music, head to Cockburn Street, home to the capital's Number 1 music shops, **Fopp** and **Avalanche**, both of which are infinitely better value than their mainstream Princes Street rivals.

Edinburgh has the largest collection of second-hand book stores in the world. So, for all you book worms, there are plenty of places to spend your days. **Till's** on Buccleuch Street, **Armchair Books** at West Port, **McFeely's** on Buccleuch Street and **MacNaughtons** at Gayfield Place are but a few of the delights in store for you.

PUB IT

Like so much of Edinburgh the key word is variety. Edinburgh's pubs and bars have the benefit of staying open until 1am every night. If a pint in a traditional pub is your aim, head to the **Blind Poet** or the **Pear Tree**. The latter boasts an impressive beer garden and many a late night can be spent clutching a pint in the cold Scottish air. If you are looking for a cheap pint then try one of the Scream pubs such as the **Tron** or **The Crags**, conveniently located next to the main Student Union halls. If you are looking for something a little more fancy then head over to New Town and enjoy the delights of **Prive Council** or **Beluga** on Chambers Street. Both offer upmarket chic surroundings and not unreasonable prices. The Royal Mile offers a plethora of bars, but often more expensive. Head to the Cowgate where you will find a virtual tunnel of bars. Of particular note is **Bannermans**, which holds live music nights for unsigned bands nearly every night of the week.

IN THE CLUB

Edinburgh has more clubs per head than anywhere else in Britain – fact. This means that you have a massive choice of venues and a huge variety of styles to choose from. For those looking for a traditional chart club night out then **City**, with its excellent lighting and sound, **Faith**, with its impressive décor and **Why Not?**, with its clean crisp image are all favourites. For the more chic amongst you, head to **Opal Lounge** or **Po Na Na** for stylish surroundings and swanky drinks. Beware the price tag that comes with the venue! Goth and Rock are catered for by **Opium** on the Cowgate and **Citrus** on Lothian Road. **Honeycomb** puts on an awesome funk night on Tuesdays, and the unique design of the club, with its literal honeycomb structure, is worth seeing anyway. **Bongo Club** offers the best hip hop and reggae in town. **Liquid Rooms** offers an excellent venue and a huge variety of nights, although it can be pricey. **Ego** on Picardy Place offers nights tailor made for gay clubbers, especially Tuesdays. With two floors of music, dirt cheap drink, and a young crowd this is an excellent night out. **CC Blooms** is the only permanent Gay Club with **Planet Out** and **Habana** providing the best of the bar scene.

Venues chop and change their nights each week, so for complete up-to-date listings pick up a copy of *The List*.

Iain Walters

UNIVERSITY OF EDINBURGH

The University of Edinburgh
57 George Square
Edinburgh EH8 9JU

TEL 0131 650 4360
FAX 0131 651 1236
EMAIL enquiries.scls@ed.ac.uk
WEB www.ed.ac.uk

Edinburgh University Student Association
Student Centre House
5/2 Bristo Square
Edinburgh EH8 9AL

TEL 0131 650 2656
FAX 0131 668 4177
EMAIL president@eusa.ed.ac.uk
WEB www.eusa.ed.ac.uk

VAG VIEW

If you are looking at the employers' surveys or parents' perceptions, it's Oxbridge then Durham and Bristol, and Edinburgh is the Scottish equivalent of these. Edinburgh, they know, is the place to be. An Edinburgh degree is a very good degree to have. It is still considered to be part of a Scottish person's birthright. They do not admit to offering a Scottish quota.

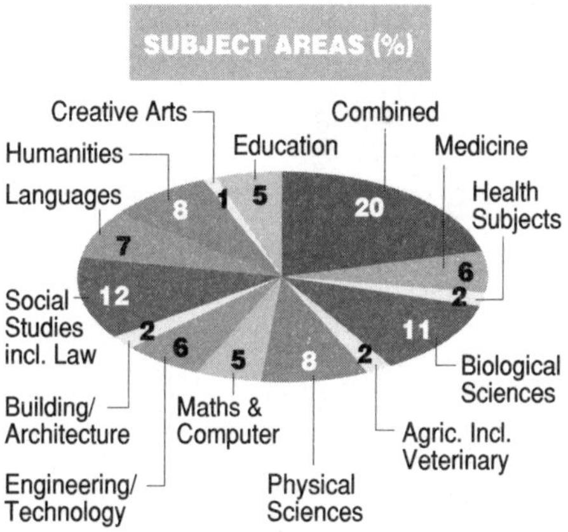

CAMPUS

'The University is primarily divided into two main campuses, two miles apart,' writes James Lumsden. 'George Square (with its central city location) for Arts & Social Science, and KB (King's Buildings) for Science and Engineering. Recently, the university has spent wads of cash reinventing KB into somewhere that you no longer want to leave before you arrive. The result reminds some of a cross-channel ferry. George Square, meanwhile, has its own brand of ugliness, in the shape of Appleton and David Hume towers. For a beautiful city that's known as the "Athens of the North", Edinburgh University seems to have done its damnedest to flout convention.'

FEES, BURSARIES

Fees for English students: £1700 p.a. for all courses at Scottish universities, except Medicine, for which you will be charged £2700 p.a. See www.ed.ac.uk for bursaries and scholarships.

STUDENT PROFILE

'Often represented by a myopic media as a toffs' university,' James continues, 'the true diversity of student and university life at Edinburgh goes

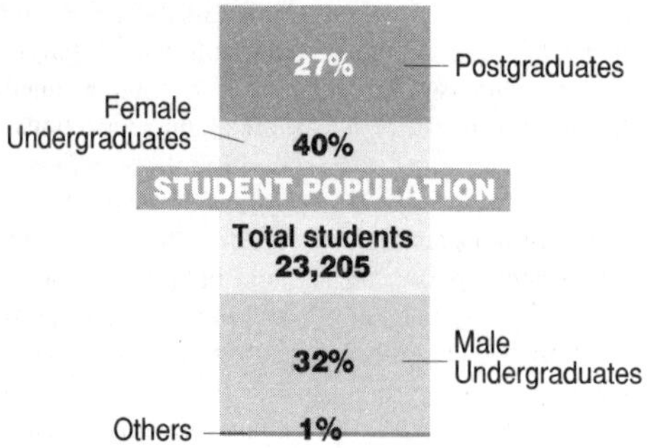

misrepresented; there are more than 20,000 students from a wide variety of backgrounds and circumstances.'

Nevertheless, the uni does have its share of rahs, and the public school girls come here in their droves. Even if the community is so huge that the young grandees are never really *IT*, we're looking at around 65% only from the state sector, and a very low take (15%) from non-traditional uni-goers.

There is a policy to target state school sixthformers interested in studying law or medicine; they're offering 75 bursaries worth £1000 per year of the degree programme; they are actively involved in LEAPS (the Lothian Equal Access Programme for Schools). Minimum grades for admission to Edinburgh are now 4 B passes at higher level or 3 at A level, but the admission procedure will take into account background and personal qualities.

UNIVERSITY/STUDENT PROFILE	
University since	**1583**
Situation/style	**Civic**
Student population	**23205**
Undergraduates	**16785**
- mature	**13%**
- non EU undergraduates	**6%**
- male/female	**44/56**
- non-traditional student intake	**15%, low**
- state school intake	**65%, v. low**
drop-out rate	**5%, low**
- undergraduate applications	**Up 13%**

ACADEMIA & JOBS

Overall, teaching assessments have been top of the range. There is an incredible 2,275,000-vol library, and excellent computer facilities and language laboratories, though there can be a problem in getting to use some of these resources. 'Queues for the Crisis Loans are lengthening ... study resources are being stretched to the limit,' said one student. One nice touch at Edinburgh is that students are assigned a Director of Studies, a guardian angel trained to guide you through your course.

Edinburgh responds to needs in a great number of graduate employment areas, but to none more strongly than in Health and Education. The degree in Medicine is the 5/6-year MB ChB. They promise 'early clinical contact' and deliver it in Year 1, together with case-based learning tutorials using problem-based learning methods. Entry AABa at A level, AAAAB at Highers. Grade B GCSE English Maths and a language other than English. It's highly competitive, however; there's only an 8% chance of acceptance; 11% is average. Teaching inspection, Highly Satisfactory. Research Grades 5*. Degrees in Podiatry are also popular and extremely efficient in terms of future employment.

Psychotherapists come in a steady stream into

ACADEMIC EXCELLENCE	
TEACHING:	
(Rated Excellent, Highly Satis. or 17+ out of 24)	
Computer Studies, Physics, Chemistry, Electrical & Electronic Engineering, Geology, Maths & Statistics, History, Finance & Accounting, Sociology, Social Work, Cellular & Molecular Biology, Organismal Biology, Veterinary Medicine.	**Excellent**
Business & Management, Civil Engineering,Music, Architecture, Geography, History of Art, Law, Philosophy, Politics, Theology, French Studies, Medicine, Nursing, English, Psychology.	**Highly Satis.**
Chemical Engineering	**19**
European Languages	**21**
RESEARCH:	
*Top grades 5/5**	
Hospital-based Clinical, Pure Maths, Computer, Electrical & Electronic Eng, Geography, Middle Eastern & African, English, German/Dutch/ Scandinavian, Philosophy	**Grade 5***
Psychology, Bio Sciences, Veterinary, Chemistry, Physics, Earth Sciences, Applied Maths, Civil Eng, Law, Anthropology, Sociology, Asian, Accounting, Celtic, French, Iberian/Latin American, Linguistics, History, Theology	**Grade 5**

the workplace from Edinburgh. There's a BSc and MA Psychology for ABB or ABBB (Highers). Teaching inspection again Highly Satisfactory. Research Grade 5. Interestingly, Languages seed jobs in social work, as at Oxford and Cambridge.

The veterinary provision actually scored better than medicine at the assessments. Edinburgh's 5-year BVM&S has a similar profile to Glasgow's degree. Entry AAB. Teaching inspection, Excellent. Research Grade 5.

The old Moray House Institute of Education is the uni's Faculty of Education. Founded in 1835, there are two campuses, Holyrood in the heart of the Old Town, adjacent to the university's central premises and, 6 miles away on the northwest edge of the city, a campus hitherto known as the Scottish Centre for Physical Education and home to PE, Leisure Studies and Applied Sports Science. The sporting facilities put Edinburgh in the Top 10 for sports trainers and coaches.

For primary or secondary teaching, they ask BCC-BBB: CC for Education Studies. They also provide lecturers for higher education: as at Leeds, it's the joint degrees that are favouring graduates in this area, and again Biological Sciences and Languages. Top-line in the research assessments; 21 points or Excellent in the teaching assessments.

> ***'There's a discernible buzz about the university, a condensed feeling of potential, and energy. This is partly due to the city itself: there's just enough of the "ivory tower" atmosphere to leave you inspired but not oppressed by your impending academia.'***

In the financial sector, Edinburgh accountants are in high demand, and their Economics graduates are main runners for jobs in banking. Their MA joint hons programmes draw in Chinese or Arabic with Economics, French or German with Business Studies, Law with either. The 4-year Business Studies & Economics looks the staple.

For merchant bankers Edinburgh is up there with Bristol and Oxford. There's a valuable range of BSc Ordinary and MA Hons combination degrees. Some 39% entered via a combined course, 28% through Business, 11% through Economics. There are also jobs galore for insurance and pension brokers/underwriters and business management consultants from Edinburgh. Teaching inspections – Finance, Excellent; Business, Highly Satisfactory.

Humanities graduates, and those studying the joint MA hons courses in particular, find work in the advertising, publicity and PR industries, and as archivists, curators, librarians, etc. Language students favour charity organisations and publishing in particular, though sciences, social sciences, law and humanities also provide here, and the extra-curricular student media will have a big effect. Masses of opportunity to hone your publishing skills on such as *Hype* (magazine) and *Student* (newspaper).

Two niche areas worth mentioning are forestry: BSc Ecological Science (Forestry), and BSc Physics with Meteorology.

SOCIAL SCENE

'I know everyone is supposed to fall in love with their university, but Edinburgh just makes it so easy,' writes Holly Crane without a hint of gush. 'It's the ideal advert for higher education: a place where you learn not only facts and formulae from your academic studies, but also about what you can do, what you want to do – and what you don't want to do – with the rest of your life.'

Holly is sensitive to 'a discernible buzz about the university, a condensed feeling of potential, and energy. This is partly due to the city itself: there's just enough of the "ivory tower" atmosphere to leave you inspired but not oppressed by your impending academia. But it's also to do with the type of students. With many doing four-year (or longer) degrees, there is, if not more time, then more reason, to get up off your arse and do something a bit different.'

WHERE EDINBURGH GRADUATES END UP

Health & Social Work: 18%; Education: 16%; Wholesale/Retail: 7%; Manufacturing: 6%; Financial Activities: 11%; Public Administration, Civil Service & Defence: 7%; Hotel/Restaurant: 4%; Transport & Communications (including Telecommunications): 2%; Construction: 1%; Agriculture: 1%; Mining/Oil Extracting: 1%; Personnel: 3%; Computer: 2%; Business & Management: 3%; Accountancy: 4%; Media (including Film): 2%; Legal 2%; Architecture: 2%; Publishing: 2%; Advertising: 1%; Artistic/Literary: 0.5%; Sport: 1%.

Approximate 'graduate track' employed **67%**

WHAT IT'S REALLY LIKE

UNIVERSITY:	
Social Life	★★★★★
Campus scene	**Diverse, active, self-assured**
Student Union services	**Good**
Politics	**Active**
Sport	**Key**
National team position	**9th**
Sport facilities	**Good**
Arts opportunities	**Good**
Student magazine	**Hype**
Student newspaper	**Student**
Journalism Awards	**1 nom, 1 award 2005**
Student radio	**Fresh Air FM**
Radio Awards	**Winner 2004; 1 nom 2005**
Nightclub	**Potterow**
Bars	**Sportsman's, Teviot, The Pleasance**
Union ents	**Cheese, comedy, Indie**
Union societies	**200**
Most popular societies	**Amnesty**
Parking	**Poor**
CITY:	
Entertainment	★★★★★
Scene	**Seething**
Town/gown relations	**Good**
Risk of violence	**Low**
Cost of living	**High**
Student concessions	**Excellent**
Survival + 2 nights out	**£150+ pw**
Part-time work campus/town	**Good/excellent**

There is opportunity aplenty to do just this – loads of clubs and societies, 200 of the latter alone, centred on **The Pleasance**, the most popular being Film Soc, The *Edinburgh Student* (newspaper, there's also a mag called *Hype* and a radio station, Fresh Air fm) and Nightline (welfare). *Edinburgh Student* is Britain's third biggest student newspaper, with a weekly circulation of 12,000 copies distributed to all the universities and higher education colleges around Edinburgh. It is also Britain's oldest student newspaper – Robert Louis Stevenson founded it in 1887. *Hype, Official Magazine of the Students' Association*, is the other student voice box.

Meanwhile the University Theatre Company draws crowds for its many productions at **Bedlam Theatre**, the site of Bristo Bedlam, where 'the mad, manic and mental' were once locked away. Now Bedlam's the UK's only student-run theatre, and every Friday in term time the Improverts do a 'Whose Line is it Anyway' style act here.

All these often win national awards, Fresh Air won Radio 1 Station of the Year award in 2004, and this year radio and magazine won national awards. Then of course there's the politics. Most active student society is Amnesty. All major political parties are represented, and level of union activity this term has been high, issues ranging from removing the honorary degree of Robert Mugabe to equality for all, from age discrimination to religious equality on campus.

For light relief Pleasance has a cabaret bar and 350-seat theatre which plays host to the best comedians from the Comedy Network.

Teviot Union, the oldest purpose-built Students' Union building in the country, has 5 levels of entertainment with 6 bars in operation, a debating hall, recently upgraded **Sportsman's Bar** with big screen and several other bars each with a different identity.

For night-time pleasure it's **The Potterow**, which has been redecorated this year, and decorations used during the Edinburgh festival retained. There's also an extra coffee bar in the Potterrow Dome. The venue has 1,200 capacity that regularly reaches capacity on weekends. Highlights include *Big Cheese* on a Saturday, the biggest student night in Edinburgh, and *Different Class* (best of Indie with guest DJs) every Thursday. Bodyrockers, Natasha Hamilton and Belle & Sebastian have all played Potterrow this Semester. Richard Herring, Dan Antopolski have all recently done comedy sets.

Down at King's Buildings, there's a £3.4 million student facility for the 7,000 science and engineering campus – catering and bar facilities, a

AT A GLANCE

ACADEMIC FILE:	
Subjects assessed	**32**
Excellent/Highly Satisfactory	**94%**
Typical entry requirements	**400 points**
Application acceptance rate	**13%, low**
Student-staff ratio	**14:1**
First/2:1 degree pass rate	**77%, high**
ACCOMMODATION FILE:	
Guarantee to freshers	**If non-local & accepted by September 1**
Style	**Halls, flats, houses**
Catered	**33%**
En-suite	**18%**
Price range pw	**£70-£140**
Approx. city rent pw	**£65-£85**

games room, squash courts, a multi-gym, a sports hall and advisory and welfare services. KB get quizzes, pool comps and film nights by way of ents.

Sport The university is pre-eminent in sport, came 9th in the UK last year. Besides its twenty-five acres of playing fields and a residential centre on the shore of Loch Tay, there's a sports centre with conditioning gymnasia, a fitness and sports injury centre, and a wide range of team and individual activities. Sports bursaries are offered through the PE Department.

Town 'When you do step out, the city offers everything,' writes James Lumsden. 'There are enough bars and pubs to see you from this life into the next, and plenty of theatres, cinemas, clubs, and 'cultural stuff' to stop at, en-route. See *Student Edinburgh* above.

PILLOW TALK

Freshers from outside Edinburgh are guaranteed a place in uni accommodation provided they apply by September 1, and that UCAS has guaranteed their place at Edinburgh by that date. There's a mix of traditional full board halls, student houses, and flats. Main accommodation for first years is Pollock Halls, a complex of houses, together with a bar, shop and dining rooms, which take around 2,000 first years. All rooms are single, but, if you pay extra, you can upgrade to a double bed and en-suite shower. Most people go for full board; breakfast and supper in the week and three meals at the weekend. However, each house has a kitchen area where you can test out your culinary talents (toast). Another residential area is Robertson's Close which consists of self-catering flats. There are also uni-run student houses.

GETTING THERE

☛ By road: M90 or M9 or A1 or M8.
☛ By rail: London King's Cross, 4:30; Glasgow Central, 50 mins; Newcastle, 1:30.
☛ By air: Edinburgh Airport.
☛ By coach: Glasgow, 1:10; London, 9:10; Birmingham, 8:10; Newcastle, 3:10.

EDINBURGH COLLEGE OF ART

Edinburgh College of Art
Lauriston Place
Edinburgh EH3 9DF

TEL 0131 221 6027
FAX 0131 221 6028
EMAIL registration@eca.ac.uk
WEB www.eca.ac.uk

The origins of this college lie in the Drawing Academy, founded by the Trustees of the Edinburgh Board of Manufacturers in 1760. From 1821 an Edinburgh School of Arts was established and thirty years later, as a tribute to the great Scottish engineer James Watt, it changed its title to the Watt Institution and School of Arts, a moment in its history remembered today in the validation of its degrees by Heriot-Watt University. Currently there are talks in progress with the university for a merger by the summer of 2001.

The college today is spread over two campuses within five minutes walk of each other at the very heart of the Old Town. Although there is institutional accommodation for very few, students coming from outside the Edinburgh and Lothian area may apply for college-managed accommodation in the city. There is an active Students' Union, and they have the city's best-loved indie night.

COLLEGE PROFILE

Founded	**1908**
Status	**Art College**
Degree awarding university	**Heriot-Watt**
Total student population	**1616**
Degree undergraduates	**1285**
ACCOMMODATION:	
Availability	**Limited**
Style	**Edinburgh uni halls**
Cost pw (no food)	**£70-£140**
City rent pw	**£65-£85**

DEGREE SUBJECT AREAS:
Art/Design (Fine Art with Edinburgh Uni), architecture, planning

UNIVERSITY OF ESSEX

The University of Essex
Wivenhoe Park
Colchester
Essex CO4 3SQ

TEL 01206 873666
FAX 01206 873423
admit@essex.ac.uk

Essex Students' Union
Wivenhoe Park
Colchester
Essex CO4 3SQ

TEL 01206 863211
FAX 01206 870915

VAG VIEW

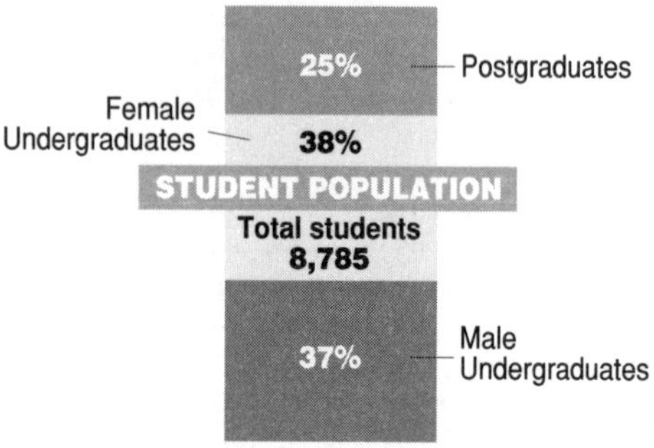

It is all too easy to underestimate Essex, a uni launched around the same time as York, Sussex, Warwick in the mid-'60s, but which, after it had marked its card as a main '60s seat of revolution, never quite found its way back into careers masters' hearts. Yet, in teaching inspections, Electronic Systems Engineering, Sports Science, Philosophy, Economics, Politics, Tourism, Molecular Biosciences, Sociology, Psychology and Art History, only dropped six marks in total. And in the research assessments, they came 10th – way ahead of the likes of Durham and Nottingham; York came 18th, Sussex 31st, and Warwick just pipped Essex into 6th.

The University of Essex is considered to be one of the best Social Science universities in the country, especially for law, politics and sociology. There are other good reasons for opting for Essex – sport, ents and student media among them. It is also convenient for London. So, why has it had to rely so heavily on Clearing to encourage applicants in?

Applications are up, though not as high as they anticipated. Investment is keeping pace. They're building a £6 million lecture hall with two new theatres holding 500 people each, but combinable into a single 1,000-seater theatre. Also in 2006 comes a new £6.9 million Social Sciences research centre, to house the Institute for Social and Economic Research (ISER) and the UK Date Archive.

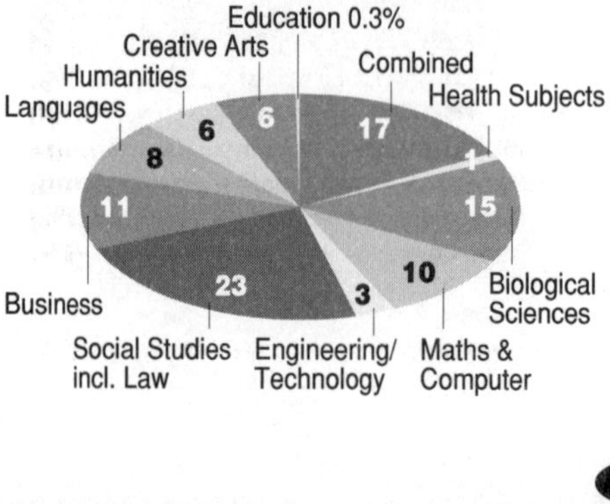

CAMPUS

Essex will never win any prizes for beauty. It is a grey, drab institution, made almost entirely of concrete. The brick, high-rise towers where students lay their weary heads are a blot on the Colchester skyline, which is not particularly nice anyway.

The campus comprises 200 acres of landscaped parkland, two miles from the centre. Colchester, capital of Roman Britain and now commuter and garrison town and base camp for Essex uni, is today a regional centre of commerce, light industry and high technology (population 150,000). It is also a dormitory city for commuters to London, an hour away by train.

FEES, BURSARIES

UK & EU Fees: £3000 p.a (£1200 for preliminary or foundation year in a 4-year course). Sliding scale bursaries dependent on parental income levels; also bursaries for athletes competing at national or international level. A new sports bursary scheme has also been launched in partnership with local solicitors Birkett Long – two £1000 donations for elite athletes who live within Essex. Bursaries of £500 for a single-honours maths students who

UNIVERSITY/STUDENT PROFILE

University since	**1965**
Situation/style	**Town campus**
Student population	**8785**
Undergraduates	**6575**
- mature	**17%**
- non EU undergraduates	**16%**
- male/female	**49/51**
- non-traditional student intake	**28%**
- state school intake	**95%**
- drop-out rate	**9%**
- undergraduate applications	**Up 9%**

ACADEMIC EXCELLENCE

TEACHING:
(Rated Excellent or 17+ out of 24)

Law	**Excellent**
Electronic Systems Eng, Sports Science, Philosophy, Economics, Politics, Tourism	**24**
Molecular Biosciences	**23**
Sociology, Psychology, Art History	**22**
Linguistics	**21**
Maths, Nursing	**20**

RESEARCH:
*Top grades 5/6**

Economics, Politics, Sociology	**Grade 6***
Psychology, Electrical & Electronic Eng, Law, Accounting, Linguistics, History, History of Art, Philosophy	**Grade 5**

obtains at least 320 points on a maximum of 21 units, including A in Mathematics at Alevel; £250 per year for a joint-honours student. Students who enrol for the 4-year Biomedical Sciences sandwich degree scheme (UCAS Code: B991 BSc/BMSP), will be entitled to financial support from the NHS during their first, second and final years. For a number of places available, this support will be equivalent to the cost of full tuition fees. Funding may also be available for students who enrol on the new Clinical Physiology (Cardiology) degree scheme (UCAS Code: BB18 BSc/CPC). The Vera Carmen Lord Fund supports Jamaican students, and there is an Essex Foundation Bursary for Refugees and the Children of Refugees. The JP Morgan Fleming Bursary is open to UK mature students normally resident in S.E. Essex.

Essex is seriously underrated. Tenth best in the country for research, consider it for social sciences – law, politics, economics, sociology; for biosciences; for sport; and much else; but close your eyes to its architecture.

STUDENT PROFILE

Nick Margerrison notes the mixed student profile as 'one of the best features – it is a small, friendly university; you will enjoy your time here, along with Sharon, Tracey and Wayne. Actually, the university has a large overseas contingent too, especially Greek.' Mixed socially, economically and nationally – almost a third of students come from overseas; people come to Essex University from almost every conceivable part of the known world. 'This provides you with a unique chance to get to know a wide variety of different cultures.'

ACADEMIA & JOBS

There are five Schools – Comparative Studies (Humanities, but with a cross-cultural, international approach), Social Sciences, Law, Maths & Computer Sciences, Science & Engineering – and consistently good teaching assessments recently – full marks for Electronic

WHERE ESSEX GRADUATES END UP

Health & Social Work: 7%; Education: 11%; Wholesale/Retail: 13%; Manufacturing: 7%; Financial Activities: 11%; Public Administration, Civil Service & Defence: 8%; Hotel/Restaurant: 4%; Transport & Communications (including Telecommunications): 5%; Construction: 3%; Mining/Oil Extracting: 0.5%; Personnel: 4%; Computer: 6%; Business & Management: 2%; Accountancy: 5%; Media (including Film): 2%; Legal 3%; Publishing: 2%; Advertising: 1%; Artistic/Literary: 4%; Sport: 1%.

Approximate 'graduate track' employed **60%**

Systems Engineering and 22 out of 24 for Psychology, Sociology and Art History. While we're on the subject, a History of Modern Art degree includes a ten-day subsidised visit to New York.

At Essex the first year is thrown open to a study of four or five courses to enable you to investigate your chosen subject from a variety of points of view. This might involve studying Sociology from an Economics point of view, History from a Psychology pov. Then in the second year you move forward to a single or joint honours degree with deeper understanding.

Economics, politics, sociology are world class – special grade 6* at the research assessments. Economics and politics also scored full marks at the teaching inspections, as did other subjects (see Academic Excellence box). What emerges from the academic statistics, taken together with the graduate employment info, is that where economics, law, politics, computer, biosciences and sociology are concerned, this uni is without doubt the place to go. The Government certainly know it, which is why they recruit intelligence officers here, as well as defence operatives and government admin. wallahs. They pick them out of social sciences, computer engineering, law, biosciences, languages (Essex has links with 50+ European unis, and exchange schemes proliferate).

In civvy street, degrees in Software Engineering, Embedded Systems & Robotics, Internet Technology, Artificial Intelligence, Computer Engineering, Electronic Engineering turn out software engineers, consultants and manufacturers, and computer games designers (there's a dedicated degree for this) by the score. Among smaller unis, Essex and UMIST are the giants in this sort of thing. Some 6% of Essex graduates enter the computer industry. New this year are BSc Computer and Network Security, BSc Internet Technology with Business, and BSc Mathematics with Network Security. See also BSc Mathematics with a Year in America.

Law is another high point. Law finds its way into all kinds of courses, and law graduates from Essex are again in demand by Government for defence and admin posts. Essex are European law specialists (and very good at languages too), and there's an interesting joint honours with Human Rights. The Human Rights Centre on campus is a leader in its field. Its teaching gets an Excellent rating and the subject an international Grade 5 for research.

With a world-class Grade 6*, Economics is another subject much in demand. More than 10% of Essex graduates go into financial activities of one sort or another, including accountancy, and some 5% into banking. See in particular, International Economics. There are single honours Accounting and Finance, but also joint honours with Finance, or Management.

Stepping aside from the kind of macho, front-line stuff we find that in the arts they have some specialist employment niches worth noting. In the Autumn of 2000 the famed East 15 Acting School merged with the uni, and so actors, directors, producers and stage managers now abound.

The programme includes a Foundation course and BA Acting and a 1-year Postgrad Diploma. There's also a Postgrad Diploma in Acting for the Media and a new BA in Contemporary Theatre Practice. Take a taste of this very impressive set-up – begun famously by Joan Littlewood in the 1960s, her Stratford East London Theatre Workshop bringing Stanislavski's method to widespread use in the UK. Here, as they boast, 'You will learn how to use the power of your mind.' New degrees this year are BA Specialist Performance Skills (Stage Combat) and BA Community Theatre. See also BA Creative Writing.

Finally, Essex makes employment waves in sport, too. the degree, Sports & Exercise Science (with Foundation), is one of a few to receive 24 points (full marks) in the teaching assessments. It has led to some very good sporting facilities.

SOCIAL SCENE

STUDENTS' UNION Being close to the metropolis has a negative effect on the uni scene at weekends, but there's no reason to leave, as far as Stephen J Peters can see: 'The SU is well run and campaigns hard on student issues. The bar is relatively big, with decent numbers of one-armed bandits and pool tables. Beer is reasonable, though prices do keep sneaking up quietly. The university magazine isn't bad, nor is the radio station.' *Parklife* is the mag, *The Rabbit* is

AT A GLANCE

ACADEMIC FILE:	
Subjects assessed	**18**
Excellent	**78%**
Typical entry requirements	**295 points**
Application acceptance rate	**16%**
Students-staff ratio	**16:1**
First/2:1 degree pass rate	**54%**
ACCOMMODATION FILE:	
Guarantee to freshers	**100%**
Style	**Flats in towers**
Catered	**None**
En-suite	**60%**
Price range pw	**£48.44-£78.68**
Town rent pw	**£55-£60**

WHAT IT'S REALLY LIKE

UNIVERSITY:	
Social Life	★★★★
Campus scene	**Diverse, fast developing**
Student Union services	**Good**
Politics	**Activity high Student issues**
Sport	**34 clubs**
National team position	**78th**
Sport facilities	**Excellent**
Arts opportunities	**Good**
Student magazine	**Parklife**
Student newspaper	**The Rabbit**
Student radio	**RED AM 1404**
Nightclub	**Underground**
Bars	**SU, Level 2, Café Mondo**
Union ents	**Full on**
Union clubs/societies	**70**
Parking	**No parking if you live on campus**
CITY:	
Entertainment	★★★
Scene	**Clubs 'n pubs**
Town/gown relations	**Average**
Risk of violence	**Low**
Cost of living	**Average**
Student concessions	**Adequate**
Survival + 2 nights out	**£80 pw**
Part-time work campus/town	**Excellent/good**

the newspaper – campus is running with them, apparently; RED AM 1404 is the radio station.'

The biggest single bar is the **SU** and there's an all-day alternative, **Café Mondo** – Monday might be *International Night/Global Music, Global People* at **Mondo** with DJ Guillermo; Tuesday *R'n'B*; Wednesday *Funky House*; Thursday *Casa De La Salsa* (with lessons); Friday **Fuse** (urban). And then there's **Level 2,** a small venue (275 capacity) with late bar extensions, comedy nights, society nights, local bands, promos, karaoke, etc, and its own club menu – e.g. *Bhangra & Desi Beats*; *Cheezy Tunes*; and Saturday night *Discord* (indie, metal & rock).

The Underground is the main venue (850 cap) – *Score* on Wednesday (sportsfed night); *Fuse* (club, commercial & party); and Saturday *The Big Cheese 999 Night* with guests and themes..

Town 'Colchester suffers from its relative proximity to other major venues in attracting big names in entertainment,' writes Stephen. 'Some occasionally grace us with their presence, but for the real stars get on the train to Cambridge or London. New talent can be seen at the local **Arts Centre**. But if you like a drink, Colchester and its environs can provide. Most tolerate students as long as you don't share your dinner with their toilet floor. The Wivenhoe Run is infamous, and has to be experienced if you reckon you can down a few. Colchester is a garrison town. Students, squaddies and alcohol are a volatile mix. Most of the time, though, you wouldn't know they are there. Find out where not to go in town when you get here (most notably the squaddie pubs).

'The nightclubs are pretty useless. Stick to the university nightclub, and only venture to town clubs for student nights. The music played on campus comes from all genres, from heavy metal to cheesy choons.

'Local transport links are average. Buses are frequent and not too expensive. Have the right change though, or the bus drivers, notoriously miserable, get a bit shirty. Trains to London are quick and reasonably reliable. And if you have a bit of money to spend, **Lakeside** and **Bluewater** are just down the road.'

At the union, besides ents, there's an excellent secondhand bookshop (student buy 'n' sell), and a good Job Shop for part-time work.

Sport Their sports facilities are among the best anywhere in the country. There's a recently extended sports hall with six badminton courts, fitness room, sauna, sun-bed, squash courts, table tennis, climbing wall, plus a sportsturf pitch, floodlit tennis courts, three cricket pitches (one artificial wicket) plus nets, Squirrel Run circuit, eighteen-hole disc/frisbee-golf, grass and synthetic pitches, and a watersports centre.

There are coaching courses in badminton, pilates, squash and tennis, and a relatively new Master's degree in Sports Science (Fitness and Health) is a sign of the commitment, and the student union website is running a poll as to how many applicants chose Essex for its sport facilities. City sports clubs offer sailing, windsurfing, canoeing. A new sports bursary scheme has just been unveiled; contact the university for details.

PILLOW TALK

More new rooms have recently been built on campus for first years. As with most other places, the private sector varies in standard and cost. More than half of students live in uni accommodation, the majority of which is on campus. Tesco is within walking distance of campus, so shopping is easy. Accommodation ranges from flats for 13 to 16 in the famous Towers (tower blocks) to smaller, en-suite flats for six people – South Courts, Houses and University Quays have smaller flats containing 4 to 8 rooms, all of which have en suite facilities.

All accommodation is networked so students can use their computer to access the internet and University network from their room free of charge. Each room also has a telephone which provides free use of the internal telephone system.

GETTING THERE

☛ By road: A12. Well served by coach services.
☛ By rail: London Liverpool Street, 1:00, every half-hour; Birmingham New Street, 3:30; Sheffield, 4:00. Ten-minute taxi run to campus.
☛ By coach: London, 2:10; Norwich, 6:15.

UNIVERSITY OF EXETER

The University of Exeter
Northcote House
The Queen's Drive
Exeter EX4 4QJ

TEL 01392 263035
01392 263030 (prospectus)
FAX 01392 263108
EMAIL admissions@exeter.ac.uk
WEB www.exeter.ac.uk

Exeter Guild of Students
Devonshire House
Stocker Road
Exeter EX4 4PZ

TEL 01392 263540
FAX 01392 263546
EMAIL enquiries@guild.ex.ac.uk
WEB www.guild.ex.ac.uk

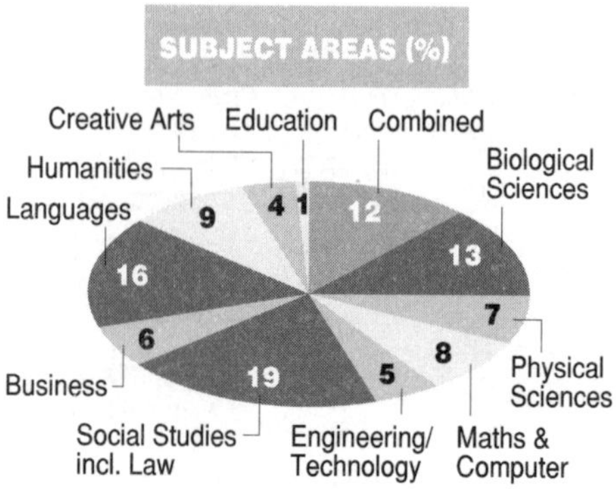

VAG VIEW

Exeter became a university in 1955, and in the 1970s, they took St Luke's College of Education into the fold.

The uni is custodian at the M5 gateway to the West Country, and has, since 2004, celebrated dominion over the region in the new Combined Universities of Cornwall, a collaborative partnership with the University of Plymouth and the Peninsula Medical School, Falmouth College of Arts, The Open University in the South West, The College of St Mark & St John, and with Cornwall's Further Education colleges - Cornwall College, Truro College and Penwith College.

The partnership has attracted massive EU and UK Government funding – £50 million for buildings at the 'Hub' (Falmouth College of Art's Tremough Campus) and a further £16 million for new buildings at the 'Rim' (the Cornish Further Education colleges). Further funding of £24.5 million has just now been secured, and Phase 2 of the scheme will be launched in 2007.

Exeter has had an interest in Cornwall for some time through its School of Mines in Camborne, and the Institute of Cornish Studies (postgraduate and lifelong learning). Now, they will become a very significant force in the West Country economy right down to Land's End.

There is also a bullish development programme at the Exeter HQ: a £1m major revamp of the students' union building and nightclub, a £19m spend on teaching and research facilities, including £5m for biosciences, £2.2m for Physics and £3m shared between Modern Languages and English. Video conferencing and AV facilities, so useful to a uni that is becoming increasingly scattered geographically, will also get a shot in the arm with a £2m upgrade.

CAMPUS

THE EXETER CAMPUS 'The university is very easy to fall in love with,' writes Jo Moorhouse. 'It has one of the most beautiful campuses in the country, in one of the most beautiful counties in Britain.' It is indeed beautifully set on a hill, 15 minutes walk from the centre of the city, which itself lies close to the sea on one side and the moors on the other.

'Students at Exeter have the best of both worlds;' writes Julie Moore, 'a cathedral city with the countryside right on the doorstep.

'Being near the beach makes the surfing society a popular choice, and with Newquay just down the road the summer terms are filled with weekend trips and beach parties.

'Many people, myself included, made Exeter their first choice uni after one tour of the campus. A lush green settlement dotted with ponds and famous sculptures, campus has a relaxed atmosphere with some perfect spots for chilling out with friends in the sun. Everything is within walking distance, which means if you have a lecture at 9am you can get up ten minutes before and still make it. There are no shortage of shops, cafés, and bars and you have no real need to leave.

'The only thing they forget to tell you is that flat roads are a rare luxury in Exeter, and some of the student halls are at the bottom of Cardiac hill, and definitely not advised for anyone with a heart condition! The other side is that you do get used to it, but tend to laugh less at the ongoing joke about "the Exeter thighs".'

St Luke's Campus The School of Education is a mile away at St Luke's College. The Students' Guild operates a frequent minibus service for the main Exeter campus.

Exeter in Cornwall Campus The £65 million campus at Tremough is on a 70-acre estate deep in Cornwall, overlooking the Fal estuary. The Fal is one of the most beautiful aspects of nature in all England and worth the trip on its own. Tremough is 10 minutes from Falmouth, a seaside town full of trippers in summer, very cheap shopping and access to coves up the Helford River. The new campus is not shared by all the participants in Combined Universities (see *VAG View* above), only by students from the University of Exeter and Falmouth College of Arts. Besides teaching facilities and resources (see *Academia*, below), there's a restaurant and bar, and a fitness studio. Sport is played at local facilities.

FEES, BURSARIES

UK & EU Fees: £3000 p.a. for all full-time undergraduate programmes, with the following exceptions: Radiography (tuition fees will be paid by the NHS); Medicine (in year 5 the Department for Health will pay fees). Sliding scale bursary of between £50 and £2000 p.a. All students with assessed income below £37425 will be guaranteed financial assistance from the scheme. Further bursary support is given to applicants from partner schools and colleges in Devon, Cornwall and Somerset: 70 bursaries of £2000 p.a. Also, science scholarships are available for applicants with 3 A grades at A Level (excluding General Studies), or equivalent points in the International Baccalaureate, taking single honours degrees in Biosciences, Computer Science, Engineering and Physics, and for those taking combined honours in Maths and Physics. Each scholarship is worth £4000 over the duration of the programme. Sports scholarships of £1000 p.a. are available – any sport, but especially cricket, football, golf, hockey,

UNIVERSITY/STUDENT PROFILE

University since	**1955**
Situation/style	**Campus**
Student population	**13554**
Undergraduates	**9969**
- mature	**13%**
- non EU undergraduates	**5%**
- male/female	**48/52**
- non-traditional student intake	**17%**
- state school intake	**71%, low**
- drop-out rate	**3%, low**
- undergraduate applications	**Down 2%**

ACADEMIC EXCELLENCE

TEACHING:	
(Rated Excellent or 17+ out of 24)	
English, Geography	**Excellent**
German, Education, Archaeology	**24**
Psychology, Politics, Theology	**23**
Drama, Dance & Cinematics, French, Italian, Maths, Physics, Classics, Business/Economics, Biosciences	**22**
Sociology, Materials Technology, Sport Sciences	**21**
Russian, Iberian Studies, Middle Eastern & African, Studies, General Engineering	**20**
RESEARCH:	
*Top grades 5/6**	
German	**Grade 6***
Hospital/Clinical, Applied Maths, Psychology, Physics, Law, Economics, Politics, Sociology, Accounting, Middle Eastern & African Studies, English, Russian/Slavonic/East European, Classics, Archaeology, History, Theology, Education, Sports	**Grade 5**

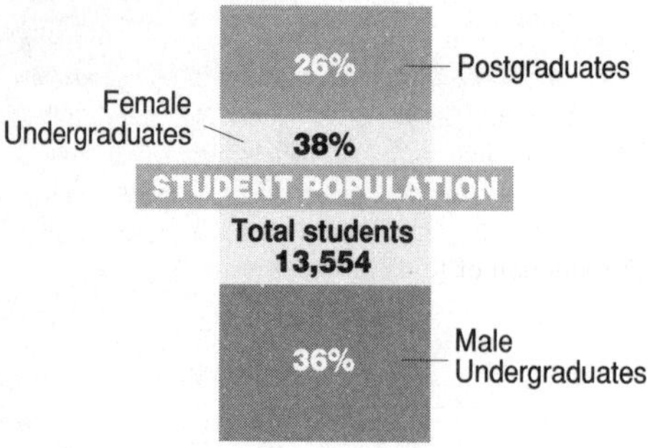

lacrosse, netball, rowing, rugby, sailing and tennis. Scholarships of £1000-1500 p.a. are open to students of the University of Exeter in Cornwall reading for BSc Applied Geology, BSc Engineering Geology and Geotechnics, BSc Environmental Science and Technology, BEng Mining Engineering or BSc Renewable Energy, while students reading for the BSc in Conservation Biology and Ecology may apply for the science and engineering scholarchips mentioned above, and all students based at Tremough may apply for a sports scholarship. The Uni also offers choral scholarships with the University Chapel Choir and other scholarships associated with the Collegiate Church of the Holy Cross, Crediton. Further details on www.exeter.ac.uk.

> ***The success of Exeter at putting graduates into the City masks other specialities – student cultural activities beyond the curriculum, which are similarly successful in launching graduate careers, especially in the media.***

STUDENT PROFILE

The uni has a reputation as a haven for the green wellie brigade, hooray Henrys careering down from London by the Golf-full, future City slickers out for a last taste of freedom in the idyllic West Country before being tethered to work stations in the Square Mile. The uni's performance in the accountancy, finance & banking fields seems to support this, and the guild's web site address used to be gosh.exeter.ac.uk.

For some time now, however, Exeter has made a concerted effort to widen participation in its degrees in other areas of the socio-economic spectrum. The most recent national statistics show that the proportion of students from state schools/ colleges increased from 66.9% to 71.2%; its take from lower socio-economic classes rose from 14.9% to 16.6%; and from low participation neighbourhoods, intake is up from 5.6% to 7.0%.

One result is a growing need to support those students who meet with financial hardship. The non-traditional intake is still not high, but it is increasing and other less Sloaney unis are commenting on it.

ACADEMIA & JOBS

Academically, Exeter is one of our premier-league establishments, and teaching assessments have been very good. Both Education and Archaeology got full marks, and German took full marks for teaching and world renown (Grade 6*) for research. This year, there are new BA degrees in German, French, Spanish and Russian with Teaching English as a Foreign Language.

'Exeter is known as a university that produces students with a wide range of skills, not merely academically sound,' writes Juliet. They produce a booklet outlining what you will require besides a degree to get a job at a worthwhile level in a competitive industry. There's a team of trainers to enable you to take those skills and training on board, and two recruitment fairs a year in Great Hall, plus a Law Fair because of strength in that area. An Innovation Centre on campus provides start-up homes for small businesses, usually hi-tech. Funding is available in the region. Finally, careers advice is given by alumni through the 'Expert' scheme, on how to get into hard-to-enter

WHERE EXETER GRADUATES END UP

Health & Social Work: 4%; Education: 14%; Wholesale/Retail: 8%; Manufacturing: 5%; Financial Activities: 11%; Public Administration, Civil Service & Defence: 6%; Hotel/Restaurant: 3%; Transport & Communications (including Telecommunications): 4%; Construction: 2%; Mining/Oil Extracting: 1%; Personnel: 10%; Computer: 2%; Business & Management: 4%; Accountancy: 7%; Media (including Film): 2%; Legal 2%; Publishing: 1.5%; Advertising: 1%; Artistic/Literary: 1%; Sport: 2%.

Approximate 'graduate track' employed **60%**

sectors like media, and non-profit organisations (charities).

School teachers were once the principal educational output, but no more. The University stopped teaching a BEd degree about 5 years ago and now offers BA in Education Studies and Youth & Childhood Studies with a typical offer of BBB-BCC.

Accountancy and finance (investment advisers, analysts) are huge here. They have had an MA in Finance & Investment for nearly 30 years. There are five dedicated courses: Accounting and Finance - 300-340 points required, the same for their Business and Accounting. Both are extended with language options. Mathematics with Accounting is a 3-year degree with at least 25% of the time spent on Accountancy. Just as many graduate accountants come from the Economics department - Economics, & Finance, & Statistics, etc, all with the Euro option of course. Teaching inspection, 22. Research Grade 5.

On the health ticket, increasingly important to the uni, the **Peninsula Medical School** is their new collaboration with Plymouth Uni and the NHS in Devon and Cornwall, the NHS hand ensuring a strong clinical element in the course. Contact: 01752 764439; medadmissions@pms.ac.uk (see also: www.pms.ac.uk).

The BM, BS degree focuses on the biological mechanisms that produce disease and its social impact. It looks very hands-on. First undergraduate intake occurred in 2002, half in Exeter (at St Luke's), half in Plymouth. Both unis already had successful postgraduate medical schools. One of the key points about the new school is that it binds them tighter into the regional community, which will be ever bigger come the CUC. Students work initially with patients in Plymouth and Exeter, then in Truro in Cornwall, finally up with the hillbillies above Dartmoor. Entry ABB-AAB, you'll need at least one science subject. There's a 10% application acceptance ratio. There is also a Diagnostic Radiography degree, through which graduates find speedy employ.

A new BSc programme in Human Biosciences this year represents an innovative collaborative teaching response to a broadening demand for graduates with skills in fields relating to medicine, chemistry, biology and physics. The programme builds on Exeter's research strengths and recognises the importance that exercise can play in the prevention and treatment of disease.

There's also a growing reputation at Exeter for getting graduates jobs in the world of sport through the Exercise & Sport Sciences degree.

Another string is a telling modern specialism in things Arabic. 'It has had a lot of inward investment from that direction,' we were told. 'It is very good on Middle Eastern languages, there's a large teaching/library facility on that side.' Arab & Islamic Studies continues to be a growth area at Exeter with rising undergrad and postgrad numbers and an expanding range of courses, including the introduction of Kurdish and Persian options.

'I did politics and there was quite a cross-over with Arab/Islamic, history of the Middle East, Middle East politics, etc,' said a graduate Guild officer, 'and the resource [the Institute of Arabic & Islamic Studies] is really good: letters, firsthand evidence... A lot of people don't realise that you don't have to know Arabic to study there. With the building of the institute - fantastic building! - we have got the largest Arabic Library and Middle East resource outside the Middle East and America. That may seem a bit random, here in Exeter, but the fact is that we are in the forefront on this thing, and it has a knock-on effect.'

2006 sees new degrees in Arabic & Middle East Studies, German & Arabic, Russian & Arabic, and Italian & Arabic.

In Law, there's an international Grade 5 for research, and they are European law specialists with LLB French Maitrise/German Magister as well as Law with European Study/International Study.

Within the Combined Universities, degrees are offered in Conservation Biology and Ecology, English, Environmental Science and Technology, Geography, Geology, Mining Engineering and Renewable Energy. £3m has been invested in new science laboratories with specialist equipment for the study of biological and earth sciences and engineering. Geography students benefit from dedicated computer labs with the latest GIS and remote sensing software and a digital map library. The research facilities include a sophisticated

AT A GLANCE

ACADEMIC FILE:	
Subjects assessed	**32**
Excellent	**78%**
Typical entry requirements	**360 points**
Application acceptance rate	**13%**
Students-staff ratio	**17:1**
First/2:1 degree pass rate	**69%**
ACCOMMODATION FILE:	
Guarantee to freshers	**100%**
Style	**Halls**
Catered	**50%**
En-suite	**50%**
Price range pw	**£57.47 - £129**
City rent pw	**£55-£65**

WHAT IT'S REALLY LIKE	
UNIVERSITY:	
Social Life	★★★★★
Campus scene	**Out-going, well-heeled, lively**
Student Union services	**Good**
Politics	**Student issues**
Sport	**Key**
National team position	**12th**
Sport facilities	**Excellent**
Arts opportunities	**Excellent, esp. theatre**
Student newspaper	**Exeposé**
Student radio	**Expression**
Student Radio Awards	**2005 winner**
Student TV	**XTV**
Nightclub	**Lemon Grove + Timepiece in town**
Bars	**Ram, Ewe**
Union ents	**Lemmy disco + live acts and nights in town**
Union clubs/societies	**190+**
Parking	**Good; permit**
CITY:	
Entertainment	★★-★★★
Scene	**Good pubs; average clubs**
Town/gown relations	**Average**
Risk of violence	**Average**
Cost of living	**Average**
Student concessions	**Good**
Survival + 2 nights out	**£80 pw**
Part-time work campus/town	**Average**

computer-controlled electron scanning microscope, QEMSCAN, currently the only one in a European laboratory and the first in any university worldwide.

Phase 2 of Combined Universities, to be delivered in 2007, will bring new degrees in law, history, politics and animal behaviour.

As for the Camborne School of Mines, an integral part of the collaboration, despite the decline of British mining, there is still high demand overseas for graduates of the BEng Mining Engineering, but the School has been developing its emphasis to environmental science and renewable energy programmes.

STUDENT SCENE

Students' Guild The **Ram** in Devonshire House is the main bar, always busy in the evenings, video juke box. Then there's the **Ewe** in Cornwall House, also home to the **Lemon Grove** (Lemmy) nightclub, a coffee bar during the day, bar in the evening (Tuesdays with karaoke) and nightclub Friday and Saturday. 'It's the biggest nightclub in Exeter with a capacity of 1,350,' my guide told me. 'A fantastic evening out, a *Double Lemmy* is a must, Friday and Saturday nights, which is why I am looking a bit rough today.

'As the Lemmy doubles as a concert venue, on Wednesday nights we put on all the campus bands – there's a tradition of that here, goes back ages, five or six bands each night. Then, afterwards, it's down to a club in town called **Timepiece**, which we work with on Athletic Union nights, the money raised going back into coaching and training, which is why we do so well in the BUSA League.' Big acts play the **Great Hall** (1,700 capacity), 'Generally we have five big name concerts a term and little ones every now and then in the Lemmy. [Recent live acts included Thrills, Feeder and Reef.]

'Then we have the university orchestra, choral society, in the Great Hall at this time of year. There's also a tradition of musicals in **Northcote** [the part-'pro' campus theatre, very good acoustics, high-banked auditorium for maximum visibility].' Footlights, Exeter Theatre Company and the Gilbert & Sullivan Society perform there, and the Exeter University Symphony Orchestra puts on termly concerts.

There is massive interest in media, too, and although the uni doesn't offer a media course, they have a surprising number of graduates going into the sector. Someone lists, 'Nick Baker, the wildlife presenter, Emma B from Radio 1, Thom Yorke of Radiohead who was a D, Isobel Lang, the weather presenter, people on the production side, like Paul Jackson who produced Red Dwarf - he came back to do a creative writing thing with the students in English, Stewart Purvis, chief exec of ITN.' Some 400 freshers attended a *Welcome to the Media* event in freshers week last year. Those who stuck with it were subjected to a period of training by the *Exeposé* team – the student newspaper is often up for national awards. As well as *Exeposé* they have Expression fm – radio, which was nominated for 3 awards in the Student Radio Awards this year and picked up the bronze Station Sound Award. In the evenings there's an on-air welfare session. 'And we've got student TV – XTV. The radio is on the Internet as well, many of the students on a year-out listen to that.'

They are proud, too. of their Community Action Group, one of the most active in the country. Student volunteering contributes over 150,000 volunteering hours per year.

Sport Their £8-million facilities definitely get the thumbs up from students. New indoor tennis facilities to LTA standards opened in 2004. Said

Julie: 'This uni is full of sports fanatics, excellent opportunities to join very competitive teams – it's all a very serious business. Also so many surfing, windsurfing and beach bum type societies to join.'

Twelfth in the BUSA team league last year, all major team games are well represented, also martial arts, watersports (rowing, canoeing, sailing – six Lark dinghies on the Exe Estuary) and ultimate frisbee. On-campus facilities include sports hall (basketball, netball, volleyball, tennis – there's a new LTA standard indoor/outdoor tennis centre – badminton, indoor cricket net), a climbing wall and traversing wall, rooms for fencing, martial arts, weights, etc. Pitches include 2 all-weather pitches, large grass pitch with nets area, and there are sixty off-campus acres of playing fields nearby.

Town 'There are certain pubs that you shouldn't really go into,' warns Juliet Oaks, 'and during Freshers Week the Guild does advise you which to avoid. Also, although Exeter is a city, it is in the West Country: clubbing is not exactly the best. However, there is at least one student night at a club every night of the week. Entry before 10:30 is usually free or very cheap. Some of the clubs distribute tickets beforehand and these are definitely worth getting. A night out can cost from £2 (only drinking water while clubbing and walking home) to £40 (drinking in town pubs and at the clubs, getting pissed and getting a taxi home)! For shopping there's enough diversity for anyone, from skaters to Goths.' A £200m retail centre just opened.

PILLOW TALK

Wide choice of good catered and self-catered accommodation. The majority of freshers take the catered option, but 250 self-catering rooms are reserved for them too. All the accommodation is either on campus or close by. There are en-suite rooms at ground level in the newer halls and flats suitable for disabled students, as well as some specially adapted rooms in the older residences. With the exception of a small number of rooms in the older residences, study bedrooms have a high-speed connection to the University data network, which can be used for e-mail and Internet access. There is a modest fixed charge for this facility.

GETTING THERE

☛ By road: M5/J30.
☛ By rail: London Paddington, 2:30; Birmingham, 3:00; Plymouth, 1:15.
☛ By air: Exeter Airport for inland, European and some trans-Atlantic flights. Fifteen mins from campus by taxi.
☛ By coach: London, 4:00; Birmingham, 4:30.

UNIVERSITY COLLEGE FALMOUTH

University College Falmouth
Woodlane
Falmouth
Cornwall TR11 4RA

TEL 01326 211077
FAX 01326 212261
EMAIL (via website)
WEB www.falmouth.ac.uk

UNIVERSITY COLLEGE PROFILE

Founded	**1938**
Status	**F/HE College**
Situation/style	**Campus**
Student population	**1990**
Degree undergraduates	**1610**
ACCOMMODATION:	
Accommodation guarantee	**42%**
Style	**Flats**
Cost pw (no food)	**£72-£79**
Town rent pw	**£50**

DEGREE SUBJECT AREAS:
Broadcasting, English with Creative Writing/Media Studies, Fine Art, Design (audio, graphic, textile, garden, interior/ landscape, ceramics, 3D), Illustration, Journalism, Photography, Film, Media & Business Management

They were granted University College status in March 2004. Degrees are offered in Broadcasting, English with Creative Writing/Media Studies, Fine Art, Design (audio, graphic, textile, garden, interior/ landscape, ceramics, 3D), Illustration, Journalism, Photography, Film, Media & Business Management. Tthere is a new Media Centre.

Campus is in some of the most lovely scenery that this country has to offer, and is hub of the new Combined Universities of Cornwall (see *Exeter* entry).

Accommodation comprises 450 rooms. Otherwise it's Falmouth student lets.

UNIVERSITY OF GLAMORGAN

The University of Glamorgan
Pontypridd
Mid Glamorgan CF37 1DL

TEL 01443 483348
FAX 01443 482925
EMAIL enquiries@glam.ac.uk
WEB www.glam.ac.uk

Glamorgan Students' Union
Treforest
Pontypridd CF37 1UF

TEL 01443 483500
FAX 01443 483501
EMAIL pres-of-glam@hotmail.com
WEB www.glamsu.com

VAG VIEW

Friendly atmosphere, pleasant setting, accessible, sporty, they lay claim that of all the Welsh universities, Glamorgan has the highest paid new graduates and one of the best graduate employment rates (though the 'graduate track' rate is lower than mid-table.

The student body is, in higher education speak, 'non-traditional'. Sixty-seven per cent of undergraduates are over 21 at inception, and almost half come from backgrounds where university has never before been an option, and many of them (17%) do not last the course.

However, the uni has a bullish investment programme, which has seen new facilities for technology and science, a £5-million refurb for maths and computing, and now a new campus in Cardiff's city centre, which will house a School of Creative & Cultural Industries and take in media, drama, cultural studies, music, archiecture and design courses.

They already have the National Centre for Writing and the Film Academy for Wales, the largest business school in Wales..

Also, we note a sparky new energy in the Union with such as a student book club and television station coming through this year.

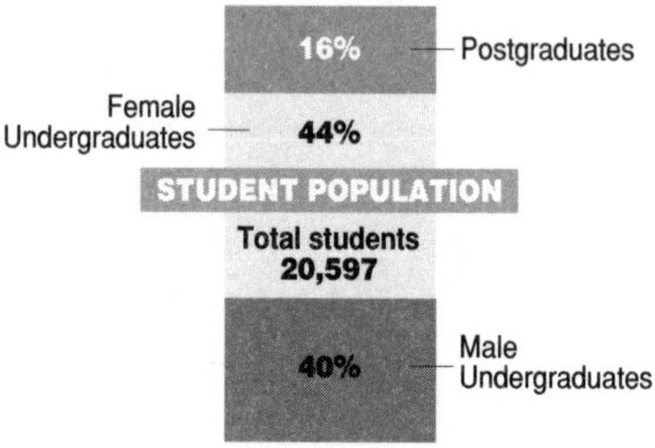

CAMPUS

The campus lies at Treforest in the Taff Valley, an ex-coal mining village, so not pretty, but the surrounding countryside is beautiful, and there are stunning views over the valley. It stands a couple of miles from the market town of Pontypridd and a mere quarter of an hour away from Cardiff by cheap trains which run every twenty minutes from just outside the university.

'Living up here isn't a drag,' writes Fiona Owen, 'it's nice to belong to a close-knit community, and the college is nearly all on one campus, apart from the Law School, which is across the road. The area is scenic and there are lots of places to go for lovely walks with your friends or your new squeeze. Pontypridd Park is open every day and it's a really nice place to chill on a sunny day.'

FEES, BURSARIES

UK & EU Fees: £1200 p.a. in 2006/7; up to £3000 p.a. 2007/8. There are a number of scholarships available to students starting in 2006 or after a gap year. in 2007, depending on whether you're Welsh or English. See www.glam.ac.uk/ money/1197.

STUDENT PROFILE

There's a high mature and state school intake and a very high number of students from new-to-uni neighbourhoods. Once on board, there's a friendly atmosphere in a pleasant setting – 'Glamorgan

UNIVERSITY/STUDENT PROFILE

University since.	**1992**
Situation/style	**Rural campus**
Student population	**20597**
Undergraduates	**17253**
- mature	**67%, high**
- non EU undergraduates	**10%**
- male/female	**52/48**
- non-traditional student intake	**43%, high**
- state school intake	**99%, high**
- drop-out rate	**17%, high**
- undergraduate applications	**Up 4%**

WHERE GLAMORGAN GRADUATES END UP

Health & Social Work: 10%; Education: 8%; Wholesale/Retail: 12%; Manufacturing: 8%; Financial Activities: 9%; Public Administration, Civil Service & Defence: 14%; Hotel/Restaurant: 4%; Transport & Communications (including Telecommunications): 4%; Construction: 3%; Personnel: 1%; Computer: 4%; Business & Management: 1%; Accountancy: 2%; Media (including Film): 1%; Legal 4%; Architecture: 2%; Publishing: 0.5%; Advertising: 0.5%; Artistic/Literary: 0.5%; Sport: 2%.

Approximate 'graduate track' employed **58%**

University is small enough to generate real warmth and a sense of close-knit community, but large enough for you to be inconspicuous when that's what you want/need,' writes Beth Smith.

ACADEMIA & JOBS

More than 200 courses are on offer – Arts & Humanities; Social Sciences; Business; Law; Design; Engineering & Construction; Computing & Technology; Sciences & Maths, Nursing, and a whole raft of joint and combined possibilities. There were 'Excellent' teaching assessments in Business Studies, Mining Surveying, Creative Writing, Theatre & Media Drama, Electrical & Electronic Engineering, Accounting & Finance, Public Sector Schemes, and Welsh, and students will tell you that the teaching is good. Their overall employment record is sound, 94% of Glamorgan students are in employment or further study within six months of graduating, a figure well above the UK average, but not that amazing in terms of 'graduate track' jobs (58%).

Getting accepted at Glamorgan is not too testing, and there are very useful foundation courses and tie-ups with colleges of Further Education to ensure it. These are listed on their web site, www.glam.ac.uk.

There's a clear line into local government administration through to Civil Service executive officer or administrative officer or assistant. The latter comes through biological sciences, business and social, economic & political studies. For executive officers it's much the same, but via law rather than biosciences.

SUBJECT AREAS (%)

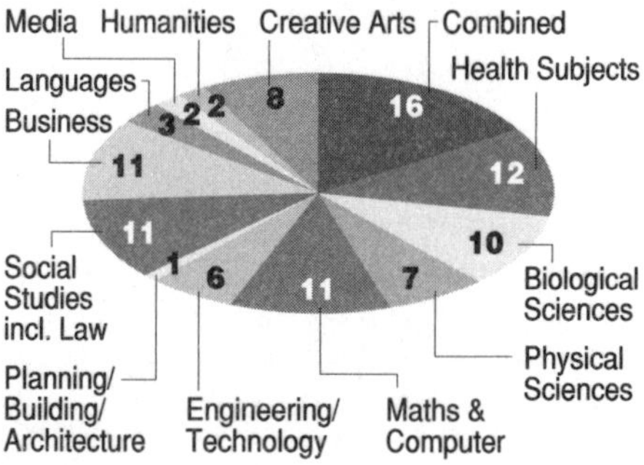

There's a Foundation available for their BA Business Administration, but you might look at Business & Public Services Management, for which there's a Public Sector Management Foundation. Note, too, the BSc Public & Social Policy (with Foundation). There are Foundations, too, in their Law department, where you can study European Law, Criminology & Criminal Justice and Legal Regulation, besides much else. Elements of all these are available in joint, major/minor and combined studies programmes.

ACADEMIC EXCELLENCE

TEACHING:	
Business Studies	**Excellent**
Mining Surveying, Creative Writing/Theatre & Media Drama, Electrical & Electronic Eng, Accounting & Finance, Public Sector Schemes, Welsh	

Glamorgan are commercial & business and European law specialists. They scored 'Good' in a recent LPC assessment. It's also worth pointing to Glamorgan's BSc Police Sciences (there's also a student society), on offer for around 200 points. See too their BSc Criminology & Criminal Justice degrees (including combos with Psychology, Sociology, Forensic Science), also BSc Forensic Chemistry and BSc Forensic Science. This is a good employment area. There's a Forensic Science Foundation Year.

For local, regional, central government administration, they have a Foundation degree in Public Policy, also Public Sector Management, Leisure & Tourism, and a HND in Public & Emergency Services, as well as the BSc Public & Social Policy, Housing & Environment, International Housing & Society, and other relevant elements in their joint hons programme,

WHAT IT'S REALLY LIKE

UNIVERSITY:	
Social Life	★★★
Campus scene	**Chummy, sporty**
Student Union services	**Good**
Politics	**Some internal**
Sport	**Competitive**
National team position	**68th**
Sport facilities	**Good**
Arts opportunities	**Good**
Student newspaper	**Leek**
Radio station	**GTFM**
TV Station	**Glam TV**
Nightclub	**Shafts**
Bars	**Baa Bar, Smiths**
Union ents	**Chart & party**
Union clubs/societies	**50**
Most popular society	**Chiropractic, LesBiGay**
Parking	**Adequate**
OFF-CAMPUS:	
Entertainment	★★
Scene	**Pubs or Cardiff**
Town/gown relations	**Mostly OK**
Risk of violence	**Average**
Cost of living	**Low**
Student concessions	**Average**
Survival + 2 nights out	**£60 pw**
Part-time work campus/town	**Average/good**

such as Environmental Management and Environmental Sustainability. You might also consider the Transport degrees.

Health is a major provision here and dead cert ground for employment. Graduates find their way into jobs as health therapists, psychotherapists, welfare, community and youth workers. Note, too, the BSc Psychology in the Life Sciences faculty, Nursing (mental health, learning disabilities, etc), and BSc Chiropractic (with Foundation).

In the Business faculty they turn out retail managers and buyers with alacrity. Look at BA Purchasing & Supply Chain Management, and there are a number of management and marketing degrees that support graduates interested in sales and marketing jobs. They have a good record in this area.

For accountancy there's also a good reputation and sound employment figures. You can have International Accounting for 220 points. See also BA Accounting & Finance.

Software engineers and computer programmers abound in a large faculty of Computing, which has dedicated Software Engineering Foundation courses, HNDs and degrees.

For budding construction engineers/managers Glamorgan is up up there with the big suppliers, as are UMIST, Napier and Paisley among the smaller unis. Look at the Built Environment Foundation year (there's also a Building Studies Foundation at Pontypridd College nearby) and consider BSc Hons Architectural Technology or Engineering, or Construction Management. The latter is also part of the Combined Studies route on which you can hold off selecting a main subject for the first year (3 to 5 subjects may be selected). This is a big area for Glamorgan, but you could get in for around 160 points.

Quantity surveyors cost building projects and must have the care for detail of an accountant. Each year nationally more than 300 graduates find employment as quantity surveyors. Glamorgan has a part of that through its dedicated BSc degree.

SOCIAL SCENE

STUDENTS' UNION 'If you're a disco queen and demand that you put your spangly dancing trousers on at least a couple of times a week, the union has a formidable entertainment schedule to tease and tantalise you,' Fiona reassures.

There's **Smiths** bar/café, which serves food, snacks and drinks, accompanied by MTV, pool and arcade machines, and the gorgeously aromatic, freshly baked cookie and baguette bar. Then there's the bar – **Baa Bar**, and **Shafts** nightclub, where there's something on every night of the week, with special participation events, talent nights, etc.

There's an active student media set-up, the student newspaper, *Leek*, and award-winning radio station, GTFM, offer plenty of challenge and opportunity, and a new society has just been set up to get Glam TV transmitting on campus and on the Internet. Besides other societies, which include the popular Chiropractic and Lesbian, Gay & Bi-sexual, Hellenic, Police Sciences and Christian Encounter – an eclectic mix – there's the uni concert band and big band, and a 40-member mixed choir. Something for everyone, you might say, but students will be students, as Stephen Harley observes: 'There are only three things that dominate every student's life: money, alcohol and sex. But if you come to Glamorgan there is a fourth thing, the mountain on which they built the university. Whenever you go down the hill from the halls of residence you should do as much as possible while you're at the bottom. The first time you go out for the evening and forget your wallet will, I promise you, be the last.

'The second point, important to note, is that the nightlife in Treforest is... well it isn't. There is a handful of good pubs which have the expected student buzz and the ents at **Shafts** make up for the short hours. Generally, life in Treforest is peaceful enough.' (See *Cardiff Student City*, page 124.)

Sport is a major part of university life, in particular rugby, though womens basketball is also big and the uni are perennially champions at golf somewhere or other. There's a Sports Centre with six badminton courts, climbing wall, all indoor sports, but no swimming pool. There's a smaller hall for keep-fit, table tennis, martial arts, fencing, plus four squash courts (one glass-backed), two conditioning rooms, sauna/solarium suite, and thirty acres of floodlit pitches - football, rugby and hockey, plus trim trail, cricket pitch, archery. Coaching and a sports scholarship scheme is available for students competing at national/international level. Nearby you'll find swimming pools, golf courses, running tracks, and Brecon Beacons for horse riding, canoeing, mountaineering, hang gliding, walking. Also sailing and windsurfing.

PILLOW TALK

The majority of accommodation on campus (halls) is reserved for first year students. They also let houses very near to the University. A meal voucher service is available. New rules allow students to stay over Christmas and Easter vacs at no extra cost. Many students live in private rented accommodation locally; others in Cardiff.

AT A GLANCE

ACADEMIC FILE:	
Subjects assessed	**17**
Excellent	**41%**
Typical entry requirements	**200 points**
Application acceptance rate	**26%, high**
Students-staff ratio	**20:1**
First/2:1 degree pass rate	**48%**
ACCOMMODATION FILE:	
Guarantee to freshers	**75%**
Style	**Halls**
Catered	**None**
En suite	**Glamorgan Court**
Approx price range pw	**£56.50-£94**
Local rent pw	**£35-£60**

GETTING THERE

- ☛ By road: M4/J32, A470. Exit Llantrisant, A473.
- ☛ By rail: London Paddington, 2:45; Birmingham, 2:15; York, 5:00.
- ☛ By air: Cardiff Airport.
- ☛ By coach: London, 4:00; Birmingham, 3:40; Bournemouth, 6:00.

STUDENT GLASGOW - THE CITY

Glasgow is a cracking city, dynamic and constantly changing. What's going on at the moment, cleaning up all the older areas, it's phenomenal. The city is packed with culture and sees little violence. There are pockets, of course, as with most towns and cities, but Glasgow is generally a peaceful place. No problems with mugging or being beaten up for students - only a couple of incidents in the past few years. The police have pretty much got the whole place tied up; you can't walk for more than thirty seconds without being on CCTV camera.

'Why Glasgow?' you'll be asked. Well, upon trying to reassure my anxious parents and friends that the whole of Scotland was not like *Trainspotting*, I began to realise that my new home for the next several years did have certain stereotypes attached to it. I think my seriously worried folks believed I would be delivered home in a body bag with a needle sticking out of my arm. To their amazement and relief, Glasgow's traditional image was a pile of cack.

In truth, it is a totally cosmopolitan city. To be honest, if Glasgow has not got it then I doubt you neither need it nor want it. Glasgow is an extremely real city, with real people and real issues. The total lack of pretension, snobbery and the general friendliness of the majority is why I love it. I think of Glasgow as my home although I was born over 100 miles away.

The city itself is a sprawling mass of offices, superb shops, fabulous bars and has by far and away the best and coolest clubbing in Scotland. And if this doesn't satisfy your thirst for adventure, just jump on a train and less than half an hour away you're in Loch Lomond or another equally beautiful rural location.

Just ensure you've packed your wellies and the stunning, moth-eaten Mac that's been lurking at the back of your wardrobe for years, for the main problem with Glasgow and most of Scotland is that the weather takes the proverbial.

CITY SCENE

Whether its cheesy pop and chart, drum 'n' bass, Latin or mainstream house, there's a scene out there for you. The legendary, newly refurbished **Sub Club** for all your underground, hard house and techno needs, **The Arches, the biggest venue in Glasgow,** finds big names like Judge Jules, Trevor Nelson and the Colours fest being hosted regularly, and the **Garage** or **Fury Murry's** for all your normal student chart classics anytime, and **The Shed** for an unpretentious good time. Itchy recommends OOT @ The Stand Comedy as a 'gay friendly comedy night'. Also, Glasgow attracts the top concerts and tours from Elton John and Meatloaf to the National Ballet.

ART & ENTERTAINMENT

Arts-wise, there's a fine selection of galleries, museums, theatres and concert halls. The theatre scene is electric - there's no one big theatre but a host (at least fourteen) offering rep (cheapest: Gorbals-based **Citizens' Theatre**), cutting edge drama (**Tramway**, **Tron**), opera (**The Royal Concert Hall**) is brilliant and not just for upper class Tosca's, ballet at the **Royal**, comedy and light entertainment at the **Pavilion**, and panto and hypnotists at the **King's**.

For art it's try the **Kelvingrove Art Gallery and Museum** - superb and wonderfully peaceful place to wander. **The People's Palace** tells of Glasgow's history, the **Botanic Gardens** is a gem in the treasure trove of lazy Sunday occupations. **The Lighthouse** is an excellent place to view numerous exhibits, constantly changing.

For cinema it's the **Glasgow Film Theatre** for everything from foreign to Hollywood gloss; plus your usual multiplex for all the latest blockbusters at student prices.

SPORT

Sports lovers can not only see two of Scotland's best football teams in action, most exhilarating on Old Firm Derby days, but there are also lower league clubs which welcome students with open arms. Partick Thistle, for example, based in Maryhill just outside the city centre, offers cheap tickets and student membership cards for wannabe Jag fans. If not football, then head to Edinburgh for your rugby international action, although local and university ties are an excellent substitute.

PUBS

There is probably nowhere better than Glasgow for pubs, and we have some of the cheapest drinks prices in the UK. Students go for **Bargo** (Merchant City), **Blob Shop** bar (Charing Cross). And how can you refuse 'buy one get one free' on Tuesday's at pre-club **Spy Bar**? Although Glasgow city centre embraces students with open arms, student heaven is a mile or so out of town. You will probably find more Glaswegians in the West End of Madrid than in Glasgow's own West End, home to many students. Student-happy bars and pubs are **Cul de Sac**, **McChills**, **Cottiers.** The Byres Road area is the ultimate student village, with Safeways, banks, underground stations and pubs all within a stone's throw.

Fionna McChlery

UNIVERSITY OF GLASGOW

The University of Glasgow
University Avenue
Glasgow G12 8QQ

TEL 0141 330 4575
FAX 0141 330 4045
EMAIL admissions@gla.ac.uk
WEB www.gla.ac.uk

Glasgow University SRC
University Avenue
Glasgow G12 8QQ

GUU: 0141 339 8697
QMU: 0141 339 9784
EMAIL enquiries@src.gla.ac.uk
WEB www.src.gla.ac.uk

VAG VIEW

This particular university – one of three in the city – enjoys the rare distinction of having been established by Papal Bull, and began its existence in the Chapter House of Glasgow Cathedral in 1451. Today it still speaks of the city's traditions, but gives an objective sense of its long history. Since 1871 it has been based next to Kelvingrove Park on the Gilmorehill campus, 3 miles west of the city centre in the fashionable West End, with its many listed buildings.

What you get is a twofold opportunity – excellent teaching in a well-respected and traditional university, and, within reach, an exciting urban culture, which may surprise the unexpected in you.

CAMPUS GLASGOW

'Glasgow itself has some wonderful sites,' writes Sharon Gaines – 'but the West End, by the university, has its own unique atmosphere. Ashton Lane winds round cobbled paths leading to the trendiest pubs in this friendly part of town, while Byres Road facilitates the most extensive pub crawl – each within spitting distance. If the opulent Merchant City is the heart of the city, Great Western Road is its lungs. An old church looms over small quaint shops while half a mile of animal-like headlights shuffle slowly towards the flyover and three colossal tower blocks stand triumphantly in the distance. An awesome sight.

'If the more tranquil appeals to you, imagine gliding through a collage of a thousand colours of trees winding down a path passing two city heroes, dodging squirrels and birds until you land on a nineteenth-century bridge where the rain crashes down into the River Clyde, gushing downstream. This is the university's Kelvingrove Park – glorious in the autumn, brimming with smiling faces in the summer as everyone collates from across Glasgow on the hills.'

Campus overlooks Kelvingrove Park. Is it always so idyllic? 'Okay, it's not all roses,' Sharon concedes – 'The park is notoriously dangerous at night as are various parts of the city, but this is true of most big cities.'

There are other, less widely-known Glasgow Uni campuses. **St Andrew's College** is the new Faculty of Education, based since summer 2002 on Glasgow Caledonian Uni's old campus on Park Drive, where the West End starts. The Vet school and outdoor sports facilities are located at **Garscube**, with an £8-million development that includes a swimming pool, cardio-vascular suites and a wide range of gym facilities. To the south, in Dumfries, is **Crichton Campus**, which offers innovative study programmes to a mixture of full-time and part-time students, the first of whom are about to graduate.

FEES, BURSARIES

Fees for English: £1700 p.a. (Medicine: £2700). The Century 21 Club has enrolled 20 firms to sponsor undergraduates at £1000 a year, as part of an arrangement to forge closer links with local business. Another ten scholarships for students from poor backgrounds will commemorate the life of Donald Dewar, Scotland's late First Minister and alumnus of the university. The Beaton Scholarship is also part of their widening access scheme. There are also a few bursaries for students tackling a

UNIVERSITY/STUDENT PROFILE

University since	**1451**
Situation/style	**City Campus**
Student population	**24750**
Undergraduates	**19385**
- mature	**14%**
- non EU undergraduates	**3%**
- male/female	**42/58**
- non-traditional student intake	**23%**
- state school sector intake	**88%**
- drop-out rate	**9%**
- undergraduate applications	**Down 2%**

second undergrad course, a tuition fee waver for self-funding 4th-year undergrads, nine choral scholarships (£300) and one organ (£850), an Italian scholarship (where the language is part of your course), Stevenson Exchange Scholarship for French, Spanish and German study, sports bursaries (www.gla.ac.uk/services/sport). The uni is also considering facilitating access for hard-pressed students with other bursaries - e-mail: L.Hamilton@admin.gla.ac.uk. See also senate.gla.ac.uk/awards/indes.html for other prizes, scholarships and endowments open to students in particular departments.

STUDENT PROFILE

Glasgow has made headway in equal opportunities – more than a fifth of students are from backgrounds new to the idea of uni, and one in six from 'low-participation neighbourhoods. They are actively seeking financial support for these groups.

There are no social divisions on campus, which is almost half made up of students local to the region. As one student commented, 'there's a sense of community – you cannot fail to walk down University Avenue without bumping into someone who wants to nick your lecture notes.'

ACADEMIA & JOBS

Thirty-three assessments and a 91% Excellent or

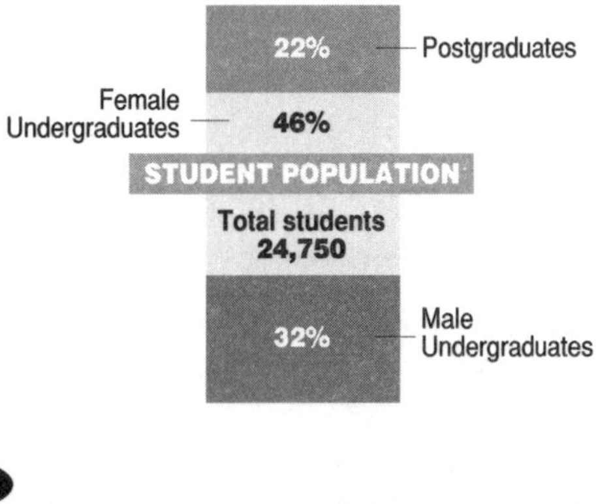

WHERE GLASGOW GRADUATES END UP

Health & Social Work: 28%; Education: 13%; Wholesale/Retail: 10%; Manufacturing: 5%; Financial Activities: 7%; Public Administration, Civil Service & Defence: 5%; Hotel/Restaurant: 5%; Transport & Communications (including Telecommunications): 3%; Construction: 1%; Mining/Oil Extracting: 1%; Personnel: 2%; Computer: 3%; Business & Management: 2%; Accountancy: 3%; Media (including Film): 2%; Legal 1.5%; Artistic/Literary: 1%; Sport: 1%.

Approximate 'graduate track' employed **65%**

Highly Satisfactory result speaks for itself. One characteristic of the syllabus is a huge programme of joint honours degrees – humanities, arts and social sciences. Research-wise, Glasgow ascended six places overall to 29th in Britain at the last research assessments, quadrupling its Grade 5* ratings (world excellence). Yet, their reputation is for being better focused on teaching their students than most. They make a deliberate effort to get more young staff in, and special needs advisers are on hand for students with disabilities and learning disadvantages.

Applications for science degrees have risen by 25% since the mid-1990s. More than a quarter of all Glasgow graduates get a job in the health industry. The degree in Medicine is a 5-year MB, characterised by clinical scenarios from Year 1, and IT featured instruction (all students are required to qualify for a Cert of Basic IT Competence). Entry AAB at A level (including Chemistry and one of Maths, Physics or Biology; General Studies not acceptable), AAAAB at Highers (including Chemistry and Biology and ether Maths or Physics. Also SG English at Grade 3). Teaching inspection, Excellent. Research Grade 5* Psychology; Grade 5 Clinical Lab Sciences, Hospital-based Clinical, Biological Sciences.

For dentists, it's a 5-year BDS. Entry ABB. Teaching inspection, Highly Satisfactory.

There's a strong call for Glasgow graduates to go into community work/counselling, they come through social studies, languages and BSc Psychology. See, too, their Podiatry degrees, which also have a sure employment basis.

After The Royal Veterinary College, Glasgow's 5-year BVMS Veterinary Medicine captures most of the graduate job market and is slightly lighter on entry, though still AAB. Teaching inspection, Excellent. Research Grade 5. They also have a Veterinary Nursing degree.

For Education, it's CCC or BBBC-BBCCC Highers for primary and secondary. They also turn out more adult education lecturers than anyone else. Languages are far and away the surest route in, perhaps because shortly after the acquisition of St Andrew's College of Education came the new School of Modern Languages & Cultures, which gives an international dimension to many degrees through six departments – Celtic, French, German, Hispanic, Italian and Slavonic. There's a world-class Grade 5* research rating for the School of English & Scottish Language.

Law, rated Grade 5 for research and coming at undergrad. level with language combos, and biological sciences are the next most certain route to employability. Biological sciences was rated Excellent at the assessments and, together with Law, has an international Grade 5 for research. Also

SUBJECT AREAS (%)

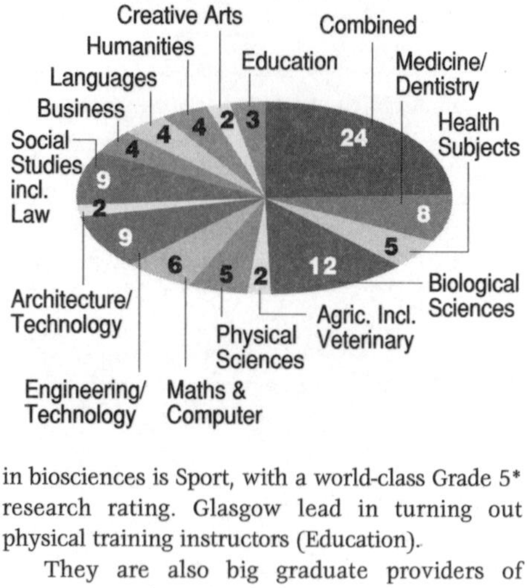

in biosciences is Sport, with a world-class Grade 5* research rating. Glasgow lead in turning out physical training instructors (Education).

They are also big graduate providers of accountants through various dedicated degrees. Note Accountancy with International Accounting in particular, but there are others – Accountancy with Finance looks tempting. The uni is also a proven launch pad for actuaries – look at the Applied Maths degrees.

Engineering and technology degrees lead, in

particular, to jobs in defence. Aeronautical, Audio & Video, Avionics, Electrical Power Engineering, Electronic & Software Engineering, etc, all pull weight in this direction and links are very tight with the Royal Air Force and the Royal Navy.

The faculty has expanded in collaboration with Strathclyde Uni over a series of Naval Architecture degrees. There are also various BEng/MEng Aeronautical, Civil, Electronics & Electrical, Mechanical Design, Mechanical (also joint with E&E, Aeronautics, Music, etc) and Product Design.

'Imagine S Club, Rage Against The Machine, Abba, 2 Unlimited, Kylie and Stevie Wonder, all mixed up, then wonder why you ever considered going anywhere else on a Friday night.'

A traditionally difficult but successful area for employment is Archaeology, available single hons/joint as part of the Science Group, or as an arts degree in the popular joint hons programme.

ACADEMIC EXCELLENCE

TEACHING:

(Rated Excellent, Highly Satis. or 17+ out of 24)

Computer Studies, Physics, Chemistry, Geography, Geology, Philosophy, Sociology, Cellular & Molec Biology, Organismal Biology, English, French, Medicine, Veterinary Medicine, Psychology, Social Policy.	**Excellent**
Civil Engineering, Music, Maths & Statistics, Mechanical + Manufacturing, Engineering, History of Art, History, Finance & Accounting, Law, Politics, Social Work, Theology, Dentistry, Nursing, Drama.	**Highly Satis.**
European Languages	**22**

RESEARCH:

*Top grades 5/5**

Psychology, European Studies, English, Sports	**Grade 5***
Clinical Laboratory Sciences, Hospital-based Clinical, Biological Sciences, Veterinary, Physics, Pure Maths, Applied Maths, Statistics, Computer, Electrical & Electronic Eng, Mechanical Eng, Town & Country Planning, Law, Politics, Accounting, French, History, History of Art, Theology	**Grade 5**

There are masses of MA joint hons possibilities, featuring Classical Civilisation, History of Art, Archaeology, Celtic Civilisation, Scottish History, Islamic Studies, etc, and the Language Department excels in its course design, too, adding depth to this joint programme with such as Polish, Czech, Russian, etc. Teaching inspection was Highly Satisfactory for History of Art, and research Grade 5, and thanks to such as this and the cultural aspect of its many courses, Glasgow leads the field in supplying museum archivists, curators and librarians.

THE CRICHTON CAMPUS Glasgow are offering seven broadly-based MAs, taught through 'virtual' and 'residential' lecturing. Cretaive & Cultural Studies, Enviro. Studies, Heath & Social Studies, Heritage & Tourism, Liberal Arts, Renewable Energy: Engineering in the Environment, and Scottish Studies. Glasgow-based expertise is on hand through video link-ups, while the benefits of one-to-one small group teaching is also maintained. *Course enquiries*: 01387 702001; Fax: 01387 702005.

SOCIAL SCENE

Glasgow, like UMIST, Imperial College, St Andrews, Edinburgh and Dundee, have cut themselves off from the National Union of Students at a saving of many thousands of pounds each year. Constant political issues this year have been anti students association and anti NUS. It's a moot point, however, whether Glasgow's own bureaucracy is better organised. 'Glasgow Uni is probably the most divided university in Glasgow,' writes Rachel Richardson with reference to the 'different bodies operating different aspects of university life. This leads to certain divisions.'

There are four union-type bodies – the Students Representative Council, Glasgow University Union and Queen Margaret Union. SRC is the political arm and administers the student societies, which are legion, supports volunteers and class representatives and is the official voice of the students on campus. Then there is GUSA, the sports association founded in 1881 that administers the sporting clubs. Adding to the confusion, postgrads have an organisation called the Research Club and there are boat clubs for both men and women, neither of which is affiliated to GUSA.

GUU operate from an impressively scary looking building at the foot of Gilmorehill. They

WHAT IT'S REALLY LIKE	
UNIVERSITY:	
Social Life	★★★★★
Campus scene	**Lively, diverse, fantastic fun**
Student Union services	**Good**
Politics	**Activity average Student issues**
Sport	**45 clubs**
National team position	**17th**
Sport facilities	**Good**
Arts opportunities	**Drama, music, art exc; dance good; film average**
Student newspaper	**GU Guardian**
Student magazine	**GUM, Qmunicate, GUUi**
Student radio	**SubCity Radio**
Radio Awards	**2005 winner**
Student TV	**G.U.S.T.**
TV Awards	**Two 2005 wins**
Nightclubs	**Qudos, Hive**
Bars	**Jim's Bar, Beer Bar, Deep-6, Altitude, Playing Fields**
Union ents	**Cheesy Pop rules + rock & indie, live**
Union clubs/societies	**120**
Most active society	**Dialectic or LGBT (lesbian, gay, bi- & transgender)**
Parking	**Poor**
CITY:	
Entertainment	★★★★★
Scene	**Very cool**
Town/gown relations	**Good**
Risk of violence	**High**
Cost of living	**High**
Student concessions	**Poor**
Survival + 2 nights out	**£80 pw**
Part-time work campus/town	**Poor/good**

AT A GLANCE	
ACADEMIC FILE:	
Subjects assessed	**33**
Excellent/Highly Satisfactory	**91%**
Typical entry requirements	**370 points**
Application acceptance rate	**17%**
Students-staff ratio	**14:1**
First/2:1 degree pass rate	**70%, high**
ACCOMMODATION FILE:	
Guarantee to freshers	**100%**
Style	**Halls, flats**
Catered	**7%**
En-suite	**23%**
Price range pw	**£65-£115**
City rent pw	**£80**

have 6 bars: **The Beer Bar** (traditional, with the names of the campus's fastest drinkers immortalised round the bar), **Altitude**, **Deep 6** (pseudo-trendy basement music bar – live bands, karaoke, juke box – open till 2am Fridays, half price cocktails, etc.), **The Playing Fields**, **Balcony Bar**, **The Hive** (the nightclub - *Lollypop* on Thursday; *Brie* (a higher class of cheese) on Friday).

QM's ents programme operates out of **Jim's Bar**, Games Room, the bottle bar and Qudos (their nightclub), 1100 capacity. The QM's main event is the long-running *Cheesy Pop* – Fridays, 10pm - 2pm, £1 members, £2 guests. Says one who knows: 'No two ways about it. Since 1993, when we invented the genre, *Cheesy Pop* has been the biggest and best student night in Scotland. Copied by many, but never equalled, the experience is still unique. Others interpret "cheesy" to mean crass, crap and often just down-right offensive, whereas *Cheesy Pop* is really about music which is fun. Imagine S Club, Rage Against The Machine, Abba, 2 Unlimited, Kylie and Stevie Wonder, all mixed up, then wonder why you ever considered going anywhere else.'

Tuesday is *Revolution* with DJ Muppet – 'rock, metal, hip hop, and a whole lot more', *Chart Attack* - Wednesday, *Style & Substance* - Thursday, and unplugged live acoustic on Sundays

Mention must be made of the lively journalistic scene at the uni: SubCity Radio (they won a Silver Award at the 2005 Student Awards), the *SRC-run Guardian* (newspaper), the *Glasgow University Magazine* (GUM, oldest student magazine in Scotland), the two Union publications, *GUUi* and *Qmunicate*, and GUST (oldest student TV station in the UK and winner of 2 awards this year as well as 2 Highly Commended).

Sport Excellent facilities, including a 25m pool, steam room and sauna, two activity halls with sprung flooring, basketball, volleyball, five-a-side soccer; a fitness and conditioning area, fully equipped. £1,500 pa bursaries offered in squash, athletics, rowing; £1,000 pa, golf: some forty courses in the area.

PILLOW TALK

Catered or self-catered halls of residence and self-catered student apartments are available, 7%

catered, 23% en suite. See *At A Glance* box for prices and look out for Queen Margaret Residences – 400 places all new, all en suite.

GETTING THERE

☛ By road: M8/J19 or J18. Good coach services.

☛ By rail: Edinburgh, 50 mins; London King's Cross, 5:00. Main campus Underground Station is Hillhead.

☛ By air: Glasgow Airport.

☛ By coach: London, 8:20; Birmingham, 6:20; Newcastle, 4:20.

GLASGOW CALEDONIAN UNIVERSITY

Glasgow Caledonian University
70 Cowcaddens Road
Glasgow G4 0BA

TEL 0800 027 9171
FAX 0141 331 3005
EMAIL helpline@gcal.ac.uk
WEB www.caledonian.ac.uk

Glasgow Caledonian Students' Association
70 Cowcaddens Road
Glasgow G4 0BA

TEL 0141 332 0681
FAX 0141 353 0029
EMAIL s.a.brady@gcal.ac.uk
WEB www.sa.gcal.ac.uk

VAG VIEW

Developments have centralised operations on one site instead of five, opened new accommodation (320 self-catering flats at Caledonian Court), a Sports Centre, a £17-million Health building and a new Learning Centre, The Saltire Centre. Now, they promise a new Student Union building, when hopefully we will see a more concentrated, student-led effort to get an extra-curricular student culture together. It is already looking up, with great success in sport over the past few years.

Meanwhile, they have been developing their on-going mission to extend access to higher education as widely as they can, by, among other things, running one of the largest summer schools in the country and sending so-called 'link students' into schools to show potential recruits what higher education is all about.

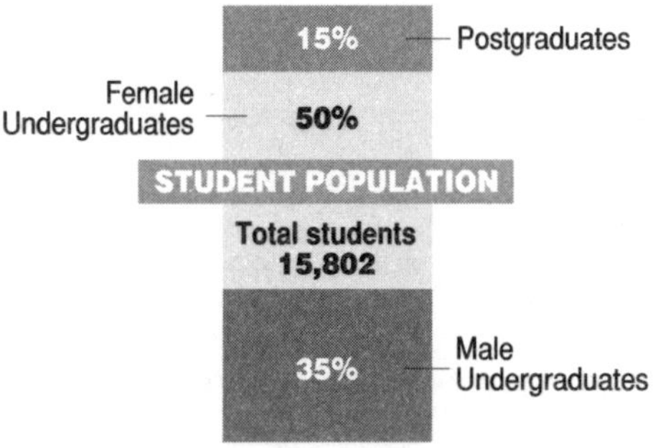

SUBJECT AREAS (%)

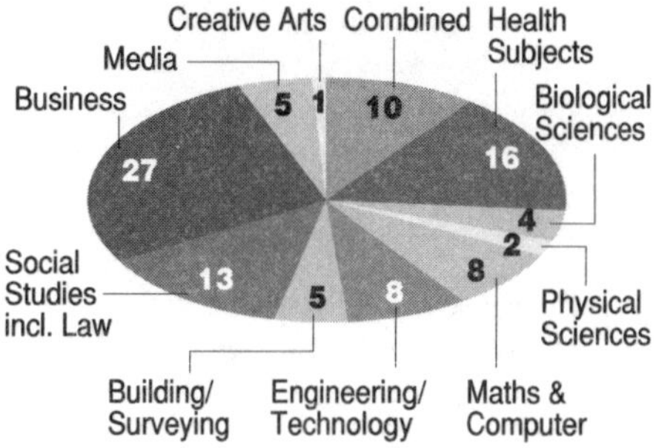

CAMPUS

City campus is on Cowcaddens Road, opposite Buchanan Bus Station, slap bang in the city centre. There is an amazing concentration of some 50,000 students here – Strathclyde University, the College of Building and Printing, the College of Food &

UNIVERSITY/STUDENT PROFILE

University since	**1992**
Situation/style	**City campus**
Student population	**15802**
Undergraduates	**13488**
- mature	**29%**
- non EU undergraduates	**2%**
- male/female	**41/59**
- non-traditional student intake	**38%, high**
-state school intake	**98%**
- drop-out rate	**12%, high**
- undergraduate applications	**Up 3%**

ACADEMIC EXCELLENCE	
TEACHING:	
Chemistry, Physiotherapy	**Excellent**
Physics, Consumer Studies, Maths & Statistics, Finance & Accounting, Mass Communications, Sociology, Social Work, Dietetics & Nutrition, Occupational Therapy, Psychology, Radiography, Biology, Nursing	**Highly Satis.**

WHAT IT'S REALLY LIKE	
UNIVERSITY:	
Social Life	★★
Campus scene	**Friendly**
Student Union services	**Average**
Politics	**Activity low**
Sport	**Some. Men's Hockey good**
National team position	**76th**
Sport facilities	**Average**
Arts opportunities	**Slim**
Student magazine	**Re:Union**
Venue	**The Bedsit**
Bars	**Main bar, Lounge, & Games Room**
Union ents	**Quiz, Caleyoke, cheesy disco, some live acts**
Union clubs/societies	**Handful**
Parking	**Poor**
CITY:	
Entertainment	★★★★★
Scene	**Cool**
Town/gown relations	**Good**
Risk of violence	**Average**
Cost of living	**Average**
Student concessions	**Good**
Survival + 2 nights out	**£70 pw**
Part-time work campus/town	**Good.**

Technology, and the College of Commerce are in the immediate vicinity.

FEES, BURSARIES

Fees for English: £1700 p.a. in 2006, but 'variable depending on programme,' so contact them. Scholarships are available in tourism and sport.

STUDENT PROFILE

'Most of Cally's recruits,' writes Rachel Richardson, 'are home-based students looking for a more vocational course.' Statistically, Cally has jumped in at the deep end, with some 38% of its entrants from groups which do not traditionally supply the university sector, and it has not been easy to get a cohesive student culture going. The drop-out rate is high - 23%.

ACADEMIA & JOBS

The university's new learning centre, The Saltire Centre - library and study facility - opened in January 2006.

Cally offer courses across six areas – Business, Engineering & the Environment (including Architectural Technology and various building and surveying courses, Music Technology with Electronics, and a host of other engineering and technology courses), Entrepreneurial & Service Sector (all kinds of management/retail/consumer courses), Health (including masses of nursing), Mathematical & Physical Sciences, and Social & Behavioural Sciences (they have recently been accredited by the Law Society of Scotland to run an LlB degree).

A new Learning Centre is planned. Meanwhile there are 350,000 volumes and extensive IT facilities in the library, including the REAL learning café.

Entry-wise, they want students who are motivated with enthusiasm and drive rather than A grades. The 24% health industry provision reveals the most measurable success story in nursing, optometry, podiatry, radiation science, ophthalmic dispensing and the like. They are the only Scottish uni to offer degrees in Optometry, and one of three that offer Occupational Therapy, Podiatry and Physiotherapy. There are also Nutrition degrees and even Medical Illustration, as well as Applied Bioscience courses.

Physiotherapy is a major career field. Over 1,000 graduates become physiotherapists each year. The route is straightforward – dedicated BSc Physiotherapy courses, which scooped the uni's best score at the assessments with an Excellent.

Their Podiatry degrees require only 120 points. the BSc Occupational Therapy is a 3-year sandwich course, undemanding at entry and highly successful in getting graduates jobs. There's a 2-year DipHE Ophtalmic Dispensing (DD at A level, BCC at Highers), and a 4-year BSc Optometry, which is more stretching, requiring BBB (BBBBB Highers, BBB Advanced Highers) to start.

For some time they have been specialists in commercial law. Now, following a new LLB, we can expect to see graduate employment taking off more in that direction. Meanwhile, bedrock Business and Finance courses continue to leave their mark on the graduate employment picture, as do Engineering and Architectural Technology and Built Environment courses.

WHERE GLASGOW CALEDONIA GRADUATES END UP

Health & Social Work: 24%; Education: 3%; Wholesale/Retail: 14%; Manufacturing: 7%; Financial Activities: 10%; Public Administration, Civil Service & Defence: 7%; Hotel/Restaurant: 6%; Transport & Communications (including Telecommunications): 4%; Construction: 4%; Personnel: 2%; Computer: 1%; Business & Management: 3%; Accountancy: 3%; Media (including Film): 1%; Legal 1%; Architecture: 3%; Publishing: 1%; Sport: 2%.

Approximate 'graduate track' employed **54%**

Nationwide, more than 4,500 graduates find work in the hotel and restaurant industry annually, and Cally are among the giants for the industry. See their Hospitality Management, Tourism Mgt, Entertainment & Events Mgt.

Property Development is another niche. Look at Property Mgt & Development/Property Studies, also such as Construction Mgt, Planning & Sustainable Development, and a good employment opportunity, BSc Quantity Surveying.

In Retail Management Manchester Met leads, followed by Ulster, but then in kicks Cally. Pre-eminent in the Business Faculty are its degrees in Retailing, Consumer & Trading Standards, Fashion Business, etc.

Finally, there is a sound employment track record in Interior Design. Explore their Applied Graphics Technology with Multimedia.

SOCIAL SCENE

Student Association It may be different when you get there, because a whole new Student Centre has been promised, but as we write, this is how it is. The **Disco Bar,** also known as the **Front** or **Main Bar** is decorated on a music theme, the wall hung with iconic rock images. Music is a constant feature, and you can even bring along your own CD's for the bar to play. There are 3 plasma screens and a pool table. Sometimes it justifies its name by turning into a club with DJ's playing cheesy pop to rock to r'n'b. Every Friday is *Funky Friday*. Such as Jamelia, Speedway, Ben from Hollyoakes, Scott Anderson, South Beach, Stu from big Brother, Trevor Nelson and Vernon Kay have visited. Then there's the **Lounge Bar**, also known as the **Back Bar** and by day a coffee bar, by night a chill zone, with *Caley Oke* (karaoke talent contest) on Wednesday, with a little help from the Bedsit's own Calley Swalley. There are 2 plasma screens, which show MTV or any large sporting event, and it has recently been refubished. Upstairs is the **Games Room** with a multitude of TV's playing MTV throughout the day, 6 pool tables and food (it's the main place for it in the union).

Then there's the **Hub**, info and resource centre for sports clubs and societies. Students use it to organise student activities for socs like Alpha for Students, Amnesty International, Chinese Students Association, Christian Union, Music Soc, Muslim Soc, GT Events, Hellenic Society, International Students, Lesbian, Gay, Bisexual Society, SSOS.

Finally, **Arc** gives access to health and fitness services and facilities, including a gym, a place to relax and de-stress at a yoga or t'ai chi class, to work out, play badminton or book in for a therapeutic massage session.

The large mature, local and part-time population is suggested as the reason for the relatively low level of action - Funky Friday is over by 7 pm. The challenge is that after nightfall and at weekends the place is deserted, while in the day, the bars are full to overflowing.

See also *Glasgow Student City*, page 195.

Sport Investment in sport facilities has been rewarded with great success in the British Uni Sport Association (BUSA) league. There are loads of sports clubs: rugby, soccer (male and female), athletics catered for alongside such as snowboarding, hillwalking and table tennis. It's the Bearsden dry ski slopes for GCU Club Ski and the real white stuff for weekends in semester two. The

AT A GLANCE

ACADEMIC FILE:	
Subjects assessed	**23**
Excellent/Highly Satisfactory	**65%**
Typical entry requirements	**275 points**
Application acceptance rate	**16%**
Students-staff ratio	**21:1**
First/2:1 degree pass rate	**59%**
ACCOMMODATION FILE:	
Guarantee to freshers	**No**
Style	**Flats**
Catered	**None**
En suite	**50%**
Approx price range pw	**£60-£80**
City rent pw	**£60-£80**

Hillwalking and Mountaineering Club is the largest – weekends away in Glen Coe.

PILLOW TALK

For lucky first years, it's Caledonian Court, adjacent to campus, 6-8 bedroom flats.

GETTING THERE

- By road: M8/J19 or J18. Good coach services.
- By rail: 50 minutes Edinburgh, 5 hours London.
- By Underground: Cowcaddens and Buchanan Street Stations are nearby.
- By air: Glasgow Airport.

GLASGOW SCHOOL OF ART

Glasgow School of Art
167 Renfrew Street
Glasgow G3 6RQ

TEL 0141 353 4512
FAX 0141 353 4408
EMAIL info@gsa.ac.uk
WEB www.gsa.ac.uk

SCHOOL PROFILE

Founded	**1845**
Status	**Art School**
Degree awarding university	**Glasgow**
Student population	**1500**
Full-time undergraduates	**1265**
ACCOMMODATION:	
Availability in college	**118 places**
Style	**Flats**
Cost pw (no food)	**£54 to £72**
City rent pw	**£80-£80**

DEGREE SUBJECT AREAS:
Art, architecture, design & humanities, engineering

This is one of the oldest and largest independent art schools in the country. It is centred on the Mackintosh Building, generally considered to be the masterwork of former student Charles Rennie Mackintosh.

There are three curricular schools: Design & Craft, Fine Art and Architecture. Teaching assessments have been Excellent for Architecture and Highly Satisfactory for Fine Art and Design & Craft.

Resources include a library, substantial art archives of international significance, two galleries and various other in-house exhibition areas. Becoming a student entails participation in the flourishing artistic community of the city of Glasgow. Tramway, one of the largest and most innovative art spaces in the UK, and The Centre for Contemporary Art (CCA), just next door to the school, provide the platform for this. An active Students' Association promotes educational and cultural activities. Limited accommodation nearby in Margaret Macdonald House (self-catering flats).

UNIVERSITY OF GLOUCESTERSHIRE

The University of Gloucestershire
Park Campus
Cheltenham
Gloucestershire GL50 4BS

TEL 01242 532825
FAX 01242 543334
EMAIL admissions@glos.ac.uk
WEB www.glos.ac.uk

Gloucestershire Uni Students' Union
PO Box 220
The Park
Cheltenham GL50 2RH

TEL 01242 532848
FAX 01242 261381
EMAIL pksu@glos.ac.uk
WEB www.ugsu.org/

SUBJECT AREAS (%)

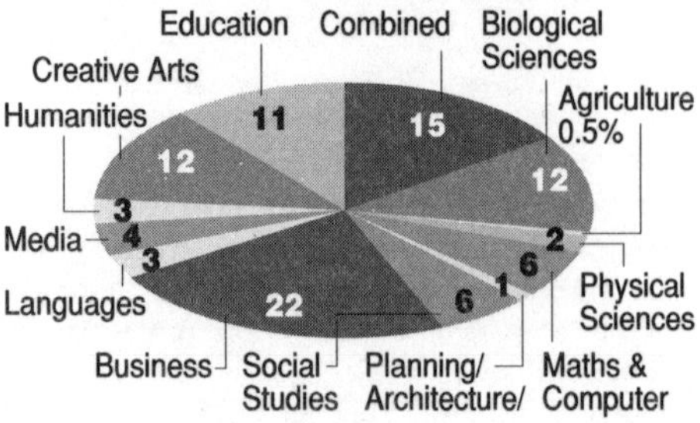

VAG VIEW

The sometime Cheltenham & Gloucester College of Higher Education, out of which Gloucester Uni was born in 2001, was established in 1990, following a merger between the College of St Paul and St Mary and the higher education section of Gloucestershire College of Arts and Technology. They now have a campus in Gloucester, too, initially for the sporting fraternity.

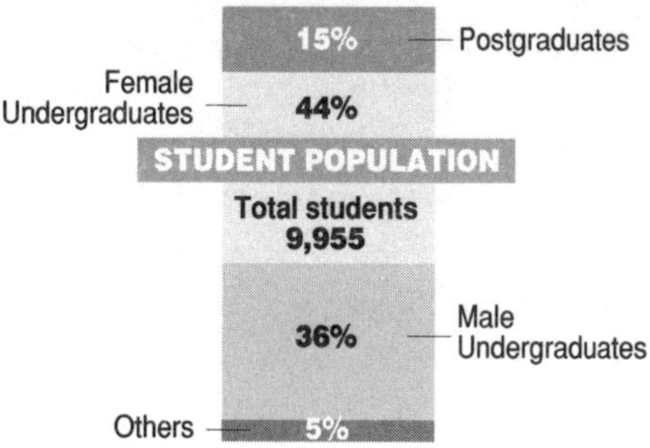

CAMPUS

There are three sites in Cheltenham. Park campus is the main site, then there's Francis Close Hall (FCH) and Pittville. When you turn up at Park, don't confuse it with the nearby Gloscat, monstrous further education establishment in crying need of a facelift. No, this is the one up the road that copped the dosh, though there academic associations with their health and teaching foundation degrees. The main campus is leafy, white, everything – halls, bars, lecture theatres – close to hand and spanking new it seems, though many of the buildings must have been here for some time. It was once a botanic garden.

UNIVERSITY/STUDENT PROFILE

University since	**2001**
Situation/style	**Town sites**
Student population	**9955**
Undergraduates	**7965**
- mature	**40%**
- non EU undergraduates	**3%**
- male/female	**45/55**
- non-traditional student intake	**30%**
- state school intake	**96%**
- drop-out rate	**9%**
- undergraduate applications	**Constant**

The newer £15-million Oxstalls Campus has opened in the cathedral city of Gloucester. It was part of their remit that they would open up there. It is being used by the School of Sport, but will be developed and the subject base widened. There's a Student Union building, halls of residence for completion this year, a refectory and astroturf, a sports science building and learning resources centre.

FEES & BURSARIES

UK & EU Fees: £3000 p.a. Relief on a sliding scale for those meeting the conditions of an Higher Education Maintence Grant.

STUDENT PROFILE

Broadly, Pittville attracts interesting/arty-types, Park besuited-&-booted business management-types, and FCH sporty-types, though presumably they're off to Oxstalls now. Like Oxford Brookes, and unusual in a new-uni demography, there was once a lean to independent school types and a very low drop-out rate. Now the intake of non-traditional uni types has tripled, independent school types are few, and the drop-out rate, which went wild for a while, has been tamed to a neat 9%. Despite big changes, students talk of the 'really great sense of community – unusual for an institute split into various campuses.

ACADEMIA & JOBS

First degree subjects fall into 3 faculties: Arts & Education (split between Park and Pittville),

WHERE GLOUCESTERSHIRE GRADUATES END UP

Health & Social Work: 5%; Education: 20%; Wholesale/Retail: 13%; Manufacturing: 6%; Financial Activities: 9%; Public Administration, Civil Service & Defence: 7%; Hotel/Restaurant: 7%; Transport & Communications (including Telecommunications): 3%; Construction: 1%; Personnel: 5%; Computer: 4%; Business & Management: 2%; Media (including Film): 2%; Legal 1%; Architecture: 0.5%; Publishing: 2%; Advertising: 1%; Artistic/Literary: 1%; Sport: 3%.

Approximate 'graduate track' employed **54%**

Business & Social Studies (Park), Environment & Leisure (FCH and Oxstalls). The programmes (BA/BSc Hons) are modular and very broad based. There is a choice of single, joint or major/minor courses, each of them composed of more than twenty modules with often less than clear synergy between subjects.

Hundreds of main subject combinations are offered, from which you will build your course. It can be quite daunting.

Sixteen per cent of its graduate output goes into primary education. The courses go from Nursery through Key Stage 2. This is the old Cheltenham & Gloucester College turned uni.

> ***There's a middle-of-the-road feel about this uni, which may be no bad thing. The huge inter-scheme modular programme continues to baffle, but the union is spot on, and the clean white lines of Park promise students the luxury to which many may well already be accustomed.***

Thereafter, managers and administrators, sales and other miscellaneous occupations proliferate from the modular degree system, with its endless but often tedious-looking combination possibilities. Business and Administrative Studies of one sort or another account for around 20% of the curriculum, even more than Education. The notably vocational interest from applicants who, for one reason or another, do choose to go to Gloucestershire is evident, too, in the recent dropping of Theology from the degree menu. Given that Lord Carey, former Archbishop of Canterbury, is the uni chairman, and that the uni is fathered by two church colleges, and that the department scored 23 out of 24 in the assessments, and Grade 4 for research, this is quite a statement. English also got a Grade 4 incidentally, nationally sound.

One significant interest point in their employment record is the category of sports trainers and coaches, graduates coming from Biological Sciences and Education. The Sport & Exercise Science courses reflect an interest rooted in one of the uni's original constituent parts, a sports college.

There's also a good record in community and youth work – see Community Studies combos, though graduates come from all over the curriculum to this. Also, the Human Resource Management degrees score well in the employment sector, again part of the Business & Admin part of the list.

Among the smaller universities who put 5% plus of their graduates into catering, Gloucester figures strongly with masses of hospitality and hotel/catering degrees on offer. Teaching inspection, 21.

Future events or conference managers should also apply. There are dedicated degree courses for this increasingly popular sector, such as Evenents Management.

Graphic artists and designers also find work and there's a fair reputation here for Film, and an emphasis recently on photojournalism.

SOCIAL SCENE

'Cheltenham & Gloucester is a fab, mad, lovely place,' I was told and didn't find much to contradict it. There are 4 bars, one on each campus. A workmanlike ents programme makes good use of the large, airy **Park Bar** with stage and seriously provocative sound and lighting systems.

Fancy dress parties figure, with *Drink Around The World* events, a different country represented at each of the three bars. There's karaoke, fun and games type *Open-the-Box* drink promo nights, **Pittville Bar** *Bingo*, various balls (the Summer Ball sells upwards of 7,000 tickets, then there's Christmas Ball, Freshers Ball, Graduation Ball) and the odd *Doctors & Nurses* night, with *Sub:Mission* the big Saturday night attraction. Also some local live bands (bigger names at balls). Sports bar, Oxtalls, at Gloucester campus is big on match days, of course.

ACADEMIC EXCELLENCE

TEACHING:	
(Rated Excellent or 17+ out of 24)	
Geography	**Excellent**
Theology	**23**
Town & City Planning, Art & Design, Psychology, Tourism, Sport	**21**
Sociology, Communication & Media Studies	**20**
RESEARCH:	
*Top grades 5/5**	**None**

It is still largely a local uni and so tends to be a bit deserted at weekends, though this *is* changing, thanks to international interest in the Business School and an ever-increasing stream of Chinese, and Norwegians for some reason.

It is fair to point out, too, that the emphasis now is on clubnights in town with the local SU bar providing a kind of pre-club, warm-up session.

WHAT IT'S REALLY LIKE

UNIVERSITY:	
Social Life	★★★
Campus scene	**Middle of the road, local**
Politics	**Interest low**
Sport	**Very competitive**
National team position	**37th**
Arts opportunities	**OK, film good**
Student newspaper	**Space**
Nightclub	**Sub:Mission @ Park**
Bars	**Park, Pittville, FCH and Oxstalls**
Union ents	**Cheesy + huge Balls**
Union clubs/societies	**52 (32 sport)**
Parking	**Poor**
TOWN:	
Entertainment	★★★
Scene	**OK clubs, pubs, good shopping**
Risk of violence	**Average**
Cost of living	**High**
Student concessions	**Excellent**
Survival + 2 nights out	**£70 pw**
Part-time work campus/town	**Good**

AT A GLANCE

ACADEMIC FILE:	
Subjects assessed	**17**
Excellent	**53%**
Typical entry requirements	**240 points**
Application acceptance rate	**21%**
Students-staff ratio	**18:1**
First/2:1 degree pass rate	**41%**
ACCOMMODATION FILE:	
Guarantee to freshers	**100%**
Style	**Halls, flats, houses**
Catered	**None**
En suite	**60%**
Approx price range pw	**£64-£85**
Town rent pw	**£60**

There is a sense of the society scene maturing. *Space* is the excellent fortnightly newspaper. The Film Society is very active. PDS (The Pittville Degree Show Society) puts on charity fund raisers throughout the year. The Art Society puts on fine shows at the end of each year in Pittville. If this is to be but the beginning of something bigger, it will take organisation and investment.

Sport They do well in the BUSA leagues. It's their big thing. There is a swimming pool, sports hall, pitches (known as ***The Folley***), a fitness suite, and at Oxstalls a sports science lab and astro turf pitch.

Town Cheltenham itself has fantastic shops (classy, unique and your high street shops too), some good pubs, the **Arts Centre** and a few clubs.

'Gold Cup Week brings the Irish to town and loadsa money,' a student confides, 'a great week for all the girls to go out. You get plied with drink after drink. This week is RAG week, just the best week of the academic calendar!! Tons of fun and misbehaviour, being on a float, driven in front of crowds of people, drunk in charge of a water pistol by 9am, expecting a lot of "cheek" from the rugby boys. And all for charity!' Is it *always* so...baby doll? I venture. 'Well, Christmas carols in FCH chapel are always a laugh...specially with all that *mulled* wine in you.'

PILLOW TALK

Apply early for the luxurious-looking, mixed, self-catered or half-board halls at Park. Priority goes to first years and overseas students. New halls in Gloucester and more planned for this year in Cheltenham.

GETTING THERE

- ☛ By road: M5/J11 or M40/A40 or M4/J15, A419. Good coach service.
- ☛ By rail: Bristol Parkway, 45 mins; Birmingham, 1.00; London Paddington, 2:30.
- ☛ By coach: London, 2:35; Birmingham, 1:10.

GOLDSMITHS COLLEGE, LONDON

University of London Goldsmiths College
New Cross
London SE14 6NW

TEL 020 7919 7766
FAX 020 7717 2240
EMAIL admissions@gold.ac.uk
WEB www.goldsmiths.ac.uk

Goldsmiths Students' Union
Dixon Road
London SE14 6NW

TEL 020 8692 1406
FAX 020 8694 9789
EMAIL gcsu@gold.ac.uk
WEB www.gcsu.org.uk)

VAG VIEW

Goldsmiths is a college of the University of London, famous for its postmodern art department, ents programme, and for the active commitment of its students to fairness and justice. It is located in south-east London, and was listed as a cool brand leader' with MTV by the Brand Council in 2004.

'Ours is one of the most exciting colleges in the country,' I was told. 'It's unpretentious [Oh, right], *set in London and neatly poised between a bad-ass ents programme and radical action. We have one of the most politically active Students' Unions in the country.'*

CAMPUS

'So, you want to know about Goldsmiths?' said Siobhan Daly. 'Well, don't come here looking for the architectural splendours of Oxbridge or the serenity of Durham. This is south-east London: bold, brash and full of embodiments of Delboy Trotter. One of my friends cried when she arrived, saying that it looked more like Grange Hill than a university.' But isn't Deptford supposed to be the new Hoxton, or is it the new Montmartre?

FEES, BURSARIES

UK & EU Fees: £3000. Bursary pf £1000 if in receipt of full HE Maintenance Grant, £300 if partial. Also academic achievement scholarships available.

STUDENT PROFILE

You don't need me to say this. The student type here is best described as 'arty'. There are no natural sciences taught at Goldsmiths and Damian 'pickled-cows' Hirst, Placebo, Julian Clary and Blur all strutted their stuff here in glorious Goldies, so you can see where the scene is at. 'This doesn't, however, mean that you have to conform to the general "I'm-finding-myself" principle of dressing,' I am reassured. 'Just do whatever you want; be yourself.

'If you are a heterosexual man, you'll love it here. If you are a homosexual woman, you'll also love it here. Goldsmiths is 65% women and the competition is hot! This is probably why *Club Sandwich* is so popular. If you are homosexual, the LGB relations here are brilliant, and there's usually a *Coming Out Night* once a term.'

UNIVERSITY/STUDENT PROFILE

College of London Uni since	**1904**
Situation/style	**Campus**
Student population	**7695**
Undergraduates	**4610**
- mature	**79%, high**
- non EU undergraduates	**8%**
- male/female	**35/65**
- non-traditional student intake	**28%**
state school intake	**91%**
- drop-out rate	**7%**
- undergraduate applications	**Up 10%**

ACADEMIA & JOBS

Local evening classes still part of the picture. The standard of teaching of Goldsmiths is variable, if one is to go by the official teaching assessments. The Psychology Department is very good, whereas the English Department didn't do so well, though it is Grade 5 for research. However, there is a Goldsmiths way of teaching, which may not always coincide with the inspectorate's, but which is part of what has led to their nomination, for the second year running, for the country's coolest brands. They are vigorously non-judgemental and the subject combinations are very much their own, interdisciplinary, encouraging innovative ideas: visual and performing arts exerting a liberating influence among mathematical and social scientists, for example.

2005 saw an ambitious new Arts Complex open, which will reflect its interdisciplinary approach. The new Centre for Cognition, Computation & Culture houses studios and teaching facilities for the Visual Arts Department, and draw on both the scientific and cultural aspects of cognition.

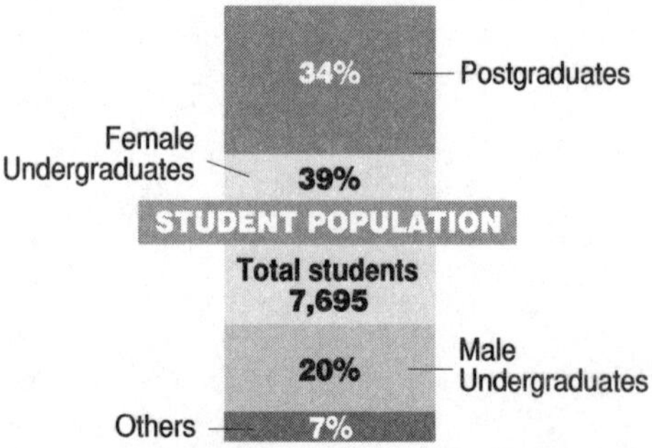

Fine Arts has the lowest work load – never arrange to meet art students in the library, they'll never find it. If they did, they'd discover some 230,000 vols, 9,500 music scores, a computer centre and language facility, all in the Rutherford Information Services Building. Investment has recently been directed to new music practice rooms for solo and ensemble work.

If the proof that it all works is not to be found in their teaching assessment record – 67%

Excellent puts it on a par with Glasgow Caledonian – it may, against the odds, be glimpsed in their graduate employment statistics in education, the arts, media, for example. Their provision excels in two classes – Library/Archival Information Services (which might be anything from museums to libraries to art galleries, etc, and will not doubt be swelled by a new Unit of Visual Cultures, attached to the History Department, which teaches history of art and visual cultures.), and in Radio/TV. Goldsmiths graduates do make waves through the Media & Communications course (22 at the assessments), so popular with students and now accompanied by International Media. Indeed, all told, some 9% of Goldsmiths graduates found positions of some sort in media, film, journalistic or artistic occupations in the end. Which is good by any standards. Also, provision to the publishing and advertising industries is always among the top in the country.

If you choose to study here you will be in London, and that gives you as many choices and opportunities as you are willing to take. A would-be journalist will be in a better position than out of town students, for example, when it comes to trying to get a placement on a London-based national paper.

At the end of it all, however, with its cutting-edge, cool appeal, it is all too easy to lose sight of the fact that Goldsmiths, the hip college of London Uni, gives most of its graduates to primary school education. Then the hard reality is that it's clerks, sales assistants, secondary school teachers, accounts and wages clerks, etc. The glamorous fashionable end of things, it seems, is also highly competitive and will never be open to all.

A host of Goldies graduate social workers highlight their BA Applied Social Science, Community Development and Youth Work (BA Social Work is currently up for approval), as well as their excellent BSc Psychology degree.

See also Computer Science, Computer & Information Systems and Internet Computing (all available as 4-year degree with work experience). These last degrees make IT consultants, software engineers and computer programmers of their students.

Creative Arts graduates either don't keep the university informed (which is likely) or very few find success. Here perhaps are the clerks, sales assistants, waiters and telephone sales persons, along with the odd editor, art gallery assistant, teacher of music or dancing, actor, entertainer, composer, artist and designer. It takes time to ply your talent as an artist of any persuasion and employment figures are recorded a mere six

ACADEMIC EXCELLENCE

TEACHING:
(Rated Excellent or 17+ out of 24)

Music	**Excellent**
Sociology	**23**
Media & Communications, Drama, Psychology, Art &	**22**
Maths	**21**
Design, Economics, Politics History of Art	**19**

RESEARCH:
Top grades 5/5/6**

Sociology	**Grade 6***
Communication/Cultural/Media,	**Grade 5***
Anthropology, English, Art & Design, Music	**Grade 5**

SUBJECT AREAS (%)

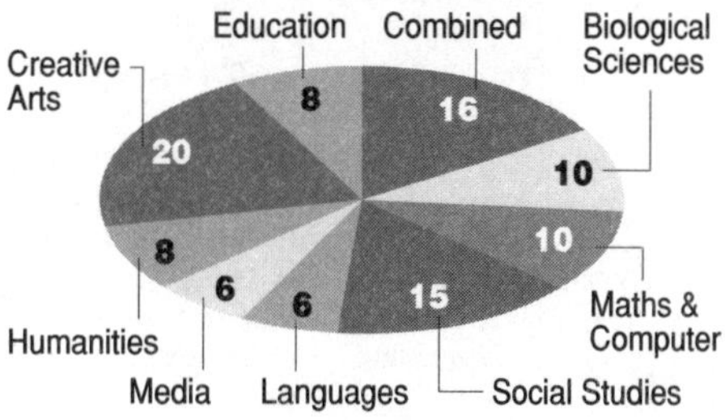

WHERE GOLDSMITHS GRADUATES END UP

Health & Social Work: 10%; Education: 22%; Wholesale/Retail: 12%; Manufacturing: 5%; Financial Activities: 6%; Public Administration, Civil Service & Defence: 10%; Hotel/Restaurant: 3%; Transport & Communications (including Telecommunications): 2%; Construction: 0.5%; Personnel: 6%; Computer: 3%; Business & Management: 2%; Media (including Film): 3%; Legal 2%; Architecture: 0.5%; Publishing: 3%; Advertising: 1%; Artistic/Literary: 3%; Sport: 0.5%.

Approximate 'graduate track' employed **61%**

WHAT IT'S REALLY LIKE

COLLEGE:	
Social Life	★★★★
Campus scene	**Trendy, radical**
Student Union services	**Average**
Politics	**Centre-to-far left: fees, racism, war**
Sport	**Relaxed; 20 clubs**
National team position	**Nil point**
Sport facilities	**Average-poor**
Arts opportunities	**Excellent film, theatre**
Student magazine	**Smiths**
2004 Awards	**Best Magazine**
2005 Awards	**Runner-up Best Feature Writer**
Student radio	**Wired**
Club venue + bar	**The Stretch**
Bar & café	**The Green Room**
Union ents	**Club Sandwich + drum 'n bass**
Union clubs/societies	**70**
Most popular societies	**African-Caribbean, Student CND**
Parking	**Non-existent**
CITY:	
Entertainment	★★★★★
Scene	**Wild, expensive, but locally pure**
Town/gown relations	**OK**
Risk of violence	**London v. high**
Cost of living	**Very high**
Student concessions	**Average**
Survival + 2 nights out	**£100 pw**
Part-time work campus/town	**Good/locally poor**

months after graduation.

SOCIAL SCENE

STUDENTS UNION Their building is called **Tiananmen, The Green Room** is the bar, and **The Stretch** is the bar/club venue – recent visitors are Roni Size, Goldie, Athlete. 'Our Students' Union may be a concrete monstrosity, but there's a fab nightlife hidden inside and rather outstanding alcohol prices,' writes Siobhan.

Especially active, besides LGB, are Afro-Carribean Soc, Student CND, Stage & Musical Society, the Student Assembly Against Racism and the Asian Cultural. They are very active politically, non-party, centre to far left.

There is also a strong culture of altruism. Goldsmiths piloted a student prison visiting scheme, just nominated for the National Student Volunteering Awards.

'If you're worried about not finding religious support groups, don't be, as there are a lot of good societies such as the Christian Union and Muslim Society, as well as local chaplains and a multi-denominational prayer room.'

Student magazine *Smiths* regularly features in the student media awards, in 2004 took Magazine of the Year and 2005 the Runner-up Award for Best Feature Writer. Student radio is Wired.

TOWN 'Apart from the wonders of the hallowed union, there are some good pubs in New Cross. I'd particularly like to point out the **Hobgoblin** on New Cross Road which has just been refurbished and is fab – there's also 20% off drinks between 3 pm and 8 pm, Monday to Friday – perfect drinking time! There's also the **Goldsmiths Tavern** (no relation), licensed until 2 am, the **Marquis of Granby** and the **New Cross Inn**, all within crawling distance of each other. The one club in New Cross is entitled **The Venue** but, personally, the all-black façade and the "A Tribute to..." nights rather put me off. Luckily, central London is only about a twenty minute journey from both New Cross and New Cross Gate stations.

'The cost of living in London is high. Travel is expensive; eating out is expensive; even food shopping is expensive.

'If you're coming from an obscure little village where everybody knows each other and they all leave their cars and houses unlocked, wise up, lock up, tie everything down, walk in well-lit areas and carry that safety alarm your Mum bought you.'

SPORT The playing fields are at least half an hour's drive away in Kent. Few seem to make it; they no points in the national team listings last year.

AT A GLANCE

ACADEMIC FILE:	
Subjects assessed	**15**
Excellent	**67%**
Typical entry requirements	**280 points**
Application acceptance rate	**17%**
Students-staff ratio	**16:1**
First/2:1 degree pass rate	**64%**
ACCOMMODATION FILE:	
Guarantee to freshers	**95%**
Style	**Halls**
Catered	**None**
Ensuite	**73%**
Approx price range pw	**£73-£94**
City rent pw	**£80-£100**

PILLOW TALK

'Halls here are quite reasonable for London [£73-£94 per week]; my flat is £80 before bills so make of that what you will,' reveals Siobhan.

Decent en-suite hall development sees Loring now satisfying 400 students and Dean House 95. 'The on-site Loring Hall is the best on offer in my opinion,' Siobhan confirms, 'every room has an en-suite bathroom, personal telephone (you will be grateful for it!) and you can get cable television. Rachel Macmillan Halls have a good reputation for friendliness but are about a thirty minute walk from college. They're also bleak and old.

'Raymont is well esteemed, but St James's (all-girls) had cockroaches a couple of years ago and Surrey House smells. I do however, recommend staying in halls during your first year, even if you already live in London, as you get to meet so many people.'

GETTING THERE

☛ By road: at the junction of A2 and A20.
☛ By rail: New Cross Gate or New Cross Underground and overland.

UNIVERSITY OF GREENWICH

The University of Greenwich
Maritime Greenwich Campus
Old Royal Naval College
Greenwich
London SE10 9LS

TEL 0800 005006
020 8331 8000
FAX 020 8331 8145
EMAIL courseinfo@greenwich.ac.uk
WEB www.gre.ac.uk

VAG VIEW

Greenwich Uni is bit by bit up-rooting from its disparate bases and focusing more keenly on its £50-million headquarters at Maritime Greenwich Campus, a setting described by the London Evening Standard *as 'one of the grandest of any university in the world'.*

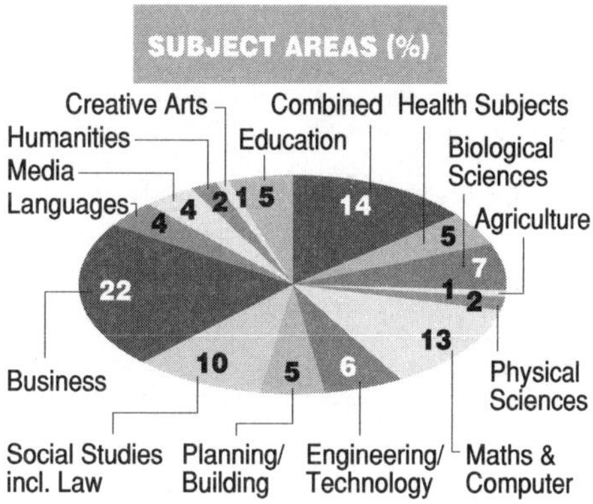

CAMPUSES

Maritime Greenwich has humanities, business, law, computing,maritime studies, maths in the Sir Chris Wren designed, former Royal Naval College, the uni's flagship campus. There's a library, computing facilities of course, some postgrad accommodation, a conference centre and the Greenwich Maritime Institute (a research/postgrad teaching facility). There's also **Bar Latitude**. Excellent party atmosphere, by all accounts, but light on ents. Drinks promos, pool competition nights, karaoke, comedy. Accommodation 10-15 minutes walk away: Binnie Court and Devonport House halls, and new Cutty Sark and McMillan Student Village en-suite residences. Student accommodation is improving greatly, but apply very early for the best.

Avery Hill Bexley Road, Eltham, London SE9 2PQ, and Every Hill Road, Eltham, London SE9 2HB. Has health & social care, social sciences, education, architecture, landscape and construction. Particularly good student atmosphere at the Village, on 86 acres of parkland. There's a magnificent library, the **Dome** nightclub, made up of **Mazey's** and **Jesters** bars – Fridays is *Dizzy* which reaches capacity (1,000). Wednesday is *Excess* (party, cheese). Saturday can be live – Trevor Nelson recently. There are also two gyms, soccer, rugby, lacrosse and hockey and cricket pitches, a running track and tennis courts. A short walk away is the **Sparrows Farm Centre,** the sporting facility, situated next door to Charlton Athletic's training ground, behind the student village. It has squash courts, fitness suite, sauna and solarium and the **Sports Bar**. Village accommodation is open to all students from Greenwich Uni (Maritime Campus is 40 mins by bus away – there's a regular peak-time service). Shared flats and maisonettes, some en suite.

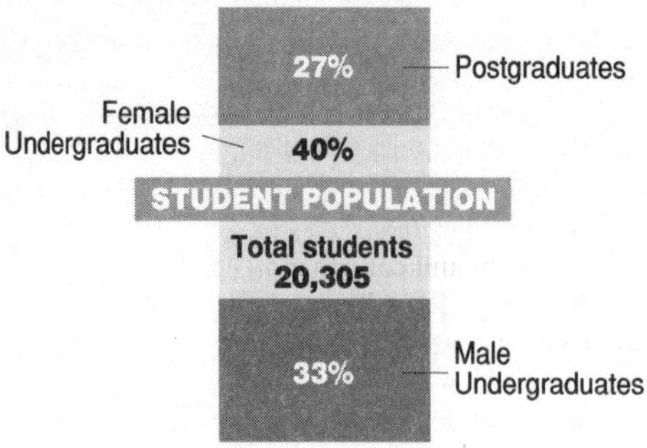

UNIVERSITY/STUDENT PROFILE

University since	**1992**
Situation/style	**City sites**
Student population	**20305**
Undergraduates	**14890**
- mature	**58%**
- non EU undergraduates	**8%**
- male/female	**45/55**
- non-traditional student intake	**46%, v. high**
state school intake	**96%**
- drop-out rate	**13%, high**
- undergraduate applications	**Up 5%**

ACADEMIC EXCELLENCE

TEACHING:
(Rated Excellent or 17+ out of 24)

Environmental Studies, Architecture.	**Excellent**
Town & Country Planning	**24**
Sociology, Pharmacology, Nursing	**23**
Psychology	**22**
Building, Land/Property Mgt, Civil Engineering, Politics, Philosophy, Theology	**21**
Molecular Biosciences, Organismal Biosciences, Educ, Economics, Agriculture, Business, Sport	**20**
Communication/Media, Maths	**19**
Subjects Allied to Medicine	**18**

RESEARCH:
*Top grades 5/5** **None**

Medway Pembroke, Chatham Maritime, Kent ME4 4AW. Has engineering, science, pharmacy, nursing, some business, and incorporates the Natural Resources Institute, a sports hall with badminton and basketball courts and a weights room. There's a friendly traditional pub-style bar, **The Drunken Sailor**, with adjacent **SUB** venue – resident DJs and regular ents. There are 2 newish halls of residence – shared en-suite flats – close to campus.

FEES, BURSARIES

UK & EU Fees: £2500 p.a. Bursaries of £500 for HE Maintenace grant holders and £500 p.a. academic achievement scholarships too.

STUDENT PROFILE

Many come from overseas and receive sterling support. The university provides immigration info concerning visas, working and health, and academic assistance: English classes, study skills, personal tutors and social events geared to integrate into the British and uni communities. There are also many mature students (58%) (and good childcare facilities) and a number of part-timers. Of full-time undergrads, 96% come from the state sector and 46% from families new to the idea of university; 13% is the projected drop out rate.

ACADEMIA & JOBS

The schools, or faculties, are: Architecture & Construction; Business; Chemical & Life Sciences; Computing & Mathematical Sciences; Education & Training; Engineering; Health; Humanities; NRI (Earth & Environmental Sciences); Social Sciences & Law (Social Science subjects).

Poor students:staff ration of 24.5:1. Best teaching is assessed as being in Pharmacology &

WHERE GREENWICH GRADUATES END UP

Health & Social Work: 8%; Education: 20%; Wholesale/Retail: 12%; Manufacturing: 5%; Financial Activities: 7%; Public Administration, Civil Service & Defence: 9%; Hotel/Restaurant: 2.5%; Transport & Communications (including Telecommunications): 2%; Construction: 3%; Personnel: 3%; Computer: 3%; Business & Management: 3%; Accountancy: 1%; Media (including Film): 2%; Legal 2%; Architecture: 4%; Publishing: 2%; Advertising: 1%; Sport: 2%.

Approximate 'graduate track' employed **59%**

WHAT IT'S REALLY LIKE

UNIVERSITY:	
Social Life	★★★★
Campus scene	**Ents-focused, disparate**
Student Union services	**Good**
Politics	**Interest low**
Sport	**11 clubs; rugby big**
National team position	**81st**
Sport facilities	**Good**
Arts opportunities	**Interest low**
Student magazine	**Sarky Cutt**
Nightclubs	**Dome**
Bars	**Bar Latitude, Drunken Sailor, Sports Bar**
Union ents	**Good club nights & comedy**
Union societies	**19**
Most popular society	**Gaelic**
Parking	**Mostly good**
CITY:	
Entertainment	★★★★★
City scene	**Go to London**
Town/gown relations	**Average-good**
Risk of violence	**Avery Hill worst**
Cost of living	**Invariably average**
Student concessions	**Locally not much**
Survival + 2 nights out	**£80-£100 pw**
Part-time work campus/town	**Good/Average**

Pharmacy, Nursing & Midwifery, Town & Country Planning. Disabled and dyslexic students benefit from a dedicated Resource Centre.

Four per cent of the graduate workforce going into architecture suggests we have a good niche area, and sure enough the department scored full marks at the assessments. There are two BA degrees, one with a landscape focus. BA Architecture with Landscape Architecture finds graduates jobs as landscape designers, Plantsmen, etc. There is also a good showing employment-wise in property development. Note their three BSc degrees in this area – Development, Management and Valuation.

Many come from overseas and receive sterling support; many are mature students and there are good childcare facilities; a number are part-timers; 46% are from families new to the idea of university; 13% is the projected drop out rate.

Far and away the biggest area for jobs is Education. Primary and secondary school teachers are trained in a department that scored 20 points at assessment. Would-be lecturers in Further Education come most out of other departments: Business and Architecture & Construction are the two faculties scoring highest in this job sector. There is also a good track record for turning out physical training instructors (Education). Besides HNDs, see degrees in Sports Science and Sports Science with Pro Tennis Coaching.

Property and construction are good areas, too. See the new course in Construction Business Management. Town & Country Planning recently too full marks at the assessments, Building and Land/Property Management scored 21 points.

The nursing (Adult Branch Registration, Children's nursing, Mental Health Registration) and midwifery degrees are responsible for the strong (8%) showing in employment. There is also a big push in the area of natural health therapy here. Degrees in Complementary Therapies, including Aromatherapy and Stress Management, are the focus.

Environmental health is another popular employment area – look at Environmental Sciences, Human Nutrition and a new BSc in Public Health, which may be extended to include industrial placement. There is also Applied Nutrition with European Studies, though this scored just 18 points at assessment.

There is a strong computer provision. Systems analysts come out of Greenwich in number. Look at the BEng Computer Networking and Computer Systems & Software Engineering degrees, which may be 3-4 years depending on industrial placement or Foundation year.

SOCIAL SCENE

STUDENTS' UNION 'The main objective at Greenwich (apart from studying of course!) is to have fun,' writes Tammy Howland. 'Our Students' Union provides an extensive range of opportunities and Greenwich cards, free to all students living in the borough, which offer free or reduced entry to many places in London. The union ents' cards are also an excellent way to save money. Your days spent at Greenwich will be memorable, exhausting, fun, hard work and exciting, so join us for the Meanest Time of your life!'

The SU manages to lay on some twenty events each week, circulating news of them in *Get Out*, a 'what's on' listing and utilitarian partner of the excellent student monthly magazine *Sarky Cutt*. A student radio station, GSR, is in the process of being set up.

Annual events include the Fresher's Ball, Fresher's Fair, Football Dinner and Dance, Christmas Dizzy and Valentine's Ball. The biggest event of the year is the May Ball. The **Café Royal** in London and **Alexandra Palace** have provided glamorous settings for this black tie evening.

There are 50 societies, the most popular being Gaelic Soc, and 30 sports clubs, the most popular being Rugby. There are no politics and no arts to speak of. The Students' Union run a leadership programme.

SPORT makes up a large part of life at Greenwich. Teams participate in thirty-six of the forty-nine national BUSA (British University Sports Association) leagues, and came 81st last year. Mens basketball team were Busa Plate Champions, 2004/2005; Medway 1st football team were Division 1East SESSA winners in 2004/2005; Avery Hill football team won Bromley and District football league, 2004/2005.

AT A GLANCE

ACADEMIC FILE:	
Subjects assessed	**34**
Excellent	**68%**
Typical entry requirements	**200 points**
Application acceptance rate	**15%**
Students-staff ratio	**25:1**
First/2:1 degree pass rate	**48%**
ACCOMMODATION FILE:	
Guarantee to freshers	**100%**
Style	**Halls, flats, houses**
Price range pw	**£73-£94**
City rent pw	**Greenwich: £68-£151 Medway: £55-£73. Avery Hill: £60-£88**

GETTING THERE

☛ By road from M25, join A2 (J2) and follow signs to Woolwich Ferry, thence Greenwich.

☛ By rail to main Greenwich site: trains to Greenwich or Maze Hill overland stations, or Docklands Light Railway from Bank.

☛ By coach: Bristol, 2:20; Birmingham, 2:40; Newcastle, 6:05; Manchester, 4:35.

HARPER ADAMS UNIVERSITY COLLEGE

Harper Adams University College
Edgmond
Newport
Shropshire TF10 8NB

TEL 01952 820280
FAX 01952 813210
EMAIL admissions@harper-adams.ac.uk
WEB www.harper-adams.ac.uk

Harper Adams is a first-class land-based college on the borders of Shropshire and Staffordshire. They have the distinction of being able to award their own degrees. The college scored 23 out of 24 points for the undergraduate provision. Learning resources include the college's 175-hectare farm, a library (38,000 volumes, 800 journals), a computer centre and the largest covered field demonstration area in the UK. All first-year students are accommodated and catered for in college. This is a very sporty place – rugby, clay pigeon shooting and mountain biking bring them national, even international gongs. Union facilities include a couple of bars.

UNIVERSITY COLLEGE PROFILE

Founded	**1901**
Status	**Uni College**
Situation/style	**Rural campus**
Student population	**1545**
Degree undergraduates	**1395**
College accommodation	**Catered halls or uni housing**
Availability to freshers	**100%**
Cost pw (incl food)	**£75-£103**
Town rent pw	**£50**

DEGREE SUBJECT AREAS:
Agriculture & land-based industries, business, leisure & tourism, countryside& environment, land & estate management

GETTING THERE

☛ By road: M6 (J 13 or J14), A518, A41, B5062.

☛ By rail to Shrewsbury: Birmingham New Street, 1:10; from London to Stafford, 1:40

HERIOT-WATT UNIVERSITY

Heriot-Watt University
Riccarton Campus
Edinburgh EH14 4AS

TEL 0131 451 3376
FAX 0131 451 3630
EMAIL admissions@hw.ac.uk
WEB www.hw.ac.uk

Heriot-Watt Students' Association
Riccarton Campus
Edinburgh EH14 4AS

TEL 0131 451 5333
FAX 0131 451 5344
EMAIL admissions@hw.ac.uk
WEB www.hwusa.org

VAG VIEW

Heriot-Watt is a research-led, technological university, high on academic, industrial and business collaboration. Sited on the edge of Edinburgh, it is small but achieves big inspection results: 73% of its teaching assessments have scored Excellent or Highly Satisfactory, and it has a sound graduate employment record, a fairly rich student culture and a lot of good sport, yet its acceptance rate is high (20%). On the downside, there is a prevalence of blokes (60%), but if you're a lass and want to study Engineering and Physical Sciences they'll pay you good money to do so. See Student Profile, *below.*

Though entry requirements can now be steep, they throw a wide net for applicants, and maintain a dogged policy of targeting 'pupils from schools where applications to university are low, students who have no family background or cultural experience of higher education and mature students with no formal qualifications who maybe want a second chance to enter university via an access course.' They have a good students: staff ratio of 14:1, which will facilitate such a policy, but only 51% get Firsts or Upper Seconds, which is relatively low these days.

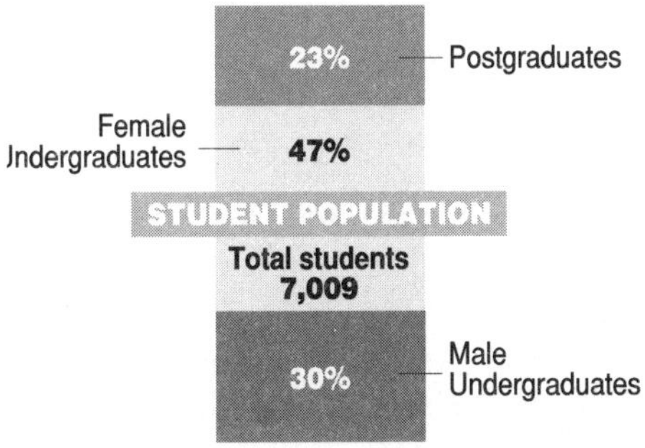

SUBJECT AREAS (%)

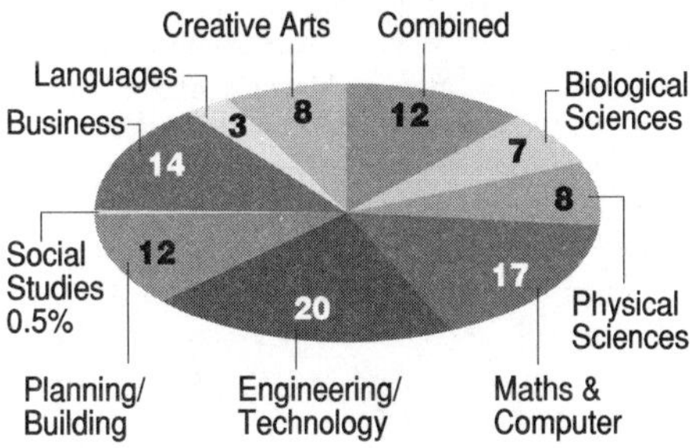

CAMPUS

The main campus at Riccarton, 6.5 miles south-west of Edinburgh city centre is an attractive 380-acre campus in a huddle with a number of independent research companies. There's a modern, almost space-age, feel to it: smart, modern buildings are set in pleasant grounds with trees, playing fields, an attractive artificial loch, squirrels, ducks and swans.

'The sense of seclusion at leafy Riccarton campus definitely aids study,' writes Richard Biggs, 'and has given rise to a community spirit that doesn't exist at inner city universities. However, the LRT buses that run to and from campus tend to be erratic – not fun in winter.'

Since the merger with **The Scottish College of**

UNIVERSITY/STUDENT PROFILE	
University since	**1966**
Situation/style	**City campus**
Student population	**7009**
Undergraduates	**5430**
- mature	**8%**
- non EU undergraduates	**8%**
- male/female	**60/40**
- non-traditional student intake	**29%**
- state school intake	**92%**
- drop-out rate	**13%**
- undergraduate applications	**Constant**

WHERE HERIOT-WATT GRADUATES END UP

Health & Social Work: 1%; Education: 3%; Wholesale/Retail: 15%; Manufacturing: 14%; Financial Activities: 17%; Public Administration, Civil Service & Defence: 6%; Hotel/Restaurant: 3%; Transport & Communications (including Telecommunications): 4%; Construction: 2%; Mining/Oil Extracting: 3%; Personnel: 2.5%; Computer: 3%; Business & Management: 5%; Accountancy: 5%; Media (including Film): 1%; Legal 1%; Architecture: 7%; Sport: 0.5%.

Approximate 'graduate track' employed **57%**

Textiles in '99, H-W also has a Scottish Borders campus. Situated in Galashiels - hence Gala, as the campus is known - a small town in the Scottish Borders, SCoT is only 33 miles/90 minutes by bus from Edinburgh, but unfortunately (if you are in a hurry) some two and a half hours by train, which detours via Berwick-upon-Tweed.

In September 2005, the University opened its Dubai Campus. Initial academic programmes include undergraduate and postgraduate courses in Management and a postgraduate course in Information Technology. It is planned to introduce further courses in the areas of science, engineering and commerce from September 2006.

FEES, BURSARIES

Following the introduction of £3000 p.a. top-up fees in England, all English students will be charged £1700 p.a. Heriot-Watt has a number of scholarships (£500 p.a.), preference given to Science and Engineering, and females studying Engineering and Physical Sciences. There are various sports scholarships funded jointly by the uni, the Alumni Fund, the Royal & Ancient Golf Club of St. Andrews and the Scottish Physical Recreation Fund (£500 to £1500 p.a.). The Wilson Scholarship for disabled athletes has just been introduced to benefit potential paralympians. A music scholarship scheme rewards talent with free tuition, and pipe band scholarships offer tuition in exchange for a commitment to the uni pipe band. Companies like Schlumberger, Agilent and MISYS also see undergraduates through.

STUDENT PROFILE

'The University,' we read, 'is committed to equal opportunities for all, irrespective of age, colour, disability, ethnic origin, gender, marital status, religious or political beliefs, sexual orientation or other irrelevant distinction.' Sounds good, and in H-W's case it *is* good. They go out of their way to pull in a diverse mix of student, being one of the elite universities who show that open access can be made to work by concentrating their efforts on relative merits and on abilities and potential. So, they can gather 29% of the uni's student body from among groups who don't normally think of going to university, hang on to more than most unis for the duration and find almost all of them jobs within six months of graduation.

The concentration of technical courses accounts for the unusually high male to female ratio - 60% male undergraduates against 40% female. So what does Heriot-Watt do about it? Equally impressively, they start up 'Women into Science and Engineering', a scheme offering taster courses, with attendant scholarships, to female pupils. It's a scheme that flows from the university's absolute commitment to equal opportunity, which lies at the heart of their 'open access' strategy. This is a caring university in the best sense, the student is the principal focus.

The concentration of technical courses accounts for the unusually high male to female ratio - a third more men than women. So what does Heriot-Watt do about it?

There is also a big foreign exchange programme - so, you'll find a rich mix of cultures, on campus. All students can choose to study abroad at some point during their course.

ACADEMIA & JOBS

The schools are Engineering and Physical Sciences; Life Sciences; Built Environment; Mathematical & Computer Sciences; Management & Languages; and Textiles & Design.

There are particular niches in photonics, actuarial maths and statistics, languages (translating and interpreting) and petroleum engineering. Recent new subjects in high demand include Applied Psychology, Chemistry with Forensic Science, Robotics and Cybertronics, Building, Architectural Engineering and Planning & Housing subjects, automotive engineering and sports science.

'Modern languages are an outstanding strength,' one sixthform adviser confirmed, and certainly their employment figures for translators and interpreters is good. 'You can walk straight out of Heriot-Watt into a job in the EC.' Also, for foreign students, the School of Management and Languages now offers a range of language support classes (MA Foreign Languages and TESOL).

School careers staff point to courses aimed at boom areas, such as microelectronics, and the pharmaceutical industry, which is equal to 27% of the UK's manufacturing industry, while their unique BSc in Brewing and Distilling is rarely short of applicants and enjoys a certain symbiosis with extra-curricular activities also popular here.

In actuarial science, three universities are head and shoulders above the rest in equating degree success with employment, namely Heriot-Watt, Warwick and Oxford. Heriot-Watt and Warwick have dedicated Actuarial Maths degrees, and together all three account for more than 20% of jobs in the sector. Nearly 5% of Heriot-Watt's graduates become actuaries. They offer a four-year BSc Actuarial Mathematics and Statistics, for which they only want 280 points. See too the new BSc Mathematical, Statistical and Actuarial Sciences.

Altogether 17% go into the financial sector, 4% into accountancy, 2% as investment advisers and analysts. Finance took a Highly Satisfactory at the assessments; Applied Maths and Statistics were rated international Grade 5 for research. Students interested in working in insurance, pension broking, underwriting should consider this uni, and look at BSc Mathematics with Psychology and BSc General Mathematics with Psychology, new this year.

On the engineering front, the teaching of Electrical & Electronic Engineering was accorded Excellent on inspection, and they have a good employment record. See also the computer and software engineering degrees in the School of Mathematical & Computer Sciences, which take more than 2% of graduates into software engineering, 1% into programming, etc.

Heriot-Watt mechanical engineers also find ready employment, as do design and development engineers, and process and development engineers. Look in particular at Chemical Engineering with Diploma in Industrial Training (Food Processing Technology) – there's a high incidence of graduate employment in this area. Chemical Engineering offers specialist routes into brewing & distilling, oil & gas production, pharmaceutical and other industries, and BSc Chemistry could take you to Australia or North America for a year.

Their strength is in the close relationship they have with industry, business and national support networks. In cahoots with the Scottish Institute for Enterprise, they deliver an enterprise-training programme, bringing entrepreneurial skills to science and engineering, from the first year of studies.

In the property context, some 6% graduates from here find employment as surveyors. Look at Architectural Engineering, Building Surveying and the two Quantity Surveying degrees in the School of the Built Environment. Note also that Heriot-Watt validates Edinburgh College of Art's degrees and that 29% of their graduates find work in architectural and related consultancies.

As for business, they excel, jobs-wise, in retail and marketing management (see Fashion below), and in business management consultancy. Look at the MA International Management or simply Management , and consider moving onto a postgrad course. If you're interested in retail management, fashion and design, note that this uni is in partnership with George Davies of 'Next', 'George at Asda' and the 'per una' collection for Marks & Spencer, to launch theGeorge Davies Centre for Retail Excellence at Heriot-Watt. There'll be in-company projects and master classes from leading academics and retailers, including George. The first postgrad course in International Fashion Marketing is running from autumn 2005.

Graduates of dedicated degrees in Fashion, Textiles and related areas, including Management, Marketing and Promotion are much in demand. Nationally, around 150 graduate textile designers move straight into the industry, some 260 clothing designers. Heriot-Watt merged with the Scottish College of Textiles in 1999. There's collaboration with industry and business in the design of the courses. They offer the employment-oriented BA Fashion Design for Industry and BSc Clothing Design & Manufacture or Textiles & Fashion Design Management.

ACADEMIC EXCELLENCE

TEACHING:
(Rated Excellent, Highly Satis. or 17+ out of 24)

Electrical & Electronic Eng.	**Excellent**
Civil Engineering, Computer Studies, Physics, Chemistry, Maths & Statistics, Mechanical + Manufacturing Eng, Finance & Accounting, Cellular & Molecular Biology.	**Highly Satis.**
Chemical Engineering	**19**
European Languages	**21**

RESEARCH:
*Top grades 5/5**

Mineral & Mining Engineering.	**Grade 5***
Applied Maths, Statistics, Built Environment	**Grade 5**

AT A GLANCE

ACADEMIC FILE:	
Subjects assessed	**15**
Excellent/Highly Satisfactory	**73%**
Typical entry requirements	**360 points**
Application acceptance rate	**20%, high**
Students-staff ratio	**14:1**
First/2:1 degree pass rate	**51%**
ACCOMMODATION FILE:	
Guarantee to freshers	**100%**
Style	**Halls**
Catered	**18%**
En suite	**62%**
Price range pw	**£46-£73**
City rent pw	**£70**

Note the Sport and Exercise Science core degree within the School of Life Sciencesand combo with psychology. See also *Sport* below.

One interesting aspect of their integrating undergraduates into the world is that they engage the support of alumni members in email and face-to-face student mentoring. The programme brings together graduates across five continents.

SOCIAL SCENE

Students' Association The Union on Edinburgh campus has three main venues: **Geordies** (bar) – the Heriot-Watt local with hustlers pool area: 3 pool tables and arcades, big screen and plasma screens, and home to the ever-popular and entertaining Monday night pub quiz. Then there's **Liberty's**, a café-bar with free wireless internet access, and **Zero°** nightclub (capacity 450). Its stage is also used for live music and Comedy Club.

Friday is *JAM* in **Zero°**: pop, chart, cheese and legendary student anthems; also *Night Train* in **Liberty's**: diverse range of 'quality music'. Every other Tuesday is Comedy Club: 'Well-established laughter session offering a changing line-up of some of the best local comics around. A bargain at only £3,' says *The List*. Saturday is *Lounge* in **Liberty's** – 'chillout to the sound of DJ's playing an eclectic mix of cool tunes" says the Student Association. 'Crayons to play with too!' Thursday in **Zero°** brings live music and, 'Often attracts Scotland's hottest band talen.' – *The List*. Thursday is *Traffic*, a crossroads of indie and alternative tunes. Every other Sunday in **Zero°**, alternating with *Your Turn* (open mic night) in *Liberty's* is *Have you got the S-Factor?*

See also *Edinburgh Student City*, page 175.

Down at Gala, they are also getting some sort of scene together. There are newish union premises, a full ents programme, a musician-in-residence and lashings of sponsorship from North Sea oil, which has led to COMA – not a state of unconsciousness due to inebriation, but the name for a network of groups available for gigs.

Sport The Edinburgh campus boasts the impressive National Squash Centre, but also has a number of large playing fields (five football, two rugby, one cricket), a floodlit training area, jogging track, three tennis courts, three sports halls, climbing wall, two multigyms, golf driving nets, weights and fitness rooms and indoor sports courts. Membership is spilt into Gold, Silver and Bronze tariffs (year, academic year and term), ranging from £18-60. The Heart of Midlothian Football Academy opened recently and includes pro-quality facilities and floodlit and indoorsynthetic pitches. The city of Edinburgh has many golf courses, a large swimming pool, ice rink and the Meadowbank Stadium. Half the city is made of parks and open spaces (including Queen's Park and Arthur's Seat). See also sports scholarships (*Fees, Bursaries* above)

WHAT IT'S REALLY LIKE

UNIVERSITY:	
Social Life	★★★
Campus scene	**Like clockwork**
Student Union services	**Good**
Politics	**Low level Student debt**
Sport	**30 clubs, hockey strong**
National team position	**55th**
Sport facilities	**Good**
Arts opportunities	**Music, film good; dance, art average, drama poor**
Student newspaper	**Watts On**
Nightclub	**Zero°**
Bars	**Geordies, Liberty's**
Union ents	**JAM (cheese) heads big ents**
Union Societies	**30**
Most popular societies	**Poker Society**
Parking	**Poor**
CITY:	
Entertainment	★★★★★
Scene	**Seething**
Town/gown relations	**Good**
Risk of violence	**Low**
Cost of living	**High**
Student concessions	**Excellent**
Survival + 2 nights out	**£60-£85 pw**
Part-time work campus/city	**Excellent**

PILLOW TALK

All freshers, with the exception of Exchange/ Erasmus students, are guaranteed a year's campus accommodation provided they are full-year, full-time students. Get your application in by September 1 and you can choose between catered and self-catered study bedrooms and self-catered flats, all a short stroll away from everything else. Of the 1,800 study bedrooms, more than 1,000 have their own shower and toilet, and there are never more than five sharing a kitchen, which comes with fridge freezer, cooker, kettle etc. Bring your own crockery, cutlery, pots and pans. Catered students have access to a pantry for snacks and hot drinks. For a small subscription, you can have access to a phone, the Internet and the Heriot-Watt Intranet. There is, in any case, free room-to-room and incoming calls, and voicemail.

GETTING THERE

☛ By road: A71 or A70; if the latter, turn off at Currie on to Riccarton Mains Road.
☛ By rail: London King's Cross, 4:30; Glasgow Central, 50 mins; Newcastle, 1:30.
☛ By air: nearby Edinburgh Airport for inland and international flights.
☛ By coach: Glasgow, 1:10; London, 9:10; Birmingham, 8:10; Newcastle, 3:10.
☛ To Gala, A7 south from Edinburgh.

UNIVERSITY OF HERTFORDSHIRE

The University of Hertfordshire
College Lane
Hatfield
Hertfordshire AL10 9AB

TEL 01707 284800
FAX 01707 284870
EMAIL admissions@herts.ac.uk
WEB www.herts.ac.uk

Hertfordshire Students' Union
College Lane
Hatfield
Hertfordshire AL10 9AB

TEL 01707 285000
FAX 01707 286150
EMAIL uhsu@herts.ac.uk
WEB uhsu.herts.ac.uk

VAG VIEW

Herts Uni is among the most impressive of the 1992 unis in rate of growth, learning resources and graduate employment. Reason for some of this is the contact with industry and the capital city which their strategically advantageous location gives them on the north-south A1, minutes from the M25 and M1, and within striking distance of four airports – Luton, Stansted, Heathrow and Gatwick. Applications were up 19% last year.

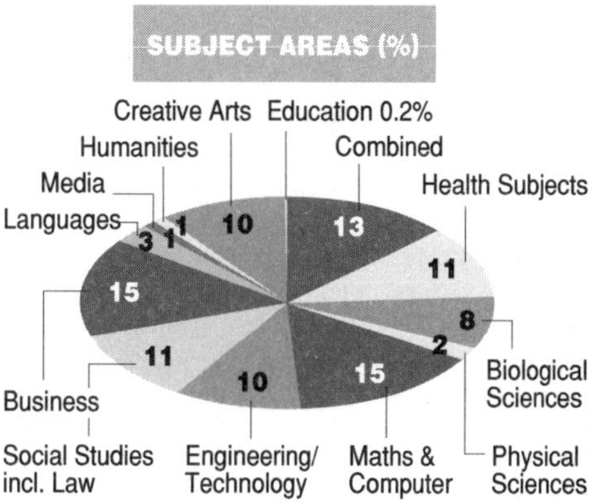

CAMPUSES

The uni is based at Hatfield and St Albans. The main Hatfield site comprises the original campus and the new de Havilland Campus, half a mile away, the two made one by cycleways, footpaths and shuttle buses.

De Havilland In September 2003 the new £120-million campus opened, housing the Business School and schools of Education and Humanities. There's a learning resources centre, a £15-million sports centre open to the public – its 3-year membership target met in the first month – an amazing 60-seater auditorium and student residences. It was an incredible undertaking and reports of 350 students having to be placed in hotels at the start of the 2003-4 session give scale to the challenge. You will be better off – the uni is at work on 1400 new en-suite rooms on its College Lane campus right this minute.

College Lane The main campus is College Lane, Hatfield, where the [original] **Learning Resources Centre** is based. With hundreds of computers, your very own e-mail and the facility to look up the George Clooney Web page, a café downstairs serving cheese toasties and banana milkshakes to eager students throughout the day and night, and copies of all the text books you need to research for those lectures you accidentally slept through, you can't complain.

Entertainment facilities include the **Elehouse** pub, which offers a wonderfully healthy food bar during the day, making a change from Pot Noodles and oven chips, and a pleasant pub atmosphere in the evenings. Downstairs there is a shop, open daily from Monday to Friday, where you can satisfy your cravings for Pringles and cream eggs, as well as allowing you to stock up on paper and pens in preparation for your lectures (you know, those things in between sleep and alcohol).

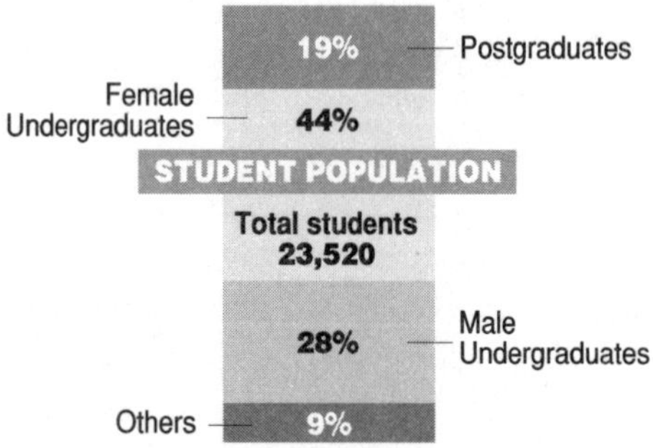

Across the courtyard is the main venue for big events, the **Font**. Weekly clubnights include *Bonk* – sports night on Wednesday; *Naughty* – main Friday club night; *Swanky* – regular house night; and *360* – alternative night. 'There's a very strong on-campus community,' a student said, 'with venues that people feel safe in. A lot of the social life is based around campus.'

The Summer Ball also offers an interesting combination of food, drink and a selection of fairground rides, only for those with iron stomachs!

Then there's the radio station, CRUSH, which is run by students for students and can be received by the majority of halls, and the *Horizon* newspaper to keep you informed of the good and the bad goings-on. The most active of 17 student societies are Christian Union, Drama and Alternative Music.

There's a 9-screen **UCI** in the **Galleria** centre, and a pub that offers cut-price drinks. The union make merry with a student night at **Pub2Club**, but generally the nightlife is poor. London beckons

St Albans The third campus is St Albans, a small campus for those studying Law. It is based in the lovely city of St Albans. It is easily accessible from Hatfield, where most first years are normally housed, and close to the town centre, which boasts many high-street chain stores, as well as a variety of specialist shops catering for the individual. There is a refectory and a Students' Union area, which although small provide good daytime facilities, such as a TV and a pool table. Oh, and the town has the oldest pub in the UK apparently, **Ye Old Fighting Cocks**.

FEES, BURSARIES

UK & EU Fees: £3000 p.a. Bursary of £1350 if in receipt of full HE Maintenance grant; if in receipt of partial grant then it's on a sliding scale down from that figure. Sports and academic scholarships are available.

STUDENT PROFILE

There is a very large student body, mainly drawn from the state sector, 40% from new to uni social groups. Twenty per cent of undergraduates are part-timers and 3% of the total population are further education students. There is also a large very local and overseas population. Given the 9% drop-out rate, the mix seems to work well.

ACADEMIA & JOBS

The award-winning learning resources centre at College and its twin at adjacent de Havilland are open 24/7. They make use of a computer system, StudyNET, their 'Managed Learning Environment', a personalised academic workspace for students on which appears information relevant to programmes

UNIVERSITY PROFILE

University since	**1992**
Situation/style	**Suburban campuses**
Student population	**23520**
Undergraduates	**18445**
- mature	**19%**
- non EU undergraduates	**12%**
- male/female	**44/56**
- non-traditional student intake	**40%, v. high**
-state school intake	**97%**
- drop-out rate	**9%**
- undergraduate applications	**Up 19%**

ACADEMIC EXCELLENCE

TEACHING:
(Rated Excellent or 17+ out of 24)

Environmental Studies	**Excellent**
Philosophy	**24**
Psychology, Business, Economics, Tourism	**23**
Mechanical, Aero & Manuf Eng, Art & Design, Subjects Allied to Medicine, Education	**22**
Maths, Molecular Biosciences, Physics	**21**
Linguistics, Elec/Electro Eng, General Eng, Nursing	**20**
Building Services Engineering	**19**
Civil Engineering	**18**

RESEARCH:
*Top grades 5/5**

History	**Grade 5**

of study, as well as a range of personal information management tools linking students to course databases.

Recently opened on College Lane is an Innovation Centre to provide incubation resources to spin out new companies, and a new Automotive Centre, dedicated to bring together academia and industry.

> ***The new £120-million campus has opened. There's a learning resources centre, a £15-million sports centre open to the public, an amazing 60-seater auditorium and student residences.***

Historically, Herts is noted for aero-engineering, computer science, areas into which they still pour graduates. They have progressed rapidly, too, in environmental sciences, in law and in health, and business – Business & Management, Economics, and Tourism picked up 23 points out of 24 in the teaching assessments recently (as indeed did Nursing).

They ask around 260 points for Aerospace Engineering and Aerospace System Engineering, and you can get in for about 200 on their top rated Aerospace Technology with Management.

They also get jobs for their civil engineers, though they come not out of engineering but the Built Environment school, which includes Architectural Engineering, Civil Eng Construction Management and Civil Eng Financial Mgt.

Prospective racing car designers and team managers should explore the BSc Hons Motorsports Technology and BEng Automotive Engineering with Motorsport. They streamline ruthlessly for employment and this is among the most impressive of the new unis, employment-wise. So, they slipped quietly out of subjects like drama, sociology, and invested heavily instead in Pharmacology, benefiting from the location in the most heavily concentrated area of pharmaceutical R&D in the country.

Hertfordshire and Nottingham Trent jostle for top place among those that feed this sector. Look at BSc Pharmaceutical Science (extended with work experience) and BSc Pharmacology, they come with the possibility of a year in Europe or the US, a dimension is a feature of other science courses. Teaching inspection 22.

Health is the most popular area of employment for Herts graduates. In nursing they are big in mental health, adult and children's. Look also at and the Health Management degree in the Business faculty and the sure-fire Paramedic Science, the first degree of its sort, which we may well look back upon as the uni's first step to a degree in medicine.

Herts' BSc Physiotherapy comes expensive BBB-ABB, but this is part of a major drive by this impressive new uni in the Health area. Their employment record speaks for itself, they are always in the Top 10, while their BSc degrees Diagnostic Radiography & Imaging and Radiotherapy & Oncology produce more than 6% of the jobs in this sector nationally. At the teaching

WHERE HERTFORDSHIRE GRADUATES END UP

Health & Social Work: 17%; Education: 12%; Wholesale/Retail: 11%; Manufacturing: 12%; Financial Activities: 8%; Public Administration, Civil Service & Defence: 6%; Hotel/Restaurant: 2%; Transport & Communications (including Telecommunications): 4.5%; Construction: 2%; Agriculture: 1%; Personnel: 3%; Computer: 5%; Business & Management: 2%; Accountancy: 2%; Media (including Film): 1%; Legal 2%; Architecture: 1%; Publishing: 2%; Artistic/Literary: 0.5%; Sport: 1%.

Approximate 'graduate track' employed **61%**

WHAT IT'S REALLY LIKE

UNIVERSITY:	
Social Life	★★★
Campus scene	**Lively community, bit spoddy**
Student Union services	**Good**
Politics	**Average: Fees**
Sport	**29 clubs**
National team position	**59th**
Sport facilities	**New/excellent**
Arts opportunities	**Good**
Student newspaper	**Horizon**
Student radio	**Crush 1278 AM**
Nightclub	**Font Bar**
Bars	**Elehouse**
Union ents	**Bonk, Naughty, Swanky**
Union clubs/societies	**17**
Parking	**Average**
CITY:	
Entertainment	★★ – ★★★
Scene	**London beckons**
Town/gown relations	**Average**
Risk of violence	**Low**
Cost of living	**High**
Student concessions locally	**OK**
Survival + 2 nights out	**£70 pw**
Part-time work campus/town	**Excellent/poor**

There is also a top-line BA Hons Fine Art, although they stress you will need to be self-motivated, ambitious and want to work as a practising artist to get a place. There's work experience and exchanges with various Western and Eastern Euro countries in the second year. Entry via a Foundation Diploma. Teaching inspection, 22.

Business-wise they place a lot of marketing and retail managers. All courses in the Business School

AT A GLANCE

ACADEMIC FILE:	
Subjects assessed	**32**
Excellent	**56%**
Typical entry requirements	**220 points**
Application acceptance rate	**23%**
Students-staff ratio	**17:1**
First/2:1 degree pass rate	**51%**
ACCOMMODATION FILE:	
Guarantee to freshers	**Apply by 31.8**
Style	**Halls, flats, houses**
Catered	**None**
En-suite	**50%**
Price range pw	**£56-£84**
Town rent pw	**£50-£65**

assesssments they scored 22 out of 24.

More than 10% of the nation's biologists come out of Herts Uni, who maintain a dominant position thanks to their excellent contacts with the expanding pharmaceutical, agrochemical and biotechnology industries. There are extended, introductory courses if you don't have the A levels to get in.

They are also in the forefront of providing graduate environment officers, their 3/4-year BSc Hons Environmental Geology/Management/ Studies or Conservation Mgt, all with a year in industry and option for a year in Europe or North America. There's also a range of Geographical Info Science degrees, and plain old Geography itself of course. Environmental Studies also features in the cross-faculty Combine Homs scheme (again with an optional year in Europe or America).

In the arts they have a new dimension in the now highly competitive world of animation. Look at their BA Model Design & Special Effects, itself designed for visual effects designers in advertising, TV and film. Graduates undertake work placements with such as Jim Henson's Creative Workshop, Artme, Asylum and the BBC Visual Effects Department. A new School of Film, Music (there are masses of Electronic Music degrees) and New Media is mooted.

modular programme are 3-4 years depending on work experience, or placing in Europe or America. Marketing may be studied as single honours or with languages, Info Systems, Accounting, Human Resources, Management Science, Tourism, etc. Management Science can be taken similarly with or without the other combos. As indeed can Tourism or any of the other combo subjects – tourism is another strong area for jobs for Herts graduates.

There are also Foundation degrees in Business with Marketing, Human Resources or Finance. Then fully-fledged degrees with the same range of employable combinations, or single honours degrees in Business Admin, Business Studies, Management, and Health Management.

The Law provision was recently assessed by the LPC Board (the Legal Practice Course is essential to becoming a solicitor) as Good.

The strong education provision is for Education Studies and an Early Years Foundation degree.

SPORT

They came 59th in the BUSA inter-university national team league last year. There's the big new, £15-million sports complex, an 8-lane swimming pool, indoor cricket nets, 100-station fitness suite, etc. American Football is key.

PILLOW TALK

Freshers are guaranteed accommodation if they send in their accommodation application forms before 'A' level results are published and have accepted an unconditional offer of a course place by August 31.

Campus accommodation means, first and foremost, halls: self-catering with single study bedrooms, shared bathrooms/showers or en suite. They have 1,600 en-suite rooms at the de Havilland campus, all with broadband internet access and refrigerator. 1,400 new rooms on the College Lane campus this year.

GETTING THERE

☛ **Hatfield** by road: A1(M)/J3. By rail: London King's Cross, 22 mins. ☛ By coach: London, 1:00. ☛ **St Albans** by road: M25/J22, A1081. By rail: London (Thameslink), 25 mins.

HEYTHROP COLLEGE

Heythrop College
Kensington Square
London W8 5HQ
TEL 020 7795 6600
FAX 020 7795 4200
EMAIL r.bolland@heythrop.ac.uk
WEB www.heythrop.ac.uk

Heythrop is an independent college within the University of London specialising in theology and philosophy and with a refreshingly evolutionary concept of higher education. For their inspiration they turn to the Swiss psychologist Jean Piaget, noted for his revolutionary work on the cognitive functions of children. Piaget wrote that 'the principal goal of education is to create people who are capable of doing new things, not simply of repeating what other generations have done... The second goal of education is to form minds which can be critical, can verify, and not accept everything they are offered.' Trawling through all that the higher educational establishments of this country can offer, such a breathtakingly simple statement seems almost unutterably bold. Their teaching is the traditional university method of tutorials and small-group seminars. They possess one of the finest collections of theological and philosophical literature anywhere to be found, their 250,000 volumes available to every one of their students without queue.

COLLEGE PROFILE	
College of London Uni since	**1971**
Full-time undergraduates	**155**
- mature	**30%**
- overseas	**11%**
- male/female	**70/30**
ACCOMMODATION:	
Availability to freshers	**100%**
Style	**Halls**
Approx cost p.w.	**£100-£130**
City rent pw	**£100+**

UNIVERSITY OF HIGHLANDS & ISLANDS

UHI Millennium Institute
Caledonia House
63 Academy Street
Inverness IV1 1BB
TEL 0845 272 3600
FAX 01463 279001
EMAIL info@uhi.ac.uk
WEB www.uhi.ac.uk

UHI Millennium Institute is a federal network of 15 colleges that makes use of information and communication technologies to overcome geographical distance. Students have a regional reference point of at least one participating college. These are further education colleges. Each UHI academic partner deals with the accommodation for students studying at their campus.

From Sabhal Mor Ostaig in Skye to North Atlantic Fisheries College in Shetland, here's a chance to learn everything from Gaelic to music to environmental studies in the lap of Nature. More than 5,000 full-time undergraduates do, and few, if any, drop out.

UNIVERSITY OF HUDDERSFIELD

University of Huddersfield
Queensgate
Huddersfield HD1 3DH

TEL 01484 472228
FAX 01484 516151
EMAIL prospectus@hud.ac.uk
WEB www.hud.ac.uk

Huddersfield Students' Union
Queensgate
Huddersfield HD1 3DH

TEL 01484 473 441
FAX 01484 432 333
EMAIL: su-comms@hud.ac.uk
WEB www.huddersfieldstudent.com

VAG VIEW

The uni traces its history back to the Young Men's Mental Improvement Society, founded in 1841. It was awarded university status in 1992 after two other incarnations, first as a technical college then as a polytechnic. Today it has a city-centre campus (Queensgate), Holly Bank campus, 2 miles to the north, and Storthes Hall, 4 miles to the south-east.

Huddersfield town is an unusual mix. Its roots in the industrial revolution are not in doubt. It is also known far and wide for its annual poetry festival, with famously the Albert pub as artistic font; folk and jazz are equally present. Sometime Heritage minister Stephen Dorrell once famously remarked that Huddersfield was the Paris of the North. One can't pretend this didn't raise a few eyebrows, but he did have a point of sorts.

The uni and the town are of a similar weave. There is this traditional, industrial, people-culture, but the academic spectrum is wide and its character modern. Major strengths are electronic engineering, IT and social work, and in health areas such as nursing and midwifery. Then you hear that they have the largest music department of any UK university, and that in the recent research assessment exercise they were awarded a coveted Grade 5 for it. Now, with new drama and media facilities, it is also developing a strong performing arts, broadcast and humanities cluster, aided by the high profile of the University's Chancellor, the film actor Patrick Stewart, who drops by to give drama workshops.

They have recently opened centres in Oldham and Barnsley to encourage participation in Higher Education in both towns.

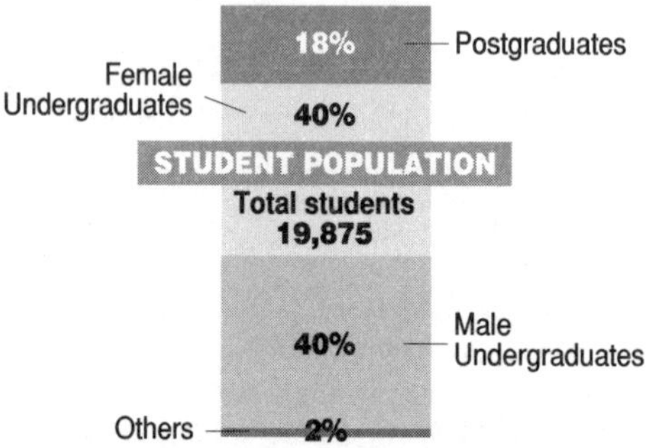

UNIVERSITY/STUDENT PROFILE	
University since	**1992**
Situation/style	**Town campus**
Student population	**19875**
Undergraduates	**15718**
- mature	**50%**
- non EU undergraduates	**9%**
- male/female	**50/50**
- non-traditional student intake	**39%, high**
- state school intake	**98%**
- drop-out rate	**11%, high**
- undergraduate applications	**Up 11%**

CAMPUS

The university has given the city-centre Queensgate campus a makeover, replacing some of the 1960s' tower blocks with the new Harold Wilson Building (natch) – HQ for the School of Human & Health Sciences. Holly Bank, two miles north is for teacher training, not a huge element in the graduate workplace – David Blunkett studied here – (now you're getting warm). Storthes Hall campus is set in 350 acres of parkland 4 miles away from the main campus and connected to it by a subsidised bus service.

The indigenous Yorkshireman is unlikely to shout much about the uni, he doesn't even look at

SUBJECT AREAS (%)

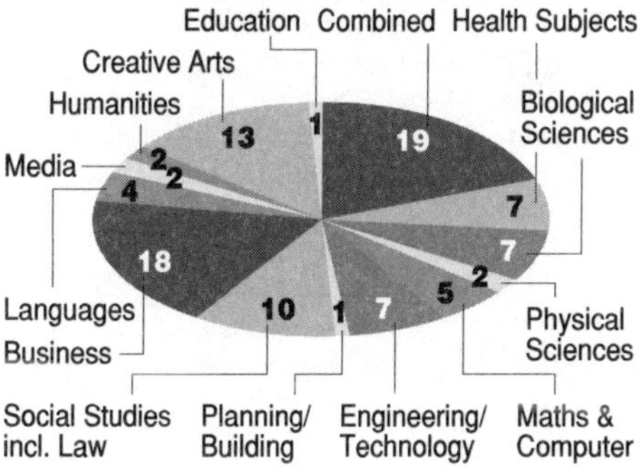

ACADEMIC EXCELLENCE

TEACHING:
(Rated Excellent or 17+ out of 24)

Social Work, Music	**Excellent**
Electrical & Electronic Eng	**24**
Politics	**23**
Nursing, Hospitality Management, Transport & Logistics, Education, Biosciences, Subjects Allied to Medicine	**22**
Design Technology, Maths	**21**
Food Sciences, Psychology, Sociology	**20**
Communications & Media	**18**

RESEARCH:
*Top grades 5/5**

Social Work, History, Music	**Grade 5**

it objectively and certainly won't waste his breath convincing a soft southerner of things he won't understand. Yet, southerners can be the very best ambassadors, should they take time to discover this uni's soul... 'I can't remember a more depressing view,' wrote student Tim Wild, a film-maker who came up from Brighton, possibly the most exciting and sunny blue city in Britain. 'In the forefront, the twin towers of the council blocks, ably supported by the dual carriageway and the gas works. Most people only have the vaguest idea where the bloody place is, so I'll attempt to clear up the confusion. Smack bang in the middle – three hours away from London by car, and about three thousand light years away in attitude. That's why this place is special – they really couldn't give a toss whether you're from Taunton or Timbuktu as long as you can hold your ale and laugh at yourself. If it's glamour and sophistication you're after, then stay away, because you'll only spoil it for the rest of us. I won't pretend it's paradise, but that's part of the appeal, in an odd way. Because it's the middle of nowhere, there are no cliques, no élite to try and be part of. It's just cold and grey and everyone here's in it together.

'Like the blitz, without the Germans.'

There are also uni centres at Barnsley and Oldham.

The Huddersfield Business Generator has created over 80 start-up businesses, half of them operated by Huddersfield graduates, with an over 80% success rate, and created two new millionaires.

FEES, BURSARIES

UK & EU Fees 2006: £1200 p.a. In 2007: £3000 (£2000 at University Centres in Barnsley and Oldham), £2000 for HND or Foundation Degree (£1,500 in Barnsley and Oldham), industrial placement year (sandwich year) free. Bursary of £1000 for students with a family income up to £17500; £750 for those with a family income between £17501 and £20000 and £500 for students with a family income between £20001 and £25000.

STUDENT PROFILE

50% are mature. Intake from classes and neighbor-

WHERE HUDDERSFIELD GRADUATES END UP

Health & Social Work: 13%; Education: 6%; Wholesale/Retail: 16%; Manufacturing: 13%; Financial Activities: 9%; Public Administration, Civil Service & Defence: 7%; Hotel/Restaurant: 6%; Transport & Communications (including Telecommunications): 5%; Construction: 2%; Agriculture: 1%; Personnel: 2%; Computer: 2.5%; Business & Management: 2.5%; Accountancy: 1%; Media (including Film): 1%; Legal 2%; Architecture: 2%; Publishing: 1%; Advertising: 1%; Artistic/Literary: 1%; Sport: 1%.

Approximate 'graduate track' employed **53%**

hoods not traditionally represented at university: 39% and 23% respectively. Those are the statistics. Huddersfield is real; social climbers need not apply; everyone has a good time.

ACADEMIA & JOBS

The university has always had a strongly vocational focus, with a quarter of students taking part in paid work-placements. They are particularly strong in Social Work, Electronic Engineering and Music, and there is a strong tradition in precision engineering and in textile design. History, Music and Chemistry also do very well in the research assessments. New drama and media facilities are developing strong performing arts, broadcast and humanities degrees. English Studies has reinvented itself with the injection of new blood and new talent and is building a reputation for linguistic analysis and poetry. Meanwhile, Music Technology and audio-engineering courses are proving particularly popular and traditional engineering and computing courses are developing new modules.

The eight academic schools are: Applied Sciences (Transport and Logistics, Chemical and Biological Sciences, Geographical and Environmental Sciences), Computing and Mathematics, Design Technology (Textiles, Architecture), Education, Engineering, Business, Human and Health Sciences, (Nursing, Podiatry, Behavioural Science, Social Work, Health Studies, Careers Guidance), Music and Humanities. It is particularly good on sandwich courses, there's 24-hour computer access, and good support for disabled students.

As well as strong links with industry, public services and the professions, the uni has a distinct vocational and entrepreneurial emphasis. The Huddersfield Business Generator has created over 80 start-up businesses, half of them operated by Huddersfield graduates, with an over 80% success rate and created two new millionaires.

They are in the Top 10 for producing architects – see the BA Architecture/Architecture (International). The artistic element is evident, too, in jobs for designers and illustrators, and their fine artists and general artists also do well. Fine Art, Drawing & Painting relates theoretical and practical through evaluation of current practice and then moves the focus of this to student concerns, aims, etc. Perhaps Stephen Dorrell had a point after all. Teaching inspection, 21.

They also make a number of graduates happy as interior designers with a dedicated degree in a department which consistently gets its graduates work. Teaching Inspection 21. The uni figures, too, in the Top 10 for set designers.

Nursing and midwifery graduates massage the Health figures, and BSc Midwifery Studies comes with an 18-month post-registration course. Teaching inspection 22 and a Grade 5 rating for Social Work. Social workers and counsellors bound out of this uni into employment. Look at BSc Social Work, BSc Social Psychology, Health and Community Studies. Chiropodists also boost the stats in Health with the Podiatry degree. Teaching inspection, 22.

In electronic engineering they are among the top three producers with Loughborough and York.

The music talent come for the BA Music Technology, also with Digital Media or Popular Music, and BSc Music Technology & Audio or Software Systems. The aim is to meld musical knowledge with electronic engineering. You'll be expected to have experience in both areas. As a result, there's a good track record for turning out producers, musicians, composers and sound recordists. 24 points at the assessments.

Fashion, clothing and textile designers should look no further. As befits a uni in the heart of the old woollen/textile industry, Huddersfield delivers more than any other except the London University of the Arts into the textile industry. MText is their Textile Design degree; there's also BA Costume with Textiles, Creative Textile Crafts and a BA/BSc alternative Textile Design. In the Fashion area: BA Hons Fashion with Manufacture, Marketing & Promotion is the main degree on offer. There's also a 1-year HND top-up, BA Fashion Design. 21 points at the assessments (19 for Communications).

Highly employable degrees in Art & Design are also BA Product Design, and BSc Product Innovation, Design & Development for students without specialist mathematical or scientific savvy beyond GSCE. See also their Computer-Aided Design and the BA Smart Design: Architecture ('the poetics of construction'). There's high energy and

AT A GLANCE

ACADEMIC FILE:	
Subjects assessed	**29**
Excellent	**57%**
Typical entry requirements	**210 points**
Application acceptance rate	**21%, high**
Students-staff ratio	**18:1**
First/2:1 degree pass rate	**45%**
ACCOMMODATION FILE:	
Guarantee to freshers	**They will advise only**
Approved city accommodation	**Halls, flats, houses**
Price range pw	**£54.95-£75.95**

WHAT IT'S REALLY LIKE

UNIVERSITY:	
Social Life	★★★
Campus scene	**Laid-back, authentic**
Student Union services	**Good**
Politics	**Interest low**
Sport	**Regional force**
National sporting position	**120th**
Sport facilities	**Average**
Arts opportunities	**Music, film; art, drama**
Student newspaper	**Huddersfield Student**
Student radio	**Ultra FM**
Nightclub & bar	**Venue**
Union ents	**2 club nights and DJ events**
Union clubs/societies	**38**
Parking	**Non-existent**
TOWN:	
Entertainment	★★★
Scene	**Pubs, music, poetry, drama**
Town/gown relations	**Good**
Risk of violence	**Low**
Cost of living	**Average**
Student concessions	**Good**
Survival + 2 nights out	**£50 pw**
Part-time work campus/town	**Good**

superb employment results at Huddersfield. Teaching inspection, 21.

They are also among the giants for the catering industry with BA Hospitality Management mixed to your taste with Tourism & Leisure/ International/Modern Languages/Licensed House Management. Teaching inspection, 22. Said a careers master, 'I have seen more enthusiasm among the staff at Huddersfield – both in the departments of Transport and Logistics and in Hotel & Catering – than at any other university in the land. I had thought, Oh, Huddersfield, can I really afford the time to go? And I was surprised, very surprised. They've looked at the market very carefully and where there's a gap they have gone for it.'

They also find employment for large numbers of IT consultants, through a series of Software Development BSc degrees that come with Artificial Intelligence, Business, Business Computing, Human-Computer Interaction, Management, Maths, Multimedia.

The education provision (primary and secondary) also favours lecturers in Further Education, where the School of Design Technology (Textiles, Architecture) again comes into its own. But look, too, at their combined BA courses, which open up Creative Writing, Journalism, Advertising, Media (18 at assessment) and much else. Languages also prove popular in this sector.

Finally, they are commercial & business law specialists, scoring 'Good' in a recent assessment by the LPC Board.

SOCIAL SCENE

STUDENTS' UNION There is a new £4-million Student Union building, the current one having been converted to studio space for drama and media. There are both alcoholic and non-alcoholic social areas, space for bands performing and administrative areas for student societies.

The advent of *X-Men* and *Star Trek: The Next Generation* star, Patrick Stewart, as the University's Chancellor has seen him take a keen interest in the Drama and English courses. He will be launching a major literature festival here in the Spring.

The Venue is the multi purpose bar which plays host to a variety of events including club and band nights. UHSU has two regularly scheduled club nights: Friday night is *Grrrr*, an indie, rock and metal night; Saturday night plays host to *Quids In*, with drinks offers and a 'party' DJ playing disco, pop and some dance music. There are also one-off DJ events, this term saw Hed Kandi play.

Student media is consistently good – the newspaper is *Huddersfield Student*, Student radio is Ultra FM. Generally students are pretty apathetic. The SU occasionally attempts to get the studemt body into a more political frame of mind, this year with a UHSU Campaigns Launch, where students voted on which campaigns they would like to see the Union run, but it didn't run beyond campus student concerns. They also launched a *Give It A Go* programme to galvanise more interest in societies. Islamic Soc remained the preferred choice.

SPORT Facilities are not extensive. There's a sports hall on campus, with a newish fitness centre and playing areas elsewhere, which provide for football, rugby (league and union), hockey, cricket and tennis. There is also a new Astroturf pitch and two new top-quality soccer pitches. Students have a discount at an Olympic standard sports centre with swimming pool in town. Rugby League players enjoy a sponsorship arrangement with Huddersfield Giants

PILLOW TALK

The uni no longer owns any accommodation, but recommends as its preferred and approved accommodation, the Storthes Hall Park Student Village and Ashenhurst Houses. These are privately-owned and operated by Ubrique Investments Limited trading as 'digs'. See www.campusdigs.com for further information.

Other hall-type accommodation and private shared houses are available around the town with rents from around £45 per week.

GETTING THERE

☛ By road: M62/J24, M1/J38-40.
☛ By rail: London via Wakefield, 3:30; Liverpool Lime Street, 1:45
☛ By air: Leeds/Bradford, Manchester Airports.
☛ By coach: London, 5:00; Leeds, 1:10.

UNIVERSITY OF HULL

The University of Hull
Cottingham Road
Kingston upon Hull HU6 7RX

TEL 01482 466100
FAX 01482 442290
EMAIL admissions@hull.ac.uk
WEB www.hull.ac.uk

Hull University Union
University House
Cottingham Road
Hull HU6 7RX

TEL 01482 445361
FAX 01482 466280
EMAIL president@union.hull.ac.uk
WEB www.hullstudent.com

VAG VIEW

The city's most famous literary son, the late poet and librarian Philip Larkin, described the city of Kingston upon Hull as 'in the world, yet sufficiently on the edge of it to have a different resonance.'

For centuries it was cut off from the rest of the country to the south by the Humber, to the north by the glorious, wide open Yorkshire Wolds (unknown to the tourist even now, thank God), and to the west by a large expanse of nothing. Then all the way from Liverpool on the opposite coast came the M62, meeting on its way the A1(M)), and suddenly Hull became part of the rest of the world, though as student Adam Ford told me, 'You'd be surprised at the number of people in Liverpool who still think that the M62 stops in Leeds.'

UNIVERSITY/STUDENT PROFILE

University since	**1954**
Situation/style	**Campus**
Student population	**21240**
Undergraduates	**16925**
- mature	**29%**
- non EU undergraduates	**6%**
- male/female	**43/57**
- non-traditional student intake	**29%**
- state school intake	**93%**
- drop-out rate	**6%**
- undergraduate applications	**Up 12%**

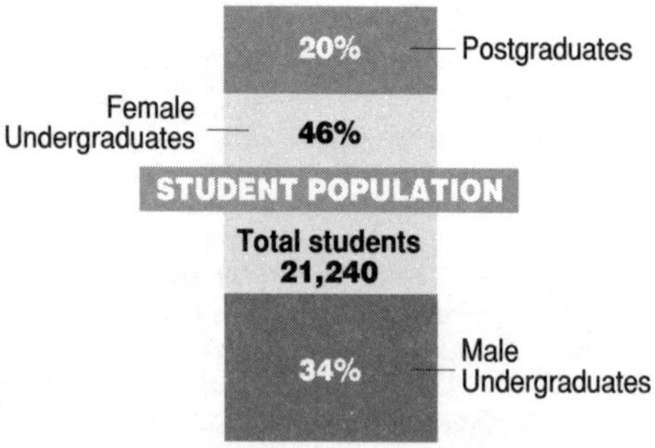

The essence of Hull is that it is distinct, not just because it has its own telephone system and white phone boxes – which might explain its students' recurring need to paint the town red – 'It is separate culturally,' a sixthform careers master said to me in hushed tones. He teaches just an hour away and still he can't find his way into it; he sends pupils to Newcastle (two hours to the north), to York (an hour to the west), to Sunderland, to Teesside, but rarely, if ever apparently, to Hull.

The point, then, is that in its insularity, Hull has developed this 'unique resonance'. For the same reason, it is a cheap place to live, more than 2% below the national average: you can buy a three-bedroom house there for what it costs to send a child to public school for two years; parents do and sell it when their darling leaves. But perhaps more important than all this is that academically the University of Hull is very strong, with high scores in teaching

SUBJECT AREAS (%)

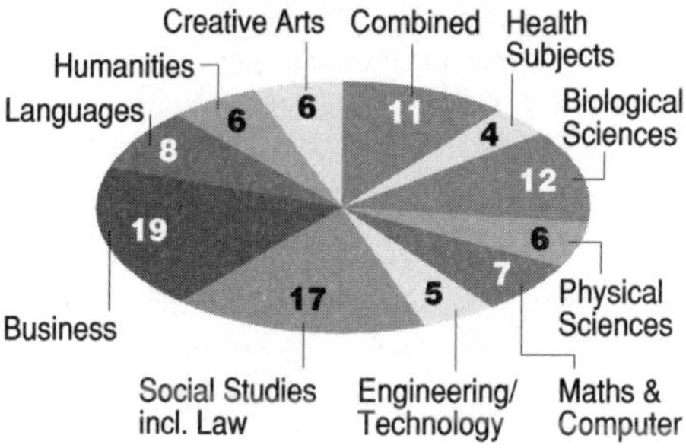

assessments, the Queen's Anniversary Prize for Social Work and Social Policy, a first class reputation for arts & social sciences – politics and languages especially – for health, for science and for business. The joint medical school is the jewel in the crown.

What's more, the campus is a friendly and creative place to be, and there's a great new Students' Union.

ACADEMIC EXCELLENCE

TEACHING: *(Rated Excellent or 17+ out of 24)*	
Chemistry, History, Social Policy, Social Work	**Excellent**
Hispanic Studies; Drama, Electron Engineering	**24**
Theology, American Studies, Physics, Psychology, Biosciences, Politics, Tourism, Sport, Business Management	**23**
Italian, SE Asian Studies, Maths, Economics, Philosophy	**22**
French, German	**21**
Sociology, Dutch, Education	**20**
Scandinavian Studies	**19**
RESEARCH: *Top grades 5/5**	
Geography, Law, Politics , Asian Studies, English, History, Music	**Grade 5**

CAMPUS

'The university is situated on Cottingham Road, about half an hour's walk, or a fifteen minute bus ride, from the city centre,' writes Albertina Lloyd. 'Cottingham Road connects Beverly Road and Newland Avenue, and you will come to know these three roads very well – Newland Avenue for shops (one claimed to sell "everything but the girl" and gave the band their name) and cafés, Cottingham Road for take-aways and Beverly Road for pubs. So, all that a student needs is situated within a short distance of the campus itself.'

'Hull prides itself on being one of the friendliest campuses in the country,' notes Danny Blackburn. 'It is a genuinely warm and welcoming environment, in which everyone feels as if they belong. The bars, corridors and lecture theatres all emanate a tremendous feeling of one-ness; it is apparent from day one. Hull's campus is, on a human scale, large enough always to be fun and exciting, but small enough to be personal, comfortable and unimposing.'

'Hull prides itself on being one of the friendliest campuses in the country,' notes Danny Blackburn. 'It is a genuinely warm and welcoming environment, in which everyone feels as if they belong.'

Now, Hull has expanded into the old and neighbouring Lincoln & Humberside Uni campus, locating Health Education there and the new Hull-York Medical School.

There is, too, Hull's **Scarborough Campus**, 40 miles north up the coast, which is known for drama, and is indeed the seat of the NUS Drama Festival, its patron Sir Alan Ayckbourn, whose plays are always premiered in the town's **Stephen Joseph Theatre**, which he runs.

FEES, BURSARIES

UK & EU Fees: £3000 p.a. If in receipt of HE Maintence grant there's a £1000 p.a. bursary, and £500-£1000 on a sliding scale if you are in receipt of a partial grant. There are also sound arrangements to encourage those from poorer postcode areas. Contact the uni.

STUDENT PROFILE

The uni has always been seen as one of this country's 'access elite' in that it enjoys a pukka academic reputation, but has been able to bring in a number of undergrads from poorer areas/classes. While others have more impressive figures for this now, they retain and develop their policy by giving 16-year-olds conditional places and running clubs for 11 and 12-year-olds. Once ensconced on campus, Hull students become stereotypical (beer, beer and more beer) or sign up as members of one of the healthy sub-groups – clubbers, metallers, crusties and skaters. At any rate, all intermingle without any trouble and relatively few drop out (6%).

ACADEMIA & JOBS

Besides Hull's very good record of excellence in teaching, there are enviable resources. The Brynmor Jones Library, named after a former Vice-Chancellor, has 850,000 volumes, subscribes to more than 3500 periodicals and contains a window-blind on which is written a poem by Stevie Smith. There are also all the usual electronics services and a 24-hour access, networked computer system reaching out from the Computer Centre to academic buildings and residences. The hub of language teaching is the Language Institute, incorporating the Open Learning Centre, where you can have a language assessment and teaching programme individually designed for you.

Says Albertina of her own experience, 'Each student is assigned a personal tutor to help with work and personal problems. Departmental deadline policies vary, but help, extensions and mitigating circumstances are considered if you contact your tutor in good time. All departments are considerate and helpful if dealt with correctly.'

Doctor, nurse, midwife, social worker – Hull now have the complete picture, particularly with biosciences and Psychology also scoring high (22 points) in the assessments.

The degree in Medicine at the Hull York Medical School (HYMS) is a 5-year BMBS (Bachelor of Medicine, Bachelor of Surgery). You may be based at either Hull or York Uni campuses (it's a dual effort, both follow the same curriculum). Hull has a decade's experience in Medicine through its Postgrad Medical School, while York's biosciences and health depts are top rated for teaching and research. Small-group clinical contact from Year 1. Equal emphasis on physical, psychological and social aspects. A low student-teacher ratio promised. Entry ABB, including Chemistry at A level and Biology at A or AS, Caring experience and interpersonal skills will be a significant separator. Tough to get in: there was only an 8% application acceptance rate in 2004

In nursing, Hull offer adult, children's, learning disability and mental health degrees, and are the second largest supplier of SRN, RGN and the third of non-hospital nurses. The school did, however, flop at the assessments. Teaching inspection, 17. Assumption is that lessons have been learned and the new broom HYMS attitude will sort it out. The BSc Midwifery suffered at the same assessment and the entry requirement (240 points) is high, though it hasn't harmed employment rates.

Nationally, more than 3,000 graduates find their way into community work/counselling annually. Over a third come through social studies departments (where you'll find Psychology and Sociology and Social Work degrees, besides a lot else). Lincoln leads the field, then comes Hull. Look at BSc Psychology with Counselling at Hull (there are other interesting Psychology parcels too), also BA Social Work (including professional qualification) and Social Policy.

Next largest graduate provision is in Education. Hull students mostly take the languages route into jobs as lecturers in Adult Education. Spanish took full marks at the assessments, Italian 22, French and German 21, Dutch 20 (you can slip over to Holland for the weekend from here), and Scandinavian Studies got 19. The hub is the Language Institute, incorporating the Open Learning Centre, where you can have a language assessment and teaching programme individually designed for you.

Over at the Scarborough campus, about 40 minutes northwards up the coast, there are masses of primary teachers busy training. But also, the character and environmental problems associated with the Scarborough coastline and seashore have become meat for a host of interesting other degrees – Coastal Marine Biology, Ecology, Environmental Science, and Tourism Management among them.

Back on the main Hull campus a sure line in accountancy jobs should be mentioned. Various degrees (BSc and BA) involving professional experience and international elements make this a very productive area. Another is computing. Programmers and games designers find work

WHERE HULL GRADUATES END UP

Health & Social Work: 17%; Education: 12%; Wholesale/Retail: 10%; Manufacturing: 9%; Financial Activities: 9%; Public Administration, Civil Service & Defence: 9%; Hotel/Restaurant: 5%; Transport & Communications (including Telecommunications): 3%; Construction: 1%; Personnel: 4%; Computer: 3%; Business & Management: 3%; Accountancy: 4%; Media (including Film): 2.5%; Legal 2.5%; Publishing: 1%; Artistic/Literary: 1%; Sport: 1%.

Approximate 'graduate track' employed **62%**

WHAT IT'S REALLY LIKE

UNIVERSITY:	
Social Life	★★★★
Campus scene	**Friendly, lively, cheap**
Student Union services	**Good**
Politics	**Average: fees**
Sport	**47 clubs**
National team position	**71st**
Sport facilities	**Good**
Arts opportunities	**Drama excellent; music good; dance, film avg; art poor**
Student newspaper	**Hullfire**
Student radio	**Jam 1575**
Radio Awards 2005	**Technical achievement nomination**
Nightclub	**Asylum**
Bars	**Resnikov, John McCarthy, Armstrong, New Sanctuary**
Union ents	**Twisted, indie, rock, cheese**
Union societies	**48**
Most popular societies	**Drama, Business, Afro Caribbean, Med Soc**
Parking	**Poor**
CITY:	
Entertainment	★★★–★★★★
Scene	**Good clubs**
Town/gown relations	**Poor**
Risk of violence	**High**
Cost of living	**Low**
Student concessions	**Average**
Survival + 2 nights out	**£50 pw**
Part-time work campus/town	**Excellent**

comes easy out of Hull. Hull comes within the top three in the employment table for programmers, software consultancy & supply. The 3/4-year BSc Computer Science with Games Development comes with a foundation year.

Finally, there is a good reputation for Law – they are European law specialists (French, German) with a Grade 5 rating for research. There's also a good line into the police. Note the BA Criminology, Criminology with Psychology, and Criminology with Law. There's also Social Policy & Criminology and now Citizenship & Social Justice, and an intriguing bunch of Chemistry with Forensic Science & Toxicology degrees.

SOCIAL SCENE

STUDENTS' UNION There's the new **Sanctuary Bar**, open 10am for coffee, 11am until 11pm for alcohol, the **John McCarthy Bar** (he was a Hull graduate) – it's recently been refurbished, but someone forgot to put any windows in, so light and airy it is not. It is renowned for its Wednesday nights of drunken debauchery, when it opens its doors to the fifty plus sports clubs for *The Tower*, music of the cheesy/r&b/old school genre. Meanwhile, at the **Asylum** nightclub there's the Armstrong bar in the main room, the union's largest, and situated on the ground floor is the **Continental Café Bar**

Asylum club nights are legendary, *Twisted* a 9-year tradition (till 2.30 a.m.) - anything you can dance to, the most popular student night in Hull. Then there's *Sweet-n-Sour*, indie, rock n roll. *Crystal* is the r&b, hip hop urban event with – one night only – Radio 1's Tim Westwood hosting this term. You''ll also get Ministry of Sound Big Tunes, Nine Black Alps, Stone Roses Experience and much more. Karaoke in **Sanctuary** on Thursday nights with DJ Ferby.

The on-campus **Gulbenkian Theatre** is the focus of a drama course which scored full marks in the teaching assessments. There is a newspaper, *Hullfire*, and a student radio station, Jam 1575. The Tech. Comm. is a parallel organisation into sound and lighting systems and gets its performance kicks at the Friday and Saturday discos. They were nominated for the top technical award in the National Radio Awards this year

Politically the union is averagely active. 'The union council is largely left wing and campaigns are well supported,' says Peter Bainbridge. Campaigns have supported Third World First, Animal Rights and Amnesty International, and there's a particularly active Women's Committee

AT A GLANCE

ACADEMIC FILE:	
Subjects assessed	**37**
Excellent	**78%**
Typical entry requirements	**280 points**
Application acceptance rate	**21%**
Students-staff ratio	**19:1**
First/2:1 degree pass rate	**56%**
ACCOMMODATION FILE:	
Guarantee to freshers	**All but late**
Style	**Halls, houses**
Catered	**41%**
En-suite	**10%**
Price range pw	**£57-£96**
City rent pw	**£45**

and Lesbian and Gay Society. 'Though the locals aren't the most tolerant of folk,' says Peter, 'there are gay-friendly places.'

Town Hull is a centre for the arts, particularly for music, poetry and theatre. The Hull Truck Company, based at **Spring Street Theatre**, is one of this country's most highly renowned creative seedbeds, and also stages one-night fringe, comedy, poetry readings and jazz productions, and galvanises the city's annual festival. The **Hull New Theatre** looks after the more conventional drama, and **May Street Theatre** is the place for dance and mime. For films, the pioneering **Take Two**, with its classic cinema fare, and the arthouse/cult cinema, **Hull Screen**, balance the more commercial ten-screen **Odeon** and eight-screen **UCI**. All these offer student discounts.

Writes Kathryn Halstead, 'Hull, an up and coming city of around 325,000 people, has a number of bowling alleys, ice rinks, swimming pools, golf ranges, gyms, and a £43-million, 25,000-seater Kingston Communications Stadium, home of Hull City Football Club and recently hosting concerts from Elton John to Lisa Scott-Lee. It also features a BBC building, **The Deep** – Europe's only submarium, a blossoming museums quarter and **Princes Quay** indoor shopping centre.'

Writes Albertina, 'Most things are, like housing, cheap in Hull. There are plenty of places to eat – chain restaurants, Indian, Thai and several vegetarian restaurants. The city also has a large number of nightclubs, all of which have student nights on different days in the week, with cheap or free entry to students and many promotional drink offers.

'Most of the larger clubs cater for a wide range of musical tastes, such as indie, drum 'n' bass, hip hop and R&B.' **The Union doews stuff with The Waterfront**.

'The scene is particularly good for alternative music fans. **Spiders** opens Fridays and Saturdays as an exclusively alternative music club. **The Adelphi Club** shows live performances from up and coming alternative music bands, as well as poetry readings and stand-up comedy. If you are into punk, rock or metal then Hull is definitely the place to come.'

As for Scarborough, where the satellite campus is, 'The town has been ruined by a Council that can often be seen lampooned in *Private Eye*,' says Peter Coon, noting that the town was the *Eye's* Rotten Borough of the Year, 'but even they can't obliterate the natural beauty of coast and moors. Nightclubs are cheesy and can get violent. Masses of watering holes, some good real ale and some very good 'locals' Old Town hostelries, though they'll never serve you. It's cheap, however, and so long as you've got something to do, you'll survive, unless you get really ill. The hospital keeps the mortuary pretty busy.' Something, perhaps the Hull-York Med School might change.

Sport Says Katherine: 'There's a fully equipped sports centre with Technogym equipment, a sports hall used for basketball and netball, and a studio area for aerobics and martial arts.' There are also 6 squash courts, a solarium, a gym, and, adjacent to the centre, pitches for football, rugby, hockey, cricket, 9 tennis courts, and a floodlit all-weather surface. The boat, canoe and sub-aqua clubs have a boathouse on the Hull. Bursaries are available, some specifically for disabled athletes.

PILLOW TALK

'You may choose traditional halls of residence or the Lawns halls, with more flexible catering options, or university or privately owned student flats and houses,' reports Katherine. The Lawns complex on the edge of Cottingham is the university's main accommodation facility. It has several halls (some self-catered, some close to a dining hall that provides an evening meal), self-catered flats and bungalows, and a bar, shop and cafeteria.

GETTING THERE

☛ By road: M62, A63, A1079, B1233.
☛ By rail: Leeds, 1:00; Manchester, 2:15; London King's Cross, 4:30; Birmingham New Street, 3:00.
☛ By air: Humberside, Leeds/Bradford Airports.
☛ By coach: London, 5:10; Manchester, 3-4:00; Newcastle, 4-5:00.

IMPERIAL COLLEGE, LONDON

Imperial College
South Kensington
London SW7 2AZ

TEL 020 7594 8001
FAX 020 7594 8004
EMAIL admissions@imperial.ac.uk
WEB www.imperial.ac.uk

Imperial College Union
Prince Consort Road
London SW7 2BB

TEL 020 7594 8060
FAX 020 7594 8065
EMAIl (see website)
WEB www.union.ic.ac.uk

VAG VIEW

Part of the federal University of London, but enjoying more independence than most, Imperial College is a world beater in the areas of medicine, engineering, technology, maths and science.

Mergers have formed its character since the beginning, where, in 1907, it arose out of the marriage of the prestigious Royal College of Science, the Royal School of Mines and the City & Guilds College.

The RCS gave Imperial pure science, *the RSM gave it* mining *(and related fields, such as geology) and the CGC,* engineering. *Mergers with three London teaching hospitals leave it with* a massive medical provision. *Now, Imperial have linked up with Thames Valley University to provide an amazing opportunity for students who have the aptitude to study medicine, but not the qualifications. They will study the first year of Human Sciences – Pre-medical Option BSc(Hons) – at TVU, and depending on their first semester exam results they can transfer to the first year of Imperial's 6-year MBBS course.*

'This has got to be the best situated college, probably in England, perhaps even in the world. If you come from a small town like I do, you'll be blown away by it. Now, the negative. If daddy doesn't own half the oil fields in Texas you are likely to hit a major financial crisis.'

There are other influences. Wye College in Kent brings the food industry, agriculture, the environment and business management into the equation.

Imperial's research record is amazing, the second best in the entire country. Make no mistake about it, if you get a place at Imperial and work hard, you will be made. It has one of the lowest drop-out rates in the country (2.9%), which shows that students appreciate the deal on offer.

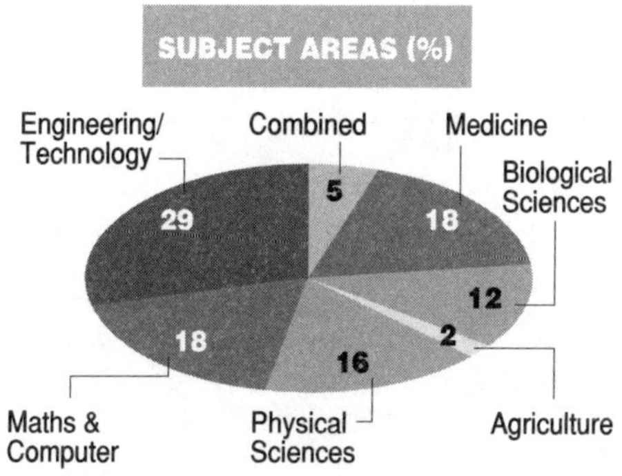

CAMPUSES

'The main campus is situated in South Kensington, Zone 1, Central London,' writes Saurabh Pandya. 'We are right next to the Victoria & Albert, Science and Natural History museums (and are granted free access to them). Travel is easy, the nearest tube is a ten-minute walk away. Generally, it is a low crime area, well lit and pretty safe for students, especially as the uni, the union and most uni accommodation are all within five minutes of each other.'

Says Sarah Playforth, 'This has got to be the best situated college in London, probably in England and perhaps even in the world. If you come from a small town like I do, you'll be blown away by it. Now, the negative. If daddy doesn't own half the oil fields in Texas you are likely to hit a major financial crisis if you eat out at anywhere other than McDonalds. Yes, central London is an extremely expensive place. By the time you graduate you'll probably have acquired an overdraft equivalent to the annual budget of a small country.'

There is an important satellite campus, too, **Wye College**, Wye Village, Ashford, Kent TN25 5AH; Tel 01233 812401. 'Quiet village surroundings and 15th-century buildings give the college a surface air of quietude and tradition,' writes Kieran Alger. It's probably as far removed from your image of London University as it could get.

FEES, BURSARIES

UK & EU Fees £3000 p.a. from 2006/07. All students in receipt of a HE Maintenance grant will receive a student support bursary up to a maximum of four years. Those receiving the maximum award, who have achieved the highest grade in at least three A-Levels and who have firmly accepted an offer of place by the UCAS deadline in May will receive a total bursary of £4000. If in receipt of partial HE Maintenance grant, at the midpoint students will receive at least £500, while if in receipt of the minimum Study Support Bursary they'll

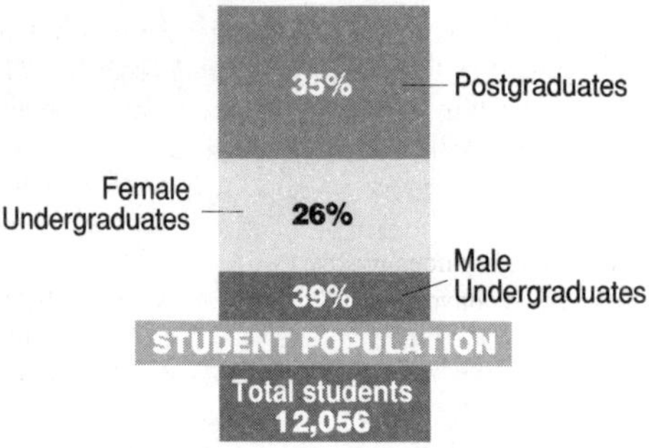

receive at least £100.

STUDENT PROFILE

There is a sense of privilege in the air. Only Oxbridge take fewer from the state sector than Imerpial. Another factor is the gender imbalance, but here things are righting themselves. Only a few years ago an Imperial student wrote: 'The male:female ratio here is about 100:1, but blokes have practically no chance of getting a woman, ever, and consequently Imperial is the sexual frustration capital of Britain!'

Sarah Playforth agreed: 'What you pull is not guaranteed to be human, but the good thing about the student body is that the college's international reputation leads to a large cultural diversity and you can make friends from all over the world.'

Such is the power of the VAG that the male:femal ratio this year is 60:40 – perfectly respectable, and if they tend to be spoddy, well what can you expect?

ACADEMIA & JOBS

'The work is hard, let's get that straight from the outset,' writes Saurabh. 'Most successful applicants have AAB or higher at A-level, and so a high standard will be expected of you. But help is always at hand should you fall behind. There are plenty of tutorials, one-to-one time with the lecturer; lecture notes are always on the web, and if you e-mail a particular lecturer they will always meet with you and explain anything that you don't understand. Most subjects have a representative, a student in your year, chosen by your vote, whose responsibility it is to ensure that you know what's going on, that the web notes are of a satisfactory standard, and so on.

'The library occupies five floors and is shared with the Science Museum. It is pretty comprehensive, and as you would expect at a science and technology uni, the computing facilities are also first rate. There are plenty of PCs, and these are upgraded every eighteen months. Staff tend to be leading figures in their field, and regardless of subject you will get a world class education by coming here.'

Ninety-three per cent of Imperial's teaching assessments have been Excellent or scored 21 or more points out of 24. Its research record is second only to Cambridge. Eleven departments were graded 6 (that's the tops), two Grade 5 (world class) and seven scored 5 (mostly world class), and all have either shown improvement or maintained their

UNIVERSITY/STUDENT PROFILE

School of London Uni since	**1908**
Situation/style	**City campus**
Student population	**12056**
Undergraduates	**7843**
- mature	**5%**
- non EU undergraduates	**27%**
- male/female	**60/40**
- non-traditional student intake	**18%**
- state school intake	**60%, v. low**
- drop-out rate	**3%, v. low**
- undergraduate applications	**Up 10%**

ACADEMIC EXCELLENCE

TEACHING:

(Rated Excellent or 17+ out of 24)

Chemistry, Business & Management, Computing, Geology.	**Excellent**
Electrical & Electronic Eng, Materials Technology	**24**
General Engineering	**23**
Chemical Eng, Mech, Aero & Manufacturing Eng, Molecular Biosciences, Organismal Biosciences, Physics	**22**
Civil Engineering, Medicine	**21**

RESEARCH:

Top grades 5/5/6**

Clinical Laboratory Sciences, Hospital-based Clinical, Bio Sciences, Physics, Pure Maths, Applied Maths, Computer, Chemical Eng, Civil Eng, Mechanical/ Aeronautical/ Manufacturing Eng, Mineral/ Mining Engineering	**Grade 6***
Chemistry, General Engineer.	**Grade 5***
Community-based Clinical, Pre-Clinical, Statistics, Electrical/Electronic Eng, Metallurgy, Business, History	**Grade 5**

position, which, as they will tell you, is a unique achievement among the top four universities in the UK.

The Medicine degree in this, the largest med-school in the country, is a 6-year MB BS (including BSc). Application acceptance rate is 13%, which is better than average, and there's a special route in via a foundation year at Thames Valle Uni (see *VAG View* above). Nearly 30% of Imperial graduates become doctors. All learning is in a clinical context. Traditional, but with special emphasis on communication skills. law, and information technology. Entry ABB including Chemistry, one other science subject or Maths + a third subject. General Studies not accepted. GCSE Biology, Chemistry, English Lang, Maths, Physics essential. At least 3 A grades and 2 B grades. Teaching Inspection 21 Research Grade 5*: Clinical Lab Sciences, Hospital-based Clinical, Bio Sciences; Grade 5: Community-based Clinical, Pre-Clinical.

From September 2006, there'll be a new degree programme in Biomedical Sciences – a 3-year BSc or 4-year MSci, a collaboration between the Faculty of Life Sciences and the Faculty of Medicine. Biomedical Sciences encompasses the principles and practice of biology and biochemistry in relation to medicine.

After doctors come financial wallahs in the Imperial job league, many becoming investment advisers and analysts. Graduates of the Faculty of Engineering/Technology lead (Information Systems Engineering, Computing, etc), then those from Physical Sciences (Maths in various guises and including Management. Far and away Imperial's most popular choice for a job in the City is followed by chartered accountancy and business analysts. Average

Around 7% of graduates become software engineers, another 4% systems analysts, more than 2% computer programmers. In the Faculty of Physical Sciences, there's a BSc and MSci in Mathematics & Computer Science, and in Engineering, MEng Computing (Software Engineering) as well as a European programme of computer study, and other degrees orientated towards Artificial Intelligence, Computational Management. Research Grade 6*. Look also at the B/MEng Information Systems Engineering degrees which come with Associateship of the City & Guilds of London Institute. See also Software Engineer.

Defence operatives and equipment engineers come along the Engineering & Technology and Physical Sciences routes.

They have one of the most exciting Physics departments in the country and a world-class Grade 5* for research. For sheer breadth of vision, look at their exciting 4-year BSc (Hons) Physics with Studies in Musical Performance, developed with the neighbouring Royal College of Music, which taps the cerebral contiguity of art and science at its most exquisite – the anatomy and astronomy of the music of the spheres, perhaps. Graduates find careers in both disciplines and also in broadcasting and recording, where the cross faculty training offers unique, if less immediately obvious, possibilities.

Imperial, in part formed out of The Royal College of Mines in 1907, has a very much more recent world-class Grade 6* for its research facility and a series of BEng/BSc degrees which offer Associateship with the Royal School of Mines; also MEng/MSci degrees with the same Associateship and including, among other degrees, Petroleum Geoscience. Jobs in oil extraction, mining, etc, proliferate. Teaching inspection, 22.

Finally, the question of Wye is answered by the college in this way: 'The future of our rural environment and how we use it to produce safe and healthy food is of critical importance in this new millennium. The Department, already widely known for its interdisciplinary approach (integrating science and management) to new technologies, strategies and policies affecting rural development worldwide, has modern laboratories and facilities, including an award-winning learning resources centre and working farm on a 350-hectare estate.'

SOCIAL SCENE

Students' Union The Students' Union, like UMIST, St Andrews, Edinburgh, Glasgow and Dundee, manage their own affairs. 'Don't worry about your student discounts,' Ed Sexton assures, 'ICU cards are

WHERE IMPERIAL GRADUATES END UP

Health & Social Work: 31%; Education: 3%; Wholesale/Retail: 3%; Manufacturing: 7%; Financial Activities: 15%; Public Administration, Civil Service & Defence: 4%; Hotel/Restaurant: 1%; Transport & Communications (including Telecommunications): 3%; Construction: 1%; Agriculture: 2%; Mining/Oil Extracting: 2%; Personnel: 3%; Computer: 4%; Business & Management: 5%; Accountancy: 4%; Media (including Film): 0.5%; Architecture: 1%; Sport: 1%.

Approximate 'graduate track' employed **79%**

WHAT IT'S REALLY LIKE	
UNIVERSITY:	
Social Life	★★★★
Campus scene	**Singular**
Student Union services	**Good**
Politics	**Low interest**
Sport	**Good**
National team position	**47th**
Sport facilities	**Good**
Arts opportunities	**Drama, dance, film excellent; art avg; music good**
Student newspaper	**Felix**
Student radio	**IC Radio**
Radio Awards 2005	**Nomination (News)**
Student TV	**STOIC**
Nightclub venues	**Da Vinci's**
Bars	**dBs, Union, Beit, Charing Cross, Wye Union**
Union ents	**Pervasive**
Union clubs/Societies	**248**
Parking	**Non-existent**
CITY:	
Entertainment	★★★★★
Scene	**Wild, expensive**
Town/gown relations	**Average-good**
Risk of violence	**London v. high**
Cost of living	**High**
Student concessions	**Good**
Survival + 2 nights out	**£100 pw**
Part-time work campus/town	**Good/excellent**

AT A GLANCE	
ACADEMIC FILE:	
Subjects assessed	**15**
Excellent	**93%**
Typical entry points	**465, v. high**
Application acceptance rate	**19%**
Students-staff ratio	**9:1, low**
First/2:1 degree pass rate	**73%, high**
ACCOMMODATION FILE:	
Guarantee to freshers	**100%**
Style	**Halls**
Catered	**Almost none**
En-suite	**A few**
Price range pw	**£57-£130**
City rent pw	**£100-£180 Zone 1, £75-£85 Zone 2**

accepted at most places in London, and you can also get a University of London Union (ULU) card, which is widely recognised.'

They have the biggest student venue in London, the cheapest bar prices in the city, the most clubs and societies and an enviable programme of some six clubnights a week and regular top-line live acts and comedy.

Union facilities feature **Da Vinci's**, a modern-style café bar – trivia nights, cocktail nights and live jazz, big screen sport, Wednesday club-nights for the sports crowd (with recent additional barbecue facilities), Saturday pre-club and a non-stop succession of Friday clubnights.

The wood-panelled **Union Bar** is a more typical pub, with reputedly the largest pewter tankard collection in Europe. The **Beit Quad bars** are in the ground floor of the Union building in Beit Quad. Then there's the **Charing Cross (med) Bar**, Fulham, and the **Union Bar,** Wye.

In addition, a **Concert Hall** is used for bigger events and there's a smaller venue, **dBs** (also known by its full name **Decibels**) or **dB's Club Bar** which is open Wednesday and Friday nights, again with big screen. Another attraction of the union is the cinema – 'the biggest student cinema in the country and the sixth biggest screen in London. It shows films much later than elsewhere but only go if you think the film is worth getting a sore bum for,' says our reporter.

The number of clubs at Imperial is pretty overwhelming – not far short of 250 from which to choose, everything from Chess, to E-commerce, to Rugby to Juggling. And just because they are a techno-based uni, it doesn't mean they don't have any arty clubs – Opera, Drama, Art, Dance, etc are all very active.

Film is rated excellent by students. Media, too, is very active both from a techno and literary pov. There's the award-winning newspaper, *Felix*, and IC Radio and STOIC, the TV arm. Politics, however, are no big deal.

Down at rural Wye, your average Wye-guy can be found not driving a tractor but done up in a penguin suit on his way to a ball, or to one of their eccentric clubs. Thursday nights see the Beaus, the Garters, the Jock-Strap Farmers and the mysterious Druids take over the union in a whirl of practical jokes, initiation ceremonies and over-consumption of alcohol. Membership of these peculiar clubs is by invitation only.

Sport Besides national competition in the uni leagues, where Imperial came 47th last year, they excel in the London University league. But in rowing – the big thing at ICS – you're talking international levels. The boathouse is at Putney Bridge.

A new sports centre, Ethos, is opening at the South Kensington campus ithis year – a 70-station fitness gym, 25m deck-level swimming pool, a sauna/steam room and spa, a five-badminton-court sports hall, a state-of-the-art climbing wall, exercise studio, and a sports injury unit. The Sports Centre at Prince's Gardens (Exhibition Road) includes a 25m swimming pool, four squash courts, a gym, a 25m rifle range, a training studio, sauna, steam room and poolside spa bath. Nearby there are tennis and netball courts, and a weights room. The 60-acre pitches are at Harlington, near Heathrow. Facilities include a floodlit multi-purpose surface and a pavilion with bar. There are a further 15 acres at Teddington (four pitches and a cricket square), 22 acres at Cobham, the boathouse at Putney and a sailing club at Welsh Harp Reservoir in North West London. In addition, its hospital sites at Paddington and Fulham Palace Road have 25m swimming pools and squash courts.

PILLOW TALK

You are guaranteed a place in either Imperial College or London University intercollegiate accommodation for the first year of study. Imperial accommodation consists of single and shared study bedrooms, with shared common rooms, kitchens, bathroom facilities and laundries. There are a small number of single and shared en-suite rooms. All accommodation is self-catering except Linstead Hall on the South Kensington campus and the Wye campus halls. 'If you are lucky,' writes London-based Saurabh, 'you'll get into one of the halls right next to campus, and you can spend all year perfecting your "get up at 8:55 and be in time for 9:00 lecture" technique. These are the Southside, Northside and Beit halls. If you are especially lucky, you will be placed in Beit Hall, which was opened recently and has brand new rooms with Ikea-style kitchens and every amenity you could possibly want. There are other halls in Evelyn Gardens (15 minutes from campus) or Pembridge Gardens (40 minutes, or 20 by tube).'

GETTING THERE

☛ By Underground: South Kensington (Circle, District and Piccadilly lines).

UNIVERSITY OF KEELE

The University of Keele
Keele
Staffordshire ST5 5BG

TEL 01782 584003/4/5
FAX 01782 632343
EMAIL undergraduate@keele.ac.uk
WEB www.keele.ac.uk

Keele Students' Union
Keele
Staffs ST5 5BJ

TEL 01782 711411
FAX 01782 712671
EMAIL sta21@kusu.keele.ac.uk
WEB www.kusu.net

VAG VIEW

Its academic strategy made it unique from the start – the emphasis on a broad education, seen in the dual honours degree, which they pioneered and which offers a rare opportunity to study from both science and arts points of view. Ninety per cent of Keele's students opt for this type of degree. A third of first years are studying a language or a related cultural module. Nearly all undergraduates at Keele, irrespective of the subject combination they are studying have the opportunity to spend a semester of their second year at one of Keele's partner institutions in North America, Australia, South Africa or another part of Europe. Keele is one of 8 British universities to have been awarded the European Quality Label for mobility.

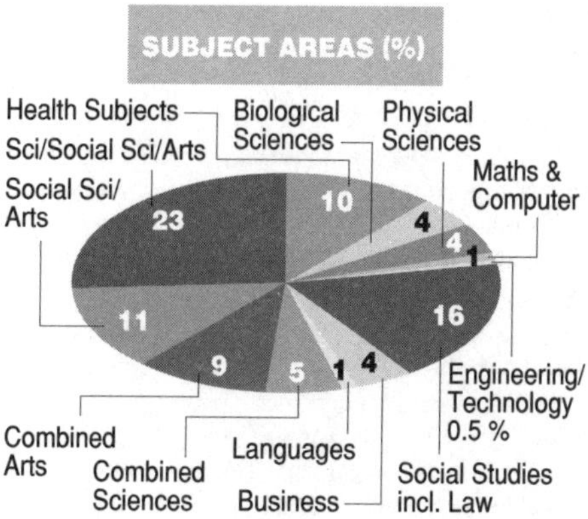

A certain sort of person thrives at Keele's isolated campus, but it might be too cosy for some.

CAMPUS

'It's the centre of England and the middle of nowhere,' write Mark Holtz and Gareth Belfield.

'Keele University's self-contained campus is a stone's throw from Stoke-on-Trent, a constant worry for those students without protective head-gear. In theory, the university is set within tiny Keele village, but the campus has grown over such a large area that saying it is part of Keele village is akin to saying that London is part of Westminster. The campus is on a hilltop and is so exposed you expect a policeman to come along and arrest it for indecency. Nearby Newcastle-under-Lyme, Hanley (Stoke) and Crewe can be reached by the bus service called (joyfully) PMT. Train-wise, Manchester is only 30 minutes away, as is Birmingham. London direct can be done in around two hours. The M6 is within earshot of the campus, and sounds like the sea if you are drunk enough.

UNIVERSITY/STUDENT PROFILE

University since	**1962**
Situation/style	**Rural campus**
Student population	**12500**
Undergraduates	**7500**
- mature	**29%**
- non EU undergraduates	**9%**
- male/female	**38/62**
- non-traditional student intake	**26%**
- state school intake	**91%**
- drop-out rate	**7%**
- undergraduate applications	**Down 5%**

**see Introduction for key to tables*

FEES, BURSARIES

UK & EU Fees: £3000 p.a. Bursary for students in receipt of full HE Maintenance grant: £300. There are also bursary schemes related to academic excellence, membership of an Ethnic Minority, domicile in rural areas, registration for certain subjects, including medicine, and access via Keele's partner schools.

STUDENT PROFILE

'Take a generous measure of "traditional" students, two heaped tablespoons of mature, nursing, international and local students, heavily season with postgraduates, add a dash of complete weirdoes and you have the recipe for the most diverse and interesting concoction of a university anywhere in the world.

'It's impossible not to fit in at Keele, with over half the students living together on campus, you're never really in danger of running out of people to borrow sugar from.'

The low drop-out rate of 7% suggests that the experiment works. Female students abound (62% of undergrads; 37% of total student population).

ACADEMIA & JOBS

The dual honours degree is a multi-disciplinary strategy which promises more than a one-plus-one benefit – at best, new, enlightening points of view on a shared subject focus, or the same skills of mind honed simultaneously by different subjects of study. If it is the analytical skills of a top-flight bioscientist that is required in the City, here you can put the theory to the test. Or you can simply look for compatibility, a vocational element that enhances your main subject interest – there are combo degrees in Marketing with Maths, Music Technology, Physics, Psychology, Statistics (as there are with Management).

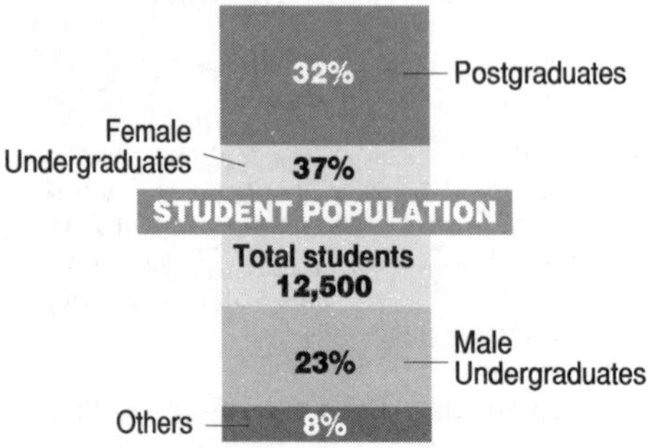

Half the Keele graduates that become marketing managers (that's 6% of all Keele graduates) ride in on these. The other half look elsewhere in the curriculum for marketing as an addendum to a subject of their choice. We find languages are an important entré into the sector – e.g. French and Marketing; and sometimes there is a good product-orientated subject given employability by the addition of Marketing, as in Biochemistry and Marketing.

Business Administration makes another highly employable mix with Psychology (or languages, law, media, or Communications & Culture). Such Business Admin combos account for nearly a quarter of jobs at Keele. Another productive multi-disciplinary course is Human Resource Management (with Psychology, Info Systems, etc) – more than 3% of Keele graduates become personnel officers. Finance, Economics and Maths combo degrees lead 10% of all Keele graduates to become accountants or to work in other financial areas.

Again, Computer Science combination degrees sustain a fine graduate employment reputation in IT consultancy, computer programing and software engineering, and Education Studies combos produce secondary and primary school teachers, while Social Studies produce high numbers of community and youth workers (almost 3%

of all graduates fall into this latter category).

Law is worth a particular mention. Part of the multi-subject curriculum, but also a single honours subject, there's an international reputation and if you want to work as a solicitor and you already have a degree in another subject, you can take the Common Professional Examination (CPE) at Keele, which you will need.

Another course available as single honours is Physiotherapy – a major career field, with some 6% of graduates becoming physiotherapists.

Keele now also offer the opportunity to study Medicine (a MBChB degree) to applicants with non-Science A levels. It is a course developed with Manchester University. The new clinical skills lab at the Dept of Nursing & Midwifery, which simulates a ward environment, is a part of this. Since 2003 they have offered a 5-year course at Keele Campus, with the first 2 years in Manchester, or a 6-year course with the pre-med year at Manchester. The 6-year is strictly for pupils taking Arts subjects at A Level (or 2 Arts and 1 Science. GCSEs Chemistry and Maths are 'desirable'). For the 5-year, you'll need AAB, including Chemistry and Biology or Physics or Maths + one other 'rigorous' subject. 8-11 GCSEs with a broad spread of subjects.

ACADEMIC EXCELLENCE

TEACHING:
(Rated Excellent or 17+ out of 24)

Applied Social Work, Music	**Excellent**
American Studies, Politics, Philosophy, Education	**24**
Economics, Psychology	**23**
Sociology, Maths, Organismal Biosciences, Physics	**22**
Nursing, Molecular Biosciences, Management	**21**
French, Russian, Subjects Allied to Medicine	**20**
German	**19**

RESEARCH:
Top grades 5/5/6**

Law	**Grade 6***
Applied Maths, General Eng, English, Politics, Social Policy, American Studies, History	**Grade 5**

STUDENT SCENE

STUDENTS' UNION Sam's Bar opens up to the Ballroom to take around 1100 on big live act nights. Apparently the KUSU building was originally designed to look like a ship with the **Ballroom** at the heart of the vessel. In the good old days the Rolling Stones used to use it as a rehearsal room and even now, on a still winter's night, faint echoes can be heard of the Eurythmics, UB40, Oasis and a young Jarvis Cocker, who graced the stage. More recent visiors were Fun Lovin' Criminals, Idlewild, Mis-Teeq, Liberty X, Atomic Kitten, Toploader, Reef, The Pet Shop Boys, Levellers, The Proclaimers.

The Lounge is – surprise – a lounge bar. **K2**, formerly **The Club**, is now KUSU's 'premier Entertainment Venue', having undergone a £250k refurbishment three years ago. With a top-specification PA & lighting system, it features a permanent 6m x 4m stage. Here, on a Monday is pop, chart & dance with resident DJ Chris; alternate Tuesdays is Comedy Club – Mark Lamarr, Peter Kay, Ed Byrne, Paul Tonkinson, Adam Bloom, Richard Morton and more. On other Tuesdays you might have *Stella Screen* – box office smashes before general release. Wednesdays – whole building is *R-wind* (retro - 80s, 90s) and indie/alternative from resident DJ The Rich. They also do monthly fancy dress nights and, in **The Lounge**, Quiz and Cocktail evenings and Sunday karaoke competitions

Keele has a history of political turbulence, but you wouldn't notice now: 'In the '70s,' write Mark and Gareth, 'Keele pre-empted Wales and Scotland by attempting to gain independence from Britain. Passports were issued, border patrols were set up, a national anthem created, and an unsuccessful attempt to enter the Eurovision Song Contest was made. More recently, they were the first university

WHERE KEELE GRADUATES END UP

Health & Social Work: 14%; Education: 8%; Wholesale/Retail: 12%; Manufacturing: 8%; Financial Activities: 10%; Public Administration, Civil Service & Defence: 13%; Hotel/Restaurant: 3%; Transport & Communications (including Telecommunications): 5%; Construction: 2%; Agriculture: 1%; Personnel: 5%; Computer: 3%; Business & Management: 3%; Accountancy: 3%; Media (including Film): 1%; Legal 5%; Publishing: 3%; Sport: 1%.

Approximate 'graduate track' employed **72%**

WHAT IT'S REALLY LIKE

UNIVERSITY:	
Social Life	★★★
Campus scene	**Isolated**
Student Union services	**Good**
Politics	**Average**
Sport	**Not impressive**
National teamposition	**109th**
Sport facilities	**Good**
Arts opportunities	**Excellent**
Student newspaper	**Concourse**
Nightclub	**K2**
Bars	**Sam's Bar, Ballroom, Lounge**
Union ents	**Cheesy + live**
Union clubs/societies	**80**
Most popular society	**Drama**
Parking	**Good**
TOWN:	
Entertainment	★★
Local (Stoke) scene	**Pubs/clubs**
Town/gown relations	**OK**
Risk of violence	**Average**
Cost of living	**Below average**
Student concessions	**Average**
Survival + 2 nights out	**£50 pw**
Part-time work campus/town	**OK/poor**

to reject the Government's tuition fees proposals.' More recently still, there was some wrangling with the uni over the union's ownership.

Sport Facilities include a gym, sports hall, floodlit synthetic pitch, 50 acres of grass pitches 'so green they'd make Kermit blush', tennis courts, fitness centre, squash courts, etc. Facilities are good, national form seems not to be. They came well down in the national leagues.

Town 'Aaarghh! Keele is in the Potteries, where the main industry is not so much in decline, as plummeting down a precipice of bankruptcy. Locals refer to you as "duck" if they like you. If they don't like you they'll just try to run over you.'

PILLOW TALK

Freshers with Keele as first choice have uni accommodation guaranteed – self-catered single study-bedrooms, 25% en suite; prices are good, see *At A Glance* box. 'There is something inexplicably nice about campus accommodation,' sigh Mark & Gareth in unison, 'even if the cleaning ladies have mastered the art of knocking, unlocking your door, opening it, coming in, and saying, "Ooh, I'll come back when you've had time to put some clothes on," all in two seconds.' The HallsNet Service allows all students direct access to the Internet.

AT A GLANCE

ACADEMIC FILE:	
Subjects assessed	**28**
Excellent	**68%**
Typical entry requirements	**300 points**
Application acceptance rate	**19%**
Students-staff ratio	**16:1**
First/2:1 degree pass rate	**55%**
ACCOMMODATION FILE:	
Guarantee to freshers	**None to Clearing**
Style	**Halls**
Catered	**None**
En-suite	**25%**
Approx price range pw	**£53-£88**
Town rent pw	**£45**

GETTING THERE

☛ By road: from the north M6/J16, A500, A531, right on to A525, right through Keele village; from south, M6/J15, A5182, left on to A53, right at Whitmore following signs.
☛ By rail: good service more or less everywhere, London 1:30 to Stoke-on-Trent station, then taxi.
☛ By coach: London, 4:00

UNIVERSITY OF KENT AT CANTERBURY

The University of Kent at Canterbury
The Registry
Canterbury CT2 7NZ

TEL 01227 827272
FAX 01227 827077
EMAIL recruitment@ukc.ac.uk
WEB www.ukc.ac.uk

Kent University Students' Union
The University
Canterbury CT2 7NW

TEL 01227 824200
FAX 01227 824204
EMAIL union@kent.ac.uk
WEB www.kentunion.co.uk

VAG VIEW

UKC is, in a nutshell, a friendly, politically correct campus, where it is easy to work hard, play hard, or do a little of both.

Writes Dominic Conway: 'If you come to this Uni you will have everything really, countryside and seaside, but still near to London; entertainment and nightlife, but still a calm working environment. For the more hard-core among you it may seem a little too relaxed, but with the facilities and the high teaching standards you should definitely get a good education, and if you don't have enough fun, it's more likely to be your fault than theirs.'

CAMPUS

UKC campus is situated on top of an alarmingly steep hill about a mile out of the main city. You will be assigned a residential college, **Keynes**, **Rutherford**, **Darwin** or **Eliot.** You can be more or less self-sufficient on campus, you could spend your entire first year without visiting the city, and many do.

FEES, BURSARIES

UK & EU Fees: £3000 p.a. If in receipt of HE Maintenance grant there's a £1000 p.a. bursary; £500-£750 if on partial grant. There are bursaries for applicants proceeding from less privileged backgrounds, and scholarships for sport and acadaemic achievement.

> ***They are pre-eminent in social sciences, with Social Policy rated world-class Grade 6* for research and Economics dropping only one point at the assessments. But bio-sciences dropped not a mark at all.***

STUDENT PROFILE

UKC is not a place for Oxbridge rejects, but it takes quite a chunk of entrants from independent schools. Intake from the poorer neighbourhoods has, however, risen sharply over the last few years (see *Fees, Bursaries*), and there are strong mature and overseas flavours, too. Indeed, Catherine Robertson goes so far as to maintain that the reason why 'many British people haven't even heard of UKC [is] the uni's dedication to attracting overseas students,' but concludes that multifarious as is its makeup is, 'what you will find is a friendly student body, and lecturers and tutors who pursue their own work as energetically as they do yours.'

ACADEMIA & JOBS

There are some clear strengths in the curriculum.

UNIVERSITY/STUDENT PROFILE

University since	**1965**
Situation/style	**City campus**
Student population	**14600**
Undergraduates	**12365**
- mature	**16%**
- non EU undergraduatess	**8%**
- male/female	**46/54**
- non-traditional student intake	**24%**
- state school intake	**89%**
- drop-out rate	**7%**
- undergraduate applications	**Up 5%**

Drama not only scored full marks at the teaching assessments, but also achieved Grade 5 at the research assessments. Focus for both student and professional theatre companies is the campus-based Gulbenkian Theatre.

In social sciences UKC are pre-eminent, with Social Policy rated world-class Grade 6* for research and Economics dropping only one point at the assessments. Meanwhile, biosciences dropped not a mark at all. Law also enjoys a reputation here, its research assessment international class Grade A. They are European law specialists, and the uni is committed to encouraging the assimilation of European culture far and wide in the curriculum – by study in Europe, by taking a European language, or by combining one of their popular artistic or media packages with advanced work in a foreign language, as in the European Arts course. 'Academically the university has a strong reputation for modern languages,' Catherine acknowledges, 'thanks to it's proximity to Europe and the encouragement to students to study abroad for a year.'

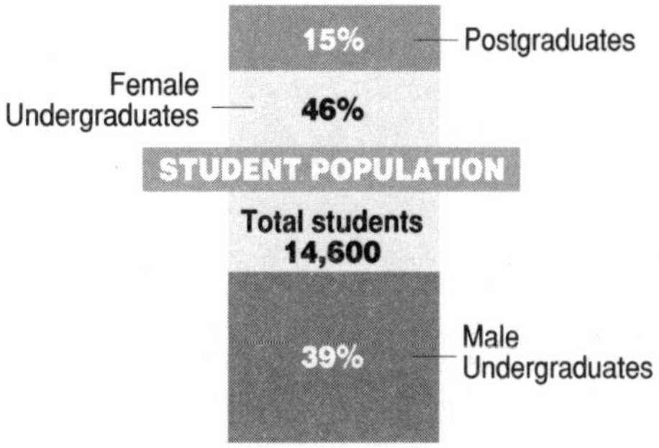

WHERE KENT GRADUATES END UP

Health & Social Work: 7%; Education: 9%; Wholesale/Retail: 11%; Manufacturing: 12%; Financial Activities: 13%; Public Administration, Civil Service & Defence: 7.5%; Hotel/Restaurant: 4%; Transport & Communications (including Telecommunications): 4%; Construction: 1%; Personnel: 4%; Computer: 5%; Business & Management: 3%; Accountancy: 3%; Media (including Film): 3%; Legal 2%; Advertising: 1%.

Approximate 'graduate track' employed **67%**

A few queries are raised when one sees the sheer number of managers, administrators, sales assistants and clerks that head off Kent's employment return. This appears to be down to their 2-subject combination courses, such as Comparative Literary Studies/Classical & Archaeological Studies, European Culture & Thought/Religious Studies, etc, which certainly don't leap out at one as likely to pay back student investment in the short term.

However, when one looks down the 'graduate track' employment table, which details numbers into real-life graduate jobs, Kent does very well. They are in the top third countrywide, positioned between Sheffield and Leeds, with 67% employed.

The first to give hope are the 8% graduates who become computer programmers, software engineers, IT consultants and the like. This is an area in which Kent is traditionally strong. Look at their department of Electronic Engineering & Computing, BEng and BSc degrees, many of them carved out with industry.

Also crucial to the graduate employment figures is the accountancy package – Accounting & Finance degrees with Business Administration, Management Science, French Business Studies, German, etc. The top-rated Economics provision brings us further into the financial sector, which is well represented, too, by Financial Mathematics, Actuarial Science, Maths and Accounting & Finance, Applied Quantative Finance. High up in the employment graph we find bank managers, financial administrators, actuaries, economists, pension advisers, and so on.

In Social Sciences, the various Industrial Relations and Human Resource Management degrees yield jobs in personnel, and community and youth workers reflect glory on the uni's well-known social studies reputation, while its Social Policy provision (on its own and with Public Management or Computing) turns out local and regional government officers.

The biological scientists and biochemists among graduates attest to the strength of physical and bio-sciences. There are foundation courses, years with industry, and promising medical bio-science aspects, as well as pharmaceutical degrees.

SUBJECT AREAS (%)

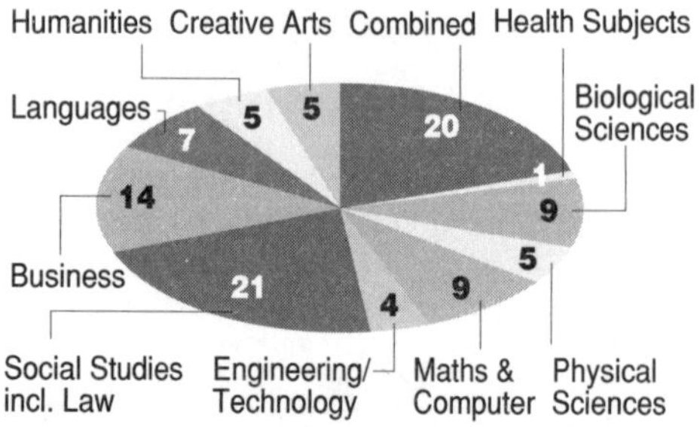

ACADEMIC EXCELLENCE

TEACHING:
(Rated Excellent or 17+ out of 24)

Computing, Anthropology, Social Policy & Administration	**Excellent**
Drama & Theatre Studies, Molecular Biosciences, Organismal Biosciences, Philosophy	**24**
Economics	**23**
History of Art, Classics, Archaeology, Psychology	**22**
Sociology, Electrical/Electron Engineering, American Studies, Subjects Allied to Medicine, Business/Management, Maths, Physics, Politics	**21**
Theology, Film Studies	**20**
Modern Languages (French, German, Italian, Euro Studies, Linguistics)	**19**

RESEARCH :
Top grades 5/5/6**

Social Policy	**Grade 6***
Statistics	**Grade 5***
English, Applied Maths, Law, Anthropology, Drama/Dance/Performing Arts	**Grade 5**

WHAT IT'S REALLY LIKE	
UNIVERSITY:	
Social Life	★★★★
Campus scene	**Friendly, southern but weekday**
Student Union services	**Good**
Politics	**Student issues**
Sport	**50 clubs, highly competitive**
National sporting position	**44th**
Sport facilities	**Good**
Arts opportunities	**Film, drama exc, music art good**
Student newspaper	**KRED**
Student radio	**UKCR**
Nightclub	**The Venue**
Bars	**Lighthouse, Mungo's, Origins, Woodies**
Union ents	**Good but few live bands**
Union clubs/societies	**80**
Parking	**Poor**
CITY:	
Entertainment	★★★
Scene	**Touristy, historic, v. good pubs**
Town/gown relations	**Good**
Risk of violence	**Average**
Cost of living	**Average**
Student concessions	**Adequate**
Survival + 2 nights out	**£80 pw**
Part-time work campus/town	**Good**

At the other end of the curriculum spectrum, employment figures for film and video activities, radio and television suggest that the longterm commitment to Film Studies – there are seven degrees (Contemporary Arts, Film, is the new one) – may be paying off, and no doubt the student media nurtures and underwrites the trend.

SOCIAL SCENE

STUDENTS' UNION 'First years tend to remain on campus to socialise,' continues Catherine, 'simply because it is cheaper and more convenient. There are 5 main bars: **Origins** is in Darwin College (trendy-type bar, good fajitas); **Rutherford Bar** – guess where that is (a drinker's bar, good juke box); **Mungo's** is in Eliot (should be better than it is, no atmosphere); and then there's **Keynes Bar** (concrete garden, popular in summer). **Woody's** at Parkwood is more of a pub than a bar and haunted by the more cliquey sports clubs (you'll see what I mean). For those of you who don't want to spend all your time drinking alcohol, there is also the **Gulbenkian Theatre** coffee bar and 2 new Wicked coffee shops this year.

'Now, what to do with your new-found friends once the bars have thrown you out into the cold, cold, night? Generally, people head onto **The Venue**, the campus club with a capacity of 1200, open six nights a week, and a café bar, **The Lighthouse** (200). Regular nights are Mondays, *Sports Fed Night*, where each sports club takes a turn as host. Thursdays are *Retro* nights Friday is dance, Saturday anything goes, from garage to pop, dance to r&b.'

Writes Dominic Conway: 'The Kent mentality is not a wild one. Although the 5 bars on campus will serve refreshingly cheap drinks nightly (£1.50 cheapest pint, £1 shot promotions) it is more common to see students sharing a few drinks at a comedy night or a salsa party than pushing the boundaries of alcohol consumption. The cultural diversity means that there is no obvious campus consensus, and the ever growing list of societies means that any student will feel well catered for.

'One thing clearly missing is an exciting music scene, the campus bands are sporadic and little talent tours these parts because there aren't any good venues for a live band. If you keep your ear to the ground, however, local groups will put on authentic, unpretentious rock shows and Whitstable (on the coast) hides a number of world class musicians playing jazz, blues, and Turkish folk music that even the most selective muso will be content with.

'Many students however don't make it as far as Whitstable and don't even trouble themselves with town very much, because the campus alone has so much to offer. The shops are a tad over priced but will stock all the essentials and some more exciting ingredients if you have a sudden urge to cook a lavish dinner. The **Gulbenkian Theatre** on campus hosts some remarkable shows, the manager is in close communication with the Drama department

AT A GLANCE	
ACADEMIC FILE:	
Subjects assessed	**31**
Excellent	**74%**
Typical entry requirements	**300 points**
Application acceptance rate	**22%**
Students-staff ratio	**18:1**
First/2:1 degree pass rate	**59%**
ACCOMMODATION FILE:	
Guarantee to freshers	**90%**
Style	**College halls, student village**
Approx price range pw	**£66-£95**
City rent pw	**£70**

and is very well informed on the acts that students want to see. Its stage is open to comedy and music, as well as some bright lights in the world of modern theatre. The multitudinous societies keep freshening up the nightlife by hiring out the various venues for evenings for a more specific audience. The hip-hop, drama and rock societies have put in the most effort so far in terms of catering for the uni as a whole. Safety on campus is ensured by Campus Watch, who offer an escort service for anyone walking around late at night on their own. '

The student radio station (UKCR) broadcasts 24/7 on 1350 AM. There are 2 studios. The student monthly magazine is *KRED*, an acronym derived from the initial letter of each of the colleges.

SPORT Sports-wise there are 50 clubs, all the usual stuff plus Choi Kwang Do, Taekwondo and Kendo (one of only five unis to offer this) and American Football (UKC Falcons). It's highly competitive. Various sports offer bursaries, some in cahoots with UKC alumni. UKC does well nationally at all the team sports, coming 44th in the national team league last year.

TOWN Writes Dominc: 'Canterbury is just a 20 minute walk away (or 10 minutes by bus, which comes regularly). Nice big cathedral, old cobbled streets, strong whiff of history in the air and a two hour walk to the beach. Although it is quite a quaint place, it is very lively and friendly – the locals never seem to mind or complain about the amount of students!'

Says Catherine: 'If you're feeling particularly adventurous then go to town for a change of scenery. It is a city because it has a famous cathedral (to which you will no doubt take your parents when they come to visit), but its size is no more than that of a large town, and if you are coming from a large, lively city you may at first be disappointed. However, Canterbury is deceiving in the sense that it appears quieter than it actually is.

'One thing it does not lack is pubs, and many of my friends have spent a happy drunken evening in the enchantingly named **Bishop's Finger** (the nun's delight apparently!). After the pubs shut, things get a bit tricky, as Canterbury is not renowned for it's club scene. **Alberry's** is recommended, but it's pretty cliquey. **The Works** is another favourite!'

PILLOW TALK

Writes Dominic: 'A lot of money has recently gone into accommodation, so the standard is fairly high. The new halls are the most spotless, but can be a little sterile. I would urge new students to brave a shared toilet for the sake of their social life.'

Surely it can't be *that* bad. Most first years opt for halls in one of the 4 colleges or their posher extensions, or in Parkwood student village, made for the purpose. The colleges tend to be the easiest way to make friends as there are usually seven people randomly thrown together in a corridor and you all just mix and match.

The colleges, Eliot, Darwin, Rutherford and Keynes, are where the majority of first years end up, although you can get a place in Tyler Court or Becket Court, both new sets of accommodation.

A problem with the colleges is that they are semi-self-catered, i.e you get breakfast included in the rent, but only until 9.30 am

Parkwood, the student village, is just off the main campus and made up of groups of houses for 4-to-6 students.

The problem here is that it is generally favoured by third years and foreign students, and they seem to get priority. The houses tend to allow more freedom than halls, but can leave you feeling a bit feel detached, as, other than **Woody's** bar, every other facility is on the main campus.

GETTING THERE

- By road: from west, M2, A2; south, A28 or A2; east, A257; northeast, the A28; northwest, A290.
- By rail: London Victoria, 85 mins; London Charing Cross or Waterloo East, 90 mins.
- By air: Heathrow and Gatwick.
- By coach: London Victoria, 1 hour 45 mins.

KING'S COLLEGE, LONDON

King's College, London
Waterloo Bridge House
London SE1 8WA

TEL 020 7836 5454
FAX 020 7836 1799
EMAIL enquiries@kcl.ac.uk
WEB www.kcl.ac.uk

King's College Students' Union
Surrey Street
London WC2R 2NS

TEL 020 7836 7132
FAX 020 7379 9833
EMAIL president@kclsu.org
WEB www.kclsu.org/

VAG VIEW

King's College London is one of London University's oldest and most prestigious colleges, founded by George IV in 1829 and one of the federal university's original colleges in 1836. Undergraduates feel part of this strong tradition, but until recently the scattered nature of the college did little to foster a sense of identity. In the course of its history it has developed through many mergers, most recently, in the summer of 1998, with United Medical & Dental Schools of Guy's Hospital (where medical teaching began in the 1720s) & St Thomas's (where Medicine has been taught since the 16th century). Since then, King's have sold off their Kensington and Chelsea campuses and, at a cost of some £200 million, completely redrawn the campus map.

UNIVERSITY/STUDENT PROFILE	
College of London Uni since	**1836**
Situation/style	**Civic**
Student population	**21315**
Undergraduates	**14880**
- mature	**16%**
- non EU undergraduates	**8%**
- male/female	**34/66**
- non-traditional student intake	**21%**
- state school intake	**67%, low**
- drop-out rate	**4%**
- undergraduate applications	**Up 11%**

CAMPUSES

There are now five campuses, four of which cluster around the Thames, close to the centre of town. With the Students' Union **Macadam** building at its core is the **Strand Campus**, on the north bank, just south of Covent Garden. Here, too, are the schools of Humanities, Law and Physical Sciences. Just across the river via Waterloo Bridge is the new **Waterloo Campus**, incorporating Education, Management, Health & Life Sciences, Nursing & Midwifery and the Stamford Street apartments with the basement gym, K4, which appeared on TV's *Watchdog* as an exemplary fitness club.

Three bridges to the east lies **Guy's Campus**. Students of Medicine and Dentistry entering King's in 1999 were the first to study at this purpose-built centre close to London Bridge. The campus incorporates a new SU building with bar, swimming pool, ballroom, shop and welfare centre, as well as accommodation.

And then there's **St Thomas' Campus** (Continuing Medical & Dental teaching), which overlooks the Houses of Parliament north across the river at Westminster Bridge, and **Denmark Hill Campus**, south of the Oval.

The only site a little out on its own, Denmark Hill is base for clinical teaching at King's College Hospital and the Dental Institute, and home to the Institute of Psychiatry.

All residences – halls (catered or self-catered), apartments or student houses (mainly for mature students) – are within London Travel Zones 1 or 2, and close to one or more of the campuses.

Word on the ground is that KCL succeeds not in spite of, but because of its location: 'Want to live and work smack in the centre of London? You got it,' write Ben Jones and Chris Wilding. 'Want high frequency bus and tube links with a 30% discount? You got it. Clubs? Pubs? Venues? Theatres? Museums? Galleries? Shops? Yeah, got them too. In fact, by nestling snugly and unassumingly within the heart of the capital, King's College London appears to students as a seventh heaven.' But at a price.

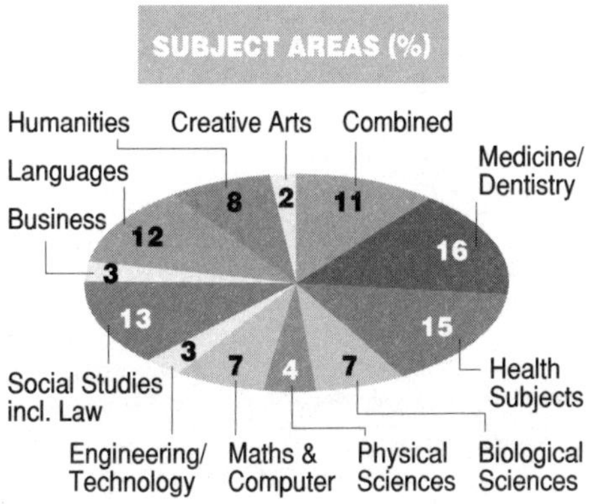

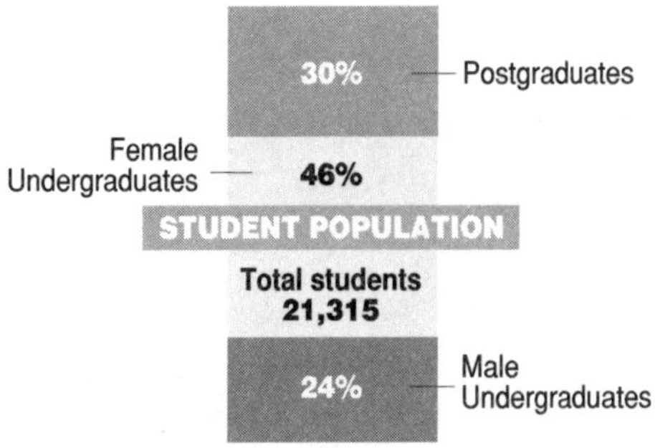

FEES, BURSARIES

UK & EU Fees: £3000 p.a. Bursary of £1350 if in receipt of full HE Maintenace grant; if in receipt of partial grant there's support up to that figure on a sliding scale.

STUDENT PROFILE

Both King's and University College, London, the mother of all London University colleges, have a high public school intake, UCL's being higher than King's. There is, at King's, what one student described as a 'friendly competitiveness' with UCL. I have heard a KCL student refer to UCL students as 'godless scum', while UCL routinely call KCL the Strand Poly. In apparent contravention of this public school profile, the uni has been digging around and found quite a healthy percentage of applicants from less traditional classes and neighbourhoods - 21% of their freshers came from the lower socio-economic orders last time. They're also encouraging mature students to their medical faculty (see *Academia* below).

ACADEMIA & JOBS

Traditional, small tutorial and seminar teaching methods are one source of the high first and upper second graduation results at KCL (71%, up 4% in 2 years). Extensive and very healthy interdisciplinary course programming (e.g. chemistry and philosophy). Music is as strong as medicine and can be found in harmony with applied computing; war studies combines with theology, and there's an international centre for prison studies within the Law School, which incidentally specialises in English, French and German law. KCL is traditional but smart and always up there with the best in graduate employment, neraly half going into the health industry and large numbers into commerce and, after further training/pupilage, into law (they are European law specialists). There are other interesting scpecialisms, however, notably media. There are no vocational media courses, just film degrees, but the student media is active and good.

The degree in Medicine is the 5-year MBBS, with a 9% application acceptance rate, which is low. There's a special Graduate/Professional entry programme for mature students (UCAS code A102.

There is full integration of medical science and clinical teaching. plus a wide range of special study modules. Fifth year includes opportunity to study abroad. Entry 3 A levels (ABB) + 1 AS (B) or 2 A levels (AB + 3 AS (AAA). Chemistry or Biology must be one of A levels, if offered at AS must be B. GCSE to include Grade B English, Maths, Physics or Double Award (if not offered at AS). Teaching

ACADEMIC EXCELLENCE

TEACHING :
(Rated Excellent or 17+ out of 24)

Law, Geography, History, Music.	**Excellent**
Classics, Dentistry, Philosophy, Politics (War Studies)	**24**
Portuguese, Subjects Allied to Medicine, Education	**23**
Spanish, Pharmacology Anatomy, Physics, Environmental, Medicine, Molecular and Organismal Biosciences	**22**
French, Nursing, Maths, Theology	**21**
German, Electronic & Elec Eng	**20**

RESEARCH:
Top grades 5/5/6**

Community/Clinical (Psychiatry), Clinical Dentistry, War Studies, German/Dutch/ Scandinavian, Portuguese, Spanish, Classics, History, Philosophy	**Grade 6***
Anatomy	**Grade 5***
Clinical Laboratory Sci, Pre-Clinical Studies, Pharmacy, Nutrition & Dietetics, Biophysics, Pure Maths, Applied Maths, Electrical & Electronic Eng, Mechanical/Aeronautical/ Manufacturing Eng, Law, Theology, Music, Education	**Grade 5**

WHERE KING'S COLLEGE LONDON GRADUATES END UP

Health & Social Work: 47%; Education: 4%; Wholesale/Retail: 9%; Manufacturing: 5%; Financial Activities: 7%; Public Administration, Civil Service & Defence: 5%; Hotel/Restaurant: 1.5%; Transport & Communications (including Telecommunications): 1%; Personnel: 4%; Computer: 3%; Business & Management: 3%; Accountancy: 3%; Media (including Film): 2.5%; Legal 1%; Publishing: 2%; Advertising: 1%.

Approximate 'graduate track' employed **80%**

Inspection 22. Research Grade 5*: Community/Clinical (Psychiatry), Anatomy; Grade 5: Clinical Lab Sciences, Pre-Clinical Studies.

They are also well represented in pathology, the branch of Medicine concerned with the cause, origin and nature of disease, biological sciences and subjects allied to Medicine come to the fore – Medical Biochemistry, etc.

With full marks at the assessments, KCL produce most dentists, followed by Manchester, Newcastle, Glasgow, Sheffield and Cardiff. The 5-year BDS plus extra Foundation year is available in Natural Sciences/Dentistry. Entry ABB+b (Chemistry or Biology except in 6-year course. Research Grade 5*. There's also a Diploma in Dental Hygiene.

Another interesting aspect of KCL concerns forensic science. You can find employment in forensic science without a degree. Forensic Scientists who want to make it up the employment ladder will need a degree. There are masses available, but the Forensic Science Society (www.forensic-science-society.org.uk) take most of their graduate members graduates from 2 universities only – Strathclyde and KCL.

For a career as musician, composer and conductor, KCL finds success with its 4-year BMus, a collaboration with The Royal Academy of Music. It combines intellectual and practical approaches, the theory being that Academy musicians benefit academically, while KCL academics benefit musically from the tie-up. Both are members of the University of London.

Among the 7% of KCL graduates that hot foot it to the City, quite a number go in as stockbrokers. There are interesting Maths degrees, but no Economics or Finance.

Specials include top-rated Classics, War Studies (10 degrees), Philosophy, and Portguguese (with, uniquely, a department to itself).

WHAT IT'S REALLY LIKE

UNIVERSITY:	
Social Life	★★★★
Campus scene	**Cosmopolitan, conservative**
Student Union services	**Average**
Politics	**Average: student issues**
Sport	**44 clubs**
National team position	**60th**
Sport facilities	**Poor**
Arts opportunities	**Good**
Student mag/news	**Roar**
Nightclub	**Tutu's, Inverse**
Bars	**The Waterfront, Guy's Bar, Tommy's Bar**
Union ents	**Phase, The Hop, Collide-a-Scope, Fuse, Score**
Union clubs/societies	**94**
Parking	**None**
CITY:	
Entertainment	★★★★★
Scene	**Wild, expensive**
Town/gown relations	**Average-good**
Risk of violence	**London v. high**
Cost of living	**High**
Student concessions	**Abundant**
Survival + 2 nights out	**£100 pw**
Part-time work campus/town	**Excellent**

STUDENT SCENE

In keeping with many student unions' apparent assumption that they can educate the masses by naming bars after prominent politicians, the showpiece attraction of King's Strand campus is its airy venue, **Tutu's**. Blessed with a stage, bar, café, dancefloor and spectacular views of the South Bank, this offers an in-house retreat for the college's loose-livered and free of fancy. A bust of the venue's namesake presides with piously disapproving glare over a feast of comedy nights, discos, live acts and all the other student malarkey.

Music is as strong as medicine and can be found in harmony with applied computing; war studies combines with theology, and there's an international centre for prison studies within the Law School.

Fave nights are typically *Phase* (cheese/dance), Saturday's indie club night, *Collide-a-scope*, *Score*, which, you may guess, is the sports night, *The Hop* (more cheese), *Fuse* (entertaining and eclectic mix: R&B, house, Bhungra) and *Comedy Basement*, Thursday's *comedy night*. Recent live acts include Green Day, Beth Orton, Pulp, Linkin Park, Haven, South.

Macadam's third floor contains the traditional student watering hole, just refurbished, **The Waterfront**, which acts as a perfectly pleasant preamble to its big brother, Tutu, upstairs. With beer nearly half the price of the non-student establishments a stumble away, it's not hard to see why it entertains a cheery crowd.

Tommy's Bar and **Guy's Bar** look after the

medics at their campuses, the latter apparently especially active on the karaoke and live music menu.

Clubs and societies are legion, with Salsa, Debating and the King's Players (theatre), popular choices. A further popular activity (although one without its own noticeboard) was reported by irreverent and controversial student tabloid, *Roar*. '*Basement Boys Use Bogs for Buggering*' ran the headline. *Roar*, incidentally, is regularly nominated for its reporting. All in all, the union keeps its flock busy – but with the bright lights of the West End topping the list of countless distractions, it will only ever deter a relatively small proportion of its students from finding ways to get deeper in debt.

At Guy's the uni's subterranean nightclub, **Inverse**, rules with its powerful sound system and fully integrated lighting system. It's *In At The Dark End*, *Wax* and *Comedy Basement* plus special events.

SPORT There are four sports grounds in Surrey and South London, rifle ranges at the Strand, the aforesaid K4 fitness club, a swimming pool and gym at Guy's, and highly successful boat and sub-aqua clubs.

Nationally, KCL's teams came 57th last year in the BUSA (uni) team leagues.

AT A GLANCE

ACADEMIC FILE:	
Subjects assessed	**30**
Excellent	**83%**
Typical entry requirements	**370 points**
Application acceptance rate	**12%**
Students-staff ratio	**11:1**
First/2:1 degree pass rate	**71%, high**
ACCOMMODATION FILE:	
Guarantee to freshers	**100%**
Style	**Hall, flats**
Catered	**18%**
Approx price range pw	**£83-£122**
City rent pw	**£100-£180 Zone 1; £75-£85 Zone 2**

GETTING THERE

☛ **Strand campus**: Temple (District Line, Circle), Aldwych (Piccadilly), Holborn (Piccadilly, Central). **Waterloo campus**: Waterloo/Waterloo East overland; Waterloo Underground (Bakerloo, Northern). **Guy's campus:** (Northern) and overland. **St Thomas' campus**: as Waterloo or Westminster (Circle, District, Northern, Bakerloo). **Denmark Hill campus**: Denmark Hill overland.

KINGSTON UNIVERSITY

Kingston University
Cooper House
40-46 Surbiton Road
Kingston upon Thames KT1 2HX

TEL 020 8547 7053
FAX 020 8547 7080
EMAIL admissions-info@kingston.ac.uk
WEB www.kingston.ac.uk

Kingston Students' Union
Main Site
Penrhyn Road
Kingston upon Thames: KT1 2EE

TEL 020 8547 8868
FAX 020 8547 8862
EMAIL president@kingston.ac.uk
WEB www.kingston.ac.uk/guild

SUBJECT AREAS (%)

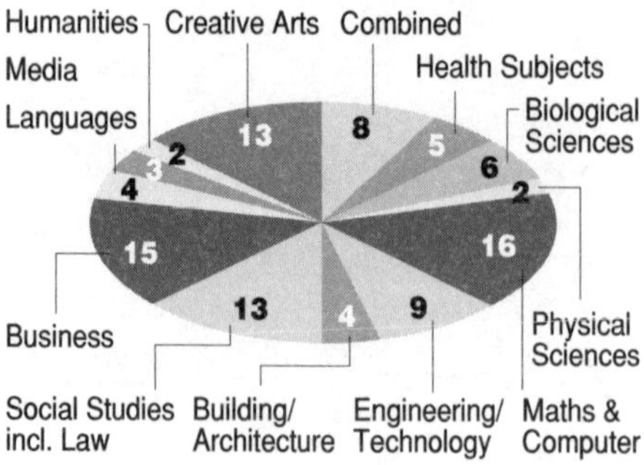

VAG VIEW

Whatever they tell you about Kingston being the oldest Royal borough, the place where Saxon kings were crowned (the Coronation stone lies in the Guildhall – King's Stone, geddit?), it is, in the cold light of reality, a suburban shopping centre/ housewife's paradise. Shoppers come from miles to the mall, the market and the endless chain-shops, while its pubs and clubs attract streams of youthful revellers and the sometime Kingston Poly delivers higher education to nineteen thousand students.

We're talking vocational at Kingston, 'even those courses that don't on the surface appear to be vocational,' says the marketing department. 'The transferable skills that students gain while they're here make them very employable.' Students say that London being only 15 minutes away facilitates the career process further.

CAMPUS SITES

The uni is based at four campuses near the A3, London's south-west outflow – Penrhyn Road, Kingston Hill, Knights Park and Roehampton Vale. However, they are planning to make a move into the prestigious local landmark building of County Hall, which will give the uni a far greater presence in Kingston. It's part of an expansion initiative which will include a new South London Institute of Art & Design with nearby Wimbledon School of Art.

They attract a mix of customer, from engineers to trendy artists, from nurses to would-be lawyers and City types, and notably a mature undergraduate body (38%). Entry is not testing. 'Graduate track' employment prospects are, however, good.

Penrhyn Road Kingston upon Thames, KT1 2EE. Tel (all sites): 020 8547 2000. **Faculties:** Science and some Technology.

Kingston Hill Kingston upon Thames, KT2 7LB. **Faculties:** Business, Education, Music, Law, Social Work, and Healthcare Sciences.

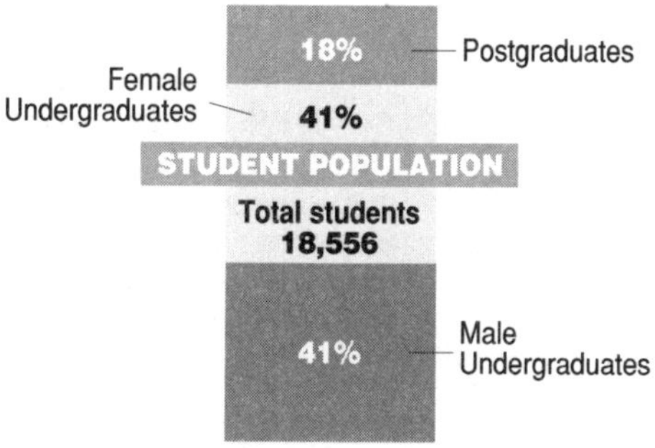

Knights Park Kingston upon Thames, KT1 2QJ. **Faculties:** Art & Design, Architecture, Quantity Surveying, Estate Mgt.

Roehampton Vale Kingston upon Thames, KT1 2EE. **Faculties:** Mechanical, Aeronautical and Production Engineering.

UNIVERSITY/STUDENT PROFILE

University since	**1992**
Situation/style	**London sites**
Student population	**18556**
Undergraduates	**15282**
- mature	**38%**
- non EU undergraduates	**7%**
- male/female	**49/51**
- non-traditional student intake	**38%, high**
- state school intake	**94%**
- drop-out rate	**8%**
- undergraduate applications	**Up 19%**

**see Introduction for key to tables*

FEES, BURSARIES

UK & EU Fees: £3000 p.a. Bursaries of between £300 and £1000 awarded to HE Maintenance grant holders, depending on level of grant. There are also bursaries for applicants availing themselves of outreach arrangement with the university, i.e. students from poorer backgrounds coming in on a special track.

STUDENT PROFILE

They attract a mix of customer, from engineers to trendy artists, from nurses to would-be lawyers and City types, most notably a mature undergraduate body (38%). A large slice of entrants (38%) come from socio-economic groups traditionally least likely to consider university. Their drop-out rate, at 8%, suggests student satisfaction levels are fine.

ACADEMIA & JOBS

Kingston is markedly vocational, into finding jobs for its graduates, even finding space for a 2-year foundation degree in Air Conditioning and refrigeration: you can't get more targeted than that.

Sandwich courses are available in science and science/business subjects, also in science/French programmes.

There's also an optional, employment-enhancing language scheme for non-language undergraduates in Mandarin, Russian, Japanese,

WHERE KINGSTON GRADUATES END UP

Health & Social Work: 7%; Education: 11%; Wholesale/Retail: 13%; Manufacturing: 9%; Financial Activities: 8%; Public Administration, Civil Service & Defence: 5%; Hotel/Restaurant: 3%; Transport & Communications (including Telecommunications): 5%; Construction: 2%; Agriculture: 1%; Personnel: 6%; Computer: 4%; Business & Management: 6%; Accountancy: 3%; Media (including Film): 1%; Legal 2%; Architecture: 3%; Publishing: 1.5%; Artistic/Literary: 1%; Sport: 1%.

Approximate 'graduate track' employed **62%**

Italian, Spanish, German and French, and a Teaching & Learning Support scheme supplies individually or group-designed study skills programmes, EFL courses for overseas students and a 'peer assisted' learning scheme for first years with advice sessions from second years. Again, with an eye to the CV, there's a skills development and certification scheme, run jointly by union and uni, the aim to develop skills such as communication, IT, teamwork and literacy.

With full marks in the teaching assessments for building, and and property management, town and country planning, you should look hard at Kingston if that's your bent. Property Planning & Development, Real Estate Management degrees, and Building and Quantity Surveying degrees (language and business combinations are available) are especially fruitful. Look, too, at the new FdEng Historic Building Conservation, which combines academic study with industrial experience.

There's a number of Applied Economics degrees, Accountancy & Finance, Business Economics, etc, but the high percentage of graduates in employment as accounts and wages clerks (more than 8%) suggests that graduates are getting in at ground level. They do also score in investment/merchant banking and financial broking, and graduates do find employment as business analysts, investment advisers, and sharedealers.

Education is more of an employment cert. The vast majority come out as primary school teachers, a smattering into secondary teaching.

Kingston excels in getting graduates into software engineering. There's a 3/4-year (with sandwich, industrial placement in year 3) BSc in Software Engineering and a new MComp Software Engineering. Kingston's new MComp qualification is a 4-year integrated Master's degree designed to provide high-calibre graduates with an in-depth, research-focused expertise. The third year of the course is split between work in industry and training for professional computing qualifications.

They produce large numbers of computer programmers, IT consultants and a handful of systems analysts. Look at the new MComp Information Systems, BSc(Hons) Cyber Security and Computer Forensics, which explores how computers can be used to prevent and solve crime. Also BSc(Hons) Games Technology. and BSc Computer Graphics Technology.

Civil Engineers out of Kingston seem most employable (4-year Civil Eng or Civil Eng Design, with industrial placement), after which the software, aeronautical, mechanical and electronic engineers impact on the Kingston job figures. There are various automative, motorcycling and motorsport BEng degrees. New in this area are BSc(Hons) Automotive Design, taught jointly by Kingston's design and engineering departments, and BSc(Hons) Motorsport Engineering, which investigates the underpinning technology and latest innovations in the motorsport industry.

Graphic artists and designers are much in demand from Kingston. Besides Fine Art in Art & Design, they offer Graphic Design, Illustration, Interior Design, Product & Furniture Design,

ACADEMIC EXCELLENCE

TEACHING :
(Rated Excellent or 17+ out of 24)

Business & Management, English, Geology.	**Excellent**
Building, Land & Prop Mgt, Town & Country Planning, Mech, Aeronaut & Manuf Eng.	**24**
Radiography, Maths, Politics	**23**
Civil Engineering, Sport	**22**
Modern Languages, Sociology, Electrical & Electronic Eng., Art & Design, Economics	**21**
Hist. Art/Architec./Design	**20**

RESEARCH :

*Top grades 5/5**	**None**

WHAT IT'S REALLY LIKE	
UNIVERSITY:	
Social Life	★★★
Campus scene	**London**
Student Union services	**Average**
Politics	**Student issues**
Sport	**Competitive**
National team position	**77th**
Sport facilities	**Could do better**
Arts opportunities	**Drama, music, film, art good; dance poor**
Student newspaper	**SUblime**
Student radio	**Stone Radio**
Nightclub	**Bar Zen**
Bars	**Hannafords, Knights Park**
Union ents	**Eclectic**
Union clubs/societies	**63 (31 sport)**
Most popular society	**Islamic/Afro-Caribbean**
Smoking policy	**Gannets, Hannafords OK**
Parking	**Adequate**
CITY:	
Entertainment	★★★★
Local scene	**Club scene OK**
Town/gown relations	**Average**
Risk of violence	**Low**
Cost of living	**Very high**
Student concessions	**Average**
Survival + 2 nights out	**£80 pw**
Part-time work campus/town	**Excellent**

and Fashion. Kingston's BA Hons Fashion produces the second largest number of graduates into the industry. There's a 21-points assessment rating, which is good. Meanwhile, the BA Interior Design scores highly on the employment graph, producing the fifth largest number of graduates into the industry. And a new BSc(Hons) Product Design Engineering combines traditional art and design modules with those offered by engineering-based programmes.

The undergraduate Health provision produces senior hospital nurses, midwives and social workers in quantity, and a new series of courses enable you to gain a degree awarded by Kingston together with the Registered Nurse qualification.. There's also an enterprising Fd Health and Medical Sciences (Paramedic Pathway) - graduates will be eligible for state registration as a paramedic with the Health Professions Council. See also BSc(Hons) Exercise, Nutrition and Health, and FdSc Pharmacy Services, designed for people working

AT A GLANCE	
ACADEMIC FILE:	
Subjects assessed	**29**
Excellent	**66%**
Typical entry requirements	**214 points**
Application acceptance rate	**21%**
Students-staff ratio	**22:1**
First/2:1 degree pass rate	**55%**
ACCOMMODATION FILE:	
Guarantee to freshers	**No guarantee**
Style	**Halls, flats**
Catered	**None**
En suite	**75%**
Approx price range pw	**£80-£95**
Local rent pw	**£75-£90**

as pharmacy technicians, and BSc(Hons) Forensic Biology, which explores the biological subjects and techniques related to biological materials associated with criminal investigations.

There's a niche for probation officers in the BA Criminal Justice Studies, which includes a diploma in Social Work. There's also BA Social Welfare Studies and various Psychology and Sociology combinations. See, too, Community Care Management, which includes a diploma in Social Work – you must be 20 to apply.

They are European law specialists, and if you do not have a Law degree, but want to become a solicitor, you can take the Common Professional Examination (CPE) here.

There are masses of media, journalism, TV and creative writing degrees here, too.

SOCIAL SCENE

Students' Union The Union offices are still located in a 20-year-old temporary structure. Of four bars, the biggest is at the main site on Penrhyn Road. **Bar Zen** is situated on the ground floor of so-called **Town House** between the union shop and the offices.

Ents comprise *Non-Stop Erotic Dancing*, *Distortion*, *Flava*, *Weak Reception*. As Kieran Alger reports, 'Ents at Kingston do little to break the mould. The mix of cheap drinks, DJs and widescreen football can be found anywhere in the country.'

History tells of visits of All Saints and DJ Paul Oakenfold, but restrictive pub licensing hours hamper the union and generally annoy the students.' Lack of social space and recreational space is high on the union's political agenda.

New-style **Hannafords** at Kingston Hill has

food and a decent coffee machine, more your 'café bar than bomb shelter', as they put it. Ents fairly humdrum, but there's a hall of residence next door, so it's more of a community bar than **Bar Zen**. **Knights Park Bar** is the arty bar, small (150 capacity) but with more of a bohemian ambience – the only bar at Kingston to sell absinthe – telling influence of the fashion, art and graphic design students. There's a varied music policy and the added bonus of a canal-side patio which makes it a popular summer venue. Again, restrictive opening hours.

Unusual amount of activity recently on the political front, albeit local student stuff: DDA Compliance, University Estates, Lack of Social space and recreational space, etc.

They've also got up and running with Stone Radio since we last visited, as well as having regular newspaper *SUblime*.

TOWN The Kingston club scene is good for students. There's **Bacchus** for indie, punk, hip hop and house to rare grooves; **McClusky's** for 'tequila-fuelled Brown-eyed girl nights'; superclub **Oceana** (5 bars, 2 nightclubs – dance, pop, r&b, disco); gay friendly club **Reflex**; and hard-to-beat **The Works** (r&b, hip hop, garage).

'Living in Kingston can be expensive,' warns Kieran. 'Students still face the London housing extortion despite missing out on some of the city benefits. Rented accommodation can cost anything from £75-90. Even at these prices, quality is not guaranteed.'

SPORT From football, rugby and hockey to Gaelic football and snowboarding, some thirty sports clubs fulfil most needs. Last year they had BUSA individual fencing champion (Women's and Men's English No.1 fencers), BUSA plate badminton champions. Much of the activity takes place at the uni's sports facility at nearby Tolworth Court. There are also fitness facilities at Penrhyn Road. Kingston runs an Elite Athlete scheme to encourage students to compete at top levels in their sport. There's rowing on the Thames.

PILLOW TALK

First years have the comfort of halls. Kingston Hill campus has on-site, en-suite facilities. There are 4 other residential sites including Middle Mill Hall, self-catering flats opposite Knights Park Campus. Most are now en suite.

GETTING THERE

☛ By road: M1/J6a, M25/J13, A30, signs to A308 (Kingston). From London: A3 to Robin Hood Roundabout, then A308.
☛ By rail: frequent trains from London Waterloo to Kingston. No Underground this far out, but well served by buses.
☛ By air: Heathrow.

UNIVERSITY OF WALES, LAMPETER

University of Wales, Lampeter
Lampeter
Ceredigion SA48 7ED

TEL 01570 424829
FAX 01570 423530
EMAIL admissions@lamp.ac.uk
WEB www.lamp.ac.uk

Lampeter Students' Union
Ty Ceredig
Ceredigion SA48 7ED

TEL 01570 422619
FAX 01570 422480
EMAIL president@lampeter.ac.uk
WEB www.lamp.ac.uk/su/

VAG VIEW

Lampeter is a small, close-knit community with a strong rootstock in higher education. They have been awarding degrees here for longer than any institution in England and Wales other than Oxbridge.

Although, today, undergraduates number less than 1000, and the entire syllabus focuses on arts and humanities, Rachel Extance recommends opting for Lampeter 'if

SUBJECT AREAS (%)

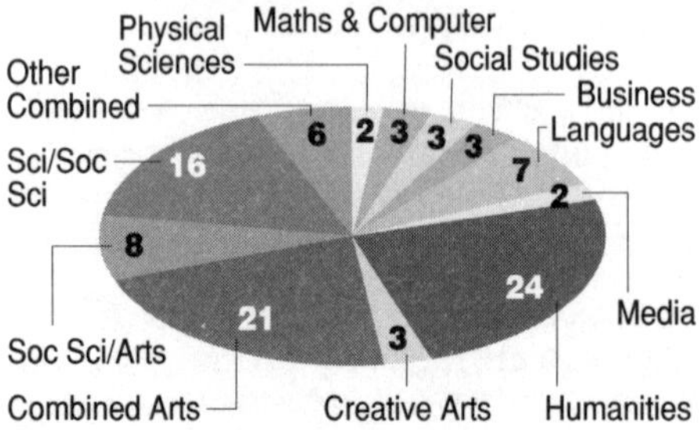

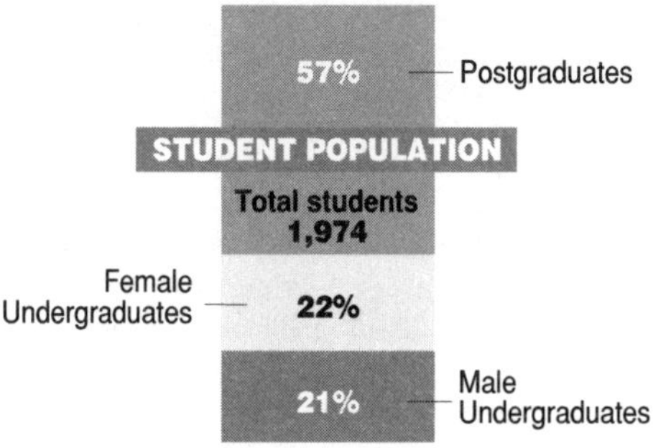

your idea of the perfect university looks like an Oxbridge college, is peaceful, friendly, tucked away in the country, and a little bit out of the ordinary.

CAMPUS

'Don't be surprised if you have only just heard of the place, it is set in the heart of mid-west Wales and its train station was removed by Beeching in the 1960s. Clearly its isolation will be a consideration. Looking at a map, you may note the distance between Lampeter and the nearest towns with more than ten houses, a post office and possibly a branch of Spar, but be advised that it is quite easy to get out of Lampeter if you know exactly when the two-hourly bus service runs.

'The theoretical advantage of being away from the shops is that your money will last longer. In practice you may spend as much money as your friends in the city because Lampeter contains fourteen pubs within a mile radius, with a cash point next to practically all of them.'

The campus is situated in a beautiful and inspirational place, not far from the Preseli Mountains, where the stones of Stonehenge, once Britain's national necropolis, were cut.

The campus is situated in a beautiful and inspirational place, not far from the Preseli Mountains, where the gigantic stones of the innermost sacred circle of Stonehenge, once Britain's national necropolis, are supposed to have been cut. This is mythic Wales, celebrated in the oldest story in *The Mabinogion*, a magical collection of eleven stories sustained orally since earliest times and written down in the fourteenth century. The story which comes from this particular area ('Pwyll, Lord of Dyfed') is probably the oldest, maybe as old as the second millennium BC.

FEES, BURSARIE

UK & EU Fees - 2006: home students up to £1200 p.a. The Welsh Assembly Government has decided not to charge variable fees in the 2006/07 academic year. A variable fee (up to £3000 p.a.) will be charged from 2007/08.

Lampeter awards numerous scholarships and bursaries up to £200 p.a.

ACADEMIA & JOBS

There is much in Lampeter's programme that reflects this backdrop. Its spiritual aspirations for a start. 'Lampeter was founded by Bishop Burgess in 1822 as a theological college for the Church in Wales,' Rachel observes. 'The Theology & Religious Studies Department continues to be strong, with Islamic Studies and Religion, Society & Ethics and Jewish Studies just some of the courses run. A mosque sits at the back of the department.'

The unique course in Religion, Ethics & Society traces the development of our multi-faith, multi-cultural society and is taught as often by lecturers in English, History and Philosophy as by lecturers in Theology. The Students Union religious societies ('older than the hills') have developed along similar lines. Also relevant to Lampeter's mythic backdrop is the emphasis on Ancient History and Archaeology. The region is littered with burial mounds and cromlechs redolent of civilisations long past.

All courses are modular in scheme and taught in small groups. A fully equipped IT facility joins a library (170,000 vols), developed over 150 years and the Founders' Library (20,000 vols printed between 1470 and 1850).

The graduate employment figures show that a

UNIVERSITY/STUDENT PROFILE

University College since	**1971**
Situation/style	**Rural campus**
Student population	**1974**
Undergraduates	**849**
- mature	**47%**
- non EU undergraduates	**4%**
- male/female	**49/51**
- non-traditional student intake	**45%, high**
- state school intake	**97%**
- drop-out rate	**7%**
- undergraduate applications	**Down 4%**

WHAT IT'S REALLY LIKE

UNIVERSITY:	
Social Life	★★★
Campus scene	**Small, friendly, relaxed, rural**
Student Union services	**Good**
Politics	**Active**
Sport	**18 clubs**
Sport facilities	**Improving**
Arts opportunities	**Drama, music, film good; art, dance average**
Student news/magazine	**1822**
Nightclub	**The Extension**
Bars	**Old Bar**
Union ents	**Discos + live acts**
Union societies	**29**
Most popular society	**Arts/Crafts, Rock, Underground, Wargames**
Parking	**Good**
TOWN:	
Entertainment	★★
Scene	**Scenic, boozey**
Town/gown relations	**OK**
Risk of violence	**Average**
Cost of living	**Low**
Student concessions	**Average**
Survival + 2 nights out	**£50 pw**
Part-time work campus/town	**Poor**

number of graduates find their way into education, mainly as instructors, further education, university and higher education lecturers, and as special school teachers.

There is also a showing of care assistants, welfare, community and youth workers, which one can imagine arises as much out of the culture of the place as any vocational degree.

Otherwise, in the short period of six months post graduation, a great number take work as sales assistants, managers, administrators, clerks, bar staff, local government officers and the like.

It is as if Lampeter has somehow managed to opt out of the commercial pressures that other universities claim they have to deal with. Perhaps there is an optimum size for doing just that.

There is a constant development of the curriculum. Modern languages have disappeared over recent years, but the apparent incursion of Business Management, Information Technology, Film, Media Studies and the like seems somehow now less intrusive, mixing as these subjects do with Greek or Islamic Studies as happily as Archaeology or Anthropology, as if here at Lampeter there is a meeting of worlds – east and west, old and new.

New courses this year are in Archaeology (Forensic) and Media Production.

STUDENT PROFILE

'The student population is incredibly diverse,' writes Rachel. 'A high percentage are mature students; there is also a sizeable band of foreign students (Greeks, Italians, French, Americans, to name just some of many nationalities you will encounter). There's a wide variety of religious groups, too. The place is simply too small for people not to get on with each other. Being in a small community, miles from anywhere is a great way of bonding people.'

STUDENT SCENE

STUDENTS' UNION At the hub, **Old Bar** is the small, warm and friendly watering hole and host to *Band in the Bar* on Tuesdays and occasionally to karaoke nights. **The Extension** is the club venue, holds the latest licence in Ceredigion on a Saturday night, and is scene of discos on Wednesdays, Fridays and Saturdays, also big bands, comedy, games and more. The alcohol is cheap and plentiful, but interestingly the union is looking very seriously at meeting what it detects to be a need for an alcohol-free environment for students in the evenings. 'The union also houses a catering outlet called **Dewi's**,' adds Rachel, 'a TV room, pool tables, a games room, and, all importantly, the pigeon holes for post.'

The summer term President's Ball is a biggie. Live acts, various guest DJs, a 20-piece jazz band and firework spectacular. It's the culmination of a

WHERE LAMPETER GRADUATES END UP

Health & Social Work: 6%; Education: 12%; Wholesale Retail: 25%; Manufacturing: 6%; Financial Activities: 9%; Public Administration, Civil Service & Defence: 13%; Hotel/Restaurant: 11%; Transport & Communications (including Telecommunications): 2%; Personnel: 2%; Computer: 1%; Business & Management: 3%; Media (including Film): 1%; Legal 4%; Architecture: 1%; Publishing: 3%.

Approximate 'graduate track' employed **61%**

AT A GLANCE	
ACADEMIC FILE:	
Subjects assessed	**11**
Excellent	**36%**
Average requirements	**230 points**
Application acceptance rate	**30%, high**
Students-staff ratio	**24:1**
First/2:1 degree pass rate	**60%**
ACCOMMODATION FILE:	
Guarantee to freshers	**100%**
Style	**Halls**
Catered	**85%**
En suite	**75%**
Approx price range pw	**£46.62-£61.21**
Town rent pw	**£40-£70**

year that has seen such as Annie Mac from Radio 1 and the Queens of Noize from NME, bands like The Hazey Janes, and Kid Carpet, plus student acoustic nights, school disco and cheesy toons.

There are 18 sports clubs and 29 societies, the most popular are Arts & Crafts, Rock, Underground, Wargames. There's also a very active Film Society (commercial and arthouse). They are not overly political, but equal rights is something they take seriously, and this year campaigns have focused on Top-up Fees. SU Disaffiliation. Nestlé. Coca Cola. 24-hour licensing. A satirical student newspaper, *1822*, carries basic union news – 'very popular, always causes a stir,' I am told. Both are always on the look-out for writers, and they are in the process of setting up a radio station. This is the brainchild of an ever-growing Media Department, working closely with the Student union.

With an eye to the sizeable mature student population (47%), the union has set up a nursery. There is even a Welsh language playgroup. All round there's a strong welfare service, including Nightline and two 'pro' counsellors.

For part-time work, the union is the main source. There are jobs available in the bar and Extension, the union shop, security and with Union Entertainments. Working for Ents can mean anything from setting up the Extension for a gig, taking money on the door, or deejaying.

Sport The 12 clubs range from surfing to Tae Kwon Do. The national uni sports organisation, BUSA, gave it a special 'most improved' award recently. 'Being small, there are brilliant opportunities for everyone to have a go,' said a student, 'and if you're half good at anything, chances are you'll get in a team. Cricket and football are particularly successful.'

Town 'Lampeter town itself is compact,' writes Rachel, 'with two supermarkets, a Boots, and a couple of New Age clothing shops. The crime rate is practically non-existent! But unlike in the big cities, entertainment is not handed to you on a plate. Of the fourteen pubs, some are famed for their lock-ins, the **Ram Tavern** is noted for its food, the **Cwmann** for its bar quiz and live music, the **Quarry** for its disco, and the **Kings Head** as the main haunt of the football team.'

PILLOW TALK

Two mainly first-year halls are full board. Most are en suite. All are on campus. Living out in the second year and third year, you can get a nice place for around £40 a week, and you don't have to pay for the summer holidays. The size of the town means you're never living too far away.

GETTING THERE

☛ By road: A485; the M4 is about 45 mins away.
☛ By rail: London Euston, 5:00; Cardiff Central, 1:30; Birmingham New Street, 4:10.
☛ By coach: London, 5:55; Birmingham, 7:25.

UNIVERSITY OF LANCASTER

University of Lancaster
Lancaster LA1 4YW

TEL 01524 65201
FAX 01524 592065
EMAIL ugadmissions@lancaster.ac.uk
WEB www.lancs.ac.uk

Lancaster Students' Union
Slaidburn House
Lancaster LA1 4YA

TEL 01524 593765
FAX 01524 846732
WEB www.lusu.co.uk

VAG VIEW

A well-thought-out curriculum, a 65% chance of ending up with a first or upper second, consistently good teaching assessments, a recent £50-million capital expenditure on resources (art gallery, libraries, union, music buildings, halls, etc.), a popular college structure, good student ents (they own their own nightclub in town), an active media, drama scene and sporting tradition, and a beautiful 250-acre, landscaped campus within sight of the Lakes – all this contributes to Lancaster remaining a special kind of choice.

It is a great university in a beautiful part of the world, with excellent extra-curricular life, and there's a strong linkage with America.

Now, they've been ripping it all apart, making a £160-million campus that will increase capacity by 50%.

UNIVERSITY/STUDENT PROFILE	
University since	**1964**
Situation/style	**Rural collegiate campus**
Student population	**11126**
Undergraduates	**8695**
- mature	**11%**
- non EU undergraduate	**10%**
- male/female	**46/54**
- non-traditional student intake	**22%**
- state school intake	**89%**
- drop-out rate	**3%, low**
- undergraduate applications	**Down 5%**

CAMPUS

The uni is far away from the industrial towns of popular imagination. It sits to the north of the county, sandwiched between the sea and the Forest of Bowland, a huge open fell space giving life to myriad becks. Lancaster itself, which is nearby, is a city, certainly, but it is small and has cobbled streets and well-maintained historic buildings, many are probably protected.

'The university has a beautiful countryside location at Bailrigg, on the outskirts of Lancaster,' writes Lis Maree. 'It is 3 miles from Lancaster city centre and set in acres of landscaped woods and parkland. On a clear day the view can extend as far as the Lakeland fells. In the centre of campus is Alexandra Square – the focus, the administrative hub, where also the Students' Union offices, the extensive and well-quipped library and shops can be found. Cultural and recreational facilities on campus include a theatre studio, art gallery, concert hall, multi-denominational chaplaincy centre and large and well-equipped sports complex.

'Lancaster is just 10 minutes away by bus, a friendly, bustling place which has all the amenities of a larger city, while retaining the unique charm of its antiquity.

COLLEGE LIFE

The essential element of the Lancaster experience is the collegiate system. Virtually everything is done with or for your college

Writes Lisa: 'The nine colleges of the university – Bowland, Cartmel, County, Furness, Fylde, Grizedale, Lonsdale, Pendle and Graduate – are a very distinctive feature of campus life. Even staff are members, many of them active in collegiate life. The colleges vary considerably in atmosphere and size, but each is a busy centre of social, recreational and educational activity. All on-campus accommodation is located within college, which makes it easy to get to know people and quickly to gain a sense of belonging in this kind of supportive community.'

You might think, with campus being a small, all-encompassing 'city' miles from anywhere, it

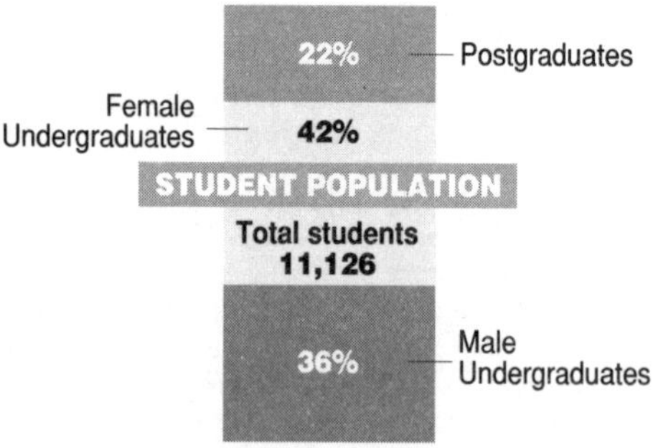

could get a bit claustrophobic in time, but that is not the experience of students. By your second year you will probably be ready to break out, but the urge is satisfied by leaving your college residence rather than the uni as a whole. For in your second

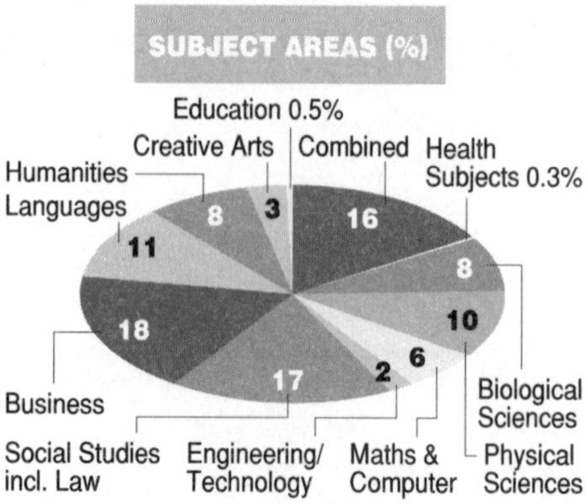

year renting accommodation in town is actively encouraged, while continuing allegiance to your college is ensured by both sporting and course activities. The result of this very successful organic experiment is that when you ask students what it's like at Lancaster University, the words that crop up time and again are 'friendly', 'relaxed', 'unintimidating'. In fact, I can't imagine that Lancaster's system of 'personal advisers' – a 1:5 staff to student welfare and educational advice service, has much to do.

FEES, BURSARIES

UK & EU Fees: £3000. Bursaries of £1000 to UK students where household income is below £17500; £500 to UK students where household income is between £17500 and £26500. 300 awards of £1000 to UK students making Lancaster confirmed UCAS choice and achieving specified grades in selected subjects. 300 awards of £1000 to both UK and EU students enrolling for specified (shortage) subjects. An extensive range of awards is in place for 2006. See: www.lancs.ac.uk/ugfinance.

STUDENT PROFILE

'The best thing about the uni is the warm, friendly atmosphere created by the students in their somewhat wind-chilled and rainy environment. The student body comprises a wide cross-section of people, including large percentages of privately educated and overseas students.'

The independent school intake is high relative to most other unis, and although they had been among the UK's 'access elite' in the matter of taking classes of student new to the idea of university, others have now overtaken them.

ACADEMIA & JOBS

Lancaster remain, however, among the leaders in the teaching and research assessments, see Academic Excellence box. But when your best teaching strengths are in Theatre Studies, Philosophy, Psychology, Theology and Education, you can't be accused of being obsessively vocational. The balance comes with their Careers Service, now the Centre for Employability, Enterprise and Careers (CEEC) better to reflect the extensive range of services delivered: careers education, enterprise skill development for budding entrepreneurs, business support services to increase the number of opportunities available to students and graduates of the university. CEEC hosts one of the largest independent career fairs in the country held every autumn.

There are 3 faculties: Arts & Social Sciences, The Management School, and Science & Technology. There's also a School for Life Long Learning and Widening Participation, andthey have recently established LICA, (Lancaster Institute for the Contemporary Arts) which brings together the departments of Art, Music and Theatre Studies.

The system is that your first year is a kind of taster year. They've woken up to the fact that a number of students study subjects at degree level that they haven't studied at school. In Part One (your first year) you take three subjects. One of these has to be what you intend to major in, but the other two can be completely off the wall. If you registered to do Politics, but, after a first year studying Politics, Law and Computing (for instance), you decide that you really should have applied to do Law all along, then so long as you get the required marks in your first year exams, transfer between departments is easy. This flexible programme in Part One is very popular.

They also have secret weapons in their educational armoury, like the Active Learning Unit, to which everyone is encouraged to submit. Special modules can be worked into your course-mix which will develop skills that employers want. And there's a first-class exchange scheme with nearly one tenth of Lancaster students exchanging with European and US institutions at some point during their degree.

Prospective business management consultants

ACADEMIC EXCELLENCE

TEACHING:
(Rated Excellent or 17+ out of 24)

History, Applied Social Work, Business & Management Studies, English, Environmental Sciences, Geography, Social Policy & Admin, Music.	**Excellent**
Theatre Studies, Psychology, Philosophy, Theology, Education	**24**
Linguistics, Art & Design, Physics, Politics	**23**
Engineering, Maths & Stats	**22**
Sociology, Molecular Sciences, Organismal Biosciences	**21**
French, Italian with Iberian	**20**
German	**19**

RESEARCH:
Top grades 5/5/6**

Statistics, Sociology, Business	**Grade 6***
Physics	**Grade 5***
Psychology, Earth Sciences, Computer, Law, Social Work, European Studies, English, Linguistics, Theology, Education	**Grade 5**

and marketing managers should look at BA Management & Organisation/North America-Australasia. Then there's the BBA European Management degrees – French, German, Italian, Spanish, North America/Australasia, and the BSc Marketing Management. They earned a top Grade 6* indicating world renown at the Research Assessments. The degrees are very popular with employers.

Accountancy is served by BA and BSc degrees, the latter offering either Computer Science or Maths with Accounting, Finance.

Employers in the advertising industry go for Advertising and Marketing, or Advertising, Economics & Marketing.

Aspiring environmental officers, cartographers and the like go for Ecology, Environmental Chemistry, Environmental Science: Earth Science with Geography

You could take the BSc Hons Combined Science for a year abroad (Biological & Environmental Sciences, for instance). There's also Physical Geography or Natural Sciences – 3/4 subjects, including one non-science.

Clearly, languages are a strength here and many go into adult education with a language degree from the uni. Humanities and social sciences are also popular routes into the sector (Psychology scored full marks at the assessments, while Politics scored 23).

They are European law specialists with an international Grade 5 rating. Look, too, at their Criminology degrees, where there's a strong line into police work. In fact, the force draws from quite a wide variety of areas in Lancaster's curriculum. They also excel in turning out social workers and counsellors. They scored full marks at the teaching assessments and there's a Grade 5 rating in Social Work. BA Social Work (including sandwich Diploma) comes out of a department with Sociology (world-class Grade 6* rating), International Relations and Peace Studies. Places on the Social Work course are in high demand.

No academic run-down would be complete without mention of Lancaster's Physics provision – world-class Grade 5*. They turn out astronomers here. Degrees include such as Physics, Astrophysics & Cosmology, and a peach of a time over four years with Physics/North America, which includes a year at an American university.

SOCIAL SCENE

'Each of the colleges also has its own JCR (Junior Common Room), complete with bar and pool table,' reports Lisa. 'Many universities have only one union bar and the nine we have on campus pro-

AT A GLANCE

ACADEMIC FILE:	
Assessments	**29**
Excellent	**86%**
Typical entry requirements	**345 points**
Application acceptance rate	**16%**
Students-staff ratio	**20:1**
First/2:1 degree pass rate	**65%**
ACCOMMODATION FILE:	
Guarantee to freshers	**100%**
Style	**College**
Catered	**None**
En suite	**52%**
Approx price range pw	**£48-£93**
Town rent pw	**£45-£60**

WHAT IT'S REALLY LIKE

UNIVERSITY:	
Social Life	★★★★
Campus scene	**Healthy, lively, college-based**
Student Union services	**Good**
Politics	**Active, not Left: fees, welfare**
Sport	**31 clubs**
National team position	**69th**
Sport facilities	**Good**
Arts opportunities	**Art, drama, music, film good; dance poor**
Student newspaper	**SCAN**
Journalism Awards	**Nominated 2005**
Student radio	**Bailrigg FM**
Radio Awards	**Nominated 2005**
Nightclub	**Sugar House**
Bars	**9 College bars**
Union ents	**Indy/Alternative, r&b, hip hop, cheesy pop, live and comedy**
Union societies	**65**
Most popular society	**Theatre group**
Parking	**No first years**
TOWN:	
Entertainment	★★★
Scene	**Excellent pubs, main uni club**
Town/gown relations	**Good**
Risk of violence	**Low**
Cost of living	**Average**
Student concessions	**Average**
Survival + 2 nights out	**£60 pw**
Part-time work campus/town	**Poor/average**

WHERE LANCASTER GRADUATES END UP

Health & Social Work: 8%; Education: 9%; Wholesale Retail: 14%; Manufacturing: 9%; Financial Activities: 9%; Public Administration, Civil Service & Defence: 10%; Hotel/Restaurant: 4.5%; Transport & Communications (including Telecommunications): 3%; Construction: 2.5%; Personnel: 5%; Computer: 3%; Business & Management: 4%; Accountancy: 3%; Legal 3%; Publishing: 1.5%; Advertising: 1%; Artistic/Literary: 1%; Sport: 1%.

Approximate 'graduate track' employed **53%**

vide perfect venues for bar crawls that last all night long. At the end of the academic year each college has its own entertainment event, affectionately named the *Extrav,* which usually results in farcically ridiculous antics and the presence of Chesney Hawkes or Abba and Elvis tribute bands.'

A poll puts **Pendle Bar** in first place in a college league of bars, followed closely by **Grizedale** (*Shite* disco on Friday) and **Lonsdale**. Most colleges organise subsidised fortnightly trips to clubs – Liverpool and Manchester are just over an hour away.

Sugar House is the union nightclub in town. It opens on Thursday, Friday and Saturday for indie, alternative to r&b, hip hop and also cheesy pop, and on other nights for live ents – bands, comedy, etc. – this year the Thrills, Fun Loving Criminals and the Dream Team.

The high-scoring Drama Department (full marks on inspection) empowers a studio theatre and the on-campus **Nuffield Theatre**, used for both student and 'pro' touring companies. The Lancaster Theatre Group is their most active society. Media-wise they are full strength with newspaper *SCAN* (nominated for Best Student Critic in the national Journalism Awards 2005) and radio station Bailrigg FM (BFM as it is known, also nominated in the national awards 2005).

'There is a huge variety of societies,' writes Lisa. 'including alternative music, Taekwando, photography, kickboxing, floorball, debating and juggling. If politics is your passion, the union is one of the most pro-active at the moment, campaigning for just about everything from abortions to AIDS. The Film Society is the largest society, and very popular are the radio station, Bailrigg fm, and *Scan*, the bi-monthly newspaper.

Sport Inter-college rivalries mean that if you enjoy sport, but aren't good enough to play at inter-university level, you will certainly be good enough to play at college level. A very high proportion of students enjoy competitive team sport, even those that aren't that good.

Lancaster have done better than they are doing currently in the national uni team sports (69th nationally last year), but the place really comes alive at Roses – Lancaster vrs York Uni, a huge weekend of sport and socials.

Town 'The social life at Lancaster should not be underestimated,' writes Guy McEvoy. 'Lancaster town itself has been transformed over the past five years by massive investment from the major brewers. Trendy pubs are now displacing the traditional Northern watering hole in the centre of town (though these can still be found on the edges if that is your thing). The union-run **Sugar House** remains the most popular club.'

Writes Lisa: 'If you are on a very tight budget I would suggest drinking in the college bars before going out into Lancaster and then clubbing dry.

'Student friendly pubs include **The Merchants**, **The Firkin**, **The Walkabout**, **Paddy Mulligan's**, **The Waterwitch** and **Blob Shop**. Recommended nightclubs are **Sugar House**, of course, and **Liquid**, **The Carleton** (host to Chesney Hawkes in the past), **Elemental**, and **Tokyo Joe's** in Preston.

PILLOW TALK

The majority of the accommodation was built in the 1960's and 1970's and is being demolished and replaced in the £160-million sweep clean. Costs are very low (approx £48-£77 per week for self-catering). All rooms have telephone and internet access, though quality does vary between colleges. In your second year, you will need to find off-campus accommodation with the help of the university housing office and in your third year you can choose whether to return to halls. Average local rent is around £45-£60 per week.

GETTING THERE

☛ By road: M6/J34, A683 or M6/J33, A6.
☛ By rail: London Euston, 3:30; Newcastle, 3:00; Sheffield, 2:30; Leeds, 2:30; Manchester, 1:30.
☛ By coach: London, 5:50; Leeds, 3:55.

STUDENT LEEDS - THE CITY

Leeds is one of the most prosperous cities in Europe, conveniently placed in the middle of the country, where two main motorways, the M1 and the M62, intersect. It has an international airport and the busiest train station outside London, but 'the Jewel of the North' is dominated by its 50-odd thousand students to the extent that it really does seem to die when they go in the vacations.

CULTURE

Leeds is the clubbing capital of the North, but has a fantastic variety on offer, from the **West Yorkshire Playhouse** (Sir Ian McKellan, Ben Elton and Irvine Welsh have all premiered productions here) to **Opera North** to **Back 2 Basics** and **Speed Queen**, with the main nocturnal student activities being based in three areas of the city, Headingley, the Union and the City Centre. The re is, too, a fantastic gay scene, it is home to some of the best urban music nights and altogether it is truly multicultural in nature.

For art truly on the cheap, there are many free galleries, some of which showcase student work. The best of these are **The Henry Moore Institute** and **The Leeds Art Gallery,** which stand next to each other in town. A quick mention must be given to **The Royal Armouries** which was given to Leeds ahead of London and contains 8,000 exhibits for under a fiver.

FILM

In the age of the futuristic multiplex the best thing about film in Leeds is that the cosy independent cinema has survived. Like most places everything is student friendly price-wise, but real value and satisfaction can be found in the cinemas, which are dotted around studentland and cost around £2.50 a pop.

The Hyde Park Picture House is eighty-five years old and the height of cool. Cult and independent films, as well as the occasional blockbuster, can be found here, and its location slap bang in the in the middle of Hyde Park ensures that it's a student favourite. Headingley has two lovely cinemas - **The Cottage Road** and **Lounge** - both quite plush and with a lovely retro feel to them. Finally **ABC** in town plays the latest that Hollywood has to offer for prices that seem to be stuck in 1987.

PUBS

A must in these parts is completing the fabled Otley Run, involving a drink in every establishment from **Boddington Hall**, four miles north of campus, to Leeds Met's **Met Bar** on the outskirts of the city centre - four miles, twenty-odd pubs and a lot of drinking. All these pubs are geared towards students and the best remain the same year in, year out. **The Original Oak** and **The Skyrack** in central Headingley are pretty much the busiest pubs in the world. No space to move, but forever popular - go on your own and you'll soon bump into someone you know. Also cheap and cheerful 24/7 are the union bars: at Leeds Uni, it's **The Old Bar** (rumoured to be the longest in Europe) and now **Stylus** (1000 capacity), and down the road, the aforementioned **Met Bar**, which hosts legendary student events.

CLUBS

A massive explosion. Just down from the uni are **Majestyk** (massive) and **Jumpin' Jaks** (cheap), **Space (mid-week)**, **The Cockpit** (indie), **Tiger Tiger** (wrinklies) Wherever you turn in the city centre there seems to be a new club springing up. Whatever you're looking for is here.

Itchy recommends student bars and pubs **Headingley Taps**, **Hyde Park** (both leaving you no doubt where they might be, **Original Oak** and **Skyrack** (both Headingley).

If you're into largin' it at every opportunity then **The Afterdark** in Morley is without doubt the best techno club north of London, with a galaxy of stars playing. Deeply fashionable and just off Leeds University campus is **The Faversham**, a pub in the week but a club on Thursday to Saturday with a crowd that is there to be seen. Situated in Call Lane, the redlight district, **The Fruit Cupboard** hosts the best R&B night in the city and is great for chilling out. Finally, no sampling of Leeds clubland can go by without mentioning the renowned hard house night *Speed Queen, a*ttracting an up for it gay/straight/TV crowd - was at **The Warehouse**, then at **Strinky's Peephouse** and now rumoured to be on the way back to **The Warehouse**, and *Back 2 Basics* - was at **Rehab**, then at **Peephouse**, a club now re-emerging appropriately enough as **My House** in February 2006. Yet there are many, many gems, many, many facets to explore before you'll find your favourites. Events details can be found in the weekly edition of *Leeds Student*, the newspaper for all students in Leeds.

SHOPPING

Leeds is often called the 'Knightsbridge of the North', but many up here think that Knightsbridge is the 'Briggate of the South'. In fact, from charity shops to **Harvey Nichols** your budget can be catered for. The main areas are in town and the best is **The Victoria Quarter**. Under a stained glass arcade independent and designer labels compete for your loan, but be prepared to spend. **The Corn Exchange** is another big hall much along the same lines, and for value, range and sheer presence the huge, Victorian, covered Kirkgate market is a joy to behold. If strapped for cash go to Hyde Park Corner and Headingley. Both have smaller independents and charity shops at the cheapest prices possible.

STUDENTLAND

While most students in most cities tend to live in the same areas, nowhere takes this to the extreme that Leeds does. There is a stretch of Leeds north of the centre which has a high percentage of students. It is a bit of culture shock to some, though, to see windows barred up – a result of a high crime rate.

Furthest away but very popular is Headingley. Famous for the cricket ground, this is still within walking distance of the university, albeit a long one. Closer in is Hyde Park, shabbier than Headingley but with more atmosphere; Burley, cheap but grim; Woodhouse, cobbled streets straight from the Hovis ad; and there are plusher places just off the city centre. Rents are cheap, as supply way outstrips demand, so the golden rule is to relax – there's enough to go round.

Karl Mountsfield

UNIVERSITY OF LEEDS

The University of Leeds
Leeds LS2 9JT

TEL 0113 233 2332 (prospectus)
0113 233 3999
FAX 0113 233 3877
EMAIL admissions@adm.leeds.ac.uk
WEB www.leeds.ac.uk

Leeds University Union
PO Box 157
Leeds LS1 1UH

TEL 0113 380 1234
FAX 0113 380 1205
EMAIL comms@luu.leeds.ac.uk
WEB www.luuonline.com

VAG VIEW

Observed a recent graduate, 'What Leeds University has to offer, which I doubt anywhere else could match, is the students themselves. There's a real atmosphere about the place. You can do whatever you want without being criticised for it. You can really get involved. And at Leeds, students do. You don't come to a place like Leeds if you're an introvert.'

What's for sure is that Leeds does offer the full thing: academic and extra-curricular, which is why students love it, and why employers warm so readily to the Leeds end product.

SUBJECT AREAS (%)

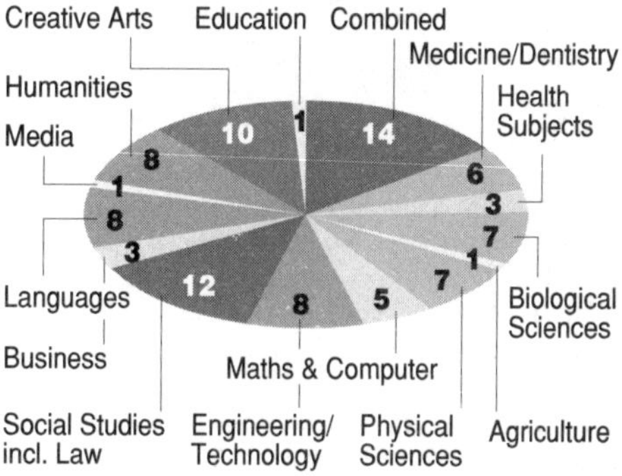

CAMPUS

The university is a mix of differing architectural styles, ranging from neo-gothic to '70s concrete to modern glass and steel, situated just to the north of the city centre before you get to the bulk of student housing areas.

Everything's within easy walking distance, and 'it's relatively safe,' writes Londoner Amy Shuckburgh. 'On the whole it doesn't have an intimidating feel to it. The same precautions should be taken as in any city: it is inadvisable to walk around late at night on your own; use taxis if possible; union night bus services are provided for girls along all routes, both girls and boys are strongly advised not to walk through Hyde Park at night.'

The union has an arrangement with a taxi service – any student can travel free on production of their union card, which is then presented by the driver to the union for payment. The union settles with the student later.

FEES, BURSARIES

UK & EU Fees: £3000. If in receipt of full HE Maintenance grant, there's a bursary of £1350; if in receipt of partial grant, there are bursaries on a sliding scale, from £300 to £1350. They also have bursaries to encourage applicants from poorer postcodes and through outreach arrangements with feeder institutions.

STUDENT PROFILE

You can expect to meet a wide range of people at Leeds. There is a huge student population, but a clear distinction at the broadest level with Leeds Met down the road: 76% from state schools as against their 93%; 20% from lower socio-economic groups as against Leeds Met's 32%... 'There is sometimes a lot of snobbery from Leeds University students towards Leeds Met,' admitted a student, 'but a lot of that is created by the Met students. We go to things there and they come to gigs here, and the newspaper [*Student Direct*] is joint with the Met, as are LSR [radio] and Community Action, Rag and Nightline.' All of which is true, but Leeds Met is mainly involved in distribution of *Student Direct*, never would Leeds let it loose on editorial policy.

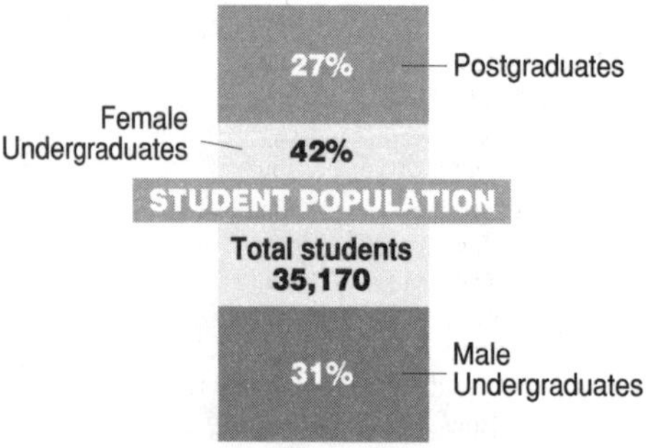

ACADEMIA & JOBS

There is a great emphasis on you and your pastoral care. As a result the drop-out rate (5%) is low. Said fresher Susan Green this year: 'What's best about this university is the very approachable lecturers. There's always someone around to help out.'

Academically, Leeds has a good reputation across the board. The Arts Faculty joint honours courses in particular distinguish the curriculum.

UNIVERSITY/STUDENT PROFILE

University since	**1904**
Situation/style	**City campus**
Student population	**35170**
Undergraduates	**25525**
- mature	**8%**
- non EU undergraduates	**4%**
- male/female	**42/58**
- non-traditional student intake	**20%**
- state school intake	**76%, low**
- drop-out rate	**5%**
- undergraduate applications	**Up 3%**

The range of these two-main-subjects programmes is wide and challenging, with Chinese, Japanese and Arabic joining the language provision, while Economics, Accounting, the Law and Politics provide some of the overt vocational elements against a rich worldwide cultural backdrop of Russian, Jewish, Roman and other civilisations. It is a heady mix. Leeds prides itself in offering some 375 of these, involving 58 subjects taught across 32 departments. First-year students divide their time equally between three subjects: the two named subjects and a third or 'elective' subject. Thereafter, they normally concentrate on two of the three. Employers take a keen interest in graduates with two named subjects from Leeds.

There's particular mention by sixthform careers teachers of languages – 'One reason we recommend Leeds is that you can do exotic languages, Arabic,' said one. They are high placed in a league of graduate interpreters and translators (a difficult field), but languages find graduates a whole range of careers, in advertising, market research, media & government research, publicity, PR, government administration and the Civil Service, and it seems more likely than not that a graduate of Leeds will leave with a language or cultural studies course in tow – Asia Pacific Studies and Economics, for instance, seems tailor-made for the new world. The breadth of the academic focus is surely the thing.

Most graduates end up in the health industry or

WHERE LEEDS GRADUATES END UP

Health & Social Work: 14%; Education: 10%; Wholesale Retail: 7%; Manufacturing: 10%; Financial Activities: 10%; Public Administration, Civil Service & Defence: 8%; Hotel/Restaurant: 3%; Transport & Communications (including Telecommunications): 3.5%; Construction: 2%; Personnel: 6%; Computer: 3%; Business & Management: 3%; Accountancy: 4%; Media (including Film): 3%; Legal 2%; Architecture: 2%; Publishing: 2%; Advertising: 1%; Sport: 0.5%.

Approximate 'graduate track' employed **67%**

in financial activities, accountancy or business/ management. But there are a number of intriguing niche areas. A huge fillip came with the merger with arts/education college, **Bretton Hall** (close to Wakefield), supported by a £9 million investment to rejuvenate the already highly regarded arts college. Directors, producers and theatre managers flow steadily out of what is now Leeds's School of Performance & Cultural Studies. You'll be on an amazing campus – 500 acres of landscaped park-land, supporting an 18th-century Palladian Mansion, lakes, woods, a nature reserve. It's a 30-minute drive down the M1 from Leeds. There is also dance and creative writing and management. The BA Performance Design & Production includes set, costume, light and sound design, learned through practical, performance-based projects.

The Leeds degree in Medicine is a 5-year MB ChB with its 3-phase focus on the fundamentals of clinical practice, clinical practice in context, professional competence. Communication skills, ethics, health & prevention of disease, community-based medicine, medical info & management are recurring themes. Entry AAB including Chemistry. Teaching inspection, 18. Application acceptance rate is 10%. Research Grade 5. A 5-year BChD allows you to become a dental surgeon. Entry 320 points. Teaching inspection, 23.

They are strong too in producing psychologists. BSc Psychology features in some of the best BSc/Undergraduate Masters joint hons courses that employers like so much: with Management, Music or Philosophy. There is also a BA Psychology-Sociology in the Arts Joint programme, and an international Grade 5 for research.

There's a nursing provision (child, adult, and midwifery. Teaching inspection, 20. Also BSc Radiography – Diagnostic. Leeds took an international Grade 5 at the research assessments and got full marks for teaching these courses – 6 points better than for its teaching of Medicine.

The city of Leeds is of course the UK's Second City for Finance. Economics holds much appeal here, the joint hons programme adding to its allure by mixing it with languages (including Russian) and Management. Investment advisers/analysts, actuaries, tax experts/consultants, stockbrokers, share-dealers and bankers flood out of this uni, as do accountants. BA Accounting comes with Finance or Management, or as joint - both subjects main - with Law. BSc Accounting-Computing or Accounting-Info Systems can be taken as a 4-year course with one year in a European university. Teaching inspection: Economics 22, Business 22. Research Grade 5: Maths (pure and applied) and Business.

There are more barristers in Leeds than any other city outside London, and it is an equally important element of the curriculum. There are 2 and 3-year LLBs and a 4-year French edition. Law was rated international Grade 5 for research, and non-Law graduates may take a 2-year full-time or 3-year part-time Senior Status law degree here.

They are, too, among the leading unis on which the publishing industry draws, indeed they are a contender wherever media is mentioned. Again it's the joint hons programme, with languages to the fore, that appeals, with the award-winning student media providing some of the expertise. Look also at BA Broadcast Journalism or BA Broadcasting, and BA Creative Writing, which covers prose, poetry

ACADEMIC EXCELLENCE

TEACHING :

(Rated Excellent or 17+ out of 24)

Chemistry, English, Geography, Music, Geology.	**Excellent**
Subjects Allied to Medicine, Philosophy, Physics	**24**
East & South Asian Studies, Pharmacology, Dentistry, Fine Art, Electrical & Electronic Eng, Molecular Biosciences, Politics, Psychology, Theology	**23**
Maths, Iberian, French, German, Communication/Media, Anatomy, Organismal Biosciences, Accounting/Finance/ Business/Economics	**22**
Arabic	**21**
Sociology, Russian, Agriculture, Nursing, Materials Technology, Food Science	**20**
Italian, Chemical Eng, Classics, Civil Engineering	**19**
Medicine	**18**

RESEARCH :

Top grades 5/5/6**

Food Science, Mechanical/Aeronautical/ Manufacturing Eng, Town & Country Planning, English, Italian	**Grade 6***
Electrical and Electronic Eng,	**Grade 5***
Clinical Laboratory Sciences, Physiology, Other Subjects Allied to Medicine, Psychology, Biological Sciences, Chemistry, Physics, Earth Sciences, Environmental Sciences, Pure Maths, Applied Maths, Statistics, Computer, General Eng, Civil Eng, Geography, Law, Social Policy, Business & Management, Asian Studies, History, Philosophy	**Grade 5**

and scriptwriting, but turns out journalists, too. There was a 22-point score at the assessments.

Business Economics and Management degrees are also key to their graduate employment success, the Management provision slotting into the joint honours programme and picking up on the Fashion and other curriculum elements. They are market leaders in Human Resource Management (BBB at entry) through their BA dedicated degree, though once again languages are an important feed here too, along with humanities – e,g. BA Management Studies-Psychology. Management Studies is also applied to biological, physical and social sciences.

Physical and biological sciences lead to a whole host of occupations. For chemistry they offer BSc/M (3-year/4-year Undergraduate Masters) and a choice of single or joint hons (various options). EaThere are courses in Medicinal Chemistry, Colour & Polymer Chemistry, Applied Chemistry (general industrial chemistry with special attention to polymer science), etc. Teaching inspection, Excellent. Research, Grade 5.

The 4-year MEng Pharmaceutical Chemical Engineering requires is equally effective job-wise. There are various Pharmacology combinations offered (Biochemistry, Chemistry, Physiology). Teaching inspection, 23. Research, Grade 5.

And they lead the way nationally in turning out environmental officers. The School of Environment tackles conservation, land management, environmental regulation, water resources and sustainable development with degrees in Earth System Science; Meteorology & Atmospheric Science; Environmental Biogeoscience, Informatics, Chemistry, Geology, Management, Pollution, Science, Sustainability, etc. Again Grade 5 for research. Meteorology is a career niche here.

A number of Environmental Science degrees look pretty sharply focused like Fire & Explosion and Food Science.

If you want to get into the Civil Service as an executive officer, biological science, law and social sciences are the main routes from Leeds. For defence operatives and equipment engineers, say in the army or RAF, it's the physical sciences route.

Mechanical Engineering is another important part of the curriculum, B/MEng and Foundation programmes in Automotive Engineering, Computing in Engineering, Management with Mechanical & Manufacturing Engineering, Mathematical Engineering, Mechatronics and Medical Engineering, in addition to the Mechanical Eng degrees themselves. In the research area they too have a world-class Grade 6* rating.

Software consultants also proliferate, as do civil engineers. Leeds mixes Civil Engineering with Transport or Structural Engineering – and there's an Architectural Engineering, too. Teaching inspection, 19. Research, Grade 5.

Ten per cent of graduates go into education – Arts Education and Childhood, Education & Culture, plus a series of named subject Education degrees. Strengths are science and maths, primary education and special needs. There's also a good track record for lecturers into higher education.

AT A GLANCE

ACADEMIC FILE:	
Subjects assessed	**43**
Excellent	**88%**
Typical entry requirements	**370 points**
Application acceptance rate	**14%**
Students:staff ratio	**18:1**
First/2:1 degree pass rate	**67%**
ACCOMMODATION FILE:	
Guarantee to freshers	**Apply by 1.6**
Style	**Halls, flats, houses**
Catered	**26%**
En-suite	**15%**
Approx price range pw	**£32-£110**
City rent pw	**£55-£70**

SOCIAL SCENE

The long-awaited overhaul of LUU (Leeds student union) has happened. A £4.8m extension has added 40% more shopping and meeting space for students and given the city a new music venue. The nightclub is called **Stylus** (capacity 1,000), which is adjacent to **Bar Coda** (capacity 290). There are then two bars jointly known as **The Terrace** (complete with sun-terrace and disabled access). Then there's the **Old Bar**, a traditional pub really, down in the basement. That leaves the **Riley Smith Hall** (capacity 600) to host productions from the students' performing societies and **The Refectory** (capacity 2,000) as the biggest venue in Leeds. There's also a nightclub opened at Bretton campus. In addition, the union now has six shops, including Leeds' second largest newsagent, an off-licence, a card and ticket shop, a copy shop, one selling past exam papers and the last union-run bookshop in the country.

They are good at much more stuff than ents, though they are tops at that. They pride themselves on their student welfare services, there's an incredible 200 clubs and societies, and there's a questioning about everything they do. 'There is a left-wing, anti-Capitalist stance at Leeds. It is very prevalent here,' I was told. Main political issues in recent years have been tuition fees, Stop The War, participation and diversity (the point of coming to Leeds as a student) and health, along with perennial ethical, environmental and international issues. 'We've got the campaign against the arms trade; the environmental group People and Planet, and things like Amnesty International and Jubilee 2000 to rid us of Third World debt. There's a huge scattering of political groups.

'At Leeds we are very, very strongly two separate institutions, the university and the union. Everybody knows that. But there's mutual respect. Community issues, drug and alcohol policy, things like that we work together on, but politically we like to be independent.'

There's an award-winning track record in media. The radio station is LSR, the weekly student newspaper, *Leeds Student*, a magazine called *Lippy*, and TV station LUUTV. What's definitive about Leeds student media is that it insists on editorial independence – even of the student union that funds it. At the national media awards last year, Lippy picked up Best Magazine; Leeds Student, 4 awards + 1 runner-up; LSR got 2 gold, 1 silver and a bronze; and LSTV got 6 awards. No-on can better that in the entire country.

Then there are the arts, and fund-raising, sport and Community Action (over 600 students are involved in this) societies. 'There are many groups within the union that work really hard. For drama, we've got **The Raven Theatre**. It seats a couple of hundred. The Theatre Group does three or four plays a term. The really big shows, musicals – *Grease, The Whizz, Hair* – are produced in The Riley Smith Hall.

'There's modern dance (they run jazz, tap, contemporary lessons), there's ballroom and salsa every Wednesday in the **Refectory**, which is packed out. You can barely move in there.

'The Symphony Orchestra and Symphonia and the chorals are all involved in the Leeds concert season, and then there's dance big bands – they've been on tour, had a CD out, played gigs in the city.

'The Film Society is very big, and the Film Making Society has really taken off. For art we've got all the resources in the city – Henry Moore Institute and the galleries and the gallery exhibition in the Parkinson Court.'

I venture to ask whether there is a personal cost, what with all this intense activity and pressure from work. 'Nightline is very high in demand... very heavily subscribed. It isn't any one thing that drives people to use it. You've got financial pressures, academic pressures, and then you've got the social pressures – to conform, to party, to pull in the grades, and then you've got other problems like housing. You don't come to a place like Leeds if you're an introvert. There's pressure from all sides.'

WHAT IT'S REALLY LIKE

UNIVERSITY:	
Social Life	★★★★★
Campus scene	**Seriously good**
Student Union services	**Good**
Politics	**Active: student & international**
Sport	**70 clubs**
National team position	**15th**
Sport facilities	**Good**
Arts opportunities	**Excellent**
Student magazine	**Lippy**
2005 Awards	**Best magazine**
Student newspaper	**Leeds Student**
2005 Awards	**Four awards**
Student radio	**LSR FM**
2005 Awards	**Four awards**
Student TV	**LUUTV**
2005 Awards	**Six awards**
Nightclubs	**Stylus, Bar Coda, K2**
Bars	**The Terrace, Old Bar, Game On, Mannygates, KB Bar**
Union ents	**Funky house & chart, drum n bass/old skool, r&b**
Union clubs/societies	**190**
Parking	**Poor**
CITY:	
Entertainment	★★★★★
Scene	**Wild**
Town/gown relations	**Average**
Risk of violence	**Average**
Cost of living	**High**
Student concessions	**Abundant**
Survival + 2 nights out	**£80 pw**
Part-time work campus/town	**Excellent**

Sport The teams came 15th in the national BUSA league last year. Women's Rugby deserve a special mention. There are facilities to match attainment at this level – two sports halls, one large enough to take 1,500 spectators. Playing fields are 5 miles from campus; there are also cricket squares, a floodlit synthetic pitch and 6 floodlit tennis courts. There's rowing both in Leeds and York, sailing on nearby lakes and reservoirs, hiking, climbing, canoeing and caving in the Yorkshire Dales. Students may use the city's international swimming pool, and golf courses in the area.

PILLOW TALK

Every first-year undergraduate student who applies for accommodation by June 1 is provided with uni accommodation. There's a variety of halls – standard, type and price very variable, from ridiculously cheap (£32) to £110, from traditional traditional hall to swanky city centre flat. Private city accommodation is reasonable (£55-£70) and certainly plentiful. Most people live in shared houses in the Headingley and Hyde Park areas of the city, the famous LS6. For people in the private rented sector there is a union and university backed housing standards authority, UNIPOL, for peace of mind. 'Burglary can be a problem,' notes Amy Shuckburgh, 'most student houses have window bars, door grates or alarms as deterrents.'

GETTING THERE

☛ By road: M62/J39, M1; or M62/J27, M621; or A1, A58; or A65, A650.
☛ By rail: Newcastle, 1:45; London Euston, 2:30; Birmingham New Street, 2:20.
☛ By air: Leeds/Bradford Airport. ☛ By coach: London, 4:00; Edinburgh, 6:00.

LEEDS METROPOLITAN UNIVERSITY

Leeds Metropolitan University
Calverley Street
Leeds LS1 3HE

TEL 0113 283 2600
FAX 0113 283 3114
EMAIL course-enquiries@lmu.ac.uk
WEB www.lmu.ac.uk

Leeds Met Students' Union
Calverley Street
Leeds LS1 3HE

TEL 0113 209 8400
FAX 0113 234 2973
EMAIL b.gibbs@lmu.ac.uk
WEB www.lmsu.org.uk

VAG VIEW

Leeds Metropolitan has full marks or near full marks for teaching vocational subjects like business management, economics, education, health, drama, sport. It is what one student called 'a centre of applied learning', and it reflects the character of the city probably better than its older uni neighbour up the hill. An active union ensures that it is a fun place to be. They were the first university to charge less than the £3000 p.a. maximum tuition fees.

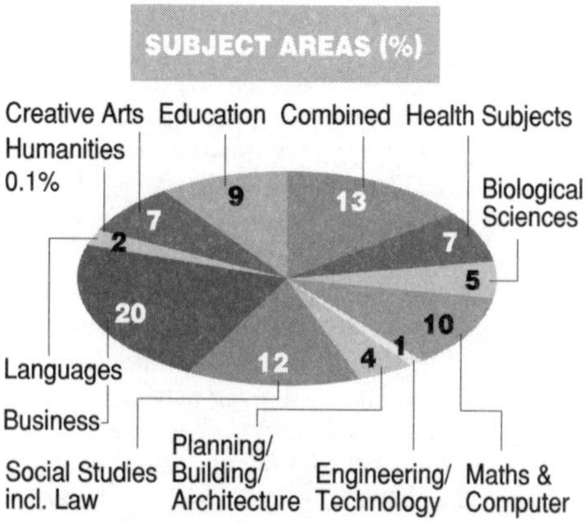

CAMPUS

City Campus, close to Leeds Uni campus, is undergoing a £100-million development. There are teaching facilities both here at Calverley Street and at nearby Queen Square. A new film school opened last year. **Headingley Campus** is three miles away in 100 acres of parkland (Beckett Park). The cultures of the two sites differ as to the type of student. Sports, business and computing students colour Headingley, while City has a lot more arts, health sciences and engineering. 'Students who play sport go out there;' said a student. 'Students who want the library and the big ents come down here.'

FEES, BURSARIES

UK & EU Fees: £2000 p.a. For scholarships, see www.leedsmet.ac.uk/internat/scholarships_fees.htm 17 students received scholarships for success in sport this year.

STUDENT PROFILE

'The demographics are quite different to Leeds University,' says student Kate Denby. 'A large proportion of students at our Leeds site are part-time. They'll come from the Yorkshire area, maybe do evening courses. The full-timers, who come from all over, tend to be more the mature type of student. People who have been out in the world.

There are also lots of international students, many of whom come on exchange. It's a more cosmopolitan atmosphere than in Leeds University.'

ACADEMIA & JOBS

Both Leeds and LMU want to get their students employed. The difference is that at LMU the approach is direct - degree names point to jobs. 'This is a centre for applied learning,' said Kate. 'I'm doing a degree in Public Relations. It's hands on. What you generally find is a lot of students go on placement. They might have a year's placement or a day each week placement. I have no lectures on a Thursday and go into a company and work one day a week. You can do that sort of thing off your own bat or you can get placements via the placements office. People who come here have a goal. They know what they want to do. We've got an Events Management course, for example, very popular, been going for about five years. And Tourism Management and people going into leisure studies. It's across the board - sport, business, computing.'

The language dimension is as significant here as at Leeds, perhaps more obviously as a skill add-on, and students also acquire skills in computing as part of a drive to employability, though sometimes there's a participating European university, which promises more. International Business Finance or European Marketing is run in cahoots with Hochschule Bremen, Germany, or the Groupe ESC Normandie at Caen, France.

Besides Events Management (a 4-year sandwich), other 'direct' vocational degrees are International Hospitality Management (with Sheffield Hallam, Manchester Met and Salford LMU are giants in this industry), International Tourism Mgt, Resort Management, Public Relations (with language add-ons: French, German, Spanish), Retailing, Urban & Regional Development, Interior Design, Garden Design (BA Garden Art & Design accounts for 25% of the landscape architect graduate employment market). There are many more, but it is not actually as widespread as elsewhere. There's no BSc Hairdressing Science as at Derby, for instance. In fact, there are plenty of named vocational degrees at Leeds Uni, too, especially in the health field.

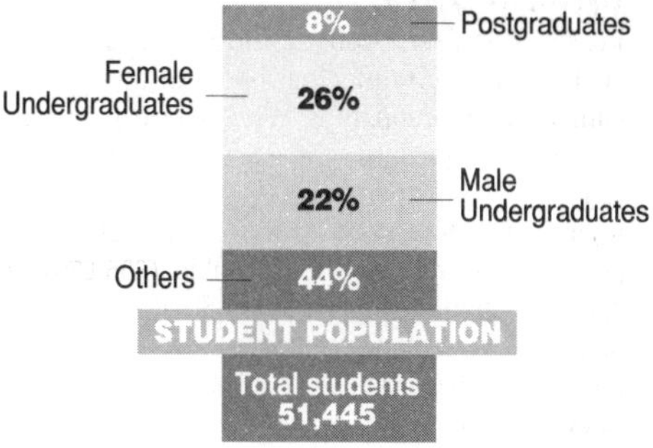

UNIVERSITY/STUDENT PROFILE	
University since	**1992**
Situation/style	**City sites**
Student population	**51445**
Undergraduates	**24260**
- mature	**42%**
- non EU undergraduates	**3%**
- male/female	**45/55**
- non-traditional student intake	**32%**
- state school intake	**93%**
- drop-out rate	**8%**
- undergraduate applications	**Constant**

ACADEMIC EXCELLENCE	
TEACHING : *(Rated Excellent or 17+ out of 24)*	
Business/Mgt, Economics	**24**
Education, Subjects Allied to Medicine	**23**
Drama/Dance/Cinematics, Sport, Hospitality Management	**22**
Civil Engineering, Building, Land & Property Mgt, Art & Design, Nursing	**21**
Psychology	**20**
Modern Languages, Communication & Media Studies	**19**
RESEARCH: *Top grades 5/5**	**None**

Perhaps the difference tells in curriculum and syllabus design, in teaching excellence and calibre of applicant - the Met is almost always among the least demanding at point of entry. Kate sees it as a question of student culture and ethos: 'There are completely different cultures in the two universities in Leeds.' I am still unclear what that means. Are we talking about titillating different parts of the cranium, or being more one-dimensional here?

Market research is one employment area where both unis, in their different ways, excel, Leeds through its languages and social studies programmes and LMU through social studies, business, and law. LMU's teaching of Psychology scored 20 points at the assessments, Business full marks (24). Note the BSc Applied Psychology.

When it comes to health, they're not turning out doctors and dentists, although, as at Leeds, there is Nursing (adult and mental health). What's strong here (and a very good employment area) is BSc Physiotherapy. This they have to themselves and such as BSc Clinical Language Sciences, designed to turn out speech therapists – it's the most popular single area for graduates in Leeds Met's Health Sciences Faculty. Teaching inspection, 23.

> ***There are completely different cultures in the two universities in Leeds. This is a centre for applied learning and the place with the reputation for nightlife. You'll find no middle-class socialism at Leeds Met.***

Both unis do well in getting graduates into the Civil Service, but while Leeds does so mainly through biological sciences, law and social science, the Met comes in strongly via computer science. BSc Computing, Computer Entertainment Technology, Computer & Digital Product Technology and the like also seed IT consultants and systems analysts in quantity. You'll be part of Beckett Park Campus in Headingley, three miles from Leeds centre.

While Leeds' School of Environment tackles conservation, etc, the Met excels in getting jobs for environmental health officers. BSc Hons Environmental Health scored 23 out of 24 points at the teaching assessments.

In the financial sector, LMU does especially well in banking. Look at BSc Economics for Business, also Accounting & Finance (there's a strong line in tax experts/consultants at LMU too). Note also the Business Computing BSc, and Business Information Systems, a Business & Finance HND + 1-year BA top-up and the BA Economics for Business. The Computer Sciences route is also popular: BA Business Info Mgt, Business Info Technology (an HND, 1-year BSc top-up), etc. Business and Economics scored full marks at the teaching assessments.

There is strong graduate employment, too, in architecture and construction. See BA Architecture, BSc Architectural Technology, Building Surveying (also Quantity Surveying), Construction Management, Project Management (Construction). There's also a Building Studies HND. Teaching merited 21 points at the assessments.

The education provision looks after around 10% of graduate output – early childhood, primary and BAQ Secondary Physical Education, the latter evincing a strength felt more strongly than at any other uni, in the employment of graduate sports trainers and coaches. BSc Sports Studies, Sport & Exercise Science and BA Sport & Recreation Development, Leisure & Sport Mgt degrees come with a health-related Exercise & Fitness Foundation. Inspection 22.

SOCIAL SCENE

'LMU's **Met Bar** hosts legendary student events.' It is a huge area, a whole floor of the building which includes an enormous bar, café and the concert hall itself, which has a stage, decent dressing rooms and a built-in DJ studio block, besides formidable sound and lighting equipment. The whole thing is fully sound proofed, floating in plastic, the Learning Centre next door remains oblivious.

'Anyone who's anyone plays Leeds Met. Leeds Uni are better at things political,' is the considered student opinion. 'Ents is a totally professional area,' Kate Denby tells me. 'Everyone who works there is a paid professional, although we do have two students who work part-time for us in an events capacity, qualified to do lighting for example. We generally do nine events a week across all three venues, so there's a lot to organise. Our main venue holds 1,500 people; it's the whole of the floor below us.

Regular Friday nights are *STAR* and *Electrichead*. Recent live acts include Mark Owen, The Darkness, Damien Rice, Funeral for a friend, Athlete, Grandaddy, The Cooper Temple Clause, Electric Six, Shed Seven, New Model Army, Howard Marx.

Then there are the comedy and movie nights, big-screen footie and private parties, all adding up

WHERE LEEDS MET GRADUATES END UP

Health & Social Work: 13%; Education: 10%; Wholesale Retail: 12%; Manufacturing: 6%; Financial Activities: 8%; Public Administration, Civil Service & Defence: 9%; Hotel/Restaurant: 6%; Transport & Communications (including Telecommunications): 4%; Construction: 3.5%; Personnel: 3.5%; Computer: 5%; Business & Management:1%; Accountancy: 1%; Media (including Film): 2%; Legal 2.5%; Architecture: 2.5%; Publishing: 1%; Advertising: 1%; Sport: 2.5%.

Approximate 'graduate track' employed **56%**

WHAT IT'S REALLY LIKE

UNIVERSITY:	
Social Life	★★★★★
Campus scene	**Sporty, spicy, action focused**
Student Union services	**Good**
Politics	**Student issues**
Sport	**60 clubs. Key**
National team position	**23rd**
Sport facilities	**Excellent**
Arts opportunities	**Drama par, rest below par**
Student Magazine	**LiMe**
Student newspaper	**Leeds Student**
Student radio	**LSR FM**
2005 Awards	**Four awards**
Nightclub	**The Met**
Bars	**Sugarwell, Kirstall Brewery, Becketts**
Union ents	**STAR, Electrichead**
Union societies	**19**
Parking	**Poor**
CITY:	
Entertainment	★★★★★
Scene	**Wild**
Town/gown relations	**Average**
Risk of violence	**Average**
Cost of living	**High**
Student concessions	**Abundant**
Survival + 2 nights out	**£80 pw**
Part-time work campus/town	**Average/Good**

AT A GLANCE

ACADEMIC FILE:	
Subjects assessed	**26**
Excellent	**58%**
Typical entry requirements	**250 points**
Application acceptance rate	**21%**
Students-staff ratio	**25:1**
First/2:1 degree pass rate	**53%**
ACCOMMODATION FILE:	
Guarantee to freshers	**60%**
Style	**Halls, flats**
Approx price range pw	**£60-£79**
City rent pw	**£55-£70**

to an ents programme rarely surpassed elsewhere.

Among societies, CALM (Community Action at Leeds Met) is expanding rapidly with over 400 students participating in student-led student projects in the community. Two students are up for National volunteering awards.

They have their own magazine, *LiMe*, and have a presence on the production side of the award-winning Leeds Uni, *Leeds Student* newspaper. They also team up with Leeds for radio – LSR, which picked up gold, silver and bronze awards at this year's National Radio Awards.

SPORT Leeds Met Chancellor is Brendan Foster, so you can expect good sport. At Beckett Park you'll find three sorts centres: the Carnegie Indoor and Outdoor centres and the £multi-million Carnegie Tennis Centre - synthetic turf pitches, gyms, dance studio, swimming pool, sports halls, athletics track, grass pitches, squash courts, indoor and outdoor tennis courts, fitness rooms, climbing wall, strength and conditioning room, gymnastics centre. Competition takes place in all sports, at all levels. 'There's also a students union out at Beckett Park,' informs Kate Denby, 'with a bar (**Becketts**), 450-500 capacity, sports theme, some accommodation.'

TOWN See *Leeds Student City*, page 260.

PILLOW TALK

Uni-owned/managed halls or flats, self-catered houses, private lodgings. The £17-million residential development, Kirkstall Brewery, has 2 squash courts, a weight training and fitness centre, a two-floor bar complex (capacity around 1,000), regular weekly and one-off events, laundry and shop.

GETTING THERE

- By road: M1, A1 or M62. Good coach services.
- By rail: Newcastle, 1:45; London Euston, 2:30; Birmingham New Street, 2:20.
- By air: Leeds/Bradford Airport.
- By coach: London, 4:00; Edinburgh, 6:00; Bristol, 5:45.

STUDENT LEICESTER - THE CITY

One of the best things about Leicester is its location right in the centre of the country. Nowhere seems too far away. No matter how much you want to get away from home, this is mentally and financially beneficial, especially in the first year. Again, whether from the north or south, you will feel comfortable in Leicester because there is a great mix of people, more than 30,000 students.

The city is still sometimes unfairly seen as having little more to it than Walkers Crisps and its most famous son, Gary Linekar, but its profile is always on the up, be it through its football and rugby teams, Comedy Festival (nationally acclaimed comedians attract a 20,000+ audience), curries or nightclubs.

Leicester is compact enough to retain a strong community atmosphere and modern enough to combine this with what you want from a city.

There is always something going on. It hosts the largest CaribbeanCarnival outside of London and the biggest Hindu Festival outside of India.

If you stay over the summer, the Abbey Park Festival is a fantastic occasion to get drunk in the sun, and that's before you look at theatre, cinema andso on.

LIVE VENUES

There are lots of live music venues around the city, the biggest of which is the very swish **De Montfort Hall** (named after the 13th-century Earl of Leicester, not the uni), popular with the bigger acts (Stereophonics, Ash, The Charlatans, Elvis Costello), and Leicester University's **The Venue** has seen Goldfrapp, Aqualung, Sophie Ellis-Bextor and the Super Furry Animals in the past 12 months. It also has very popular club nights (*Madfer-It*, *Reagans & Brighton Beach*). The world-famous **Princess Charlotte** has hosted Sebadoh, Gay Dad, Add n to (x), E-Z Rollers, Badly Drawn Boy and Arab Strap, and features numerous club nights. The Factory and The Shed book small and local acts and are supportive of student bands, so get your tapes in!

PUBS & CLUBS

Leicester has a diverse range of clubs and pubs. Everybody has their own favourite and new pubs are opening all the time. Go to **Market Square** for-traditional pubs and for Irish – **O'Neill's** and **Molly O'Grady's**. It's a case of take your pick.

For the more discerning sophisticate there are a wide range of cocktail bars and restaurants in the area of town known as **Braunstone Gate**.

There are numerous clubs catering for all tastes ranging from **Lounge One**, which regularly hosts Goodbye Cruel World and has featured DJs such as Boy George, Brandon Block, Pete Heller and Phats and Small, to **Junction 21**, with an eclectic mix of different dance music styles.

Streetlife is Leicester's main gay nightclub and has the soundest door policy in the city. You can lose the plot at various all-nighters, but it's best to check flyers for one-off events.

Fans of less specialist, more mainstream clubs should check out **Zanzibar** (Leicester Uni has Monday night promotions here), **Creation** or **Life**. Among alternative clubs try **Mosh Rock**, **The Fan Club** (indie and alternative), and **The Attic** (also a live venue).

CINEMA, THEATRE, COMEDY

Leicester has three main theatres: **The Phoenix** swaps between performance and cinema in a jammed weekly programme that features dance, film festivals, operas and comedy. The **Y Theatre** also has a diverse programme that is always worth checking out and occasionally has nicely relaxed music nights. A gem. Most of the national tours feature at **De Montfort Hall**, which also plays a big part in the Leicester Comedy Festival.

There are numerous other smaller venues that host live performances and comedy, including **The Looking Glass** in Braunstone Gate, the **Little Theatre** on Dover Street and Granby Street has a **Jongleurs**.

There are two multiplexes in Leicester. **Vue** at **Meridian Leisure** is 20 minutes drive away and next door to a **Fatty Arbuckles** and **McDonalds**, if you want to make a night of it. A very similar arrangement can be found at Freemans Common where there are two pubs, a restaurant and a 12-screen **Odeon**.

SHOPPING AROUND

You can't talk about Leicester and shopping without mention of Europe's largest covered market. From clothes to food, some days are better than others and you'll have to be prepared to get to know when to go there for what, but this is where Leicester's real roots are, and their vegetables aren't bad either. Ask the Linekars, Gary used to work here and the family still maintains a stall.

Alternative shopping may be had in St Martin's Square, just behind the market and in Silver Street and the surrounding lanes. Leicester benefits from many specialist international food stores due to its highly diverse population.

Katherine Irving

UNIVERSITY OF LEICESTER

The University of Leicester
Mayors Walk
University Road
Leicester LE1 7RH

TEL 0116 252 5281
FAX 0116 252 2447
EMAIL admissions@le.ac.uk
WEB www.le.ac.uk

Leicester Students' Union
Percy Gee Building
University Road
Leicester LE1 7RH

TEL 0116 223 1111
FAX 0116 223 1112
EMAIL lusu@le.ac.uk
WEB www.leicesterstudent.org

VAG VIEW

Leicester is 50 years old as a uni in 2007 and is celebrating it by spending £25 million on the library. Applicants may be relieved to hear that a good deal more has already been spent recently on the leisure facilities. The uni is flanked by 20 acres of parkland a short walk from the city centre. They see themselves as the more pukka of the city's two unis, student attitude being, 'De Montfort's the Poly,' and the De Montfort attitude being, 'There is still something of an air of institutional superiority, them being Leicester's redbrick.' However, there's no real snobbery involved, for Leicester now takes a quarter of their students from new-to-uni social groups. What undergraduates do appreciate is that Leicester has one of the best Student Unions in the country, and not just for the excellent ents laid on – though that, most definitely, too.

CAMPUS

'The main university campus is situated close to the city centre and within walking distance of all university halls of residence,' writes Christina McGear. 'But, unlike many inner city universities, everything you need is situated on campus including banks, restaurants, cafés, shops, the university library and union. This means that you never have far to walk between lectures.'

FEES, BURSARIES

UK & Eu Fees: £3000. If eligible for a full HE Maintenance grant, you also qualify for a bursary of £1300 from the uni.

Alternatively, freshers may opt for a £1300 package: loan of a laptop computer, with an option to purchase; £200 reduction in accommodation fees; local bus pass; a sum credited to the University SNAP Card for meal purchase; University print card (value £50); sum credited to

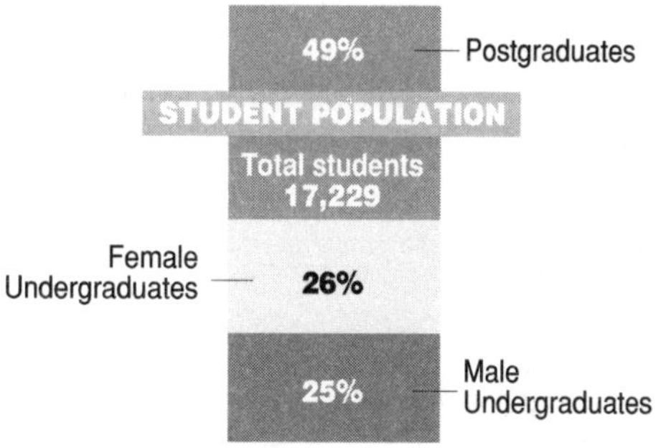

the University bookshop account and sports card; SU credits and £300 cash. Students on partial grants get bursaries on a sliding scale.

STUDENT PROFILE

Student type? They'll tell you many are from the Southeast – which is true, with a number from independent schools, good, white middle-class kids – and then they'll admit that there's a huge contingent from Wales. Why Wales? Because Leicester is far enough from Wales to make you feel like you are away and yet not too far for discomfort. And maybe that's as much of the truth as you are likely to get. For Leicester is the choice of students from more than 100 countries and has always been convenient to a wide cross-section of UK journeymen, being sited along that zippy M1 corridor and not too far north even for the softest southerner. They have a high intake from public schools.

ACADEMIA & JOBS

With 82% of their teaching assessments either Excellent or scoring 18+ out of 24, Leicester's teaching record is first class and backed by an annual £3 million spend in the university library, a Student Learning Centre with workshops and self-learning materials designed to develop study skills and a well-equipped Language Centre supporting the uni's policy of 'languages for all'.

There are five faculties – Arts, Law, Medicine, Science, Social Sciences. Top teaching assessments

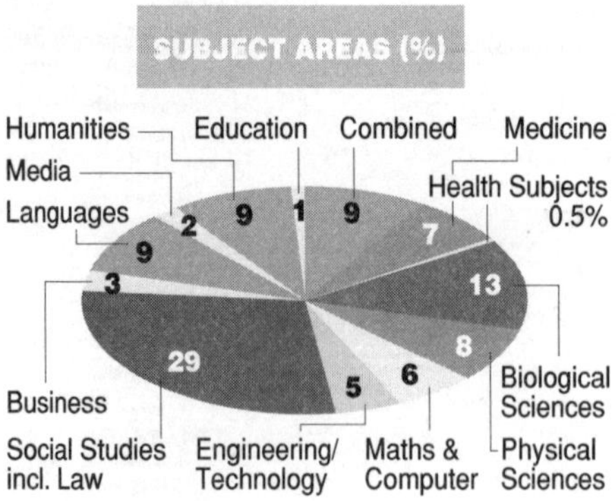

are in Economics, Sport, Psychology, Physics, Politics, History of Art, Maths, and Biosciences. They are widely targeted by employers. An on-line database keeps all students up to date with the latest job vacancies

The Faculty of Medicine, which, with Physics and American Studies, recently clocked 23 out of a maximum 24 points on inspection and a 13% application acceptance rate (which is high) would be a jewel in anyone's crown, and was one of three medical schools given the go-ahead to form new joint schools with other universities. Leicester's partner is Warwick. Part of the deal is a fast track medical degree for biological sciences graduates.

The 4/5-year MB ChB is in fact the backbone of Leicester's curriculum in terms of graduate employment. The civil service (chiefly from social studies, languages and humanities), education, finance, accountancy and computing make a showing, but medicine is far and away the most stable element of their employment profile. Entry requirements are four AS levels in first year, including Chemistry and Biology, excluding General Studies. Three A levels at AAB, including Chemistry, excluding General Studies. GCSE English Lang and sciences if not held at AS level.

Leicester has a world-class genetics research record – it was here that genetic fingerprinting was first developed. The career pathways of biological science graduates from Leicester are various, but in a given year15% or so (the biggest proportion of the department) become biochemists, medical scientists, biological scientists or biochemists. Another strength in research is Pharmacology, and there is BSc Pharmaceutical Chemistry at undergraduate level, but few chemists result.

Student type? They'll tell you many are from the southeast – which is true, with a number from independent schools, good, white middle-class kids – and then they'll admit that there's a huge contingent from Wales. Why Wales?

3.5% of graduates become accountants, more begin at the bottom as accounts or wages clerks. Theirs are nothing like the bullish figures in this area that you get from Birmingham, Warwick, Durham, Sheffield, Manchester, Leeds, etc, and no named accountancy courses.

Instead, there are BA and BSc Financial Economics and Business Economics degrees and a range of interesting Maths degrees, such as the 4-year Maths with Computer Science. There are placements in Europe and USA, as well as matches with Management, on the one hand, and Astronomy on the other.

There is a particular reputation in the fields of physics and astronomy, and they claim the largest uni-based space research centre in Europe. The Beagle 2 Mars Probe, the UK's first mission to another planet, had its Operation Control Centre at Leicester. There is a newish Space Research and Multi-disciplinary Modelling Centre.

Look at the BSc/MPhys degrees like Physics with Space Science & Technology; Physics with Planetary Science; Physics with Astrophysics. They scored 23 points and an international Grade 5 for research in the assessments, and have a certain place in the Top 10 for employment.

Computer operators, software engineers, IT consultants and systems analysts flow in a steady stream from Leicester, and there is an impressive looking series of Electronic & Software Engineering degrees, again with a year out in USA.

They are an employment leader in

UNIVERSITY/STUDENT PROFILE

University since	**1957**
Situation/style	**City campus**
Student population	**17229**
Undergraduates	**8781**
- mature	**10%**
- non EU undergraduates	**9%**
- male/female	**50/50**
- non-traditional student intake	**25%**
- state school intake	**87%, low**
- drop-out rate	**11%**
- undergraduate applications	**6% up**

Archaeology. BA degrees only are available, though you can take BSc Geography & Archaeology, and there's a BA Arch. Combined Studies degree with Art History, also BA Histoyr or Ancient History with Arch. The department scored full marks in the teaching assessments. Research Grade 5. Geography is also hot at Leicester, BA and Bsc degrees, and links with History or Geology as well as Archaeology.

Finally, there's an interesting law provision, for which they have another international Grade 5 for research; they are specialists in French law. Explore the difference between English & French Law (LlB/Maitrise) and Law with French Law and Language. The latter lasts four years.

SOCIAL SCENE

Unlike at nearby self-contained Nottingham or Loughborough, there is competition here, entertainment-wise, with the city. When we appeared, the union was taking the challenge of a couple of new pubs seriously, but with a confident gleam in its eye, for when it comes to home-grown ents Leicester SU has a pedigree.

When the house scene was in its infancy their *High Spirits* club night travelled to **Es Paradis** in Ibiza, to the **Queen Club** in Paris and the **Venue** in Jersey. There must have been some energy around in those days. Even today, Leicester maintains a full-time, non-student ents manager with two assistants, though, along with student taste, the focus has shifted – to the *Mega*, with theme nights and giveaways, and *Reagans*, an '80s sell-out night.'

Union ents happen at the **Venue**, at modern, minimalist **Element** and the **Redfearn** pub. There's a Monday contract with **Zanzibar** in town (*SHAG*), a good pub quiz in the **Redfearn** on Tuesday. The most popular union night is Wednesday's night, *Reagans*, it takes place in the Venue. *Madfer-It* is Friday's big deal, which takes over the entire building. Saturday is *Brighton Beach* – 'mods, rockers, pills and '60s sun, sea and sand...a chance for Leicester's perpetually drunk undergrads to escape the endless hell of '80s cheese and '90s pop,' as student newspaper *Ripple* puts it. There are also many special events.

ACADEMIC EXCELLENCE

TEACHING :
(Rated Excellent or 17+ out of 24)

History, Law, Chemistry, English.	**Excellent**
Economics, Leisure & Sport, Psychology, Archaeology, Education	**24**
Physics, Politics, Medicine, American Studies	**23**
History of Art, Maths, Biosciences	**22**
German, Communications/Media	**21**
Italian, General Engineering	**20**
Sociology, French	**19**

RESEARCH:

Genetics,	**Grade 5***
Pharmacology, Biochemistry, Biology, Physics, Pure Maths, Applied Maths, General Eng, Law, Economics, English, Archaeology, History	**Grade 5**

'There are also endless sports clubs (30) and societies (95 – academic, campaigning, performance, recreational ,religious and cultural) to join,' writes Christine, 'ranging from Dance and Drama to religious societies to completely obscure ones.'

There's a good campaigning arm and lively media – *Ripple* is the newspaper, Lush FM the radio station. LUST, the TV, is also back with us now.

Sport is big, though local competition is with Nottingham rather than international-level Loughborough, and developments are now afoot to lock horns more meaningfully with De Montfort University. Slipping to 92nd place last year in the national leagues suggests a dip in performance levels. There's a sports hall, Greenhouse 1, in the Charles Wilson Building on campus, and new rugby, lacrosse and football pitches at Stoughton Road, east of campus, close to Manor Road Sports

WHERE LEICESTER GRADUATES END UP

Health & Social Work: 20%; Education: 8%; Wholesale Retail: 8%; Manufacturing: 7%; Financial Activities: 12%; Public Administration, Civil Service & Defence: 11%; Hotel/Restaurant: 2.5%; Transport & Communications (including Telecommunications): 4%; Construction: 1%; Personnel: 5%; Computer: 2.5%; Business & Management: 1.5%; Accountancy: 3.5%; Media (including Film): 1%; Legal 2%; Architecture: 0.5%; Publishing: 2%.

Approximate 'graduate track' employed **63%**

WHAT IT'S REALLY LIKE	
UNIVERSITY:	
Social Life	★★★★
Campus scene	**Lively, traditional, excellent vibes**
Student Union services	**Good**
Politics	**Involved**
Sport	**30 clubs**
National team position	**92nd**
Sport facilities	**Good**
Arts opportunities	**All excellent**
Student newspaper	**Ripple**
Student radio	**LUSH FM**
Student TV	**LUST**
Nightclub	**Element**
Bars	**Redfearn**
Venue	**Venue**
Union ents	**Reagans, Madfer it, Brighton Beach**
Union societies	**95**
Parking	**Poor**
CITY:	
Leicester Nightlife	★★★★★
City scene	**Top town - clubs, pubs, curries**
Town/gown relations	**OK**
Risk of violence	**Average**
Cost of living	**Average**
Student concessions	**Good**
Survival + 2 nights out	**£70 pw**
Part-time work campus/town	**Excellent**

Centre (Greenhouse 2) and the accommodation halls.

AT A GLANCE	
ACADEMIC FILE:	
Subjects assessed	**28**
Excellent	**82%**
Typical entry requirements	**330 points**
Application acceptance rate	**15%**
Students-staff ratio	**17:1**
First/2:1 degree pass rate	**67%**
ACCOMMODATION FILE:	
Guarantee to freshers	**100%**
Style	**Halls, houses**
Catered	**40%**
En suite	**25%**
Approx price range	**£55-£108**
City rent pw	**£50**

TOWN See *Leicester Student City*, page 269.

PILLOW TALK

'All halls are within walking distance,' writes Christine, 'and are served regularly by the number 80 bus. Beaumont Hall in Oadby is one of the most attractive, set amongst beautiful botanical gardens.'

GETTING THERE

☛ By road: M1/J21 or J22. Good coach services.
☛ By rail: London St Pancras, 1:20; Manchester Piccadilly, 1:30; Sheffield, 1:30; Birmingham New Street, 1:00; Nottingham, 0:30.
☛ By air: Bus from Birmingham International and East Midlands International Airports.
☛ By coach: London, 2:30; Leeds, 3:00; Cardiff, 4:10.

UNIVERSITY OF LINCOLN

The University of Lincoln
Brayford Pool
Lincoln LN6 7TS

TEL 01522 882000
FAX 01522 886041
EMAIL enquiries@lincoln.ac.uk
WEB www.lincoln.ac.uk

Lincoln Students' Union
Brayford Pool
Lincoln LN6 7TS

TEL 01522 882000
FAX 01522 882088
EMAIL (see website)
WEB www.lincoln.ac.uk

VAG VIEW

Lincoln has arrived. No-one can remember Humberside University or the fact that Hull was once its main base; and the bandwaggon still keeps rolling on.

Its superb Brayford Pool Campus now has a £5-million library, and a further £30 million is being spent – £6m on a new Student Centre, which will open this year, and a similar amount on developing the city's Lincoln Centre UK *as a performing arts venue.*

Meanwhile, Media, Humanities and Applied Computing Sciences are being enhanced with a new extension, and the Riseholme Park Campus, which looks after the agriculture and equine provisions, is going to see new teaching facilities, a conference centre and a science park.

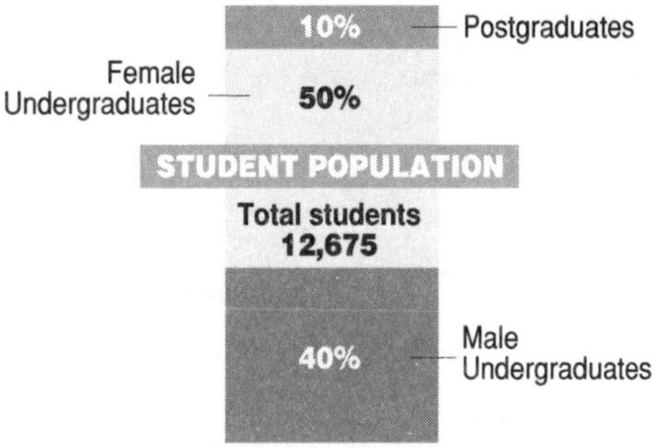

CAMPUS

The main **Brayford Pool Campus** in Lincoln is situated on the riverside in this picturesque cathedral city and cost £32 million; it's pretty impressive, although, reports Paula McManus, 'sometimes it feels more like an airport or shopping centre than a university: security guards are constantly on patrol to stop any damage being done to this sparkling new building.' How can they win!

A city-centre **Hull Campus** retains illustration, graphics, social work and community studies degrees, as well as computer games, animation and TV and film design and media technology degrees.

The agriculture and equine provision (once part of De Montfort Uni) is at the 1000-acre **Riseholme Park Campus**, near Lincoln, while Lincoln's Art & Design is at the old pre-uni college site in the city.

FEES. BURSARIES

UK & EU Fees: £3000. There's a £600 p.a. bursary for students in receipt of the full HE Maintenance grant, and a pro-rata bursary for thos in receipt of a partial grant. A £500 scholarship will be available to all students enrolling in September 2006 for each completed year of their course, and there'll be a £500 Faculty Scholarship for each year studiedat the university. Qualification for these awards depends on exam results.

STUDENT PROFILE

Recruitment has been successful among social groups that do not traditionally consider university. More than a third of undergraduate entrants come from the middle to lower end of the social spectrum and from new-to-uni social groups. Many are mature; few from the publci school sector.

UNIVERSITY/STUDENT PROFILE	
University since	**1992**
Situation/style	**City campus**
Student population	**12675**
Undergraduates	**11447**
- mature	**49%**
- non EU undergraduates	**1%**
- male/female	**45/55**
- non-traditional student intake	**34%**
- state school intake	**97%**
- drop-out rate	**9%**
- undergraduate applications	**Down 5%**

ACADEMIA & JOBS

Particular strengths, or niche areas, are Social Work, Journalism, Media and Human Resource Management. The Lincoln Business School, the Lincoln School of Architecture and the Institute of Medical Sciences were launched as recently as 2003, yet they are now heavily subscribed, firm fixtures. They were joined by the Lincoln School of Journalism in 2004.

SUBJECT AREAS (%)

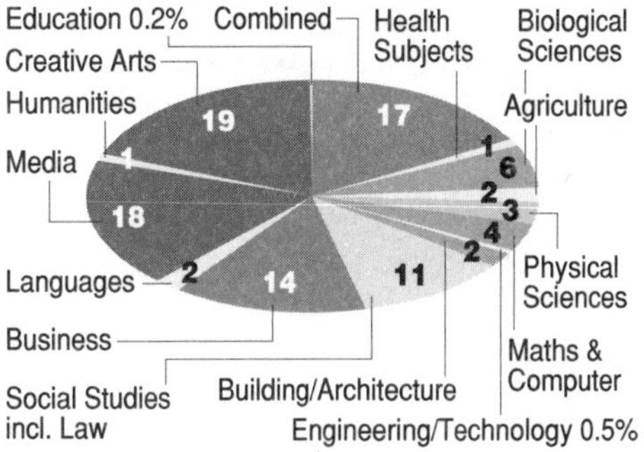

Faculties now offered are Health & Life Sciences; Social Sciences & Law; Business & Management; Art, Architecture & Design; Computing Sciences; Media & Communication. Language and cultural experience is an integral part of the academic recipe. Study abroad arrangements are made in Europe and Australia; formal exchange arrangements are made with sixty-two EU universities or colleges; 25% of first degree students take a language as part of their course and 15% spend six months or more abroad.

In the health faculty, Health Studies (how the health service works) was the staple, and it is still

ACADEMIC EXCELLENCE

TEACHING :	
(Rated Excellent or 17+ out of 24)	
Education	**24**
Politics	**22**
Tourism, Health Studies, Psychology	**21**
Food Science, Art & Design	**20**
Agric/Agricultural Sciences	**19**
Engineering (E & E, General, Mechanical, Aeronautical)	**18**
RESEARCH :	
*Top grades 5/5**	**None**

available. But they now also have Nursing, BSc Psychology, Psychology with Clinical Psychology and BSc Western Herbal Medicine. Last year came B.Sc Acupuncture and B.Sc Herbal Medicine. In Hull they still have BSc Social Work and BA Child & Youth Studies or Early Childhood Studies. And now Social Work is also available at Lincoln.

Particular strengths, or niche areas, are Social Work, Journalism, Media and Human Resource Management

Prospective animal health technicians should also be aware that Lincoln lead in this field, too, followed by Bristol West of England, Aberystwyth and Leeds. Lincoln have a range of degrees in Animal Management & Welfare, Animal Nutrition, Applied Animal Behaviour, as well as an interesting HND and BSc in Conservation Biology (Animal Behaviour). Since taking on De Montfort's Lincoln-based agric operation, they have become a place to watch in this sector. BSc Forestry & Biological Science – teaching inspection 19 – is also high up in the graduate employment stakes.

They also offer a sure track for probation officers through their Criminology degrees, which ties up interestingly with anything from Psychology to Journalism to Forensic Science.

But what's really causing ripples is the art and media provision, the degrees in Animation, Games Design, Architecture, Fine Art, Graphic Design (including design for TV and film), Illustration, Interactive Design, Fashion, Interior Design, Museum/Exhibition Design, Journalism, Media Technology and Media Production (aimed at producing writers and producers), and many others. It really is worth taking the time to look. Phonic Art (a sound-based fine art course), alas, did not stay the distance, but there's a BSc Audio Technology up at Hull, which seems much well placed.

These, and other degrees like them, are responsible for a whole lot of employment niches – such as TV and film industries, radio, architecture, advertising and industrial design.

Look especially at the Lincoln-based Advertising degrees – art direction, fashion, illustration, which will impact heavily on their employment figures. Also, the School of Architecture is going from strength to strength in its £10 million building, designed by Rick Mather for the purpose.

Again, Lincoln's BA Public Relations is clearly adding to its employment success in this artistic area. And the modular degree adjunct Media Culture & Communications leads the way for a host of students in the BA/BSc Joint Honours School. All this may well, with the health provision, be the making of Lincoln. Note, the media, art and design is a split provision, some on the George Street Hull Campus (animation, TV & film, games design, etc).

The BA Hons Journalism, now well established in the Top 10 media lists, is worth dwelling on. It covers print, internet, radio and TV and helped capture 4% of the graduate employment market last time. There is also a host of BA/BSc Journalism tie-ups with Politics or Public Relations. See, too, their Media and Multimedia Production courses – would-be printers and publishing production manager are lining up for them.

Finally, soon to come out of the health faculty is a series of sports degrees – one, Sport & Exercise Science, being developed with nearby Lincoln

WHERE LINCOLN GRADUATES END UP

Health & Social Work: 11%; Education: 8%; Wholesale Retail: 13%; Manufacturing: 13%; Financial Activities: 7%; Public Administration, Civil Service & Defence: 7%; Hotel/Restaurant: 3%; Transport & Communications (including Telecommunications): 7%; Construction: 1%; Agriculture: 1%; Personnel: 6%; Computer: 3%; Accountancy: 1%; Media (including Film): 5%; Legal 4%; Architecture: 1%; Publishing: 1.5%; Advertising: 1%; Artistic/Literary: 1%; Sport: 0.5%.

Approximate 'graduate track' employed **55%**

WHAT IT'S REALLY LIKE	
UNIVERSITY:	
Social Life	★★★
Campus scene	**Expanding, diversifying**
Student Union services	**Good**
Politics	**Student issues**
Sport	**Good, 13 clubs**
National team position	**84th**
Sport facilities	**OK**
Arts opportunities	**Film OK**
Student magazine	**Bullet**
Student radio	**Fuse**
Venue	**Engine Sheds**
Bars	**Delph, Riseholme**
Union ents	**Cheese**
Union societies	**40**
Most active society	**Afro-Caribbean Society**
Parking	**Poor**
CITY:	
Entertainment	★★-★★★
Scene	**Good pubs; average clubs**
Town/gown relations	**Average**
Risk of violence	**Average**
Cost of living	**Average**
Student concessions	**Average**
Survival + 2 nights out	**£60 pw**
Part-time work campus/town	**Average**

College. The other a neatly specific, Sports Development & Coaching.

SOCIAL SCENE

STUDENTS' UNION The new £6 million **Student Centre** opens this year and will include bars, food, shops and a music venue with a capacity of 1500. This is also where the SU's clubs and societies will hang out, the new building incorporating the historic railway engine sheds in, they promise, 'an innovative and exciting design'.

Bars are **Engine Sheds**, **Delph Bar**, and **Riseholme** (agrics) **Bar**. Regular club/disco nights are *Fuse, Essential*. Magazine is *Bullet*. Radio station is Fuse. Most active society (there are 40, plus 13 sports clubs) is Afro-Caribbean Soc.

SPORT There are hockey, football, and rugby teams, and a Sports Centre with pitches and a gym. Four years ago a student could say, 'We are not major contenders yet against other universities.' They were nowhere, but this year they came 84th nationally (our of 130+ in the BUSA league), and with the new academic sporting provision we can expect the graph to continue in the same direction.

TOWN Think of the city of Lincoln, doesn't it remind you of Canterbury or York, both highly successful olde worlde cathedral seats of learning? To fresher Caroline Stocks, when she first set eyes on it, the place seemed promising if rather sedate: 'It's easy to see why so many pensioners flock to Lincoln during the summer, or why the annual Derby-and-Joan Christmas outing is to the town's festive market. There's the majestic cathedral and ancient castle, which sit on a hill overlooking the town, with its tiny old shops on cobbled streets. There are the visitors who stroll along the castle ramparts before taking a look at the 19th-century prison museum. There's the Brayford Pool, where swans paddle lazily, pausing only to let pleasure boats or brightly painted barges pass. And overlooking this pool... there are the university buildings... very modern.

AT A GLANCE	
ACADEMIC FILE:	
Assessments	**20**
Excellent	**45%**
Typical entry requirements	**240 points**
Application acceptance rate	**26%, high**
Students-staff ratio	**23:1**
First/2:1 degree pass rate	**49%**
ACCOMMODATION FILE:	
Guarantee to freshers	**30%**
Style	**Halls, flats**
Catered	**10%**
En-suite	**80%**
Price range pw	**Brayford Pool £69-£83. Riseholme Park £85-£118**
City rent pw	**£50-£60**

'At the moment students have made a limited impact: businesses are only just beginning to cater for them, and the university is itself so new that organising social events seems to be a difficult task. Basically, Lincoln is a safe, quiet town; perfect if you don't want to be in the centre of the action. It has many pubs, the best are the **Varsity** (which always has student offers), **Yates** (somewhere to take your parents for dinner when they visit), **Walkabout** (a great place to watch sport), and the **Vaults** (an underground establishment where you can't use your mobile phone without a bearded biker-type shouting at you, though their Czech Republic beer is cheap).

'The best of the clubs (of which there are few)

is **Pulse & Ritzy**, which plays pop. **The Avenue** also plays pop music and has R&B nights, but the décor can be off-putting. **Po-na-na** has '80s, indie and rock nights, and for *Gatecrasher* wannabes there's dark and dingy **Sugar Cubes**.

'Visiting Nottingham for a night out is easy and cheap travel, and although Lincoln has no motorways to let you travel anywhere quickly, it is easy enough to follow the country roads to Newark, Sheffield, or Skegness for a day beside the sea.'

PILLOW TALK

30% of freshers live in university-owned accommodation: 953 state-of-the-art en-suite bedroom apartments in courts on campus, 84 non-en-suite rooms, 159 places in traditional halls of residence, as well as 2229 beds in privately owned halls of residence. Most of these are new-builds and all are within easy walking distance of the campus. There are also around 1000 beds in privately-owned flats and houses available to freshers. There is catered accommodation on Riseholme Park Campus.

GETTING THERE

☛ By road: from north, A15; northwest, A57, A46 Lincoln by-pass.
☛ By rail: King's Cross, 2:00; Nottingham, 1:00.
☛ By coach: London, 4:10.

STUDENT LIVERPOOL - THE CITY

Visitors to Liverpool are constantly amazed by the rich tapestry of theatres, concert halls, museums, galleries, bars, shops and restaurants which the city centre has to offer. Liverpool also offers an abundance of parks and gardens, including Sefton Park with its beautifully restored Palm House. A short ferry journey across the Mersey will take you to the more rural surroundings of the Wirral.

The city celebrates its 800th Birthday in 2007 and becomes European Capital of Culture in 2008 with the special theme of *Performance* to highlight iys cultural and sporting achievements. As the birthplace of The Beatles, Liverpool is renowned for its musical talents. The *Mathew Street Festival*, *Liverpool Summer Pops* and *Creamfields* are some of the annual music events which take place around the city, with The Royal Liverpool Philharmonic Orchestra providing classical music performances throughout the year.

All three universities will be playing their part in this, as will cultural institutions like the **Playhouse** and **Everyman** theatres, **The Tate** and **Bluecoat** art galleries, the 4th Liverpool Biennial, The Royal Liverpool Philharmonic Society, FACT, the **European Opera Centre** and numerous smaller galleries and theatre companies, several of which are run by Liverpool graduates.

The city's thriving alternative student scene is clustered around three main epicentres: the city centre, Lark Lane and Penny Lane/Smithdown Road. Here's a whistle-stop guide to some of the hidden gems.

STAR PUB

Despite being part of the *It's a Scream* chain of pubs, the **Brookhouse** (Smithdown Road) is one of Liverpool's most popular student pubs, due to its proximity to the centre of student population. **Kelly's**, again on Smithdown, is a regular haunt for second and third years. **The Caledonia** on Catherine Street is always good for a few pints. Most decent nights have a pre-party here. **The Pilgrim** in Pilgrim Street offers cheap beer and passable Sunday lunch fare. It's quiet, safe and pleasant – a good place to chill the morning after the night before. Lark Lane's **Albert Hotel** is a busy, smoky student local with a friendly atmosphere and good draught beers.

STAR BAR

L'agos (or Lago's) is by far the star bar. Trendy decor, wonderfully cheap drinks, soulful music and a good mix of students and locals. **The Magnet** on Hardman Street co-exists with a restaurant, club and a vintage clothing shop. The food not always the best but the atmosphere is always brilliant, and the club is home to some very popular nights. **Hannah's Bar** on Hardman Street has an unpretentious atmosphere, live music or DJs most evenings and good looking bar staff. Fleet Street's **Rocomodo's** (**Modo's**) is suave and modern. It serves posh cocktails at decent prices, is often filled with beautiful people and opens until 2. Also in Fleet Street, is **Baa Bar**, which serves £1 cocktails called 'shooters' and is a common first stop on nights out in the city centre. **The Penny Lane Wine Bar** is friendly and small, with a good summer beer garden.

STAR EATERY

The new **Bluu Bar**, often with big queues (only a good thing?) has really tasty food, with a laid back atmosphere, leather sofas, perfect for a swish lunch.

The Everyman Bistro on Hope Street is attached to the famous theatre set up by graduates of the Liverpool Uni in the 1960s. At moderate prices the food is healthy, well presented and often veggie friendly. The adjacent bar was one of the first places in Liverpool to stock the legendary spirit absinthe – scourge of the Romantics and very trendy. **The Tavern Company** on Smithdown Road is a superb Mexican restaurant loved by students and parents alike. **Maranto's** (Lark Lane) is a large restaurant with a huge bar serving good, moderately priced international cuisine. More expensive is nearby **Viva**, but well worth it as a treat (or when the parents are in town). Best take-away in Liverpool is Smithdown Road's little-known **Pizza Parlour** – authentic pizzas at decent prices, with wine or Italian beer to drink at the counter while your order is prepared.

CLUBS

If it's clubbing you want then Liverpool is the place to come. **Cool Seel Street club The Masque was** started by 3 students 6 years ago and is intensely popular, full of beautiful people and attracts the biggest DJs around. It has won *Mixmag's* Club of the Year award.

Cream @ **Nation**? A distant memory... Today, **Nation** hosts *Bugged Out* on a Saturday, and the raucously fabulous student night *Medication* on a Wednesday (probably what it's most well known for now), as well as the drum 'n' bass fest *X*.

But the people behind Cream are back in a lounge bar/restaurant, **Baby Cream**, at Albert Dock.

At the other end of the spectrum is Tuesday night **The Blue Angel** (108 Seel Street) – 'even Johnny Vegas could pull here,' says Itchy. **The Raz,** as it is affectionately known, is Liverpool's cheesiest student dive, but alumni look back with tender memories – 'Best chat up line from a very pissed Welshman:' says Lotty. '"I saw you coming down the stairs and I thought you were a vision of loveliness" – I did snog him and my mate snogged him the week after! Happy days...' Others can't imagine why you don't go looking for somethiung finer, like **Le Bateau** on Duke Street, known for its indie.

Look, too, at **L2** (The Lomax) for live and alternative dance nights, **Krazy Horse** for indie and hard rock, **Cavern Club** for Beatles nostalgia. Another outstanding club is the gay friendly **Garlands** (Eberle Street), also a winner of *Mixmag's Club of the Year Award*. Temporarily, **The State** is home to Garland's nights. Meanwhile, Monday's student night is *Double Vision* at **The Guild of Students**, Saturday's is *Time Tunnel* (city centre).

SHOPS

The one shop students couldn't live without is **WRC** (West World Retail Corp.) on Bold Street. For labels and good trainers for boys and girls visit **Open** (city centre) and **Drome** women (sorry lads). Hardman Street's **Bulletproof** is a good retailer of pretty much passé '70s clothing; it sells clothes by weight. Slater Street's **Liverpool Palace** and School Lane's **Quiggins** are *pot pourris* of student goods and services – from tatooists to African art. The University of Liverpool's *Monday Market* taps the same market for books, wall hangings and plants, but some stallholders provide products as diverse as PCs and collector's items.

THEATRE & MOUTH ART

The Everyman, Hope Street, is one of the most student-friendly venues around, is known for giving local writers a break, and has started the careers of several big-name Liverpudlian actors, like Pete Postlethwaite and Julie Walters. The more 'street level' **Unity Theatre** nearby does workshops and alternative theatre experiences. Currently, Hanover Street's **Neptune** is a cosy venue favoured by touring shows and comedy acts. **The Egg Café** (Newington, top floor) has bags of atmosphere and features open floor slots for local poets. **The Everyman Bistro** hosts the Dead Good Poets Society, a collective of performance poets, twice a month.

FILM, MUSIC & COMEDY

The new **FACT** centre – a gateway to the city's **Ropewalks** development, which is regenerating a sadly neglected area of the city – is an arts complex showing a wide range of films from quality blockbusters to the most obscure Eastern European cinema as well as media exhibitions and art installations. There are a few good chain cinemas on London Road, Switch Island and Edge Lane. **The Philharmonic**, Hope Street, shows a series of classic films on its unique raising screen, with its traditional cinema organist.

Probably the two best venues for live music are **Liverpool Academy** at the University and **The Picket** (Hardman Street). The former has three venues with the largest having a 2,000+ capacity and has played host to many big names including Coldplay, Groove Armada, The Hives, Faithless. **The Picket** is famed for showcasing loads of local bands, but at present is under threat of closure.

The Rawhide Comedy Club at **Blue Bar** (the Docks) specialise in the field – essential to book ahead. With the **Everyman** they stage mainly established comedians. Sniggers Comedy at the Guild of Students hosts some decent comedians.

VISUAL ART

The Tate Gallery on Albert Dock has 3 floors featuring major touring exhibitions. **The Walker Gallery** (William Brown Street) offers traditional fare. Liverpool Uni has a small gallery by Abercromby Square. **The Open Eye** (Wood Street) exhibits touring photographic shows. Seek out also a plethora of little-known galleries, like the **Bluecoat Chambers** (School Lane).

Anne Fuell

UNIVERSITY OF LIVERPOOL

The University of Liverpool
Student Services Centre
150 Mount Pleasant
Liverpool L69 3GD

TEL 0151 794 5928
FAX 0151 794 2060
EMAIL ugrecruitment@liv.ac.uk
WEB www.liv.ac.uk

Liverpool Guild of Students
PO Box 187
160 Mount Pleasant
Liverpool L69 7BR

TEL 0151 794 6868
FAX 0151 794 4174
EMAIL guild@liv.ac.uk
WEB www.guildofstudents.com

VAG VIEW

Established in 1881, this is the original redbrick university, a great big bustling traditional university, which far from feeling a need to keep up with the times seems somehow to absorb government exigencies and move at its own pace and in its own space.

Liverpool is a well-balanced university and what you might call a safe bet, if you're up for a uni among those at the very top.

There is huge investment in the main campus, rising applications, a testing 14% acceptance rate, an ever better staff to student ratio and healthy chance of getting a good degree at the end. That you'll have a good time at Liverpool goes without saying, but don't expect all mod cons.

UNIVERSITY/STUDENT PROFILE

University since	**1881**
Situation/style	**Civic**
Student population	**21660**
Undergraduates	**16970**
- mature	**7%**
- non EU undergraduates	**6%**
- male/female	**46/54**
- non-traditional student intake	**25%**
- state school intake	**85%, low**
- drop-out rate	**5%**
- undergraduate applications	**Up 11%**

SUBJECT AREAS (%)

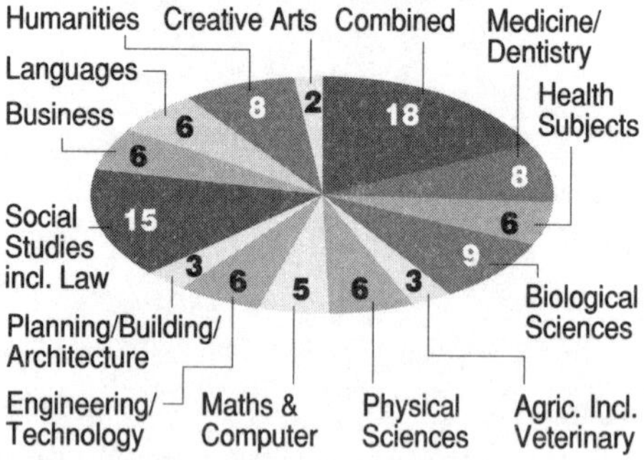

CAMPUS

The campus **Precinct** is a few minutes' walk from the centre of this city, famous for football, the Beatles and the Mersey ferry. With Liverpool Uni, John Moores, Liverpool Hope and Sir Paul McCartney's Lipa, Liverpool is now, also, one of the major centres of higher education in Britain, home to three universities.

FEES, BURSARIES

UK & EU Fees: £3000 p.a. Bursaries of £1350 if in receipt of full HE Maintenance grant; £1000 if in receipt of partial grant. Bursaries also available for students from local and specified postcodes, and for academic achievement, and scholarships for sporting attainment.

STUDENT PROFILE

Liverpool Uni is popular with state and public school kids and students from a whole range of backgrounds – 25% are from new-to-uni social

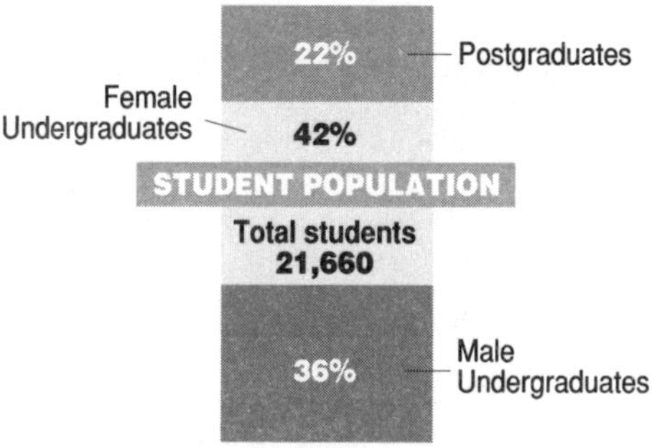

groups; 15% are from private schools. The low drop-out rate (5%) shows that they know how to hang on to them.

ACADEMIA & JOBS

Medicine, Philosophy, Physics, Veterinary, Town/ Country Planning, Maths, Anatomy, Politics & Media, and Management are the top scorers, and for research, it's Physiology, and Engineering.

Faculties include Arts, Engineering, Law, Medicine & Dentistry, Science, Social & Environmental Studies, and Veterinary Science.

For Arts, Science, and Social & Environmental there are Combined Hons Studies interdisciplinary groups, making for some interesting combinations, such as Maths & Philosophy. Study these carefully for the enlightened combinations they make possible.

Within Social & Environmental faculty we find accounting (BA) and economics (BA and BSc) degrees. Liverpool is highly productive career-wise in this area, as it is for insurance and pension brokers and underwriters. Around 9% of Liverpool's graduates go into the financial sector, most popular avenue after Health and Manufacturing, a little less than a third of these into Insurance and pension funding. Economics scored 22 points at the assessments.

Health soaks up not far short of 30% graduates. Liverpool is one of four med-schools awarded 24 points (full marks) for its teaching. The others are Manchester, Newcastle and Southampton (Cardiff was Excellent on the Welsh criteria). The degree is a 4/5-year MC ChB. Clinical skills are introduced in Year 1. Entry 340 points: Chemistry + one other science + one other. There is a 13% acceptance rate, which is high.

The 4-year course is for graduate entry if you have a 2:1 in an approved biomedical discipline or health/social care profession, and it focuses particularly on the ability to use and apply information in the clinical setting. Research Grade 6*: Physiology; Grade 5: Clinical Lab Sciences and Biological Sciences.

Dentists go for the 5-year BDS – entry 360 points; teaching inspection, 21 points. Vets meanwhile opt for the 5-year BVSc, which requires relevant work experience. There's a 6-year BSc Intercalated Honours Year. Look also at the BSc degrees: Bioveterinary Science and Veterinary Conservation Medicine. Teaching inspection, 24. Research Grade 5.

The uni also places quantities of educational psychologists in work – there are four BSc degrees with a 22 out of 24 points rating. There are healthy employment stats, too, for the degrees in Diagnostic Radiography, Radiotherapy, Physiotherapy and Occupational Therapy. Nursing struggled on its first teaching assessment, but came through with 22 points in the end.

Architecture leads to Top 10 graduate employment figures, and the planning theme continues into BA Urban Regeneration & Planning and

ACADEMIC EXCELLENCE

TEACHING:
(Rated Excellent or 17+ out of 24)

History, Law, English, Geology & Environmental Sciences.	**Excellent**
Medicine, Philosophy, Physics, Veterinary	**24**
Town/Country Planning, Maths Anatomy, Politics & Media, Management	**23**
French, Civil Eng, Psychology, Economics, Pharmacol, Nursing, Arachaeology, Classics	**22**
Iberian Studies, Sociology Materials Technology, Dentistry, Electron & Electric Eng	**21**
General, Manufacturing & Aerospace Eng, Subjects Allied to Medicine	**20**
German, Organismal Biosciences, Molecular Biosciences	**19**

RESEARCH:
Top grades 5/5/6**

Physiology	**Grade 6***
Mech/Aero/Manufacturing and Civil Engineering	**Grade 5***
Clinical Laboratory Sciences, Pharmacology, Biological Sciences, Veterinary, Chemistry, Physics, Earth Sciences, Pure Maths, Applied Maths, Computer, Electrical & Electronic Eng, Metallurgy, American Studies, English, French, German/Dutch/Scandinavian, Archaeology, History	**Grade 5**

MPlanning Town & Regional Planning – all of which make their graduate would-be town planners irresistible, it seems. There's also a combined hons Environment and Planning. Entry 320 points. Teaching scored 23.

Liverpool Humanities graduates find quality jobs in the Civil Service apparently, and in charity organisations. Law is also a reliable pathway into the former, as are languages.

They are, too, European specialists in law, and recently were assessed 'Good' in this department by a reporting assessor for the LPC (the Legal Practice Course) Board. See, too, theirBA Legal & Business Studies.

Biological sciences cut a path through to higher education lecturer in the careers market (only 19 at teaching assessment, but Grade 5 at research), also into Defence. Liverpool turns out more than most defence operatives and equipment engineers. For a career in the Royal Navy or RAF (a popular choice here), look at their Engineering Group of degree programmes, from Aerospace Engineering to Digital Signal Processing & Communications to Civil & Maritime Engineering. Teaching assessments range from 20 to 22 and there's a Grade 5* for research into Mechanical, Aeronautical and Manufacturing Engineering.

Liverpool is a great big bustling traditional university with some of the best teaching in the country, not least in Medicine. But mythic status is accorded the city when they start talking about it.

Also out of the Engineering Faculty comes a host of furniture designers to help make them the sixth biggest supplier in the country. Look at the BSc Product Design with Multimedia, and Design & Technology with Multimedia. Consider, too, the BEng Materials, Design & Manufacture. 21 points at assessment.

They also have a reputation for producing chemists. BSc/MChem Chemical Sciences comes with numerous combinations, such as Pharmacology, Industrial Chemistry, Industrial Management, Management, Materials Science, Oceanography or a European language. Research Grade 5. Leeds, Nottingham, Bath and Liverpool, are the only traditional unis in the top league when it comes to careers in pharmaceutical manufacture.

SOCIAL SCENE

Students' Guild The Guild has four live music venues which go by the name of **Liverpool Academy**, the biggest capacity venue in the city. Last year they ran in excess of 180 live music events. BLOC Party, Rooster, Subways, Motorhead, Texas, The Kills have all played here recently and Goldfrapp, The Coral and KT Tunstall are all due to play shortly, as we write. They have two weekly club nights, called *Time Tunnel* (Saturday) and *Double Vision* (Monday) and the capacity for these is 2600. In total, the Guild has nine bars, of which, **The Gilmore**, **The Liver Bar** and the **Saro Wiwa** are open throughout the day.

The student newspaper, *Liverpool Student*, like other top student city newspapers, *Leeds Student*, Manchester's *Student Direct* and *London Student*, has become a virtual passage into the media. If that's your thing, get involved. ICON is the radio station.

As elsewhere, there are all kinds of societies with which to get involved – 90 at the last count and 45 sports clubs. Among the former, the most popular are Islamic Soc, Drama, RockSoc, and LUST – that's Liverpool Uni Show Troupe.

The Guild runs LUSTI (Liverpool Uni Student Training Initiative) to train students in key transferable skills such as communication, assertiveness, time and stress management, meeting skills etc.

PULSE is a new job-centre service that has been set up by the uni to help students find part-time jobs with local employers during term and more full-time during the vacations.

WHERE LIVERPOOL GRADUATES END UP

Health & Social Work: 28%; Education: 7%; Wholesale Retail: 7%; Manufacturing: 10%; Financial Activities: 9%; Public Administration, Civil Service & Defence: 8%; Hotel/Restaurant: 3%; Transport & Communications (including Telecommunications): 2%; Construction: 2%; Personnel: 4%; Computer: 2%; Business & Management: 2%; Accountancy: 3%; Media (including Film): 2%; Legal 2%; Architecture: 2%; Publishing: 2%.

Approximate 'graduate track' employed **66%**

Sport They are nationally strong. The **Sports Centre** – extended and renovated in 2004 – includes swimming pool, squash courts, weight training, indoor cricket nets, climbing wall, sunbeds, facilities for aerobics, dance, trampolining. There's a hall at the gym for judo, fencing, archery, four additional squash courts, rifle and pistol range and a weights room. The main sports ground, near the halls, includes two floodlit artificial turf pitches for hockey, field sports, five rugby and six soccer pitches, four tennis courts, a lacrosse pitch, two cricket squares and two artificial wickets, bar and cafeteria. Two other grounds add a further six soccer pitches, and there's a base for climbing, walking, canoeing and field studies in Snowdonia, which accommodates eighteen.

Town See *Liverpool Student City*, page 278.

PILLOW TALK

Most first years dwell in massive catered halls (Greenbank or Carnatic) 3 miles out. All freshers who apply by August 31 are guaranteed a place. See *At A Glance* box for prices. If you're expecting luxury accommodation you'll be sorely disappointed, though the community spirit which grows up in halls like Rankin on the Carnatic site stand you in great stead. They have bars and ents, and are linked to uni and city centre by a regular bus service.

GETTING THERE

☛ By road: M6/J21a, M62, A5080, A5047. Well served by National Express coaches.
☛ By rail: Manchester, 40 mins; Sheffield, 1:45; Leeds, Birmingham, 2:00; London King's Cross, 3:00.
☛ Liverpool airports for inland/Ireland flights.
☛ By coach: London, 5:00; Manchester, 50 mins.

AT A GLANCE

ACADEMIC FILE:	
Subjects assessed	**37**
Excellent	**84%**
Typical entry requirements	**330points**
Application acceptance rate	**14%**
Students-staff ratio	**15:1**
First/2:1 degree pass rate	**62%**
ACCOMMODATION FILE:	
Guarantee to freshers	**95%**
Style	**Halls**
Catered	**62%**
En-suite	**3%**
Approx price range pw	**£65-£104**
City rent pw	**£50-£70**

WHAT IT'S REALLY LIKE

UNIVERSITY:	
Social Life	★★★★★
Campus scene	**Great time, unpretentious, rich opportunity**
Student Union services	**Good**
Politics	**Activity high: student issues**
Sport	**45 clubs**
National team position	**40th**
Sport facilities	**Good**
Arts opportunities	**Excellent**
Student newspaper	**Liverpool Student**
Student radio	**ICON**
Nightclub venue	**Academy**
Bars	**9 bars, Gilmore, Liver Bar, Saro Wiwa...**
Union ents	**Time Tunnel, Double Vision, major live gigs**
Union societies	**90**
Most popular societies	**Islamic**
Parking	**Adequate**
CITY:	
Entertainment	★★★★★
City scene	**Fab**
Town/gown relations	**Good**
Risk of violence	**Average**
Cost of living	**Low**
Student concessions	**Excellent**
Survival + 2 nights out	**£70 pw**
Part-time work campus/town	**Good/Excellent**

LIVERPOOL HOPE UNIVERSITY

Liverpool Hope University
Hope Park
Liverpool L16 9JD

TEL 0151 291 3295
FAX 0151 291 2050
EMAIL admissions@hope.ac.uk
WEB www.hope.ac.uk
SU WEB www.hopesu.co.uk

Liverpool Hope University has a reputation as a major provider in the field of Education, although this is anything but the whole story. For years they offered degrees in a variety of subjects, all of them awarded by Liverpool University. In those days, the Pro-rector's introduction – 'Hope is a great virtue with both sacred and secular connotations,' - sounded a bit like a sermon, and we should not be surprised, for Liverpool Hope, once the Liverpool Institute, has its roots in an ecumenical amalgamation of two colleges with religious foundations – St Katherine's, an Anglican foundation, and Notre Dame, its Roman Catholic neighbour – a union championed years ago by the then Bishop of Liverpool – the cricketing David Sheppard. In 2005, when Hope became a university, its first Vice-Chancellor, Professor Gerald John Pillay, was fittingly a theologian.

Liverpool Hope offered Liverpool University course elements, such as Theology and Religious Studies, which the it lacked. At the same time, Liverpool offered Hope top-notch facilities for its Sport, Recreation & Physical Education courses, which are still part of the syllabus today. It was a good marriage – made in heaven you might say.

But Hope was always bound to come good in its own right in these days of 'widening participation' because at the heart of its mission is a determination to make higher education more widely available, not for political correctness, but because it is an essential part of its ethos, and always has been. It was doing it already – for real.

Springing from its religious roots is a determination to provide for 'those who have hitherto not had the most distinguished or easy path to academic honours.' Foundation courses prepare students without the required grades to study a degree course. Lecturers go out into the community and preach, sorry teach, those who for one reason or another can't take up a place at Hope. They called it their 'Reach Out' degree route long before Blair's Labour called it 'out-reach'. At Everton, a £15.5-million development was set up to house Hope's community-education strategy. More recently, they developed what they call a Network of Hope, a partnership with communities further afield that would otherwise not have had such a provision. It is now possible for students to undertake full- and part-time degree level study in Hope courses at colleges within the bounds of their local communities.

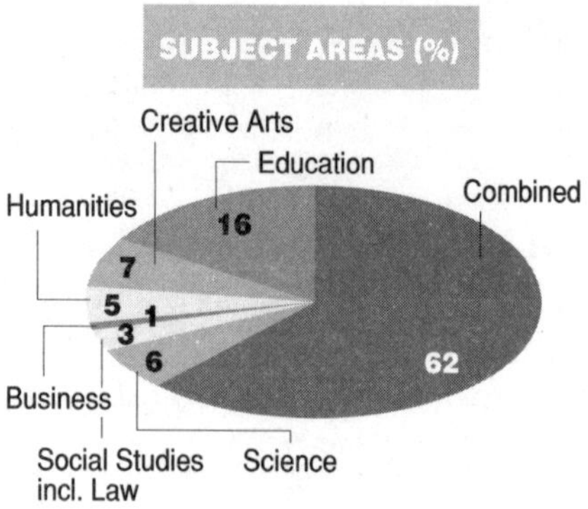

CAMPUS

With such an eternally optimistic agenda, how disappointing that its name comes from its situation in Hope Park, Childwall, some 3 miles from the centre of Liverpool, the original buildings of the two constituent colleges forming the basis of a campus none too exhilarating architecturally.

This is the centre of operations, however, and where you'll find the student union HQ. Hope at Everton, a few miles away, has two Grade II Listed buildings, a hall of residence offering self-catering en-suite accommodation for 180 students and the refurbished St Francis Xavier's Church. It is well-established as one of the most important arts venues on Merseyside.

Here, students study Creative & Performing Arts subjects, Fine Art & Design, Film Studies, Dance, Drama & Theatre Studies and Music. Wholly appropriately, they share with the European Opera Centre, the Music Space Trust and

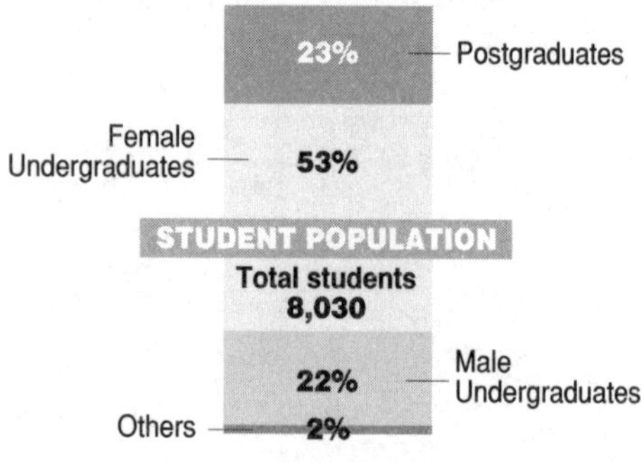

UNIVERSITY/STUDENT PROFILE	
University since	**2005**
Situation/style	**Civic**
Student population	**8030**
Undergraduates	**6050**
- mature	**28%**
- non EU undergraduates	**6%**
- male/female	**30/70**
- non-traditional student intake	**42%, high**
- state sector intake	**98%**
- drop-out rate	**16%, high**
- undergraduate applications	**Up 19%**

The Cornerstone Gallery, with its continuous exhibition of professional art. Playwrights, artists and musicians, including Visiting Professors Willy Russell and John Godber, Alan Bleasdale, Julian Lloyd Webber, Joanna McGregor and ex-Beatle Stuart Sutcliffe complete the scene.

The Reach Out Community Forum ties up with such as the Everton Development Trust, the Rotunda Community Arts Centre, local churches and secondary schools. The Hope Community Youth Theatre is based here, and The Royal Liverpool Philharmonic Orchestra, the 10:10 Ensemble and youth and community choirs all practise here.

Hope is running with a strong current in this vibrant, ever evolving city, and it was rewarded first with university college status and then university status because it is running with it rather well. Numbers of applicants are leaping (up 19%), but the drop-out rate in the transformational process is also running high (16%).

FEES, BURSARIES

UK & EU Fees: £3000 p.a. If in receipt of full HE Maintenance grant there's a bursary of £1000; if in receipt of partial grant, it's £700. Students with a family income above £32000 will receive Liverpool Hope bursary payments of £400. There are also academic achievement scholarships and other bursaries designed to improve student retention and nurture the curriculum. Contact the university.

STUDENT PROFILE

28% of undergraduates are mature, 70% of them are female, which is apt, because its constituent colleges were both women's colleges; 20% are part time, 98% are from the state sector and 42% from classes new to university. Many, of course, are also local. Beyond statistics, there is a spirit about the place – a relaxed, focused, community spirit – which is Hope's own, although campus can be a bit lonely at weekends.

ACADEMIA

Subjects at Liverpool Hope are grouped into four *Deaneries*: Arts & Humanities, Education, Business & Computing, and Sciences & Social Sciences. All of the undergraduate programmes are modular. There are BA and BSc single honours, BSc combined honours (major/minor), BA combined honours (major/minor), and equal weight combined honours for both BA and BSc subjects. There are also a load of 1-year Certificates in HE, the BA with QTS teacher training degrees, and a BDes (Design), the first year of which can be studied on the Isle of Man. Characteristically, students are stimulated by the content and sympathetic delivery of the programme, and produce some imaginative work in response.

Theology is, of course, still on offer and scored 23 points at the teaching assessments and a Grade 4 at the research assessments. Business, however, scored full marks at the assessments and features in the BA single honours and widely throughout the 450 combination courses offered. There is also an apparently improbable course called Gaming Technology, which has in fact nothing to do with gambling, but computer games technology.

Art and Design, and performing arts – Dance, Drama & Theatre Studies, music, are a core provision at Everton, and were rewarded with a 20-point teaching assessment. Teacher Training focuses on primary teaching (English lang/lit, art/design, geography, history, information technology, maths, music, special needs, sport studies, religion, and a series of Advanced Study of Early Years is part of the BA Hons combined course strategy.

ACADEMIC EXCELLENCE	
TEACHING: *(Rated Excellent or 17+ out of 24)*	
Geography & Environmental Studies.	**Excellent**
Business	**24**
Theology	**23**
Psychology, Sociology	**22**
Maths, Biosciences	**21**
Art & Design	**20**
Modern Languages, American Studies, Drama & Theatre, Leisure and Sport degrees	**19**
RESEARCH:	
*Top grades 5/5**	**None**

Among social sciences, Psychology is recommended and Sociology (both with a 22-point assessment), and clearly their Childhood & Youth Studies,

Social Work, Special Needs and Pastoral Leadership programmes are central to the Hope's ethos. Note, too, the BSc Health & Fitness, Sports Psychology, Sport Studies and Sustainable Sports Management (19 points at the assessments). There is a new air-conditioned fitness suite, equipped withstate-of-the-art cardiovascular and resistance equipment.

The £5.3 million Sheppard-Worlock Library houses 250,000 books, many PCs and 500 study places. There is an on-site nursery that even provides for children younger than two years, and the future prospects of both its many mature and more youthful students are encouraged by elective modules in languages and IT, and by modules which take students out into the workplace and community, both in the UK and overseas.

SOCIAL SCENE

STUDENT UNION The two student bars are **D2** (with video wall) on the ground floor of the Union, and the lounge-style **Derwent Bar** upstairs.

There is also a Union presence (and bar) at Everton. Ents are traditional fare - bands (of the tribute variety), comedians (Jack Dee and Lee Evans have played here), karaoke, jazz nights, and a multitude of society thrashes. Tuesday takes students out to **The Blue Angel** in town (108 Seel Street) – 'even Johnny Vegas could pull here,' says Itchy. **The Raz,** as it is affectionately known, is Liverpool's cheesiest student dive, but alumni look back with tender memories – 'Best chat up line from a very pissed Welshman:' says Lotty. '"I saw you coming down the stairs and I thought you were a vision of loveliness" - I did snog him and my mate snogged him the week after! Happy days...'

Regular DJ Welsh Dave of the **Derwent** grooms Hope students for such antics. Wednesday is sports or societies night. 'It's always a popular night in **D2** with each team coming up with a weekly theme to get ya involved.' On Friday comes 'The WORLD Famous all day party. Music and fun throughout the day in the **Derwent** bar from 12 with Karaoke and DJ's starting at 6. Getting you warmed up and in the mood for our Flagship night *Reload*, starting at 9.' It's DJ Welsh Dave again plus up and coming DJ's eager to fill his shoes. Saturday most people have gone home and it's live football and rugby on the screens. Then it's the *Sunday Night Social* – quiz, bingo, sing-a-long, 'with great acts every week'.

There are plenty of societies and an opportunity to be part of the team that produces the award-winning *Liverpool Student* newspaper that serves all 3 unis.

SPORT They have recently installed a floodlit, all-weather astroturf pitch for hockey, tennis, football; there's a gym, and the Athletics Union is involved in all the usual inter-Uni competitions, with not at all a bad record, given the size of the student population. They came 82nd nationally last year.

Hope Park Sports is managed by Healthworks, an outside firm. Facilities include a multi-purpose sports hall for 5-a-side football, badminton, basketball and tennis, volleyball, netball and hockey. There's access to football and rugby pitches and squash courts and the new fitness suite mentioned under *Academia* above. There are exercise classes and coaching courses for all abilities and levels of fitness,.

Among a handful of unusual clubs is Kick

WHAT IT'S REALLY LIKE

UNIVERSITY:	
Social Life	★★★
Campus scene	**Friendly, focused**
Student Union services	**Good**
Politics	**Caring**
Sport	**Competitive**
National team position	**82nd**
Sport facilities	**Good**
Arts opportunities	**Excellent**
Student newspaper	**Liverpool Student**
Bars	**D2, Derwent**
Union ents	**DJs, cheese, karaoke, quiz**
Union clubs/societies	**45**
Parking	**Adequate**
CITY:	
Entertainment	★★★★★
City scene	**Fab**
Town/gown relations	**Good**
Risk of violence	**Average**
Cost of living	**Low**
Student concessions	**Excellent**
Survival + 2 nights out	**£70 pw**
Part-time work campus/town	**Good/Excellent**

AT A GLANCE

ACADEMIC FILE:	
Typical entry requirements	**200 points**
Application acceptance rate	**24%, v. high**
Students-staff ratio	**26:1 v. high**
First/2:1 degree pass rate	**45%**
ACCOMMODATION FILE:	
Guarantee to freshers	**100%**
Style	**Halls**
Price range pw	**£70-£82**
City rent pw	**£50-£70**

Boxing, and the Mountaineering club is worth a mention not least because of **Plas Caerdeon**, Hope's Outdoor Education Centre. This old manor house in 18 acres of woodland overlooking the glorious Mawddach Estuary (Snowdonia) hosts field and study trips, but it's also a bolt hole for music students on Composition weekend, Drama students for rehearsals and anybody for simpler regenerative pleasures. There is good accommodation.

CITY See *Liverpool Student City*, page 278.

GETTING THERE

- ☛ By road: easy access M62 (east/west), which connects with M6 (north/south) at Junction 21a.
- ☛ Well served by National Express coaches.
- ☛ By rail: Manchester, 0:40; Sheffield, 1:45; Leeds or Birmingham, 2:00; London Kings Cross, 3:00.
- ☛ Speke Airport 5 miles away.

LIVERPOOL INSTITUTE FOR PERFORMING ARTS

Liverpool Institute for Performing Arts
Mount Street
Liverpool L1 9HF

TEL 0151 330 3000
FAX 0151 330 3131
EMAIL admissions@lipa.ac.uk
WEB www.lipa.ac.uk

INSTITUTE PROFILE

Founded	**1996**
Status	**HE College**
Degree awarding university	**Liverpool JM**
Full-time undergraduates	**598**

DEGREE COURSES:
Performing Arts, Sound Technology

Sir Paul McCartney, Dame Judi Dench, Mark Knopfler, Richard Branson, Carly Simon, Sir George Martin are all patrons of Lipa. Performing Arts degrees, awarded by Liverpool John Moores University, are available in Acting, Community Arts, Dance, Enterprise management and Music, and there's a degree in Sound Technology.

All students follow the same core programme: IT (including light, sound and video), Professional Development and Contextual Studies, plus specialist classes in their chosen subject. All must take part in performance projects, workshops and electives. Magnificent learning resources, editing suites, production gear, plus 5 large rehearsal rooms.

Students have ready access to the uni's **Cooler** and **Scholar's** bars, and the **Base** (the gym). The ISPB provides entertainment in the bar or canteen most nights.

They have no accommodation of their own, but places, including student halls, can be lined up.

LIVERPOOL JOHN MOORES UNIVERSITY

Liverpool John Moores University
Roscoe Court
4 Rodney Street
Liverpool L1 2TZ

TEL 0151 231 5090
FAX 0151 231 3462
EMAIL recruitment@ljmu.ac.uk
WEB www.ljmu.ac.uk

Liverpool John Moores Students' Union
The Haigh Building
Maryland Street
Liverpool L1 9DE

TEL 0151 231 4900
FAX 0151 231 4931
EMAIL lsujmill@livjm.ac.uk
WEB www.l-s-u.com

VAG VIEW

Liverpool John Moores (JMU) is Liverpool's metropolitan university, more part of the city than the older campus-based university. JMU's many buildings are strewn all over the city, and the 3-bar Students' Union building, **The Haigh**, *is an integral part of the Liverpool scene. Through the uni's affiliation with Sir Paul McCartney's Liverpool Institute for*

Performing Arts (see above), JMU has a proud association with the city's most influential artists of all time. Also, they draw many students from the region, and the institution's roots run deep into the city's industrial history.

Origins go back to 1823 as the Liverpool Mechanics' and Apprentices' Library. As poly, the institution brought together the City Colleges of Art and Design and Building, Commerce, and the Regional College of Technology, the City of Liverpool College of Higher Education, the IM Marsh College of Physical Education, the FL Calder College of Home Economics and the Liverpool College of Nursing and Midwifery – all of which give a good clue to the uni's academic profile today.

Finally, JMU owes its name and ethos to one of the city's most famous entrepreneurs. Sir John Moores CBE (1896-1993) built Littlewoods – the football pools organisation – from scratch. 'Sir John's business success was built upon his philosophy of the equality of opportunity for all,' the uni says. 'This fundamental belief... is a reflection of the university's commitment to higher education, to access, to flexibility and to participation.' Most of all, perhaps, it gives the clue to the underlying ethos – applied learning – they are very hot, across the board, on how what is learned and imbued here can be applied on graduation in the world of work.

Students are requested to identify any disabilities including Dyslexia as early as possible, so as to take advantage of JMU's rigorous support programme.

CAMPUS

JMU is roughly three main sites: Mount Pleasant, Byrom Street/Henry Cotton campus and IM Marsh. Each has lecture theatres, seminar rooms, laboratories, editing suites, individual study and computer rooms, as well as union bars, shops and sports facilities. Everything is in and around the city, accessible to public transport and in easy reach of the city centre and halls of residence.

Writes Emma Hardy: 'JMU buildings are scattered across the city, many are impressive. The School of Media, Critical and Creative Arts, where I study, is one of the most impressive buildings in Liverpool. Located next to the Anglican Cathedral, the views from it are spectacular and the facilities are exemplary. The main library is a great glass structure of imposing stature and, like much of the rest of the university, likely to take your breath away when you first see it. But there are some grim high rise blocks too. Prospective students do well to bear in mind that what they see on Open Day are the best bits.'

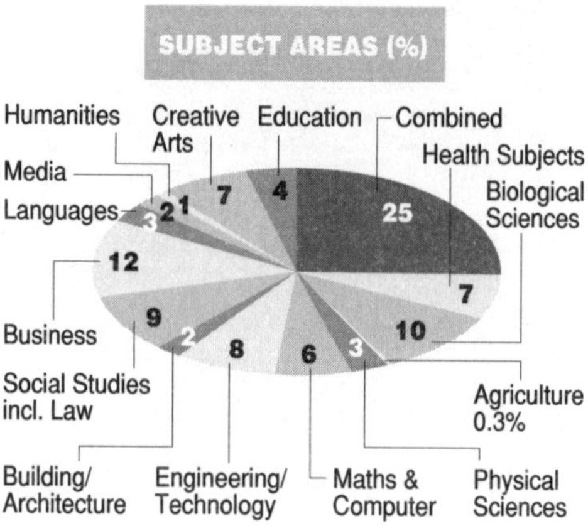

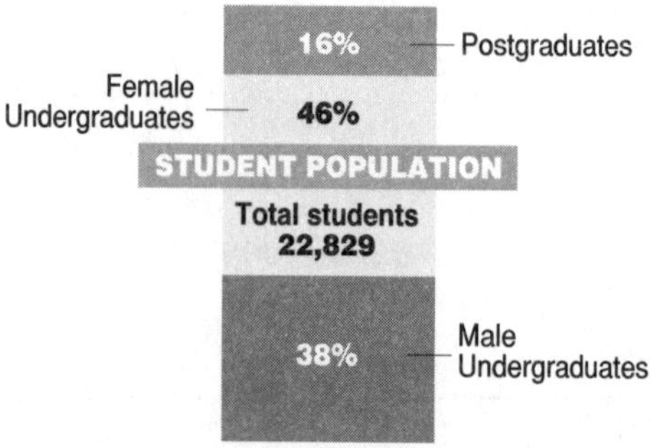

UNIVERSITY/STUDENT PROFILE

University since	**1992**
Situation/style	**Civic**
Student population	**22829**
Undergraduates	**19274**
- mature	**35%**
- non EU undergraduates	**9%**
- male/female	**46/54**
- non-traditional student intake	**35%**
- state school intake	**94%**
- drop-out rate	**10%**
- undergraduate applications	**Constant**

FEES, BURSARIES

UK & EU Fees: £3000. If in receipt of full HE Maintenance grant there's a bursary of £1000; if in receipt of partial grant, it's £400. There are sports

ACADEMIC EXCELLENCE

TEACHING :
(Rated Excellent or 17+ out of 24)

Health Studies, Food & Nutrition, Sport, Tourism	**24**
Pharmacology, Organismal Biosciences	**23**
Communication & Media, Building, Land & Property Management, Nursing, Politics, Molecular Biosciences, Business & Management, Economics	**22**
Drama & Dance, American Studies, Maths, Education	**21**
Civil Engineering	**20**
Modern Languages (French, German, Russian, Spanish), Psychology, Art & Design	**19**
Sociology, Town & Country Planning, Electric & Electron Eng, General Eng	**18**

RESEARCH :
*Top grades 5/6/6**

Sport	**Grade 6***
General Engineering	**Grade 5**

scholarships - contact Sports Scholarship Manager (David McDermott); also Dream Plan Achievers for those getting three As at A level – £1000 per year. Achievers award, connected to 'link' schools are £1000 p.a.

STUDENT PROFILE

Asked to give us a profile, Emma concluded, 'Despite the huge diversity in matters of taste and style, your JMU student is a mellow person, out to enjoy their time at university. The general atmosphere is far from snobbish, and with such a wide range of people studying here, friends are not hard to find, no matter what your age, or what your interests.'

The statistics show that 94% of applicants come from the state sector and 35% from new-to-uni social groups. There is also a 35% mature population and a significant overseas presence. JMU's problem has not been getting students so much as hanging on to them, but they have this under control now: their drop-out rate is running at 10%.

ACADEMIA & JOBS

Writes Emma: 'JMU are big on student feedback. Tutors are approachable and changes do get made. Questionnaires regarding each and every module taught are distributed to students and the uni does listen to complaints. The emphasis is on making the experience as enjoyable as possible.'

Vocational bias, strong on sandwich courses, good contacts with industry – professional associations offer direct employment routes, for example, in pharmacy, surveying and engineering. And now they've established a business club for graduates called NEXUS, through which you'll be able to network and tap into uni-based expertise and resources.

Faculties include: Business & Law; Education, Community & Leisure; Health & Applied Social Sciences; Media, Arts & Social Science; Technology & Environment.

Education is a defining provision – 59% from the faculty go into secondary teaching; 32% into primary. There are also ESOL and TESOL courses – English for non-English speakers and courses for teachers of same. Teaching inspection, 21 points.

Among engineering graduates in a department that won a Grade 5 listing for research (international level), civil engineers proliferate, then it's design & development engineers, computer programmers and systems analysts, sound recordists, IT consultants, software engineers, process and production engineers and construction engineers. Radio & TV broadcasters and sound recordists love JMU, in particular their BSc Broadcast Technology. There's Granada TV partnership status and great tie-ups with Sky TV.

Look, too, at BA Hons Journalism, which includes practical TV Journalism (there's also International Journalism) and Media Professional Studies for TV production, business and management enterprise, info technology and media theory.

WHERE LIVERPOOL JOHN MOORES GRADUATES END UP

Health & Social Work: 10%; Education: 17%; Wholesale Retail: 12%; Manufacturing: 8%; Financial Activities: 7%; Public Administration, Civil Service & Defence: 8%; Hotel/Restaurant: 4%; Transport & Communications (including Telecommunications): 4.5%; Construction: 2%; Personnel: 4.5%; Computer: 3%; Business & Management: 2%; Accountancy: 0.5%; Media (including Film): 3%; Legal 2%; Architecture: 2%; Publishing: 1%; Advertising: 0.5%; Artistic/Literary: 1.5%; Sport: 1%.

Approximate 'graduate track' employed **64%**

The latter is run in partnership with Mersey Television (*Brookside* and *Hollyoaks* producer, Phil Redmond, is their Honorary Professor). Teaching inspection, 22.

Prospective social worker/counsellors also treat JMU with respect. They are in the top echelon of graduate providers in this sector through a series of Applied Community Studies/Social Work/ Youth & Community Work Studies BA degrees.

Nursing and midwifery students now benefit from 'SimMan' – a high-tech 'universal patient simulator' mannequin, which is part of the new Clinical Practice Suite, developed in partnership with the Cheshire and Merseyside Strategic Health Authority: 6 rooms designed to function like real hospital wards.

Students are requested to identify any disabilities including Dyslexia as early as possible, so as to take advantage of JMU's rigorous support programme.

There are good career figures too for animal health technicians, carers, nurses. They leave the vet degrees to their neighbour and position themselves instead with the likes of BSc Animal Behaviour and Zoology.

Another key area can be gleaned from the *Academic Excellence* box (page 289). Full-mark scores (24 points) were had for Food & Nutrition, and 23 points for Biosciences. A 4-year sandwich BSc Hons Applied Microbiology is one of a range of similar courses, from Applied Biochemistry to Nutrition, all with foundation years. Many go on to become bacteriologists or microbiologists, who work with living organisms, focused on human health and environmental issues, food poisoning, drugs, viruses, bacteria, etc. See also BSc Nutrition.

There's a good employment track record, too, for prospective chemists and those planning a career in Pharmaceutical Manufacture. There are degrees in Industrial Pharmaceutical Science, Pharmaceutical Science or Analysis, as well as an MPharm. JMU take 3%+ of the graduate employment market. Teaching inspection – 23 out of 24 points.

In computing, the degree that opens doors is BSc Computer Games Technology degree. Computer programmers (also highly in demand from here) should look at their BSc Computer Aided Design or simply BSc Computer Studies.

The BA Architecture attracts employers, and JMU is in the Top 10, too, with its Property Management degree (see also the Real Estate Management degrees and BSc Quantity Surveying).

This year sees work begin on The Design Academy, the new £21million home for Art and Design, designed by Rick Mather Architects.

In Law, JMU was assessed 'Good' on a scale of Excellent, Very Good, Good, Satisfactory or Unsatisfactory by a reporting assessor for the LPC Board – the Legal Practice Course is essential for becoming a solicitor. Moot Court is or 'mock' courtroom to give law degree and legal practice students the chance to gain intensive trial practice There is no dedicated policing degree – you'd have to go to Central Lancashire, Glamorgan, Central England in Birmingham or Buckinghamshire Chilterns University College for one of those, but as is so often the case in a city uni with good Criminology, Forensic Science and Youth & Community degrees and a strong sporting provision, jobs come easy with the police.

JMU have the only Sport & Exercise Science department in the UK with a maximum teaching assessment rating of 24, and a maximum research assessment rating of Grade 6*. Prospective pro players and officials should look at BSc Sport Science, Sport Technology, Applied Psychology and BA Sport Development & Physical Education. JMU will be awarded around £4.5 million over the next five years in recognition of its teaching excellence in the fields of PE, Dance, Sport and Exercise Sciences, to create a new Centre of Excellence in Teaching and Learning.

AT A GLANCE

ACADEMIC FILE:	
Subjects assessed	**37**
Excellent	**68%**
Typical entry requirements	**235 points**
Application acceptance rate	**19%**
Students-staff ratio	**19:1**
First/2:1 degree pass rate	**51%**
ACCOMMODATION FILE:	
Availability to freshers	**100%**
Style	**Halls**
Catered	**None**
En suite	**80%**
Approx price range pw	**£58-£85**
City rent pw	**£45-£95**

Finally, drama students and local community groups Black Box Theatre Company, Momentum Theatre Company, Liverpool Youth Service and Unity Theatre will benefit from a £200,000 refurbishment of the uni's Joe H Makin Drama Centre.

SOCIAL SCENE

STUDENTS' UNION As a prospective student, bear in mind that it is up to you to make the most of your time at JMU. This means finding out about what is going on and getting involved in what interests you. Radio stations, newspapers, clubs, societies and events need student support.

The union building, the Haigh, has a bar – **Scholars**, the newest venue, designed trad. pub-style with pool tables, jukeboxes and three televisions – and a club, **The Cooler** – a 500-capacity nightclub with new air-conditioning system, hence its name, and late bar, disco, stage facilities, Playstation and a giant television screen for sport and films. Entry is free. Every night of the week there is a different music theme in **The Cooler – from Doctors & Nurses to Ann Summers**, and there are screenings of recent movies and big screen football.' Saturday's *Loveshack* ('60s, '70s, '80s, '90s) has long been rated the best retro night in town. Now, too, there's Lush (funky dance) and drinks promos like *Vodipop*.

Another popular meeting place is **Sanctuary**, a café bar, chill-out zone with sofas, speciality coffees, etc. There are also bars at the IM Marsh (Education) and Byron Street sites.

Among the most successful student societies is the radio station, Shout fm, and now there's a student magazine, *Re:load*, which in its previous incarnation as *Shout* figured in many a national awards ceremony.

Situated in the Haigh is UNITEMP, JMU's own employment agency. It does offer some exclusive Unitemp related jobs, but doesn't beat getting the local newspaper, visiting the job centre, or simply asking around for vacancies.

WHAT IT'S REALLY LIKE	
UNIVERSITY:	
Social Life	★★★★
Campus scene	**Local, top scene**
Student Union services	**Good**
Politics	**Active: safety, sex, housing**
Sport	**19 clubs**
National team position	**52nd**
Sport facilities	**Good**
Arts opportunities	**Music excellent; drama, dance, film, art good**
Student magazine	**Re:Load**
Student radio	**Shout fm**
Nightclub	**The Cooler**
Bars	**Scholars, Sanctuary, IM Marsh, Byron Street**
Union ents	**Pop, retro, funky dance**
Union clubs/societies	**72**
Most popular societies	**Ski/Snowboard, Afro-Carribean, Christian Union**
Parking	**Poor**
CITY:	
Entertainment	★★★★★
City scene	**Fab**
Town/gown relations	**Good**
Risk of violence	**Average**
Cost of living	**Low**
Student concessions	**Excellent**
Survival + 2 nights out	**£70 pw**
Part-time work campus/town	**Good/Excellent**

SPORT Good facilities for uni team sports, most are 3 miles from the city centre at the Education & Community base – gym, dance studios, sports halls, indoor swimming pool, pitches, all-weather athletics track – and at the St Nicholas Centre by the cathedral – sports hall, gym, weight training room. JMU's proudest boast is its Base Fitness Centre, well equipped and professionally staffed. There's a student sports pass for free/reduced price access to facilities – badminton courts, swimming pools, squash courts, athletics tracks.

TOWN See *Liverpool Student City*, page 278.

PILLOW TALK

'Pretty much all university halls and JMU residences are fine except Crete and Candia Towers, which should be avoided at all costs,' said a student. 'You have been warned.'

All freshers are now guaranteed university owned or private specialist student accommodation - modern halls of residence (shared flats).

GETTING THERE

- By road: M62, M6/J21a. Well served by coach.
- By rail: Manchester, 40 mins; Sheffield, 1:45; Leeds, Birmingham, 2:00; London King's Cross, 3:00.
- Liverpool airports for inland/Ireland flights.
- By coach: London, 5:00; Manchester, 50 mins.

STUDENT LONDON - THE CITY

London is an expensive place to live. Everything from shopping to travel can bite huge chunks out of your student loan. Sometimes it can feel like the only thing you've achieved during your course is a hefty debt. That is unless you learn to flash your student card at every opportunity. Although you may face ridicule for being a 'bake bean loving, beer-swilling creature of the night', you will be the envy of every non-student when you get offered a rather nice discount just about everywhere you go.

With a population of over seven million, London is one of the most diverse cities in the world - 30% of residents were born outside England. Greater London not only covers a lot of multicultural ground, but also physical, as it spans 1584 square kilometres. That space is filled with so many interests and attractions that you could not visit them all in one lifetime; London plays host to more than 200 carnivals and festivals annually. With its mixture of historical landmarks and modern masterpieces, London is a great place to learn, and not just in the lecture theatre.

THEATRE

On an average day in London you will be able to watch one of 76 plays, 33 musicals, 19 operas or 16 dance performances. If you were to go to one a day starting on the first of January, you wouldn't be finished until the end of May. The West End is one of the UK's biggest attractions: the choice of plays and shows is superb, but you often end up paying more up there. **The National Theatre** (Southbank, Embankment tube, +44 (0)20 7452 3000) and **The Globe Theatre** (21 New Globe Walk, Mansion House tube, +44 (0)20 7902 1400) are two of the most popular repertory companies. Playing less commercial performances, they often have the best offerings. The NT is subsidised. Otherwise there are countless fringe theatres showing allsorts for allsorts.

TKTS is the place to go for theatre on a budget. As the only official half price and discounted theatre ticket operation in London, they offer tickets on the day of the performance only, and have no phone number, so you have to visit. They are based in both Leicester Square and Canary Wharf DLR Station. Many theatres offer student tickets with proof of ID, otherwise it can be worth waiting at the venue box office for returns or standby tickets before the performance.

DANCE

Whether you're up for a class or just sitting back and watching somebody else shake their thang, London is a great place for dance.

The Barbican Centre (Silk Street, +44 (0)20 7638 4141, Barbican tube) is Europe's largest arts venue and a key member of the dance scene, especially the unconventional. Students get half price tickets in advance for all Wednesday evenings. **The London Coliseum** (St Martin's Lane, +44 (0)20 7836 0111, Leicester Square tube) is home to the English National Opera and is the London base of the English National Ballet. Standby tickets are available to students. There are many more major venues including **The Place**, Riverside Studios, Royal Opera House and Sadler's Wells.

To get involved yourself, there are classes of many different styles held in many venues. **Dance Attic** (Old Fulham Baths, 368 North End Road, +44 (0)20 7610 2055, Fulham Broadway tube) costs £50 a year for students to join, you then just pay per class. **Pineapple Dance Studios** (7 Langley Street, +44 (0)20 7836 4004, Covent Garden Tube) costs £70 a year, that's half price for students. For full Dance listings visit www.londondance.com.

COMEDY

A comedy club is a great choice for an evening out in London. There are dozens of great venues scattered around, but here are a few of the more student friendly offerings.

Backyard Comedy Club, 231 Cambridge Heath Road, +44 (0)20 7739 3122, Bethnal Green tube. This converted factory is now a club owned by comedian Lee Hurst, who quite often acts as host. There is also a restaurant and disco after the show for anyone wanting a full night out.

Chuckle Club, London School of Economics, Houghton Street, +44 (0)20 7476 1672, Holborn tube. For less than a tenner you can see a host of comedians, including household names. Being a student union bar the drinks are all fairly cheap.

The Cosmic Comedy Club, 177 Fulham Palace Road, Hammersmith tube. This club is free to get in. You just have to pay what you think it was worth afterwards. Also, every week the BBC makes comedy programmes for radio. It's free, so anyone can go along. Call BBC Radio Theatre +44 (0)20 8576 1227.

CLUBS AND VENUES

London has around 15% of all the clubs in Britain. That means that you are never lost for a place to go for a spot of late night drinking. The biggest clubbing nights are still Friday and Saturday, but any day is a good day. Some of the bigger names include **Fabric**, **Ministry of Sound** and **The Cross**, but there are hundreds of other venues catering for every taste. www.londonnet.co.uk has a great clubs section where you can select which day of the week you want to go out, or which style of music, and see complete listings. For free entrance into 25 London nightclubs, including **Café de Paris** and **Elysium**, become a Circle Club member, for just a £5 admin fee. It gives you free admission during the week and half price at weekends, and you can also purchase 2-4-1 drinks vouchers in advance. Visit www.circleclubcard.com for full details.

CINEMA

London has almost 500 cinema screens and a choice of over 100 films showing at any time. Leicester Square is the centre for cinema in London. Every year it hosts numerous star-studded premieres on the many huge screens. But it isn't particularly student friendly with rather expensive ticket prices, making London's independent cinemas the better option. The **Prince Charles Cinema** (7 Leicester Place, Leicester Square tube) is one such place. *Feel-good Fridays* cost just £1 and the most non-members have to pay for a regular performance is £4. Annual Membership is just £7.50. For a search that allows you to find a cinema by a particular postcode, tube location or where a certain film is showing visit www.viewlondon.co.uk. Alternatively most of the chain cinemas in Greater London offer student prices. **UGC** offers an unlimited monthly card for £13.99. Orange mobile customers can text FILM to 241 on Wednesdays and receive a code allowing them two tickets for the price of one.

ART

In London there are around 50 exhibitions open to the public each day. 17 national museums and galleries, as well as many other smaller, local galleries, allow free entrance. These include the **British Museum**, **National Gallery**, **Tate Modern** and **V&A Museum**. London exhibits countless works or all kinds, both permanent and temporary collections. For a list of all the contemporary exhibitions London has to offer at any time, visit www.newexhibitions.com. For more details about all the major London galleries go to www.londontourist.org/art.

MUSIC

There are 9 major concert halls in London – **Barbican** (where they often hold free events), **Purcell Room**, **Royal Albert Hall**, **Royal Festival Hall**, **Royal Opera House**, **Queen Elizabeth Hall**, **St John's Smith Square**, **Wembley Arena** and **Wigmore Hall** - as well as 47 major rock and pop venues, including **Astoria**, **Barfly**, **Brixton Academy**, **Forum and Garage**. From ultra-trendy to cheesy and trashy, international superstars to local legends, you will find whatever type of music you are after in London, and all of your favourite musicians will have played here, or will play here at some time. www.bbc.co.uk/music/whatson has regularly updated information covering all kinds of music. For the cheapest tickets go direct to the venue box office and avoid those booking fees, but for the best tickets visit www.gigsandtours.com or www.ticketmaster.co.uk

SHOPPING

London has over 40,000 shops and around 80 markets making it one of the world's best places to buy. Whether you want to seriously damage your loan in a designer boutique or pay as little as possible for living essentials, London has it all. **Camden** is a great place to shop. The cheap goods and cosmopolitan atmosphere make it a unique experience. You can find just about anything there and can easily spend a day wandering the many shops and stalls. The market is open seven days a week and the nearest tube station is Camden Town. Covent Garden market offers more specialist goods with many arts and crafts. This historic setting is full of street entertainers and is easily accessed from a number of tube stations including Covent Garden and Leicester Square. **Portobello Road**, in the trendy Notting Hill area and accessed through Notting Hill Gate tube, is also worth a mention (open on Saturdays). **Oxford Street** is a great place to shop with many highstreet and department stores, the biggest of which is **Selfridges** with 40 retail departments and over half a million square foot of space. www.streetsensation.co.uk has photographs and maps of Oxford Street as well as many other major shopping areas including Knightsbridge (home to **Harrods**) and Regents Street (where you'll find toyshop **Hamley's**). Most of the High Street stores offer a student discount, just remember, always flash your student ID, and don't be afraid to ask.

Paul Stephen

LONDON METROPOLITAN UNIVERSITY

London Metropolitan University
31 Jewry Street
London EC3N 2EY

TEL 020 753 3355
020 7753 3355 (Campus North)
EMAIL admissions@londonmet.ac.uk
WEB www.londonmet.ac.uk

London Metropolitan Students' Union
2 Goulston Street
London E1 7TP

TEL 020 7320 2233
FAX 020 7320 2244
EMAIL su@londonmet.ac.uk
WEB www.londonmetsu.org.uk

VAG VIEW

North London and London Guildhall unis have become one. 'The new university is one of the biggest in the UK,' writes John Shaw, who was on the future strategy task group. 'With 13 main sites, grouped into two campuses (London North and London City),' it was Mr Shaw's job to identify the 2 unis' very different histories and cultures and direct the way forward.

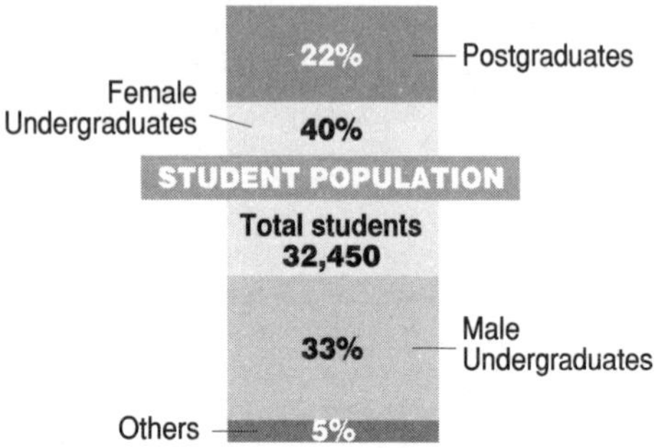

CAMPUS SCENE

City Campus It is an unusual set-up for a uni, with its sites strewn around London's Square Mile financial district – 8 sites: Calcutta and Central Houses, Jewry Street, Moorgate, Goulston Street, Whitechapel, Tower Hill and Commercial Road.

The East End is a racially diverse area with, in particular, a thriving Bangladeshi community giving the cultural flavour to the eating and shopping delights of Brick Lane.

The campus's main Moorgate site is built on what used to be one of the most (in)famous insane asylums in England. The Bethlem Royal Hospital (originally based at nearby Liverpool Street Station) moved to the site in the late 1670s.

Campus North comprises a collection of sites around the Holloway Road. Writes Maureen Okolo: 'We is in the right place for a great, big, delicious slice of London's night life. Step outside and find yourself in the infamous Holloway Road. Packed with takeaways, cafés, restaurants and shops. Totally student friendly in prices. At one end [south] is Highbury and Islington; at the other, Archway (very long road, this, but with day and night bus routes galore, tube and train stations close to uni and halls, you'll be able to get around)...'

Campus North doesn't just preach wider access to higher education, it ensures it. It is as far away from the punts and gowns of Oxbridge as you can get. It is a people's university, as much a part of the local scene as the Arsenal up the road. 'Uni life is great, if you like that sort of thing. You get everyone who's into everything,' promises Maureen. 'Just expect constant rounds of socialising with chic, retro, funky, cool, funny individuals from all walks of life.'

So there we have it. Chapel Market and Camden Lock meet Aldgate, Petticoat Lane and Spitalfields.

FEES, BURSARIES

UK & EU Fees: £3000. If in receipt of full HE Maintenance grant there's a bursary of £1000; if in receipt of partial grant, bursaries are on a sliding scale up to £975.

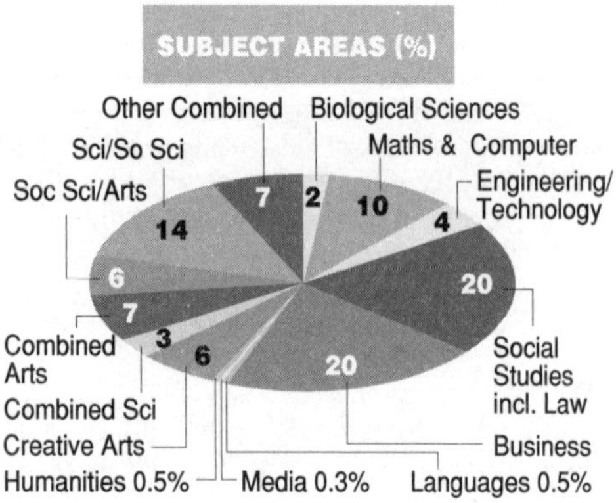

STUDENT PROFILE

A century and a half after London Guildhall started out by offering 'evening classes for young men',

UNIVERSITY/STUDENT PROFILE	
University since	**1992**
Situation/style	**Civic**
Student population	**32450**
Undergraduates	**23665**
- mature	**47%**
- non EU undergraduates	**12%**
- male/female	**46/54**
- non-traditional student intake	**43%, high**
- state schhol intake	**96%**
- drop-out rate	**15%, high**
- undergraduate applications	**Down 8%**

there is still a significant student population on part-time courses. The uni is one of the largest providers of part-time business courses in the country. It's this part-time population that boosts the mature student percentage, and you will in fact meet many youthful full-time undergrads, as well as many students studying subjects other than business.

Besides Barings broker and breaker, Nick Leeson, and multi-millionaire Mark Thatcher, the former Tory PM's son, both of whom did time at City, the mass of its students are very interesting. 'A high proportion originate from London and the surrounding Southeast, but the melting pot,' confides Stuart Harkness, 'is fuelled by those from farther afield, to the tune of 110 countries. The cosmopolitan flavour makes LGU a truly multi-cultural university. Multiple faiths are therefore evident and well catered for with prayer rooms at various university sites, a chaplaincy and numerous students' union-funded cultural societies, including Christian, Islamic, Muslim, Afro-Caribbean, to name but a few. All seem to respect each others' practices under the umbrella of LGU brotherhood.'

It is true. They have more international students than any other new university in the UK and they run their own offices in China, India, Pakistan and Bangladesh. They provide a three-day orientation course for international students each September. There is also a successful peer support scheme, involving language support, a buddy system and subject area support. But all that aside, what we have is a cultural recipe with flavour, which is also what we have at Campus North, whose undergraduate body is to a large extent drawn from the local, notably ethnic population.

SOCIAL SCENE

Students Union London Met's **Rocket** has a fascinating history, worth a book of its own. It has been around since the inception of the North London Poly itself. It began as the Great Hall when the first students arrived in 1896. Some of the concerts there were actually conducted by Proms inventor Sir Henry Wood. Since then it became a proscenium arch theatre, the arch picked up for a song from the old **Marlborough Theatre** down the road opposite the **Nag's Head**, after which it was used as a cinema, whose organ was played by William Lloyd Webber, father of millionaire musical maestro Andrew... And so the tale goes on. Today, the **Rocket Complex**, as it is known, is a meeting place of some style, cool enough for like-minded City students, used to their ground-floor **Sub Bar** in Goulston Street (where one of Jack the Ripper's victims was found) to get up and out, and go along. Certainly the **Rocket**'s entertainment list looks suitably enticing.

ACADEMIC EXCELLENCE	
TEACHING - CAMPUS NORTH: *(Rated Excellent or 17+ out of 24)*	
English	**Excellent**
Business/Management	**24**
Film Studies, Art & Design, Electric /Electron Eng, Philosophy	**22**
Modern Langs (Dutch, French, German, Iberian Studies), Education	**20**
Maths, Nursing, Other subjects Allied to Medicine	**21**
Materials Technology, Food Sciences, Psychology	**19**
Library/Info, Biosciences,	**18**
TEACHING - CITY CAMPUS: *(Rated Excellent or 17+ out of 24)*	
Social Policy & Admin	**Excellent**
Art & Design, Economics	**23**
Business/Management, Politics, Psychology	**22**
Materials Technology	**20**
Modern Languages (French, German, Spanish)	**19**
Maths	**18**

However, and this may need to be addressed, neither this nor the facilities at City campus are run by the Student Union; they are run by the university. The union has no venues of its own.

'The award-winning venue the **Rocket Complex** comprises a nightclub, live music venue (with the latest turbo sound floodlight system), 2 licensed bars, external courtyard, pool and games room, coffee bar and shop,' chirps a union wallah only barely hiding his true revolutionary mission from our star-struck eyes. 'The weekly events programme includes *The Big Fish* ("the best student night in London" - *Time Out*), *Pint Sized Comedy Club* and regular events showcasing music and culture from around the globe. Recent headliners... Trevor Nelson, Jools Holland, Punjabi Hit Squad, Asian Dub Foundation, Kele le Roc, Ms Dynamite, Artful Dodger, Timmi Magic, DJ Hanif, DJ Luck + MC Neat, Jah Shaka, Latina Max + London's largest Brazilian Carnival.'

Sounds even more enterprising than the ents down in City campus's **Sub Bar** – *Cheese and Teese*, *Funk da House* and *Silver Tonic*, and the latest pool and games machines in the bar. Student night specials include *S*M*A*S*H*E*D*, *Funkin' Fridays*, *Time of the Month*, and recent headliners... Kele le Roc, Terri Walker, DJ Fidgit (Missy Elliott UK Tour DJ), DJ X Ray.

There's a student mag: *Independent Student Metro*, and a radio station is scheduled for this year, Ear Fm. There are internal media and arts awards aplenty and excellent departments in these areas. There is also political activity (and a tradition of that). This term there was a campaign about the enforced closure of the Islamic Students Library. Apparently Islamic Soc is the most active society.

SPORT The sports teams do very well (21st nationally!) on account of the excellence of the sports department, and good players are given scholarships.

Sports facilities are shared with Arsenal FC and Essex CC. The new Arsenal stadium is right behind one of the university buildings. Pitches, courts, sports halls, all the usual requirements are to a high standard.

WHAT IT'S REALLY LIKE	
UNIVERSITY:	
Social Life	★★★★
Campus scene	**Mature, local, urban, easy going**
Student Union services	**Average**
Politics	**Internal**
Sport	**Very competitive**
National team position	**21st**
Sport facilities	**Professional**
Arts	**Available**
Student magazine	**Independent Student Metro**
Student radio	**Ear Fm**
Nightclub venues/bars	**Sub Bar, Sub Club (Aldgate), Rocket (Holloway Road)**
Union ents	**Big Fish (Rocket), Time of the Month (Sub)**
Union societies	**44**
Most active	**Islamic Soc**
Parking	**Non-existent**
CITY:	
Entertainment	★★★★★
Scene	**Wild, expensive**
Town/gown relations	**Average-good**
Risk of violence	**'Average'**
Cost of living	**Very high**
Student concessions	**Locally adequate**
Survival + 2 nights out	**£100 pw**
Part-time work campus/town	**Good/excellent**

ACADEMIA & JOBS

Around a third of Campus North students graduate in business subjects (they scored full marks at the teaching assessments for Business Management), and there is a dominant but well thought-out joint degree series, which accounts for just less than a quarter of graduates and explores, amongst much else, particular possibilities in employment for business-minded students. Down at City around a third of students graduate in a very similar joint vocational degree system and more than a quarter graduate in business subjects. From both campuses, many go into retail.

Some joint courses require travel to both campuses – Economics & International Business and International Relations and Peace & Conflict Studies among them. Check out where you'll be.

Meanwhile, aspiring accountants should consider the flagship Accounting & Finance (City and North), which leads to complete exemptions from professional examination, but also the joint degree extrapolations of that – such as Accounting & Business Economics (City and North), Accounting & International Business or Accounting & Banking (North), Accounting & Investment (City) – and most important Professional Accounting (City), a degree that incorporates examinations of the Institute of Chartered Accountants of England and Wales.

Another strength is in computing, with such as Computer Science, Computer Visualisation & Games, and Computer Animation. There is also a mass of Music Management and Technology/Audio Systems/ Audio Electronics, a retail management dimension, and a niche area in radio and TV broadcasting, City campus popping up in the Top 10 nationally for employment in this.

Then we have another important area – health, with degrees such as Herbal Herbal Medicine Science alongside Pharmaceutical Science and Pharmacology, and Biomedical Sciences, a programme that scores particularly strongly in the employment table. There is also a notable lean at North towards the therapeutic care side, with degrees in Social Work and BSc Psychology (Applied) & Health Studies.

Still on the professional front, look to either campus for LlB Law. While City are commercial & busi-

AT A GLANCE

ACADEMIC FILE:	
Subjects assessed	**44**
Excellent	**61%**
Typical entry requirements	**250 points**
Application acceptance rate	**14%**
Students-staff ratio	**21:1**
First/2:1 degree pass rate	**n/a**
ACCOMMODATION FILE:	
Guarantee to freshers	**OK if from 25 miles away**
Style	**Halls, flats**
Catered	**16%**
En suite	**None**
Approx price range pw	**£80-£100**
City rent pw	**£75-£85 Zone 2**

ness law specialists, North have LlB (Social Justice).

Another string to North's bow is sport – BSc Sports Nutrition, Psychology & Performance, Science, Science & Coaching, Therapy, as well as Management and Technology modules in the joint course series.

Another defining niche at City, for which they scored a near perfect score at the assessments, is Fine Art, Design, and Silversmithing, Jewellery & Allied Crafts), appropriate to the traditional strength of this area of London in the art and craft movement. Writes Sam Hall: 'The university is gaining a reputation for artistic excellence, with well-respected jewellery-making and furniture departments, and many student-led initiatives leading to national awards.'

Jewellery design/making may be a small, specialist field, but City hits the spot employment-wise. The Art Foundation course is the required entry point for the BA Hons Silversmithing, Jewellery & Allied Crafts.

Furniture design and manufacture is another area of supreme confidence here. There's the 3D Design (Furniture & Product), but also a huge number of combinations with Textile Furnishing Design – elements as diverse as Art & Design History, Computer-Aided Design, European Studies, etc. There are also Design & Realisation and Restoration HND routes.

North's response in this area is the BA Interior Architecture & Design, and a very sound employment record in architectural consultancy and construction with BA Architecture.

PILLOW TALK

Students have access to over 1300 rooms in halls, each situated close to either the London City or London North campuses. Accommodation is guaranteed for all first years who live more than 25 miles away and who accept a conditional or unconditional offer of a course and return their halls application by the 8th August. For more detail go via the web address or email accommodation@londonmet.ac.uk

GETTING THERE

☛ By Underground to City Campus: Aldgate (Metropolitan and Circle lines), Aldgate East (District and Hammersmith & City).

☛ By Underground to Campus North: Holloway Road (Piccadilly Line).

LONDON SCHOOL OF ECONOMICS & POLITICAL SCIENCE

The London School of Economics
& Political Science
Houghton Street
London WC2A 2AE

TEL 020 7955 6613
FAX 020 7955 7421
Email stu.rec@lse.ac.uk
WEB www.lse.ac.uk
LSE Students' Union
East Building
Houghton Street
London WC2A 2AE

TEL 020 7955 7158
FAX 020 7955 6789
EMAIL su.gensec@lse.ac.uk
WEB www.lse.ac.uk/union

VAG VIEW

LSE is part of the federal University of London. It is famous the world over for research. It may have been pipped into fourth place after Oxbridge and Imperial in the research assessments, but by any standards that is good, particularly when you consider that the proportion of staff selected for assessment was higher than at any other establishment. Teaching inspection results have been high, and the LSE is as secure as the British

Establishment, with which, despite the school's history of '60s student revolt – Mick Jagger, Grosvenor Square and the Vietnam War and all – it is, indeed, synonymous.

LSE goes hand in hand with Westminster, with Whitehall, with the City and with the legal and the media sub-strata too. In fact, its geographical position ensures it closer contact with all departments of the Establishment than either Oxford or Cambridge, and its specialist areas – Economics, International Relations, Government, Law, Finance – are what you might call the active ingredients of life in the Establishment. That is why many of its academic gurus are recognisable faces or bylines in the media. If analysis is required, it's the LSE they call up.

It is difficult to see what better finishing school you could find than that. Concludes our student mole: 'The LSE is no Utopia, but it is definitely one-up with its individual culture, school of thought, and world of opportunities.'

CAMPUS

'The LSE is the filling in a sandwich,' writes Dominique Fyfe, a student from America. 'On one side (the capital's financial and legal district) the air is serious and the suits Armani, and the *FT*-reading societal stress-set is on the go until long after the sun is down. On the other, west of Kingsway (the dividing line, a road where all those who cannot drive test their inabilities), lie the expensive, funky, multi-purpose Covent Garden and London's theatreland and Soho, haven for sex addicts and non-traditionalists, and the book lovers' paradise of Charing Cross Road.'

In translation, LSE is situated between Kingsway and the Strand, at the heart of London culture and the legal establishment, and not far from the City or Westminster either. It is a campus crowded with buildings, the so-called Old Building being on the site of the small hall, where it all began and from which it has steadily expanded into buildings close by – the East Building, Clare Market, St Clement, St Philips, Clement House, all built on land which is among the most expensive per square foot in the world.

UNIVERSITY/SCHOOL PROFILE

School of London Uni since	**1900**
Situation/style	**City campus**
Student population	**8570**
Undergraduates	**3810**
- mature	**7%**
- non EU undergraduates	**37%, high**
- male/female	**53/47**
- non-traditional student intake	**17%**
- state school intake	**64%, v. low**
- drop-out rate	**6%**
- undergraduate applications	**Constant**

FEES, BURSARIES

UK & EU Fees: £3000. If in receipt of full HE Maintenance grant, there's a bursary of £2500; if in receipt of partial grant, there are bursaries up to £1700.

STUDENT PROFILE

They come from all over the world, about a quarter from North America, over a third from Europe, another quarter from Asia... This is the cream of students anxious to acquire the LSE cachet, and there is a snobbery attached Last year it took fewer from the state sector in the UK than all but Oxbridge, Imperial and University College London.

'Interesting conversation is one thing you will not find a lack of at the LSE,' writes Dominique. 'The students here think critically in the classroom

SUBJECT AREAS (%)

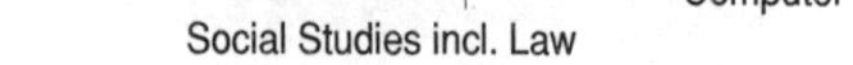

but also have a point of view in friendly discussion outside. Many are highly driven, always ready for an intellectual challenge and very competitive. However, not all are so intense; some don't even find the library until summer exams!

'Naturally, most of the students you will meet here are reading for a degree in Economics, but what makes the school a fascinating place is that there are so many studying other subjects, like anthropology, finance, social psychology and philosophy, and you learn from everybody.

'The LSE is a breeding ground for global nomads. In between lectures, the Houghton Street hub of LSE activity overflows with student representatives of all races of our world. Languages you will begin to learn in this global microcosm are Indian, French, Italian, Spanish, Russian, German,

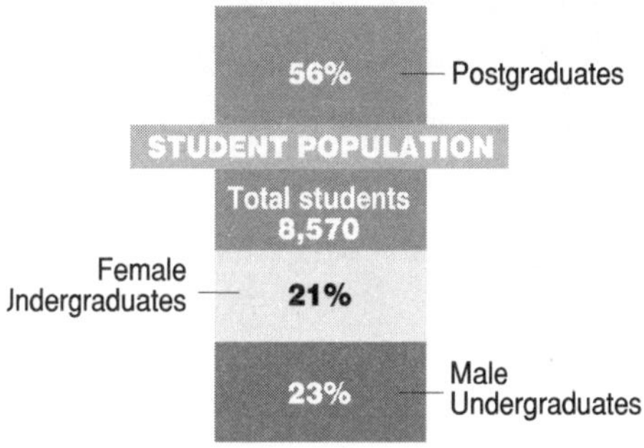

not to mention English of course. Not only do these students of all cultures bring their traditions but they also bring the trendy, money-sucking, modern fashions, but don't worry if your wardrobe didn't appear in the latest issue of *Cosmo* or *GQ*; nobody really cares whether its Oxfam or Armani.'

ACADEMIA & JOBS

Writes Dominique, 'Lectures and classes are well enough taught. In fact I find myself wanting to go to them – a truly novel experience for me! Don't be surprised if the reading list for a class is more like a library's inventory record! The lectures are monologues, but the classes are interactive and "cosy" in size (maximum fifteen students). Essays are written for classes but not always formally assessed or given a definitive deadline, which can make procrastination seem dangerously attractive.'

The LSE library, the British Library of Political and Economic Science, contains one million volumes, 28,000 journals (10,000 on current sub.), numerous specialist manuscripts – all totalling some three million items. Founded in 1896, it recently enjoyed a multi-million pound overhaul by architects Foster and Partners. Even so, it is not immune to student criticism: 'LSE's library is overwhelming and quite frankly I would not go there if I didn't have to. The process is as follows: when you reach the library half of the books you are looking for are not there and if they are, there is only one copy of the main text for about twenty to forty-plus students and are titled as set texts, which means that they can only be borrowed for twenty-four hours. Return it twenty-four hours too late and the librarians grow the devil's tail and horns and collect a large amount of your own precious money! If that seems a tough sentence, it is and is meant to be.'

Graduates of LSE make their careers in investment advice and analysis, in accountancy, as economists and business analysts, management consultants and merchant bankers, as computer/IT consultants and secondary school teachers, as actuaries, stockbrokers and sharedealers. A few recalcitrants – about 1% – become social workers.

Many of the accountants get there via the Accountancy & Finance degree in a department which has been teaching the subject since 1896. It is one of only two provisions nationally that received a top Grade 6* in the research inspection exercise (the other is Manchester). Some 30% of LSE accountants arrive via the economics route – BSc Economics or with Economic History or Econometrics & Mathematical Economics (there's a host of other possible combos).

More than a quarter of graduates go into banking. Some 50% choose Economics, which dropped only one point at the teaching assessment and has

ACADEMIC EXCELLENCE

TEACHING:	
(Rated Excellent or 17+ out of 24)	
History, Anthropology, Applied Social Work, Business, Law, Social Policy & Admin.	**Excellent**
Industrial Relations	**24**
Psychology, Economics	**23**
Politics, Philosophy, Maths, Media	**22**
Sociology	**20**
RESEARCH:	
*Top grades 5/6**	
Economics, Law, Anthropology, Social Policy, Accounting, International History, Philosophy	**Grade 6***
Politics, Sociology, Geography, Management, Economic History	**Grade 5**

WHERE LSE GRADUATES END UP

Health & Social Work: 5%; Education: 5%; Wholesale Retail: 5%; Manufacturing: 2%; Financial Activities: 32%; Public Administration, Civil Service & Defence: 7%; Hotel/Restaurant: 2%; Transport & Communications (including Telecommunications): 2.5%; Personnel: 3%; Computer: 2%; Business & Management: 5%; Accountancy: 18%; Media (including Film): 2%; Legal 2%; Publishing: 1%; Advertising: 1%; Sport: 1%.

Approximate 'graduate track' employed **78%**

a world-class Grade 6* research rating. Thirty per cent opt for the Business route, Management, Management Sciences, etc. These degrees produce many business management consultants as well - see in particular Human Resources Management & Employment. Teaching inspection: Economics 23, Business 24. Research Grade 6*: Economics. Grade 5: Management.

More than 3% of graduates end up in merchant banking via business degrees such as Business Mathematics & Statistics, and via economics and maths - see Business Mathematics & Statistics, Econometrics & Mathematical Economics, Mathematics & Economics. Maths scored 22 out of 24 points at assessment.

Then there is the core of graduates who become investment advisers and analysts. More than 16% choose this sector; it is in fact the single most popular LSE graduate occupation, many choosing from the range of economics degrees, about a third preferring the business route.

Sharedealers come via business, stockbrokers via economics. There is no dedicated degree for computer/IT consultants, who come via business and social studies, mainly the latter.

A dedicated Actuarial Science degree finds some 2% of LSE graduates jobs with insurance companies, their function of course to calculate risk.

Law is rated world-class Grade 6*, and there is a specialist French Law degree. There is no social work degree as such. Besides Sociology, they offer Social Policy and four combinations - with Economics, Sociology, Government, and Criminal Justice & Psychology. Ther's also an interesting BA Anthropology & Law.

A language Centre specialises in creating courses targeted to the particular needs of students and offers EAP, French, German, Italian, Japanese, Russian, Spanish, Arabic, Chinese, Portuguese, Norwegian, Basque, Turkish.

WHAT IT'S REALLY LIKE

UNIVERSITY:	
Social Life	★★★★★
Campus scene	**Small: driven, global nomads**
Student Union services	**Good**
Politics	**Active: weekly debates, local, national & internat. issues**
Sport	**30+ clubs**
National team position	**51st**
Sport facilities	**Average**
Arts opportunities	**Limited**
Student magazine	**The Script**
Student newspaper	**The Beaver**
Student radio	**PuLSEfm**
Student TV	**LSETV**
Venue/bars	**Three Tuns, Underground Bar, Quad bars**
Union ents	**CRUSH, Comedy, live events**
Union societies	**150+**
Parking	**Non-existent**
CITY:	
Entertainment	★★★★★
Scene	**Wild, expensive**
Town/gown relations	**Average-good**
Risk of violence	**'Average'**
Cost of living	**Very high**
Student concessions	**Good**
Survival + 2 nights out	**£100 pw**
Part-time work campus/town	**Excellent**

SOCIAL SCENE

STUDENTS' UNION The Three Tuns, **Underground Bar**, **Quad** and shop are all newly refurbished. 'Many students drift in the direction of the pub, **The Three Tuns**,' says Dominque, 'which has a "cool" atmosphere. The drinks are cheap, the company is friendly and the music plays at a level that doesn't reach eardrum-damaging decibels.

The LSE is a breeding ground for global nomads. The Houghton Street hub of LSE activity overflows with student representatives of all races of our world.

'The Students Union offers a wide range of societies at the Freshers' Fair! The Socialism Society and other political groups will attack in a desperate attempt to sway you, but other societies adopt a less obtrusive approach. There are plenty of opportunities to get involved, be it through the arts, politics, radio, religion (most religions and denominations are observed), business, or cultural groups. Sports teams exist, but I can give you little information about them, as I am motivationally challenged as regards any kind of physical activity.'

LSE claims the only weekly Students Union General Meeting in the country. More than 200 students regularly attend to hold union officers to acount and to debate campus level, national and international issues. 'Those who get involved in the SU are usually left-wing,' says one who does; 'those who focus on careers are right-wing. Occasionally there are clashes.'

Excellent media: magazine *Script*, newspaper *Beaver*, radio station PuLSE FM, and TV LooSE TV.

LSE also has its own dedicated ents manager and the Friday night clubnight, *Crush*, is one of the most popular student nights in London every Friday. TOther regular ents are *Mind the Gap*, and for LGBT students - gays - there;s a gay salsa night, *Exilo*; *Afta Skool* (indie) is a Saturday clubnight at **Quad**. They can get 1000 bodies in to the 3-room club, made up of the **Tuns**, the **Quad**, with its sofa-strewn mezzanine, and the smaller venue, the **Underground**. There are also students nights at selected sites in London's clubland.

Town Top tip from Dominique: 'On arrival in London, buy the *London A-Z* (to avoid looking like a tourist only whip it out in times of emergency) and the student's bible, *Time Out*, essential to anybody's social survival kit. Manage limited finances by drinking your fill at the cheapest union bar before a night out.'

Sport In the basement of the Old Building there's a training room and multigym. The school also has its own sports grounds in South London. There are also netball, tennis courts and four large swimming pools within two miles of Houghton Street. The University of London Union has facilities for squash, basketball, rowing and swimming. LSE cricketers may use the indoor facilities at Lords. LSE sports teams came 89th nationally last year in the national team league.

PILLOW TALK

All first year students are guaranteed a place in LSE or London University accommodation – basically halls and one block of self-catering flats. 'Residence halls are cheap and easy,' writes Dominique, 'but in my opinion the London University intercollegiate option is preferable. You will find the quality of food to be not much better than that of pig slop, but living next door to two vets, across the hall from a nurse, next door to a musician, down the hall from an opera singer, and one floor above a physiotherapist could only happen in an intercollegiate hall (see *Introduction*). This option definitely widens your social circle. Rooms are basic with a small single bed (not much room for two if you have big plans), a desk and a wardrobe. Your room is your home and you make it your own.'

AT A GLANCE

ACADEMIC FILE:	
Subjects assessed	**15**
Excellent	**93%**
Typical entry requirements	**445 points**
Application acceptance rate	**9%, low**
Students-staff ratio	**13:1**
First/2:1 degree pass rate	**75%, high**
ACCOMMODATION FILE:	
Guarantee to freshers	**100%**
Style	**Halls**
Catered	**45%**
En-suite	**Some**
Price range pw	**£65-£90**
City rent pw	**£100-£180 Zone 1; £75-£85 Zone 2**

GETTING THERE

☛ Holborn (Piccadilly, Central lines), Temple (District, Circle lines), Charing Cross (Jubilee, Northern, Bakerloo lines).

LONDON SOUTH BANK UNIVERSITY

London South Bank University
103 Borough Road
London SE1 0AA

TEL 020 7815 7815
FAX 020 7815 8273
EMAIL (go via website)
WEB www.lsbu.ac.uk

London South Bank Students' Union
Keyworth Street
London SE1 6NG

TEL 020 7815 6060
FAX 020 7815 6061
EMAIL vpcomms@lsbu.ac.uk
WEB www.lsbu.org

VAG VIEW

London South Bank projects you into the big city, where the streets are paved with whatever you want them to be paved with. You come to South Bank University, you come to London... for a bit of gritty realism.

CAMPUS

Much of it is clustered around a triangle formed by Borough Road, London Road and Southwark Bridge

Road, just south of the Thames at Elephant and Castle. The learning resources (including a library) and the students union is on nearby Keyworth Street, where last year the brand new 9-storey Keyworth Centre opened. There are yet two other sites further away – the Faculty of Health & Social Care at Harold Wood Hospital (Romford) and Whipps Cross Hospital (Leytonstone) – a situation rather optimistically 'solved' by calling these two distinct sites the Redwood Campus.

'Don't come to South Bank if you are expecting a campus lifestyle, come to South Bank if you want the excitement of studying in London. Location – prime,' reports Lola Brown. 'Situated in Zones 1/2, the main campus of LSB is ideally located on the uber trendy South Bank, in walking distance of London Bridge and Waterloo stations. Elephant & Castle itself is a bit of a hole but is improving rapidly with some major urban regeneration happening. It has its own tube station (Bakerloo & Northern lines), a new bowling alley and a Tesco Metro.

'South Bank is good for gritty realism. Many of the university buildings are quite grim and old, the Students' Union is situated next to the DHSS, there are plenty of colourful local characters shouting at students, and there are no real open spaces unless you are based at Redwood Campus (some Faculty of Health courses), which is in the middle of nowhere and can feel isolated.'

FEES, BURSARIES

UK & EU Fees: £3000. If in receipt of full HE Maintenance grant there's a bursary of £300.

STUDENT PROFILE

70% undergrads are mature, the majority come from the locality, which includes a colourful tapestry of ethnicity; 97% come from the state sector, 41% from new-to-uni social groups. A very large section (16%) drop out before finishing their degree.

UNIVERSITY/STUDENT PROFILE

University since	**1992**
Situation/style	**City sites**
Student population	**18000**
Full-time undergraduates	**13500**
- mature	**70%, v. high**
- non EU undergraduates	**35%**
- male/female	**42/58**
- state sector intake	**97%**
- non-traditional student intake	**41%**
- drop-out rate	**16%, v. high**
- undergraduate applications	**Up 8%**

'A real cross section,' says Lola. 'South Bank has many mature students and a diverse ethnic mix. Freshers here are not generally middle-class white kids, though there are a fair few of those too.

'We have several famous students, high numbers of sporting achievers (including members of the British Commonwealth Team) and of course Louise Woodward – but you probably won't see her, as she never hits the union for a night out.'

ACADEMIA & JOBS

Interestingly (see *At A Glance* box), despite the high acceptance rate of applicants and the low points requirements, they have a decent First/2:1 degree pass rate (52%).

The portfolio of degrees is markedly vocational. There's a feel of Salford Uni about it – the health – nursing (child, adult, mental care), the nutrition, occupational health & safety, sociology, engineering, media, computing, business, sport, built environment – South Bank is No 5 and Salford is at No 6 nationally in our Employment Top 10 for the construction industry. Again, as at Salford, many undergraduates are on sandwich courses. There's a taste of the workplace about much on offer, though the course list is not as well developed as Salford's: there's not such a priority language pro-vision, for

SUBJECT AREAS (%)

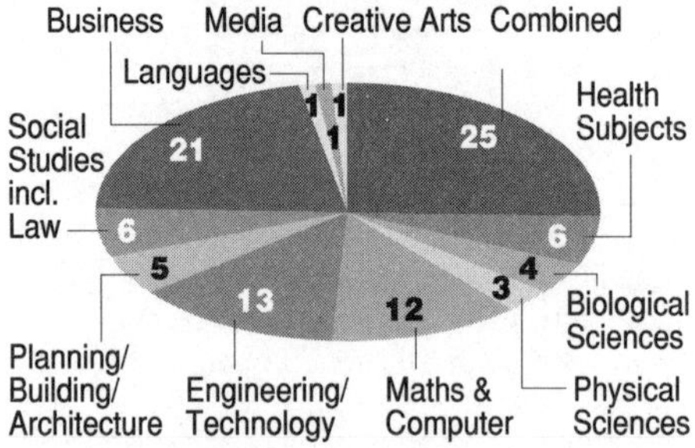

example – Salford's is first class and all-pervasive – and the media is more general and bland. There are some good BA/BSc combinations of the subjects that are on offer, and our advice is to pick subjects where skills content is high.

Besides Built Environment, faculties include Business & Management (by far the largest), Engineering, Computing, Design & Technology, Science, Humanities & Social Science and Health & Social Care. The course programme is modular in structure. There are decent learning resources, a centre has 400 Pentium PCs with Internet facility and allows access to a CD-ROM network. In addition, there are four libraries, one at each of the four sites, with a total of 300,000 books. The teaching

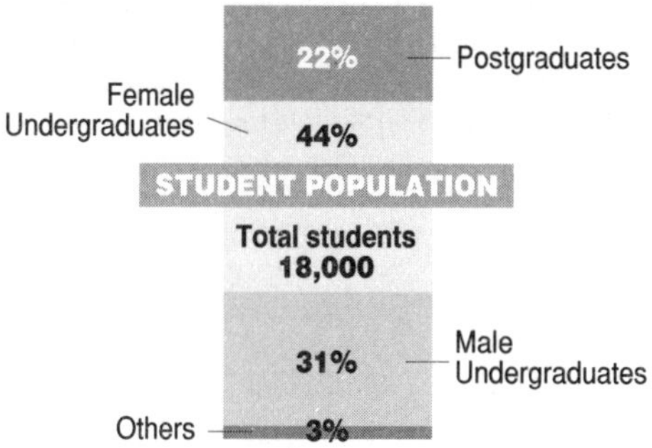

picture is very good., while asking grades are low.

Health steals the scene career-wise - 17% of LSB graduates go for it. Hospital staff nurses, non-hospital nurses, medical radiographers, medical practitioners dominate the employment figures. Look at BSc Nursing (Adult Health, Mental Health, Learning Difficulties, Child Care), various psychology BSc degrees, including Psychology with Sexuality.

There are, however, far more business graduates emanating from LSB each year, and a less than certain employment pathway. A large number enter employment as general administrators, sales assistants, and accounts and wages clerks. Accountancy, market research, personnel and travel/tour agency business are probably the brightest opportunity areas. Look at Accounting & Finance and the BA/BSC combined hons programme (another seven degrees there). Similarly there's Tourism & Hospitality Management and various Human Resources or Tourism tie-ups (perhaps the best with Marketing) in the list of combined BA/BSc degrees. Marketing comes with Tourism, Sociology, Social Policy, but not Psychology, which is a pity. There's also Management & Marketing. 20 points at assessment. Average entry requirements 160 points.

For aspiring property developers the fount is BSc Building Surveying & Property, Commercial Management (Quantity Surveying) and similar. There's a traditional focus on Built Environment, Planning and Property Management here. Look also at Architectural Engineering, also Technology, Building Services Eng, Commercial Management (Quantity Surveying), Construction Management, etc. Teaching Inspection 18-22.

A smattering of computer graduates find employment as IT consultants, computer engineers, software engineers and computer programmers, and it's a useful line into the civil service and local government.

Law. Recently a Reporting Assessor for the LPC Board (a Legal Practice Course is essential to becoming a solicitor) rated them as *Good* on a scale of Excellent, Very Good, Good, Satisfactory or Unsatisfactory.

Finally, there are the sports courses - Sport & Exercise Science and Sports Product Design. It is very likely that this will be an expanding area, considering the incredible success the uni Athletic Union has enjoyed this year. See *Sport*, below.

SOCIAL LIFE

'It's London, innit,' exclaims Lola. 'Anything, anytime, whatever you like to do. The South Bank itself has a buzzing vibe every night and there are some fantastic restaurants in the Elephant - **Pizza Castella**, Ivory Arch (Indian cuisine) and Tai Won Mein (super cheap scrummy noodle bar). We're close to both the **Old Vic**, Shakespeare's **Globe** theatres and the famous South Bank arts complex, **National Theatre** and **Royal Festival Hall**, which'll inject you with culture. There's the **IMAX** cinema and it takes only about five minutes on the tube to get to Oxford Circus so the whole of London is your oyster.

'Elephant is not, however, the nicest of areas, but keep your wits about you and everything's cool.

'On campus the **Isobar** is used for clubnights and parties - Oblivion, Wednesdays; once-a-month *Raise the Roof* (garage) whilst the **Arc** (which is huge) hosts bigger do's. Several big name acts have played.

'Just around the back of the students' union is the **Ministry of Sound**, an experience everyone has to try once so they can see London's entire tourist population crammed into one small space. Ministry are starting a student night soon, though if

ACADEMIC EXCELLENCE

TEACHING:	
(Rated Excellent or 17+ out of 24)	
Education	**23**
Modern Languages, Town & Country Planning	**22**
Subjects Allied to Medicine, Politics	**21**
Communication & Media, Civil Eng, Anatomy, Biosciences, Business/Management, Economics, Nursing, Psychology	**20**
Sociology, Electrical & Electronic Engineering.	**19**
Chemical Engineering, Land & Property Mgt, Mechanical & Manufacturing Engineering, Building, Food Sciences.	**18**
RESEARCH:	
*Top grades 5/5**	**None**

WHAT IT'S REALLY LIKE

UNIVERSITY:	
Social Life	★★★
Campus scene	**More of a London than a uni scene**
Student Union services	**OK**
Politics	**Student issues, activity low**
Sport	**20 clubs**
National team position	**49th**
Sport facilities	**Improving**
Arts opportunities	**Music excellent, drama, dance, film good; art poor**
Student newspaper	**Scratch**
Nightclub	**Isobar**
Bars	**Tavern**
Union ents	**Oblivion**
Union clubs/societies	**35**
Most popular societies	**Afrikan, Islamic, Forensic Science**
Smoking policy	**Union, halls OK**
Parking	**Poor**
CITY:	
Entertainment	★★★★★
Scene	**Excellent**
Town/gown relations	**Average**
Risk of violence	**'Average'**
Cost of living	**Very high**
Student concessions	**Excellent**
Survival + 2 nights out	**£100 pw**
Part-time work campus/town	**Average/excellent**

past experience is anything to go by the drinks will still cost a high percentage of your student loan.

'In the main Students' Union building there are three bars, the **Tavern** (traditional pub type, TV screens for sport, pool table), the **Snug** (a cosy no smoking zone) and the **Isobar**, with a café area and pool tables by day then turning into a club by night. These are always fairly busy and there is usually plenty of free entertainment. Alcohol is relatively cheap compared to drinking in the rest of London.

'Generally, coming to study at South Bank will not be cheap, but it depends how you want to spend your time. There is plenty of opportunity to find a job however, so you can earn to support whatever habits you acquire living in the city.'

A social life can also be lived through one of the clubs & societies – not a great number, twenty of the former and 15 societies only – but there are some very successful cultural societies at South Bank, such as the Afrikaan society with its hugely successful club night, *Black Pepper*. Islamic is also big – there are prayer rooms for Islamic students, a Chaplaincy service and several religious societies – oh, and Forensic Science, I kid you not (and this is a good degree course to get on if you can). There is also plenty of scope for students to get involved with the student magazine, *Scratch*, or the new radio station, A-cape, or indeed to organise your own thing – as elsewhere, if you get a quorum, the union will fund it.

'Politically,' writes Lola, 'we're verging on the left wing, but the most political thing to happen is an occasional guest speaker or a meeting.'

Sport There has been a spectacular enhancement of the fortunes of LSB's Athletic union. Last year they finished above half way (49th) in the national leagues. The union was awarded the H G Messer Trophy for 'most improved university in 2003' from BUSA. Now the uni has created an Academy of Sport, Physical Activity & Wellbeing. The indoor sports facilities on the main campus includes a 40 + station fitness suite, weights room, sports hall and injury clinic.

The sports ground is a 21-acre site at Turney Road, Dulwich, with pavilion and bar. There are coaching courses and sports scholarships.

PILLOW TALK

There are several halls of residence available to first years; Dante Road or New Kent are by far preferable to McLaren House, which is famed for its Nazi-like wardens and strict regimes apparently, though its 620 en-suite rooms sound very nice and are close to home. See *At A Glance* box for prices.

GETTING THERE

☛ By Underground: Elephant and Castle (Bakerloo and Northern Lines) or mainline Waterloo station.

AT A GLANCE

ACADEMIC FILE:	
Subjects assessed	**28**
Excellent	**75%**
Average requirements	**180 points**
Application Acceptance	**21%, high**
Students-staff ratio	**19:1**
First/2:1 degree pass rate	**52%**
ACCOMMODATION FILE:	
Guarantee to freshers	**75%**
Style	**Halls**
Approx price range pw	**£73-£92**
City rent pw	**£100-£180 Zone 1; £75-£85 Zone 2**

LOUGHBOROUGH UNIVERSITY

Loughborough University
Ashby Road
Loughborough
Leicestershire LE11 3TU

TEL 01509 223522
FAX 01509 223905
EMAIL admissions@lboro.ac.uk
WEB www.lboro.ac.uk

Loughborough Students' Union
Ashby Road
Loughborough
Leicestershire LE11 3TT

TEL 01509 635000
FAX 01509 635003
EMAIL president@lborosu.org.uk
WEB www.lufbra.net

VAG VIEW

When people think of Loughborough, which has been a university since 1966, they think of its engineering capability – it came out of Loughborough Technical Institute – and they think of sport, for today it is the best UK university at sport by such a long way that some of its teams can't find decent opposition on the university circuit and turn to professional clubs to sharpen their teeth yet further.

Surprise then that the weekly student magazine, Label, *received a letter from a reader complaining that coverage favoured the arts at the expense of sport. Surprise that the official uni line is: 'Contrary to popular belief, sport does not pervade everything at Loughborough – couch potatoes are also welcome, and there are plenty of non-sporting activities for students to get involved in.' Surprise, too, that alongside aeronautical and electronic and electrical manufacturing, and sport, and defence, and the construction industry, we find artistic/literary, film/video and publishing as categories of graduate employment in which Lboro students excel.*

The uni is now pre-eminent in social science, in English, in library & information management – these are all areas in which it has been adjudged a research institution of renown. Meanwhile, Psychology, Drama and Art & Design are among its top teaching subjects at inspection.

CAMPUS

Loughborough is a campus university situated just off the M1. 'It is one of the largest campuses in Europe,' writes Vicky Cook, 'and conforms to the stereotype of a leafy, green, self-contained campus. This has its advantages, everything is located within walking distance from halls (though the free campus bus is worth remembering on rainy days). There are bars, restaurants (although nothing gourmet) and three food shops to buy overpriced essentials when a walk into town is too great an effort. And, should campus and small market town become too claustrophobic, Leicester and Nottingham are mercifully close.

The uni recently acquired the Holywell Technology Park on the edge of the campus, making it one of the biggest campus universities in the UK, with a total area of 410 acres. The new space is used to enhance its research portfolio and links with industry.

FEES, BURSARIES

UK & EU Fees: £3000. Bursary for UK students with residual household income up to £17,500: £1,300 . Bursary for UK students with residual household income between £17,501 and £33,000: £200 - £1,100. Sports Scholarship of £1,000 plus specialist coaching. £1,000 merit scholarship for new UK students in selected subject areas who receive specific A level grades. 2 music awards of £500, plus 880 music tuition bursaries of £150 each. Mature students bursaries of £400-£2,600, depending on household income.

STUDENT PROFILE

Mostly male (60/40), many from independent schools, 'A typical Lboro student,' Vicky continues, 'is one who enthuses about sport and thrives on

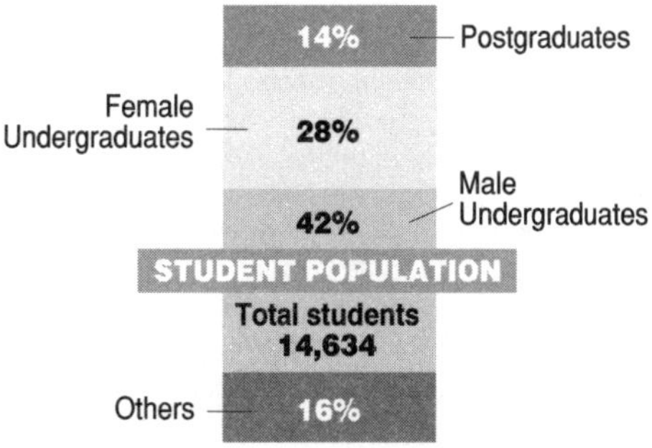

competition, and appears to be a walking advert for sportswear companies. There are students who are not like this, but they make less noise and therefore attract less attention. Sport at Lboro is impossible to ignore. This enthusiasm is not a bad thing, but if you don't share a love of sport it can become a tad irritating.'

Writes Jennie Byass: 'The only problem that comes with such a high standard of facilities is the limited times non-elite athletes can use them. The focus here is undoubtedly on the elite athlete, and I've found it quite hard coming here after being towards the top standard of sports back home to being right at the bottom of the pile here. That's not to say there aren't opportunities, and if you don't get into the university team for your sport there are intramural games which are good fun. Matches take place on an evening and with the support of your whole hall the games are thoroughly enjoyable and very competitive.'

Despite welcome to couch potatoes, it seems you'll be in a minority if you don't like sport, and in a two-thirds minority if you are female.

ACADEMIA & JOBS

There's a tough-ish average points requirement at A level (345), but a poor-ish staff-student ration of 20:1. Nevertheless, a high 68% of graduates get Firsts/2:1s, and the employment picture is good.

> ***'The focus here is undoubtedly on the elite athlete... I've found it quite hard coming here after being towards the top standard of sports back home to being right at the bottom of the pile here.'***

Though known for engineering, business and built environment, the uni is pre-eminent in art & design, in social sciences (notably Bsc Social Psychology, Sociology, Psychology, Psychology with Ergonomics), and in drama (also publishing/English). These faculties or departments achieving either full marks or 23 out of 24 points in recent inspections by the QAA or featuring at world class level in the recent research assessments, which put the uni up in the top third of the national league table. More than a fifth of graduates go into some sort of manufacturing. Sport is obviously a niche area, but they do not enjoy the dominance in the work place that they do in the undergraduate sports ratings.

'How much help is given to find a career and key skills taught appears to depend greatly on the department you are in,' says Vicky. 'The university does run seminars on such issues, though they are few and far between and take some tracking down.'

For prospective aeronautical engineers, the big four players are Loughborough, Bristol West of England, Hertfordshire and Sheffield Hallam. At Loughborough they'll ask you for around 340 points, but that's less than at Cambridge and Southampton.

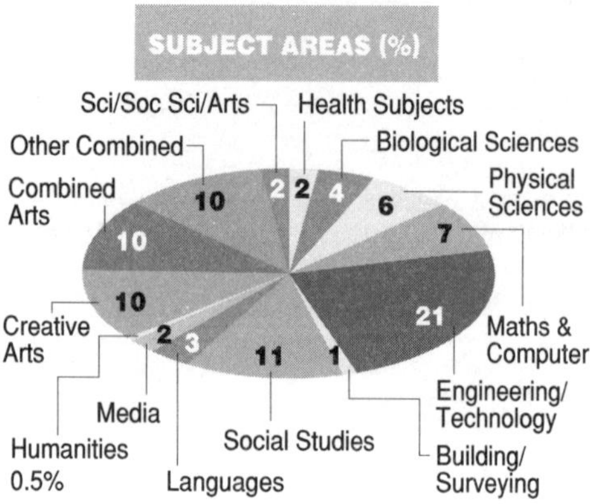

Look for Aeronautical Engineering, the 4-year Aeronautical Engineering or 4-year sandwich MEng Aeronautical Engineering, or the 5-year Aeronautical Engineering. Teaching inspection 23. Research Grade 5.

Automobile engineers are similarly well placed careers-wise – look at BE/MEng Hons 3-5-year (sandwich) Automative Engineering and a range of Automative Materials degrees. Entry 280 points.

Again would-be civil, mechanical and construction engineering graduates are served well here, Loughborough enjoy a Top 10 position in the employment league table for all these core areas.

UNIVERSITY/STUDENT PROFILE

University since	**1966**
Situation/style	**Town campus**
Student population	**14634**
Undergraduates	**10171**
- mature	**6%**
- non EU undergraduates	**7%**
- male/female	**60/40**
- non-traditional student intake	**25%**
- state school intake	**85%, low**
- drop-out rate	**4%, low**
- undergraduate applications	**Up 4%**

The BEng Hons Mechanical Engineering is 3-4 years depending on the extra sandwich year; MEng is 4-5 years. It's a balanced theoretical/practical course. There are also Materials Eng degrees, the latter with a Management Studies component. Note, too, the 4-year sandwich BSc Construction Engineering Management. Again teaching worth 22 points at the assessments and world-class Grade 5* rate research.

Prospective electrical and telecommunications engineers can spend up to 5 years on an MEng and combine with French or German, or there's a 4-year sandwich BEng & Diploma in Industrial Studies, or the 3-year BEng. Teaching inspection, 22. Research Grade 5.

Look also at Computer Systems and Software Engineering orientations. Many graduates become software engineers and consultants – they are up there with Brunel as the largest suppliers to the sector. They come not only off the computer courses but also through maths.

IT consultants also boost their graduate employment figures. There are 4-year BSc sandwich degrees in Computer Science, CS & E-Business, Computing & Management, and new - Computer Science & Artificial Intelligence. The first two can also be taken as 4/5-year MComp degrees, the 5-year course with industrial placement – you get a Diploma in professional studies as well.

Many of these engineering and technological strengths forge pathways into Defence, either as operative or equipment engineer. They lead with the likes of Southampton, Bristol, Nottingham, Bath, Durham, Imperial and Glasgow in this regard. Look, too, at their BA/BSc Industrial Design & Technology.

Meanwhile, their Visual Communication: Illustration degree makes graphic artists, designers, illustrators in quantity, and textile design is a particular speciality. For a few years now the old Art College down the road has been making a welcome impact on the engineering/techno-based population, both socially and academically. The strength in textiles was awarded full marks at the teaching assessments: Multi-Media Textiles, Printed Textiles, Woven Textiles are the three BA degrees on offer.

Aspiring bankers/ merchant bankers should look at BSc Business Economics & Finance and,at BSc Management Sciences and the economics, languages and computer sciences areas, each of which contributes some 10% of the graduate feed into this area.

Accountants (see Economics with Accounting) and stockbrokers also graduate in quantity from here. In fact, the 6% of graduates who become accountants make up the single largest group by destination. Economics dropped only one point at the assessments.

ACADEMIC EXCELLENCE

TEACHING: *(Rated Excellent or 17+ out of 24)*	
Business & Management	**Excellent**
Anatomy & Physiology, Other Subjects Allied to Medicine, Psychology	**24**
Art & Design, Sociology, Drama, Mechanical, Aeronautical, Manufacturing Eng, Politics, Economics, Tourism, Physics	**23**
Maths, Chemical Eng, Electron/Electric Eng, Civil Eng, Business & Management, Building	**22**
Materials Technology	**21**
RESEARCH: *Top grades 5/5*/6**	
Sociology	**Grade 6***
Built Environment, Sports	**Grade 5***
Electrical and Electronic Eng, Mechanical/Aeronautical/ Manufacturing Eng, Geography, European Studies, English, Library & Info Management	**Grade 5**

WHERE LOUGHBOROUGH GRADUATES END UP

Health & Social Work: 3%; Education: 4%; Wholesale Retail: 8%; Manufacturing: 21%; Financial Activities: 12%; Public Administration, Civil Service & Defence: 5%; Hotel/Restaurant: 2%; Transport & Communications (including Telecommunications): 4%; Construction: 5%; Mining/Oil Extracting: 1%; Personnel: 3%; Computer: 6%; Business & Management: 4%; Accountancy: 6%; Media (including Film): 1%; Legal 1%; Architecture: 1.5%; Publishing: 1%; Advertising: 1%; Artistic/Literary: 1%; Sport: 3%.

Approximate 'graduate track' employed **68%**

Loughborough's Business School has the cornerstone 4-year sandwich degree, International Business, but the choice of degrees suggests an eye for business in every aspect of the curriculum, from engineering to fashion. Look at Retail Management in this regard.

In Built Environment, Loughborough are Top-10 rated for the deployment of quantity surveyors. The 3-year BSc Commercial Management & Quantity Surveying has a good teaching assessment, a world-class rating for research. In both Management and Construction industries Loughborough is a classy product. Entry 280 points. Teaching inspection, 22. Research Grade 5*.

Unis with a Grade 5*/6* research rating for sport are Loughborough, Manchester Met, Glasgow, Liverpool John Moores and Birmingham. For pro athletes, sportsmen, players and sport officials it's Surrey Roehampton then Loughborough. For sports trainers and coaches, it's Leeds Met, Abertay Dundee, Sheffield Hallam, De Montfort, Gloucestershire, St Mary's, Manchester Met, then Loughborough. But overall they lead: BSc Sport & Exercise Science. Sports Science mixes with Management, Physics, Social Science, Chemistry, Humanities, also BSc Sports Technology and Sports Science & Physics. Teaching inspection, 23.

SOCIAL SCENE

STUDENTS' UNION Writes Jennie: 'The union club has much to offer, primarily *Friday Night Disco (FND)* and *Envy* (r&b) on a Saturday night; both are wicked nights out. By far the best night, however, is *Hey Ewe* on a Wednesday Night after all the sports matches have been played (and usually won!) during the afternoon. We all meet up with our sports or social clubs for an hour or so for some social drinking, and then proceed onto **Fusion**, where the key theme to the night is 'cheesy music' and lots of dancing. Midnight Madness happens between half 11 and half 12 at which time all drinks are only one pound!

'**JC's** is the sports bar, where everyone goes to celebrate victories. **Cognito** – bar – flashing dance floor, what more can I say? Recent live acts include Girls Aloud for the Freshers Ball, DJ Spoony, and Navi, a Michael Jackson impersonator, amazing!'

I asked an anonymous student about that hour's drinking on match night. 'There are certain rituals and traditions which we here in Loughborough have developed and institutionalised over the years,' I was told: 'The rugby shirt worn with jeans, AV's, collars up, *Hey Ewe* mayhem on a Wednesday evening, drinking games and of course Nasty...the Lufbra drink...' This latter, though increasingly at risk to the almighty Red Bull/voddie alternative (decried by purists as expensive and injurious to health), remains the people's choice.

There are 40 societies, the more traditional such as the International Students' Association and the LGBT Association, while quirkier ones, like the Hot Air Balloon club, the Breakdancing club and the circus society, Fever, show the possibilities.

Recent expansion reveals a **Media Centre**, various franchise shops, banks, etc. The venue itself is open for event nights every night of the week, with 9 bars and the newly refurbished **Room 1**.

The **Media Centre** houses the 24/7 student radio station (LCR), the student magazine offices (*Label*) and a TV/video editing suite. LSUTV won the Light Entertainment award in the 2005 national judgings and were runners-up for News & Current Affairs. The 'talk' studio and production studio (drum booth, guitar booth) beyond leave you in no doubt that these students have not been overcharged at £1.4 million. Sound, vision, print, web, all of it together on a single floor and serviced by student engineers who know their stuff. The uni looks after its engineers, who make up the largest single group of undergrads in this university.

The union also has a student advice centre and employment exchange, and adjacent nursery with subsidised places for students' children.

SPORT Lboro teams beat everyone each year. Which other uni could entertain an annual competition with the Amateur Athletics Association of Great Britain? Recently, £25 million was earmarked for a new 50m swimming pool, a 5000+ square metre indoor athletics training area, a new 12-court sports hall, a sports science, sports medicine and conditioning facility (including a hockey and gymnastics analysis centre) and a water-based astro turf.

AT A GLANCE

ACADEMIC FILE:	
Subjects assessed	**20**
Excellent	**85%**
Typical entry requirements	**345 points**
Application acceptance rate	**17%**
Students-staff ratio	**20:1**
First/2:1 degree pass rate	**68%**
ACCOMMODATION FILE:	
Guarantee to freshers	**100%**
Style	**Halls**
Catered	**60%**
En suite	**10%**
Cost pw (no food/food)	**£54-£128**
Town rent pw	**£50-£75**

TOWN Writes Jennie: 'Loughborough is quite a small market town, with 12,500 students dominating a 60,000 population. The town itself is pleasant, with all the basic shops you need, and plenty to offer. Also, Loughborough offers a greater sense of security when compared to the majority of the big cities. But it is quite a different proposition to the other cities of sport, such as Manchester or Sheffield...

PILLOW TALK

'All freshers are guaranteed hall accommodation and it is usually possible to remain in hall throughout your time at Lboro, although a lot of people choose to spend a year in town. The halls are very varied. Don't set your heart on a particular one, the allocation process appears random.'

Says Jennie: 'I am in catered accommodation and my hall is situated in the heart of the student village, with food, washing rooms and leisure facilities all with in about a minute's walk. Some people are not so fortunate and I have seen some of the halls which could certainly do with some attention.'

Accommodation in town is more expensive, because of the utility bills, but it is quieter, less claustrophobic and less intrusive as you choose who you live with. All hall rooms are computer networked and carry phone sockets. There's something to suit every pocket, 'and the sense of loyalty and community spirit in these halls is of an intensity usually reserved for centuries-old universities.'

WHAT IT'S REALLY LIKE	
UNIVERSITY:	
Social Life	★★★★
Campus scene	**Well resourced, sports crazy**
Student Union services	**Good**
Politics	**Light**
Sport	**Simply the best**
National team position	**Always 1st**
	53 clubs
Sport facilities	**Excellent**
Arts opportunities	**Very good**
Student magazine	**Label**
Student radio	**LCR**
Student TV	**LSUTV**
2005 TV Awards	**1 win, 1 highly commended**
Nightclub	**Fusion + bar upstairs**
Bars	**JC's, Cognito**
Union ents	**FND (disco), Hey Ewe (cheese), Envy (r&b) + live**
Union societies	**40**
Most popular society	**International**
Parking	**No 1st years**
TOWN:	
Entertainment	★★
Scene	**Market town, good pubs**
Town/gown relations	**Good**
Risk of violence	**Average**
Cost of living	**Average**
Student concessions	**Excellent**
Survival + 2 nights out	**£70pw**
Part-time work campus/town	**Good/average**

GETTING THERE

☛ By road: M1/J23, A512.

☛ By rail: London St Pancras, 1:45; Birmingham New Street, 1:30; Sheffield, 1:30; Nottingham, 0:20; Leicester, 0:15.

☛ By air: East Midlands Airport close by.

☛ By coach: London, 2:45; Exeter, 6:50; Newcastle, 8:10; Manchester, 4:30.

UNIVERSITY OF LUTON

The University of Luton
Park Square
Luton LU1 3JU

TEL 01582 489262
FAX 01582 743400
EMAIL admissions@luton.ac.uk
WEB www.luton.ac.uk

Luton University Students' Union
Europa House
Luton LU1 3HZ

TEL 01582 743265
FAX 01582 457187
EMAIL kelly.paul@luton.ac.uk
WEB www.ulsu.co.uk

VAG VIEW

Luton is exemplary in its widening access to students beyond traditional socio-economic uni boundaries: 45% undergraduates are classed as non-traditional student intake, while their drop-out rate, at 9%, is OK.

Now they are about to get a boost. In

August of this year, De Montfort University's Faculty of Education, Bedford campus, will become part of a new university for Bedfordshire due to be created with Luton University.

For the first time, the county will have a single, major provider of undergraduate and postgraduate education, with a strong emphasis on meeting local and sub-regional needs.

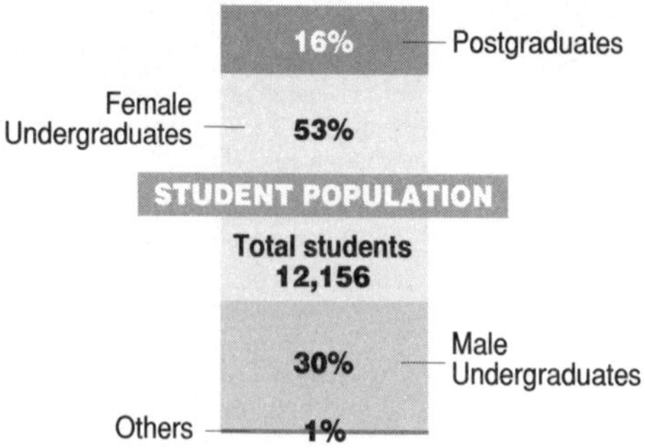

CAMPUS

PARK SQUARE is the main campus in the centre of town. There's a rural mansion a few miles away (Putteridge Bury), a conference centre and home to the Faculty of Management. Then there's a site in Castle Street in town for Humanities.

BEDFORD CAMPUS The new Bedford site is 20 miles away. It used to be Bedford's Sports College. It is undergoing a £14million redevelopment, including two new gymnasiums, sports science labs, a new Campus Centre with a 300-seat auditorium and student accommodation.

FEES, BURSARIES

UK & EU Fees: £3000. If in receipt of full HE Maintenance grant there's a bursary of £1750; if in receipt of partial grant, between £300-£1000.

STUDENT PROFILE

Luton has one of the most diverse student populations in the country – 22% of undergraduates are mature, 30% are from ethnic minority groups, many are from overseas, and there are also plenty of locals. It is a mix of students bent on developing their own idea of what a uni should be.

The positive point in all this is that everybody who comes to Luton, comes for a purpose. They are not living out someone else's blueprint for life. They have concluded that these days, to get on, you are going to have to get a degree. University may be a bit of a novel thought for many of them, but very likely it is part of their own plan, often after they have been out in the workplace and seen what's missing.

Someone once joked that all you needed to get into Luton in 1993 was two Es, but now you need two Es and a bag of amphetamine... Just to keep up. Many don't keep up (9% fall away), but for those who do, there's plenty on offer.

ACADEMIA & JOBS

Luton operates through six faculties: Business, Design & Technology, Health Care & Social Studies, Humanities, Management, Science & Computing, and now the new Bedford provision.

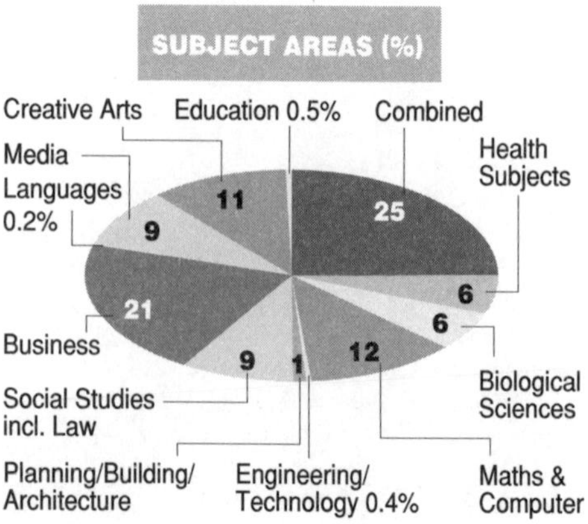

The new faculty comprises two schools: Education (one of the largest providers of Initial Teacher Training in the UK) and Physical Education & Sport Sciences (with over 100 years teaching experience and a 23 out of 24 teaching ssessment); and two departments: Business & Applied Social Sciences and Performing Arts & English.

In the old days, you thought of Luton, you thought of Vauxhall Motors. Luton has always been heavily into links with commerce and industry, and it is ideally placed, between Junctions 10 and

STUDENT POPULATION

Total students 12,156

- Postgraduates 16%
- Female Undergraduates 53%
- Male Undergraduates 30%
- Others 1%

SUBJECT AREAS (%)

- Creative Arts 11
- Education 0.5%
- Combined 25
- Health Subjects 6
- Biological Sciences 6
- Maths & Computer 12
- Engineering/Technology 0.4%
- Planning/Building/Architecture 1
- Social Studies incl. Law 9
- Business 21
- Media 9
- Languages 0.2%

UNIVERSITY/STUDENT PROFILE

University since	**1993**
Situation/style	**Town sites**
Student population	**12155**
Undergraduates	**10140**
- mature	**22%**
- non EU undergraduates	**17%**
- male/female	**36/64**
- non-traditional student intake	**45%, high**
- state school intake	**99%, high**
- drop-out rate	**9%**
- undergraduate applications	**Constant**

ACADEMIC EXCELLENCE

TEACHING:
(Rated Excellent or 17+ out of 24)

Nursing, Health Science	**23**
Anatomy, Art & Design, Pharmacology, Psychology, Organismal Biosciences, Molecular Biosciences, Media Studies, Building Surveying/Construction Mgt	**22**
Linguistics	**21**
Modern Languages, Electrical & Electronic Engineering.	**20**
Sociology	**18**

RESEARCH :

*Top grades 5/5**	**None**

11 on the M1, 20 or so miles north-west of London. But while good relations with the business and industrial sectors remains at the heart of its education strategy (not complete until the graduate has a job), over a decade it has been expanding in other important areas – £2 million on an art design studio, £5 million on a computer centre, £500,000 on a research centre, and £250,000 on a media centre.

'Media and sport are the big attractions,' one student said. They are indeed Top 10 providers in the radio/TV sector, and film and video operatives and producers come out of such as their Film Studies, Media Production and Photography & Digital Art degrees. Creative Writing is a popular minor in their modular credit scheme, in which combinations may involve two joint subjects or a major subject with a minor. Media is strongly represented on this scheme and scored 22 points at the teaching assessments. An investment of some £2 million hs provided a new broadcast television studio, three digital radio studios, a performance studio and editing facilities. New this year is a BSc Television Production.

Media and sport are the attractions, they are Top 10 providers in the radio/TV sector, and film and video, and their BSc Sports Therapy is one of the most sought-after in sport.

'Besides the broadcasting studio, we've got a massive fitness suite and new scientific body fitness analysis equipment,' our mole continued, and this is surely bound to be put together with the Bedford provision soon. it was only a few years ago that the BSc Sports Therapy appeared on the course list, yet sport scores big in the research assessments. BA Sport & Fitness (Management or Studies), Sport Development, Marketing, Tourism, etc, should command an interest, 2-3% becoming physical training instructors (Education), 1%+ pro-athletes of one sort or another. Sports Therapy is one of the most sought-after degrees in sport, and Luton is one of only a handful to provide it.

The Tourism dimension reminds that the subject scored a high research Grade 4 (max 5) in the research assessments and feeds through as an important niche area in their employment stats.

See, too, the nursing provision, which dropped only one point in the teaching assessments. A popular route for non-hospital nurses is BSc Mental Health Nursing, BSc Midwifery, etc, which sit alongside Health Science, Health Psychology, and BSc Psychology.

They're commercial & business law specialists at Luton, and Law is a recognised pathway from here into the Civil Service.

For market research, another sector where they score in graduate employment, law again figures. See also their BA Advertising & Marketing Communications and BA Adverising Design.

Graduates of the various Management degrees, Business Decision Mgt, Psychology & Business, tend to become managers in large retail operations (2%), marketing managers (1%+) and sales managers (1%). Around 5% of graduates go into personnel, their line into the sector via BSc Hons Human Resource Management.

WHERE LUTON GRADUATES END UP

Health & Social Work: 9%; Education: 5.5%; Wholesale Retail: 15%; Manufacturing: 7%; Financial Activities: 6%; Public Administration, Civil Service & Defence: 9%; Hotel/Restaurant: 7%; Transport & Communications (including Telecommunications): 8%; Construction: 2%; Personnel: 4%; Computer: 1.5%; Business & Management: 1%; Media (including Film): 3%; Legal 4%; Architecture: 1%; Publishing: 2%; Advertising: 1%; Artistic/Literary: 1%; Sport: 3%.

WHAT IT'S REALLY LIKE

UNIVERSITY:	
Social Life	★★★
Campus scene	**Urban good timers**
Student Union services	**Average**
Politics	**Some**
Sport	**18 clubs**
National team position	**112th**
Sport facilities	**Good**
Arts opportunities	**Good drama; average art**
Student magazine	**Streaker**
Student newspaper	**Flasher**
Student radio	**Luton FM**
Nightclub	**Sub Club**
Bars	**Main Bar**
Union ents	**Cheese & chart, r&b. Massive May ball's back.**
Union clubs/societies	**50**
Most popular society	**African Caribbean**
Parking	**Adequate**
TOWN:	
Entertainment	★★★
Scene	**Pubs, clubs**
Town/gown relations	**Poor**
Risk of violence	**Average**
Cost of living	**Average**
Student concessions	**Good**
Survival + 2 nights out	**£80 pw**
Part-time work campus/town	**Average/good**

Finally, there's a range of computing degrees and jobs aplenty for graphic artists, designers and Illustrators who follow their BA Graphic Design and Interior Design.

SOCIAL SCENE

STUDENTS' UNION/LUTON **Main Bar** is the focal point, replete with all the usual trappings – arcade machines, a juke box, tellies and the like vie for attention. An adjacent, courtyard, beer garden is very popular in the more clement months. The venue for most of the organised hedonism is **Sub Club**, in the basement of the building. Wednesday is Sports Night: *Sin*, re-launched this February (best in cheese and chart). *Cyber Dirk* or *Tush* do the business on Friday, on alternative weeks. On Saturday, it appears everyone goes home. The brain-damaging effects of such revelry can be put to the test at the regular Quiz Nights, and students with bright ideas can also put the facilities to their own use if they can convince the powers that be that enough people will attend.

Undisputed highlight of the year is the May Ball, which attracts thousands of the Luton faithful. The gowned and tuxedoed masses arrive in such numbers that the event is one of the country's largest student balls, and reckoned to be the best. For just over £30, the likes of Prodigy, Tim Westwood, Jeremy Healy, Dodgy, Space and the Bootleg Beatles have rocked their world, while casinos, funfairs and top nosh add to the experience.

Societies, of which there are 30-odd, include the huge Cocsoc, which aims to get punters drunk in style once a term on a variety of brightly coloured booze. Media-wise, there's magazine *Streaker* (student life laid bare), newspaper *Flasher*, as well as radio station, Luton FM.

SPORT/LUTON Besides access to pitches, there's the fitness centre, sauna, steam room and solarium. Sport is competitive here, not only an important academic subject, but there was a bit of a dive in form last year, they came 95th in the national league.

TOWN/LUTON 'Luton is a brilliant in-between town,' said Becky Hill. 'We have access to London in less than an hour, and Milton Keynes is brilliant for shopping.' If this sounds a bit of a back-handed compliment, it is. Luton is not a place you'd go out of your way to spend time in. But there are pubs galore and a handful of clubs, like **Edge** and **Liquid**, who do a Student Night. Otherwise, it's the **Galaxy Centre**'s screens, eateries, art gallery and café. Oh, and there's **The Hat Factory**, an arts venue run by the Council.

AT A GLANCE

ACADEMIC FILE:	
Subjects assessed	**26**
Excellent	**54%**
Typical entry requirements	**190 points**
Application acceptance rate	**24%, high**
Students-staff ratio	**24:1**
First/2:1 degree pass rate	**52%**
ACCOMMODATION FILE:	
Guarantee to freshers	**100%**
Style	**Halls**
Catered	**None**
Approx price range pw	**£60-£72**
Town rent pw	**£45-£65**

STUDENTS' UNION/BEDFORD The £14-million redevelopment brings a new Campus Centre with a 300-seat auditorium, in addition to sport facilities and accommodation. there is an exceptional sense of community. Bedford students spend a lot of their time at the union bars. Wednesday nights are the stuff of legend. Bedford also traditionally has Freshers', Christmas and Summer balls.

SPORT/BEDFORD features regularly in the BUSA finals. They've been finalists in Women's Rugby at Twickenham and in Men's Football at Walsall FC, and were the first student Men's Hockey finalists. Gongs in BUSA Mountain Biking Championships and White Water Kayak Championships give the spread. The annual Rugby Sevens is as famous as it is notorious. Besides the new gym and fitness suites on campus, the town is home to the international standard Bedford Athletic Stadium and has three swimming pools.

TOWN/BEDFORD is now a place for pubs and bars more than clubs. **The Forresters** (traditional), **Pilgrims Progress** (excellent value with decent food), the **Bull Nosed Bat**, **The Bedford Lounge** (with dancefloor), the **Litton Tree**, **The Rose** (pop venue with dancefloor), **Venom** for r&b, **New York, New York** (bit cheesy). Late licensing to 2 or 3 a.m. is the thing. There are off-campus club nights at places like **Nexus**, and what was **Limehaus** is now a cool venue called **The Pad** – dance nights, big names, small but intimate. Nightclubs big with students are **Oxygen** (4 floors, masses of rooms, **Bar Soriet** (a student affiliated bar witrh themed nights), **Time Out** (small & funky, open till 5 a.m.) A bar called **Esquires** is a live music venue with a reputation for hosting new bands – even Cold Play and Oasis – before their time. **Corn Exchange** is a live venue for theatre, music and comedy.

PILLOW TALK

They invested £60 million in new facilities during the past decade – much of it on accommodation. The Student Village lies within staggering distance of the union, town centre and lecture halls, and offers secure accommodation to 1,600 students in eleven separate halls.

Halls are divided into single-sex and mixed flats, each with shared kitchen, laundry facilities, and bathroom. Several flats are designed for students with disabilities.

With around 25% of students living in uni-managed accommodation close by, the town centre feel almost like a campus.

Brand new accommodation at Bedford.

GETTING THERE

☛ By road: M1/J10t.
☛ By rail: London King's Cross Thameslink, 40 mins; Nottingham, 1:45; Oxford, 2:15; Birmingham New Street, 2:30.
☛ By air: London Luton Airport.
☛ By coach: London, 1:15; Manchester, 5-6:00.

STUDENT MANCHESTER - THE CITY

Since the **Hacienda** closed in 1997 a number of clubs have tried to replace it. **Sankey's Soap** seemed to be the best contender, then closed, and has now reopened, the legend redoubling upon itself in the process, though it's quite a bit different to how it used to be. Another popular club, with students and locals is the hardcore **Music Box**, which hosts a variety of regular and one-off nights.

Right beside this is **Jilly's**, which is the club for alterna-kids and aged hard rockers. Although a tad on the gloomy side, **Jilly's** boasts three rooms which each play different veins of rock and metal (all equally heavy). Most challenging is perhaps the Friday night all-nighter. **The Ritz** and **5th Avenue** are still student favourites and the stainless steel and white-walled **Elemental** (house and garage) is an up & coming club with a good atmosphere. Itchy describes **5th Avenue** as 'out-and-out student bliss...tongue-in-cheek playlist from Queen to Madness'. All play a blend of indie, rock and Brit Pop.

Popular late-night bars are the sci-fi themed **Fab Café** (with real daleks!), the fascinatingly-shaped **Contact Theatre** and the host of bars on Canal Street, the central point of Manchester's renowned **Gay Village**. Bars to look out for in the gay village include pre-club **Tribeca**, **Via Fossa** and the newly opened **Queer** bar.

For a more mainstream student night out, try the infamous *Owens Park Bop* in Fallowfield every Friday, alternatively *Club Trop* at **The Academy** on a Tuesday is a must do for all freshers. **The Academy** also runs weekly nights which, being part of Manchester University, attracts a big student crowd. Itis also one of the main live venues for touring bands. The city's other concert venues are **The Apollo**, **The Manchester Evening News Arena** and **The G-Mex**. For jazz fans, **Matt and Phred's Jazz Club**, **Band on the Wall** and **Jumpin' Jack's Piano Bar** are all worth a mention.

THEATRE

The Royal Exchange Theatre offers 2 stages (one in the round) and a combination of modern and traditional plays (all at student discounts). Situated in a rather nice area right in the city centre, it's also a good place to pop in for a cuppa during the day. Another of Manchester's major venues is **The Palace Theatre** in Oxford Road. Although designed for more family-friendly showings, they offer a good mix of shows (recent plays have included Grease, Vagina Monologues and Cinderella) and fairly big names. **The Contact Theatre** caters more to the student market and has occasional art exhibits as well as writing, DJ and drama workshops. Resplendent with vibrant orange décor, **The Contact** also features the **Café Deluxe**, which makes hearty sandwiches and a mean cup of coffee. **The Green Room** is another avant-garde venue which, like **The Contact**, boasts its own nightclub nights, a small theatre and a small café-bar. **The Lowry** is also worth a mention here. Although a little more out-of-the-way than its rivals, it offers the largest stage outside of London, with Ferrari-designed seating! On a more low-key note, **The Library Theatre** offers a range of events from jazz to comedy, and traditional plays.

CINEMAS

Going to the cinema in Manchester costs about £4 pretty much everywhere. **The Filmworks** is by far the most popular, and despite seeming a little like an airport, boasts a ridiculous number of screens, some of which show IMAX 3D movies as well as arthouse and mainstream films. **The Odeon** is the city centre's only mainstream cinema, a quieter venue. In his days as Manchester United's captain, Eric Cantona used to get his French film 'fix' at the **Cornerhouse**, the best place for arthouse, foreign and small budget films. It also features a small but interesting art gallery and what is arguably the first modern-style bar in Manchester. Opened in 1985 it has an arty clientele and Belgium beers.

There is also the **AMC** situated in the Great Northern building on Deansgate, which usually shows all the latest releases. Although quite a way to travel out of the city and relatively expensive, **The UCI** at The Trafford Centre is also a nice little cinema complex (the outer facia has Islamic pillarsbeside the centre's themed foodcourt).

COMEDY

Manchester knows how to have a laugh and **The Comedy Store**, situated on Deansgate Locks is definitely the best for doing that. *The Best In Stand-Up* on Friday and Saturday provide a fantastic night out and offer great student concessions, just make sure you buy tickets in advance the night is known to sell out. **The Frog and Bucket** is another popular comedy venue, although different in style, less slick and more traditional in its humour. They offer open mic nights on Mondays. **The Buzz** is possibly the longest running venue and has featured many a great, such as Jack Dee. **The Dancehouse Theatre** is also known to host occasional comedy nights, as is **The Contact**, known for its up-and-coming, very modern acts). Other popular comedy venues include **Bar Risa** and **Jongleurs**.

SPORT

Manchester United memorabilia is everywhere and the ticket price is extortionate! Manchester City offers a more accessible option offering discounts for students and, to be truthful, attracting more Mancunian fans, however their newly acquired grounds located north of the city can be difficult to get to from university campus. Manchester Storm ice hockey is another favourite, and the Manchester Giants basketball team offer a student deal of £4 for a game.

The Aquatics Centre, ideally located on Oxford Road is another sports venue to have come out of the 2002 Commonwealth games. This purpose-built swimming pool & leisure complex, partly owned by the university, gives a substantial discount to students as well as good rates on membership. University-owned sports complexes are the Armitage, Sugden and McDougall Centres. They offer a variety of sports, cricket and football grounds as wells as gyms and tennis courts.

A little further out of town you can find the Manchester velodome for bike enthusiasts and the Sale Water Park for those who prefer watersports.

SHOPPING ON A LOAN

Affleck's Palace alone features more interesting little stalls than you can shake an oversized stick at, and is quite a Manc institution. A maze of a place it offers piercings, tattoos, t-shirts, CDs, vintage clothing, condoms, fancy dress, fetish wear and the ever popular rainbow-coloured hair extensions. **The Coliseum** is similar, situated behind **Affleck's**, on a smaller scale and with more of a gothic twist. **The Arndale Market** is handy for picking up cheap, fresh food as well as clothes, shoes and practical jokes – all fairly cheap.

The Student Market in the Academy sells bikes, clothes, hippie items, discount CDs and a variety of other stuff and is a favourite haunt on a Tuesday lunchtime. **The Trafford Centre** is the second biggest shopping centre in England and has literally miles of shops, but it's so big that your funky new purchases will probably have gone out of fashion by the time you leave.

Most chain shops can be found in the city centre. Student discounts are ubiquitous. A little more up market are **Harvey Nichols** and **Selfridges**, as well as the King Street area of the city centre which also features **DKNY**, **Max Mara** and **Hermes**.

Elka Malhotra

UNIVERSITY OF MANCHESTER

The University of Manchester
Oxford Road
Manchester M13 9PL

TEL 0161 275 2225
FAX 0161 275 8278
EMAIL ug.admissions@man.ac.uk
WEB www.manchester.ac.uk

Manchester Students' Union
Oxford Road
Manchester M13 9PR

TEL 0161 275 2930
FAX 0161 275 2936
EMAIL comms@umsu.man.ac.uk
WEB www.umu.man.ac.uk

VAG VIEW

Manchester University and UMIST, the world-famous Institute of Science and Technology, are now one university. UMIST's sometime Sackville Street address, a walk away from the mother site, is now known as North Campus. They are, of course, joined in this feverishly studenty neck of the woods by another university, Manchester Met; and Salford University is only a 15-minute bus ride away.

So it is that whole areas of this elegant, busy city are, to all intents and purposes, campus. With the Royal Northern School of Music and Manchester Business School also here, it must be the largest conglomeration of students anywhere in the world.

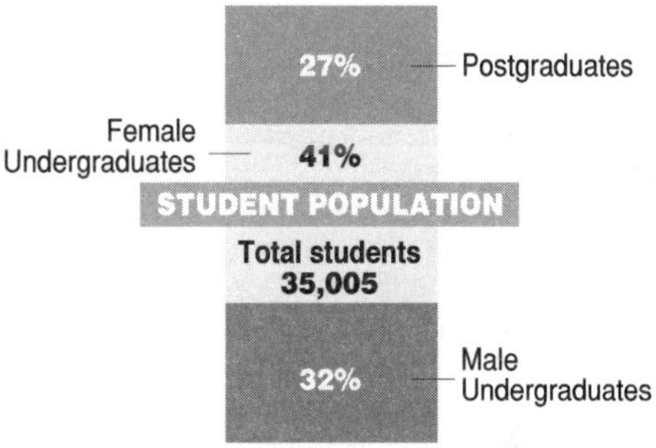

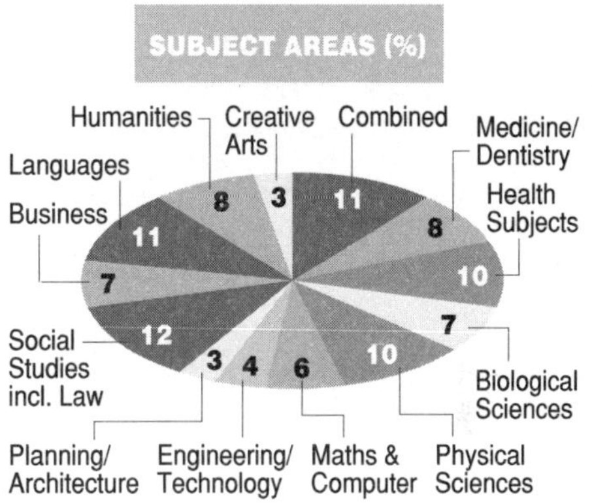

CAMPUS

Manchester Uni has grown up with the city. The Wilmslow/Oxford Road runs right through the centre of campus, linking it at the top end with Manchester Met, Whitfield Street (gateway to the city's legendary Gay Village) and UMIST, and at the bottom end with the most populous areas of student residences – Rusholme, Fallowfield, etc.

The whole street is campus, but it is also city.

UNIVERSITY/STUDENT/PROFILE	
University since	**1903**
Situation/style	**Civic**
Student population	**35005**
Undergraduate	**25683**
- mature	**13%**
- non EU undergraduates	**10%**
- male/female	**45/56**
- non-traditional student intake	**21%**
- state school intake	**80%, low**
- drop-out rate	**8%**
- undergraduate applications	**Up 3%**

Manchester University has a theatre (**Contact**) and a premier gig venue (**The Academy**) and a museum (**Manchester Museum**, currently undergoing a £20-million facelift) and an art gallery (**Whitworth**) which are all key sites of this city (see *Manchester Student City*, page 313).

City and university are absolutely inseparable, not least because they share the same vibe. It is an active, buzzing scene, a place some parents dread their children choosing.

FEES, BURSARIES

UK & EU Fees: £3000. If in receipt of full HE Maintenance grant there's a bursary of £1000; if in receipt of partial grant, £5000 p.a. if also attain 3 A grades at A level or equivalent with annual household income of around £17500 or less. £1000 p.a. if 3 A grades at A level (or equivalent) regardless of household income, and choose designated degree programmes (see www.manchester.ac.uk for more details). £2000 p.a. if on their special Access Programme. There's also a range of subject-specific schemes, and financial support for students with disabilities, students who may find themselves in financial hardship and scholarships awarded to talented athletes and musicians. See www.manchester.ac.uk.

STUDENT PROFILE

There is a socially well-balanced population with a sizeable portion (21%) now coming from non-traditional areas of supply, and a bigger state school intake than at Durham, Bristol, Exeter or Oxbridge. In general, Manchester is a university for kids who like to make things happen – they're an intelligent, resourceful, lively crew, not afraid or too lazy to lay themselves on the line and apply themselves, and not averse to letting their hair down either. In a survey by the Adam Smith Institute (*The Next Leaders?*) they came out top for sex and drugs, leaving Cambridge to take the honours on booze.

ACADEMIA & JOBS

There is no limit to the number of top-rated course assessments – 96% make our criteria of Academic Excellence, and research here has a pedigree of its own – this is where Ernest, First Baron Rutherford did the work which led to the splitting of the atom, and where the computer was invented. They are still pre-eminent (with the likes of Birmingham, Bath and Imperial College) in the provision of graduate physicists. Overall, the uni came 9th in the research assessments and claims the top grade 5, 5*or 6* ratings in 37 out of 46 subjects.

On-campus resources include the John Rylands Library, the third largest uni library in the country with more than 3.5 million books. There is no shortage of computer technology – there are now 6000 PCs in public clusters on campus.

There are 4 Faculties: Engineering & Physical Sciences; Humanities; Life Sciences; Medical & Human Sciences.

With more than half graduates entering the Health sector, and Manchester creating Europe's premier biomedical campus, a series of linked scientific and hospital facilities on Oxford Road, it is right to open with the 5/6-year MB ChB, which scored full marks at the teaching assessments. There has long been a medical faculty at Manchester Uni. Now, 50 students can also study an identical programme at Keele University (see entry). Critical faculties and communication skills are to the fore, as is constructing a methodology of self-education. There is also MBChB with European Studies – six months at a partner institution in France (Rennes), Switzerland (Lausanne) or

ACADEMIC EXCELLENCE

TEACHING:
(Rated Excellent or 17+ out of 24)

Chemistry, Law, Mechanical Engineering, Anthropology, Business & Management, Computer Studies, Music, Geography, Social Policy & Administration, Earth Sciences	**Excellent**
Physics, Management, Politics, Economics, Philosophy, Dentistry, Medicine, Pharmacology, Classics, Theology	**24**
Anatomy, Archaeology, Biosciences, Nursing, Education	**23**
Psychology, Maths, Leisure, Subjects Allied to Medicine	**22**
German, Linguistics, Sociology, Materials Technology, Drama, History of Art	**21**
Iberian Studies, Electrical & Electronic Eng, Aerospace Eng, Town & Country Planning, Middle Eastern Studies	**20**
French, Italian	**19**
Civil Engineering	**18**

RESEARCH:
Top grades 5/5/6**

Pharmacy, Biological Sciences, Computer, Metallurgy , Sociology, Accounting, Iberian/ Latin American, Theology, Music	**Grade 6***
Pre-Clinical Studies, French, German, Dutch/Scandinavian	**Grade 5***
Community & hospital-based Clinical Subjects, Nursing, Subjects Allied to Medicine, Psychology, Chemistry, Physics, Earth Sciences, Pure Maths, Applied Maths, Civil Eng, Mechanical/Aeronautical, Manufacturing Eng, Law, Anthropology, Politics, Social Policy, Management, Middle Eastern and African Studies, English, Italian, Linguistics, Classics, History, History of Art, Drama/Dance/Performing Arts	**Grade 5**

Germany (Homberg). Entry AAB including Chemistry, one of Maths/Physics/Biology + one other, not necessarily Science, not General Studies, Media, Theatre or Home Economics. Grade A GCSE Chemistry, Physics, Biology, Maths. Grade B English Language.

Biological Sciences are of course key elements in the same faculty and attracted the highest listing – Grade 6* – in the research assessment.

Manchester also scored full marks at the teaching assessment of its 5/6-year dental degree. Entry ABB. Prospective dental hygienists and nurses note the BSc Oral Health Science (BBC to get in).

City and university are absolutely inseparable, not least because they share the same vibe. It is an active, buzzing scene, a place some parents dread their children choosing.

Finally, Manchester is one of only three unis to be awarded Grade 5 for research in nursing, Pharmacy took full marks at the teaching assessments and is a Top 10 job provider, and there is a BSc Physiotherapy taught at the Manchester Royal Infirmary.

For psychology there's a 22-point teaching assessment and international Grade 5 for research, and they are among a few unis whose postgrad provision is approved by the British Psychological Society for career psychologists.

Manchester's *Student Direct* is the city's No. 1 student newspaper. Fuse FM and MSTV complete the media picture, and they are high in employment league for editors – languages and humanities being the main graduate sources, while Mancunian publishers come to publishing from more parts of the curriculum than in any other uni at the top of the employment league.

There is a sterling reputation for both English and Drama.

For would-be accountants, there's a flexible option within Humanities. Accounting or Accounting & Economics/ Finance/Law (4 years), or Accounting with Business Information Systems are among the degrees on offer. See also the Management degrees, one of which focuses on accountancy & Finance. Teaching inspection: Economics 24, Business 24. Research: Grade 6*. Research Grade 5 for Management.

IT consultants also proliferate, see BEng, MEng and BSc degrees.

The defence industry plunders many a Manchester graduate from the School of Biological Sciences, while the Royal Air Force Officer concentrates on Aerospace Engineering (B/MEng), the MEng Avionics degrees and the Computer Science and Engineering degrees: international Grade 5 for research. Manchester are perennially among the Top 10 providers of aeronautical engineers, and offer enticing combinations involving Business and/or European industrial experience.

Within the education provision, both adult and higher education sectors are particularly well served. By far the most popular route is via the joint hons Languages, from which there's also a Top 10 provision of translators and interpreters. At the teaching assessments they scored 19 for French, Italian; 20 for Spanish; 21 for Linguistics and German. French and German were awarded a world-class Grade 5* rating at the research assessments; Iberian Grade 6*. Look, too, at the series of Middle Eastern studies degrees, including Arabic, Hebrew (& Jewish Studies), Persian, Turkish, Islamic. There's an international Grade 5 for research.

Manchester send many languages graduates into personnel. Sciences and Social Studies are also strong in this employment area. Note an excellent series of Social Policy (international Grade 5 for research), Sociology and Social Anthropology degrees and combinations, also the BA and BSc Psychology degrees (22 at assessment).

Architecture, town planning and property development are all rich employment seams out of Manchester. There's BA Architecture, but also an interesting series of MEng Structural Engineering & Architecture. See, too, the 4-year MTCP Town &

WHERE MANCHESTER GRADUATES END UP

Health & Social Work: 26%; Education: 6%; Wholesale Retail: 8%; Manufacturing: 7%; Financial Activities: 9%; Public Administration, Civil Service & Defence: 6%; Hotel/Restaurant: 3%; Transport & Communications (including Telecommunications): 3%; Construction: 1%; Mining/Oil Extracting: 1%; Personnel: 5%; Computer: 4%; Business & Management: 5%; Accountancy: 5%; Media (including Film): 1%; Legal 2%; Architecture: 1%; Publishing: 2%; Artistic/Literary: 0.5%; Sport: 0.5%.

Approximate 'graduate track' employed **67%**

WHAT IT'S REALLY LIKE

UNIVERSITY:	
Social Life	★★★★★
Campus scene	**Big, busy, self-assured**
Student Union services	**Good**
Politics	**Active & widely representative: fees, war, housing, racism**
Sport	**Key**
National team position	**14th**
Sport facilities	**Good**
Arts opportunities	**Excellent; high profile drama, dance, film**
Student newspaper	**Student Direct**
2005 National Awards	**2 wins**
Student radio	**Fuse FM**
2005 National Awards	**1 win: Fashion**
Student TV	**MUSTV**
Nightclub and venues	**Cellar, Academy 1,2 & 3**
Bars	**Solem, Hop & Grape, Lunar**
Union ents	**Club Tropicana, Horny and much much more live**
Union clubs/societies	**200**
Parking	**Poor**
CITY:	
Entertainment	★★★★★
City scene	**Legendary**
Town/gown relations	**Average-poor**
Risk of violence	**High**
Cost of living	**Average**
Student concessions	**Good**
Survival + 2 nights out	**£90 pw**
Part-time work campus/town	**Average/good**

Country Planning and BA City & Regional Development. Teaching inspection 20.

Finally, they are European law specialists and were awarded an international Grade 5 for research in this area.

SOCIAL SCENE

Students' Union It is an unadventurous soul who appears at the foot of MUSU's steps any day in term time and resists propulsion inside – bodies hurry purposefully like ants, while as alien visitors we were drawn irredeemably by the sights and sounds of the new **Solem Bar**. The sound inside is the city and has the power during the day to reconfigure the cranium back into last night's form. The bar's design – 'Swedish sauna meets trendy metal,' sourpussed someone in earshot – actually makes for a cosy place to hang out, and perhaps shoot some pool on the new tables. It's a vast improvement on the old Serpent Bar.

'Next door to the union is the **Academy,** a 1200-capacity live band venue,' Leonie Kenyon tells us, 'and, on the top floor of the union, is the **Hop & Grape**, not actually a pub despite it's name, but a small bar and occasional venue for live bands. These venues have recently been visited by Placebo, Pitchshifter, Eels, and Ash, and the Academy has the infamous *Club Tropicana* cheese nights on Tuesdays, pulling itself round in time for the Student Market during the day. It's a prime spot for posters, bikes, CDs, clothes and hippy items, a favourite haunt of students especially at lunchtime when the homemade chocolate cakes are rather popular! Another union nightclub is the **Cellar**, which features *Horny* on Friday, and plays a mixture of pop and cheese. On weekday afternoons it is also used as a café.'

Twice a year comes *Club Trop All Nighter*, which takes over the entire union, including the Academy next door, in a multi-faceted romp with casino and dodgems and all the rest. Early this year the gig guide to the Academy – the veritable summit of achievement of full-time ents manager Sean Morgan and his sidekick, Sarah – saw twenty-two acts between October and December.

Meanwhile, students galvanise themselves into national prominence with their media, though they don't match Leeds, with its 15 wins last year across paper, radio and TV. Manchester took a Gold for Presenter on Fuse fm, which, with MSTV, is going from strength to strength. Meanwhile *Student Direct* – the student newspaper with a 60000 readership, won twice - Fashion and Travel Reporters.

In the area of drama, the uni is a major force,

AT A GLANCE

ACADEMIC FILE:	
Subjects assessed	**47**
Excellent	**96%**
Typical entry requirements	**370 points**
Application acceptance rate	**11%**
Students-staff ratio	**13:1**
First/2:1 degree pass rate	**69%**
ACCOMMODATION FILE:	
Guarantee to freshers	**100%**
Style	**Halls, flats**
Catered	**30%**
En-suite	**30%**
Price range pw	**£50-£112**
City rent pw	**£50-£65**

the annual springtime student festival still reigns supreme. And politically, the union's campaigning reputation still goes unquestioned.

North Campus The old UMIST SU, the Barnes Wallis Building on the North Campus off Sackville Street still has ground floor **Harry's Bar** and **Paddy's Lounge**, U-Print, a Union Shop, the North Campus Advice Centre, and the RAG and Student Action Office. Meanwhile, **Club Underground** still attracts a faithful few in the basement.

Sport The teams came 14th in the national uni team ratings last year. Facilities include a boat house on the Bridgewater Canal, Yacht Club at Pennington Flash, Leigh, 18 miles west of the city. Pitches (31 acres) for rugby, soccer, hockey, lacrosse, cricket, netball, are close to the student village at Fallowfield, also tennis courts, all-weather, artificial grass areas and pavilion. In Fallowfield, too, is the **Armitage Centre** with sports hall and squash courts close by. A further 90 acres lie ten miles south, below the M63, at Wythenshawe sports ground. On campus itself is the **McDougal Centre**, which has a swimming pool, indoor games hall, gym, squash and fives courts, an outside five-a-side court, rifle range, climbing wall, bowls carpets, sauna and solarium. The new Commonwealth Games swimming pool is open to students. There are bursaries, two offered by the exclusive XXI, an elite sports club founded in 1932.

Town See *Manchester Student City*, page 313.

PILLOW TALK

All freshers are guaranteed a place in halls and flats. The most populous areas of student residences - Rusholme, Fallowfield, etc - are at the bottom end of the Oxford Road corridor. Writes Leonie: 'Under the railway line and through Rusholme's Curry Mile - which, as the name would suggest, is full of curry houses and interesting Eastern-style shops. Although located next to the infamous Moss Side, it's quite safe.

'Fallowfield is the ideal place to live as it is secure, lively, and features some very nice little houses. The student halls range from very nice to eyesore (The Oak House Tower - eek!), and are backed by the university-owned Armitage Sports Centre, which offers student discounts on a range of sporty activities. The road here is lined with bars and pubs (including the oft-frequented vodka bar, **Revolution**) and has buzzing, student-orientated nightlife. Withington is a little quieter, a little more expensive, and that little bit further away from the universities and the town centre, but has a good variety of pubs, shops and coffee shops. Similarly Didsbury (home of the "Disbury Dozen" series of pubs – a pub crawl classic) has a good deal to offer, but is more expensive than the wholly studenty Fallowfield area.

'Victoria Park is seen as the posh alternative, probably because most of its halls are large, leafy, Victorian buildings. It's an area between Fallowfield and the main campus - approximately 15 minutes walk from the main university buildings. The Students' Union is located at the top of the Victoria Park area, as is Whitworth Park Hall, affectionately known as the Toblerone building and the perfect choice for Arts students, since you can stagger out of bed and be right outside the Faculty of Arts. These halls tend to be a tad more expensive because the rooms are nicer and most are catered.

'There are also private halls of residence in the city centre Student Village, popular with students at Manchester Met since it is right on their doorstep. Victoria Hall is another privately owned student residence near the city centre.'

GETTING THERE

☛ By road: M63/J10, A34.
☛ By rail: London Euston, 2:30; Leeds, 1:45; Liverpool Lime Street, 0:50.
☛ By air: Manchester Airport for international and inland flights.
☛ By coach: London, 4:35; Bristol, 5:00; Newcastle, 5:00.

MANCHESTER METROPOLITAN UNIVERSITY

The Manchester Metropolitan University
All Saints
Manchester M15 6BH

TEL 0161 247 1035-8
FAX 0171 247 6871
EMAIL prospectus@mmu.ac.uk
WEB www.mmu.ac.uk

Manchester Met Students' Union
99 Oxford Road
Manchester M1 7EL

TEL 0161 247 1162
FAX 0161 247 6314
EMAIL mmsu@mmu.ac.uk
WEB www.mmsu.com

VAG VIEW

Manchester Met, formerly Manchester Poly, is situated on various sites in Manchester and in Crewe and Alsager, two towns either side of the M6 between junctions 16 and 17.

People pick MMU for its reputation as a party-till-you-die university. When you visit, they do not disappoint: 'Everyone gets very focused on what's going here, which is massive,' confessed a student.

UNIVERSITY/STUDENT PROFILE

University since	**1992**
Situation/style	**Civic**
Student population	**33500**
Undergraduates	**26245**
- mature	**62%**
- non EU undergraduates	**3%**
- male/female	**42/58**
- non-traditional student intake	**36%**
- state school intake	**95%**
- drop-out rate	**11%**
- undergraduate applications	**Up 4%**

CAMPUS

The Manchester base is centred at the All Saints site on Oxford Road, very close to Manchester Uni, making, with UMIST and a couple of other colleges in the vicinity, a quite extraordinary concentration of students (around 100,000) within the square mile.

Crewe & Alsager are towns about 6 miles apart, some 35 miles south of Manchester, their semi-rural campus environments a million miles away in spirit from heaving Oxford Road. 'There's not a lot of contact with Crewe & Alsager,' my guide admitted. 'They always say there is, but in practice there's not. They have their own set-up down there. They're very sports and drama orientated. I think you still get some who enrol for C&A and are quite surprised that it's not just down the road and you can't always get up here on a Saturday night! I understand quite a few drop out over that.'

FEES, BURSARIES

UK & EU Fees: £3000. If in receipt of full HE Maintenance grant there's a bursary of £1000; if in receipt of partial grant, there's a slodong scale of awards.

STUDENT PROFILE

At MMU there is a high percentage of mature and part-time students, more from state school and far more the lower socio-economic reaches. Bruce McVean sees only advantage in this. 'MMU is perceived to be the younger more dynamic university because it is not as staid as Manchester University.' Bruce was an engineering student at Manchester Uni and, seeking a course change to Geography, was turned down and then accepted by MMU. 'But I now know people doing Geography at Manchester and there's not a lot of difference between the two departments. When students are actually here, I don't think they perceive much difference between the two establishments.'

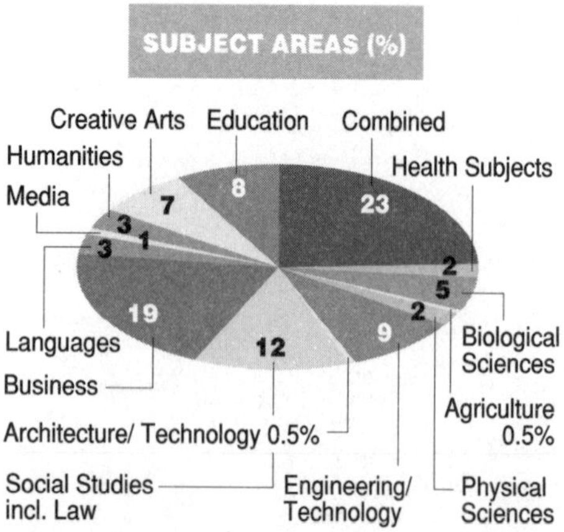

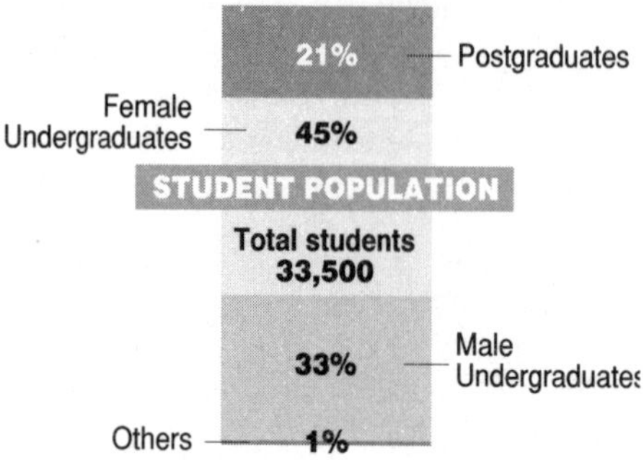

ACADEMIA & JOBS

The modular courses have a practical emphasis, tracing a clear vocational line to jobs in industry, where their employment rate is good.

More than 400 courses are offered from within Art & Design; Community Studies, Law & Education; Food, Clothing & Hospitality Management; Humanities & Social Science; Management & Business; Science & Engineering.

At Alsager there's a range of sports science subjects available, plus the departments of Humanities & Applied Social Studies (Sociology scored an excellent 21 on inspection) and the Modular Office, which looks after all inter-departmental modular mixes. At Crewe, the Business & Management Department sits alongside the Department of Environmental & Leisure Studies with its own stream, woodland and conservation habitats. Other than that, there is the School of Education (PGCEs and Primary and Secondary degrees)

For jobs in retail management Manchester Met leads. There's a retail marketing Foundation and application in a variety of areas. For example, Fashion Buying For Retail (HND and BSc) is a major contribution to employment figures in the fashion sector, even though in textile design the designers themselves make waves almost as big as the London Uni of the Arts and Huddersfield.

'It's true, we still have a really strong gay scene. Gays won't need to be told about Manchester's Mardi Gras... but the hub – day in, day out – is the Village: late licensing, all-night cafés and a huge choice of venues.'

BA degrees: Fashion, Fashion Design Technology and Embroidery degrees are joined by BA Clothing Design & Technology and Textiles for around 180 points. There's a 22-point assessment.

Meanwhile, in furniture design, Manchester Met's involvement is more markedly on the non-artistic side, through business courses and Marketing and Retail Management, only lightly through the Art & Design facility. These also turn out numbers of graduates into market research, where again they are among the sector leaders. See also Food Marketing (with Foundation).

In advertising, their Art & Design Faculty *is* to the fore, with such as Design & Art Direction. Graphic artists, designers, illustrators (including Illustration with Animation) also proliferate. Set design is another niche.

Meanwhile, in their Department of Contemporary Arts, positive employment figures in a difficult area point up Dance, which may be studied in combination with another Arts subject or as a single subject. There's also an interdisciplinary BA Contemporary Arts degree or a joint hons with a subject available in the Joint Hons faculty. No formal academic qualifications required. Teaching inspection 23.

There is a sound track record, too, in architecture. BA Hons Architecture cane be combined with Structures, Construction, Environmental Studies, or with humanities (History, Social, Cultural, Urbanism, etc), and is required to move onto the postgrad BArch, a 2-year degree, unless you have ARB/RIBA Part 1. Teaching inspection 20.

MMU is also up there with a top league of landscape architects led by the likes of Sheffield, Leeds Met and Greenwich. BA Landscape Architecture is the degree. Teaching inspection 22.

In Law only 8 institutions undertake the BVC (Bar Vocational Course), and MMU is one. They were rated 'Good' recently by the LPC Board.

They are, too, major providers of health sector graduates, though on a different wicket to the uni up the road. MMU supplied more than half the dental technicians registered as finding employment last time. See their BSc Dental Technology and BSc Dental Technology with Study in Industry. There are Foundation courses; otherwise, it's 160-220 points at A level. Speech therapy is another proven slot. It's BSc Speech Pathology & Therapy or BSc Psychology & Speech Pathology. Teaching inspection 22.

BSc Environmental Health sits with various Enviro Management and Protection degrees and Enviro Science or Studies programmes, which have the possibility of time in North America – perfect for budding environmental health officers. Look, too, at the Food Technology/Nutrition degrees.

There's a Foundation, too, for their list of Hospitality Management degrees and a sterling record in employment in the catering industry.

ACADEMIC EXCELLENCE

TEACHING:
(Rated Excellent or 17+ out of 24)

Mechanical Engineering	**Excellent**
Drama, Business & Mgt, Philosophy	**23**
History of Art & Design, Materials Technol, Psychology, Subjects Allied to Medicine, Anatomy, Art & Design, Tourism, Molecular & Organismal Biosciences, Politics, Sport	**22**
Sociology, Modern Languages, Electron & Elect Eng, Dental Technol, Nursing, Information Library Management	**21**
Maths, Town/Country Planning, Education, Economics	**20**
Food Science	**19**

RESEARCH:
Top grades 5/5/6*

Sports-related Subjects	**Grade 6***

WHERE MANCHESTER MET GRADUATES END UP

Health & Social Work: 9%; Education: 18%; Wholesale Retail: 13%; Manufacturing: 8%; Financial Activities: 9%; Public Administration, Civil Service & Defence: 7%; Hotel/Restaurant: 5%; Transport & Communications (including Telecommunications): 4%; Construction: 1%; Personnel: 5%; Computer: 3%; Business & Management: 1%; Accountancy: 1%; Media (including Film): 1%; Architecture: 3%; Publishing: 0.5%; Advertising: 1%; Artistic/Literary: 1%; Sport: 1%.

Approximate 'graduate track' employed **54%**

Courses include Culinary Arts, Tourism, International and Licensed Retail Management by way of orientation. Teaching Inspection 22.

Their Human Resource Management programmes are also to the fore (200 points required at entry). There's a host of possible combinations, Psychology and Sociology being two clearly relevant.

Finally, sports trainers and coaches, and physical training instructors (Education) need look no further than MMU's Alsager Campus. There's a world-class Grade 5* research rating and a very strong track record in employment.

WHAT IT'S REALLY LIKE

UNIVERSITY:	
Social Life	★★★★★
Campus scene	**Huge, diverse happening place**
Student Union services	**Average**
Politics	**Low interest**
Sport	**Competitive**
National team position	**62nd**
Sport facilities	**Good**
Arts opportunities	**Music, film excellent; rest good**
Student newspaper	**Student Direct**
Student magazine	**Pulp**
Nightclub	**K2**
Bars	**MancUnion**
Union ents	**Double Vision**
Union clubs/societies	**70**
Parking	**Poor**
CITY:	
Entertainment	★★★★★
City scene	**Legendary**
Town/gown relations	**Average-poor**
Risk of violence	**High**
Cost of living	**Average**
Student concessions	**Good**
Survival + 2 nights out	**£90 pw**
Part-time work campus/town	**Good**

SOCIAL SCENE

STUDENTS' UNION There are of course many collaborations between Manchester Uni and Manchester Met, the unions being but a walk apart on Oxford Road, the most visible of which is *Student Direct*, the paper which won 2 national awards last year. *Student Direct* and Manchester Met's *Pulp* magazine now get distributed to all three unis (Salford included).

There are, nevertheless, marked differences between the two unis. There is great activity within student societies at Manchester Met – 70 all told, but, as one student said to me, 'Politics is a dirty word... We don't have a very political union. We have political groups – Socialist Workers and so on, but that whole scene is more active at Manchester University. It's a lot more that our union here provides a service, it's more of a social and representational thing.

'It's true, we still have a really strong gay scene within the union.' Gays won't need to be told about Manchester's *Mardi Gras*, an unforgettable weekend of parades and parties. But the hub – day in, day out – is the Village: late licensing, all-night cafés and a huge choice of venues, all within walking distance of one another and MU and MMU.

Watering holes at union headquarters on Oxford Road include **Blue Café**, open from 8.30 am Monday to Friday for breakfast, lunch. Then, there's **MancUnion Bar** with big screen TV and bar promotions. **K2** is the nightclub. They say that when **K2** is open till 2, **MancUnion** is also open till 2, but then MancUnion has a licence till 2 every day except Sunday. Almost every major DJ has graced the K2 decks.

The MancUnion is a 450-capacity bar open 7 nights a week on the 2nd floor of the Student Union building on All Saints Campus, Oxford Road. **K2's** the 900-capacity nightclub downstairs, where after-match joys and blues are danced away on a Wednesday. Friday is *Double Vision* (party toons) – 2 floors of 'utter madness' – in the main room, commercial dance and chart stompers from past to present, plus r&b, soul and jazz upstairs and hip hop

AT A GLANCE

ACADEMIC FILE:	
Subjects assessed	**35**
Excellent	**74%**
Typical entry requirements	**250 points**
Application acceptance rate	**17%**
Students-staff ratio	**21:1**
First/2:1 degree pass rate	**49%**
ACCOMMODATION FILE:	
Guarantee to freshers	**70%**
Style	**Halls, houses**
Catered	**4%**
Approx price range pw	**£50-£80**
City rent pw	**£50-£65**

treats and laid back beats in the back room. On Saturday, it's *Rock Kitchen* and 'rock music played loud' through 2 rooms, 'hosted by DJs Stevie B, Adam, the Rock-It-Crew, and Boxer.' Plus specials like *Sex Lies and R&B*, and *Skool Disco* – 'free sweets, soggy school dinners and prizes for the best fancy dress', and live acts like Timmy Mallett and Pat Sharp. All of which culminates in the Summer Ball at the Palace Hotel, Manchester.

Down in Crewe + Alsager there is a union presence, and bars, shops, clubs and societies at both campuses, and even a nightclub at Crewe. Currently they're running a competition to name their bars, and advertising for students to come help run ents. It is not Manchester, so don't come here if that's what you're after, but there are bus nights to city clubs and among a handful of societies may be found four – Live Music, Alternative Music, Music and Film – which suggest a commendable do-it-yourself artistry to life.

Alsager has an **Arts Centre** with a resident theatre company and a packed programme of performance and literary arts. There are two theatres (the **Axis Theatre** seating 500), a dance studio and an art gallery, and it is here that is run a Drama course so good that it was awarded 23 points out of 24 after a recent inspection. The mind/body balance is made at Alsager by one of the best sports outfits in the country. There are 32 acres of playing fields, an athletics track, swimming pool, indoor facilities galore and a 1,000 square metre laboratory complex, which features a 33 x 6m track for performance data collection, regularly visited by top athletes.

PILLOW TALK

The university halls are good for first years wanting to meet people, but are not cheap and it is fairly difficult to get your first choice. The halls at All Saints have the best location; those at Didsbury require a considerable bus journey. See *Manchester Uni* entry, Pillow Talk, for city accommodation.

GETTING THERE

☛ By road: Manchester, M63/J10, A34. Coach services good. Crewe/Alsager, M6/J16.
☛ By rail to Manchester: London Euston, 2:30; Leeds, 1:45; Liverpool Lime Street, 0:50. Crewe, connections from Manchester Piccadilly.
☛ By air: Manchester Airport for international and inland flights.
☛ By coach: London, 4:35; Bristol, 5:00; Newcastle, 5:00.

MIDDLESEX UNIVERSITY

Middlesex University
Trent Park
London N14 4YZ

TEL 020 8411 5898
FAX 020 8362 5649
EMAIL admissions@mdx.ac.uk
WEB www.mdx.ac.uk

Middlesex University Students' Union
Trent Park
London N14 4YZ

TEL 020 8411 6473
FAX 020 8440 5944
EMAIL r.banford@mdx.ac.uk
WEB www.musu.mdx.ac.uk

VAG VIEW

There are many impressive elements in Middlesex's strategy, not least their Able Centre, *a disability support centre with recording studios turning out audio texts for blind students, a dyslexia support co-ordinator and a sign language bureau, which has appealed to thousands beyond campus too. But there is a huge locally based and mature student population and it would be a mistake to believe that this uni picks you up and takes you out of life in quite the same way as a traditional campus university like Nottingham, Kent or Sussex.*

Most people who come to Middlesex are

not that bothered that the extra-curricular scene at the Students' Union is second rate, or that much of what is on offer has been taken out of the hands of the students, but it may be that this aspect of a traditional university education is precisely what will be seen to be important to the applicant. The drop-out rate is certainly high (12%).

CAMPUS

Getting to grips with this university has been like wrestling with a family of octopuses, so many tentacles are there reaching out across North London and beyond. At one time there were some 18 sites and campuses, but now they concentrating their energies on 3 main-campus sites and pulling the whole operation together onto Trent Park, Hendon and Tottenham in a £100-million strategy.

Tottenham White Hart Lane, London N17 8HR Tel (for all sites): 020 8362 5000. Wood Green tube (Piccadilly line), then W3 bus. Humanities, Business Studies, Law, Sociology, Women's Studies, Computing Science.

Hendon The Burroughs, London NW4 4BT. Hendon Central (Northern line). Business Studies, Management, Accounting & Finance, Economics, Law. A new £17-million learning resource centre opens here this year.

Trent Park Bramley Road, London N14 4YZ. Set in 900 acres of woodlands and meadows. Cockfosters or Oakwood tubes (Piccadilly line). Performing Arts, IT, Cultural Studies, Education Product Design & Engineering, Biological Science.

Cat Hill Barnet, Herts EN4 8HT. Cockfosters (Piccadilly line). Department is Art & Design, Cinematics and Electronic Arts.

UNIVERSITY/STUDENT PROFILE	
University since	**1992**
Situation/style	**Campus/ city sites**
Student population	**22415**
Undergraduates	**16660**
- mature	**43%**
- non EU undergraduates	**14%**
- male/female	**41/59**
- non-traditional student intake	**44%, high**
state school intake	**99%**
- drop-out rate	**12%, high**
- undergraduate applications	**Up 6%**

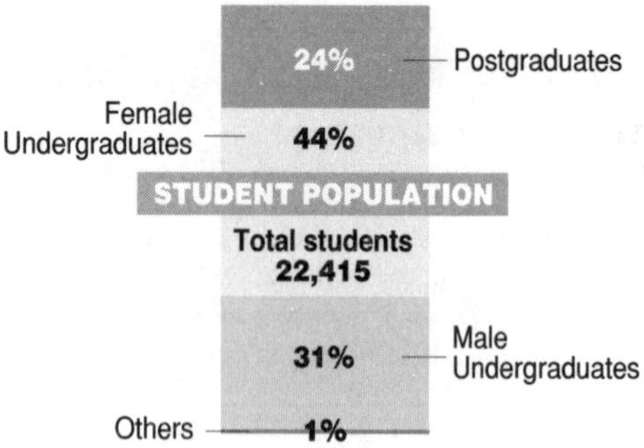

Enfield Queensway, Enfield EN3 4SF. Overland to Southbury Station. Social Sciences, Health Sciences.

FEES, BURSARIES

UK & EU Fees: £3000. If in receipt of full HE Maintenance grant there's a bursary of £1000. Also scholarships of £1000 if you get 300 points at A level or equivalent.

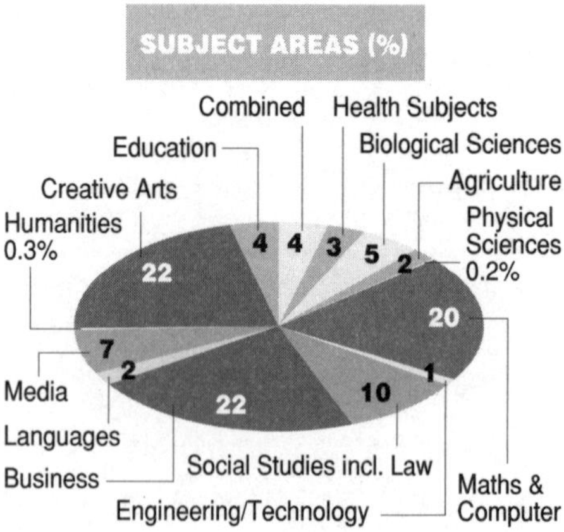

STUDENT PROFILE

Middlesex is a large university and has anything but a traditional university clientele. Many undergraduates are mature, many come from new-to-uni social groups. There is also a large number of part-timers among non-degree (HND) undergraduates. Where numbers have escalated since 1995 is in overseas recruitment. They have won awards for attracting students in from Europe and further afield. Language support is an essential requirement – there's a series of courses incorporating a Foundation year for non-EU international students. Coping with the high drop-out rate that their open-doors policy has helped create is clearly the thought behind the £1000 bursaries for applicants with 300 points at entry, mentioned in *Fees, Bursaries* above.

ACADEMIA & JOBS

The five academic schools are Arts, Computing Science, Health & Social Sciences, Lifelong Learning & Education, and Business.

Jobs for graduates in Art & Design proliferate for graphic artists, designers and illustrators, and elsewhere there's a dedicated BSc Computing Science Graphics & Games which puts them up there in the Top 10 for computer game design. Back in the arts area, BA Interior Design is a fast track to employment, while among Fine Art, Fashion (also Knitwear and Textiles), Product Design, and Jewellery, the latter stands out as a good niche.

Musicians, composers, music industry managers are all well served here, too, and Dance, Drama, Music & Performing Arts are a thoroughly practical niche area, with a good (22-point) teaching rating. Be aware, also, of the Jazz specialism at Middlesex.

For actors, directors, producers there are two BA degrees: Drama & Theatre Studies and Technical Theatre Arts.

They also make arts administrator/managers in quantity – they've cornered 5% of the employment market in this area. Look at the BA Music & Arts Management degree. And Journalism, Publishing and TV Production have dedicated degrees.

Health is another strong area jobs-wise (again a 22-point assessment). They do brisk business with their top-up diploma and foundation course programmes – Nursing, Pre-Registration Midwifery, and Veterinary Nursing, a joint course with the Royal Veterinary College (the best in the field). See, too, the Herbal Medicine and Traditional Chinese Medicine degrees, where Middlesex was a pioneer. The BSc Vet Nursing also leads to the RCVS Vet Nursing Certificate.

There's also a strong line in psychotherapists at the graduate job bank. Look at the Social Sciences with Communication & Language Studies and the BSc Psychology, which carries British Psychological Society accreditation.

ACADEMIC EXCELLENCE

TEACHING:
(Rated Excellent or 17+ out of 24)

Philosophy	**23**
Drama, Dance, Cinematics, History of Art, Architec & Design, American Studies, Education, Nursing, Subjects Allied to Medicine, Politics, Sport, Marketing/Management, Tourism	**22**
Art & Design, Economics, Psychology	**21**
Maths	**20**
Sociology, Modern Langs, Electric & Electron Eng	**19**

RESEARCH:
*Top grades 5/5**

History of Art, Architecture & Design, Philosophy	**Grade 5**

Finally, there is a discernable pattern of careers in environmental health and a whole range of Health & Policy Studies degrees in the BSc joint degree series, also Occupational Health & Safety and BSc Environmental Health. The latter is a joint course with the College of North East London – 22 points at the assessments.

Middlesex have plenty of Management degrees with such as Marketing, Business, Info Systems, and International-style biases, and their joint hons programme allows Management combinations in a whole host of areas. Sales managers proliferate, most of them with an Art & Design bias – textiles, knitwear, jewellery, fashion providing the focus.

They are also commercial and business law specialists incidentally, a subject that carries some useful management and other tie-ups.

SOCIAL SCENE

Students' Union Shame, the bars and ents are now

WHERE MIDDLESEX GRADUATES END UP

Health & Social Work: 12%; Education: 11%; Wholesale Retail: 16%; Manufacturing: 6%; Financial Activities: 8%; Public Administration, Civil Service & Defence: 8%; Hotel/Restaurant: 2%; Transport & Communications (including Telecommunications): 3%; Personnel: 3%; Computer: 4%; Business & Management: 1%; Accountancy: 1%; Media (including Film): 1.5%; Legal 2%; Publishing: 1%; Advertising: 1%; Artistic/Literary: 1%; Sport: 0.5%.

Approximate 'graduate track' employed **54%**

WHAT IT'S REALLY LIKE

UNIVERSITY:	
Social Life	★★
Campus scene	**Friendly, mature, colourful, not campus focused**
Student Union services	**Average**
Politics	**Active**
Sport	**Competitive**
National team position	**67th**
Sport facilities	**Good**
Arts opportunities	**Excellent**
Student magazine	**MUD: Middlesex Union Direct**
Nightclub	**Enfield forum**
Bars	**1 on each campus**
Union ents	**Not a lot**
Union clubs/societies	**30 max.**
Most active society 2005	**Stop The War**
Parking	**Poor**
CITY:	
Entertainment	★★★★★
City scene	**Wild, expensive**
Town/gown relations	**Average-good**
Risk of violence	**Average**
Cost of living	**Very high**
Student concessions	**Good**
Survival + 2 nights out	**£100 pw**
Part-time work locally	**Fair**

AT A GLANCE

ACADEMIC FILE:	
Subjects assessed	**29**
Excellent	**62%**
Typical entry requirements	**200 points**
Application acceptance rate	**15%**
Students-staff ratio	**18:1**
First/2:1 degree pass rate	**52%**
ACCOMMODATION FILE:	
Guarantee to freshers	**No**
Style	**Halls, flats**
Catered	**None**
En suite	**65%**
Approx price range pw	**£68-£82**
City rent pw	**£75-£85 Zone 2**

run by a private contractor (Scolarest) and competitive sport is run directly by the University. This is no way to encourage a strong student culture. The four bars – Enfield, Tottenham, Trent Park and Cat Hill – provide drinks promos and ents during the week, but they close at weekends. There's a Freshers' Ball, of course, and some tell of a Middlesex extravaganza, a 36-hour festival in the summer at Trent Park, and there's a student magazine called *MUD – Middlesex Union Direct*.

SPORT Gym facilities exist on all campuses. Sport is an area of continual investment. Recent large projects include a £2.5m state-of-the-art gym, the Real Tennis Centre at Hendon, and two artificial hockey pitches at Trent Park. Students have access to uniswimming pools, indoor and outdoor, football and rugby pitches and a golf club.

PILLOW TALK

There are 2400 places in halls, all of which are self-catering. The vast majority have been built over the past five years; all are within easy reach of their respective campuses. See *Campus* notes above for how to get there.

NAPIER UNIVERSITY

Napier University
Craiglockhart Campus
10 Colinton Road
Edinburgh EH10 5DT

TEL 0500 35 35 70
FAX 0131 455 2588
EMAIL info@napier.ac.uk
WEB www.napier.ac.uk

Napier Students' Association
12 Merchiston Place
Edinburgh EH10 4NR

TEL 0131 229 8791
FAX 0131 228 3462
EMAIL nsa@napier.ac.uk
WEB www.napierstudents.com

VAG VIEW

Napier has a strong reputation for getting its graduates jobs. Its difficulty has always been that it is a bit of a local uni, with a weekday frame of mind. As that began to change, students cheered in the process and Napier's traditionally high drop-

out rate fell by a third in just two years. But now, at 21%, it is not looking so good. They and Abertay Dundee had the worst drop-out results at the last count, and there was a 10% drop in applications recently. Rather oddly, at the same time, a whopping 61% graduated from here with Firsts or 2:1s.

CAMPUS

'Napier is not a campus university,' writes Gareth L Mackie. 'Instead it has 4 major sites [whose faculties are currently in flux] – **Merchiston** [engineering, arts, social sciences], **Sighthill** [business and languages], **Craiglockhart** [computer, electrical & electronic engineering and maths] and **Craighouse** [management, tourism, music, media, communications, etc.] – and 5 minor ones, spread out mostly through the south and west of Edinburgh. This can be a pain if you have lectures at more than one site, though generally you'll be based in one place.

'Each site has an atmosphere of its own: Merchiston is probably the busiest and liveliest, as it is the nearest to the city centre. Craighouse only received a student bar in November 1998. There is no one place where Napierites congregate.'

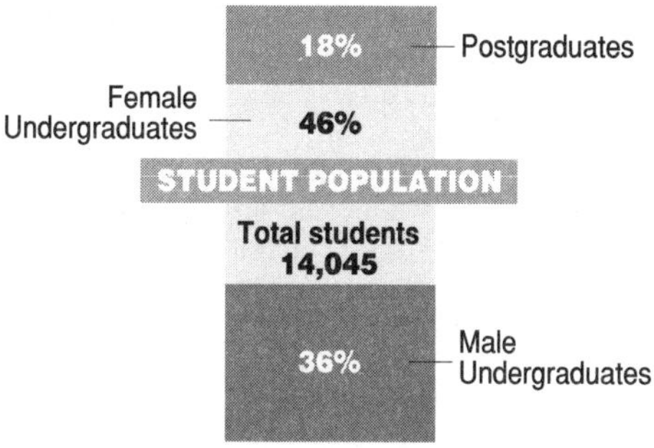

FEES, BURSARIES

Fees for English students: £1700 p.a.

STUDENT PROFILE

The student profile shows a fair mix of state and public school for a new uni, and given the number of independent school entrants there is a healthy balance in 35% of the undergraduate population coming from new-to-uni backgrounds, 25% from 'low-participation neighbourhoods'. This fact, were it combined with a low drop-out rate, would surely make it one of the government's elite 'access universities'. There is also a sizeable mature population (50%), a number of HND students and a smattering of part-timers, the local element perhaps tending to

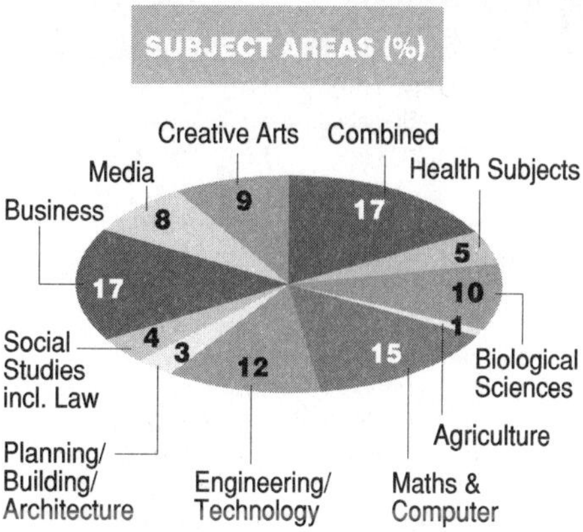

limit Napier to something of a day-time college, rather than university.

ACADEMIA & JOBS

Its roots are in science and engineering – the broad-based BEng in Energy and Environmental Engineering is one of many courses typically well conceived for a job in industry. The uni is known for business, too, and for built environment. Their graduate placement record in engineering and industrial design, in manufacturing (particularly in electronic & electrical manufacturing), in finance and in the construction industry, reflect these preoccupations.

Look also at Civil Engineering. Given that it's a small uni, Napier has done well to find employment for sufficient graduates in this area (some 3% of its annual output) to make the national Top 10. There are some specialist niches, as you might expect from a uni focused on getting its graduates jobs: Civil & Transport Engineering, Civil Eng. & Computing, Civil & Timber Eng (there's a spin-off here into forestry as a career path) – you can bet they know exactly where to place you. Note also

UNIVERSITY/STUDENT PROFILE

University since	**1992**
Situation/style	**Civic**
Student population	**14045**
Undergraduates	**11470**
- mature	**50%**
- non EU undergraduates	**4%**
- male/female	**43/57**
- non-traditional student intake	**35%**
-state school intake	**95%**
- drop-out rate	**21%, v. high**
- undergraduate applications	**Down 10%**

ACADEMIC EXCELLENCE

TEACHING:
(Rated Excellent, Highly Satis. or 17+ out of 24)

Civil Engineering, Building & Surveying, Chemistry, Hospitality Studies, Mass Communications, Maths & Statistics.	**Highly Satis.**
European Languages	**19**

RESEARCH :

*Top grades 5/5**	**None**

BSc Architectural Design & Civil Eng. Teaching inspection, Highly Satisfactory.

There is a range of architectural design and technology degrees, of construction industry and surveying degrees, bringing it Top 10 status in the area of Construction Engineer/Manager. A quantity surveyor costs the building of our constructed environment and must have the care for detail of an accountant. This is a very effective niche area too (around 2% of graduates find jobs in it), and an accessible opportunity at point of entry. They have the BSc Single Hons and BSc Quantity Surveying with Computing. Teaching inspection, Highly Satisfactory. Jobs are also plentiful in Electronic or Telecommunications Engineering for Napier graduates, most come from dedicated Engineering degrees, a handful via Computer Science and Physical Sciences.

> ***So great has been their employment muscle that a few years ago the*** Financial Times ***named Napier Scottish Uni of the Year.***

The uni is also big on the engineering design consultant front. Nationally, entry is mainly via Engineering (67%) and Architecture (8%) or a blend of the two, design being an aspect of many an Engineering degree of course. Napier's BEng and BSc degree courses range from Computing Networks & Distributed Systems to Polymer Engineering, Architectural Design & Information Systems, Computer-Aided Design & Business Studies and Product Design Engineering. Average

The uni is pre-eminent, too (more than 2% of graduates), in software engineering via its BEng and BSc software degrees.

Next, cut to the uni's extraordinary success in journalism – more than 2% of its graduates are finding jobs in the sector. There is a dedicated degree, and one in publishing, too, Napier now mount an amazingly strong challenge in these areas, being right up there in employment terms with unis that have double their number of undergraduates. Look, too, at their Art & Design courses, with Photography and Film. These are very popular areas for applicants, and you will likely be interviewed. There is also a new £22-million Scottish Centre for Creative Industries, which will pull together all the faculty elements and bring a studio and recording space into the picture. On tyhe music front, there's a BMus and BA Pop Music.

Prospective investment advisers and analysts in the insurance and pension fields should be interested that 27% of Napier's applicants are taken into the Business Faculty and 18% of all their graduates get a job in the financial sector (more than any other single sector), a third of these into the insurance and pensions fields. Note also in the Business School the marketing degrees, which are bringing 2% of their graduates work as marketing managers or in related occupations. Business Studies links also with Finance, Entrepreneurship, Languages, Psychology, Operations Management. Accounting comes with Finance or Economics. Nearly 2% of their graduates find jobs in the hotel and restaurant management sector – look in particular at the Tourism Management with Entrepreneurship and similar degrees.

Nearly 2% of their graduates find work as bacteriologists and microbiologists. There is a BSc

WHERE NAPIER GRADUATES END UP

Health & Social Work: 7%; Education: 3%; Wholesale Retail: 10%; Manufacturing: 10%; Financial Activities: 18%; Public Administration, Civil Service & Defence: 6%; Hotel/Restaurant: 8%; Transport & Communications (including Telecommunications): 4%; Construction: 5%; Agriculture: 1%; Mining/Oil Extracting: 9%; Personnel: 1%; Computer: 2%; Business & Management: 4%; Accountancy: 1%; Media (including Film): 3%; Legal 2%; Architecture: 4%; Publishing: 4%; Advertising: 2%; Sport: 1%.

Approximate 'graduate track' employed **57%**

WHAT IT'S REALLY LIKE

COLLEGE:	
Social Life	★★
Campus scene	**Weekday and disparately focused**
Student Union services	**Average**
Politics	**Interest low**
Sport	**Improving**
National team position	**89th**
Sport facilities	**Improving**
Arts opportunities	**Average**
Student mag/news	**Veritas**
Bars	**Twelve, Asylum/**
Union ents	**DJs**
Union clubs/societies	**20**
Most popular society	**Gaelic**
Parking	**Poor**
CITY:	
Entertainment	★★★★★
Scene	**Seething**
Town/gown relations	**Good**
Risk of violence	**Low**
Cost of living	**High**
Student concessions	**Excellent**
Survival + 2 nights out	**£150+ pw**
Part-time work campus/town	**Good/excellent**

Microbiology & Biotechnology.

Meanwhile, word is spreading about the degrees in natural health therapies – Aromatherapy, Reflexology and Herbal Medicine. Recently another popular niche development has been the Veterinary Nursing.

SOCIAL SCENE

There are two student bars – **Bar Twelve** at Merchiston and **BaseRate** at Craiglockart – but short opening hours and limited capacities inhibit what can be done ents-wise. **Twelve** (at 12 Merchiston Place) is a café bar during the day and a pre-club (DJs, theme nights, live music) from late afternoon – latest licence is Monday to Friday at 1 am, midday to 6 pm Saturdays. There are three pool tables and games machines. At Merchiston, too, the **Apex** café recently opened to complement the **Triangle** restaurant.

Writes Gareth: 'Drinking aside, there are several clubs and societies worth joining, the most popular the Gaelic Society, and it's relatively easy to form your own, so long as you can find enough like-minded people. Through the NSA, there are teams and clubs for just about every sport imaginable; from sub-aqua to mountaineering. Napier used to have the best student football team in Scotland, but it's not too hot right now. Our netball team is doing rather well, though!' They sat 89th in the BUSA league last year. There's a sports centre at Sighthill.

TOWN See *Edinburgh Student City*, page 175.

PILLOW TALK

Uni accommodation in apartment developments in the city centre is guaranteed to freshers coming 'outwith a thirty-mile radius of Edinburgh'. There is no catered accommodation. Four-person flats have one shared bathroom; five-person flats have two shared bathrooms.

Says Gareth: 'Napier provides housing for over 1,000 students, it's quite expensive but is quickly snapped up. Edinburgh has an abundance of reasonably priced flats, so it should be easy to find one in an area that suits you and your pocket. Areas to consider include Tollcross, Gorgie/Dalry, Marchmont and Bruntsfield. You may see cheaper areas, but they may not be student-friendly.'

GETTING THERE

AT A GLANCE

ACADEMIC FILE:	
Subjects assessed	**18**
Excellent	**50%**
Typical entry requirements	**220 points**
Application acceptance rate	**30%, v. high**
Students-staff ratio	**22:1**
First/2:1 degree pass rate	**61%**
ACCOMMODATION FILE:	
Guarantee to freshers	**Non-local applicants**
Style	**Flats**
Catered	**None**
Price range pw	**£65-£70**
Approx. city rent pw	**£65-£85**

☛ By road: from north, M90; from Stirling, M9; from Newcastle, A1; from Glasgow, M8.
☛ By rail: London King's Cross, 4:30. Glasgow Central, 50 mins; Newcastle, 1:30.
☛ By coach: Glasgow, 1:10; London, 9:10.

STUDENT NEWCASTLE - THE CITY

Newcastle is a city at the cutting edge of student life. Offering the very best in entertainment, its lively and vibrant atmosphere, progressive and diverse character make it an essential stop for any fun lovin' student. Ranked as the 7th best party city in the world, the 'toon', as it is affectionately known, is also heading up the field in all things cultural. Along with Gateshead, its neighbour on the Tyne, recent years have witnessed a massive boom for Newcastle Arts. 2002 saw the development of the world renowned **Baltic Centre for Contemporary Art**, a 4- storey converted flour mill which houses numerous temporary exhibitions, and now the **Sage Music Centre** on Newcastle's very own south bank.

NIGHTLIFE

Geordie attitude turns on the old adage, 'work hard, play hard', and be it the legendary **Bigg Marke**t, the swanky watering holes of the Quayside or the cosmopolitan bars of Jesmond's Osborne Road and the area around Central Station, there is opportunity for everyone to play as hard as they like, often at a price most students can afford.

When it comes to clubbing and live acts, both universities are up there with the best in live entertainment. The Darkness, Coldplay, Kosheen, Shed 7, Elbow, Starsailor, Mark Owen and Jools Holland are just a few of the big name acts to have played . **The Telewest Arena** attracts all the major national tours, from Justin Timberlake, Beyonce and Blue to Stereophonics and Craig David, while the **City Hall** has it's own share of the stars, the likes of Norah Jones and Travis The only downside is that our location means a lot of small tours do not visit. Don't expect to see everyone.

If you want to sample musical delights a little closer to home there are also smaller more intimate live venues such as **The Cluny** and **The Head of Steam** which showcase the cream of Newcastle's homegrown musical talent.

The city's club scene has rocketed to success in recent years with the launch of numerous highly acclaimed club events. **Shindig**, which celebrated its tenth birthday in 2002 still has the edge as it continues to attract a huge variety of big name DJs with Erick Morillo, Roger Sanchez, Sister Bliss, Steve Lawler and Danny Rampling among those to have graced their decks. It was voted *Muzik Magazine's Underground Club Night of the Year* in 2001. *Promise* on Friday @ **Foundation** does a similar job for the harder and progressive house scene, while other notable nights include: *LoveDough* @ **Ikon**, *Positive* @ **Newcastle Student's Union** and *Traveller* @ **Northumbria University Student's Union.** Also look out for Newcastle University's once termly *Arcane*, which has a reputation among students and locals alike.

The most notorious student-only nights are held at **Blue Bambu**, **Tiger Tiger**, **Ikon**, **Sea**, **Baja Beach Club** and **the Tuxedo Princess**, the latter being a permanent floating fixture of the Quayside.

The gay scene is well served in the city's pink triangle (behind the **International Centre for Life**), with **Powerhouse** the most popular night club having opened its doors to the likes of Holly Valance and Lisa Scott-Lee.

SPORT

The whole city revolves around the fortunes of Newcastle United, so get informed. St James's Park is the most imposing landmark on the city skyline and the second largest stadium in the Premiership. Getting tickets can be a problem, however, despite the 52,000 capacity, but well worth trying for.

Elsewhere, Johnny Wilkinson (occasionally) and the rest of the Newcastle Falcons offer a student friendly environment for rugby fans, while the Newcastle Eagles do the same for basketball followers. Wherever you go, don't mention any allegiance to Northeast rivals Sunderland or Manchester United or you are liable to end up in a bit of bother.

CINEMA

The Odeon is the most central cinema and with its brand new multiplex having recently opened in **The Gate** on Newgate Street, you can enjoy all the top films at student prices right on your doorstep. Also in the city centre is a 12-screen **Warner Village**, while a short drive will take you to **UCI Silverlink** or **MetroCentr**e. For the more artistic, the **Tyneside Cinema** on Pilgrim Street is one of the best independent cinemas in the country.

THEATRE AND COMEDY

Newcastle is one of the Royal Shakespeare Company's second homes. In the autumn, it doth take over most of the city's stages for a month of highbrow entertainment. The major venue is the **Theatre Royal**, the poshest of Newcastle's theatres. For a smaller, cheaper alternative, try the **Live Theatre**. If it's a more relaxed, studenty atmosphere you're after you can't beat the **Playhouse** and **Gulbenkian Studio** to get the best in up and coming talent. Both theatres are housed in the same building at the edge of Newcastle University's campus, and are home to the more cutting-edge Northern Stage company.

For comedy look no further than the fantastic

Hyena Café, open 12 months of the year, and the annual Newcastle Comedy Festival, which plays a number of venues across the city for a two-week spell. **Newcastle Student Union** also puts on a comedy night every Monday during term-time, in it's **Global Café** venue.

SHOPPING

The only major studenty shop is **Period Clothing**, with some fantastic stuff in store. Otherwise Newcastle blends high street stores with smaller designer boutiques well. On Northumberland Street you can check out all the highstreet brands such as **H&M**, **Zara** and **Warehouse**, whilst **Eldon Square Shopping Centre**, just off Northumberland Street is home to **TopShop**, **USC**, **Oasis** and all the major department stores. Grainger Town is where you'll find the 'trendier' and more expensive shops as well as some quality boutiques. Check out **Mint**, just off Grey Street, it's a truly awesome shopping experience. A short journey will take you to the Gateshead **MetroCentre** and the major stores/labels. For music, **Steel Wheels**, **RPM** and **Flying Records** offer good independent options.

Jess Gooch

UNIVERSITY OF NEWCASTLE UPON TYNE

The University of Newcastle upon Tyne
Kensington Terrace
Newcastle upon Tyne NE1 7RU

TEL 0191 222 5594
FAX 0191 222 8685
EMAIL enquiries@ncl.ac.uk
WEB www.ncl.ac.uk

The Newcastle University Union Society
Kings Walk
Newcastle upon Tyne NE1 8QB

TEL 0191 239 3916
FAX 0191 222 1876
EMAIL comm.union@ncl.ac.uk
WEB www.unionsociety.co.uk

VAG VIEW

Academically, Newcastle is good right across the board. 'Those who live in the north perhaps understand how good it is better than those from the south,' said one Yorkshire-based school careers teacher, adding with weight, 'It is very popular among students who go there.'

Good across the board, certainly, but at the very height of academic excellence sit Medicine, Physiological Sciences, Psychology, Molecular Biosciences, Pharmacology and subjects allied to Medicine. These are the departments that scored full marks in the assessments. True, nothing has scored less than 20 points out of 24, but these did not drop a point. The subjects allied to Medicine are speech language sciences. All the top ratings are sciences with a medical tinge. In the national research assessments, high among the departments adjudged world class are Clinical Laboratory Sciences, Psychology, Biological Sciences... and Music, the latter reminding us that there are dimensions to the Newcastle experience beyond clinical laboratories.

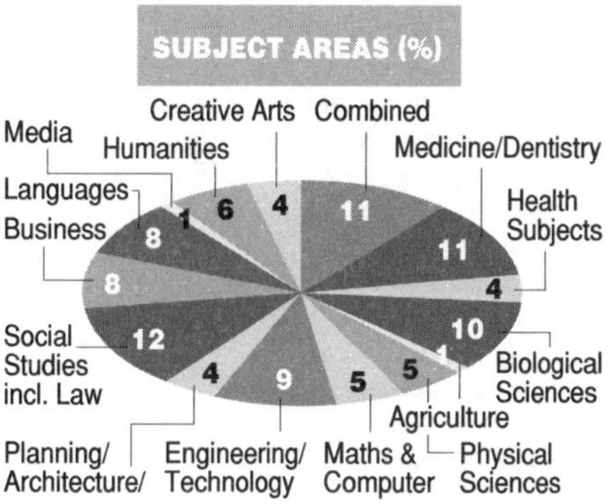

Last year they bid successfully for £9m of Government funding to establish two Centres of Excellence in music and healthcare. One project will run workshops for student composers and performers together with leading musicians at the newly-opened Sage Music Centre on Newcastle's very own south bank. Another project will network hospitals and universities in the North to enhance the clinical aspects of teaching medicine.

Where Newcastle scores over London and, yes, over Manchester, is in its packing an incredible array of cultural, artistic and hedonistic power centres into a very small space (and at relatively low cost). So much is going on, and all of it so concentrated, that the buzz on the street at night is ten times what you will feel in the greater, but more dispersed metropolis.

Newcastle's undergraduates have a real and vibrant city to discover, but the loyalty of its students is down to what goes on in the Students' Union.

Go there and see. What you notice on campus is people doing, things happening, students in control... of themselves and what they are about. 'We actually own the whole set-up,' they say. They do – union building and all.

CAMPUS

Newcastle is a campus university situated right in the heart of this compact and compelling city, within walking distance of theatres, cinemas, shops, bars, pubs, restaurants, but equally only a short way from the eye-catching north-east coast.

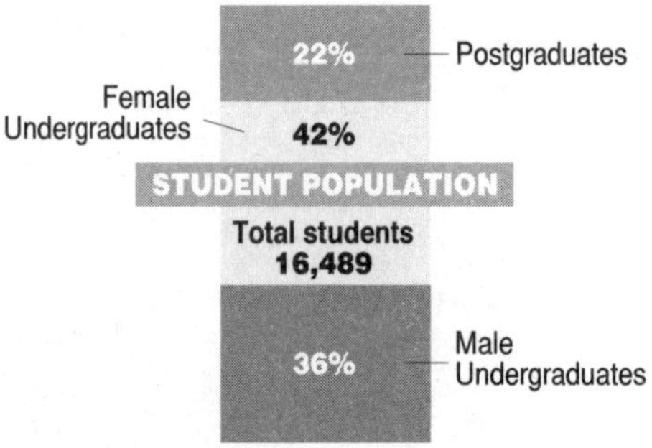

FEES, BURSARIES

UK & EU Fees: £3000 p.a., with some exceptions: Speech and Language Sciences (no fee), Medicine and Dentistry (no fee for final/5th year), Placement Years (charged at usually 25% of full tuition fee). For all 2006 Finance Information at Newcastle University see www.ncl.ac.uk/ undergraduate/finance. Bursaries, see www.ncl.ac.uk/ undergraduate/finance/bursary.phtml.

'From 2006,' they say, 'we will be offering a wide range of scholarships and other awards to recognize and reward outstanding achievement and ability... 194 scholarships worth £465,000 in total.' See www.ncl.ac.uk/undergraduate/finance/scholarships/index.phtml. Elite Athletes Bursaries - 15 of £500 p.a. Performance Sport Bursaries - 20 of £500. Royal and Ancient Golf Club at St Andrews Golf Bursaries are also available. The University spends over £20000 on its golf programme. There are other grants available for particular categories of students e.g. students with children, adult dependants, or students with disabilities.

STUDENT PROFILE

The student profile reveals a low proportion of state school entrants: 'The pink pashmina and boat shoe brigade do seem to claim the majority,' as a student put it, 'but people tend to separate into their own different groups according to individual taste. There is enough to do to keep all parties happy. Freshers Week tends to be the only time when you have to put up with people who aren't necessarily "your kind of people", to quote Michael Barymore.'

Statistics apart, after it has been well and truly done by Freshers Week this student body soon gets focused on making things happen, a lot of it through the union's 150+ clubs and societies, but not only through them; the typical Newcastle student likes to make it happen, it is part of the culture of Newcastle University, an organic thing perhaps. When recently the uni was approached by London-based Winning Moves, the makers of Monopoly to pilot a game of monopoly, for purchase by Newcastle students and alumni, they said they chose Newcastle beacuse: 'Students have the time of their lives at Newcastle, so its graduates have fond memories. We knew we were onto a winner.'

Everyone seems to be happy – the drop-out rate, at 3%, is very low.

ACADEMIA & JOBS

'The general ethos seems to be work hard, play hard,' writes Geraldine Englard. 'The standard of teaching is generally high, some lecturers being able to communicate with their students better than others. Workloads differ, but as a rule, students doing a science degree have a whole lot more lectures than do arts students. However, when it comes to coursework and exams, the pressure seems to equalise, as all courses are based on a

UNIVERSITY/STUDENT PROFILE

Independent university since	**1963**
Situation/style	**City campus**
Student population	**16489**
Undergraduates	**12899**
- mature	**11%**
- non EU undergraduates	**9%**
- male/female	**46/54**
- non-traditional student intake	**21%**
- state school intake	**69%**
- drop-out rate	**3%, low**
- undergraduate applications	**Up 5%**

similar modular system.

'There are two main libraries, the Robinson library and Medical library, both are well resourced, well staffed and fully computerised, but be prepared for a massive demand on books when it comes to exam time. Don't think that you will be able to pop into the library a day before the holidays and find all the books you need, because you won't. The geeks will have got there first.

'Computing facilities at Newcastle are excellent, each department having a number of its own computer clusters, all linked to the net, in addition to those available in the libraries. There is even a large 24-hour access cluster, a godsend because, though you might find it difficult to imagine now, you may well have to work through the night.'

An Enterprise Centre turns ideas into action by creating new business, using public and private sector experts as mentors for students, brokering industry expertise in curriculum development and inviting entrepreneurs and other professionals to lecture to students. The culture enabled student companies from Newcastle to win four awards in the national final of the Graduate Enterprise Programme in Leicester this year.

Almost one fifth of undergraduates go into the health sector, and the medical school took full marks at assessment and is regarded by many as the best in the country. There's a 10% chance pf gettin, but that's only a tad below average. Besides the 6-year MB BS (with pre-med year for students without the necessary science background), there's a 4-year accelerated MB BS designed for graduates and a 5-year MB BS, Phase 1 of which can be undertaken here or at Durham Uni's Stockton Campus (south down the A1 on the outskirts of Middlesbrough); 245 places at Newcastle, 95 at Stockton – all come together at Newcastle for Phase II training in cahoots with the NHS. Clinical relevance is emphasised throughout. Entry The 6-year course requires AAB excluding General Studies + 5 passes at GCSE including English, Maths and a science subject. For the 5-year Stockton/Newcastle degree, it's AAB including Chemistry or Biology but not General Studies (2 AS levels are accepted in place of 1 A). GCSE Biology, Chemistry, Physics, Maths, English. Teaching inspection 24. Research Grade 5*: Clinical Lab Sciences, Psychology,

ACADEMIC EXCELLENCE

TEACHING:

(Rated Excellent or 17+ out of 24)

Architecture, English, Geology, Social Policy & Administration	**Excellent**
Medicine, Physiological Sciences, Psychology, Molecular Biosciences & Pharmacology, Subjects Allied to Medicine	**24**
Dentistry, Maths, Economics, Politics	**23**
Modern Languages, Linguistics Agric, Forest & Agric Sciences, Organismal Biosciences, Classics, Education, Theology	**22**
Chemical Engineering, Electrical & Electronic Eng, Town & Country Planning, Physics, Archaeology	**21**
Civil Engineering/Geomatics, Marine Technol, Art & Design	**20**

RESEARCH :

Top grades 5/5/6**

Clinical Laboratory Sciences,. Psychology, Biological Sciences, Music,	**Grade 6***
Community-based Clinical, Hospital-based Clinical, Clinical Dentistry, Physiology, Nursing, Earth Sciences, Pure Maths, Statistics, Computer, Chemical Eng, Civil Eng, Electrical/ Electronic Eng, Town /Country Planning, Geography, Law, Politics, Accounting, English, Iberian and Latin American, Linguistics, Theology	**Grade 5**

WHERE NEWCASTLE GRADUATES END UP

Health & Social Work: 19%; Education: 5%; Wholesale Retail: 8%; Manufacturing: 9%; Financial Activities: 7%; Public Administration, Civil Service & Defence: 10%; Hotel/Restaurant: 3%; Transport & Communications (including Telecommunications): 3.5%; Construction: 1%; Agriculture: 2%; Mining/Oil Extracting: 1%; Personnel: 4%; Computer: 2.5%; Business & Management: 2%; Accountancy: 3%; Media (including Film): 1%; Legal 1.5%; Architecture: 2%; Publishing: 1%; Advertising: 1%; Artistic/Literary: 0.5%; Sport: 1%.

Approximate 'graduate track' employed **75%**

Biological Sciences; Grade 5: Community-based Clinical, physiology. The dental degree is a 5-year BDS. Entry ABB. Teaching inspection 23. Research Grade 5.

The 10% provision of graduates to public admin, the civil service and defence points us in other directions. Look especially at the 4-year Government & European Union Studies degree. The Law is a recognised pathway for defence executives from Newcastle, while defence operatives and equipment engineers often come the biological sciences route, look at Biological Sciences, Biomedical Sciences, Medical Microbiology & Immunology, Biochemistry with Immunology, etc. There's full marks at the assessments for biosciences and subjects allied to medicine, and world class, Grade 5* ratings for Clinical Laboratory Sciences and Biological Sciences, too. The army and Royal navy are popular among Newcastle graduates, and there's a good track record for government researchers.

> ***Where Newcastle scores over London and, yes, over Manchester, is in its packing an incredible array of cultural, artistic and hedonistic power centres into a very small space (and at relatively low cost).***

The 3% provision into accountancy points up BA Accounting & Finance and Business Accounting & Finance with a business placement (4 years). There are also BSc joint hons degrees in Accounting with Computer, Info Systems, Maths, or Statistics – a department where you'll also find Economics & Maths or Statistics. Graduate stockbrokers proliferate at Newcastle.

Architecture is a strength that converts into jobs on a big scale. There's BA Architectural Studies (recognised by RIBA) and a raft of interesting nautical developments in the Newcastle and Strathclyde University Engineering faculties, both names traditionally associated with shipbuilding. Engineering design consultants proliferate. Cartographers should look to the Geomatics Department and its Surveying & Mapping Science degree.

Electrical and telecommunications engineers at Newcastle find careers come easy, and entry is no problem thanks to Foundation courses available for both the BEng and MEng routes. Teaching inspection 21. Research Grade 5.

IT consultants pour out of Newcastle. Look in particular at the B/MEng Computer Systems Engineering and the BSc Computing Science, and Software Engineering.

The language provision at Newcastle is first class, and very often they lead the way in finding employment for graduate translators, and many also find jobs in advertising. Newcastle offer Chinese, Japanese, European and Modern Languages with all sorts of orientations. There's a teaching assessment of 22 points out of 24.

In farming there's the top employment-rated Agri-Business Management and other Management courses – Farm Business, Rural Resource, also mainstream Agriculture, Applied Biology and the non-practical Agronomy, plus a host of animal science degrees. There's also a tie-up with Tesco on the organic food production wicket. Teaching inspection, 22.

Finally, two courses command serious attention. Newcastle and Nottingham Trent lead in what is not

WHAT IT'S REALLY LIKE

UNIVERSITY:	
Social Life	★★★★★
Campus scene	**Lively, aware, middle-class**
Student Union services	**Good**
Politics	**Active, mainly student issues**
Sport	**57 clubs**
National team position	**19th**
Sport facilities	**Good**
Arts opportunities	**Drama excellent; rest good**
Student magazine	**Pulp**
Student newspaper	**The Courier**
Student radio	**NSR**
Nightclubs	**Global, Beats, Bassment**
Bars	**Mens Bar, Green Room, Cochrane**
Union ents	**Chart, dance, Indie, drum 'n bass, live**
Union societies	**100**
Most popular societies	**NUTS (theatre), Cheerleading, Jazz**
Parking	**Adequate**
CITY:	
Entertainment	★★★★★
Scene	**Vibrant, fun**
Town/gown relations	**OK**
Risk of violence	**Low**
Cost of living	**Low**
Student concessions	**Good**
Survival + 2 nights out	**£70 pw**
Part-time work campus/town	**Average/excellent**

(unfortunately for the consumer) a crowded field. Their MEng Mechanical & Railway Engineering is, as far as we can tell, one of only two degrees in this field. It has been developed with a whole lot of operators and equipment manufacturers, including Virgin Trains, Bombardier Transportation, The Engineering Link & Arriva Trains Northern. Get on it as quickly as you can and pray it arrives on time.

SOCIAL SCENE

Students' Union It's the central point of social life here, with 6 bars and 3 clubs, **Global**, **Bassment**, and **Beats**. It plays host regularly to big name bands and DJs.

Every Friday there's *Solution*: cheesy main room, indie side room, lots of drinks offers. Recent guests include: Futureheads, Goldie lookin chain, elbow, Hard fi, 2manydjs.

There are also monthly music events, *Turbulence*, which has been rated the best drum 'n' bass night in the North, *Brighton Beach* (indie), *Substance* (eclectic breaks and beats), and *Universal* – chart 'n' cheese.

The Bassment takes about 1000 and then they've got the 300-capacity **Global Café**. Once a term they have *Arcane* – all the proceeds fund a student from some underprivileged area of the dark continent. *Arcane* lasts from about 8pm until 6am. As well as the two main dancefloors (**Bassment, Global**), there are specialist drum 'n' bass areas and chill out rooms.

There's a comedy night every Monday during term-time in the **Global Café** venue, and monthly local band showcases – student and local bands do gigs, and there's an annual battle of the bands when they invite A&R men to seed record deals. Then there's also a weekly quiz night.

Whatever's on, they open all the bars in the building (total capacity 2200), and with a new lift installed they have open access to all floors, which makes for a climactic scene. When one bar shuts down – the **Men's Bar** and the smoke-free **Cochrane Lounge** seem first to go, everyone goes on to wherever the action is. Other bars are **Subterranean**, **Subversions**, **Beats** and **The Irish Bar**. **Beats** has recently been renovated – meals during the day, venue at night.

'With all these great nights out, some extra cash is bound to come in handy,' writes Geraldine in practical mode. 'The SU provides a job shop, advertising all kinds of part-time vacancies with accredited employers. It also offers welfare and advisory services in addition to supporting over 100 different societies and more than sixty sports clubs.'

Ents are, indeed, but the beginning. Much is done in the context of the real world outside. Student drama producers, for example, have to survive in real terms, are dependent on public audiences, arrange sponsorship and all the rest. Two or three student-produced plays appear each year at **The Gulbenkian**, a small, vigorously experimental studio-type place. There might be a production at **Live**, the theatre on the Quayside.

Student **C**ommunity **A**ction **N**ewcastle SCAN – 'is very big,' I was told. 'At the moment we're working on a children's outdoor experience area and a community gym-type area in the city. Our policy is that students are not just here to go to lectures but to develop skills. Volunteer work is one area for that. We find SCAN just about the easiest thing to get students involved in, and the SCAN ball is one of the best. Nightline is popular as well – telephone counselling by student volunteers.'

The SU Debating Chamber, looked to us uncannily like the House of Commons, when we visited, but the campaigning seems pretty much non-party.

The *Courier* office is a crammed galley of a room, space enough for the award-winning student weekly to be committed to Quark. Now there's a magazine (*Pulp*) too and radio station, N.S.R.

Sport There's a Talented Athlete Sports Scholarship (TASS) scheme and a new £5.5m indoor sports facility, opened in August 2005. There are 57 sports clubs on offer and the uni came 19th nationally last year out of all universities (observe: 9 places below Northumbria). The much-respected American Football team is called Newcastle Mariners or Crazy Blue.

On-campus s**ports centres** provide for aerobics, badminton, basketball, indoor hockey, soccer, netball, squash, tennis, trampolining, volleyball, fitness training, martial arts, dance, gymnastics.

Track and field athletes use the **Gateshead International Stadium**. There are pitches and

AT A GLANCE

ACADEMIC FILE:	
Subjects assessed	**36**
Excellent	**78%**
Typical entryl requirements	**365 points**
Application acceptance rate	**15%**
Students-staff ratio	**17:1**
First/2:1 degree pass rate	**67%**
ACCOMMODATION FILE:	
Guarantee to freshers	**100%**
Style	**Halls, flats**
Catered	**40%**
En-suite	**10%**
Price range pw	**£45.01-£97.86**
City rent pw	**£30-£65**

courts at Cochrane Park, Heaton (Medicals), Longbenton (with its new all-weather pitch), and at Close House, the uni estate ten miles to the west. Rowing is also popular and successful.

TOWN See *Newcastle Student City*, page 330.

PILLOW TALK

Newcastle have a torturously worded test for uni accommodation, but as it allows first year undergraduates 'who will be coming alone to the University for the full academic year', the policy is effectively pretty inclusive. Local students will have more of a problem than those from afar, and be sure to get the application form in by 30 June.

Castle Leazes Halls and Henderson Hall are catered. Self-catered flats include: Richardson Road, Marris House, St Mary's College, Windsor Terrace, Leazes Parade, and Bowsden Court Shared Flats. There's also couple and family accommodation, and places adapted for students with disabilities.

Close to campus city-centre rents range from £50-£58 p.w. But at Fenham, close to the Medical School, it's less, around £30-£38. Further out, at Gosforth, it's £43-£48 per person per week. Heaton has a long tradition of housing students; rents are currently £42-£47. Leafy Jesmond, which is close to the uni, served by the Metro and with good shops and pubs, costs £52-£65. Sandyford, very close to uni, is rapidly catching up to Jesmond in popularity. Rents are £48-£58 p.w.

GETTING THERE

☛ By road: A1, A167/A696; A167 exit.
☛ By rail: Edinburgh, 1:30; Leeds, 1:45; London King's Cross, 3:00; Manchester Piccadilly, 3:00; Birmingham New Street, 4:00.
☛ By air: Newcastle International Airport.
☛ By coach: London, 6:05; Birmingham, 4:25.

UNIVERSITY OF WALES, NEWPORT

University of Wales, Newport
Caerleon Campus
PO Box 179
Newport NP6 1YG

TEL 01633 432030
FAX 01633 432850
EMAIL admissions@newport.ac.uk
WEB www.newport.ac.uk

Newport Students' Union
College Crescent
Caerleon
Newport NP18 3YG

TEL 01633 432076
FAX 01633 432688
WEB www.newportunion.com

VAG VIEW

University of Wales, Newport, comes out of Gwent College of Higher Education. It became a University College in 1996 and a fully fledged university in 2003. During this period we watched it achieve huge success in a particular area, oblivious to Government assessment that most of its courses were merely Satisfactory. While the wheels of bureaucracy ground it down, Hollywood beckoned, and its students were being nominated for Oscars and winning BAFTA awards. Finally, in 2001, the Establishment had to take notice, and awarded its Art, Media & Design provision a Grade 5 rating for research, recognising its international importance. In the 2008 assessment exercise, we can expect it to do even better. Meanwhile, applicants are flooding in. Up 15% in 2004, and a figure of 41% for 2005 is reported.

UNIVERSITY/STUDENT PROFILE	
University since	**2003**
Situation/style	**Campus**
Student population	**9340**
Full-time undergraduates	**7235**
- mature	**41%**
- non EU undergraduates	**2%**
- male/female	**43/57**
- state sector intake	**99%**
- non-traditional student intake	**42%, high**
state sector intake	**98%**
drop-out rate	**14%, high**
- undergraduate applications	**Up 15%**

CAMPUS

Newport, Gwent, lies half way between Bristol and Cardiff; it is the first town of any size you come to travelling west along the M4 from England. Activities are split between two campus sites: Newport itself and, 10 mins to the north, **Caerleon** – 'City of Legions and Court of King Arthur,' according to Geoffrey of Monmouth. Caerleon is where all the real stuff goes on.

The village of Caerleon, supposed site of Camelot, takes us back into the mists of time, but the area is a tourist draw as much for its beauty. To the east lies the Wye Valley and the Usk, on whose banks lie the ruins of Tintern Abbey, which inspired Wordsworth to write one of his most important poems. To the west are the Welsh valleys, industrial heartland of South Wales.

Today at Caerleon Campus there are some of the best art and design facilities in Europe, whose students are taking the world of film animation by storm, with one film, *Famous Fred*, being nominated for a Hollywood Oscar, others, such as *Human Traffic* and *Waking Ned* enjoying great commercial success, and *The Gogs* winning its student makers a clutch of BAFTA awards.

The second campus, **Allt-yr-yn**, is home to the Newport Business School, to computing, engineering and the School of Health and Social Sciences. It has none of the mystery of Caerleon, but seems to be enjoying Newport's rise just as much. There's an hourly shuttle between the two.

FEES, BURSARIES

Fees: £1200 p.a. in 2006/7; up to £3000 p.a. 2007/8. There are £8,000 scholarships available to students who have represented their country or region in sport. An assault on the BUSA league – the national UK students sports league – is Newport's next move.

STUDENT PROFILE

They are broadly a new-university crew, and there's a markedly local 'take' overall. With the huge recent expansion in numbers, however, some of the statistics may speak more of the past than

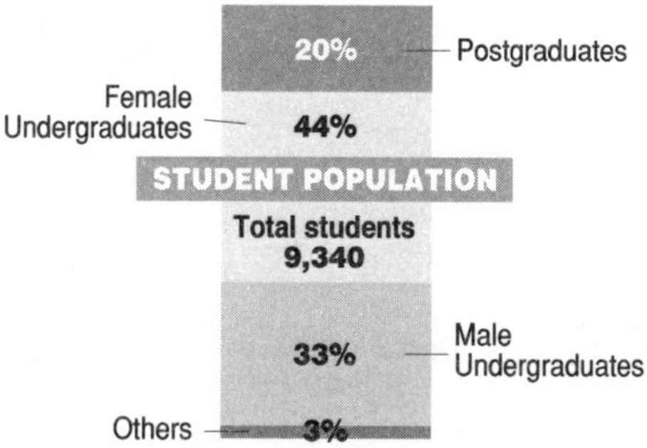

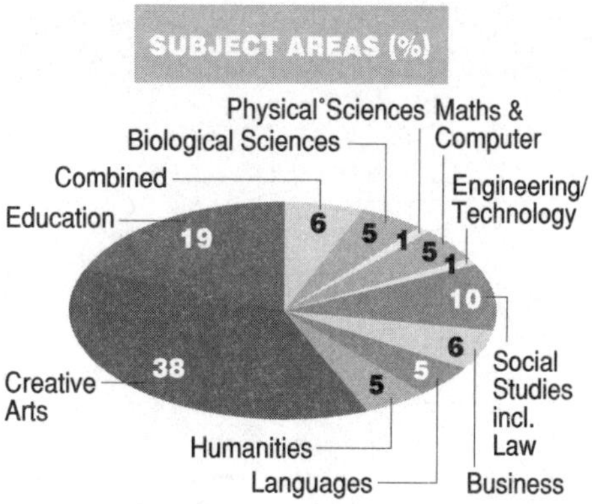

the present. More than a fifth of the undergraduate population is mature. The balance between male and female is pretty healthy (43% male).

ACADEMIA

The faculty or school that is causing all the fuss is the Newport School of Art Media and Design. It offers courses under the banners, Art & Photography, Film and Animation, Performing Arts, and Design.

Camelot has become the International Film School, Wales, with BA (Hons) Animation, Cinema Studies & Scriptwriting, Computer Games Design, Documentary Film &Television, Film & Video, Performing Arts, MA Animation, and MA Film, BA Creative Sound & Music, Documentary Photography (BA and MA), Fine Art, Photographic Art, Photography for Advertising & Fashion, New Media Publishing, and MA Art.

If this is your bent, go for it, not least because they are among the top graduate providers to the film industry. Eight years ago, we wrote: 'What comes across is that Newport provides an imaginative environment. Subtlety, humour and creative thinking are to the fore.' We can find no reason to change that view.

Meanwhile, there's the Newport Business School, the School of Health & Social Sciences, the Centre for Community and Lifelong Learning, and Education – Primary Initial teacher training at the uni was designated as 'Excellent' by the Higher Education Funding Council for Wales in 2000.

Foundation courses leading to direct entry into the uni are available in Science, Technology, Info Technology (Computing, Business Studies, Statistics), Humanities (English, History, Media Studies), Labour Studies, Business Studies, Social Studies, Youth & Community Work and Politics.

SOCIAL SCENE

Students' Union For ents there's a 500-capacity venue in the **Main Hall** and the university-owned

WHAT IT'S REALLY LIKE

UNIVERSITY:	
Social Life	★★★
Campus scene	**Lively**
Student Union services	**Fair**
Politics	**Active**
Sport	**Relaxed**
National team position	**120th**
Sport facilities	**Good**
Arts opportunities	**Good**
Student newsletter	**Grapevine**
Venue	**Main Hall**
Bar	**The Clarence**
Union ents	**Chees and live; good May Ball**
Union clubs/societies	**323**
Most popular society	**Rugby**
Parking	**Adequate**
TOWN:	
Entertainment	★★
Scene	**Pubs, clubs**
Town/gown relations	**OK**
Risk of violence	**Low**
Cost of living	**Average**
Student concessions	**Good**
Survival + 2 nights out	**£60 pw**
Part-time work campus/town	**Good**

Clarence Bar. There's also a restaurant and café. The most popular society is Rugby, so Wednesday's post-match disco is one big focus, as are Sky big screen nights. High point of the year is the May Ball. Drawing biggest audiences currently among the student throng, however, is live music in the **Clarence**, which also hosts karaoke, Chris Tarrant-inspired 'Who wants to win a crate of beer?' and other quizzes. Also figuring large in students' lives is Newport's own **TJ's** – bar, disco and music venue. Others stagger down the road into Cardiff (see *Cardiff Student City*, page 118).

The union is active on student and awareness campaigns, which have included breast cancer, access & equality, anonymous marking, sexual health and drug awareness. There is, of course, a good focus on theatre, dance, etc, through the Performing Arts department, and Newport's **Riverfront Arts Theatre** figures strongly.

It is all a surprisingly eclectic and energetic mix, with regular art exhibitions vying with sporting nights, e-culture (cyber café) and student concern (a student development officer is in place).

Societies are, however, so far fairly thin on the ground: Lesbian, Gay, Bisexual, Trans-gender (LGBT), Socialist Workers, Circus Skills, Students Against Anti Social Behaviour, Literate Soup, Christian Union, Photographic Society, and Film Makers Soc. is the mix.

Sport There are 15 clubs, from Surf to Skiing, Rugby to Mountain Sports, boosted on Caerleon with a Sports Centre, hall, gym, fitness suite; also a rugby pitch and 2 floodlit tennis (there's a popular Tennis Academy) and netball courts. They get involved with the Welsh Rugby Union and Cricket Association, and run courses to enable students to pick up nationally recognised coaching qualifications. Within easy reach are facilities for sailing and windsurfing, dry-slope skiing, caving, canoeing, mountain biking, rock climbing, orienteering and hill walking. There is an ambition to build success to regional, national and international standard. There is everything to play for. Last year's BUSA ranking accorded them Nil Points.

PILLOW TALK

They have 650 self-catered single study bedrooms on Caerleon. Every first year student who applies before September 1 will be satisfied. 447 en-suite rooms cost £60 p.w.; traditional halls Abergavenny, Blaenavon, Camelot cost £51, while Dolaucothi, more bog standard than most, comes in at £49.

GETTING THERE

☛ By road: M4/J25. If approaching Caerleon from Cardiff, there is no direct exit from the J25. Either exit at J26, or take J24 and U-turn at r/about to approach Junction 25 from the East.
☛ By rail: London Paddington, 1:50; Birmingham New Street, 2:00; Cardiff, 40 mins; Bristol Parkway, 25 mins.
☛ By coach: London, 2:45; Manchester, 5:15.
By air: Heathrow, 2 hours; Cardiff and Bristol, 1. Direct coach service from Heathrow and Gatwick.

AT A GLANCE

ACADEMIC FILE:	
Subjects assessed	**8**
Excellent	**Education**
Art and Design	**Grade 5 Research**
Typical A level requirements	**195 points**
Students-staff ratio	**22:1**
First/2:1 degree pass rate	**48%**
ACCOMMODATION FILE:	
Guarantee to freshers	**100%**
Style	**Halls, student village**
Cost pw (no food)	**£51-£60**
Town rent	**£45**

UNIVERSITY OF NORTHAMPTON

The University of Northampton
Boughton Green Road
Moulton Park
Northampton NN2 7AL

TEL 0800 3582232
FAX 01604 713029
EMAIL admissions@northampton.ac.uk
WEB www.northampton.ac.uk

Northampton Students' Union
Boughton Green Road
Moulton Park
Northampton NN2 7AL

TEL 01604 734567 X2818
FAX 01604 719454
EMAIL [firstname.surname]@ucnu.org
WEB www.ucnu.org

VAG VIEW

University College Northampton became Northampton University in October 2005. But it nearly didn't happen. Apparently, Henry III dissolved the original Northampton University in 1265, for no other reason than that it posed a direct threat to the University of Oxford – he had been advised by his bishops that many students from Oxford had migrated to it. A Royal command is law, but UCN put their legal beavers onto it, and the way was made clear. Oxford must be quaking in anticipation of the application backlash.

CAMPUS

The main Park campus, an 80-acre estate on the edge of town, has been well designed. What strikes the visitor immediately is the careful architectural integration of facilities and services, none of which limit or indeed offend the eye. Halls are in among lecture theatres, sports centre by the nightclub, eaterie and bar; a rugby pitch in the centre of things gives a welcome sense of space and a reminder that rugby is a religion both here and in town, which has one of the best teams in the Premier League.

Close by is the intriguing Leather Conservation Centre – (Northampton is the centre of the shoe industry; the football ground is called **The Cobblers**). Some buildings are named after villages in the county, the halls after notable people of the area, including the tragic Northamptonshire poet John Clare, whose parents were illiterate, but who achieved national renown in his day by imbibing the spirit of this place before going insane.

Artistically, the focus is at UCN's Avenue campus in town, however. This 24-acre site – 20 mins. away from Park and linked by a free bus service – houses Art, Design, Technology and Performance Arts. In particular there's quite a theatre tradition. A few years ago they won the Playwright Bursary at the NUS Drama Festival.

ACADEMIA

There are three faculties. **The Faculty of Applied Sciences** includes schools of Leather Technology, Built Environment, Engineering & Technology, Environmental Science, Health & Life Sciences, and Nursing & Midwifery. Medical sciences have links with the General Hospital in Northampton and with Milton Keynes, 'Nursing courses are always over-subscribed,' I was told.

The Faculty of Arts & Social Sciences includes Art & Design, Behavioural Studies (including a BSc in Psychology), Cultural Studies (such as a cross-cultural degree in Performance Studies – Drama, Dance, Music), Education (BA Hons QTS Primary), and Social Studies (American Studies, History, Sociology).

UNIVERSITY/STUDENT PROFILE	
University College since	**1999**
Situation/style	**Town campus**
Student population	**11255**
Undergraduates	**9915**
- mature	**29%**
- non EU undergraduates	**4%**
- male/female	**36/64**
- non-traditional student intake	**37%, high**
- state sector intake	**98%**
- drop-out rate	**10%**
- undergraduate applications	**Down 10%**

The Faculty of Management & Business includes the schools of Business, Information Systems, Law & International Business, Professional Studies (Finance and Accounting) and Management (MMB, MSc Management Studies).

Career strength in the health sector comes out of the occupational therapy and podiatry degrees. Countrywide, Salford and Northampton probably offer the best value – entry requirements to job satisfaction. There are strong links with the General

ACADEMIC EXCELLENCE

TEACHING:
(Rated Excellent or 17+ out of 24)

Art & Design	**23**
Anatomy, Nursing & Other Subjects Related to Medicine, Materials Technology	**22**
Communication & Media Drama, Dance, Cinematics, Education	**21**
Psychology, Sociology	**20**
Building & Civil Engineering	**19**
American Studies, General Eng & Electric/Electron Eng	**18**

Hospital in Northampton and Milton Keynes, a top notch teaching assessment result and a low entry requirement as well as the strong employment reputation that puts them in the Top Ten. Teaching inspection 22

Furniture design and manufacture is another niche employment strength. Northampton is in the heart of the leather industry, and furniture was probably always on the agenda for Product Design students. There is also a fast employment flow into these industries out of the Management & Business faculty up at Park (design being at Avenue Campus).

Graphic artists are parrticularly employable through BA Graphic Communication, and designers and sculptors also register with relatively strong prospects in the employment league.

In the business sector personnel officers/managers are particularly well served, the rush of graduates into the sector coming from a range of courses featuring Human Resource Management, like the 4-year sandwich BA Human Resource Management.

92% of the education provision finds expression in primary school teaching. You'll be at Park. Teaching inspection 21.

AT A GLANCE

ACADEMIC FILE:

Subjects assessed	**21**
Excellent	**48%**
Typical entry requirements	**205 points**
Application acceptance rate	**21%**
Students-staff ratio	**21:1**
First/2:1 degree pass rate	**56%**

ACCOMMODATION FILE:

Guarantee to freshers	**95%**
Style	**Halls, flats**
Catered	**None**
En-suite	**67%**
Approx price range pw	**£41-£66**
Town rent pw	**£45**

SOCIAL SCENE

Students' Union All the chat was of the opening of the new £1.65m 'Student Centre' on Park Campus in 2006, as yet unveiled when going to press.

Pleasure-seeking students have moulded town and uni alike. 'In the last two years no end of new pubs have opened,' a student told me. Lots of clubs offer student nights. There are free buses from Park into town.

There are two bars on Park, **Pavilion**, with views over games pitches and Sky TV, and the main union bar with drinks promos, etc – **nn2.** By night, the newly refurbed bar becomes a nightclub, with a storming new lighting and sound rig and a 12 foot big screen. By day, **nn2 is a** stylish diner.

Thursday night's *Shots in the City* is the main ents fare. Saturdays you get discos, live bands, theme nights and foam parties.

Then there's **Laidback** on the ground floor, relaxed café-bar, Sky TV, pool, games machines and music of course. **Laidback** also does events, such as 'open mike', quiz and karaoke.

At **George's**, the hub of Avenue Union, a bar is open till 2 am Fridays for the regular clubnight, variously known as *Club Friday* and *Friday the 13th*. While we were there they had a hypnotist and comedian and *Bar Footsie* (Stock Exchange drinks promo).

The student nespaper is *Wave*, the newsletter *Xpress*, and altogether 20 societies, the most active being Christian Union, kickboxing and Islam, and there are 20 sports clubs and some 50 teams. Music is prolific and student led. There is a choir, chamber orchestra and other ensembles. Students play in the Northampton Symphony Orchestra, and sing in the acclaimed Central Festival Opera.

PILLOW TALK

Uni accommodation is guaranteed to 'first and firm choices' in halls or flats (some 67% are en suite. Price per week ranges from £41 to £66, while average town rent is £45 per week.

GETTING THERE

☛ By road: M1/J15/15a/16; easy access to M5/6/25/40, A1 and A45.

☛ By rail: London and Birmingham, 1:00.

☛ By coach: London, 2:00; Birmingham, 1:35; Leicester, 1:00.

UNIVERSITY OF NORTHUMBRIA

University of Northumbria
Ellison Place
Newcastle upon Tyne NE1 8ST

TEL 0191 232 6002
FAX 0191 227 4561
EMAIL ca.marketing@northumbria.ac.uk
WEB www.northumbria.ac.uk

Northumbria Students' Union
2 Sandyford Road
Newcastle Upon Tyne NE1 8SB

TEL 0191 227 4757
FAX 0191 227 3760
EMAIL su.president@unn.ac.uk
WEB www.mynsu.co.uk

VAG VIEW

The two universities in the city of Newcastle are situated within walking distance of one another. Health is now a crucial provision of both, having overtaken Business as Northumbria's defining interest. While Newcastle Uni has medicine, Northumbria has nursing (which achieved full marks at the teaching assessments), midwifery, physiotherapy, occupational therapy.

There are also some excellent social science courses, including a key Law degree, a 4-year 'fast-track' Exempting degree. Another defining mark of Northumbria is its fashion department.

But that is not all. Some 1992 unis have not taken on board the significance of the student culture in student development. Northumbria has, and took big strides. Then it seemed to lose steam. Now it's back on top again with more than 50 student societies, a refurbished Students' Union, and sports teams that came 10th nationally last year, while Newcastle, which puts much store by sport, managed only 19th.

CAMPUSES

City campus (address above) Student Union, library, sports centre, language laboratories, art gallery. A wireless computing network, providing internet access for laptops has been instituted

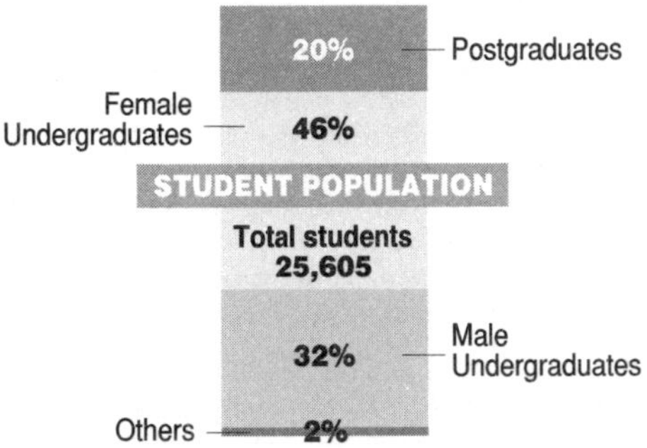

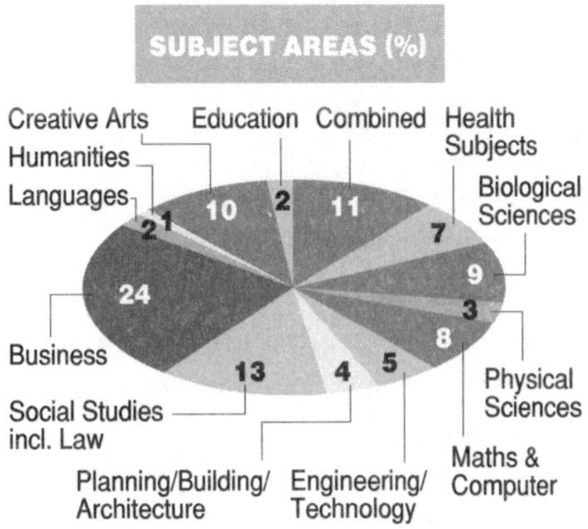

across the uni.

Coach Lane campus Coach Lane, Benton, Newcastle upon Tyne NE7 7XA. Tel: 0191 215 6000. Recent beneficiary of a £40-million development. Health, Social Work & Education are here. Coach Lane also has a union, library and computing facilities, a sports hall, fitness suite, activity studio and all-weather hockey pitch.

FEES, BURSARIES

UK & EU Fees: £3000 p.a. except for nursing, midwifery, social workd, physio. and occupational therapy, where they are picked up elsewhere. Law students on the Exemption course pay an extra £900. On a year out in a sandwich course, you pay only £750. Built Environment Foundation year is £1500. There's a Northumberland Scholarship, worth between £250 and £1000 in first year, not dependent on household earnings, but on course studied (see web site for listing). In subsequent years it's dependent on your exam results.

STUDENT PROFILE

Relative to many other unis, there's a sound balance between applicants from state and private sector (considerably fewer public school boys than Newcastle Uni, but more than many a newish uni) and an average sort of take from socio-economic

UNIVERSITY/STUDENT PROFILE	
University since	**1992**
Situation/style	**Civic**
Student population	**25605**
Undergraduates	**19935**
- mature	**35%**
- non EU undergraduates	**7%**
- male/female	**41/59**
- non-traditional student intake	**31%**
- state school intake	**90%**
- drop-out rate	**9%**
- undergraduate applications	**Down 4%**

classes new to the idea of university. More notable are the figures for mature undergraduates (35%) and part-timers (25%), part of their Lifelong Learning policy. Basically, the mix works; everyone has a cool time in a very cool place. 'Best thing,' said Jack Ford when he alighted there for the first time, 'was the relaxed atmosphere that enables students to bond and make lots of new friends.'

ACADEMIA & JOBS

Seriously good reputation on graduate employment and less demanding at entry than many. Contact with firms in the North East region is facilitated by all sorts of strategies, not least Northumbria's e.Business Centre, which dispenses advice and support to small and medium sized businesses, utilising uni expertise in law, technology, marketing and business.

Property developers, architects, construction managers, quantity surveyors and estate agents pour out of Northumbria. The big four for property development nationwide are Sheffield Hallam, Northumbria, Nottingham Trent and Manchester Met. At Northumbria there's a mix of Business and Building/Engineering graduates boosting employment figures in Property Development. The uni's Business & Management expertise is second to none – see the new 3-year Corporate Management degree, broken down into one year intensive learning, then two years on a work placement followed by a final six months to complete a dissertation. Also BA Business Management, Business Admin top-up ('Excellent' in the assessments), qand various Joint Business degrees.

In building, BA Architectural Design & Management sits alongside BEng Building Services Engineering, and BSc Architectural Technology, Building Design Mgt, Building Project Mgt, Commercial Quantity Surveying, Building Surveying, Construction Management, Estate Management, etc (foundation degrees available in many of these). Teaching inspection 22.

Meanwhile, prospective engineer design consultants leap at their computer-aided design degrees, such as BEng Computer Aided Engineering and Manufacturing Systems Engineering, as well as BSc Computer & Network technology.

Electrical, electronic and telecommunications engineers are especially well served by a strong 22 points out of 24 at the assessments, and Northumbria came top among those unis that offer games degrees for getting programmer graduates employment. Have a close look at their 4-year sandwich BSc Computer Games Software Engineering. See also Computer for Business and Computer Studies degrees: it's a very strong employment area.

Northumbria's School of Law is authorised by both the Law Society and the Bar Council to run the only 4-year Exempting LLB degree, in the UK

The School of Law is authorised by both the Law Society and the Bar Council to run the only 4-year Exempting LLB degree, in the UK, which gives students the opportunity to work on real client cases through the Student Law Office. This exempts from the need for further professional vocational training, namely the

WHERE NORTHUMBRIA GRADUATES END UP

Health & Social Work: 13%; Education: 11%; Wholesale Retail: 10%; Manufacturing: 9%; Financial Activities: 6%; Public Administration, Civil Service & Defence: 9%; Hotel/Restaurant: 4%; Transport & Communications (including Telecommunications): 5%; Construction: 2%; Agriculture: 1%; Personnel: 5%; Computer: 3%; Business & Management: 5%; Accountancy: 2%; Media (including Film): 0.5%; Legal 4%; Architecture: 2%; Advertising: 0.5%; Artistic/Literary: 1%; Sport: 1%.

Approximate 'graduate track' employed **66%**

ACADEMIC EXCELLENCE

TEACHING: *(Rated Excellent or 17+ out of 24)*	
Business & Management, English, Law.	**Excellent**
Nursing, Education	**24**
Languages (French, German, Russian, Spanish), Physics, Subjects Allied to Medicine	**23**
Drama/Dance /Cinematics, Built Environment, Electrical & Electronic Eng, Art, Economics, Library/Info Mgt, Politics & Design, Business, Psychology	**22**
History Art/Design & Film, Town/Country Planning, Maths, Sport, Molecular Biosciences	**21**
Sociology	**20**
RESEARCH : *Top grades 5/5**	**None**

Legal Practice Course and the Bar Vocational Course, both of which are also offered as stand alone programmes.

Government administration (local, regional, central) is another sector served well by Northumbria – various Politics degrees, BSc Social Work, and Social & Public Policy. Probation officers proliferate, and most graduates into government

AT A GLANCE

ACADEMIC FILE:	
Subjects assessed	**30**
Excellent	**77%**
Typical entry requirements	**260 points**
Application acceptance rate	**22%, high**
Students-staff ratio	**18:1**
First/2:1 degree pass rate	**49%**
ACCOMMODATION FILE:	
Guarantee to freshers	**100%**
Style	**Halls, flats, houses**
Catered	**18%**
En-suite	**13%**
Price range pw	**£78-£105**
City rent pw	**£30-£65**

admin come from the Social Studies area. Look closely at the Professional Practice Studies & Advice Guidance & Counselling, Childhood Studies, Disability Studies, etc. While on the social studies ticket, note, too, Drama scored 22 out of 24 at the assessments – it's a performance-related course with a community focus,

One fifth of intake goes into business and employability is high, but one interesting scoop in the transport business is a design pathway. You'll need to go through the Foundation Art course (portfolio required) to join the BA Transportation Design, which builds on a tradition of supplying Design graduates into the automotive, marine, rail and aviation industries. Teaching inspection 22.

Another excellent career niche degree is their 4-year sandwich BA Human Resource Management, which looks after a third of their large contingent going into the sector. Sciences and Social Sciences are also popular routes (all 22 points at assessment). Psychologists find the BSc degree (and another with Sports Science) very efficient career-wise, both accredited by the British Psychological Society.

There's also a dedicated Physiotherapy degree. The nursing, midwifery, physiotherapy, occupational therapy side helps to find some 13% of its graduates jobs, and Northumbria is one of only four institutions to attain full marks in the teaching assessments for nursing. They cover adult, children's nursing, learning disabilities and mental health. Most graduates are SEN and half as many, non-hospital nurses.

The Pharmacology and Pharmacy degrees spawn pharmaceutical manufacturers and chemists in number. Passport to success here is BSc Pharmaceutical Chemistry. Teaching inspection 23.

The fashion department excels. They have two degrees, Fashion and Fashion Marketing, a 4-year sandwich. Excellent careers track record here, as there is for graphic artists and designers and set designers.

SOCIAL SCENE

At City Campus the **Venue Bar**, on the first floor, is the place for live music (capacity now 3000), while **Reds** (circular bar, 550 capacity), on the second floor, is for discos. There's also **Bar One,** on the ground floor. Coach Lane campus has a big hall, one bar and one major clubnight on a Thursday.

Reds has new night *Hype* on a Friday – indie, electro, rock, r&b, soul – at **Reds**. On Saturday, *Wiggle* survives: it's a tradition, it's the biggest night of the week – 'pulling not posing' – both upstairs in **Reds** and downstairs in the **Venue**. 'Last year we had it upstairs only and we'd sell out in the first fifteen minutes,' we were told. It's chart, cheese and party + £1.50 VK flavours all night.

They boast live gigs this term from Junco Partners, Julian Cope, Death Cab for Cutie, and the usual run of hypnotists and ceilidhs. 'We promote our own DJs in Reds.' There are also good opportunities for DJs to make the transition to city clubs. 'One of our DJs, who does Saturday night *Wiggle*, was a student here, and now he's working six nights a week in bars and nightclubs in town.'

There's also a decent drama society – 3 or 4 productions a year, a monthly newspaper (*Northumbria Student*) looking for contributors, and they're part of Newcastle Uni's LSR radio station.

Probably the most active of the 30 societies is Community Student Action. GLOBE – Gay, Lesbian & Bisexual – get involved in national campaigns. Three years ago they invested £1 million in the Student Services department – the counselling, careers and study skills services.

Sport Lots to offer, well-equipped sports hall, gym and indoor tennis courts, options to do anything from scuba diving to rugby, which has some very high-class teams and regularly trounces Newcastle Uni, good hockey, football and tennis. They run an Elite Athlete Programme – Team Northumbria – which offers practical and financial support to students with particular potential. Maybe too high class, one student complained that there's only 3 uni football teams and it's hard to get a trial date.

PILLOW TALK

They guarantee approximately 95% freshers uni accommodation, with priority given to non-local first-years. Local students can apply for rooms only after the start of term. First-year accommodation consists of halls and flats. Claude Gibb is the most popular hall, being in crawling distance of town and lectures – 'more of a public school crowd here,' said one. The Larches is the one to avoid (rough area). Lovaine, also on campus, is handy but poky. Of flats a student said that Glenamara and Stevenson both have the advantage of a very central location. Only 18% of accommodation is catered and 13% en suite. Last new residences with en-suite and internet sockets have opened adjacent to City Campus in September 2002, before the opening in autumn 2005 of two large residential develepments, which will boost the en-suite complement considerably.

WHAT IT'S REALLY LIKE

UNIVERSITY:	
Social Life	★★★★
Campus scene	**The lively, less self-conscious one**
Student Union services	**Average**
Politics	**Average**
Sport	**Key**
National team position	**10th**
Sport facilities	**Good**
Arts opportunities	**Drama, music, film good; dance, art average**
Student newspaper	**Northumbria Student**
Nightclubs	**Venue**
Bars	**Reds, Bar One, Coach Lane**
Union ents	**Big club nights and live**
Union societies	**53**
Parking	**Poor**
CITY:	
Entertainment	★★★★★
Scene	**Vibrant, fun**
Town/gown relations	**OK**
Risk of violence	**Low**
Cost of living	**Low**
Student concessions	**Good**
Survival + 2 nights out	**£70 pw**
Part-time work campus/town	**Average/excellent**

GETTING THERE

☛ By road to Newcastle: A1(M) from the south and north; A19 from York; A69 from the west; M6 from the southwest.
☛ By road to Carlisle: A7 from the north; M6 from the south; A69 from Newcastle (the east).
☛ By rail to Newcastle: Edinburgh, 1:30; Leeds, 1:45; London King's Cross, 3:00; Manchester Piccadilly, 3:00; Birmingham New Street, 4:00.
☛ By rail to Carlisle: Edinburgh, 1.25; Leeds, 3.15; London King's Cross, 4.45; Manchester Piccadilly, 2.20; Birmingham New Street, 2.57.
☛ By air: Newcastle International airport.
☛ By coach: London, 6:05; Birmingham, 4:25.

STUDENT NOTTINGHAM - THE CITY

Nottingham is without doubt, the best city in the country for a student. Situated in the Midlands, it's never too far UK students to get home, and being in the middle of the country, you get a really good mix of both southern and northern students along with the grounded Nottingham locals themselves.

There are two universities and eight further education colleges in Nottingham, a bustling city that has come into its own, it almost seems, in the very process of catering for the huge number of students it attracts.

LIVE MUSIC

For its sheer size and the big names it attracts, the best venue for live music has to be the **Ice Centre**, situated in the **Lace Market**. The Strokes, Kelly Clarkson and the Little Britain Tour have all been there recently. The drinks are extortionately priced, but if you want to see the big names it generally does mean big bucks.

A venue for live music acts with more *cred.* is the less-commercial **Rock City**. City centre situated, and a lot more edgy, **Rock City** has hosted such as The Killers and Oasis in this small but very atmospheric club. With student club nights throughout the week, this is a *must* if you want to dodge the cheese and get heavily into eyeliner.

If its un-discovered talent you're after, then look no further than the **Rescue Rooms**, which is just round the corner and almost a pint-sized version of **Rock City**.

Live music is really taking off in Nottingham and even Trent's Student Union is jumping on the bandwagon, hosting its very own live music night with some great up-coming bands every second Friday.

CLUBBING

Nottingham is now seen as a bar city, not first and foremost club orientated. Yet, with the mix of clubs it has, catering for all wants and tastes, you will be hard pushed to find better elsewhere. The newly opened **Oceana** is very popular with students – 5 rooms filled with different atmospheres and music – but again be prepared to spend a penny or two. The city also has **Mode** nightclub and **Lost Weekend**, both with great student nights, cheap drinks and cheesy tunes.

But the clubs of all clubs remains the mighty **Ocean** nightclub. Not to be confused with **Oceana**, it has just become solely a student nightclub every day of the week, with both universities holding nights. You're guaranteed a good night out, if drunken sportsmen, scantily clad ladies and cheap drinks and cheese is your cup of tea.

For an alternative night, try **Stealth**, **The Cookie Club** and **The Bomb**. The venues are slightly more intimate, a lot smaller, but by no less lively.

DRINKING

Nottingham Trent Students Union offers a fantastic place to drink with its **Glo** bar being well equipped for both chilling out and dancing, and its **Sub** bar to kick back and play some pool. **The Ark** at Nottingham Uni's Students Union is no way near as big, but still offers the usual guarantee of cheap drinks and cheese.

In the city centre, **The Horn in Hand**, **Varsity**, **Templars**, **Up and Down Under** and **Walkabout** are very student populated, give student discounts and offer a relaxed atmosphere. Each has a new deal each week.

For more sophistication, try Hockley and the Lace Market, where most of the following are situated – **Revolution** (over 100 different vodka shots can be tried and consumed), **Tantra** (you can hire out beds for the evening), **Quilted Lama** (with its enormous fish bowls), and the sometime church come bar, **Pitcher and Piano**. But be warned, it it won't come cheap.

The Waterfront takes it home at the other side of town, and has 7 bars spread across 7 floors. In summer time, the canal-side terrace is packed.

SHOPPING

Prepare to spend, spend, spend when you come to Nottingham and hit the shops. It is worryingly easy to blow your student loan on the incredible shopping experience that Nottingham offers. There are all the chain stores, many cool trendy shops and it's rife with factory shops. Go to the **Victoria Centre** for day-to-day student favourites, the brand new **Topshop**, **La Senza**, **Republic**, and such as HMV, Boots... Along with its market, department store and supermarket, it caters for everyone. **The Broadmarsh** is at the other end of town and is again a shopping complex, but offers fair-priced **H&M**, **TK Max** and **New Look**. **The Broadmarsh** is very handy for fancy dress outfits at a cut rate, too.

If you want to spend that bit more, then walk down Bridlesmith Gate to **Flannels**, **Diesel** and **Kurt Geiger**. You really can get your heart desire, from retro gear at **Ice Nine** and **Wild Clothing** to everyday fashions at **Warehouse** and Zara.

EATING

Whether you are looking for quality (somewhere to drag your parents), quantity (eat all you want), or somewhere to bring your own wine, Nottingham does not disappoint. The **Corner House** in the city centre offers an array of different cuisine from Flaming Dragon, the Chinese buffet, to Bella Italia, a very fair priced and tasty Italian. American style diners proliferate around the city centre, including **Hard Rock Café** and **Frankie and Benny's**, while Hockley has **Fresh**, a great place to eat and very healthy, and some great bars that offer good, extravagant bar meals, like **Browns** and the **Hog's Head**.

For daytime snacking, it's **Subways**, the individual outlets scattered across the city, and you'll find a favourite dive among a whole host of small, reasomnably priced city café's.

Whatever you're in the mood for, whatever your needs and requirements, Nottingham really does have something for everyone.

Annabel Woollen

UNIVERSITY OF NOTTINGHAM

The University of Nottingham
University Park
Nottingham NG7 2RD

TEL 0115 951 6565
FAX 0115 951 6566
EMAIL enquiries@nottingham.ac.uk
WEB www.nottingham.ac.uk

Nottingham Students' Union
University Park
Nottingham NG7 2RD

TEL 0115 935 1100
FAX 0115 935 1101
EMAIL studentsunion@nottingham.ac.uk
WEB www.students-union.nottingham.ac.uk

VAG VIEW

Nottingham is a top university with a 91% Excellence rating, and Nottingham students have a 77% chance of graduating with a first or upper second class degree.

More than this, it is one of the most employer-friendly universities in the world, and students are happy here: its drop-out rate, at 3%, is very low.

Known, among much else, for its medical provision, the uni is launching a School of Veterinary Science this year, a landmark – it will be the UK's first new Vet School since the 1950s.

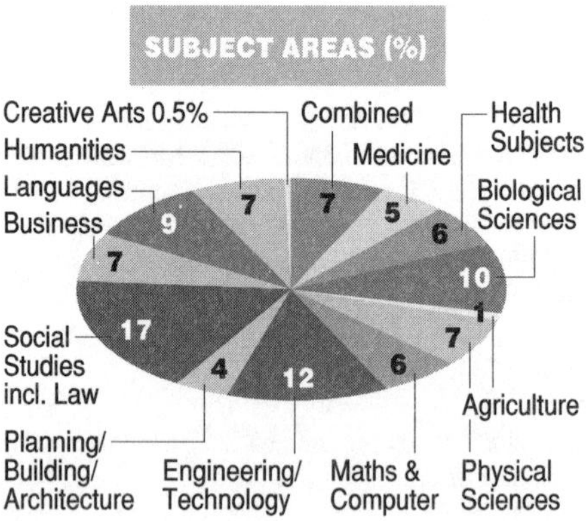

CAMPUSES

The 300-acre **University Park**, home to 3,000 students, workplace to a further 26,000 students and staff, and located just a short bus or bike ride from Nottingham city centre, is the main campus – huge lake, views over Trent valley, rolling Downs that sweep away into the distance, all a neat ten minutes by bus from town.

There is a 16-hectare satellite campus at **Sutton Bonington**, 10 miles distant, for the School of Biological Sciences. This is also where the new Vet school will function. Besides teaching and research facilities, the James Cameron-Gifford Library and student residences, there's a sports centre, bank and bookshop. A free shuttle-bus service runs between it and University Park during the day.

The **Jubilee Campus**, on a site close to University Park, houses the Schools of Education, Computer Science and Information Technology, as well as The Business School. The site is also the home of The National College for School Leadership. Green in concept and design, an impor-

UNIVERSITY/STUDENT PROFILE	
University since	**1948**
Situation/style	**Edge of city campuses**
Student population	**29726**
Undergraduates	**23817**
- mature	**8%**
- non EU undergraduates	**12%**
- male/female	**49/51**
- non-traditional student intake	**16%**
- state school intake	**67%**
drop-out rate	**3%, v. low**
- undergraduate applications	**Down 6%**

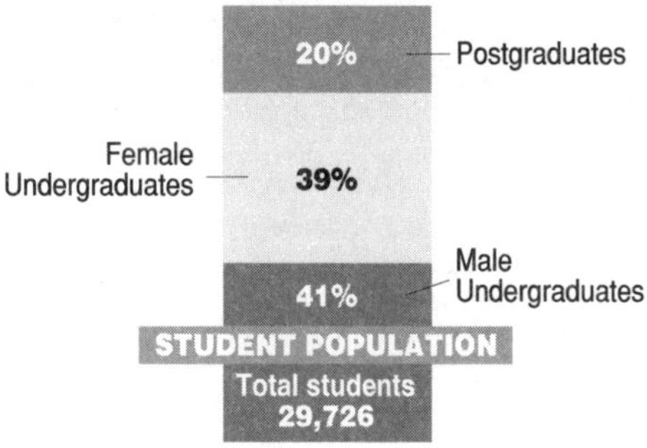

tant feature is the series of lakes which, as well as being home to wildlife, provide cooling for the buildings in the summer and receive all surface water. Less visible – but equally important to this model of a sustainable campus – are the roofs which are, quite literally, green. A carpet of low-growing alpine plants helps maintain steady temperatures within the buildings throughout the year and is more effective than traditional insulation. Buildings also feature a super-efficient mechanical ventilation system, lighting sensors to reduce energy consumption, and photovoltaic cells integrated into the atrium roofs. The environmentally-friendly nature of the campus and it's buildings have been a big factor in the awards that it has received, including the Millennium Marque Award for Environmental Excellence, the British Construction Industry Building Project of the Year, the RIBA Journal Sustainability Award and the Civic Trust Award for Sustainability.

'When I first visited the university, all fresh-faced and eager,' recalls Mark Tew, 'I couldn't help but be struck by the sheer size of the place. It's BIG. Put it this way, when embarking on the almost weekly drinking binge known as "Campus 14" (a foolish display of drinking prowess in which several people of varying levels of commitment attempt all fourteen bars on campus), it's not so much guzzling the gallons of snakebite-and-black that poses a problem as the trudging round several miles of semi-mountainous campus in the driving rain. It's a tough life!'

FEES, BURSARIES

UK & EU Fees: £3000 p.a. You will not need to pay course fees if you are studying B160 Physiotherapy, B401 MNutr Nutrition, B700 Nursing (Masters) or the Diploma of Nursing, or NMAS 1800 Midwifery. Equally, you will not be eligible for a uni bursary, but you may be eligible for a bursary from the National Health Service. University bursaries come in the shape of a means test. Where household income is less than £32000, a bursary of £1000 is available. Thereafter the bursary reduces on a sliding scale to £250 if there's a residual household income of £41500. Additional bursaries worth up to £3000 a year are available, depending on where you live, your personal circumstances and your academic route into University. You will know before you start studying whether or not you are eligible. If you are a local student and on a lower income, you can apply for a First in the Family scholarship or an Ethel and Kevin B. Malone scholarship. Each of these offers £1000 a year. Finally, a number of academic schools will be making scholarships available to students.

STUDENT PROFILE

The uni has among the lowest intakes from the state sector and from so-called non-traditional uni heartlands (lower socio-economic groups and neighbourhoods). However, they want to change this. To encourage applicants from poor areas of the local community with potential, they have an outreach programme offering summer schools, drama workshops, campus tours, coaching in study skills and interview techniques. Last year almost 10000 young people participated, and over 4000 people participated in activities run through community groups or with mature learners.

'I was told to expect a lot of bitter and twisted Oxbridge rejects with a big fat chip on the shoulder, but this hasn't been the case,' Mark recalls. 'The "rah-rah, sooo drunk!" toff brigade, however, is definitely out in full force! Being from up t' North, it was a culture shock to say the least. But it's well worth being here if just to take the piss. "Another bottle of champers Roger?"'

ACADEMIA & JOBS

The medical degree, BMBS, is rigorous – 3 years to BMedSci, then 2 increasingly clinical years. It is also highly competitive at entry – AAB, 9% chance of getting in. Must have Chemistry and Biology (A).

There's also a fast-track graduate entry version based at Derby, a £12 million Medical School and Clinical Sciences building opened on a site at Derby City General Hospital. GEM – Graduate Entry Medicine is for graduates of any discipline with a 1st or 2:1 (no fixed upper age limit). Typical offer for the traditional degree is ABB: Chemistry + one other science + one other. Teaching inspection, 21.

The Nottingham Law degree was recently assessed by the LPC Board, and it was among the very few to be rated Excellent. International Grade 5 for research. All candidates must sit the National Admissions Test for Law (LNAT).

Some 11% of Nottingham graduates go into Finance. Most become chartered accountants, investment analysts and actuaries. They offer BA Finance, Accounting & Management, while the

Social Sciences Faculty has such as BSc Economics & Econometrics, and the joint hons. programmes have BSc Maths & Economics, Maths & Management Studies, and BC Economics and Philosophy. Teaching inspection: Economics 24, Maths 23, Philosophy 22. Research Grade 5: Maths, Economics and Philosophy.

There's a BA Industrial Economics with Insurance degree, also productive of jobs in the investment analyst sector, in which this uni seems particularly to excel.

Would-be business management consultants look at BA Management Studies and a range of joint degrees with French, German, Spanish, Asian or Chinese Studies. There's a research Grade 6* for some of these. There are interesting language and management tie-ups, too, with engineering.

Industrial relations are good. Blue-chip companies that maintain ongoing research relationships include Powergen, The Boots Company and GlaxoSmithKline. The Ford Motor Company and AstraZeneca have both been involved with the University for over 30 years. The University's relationship with Rolls-Royce includes hosting two Technology Centres in the areas of gas turbine transmission systems and manufacturing technology. They are also working together on a research programme aimed at improving the performance of aerospace engines for which the uni will receive £2.2 million.

Look closely at BA Industrial Economics. This is Jessie Boot territory, so expect jobs, too, for chemists. Nottingham's eco-friendly philosophy, a main principle behind the Jubillee campus is evident in their Green Chemistry & Process Engineering, their aim to produce graduates with a blend of knowledge and skills that will enable chemical industry to move in harmony with the environmental sustainability that is on everyone's longterm strategy.

Aspiring Pharmacists read Pharmacy, and the uni's 23 points out of 24 in the assessments for the 4-year MPharm, and Grade 5 for research, confirm its status at the top.

Aspiring biologists and physicists also find their needs met here. There's a 23-point assessment score in these areas and strong bio-medical-agri links within the wider curriculum, as well as a

ACADEMIC EXCELLENCE

TEACHING:
(Rated Excellent or 17+ out of 24)

Chemistry, Law, Mechanical Engineering, Architecture, Business & Management, English, Geography, Music. German,	**Excellent**
Manufacturing Engineering & Operations Mgt, Classics, Psychology, Economics, Politics	**24**
Agriculture & Food Sciences, Art History, Urban Planning, Pharmacology, Biosciences, Physics, Maths, Theology	**23**
Civil Eng, Nursing, Anatomy Electrical & Electronic Eng, American Studies, Philosophy, Education	**22**
Sociology, Chemica Eng, Materials Technology, Subjects Allied to Medicine, Archaeology, Medicine	**21**
Russian & East Euro Langs	**19**

.RESEARCH:
Top grades 5/5/6**

American Studies, German/ Dutch/Scandinavian, Iberian/ Latin American, Theology, Music	**Grade 6***
Pharmacy, Psychology, Genetics, Agriculture, Food Science, Chemistry, Physics, Pure Math, Applied Math, Statistics, Computer, Civil Eng, Mechanical/Aeronautical/ Manufacturing Eng, Geography, Law, Economics, Management, English, French, Russian/Slavonic/ East European, Philosophy	**Grade 5**

WHERE NOTTINGHAM GRADUATES END UP

Health & Social Work: 22%; Education: 5%; Wholesale Retail: 7%; Manufacturing: 9%; Financial Activities: 11%; Public Administration, Civil Service & Defence: 7%; Hotel/Restaurant: 2%; Transport & Communications (including Telecommunications): 4%; Construction: 1%; Agriculture: 1%; Personnel: 3.5%; Computer: 5%; Business & Management: 4%; Accountancy: 5%; Media (including Film): 1%; Legal 2%; Architecture: 0.5%; Publishing: 1%; Advertising: 1%

Approximate 'graduate track' employed **69%**

Grade 5 for Genetics.

Engineering is a big strength for Nottingham, 15% graduate in it. It's a route into Defence, among many other areas, but there's an interesting employment strength in design here. They have long had a lean towards interesting eco-friendly structural design through such as the Institute of Environmental Science and the Institute of Building Technology, and now strong prospects for all sorts of design-orientated courses, from the arts group BArch degree through B/MEng Architectural Environment Engineering and Architecture & Environment Design. Note also MEng Mechanical, Design, Materials & Manufacture. They're similarly productive of civil engineers. Full marks in the teaching assessments, 22 points for Civil Eng. International Grade 5 for research.

Again, they are among the leaders in the field for finding jobs in computer programming. BSc degrees include Computer Science, e-Commerce & Digital Business and Computer Science & Management Studies. Research Grade 5.

Jobs also abound in forestry and agriculture through their degrees in Plant/Animal Science, Food Science/Microbiology, Zoology, Ecology, Botany, etc. Note, too, the new Veterinary Medicine/Science degree and 1-year Pre-Vet Science Certificate.

Finally, Nottingham's top-rated BSc Psychology leads graduates into all sorts of areas, including market research, publicity and PR, choice too of many of Nottingham's sought-after graduates in languages, social studies, business and humanities.

WHAT IT'S REALLY LIKE

UNIVERSITY:	
Social Life	★★★★★
Campus scene	**Well-heeled, bright, sporty, creative**
Student Union services	**Good**
Politics	**Activity high**
Sport	**Key nationally & v. active inter-hall. 67 clubs.**
National team position	**7th**
Sport facilities	**Good**
Arts opportunities	**Drama excellent; music, art good; dance, film great**
Student magazine	**Impact**
Newspaper	**Grapevine**
Student radio	**URN**
Venue	**The Ark**
Bars	**D H Lawrence + in all 14 halls**
Union ents	**College & town club based**
Union clubs/societies	**207**
Most popular society	**Christian Union, Cock Soc, Dance Soc**
Parking	**Adequate**
CITY:	
Entertainment	★★★★★
Scene	**Serious nightlife, good arts**
Town/gown relations	**OK**
Risk of violence	**High**
Cost of living	**Average**
Student concessions	**Good**
Survival + 2 nights out	**£90 pw**
Part-time work campus/town	**Good/excellent**

SOCIAL SCENE

STUDENTS' UNION This is housed in the newly extended Portland Building, which overlooks the lake and which at long last has undergone a multi-million pound makeover, with a new SU shop, banks, Blackwells and Boots outlets, and a type of revolving door that spews students with armfuls of books out onto the steps. The renamed **Buttery** bar, **The Ark,** has also had a makeover, but, according to one student 'with little discernible difference other than a coat of paint and a cashpoint, although the hatch serving food – healthy sandwiches by day, greasy chips by night – is very welcome.' In addition, the **D H Lawrence** bar can be found in the Lakeside **D H Pavilion**, where exhibitions and stage productions run as prolifically as in the **New Theatre**, which is elsewhere, tucked up behind Portland and as old as the hills.

There are also bars in the 14 halls of residence, and no difficulty in seeing how the drinking binge known as "Campus 14" became so popular. First-year social life spins off halls, off societies, off departments and off sport, rather more than off the Union: 'It still amazes me how such fine, upstanding, intelligent people, who clearly had the "right stuff" to get into Nottingham University, all seem mystically drawn to the Union on a Friday night,' writes Mark. 'Why? It's a *dive*! Maybe that's harsh. It's actually really nice during the day, its only real crime may be overcrowding on the weekend.'

Lurve Machine @ **The Ark** has been a perennial fave. They've also had Blues Brothers Experience and Chesney Hawkes, Feeder and Queens of the Stone Age, and the Comedy Society does a regular-stand-up open mic session there and plays host to such as Ross Nobel and Johnny Vegas.

AT A GLANCE

ACADEMIC FILE:	
Subjects assessed	**43**
Excellent	**91%**
Typical entry requirements	**420 points**
Application acceptance rate	**11%**
Students-staff ratio	**16:1**
First/2:1 degree pass rate	**77%**
ACCOMMODATION FILE:	
Guarantee to freshers	**100%**
Style	**Halls, flats**
Catered halls	**55%**
Approx. price per 31 weeks	**£2600-£4300**
City rent pw	**£45-£70**

The Ark was also home to Radio 1's Live in Nottingham gig – both Emma B and Jo Whiley in attendance. Nottingham radio is quite a big deal. The students have won more national awards than any other university. Last year, something of an 'off' year, they had 9 nominations, 1 bronze, 4 silvers and 1 gold award, and as two of the nominations were for best newcomer, the tradition is clearly in good hands. The student magazine is *Impact*.

Nottingham has also long had an enterprising drama society. **The New Theatre**, which once exuded all the spit-and-sawdust appeal of true fringe theatre, now more suits its name. They write, produce and direct up to twenty plays a year and invariably take a production or two to Edinburgh. Theatre has always been big in this city, the **Playhouse**'s deep-rooted reputation to the fore, and **Malt Cross Music Hall** offers an eerie alternative with drama, music hall, comedy, jazz and folk, with poltergeists in attendance and spooky goings-on that no one seems able to explain. Then there's the **Theatre Royal** of course (Gilbert & Sulivan, *Rocky Horror*, Arthur Miller, *My Fair Lady*, etc.), and music and dance at the **Palace Theatre**, Mansfield.

The New Theatre, which once exuded all the spit-and-sawdust appeal of true fringe theatre, now more suits its name. They write, produce and direct up to 20 plays a year.

On campus, music societies proliferate, such as Blow Soc (wind, to be sure), and for music and art there's the **Arts Centre** – a superb art gallery (with artist in residence) and recital hall next door.

Students may come from comfortable backgrounds and rarely set the firmament alight with radical political action, but they apparently have a caring nature, expressed in the extraordinary agenda of Community Action, some 2000 student volunteers getting involved in arts projects (drama, music), welfare projects (including prison visiting), health, education, housing, sport, environmental projects.

Sport Notttingham teams came 7th nationally last year, but they also claim the largest and most comprehensive inter-hall league. There is opportunity at all levels to participate in as many as 67 clubs. Facilities include two sports halls, rooms for martial arts, aerobics, etc., climbing wall, fitness/weights room, **Champions** bar and restaurant, six squash courts, and at long last they have their own swimming pool (25 x 18m). Outside, there's a floodlit, artificial turf hockey pitch and athletics track. Boating (with boathouse) on the tidal Trent. Sutton Bonington has its own sports centre, squash and tennis courts, rugby, football and cricket pitches. Bursaries are available.

PILLOW TALK

Freshers are guaranteed a place in halls if they receive your Preference Form by August 1. You're talking fully catered halls & self- catering flats. about a third are en suite. There's lots of other accommodation in flats, but catered halls it probably will be, unless you're at Sutton Bonnington. There are 14 halls in total, home to approximately 4,000 students, across two sites – Jubilee Campus and University Park. All of the halls provide three meals a day, every day during term time, as part of the accommodation fee. There are 5 different room-types, ranging from sharing a bedroom to your own bathroom. Each hall offers great amenities – coin-operated laundry facilities, pantries to make snacks, chill-out areas like a bar, Junior Common Room, TV and games room, plus a mini library and computer suite.

Writes Mark: 'To be fair, all the halls are pretty nice. Being a former Lincolnite, my totally unbiased opinion is that it is by far the best hall in the world. Small, yet cosy bar, good food, big rooms, our very own library and even cheese and wine nights in the SCR! What more could you want? OK, so Hugh Stu has the best bar, Derby has the best women and Sherwood has a slide shaped as a dragon. So what!'

Check web site for the latest on the new Veterinary Medicine and Science school's purpose-built accommodation.

If you have a disability and need accessible accommodation, you'll be guaranteed a suitable room. Email: disabilityadviser@nottingham.ac.uk

GETTING THERE

☛ By road: Nottingham, M1/J 25, A52. Sutton Bonington, M1/J24, A6, then left turn.

☛ By rail: London St Pancras, 1:50; Edinburgh, 4:30; Exeter, 4:00; Birmingham New Street, 1:30.

☛ By air: East Midlands Airport.

☛ By coach: London, 2:55; Birmingham, 1:30; Newcastle, 5:00; Exeter, 6:30.

NOTTINGHAM TRENT UNIVERSITY

The Nottingham Trent University
Burton Street
Nottingham NG1 4BU

TEL 0115 941 8418
TEL 0115 848 6868 (prospectus)
FAX 0115 848 6503
EMAIL marketing@ntu.ac.uk
WEB www.ntu.ac.uk

VAG VIEW

Centred on the building in Shakespeare Street where, in 1887, the foundation stone was laid by Gladstone for University College Nottingham, later to become Nottingham University (the one that D H Lawrence actually attended), this particular institution began life as Trent Poly in 1970, but today has arrived on the scene as one of the most impressive of our new universities.

CAMPUS SITES

City Campus Burton Street is the location of the central admin building, 'front' for a whole load of buildings in neighbouring streets. The Students' Union headquarters (Byron House) is here, along with the new Boots Library, student residences and six of the uni's nine faculties: Art & Design, Business, Environmental Studies, Law, Economics & Social Sciences, Engineering & Computing.

Clifton Campus Clifton Lane, Nottingham NG11 8NS. This is a spacious, green field campus some four miles southwest of the city centre along the A453. It is wholly self-contained with its own SU, sports grounds and student residences, and is home to the Humanities and Science & Mathematics faculties.

'Clifton is the smaller of the two campuses with around 5000 students,' writes Daniel Ashley, 'and still thrives on the community atmosphere. A new student village and all-weather Astroturf allows the Clifton student to become almost self-sufficient within the campus. Probably not a bad thing, as the Clifton locals are not famed for their tolerance of us.'

Clifton Hall Clifton Village, Nottingham NG11 8NJ. This is a Georgian manor house a few minutes walk from Clifton campus and includes lecture halls for use by the faculty of Education, a resource centre, dance studio and refectory.

Brackenhurst College is their Department of Land-based Studies near the historic town of Southwell, 10 miles north east of Nottingham, which for years has offered Trent degrees and comes with a 200-hectare farm. There's a whole Student Association set-up here, bar, sports, ents, etc and special things with clubs in town.

FEES, BURSARIES

UK & EU Fees: £3000 p.a. If in receipt of full HE Maintenance grant there's a bursary of £1000; if in receipt of partial grant, it's £250. There are bursaries to encourage applications from poor neighbourhoods, and there are academic achievement scholarships.

STUDENT PROFILE

The student body is better balanced class-wise than at Nottingham Uni. State school intake is 92%, as against 67% at Nottingham; the take from

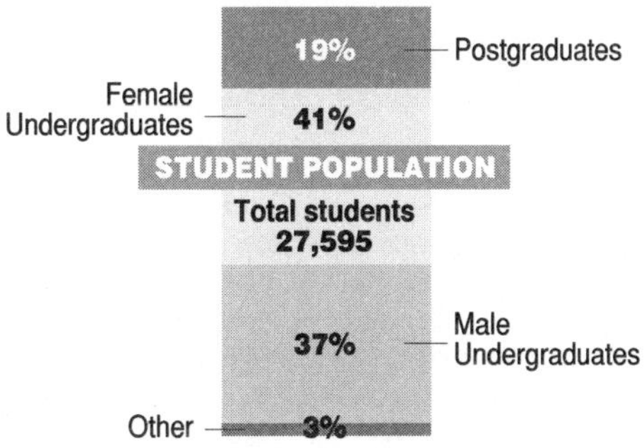

UNIVERSITY/STUDENT PROFILE	
University since	**1992**
Situation/style	**Campus & city site**
Student population	**27595**
Undergraduates	**21390**
- mature	**15%**
- non EU undergraduates	**3%**
- male/female	**48/52**
- non-traditional student intake	**31%**
- state school intake	**92%**
- drop-out rate	**7%**
- undergraduate applications	**Down 7%**

the lower socio-economic brackets is 31%, as against 16% at Nottingham. There's also a much larger mature undergraduate population at Trent.

At the city site there is enthusiasm and a high focus. We had the impression that students make the most of their three or four years here.

ACADEMIA & JOBS

They claim more students on sandwich courses than any other unis, students experiencing the real world of work as part of their courses. This and the uni's strong links with employers, is the basis of their strength in graduate employment. Trent is a hive of industry, hence the name of its enterprise centre, The Hive, its purpose to encourage and develop ideas into sustainable businesses

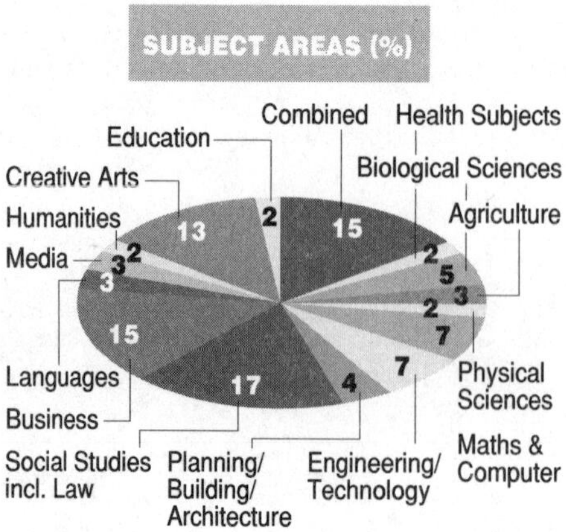

Trent University and industry scratch each other's backs in a way that gets right to the spot. In particular, graduates from the School of Property and Construction attract some of the highest starting salaries in the country. With their Architectural Technology BSc they have the edge. It sits comfortably among their Building, Design and BSc Construction Management degrees. The architectural input brings social, political, economic, environmental features to the fore in an otherwise out-and-out technological degree. It can get you a job with an architectural practice, a building contractor, a local authority or a large property developer. There's now also BA Architecture. Teaching inspection 22.

Big in property developing are Sheffield Hallam, Northumbria, Manchester Met and Trent. Look at BSc Planning & Property Development, Property & Management, Building Surveying, Quantity Surveying (two degrees, the Single BSc Hons and Quantity Surveying & Construction, which suggests an even more hands-on approach), and Real Estate Management. Teaching inspection 23.

Prospective construction engineers look at BEng Civil & Structural Engineering.

For numbers of graduates, government administration, Trent lead the way nationally. Look at their Euro Studies, Global Politics, Politics, Political Economy, International Studies. A high level of public administration jobs comes down to Social Studies and Education (which dropped only one point at inspection) in the end.

ACADEMIC EXCELLENCE	
TEACHING: *(Rated Excellent or 17+ out of 24)*	
Chemistry, Business & Management	**Excellent**
Physics, Molecular Biosciences, Organismal Biosciences	**24**
Subjects Allied to Medicine Education, Politics, Sport	**23**
Building, Psychology, Art & Design, Economics	**22**
Communication/Media, Maths	**21**
Electric/Electron Engineering, Civil Eng, Land & Property Mgt Materials Technology	**20**
Sociology	**19**
RESEARCH : *Top grades 5/5**	
Subjects Allied to Medicine , English, Media Studies, Drama/ Dance/Performing Arts	**Grade 5**

In teaching, there's a primary specialism, also advanced early years, and Design & Technology (secondary), while graduates to further education tend to come (in quantity) mostly from biological sciences (full marks in the assessments) and creative arts (22 points at assessment – from Fashion to Furniture to Photography). Then it's Social

Sciences (there's a very good Euro Law degree), Education (23 points at the assessments), and animal and horsey things out at the land-based department, Brackenhurst College, north east of the city.

For aspiring environmental health officers, BSc Environmental Health hits the spot in a cluster of BSc degrees, which tie in Biology, Chemistry, Physics, and Enviro Science.

For prospective environmental officers there's BSc Environmental Conservation & Countryside Management at Brackenhurst, where a new £3-million teaching and laboratory facility has been completed. Other Brackenhurst degrees are Physical Geography, Landscape & Heritage, Equine Sports Science (one including Equestrian Psychology), Wildlife Conservation - and there are foundation degrees to see you in.

Meanwhile, back in the city, chemical company BASF has donated a research and development facility, probably the largest known corporate gift to a new university. It's to be the base for BioCity Nottingham, destined to be the UK's largest bioscience and healthcare innovation centre – 12,000 square metres of labs, equipment and office space for bioscience start-ups and established ventures.

They claim more students on sandwich courses than at any other uni. Their strong links with employers is the basis of their strength in graduate employment.

In the heady realm of pharmaceuticals, Hertfordshire and Trent jostle for top place as biggest graduate provider, followed by Leeds and Nottingham. Trent has a 3/4-year BSc/MSci Pharmaceutical & Medicinal Science, BSc Pharmacology & Neuroscience, BSc Physiology & Pharmacology. Teaching inspection 23. Research Grade 5.

For banking Trent are again among the leaders, their degrees far more accessible than many others. There's a 4-year sandwich Business & Financial Services BA. Look also at the Business Economics BA at 240 points, as well as a raft of European Economics BAs. Computer Sciences is also a popular route into banking. The BA Business Info

AT A GLANCE	
ACADEMIC FILE:	
Assessments	**25**
Excellent	**68%**
Typical entry requirements	**265 points**
Application acceptance rate	**19%**
Students-staff ratio	**18:1**
First/2:1 degree pass rate	**57%**
ACCOMMODATION FILE:	
Guarantee to freshers	**70%, apply early**
Style	**Halls + flats**
Catered	**None**
En-suite	**69%**
Price range pw	**£68-£82**
City rent pw	**£45-£70**

Systems asks 260 points, BSc Business & Info Communications Technology, 240. Jobs also go in quantity to investment adviser/analysts.

Showing faith in Trent's business provision, in 2002, auto-giant Toyota joined forces with them on Clifton campus to build a £3-million training centre, the only one of its kind in Europe. The uni's so-called Nottingham Business School will work with the company on a portfolio of formal qualifications and professional programmes.

In Law, there is a choice of eight institutions where the Bar Vocational Course may be undertaken, Trent's Nottingham Law School is one of them. The BVC course lasts for a year and is followed by a year's pupillage – practical training under the supervision of an experienced barrister.

Their Art & Design Faculty lead many into advertising, Design for Television is a particular niche in dedicated design/IT studios. Look, too, at the BA Communications and the Media & Cultural

WHERE NOTTINGHAM TRENT GRADUATES END UP

Health & Social Work: 4%; Education: 6%; Wholesale Retail: 11%; Manufacturing: 14%; Financial Activities: 9%; Public Administration, Civil Service & Defence: 13%; Hotel/Restaurant: 3%; Transport & Communications (including Telecommunications): 4%; Construction: 4%; Personnel: 6%; Computer: 4%; Business & Management: 3%; Accountancy: 1%; Media (including Film): 2%; Legal 2.5%; Architecture: 3%; Publishing: 1%; Advertising: 1%; Artistic/Literary: 1%; Sport: 0.5%.

Approximate 'graduate track' employed **60%**

Studies, and a new course for 2004, English with Writing.

In the same faculty, Theatre Design put students to work in set design, and you could get to study Fashion, Knitwear or Textile design. No suprise that such a construction-intensive uni should come up with the highly vocational 4-year sandwich BA Furniture & Product Design (engineering design students have a hand in it too). Always there is this lean towards a job, even in difficult art and design. Teaching inspection 20.

For radio and TV broadcasting, it's Leeds, Bournemouth and Nottingham Trent. Their Centre for Broadcasting & Journalism is housed in the old BBC studios in Nottingham, making it the only training centre in the UK to have access to authentic broadcasting facilities, so we should not be surprised to find an international Grade 5 rating for research in this area. In the BA (Hons) Broadcast Journalism there's a healthy lean towards ethics, too. Constantly award-winning student radio station Fly FM plays its part. Teaching inspection 21.

Finally, their sports provision (BSc Sport Science & Management, Sport & Exercise, etc) produces more physical training instructors than any uni outside of Brighton.

SOCIAL SCENE

The Students' Union bar at City has undergone a £300,000 facelift, giving a new continental café bar and late-night (2 am at weekends) drinking spot, **Glo** bar, in addition to **Sub** bar, itself refurnished this year. At Clifton campus there's the **Point** bar and at Brackenhurst, it's the **Museum** bar.

Says Annabel Wollen: 'Once a month we have a legendary fancy dress night called *Kinki* at **Ocean** nightclub in town, each month with a different theme. It is somewhat infamous (a bit of a religion at Trent). Also at **Ocean** we have a Wednesday sports and societies night called *Campus*. Then there's a Thursday night called *DV8* at **Walkabout**. Both these mid-week nights play mainly commercial music and a big dollop of cheese is always on offer. On Fridays we hold *Flirt* at Clifton campus and alternate between *Asault* (a rock night) and *The Tone* club (live) at City, **Sub** bar being transformed into a late bar, chilled out and relaxed. Finishing the week is Saturday night – *Climax* – where our City site venue is transformed into a nightclub holding 2500 people. Nusic policy is cheese and golden oldies downstairs with a mix of r&b and garage upstairs. All our nights are NUS only, and packed to the rafters, but on a Saturday we do allow our members to sign townies in as guests.

The city is very popular with students – see *Nottingham Student City* by Annabel (page344).

Platform is the weekly paper, which the *Nottingham Evening Post* prints for them. 'They have nothing to do with editorial, well ... they sort of peruse it, nick some of our stories.' It has won many awards. The Trent student radio station isFly FM.

The Students' Union is also proving that what it has long been doing for student entertainment it can do equally well for more serious pursuits: a Community Action Group was set up, an Employment Store has grown from one small office to two massive departments that together will deal with upwards of 9,000 placements in part-time employment this year, and the SU employment skills training programme, Stride, has broken all expectations, with every programme either full or over-subscribed.

SPORT Their teams came overall 27th in the nation last year, and won the annual Varsity series against arch rivals Beeston Tec, as Nottingham University is known. Already in 2006 half of their 38 teams are top of their BUSA national leagues. Rugby League 1st and men's Hockey 1st have played so well that

WHAT IT'S REALLY LIKE

UNIVERSITY:	
Social Life	★★★★
Campus scene	**Streetwise, fun**
Student Union services	**Average**
Politics	**Interest low**
Sport	**42 clubs**
National team position	**27th**
Sport facilities	**Average**
Arts opportunities	**Drama,art, music, good; dance avg; film poor**
Student newspaper	**Platform**
National awards 2005	**1 nomination**
Student radio	**Fly FM**
Venue/bars	**Glo, Sub, Point, Museum**
Union ents	**Wild**
Union societies	**70+**
Parking	**Clifton good, City campus poor**
CITY:	
Entertainment	★★★★★
Scene	**Clubby, pubby, good arts**
Town/gown relations	**OK**
Risk of violence	**High**
Cost of living	**Average**
Student concessions	**Good**
Survival + 2 nights out	**£90 pw**
Part-time work campus/town	**Good/excellent**

they have already won their leagues. They have many TASS athletes and also a handful who represent the country – in hockey, archery and canoe.

A £2 million sports hall plus all-weather pitch opened in 2001 at Clifton. There are 42 clubs, offering everything from circus skills to rugby league, traditionally the most successful club in the university.

PILLOW TALK

They accommodate 70% of first years; 25% live in flats and shared houses in the private sector. Not sure where the residual 5% end up. All halls are self-catered, approximately 69% of rooms are en suite. New residence of approximately 440 en-suite rooms were made available in 2005.

'City site freshers are likely to find themselves in one of the many halls scattered within a mile or so,' writes Daniel, 'so it is possible to get to college both on foot or by bike. Early enthusiasm for this does tend to wane as it gets a bit colder. However, the parking facilities in City are not brilliant, and a permit must be applied for. Do this as soon as you arrive. At Clifton nearly all first-year students are accommodated in the on-site, en-suite Peverell halls of residence. Halls may not be the cheapest form of accommodation, but they are certainly the best. As well as meeting all sorts of people, that £70 includes all your bills. Three warm showers a day are rarely a possibility in a shared student house!

GETTING THERE

☛ By road: M1/J25/6. Good coach service.
☛ By rail: London St Pancras, 1:50; Edinburgh, 4:30; Exeter, 4:00; Birmingham New Street, 1:30.
☛ By air: East Midlands Airport 12 miles away.
☛ By coach: London, 2:55; Birmingham, 1:30.

UNIVERSITY OF OXFORD

The University of Oxford
Wellington Square
Oxford OX1 2JD

TEL 01865 288000
FAX 01865 270708
EMAIL undergraduate.admissions@admin.ox.ac.uk
WEB www.ox.ac.uk

OUSU
28 Little Clarendon Street
Oxford OX1 2HU

TEL 01865 270777
FAX 01865 270776
EMAIL info@ousu.org.uk
WEB www.ousu.org

VAG VIEW

As a sixthformer, the great thing is not to be fazed by the clichéd reputation. If you fancy the trademark one-to-one tutor system (and who wouldn't?), simply apply. So few do apply that there's straightway a one-in-four chance you'll get in, which is way better than any other university but Cambridge.

FEES, BURSARIES

UK & EU Fees: £3000 p.a. If in receipt of full HE Maintenance grant there's a bursary of £4,000 in year 1, £3000 p.a. thereafter; if in receipt of partial grant, bursaries are on a sliding scale. If household income is between £22500 and £37425 p.a. you will receive between £2500 and £100 p.a. on a sliding scale according to income: if household income is below £22499, it's £3000 in year 1 and £2600 p.a. thereafter. In addition, individual colleges make available from their own resources a wide range of scholarships and financial support.

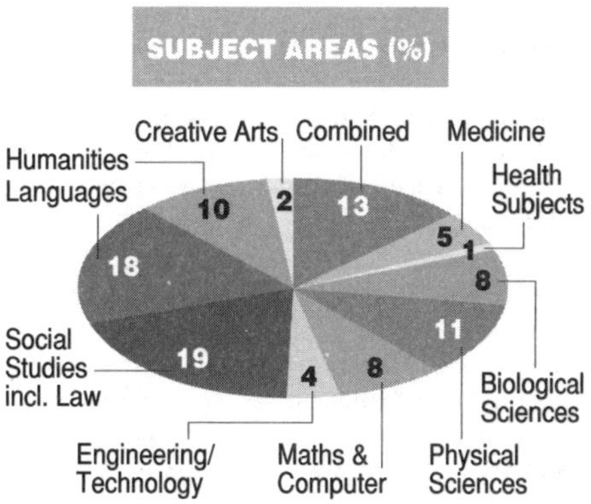

STUDENT PROFILE

'Oxford as a vanguard of elitism and discrimination has made the headlines countless times in the past few years. Personally, I haven't experienced any discrimination,' writes history undergraduate Rachel Cocker, 'but as a white, middle-class girl from an independent school in the North West I am not exactly a member of a minority group here.'

Rachel will tell us more, but perhaps Christabel Ashby, from a different background, may have a different story: 'I'm Christabel Ashby, I'm from London. I went to a state school, and I'm a final-year student at Keble, studying Theology. I'm not going to lie; my first few days in Oxford were terrifying. In Freshers Week we were inundated with information and events. There were both the university and the college fresher fairs [presentations to freshers by sports clubs and societies], and we were forced into going out and getting drunk by well meaning second-year students. Despite this it was really easy to make friends, and after two weeks I felt as at-home and confident as if I'd been there for years.

'The nice thing about the Oxford student scene is that it is so *inclusive*. Whatever you're into, you are bound to find people to hang out with. You will probably meet a few people who are a bit elitist or arrogant, but I suspect that is true of any university.'

ACADEMIA & JOBS

'The myth that Oxford students have no time for a social life is false, but that we have a very heavy workload is, however, perfectly true,' continues Rachel. 'Eight weeks is a short period for a term and a lot of work is packed into it. Scientists, medics and lawyers have by far the most to do. Historians get off relatively lightly. Still, it's hard when you hear your mates at other unis talk of two-month deadlines when you're going through the weekly essay grind. It *is* stressful, but none of my friends have, as yet, launched themselves off Magdalen Bridge. Tutors are generally willing to give more guidance and leeway than you might imagine. At the end of every term you will be given a feedback form, and although for some this may be simply a faculty-proscribed exercise, for others students' comments have shifted the focus and structure of the course they teach.

'All colleges have computer facilities where you can type up your work or check your e-mail, an Oxford e-mail address is provided for everyone upon arrival.

Oxford has some of the best libraries in the world, the state of your college library depends on its personal wealth but as the Bodleian has a copy of every book ever written, or something like it, you don't have much of an excuse for not reading that "essential" item on the reading list.'

UNIVERSITY/STUDENT PROFILE

University since	**1096**
Situation/style	**City collegiate**
Student population	**18113**
Undergraduates	**11225**
- mature	**5%**
- non EU undergraduates	**7%**
- male/female	**45/55**
- non-traditional student intake	**12%, v. low**
- state school intake	**54%, v. low**
- drop-out rate	**1%, v. low**
- undergraduate applications	**Up 5%**

The uni is developing a rich diversity of online resources and course materials – full details can be found at http://www.online.ox.ac.uk/. There are also little known welfare resources – a disability service, for example, even grants available from such as the Dyslexia Fund. Again, the Oxford University Resources for the Blind provide tape recordings for students with a print impairment, including dyslexia sufferers. Note-takers or readers are also available.

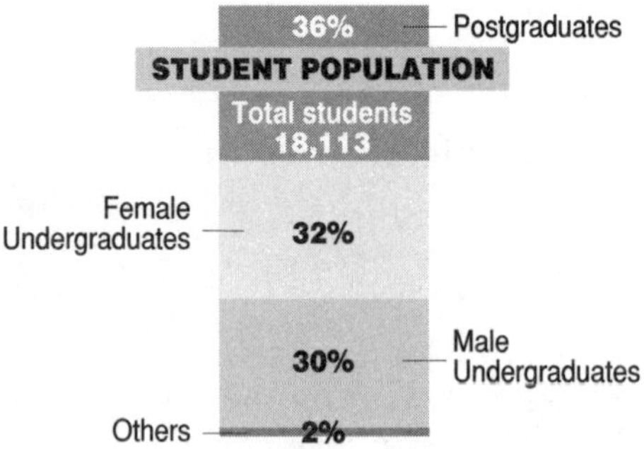

To become a doctor at Oxford you will need the 4 or 6-year BM BCh. Oxford now stipulate that all candidates applying to read Medicine will sit a written test called the Biomedical Admissions Test (BMAT). The test is being used to assess scientific aptitude, not fitness to practise medicine (which will continue to be assessed in other ways, including interview) and focuses on scientific abilities relevant to the study of medicine. There's a 12% chance of acceptance, which is a better application acceptance rate than most.

For the degree they have retained a 3-year preclinical course with small group tutorial teaching (often pairs). There are regular GP visits, too, and clinical experience. Nearly 20% of those who apply get in. Entry AAA: Chemistry with either Maths or

Biology or Physics. Humanities subject welcomed. Teaching inspection 21.

The Law Faculty has a world-class Grade 5* for research. They are European Law specialists. Non-Law graduates may opt for a 2-year Senior Status Law Degree. All candidates must sit the National Admissions Test for Law (LNAT).

The appearance of Oxford University among the Top 10 providers to accountancy gives the lie to the proposition that vocational courses are what is needed in this area (in fact a degree is not needed at all). What they have is a small number of very high-powered courses in physical and biological sciences, which dispense skills of analysis so commanding as to question the wisdom of too early a specialisation. These, together with abilities honed in departments of Modern Languages, Mathematics and even Humanities, provide 90% of Oxford's graduate accountants.

Likewise, analysing and understanding how people think, how communities respond, is what is required at the sharp end of market research, which is why 25% of Oxford graduates into this area have analytical minds honed in the study of biological sciences.

For anyone wanting to become an actuary three universities are head and shoulders above the rest in equating degree success with employment, namely Heriot-Watt, Warwick and Oxford. Again, there are no dedicated degrees, but look at maths, of course, and also the Physics Department, which is also where Oxford's actuaries come from.

It may seem strange to choose Oxford particularly if you want to be a management consultant, there being many more vocational courses elsewhere, but they are way out front in the stats for graduates into this sector. The degree that causes all the fuss is BA Economics & Management. There are also combinations with Engineering or Materials.

Bankers, merchant bankers, stockbrokers, sharedealers, investment advisers and analysts all proliferate out of Oxford. The Arts & Social Studies BA hons programme accounts for more than a third of them. This includes Economics & Management, but also a number of Classics combinations, and Oxford Classics graduates have always been much in demand in the City. Then it's Physics and Languages and Mathematics. Employers are after analytical and flexible thinking.

Plenty of their language graduates make it into translating/interpreting, but how interesting, too, that Oxford language graduates get jobs as social worker/counsellors in number, and probably at levels higher than those reading Social Work degrees elsewhere.

At the same time, many of their language graduates are sought by advertising agencies – any European Language adjunct goes down well in this sector from Oxford. Languages are to the fore again in jobs for government and media research. As at Durham, there is an interesting focus here on European and Middle/Far Eastern Languages.

For jobs in publishing, Oxford is No. 1, and languages are again the most popular route, followed by the Arts & Social Studies combos (everything from English Language & Literature or Classics & English to Archaeology & Anthropology), followed by humanities.

ACADEMIC EXCELLENCE

TEACHING : *(Rated Excellent or 17+ out of 24)*	
Chemistry, History, Law, Anthropology, Social Work, Computing Science, English, Geography, Geology.	**Excellent**
Organismal Biosciences, Forestry & Agric Sciences, Classics, Philosophy, Politics, Psychology, Biochemistry, Fine Art	**24**
Engineering, Materials Tech., Economics, Physics, Theology	**23**
Asian/Mid-East/African Studies, Archaeology, Oriental Studies, Maths	**22**
Modern Languages, Medicine, Anatomy	**21**
RESEARCH : *Top grades 5/5*/6**	
Pharmacology, Pathology, Community & hospital-based Clinical Subjects, Psychology, Chemistry, Physics, Earth Sciences, Pure Math, Statistics, General Eng, Metallurgy, Law, Politics, Asian Studies, English, French, Italian, Russian/Slavonic/ East European, Linguistics, Classics, Archaeology, Philosophy, Theology, Music	**Grade 6***
Clinical Lab. Sciences, Anatomy, Physiology, Zoology, Biochemistry, Applied Math, Computer, Anthropology, Economics, Sociology, Management, Middle Eastern/ African Studies, Celtic Studies, German/Dutch/Scandinavian, Iberian/Latin American, History, Education	**Grade 5**

WHERE OXFORD GRADUATES END UP

Health & Social Work: 13%; Education: 10%; Wholesale Retail: 5%; Manufacturing: 8%; Financial Activities: 12%; Public Administration, Civil Service & Defence: 6%; Hotel/Restaurant: 2%; Transport & Communications (including Telecommunications): 2%; Construction: 1%; Personnel: 4%; Computer: 3%; Business & Management: 7%; Accountancy: 6%; Media (including Film): 2%; Legal 2%; Publishing: 4%; Advertising: 1.5%; Artistic/Literary: 2%

Approximate 'graduate track' employed **78%**

They also turn out more graduate editors than most – nearly half are languages graduates again, then come students of humanities, biological sciences and law. Similar areas train a good number of those that take up journalism after Oxford – another powerful graduate employment area.

Languages and humanities graduates also find work in charities, and dominate the civil service and adult education sectors, and, as elsewhere, it's the arts & social studies joint degrees, languages, biological sciences and humanities that lead the way for lecturers into higher education .

Finally, Oxford is one of the top graduate providers to automobile engineering, with Loughborough, Oxford Brookes, Bath, Swansea Institute and Coventry University. Good to think of them hand in glove with the Swansea Institute. All engineering students here follow a general course for the first year before naming a MEng specialism.

SOCIAL SCENE

Students' Union 'Once you've made your new-found friends, there is a reasonable social life to be had with them. A lot of it is college based; most have weekly bops. One thing Oxford seriously lacks is a central student venue, but once you venture outside the walls of your cosy college environment there are plenty of university-wide activities in which to get involved. Theatre, journalism, music, student politics and Anglo Saxon re-enactment (apparently) are all strong. Cherwell, ISIS and *The Oxford Student* were shortlisted 5 times in the national student jouranlism awards last year, and Oxide, the student radio station won a Gold award in its section. Every year the Oxford University drama festival, 'Cuppers', sees around 30 productions performed, directed and often written by freshers. Hacks tend to gravitate towards the famed Oxford Union, where they can fine tune their debating and back-stabbing skills, and it is possible either to infiltrate or avoid their number at will.

Sport... 'is a big deal from football to ultimate frisbee. There are college leagues for every sport you can think of; even pool. Most colleges have their own sports ground and of course there are the university facilities down Iffley Road, the 25-metre, eight-lane Rosenblatt swimming pool has now opened. The pool is part of the training facilities for the OU Swimming and Water Polo Clubs, but it's available for recreational use too. Most people try their hand at rowing at some point during their university career and many, many join the ranks of "boaties", consigning themselves to years of early morning outings and gruelling weights sessions. All very rewarding, especially for all who get to cheer them to victory during Eights Week, while getting pissed on Pimms.

Town 'There are some great pubs; the most studenty of which are the **Kings Arms** and **The Turf**, both rammed to the rafters after exams. The city is also a haven for cocktail bars, and the **Duke of Cambridge** is immensely popular for its very happy "happy hour", which lasts from 5 till 8.30pm every single day of the week. Oxford also boasts some fantastic restaurants, although some of these are so fantastically priced you might have to wait until your real Mummy and Daddy come to take you home before sampling them.

'**Oxford Brookes**' Union hosts live touring bands and probably the best student nights to be had in the city on Fridays and Saturdays. College balls also feature largely in Oxford life and for an average non-dining ticket you are looking at around £50. The larger balls, such as Merton in the winter and Magdalen, New, Trinity and Worcester in the summer can set you back up to £110 per person. Luckily, these only take place once every three years so a lot of people attend but one during their time here. Once you get in there, of course, everything is free.

'*Cost of living*: if you take into account that the average student here goes out at least twice a week (most people's workloads make it hard to manage more) then I would say someone with stronger self-discipline than myself might survive on £50.'

Note, if you're a home/EU publicly-funded first-year who has been granted full fee remission by your LEA, you are eligible for a bursary worth £1,000 in the first year, £500 in each subsequent year. Go to www.admissions.ox.ac.uk/finance/bursaries/index.shtml

'*Safety*: everything being just down the road encourages a feeling of safety, but there have been several attacks on students since I've been here. You do still need to be on your guard. Town/gown relations don't seem to be anywhere near as bad as in Durham, but there are a few unofficially designated townie pubs and clubs, which students avoid, though not through fear for their lives.'

PILLOW TALK

All freshers are guaranteed college accommodation for their first and at least one additional year. Facilities offered by the college include a library, bar, common room, laundry facilities, computer room, sports ground and dining room, where three meals are offered every day. Costs vary from college to college – as a rough guide, £600-£800 per term usually to include rent, cleaning, heating, water and electricity. If you were to take three meals a day in college, it might cost you an addtional £325-£425 a term.

COLLEGE CAMEOS

by Caroline Rowe & Sacha Delmotte

BALLIOL
Broad Street, Oxford OX1 3BJ
TEL 01865 277777
WEB www.balliol.ac.uk
Founded in 1263, Balliol has a claim to be the oldest Oxford college and is situated right in the centre of town, so access and convenience are optimum. Balliol has very high academic standards, and is proud to boast its 'effortless superiority'. Today its main strengths lie in Classics, PPE, Physics and Philosophy. The college used to be very left-wing, which is still evident today in one of the most active JCRs in the university, and the bar being entirely student-run (only Hertford does this as well). There is also a notable absence of Balls or even formal hall.

Balliol has, however, always been very liberal, and was the first college to admit international students (today it has the highest percentage of overseas students of all colleges), and the first to allow women into Oxford academia. There is a fairly high proportion of state-school students, and social elitism is not rife, despite the existence of the Annandale Society (a pretentious, all public school gentlemen's club of sorts).

Balliol provides a JCR Pantry, which is open all day, serving breakfast until 11:30, and provides colossal portions. College ents are of high standard, rent is second lowest in Oxford and the bar is small but relaxed. There is a long-standing feud between Balliol and Trinity, orchestrated by a (rather rude) song, the 'Gordouli'. College gossip is assured instantaneous propagation via the *John de Balliol* bogsheet.

BRASENOSE
Radcliff Square, Oxford OX1 4AJ
TEL 01865 277510
WEB www.bnc.ox.ac.uk
Founded in 1509, BNC, as it is known, is renowned for its tourist-friendly location and its sporting exploits rather than for academic excellence. Rugby is very big and indeed sports in general tend to be edified, though to be fair it does have a good reputation for PPE and Law. The main social focus of the college is the infamous Gertie's Tea Bar, and it has a medium-size May Ball every summer term. BNC has a fairly low profile within the university, but is interestingly named after the brass door-knocker in hall.

CHRIST CHURCH ('The House')
St Allgates, Oxford OX1 1DP
TEL 01865 276150
WEB www.chch.ox.ac.uk
Founded in 1546, Christ Church is the biggest college (both in number of undergrads and in area), and still to this day has an (entirely undeserved) reputation of being a haven for rich Etonians and other public-school types. Typically, Christ Church students are fairly good at sport,and have the best kept and most central sportsground. The college does well academically and has a strong reputation for law with a specially dedicated library. Christ Church is also the second richest college after St

AT A GLANCE

ACADEMIC FILE:	
Subjects assessed	**30**
Excellent	**97%**
Typical entry requirements	**500 points**
Application acceptance rate	**24%, high**
Students-staff ratio	**13:1**
First/2:1 degree pass rate	**86%**
ACCOMMODATION FILE:	
Availability to freshers	**100%**
Style	**College rooms**
Catered	**100%**
En-suite	**Some**
Average price pw	**£90**
Average city rent pw	**£70**

John's and thus welfare and accommodation provisions are excellent, with rooms available for all your time in Oxford. The college is extremely beautiful, with extensive meadows, Oxford's mediaeval cathedral and an art gallery containing works by Leonardo da Vinci and Michelangelo. It holds a yearly impressive ball. Pembroke as its rival, not surprising as it technically owns the college. Film wise, while Magdalen has *Shadowlands*, Ch Ch can boast being the location for much of the new Harry Potter film!

CORPUS CHRISTI
Merton Street, Oxford OX1 4JF
TEL 01865 276693
WEB www.ccc.ox.ac.uk
Founded 1517, Corpus is tiny, really tiny, both in land area and in student number. This feature gives it a sense of intimacy that other colleges cannot claim, and accommodation is guaranteed for all students. Corpus excels academically and is quiet as a result of all the hard work. Recently it has introduced a new tradition, the Tortoise Race, where the Corpus reptile races against the demon speed-machine from Balliol. Corpus puts on a small-scale Summer Event (advertised as the cheapest Oxford Ball) at the beginning of every Trinity term, but on the whole it has a low profile in the university.

EXETER
Turl Street, Oxford OX1 3DP
TEL 01865 279660
WEB www.exeter.ox.ac.uk
Founded 1314, Exeter is a compact college and is so close to the Bodleian Library it may as well be part of it. Public perception is that it contains rowdy, sport-playing types. This certainly appears to be the case as the bar is very active, with lots of cool, outgoing people, and intimate ents – the JCR is famously apathetic, and one rarely hears of political activism from within Exeter's walls. The college has a long-standing rivalry with its neighbour, Jesus, also on Turl Street.

HARRIS-MANCHESTER
Mansfield Road, Oxford OX1 3TD
TEL 01865 271009
WEB www.hmc.ox.ac.uk
Founded in 1786, there is very little to be said about this college since it only admits mature students, mostly to read an Arts degree. The college was founded in Manchester to provide education for non-Anglican students, who at the time were not allowed into Oxbridge. Following a move to Oxford, it was granted Permanent Private Hall status, and only recently (1996) become a full college. Currently the college faces longterms financial and governance problems. In 2003 they asked Derek Wood QC to review resources, particularly for history, PPE and related subjects. The upshot was to ditch history. Pleasant Gothic Revival buildings.

HERTFORD
Catte Street, Oxford OX1 3BW
TEL 01865 279400
WEB www.bertford.ox.ac.uk
Founded in 1740, Hertford has had a tumultuous past with various changes of name, owner and status over its 250-year history; it used to be a subdivision of Magdalen. Hertford is very central and opposite the ever-popular **King's Arms** pub. Hertford students really know how to party (their bar is rumoured to have the highest fiscal turnover in the university). Whether this is explained by its large population of state-school students, and the distinct Northern flavour of the undergrad body in particular, would not be PC to enquire. Altogether it is a progressive establishment and was one of the first all-male colleges to admit women and the first to make the entrance exam optional. Students enjoy full accommodation, an excellent atmospheric JCR bar, which is entirely student run and concocts brilliant, toxic cocktails.

JESUS
Turl Street, Oxford OX1 3DW
TEL 01865 279720
WEB www.jesus.ox.ac.uk
Founded in 1571, Jesus is small, beautiful and wealthy, and has a reputation for being the 'Welsh College', which is perfectly fair since a not insignificant proportion of students come from Wales. The college bogsheet is *The Sheepshagger*. The college is quite insular and politically unmotivated. Jesubites have it easy: accommodation is excellent and hall food is cheap. Recently Jesus is feared in rugby circles, and does well in other sports too. It has a feud with Exeter.

KEBLE
Parks Road, Oxford OX1 3PG
TEL 01865 272711
WEB www.keble.ox.ac.uk
Founded 1870. Writes Christabel Ashby: 'Keble College is notable for being the only redbrick, Victorian college. It is ideally placed for town and most university facilities, and is right opposite the University parks. College facilities are good; we have phone and internet lines in every room, and all the rooms are nicely furnished. The college guarantees you two years accommodation.

'Keble is also rather traditional, there is formal hall every night, which means you wear your gown to dinner, which has waiter service. On the social side, there's a mixed bag. It has one of the largest undergraduate populations of Oxford colleges, which means there are lots of people with whom to make friends, but also means you will never know everyone, and seeing people you don't recognise all over the place can be a little disconcerting.

'Keble is sporty, there are lots of teams and clubs, and the bar is also fairly popular. Ents are predictable however, usually consisting of a live band or karaoke nights. These events happen once or twice a term. The JCR is well stocked with electronic games, pinball, table-footy and pool, and also has sky TV. Unlike some of the other colleges, however, there is no JCR shop.

'There is a strong sense of equality at Keble, both in terms of women's and men's rights and in gay/lesbian rights. The environment is welcoming and friendly to anyone and everyone, but at the same time its size means you are able to retain a degree of anonymity not possible in many of the other colleges.'

LADY MARGARET HALL
Norham Gdns, Oxford OX2 6QA
TEL 01865 274300
WEB www.lmh.ox.ac.uk
Founded 1878. LMH was the first college founded solely for women in the university. Since there was no vacant land in the centre of town, LMH is fairly far out of town, but this has resulted in the luxury of extensive gardens. The college began admitting men in the '70s, and since that day and age LMH has achieved an unparalleled male/female ratio of 1:1 at levels of college hierarchy. LMH is socially self-sufficient and has a low profile in the university. It is neither renowned for scholastic or sporting brilliance, and has no great political aspirations. Its sole reputation is for producing Thespians, who tend to hang out in cliques with other college actors (read 'actoars'). Otherwise unpretentious and unintimidating.

LINCOLN
Turl Street, Oxford OX1 3DR
TEL 01865 279800
WEB www.linc.ox.ac.uk
Founded in 1427, Lincoln is the smallest of the three colleges on Turl Street, but beautiful. The college is a rather wealthy one, which is evident from the extensive facilities provided to students: good accommodation, excellent sporting facilities, and allegedly the best hall food in the university. This comfort of college life means that very few Lincolnites emerge from their cushy environment to participate in university-wide activities, and thus charges of insularity are fair and merited. Overall, the college is a rather 'shy' one on the university scene, and is not really noted for spectacular achievement in any academic, political or sporting field. Tradition has it that on Ascension Day, Lincoln undergrads stroll around town in subfusc (formal wear) with the vicar of St Michael's in the Northgate and a gang of choristers 'beating the bounds', or thrashing at the town limits with canes. Then the students drink lots of ivy beer and toss hot pennies at the choirboys.

MAGDALEN
High Street, Oxford OX1 4AU
TEL 01865 276063
WEB www.magd.ox.ac.uk
Founded in 1458, Magdalen (read 'Maudlin') is a gorgeous college in every respect. It is one of the oldest, richest and most beautiful. Its buildings, extensive grounds (including the famous Deer Park), beautiful cloisters, and Magdalen Tower, and location on the banks of the River Cherwell are stunning, breathtaking. On May Day the choir sings from the top of Magdalen Tower and the tradition is to jump off the bridge into the river, although the police keep deciding to cordon it off. The film *Shadowlands* was shot there, and the money earned was spent on renovating certain college rooms. Accommodation facilities are second to none (everyone can live in throughout their whole student career), and some of the sets offered are simply amazing (bedroom, living room, and bathroom!). The college has a huge and lively bar, and puts on very good ents events, but is pretty insular (the **Lower Oscar Wilde Room** is often the site of debauched and drunken student carnage). Magdalen, like Christ Church, owns its own punt. It is academically successful and socially intense, but rather uninterested in political and JCR issues.

MANSFIELD
Mansfield Road, Oxford OX1 3TF
TEL 01865 270970
WEB www.mansfield.ox.ac.uk
Founded in 1886, Mansfield only obtained its college status in 1995; prior to that it was a Permanent Private Hall. It is among the smallest of colleges, only admitting about sixty undergrads every year. This leads to a very close-knit yet appreciably claustrophobic community. Due to the small size of the college many students explore extra-curricular opportunities in the university, and the college is famous for drama. The college is very poor and thus room rents are relatively high. Mansfield has a reputation for tolerance and is sometimes known as the LGB (Lesbian Gay Bisexual) college. Ents are diverse, with bops, karaokes, trips to the theatre, Laserquesting, and there is a triennial Venetian

Masked Ball held in the seventh week of Michaelmas term.

MERTON
Merton Street, Oxford OX1 4JD
TEL 01865 276329
WEB www.merton.ox.ac.uk
Founded in 1264, Merton, along with Balliol and University, has a claim to be the oldest Oxford college, and is very rich and beautiful, containing the oldest surviving Oxford quad (Mob quad). The college has an undisputed reputation for being a centre of academic excellence, fuelled by SCR encouragement and a competitive spirit among the student population. Socially Merton appears to be fairly insular, and one rarely meets Mertonites around the university; in fact it would seem that Mertonites are quite dull. Nonetheless every year Merton puts on the only Christmas Ball in Oxford, on the last day of Michaelmas term, which is usually a roaring success. It is particularly popular with Freshers who are able to finish their first term at Oxford with style and panache (and a random snog perhaps!). Merton's tradition, the Time Ceremony, has existed for barely fifteen years, but is now firmly implanted in the college calendar, and for a day lifts the veil of seriousness which rests upon the college. It involves students walking backwards around Merton's Mob Quad while continuously downing port, on a particular day of each year.

NEW COLLEGE
Holywell Street, Oxford OX1 3BN
TEL 01865 279590
WEB www.new.ox.ac.uk
Founded in 1379, here's another beautiful college, and very inappropriately named too! New is one of the oldest, largest and most impressive colleges in Oxford and takes in part of the city walls, as well as a few ancient plague-heaps. Widely accepted as having the best and most beautiful student bar, New puts on great ents: the bops are legendary, and the Long Room is as much a site of drunken mayhem as the Lower Oscar Wilde Room at Magdalen, with many different societies hiring the room to throw crazy parties. New also puts on a gargantuan Commemoration Ball every three summers, described by many as the best ball in Oxford. Scenes from the Bond film *Tomorrow Never Dies* were filmed at New College, and the college has a fair share of Bond-girl lookalikes. New is particularly accomplished in musical matters: the college choir is one of the best in Oxford. New has been described as 'one of Oxford's least stressful places to live'.

ORIEL
Oriel Square, Oxford OX1 4EW
TEL 01865 276555
WEB www.oriel.ox.ac.uk
Founded in 1326, Oriel is mostly famous for its monotonous and undeniable domination of the river: it's a boatie's college. Apparently Oriel brings in students from America especially for their rowing prowess, regardless of their academic (in)abilities, and provides them with the best en-suite rooms in college and lavish free meals. Every extra year that sees Oriel come out victorious of the Summer Eights rowing race, another of its old boats is religiously burnt in the middle of their quad (that's Oxford tradition for you!). Architecturally the college is something of a rabbit warren. The distinctive front quad sees a Shakespeare production every summer, and the college is strong musically, with its own orchestra and choir. Academically very relaxed, the college reveres sport: those who can participate, do, and those who can't, support from one of the best boat houses on the river.

PEMBROKE
St Aldates, Oxford OX1 1DW
TEL 01865 276412
WEB www.pmb.ox.ac.uk
Founded in 1624, Pembroke is one of the poorest colleges in Oxford, and allegedly the college Boat Club Trust Fund is richer than the rest of the college put together! This astonishing fact holds its currency in donations from rich alumni rowers. Thus Pembroke is very strong at rowing, and the only plausible pretender to Oriel's rowing crown. In fact in the fifteen or so years of Oriel dominance on the river, Pembroke has been the only college capable of beating them once, several years ago; now the college is regularly second behind Oriel. Socially Pembroke is rather insular, has a low profile in the university, and academically it is laid back. A college rivalry exists with Christ Church.

QUEEN'S
High Street, Oxford OX1 4AW
TEL 01865 279167
WEB www.queens.ox.ac.uk
Founded 1624. Despite having a very high-profile location, right in the middle of the High, the college has a very low profile in the University; one rarely meets students from Queen's. It has some of the most obviously dramatic architecture in Oxford, ranging from the classical cupola to the UFO-like Florey building off St Clement's. Queen's is very rich and is one of the cheapest colleges to attend, offering full accommodation for all your Oxford years. There is also a particularly good

library. Excluded are undergrads wanting to read Single Hons English, however, a fact unconnected with the college being a home from home to Northerners. Quirkily, Queen's has an annual dinner to celebrate the survival of an undergraduate who in 1935 was viciously attacked by a boar and defended himself by driving a tome of Aristotle into the boar's mouth.

ST ANNE'S
Woodstock Rd, Oxford OX2 6HS
TEL 01865 274825
WEB www.stannes.ox.ac.uk
Founded 1879. St Anne's, very far away from the city centre, is atypical – laid back and unpretentious and lacking in the pomp and archaic traditions of older colleges. Isolation breeds self-sufficiency, and the college has a low profile in the university. A large proportion of the undergraduate community come from a state-school background, and the college is now one of the largest in terms of undergraduate numbers. Despite being a poor college, the library has around 100,000 volumes for current use, and is one of the two largest undergraduate college libraries in Oxford. The architecture is modern and unusual for Oxford, and the gardens are pleasant in the summer.

ST CATHERINE'S (St Catz)
Manor Road, Oxford OX1 3UJ
TEL 01865 271703
WEB www.stcatz.ox.ac.uk
Founded in 1963, St Catz possesses some breathtaking architecture, much of which is Grade 1 listed. Designed by Arne Jacobsen, the famous Danish architect, a spirit of openness infuses the place, with quads having no enclosing ends. It is located just outside the tourist-infested city centre, lending it some peace and tranquillity, but is still within a convenient distance of all central facilities. St Catz has exceptional resources, including the largest student theatre in Oxford, an extensive JCR building, and a moat. It is the youngest college, and, though obviously lacking traditions, has a very friendly atmosphere. Every summer St Catz has a Summer Ball which is a big success, and good bops are laid on regularly.

ST EDMUND HALL (Teddy Hall)
Queen's Lane, Oxford OX1 4AR
TEL 01865 279008
WEB www.seh.ox.ac.uk
Founded 1278. Teddy Hall, as it is informally known, is a very poor college, and rumours abound that it has been financially helped by its close neighbour Queen's. Its main reputation across the university is for being very good at sports: men excel at rugby in particular. Despite not being one of the highest profile colleges, Teddy Hall students still manage to get involved at most levels of university life, and are particularly good at drama and music. Teddy Hall is known for being the party college, where academia is not taken too seriously, and it puts on good ents.

WHAT IT'S REALLY LIKE

UNIVERSITY:	
Social Life	★★★★
Campus scene	**Intense, challenging, satisfying**
Student Union services	**Well organised, but no venue**
Politics	**Active**
Sport	**Key**
National team position	**8th**
Sport facilities	**Good**
Arts opportunities	**Excellent**
Student mag/news	**Cherwell, Isis, Oxford Student, The Word**
2005 National awards	**Shortlisted 5 times**
Student radio	**Oxide**
2005 National awards	**1 Gold award**
Nightclub	**None**
Bars	**College bars**
Union ents	**College-based**
Union clubs/societies	**200+**
Parking	**Buy a bike**
CITY:	
Entertainment	★★★
Scene	**Small, good pubs, OK clubs**
Town/gown relations	**Average**
Risk of violence	**Average**
Cost of living	**High**
Student concessions	**Good**
Survival + 2 nights out	**£70 pw**
Part-time work campus/town	**Good**

ST HILDA'S
Cowley Place, Oxford OX4 1DY
TEL 01865 276816
WEB www.sthildas.ox.ac.uk
Founded in 1893, St Hilda's is an all-women college, not only at the JCR level, but also across the OCR and SCR, although this year it has been teetering on the edge of going bi. The college is home to the notorious, roaming 'Hildabeasts', which are among the most active members of the university, getting involved in many sports, societies and other extra-curricular pursuits. College buildings are bland but pleasant, and the site is on the banks

of the Cherwell, with beautiful gardens adding a colourful touch to the landscape. The college is fairly poor, and facilities are limited. St Hilda's is strong at rowing. Lots of ents are put on, with something to keep the lasses happy every weekend. The bar is unexciting, despite being the cheapest in Oxford. Being next to the river, the college owns its own punts, which are free for use by St Hilda's students and their guests. The college is seldom visited by tourists, which is a good thing.

ST HUGH'S
St Margaret's Rd, Oxford OX2 6LE
TEL 01865 274910
WEB www.st-hughs.ox.ac.uk
Founded in 1886 St Hugh's is so far out (geographically) it may as well be part of another university, and the walk into the centre of town can be long and laborious, although buses are very frequent. This is both an affliction and an attraction: St Hugh's has huge grounds (including croquet lawns and tennis courts) and there is (unfortunately small and ugly) on-site space to accommodate all students. College facilities are good and social life is tumultuous and intense. Ents are good, with a large-scale bop including a bouncy castle and barbecue organised during the summer. Despite being so far out of town, St Hugh's students are reasonably involved across the university activities, especially in art and drama.

ST JOHN'S
St Giles, Oxford OX1 3JP
TEL 01865 277317
WEB www.sjc.ox.ac.uk
Founded 1555. This is the richest college in Oxford. St John's provides excellent facilities: there are financial rewards for the academically strong (1st, Norrington Table 1999): on-site accommodation (including luxurious sets and the strange honeycomb structures for Freshers) is guaranteed for everyone, there is a modern conference centre, and beautiful gardens adorn the quads. St John's is academically very strong and there is considerable pressure on students to work hard. The college performs well in sports as well, at rugby and rowing in particular. On the social front St John's doesn't deliver quite as well: students tend to be quite dull, a fact reflected by the college bar which is very nice and spacious, but rarely alive and kickin'.

ST PETER'S
New Inn Hall Street, OX1 2DL
TEL 01865 278892
WEB www.spc.ox.ac.uk
Founded in 1929, St Peter's is a relatively new college in Oxford history, and covers very small grounds in the centre of town. Priorities here are much higher on social issues than on academic matters, and St Peter's doesn't excel at sports either. Nevertheless students seem fairly involved around the university, and the JCR is very active. St Peter's is very poor, which is obvious from the blatant lack or inadequacy of certain facilities. The college has a reasonable bar and puts on good ents events. Every year a middle-size Summer Ball is organised.

SOMERVILLE
Woodstock Road, Oxford OX2 6HD
TEL 01865 270629
WEB www.some.ox.ac.uk
Founded in 1929, Somerville is the most recent of colleges to have gone mixed (1994) and is located just beyond the reach of annoying tourists, yet close enough to the city centre for convenience. The generally left-wing college [with some notable exceptions – this was Margaret Thatcher's college] has always been politically very active and JCR members voice their opinions loudly. Indeed, Somervillians are active in every respect of university life, and the college has a fairly high profile amongst university students. College atmosphere is easygoing though the number of political hacks and activists can sometimes be distressing. Somerville has good ents although the college bar is dull and bare.

TRINITY
Broad Street, Oxford OX1 3BH
Tel 01865 279910
web www.trinity.ox.ac.uk
Founded in 1554, Trinity is centrally located, next door to its arch-rival Balliol. The college has spacious and attractive grounds (which it leases from Balliol!) and elegant buildings. The undergraduate body is fairly small which lends to an intimate college atmosphere. Trinity used to be dominated by public-school types, but this has now changed. Accommodation provisions are good, and the college flats on Woodstock Road are regarded as among the best and poshest in Oxford. Trinity students have a high profile in the university, and are popular and involved in many activities. A Commemoration Ball is organised every three years in the summer and, on a more day-to-day basis, ents is good with fun bops, and Trinity men and women enjoy a lively and atmospheric bar.

UNIVERSITY
High Street, Oxford OX1 4BH
TEL 01865 276602
WEB www.univ.ox.ac.uk
Founded 1249. University is one of the colleges

Oxford students hear the least about: it has an extremely low profile and is very quiet. This is despite the fact it is one of the oldest colleges (holding a claim, with Balliol and Merton, to being the oldest, although there is evidence that the college forged some deeds in 1381 to prove that it was founded in advance of Merton). The college is undeniably ancient, however, and very beautiful. Like St John's, it has a reputation for being full of bookworms who take life far too seriously and are unaware of the existence of the words 'fun' and 'enjoyment'. College life is said to be a little slow, although the alleged existence of bops and a good bar do redeem it a little.

WADHAM
Parks Road, Oxford OX1 3PN
TEL 01865 277946
WEB www.wadham.ox.ac.uk
Founded in 1610, Wadham is a bastion of the left, with an even greater lefty image than Balliol. Getting involved in JCR and student affairs is a great springboard into the political limelight. It has always been liberal, and is very involved in LGB affairs: it hosts Queer Week, which culminates in an S&M and Fetishes Bop (where you get to see some quite outlandish costumes...). The college is also strong in music and drama (helped by the fact that Wadham has one of the university's only reasonably sized theatres), and the Saturday night bops are legendary.

WORCESTER
Worcester Street, Oxford OX1 2HB
TEL 01865 278391
WEB www.worcester.ox.ac.uk
Founded 1714. Worcester possesses huge and beautiful grounds, including tennis courts, sports grounds and a lake. Beautiful gardens decorate the college and provide a suitable backdrop to the medieval cottages and classic colonnade. All students are accommodated on the main college site. The college is presently enjoying some success at rowing and rugby, but is not known for any academic excellence. Lord Sainsbury was a Worcester student, thus hall food is very cheap and also very good. Every three years the college hosts a huge Commemoration Ball in the summer. Worcester is lively, fairly rich and somewhat self-contained.

OXFORD BROOKES UNIVERSITY

Oxford Brookes University
Gipsy Lane Campus
Headington
Oxford OX3 0BP

TEL 01865 483040
FAX 01865 483983
EMAIL admissions@brookes.ac.uk
WEB www.brookes.ac.uk

Oxford Brookes Students' Union
Helena Kennedy Student Centre
London Road
Headington
Oxford OX3 0BP

TEL 01865 484715
FAX 01865 484799
EMAIL obsu.president@brookes.ac.uk
WEB www.theSU.com

VAG VIEW

If you are looking for a university not too demanding at entry, which offers a host of well-conceived modular courses in some interesting niche areas, and which enjoys the atmosphere of one of the world's true student cities, then Brookes might well be for you.

CAMPUS

Brookes is based over three main campuses; two in Headington (approx. 1.5 miles from city centre) and one at Wheatley (5 miles away). A free inter-site bus service runs every half hour during the day. The Helena Kennedy Student Centre (HKSC), the main Students' Union, is housed with teaching facilities and accommodation across the road from

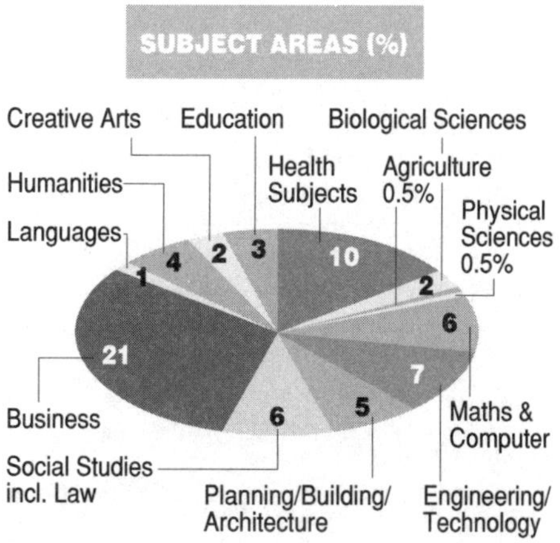

UNIVERSITY/STUDENT PROFILE	
University since	**1992**
Situation/style	**Campus**
Student population	**18345**
Undergraduates	**12860**
- mature	**27%**
- non EU undergraduates	**12%**
- male/female	**41/59**
- non-traditional student intake	**42%, high**
- state school intake	**73%**
- drop-out rate	**9%**
- undergraduate applications	**Up 12%**

Gypsy Lane on the Headington Hill site, formerly the house of tycoon Robert Maxwell, who called it the largest council house in England, which indeed it was. He never owned it.

FEES, BURSARIES

UK & EU Fees: £3000 p.a. If in receipt of full HE Maintenance grant there's a bursary of £1200; if in receipt of partial grant, bursaries are on a sliding scale from £200 to £1200, according to household earnings. There are also bursaries to encourage applications from areas new to the idea of going to uni, and some scholarships, too. See web site.

STUDENT PROFILE

Oxford Brookes is uncharacteristic of most recently founded universities because of its high independent school intake (27% of undergraduates). There's a statistical lurch towards the middle class, which serves to prompt the stereotypical image of the uni as a hang-out for air-head Sloanes who couldn't get a place at Durham. However, there is, too, a large overseas body of students, and Giles Balleny insists that whatever the statistics indicate, on the ground the perception is of a rich tapestry of life. Certainly they have doubled their quota of undergraduates from socio-economic classes new to university.

'Brookes has an unusually varied cross section of students, which gives it a cosmopolitan outlook in everything it does,' writes Giles. 'Among the more prominent groups, public-school student types are not as dominant as people suggest, although there probably is a larger public school contingent than at any other of the new universities. Most ignore their fraternising and get on with doing their own thing. Whether you are from an independent school or from a state school you will undoubtedly find "your type".

'There is also a large proportion of foreign students from a huge range of countries. Ethnic minorities from the UK are also very well represented and play a large part in the overall feel of the place.'

There are also quite a few part-timers, further education students and mature students in the mix.

ACADEMIA & JOBS

There are 8 academic schools: Arts & Humanities, Built Environment, Biological & Molecular Sciences, the Business School, the Westminster Institute of Education, the School of Technology, Health & Social Care, Social Sciences & Law.

Modular joint hons degrees characterise the curriculum, and an academic year-structure made up not of terms but semesters. Ground-breaking when first launched more than a quarter of a century ago, the modular system can be made to work to your advantage, but individuals are left pretty much to design their own courses, and, so student Emily Waller says: 'All the rules and regulations can be confusing, so get help if you need it.

'The work load is manageable, but depends on the course that you are taking. Work placements both abroad and in Britain are common. Teaching staff are generally very helpful (if you can find them). Each student is assigned a personal tutor for their years of study.

'There are 3 libraries, well stocked with up-to-date and ancient texts and an easy-to-use computerised catalogue; friendly individual subject librarians are always willing to help. The main library has over 1,000 private study desks and some group study rooms (great for catching up on gossip, if not for study!). It is open until 10.00 pm weekdays. Every student has free Internet and e-mail access, and com-puters are accessible 24/7. Computer Services – in particular the help desk – are invaluable, as the network has an annoying habit of crashing (normally about five minutes before an assignment is due in!).'

The Disability team includes a Dyslexia Support Tutor. Her work encourages dyslexic students to develop 'their innate, non-language intelligences and explore how to use them as study skills'; there's also extra time for exams, etc.

More than a quarter of graduates go into the health field. They educate by far the largest number of graduate nurses, the majority SEN. There are BA degrees in midwifery, learning disability, mental health, specialist interest community practitioner (district nursing, school, etc), and BSc also in midwifery (post-experience), adult, children's. cancer care, palliative care, rehabilitation. 'Post Experience' means an 18-month programme for Registered

WHERE OXFORD BROOKES GRADUATES END UP

Health & Social Work: 29%; Education: 13%; Wholesale Retail: 7%; Manufacturing: 10%; Financial Activities: 2%; Public Administration, Civil Service & Defence: 5%; Hotel/Restaurant: 4%; Transport & Communications (including Telecommunications): 3%; Construction: 2%;; Personnel: 4%; Computer:2.5%; Business & Management: 2%; Accountancy: 1.5%; Media (including Film): 0.5%; Legal 1%; Architecture: 2%; Publishing: 3%; Artistic/Literary: 1%; Sport: 1%.

Approximate 'graduate track' employed **68%**

Nurses. Teaching Inspection 20. Entry BB.

Aspiring occupational therapists note, they take nearly 6% of the annual graduate employment market.

Brookes also has a large primary teaching provision: BA Primary (Work-based) and BA Initial Teacher Training – 13% of their graduates go into teaching.

Their engineering graduates are among the most popular in the automobile industry. The B/MEng 3/4-year Hons degrees in Automative Engineering take 16% of the jobs in the sector. There's also a BSc Motorsports Technology and an HND in Motorsports Engineering. Civil engineers also find ready employment.

Environmental Biology, WEnvironmental Science, and Public Health Nutrition also find graduates certain jobs in the public sector.

They are of course renowned for their Publishing degrees, having produced the prototype. Some, like Accounting/Publishing in the Joint Hons programme have obvious relevance, others less so, but the single hons BA Publishing is undoubtedly the industry's favoured vocational entré. It illuminates the entire process: editorial, production and marketing. Teaching inspection 21.

Estate agent/managers also proliferate. look at BSc Real Estate Management, also BA Business of Real Estate. Real Estate Management only dropped one point at the teaching assessments; Business and Economics took full marks. So, you are in good hands. Planning is big here, too, and also scored full marks: see BA Cities - Environment, Design & Development or BA City & Regional Planning. There are jobs in the construction industry too for students of such as BSc Construction Management or Foundation Built Environment.

They are also management leaders in the catering and hotel trade. The choice degrees here are the 4-year sandwich BSc Hotel & Restaurant Management and the two International Hospitality/Tourism Management, again 4-year sandwich BSc.

Graduates of Marketing and Languages find employment in market research, and aspiring marketing managers finding ready work armed with their Marketing Management Communication and Business & Marketing Management BA degrees, available in combination with a host of interesting focuses – Publishing, Psychology, Performing Arts, Retail, Sociology, Tourism look like good synergy.

SOCIAL SCENE

STUDENTS' UNION There's an active ents programme with regular clubnights, film nights, comedy nights and termly balls. Wednesday is *Playground* (new themes and promos each week); Friday is *Pleasuredome* (9 pm-2 am) – 'the best sound system, lighting and dance tunes in Oxford', a mixture of styles at the main SU **Venue**, which has a capacity of over 1,200.

The main union bars based around the university are the **Harts** lounge bar, **Morals Bar** and the **Mezannine**. **Morals Bar** is the home of *Blitz* (9 till 2 pop tunes), *Chalk & Cheese* (from live jazz to comedy) and the SU's rock and indie night *Feedback* –

ACADEMIC EXCELLENCE

TEACHING:
(Rated Excellent or 17+ out of 24)

Law, Anthropology, English, Geography.	**Excellent**
Planning, Business, Economics	**24**
History of Art, Real Estate Mgt, Building, Psychology, Biology & Enviro Science, Art & Design, Theology	**23**
Italian & Spanish, French, Maths, Politics, Tourism	**22**
Sociology, Publishing, Civil Eng, Education	**21**
Food Science, Nursing, Subjects Allied to Medicine	**20**
German, Electronic Eng	**19**

RESEARCH:
Top grades 5/5/6**

History	**Grade 6***
English, French	**Grade 5**

WHAT IT'S REALLY LIKE

UNIVERSITY:	
Social Life	★★★★
Campus scene	**Cross section**
Student Union services	**Good**
Politics	**Average**
Sport	**Competitive**
National team position	**54th**
Sport facilities	**Good**
Arts opportunities	**Drama, music, art excellent; film good; dance avg**
Student newspaper	**OBScene**
Nightclub	**The Venue**
Bars	**Morals, Harts, Mez**
Union ents	**Pleasuredome, pop, jazz, comedy**
Union clubs/societies	**60**
Most popular society	**Cocktail**
Parking	**Poor**
CITY:	
Entertainment	★★★
Scene	**Small, good pubs, OK clubs**
Town/gown relations	**Average**
Risk of violence	**Average**
Cost of living	**High**
Student concessions	**Good**
Survival + 2 nights out	**£70 pw**
Part-time work campus/town	**Good**

AT A GLANCE

ACADEMIC FILE:	
Subjects assessed	**37**
Excellent	**76%**
Typical entry requirements	**250 points**
Application acceptance rate	**15%**
Students-staff ratio	**16:1**
First/2:1 degree pass rate	**57%**
ACCOMMODATION FILE:	
Guarantee to freshers	**95%**
Style	**Halls**
Catered	**23%**
En suite	**43%**
Approx price range pa	**£2600-£4200**
City rent pw	**£70**

the best grunge, rock, metal, punk, alternative with resident DJs Sht Chaos and Hell. High above **The Venue**, the **Mez Bar** is the home of the Sunday Session.

'A free and confidential advice and counselling service is on offer, as is representation for all students on academic, personal and financial issues. Over sixty clubs and societies ensure that there really is something for everyone. Currently the most popular society is Cocktail.'

There's a monthly student paper called *OBScene*.

Sport Facilities are excellent and include Astroturf, squash courts, health suite, heavy weights gym, tennis courts, rugby, football, cricket and hockey pitches, fitness trails, two boat houses and a multi-purpose sports hall for aerobics, martial arts, women's boxing, circuit training, etc. The Centre for Sport is open from 7.30 am to 11.00 pm. The university teams came 41st overall last year.

Town 'The night life in Oxford, always busy and full of tourists and students, is varied but expensive, even with the student discount that most clubs, pubs, bars and restaurants offer.

There is a great music and theatre scene with lots of theatres, gig venues and cinemas, but the clubbing scene is definitely mediocre (unless you are a big cheesy '60s to '80s fan). Travel around the city is regular and simple, and for women the Students' Union runs a special Safety Bus from campus to doorstep. As long as 'home' is within the Oxford Ring Road, this is a free service. Coaches run every ten minutes to London, Gatwick, Heathrow and Cambridge. Student discounts are available.

PILLOW TALK

There are nine halls of residence, all with easy access to the university, and many, but not all, with an internet facility available in each room. Clive Booth Hall was opened last autumn, and Cheney Student Village in the spring. Although in practice most freshers live in halls, priority is given to those living farthest distant from Oxford. Facilities generally accommodate both sexes, although single sex accommodation is available on request. With the exception of two halls, it's a condition of residency not to keep a car.

GETTING THERE

☛ By road: from north, A423 or A34 or A43; London, M40; south, M4/J13, A34. Wheatley campus, M40/J8, A418. Good coach service.

☛ By rail: London Paddington, 1:00; Birmingham, 1:30; Bristol, 1:45; Sheffield, 3:30.

☛ By air: Heathrow/Gatwick; coaches/buses will stop outside Gypsy Lane campus on request.

☛ By coach: London, 1:40; Birmingham, 1:30; Leeds, 5:30; Bristol, 4:30.

UNIVERSITY OF PAISLEY

The University of Paisley
High Street
Paisley PA1 2BE

TEL 0141 848 3727
0800 027 1000 (prospectus request)
FAX 0141 848 3623
EMAIL alison.copeland@paisley.ac.uk
WEB www.paisley.ac.uk

Paisley Uni Students' Association
Storie Street
Paisley PA1 1DN

TEL 0141 849 4169
FAX 0141 849 4158
EMAIL theunion@upsa.org.uk
WEB www.upsa.org.uk

VAG VIEW

Paisley University came out of Paisley Technical College, founded in 1897. In the same year as it became a fully fledged university (1995) it began its development into nursing and midwifery, a faculty largely to be found at its campus to the south, in Ayr – Robbie Burns country. The main university campus is in Paisley itself, the largest town in Scotland and just a mile or so from Glasgow Airport. Only a few years old is a third campus, a joint venture with Glasgow Uni and Dumfries & Galloway College, on an 80-acre parkland site half a mile from the centre of Dumfries, which is many miles to the south, close to the Solway Firth.

While most unis are struggling to meet government targets to diversify their student body by delving into sections of the public that haven't traditionally gone to university, Paisley has plenty of those and there's a very high drop-out rate. Nevertheless, loads is going on that is bright and new.

UNIVERSITY/STUDENT PROFILE	
University since	**1995**
Situation/style	**Town campuses**
Student population	**11450**
Undergraduates	**9415**
- mature	**43%**
- non EU undergraduates	**3%**
- male/female	**36/64**
- non-traditional student intake	**43%, high**
- state school intake	**98%**
- drop-out rate	**21%, v. high**
- undergraduate applications	**Constant**

CAMPUS

Paisley Campus takes getting to know: 'It would be really easy for a fresher, such as yourself, to mistake the main campus for a hospital wing in need of a cosmetic facelift,' writes Nausheen Rai. 'The "traditional" building has a blend of lino-type tiled floors, a supposed up-to-date glass "hamster" tunnel walkway (for fashion purposes *darling*), a surgical hospital smell that leaves one feeling oddly confused, and a brand new, £6-million, out-of-sync library with glass lift, plush pink carpets, novelty chairs and lots of space.'

Ayr Campus (known as 'Craigie') Tel 01292 886000. Opines Nausheen: 'This is definitely the more friendly campus (if that were to make the choice). Being smaller, it's more cosy. Males may count themselves fortunate to study in this sister campus tucked away on the west coast. There's an estimated ten women to every one of them.'

Dumfries Campus Tel 01387 702060. It is situated beside the Crichton Business Park in eighty-five acres of parkland and gardens. A £1.8-million grant from the Scottish Funding Council is underwriting the development, which builds on franchise links which Paisley has had with Dumfries & Galloway College since 1994. The campus is an element in their open-access strategy, an attempt 'to widen the provision of higher education in the south west of Scotland.' It's worked.

SUBJECT AREAS (%)

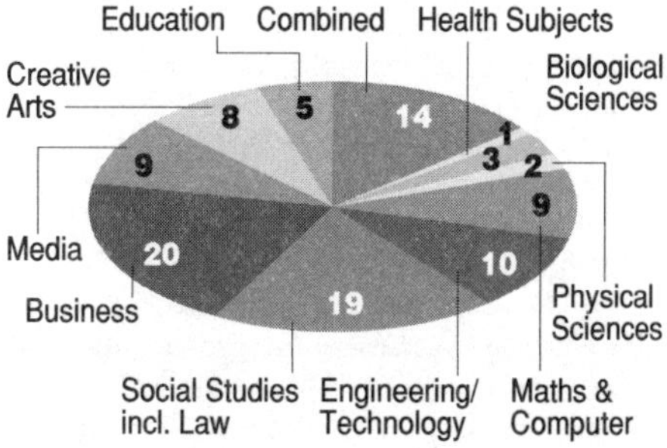

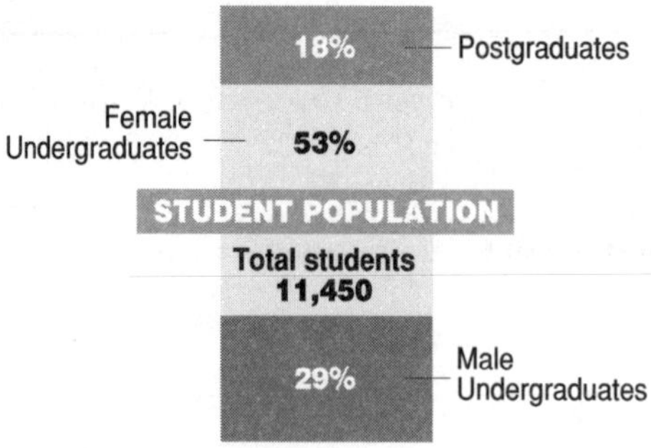

FEES, BURSARIES

Fees for English students: £1700 p.a. Contact uni direct for bursaries, etc.

STUDENT PROFILE

Many students are local, mature and/or part-timers (35%) and almost exclusively come to Paisley from the state sector, flooding in from neighbourhoods which haven't traditionally supplied universities.

ACADEMIA & JOBS

Faculties at Paisley include Engineering, Information Sciences, Science & Technology, Social and Management Sciences (and some midwifery and nursing). Faculties at Ayr are Education, Media Studies, Business, Nursing & Midwifery (apply through CATCH: 0131 220 8660). Subjects at Dumfries include Computing, Business & IT, along with Childhood Studies.

The big swell here is the increase in degrees in media, computing and technology. There has been a transformation at Ayr, where the largely female body of primary school teachers (Education is the most popular employment sector, 11% of graduates) and nurses have been getting cosy with the largely male students of BA Digital Art, BA Commercial Music, and BA degrees in Cinema, Media and Screen Practice. There are great media and broadcasting facilities at Ayr. They even run their own digital radio station.

Nevertheless, the real powerful computer and technology courses are still at Paisley, such as BSc Computer Games Technology, BA Computer Animation & Digital Art, BSc degrees in Computer-Aided Design, Digital Modelling, Computer Animation, Multimedia with Interactive Entertainment Technology, etc, and BEng degrees in Design and Product Design & Development, as well as BSc Music Technology.

Civil engineering is still a major focus, too, and they make as good a showing as Manchester Uni in the employment league. You get a BSc/BEng option in the single hons and three additional orientations for the BEng – Project Management, Environmental Mgt, Architectural Studies. Teaching inspection, Highly Satisfactory.

See also the Business IT & e-Commerce Department – BA Business Info Technology with either Accounting (there's an international Grade 5 in Accounting & Finance for research), Human Resource Management, Management or Marketing; or BSc with Multimedia or e-Business.

Note also an employment strength in social work, community and youth work – around 5% of graduates. See their Social Sciences faculty, which has a common first year before specialisation: Social Work, Sociology, Social Policy, Psychology, etc.

ACADEMIC EXCELLENCE

TEACHING :
(Rated Excellent, Highly Satis. or 17+ out of 24)

Civil Engineering,	**Highly Satis.**
Chemistry, Maths & Statistics, Mechanical (incl Manufacturing) Engineering, Teacher Education Sociology, Social Work, Cellular & Molecular Biology, Organismal Biol, Psychology.	
European Languages	**19**

RESEARCH:
*Top grades 5/5**

Accounting & Finance,	**Grade 5**

Paisley degree courses are designed with input from industry and commerce. Languages, IT training and work placements are key. IBM, M&S, BBC, Volkswagen, Standard Life and BAe all take Paisley undergrads on annual placements.

Another boost recently has been the offer of a BSc Sports Studies, with its dedicated option routes. It's designed for students building on HNDs to degree level. Special focus areas are sports therapy, exercise, health and fitness, sports development, outdoor recreation administration.

SOCIAL SCENE

Students' Association UPSA have been campaigning for a proper union building since 1971. Now, following a new union at Ayr – café-style, chrome tables, Chesterfield sofas, very slick – they have one, a £5-million town centre HQ.

Hitherto they have held comedy and home-grown theme nights, karaoke, quizzes and talent contests.

WHERE PAISLEY GRADUATES END UP

Health & Social Work: 8%; Education: 11%; Wholesale Retail: 17%; Manufacturing: 10%; Financial Activities: 7%; Public Administration, Civil Service & Defence: 9%; Hotel/Restaurant: 5%; Transport & Communications (including Telecommunications): 4%; Construction: 4%; Personnel: 2%; Computer: 4%; Business & Management: 1%; Accountancy: 1%; Media (including Film): 1.5%; Legal 0.5%; Architecture: 3.5%; Publishing: 1%; Sport: 1%.

Now they do much the same. but with **Big Bar** the venue – a massive hanger of a place – and *Salamander* returns with resident DJs Brad and Anthony as the official Friday night extraveganza. Monday is pub quiz, *Universally Challenged;* Tuesday is Karaoke; Wednesday is Games Nights. A trip the six miles into the centre of Glasgow is a regular alternative.

At Craigie there are two or three discos, a Saturday party, quizzes, karaoke, etc, and a popular live act Accoustic Night. In town there's the **Wulf & Whistle** and **O'Briens**, virtually union property by adoption, and three cheesy nightclubs with weekly student nights.

Sport The Robertson Trust Sports Centre is located in the student village in Paisley and has had a £1.5-million facelift. Some 1,500 students are members. Recent improvements include turf pitches for rugby and soccer and floodlit synthetic pitches. There are also facilities for squash, multigym workouts, badminton, hockey, netball, tennis, basketball, volleyball and table tennis.

There's not much sport in Ayr.

WHAT IT'S REALLY LIKE

UNIVERSITY:	
Social Life	★★★
Campus scene	**Friendly, local, urban cowboys**
Student Union services	**OK.**
Politics	**NUS issues**
Sport	**Relaxed**
National team position	**122nd**
Sport facilities	**Average**
Arts opportunities	**Few**
Student newspaper	**Banter**
Student radio	**UCA Radio**
Venue bar	**Big Bar**
Union ents	**Games, karaoke, clubnights**
Union societies	**12**
Parking	**Poor**
TOWN:	
Entertainment	★★
Local scene	**Clubs, pubs**
Town/gown relations	**Poor**
Risk of violence	**Average**
Student concessions	**Adequate**
Survival + 2 nights out	**£60 pw**
Part-time work campus/town	**Fair/good**

AT A GLANCE

ACADEMIC FILE:	
Subjects assessed	**17**
Excellent/Highly Satisfactory	**65%**
Typical entryl requirements	**235 points**
Application acceptance rate	**26%, high**
Students-staff ratio	**16:1**
First/2:1 degree pass rate	**52%**
ACCOMMODATION FILE:	
Guarantee to freshers	**90%**
Style	**Halls, flats**
Cost pw (no food)	**£40-£48**
Town	**£40**

PILLOW TALK

Apply early for accommodation; it's in short supply, though at Paisley unbelievably cheap. Most students bed down in flats or 'villas' in the student village at Thornly Park, two miles from campus, hard by the uni's sports facilities. Other residences are more central; all are self-catering.

Accommodation at Craigie comprises catered single or shared study-bedrooms. No accommodation at Dumfries.

GETTING THERE

☛ By road to Paisley: M8 – M74, A726, A737. For Ayr, M77/A77. For Dumfries, A76 or A701 from the north; A75 from the south.

☛ By coach to Glasgow: London, 8:20; Birmingham, 6:20; Newcastle, 4:20.

☛ By rail to Paisley: Ayr, 45 mins; Glasgow Central, 15 mins. Glasgow to London, 6:00; For Dumfries: Glasgow, 2:00; Ayr, 1:50.

☛ By air: Glasgow International Airport.

UNIVERSITY OF PLYMOUTH

The University of Plymouth
Drake Circus
Plymouth
Devon PL4 8AA

TEL 01752 232 232
FAX 01752 232 141
EMAIL prospectus@plymouth.ac.uk
WEB www.plymouth.ac.uk

Plymouth Students' Union
City Site
Drake Circus
Plymouth PL4 8AA

TEL 01752 238500
FAX 01752 251669
EMAIL
presplymouth@su.plymouth.ac.uk
WEB www.upsu.com

VAG VIEW

Plymouth has made a vigorous rise since gaining university status – teaching assessments, if not amazing, are consistently good.

The uni majors in marine and maritime courses, water sports and Australians – there's even a Surf Science & Technology degree – believe it, dudes, this really does exist. Sand, sea, surf is what Plymouth is about, and it shows: 'Wherever we go,' said a student, 'people say, "You look so well!"'

Then, back in 2004, they all of a sudden took a new direction. Under the influence of a new Vice Chancellor, who came down from the mighty Imperial College, London, they laid out a strategy to become a university of world-class excellence that served the region and began by galvanising local colleges in partnership schemes, and then nearby Exeter Uni and the regional NHS in the £16 million Peninsula Medical School at Derriford, Plymouth, which has been an unqualified success. Now they are building a £4-million Allied Health Centre to go with it – for students of dietetics, physiotherapy, podiatry, midwifery and speech & language therapy. There's also to be a new £8-million library extension, with a new café, 24/7 access computing and media area, extended stock to cater for students moving to Plymouth from other campuses. And in 2007 a £27-million Faculty of Arts building will open, for arts, architecture and humanities.

Meanwhile, millions of pounds have been and are being spent on a centralisation project that will bring their scattered satellite campuses home. Last year, their famous Agric arm (Agriculture, Tourism, Hospitality, Food Science, etc) moved from Seale-Hayne, Newton Abbot, to the Plymouth campus. Now, there's an ´in principle´ decision to relocate the Faculty of Education from Exmouth to the heart of the Plymouth campus, from autumn 2008. The word is that an early movement of humanities (from the Exmouth campus) and media arts (from the Exeter ampus) to Plymouth has increased recruitment by 20%.

No doubt students can't wait for the dust to settle.

SUBJECT AREAS (%)

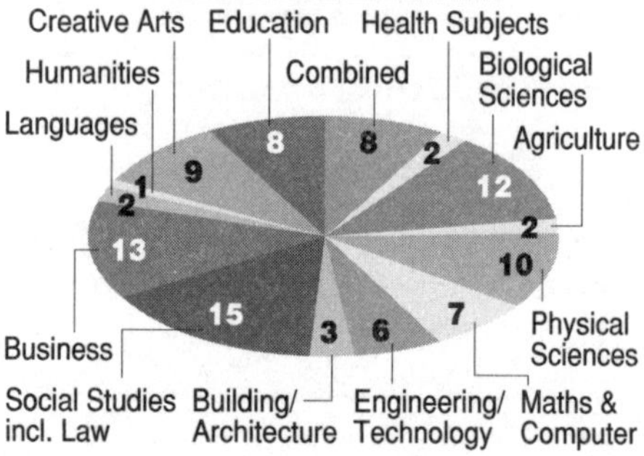

UNIVERSITY/STUDENT PROFILE	
University since	**1992**
Situation/style	**City/town campuses**
Student population	**28420**
Undergraduates	**23570**
- mature	**24%**
- non EU undergraduates	**4%**
- male/female	**38/62**
- non-traditional student intake	**29%**
- state school intake	**92%**
- drop-out rate	**7%**
- undergraduate applications	**Up 4%**

FEES, BURSARIES

UK & EU Fees: £3000 p.a. If you qualify for the full HE Maintenace grant, i.e. there's a household income of below £17500, you get £300 p.a. The Peninsula Regional Bursary makes a one-off payment of £500 if family income is less than £30000 per annum, and you are in your final year of study in a school/college in the South West Peninsula region (Cornwall, Devon, Somerset, Bristol and Bath) anddo not qualify for an Access or Compact Bursary. The latter is £500 p.a. for school pupils on the Compact scheme. The Access bursary is a scheme (also £500) for mature students of the Open College South West Region that do not qualify for an Peninsula Regional Bursary or Compact Bursary.

STUDENT PROFILE

There's a big mature and international student draw from 100 countries and an active international office and International Students' Society. Applicants from the UK tend to be drawn from below a line drawn south of the Midlands through Wales, Bristol and London, and from the surf cities of the world. Is that why there is a preponderance of female undergraduates (62%)? Whatever, it's easier on the eye.

CAMPUSES

PLYMOUTH CAMPUS (address on page 372) **Faculties:** Science, Technology, Human Sciences, Business. But now the agrics, and goodness who else is going to pour in any day. See *Social Scene*, page 375.

EXMOUTH Douglas Avenue, Exmouth EX8 2AT. Tel: 01395 25509. There's an 'in principle' decision to relocate the Faculty of Education from Exmouth to the Plymouth campus, from autumn 2008. A final decision will be made in October, 2006. What will become of the new £2.1 million centre with performance space, lecture theatre and seminar rooms? **Ents, campus & city:** second biggest campus (approx 1,000 students). Ents facilities exist: **S.U.B. Station** – two bars, but if you're expecting the bright lights and big sailors of Plymouth, you'll be disappointed. Exmouth is the relaxed, seaside campus. The **S.U.B. Station** bars provide theme nights, discos, live bands, hypnotists, club trips to Plymouth, etc.; LGB to **Boxes** or **The Loft** in Exeter. Popular local nightclub is **Samantha's**; there's a strong local live music culture. **Sport:** playing fields with pavilion close to campus. Rolle Rovers (soccer), men's and women's rugby teams, netball, basketball and cricket all perform well within their respective leagues. Diving, sailing and windsurfing facilities locally. **Media:** *Rolle-Up* is the student magazine 'because our full title is University of Plymouth: Rolle College Faculty of Arts & Education.'

EXETER Earl Richards Road North, Exeter EX2 6AS. Tel: 01392 475004/9. Faculties of Arts (art, design, media, photography, humanities), and Health & Social (nursing, midwifery, occupational therapy). **Ents facilities:** bar, 266 ents capacity. Ents, campus & city: regular ents – Wednesday Film Club, Thursday pool competition, Friday theme nights – *Tarts & Trannies*, '70s, etc. A busy arts schedule includes trips to London, Birmingham, Cardiff and Cornwall art galleries and theatres. See *Exeter Uni* entry for lively student city nightlife. **Media:** *Illuminate* magazine. **Sport:** local sports facilities only; uni teams include football, hockey, rugby.

ACADEMIA & JOBS

The new faculty structure is as follows: Arts (arts, architecture and humanities), Education, Health & Social Work, Science, Social Science & Business, Technology. Plymouth is also a partner in the

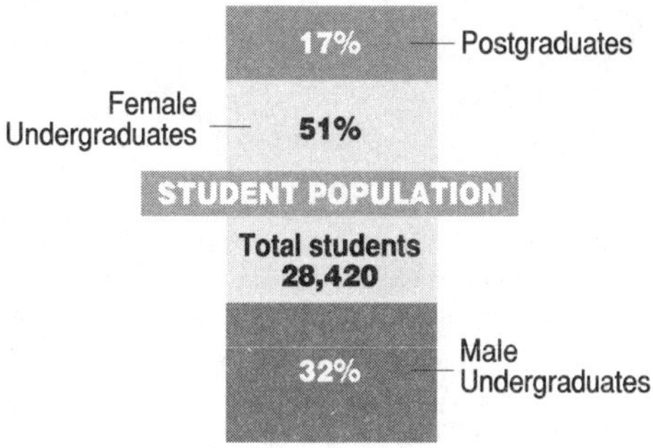

Peninsula Medical School (see below). The final faculty, formed last year, is a network of partner colleges in Cornwall, Devon and Somerset, known as the University of Plymouth Colleges (UPC). Plymouth is also part of the Combined Universities of Cornwall project (see separate entry).

They are hot on study skills support programmes. There are disability services, support for dyslexia, specialist assessment for students applying for the Disabled Student Allowance, and training in the use of specialist technical equipment. They boast a higher percentage of disabled students than any other university.

So, what was that about a degree in surfing? 'This is the first academically rigorous surf science course in the world,' boasts Dr Malcolm Findlay of the Institute of Marine Studies. The first year dwells on oceanography, surfing materials and business studies. The second moves uncontrover-

ACADEMIC EXCELLENCE

TEACHING:
(Rated Excellent or 17+ out of 24)

Environmental Science, Geography, Geology, Oceanography.	**Excellent**
Psychology, Civil Eng, Building, Nursing	**23**
Food/Agriculture, Biosciences, Politics, Sport, Tourism, Education	**22**
Art & Design, Media, Drama, History of Art	**21**
Sociology, Subjects Allied to Medicine, Maths	**20**
Materials Technology	**19**
Electronic & Electrical Eng	**18**

RESEARCH :
*Top grades 5/5**

Psychology, Computer, History Art/Architecture/Design	**Grade 5**

sially into areas like human biology and human performance, but in the third year you develop your own specialism. Head for the beach presumably.

There is all sorts of marine interest (the Nautical School, the original fount of this uni, was established in 1862, and marine courses account for almost a quarter of Plymouth's undergraduate programme) – Aquaculture, Marine Biology, Marine Navigation, Applied Marine Sport Science, Nautical Studies and Ocean Science, Civil & Coastal Engineering, Geography or Geology with Ocean Science, Ocean Exploration. This year, degrees in Marine Studies appear with options to specialise in Ocean Yachting, Merchant Shipping or Navigation.

There's also a trio of Maritime Business degrees, and, they have a BSc in Cruise Operations Management, with support from Princes Cruises (hospitality, marine studies, business plus a year on a cruise liner!), directing our interest into their hospitality and tourism programme: Business & Tourism, Hospitality & Tourism, International Tourism Mgt, etc. Plymouth takes up the challenge from the Devon Riviera, excellent International and Euro Business degrees, plenty of sea air and extracurricular encouragement.

But most especially, the marine bias takes the uni deep into biological sciences. Biologists are made aplenty here in courses with a 23 out of 24-point success rate at the assessments. There are interesting medical, agricultural and computer applications, as well as marine. And now, the new Peninsula Medical School, a partnership with Exeter Uni and the NHS in Devon and Cornwall, is a wholly compatible development. Plymouth's Institute of Neuroscience opened as the new £30-million Portland Square building opened to student doctors, nurses and all the other health care professionals.

Tying up with the NHS ensures a strong clinical element. The medical course focuses on the biological mechanisms that produce disease and its social impact. It looks very hands-on. Entry ABB-AAB, at least one science subject. There are various sites, Exeter, Plymouth, Truro, Barnstaple, Torbay, and you will move around during the course. Applications have soared, but there's still a 10% application acceptance rate.

Well over 2500 graduate nurses pour out of our universities each year, many off the Plymouth degrees in Adult Nursing, Community Health Care, Mental Health, Midwifery, Physiotherapy and Podiatry, Dietetics, and Occupational Therapy.

Again, clinical psychologists abound from their BSc Psychology, which also comes with a host of adjuncts. The psychology and mental health provisions lead to an employment track record in psychotherapy.

Meanwhile, graduates in BSc combinations with their Criminal Justice Studies, Psychology, Social Policy, Social Research, Law, Sociology, Statistics, etc, find a variety of jobs, often probation officers. Plymouth accounts for 13% of the total nationwide.

The Faculty of Agriculture, like Harper Adams, covers the whole gamut of courses, from

WHERE PLYMOUTH GRADUATES END UP

Health & Social Work: 8%; Education: 11%; Wholesale Retail: 9%; Manufacturing: 11.5%; Financial Activities: 6%; Public Administration, Civil Service & Defence: 12%; Hotel/Restaurant: 4%; Transport & Communications (including Telecommunications): 6%; Construction: 3%; Agriculture: 2%; Mining/Oil Extracting: 0.5%; Personnel: 3%; Computer: 3%; Business & Management: 3%; Accountancy: 1%; Media (including Film): 0.5%; Legal 1.5%; Publishing: 1%; Advertising: 0.5%; Artistic/Literary: 0.5%.

Approximate 'graduate track' employed **56%**

Management to Nutrition, from Agriculture to Estate Management, and there's a Wildlife Conservation option too. Teaching inspection 22. A recent popular development has been the Veterinary Nursing & Management degree.

Foresters also find jobs in quantity from Plymouth, and aspiring environmental officers enjoy a strong niche (see their Enviro. Science degrees).

Besides the BSc Civil & Coastal Engineering, in the same faculty you'll find BSc Civil Eng & Computer-aided Design, Construction Mgt and the Environment and Environmental Construction Surveying, all of which put Plymouth into the Top 10 for supplying construction engineer/managers. 23 points at the assessments. An international Grade 5 for research covers their Architecture degrees, too, which include BA Architectural Design with Digital Media, one source probably for their strong employment line int town planning.

Cartography is another niche – they are leaders in the field at Plymouth. See degrees like Design: Graphic Communication & Typography (or Illustration or Photography). Others in 3D Design, with 'Designer-Maker' or 'Furniture & Interior Design' or 'Product Design' are especially productive of careers – 21 points at assessment. But there are as many graduates finding their way into the furniture manufacturing business through Plymouth's excellent International Business faculty. Aspiring market researchers and marketing managers build careers out of the BA Marketing (260 points), which comes with a 2-year Foundation at Plymouth College of Further Education.

Meanwhile, computer science finds Plymouth graduates jobs in media and government research. Look , for example, at their Computing Informatics and Statistics (Applied) & Management Science with Computing BSc degrees.

More than 10% of graduates go into education: 86% of them become primary teachers. Teaching inspection, 22.

WHAT IT'S REALLY LIKE

UNIVERSITY:	
Social Life	★★★★
Campus scene	**Lively ents, water sporty**
Student Union services	**OK**
Politics	**Interest low**
Sport	**47 clubs**
National team position	**56th**
Sport facilities	**Average**
Arts opportunities	**Drama, dance, music, art avg; film poor**
Student magazine	**Fly!**
Nightclub/bars	**Ignition, Illusion**
Union ents	**Party, cheese, indie**
Union clubs/societies	**78**
Most popular society	**Football**
Parking	**Non-existent**
CITY:	
Entertainment	★★★★
Scene	**Clubs, pubs OK**
Town/gown relations	**Poor**
Risk of violence	**Average**
Cost of living	**Below average**
Student concessions	**Average**
Survival + 2 nights out	**£70 pw**
Part-time work campus/town	**OK**

SOCIAL SCENE

Students' Union The Plymouth Students' Union has undergone a refurbishment and now boasts leather sofas, Sky TV and new games machines. A new **DJ** bar has met expectations.

They have a dynamic ents manager, digging out new local bands, and as a result Plymouth is featured in many a uni tour. The May Ball, we are told, 'attracted 3,500 to a field', actually Newnham Park, the classical Georgian manor between the outskirts of Plymouth and the foothills of Dartmoor National Park.

Friday night's *Burn* sets the scene for the weekend on the main campus – two dance rooms, 1,450 capacity – cheese and party in **Ignition**; indie to rock, ska to punk in **Illusion**. Saturday is regulation SU fare: *Flirt* in Ignition. Comedy nights (*Laughing Goldfish*) are especially popular, as are *Spin What You Bring* and *Open Mic Night*. *S.I.N.* is the official sports & societies DJ night, then it's on to **C103** in town for more, where Wednesday is *Boogie Nights* (chart & cheese; Friday is *Total Rock* (Room 1: rock; Room 2: heavy metal).

They say the superclubs are closing down in Plymouth and students are going more for the pub music scene. The union still team up with clubs for student nights – **C103** in Union Street is the present choice, and the Plymouth **Walkabout** does good business with them.

When not clubbing and surfing, there are society activities, notably *Fly* magazine and SCAP, Community Action, which has BIG ideas, last year an international project in Thika, a small town in Kenya no less.

Now, in line with Plymouth's bid to become a 'European City of the Sea', they are planning to develop a 'cultural quarter'. The idea came simultaneously to Newcastle, and it's a good one – a conglomeration of galleries, cinemas, exhibition areas

AT A GLANCE

ACADEMIC FILE:	
Subjects assessed	**24**
Excellent	**75%**
Typical entry requirements	**250 points**
Application acceptance rate	**22%, high**
Students-staff ratio	**13:1**
First/2:1 degree pass rate	**53%**
ACCOMMODATION FILE:	
Guarantee to freshers	**Medics & overseas**
Style	**Halls, flats, houses**
Catered	**None**
En-suite	**50%**
Approx price range pw	**£50-£99**
City rent pw	**£45-£65**

theatre space, and a café. The first building, due to open in 2007, will be a base for the Faculty of Arts and a new home for the Plymouth **Arts Centre**.

SPORT £850,000 has been invested in a new fitness complex with squash courts and resistance and cardiovascular training equipment, and over £70,000 has gone into new boats and dinghies for the University's own Diving & Sailing Centre. There's national/world-class water-sport – sailing, diving, surfing, windsurfing, power-boating, wakeboarding, canoeing and waterski. A fleet of dinghies and yachts provide sailing opportunities. Plymouth is the only UK uni to have its own diving and sailing centre. Students can learn to dive pro-fessionally as part of their course (selected disciplines only) or take a recreational diving course, which is open to all students.

There's also the usual land-based team stuff. They came 56th nationally last year – most popular club is soccer, though it was their American football squad that was named 'Team of the Year' by the British Collegiate American Football League last year.

TOWN Plymouth – destroyed during the war and rebuilt at a low point in British architecture – has been designated second poorest ward in Europe, but you wouldn't know it since it has won huge EU investment. There's a surfeit of accommodation which costs upwards of £40 per week, you can walk anywhere, it is a safe, friendly, smiley place. When the sun shines it is unbeatable, the beach is 10 minutes away, and when it doesn't shine, maybe the snow on the nearby moors is not so bad an option.

Like nearby Exeter, Plymouth has recently become more cosmopolitan. Think huge shopping centre and **Barbican**. **The Barbican** is, of course, waterside, the olde worlde bit of town – boats, fish and tourists, but more to the point, pubs, clubs and restaurants. Arts-wise, there's the **Theatre Royal**, which had the Royal Shakespeare Company in residence when we were there, and the alternative **Drum Theatre** for more progressive fare. If you're seriously into painting, why not cross the border into Cornwall – many do so as to chase the surf in Newquay (current international surf and clubland Mecca) – but continue west, down to St Ives, the 'Tate of the South West,' as it is known.

PILLOW TALK

Freshers are guaranteed a room in halls if they live more than 25 miles from the campus at which they will be studying, if Plymouth is your first choice uni, if the academic criteria of your original offer are met, and if your application for a halls place is received before July 9. So they don't ask much then! In fact, there are even more ifs and buts, so you'd better speak to them, or their lawyers, personally...and get in quick! Note, all medical students are guaranteed an offer of a place in halls for their first year of study.

There are mixed-sex halls, flats and houses, all self-catering. New halls planned for 2007 – 450 rooms on Plymouth campus.

GETTING THERE

☛ By road: M5, A38 Exeter, Plymouth; Newton Abbot, A38, A383; Exmouth M5/J30, A376. Good coach services to Exeter and Plymouth.

☛ By coach to Plymouth: London, 4:40; Bristol, 2:30; Exeter, 1:05. To Exeter: London, 4:00; Birmingham, 4:30.

☛ By rail to Plymouth: London Paddington, 3:30; Bristol Parkway, 3:00; Southampton, 4:00; Birmingham New Street, 4:00. Exeter from London Paddington, 2:30; Bristol Parkway, 1:30; Birmingham New Street, 3:00.

☛ By air: Exeter or Plymouth City Airports.

UNIVERSITY OF PORTSMOUTH

The University of Portsmouth
University House
Winston Churchill Avenue
Portsmouth PO1 2UP

TEL 02392 848484
FAX 02392 843082
EMAIL admissions@port.ac.uk
WEB www.port.ac.uk

Portsmouth Students' Union
Cambridge Road
Portsmouth PO1 2ET

TEL 02392 843640
FAX 02392843667
EMAIL student-union@port.ac.uk
WEB www.upsu.net

VAG VIEW

Portsea behaves like an island, it has its own microclimate, slightly warmer than nearby Brighton or Bournemouth, as it sits snugly behind the Isle of Wight. For centuries, because of its strategic position, it was an important naval base, but now the focus is moving away from the military, the old naval dockyard giving itself to a pleasure zone of shops, nightclubs, bars, called Gun Wharf.

What once we detected as a military ethic in the university's 'Code of Student Discipline' seems also to have slipped away – though there remains an active OTC (Officer Training Corps), and a high input of graduates into the defence arena from a variety of departments. Today, however, military-style disciplines seem to have been sublimated in a caring ethos, modern, civilian, and maybe a slip laden with PR. They describe themselves as 'a hands-on student university: we care that our students turn up at lectures.' There is no clock-watching, but they want to find out why a student's interest is dropping away, if it is.

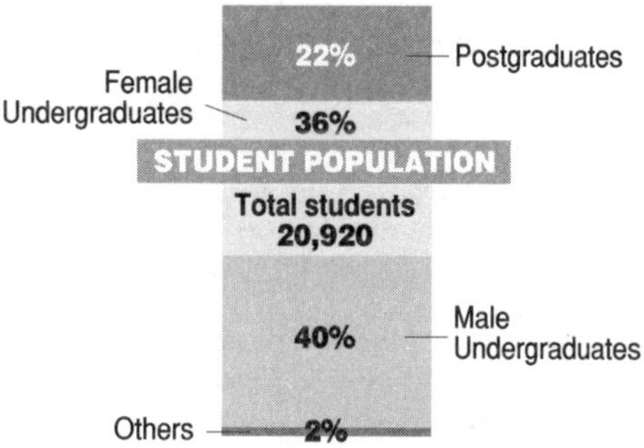

The uni serves up business, engineering, science, and media, art & design – vocational fare, true to its roots that lead us back to 1869, foundation year of Portsmouth & Gosport School of Science & Art. It was 100 years later that the college became Portsmouth Polytechnic, before receiving its Royal Charter as a university in 1992.

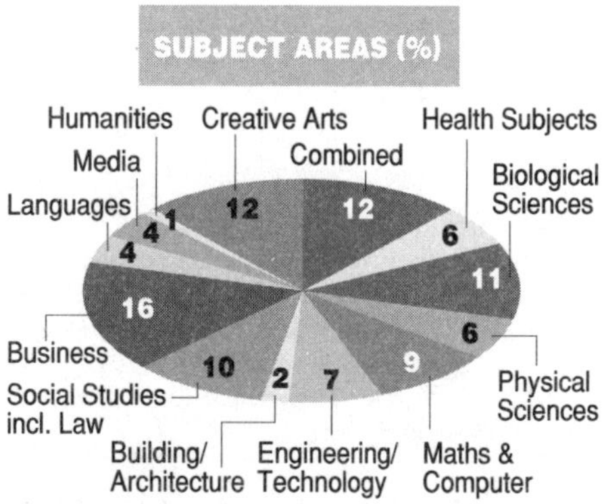

CAMPUS

Guildhall Campus is the name they give to the collection of sites in the centre of town, which has a European, café-style feel to it, and there are so many students marauding about that it seems not so much town as university precinct. When students go down in the summer they are replaced by as many tourists. Two other campuses, Milton and Langstone two and three miles away, are less and less significant. The Business School is now in its new building on campus.

FEES, BURSARIES

UK & EU Fees: £3000 p.a. If in receipt of the HE Maintenance grant there's a bursary of £500.

STUDENT PROFILE

It is a predominantly male student body. A lot of mature students come here too. They tend to recruit from the south of England. For many, Portsmouth is the local university. There is a high

UNIVERSITY/STUDENT PROFILE	
University since	**1992**
Situation/style	**Civic campus**
Student population	**20920**
Undergraduates	**16060**
- mature	**24%**
- non EU undergraduates	**9%**
- male/female	**53/47**
- non-traditional student intake	**29%**
- state school intake	**94%**
- drop-out rate	**9%**
- undergraduate applications	**Up 9%**

state-school intake, and 29% of the undergraduate population come from sections of society new to university. Given the unpractised element, their drop-out rate of 9% should suggest there's something to stay for.

Support for the new uni intake is as good as they claim. 'There's a full-time counselling service,' a student tells me. Why? 'Students find it hard at this...at university, money problems, pressures. People think being at university is easy. It is not. I am the only child of five in my family to have gone to university. It wasn't part of the culture of my family. I have struggled here, had to get jobs. People have this concept of university, students getting drunk all the time, having a good time...I have heard about that, but never experienced it.'

Portsmouth is massive in software engineering and systems analysis, coming third nationally for producing software engineers and fourth for software consultants.

ACADEMIA & JOBS

Faculties are Humanities and Social Sciences; Science; Technology; Environment; and Business. Their Grade 5 for research in European Studies and Russian/Slavonic/East European languages gives a hint of the special dimension. There are sound degrees in Applied Languages, Combined Modern languages, Euro Studies with various combination subjects, international dimensions to Business or International Trade, language add-ons to everything from American Studies to Creative Writing to Film Studies. And there is a strong contingent (5%) among undergraduates from elsewhere in Europe.

Accountants do well here. There's a range of BA degrees with Business, e-Business, and Business Law. Then there's Accountancy Studies or Accountancy & Financial Management for students with sufficient experience or qualifications to miss out on Year 1 of a regular accountancy degree.

They produce a big share of architects, too. Causing a stir is the BA Hons Architecture which comprises 50% design projects and 50% taught courses. It earns exemption from Part 1 RIBA. Likewise, property and construction employment markets like stocking up from this uni. Portsmouth has been No. 1 in the field of quantity surveying. The dedicated degree has been replaced by BSc Property Development with Quantity Surveying. There's also a good employment record (Top 10) for civil engineers and construction engineer/managers – the B/MEng Civil Engineering is accredited by the appropriate Institute. Teaching inspection 20.

Meanwhile the School of Pharmacy & Biomedical Sciences is recommended by both teaching assessments and employment data. Look at the 4-year MPharm, also Pharmaceutical Science and Pharmacology degrees (full marks at the assessments). Teaching inspection 22 for biosciences.

The Faculty of Humanities & Social Sciences has a tie-up with Southampton University to train health care professionals to work together: trainee nurses alongside trainee pharmacists and trainee radiographers, and so on. Health subjects, such as nursing, radiography were also top scoring at the teaching and research assessments.

WHERE PORTSMOUTH GRADUATES END UP

Health & Social Work: 7%; Education: 5%; Wholesale Retail: 12%; Manufacturing: 13%; Financial Activities: 8%; Public Administration, Civil Service & Defence: 9%; Hotel/Restaurant: 4%; Transport & Communications (including Telecommunications): 5%; Construction: 3%; Personnel: 5%; Computer: 5%; Business & Management: 3%; Accountancy: 2.5%; Media (including Film): 1%; Legal 3%; Architecture: 8%; Publishing: 0.5%; Sport: 1.5%.

Approximate 'graduate track' employed **57%**

Clinical and educational psychologists find jobs in number from here. Their BSc Psychology is accredited by the British Psychological Soc., and if you get at least a second class degree you've taken the first step to becoming a chartered psychologist.

There's also BSc Psychol. with Criminology. Many graduates find careers with the police and the probation service. One little gem is the Institute of Criminal Justice Studies, whose work on counter-fraud, benefits fraud and so on, has brought it links with TV's *Crimewatch*. Teaching inspection, 23.

There's a useful niche here, too, for cartographers – BSc Geographical Information Science scores highly in the employment league.

There's a traditional tie-up with the navy, excellent career prospects with the army and a good number of jobs, too, for defence operatives and equipment engineers. The Institute of Maritime Heritage Studies preserves the tradition, it's based in an old boathouse in the naval dockyards area.

ACADEMIC EXCELLENCE

TEACHING :	
(Rated Excellent or 17+ out of 24)	
Geography	**Excellent**
Pharmacology	**24**
French, Psychology, Politics, Subjects Allied to Medicine, Education	**23**
Maths, Biosciences, Nursing	**22**
German, Economics, Leisure/Sport	**21**
Sociology, Italian, Civil Eng, Electric & Electron Eng, Building, Land & Property Mgt, Physics, Art & Design	**20**
Russian, Iberian Studies	**18**
RESEARCH:	
*Top grades 5/5**	
Studies/Professions Allied to Medicine, Applied Maths, European Studies, Russian/ Slavonic/East European	**Grade 5**

Portsmouth is of course famous for being the site where the Mary Rose is docked.

Portsmouth lead the field in supplying to the Electrical and Electronic manufacturing industry. Computing degrees are also very strong, information and internet systems and much else besides. Aparticular strength in the employment sector being computer games technology. The BSc Computer Animation is aimed primarily at the implementer of a system rather than the conceptual/creative designer. There's a new BSc called Enterprise Dynamics in Computer Games Technology.

AT A GLANCE

ACADEMIC FILE:	
Subjects assessed	**32**
Excellent	**72%**
Typical entry requirements	**230 points**
Application acceptance rate	**20%**
Students-staff ratio	**20:1**
First/2:1 degree pass rate	**46%**
ACCOMMODATION FILE:	
Guarantee to freshers	**80%**
Style	**Halls, flats, Houses**
Catered	**25%**
En suite	**84%**
Cost pw (no food/food)	**£65-£100**
Town rent pw	**£55**

Portsmouth is also massive in software engineering and systems analysis, coming third nationally for producing software engineers and fourth for consultants. There's a BSc Software Engineering (and an HND if you need it). Look, too, at their BSc Computer Science(s), Systems Eng, Management & design. On the BEng route there's Computer Eng or Technology (the former also an MEng).

The Portsmouth Business School accounts for around 18% of students at undergraduate level. International and European options are legion. There's also BA Marketing, Marketing & Psychology or Leisure Management & Marketing. Sales managers pour out of this faculty, but also out of biological sciences, where there is that in-depth strength and opportunity for sales focus in the pharmaceutical/biotech industry, medical sales, etc, mentioned above. Finally, they are commercial & business law specialists.

Designers, illustrators, set-designers and film/video producers do well jobs-wise, which will be why they have just just created a new School of Creative Arts, Film and Media. There' are Photography, Video Production and various Film Studies degrees, plus a Media Development Centre with broadcast TV facilities and a digital development laboratory.

There are three BSc degrees in Sport – Sports Development, Sports Science, Water Sports Science. They are up there with the top providers to the industry.

STUDENT SCENE

Students' Union The new SU building gives them

a 2500 capacity. The investment is some £8 million. The nightclub, **LUX**, alone can take in 1100. This year it's getting a new lighting and sound system. Then there's the sportsbar **Waterhole** (500), chill-out bar **CO2** (500) and international bar **Embassy** (400). Regular ents are *Purple Wednesdays*, *Forbidden Fruit* (Fridays), *Flirt* (Saturdays)

Top of the ents menu are their mammoth balls – a new Presentation Ball for Purples (full/half colour awards: sport is big here), various societies' balls, Graduation Ball (Republica played last year) and so on.

Media-wise, students are active with monthly mag *Pugwash*. Pure Radio has been enjoying its most popular year with daily Internet broadcasts..

SPORT Men's sports teams are consistently high in the BUSA league. Geographical position gives them special potential – sailing (larks and lasers), windsurfing and canoeing. Applications for scholarships in hockey, rugby, swimming, water sports, gymnastics and netball are encouraged.

TOWN 'If you work in London and don't want to live there... Hence the excellent night life, large number of cafés...' Student and singer Genna Hellier was enthusing about the place: 'It is part of the reason I came here to be quite honest. It was a really nice summer's day and I saw the cafés lining the streets. It looked beautiful. I love it here. I came here shy and now I am going into PR! I never did any sport and now I work out every day. This union here provides amazing sporting opportunities. We have over 120 sports clubs and societies.'

South of campus is **Gun Wharf**, reclaimed from the MoD – 'Really nice,' Genna went on, 'all the London-based clubs are here. There is no rivalry between locals and students. It is a very safe place to live, music is especially good here. More locally we have the **Wedgwood Rooms** and **The Pyramid**. There's a place called **Havana** for student bands, and we organise open mic nights at the union and so on. The local theatre is the **Theatre Royal**, nice little theatre in the **Guildhall**, often used for student productions. The uni also built **Wiltshire Studios**, where a lot of student productions are done.'

There's a bountiful supply of clubs, cafés and wine bars in the Guildhall area. Other student hang-outs, such as the Havana Café Bar and the **Frog on the Front**, are within walking distance.

The club scene ranges from cheesy handbag to razor-tuned, techno beats. The Wedgwood Rooms in Albert Road offer a fine selection of dance music and bands, making it one of the premier music venues in the city. With its restaurants, cafés and bizarre shops, Albert Road is fast becoming the Soho of this city. Commercial Road, with its huge shopping mall is perhaps better suited to those drawn in by the consumer tractor beam, while **One Legged Jockey**, which resides in this area of the city, can only be described as the Style HQ of Portsmouth.

WHAT IT'S REALLY LIKE

UNIVERSITY:	
Social Life	★★★★
Campus scene	**Good mix**
Student Union services	**Good**
Politics	**Average**
Sport	**50 clubs**
National team position	**41st**
Sport facilities	**New sports hall**
Arts opportunities	**Plenty dance, music, film**
Student magazine	**Pugwash**
Student radio	**PURE FM**
Nightclub	**LUX**
Bars	**Waterhole, CO2, Embassy**
Union ents	**Rock, cheese, r&b, comedy**
Union societies	**40**
Most active societies	**People & planet, Breakdance**
Parking	**Poor**
TOWN:	
Entertainment	★★★
Scene	**Good: pubs, clubs**
Town/gown relations	**Good**
Risk of violence	**Low**
Cost of living	**Average**
Student concessions	**Excellent**
Survival + 2 nights out	**£70 pw**
Part-time work campus/town	**Average**

PILLOW TALK

Around 3000 places are available. 710 en-suite, self-catered beds are now up for grabs at James Watson Hall, which opened recently. Every first year who makes the uni their first choice by end April will qualify for a place in hall. If you don't get a place with them, then the uni will sort you out: 'It is our philosophy to care all the way through.'

GETTING THERE

☛ By road: A3(M), 2 hours from London.
☛ By rail: London Waterloo, 1:30; Bristol Parkway, 2:15; Birmingham New Street, 3:30; Sheffield, 4:45.
☛ By coach: London, 2:30; Exeter, 6:45.
☛ By air: Southampton Airport.

QUEEN MARGARET UNIVERSITY COLLEGE

Queen Margaret University College
Clerwood Terrace
Edinburgh EH12 8TS

TEL 0131 317 3247
FAX 0131 317 3248
EMAIL admissions@qmuc.ac.uk
WEB www.qmuc.ac.uk

COLLEGE/STUDENT PROFILE

Founded	**1875**
Status	**HE College**
Situation/style	**City campus**
Student population	**4645**
Degree undergraduates	**3690**
ACCOMMODATION FILE:	
Guarantee to freshers	**70%**
Style	**Halls**
Cost pw (no food/food)	**£58-£85**
City rent pw	**£65-£85**

Queen Margaret's began in 1875 as the Edinburgh School of Cookery and was re-named in 1930 The Edinburgh College of Domestic Science. Today there are four faculties: Arts, Business & Consumer Affairs, Social Sciences & Health Care, and Health Sciences, and they have become a university college with direct line into a number of career opportunities. They are located at three sites in Edinburgh. At the main Corstorphine campus near Edinburgh Airport, in the grounds of a former stately home, are the departments of Business & Consumer Studies, Communication & Information Studies, Hospitality & Tourism Management, Management & Social Sciences, Dietetics & Nutrition, Health & Nursing and Speech & Language Sciences. Leith Campus in old Edinburgh is home to the departments of Occupational Therapy, Physiotherapy, Podiatry and Radiography, while The Gateway Theatre in nearby Elm Row is the base for Drama.

5% plus of their graduates go into the hotel and restaurant trade. In the Health Sciences faculty, they produce 17% of all graduate physiotherapists nationwide; also from here come 6% of the entire provision of speech therapists. BSc Speech Pathology & Therapy is the course.

Accommodation at Corstorphine is in 3 halls. They have a swimming pool, gym, squash courts and all-weather surface for tennis, football, hockey and netball. The Students' Association has a bar.

QUEEN MARY, UNIVERSITY OF LONDON

Queen Mary College
University of London
Mile End Road
London E1 4NS

TEL 020 7882 5511
FAX 020 7975 5588
EMAIL admissions@qmw.ac.uk
WEB www.qmw.ac.uk

Queen Mary College
Students' Union
432 Bancroft Road
London E1 4DH

TEL 020 7882 5390
FAX 020 8981 0802
EMAIL su-genoff@qmw.ac.uk
WEB www.qmwsu.org

VAG VIEW

A constituent college of the federal University of London, QMW arose out of the merger (in 1989) of two colleges: Westfield College, a 19th-century pioneer in higher education for women, and Queen Mary College, founded in 1885 and located at the People's Palace in Mile End Road, ideally situated for its essential purpose, namely to educate the East End poor. This is the uni's base in Mile End Road today. A later, medical foundation arose out of a merger in 1995 between the Royal London School of Medicine & Dentistry and St Bartholomew's Hospital Medical School, now QMW's Medical School. Medical students undergo their clinical training at the Royal London in Whitechapel and Barts in West Smithfield.

QMW's location thus keeps it true to its roots, while its large overseas student contingent – they draw from some 100 countries

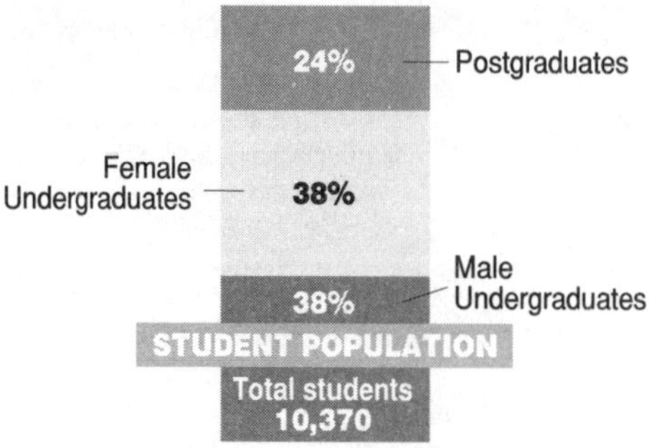

worldwide – reflects the multi-cultural character of the area as it is today. Central to this strategy is a Study Abroad programme. Languages are to the fore throughout the curriculum, and have scored highly in both teaching inspections and research assessments.

FEES, BURSARIES

UK & EU Fees: £3000 p.a. If in receipt of full HE Maintenance grant there's a bursary of £1000; if in receipt of partial grant, £800. They also offer academic achievement scholarships.

STUDENT PROFILE

'Integration between medical students and the rest of the college leaves a lot to be desired,' writes Kieran Alger, 'the two groups preferring to indulge in separate activities, the medical students enjoying their own bar, for example, and playing for separate sports teams while the main body of students mixes well, regardless of subject.'

As at other medical schools, the medical students sharply increase the public school quota and give QMW a state/public school ratio akin to Reading's or Southampton's, Warwick's or York's.

UNIVERSITY/STUDENT PROFILE	
School of London Uni since	**1915**
Situation/style	**Campus**
Student population	**10370**
Undergraduates	**7915**
- mature	**21%**
- non EU undergraduates	**12%**
- male/female	**51/49**
- non-traditional student intake	**31%**
- state school intake	**85%, low**
drop-out rate	**9%**
- undergraduate applications	**Up 6%**

The Mile End Road student population is another story. 'Queen Mary proper is a cultural melting pot,' agrees Kieran – 'a fascinating blend of overseas students, a large ethnic contingent and UK residents,' and a 31% draw last year from the new-to-uni social groups. There are also larger than average local and mature populations (they even have 'mature student socials' at the student union), which serve to distinguish the clientele from what Kieran describes as 'the stereotypical beer and beans, lazy student'.

CAMPUS

'QMW, with its modern architecture, is one of the few universities to combine the class of the well established with the youth, vigour and dynamism of an ex-polytechnic,' continues Kieran. 'In many ways this college is the orange Kit-Kat of academia – all the chocolatey, biscuity re-assurance of our nation's biggest selling snack, but with a little twist of fruity diversity.

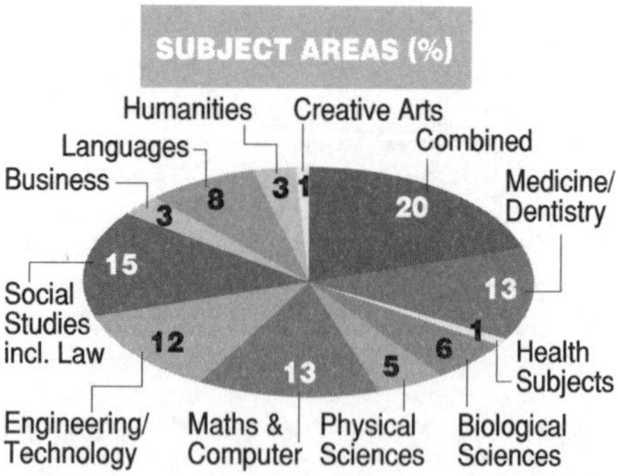

'Set in the heart of the multi-cultural hotchpotch which forms the East End, the student population reflects its intriguing surroundings. The East End, home of imports, the cloth trade, Phil, Grant and the Kray twins, has an illustrious history of intermingling races. From jellied eels at Spitalfield's Market to chicken balti in one of Brick Lane's curry houses, this area caters for a huge range of tastes. Just now it is also asserting its own brand of sophistication in the stunning and ever-encroaching Docklands development. The combination of Canary Wharf Tower dominating on one side and the trendification of the E1, E2, and E3 postal areas is causing a surge in social and cultural activity. The East End, with its fashionable gangster land history and eerie Jack the Ripper connections, is becoming the place London's affluent young professionals want to live. In Bethnal Green, comedian Lee Hurst has opened a comedy club. Neighbouring areas, such as Bow and Aldgate, are being inundated with new eateries, coffee houses, galleries and nightclubs.'

Clinical students head for Bart's on the Smithfield site, a square deep in the heart of the City, close to the Barbican. It is the oldest member of the college. The hospital was founded in 1123 by a jester turned monk by name of Rahere. Halls of residence cluster around it. On-site is a clinical library, research and computer facilities, a theatre, sports facilities, and a bar. The Royal London, at Whitechapel in the East End, is one of the busiest and largest hospitals in the capital. There is a £33.5-million plan to re-house Barts and the London Medical School.

ACADEMIA & JOBS

Forty per cent of QM graduates are destined for the health sector. The medicine degree, a 5-year BM BS (Medicine, Surgery), stresses clinical method and communication skills and the experience of the patient in the community, and there's a significant element of problem-based learning (small-group explorations of particular scenarios). First 2 years at the Mile End campus, final three at the the Royal London Hospital, Whitechapel Campus. There's a 4-year graduate entry, too. Entry AABB including Biology and Chemistry. Teaching inspection 21.

Of interest to future dentists, the dental schools with full marks at the assessments are King's College London, Manchester University, Queen's Belfast and Queen Mary College London. It's a 5-year BDS plus a B/MEng Dental Materials. Entry AAAb including a science subject + Chemistry/Biology. Research Grade 5.

Safe ground, too, is Law. QM are world-class European law specialists, and non-Law graduates may opt for a 2-year full-time or 3-year part-time Senior Status Law degree here.

Investment advisers/analysts, accountants are also to the fore, and there's a bunch of good Economics and Finance degrees. So, too, IT consultants, software engineers, programmers, who attest to the sound Computer Science, IT Science and Computer Engineering degrees. There is a foundation programme attached to all BEng, BSc and BSc (Eng) degrees.

Languages feature strong. Graduate jobs for language students vary widely, some find a use in community and youth work, others take a vocational direction from a subject studied in combination, as in chartered accountancy, investment, management, etc. Others become teachers (5%), but there is a great mass of language graduates here who become sales assistants, clerks, etc, and one cannot help but advise applicants to stick to QM's mainstay areas if, that is, paying back fees and loans are uppermost in mind.

One interesting novelty is a degree in Journalism & Contemporary History, run jointly with City University. City is a world leader in journalism.

ACADEMIC EXCELLENCE

TEACHING:
(Rated Excellent or 17+ out of 24)

English, Geography	**Excellent**
Dentistry	**24**
Politics, Modern Languages	**23**
Biosciences, Subjects Allied to Medicine	**22**
Medicine, Electric/Electron Eng, Maths, Physics, Drama	**21**
Materials Technology	**20**
General Engineering	**19**

RESEARCH:
Top grades 5/5/6**

Law, Linguistics, Iberian/LatinAmerican	**Grade 6***
Clinical Dentistry, Physics, Pure Maths, Statistics, Mechanical/Aeronautical/ Manufacturing Eng, Metallurgy, Geography, Law, English, French, German/Dutch/ Scandinavian, Russian/ Slavonic & E. European Languages., History	**Grade 5**

SOCIAL SCENE

The medics have their own union – SoMaD Students' Association. There are two bars: the

WHERE QUEEN MARY GRADUATES END UP

Health & Social Work: 39%; Education: 5%; Wholesale Retail: 9%; Manufacturing: 5%; Financial Activities: 10%; Public Administration, Civil Service & Defence: 7%; Hotel/Restaurant: 2%; Transport & Communications (including Telecommunications): 2%; Construction: 0.5%; Personnel: 3%; Computer: 2%; Business & Management: 1%; Accountancy: 3%; Media (including Film): 1.5%; Legal 1.5%; Publishing: 1%; Advertising: 0.5%; Artistic/Literary: 1%; Sport: 1%.

Approximate 'graduate track' employed **69%**

Clubs Union Bar at the Royal London Hospital (Whitechapel), and **Bart's Bar**, close to Bart's Hospital in Charterhouse Square (where there is also a swimming pool, squash, tennis and badminton courts). There's also a glass-fronted bistro bar, **BarMed**, in the Medical Science building looking out on to Library Square. Regular high jinks are the Association Dinner, the Christmas Show, Burn's Night and the sporting cup finals. There's a flourishing drama society – plays, a Christmas Show, a production for the Edinburgh Fringe – a Gilbert & Sulivan Society, a choir and orchestra, and of course Rag. Otherwise, they bounce around at *Toga Nights*, *Star Wars Night*, *Austin Powers Night*, and *Mummies and Daddies Night*. I guess *Doctors & Nurses Night* is simply 'too day-time' to compete.

In Mile End Road, the more dissipated wind up rather than down at looking for 'the best student nightclub in London' (the Union's boast) at **Club e1**. Complete with 12K JBL sound system and state of the art computer-controlled lighting rig it is open till 2 am from Thursday through Saturday. Then, there's **The Drapers Arms**. The **e1** nightclub has a 750-capacity, top sound and lighting systems and a reputation built on the sometime, much-vaunted, *Time Out*-supported *Time Tunnel* ('60s to '90s) on Saturdays, a once regular Saturday pop ('70s to the present day) extravaganza, *ROAR*, and more recently, *FIZZ*, on Saturday night, *Gagging for it* on Tuesday, *Hail Mary* on Wednesday, *Now Music* on Thursday, *Take a Ride* on Friday... However, this year there's a more basic menu of *Flirt! Toga & Tequila Party*, *Ann Summers Night* followed by *Flirt*, *Saints + Sinners Flirt*, *Flirt! Halloween*, *Mary's Cheese*, *Hail Mary*. *Flirt* is a national SU package, and the cheesy home-bred stuff suggests QM may have lost its way a bit. Mind you, they had a long way to fall, and they're feeling very defensive this year, what with Ismail Malik's article in *London Student* suggesting that 'a whole host of students who fail to get into other University of London institutions go to Queen Mary'. The pages of QMSU's newspaper, *CUB*, have been putting Ismail right.

No stranger to student media awards, *CUB*, founded in 1947, is one of the oldest student papers in London. There's a clubs and societies resource centre.

WHAT IT'S REALLY LIKE

UNIVERSITY:	
Social Life	★★★★
Campus scene	**Lively**
Student Union services	**Average**
Politics	**Apolitical**
Sport	**19 clubs**
National team position	**59th**
Sport facilities	**Average**
Arts opportunities	**Drama excellent**
Student newspaper	**Cub**
Nightclub	**Club e1**
Bars	**The Drapers Arms, Barts, Union Bar**
Union ents	**Flirt**
Union clubs/societies	**52**
Most active siocieties	**Islamic Soc, Friends of Palastine**
Parking	**Poor**
CITY:	
Entertainment	★★★★★
Scene	**Wild, expensive**
Town/gown relations	**Average-good**
Risk of violence	**London**
Cost of living	**High**
Student concessions	**Good**
Survival + 2 nights out	**£100 pw**
Part-time work campus/town	**Excellent**

AT A GLANCE

ACADEMIC FILE:	
Subjects assessed	**21**
Excellent	**71%**
Typical entry requirements	**290 points**
Application acceptance rate	**14%**
Students-staff ratio	**13:1**
First/2:1 degree pass rate	**59%**
ACCOMMODATION FILE:	
Guarantee to freshers	**Non-locals OK**
Style	**Halls, houses, flats**
Catered	**10%**
En suite	**Some**
Approx price range pw	**£80-£110**
City rent pw	**£100-£180 Zone 1; £75-£85 Zone 2**

SPORT Sports fields are at Chislehurst. 'Sports are abundant,' Kieran writes, 'from rock climbing, netball and fencing, to the somewhat more comfortable pastimes of rowing and rugby. The football club is of a particularly high standard, as is the women's football team. Collegiate London Uni delivers many an opportunity for battle.'

PILLOW TALK

For first years it's London University 'intercollegiate halls' (catered), where you could be with anyone, or QM's own (self-catered) at the Mile End campus (2109 places), where now, from this year, there's a new Student Village - 995 rooms (15 for wheelchair users), all with computer connections, village shop, café bar... Mile End Park has single rooms, en-suite facilities, arranged in flats - lawns, woodland courtyards. The older (pre-Village) accommodation at Mile End is the cheaper.

50 rooms available at Dawson Hall, Charterhouse Square, close to Barts, and at Floyer House on the Whitechapel campus.

GETTING THERE

☛ By Underground: QMW, Stepney Green (District, Hammersmith & City) or Mile End (+Central line). The Royal London, Whitechapel tube (East London, District, Hammersmith & City lines); nearest Bart's is Barbican. St Paul's (Central).

THE QUEEN'S UNIVERSITY OF BELFAST

The Queen's University of Belfast
University Road
Belfast BT7 1NN

TEL 028 9033 5081
FAX 028 9024 7895
EMAIL admissions@qub.ac.uk
WEB www.qub.ac.uk

Queen's University Students' Union
University Road
Belfast BT7 1PE

TEL 028 9027 3106/8
FAX 028 9023 6900
EMAIL info@qubsu.org
WEB www.qubsu.org

UNIVERSITY/STUDENT PROFILE	
University since	**1908**
Situation/style	**Civic**
Student population	**24178**
Undergraduates	**19643**
- mature	**19%**
- non EU undergraduates	**5%**
- male/female	**42/58**
- non-traditional student intake	**36%**
state school intake	**99%, high**
- drop-out rate	**7%**
- undergraduate applications	**Up 12%**

**see Introduction for key to tables*

SUBJECT AREAS (%)

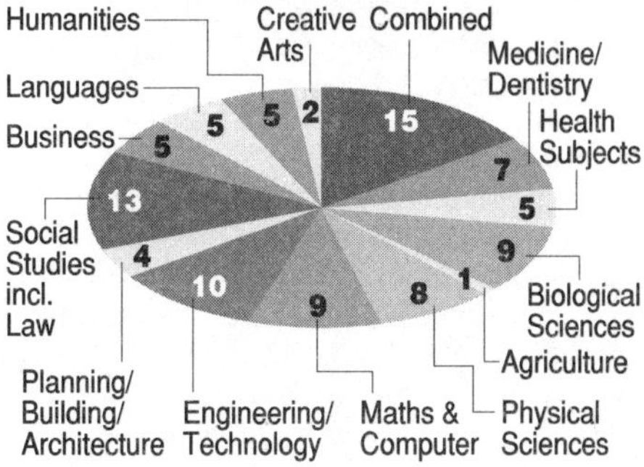

VAG VIEW

Northern Ireland's leading educational institution has its origins in the Queen's College, Belfast, founded in 1845. There is a traditional Oxbridge-style reputation, with good lines into the professions, medicine, dentistry, the City and law.

Now, under the leadership of Vice-Chancellor Professor Peter Gregson, who took up office in August 2004, Queen's is implementing an ambitious Vision for the Future, beginning with a new academic framework (see Academia *below), a £200 million investment in staff, students and facilities, including a £44-million library project, a £45-million student village, replacing the present high-rise catered tower blocks with self-catered three-storey villas in a village setting by 2009/10, and an extensive refurbishment to the Students' Union and the Physical Education Centre.*

CAMPUS

Set a few kilometres from the city centre in a so-called 'safe' area of Belfast, the campus encompasses the Botanic Gardens and Ulster Museum. Areas around Queen's University, Stranmillis and Botanic Avenue are now busier than ever and spilling over into the once isolated city centre.

Writes Laura Cattell: 'The big red buses that pass by Queen's every few minutes are packed with camera-happy tourists snapping a shot of the redbrick Lanyon hall. The impressive building (apparently modelled on Oxford University's Magdalen College), is at the heart of the city campus and though few actual lectures take place in the building it's the focus for academic and ceremonial life at Queen's. Set in the southern and leafier part of Belfast, most of the departmental buildings are housed in the Georgian terraces along University Square, opposite Lanyon hall or in the larger more modern Ashby Hall further along Stranmillis Road. As a student, most of your

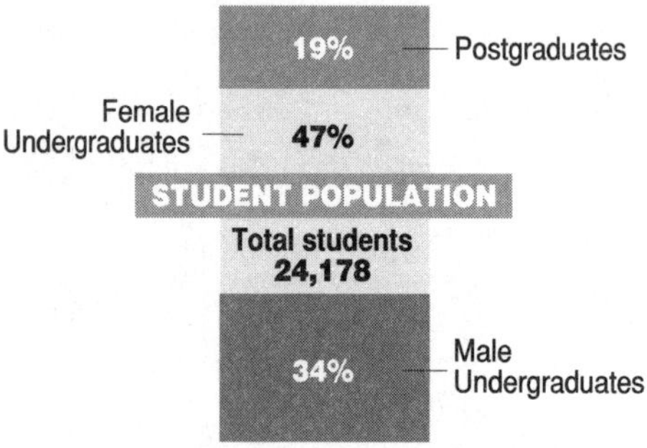

social life will be based in this area - from Eglantine to Botanic Avenue. The Student Union is located opposite the Lanyon buildings and as with most 1960s university structures it's not architecturally stunning, but it has everything you need - from banks, second-hand bookshops, convenience stores and a laundry, to cafes, bars, toilets and a nightclub. Although much of Belfast has been affected by the troubles in recent years this part of the city remains largely untouched by sectarianism.'

FEES, BURSARIES

UK & EU Fees: £3000 p.a. If in receipt of full HE Maintenance grant there's a total possible bursary of £4300, including sport and books allowances, etc; if in receipt of partial grant, this decreases according to size of household income on a sliding scale to £250. There are also Guinness Sports Scholarships and 27 Entrance Scholarships.

STUDENT PROFILE

Queen's claim to be 'one of the most socially inclusive universities in the United Kingdom. It consistently out-performs national benchmarks in attracting students from poorer backgrounds.' Perhaps they should do more for the beleaguered English public school boy and girl who, for example, find themselves victims of discrimination too. Certainly there are some opportunities for them here. For example, Queen's Uni's medical school is one of the best in the world, and the application acceptance rate is three times what you'll find in most English med schools.

The fact is that most of the student population is local, and 31% of undergraduates are part-timers. There is, however, a very low (8%) take from underprivileged so-called 'low participation neighbourhoods', but a high take (36%) from socio-economic classes new to going to university. Almost all that come here had a state school education, but this is not the land of the English public school after all.

ACADEMIA & JOBS

'Academically,' Laura continues, 'Queen's is Northern Ireland's best University and lies in the top three of Ireland's higher education institutions. It is still overlooked by many students in mainland Britain not only because of its location, but also because of its lowly ranking alongside U.K institutions. It is let down by a few weak departments, but this is counteracted by other world-class departments: Medicine, Engineering, English and Politics.

'There is a thriving literary scene, forefronted by the excellent teaching and research record of the English department. The School of English has some of the best academics in their field and is of course well-known for being the alma mater of Northern Ireland's most celebrated poets: Seamus Heaney and Paul Muldoon.'

Queen's is an artistic hub, home to Belfast's International Festival and to Northern Ireland's sole arthouse cinema in the Queen's Film Theatre, and to the region's newest museum, the Naughton Gallery. The University runs a host of musical

WHERE QUEEN'S BELFAST GRADUATES END UP

Health & Social Work: 24%; Education: 7%; Wholesale Retail:15%; Manufacturing: 8%; Financial Activities: 7%; Public Administration, Civil Service & Defence: 5%; Hotel/Restaurant: 3%; Transport & Communications (including Telecommunications): 3%; Construction: 2%; Agriculture: 1%; Personnel: 1%; Computer: 3%; Business & Management: 1%; Accountancy: 7.5%; Media (including Film): 0.5%; Legal 2%; Architecture: 3%; Publishing: 0.5%

Approximate 'graduate track' employed **75%**

events, including an annual international festival of Contemporary Music. Courses in drama and film studies underpin its cultural contribution and the Seamus Heaney Centre for Poetry reinforces the university's reputation as a world literary force.

'Famous-Seamus has also given his name to several buildings around campus and is an occasional visitor at the university,' writes Laura. 'The Heaney Centre, found at the back of the School of English, organises regular literary events - most of which are free and usually boast free wine as an incentive (if you need one!). Recent guests to the centre have been Jackie Kaye, Nick Laird, Ali Smith, Paul Durcan and Terry Eagleton. There's also a lively English Society and several reading and writing groups. Last year's poet-in-residence was Sinead Morrisey, who ran the writing group, while this year sees young poet Leontia Flynn as chair.'

The new academic framework consists of 21 large schools within 3 faculties: Arts, Humanities & Social Sciences; Engineering & Physical Sciences; and Medicine, Health & Life Sciences. It is too early to say how successful the reorganisation will be, though there have been criticisms about the organisational sense of the reshuffling of some schools into super-schools. The new library is due for completion in 2009 and will accommodate 2000 reader places and house 1.5 million volumes. There will also be an exhibition space, café, language laboratory, information points and multimedia resources.

A quarter of graduates enter the health sector. The 5-year MB has a pre-med year for applicants with broader based qualifications than A levels, but only 5 places on it. A 28% application acceptance rate to the MB in 2004 (latest available), makes it look the easiest medical school to get into by far (the average AAR is 11%), but the A levels requirement is the highest. Scientific and Clinical Medicine is taught for each system of the body – system by system, rather than Physiology, Anatomy, etc. Strong emphasis on clinical skills. Average Entry Requirements AAA including Chemistry A + Physics ir Biology or Maths, or AAB including Chemistry A + A at AS level. Teaching Inspection 22. Research Grade 5 for Community-based Clinical subjects. The Dental School scored full marks at the assessments, the 5-year BDS requires AAB at entry. For midwifer Queen's look all round the best bet. They produce around 7% of graduate midwives, not with a dedicated Midwifery degree, but through BSc Hons/Higher Diploma in Nursing Science. The entry requirements in this instance are surprisingly low. Take advantage! The reputation in engineering is world class: Mechanical, Aeronautical and Manufacturing Engscored Grade 5* at the assessments. Jobs are legion in aeronautical, and note the Mechanical with Food Engineering speciality. Electrical and telecommunications engineers proliferate and benefit from Electrical & Electronic Engineering taking full marks for teaching, and a Grade 5 (international reputation) for research. There are good sandwich/professional experience opportunities.

Architecture, Environmental Planning, Structural Engineering with Architecture, Civil Engineering, Environmental & Civil Engineering are B/MEng sandwich courses speak of their employment strengths in built environment. There are decent teaching assessments and an international track record in research. Teaching inspection, 22. Research Grade 5.

ACADEMIC EXCELLENCE

TEACHING: *(Rated Excellent or 17+ out of 24)*	
Applied Social Work, History, Law, English, Geology, Music.	**Excellent**
Elec & Electron Engineering, Dentistry, Psychology, Economics/Accountancy	**24**
Management , Archaeology, Education, Physics, Politics, Classics, Celtic Studies	**23**
Civil Eng, Enviro Planning, Medicine, Anatomy, Maths, Nursing, Theology	**22**
Iberian Studies; Chemical Engineering; Mechanical, Aeronautical & Manufacturing Engineering, Food Sci, Agric, Podiatry, Biosciences, Philosophy	**21**
French	**20**
Sociology, Modern Languages (German, Italian, Russian & E. Euro languages).	**19**
RESEARCH: *Top grades 5/5**	
Mechanical/Aeronautical/ Manufacturing Engineering.	**Grade 5***
Community-based Clinical Subjects, Physics, Civil Eng, Electrica & Electronic Eng , Law, Anthropology, Politics, Sociology, European Studies, Irish Studies, Celtic Studies, English, Archaeology, History, Music	**Grade 5**

Accountants are legion in the Management & Economics School, the named degree coming also with French, German or Spanish – 7.5% of all Queen's graduates become accountants. The Managment degree also comes with three language options and Information Systems. They put very high numbers into retail management.

They are also high up among unis producing actuaries. Look at the Economics and Finance degrees, but especially the Maths (Pure/Applied) and extended for a year in Europe.

Note also Law & Accounting, one of an interesting bunch of degrees, which includes Common & Civil Law with French/Spanish (4 years). There's also a Law with Politics, and non-Law graduates may opt for a 2-year full-time or 3-year part-time Senior Status Law Degree here.

AT A GLANCE

ACADEMIC FILE:	
Subjects assessed	**44**
Excellent	**84%**
Typical entry requirements	**350 points**
Application acceptance rate	**17%**
Subjects assessed	**18:1**
First/2:1 degree pass rate	**60%**
ACCOMMODATION FILE:	
Guarantee to freshers	**Most get in**
Style	**Halls**
Catered	**None**
En suite	**40%**
Approx price range pw	**£53-£75**
City rent per month	**£170-£220**

WHAT IT'S REALLY LIKE

UNIVERSITY:	
Social Life	★★★★
Campus scene	**Craic is good**
Student Union services	**Good**
Politics	**Yes**
Sport	**Competitive**
National team position	**71st**
Sport facilities	**Improving**
Arts opportunities	**Cinema excellent; theatre poor**
Student newspaper	**The Gown**
Venue/bars	**Speakeasy, Bunatee, Bar Sub, Mandela Hall, Varsity**
Union ents	**Shine (infamous house), Good Friday + live acts**
Live venue capacity	**1,000**
Union clubs/societies	**100**
Parking	**Adequate**
CITY:	
Entertainment	★★★
City scene	**Clubs, pubs, arts**
Town/gown relations	**Generally OK**
Risk of violence	**Average-high**
Cost of living	**Low**
Student concessions	**Good**
Survival + 2 nights out	**£65 pw**
Part-time work campus/town	**Average**

Computer programmers pour off a 4-year sandwich Business Information Technology BSc, there are BEng and BSc Computer Science, both 4-year sandwich, and a 4/5-year MEng Computer Science (the extra year in industry).

For teaching, it's largely St Mary's University College, Belfast. Output: 23% Secondary, 77% Primary. Roman Catholic teacher training college recently given UC status with a broader, less vocational syllabus including such as BA Liberal Arts. Degrees awarded by Queen's. Stranmillis University College is another Belfast university college closely involved with training Queen's Uni students to become teachers. Output: 20% Secondary, 80% Primary.

SOCIAL SCENE

STUDENTS' UNION There are various SU pleasure zones – the plush **Speakeasy Bar** with big screen sport, pub quizzes, Playstation challenge and hedonistic nights on the pull, the subterranean **Bunatee Bar** and intimate venue, **Bar Sub**, **Mandela Hall** (capacity: 1000, one of the best live venues in Belfast, home to the **Underground** and the Comedy Network) and **Varsity** (just round the corner from the Union buidings).

Writes Laura: 'The Union is a hub of activity during term time and the long opening hours mean you can always pop in to grab something to eat or drink or even to buy some paper to print those essays on... Every night there is something going on - usually in the dingy **Speakeasy**, or there are cheap comedy nights in **Mandela Hall**. Although the **Mandela Hall** supports local talent by showcasing local acts on Thursday's, the best music venues are to be found in the city. Northern Ireland's Ash as headlining act meant that last year's Fresher's ball was a big success. Every department within the university seems to have its own social events so there's no shortage of pub crawls/balls to attend.

'A typical week's ents is Monday: *Student Anthems* in **Speakeasy**; Tues: *Motherfunk*, free before 11pm and very cheap spirits; Society's Quiz

Night; Wed: hip hop and r&r; Comedy Night in **Mandela Hall**; Thurs: *Radar Live* (showcase of local bands); Fri: *Good Friday* (all drinks £1.50 from 4pm till close); Sat: *Shine* - infamous house night (non-Union run). Recent live acts were Babyshambles and Fun Lovin' Criminals. Altogether the union building can take 2500 for entertainments.'

Naturally students are highly politicised, with a strong focus on Northern Ireland politics, but also on student issues. The union is generally characterised as nationalist and left of centre.

Student media is generally rather poor. Newspaper is *The Gown* (Laura gives it 4/10). More independent publications are such as the polemic, *The Vacuum* ('had many run-ins with Belfast City council resulting in a 'Sorry' day about the city earlier this year...)'. A radio station is just setting up and going on air.

Queen's clubs and societies are legion, but most of the Irish students at Queen's clear off home at the weekend to get their washing done and to raid the family fridge. There's a very good cinema on campus - called Queen's Film Theatre - which runs a film club, a short films festival, and lots of arthouse films every day of the week. £2.50 on Monday, as it's student night. Its also £2.50 on Tuesdays (*Crazy Tuesday* it's called) at the Moviehouse on Dublin Road - for all films.

SPORT They have two swimming pools (diving, subaqua, water polo and canoeing facilities), conditioning rooms, squash courts, badminton, basketball, tennis courts, volleyball, handball, hockey, netball courts, two judo squares, cricket nets, a purpose-built mountain wall and facilities for gymnastics, athletics, fencing, golf, karate, bowls, yoga and archery, seventeen pitches for rugby, soccer, gaelic, hockey, hurling, camogie and cricket, netball and tennis courts, a floodlit training area and an athletics arena where the Mary Peters Track is situated. Opportunities for golf at Malone Golf Club (3 miles away), sailing at Belfast Lough and Lough Neagh, waterskiing at Craigavon, gliding and parachuting at Magilligan, mount-aineering in the Mourne mountains, caving in Fermanagh and rowing on the nearby River Lagan. Fifteen sports bursaries are available, sponsored by Guinness. Use of the pool or gym costs a mere £1 and is located a 5-minute walk from campus. When renovations to the P.E.C are complete, they'll have Northern Ireland's largest sports facility on the doorstep.

PILLOW TALK

150 new en-suite rooms opened in Sept 2005, 33 en-suite rooms due in January 2006, 180 en-suite rooms in Sep 2006 and a further 120 en-suite rooms in Sep 2007.

'Most freshers are allocated rooms in the Queen's Elms halls of residence,' writes Laura. 'These 60s monstrosities are a 20-minute walk from campus and although the tower blocks can seem rather bleak there are new cafés and bars being built on the site, which will create a better atmosphere. All the room facilities such as internet connections and en-suite bathrooms are excellent. If you're lucky enough to get a place in any of the university-owned houses then Mount Charles just off Botanic Avenue or Guthrie house on Fitzwilliam Street are the best of the bunch.

'In general, though, living in privately-owned accommodation is much cheaper so most students move out once they finish the first year. Most students live in South Belfast, along or off the Lisburn or Ormeau Road and rent per month varies from as little as £130 to £200 a month. Stranmillis, just a ten minute walk from the campus, is the most sought-after area, though naturally as a result it's a bit pricier - all to be expected if you want a BT9 postcode.'

GETTING THERE

☛ An hour by air from London, with at least 24 flights a day each way.

STUDENT BELFAST - THE CITY

TENSIONS

Town/gown relations are good and local businesses tend to recruit heavily from the university. Recent tension in the Holylands between students and residents has meant that the university comes down very hard on any students thought to be displaying 'anti-social behaviour'. Good community relations are very important and as such there are many local volunteering and work experience opportunities on offer at the uni careers service.

Belfast is one of those places that is stereotyped over and over again - descriptions such as 'divided', 'troubled', 'industrial' and 'the wettest place on earth' all come to mind. There are re-occurring sets of binaries that fracture the city: politically, socially and religiously. And whether you are from Northern Ireland or not, these fractures cannot be ignored, but this doesn't mean the city can't overcome such problems and enjoy itself.

Despite the tensions and occasional setbacks (the riots and fires of last October caused blockades and chaos around the city for several days), Belfast is a lively and great place to live. It's a small and compact city so you'll soon find your way around. The new bus system is cheap and efficient and as such you'll rarely find it necessary to get a train anywhere – they're far too pricey anyway. Unless you have a car already, don't get one to live in Belfast – driving around the city can be a nightmare.

Central and South Belfast is the focus for most of student life. Botanic gardens are a haven away from the busy city; the green is packed in the summer and there's often a brass band playing on the bandstand by the rose garden. Inside the gardens you'll find the pretty **Palm House** and also the **Ulster Museum**, which tends to show interesting contemporary art and houses the permanent 'Ireland in Conflict' exhibition. Botanic Avenue and Dublin Road lead the way from the city to the University area – a mere 15-minute walk.

Apart from the stunning white marble **City Hall** and several redbrick Victorian buildings (**The Linen Hall** and **Marks & Spencer**), the rest of the centre is fairly unspectacular. The waterside is still being developed although the **Waterfront Hall** and the **Odyssey Complex** are already good music and entertainment venues, and along and near Royal Avenue there are the usual High Street stores, lots of secondhand bookshops, plus, off Queen's Street, some pricier boutiques. But if you want to do any serious shopping, take the 2-hour train journey to Dublin. It is well worth it.

CRAIC

As a newcomer to Belfast you'll soon learn the true meaning of the famous 'craic'. People really know how to go out and have a great time here. Bars and pubs are plentiful (though very smoky!) – from trendy 'sit-in-and-be-seen' cocktail bars, such as **The Apartment**, to traditional taverns such as **Whites**. In the city centre the Cathedral quarter contains the lovely **John Hewitt** pub (with an excellent choice of ales & beers) and **The Spaniard** – a great bar with quirky décor and fantastic music – serves tapas and light meals. **The Kitchen Bar** in the nearby **Cornmarket** is very classy and holds a jazz night every Monday. Going away from the city centre and leading towards the uni area, **Katie Daly's** and the **Limelight** are well known for their student-orientated theme nights. Closer to Queen's there's always a good atmosphere in **Auntie Annies** while **The Bot** and **The Egg** (off Eglantine Avenue) are convenient and cheap student dives (**The Egg** does a £5 Sunday roast). Though the variety of nightclubs doesn't really rival that of pubs, there are a couple worth checking out – **Milk** and **The Pothouse** being the best of the bunch. Although there isn't much of a gay/lesbian scene in Belfast there are a couple of sympathetic clubs in the cathedral quarter: **The Cremlin** and **The Nest**.

ART

Belfast is full of poets and musicians and as such there's always a poetry reading or a band playing in a pub nearby. All music events are listed in the free pamphlet – *The List*, or you can find full entertainment listings in the *Belfast Telegraph* on a Friday. Traditional music sessions can usually be heard at **Whites**, **The John Hewitt** or **Kelly's Tavern**, while folk or rock bands often play in **Katie Daly's**, **The Empire** or **Auntie Annies**. **The Limelight**, **The Ulster Hall** and **The King's Hall** all host bigger bands – such as The Magic Numbers, K.T. Tunstall and Gabriel y Rodrigo.

Spring and autumn see lots of festivals in Belfast – such as the big Belfast Festival (all over the city), Between the Lines (literature & music – at **The Crescent Arts Centre**), Belfast Film Festival, the Cathedral Quarter Arts Festival and the new Holylands Arts Festival. Throughout the summer there are Irish festivals or fleadh held in West Belfast, and the **An Cultural Ann** (Culture Centre) on the Falls road has a lovely café and an Irish language book shop, where you can often hear local musicians.

Laura Cattell

UNIVERSITY OF READING

The University of Reading
Whiteknights
Reading RG6 6AH

TEL 0118 378 6586
FAX 0118 378 8924
EMAIL schools.liaison@rdg.ac.uk
WEB www.reading.ac.uk

Reading University Students' Union
PO Box 230
Reading RG6 2AZ

TEL 0118 986 0222
FAX 0118 975 0337
EMAIL (see website)
WEB www.rusu.co.uk

VAG VIEW

The student body is far from being limited to the marauding agrics of popular legend. Reading's areas of academic strength cover a wider spectrum than many imagine – cybernetics, classics, environmental sciences, agriculture, meteorology, film & theatre.

What's more, £500,000 has been lavished on the union pleasure dome. Reading, we are told, is now 24/7.

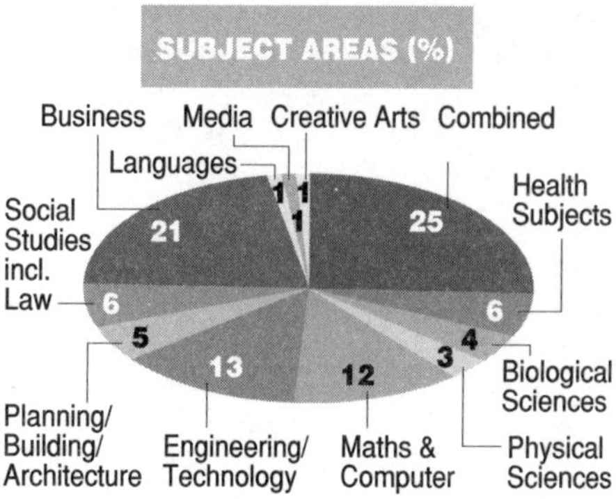

CAMPUS

Writes Laura Cattell: 'Set in the leafy Whiteknights grounds on the outskirts of the town Reading maintains a close campus atmosphere while being only a stone's throw from the bright lights of London. One and a half miles from the town centre the University actually has two campuses – the larger Whiteknights where most undergraduates study and live and then the smaller Bulmershe, a further mile out of the city (home of Education faculty and unlucky Erasmus students who didn't get a place in halls on the main campus).'

FEES, BURSARIES

UK & EU Fees: £3000 p.a. If in receipt of full HE Maintenance grant there's a bursary of £1300; if in receipt of partial grant, bursaries are on a sliding scale from £325 to £1300, according to household earnings. There are also sport and (in designated subjects) academic scholarships available, and pre-application bursaries are available to the disabled.

STUDENT PROFILE

Life is relaxed and sport-orientated at Reading and the majority of students are southern and well-heeled, many of them from public schools. However, there is also a large take from overseas, and an increasing take (24%) from among families new to the idea of university. 'Nevertheless,' says Laura, 'despite the government's widening participation scheme and a huge influx of international students, the uni still retains an upper to middle class/middle England feel.'

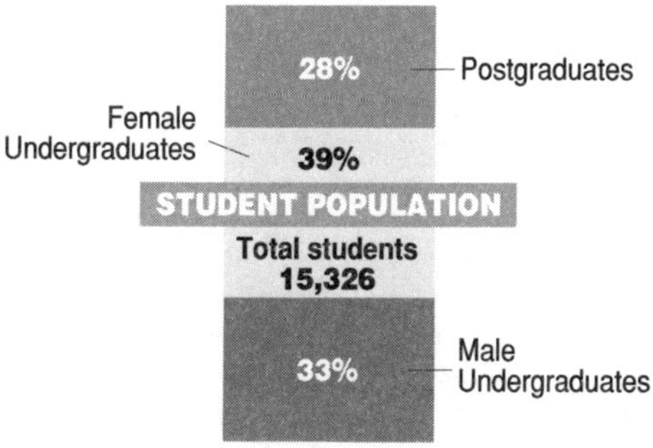

ACADEMIA & JOBS

Reading's reputation may be for agriculture, land management, cybernetics, food and soil sciences, but there's a huge range of arts, humanities, education, languages, and social studies courses, and Education is the single biggest graduate job market at Reading. Still, the sparkling exterior of the ISMA building (Investment Banking, International Security, and Finance) and the hi-tech Agri Department dominate one's image of the place.

UNIVERSITY/STUDENT PROFILE	
University since	**1926**
Situation/style	**Campus**
Student population	**15326**
Undergraduates	**10987**
- mature	**16%**
- non EU undergraduates	**14%**
- male/female	**45/55**
- non-traditional student intake	**24%**
-state school sector	**82%, low**
- drop-out rate	**7%**
- undergraduate applications	**Up 8%**

All undergraduates are matched with a personal tutor, a constant for the duration. This can work well as long as you attend some lectures and meet with him/her when you're meant to. Within your undergraduate degree it's possible to take courses in other departments and taking on a free language class (part of the IWLP - Institution-wide Language Programme) is also a good way to supplement your studies and gain a further qualification. You can

ACADEMIC EXCELLENCE

TEACHING:
(Rated Excellent or 17+ out of 24)

Geography, Mechanical Engineering, Environmental Sciences, Geology.	**Excellent**
Drama, Dance & Cinematics, Physics, Philosophy, Nursing, Psychology	**24**
History of Art, Typography, Archaeology	**23**
Sociology, Land & Property Mgt, Town/Country Planning, Food Science, Maths, Politics, Classics	**22**
Economcs, French, Building, Forestry & Agric Sciences, Anatomy, American Studies, Business, Biosciences, Elec/Electron Eng.	**21**
Italian, German	**20**
Linguistics, Art & Design	**19**

RESEARCH:
Top grades 5/5/6**

Psychology, Environmental Sciences, English, Italian, Archaeology	**Grade 6***
Agriculture, Plant Sciences, Food Science, Applied Maths, Electrical and Electronic Eng, Built Environment, Town/Country Planning, Law, Politics, Business, French, Philosophy, Typography, Drama/Dance/Performing Arts	**Grade 5**

also take more free courses in the Library if you feel the need to update your computer skills or learn to use electronic databases more effectively.

They are big providers in accountancy – three degrees, two with Economics (one BSc), the other with Management, and there is great employment strength in both finance and business management.

Five per cent of Reading graduates go into architecture, and more into the construction business. We are talking here about a BSc in Building Construction & Management and one in Construction Management & Surveying that gives you the entire construction process, from brief to architect through design, planning and project completion. The Chartered Institute of Building (CIOB) grants membership after two years experience. Teaching inspection Excellent. Research Grade 5. See also BSc Building Surveying

Electronic Engineering – B/MEng – with Computer Science, Cybernetics, etc ensures a fast flow of graduates into electronics and telecommunications engineering, and if you fancy tinkering with control systems in electronic devices, look at their Cybernetics & Control Engineering (also 4-year MEng) – there's been a lot in the press about this. This year there's a new BSc Systems Engineering and BSc Robotics. Cybernetics also mixes with Computer Science (BSc or MEng). Reading scores highly with employers for software consultancy & supply and in IT consultancy.

Farmers know this as the top-rated research establishment, and very strong on Agricultural Business Management, but also other sorts of management - Rural Resource, Landscape, Habitat & Soil. Also very big in Food Science, with Business, or Food Technology.

Aspiring curators study Zoology, Botany & Zoology for certain careers, and aspiring animal health technicians/nurses take Animal Science. Reading is also among the country's leaders for finding employment for landscape designers, plantsmen, gardeners. BSc Horticulture joins one of the best agric departments in the country with a Grade 5 international rating for research in Agriculture and Plant Sciences. See also the 4-year sandwich BSc

Life is relaxed and sport-orientated at Reading and the majority of students are southern, many of them from public schools.

WHERE READING GRADUATES END UP

Health & Social Work: 8%; Education: 14%; Wholesale Retail: 8%; Manufacturing: 11%; Financial Activities: 9%; Public Administration, Civil Service & Defence: 8%; Hotel/Restaurant: 3%; Transport & Communications (including Telecommunications): 3%; Construction: 1.5%; Agriculture: 2%; Personnel:3.5%; Computer: 5.5%; Business & Management: 4%; Accountancy: 5%; Media (including Film): 1.5%; Legal 1%; Architecture: 5%; Publishing: 2%; Advertising: 1%.

Approximate employed **93%**

WHAT IT'S REALLY LIKE

UNIVERSITY:	
Social Life	★★★★
Campus scene	**Middle class, southern, sporty.**
Student Union services	**Average**
Politics	**Strong internal**
Sport	**55 clubs**
National team position	**31st**
Sport facilities	**Good**
Arts opportunities	**Good, esp. drama**
Student newspaper	**Spark**
Student radio station	**Junction 11**
Student TV station	**RUSU TV**
Nightclub	**3sixty**
Bars	**Mojo's, Bar Breeze, Café Mondial**
Union ents	**6 nights eclectic**
Union societies	**45**
Most active societies	**RUDS - drama**
Parking	**Adequate**
TOWN:	
Entertainment	★★★★
Scene	**Pubs, clubs OK**
Town/gown relations	**Average**
Risk of violence	**Average**
Cost of living	**High**
Student concessions	**Good**
Survival + 2 nights out	**£90 pw**
Part-time work campus/town	**Excellent/good**

Landscape Management. Teaching inspection 21. Research Grade 5.

Geography, Rural Environmental Science, Rural Resource Mgt, Land Mgt – this is all mainstream Reading. This year there's a new BSc Applied Ecology & Conservation. Other useful niches for jobs include cartography – Physical Geography and meteorology. Reading's BSc Meteorology sits alongside one with a year in Oklahoma, and there's a Foundation year opportunity. Meteorology is also to be found in concert with Physics (BSc or 4-year MPhys) and Maths (BSc or MMath).

Physics is a big thing at Reading, one of the five departments that scored full marks at the assessments. There are BSc and 4-year MPhys degrees (like MPhys Physics & the Universe), one with a year in Europe.

Other top scoring assessments include Psychology. There are BA and BSc degrees, pairing with such as Biology, Philosophy, Childhood & Ageing, Mental & Physical Health. Also Drama, which finds its place among Film & Theatre degrees and BA Theatre Arts Education & Deaf Studies, and with Englih, of course, which has a world class Grade 6* for research.

Educational Studies with Art/Music/English to primary level is only part of the story for teachers. Language graduates find jobs as lecturers in further education (French 21 points at assessment, Italian and German 20, Linguistics 19), as do many graduates from the famous Faculty of Letters & Social Sciences with its unique set of arts and social science mixes.

Humanities pack them into libraries and museums as curators, librarians, archivists; archaeologists abound (the dedicated degree leaving few hungry), and publishing is a very popular recourse from Reading. There's also a good track record for musicians. Music comes with languages and with History of Art – practical attainment important.

Library and computer resources are brilliant and there are 200 networked PCs in the main library and several other computer suites, some offering 24-hour access.

There are three main libraries – the main library on Whiteknight's campus, the music library, and Bulmershe library. The first is the largest with longest opening hours although Bulmershe can be a quieter choice to study in if you need to get away from any distractions.

That said there are plenty of big tables and study booths to be found on three floors of the main library. The demand for set texts is served by a short loan system and popular books are loaned out for 4hr/7day loans.

SOCIAL SCENE

STUDENTS' UNION 'The RUSU houses a student advice centre, large shop, off-licence, insurance outlet, student travel agency and three entertainment venues,' writes Laura. 'By day there are plenty of eateries and cafes open to grab a cheap lunch while by night the impressive Union offers up **Mojos**, **Café Mondial** and **3sixty** as watering holes/dance floors. Wednesday and Saturday are the biggest nights at the Union - and the most expensive too. For a majestic £4 the Union offers up cheesy chart music, r&b, retro '70/'80s hits - and all with a few rugby/hockey players covered in snake bite&black thrown in for good measure. A cheaper alternative is Friday night at the refurbished **Breeze Bar** on Bulmershe campus. Before 11pm it's free and vodka shots cost just £1.

'The Union also occasionally attracts big bands such as Kosheen, Goldie Lookin' Chain and Travis, but regularly gets local bands to perform as well.

'The lively music department organises regular choir recitals and concerts. RUMS (Reading University Music Society) has a Choral Society, Gospel Choir and the also the more relaxed University Singers. There's also an orchestra, con-

AT A GLANCE

ACADEMIC FILE:	
Subjects assessed	**41**
Excellent	**81%**
Typical entry requirements	**315 points**
Application acceptance rate	**12%**
Students-staff ratio	**15:1**
First/2:1 degree pass rate	**65%**
ACCOMMODATION FILE:	
Guarantee to freshers	**96%**
Style	**Halls, flats**
Catered	**40%**
En-suite	**40%**
Price range pw	**£52-£121**
City rent pw	**£56-£75**

cert and jazz band, and it's home to the infamous Reading Rock Festival and the WOMAD world music festival, which liven up the town in the summer and offer up volunteer opportunities if you want a chance to see your favourite band for free.

'There is a student newspaper – *The Spark* – and the Union claims a 3000 weekly run, but the quality has slipped over the years. Nevertheless, it is a good opportunity to improve your writing skills and to learn how to use some of the computer software important for journalism today. Junction 11, the student radio station is accessible on campus and in halls though again isn't as popular as it perhaps should be. This Media blindspot isn't exactly due to the inability of the students involved, but more to do with the general mood of apathy within the student body at Reading. Perhaps the new RUSU TV, broadcasting across Union venues, will galvanise students more.

Sport 'Sport is an integral part of life on campus. The sports facilities are excellent and most of the playing fields are on campus so whenever there's a big match there's a great atmosphere and everyone goes along to watch. The Wolfenden Sports Centre has a flashy gym and there are squash courts and several halls where most of the fitness classes and clubs/societies take place. £120 for six months may seem a bit steep at the beginning of term, but it does entitle you to use all facilities in the centre at any time you like and you don't have to pay another penny after that. The team standards are pretty high, especially for women's netball and hockey. But there is also a friendly Intramural programme.

Town 'Reading is set in picturesque countryside and pretty villages such as Sonning or Pangbourne are never far away if you fancy a walk along the river. Reading has bowed to the fashion for making every British town centre look exactly the same. There is the standard riverside development, known as the **Oracle**, full of chain restaurants and High Street stores. Look beyond the main High Street – to places like the Chinese supermarket or the **Global Café**. There are lots of good restaurants, especially Indian ones, but the best ones in town are **La Tasca** (Spanish/tapas style) and **Ninos**. Pubs and clubs-wise there's plenty of choice – **Café Iguana**, **Purple Turtle**, **Mangos** and the **Vodka Revolution** bar being among the best. And of course London and Oxford are only a 25-minute train ride away if you're looking for a bit more excitement.'

PILLOW TALK

60–70% of first years are allocated catered hall accommodation, and if you want to make lectures in your first year, it's no bad idea. The best has to be Whiteknights, but equally fun and popular halls are Wantage, an Oxbridge-style building just off campus, but very close, St Patricks, and, for friendliness, Bridges. A redevelopment of St Georges Hall recently opened - 426 bedrooms, majority en-suite. If you're studying Education or Film & Drama you may be placed in modern Bulmershe halls, where there's a closer, friendlier, if quieter, atmosphere.

GETTING THERE

☛ By road: M4/J11, A33. An express bus service to London leaves from outside the university.
☛ By rail: London Paddington, 0:30; Birmingham, 2:15; Oxford, 0:40; Bristol Parkway, 1:00.
☛ By air: Heathrow and Gatwick.
☛ By coach: London, 1:20; Brighton, 3:45; Exeter, 3-5:00; Leicester, 5:00.

THE ROBERT GORDON UNIVERSITY

The Robert Gordon University
Aberdeen AB10 1FR
TEL 01224 262105
FAX 01224 262185
EMAIL admissions@rgu.ac.uk
WEB www.rgu.ac.uk

Robert Gordon Students' Association
Aberdeen AB10 1JQ
TEL 01224 262262
FAX 01224 262268
EMAIL rgusa@rgu.ac.uk
WEB www.rgunion.co.uk/

VAG VIEW

Robert Gordon is consistently in the UK Top 20 for getting its graduates real, 'graduate track' jobs. It owes its foundation to philanthropist Robert Gordon, from whose estate the Robert Gordon's Hospital was created in 1750, and which developed into a college half a century later. It is also the beneficiary of another Aberdeen entrepreneur, an architect by name of Tom Scott Sutherland, who presented them with the grounds and mansion at which the Scott Sutherland School of Architecture is based, a beautiful site overlooking the River Dee. Another of RGU's constituent parts is the Gray's School of Art, named after Aberdeen engineer John Gray; it was founded in 1885.

CAMPUS

While the Students' Association and uni are based at the Schoolhill site in Aberdeen, 75% of RGU students are now taught at the Garthdee Campus on the south side of the city on the banks of the Dee. Over £60 million has been invested in the development of this campus in the last four years.

FEES, BURSARIES

Fees for English students: £1700 p.a.

STUDENT PROFILE

There is a large state sector intake, many local (though a rapidly growing overseas contingent), many part-timers, a large (38%) intake from families new to university and a relatively high proportion of students (16%) from so-called low participation neighbourhoods. There are also a number of participants in RGU's Virtual Campus courses (for info, visit www.campus. rgu.com).

ACADEMIA & JOBS

The university has three faculties: The Aberdeen Business School, The Faculty of Health & Social Care and The Faculty of Design & Technology.

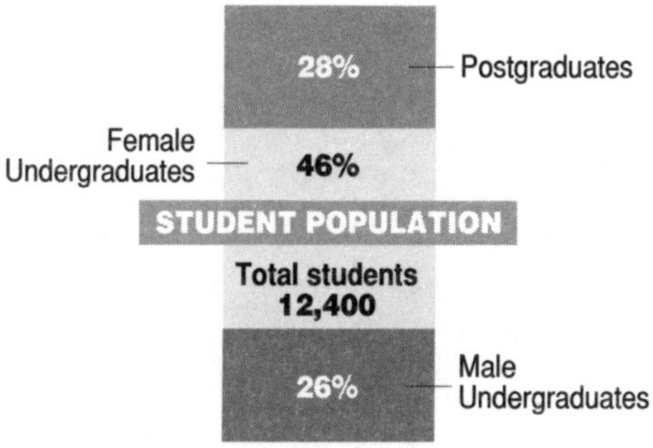

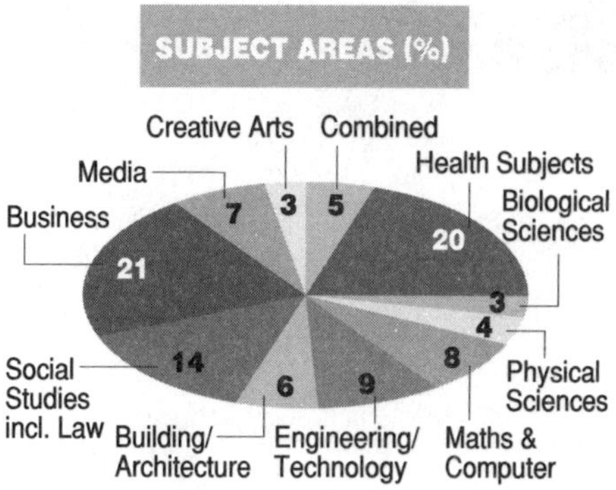

They make their traditional contribution to oil extraction and mining consultancy through Mechanical & Offshore Engineering, Mechanical & Environmental Engineering, etc, but that is no longer their defining area. There's now a major career focus in the area of health – nursing (adult, children, mental) radiography, nutrition, occupational therapy, physiotherapy are among the best from an employment point of view. There is a new, purpose-built Faculty of Health & Social Care building. See also their Biomedical Sciences degrees and the new MPharm Pharmacy; also Forensic Science (there's a traditional fast track into police work); and the BA and MSc (postgrad) Social Work.

UNIVERSITY/STUDENT PROFILE

University since	**1992**
Situation/style	**Civic**
Student population	**12400**
Undergraduates	**8895**
- mature	**18%**
- non EU undergraduates	**3%**
- male/female	**36/64**
- non-traditional student intake	**38%**
state sector intake	**94%**
- drop-out rate	**12%**
- undergraduate applications	**Up 7%**

In the Aberdeen Business School, they have great strength in the tourism and hospitality area – they are regularly No. 1 in Britain as graduate suppliers to the catering industry through dedicated degrees. Also, there's BA Retail Management, which accounts for a strong showing in retail (15% of graduates) and BA Accounting & Finance.

Look, too, at their in-depth strength in Computing – Artificial Intelligence, Electronic Engineering, Robotics, Computing for Graphics &

AT A GLANCE

ACADEMIC FILE:	
Subjects assessed	**21**
Excellent	**57%**
Typical entryl requirements	**295 points**
Application acceptance rate	**25%, high**
Students-staff ratio	**18:1**
First/2:1 degree pass rate	**58%**
ACCOMMODATION FILE:	
Guarantee to freshers	**100%**
Style	**Flats**
Catered	**None**
En-suite	**20%**
Price range pw	**£65-£80**
City rent pw	**£55-£70**

Animation, Computer for Internet, for Mobile Applications, for Business.

And then there's the traditional good showing employment-wise in Built Environment – BSc Architectural Technology, Construction Design, Surveying (Quantity Surveying, a dedicated degree, is a particular strength). Three degrees: BSc Architecture, Architec. (European Practice) and Interior Architecture are recognised by RIBA. See, too, their Design for Industry programme – Digital Media, Graphic, Product Design degrees.

A longterm specialism in Law & Management has now been joined by a fully fledged LLB, recognised by the Law Society of Scotland.

Finally, there is now, too, a Sports Science degree, backed up by a multi-million pound sports and leisure centre at its new Garthdee Campus.

SOCIAL SCENE

Students' Association RGUnion has two bars in the Union building at Schoolhill which provide a wide range of entertainment 7 nights a week. Regular nights include: open mic, *Karaoke Idol*, r&b hip hop, *The Master Chill*, and everyone's disco favourite, *Thursday Night Fever*. The downstairs bar is available for private functions on Tuesdays and Sundays; students have recently used these nights for events such as speed dating and games like *Play Your Cards Right*.

ACADEMIC EXCELLENCE

TEACHING:	
(Rated Excellent, Highly Satis. or 17+ out of 24)	
Chemistry, Dietetics & Nutrition	**Excellent**
Physics, Business & Management, Graphic/Textile Design, Maths & Statistics, Mechanical & Manufacturing Eng, Architecture, Social Work, Pharmacy, Physiotherapy	**Highly Satis.**
European Languages	**19**
RESEARCH:	
*Top grades 5/5**	**None**

WHAT IT'S REALLY LIKE

UNIVERSITY:	
Social Life	★★★
Campus scene	**Part-time, local but increasingly cosmopolitan**
Student Union services	**Poor**
Politics	**Interest low**
Sport	**Relaxed**
National team position	**101st**
Sport facilities	**New centre**
Arts opportunities	**Drama, dance, music good; film, art average**
Student magazine	**Cogno**
Nightclub/bars	**U-bar, Blue Iguana**
Union ents	**7 nights a week**
Union clubs/societies	**39(9 sport)**
Most active society	**Cogno**
Parking	**Adequate**
CITY:	
Entertainment	★★★★
City scene	**Intoxicating**
Town/gown relations	**OK**
Risk of violence	**Low**
Cost of living	**Average**
Student concessions	**Adequate**
Survival + 2 nights out	**£70 pw**
Part-time work campus/town	**Good/excellent**

The whole building is currently being refurbished and now provides a Volunteering Centre to help students gain recognition for unpaid work. The Union actively encourages students to get involved in university life by awarding recognised certificates for their volunteering efforts. A new Marketing and Communications Centre opened in January 2006, with up to date software that'll be used to develop the re-vamped student magazine, which goes by the name of *Cogno*.

Sport The new Sports Centre will revolutionise things. There's hockey, athletics, rugby, rowing, football, archery, badminton, basketball, and of course all those outward bound activities – skiing, hillwalking, etc, naturally available in this area.

PILLOW TALK

Accommodation is thin on the ground, and students' advice is to get in quick. There is a commendable lack of fuss, however, at the uni: 'Everyone who applies for accommodation,' they say, 'is usually allocated accommodation.' It consists of self contained, self-catering flats, six to eight sharing, all with own bedroom, 20% en suite. Price per week ranges from £65 to £80.

GETTING THERE

- ☛ By road: from south, A92, thence ring road for signs; from north, A96 or A92.
- ☛ By coach: London, 11.30; Newcastle, 7.35.
- ☛ By rail: London King's Cross, 7:00; Glasgow, 2:45; Edinburgh, 2:30; Newcastle, 4:30.
- ☛ By air: Aberdeen International Airport.

WHERE ROBERT GORDON GRADUATES END UP

Health & Social Work: 16%; Education: 3.5%; Wholesale Retail: 15%; Manufacturing: 6%; Financial Activities: 4%; Public Administration, Civil Service & Defence: 7%; Hotel/Restaurant: 4%; Transport & Communications (including Telecommunications): 3.5%; Construction: 2%; Mining/Oil Extracting: 18%; Personnel: 1%; Computer: 3%; Business & Management: 1.5%; Accountancy: 4%; Legal 1%; Architecture: 2%; Sport: 1%.

Approximate 'graduate track' employed **70%**

ROEHAMPTON UNIVERSITY

Roehampton University
Erasmus House
Roehampton Lane
London SW15 5PU

TEL 020 8392 3232
EMAIL enquiries@roehampton.ac.uk
WEB www.roehampton.ac.uk

Roehampton Students' Union
Froebel College
Roehampton Lane
London SW15 5PJ

TEL 020 8392 3221
EMAIL info@roehamptonstudent.com
WEB www.roehamptonstudent.com

VAG VIEW

Roehampton University offers vocational courses in the arts, education, social sciences, sciences and sports areas, but with a rather attractive, artistic and caring ethos, which is part and parcel of the place.

Of its four constituent colleges, Digby Stuart College (Arts & Humanities) has a Roman Catholic foundation; Froebel College (Education) follows the teachings of Friedrich Froebel, the caring chappie who invented kindergartens; Southlands College (Social Sciences) has a Methodist base; and Whitelands College (Science) has a Church of England base.

They are not, however, in the business of shoving this down your throat.

It seems but a moment ago that the chief executive of the sometime Roehampton Institute was congratulating his staff for winning the right to award their own research degrees by saying, 'It is the fulfilment of a collective ambition and the penultimate step on the road to university status.' Now, they have that status, the university has fathered its sometime scattered colleges into one campus in south west London, and things are looking very bright indeed.

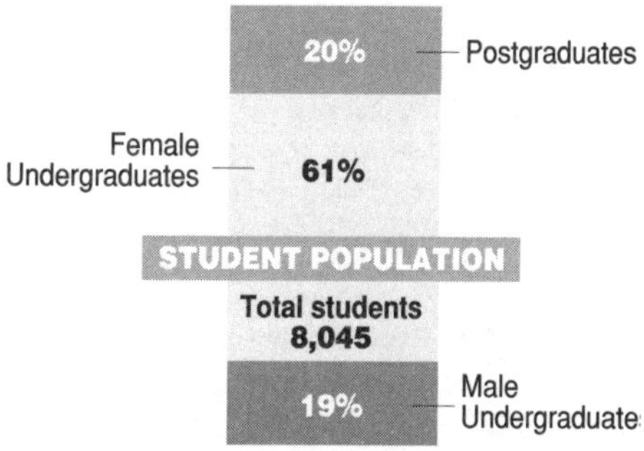

CAMPUS

The uni's four colleges are cosily set together on the edge of Richmond deer park. 'Roehampton

UNIVERSITY/STUDENT PROFILE	
University since	**2004**
Situation/style	**City campus**
Student population	**8045**
Undergraduates	**6450**
- non EU undergraduates	**6%**
- male/female	**24/76**
- non-traditional student intake	**35%**
state school intake	**93%**
- drop-out rate	**10%**
- undergraduate applications	**Down 1%**

combines the best aspects of living in London,' writes Gina Wright. 'I cannot imagine a more perfect site – a peaceful green campus set in landscaped grounds with lakes and trees, yet near enough to buses and tubes to make the journey into central London in about half an hour.'

Digby College has the **Belfry Bar**, a **Learning Resource Centre**, self-catering flats and a warm, welcoming atmosphere. Froebel College is dominated by the imposing, **Georgian Grove House**, its period feel making it popular with students and TV productions such as *Inspector Morse*. It also has the music venue, Montefiore Hall.

Southlands, relocated from Wimbledon in 1997, is clean, modern and the musical pulse of USR, with studios, a Steinway concert grand and a double-manual French harpsichord.

Whitelands founds its way here in 2004, and occupies an 18th-century Palladian mansion, Parkstead House, at the heart of campus.

FEES, BURSARIES

UK & EU Fees: £3000 p.a. If in receipt of the Higher Education Maintenance grant, there's a £300 p.a. bursary. There are also academic achievement scholarships worth £1000.

STUDENT PROFILE

16% of undergraduates are part-time, more than a third come from families for which higher education is a new idea, and 12% from so-called 'low participation' neighbourhoods. Only about 7% come from the independent school sector. The application acceptance rate is necessarily high.

ACADEMIA

Faculties include Arts & Humanities, Education, Sciences, Social Sciences.

When it comes to graduate supply to primary teaching, Roehampton mounts a very strong case. Output: 93% Primary. They are renowned for their Drama and QTS courses and dropped only two points at their assessment (22 out of 24).

The teaching for biosciences is even better – 23 points at the assessments: BSc Biological Sciences, Biological Anthropology, Biomedical Sciences, Biology, Conservation Biology.

The religious background to the constituent colleges comes through in courses for the caring professions, such as healthcare and therapeutic work (and teaching too, under their particular educational regime). Look at the foundation course, Childcare and Early Years Education, and BSc Integrative Counselling, Counselling, Psychology & Counselling, Psychology, Psychology & Health, BA Early Childhood Studies, BSc Health & Social Care, Health Studies, and BA Human Rights.

Dance is outstranding. Their reputation is rated international Grade 5. Besides BA Dance Studies, BA Drama, Theatre & Performance Studies is also rated high, and their music and film courses are very popular. New to media, and much vaunted, is BA Journalism and News Media.

They are also among the leaders in getting jobs for graduates in sport – as players or sport officials. The BSc Sport & Exercise Science is the prototype, a good balance of Physiology, Biomechanics and Psychology.

SOCIAL SCENE

Each of the four campuses has its own bar. Ents are OK. In the week this is being written, Thursday is Bands Night, featuring, for example, Last Gang In Town, Blue Mojo, Dancing Bears at **Belfry Bar**, Digby. Friday, at Froebel, is invariably *The Bop: Heaven or Hell*, or *Vicars and Tarts*, or some other theme. Monday might be comedy at the **Lounge**. Wednesday, Sports Night, is held at **Fez Club**, in nearby Putney. They have things with **Hammersmith Palais**, too. Events, such as fashion shows or the long-running *Roehampton Idol*

ACADEMIC EXCELLENCE	
TEACHING: *(Rated Excellent or 17+ out of 24)*	
English	**Excellent**
Biosciences	**23**
Psychology, English & Linguistics, Education	**22**
Drama, Dance & Cinematics, Hospitality, Religious Studies	**21**
Sociology, Health	**20**
Modern Languages (French, Spanish), Art & Design	**19**
RESEARCH: *Top grades 5/5**	
Drama, Dance & Cinematics	**Grade 5**

WHAT IT'S REALLY LIKE

UNIVERSITY:	
Social Life	★★★
Campus scene	**Diverse, friendly**
Student Union services	**Good**
Politics	**Apathetic**
Sport	**Keen**
National team position	**106th**
Sport facilities	**Poor**
Arts opportunities	**Very good**
Student newspaper	**Fresh**
Venue	**Monte Hall, RSU Lounge, Belfry Bar**
Bars	**College bars**
Union ents	**Chav Night, Heaven or Hell + live bands**
Union clubs/societies	**25**
Parking	**Poor (permit)**
CITY:	
Entertainment	★★★★★
Scene	**Wild, expensive**
Town/gown relations	**Average-good**
Risk of violence	**High**
Cost of living	**Very high**
Student concessions	**Abundant**
Survival + 2 nights out	**£100 pw**
Part-time work campus/town	**Excellent**

AT A GLANCE

ACADEMIC FILE:	
Subjects assessed	**16**
Excellent	**69%**
Typical entry requirements	**225 points**
Application acceptance rate	**25%, high**
Students-staff ratio	**20:1**
First/2:1 degree pass rate	**51%**
ACCOMMODATION FILE:	
Guarantee to freshers	**60%**
Style	**Halls, houses**
Catered	**13%**
Price range p.w.	**£85-£105**
City rent pw	**£100-£180 Zone 1; £75-£85 Zone 2**

might be held at **Monte Hall**. There are also balls, the year culminating in the infamous, extravagant Summer Ball. Froebel boasts the second largest ball after Oxford and Cambridge.

Societies tend to be transient. Large and long-standing socs are RIACAS, which promotes Afro-Caribbean and Asian culture, and top soc. Open Mic. There's a monthly newspaper, *Fresh*, and other societies spin off undergraduate courses.

Writes Gina: 'I enjoy the many reasonably priced concerts promoted by the active Dance Department. A series of open events in the outstanding **Michaelis Theatre** attracts audiences from both inside and outside the university. Students are given every opportunity to perform their own works, view professional companies and share the results of collaborating with well known dance companies.'

SPORT Roehampton competes in the BUSA leagues, and a local rivalry with Kingston Uni adds spice to the rugby especially. Also popular are tennis, football and rowing on the Thames. Each college has its own teams, and the football battles between the Digby Lions and their 'natural prey', the Froebel Zebras, are legendary.

PILLOW TALK

Two new student residences opened in 2004, which took the promise of accommodation for freshers up from 60% by about 20 points. There's a mix of catered and self-catered. Each college's halls of residence have basic utility rooms. There are also coffee and snack bars, Students' Union facilities and shops. All Colleges cater for vegetarians. There are some en-suite ground floor rooms for students with disabilities. They allocate rooms on a 'first come, first served basis', so get there fast.

GETTING THERE

☛ US Roehampton, Barnes British Rail station or No. 72 bus from Hammersmith Underground; No. 265 runs from Putney Bridge.

☛ Whitelands College, East Putney or Southfields Underground or Clapham Junction British Rail and No. 170 bus

ROYAL ACADEMY OF MUSIC

The Royal Academy of Music
Marylebone Road
London NW1 5HT

TEL 020 7873 7373
FAX 020 7873 7374
EMAIL registry@ram.ac.uk
WEB www.ram.ac.uk

A collaboration between the Royal Academy and King's College, both of London University, is what distinguishes the BMus degree. Academy musicians benefit academically by attending lectures at KCL, King's undergraduates from the performance culture at the Royal Academy. There is a diverse student mix, with 40+ countries represented. London University halls of residence are available.

ROYAL AGRICULTURAL COLLEGE

The Royal Agricultural College
Cirencester
Gloucestershire GL7 6JS

TEL 01285 652912
FAX 01285 650219
EMAIL admissions@rac.ac.uk
WEB www.rac.ac.uk

The college runs the largest agri-student European exchange programme in the country, and it's the principal's boast that there's 'hardly a major farming/business or land-management employer in the UK and beyond that who doesn't have a former RAC student in a decision-making position.'

Accommodation is guaranteed for first years. There is a bar, a union, and sport is big news.

ROYAL COLLEGE OF MUSIC

The Royal College of Music
Prince Consort Road
London SW7 2BS

TEL 020 7589 3643
FAX 020 7589 7740
EMAIL info@rcm.ac.uk
WEB www.rcm.ac.uk

The famed 4-year BMus is joined by BSc Hons Physics with Studies in Musical Performance, an exciting cross-faculty joint venture with world-class Imperial College nearby. Halls accommodation is available. A Student Association promotes ents. Students use Imperial's local Sports Centre.

ROYAL HOLLOWAY, LONDON UNIVERSITY

Royal Holloway College
Egham
Surrey TW20 0EX

TEL 01784 434455
FAX 01784 473662
EMAIL liaison-office@rhbnc.ac.uk
WEB www.rhul.ac.uk

Royal Holloway Students' Union
Egham
Egham TW20 0EX

TEL 01784 486300
FAX 01784 486312
EMAIL reception@su.rhul.ac.uk
WEB www.surhul.org.uk

VAG VIEW

Royal Holloway, a college of London University, is situated on a 120-acre campus at Egham in Surrey, far enough to the south west of London's bright lights to favour a well-focused regime. Students almost uniformly mention the workload, although there is a lively campus social scene too. The regime is very productive: there's a 12:1 student: staff ratio and 65% of students obtain firsts or upper second class degrees.

CAMPUS

'Holloway, isn't that a women's prison?' iterates Sarah Toms with a sigh which suggests she has heard the jibe many times before. 'It is of course, but not here, it's in South London! You'll get used to that question. This is *Royal* Holloway, University of London – yes, the one with THAT building (Founders Hall). Located a train ride from central London – forty minutes on a good day, barring leaves on the line or the wrong kind of snow.'

It has been called 'London's Country Campus', and it is certainly a beautiful spot, made distinctive by Founder's Building, a copy of the Chateau de

UNIVERSITY/STUDENT PROFILE	
School of London Uni since	**1800**
Situation/style	**Campus**
Total student population	**7600**
Undergraduates	**5670**
- mature	**11%**
- non EU undergraduates	**13%**
- male/female	**40/60**
- non-traditional student intake	**23%**
- state school intake	**78%, low**
- drop-out rate	**5%**
- undergraduate applications	**Up 9%**

Chambourd in the Loire built by Thomas Holloway, who in 1886 founded a college for women there. Nearly a century later it merged with another all-female foundation, Bedford College, creating Royal Holloway and Bedford New College. You may be interested to know that there is still a preponderance of females here today.

FEES, BURSARIES

UK & EU Fees: £3000 p.a. If in receipt of HE Maintenance grant there's a bursary of £500. There are also scholarships for academic achievment.

STUDENT PROFILE

The student body is small, little more than a third the size of King's College or University College, London. Public school intake is high, as it is from overseas (the relatively new African-Caribbean society is among the strongest in the union). They're a very happy crew: only 5% don't finish.

ACADEMIA & JOBS

University of London degrees are offered in biological and physical sciences, maths, computer science, humanities, languages, arts, social sciences and management. Their success in the teaching assessments include full marks for Psychology and Biosciences, 23 points out of 24 for Drama, Physics and Classics, 22 for Maths, and 21 for languages, Sociology, and Business.

It's a well balanced mix, more so when you see that they have developed a course unit method study that allows groupings of subjects across an often imaginative spectrum. For example, Latin is offered as a BA single hons, but also with English (a tantalising prospect for students of syntax and etymology). The English department has a national reputation for research. The Creative Writing course has benefited from the attentions of poet laureate Andrew Motion.

Languages are clearly another strength. French and German were rated world class at the research assessments. The International Building incorporates the English, French, German, Hispanic and Italian departments, a dedicated Japanese Studies section (including the Noh theatre – donated by the Japanese government), and a stylish café. Languages and European Studies, Literature, Culture are frequent course elements.

The Drama & Media Arts provision (which took an international Grade 5 for research) lands graduates real jobs in such as publishing, radio, TV, film, advertising and market research. Music also has a world-class reputation (Grade 6* for research; there's a link with the Royal College of Music) and can be studied as a single hons or with Maths or BA Psychology, or taken with a year abroad, a language thrown in.

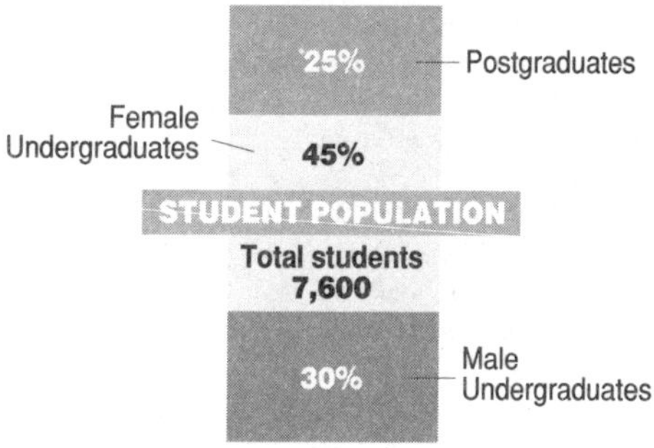

The preponderance of humanities, languages and arts degrees can make the immediate graduate employment picture look a bit bleak for some: we find a preponderance of secretaries alongside the more targeted occcupations: local government administrators, researchers, personnel officers, librarians, actors, stage managers, etc. They sit 69th in the 'graduate track' employment table.

One professional carrer area is noticably well served. Accountants proliferate. The number of independent school applicants and strength of Maths, Management (note BSc Management with

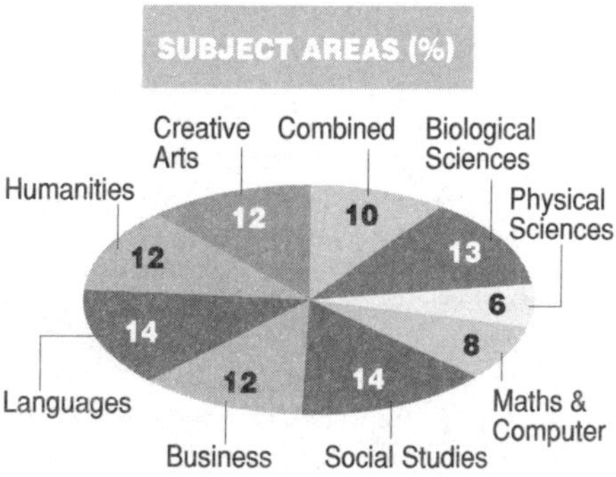

ACADEMIC EXCELLENCE

TEACHING:
(Rated Excellent or 17+ out of 24)

History, Geology,	**Excellent**
Psychology, Organismal Biosciences	**24**
Drama, Theatre & Media Arts, Physics, Classics	**23**
Maths	**22**
French, Italian, Sociology, Molecular Biosciences, Business	**21**
German	**19**

RESEARCH:
Top grades 5/5/6**

Geography, French, Music	**Grade 6***
German/Dutch/Scandinavian	**Grade 5***
Drama/Dance/Performing Arts, History, Classics, English, Computer, Pure Maths, Earth Sciences, Biology, Physics, Psychology	**Grade 5**

Accounting) and Economics help to ensure this.

Management also hooks up with Marketing (some 2% of graduates find jobs in this sector), with Human Resources (another strong take-up for jobs), and with Information Systems and Technology & Operations. While the Computer Science facility produces numbers of software engineers, computer analysts/programmers, systems analysts, IT consultants, etc.

Science looks to be the new way forward here, with interesting developments in biological science – a degree in Molecular Biology & Genetics recently. And the 23/24 teaching rating (and Grade 5 for research) for Physics is leading to a new BSc degree in Astrophysics and another in Physics with Particle Physics, which already figures in a fine list of MSci degrees.

Geography is another science with a world class reputation here (Grade 6* for research).

That science is now a main current of academic policy here is confirmed in their offering a science foundation course to partner colleges in the region.

The student body is small; public school intake is high, as it is from overseas. They're a happy crew: only 5% don't finish.

SOCIAL SCENE

Students' Union The college is largely self-sufficient and most students spend their social hours on site, rather than succumbing to the distant twinkling lights of London. Frankly, the hour-long hike to the capital is seen as a hassle by most, as the last train back is at 11:30 pm, with no more links until 6 am the next day.

In contrast to the friendly, welcoming campus, the nearest town, Egham, remains aloof, a cultural and social pit of suburban blandness.

To compensate for the paucity of local entertainment, the SU serves up a social calendar of unprecedented fullness for an establishment of this size.

Every night is an ents night of some description, ranging from the usual pub quizzes on quiet Sundays to the late bars and DJs which dominate weekends and have a significant foothold in the working week as well.

There's a late licence five nights a week, main hall functions two to three times a week, bar ents every other night. How many unions boast two resident DJs poached from the brighter lights of London? Both Brandon Block and DJ Swing are employed to keep the body student moving, and the latter has been known to hurl the crispest of currency into the crowd too, enhancing popularity and drinks consumption in equal measure. Imported additions include Ministry of Sound, A1, Trevor Nelson, Apollo 440.

Tommy's is the newest bar in the union, and the most popular haunt of the socialites. Only Tuesday and Sunday see it shut before midnight, so the quiet beer with a friend at nine has a sneaky habit of turning into eight loud beers with a roomful of pissheads by kicking out time.

The **Dive Bar**, attached to Tommy's, isn't as seedy as it sounds, and offers a cosier venue. The **Union Bar** is a pretty standard affair, and it is these three which combine to hold 1200 for the big function nights – it has its own in-house technical crew.

Also on campus is the strangely named **Stumble Inn** ('Stumble Out' would surely have been more appropriate), a pub to all intents and a popular one at that, ideal for those nights when aggravating your tinnitus shies you from Tommy's.

Holloway's Bar houses sixteen pool tables, dart boards and a host of ever-changing video games, a free Playstation for the deprived, and live sports courtesy of the ubiquitous Sky TV.

There is also the coffee bar, **TW20's**, a food and caffeine establishment that, according to some, is lamentable, but being dirt cheap and on campus attracts students like flies around the proverbial.

Every June they run a Summer Ball in the quads of Founders: 2000 tickets are sold in

WHERE ROYAL HOLLOWAY GRADUATES END UP

Health & Social Work: 7%; Education: 8%; Wholesale Retail: 14%; Manufacturing: 9%; Financial Activities: 12%; Public Administration, Civil Service & Defence: 8%; Hotel/Restaurant: 3%; Transport & Communications (including Telecommunications): 4%; Personnel: 6%; Computer: 4%; Business & Management: 5%; Accountancy: 4%; Media (including Film): 3%; Legal 2%; Publishing: 3%; Advertising: 1%.

Approximate 'graduate track' employed **60%**

exchange for big name acts, cocktail bar, Champagne bar, Glastonbury stage, dance tent, fairground rides, hog roast – it runs from 7 until 7 all through the night.

Media, drama and entertainments in general, are of a high standard. The Musical Theatre Society goes to the Edinburgh Fringe. The radio station, Insanity, wins national awards – this year it was nominated for awards three times and won two, and the student mag, *Orbital*, has featured too. Politics are not so much of a preoccupation.

SPORT The college has a reputation as the best sporting college in London University, and it does well in inter-LU leagues, though it languished at 70th position nationally last year.

A new sports complex has lifted it above its neighbours. Cricket, women's football have bossed the London indoor leagues for three years, and men's rugby supplies players to senior sides, such as Harlequins and London Welsh.

TOWN 'Sadly, the surrounding area, quaint little Egham, with as many useful shops as you are likely to see students at a nine o'clock lecture, fails to happen,' Sarah Toms reports, 'though it does have three supermarkets, a covey of takeaways, a bevy of student-friendly pubs, and **The Staines Massive**, which boasts not only a cinema, but wait for it... a *nightclub*! Those for whom the excitement proves too much, worry not. Royal Holloway is positioned a train ride away from the capital – deliberately, strategically even, to enable you to enjoy London life without paying a high price.

'Sure, the prices locally are higher than average, but not too damaging, and there is the advantage of the London loan rate and that both campus and surrounding area are fairly safe.

PILLOW TALK

'On the one hand, there is Founders Hall,' writes Sarah. 'Its rooms are fairly large and filled with an odd assortment of furniture from across the centuries. On the other, we have New Halls, built in the 1950s by an architect who won a prize for designing a Swedish prison! Affectionately known as 'Cell Block H', the rooms are, let us say, cosy...'

New Halls – Athlone, Cameron and Williamson – are catered and come with common rooms, bar, snack bar (**Times Square**), and a good community spirit. Founder's comes with common rooms, TV rooms, bar/snack bar (**Crossland Suite**); it's hard to get a room here. Reid Hall, near New Halls, is

WHAT IT'S REALLY LIKE

UNIVERSITY:	
Social Life	★★★★
Campus scene	**Active, friendly, artistic, female**
Student Union services	**Good**
Politics	**Big right now**
Sport	**36 clubs**
National team position	**70th**
Sport facilities	**Good**
Arts opportunities	**Drama excellent; music, film good; dance, art avg**
Student magazine	**The Orbital**
Student radio	**Insanity**
2005 National Awards	**3 nominations; 2 awards**
Nightclub	**Union +Tommy's**
Bars	**Union, Tommy's, Stumble Inn, Holloway's, Dive**
Union ents	**Cheese, Spaced, Orgasmatron, etc**
Union clubs/societies	**99**
Most popular society	**James Bond Appreciation Soc**
Smoking policy	**No smoking**
Parking	**Adequate**
CITY:	
Entertainment	★
Scene	**Good pubs, but London beckons**
Town/gown relations	**Good**
Risk of violence	**Low**
Cost of living	**High**
Student concessions	**Average**
Survival + 2 nights out	**£40 pw**
Part-time work campus/town	**Good/poor**

catered with en-suite rooms. Runnymede is self-catered, flat-style around a central kitchen/social area, en-suite.

Three halls - Beeches, Chestnuts, Elm Lodge - are converted Victorian houses, catered but with small kitchen/pantries and laundries. Kingswood is catered, off campus (but less than a mile away and with a free bus service to campus during the day) and has rooms and flatlets on a hillside overlooking the Thames at Runnymede with squash and tennis courts, TV/common room, tapas bar and dining room.

GETTING THERE

- By road: M25/J13, A30.
- By rail: London Waterloo, 35 mins; Reading, 40.

AT A GLANCE

ACADEMIC FILE:	
Subjects assessed	**19**
Excellent	**74%**
Typical entry requirements	**345 points**
Application acceptance rate	**20%, high**
Students-staff ratio	**12:1, low**
First/2:1 degree pass rate	**65%**
ACCOMMODATION FILE:	
Guarantee to freshers	**100%**
Style	**Halls, flats, houses**
Catered	**46%**
Approx price range pw	**£51-£95**
Average local rent pw	**£75**

ROYAL SCOTTISH ACADEMY OF MUSIC & DRAMA

Royal Scottish Academy of Music & Drama
100 Renfrew Street
Glasgow G2 3DB

TEL 0141 332 4101
FAX 0141 332 8901
EMAIL registry@rsamd.ac.uk
WEB www.rsamd.ac.uk

RSAMD is the only school for music and drama in Scotland. The curriculum explores Scottish music, in particular piping, as well as opera, composition and conducting. In theatre, there are degrees in Technical & Production Arts, Digital Film & TV, and a Master of Performance in Musical Theatre.

Accommodation is available in halls. See Glasgow universities and Student City entries.

ROYAL WELSH COLLEGE OF MUSIC & DRAMA

The Royal Welsh College of Music & Drama
Cathays Park
Cardiff CF1 3ER

TEL 029 2034 2854
FAX 029 2039 1304
EMAIL info@rwcmd.ac.uk
WEB www.rwcmd.ac.uk

Music teaching involves the Welsh National Opera and the BBC National Orchestra of Wales. Performance is central; every student has a personal tutor. The Grade 2 listed Castle Mews next to the Welsh conservatoire opened as the Anthony Hopkins Centre a year ago, providing new teaching, rehearsal and performance facilities.

No college accommodation available.

ROYAL VETERINARY COLLEGE

The Royal Veterinary College
Royal College Street
London NW1 0TU

TEL 020 7468 5148/9
FAX 020 7468 2342
EMAIL registry@rvc.ac.uk
WEB www.rvc.ac.uk

The RVC is a specialist college of London University that achieved full marks in the teaching assessments. All candidates must sit the Biomedical Admissions Test (BMAT) to assess scientific aptitude. The undergraduate programme includes Batchelor of Veterinary Medicine, BSc (Hons) Veterinary Pathology, BSc (Hons) Veterinary Sciences, BSc (Hons) Veterinary Nursing, BSc Intercalated courses, BSc (Hons)/BVet Med Combined Degree Programme. They excel, too, at extra-curricular activities, especially in Women's Rugby.

Your first two years are based in Camden, a fun place with its outdoor market, some very good pubs and well placed for city nightlife. Accommodation is in London University intercollegiate halls (see Introduction). In Year 3 it's off to 230-hectare Hawkshead campus, Potters Baaa, with its new Learning Resource Centre and Diagnostic Imaging Unit with the first uni-based CT scanner.

UNIVERSITY OF ST ANDREWS

The University of St Andrews
Old Union Building
St Andrews
Fife KY16 9AJ

TEL 01334 462150
FAX 01334 463388
EMAIL admissions@st-andrews.ac.uk
WEB st-andrews.ac.uk

St Andrews Students' Association
St Mary's Place
St Andrews
Fife KY16 9UZ

TEL 01334 462700/1
FAX 01334 462740
EMAIL pres@st-andrews.ac.uk
WEB www.yourunion.net

VAG VIEW

St Andrews has a very old foundation (1410) and appeals almost as much to English students as to Scots as an alternative to Oxbridge. It is a small, very traditional university, set in an out-of-the-way seaside place known for its golf.

Jargon is as prevalent here as in the great Imperial days of the public school system, whence many of its students come. Some of its practices earmarked as traditions are in fact only a few years old, so the tradition of being traditional is not about to change.

The appearance of a future King of England on the list of undergraduates was, therefore, no great surprise. Prince William's arrival brought a 45% increase in undergraduate applications, but it was useful publicity: applications were up again last time.

Within its rather tight academic straightjacket, one of St Andrews' great attractions is the student/staff ratio, 10:1 (third best in Britain). There's a 78% chance of a first or 2:1.

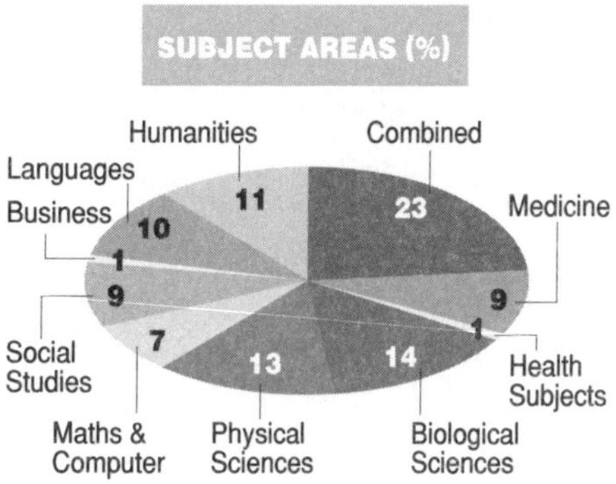

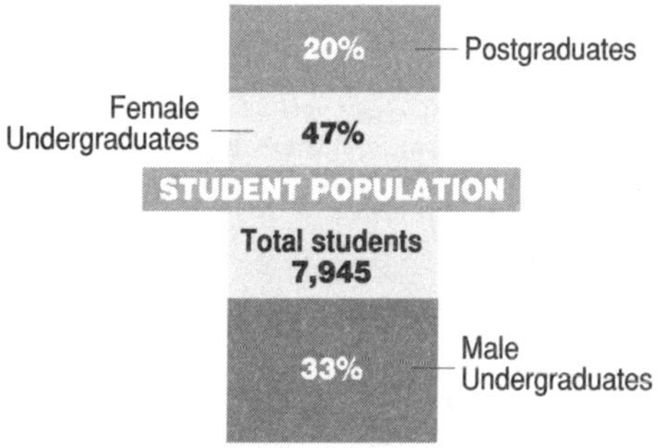

CAMPUS

St Andrews is out on its own, a small seaside town in the northeast of Scotland, surrounded by open countryside and sea, twelve miles from Dundee and around fifty from Edinburgh.

FEES, BURSARIES

Fees for English students: £1700 p.a. (Medicine: £2700). Confirm fees and bursaries on web site.

STUDENT PROFILE

The student body is dominated by public school types, but there's also an unexpectedly high intake from countries beyond the EU (almost a fifth of undergraduates). For a Scottish university there is also a surprisingly large percentage of English students (around 40%), and, having a fine, traditional reputation, it attracts those who failed to get into Oxbridge, though quite a few do make St Andrews their first choice.

Above all, it is a friendly community. 'You can almost guarantee that every time you leave your front door, you'll see someone you know,' writes Melanie Hartley. 'When you've just crawled out of bed for a 9 am tutorial and you've only had four hours sleep, it's debatable whether that's a good thing or not! But St Andrews is a pretty close-knit society. Indeed, once people get here they don't tend to leave. They'll even tell you that one in three graduates end up marrying other St Andrews graduates!'

UNIVERSITY/STUDENT PROFILE

University since	**1410**
Situation/style	**Town campus & sites**
Student population	**7945**
Undergraduates	**66340**
- mature	**9%**
- non EU undergraduate	**19%, high**
- male/female	**41/59**
- non-traditional student intake	**18%**
- state school intake	**65% low**
- drop-out rate	**7%, low**
- undergraduate applications	**Up 16%**

ACADEMIC EXCELLENCE

TEACHING:
(Rated Excellent, Highly Satis. or 17+ out of 24)

Physics, Chemistry, Economics, Geography, Maths & Statistics, History, Cellular & Molecular Biology, Organismal Biology Psychology.	**Excellent**
Computer Studies, Business & Management, Geology, History of Art, Philosophy, Theology, English, Medicine.	**Highly Satis.**
European Languages	**22**

RESEARCH :
*Top grades 5/5**

Psychology, English	**Grade 5***
Chemistry. Biological Sciences, Physics, Pure Maths, Applied Maths, Statistics, Computer, Anthropology, Politics, Iberian/ Latin American, Classics, History, History of Art, Philosophy, Theology	**Grade 5**

ACADEMIA & JOBS

When we look at graduate careers, we find an emphasis on analysis, management science and interpersonal skills, which St Andrew's clearly teaches well in whatever subject form.

When we look at graduate careers, we find an emphasis on analysis, management science, interpersonal skills, which St Andrew's clearly teaches well in whatever subject form.

But this is a small uni, with nearly a fifth of graduates on humanities degrees and another fifth on combined subject degrees, many of them involving languages and humanities, and one fears that job hunting, for some at least, might be a lottery.

Do subjects like Mediaeval History, Hebrew, Biblical Studies, Classical Studies, Art History and the like find their graduates jobs, however well taught? After six months a tidy number of St Andrews graduates appear in the statistics as secretaries, sales assistants, clerks, bar staff and receptionists. However, their showing in the 'graduate track' employment chart (26th) shows that in time graduates find their feet.

Originally, the more vocational degrees were based in Dundee and became the curriculum of Dundee University, when the split came in the 1960s. Recently, the two have moved closer again with the launch of a joint degree in engineering – Microelectronics & Photonics (there had already been a parlay through their pairing of Art History with Dundee's excellent school of Art & Design). But there is evidence, too, that this very traditional university somehow gets behind the new-uni 'how-to' ethos into a kind of 'can-do', that in their hands the business of university is, as it was originally meant to be, a training of the mind per se, that far from being out-of-date, they are moving forward with insight. They show this not least in their inspired cross-faculty strategy.

WHERE ST ANDREWS GRADUATES END UP

Health & Social Work: 8%; Education: 14%; Wholesale Retail: 8%; Manufacturing: 7%; Financial Activities: 16%; Public Administration, Civil Service & Defence: 9%; Hotel/Restaurant: 4%; Transport & Communications (including Telecommunications): 2.5%; Computer: 2%; Business & Management: 6%; Accountancy: 6%; Media (including Film): 2%; Legal 2%; Artistic/Literary: 2%; Sport: 1%.

Approximate 'graduate track' employed **69%**

Besides an increasing range of sciences with language degrees, there are some tantalising combinations such as Arabic-International Relations, Classics-Integrated Information Technology, Hebrew-Mathematics, and Economics-Social Anthropology. There is even the ultimate cross-faculty mesh – Integrated Information Technology and Theological Studies, which if not exactly offering a fast-track to the meaning of life, suggests a challenging examination of the traditional tensions between science and humanities.

End result is a sound training for whatever you do, and a good record for jobs that do not require specific training at degree level – journalists and editors abound, for instance.

Elsewhere on the list, education and financial activities are to the fore. Instructors and secondary school teachers come from here in great number, the languages and humanities provision serving them well. For finance, Financial Economics MA Hons points the way. MA Management is also a popular route. Economics, Financial Economics, Economics in combination with Russian (and including a year there), International Relations, Euro languages, Management, Mathematics, etc, sustain a reputation in the job market for chartered, certified and management accountants, investment advisers/ analysts, merchant bankers and business analysts. There's a top – Excellent – rating for Economics.

The medical degree asks ABB including Chemistry + Physics or Maths; GCSE grades A*, A or B.. There's a good chance of getting in – the application acceptance rate was 22% in 2004, 11% better than average. And there's also a good vocational reputation for psychologists and care assistants, BSc Psychology providing the harder edge to what is offered in the MA joint hons system, where a good combo may be had with, say, Social Anthropology. Look also at Physiology, Neuroscience, Medicinal Science, Medicinal Chemistry.

There is also a fair number of graduates getting jobs as software engineers, IT consultants, computer programmers, which shows that where they do go for a vocational dimension they can get it right. Computer Science comes with languages, Maths, Linguistics, Philosophy, Management, Physics, or Statistics. A new computer building opened in 2004.

Finally there's traditionally a close relationship with the army, and a big take-up in the civil service and defence.

A Learning and Teaching Support Unit (LTSU) works closely with the academic schools to co-ordinate and advise.

SOCIAL SCENE

STUDENTS' ASSOCIATION The student population makes up a large proportion of the town and the social life is created by students. Location denies them any big bands at the union.

Reports Melanie: 'There is no club as such; the union doubles up as a venue (**Venue 1** and **Venue 2**: 1,000 capacity), hosting events all through the week. Every Friday is the *bop* – a cheesy night [*Red Not Bed*], very reminiscent of your old school discos, but a particularly revered part of student life. **Venue 2** hosts a range of different nights; *Rock-soc*, *Bulletproof* (alternative music) and *Jazz-soc* are regulars.' Saturday clubnights include *Squeeze* ('80s), *Explosion* (R&B), *Ebenezer* ('90s) or *Retro*.

'Pre-Sessional week – known as Freshers Week everywhere else – is non-stop events, including some biggish acts: recent weeks have hosted Space, Toploader and Euphoria. There are lots of 2nd, 3rd and 4th years willing to make friends – (some a bit too willing!) – and to show you around. Some will become your academic parents, a tradition that involves a weekend of parties with them, some time in November, before you get dressed up – many wittily/ridiculously as as bottles of wine, Care Bears or condoms – and are frogmarched to the Quad on the Monday morning for a huge shaving foam fight. So fondly do many look back on their *Raisin* experience that they try to recreate it every year. [It can in fact degenerate into a mass piss-up and/or an excuse to pull: "Remember not to be forced into anything ..." warns the SA's *Alternative Prospectus*.]

'Student life is very much centred around the pubs. There are reputed to be more pubs per square mile than in any other university town, which means you're never stuck for choice: **Broons** or **Bridges** if you want to hang with the yahs, **Ogstons** or **The Raisin** if you want large and loud, **Drouthy Neebors** or **The Cellar** if you're into Real Ale. Such is the pace of life that by the time you've been here a fortnight, you should have an encyclopaedic knowledge of what's available, and your weekly "happy hour'" schedule will be sorted!

'There are lots of ways in which this is a relatively cheap place to live, not least because it's small, though in fact taxis do a healthy business with flat fares anywhere in the town.

'For entertainment other than pubs, most students look to student societies. Everybody is a member of at least one, and most people more. Options range from academic to music to political. The International Politics society recently had Michael Douglas to talk on behalf of the United Nations. You might prefer the Tunnocks Caramel Wafer Appreciation society or Quaich (whisky appreciation). You could also get involved with *The Saint* (student newspaper), which often wins awards, or the new radio station: Star FM.'

The Union also has one of the oldest debating societies in the world, and drama is an active aspect of student life. Each year Mermaids, a sub-committee of the Students' Association, gives financial assistance to several productions, some of which go to the Edinburgh Festival.

Part-time work opportunities are poor, but, 'if you're looking for a bit of extra cash, the Dunhill Cup creates the possibility of a job washing up or directing traffic for the weekend,' Melanie reports. 'The attitude of most students is that term time isn't for working, but there are occasional jobs behind bars. Most of the shops, however, seem to favour 16-year-old Madras College kids over us students when it comes to weekend work.'

AT A GLANCE

ACADEMIC FILE:	
Subjects assessed	**18**
Excellent	**100%**
Typical entry requirements	**415 points**
Application acceptance rate	**17%**
Students-staff ratio	**10:1**
First/2:1 degree pass rate	**78%**
ACCOMMODATION FILE:	
Guarantee to freshers	**If single and apply before 31.5**
Style	**Halls**
Catered	**55%**
En-suite	**19%**
Price range pw	**£45-£127**
City rent pw	**£60-£100**

WHAT'S ITS REALLY LIKE

UNIVERSITY:	
Social Life	★★★
Campus scene	**Conservative, traditional, uni by the sea**
Student Union services	**Good**
Politics	**Student issues; activity high**
Sport	**50 clubs**
National team position	**36th**
Sport facilities	**Excellent**
Arts opportunities	**Drama excellent; performing arts all very popular**
Student magazine	**The Vine**
Student newspaper	**The Saint**
Student radio	**Star FM**
Nightclub	**Venue 1**
Bars	**Main Bar, Venue 2**
Union ents	**Disco dance, retro, live acts massive & refined**
Union clubs/societies	**130**
Most popular society	**Breakaway (outdoor pursuits), Debating**
Parking	**Adequate**
TOWN:	
Entertainment	★★
Scene	**Pubs, coffee houses**
Town/gown relations	**Average**
Risk of violence	**Low**
Cost of living	**High**
Student concessions	**Average**
Survival + 2 nights out	**£100 pw**
Part-time work campus/town	**Poor**

SPORT Golfers' paradise – the student team is one of the best in Britain. 'If this isn't your thing,' says Melanie, 'you still get to see the likes of Hugh Grant and Samuel L. Jackson strutting their stuff around town at the Dunhill Cup every October.'

In the national team championships they came 33rd last year. There's a sports centre with sports hall, gym, activities room, weight training room, squash courts, solarium. Extensive playing fields, jogging and trim tracks. Golf bursaries are funded by the Royal and Ancient Golf Club.

PILLOW TALK

'Most of the halls are in the centre of town, and are steeped in traditions,' writes Melanie. 'Most first years procure an undergraduate gown soon after arrival – a tasteful red fleece type-thing and a bit pricey. Although it varies from hall to hall, there will be occasions throughout the year when you can wear these – hall dinners, photographs, chapel. Most of the halls are catered, and the food is pretty reasonable, although you'd be well advised to avoid the universally acclaimed lemon "toilet duck" mousse. Self-catering accommodation can be found in Albany Park and in Fife Park, which provide some of the most economical student accommodation in the country. "Simplistic" isn't the word for these flats, but they're cheap.'

Around half St Andrews students live in halls or other uni-owned accommodation – 55% of it catered, 19% of it en suite. Freshers are almost automatically given a place, but you must apply for it by May 31 in the year of entry. From then on there is no guarantee and the hunt for flats, particularly near the centre of town, can begin around the middle of January. Accommodation is quite expensive for such a small town – £60+ per week – largely because students make up a high proportion of the population.

GETTING THERE

☛ By road: Forth Road Bridge, M90/J3, A92 to Kirkcaldy, A915 to St Andrews; or M90/J8, A91.
☛ By rail: Nearest station on main line London (King's Cross) – Edinburgh – Aberdeen line is Leuchars (5 miles). Then bus or taxi.
☛ By air: Edinburgh Airport, airport bus to Edinburgh, thence by rail.

ST GEORGE'S, UNIVERSITY OF LONDON

St George's, University of London
Cranmer Terrace
Tooting
London SW17 0RE

TEL 020 8725 5201
FAX 020 8725 5419
EMAIL adm-med@sghms.ac.uk
WEB www.sgms.ac.uk

MEDICAL SCHOOL PROFILE	
Founded	**1751**
Status	**Associate of London Uni**
Situation/style	**City site**
Student population	**3430**
Full-time undergraduates	**2845**
ACCOMMODATION:	
Availability to freshers	**100%**
Style	**Halls**
Cost pw (no food/food)	**£59-£96**
City rent pw	**£80-£180+**

A college of London University, St George's entry policy is one science A level; it can be Chemistry or Biology; if Biology then AS Chemistry is required; but if Chemistry the other two A levels can be a modern Euro language and a Social Science. Leisure-wise there's a Friday disco at the Med School Bar (650 capacity) and 42 clubs and societies, Rowing and Film being the most popular. The sports grounds are in Cobham, Surrey – 9 winter pitches and 2 cricket squares, grass and hard tennis courts. They also keep an eight and a four in the London Uni boathouse and have facilities for sailing. Back at the hospital there's the Lowe Sports Centre, 6 squash courts, gym and areas for badminton, basketball, etc.

ST MARY'S COLLEGE

St Mary's College
Waldegrave Road
Strawberry Hill
Twickenham TW1 4SX

TEL 020 8240 4029
FAX 020 8240 2361
EMAIL admit@smuc.ac.uk
WEB www.smuc.ac.uk

St Mary's is a self-contained campus situated south of the England rugby ground at Twickenham, between Richmond and Kingston. Many undergraduates are destined to become teachers, but there is a wide range of subjects on offer – drama, English, theology, Irish culture, sport, biology, health, environment, sociology, classical studies, media, geography, history. It is a Roman Catholic foundation and they are good at sport – they came 28th in the national uni team ratings last year, a fantastic result for the college's size.

Two halls (Cashin and Cronin) offer en-suite facilities. Students' Union bars include **SU Bar** (600-800 capacity) and **Tartan Bar** (100-150) – 2 weekly discos, theme nights or live gigs.

COLLEGE PROFILE	
Founded	**1850**
Status	**HE College**
Degree awarding university	**Surrey**
Situation/style	**City campus**
Total student population	**3440**
Full-time undergraduates	**2710**
ACCOMMODATION FILE:	
Availability to freshers	**100%**
Style	**Halls**
Cost pw (no food/food)	**£68-£115**
City rent pw	**£80-£100+**

UNIVERSITY OF SALFORD

TheUniversity of Salford
Greater Manchester M5 4WT

TEL 0161 295 4545
FAX 0161 295 4646
EMAIL course-enquiries@salford.ac.uk
WEB www.salford.ac.uk

Salford Students' Union
University House
The Crescent
Salford M5 4WT

TEL 0161 736 7811
FAX 0161 737 1633
EMAIL president-ussu@salford.ac.uk
WEB www.susu.salford.ac.uk

VAG VIEW

Everyone knows that Salford is good at built environment, at science, engineering, computer and business, but a closer look reveals a developing picture – in particular into the arts, languages (also feted in the research assessments) and media – now eminently worth considering.

SUBJECT AREAS (%)

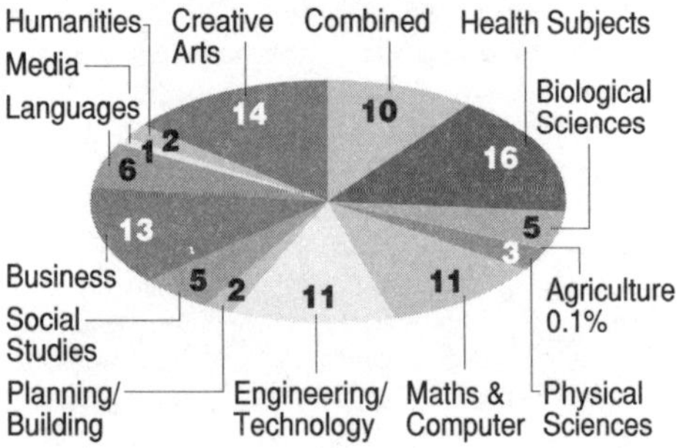

CAMPUS

'The main campus, Peel Park, is 2 miles from Manchester City Centre,' reports Shauna Corr. 'There are 3 main campuses: Adelphi, Frederick Road and the main campus: which is known as Peel Park.'

'So what do you know about Salford? Well, have you ever seen the opening credits of *Coronation Street*? That's Salford,' informs Lindsay Oakes. 'It's where *Corrie* is set and filmed. You may also have heard that it's a rough area with a high car crime rate. Sadly, Salford is known more by its bad reputation than for any of its good points. Of course I'd be lying if I told you that there aren't any negative aspects to living here; it's like any suburban city area: if you're not sensible then it could be dangerous. But where better to spend three or four years of your student life than in the student capital of Britain – Manchester? Salford University actually lies closer to the centre of Manchester than Manchester University itself. It is only a fifteen-minute bus ride away, or five minutes in a taxi, the way they drive round here!

FEES, BURSARIES

UK & EU Fees: £3000 p.a. If in receipt of full HE Maintenance grant there's a bursary of £300.

Scholarships worth £3,000 are available for undergraduate study, two reserved for local students.

STUDENT PROFILE

'There are students from all walks of life here, and from practically every continent. There is a real international feel to Salford because of all the links we have with universities abroad [see *Academia*, below]. And it may be true of many universities, but there is a real community among Salford students,' notes Lindsay, in particular among freshers in the student village. There is also a high percentage of mature students.

ACADEMIA & JOBS

They are a pioneer of sandwich courses, work placement schemes, and their links with local firms are legendary. 'There are certainly strong links with industry,' says Shauna, 'and opportunity on many courses for industrial sandwich years, home and abroad.' The culture is fostered by Academic Enterprise their 'integrated third strand alongside teaching and research. Many students experience a work placement as part of their course and 50% of programmes offer the chance to work or study abroad. Our Business Enterprise Support Team (BEST) encourages staff and students to build upon their ideas for self-employment,' they say.

Graduates pour out of Salford to be lecturers in higher education, and interest is directed at their School of Languages and its contemporary Euro culture degrees with a language, Linguistics with a language, three language mixes, languages with Marketing, Translation and Interpreting Studies. A new £1-million, campus-based Language Resource Centre offers advanced multimedia and language facilities. Biosciences is another popular route into higher education teaching - full marks at the assessments.

Meanwhile the faculty's School of Media, Music & Performance has employment success with dedicated degrees in radio/TV, journalism, music & recording. The 23/24 assessment for Drama/Dance/Cinematics shows that they, too, are performing well.

Aspiring music producers should look at the Faculty of Science, Engineerinf & Environment – the BA Acoustics, which prepares students for jobs with such as Philips (Holland) and Bang & Olufson (Denmark). Sound recordists and technicians look to the BSc Audio, Video & Broadcast Technology. Strong emphasis on practical work. BSc Audio Technology includes industrial placement. Meanwhile, in Media, Music & performance BA Popular Music & Recording is the business.

A new BA Journalism & Broadcast joins BA Hons Television & Radio (theoretical elements

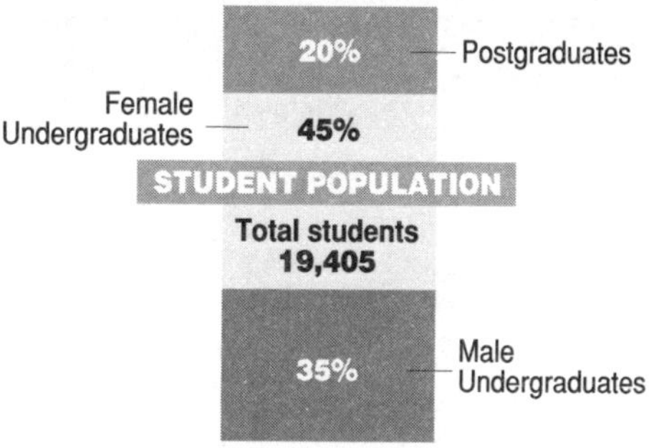

married to practical modules, such as editing, producing, directing). There are 5 other Journalism combinations. Look, too, at their BA Media & Performance and BSc Media Technology, the latter aimed at technical operators and operational engineers. Great student media – Shock FM and Channel M (TV). Teaching inspection, 20.

In the bedrock subjects, aspiring property developers still flock to Salford's world-class School of Construction & Property Management. Look at BSc Property Management & Investment. There's a world class Grade 6* rating for research. Teaching inspection, 18. Construction engineers/managers should consider the 4-year BSc Construction Mgt, or Construction Project Mgt. There's a dedicated degree in Quntity Surveying.

Salford's civil engineers also get jobs in number. There's a BSc or B/MEng route plus an option to mix with Environmental Engineering. Teaching assessment for Civil Eng (19 points) is less overpowering however.

Other sure-fire career hits are for aeronautical engineers. Salford places more graduates than most in the industry with its Aerospace courses, including the interesting e-design/Aerospace.

Health care professionals are equally well served by courses in Radiography, Midwifery, Occupational Therapy, Physiotherapy, Podiatry, Prosthetics/Orthotics, Sport Rehab – all 22 points

ACADEMIC EXCELLENCE

University since	**1967**
Situation/style	**Campus**
Student population	**19405**
Undergraduates	**15545**
- mature	**31%**
- non EU undergraduates	**5%**
- male/female	**44/56**
- non-traditional student intake	**37%**
- state school intake	**97%**
- drop-out rate	**10%**
- undergraduate applications	**Down 3%**

ACADEMIC EXCELLENCE

TEACHING: *(Rated Excellent or 17+ out of 24)*	
Music	**Excellent**
Organismal Biosciences, Politics, Molecular Biosciences	**24**
Drama/Dance/Cinematics, Physics	**23**
Housing, Subjects Allied to Medicine, Nursing	**22**
Art & Design, Maths	**21**
Economics, Sociology, Media, Modern Languages & Arabic	**20**
Civil Engineering, Tourism	**19**
Building & Land/Property Mgt	**18**
RESEARCH: *Top grades 5/5*/6**	
Built Environment, Library & Information Management	**Grade 6***
Statistics, European Studies	**Grade 5**

at assessment; they also offer one of the few Traditional Chinese Medicine/Acupuncture degrees.

Their Faculty of Business & Informatics is a leading edge into employment, with Business Decision Analysis (study in North America a possibility), Business Economics (with Gambling Studies – yes, you read right!), and a raft of Management Science degrees, with study in North America.

Serious employment strengths in the business sector include retail management and buying. Look at the School of Leisure, Hospitality & Food

They are No. 1 countrywide for jobs in sales management. The Art Department, Product Design, Sports Equipment Design and Fashion provide the focus for this. Engineering/business is another popular route into sales management.

They score well, too, with jobs in government admininistration (local, regional and central) – degrees such as BSc Environmental Health helping graduates in. See also the environment and conservation

Many courses have an international dimension, most offer the chance to study abroad. Excellent relationships with Europe and farther afield have produced interesting curriculum groupings

Not surprisingly translators and interpreters come in number from Salford, though it is not a crowded profession. Look at their Translation and Interpreting degrees – Arabic/English, Italian/ Portuguese, German/Spanish require Teaching inspection, 20. Research Grade 5.

SOCIAL SCENE

STUDENTS' UNION 'The union runs 4 bars (one being a nightclub-come-bar),' writes Shauna. '**The Pav** (at Castle Irwell student village) has two main nights: Tuesday and Friday. Tuesday's *Flair*, '60s, '70s and '80's music, is a constant, and whatever they call Friday night when you get there, it won't be retro. **The Lowry Bar** on Peel Park is situated in University House, it's a good day-bar. So far this year we have had a Ministry of Sound night, at which Youseff played, and we've had Jason Donovon, Timmy Mallet and Tymes Four as well as student bands and DJs. We also have the **Wallness Tavern**, recently refurbished, open all day. **The Sub Club**, Frederick Road, is a good day bar for students on site. All bars have games' machines and pool tables. Local pubs are a bit rough and not always safe for students.

'One thing I should point out,' writes Lindsay, 'is that unlike most unis, beer and food at Salford are *not* subsidised.'

Especially active among numerous sports clubs and societies is the LGB group – lesbian/gay. '*Student Direct* is our weekly publication,' Shauna continues, 'shared with both Bolton Uni and Manchester University.' The union rates most active societies as Plastic Surgery/Shock fm, both music societies: 'Plastic Surgery is the DJ soc, and Shock fm deals with the student radio station.' The campus-based (TV) Channel M broadcasts to half a million people in the Manchester region with pro-

WHERE SALFORD GRADUATES END UP

Health & Social Work: 13%; Education: 5%; Wholesale Retail: 10%; Manufacturing: 11%; Financial Activities: 7%; Public Administration, Civil Service & Defence: 9%; Hotel/Restaurant: 6%; Transport & Communications (including Telecommunications): 5%; Construction: 4%; Mining/Oil Extracting: 1%; Personnel: 2%; Computer: 5%; Business & Management: 2%; Accountancy: 2%; Media (including Film): 2%; Legal 1%; Architecture: 1%; Publishing: 0.5%; Advertising: 0.5%; Artistic/Literary: 0.5%; Sport: 1%.

Approximate 'graduate track' employed **62%**

grammes developed and made at Salford's media facilities. Channel M recently beat BBC and Sky One to a Royal Television Award.

Reflecting the growth in arts degrees – note the 23 points out of 24 for Drama at the teaching assessments – students describe extra-curricular arts opportunities as excellent too. The **Robert Powell Theatre** was opened by namesake Salfordian actor, Robert Powell.

> ***Salford has all the advantages of a small town – cheap rent, everything close by, a friendly atmosphere – yet with the facilities of a city nearby. But don't expect cheap beer – unlike most unis, it is not subsidised.***

The central, Peel Park Campus contains the Lowry Museum and Art Gallery. L S Lowry was born in the town.

Salford Community Action Project (SCAP) is a student project involved with children in the locality, and senior citizens, the disabled, ex-offenders, and in giving English lessons to overseas students and others.

SPORT 'The union runs a very cheap Leisure Centre which provides a swimming pool, climbing wall, weights room, badminton, tennis and squash courts, five-a-side football pitches, sun beds, sauna and jacuzzi. There is a large sports hall with just about every indoor pitch marked down, facilities for trampoline, and sports pitches at Castle Irwell for rugby, football, hockey and cricket.'

TOWN Cost-wise, as Suzanne Ashton points out, 'Salford has all the advantages of a town – cheap rent, everything close by, a friendly atmosphere – and yet still with the facilities of a city nearby.' See *Manchester City* article. 'There's part-time work in union bars, in ents, in the library and in Manchester,' notes Shauna, 'and a Job Shop to help you find reliable and safe, part-time or holiday work. There are loads of part-time jobs to be had.

PILLOW TALK

They guarantee a place in one of the 4,000 study bedrooms to all freshers who have an unconditional offer and whose accommodation application form has been received by 12 noon on the September 1 in the year of admission.

The 3 main campuses (Peel Park, Frederick Road, Adelphi) are within walking distance of the residences. 'There is a good selection of accommodation ranging from Castle Irwell Student Village to blocks of flats and on-campus catered accommodation,' Shauna reports. 'Castle Irwell has 1,612 rooms and is 25 minutes walk from Peel Park campus. It

AT A GLANCE

ACADEMIC FILE:	
Subjects assessed	**26**
Excellent	**69%**
Typical entry requirements	**260 points**
Application acceptance rate	**22%, high**
Students-staff ratio	**18:1**
First/2:1 degree pass rate	**52%**
ACCOMMODATION FILE:	
Guarantee to freshers	**100%**
Style	**Student village, houses, flats**
Catered	**7%**
Price range pw	**£50-£95**
City rent pw	**£65+**

WHAT IT'S REALLY LIKE

UNIVERSITY:	
Social Life	★★★
Campus scene	**Friendly, boozy**
Student Union services	**Good**
Politics	**Interest low, but SWSS & Anti-Nazi League**
Sport	**19 clubs**
National team position	**102nd**
Sport facilities	**Good**
Arts opportunities	**Excellent**
Student newspaper	**Student Direct**
Student radio	**Shock fm**
Student TV	**Channel M**
Nightclub	**The Pav**
Bars	**Lowry, Sub Club, Wallness Tavern**
Union ents	**Themed, requests, tours**
Union societies	**19**
Most popular societies	**Plastic Surgery**
Parking	**Adequate**
CITY:	
Entertainment	★★★★★
City scene	**The best**
Town/gown relations	**Average-poor**
Risk of violence	**High**
Cost of living	**Locally low**
Student concessions	**Low**
Survival + 2 nights out	**£70 pw**
Part-time work campus/town	**Average/excellent**

boasts numerous playing fields, an astro-turf pitch, and **The Pav**. There is also a laundrette, taxi rank and a house with disabled access.'

Writes Lindsay: 'In the summer, the entire village turns out on to the playing fields to play sports, sunbathe or even have barbecues. In the winter, you'll find yourself having a snowball fight with someone you've never met before.'

GETTING THERE

☛ By road: M62 (which connects with the M6, M63)/M602. Coach services good.
☛ By rail: Salford Crescent station is on-campus; Manchester Oxford Road is a few minutes away; Liverpool, 1:20; Sheffield, 1:30; Birmingham New Street, 2:30; London Euston, 3:30.
☛ By air: Manchester Airport,.
☛ By coach: London, 4:35; Bristol, 5:00.

SCHOOL OF ORIENTAL & AFRICAN STUDIES, LONDON UNIVERSITY

School of Oriental & African Studies
Thornhaugh Street
Russell Square
London WC1H 0XG

TEL 020 7898 4034
FAX 020 7898 4039
EMAIL study@soas.ac.uk
WEB www.soas.ac.uk

SCHOOL/STUDENT PROFILE

School of London Uni since	**1916**
Situation/style	**City site**
Student population	**3451**
Undergraduates	**2160**
ACCOMMODATION:	
Guarantee to freshers	**100%**
Style	**Halls**
Cost pw (no food)	**£100-£200**
City rent pw	**£100+**

SOAS, part of of the University of London, is situated in Bloomsbury and has a close working relationship with branches of the Civil Service, especially the Foreign Office (SOAS actually teach their staff). Teaching assessments are first class. Connections with overseas governments, industry and commerce facilitate, among other things, the college's study-abroad programmes. SOAS does all the usual disciplines, but with specific reference to Africa and Asia.

This means that in Geography you're more likely to be looking at the 'Bio-geography of Savannahs in Sub-Saharan Africa' than the spatial planning of Birmingham town centre. It's strong on languages, from Chinese and Japanese to a whole lot you may not have heard of. Colloquial Cambodian, for example, looks great on your CV.

The bar, capacity 200, is renowned the world over (by a discerning few). Student accommodation is provided as 500 single, en-suite study-bedrooms in cluster flats 15 minutes' walk away on the Pentonville Road. Alternatively, students may use London Uni's intercollegiate halls (see Introduction).

There are two squash courts on site and a sports ground at Greenford. London Uni Students' Union aport and fitness facilities are nearby.

GETTING THERE

☛ Underground: Russell Square (Piccadilly line).

SCHOOL OF PHARMACY, LONDON UNIVERSITY

School of Pharmacy
29-39 Brunswick Square
London WC1N 1AX

TEL 020 7753 5831
FAX 020 7753 5829
EMAIL registry @ulsop.ac.uk
WEB www.ulsop.ac.uk

The School of Pharmacy is a specialist school of the University of London. A Grade 5 in the research assessments confirms its national and international reputation. Ssituated within walking distance of the British Museum, it has a small amount of its own accommodation, otherwise it's London Uni's intercollegiate halls, or living out. For sport, the school shares grounds out at Enfield with the Royal Free Hospital Medical School (now part of University College, London); closer to home are facilities for squash, badminton, swimming, etc., and the London University Union is close at hand. There is a union bar, a theme night on Friday, and facilities for table tennis, pool, etc.

SCHOOL PROFILE	
Founded	**1842**
Status	**School of London Uni**
Situation/style	**City site**
Total student population	**1345**
Full-time degree undergraduates	**675**
ACCOMMODATION FILE:	
Availability to freshers	**50%**
Style	**Halls**
Approx cost pw (catered)	**£90-£110**
City rent pw	**£100+**

GETTING THERE

☛ By tube: Russell Square (Piccadilly line); overland stations (King's Cross, St Pancras and Euston) are all within a short walk.

SCOTTISH AGRICULTURAL COLLEGE

Scottish Agricultural College
Ayr Campus
Ayr KA6 5HW

TEL 0800 269453
FAX 01292 525357
EMAIL recruitment@sac.ac.uk
WEB www.sac.ac.uk

SAC is a small college based at three sites, in Aberdeen, Edinburgh and Ayr. Halls accommodation is available. Technical and management skills required to manage livestock or crop enterprise are to the fore; it's a three-year course, four for an honours degree. Degrees in related specialisms are also available. *Aberdeen* has BTechnol Agriculture, BTechnol Countryside Management and BTechnol Business Management; *Ayr* BTechnol Agriculture, BSc Horticulture or Horticulture with Horticulture Mgt (first 2 years at Strathclyde Uni), BSc Landscape Management, BTechnol Environmental Protection & Management (years 3 & 4 in Edinburgh), BTechnol Countryside Management, BTechnol Leisure & Recreation Management, BSc Applied Plant & Animal Science, and BTechnol Food Technology; *Edinburgh* has BTechnol Agriculture, BTechnol Rural Resources Management, and BTechnol Environment Protection & Mgt (first 2 years at Ayr).

STUDENT SHEFFIELD - THE CITY

Steely Sheffield is a born-again cosmopolitan city offering pretty much anything you desire. For some it may never rival Leeds, Manchester or Nottingham, but come here and you will soon discover that it has its own inimitable charm. People are friendly to all, even if you are a student! And many students choose to stay after graduation, which proves that it is a place to live and work in, not just somewhere to pass through.

CLUBS

Sheffield placed itself in the vanguard of the club revolution with several big names – **Gatecrasher**: '**Gatecrasher One** has taken over *Skool Disco* duties, providing salivating perverts a new location to drool over girls in pigtails and pleated skirts,' writes Itchy, 'while *Blessed* @ **Republic** on a monday night is absolute quality, if you like r&b and hip hop.' With major acts and DJ's plying their trade, there are no end of nights to check out and something to suit everyone's taste. Sheffield Hallam's **NMB** also provides, and sells out its *Stardust* and *Sheff 1* clubnights on a weekly basis.

The alternative scene is not to be missed though, with Sheffield University's Student Union offering a great live venue in the **Octagon** (yes, it has 8 sides) for touring bands. They are even kind enough to put on indie clubnights to fill the gaps between gigs. Look in particular for the *Fuzz Club* on a Thursday night.

Other venues includevenue and indie haunt **Leadmill** (voted best venue outside of London a while back) and **City Hall** for the more 'cultured' acts. While Hallam's **Arena** and the **Don Valley**

Stadium provide the capacity required by the really big bands, like recent Paul McCartney and Eric Clapton.

GALLERIES AND THEATRES

The Crucible and **Lyceum** are Sheffield's 2 major playhouse venues, they have shows running all year round, ranging from pantomime, to ballet to Shakespeare. Both offer discounts for students, who also have their own productions at the **Drama Studio** on Glossop Road.

Among major arthouses, the star attraction is the **Millennium Galleries**. **Graves Art Gallery** has smaller, but still great, exhibitions, a recent highlight the William Blake show from the Tate in London.

SCREENS

Film buffs love the **Showroom** on Paternoster Row, an arty cinema with bar attached; it even does a 'film and meal deal'. Cheap and cheerful in-town cinema is the 10-screen **Odeon**, while out at **Meadowhall** there's a 15-screen multiplex, where a film can be incorporated into a day out shopping. The **UGC, also** outside the city centre, boasts a huge 'Full Monty' screen, perfect for watching the latest blockbuster.

SPORT

Sheffield is home to 2 football teams - Sheffield Wednesday, who play at **Hillsborough**, and Sheffield United at **Bramall Lane**. Whatever you do, don't confuse the two. We also have ice hockey team and basketball teams. The Sheffield Steelers glide across the ice at **The Arena,** and the Westfield Sharks shoot the hoop there on non-ice days. Look, too, for the world-class swimming pool at **Ponds Forge**. And, of course, the **Crucible** is transformed once a year into a sporting venue, when it hosts the Embassy World Snooker Championship. Alternatively, many like a flutter at **Owlerton Greyhound Stadium** on Penistone Road.

STUDENT GHETTOES

As with most cities, students have monopolised a couple of areas. Broomhill, a paradise of pubs, takeaways, a supermarket and the ever popular **Record Collector** - whatever your taste in music, they'll stock it. Convenient for the Sheffield Uni campus - 10 minutes away on foot - it's reasonably cheap and pretty safe. Hallam students, meanwhile, tend to congregate around the Ecclesall Road area, or roads just off the city centre, being just a stone's throw away form their 3 campuses. Again, these areas have everything a student needs - supermarket, pubs and the odd bookshop or two.

There are endless pubs and bars, in particular in the student areas of Broomhill, Crooks and Ecclesall Road. Division Street also has a good dozen, while outside the city centre there are loads of vast watering holes.

CONSUMERISM

The debt-riddled student gets a lifeline from Broomhill's array of charity shops, also from **Castle Market** - brilliant for cheap veg, fish and meat. Those past caring visit Division Street, where all the latest trendy and alternative gear purveyed in chic boutiques and the **Forum Shopping Centre**. Chapel Walk is full of small shops with large price tags, and although Ecclesall Road is a student area, it, too, has shops generally far too expensive for a student's pocket. Then there is the experience of **Meadowhall** (Meadow 'hell' on a Saturday) - shop after shop selling its wares, all under one roof, again sometimes at high prices.

Ellen Grundy

UNIVERSITY OF SHEFFIELD

The University of Sheffield
Western Bank
Sheffield S10 2TN

TEL 0114 222 2000
FAX 0114 222 1234
EMAIL www.sheffield.ac.uk/asksheffield
WEB www.sheffield.ac.uk

Sheffield University Students Union
Western Bank
Sheffield S10 2TG

TEL 0114 222 8610
FAX 0114 275 2506
EMAIL union@shef.ac.uk
WEB www.sheffieldunion.com

VAG VIEW

Sheffield is a top university across the board. Whichever one of our statistical boxes you care to consult – 'Where Sheffield Graduates End Up', 'Academic Excellence', 'What It's Really Like' – they excel.

As student Rose Wild wrote: 'In today's

cut-throat world, where new students have to pay just to enter this carnival of hedonistic abandon, and thereafter graduate to a future in which security is not guaranteed, it is probably worth choosing a university which gives you best value for your dosh and which has a reputation that will outshine the competition. That university is Sheffield.'

CAMPUS

The city of Sheffield is roughly in the centre of England. The uni and student ghettoes are all on one side of it and there's a friendly community-feel, although Sheffield is most definitely not a campus university. One word describes Sheffield, and that's 'hilly'. Most students walk everywhere, but public transport is reliable and cheap, and there's also Supertram, which runs from the centre to numerous places, including Meadowhall, the famous, out-of-town shopping centre. Having your own transport enables you to enjoy weekends, though. When you come here you'll be on the edge of the Peak District, one of the last great, beautiful wilderness areas of England.

FEES, BURSARIES

UK & EU Fees: £3000. If in receipt of full HE Maintenance grant there's a bursary of £3000 p.a. There are three types of bursary, and students can qualify for more than one type, to the maximum of £3,000: £650 for household incomes under £16000; £400 for incomes between £16000 and £33000. Awards also (£250 to £1550) for pre-uni academic achievement and if a Graduate Priority Subject is chosen. Support, too, if applying from partnership colleges or schools. There are also sports bursaries and several funds available for students who face unforeseeable costs associated with study or who fall into the following categories, mature students, lone parents, students with dependants, and students with a disability.

UNIVERSITY/STUDENT PROFILE

University since	**1905**
Situation/style	**Civic**
Student population	**25526**
Undergraduates	**19888**
- mature	**41%**
- non EU undergraduates	**13%**
- male/female	**43/57**
- non-traditional student intake	**20%**
- state school intake	**83%**
- drop-out rate	**3%, low**
- undergraduate applications	**Up 3%**

SUBJECT AREAS (%)

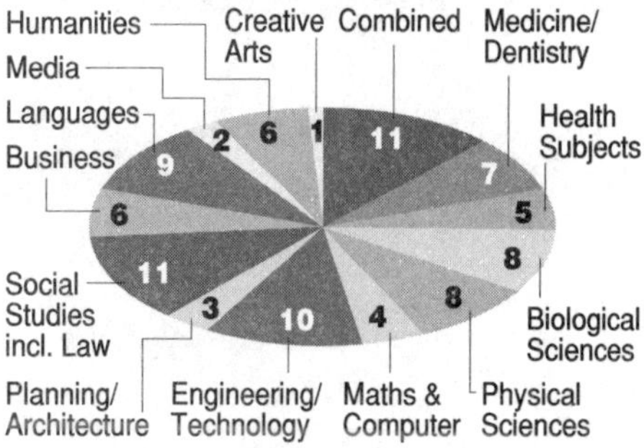

STUDENT PROFILE

There are plenty of bright undergraduates, most of them capable of 400 points at A level. There's a high proportion of public school type, but there is a growing number, too, of new-to-uni social groups (20%). The mature population at 41% (includes both full-time and part-time undergraduates) is unusually large. So, students come from a variety of backgrounds and together they are happy enough to achieve a mere 3% drop-out rate. Writes Rose:

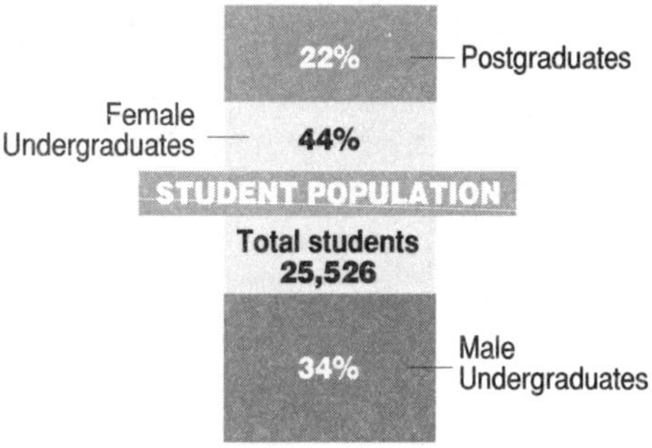

'One of the most striking and pleasing things about the cosy little cocoon of life, which makes this university a very pleasant place to be, is that you will rarely – if ever – come across prejudice of any sort. The union's absolute tolerance of the sizeable gay community is but one reflection of this. Another striking feature is the high visibility of the university's religious community. A small but significant proportion of Sheffield's students, embarking upon their journey of self-discovery, stray off more well-trod paths and instead find God.'

ACADEMIA & JOBS

A new £16-million Learning Resource Centre will be completed in late 2006, with provision for nearly 1,000 study places, state-of-the-art IT facilities and 100,000 undergraduate textbooks.

Almost a fifth of graduates go into health. A

new £3.1-million Health Centre opened in September 2004. £26 million was spent on the refurbishment of teaching and research facilities in the Medical School.

ACADEMIC EXCELLENCE

TEACHING:
(Rated Excellent or 17+ out of 24)

History, Mechanical Engineering, Law, Sociology, Social Work, Architecture, English, Geography, Music, Social Policy, Initial Teacher Training.	**Excellent**
Russian, Automatic Control & Systems Engineering, Electron/Electric Eng, Mechanical Eng, Theology, Education, Anatomy, Biosciences, Philosophy, Politics	**24**
Landscape/Town & Regional Planning	**23**
Linguistics, East Asian Studies, Materials Technology, Physics, Archaeology, Library/Info, Psychology	**22**
Hispanic Studies, Chemical Engineering, Civil Eng, French, Maths, Pharmacology, Other Subjects Allied to Medicine, Nursing, Economics	**21**
German	**20**
Medicine	**19**

RESEARCH:
Top grades 5/5/6**

Pre-Clinical Studies, Electronic/Electrical Eng, Metallurgy, Politics, Russian/ Library/Info Mgt.	**Grade 6***
Animal & Plant Sciences, Molecular & Cellular Biology, Automatic Control/Systems Eng,	**Grade 5***
Hospital-based Clinical Subjects, Clinical Dentistry, Nursing, Psychology, Chemistry, Physics, Medical Physics & Clinical Eng, Pure Maths, Statistics, Computer, Civil Eng, Mechanical/Aeronautical/ Manufacturing Eng, Built Environment, Town/Country Planning, Geography, Law, Social Policy, English, French, Iberian/Latin American, Archaeology, History, Philosophy, Theology, Music, Education	**Grade 5**

In the 5/6-year MB ChB there's an emphasis on self-learning and computer-aided learning packages. Wide clinical experience offered. The 6-year course includes a pre-med year for students with non-scientific backgrounds. Entry requirements ABB – AB in 2 science subjects, one of which must be Chemistry. Grade B in any other subject. With a well-below average of 8%, the 2004 application acceptance rate onto this marks the medical provision out as one of the most popular and demanding at entry.

Another noticeable career strength within the sector is BSc Psychology, fully accredited and first step to becoming a Chartered Psychologist. And for nurses, Sheffield is one of only three universities to be awarded Grade 5 for research. Speech therapists also thrive on the BMedSci Speech Science.

Accountancy is also very big at Sheffield. BA Accounting & Financial Mgt degrees combine with Business Mgt, Economics, Info Mgt, or Maths. Tax consultants also thrive, and aspiring actuaries get happy with their Maths degrees especially BSc Financial Mathematics.

Sheffield claim to attract more undergraduates in their School of Architecture than any other. There are 7 courses, a single hons – BA Architectural Studies, and landscape and urban environment degrees. Also, in Engineering, MEng Structural Engineering & Architecture. Teaching inspection, Excellent. Research, Grade 5. As for landscape architecture they find more graduates employment than any other uni. Teaching inspection, 23.

A new £25 million multidisciplinary science and engineering campus is being developed, the first stage of which opened in June 2005.

Engineering design consultants find their way from all over the Engineering faculty. Look at their 3 to 5-year B/MEng Civil Engineering degrees, but also a range of design engineering degrees, such as B/MEng Medical Systems Engineering, Computer Systems Engineering, Systems & Control Engineering. There's also Biomedical Engineering, which gets into design for prosthetics.

The Faculty of Engineering, which took full marks at teaching inspection and world class Grade 6* for research, has established the Advanced Research Manufacturing Centre with Boeing and opened its third Rolls-Royce Technology centre in Advanced Electrical Machines and Drives. They are also collaborating with British Aerospace.

The Sports Engineering degree (introduced in 2004) has now been joined by a degree in Motor Sports Engineering Management, and a new degree course in Aerospace Engineering with Private Pilot Instruction is proving popular.

Electronic and telecommunications engineers abound. A number of army officers come out of this department, as they do from physical sciences, where in civvy street chemists (research grade 5) and archaeologists (teaching assessment 22, research grade 5) flow in greatest number, then software engineers and computer operators.

Sheffield's Faculty of Pure Science offers a whole range of 3/4-years BSc and Masters degrees, Chemistry, for example, coupling with Chemical Engineering, Maths, study in Europe or Australia or Japan or the US or in industry.

'In today's cut-throat world, where new students have to payto enter this carnival of hedonistic abandon, and thereafter graduate to a future in which security is not guaranteed, it is probably worth choosing a university which gives you best value for your dosh. That university is Sheffield.'

Computer Science (with Foundation year if you want it) has various language possibilities and Physics might come with Medical Physics, Maths, Study in Europe, or there's a 4-year MPhys in Theoretical Physics. There's also a BSc Science Foundation (4/5 years).

The Faculty of Social Sciences mixes social and political studies and reaches into China, Korea and Japan, and this is also where you'll find a raft of Economics degrees and Accountancy & Finance. Researchers for media & government come out of here, and out of language degrees. Aspiring translator/interpreters note the 4-year BA Modern Languages with Interpreting.

Languages and Sciences produce editors, too, and look out for BA Journalism Studies (backed by superb student media). Sheffield is also good for publishing.

Instructors by the dozen come out of Sheffield and would-be adult education lecturers find a certain route via languages, where Russian is a particular strength, with full marks at the teaching assessments as well as Grade 6* (world class) for research. Also popular ways into adult education are biological sciences (full marks at the assessments) and social sciences (Politics full marks, Psychology 22. Law is Excellent).

SOCIAL SCENE

Students' Union If you arrive by train or bus you'll be met by Student Reception; volunteer students will beard you in the bars, in halls – every fresher will get a visit, even those in private accommodation. The next impressive feature is the union concourse with large open-plan sports and activities Workspace, which includes the Viglen Computer Suite with 16 high-spec PCs for publishing promotional material.

Then there's **The Auditorium** with 380 seats and state-of-the-art audio/visual system, it's a venue for four films a week selected by student ballot, for live jazz and comedy, and for a rolling programme of guest speakers. Fulcrum of the ents scene is **Bar 1**, which recently had a £500,000 makeover. It serves over thirty varieties of beer and takes more in a night than most pubs do in a week.

It also has **Griddles,** meat and veggie fast food emporium, and the **Pizza Bar**. **Interval** (600 capacity) is the continental style café bar – pasta, baguettes, pastries and cabaret acts. **Fusion** (600 capacity) is the intimate venue for live bands and clubnights. Recently Ash, Orbital, Placebo, David Gray, Starsailor, Elbow, Pulp, Basement Jaxx, Wheatus.

Then there's **The Foundry** (1,000), which, with Fusion, is host to an amazing series of clubnights. *Tuesday Club* is drum 'n' bass/hip hop, Wednesday's *The Big One,* with top line DJs, Grooverider and LTJ Bookem, Thursday's *The Fuzz Club* (indie/metal in two rooms). Then there's *Loveshack*'s traditional roof-raising eclectic mix on Friday, and *Pop Tarts, Saturday,* the ultimate '60s/'70s retro party – which now

WHERE SHEFFIELD GRADUATES END UP

Health & Social Work: 19%; Education: 8%; Wholesale Retail: 7%; Manufacturing: 9%; Financial Activities: 9%; Public Administration, Civil Service & Defence: 8%; Hotel/Restaurant: 3%; Transport & Communications (including Tele communications): 4%; Construction: 1%; Personnel: 3%; Computer: 2%; Business & Management: 3%; Accountancy: 5%; Media (including Film): 1%; Legal 2%; Architecture: 5%; Publishing: 1%.

Approximate 'graduate track' employed **67%**

WHAT IT'S REALLY LIKE

UNIVERSITY:	
Social Life	★★★★★
Campus scene	**Diverse, lively, sporty, happening and safe**
Student Union services	**Excellent**
Politics	**High level: fees, war, abortion, fair trade**
Sport	**Key, 48 clubs**
National team position	**30th**
Sport facilities	**Good**
Arts opportunities	**Film excellent, drama, dance music, art good**
Student magazine	**Stainless**
Student newspaper	**The Steel Press**
2005 National Awards	**2 nominations**
Student radio	**SURE FM**
2005 National Awards	**1 nomination**
Nightclub	**Fusion & Foundry, Octagon**
Bars	**Bar One, Interval + SU pubs in town**
Union ents	**Drum 'n bass, hip hop, dance, pop, Indie, rock&roll electro punk, retro + live**
, Union clubs/societies	**188**
Parking	**Poor**
CITY:	
Entertainment	★★★★★
Scene	**Seriously good**
Town/gown relations	**Good**
Risk of violence	**Low**
Cost of living	**Low-average**
Student concessions	**Good**
Survival + 2 nights out pw	**£80**
Part-time work campus/town	**Good**

employs two dancefloors. The monthly *Climax* is LGB night, now a widely known favourite on the gay scene. The **Octagon Centre** is the major, national-circuit venue (1600 capacity), just recently feted *Club Mirror* 'Venue of the Year'.

Societies cover almost everything, as Rose discovered: 'Whether you're one of the rare few who actually come here to learn, or you're one of the many who come to play rugby, edit a newspaper, watch bands, worship God, fight injustice, walk up big hills, practise politics, become an actor or do any number of diverse and often bizarre activities – (I'm talking about *you*, Dungeons and Dragons Society!) – you can not only do them here, but you can meet a load of people who'll do them with you.'

A recent initiative this year is Sheffield's *Give It A Go* programme. The idea is to encourage you to dip in to a whole host of activities – suck it and see before making a long-term commitment.

The Radio Society, SURE fm, started as an individual's idea and they're now broadcasting around the union from their own studio. *Stainless* is the new magazine and the student newspaper, *Steel Press*, won Newspaper of the Year more times than one cares to remember.

The Workspace is the heart of sports clubs and societies and consists of meeting rooms and work areas with telephones and computing facilities that members can use to contact each other, meet and organise events.

The Theatre Company uses the **Drama Studio** for productions ranging from Shakespearean tragedy to student-written plays on pornography to musicals.

A 400-seat auditorium, extension to the union, is used by the Film Unit as a cinema four times a week, showing films prior to release on video.

AT A GLANCE

ACADEMIC FILE:	
Subjects assessed	**47**
Excellent	**89%**
Typical entry requirements	**400 points**
Application acceptance rate	**14%**
Students-staff ratio	**15:1**
First/2:1 degree pass rate	**72%**
ACCOMMODATION FILE:	
Guarantee to freshers	**98%**
Style	**Halls, flats, houses**
Catered	**59%**
En suite	**18%**
Approx price range pw	**£59-£118**
City rent pw	**£38-£68**

Sport The Goodwin Sports Centre, which includes a first-class (but cold) swimming pool, gym and numerous astro-turf pitches, has had major improvements to its facilities recently at a cost of £14 million. There are currently some 40 sports clubs with the policy 'sport for all', covering traditional sports like rugby, hockey and cricket and newer sports like frisbee, step and skiing. You can be as involved as you like, many aerobics classes work a 'pay as you go' system for example.

Town 'Roughly a third of all Sheffield University students stay in the city after they graduate,' notes

Rose, 'which indicates either a staggering lack of imagination or a real affection for the place.' See *Sheffield Student City*, page 415.

PILLOW TALK

Get in their quick, because it's a 97% guarantee only. 'Ranmoor is the biggest hall and has a bar to rival no other, although smaller halls like Stevenson or Halifax are friendlier. Self-catering flats are popular with those who appreciate their independence and enjoy cooking. Some, like Crewe Flats, offer entertainment like a hall, others like Riverdale Flats are cheaper and quieter.'

GETTING THERE

☛ By road: M1/J33, A630, A57.
☛ By rail: London, 2:30; Liverpool Lime Street, 1:45; Manchester Piccadilly, 1:00; Nottingham 1:00; Leeds, 30 mins.
☛ By air: Manchester Airport.
☛ By coach: London, 3:45; Newcastle, 4:45;.

SHEFFIELD HALLAM UNIVERSITY

Sheffield Hallam University
City Campus
Sheffield S1 1WB

TEL 0114 225 5555
FAX 0114 225 2042
EMAIL undergraduate-admissions@shu.ac.uk
WEB www.shu.ac.uk

Sheffield Hallam Union of Students
The HUBS
Paternoster Row
Sheffield, S1 2QQ

TEL 0114 225 4111
FAX 0114 225 4140
EMAIL [initial.name]@shu.ac.uk
WEB www.hallamunion.com

VAG VIEW

Hallam is big business, its work-orientated courses suggest that it is bent on stoking the nation's economy. Recently they have made a huge investment in reorganisation, shedding one campus site and boosting two others, one in the city centre, the other in the suburbs. Last year, following the opening of the Adsetts Centre, *a multimedia Learning Resources Centre, their new 'beacon for health and social care education', the £15-million Health and Wellbeing building opened on Collegiate Campus, and now this year the Faculty of Arts, Computing, Engineering and Sciences has moved from depressing Psalter Lane to the Students' Union building on City Campus.*

Worry not, however, the SU has itself moved to the former National Centre for Popular Music, which couldn't be more appropriate, and was up and running in time for Easter term 2006.

SUBJECT AREAS (%)

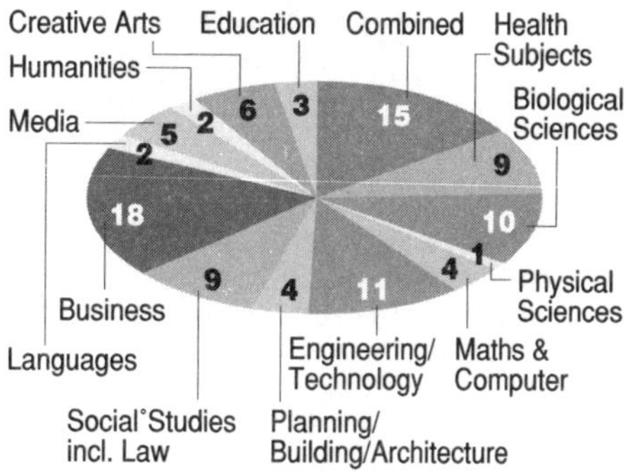

CAMPUSES

SHU is based around 3 sites, City, Collegiate Crescent, and Psalter Lane. The latter, the runt of the litter, with it's school-like corridors and grim exterior, will close on completion of a new city-centre site adjacent to Sheffield's Cultural Industries Quarter, when the Students Union will also move into the former National Centre for Popular Music. Now – this year – an £8-million School of Health and Social Care will open on the Collegiate Crescent site.

'Collegiate campus is really quite good,' writes Chris Gissing. 'It's a traditional, leafy campus, ideally placed on the *revelation* that is Ecclesall Road. Sheffield's Eccy Road is the hub of student ents, with about 830 bars and 6,000 coffee houses (well, maybe not as many as that, but after the first 5 pubs, who cares?).

'City Campus is excellent too, centrally located and based around 4 or 5 disparate buildings, connected by the stunningly designed **Atrium**. This glass/steel construction has masses of open space, and is like a cosmopolitan street café with tables and chairs and...well...a café. The Adsetts Centre is based here and offers 24-hour access to computers, Internet, books, photocopying etc. Fortunately, the library staff who seemed to fine me on a weekly basis don't work twenty-four hours.'

FEES, BURSARIES

UK & EU Fees: £3000. If in receipt of full HE Maintenance grant there's a bursary of £700. Support, too, if applying from partnership colleges or schools.

STUDENT PROFILE

'We have the whole range,' Chris continues, 'from working-class-kid-scraped-through-on-a-BTEC/through-Clearing sort, to Mummy-and-Daddy-paid-for-my-flat-and-course-fees-darling sort. They're all here in this city – 12% of the city's population are students. Sheffield Hallam has more working-class students than Sheffield University does.' In fact, the 31% figure is now no longer a big deal in the context of UK unis, and, as Chris says, 'we all seem to get along fairly well, and we are of course allowed to use each others' union bars/women/blokes (delete as appropriate).'

'Hallam is a place of two halves,' writes Mark Cordell. 'There are a lot of mature students, but they aren't exactly grey-haired men with sticks scooting around, though Hallam does have a calmer, more serious environment than other institutions.'

ACADEMIA & JOBS

Tom Bilton writes: 'Your degree will find you a job, but 'you will need to be self-motivated. If you're after close-knit tutorials with tutors that take a thorough interest in you, you'd be better off at Sheffield University.' At Hallam the student:staff ratio is nearly 22 to 1; at Sheffield it's below 15:1.

Back-up resources are increasingly good, however, and Chris Gissing concludes: 'The teaching within my school (Computing & Management Science) was on the whole very good. I cannot fault the department for what they offer in terms of specialist knowledge and resources. On the IT courses there is a strong bias towards industrial placements and business skills, invaluable when going into the real world of work.'

More than 10% of graduates go into education – secondary and primary. Top scoring at the teaching assessments, it's not too difficult to get in, and Education is one of three subjects to score 23 points out of 24 for teaching. The others were maths and health.

Graduates of Computer Science, Health, Business, Social Science, and Creative Arts also march confidently into the higher education sector as lecturers. Art & Design and Social Science scored 22 points at the teaching assessments and Art an

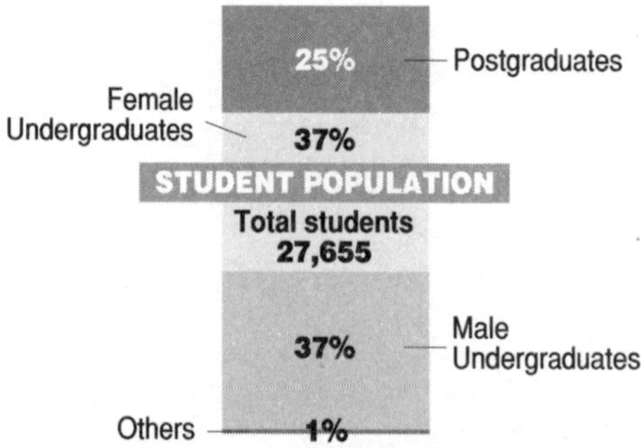

ACADEMIC EXCELLENCE

TEACHING: *(Rated Excellent or 17+ out of 24)*	
English	**Excellent**
Psychology, Physics, Tourism	**24**
Maths, Education, Subjects Allied to Medicine	**23**
Sociology, Materials Technology Art & Design, Molecular Biosci., Business/Finance	**22**
General Engineering; Mech, Aeronautical & Manufacturing Engineering, Nursing, Building	**21**
History of Art, Design & Film	**20**
Modern Languages (French, German, Italian, Spanish) Communication Studies.	**19**
Civil Eng, Elec & Electron Eng.	**18**
RESEARCH: *Top grades 5/5**	
Metallurgy, History, Art & Design	**Grade 5**

UNIVERSITY/STUDENT PROFILE

University since	**1992**
Situation/style	**City campus**
Student population	**27655**
Undergraduates	**20545**
- mature	**19%**
- overseas	**4%**
- male/female	**50/50**
- non-traditional student intake	**31%**
-state school intake	**95%**
- drop-out rate	**7%**
- undergraduate applications	**Down 2%**

international, Grade 5 rating for research.

Hallam is among the leaders for sheer numbers of graduates into banking, a 3/4-year sandwich BA in Banking & Finance requires 240 points only. A BSc Business & Finance is a top-up alternative. Hallam is again the place for insurance/pension brokers/underwriters. These sectors account for between 2% and 3% of all graduates from here.

Business scored 22 out of 24 points at the assessments. They have recently launched an Enterprise Centre to imbue the whole uni with an enterprise culture. There are Finance, Human Resources Mgt, Marketing or Financial Services adjuncts and a series of International Business Studies (French, German, Italian, Spanish) and languages with e-Commerce degrees.

> ***'I cannot fault the department for what they offer in terms of specialist knowledge and resources. On the IT courses there is a strong bias towards industrial placements and business skills, invaluable when going into the real world of work.'***

Employment figures show success in personnel in particular through the 4-year sandwich BA Hons Business & Human Resource Management. Look, too, at transport, where Hallam is out in front for graduate employment. BA Planning & Transport or Geography with Transport are the degrees. For the catering trade (another key graduate employment area) there's BSc Hons Hospitality Business Management with Conference/Events or Culinary Arts possibilities, or Leisure Events Management with Arts & Entertainments, Outdoor Recreation, or Tourism. They scored full marks at the assessments.

Marketing is also a strength and there is a steady flow of graduates into advertising. See the BA Communication and Information degrees – Communication Studies, and in the Art & Design Faculty, Information Design & Multimedia.

Engineering has always been a strength. For mechanical engineers they ask least at entry among the employment leaders. BEng Hons include Mechanical & Computer-Aided Eng and Mechatronics, and there's a major/minor route for Mechanical Engineering with minor options being Automotive, Control, Environmental Management, Business Management or Electrical Eng. 21 points at the assessments.

Again, like Bath Uni, they lead the way in guiding Electrical Engineering graduates into telecommunications. Look at the E & E and Computer Aided Engineering & Design degrees. There may be a low teaching assessment, but employers still love them. Teaching inspection 18.

Computer programmers come thick and fast off the Hallam production line with BSc Computing and its applications – Networks, Software Eng, Visualisation, Web Info. Systems & Services, or with Management Science.

BSc Pharmaceutical Sciences puts the uni into the Top 10 for finding graduates work in the pharmaceutical manufacturing industry. Meanwhile, health subjects make a huge impact on their employment figures – degrees in Physiotherapy, Occupational Therapy, Radiotherapy, Oncology, Nursing... They have opted for areas where the other Sheffield university doesn't tread, and they dropped only one point at the assessments. The Diagnostic Radiography and Radiography & Oncology BSc degrees corner well over 4% of the national employment market in this sector at a low asking rate. Teaching inspection, 23.

They're among the leading providers, too, for social workers/counsellors. The BA Social Work Studies hits the spot, but see, too, Social Policy, Social, Cultural and Psychology mixes.

See also the BSc Psychology, fully accredited by the British Psychological Society and first step to becoming a Chartered Psychologist.

Stats show, too, that BSc Architectural Technology or Architecture & Environmental Design are both solid lines into a career. Look also at Construction Management, Construction Commercial Management and Building Surveying. There is employment strength in-depth at Hallam

WHERE SHEFFIELD HALLAM GRADUATES END UP

Health & Social Work: 12%; Education: 11%; Wholesale Retail: 9%; Manufacturing: 10%; Financial Activities: 9%; Public Administration, Civil Service & Defence: 10%; Hotel/Restaurant: 6%; Transport & Communications (including Telecommunications): 2%; Construction: 3%; Personnel: 4.5%; Computer: 4%; Business & Management: 2%; Accountancy: 1%; Media (including Film): 1%; Legal 4%; Architecture: 1.5%; Publishing: 1%; Advertising: 1%; Artistic/Literary: 0.5%; Sport: 1%.

Approximate 'graduate track' employed **59%**

for jobs in the construction industry and BSc Quantity Surveying is no exception. Teaching inspection, 21. There's a track record, too, in property – look at BSc Property Studies.

Law also has a good reputation. Note the LLB /Maitrise En Droit (Francaise) – 2 years in Paris – and the joint degrees with Criminology, Business, Psychology. It is not difficult to see why more probation officers come out of Hallam than anywhere. You can study BA Criminology and Psychology/Sociology, Social Work Studies, Society & Cities, Social Policy, Social Policy & Sociology.

The Law is also a recognised pathway into Civil Service administration from here, while local and regional government administration call on Hallam graduates in such as Social Policy, Society & Cities, Urban Regeneration, Education, Architecture, Building & Planning, and Business & Administration. BA Business & Public Policy is clearly useful. Note also their BSc Public Health Nutrition, and the Planning & Transport BA.

Finally, they are employment leaders in sport, a fact which knits academia together with student leisure – they came 18th in the national sporting league last year. The department was among the few nationwide to score 24 points (full marks) in the teaching assessments.

WHAT IT'S REALLY LIKE

UNIVERSITY:	
Social Life	★★★★
Campus scene	**Mature, diverse**
Student Union services	**Good**
Politics	**Activity high**
Sport	**35 clubs**
National team position	**18th**
Sport facilities	**Good**
Arts opportunities	**Few**
Student magazine	**SHU-Print**
Student radio	**RUSH**
Nightclub/bars	**Bar Phoenix**
Union ents	**Cheese, indie**
Union clubs/societies	**65**
Most popular society	**RUSH fm**
Parking	**Poor**
CITY:	
Entertainment	★★★★★
Scene	**Seriously good**
Town/gown relations	**Good**
Risk of violence	**Average**
Cost of living	**Average**
Student concessions	**Good**
Survival + 2 nights out	**£80 pw**
Part-time work campus/town	**Good/excellent**

AT A GLANCE

ACADEMIC FILE:	
Subjects assessed	**27**
Excellent	**78%**
Typical entry requirements	**250 points**
Application acceptance rate	**20%, high**
Students-staff ratio	**22:1**
First/2:1 degree pass rate	**47%**
ACCOMMODATION FILE:	
Guarantee to freshers	**100%**
Style	**Halls, houses, lodgings**
Catered	**10%**
En-suite	**30%**
Price range per annum	**£58-£91**
City rent per week	**£38-£68**

SOCIAL SCENE

STUDENTS' UNION The stunning silver drums of the new Union Building (known as HUBs) beat a fanfare to what the uni describes as 'a unique and unrivalled welfare and social facility for 28,000 students'. It cost them £5 million, so we should allow them that. There's a student advice centre and volunteering team, a shop, social space and activities area, plus 3 multi-functional entertainment rooms and a café/bar. **Bar Phoenix** is the focal point, downstairs from the club nights. Ents come on weekday nights in the shape of *Souled* – 6ts guitar, Motown and northern soul, and *You Bring We Spin*, pub quiz etc. On Fridays, it's *Stardust* (6ts/7ts - geddit?), back from its intergalactic break, while Saturday is, and always has been, *Sheff 1* (chart and dance favourite choice of the city).

Stardust and Sheff1 have been so popular that battles have been known with ticket touts re-selling tickets bought at cheaper advance prices.

Meanwhile, if the thought of another night of cheesy chart music 'sends a chill down your spine,' says the increasingly sassy union, 'you'll be glad to know that every Tuesday the HUBs become home to the weekly indie rock'n'roll ruckus that is *Plan B*!'There's also Feliz: Sheffield's newest Gay friendly night, Feliz (fi-leeth), Spanish for 'happy and gay'.

There are 30 student societies, Media = the weekly *HUGE - Hallam Union Guide to Events*, also *SHU-Print* their monthly paper, and RUSH radio, 'with a brand new look and a brand new attitude!'.

War, fees housing and 'Free Wednesdays from lectures' have been the substance of highly active campaigning. Amazing to think that they have to free Wednesdays, given that it's sports day and they are one of the most competitive in the country – there are 35 sports societies and thoroughly professional facilities are available.

Sport The new fitness suite spans 600 square metres and has more than 70 fitness stations, an array of the latest equipment, and an advanced weights and training area. The changing facilities are fully equipped for the disabled, and there's also 'a sunbed, assessment rooms and full audio and satellite TV system' – they call that exercise? There's another suite on Collegiate Campus.

Town See *Sheffield Student City*, page 415.

PILLOW TALK

Catered halls and self-catered purpose-built complexes are available. Some catered – about 10%

Besides halls, there are partnership schemes in the private sector.

GETTING THERE

☛ By road: M1 (J33), A630, A57.
☛ By coach: London, 3:45; Newcastle, 4:45; Exeter, 6:30-7:30; Manchester, 3:00.
☛ By rail: London, 2:30; Liverpool Lime Street, 1:45; Manchester Piccadilly, 1:00; Nottingham, 1:00; Leeds, 0:30.
☛ By air: Manchester Airport.

UNIVERSITY OF SOUTHAMPTON

The University of Southampton
Highfield
Southampton SO17 1BH

TEL 023 8059 5000
FAX 023 8059 3037
EMAIL prospenq@soton.ac.uk
WEB www.soton.ac.uk

Southampton Students' Union
Highfield
Southampton SO17 1BJ

TEL 023 8059 5201
FAX 023 8059 5252
EMAIL susu@soton.ac.uk
WEB www.soton.ac.uk/~susu/

VAG VIEW

Southampton has one of the best academic records in the country, but has suffered a poor reputation for student satisfaction beyond academia – historically the social side of things has been a bit limp. Now it has been revitalised by a huge investment in the Students Union.

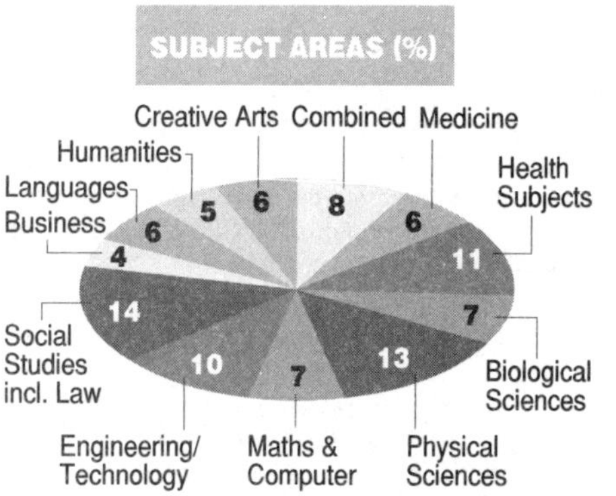

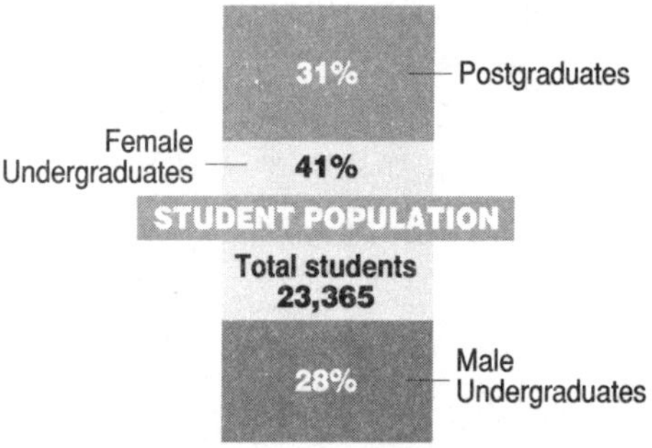

CAMPUS

Highfield Campus From east or west you rattle along the M27 until you hit Junction 5, whereupon you dive down south, following the uni signs, and suddenly, 2 miles from the centre of the city, there you are in it. You don't *enter* the main Highfield campus as you might Sussex campus or Nottingham. It is a campus split by University Road, a public road with uni buildings off to the left and right, so that you're not sure whether the city has wandered onto the campus or the campus has not yet quite commandeered its piece of the city (there is nothing of the excitement of Manchester's Oxford Road, where such questions would never occur).

There's a chemically, sciency feel to it. It's all rather laboratorial, claustrophobic, bursting at the seams, for such an eminent university. And then you are transported into some carefully landscaped botanical gardens with stream, and on, across The Avenue, eventually to be released onto the huge open acreage of Southampton Common, where you can...breathe!

Arts are at The Avenue Campus nearby. Finally, you arrive at their internationally renowned **Waterside Campus**/Oceanography Centre.

FEES, BURSARIES

UK & EU Fees: £3000 p.a. If in receipt of full HE Maintenance grant there's a bursary of £1000; if in receipt of partial grant, bursaries are on a sliding scale up to £1000, according to household earnings. There are bursaries to wncourage applications from a wider section of the population and scjolarships for academic achievement.

STUDENT PROFILE

The tradition is that, apart from a small scattering of minority groups and locals, Southampton students are middle-class, although the public school kid intake is in fact similar to that of Reading or Warwick, and less than at Bristol, Durham or Exeter. In a survey of student drug-taking habits by the Adam Smith Institute, they came out 'most abstemious'. The survey was undertaken before the opening of the new on-campus pleasure dome (see *Social Scene* below). It is as yet unclear whether students' habits have changed, only that everyone is having the time of their lives at Highfield.

ACADEMIA & JOBS

The 5-floor Hartley Library on the main Highfield campus has recently undergone a massive refit, making it one of the most advanced university libraries in Britain. Access to resources has been improved and personal study areas have been restyled to allow more privacy.

The Medical Faculty was rated full marks in the teaching assessments. It's a 5-year BM with integrated course structure and clinical contact from first year. A 4th-year 8-week period of clinical experience may be had in subject and place of your choice (many opt to go abroad). In 2004 there was a 9% application acceptance rate, makig it more competitive than most. Entry AABb, including Chemistry A. 7A/B at GCSE to include Maths, English and Double Award Science. Teaching inspection 24 (full marks). Research Grade 5: Clinical Lab Sciences, Hospital-based Clinical, Psychology, Biological Sciences. They are looking for the committed, well-rounded applicant capable of approaching problems with a certain flair, not confined by specialism. Coursework is geared towards problem-solving; patient contact is made in the first term in order to develop communication skills.

Other departments that scored full marks for teaching are: Education, Philosophy, Economics, Electrical & Electronic Engineering, Archaeology and Politics.

If you look at another area in which the uni is

ACADEMIC EXCELLENCE

TEACHING: *(Rated Excellent or 17+ out of 24)*	
Chemistry, Applied Social Work, Computer Studies, Geography, English, Oceanography, Geology, Music.	**Excellent**
Philosophy, Electric/Electron Eng Economics, Education, Medicine, Archaeology, Politics	**24**
General Eng, Management Ships Science, Biosciences	**23**
Art & Design, Nursing, Physics	**22**
Psychology, Sociology, Civil Eng, Mech, Aeronaut & Manuf Eng	**21**
History of Art, Maths, Subjects Allied to Medicine	**20**
Modern Languages (French, German, Iberian Studies).	**18**
RESEARCH: *Top grades 5/5*/6**	
Computer, Electrical/Electronic Eng, Mechanical/Aeronautical/ Manufacturing Eng, Law, European Studies, Music	**Grade 6***
Physics, Civil Eng,	**Grade 5***
Clinical Laboratory Sciences, Hospital-based Clinical, Psychology, Biological Sciences, Chemistry, Environmental Sciences, Pure Maths, Applied Maths, Statistics, Operational Research, Geography, Economics, Social Policy, English, Archaeology, History	**Grade 5**

UNIVERSITY/STUDENT PROFILE

University since	**1952**
Situation/style	**Campus**
Student population	**22365**
Undergraduates	**16030**
- mature	**14%**
- non EU undergraduates	**4%**
- male/female	**40/60**
- non-traditional student intake	**20%**
- state school intake	**80%**
- drop-out rate	**4%, low**
- undergraduate applications	**Up 9%**

renowned – Geography – you see a similar sort of picture. Analytical skills, problem-solving and written and oral expression are to the fore – it's an approach to which employers relate.

Physiotherapy, Occupational Therapy and Podiatry degrees further boost the health sector. There's also Nursing (Adult, Child, Learning Disability, Mental) and Midwifery. Psychotherapists also bound out of here. Look at their Applied Social Science degrees (Anthropology, Criminology), as well as the BSc Psychology and BSc Social Work.

After health, the City claims most of Southampton's graduates. Accounting & Economics or Finance ensure good employment figures, and there's a leaning to careers for tax expert/consultants and actuaries. For the latter, look especially at Economics with Actuarial Studies and Mathematics with Actuarial Studies. Teaching inspection 20. Research Grade 5.

Economics, Maths and Business are the main routes for aspiring bankers, financiers and investment advisers/analysts. Economics took full marks at the assessments and an international Grade 5 for research; Management scored 23. Maths 20 and again a Grade 5 for research.

Analytical skills, problem-solving and written and oral expression are to the fore – it's an approach to which employers relate.

Southampton are hot on student enterprise. 'Spin out' companies have raised more than £20 million of private funds. More than 60 students enrolled with the Student Entrepreneurs Club. SETsquared is a dedicated support and mentoring facility for entrepreneurs and fledgling enterprises.

In the Oceanography Centre at Southampton's Dockside, Marine Science students again have access to exceptional analytical and research facilities. The faculty produces partnership degrees with Biology, Geology, Geography, Maths, Physics, which have led to Excellent ratings in the assessments. Ellen MacArthur's stunning performance in Kingfisher, in the Vendee Global Challenge, carried with it tank and wind-tunnel research work done by the university. The yachtswoman was closely involved in the design and testing processes.

Defence is clearly a priority. Like Portsmouth along the coast, Southampton has an active OTC. There's a University Air Squadron and Royal Naval Unit. Many Southampton graduates bound for the Defence industry come from the Faculty of Engineering & Applied Science, which gained world-class ratings in the research assessments, and Electronics scored full marks in the teaching assessments: Acousitical, Aerospace, Civil, Electrical & Electronic, Electromechanical and a number of Engineering Management degrees, also Computing Engineering.

The uni has more than a 27% share nationally of RN officers. See in particular the B/MEng Ship Science, the MEng comes in various orientations: Yacht & Small Craft, Naval Architecture, Inter-Disciplinary, and the 4-year Advanced Materials. There's a 23-point assessment for Ship Science and an international Grade 5 level for Operational Research. For RAF officers, there's a BEng Foundation year and everything from Computer Science/Engineering through MEng Aerospace Engineering with European Studies. Army officers' interest tips in favour of Physical Sciences, where there are 4-year Masters degrees and 3-year BSc Hons from which to choose. There are good joint Chemistry or Physics courses with specialisms such as Laser Science, Maths and Theoretical Physics (5* world-class research rating).

No mention of Southampton ever goes without a nod to Medicine, and in this context, some 8% of graduates going into Defence do so with some medical science background – Medicinal Chemistry, Biomedical Sciences, etc.

Computer programmers and software engineers also proliferate. They offer BSc Computer Science and various orientations – with AI, Distributed Systems & Network, Image &

WHERE SOUTHAMPTON GRADUATES END UP

Health & Social Work: 21%; Education: 4%; Wholesale Retail: 7%; Manufacturing: 9%; Financial Activities: 11%; Public Administration, Civil Service & Defence: 9%; Hotel/Restaurant: 4%; Transport & Communications (including Telecommunications): 4%; Construction: 1%; Personnel: 5%; Computer: 3.5%; Business & Management: 3%; Accountancy: 4%; Media (including Film): 1%; Legal 2%; Publishing: 1.5%; Advertising: 0.5%; Sport: 1.5%.

Approximate 'graduate track' employed **64%**

WHAT IT'S REALLY LIKE	
UNIVERSITY:	
Social Life	★★★★★
Campus scene	**Active, impressive**
Student Union services	**Good**
Politics	**Tory heartland**
Sport	**70 clubs**
National team position	**13th**
Sport facilities	**Excellent**
Arts opportunities	**Drama, film excellent**
Student newspaper	**Wessex Scene**
Student radio	**Surge**
Nightclub	**The Cube**
Bars	**Bridge Bar, Stag's Head**
Union ents	**Kinki, Generator, Fat Poppadaddys**
Union clubs/societies	**160+**
Most active society	**Theatre Group**
Parking	**No first years**
CITY:	
Entertainment	★★★
Scene	**Pubs, clubs, water**
Town/gown relations	**Average-poor**
Risk of violence	**Average**
Cost of living	**Average**
Student concessions	**OK**
Survival + 2 nights out	**£80 pw**
Part-time work campus/town	**Good/excellent**

Multimedia Systems, Software Eng. There are also two MEng degrees: Software Engineering and the 4-year Computer Engineering, and a facility, too, to study Computer Science for a BEng with Foundation year.

For would-be sound recordists Southampton leads the employment field with B/MEng Acoustical Engineering. Look at course links between their Institute of Sound & Vibration and the Dept of Music: BSc Acoustics and/with Music and the Acoustical Engineering Foundation course. Full marks and a world class reputation for Electronic Engineering and an 'Excellent' for teaching Music and Grade 6* for research give one confidence.

Boat/ship designers/surveyors/brokers are all served well. Southampton satisfies through design, construction and operation in its Department of Engineering. Maths and a science (preferably Physics) or a techno subject are essential for the various Ship Science courses. Among the Masters and Bachelor degrees on offer is Ship Science/Yacht & Small Craft and SS/Naval Architecture asking the same; 350 points will get you the main BEng, Ship Science, and there's a 4-year version with Foundation if you need it. Teaching inspection 23.

For aspiring environmental officers the 4-year MEnvSci Environmental Sciences does the trick. Similar Masters degrees are available in Geology, Geophysics, and Oceanography, and then a whole range of BSc degrees variously offering French or German options, and there's an Environmental Sciences Foundation year too.

Humanities spawn their fair share of librarians and museum curators from here, while in the business sector a number become sales or travel agency managers.

Their Sports Management & Leadership and Sport Studies degrees put them in the Top 10 for athletes, sportsmen, players and officials, and ensure a very healthy spin-off in performance levels in the BUSA league (13th this year).

Finally, Law is also a big draw, they have a world-class Grade 6* rating for research.

Winchester School of Art Park Avenue, Winchester SO23 8DL. Tel 01962 842500 is Southampton's Art & Design faculty and has been part of the uni since 1996. They are only about 12 miles apart, but really quite separate. There has been considerable investment – £3 million bought new studios, a library (20-25,000 volumes, 100,000 slides, 4,000 videos), a lecture theatre, photo and digital workshops, seminar rooms and a Students' Union. Degrees are offered in Fine Art, Practice & Theory and Textiles, Fashion & Fibre. Teaching inspection 22.

SOCIAL SCENE

Students' Union A new Student Services Centre, site for SUSU's Advice & Information Centre opened in October 2005.

For the past few years SUSU has been a bit of a building site, but now boasts a new cinema and nightclub with three bars collectively known as **The Cube**, increasing capacity to 1700. At the Friday night *Kinki* event – low drinks prices and music across three floors (from cheese, to dance, to indie) – it's heaving.

The Cube is open until 2 am, three nights a week. **The Stag's Head** is a pub-style bar with license until midnight, and runs events such as Karaoke and the Sunday Quiz.

There is also the **Bridge** bar, located at the top of the Union building and with a view of campus and stream below. **The Bridge** hosts the *Jazz Lounge*, the *Laughter Lounge*, and the chill-out *Living Room* events.

Fat Poppadaddys comes to town on Saturday (funk, 60s, hip hop, reggae, drum 'n' bass). Thursdays hosts *Generator* – their indie and rock night, which feature live bands, like Arab Strap.

Over the past couple of years, SUSU has also hosted big name DJs such as Dave Pearce, Carl Cox and Judge Jules. The Cut Up Boys kept the Grab Ball pumping, and Colin Murray took to the decks in Freshers' Week last year. Radio 1 Zane Low's *In New Music We Trust* tour came to the Union as well and Razorlight played live. More recently, Zane hijacked the student radio station, Surge, and took over the Saturday night show.

Societies have always been strong at Southampton. *Wessex Scene*, the student paper, and Surge Radio remain a feature, as does *The Edge*, the ents paper. *Wessex Scene* won the 2004 *Guardian* Media Award for Website of the Year and has been nominated in that category for 4 successive years. Surge, which has recently benefited from a new £20k studio, scooped 2 gold awards at the National Student Radio Awards in 2005 – for best newcomer and best news and talk. They also received nominations for best technical achievement, best male and best off air marketing and publicity.

For Drama, there's the highly rated **Nuffield Theatre,** and there's a thriving Film Society. They have a 400-seat cinema showing second-release films through Dolby surround sound. There's also a tradition of student bands.

Sport Sport is huge at Southampton. Last year saw the opening of a brand new sports centre on the campus, complete with swimming pool, gym, 8-badminton court sports hall and 140-station fitness suite. And in Autumn 2005 the new Wide Lane Sports Complex was opened by John Inverdale. This £4.3m complex boasts 76 acres of pitches (including 2 floodlit synthetic pitches), 24 changing rooms, meeting rooms and a fully-licensed bar. There's also a boatyard for watersporters. The sailors have won the BUSA championship more times than Portsmouth care to recall.

Town While Southampton itself has neither the size nor vigour of Manchester or its football team, nor yet the groovy cuts of Brighton or even Bournemouth, it's a lively enough place to live. Having been a Regency holiday resort, the city centre has a large number of spacious parks and waterfront attractions.

'If Southampton were a person, it would be a dedicated alcoholic,' said a student. 'The city centre and waterfront have a network of colossal alcohol palaces (including Britain's largest pub, the **Square Balloon**), yet the city lacks a twilight zone, for, owing to a local statute, even nightclubs are not allowed to open later than 2.'

There are three cinemas and the **Mayflower Theatre**, which plays host to several major West End shows. Musically, Southampton lacks a major venue and is often ignored by the larger acts: consult your Bournemouth train timetable.

AT A GLANCE

ACADEMIC FILE:	
Subjects assessed	**34**
Excellent	**91%**
Typical entry requirements	**360 points**
Application acceptance rate	**12%, low**
Students-staff ratio	**15:1**
First/2:1 degree pass rate	**69%**
ACCOMMODATION FILE:	
Guarantee to freshers	**If uni first firm choice**
Style	**Halls, flats**
Catered	**25%**
En-suite	**45%**
Price range pw	**£65-£128**
City rent pw	**£48-£70**

PILLOW TALK

University accommodation (halls and flats) is guaranteed to all first year undergraduates who meet the terms of their offers, and name Southampton as their firm choice.

There are new and notably enlightened residences now for couples, too: Shaftesbury Avenue and Edwina House. Facilities may include a library and music room, and computer, TV and games rooms. Some halls have sports facilities, all have launderettes and many have shops and bars. Every room has a phone. Avoid Bencraft and Stoneham halls. Bencraft is miles from anywhere and Stoneham is Southampton's answer to the walled city of Kowloon apparently.

GETTING THERE

☛ By road to Southampton: M3/J 14, A33. To Winchester: M3/J10 or A34.

☛ By coach to Southampton: London, 2:30; Bristol, 2:45; Birmingham, 3:40. To Winchester: London, 2:00; Birmingham, 5:30.

☛ By rail to Southampton: London Waterloo, 1:40; Bristol Parkway, 2:15; Birmingham, 3:30; Sheffield, 4:45; Winchester, 20 mins.

☛ By air: Southampton International Airport.

SOUTHAMPTON SOLENT UNIVERSITY

Southampton Solent University
East Park Terrace
Southampton
Hampshire SO14 ORT

TEL 023 8031 9039
FAX 023 8022 2259
EMAIL enquiries@solent.ac.uk
WEB www.solent.ac.uk/

VAG VIEW

Southampton Institute, out of Southampton's College of Art and College of Higher Education, and the College of Nautical Studies at Warwash, looks an attractive thoroughbred in its own right. There is an innovative vocational portfolio, an enviable record of excellence in teaching assessments, a lively student scene, and it is not too demanding at entry. What's more, its investment in student residences (they tell us they can meet 'all demand') even three years ago indicated an appeal not restricted to a local clientele. As we said at the time: 'We should not be surprised that the institute has on its longterm plans the desire for University status.'

Well, now they have it. On August 15, 2005, they became a university. They say: 'We have no intention of changing our mission or ethos. Our focus will remain on accessibility and teaching strongly underpinned by research and community engagement. We will continue to offer and develop innovative courses with an emphasis on preparing students for the world of work.'

FEES, BURSARIES

UK & EU Fees: £3000 p.a. All sub-degree courses (HNDs and Foundation Degrees): £1950 p.a.; Foundation year: £1600 p.a. Bursary for students in receipt of full HE Maintenance grant £1000 (£300 for HND); £500 for 50% grant; £250 for 25%. Sports scholarships are available, as are the Lisa Wilson scholarship and Toft Scholarship for students 'who have overcome adversity or can demonstrate why he/she needs extra financial help with his/her studies' (£1000).

STUDENT PROFILE

Writes Tanver Hussain. 'The blokes all look like fugitives from just about any boy band and the girls could form All Saints 100 times over. This excludes Art students and the rugby team, as you will find that they are in worlds of their own!

SUBJECT AREAS (%)

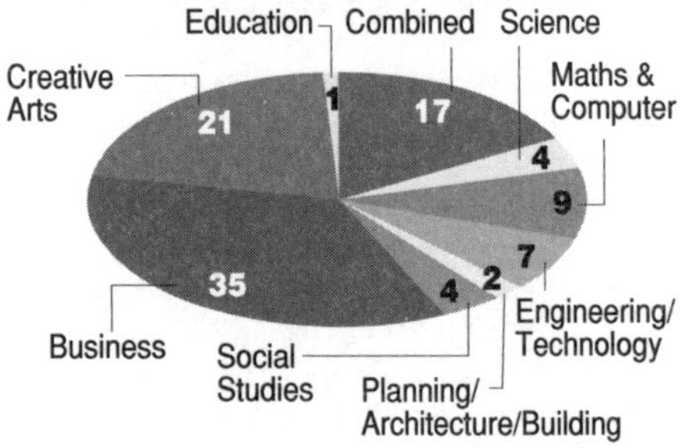

Don't be frightened! You'll find a group of people you will naturally slot into and pretty soon you will go drinking with them every night until you run out of money or are barred from every club, pub or bar in the city.'

Tanver's judgement may have been swayed by the thousands of FE students that inhabit Solent. There are, too, among undergraduates, some 18% part-timers.

ACADEMIA & JOBS

The faculties are: Business; Media, Arts and Society; and Technology. Recently they opened a £9-million centre with information technology suite, lecture theatres and admin offices. Besides Maritime (including yacht and powercraft design), departments include Design (Fashion, Fine Art, Graphic Design, Interior, etc); Built Environment

UNIVERSITY/STUDENT PROFILE

University since	**2005**
Situation/style	**Civic**
Student population	**11000**
Undergraduates	**10060**
- mature	**40%**
- non EU undergraduates	**6%**
- male/female	**54/46**
- non-traditional student intake	**32%**
- state sector intake	**95%**
- drop-out rate	**9%**
- undergraduate applications	**Constant**

(big strength in Architectural Technology degrees, Construction Management, etc); Business (Tourism Management is new with options like Cruise and Travel Operations); Law (Commercial Law degrees); Media Arts (Film, Fiction, Journalism, Advertising); Social Science (Community Studies, Psychology, Criminology, Politics); Systems Engineering (masses of computer courses and a tasty specialist degree in Media Technology for the broadcast, film & entertainment industries). The curriculum is exciting, innovative, expanding fast.

To be an advertising account executive, you can hardly do better than this university. They place more graduates into the sector than virtually any other. Look at the Design courses and the 3-year Advertising BA or the 1-year Creative Industries top-up for their 2-year HND, Advertising and Media Communication.

Emphasis is on developing the creative faculties by means of idea generation exercises and creative thinking workshops. Budding art directors or copywriters will also get genned up on campaign planning, media buying, targeting and brand positioning. Conversely, if you want to play a strategic role as account planner, handler, media buyer or brand manager, you get a chance to produce campaign concepts for a creative portfolio of work. There's a twinning with a London ad agency, and terrific hands-on experience available from tutors.

Creative writing is a developing area. new this year is BA Popular Fiction, Screenwriting, Magazine Journalism & Feature Writing, Comedy - Writing & Performance, Sport Writing. Generally, for journalism it's the BA dedicated degree, while for scriptwriting it's BA Media Writing. Nationwide, the three scriptwriting degrees are Scriptwriting for Film & TV at Bournemouth, Writing (Scripted Media) at Dartington College of Arts, and this one at Southampton Solent. It offers a thorough knowledge of the contexts in which you could put the skills it teaches to work – Theatre, Television, Publishing, Editing, Journalism, PR, or Advertising.

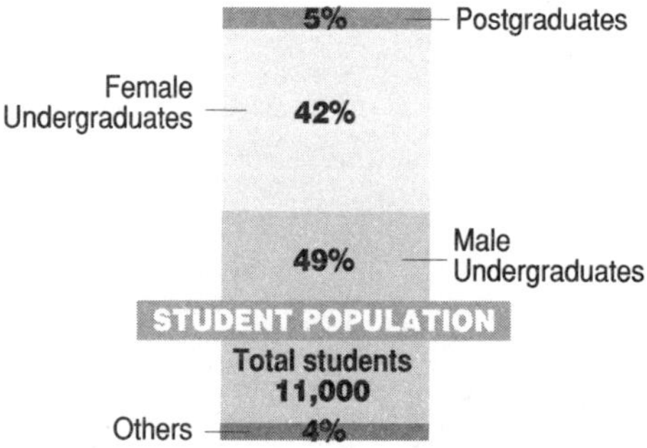

ACADEMIC EXCELLENCE

TEACHING :
(Rated Excellent or 17+ out of 24)

Civil Eng, Building, Land & Property Mgt, Business	**22**
Drama, Dance & Cinematics, Leisure/Sport	**21**
Psychology, Sociology, Electric & Electron Engineering, General Eng, Mechanical & Manuf Eng, Aero Eng, Materials Tech.	**19**
Town & Country Planning, Communication & Media	**18**
Art & Design	**17**

Teaching inspection, 18, is low, but results are good.

Among the smaller student populations Solent and Napier (Edinburgh) mount an amazingly strong challenge to the big boys in getting graduates into publishing, being right up there with universities that have double their number of undergraduates. Solent mounts its strategy through Media with Cultural Studies, Media Writing, Advertising, Journalism, Marketing with Media & Design, and through its Graphics, Design Studies, Product Design with Marketing, etc degrees. Its general Marketing, Management and Communications degrees are also a gateway.

'Solent's already good media production facilities are being remodelled to produce a complete digital media centre,' they say: 'four new digital radio studios came on stream this year and work underway will see digital television studios and a brand new recording studio complex ready for this year. This will complement the Centre of Excellence for Broadcasting and Multimedia Production, to be opened early in 2006.'

Film cameramen/women (TV & Film) look to their BSc Film & Video Technology. This year, too, comes BA Television & Video Production. BSc Media Technology & Music, and BSc Studio Technology find graduates jobs in the music business. Now comes BA Popular Music Studies & Record Production.

Meanwhile, trainee antique dealer/restorers revel in BA Antiques (History & Collecting) – fine arts valuation and appraisal with sharp focus on collecting and the history of collecting from an aesthetic, cultural and financial viewpoint. That's how vocational the set-up is. If you're interested, look at their BA Fine Arts Valuation, too. Both courses are linked to national auction houses.

There's constantly new things going on in art and design – a whole host of new fashion, fashion photography, interiors degrees this year – and recently Muti-media Design and Digital Imaging degrees have led to a big increase in jobs. BA Illustration with Animation also scores high in the world of computer games design.

BSc Mobile Web Technology is new this year, and Electronic Engineering is another big strength. Many come through the HND or Foundation years, their destination almost exclusively telecommunications. Employment figures are good.

Finally, boat/ship designer/surveyor/brokers find their way to courses dedicated to their interests – such as Merchant Ship Operations, Maritime Business, Shipping Operations BSc, Yacht Manufacturing & Surveying and Yacht & Powercraft Design. Foundation years are invariably available, if necessary.

AT A GLANCE

ACADEMIC FILE:	
Subjects assessed	**20**
Excellent	**70%**
Typical entry requirements	**180 points**
Application acceptance rate	**30%, high**
Students-staff ratio	**n/a**
First/2:1 degree pass rate	**45%**
ACCOMMODATION FILE:	
Guarantee to freshers	**95%**
Style	**Halls**
Catered	**None**
En suite	**45%**
Approx price pw (no food)	**£46.65-£91**
City rent pw	**£48-£70**

SOCIAL SCENE

STUDENTS' UNION The union has two bars, renovated within the not so distant past, the imaginatively-named **Bottom Bar** (downstairs) opens during the week, 11am-5pm, and on Saturday 7pm-11pm in concert with **Top Bar** (11am-11pm in week, 7pm-11pm Saturday). Saturday is the same here as it is at the other uni in Southampton – *Fat Poppadaddys* (funk, 60s, hip hop, reggae, drum 'n' bass). *Fridays @ Solent* are £1-a-shot funky house nights. Thursdays are *Paper Scissors Rock* (alternative). Wednesdays, there's *Loaded*, 9-10pm @ Top Bar, pre-club for *Cheeky Monkey* @ **Ikon Diva** or **Kaos** in town (with an Express Pass which beats the inevitable queue at these the biggest nightclubs).

This union/town tie-up is typical of the weekly ents menu. Tuesday is *Funkie Junkie* (mainstream r&b, house & party anthems) at newest club, **Junk**, on the London Road, again after a **Top Bar** warm-up. Monday, meanwhile, is *Acoustic Night* at Top Bar, a 'bring mates, bring a guitar' affair.

Media-wise there's SIN Radio and Re:SUS magazine. There are 28 societies in operation, not counting course-related efforts.

WHAT IT'S REALLY LIKE

UNIVERSITY:	
Social Life	★★★
Campus scene	**Avtice, diverse**
Student Union services	**Good**
Politics	**Not much**
Sport	**Competitive**
National team position	**43rd, 31 clubs**
Sport facilities	**Good**
Arts opportunities	**Available**
Student magazine	**Re:SUS**
Student radio station	**SIN Radio**
Nightclub	**In-town clubs**
Bars	**Top Bar, Bottom Bar**
Union ents	**Fat Poppadaddys, city student nights**
Union societies	**28**
Parking	**Poor, permiy**
CITY:	
Entertainment	★★★
Scene	**Pubs, clubs, water**
Town/gown relations	**Average-poor**
Risk of violence	**Average**
Cost of living	**Average**
Student concessions	**OK**
Survival + 2 nights out	**£80 pw**
Part-time work campus/town	**Good/excellent**

SPORT There were 31 sports clubs up and running this year, from Capoeira to roller hockey, and triathlon to taekwon do, as well as the more usual – rugby, rowing, American Football, and, as expected in a college dedicated to maritime subjects, water plays a key part.

Solent is improving rapidly in its strength in sports and is now 43rd in the national BUSA leagues. Sailing is the strongest sport – they've been national champions three times in the past four years (came second the other time) and three times in the top three in the world. Students come to the university because of its reputation in this sport. Sports scholarships were introduced to attract top performers in all sports. Ground-based sports facilities include a sports hall and fitness suite, sauna and solarium. Playing fields are 4 miles from the city. There's a licensed pavilion, the **Budweiser Sports Bar**.

PILLOW TALK

Cream of the halls crop would have to be Lucia

Foster Welch, not only is it the biggest, but it has the advantage of having Ocean Village on its doorstep. The downside is that you are 15 minutes away from the main campus and there is no common room. The other halls all have their plus points, Kimber and its spangly new kitchens or Deanery, one of the newest. All have their own laundry, and all have recently been wired for intranet and intranet access, giving students 24-hour on-line access to the university's managed learning environment and email and internet. You can't choose where you live, but you can choose to have an en-suite bathroom or not.

GETTING THERE

- ☛ By road: M3/J 14, A33. Warsash: M27/J8, A27.
- ☛ By coach to Southampton: London, 2:30; Bristol, 2:45; Birmingham, 3:40.
- ☛ By rail: London Waterloo, 1:40; Bristol Parkway, 2:15; Birmingham, 3:30; Sheffield, 4:45.
- ☛ By air: Southampton International Airport.

STAFFORDSHIRE UNIVERSITY

Staffordshire University
College Road
Stoke-on-Trent ST4 2DE

TEL 01782 294000
FAX 01782 292740
EMAIL admissions@staffs.ac.uk
WEB www.staffs.ac.uk

Staffordshire Students' Union
College Road
Stoke-on-Trent
Staffs ST4 2DE

TEL 01782 294629
FAX 01782 295736
EMAIL theunion@staffs.ac.uk
WEB www.staffsunion.com

VAG VIEW

There is clear alignment between their academic strengths and their nationally excellent employment record. There's also good sport, a strong local ents scene and plenty of student activities to widen your perspective on life. Yet, be aware, Staffordshire is very different from neighbouring Keele

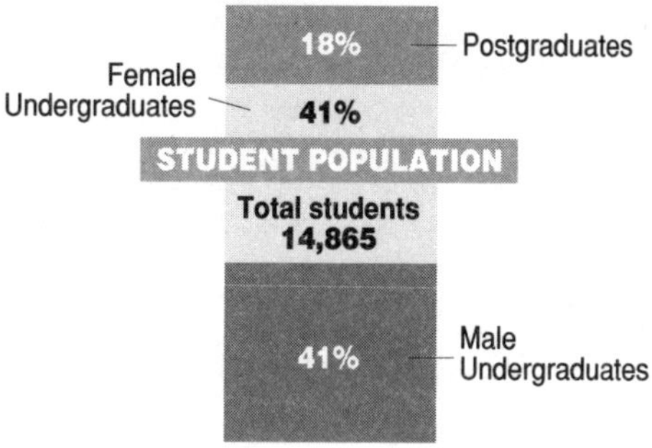

CAMPUSES

There are sites in Stoke and Stafford, 12 miles to the south, opposite the railway station. This is an area known as the Potteries, a borough incorporated in 1907 to include Stoke-on-Trent, Hanley, Burslem, Tinstall, Longton and Fenton. Its most famous son, Arnold Bennett (author of *Clayhanger*, *Anne of the Five Towns* – he preferred the sound of five, so left out Fenton) couldn't get away fast enough, but that had nothing to do with the university, which only gained its status in 1992.

FEES, BURSARIES

UK & EU Fees: £3000 p.a. If in receipt of full HE Maintenance grant, there's a bursary of £1000; if in receipt of partial grant, bursaries are on a sliding scale from £500 to £1000, according to household earnings.

STUDENT PROFILE

The student profile is as you would expect. There's a sizable mature population and a sizable local intake. Most entrants are from state schools, and a third of non-mature entrants from social groups least represented at university. The uni appeals to

UNIVERSITY/STUDENT PROFILE	
University since	**1992**
Situation/style	**Campus/ town sites**
Student population	**14865**
Undergraduates	**12235**
- mature	**30%**
- non EU undergraduates	**4%**
- male/female	**51/49**
- non-traditional student intake	**37%**
- state sector intake	**97%**
- drop-out rate	**10%**
- undergraduate applications	**Down 2%**

WHERE STAFFORDSHIRE GRADUATES END UP

Health & Social Work: 7%; Education: 7%; Wholesale Retail: 15%; Manufacturing: 11%; Financial Activities: 6%; Public Administration, Civil Service & Defence: 10%; Hotel/Restaurant: 4%; Transport & Communications (including Telecommunications): 5%; Construction: 1%; Mining/Oil Extracting: 0.5%; Personnel: 5%; Computer: 6.5%; Business & Management: 6.5%; Accountancy: 1%; Media (including Film): 2.5%; Legal 2.5%; Architecture: 1%; Publishing: 1%; Advertising: 0.5%; Sport: 0.5%.

the region with a priority application scheme.

ACADEMIA & JOBS

The faculties are Arts, Media & Design; Business & Law; Computing, Engineering & Technology; Health & Sciences; the Staffordshire University Business School; and the Staffordshire Law School. At Stoke there's Art & Design, Business, Law, Humanities & Social Sciences and Sciences. At Stafford, Computing, Engineering & Advanced Technology and Health. But what's novel is the HE-FE federation being developed with Tamworth & Lichfield College and other further education colleges. There is a Lichfield Campus for the purpose and a whole range of courses, degrees and HNDs with links to what's going on at the mother house.

There are top teaching assessments in Economics (full marks), Psychology, Philosophy, Art & Design, Physics, Sport, Biosciences, Nursing and other subjects allied to Medicine – the latter featuring midwifery and the nursing (adult, child and mental health). A new healthcare facility opened in 2004 at the Stafford campus to provide NHS care to students, staff and the community. There are doctors' consulting rooms, a practice nurse physiotherapy service and a retail pharmacy.

Meanwhile, Staffs' IT & Computing faculty is brimming with opportunity: Graphics/Imaging /Visualisation, Science, Systems, Applicable Maths, Internet Technology, Intelligent Systems, Software Engineering, Forensic, Mobile, computer Design, Games Design, Network Engineering... Aspiring computer programmers and IT consultants (they lead the employment field nationally) should go through it with a toothcomb, Staffordshire Uni is the top graduate supplier to this sector. Entry 240 points. Resources in computing are especially good – two IT centres, the £5-million Octagon centre being a central focus with 800+ workstations.

SUBJECT AREAS (%)

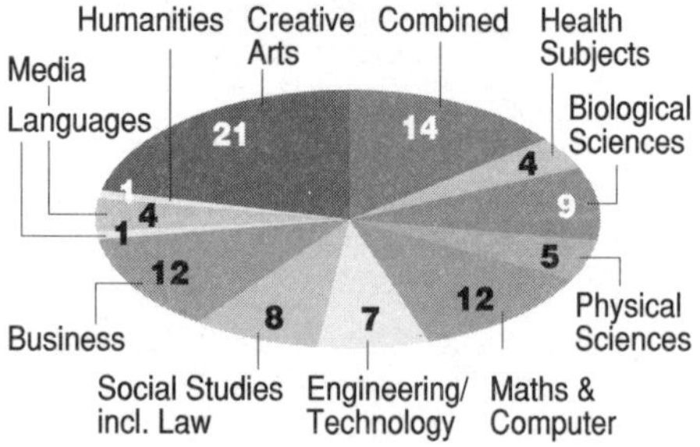

Graduates acquire accounting knowledge with computer-based analytical, management and design skills. The single honsBA Accounting is joined by combos with Business, Economics and Law.

There's a £1.25-million incubation business project at the Stafford Business Village, with 'high specification incubation' for 40 businesses. Marketing is one highly successful employment area at the Business School, which also explores management and entrepreneurship in areas such as personnel, travel and tourism, as well as having a clutch of degrees in business, computing and IT.

A large number of graduates go into welfare, community and youth work. Look at the Applied Social Studies top-ups, the Sport degrees and high-flying BSc Social Psychology, or the Psychology degrees, which can be done alonc or with

ACADEMIC EXCELLENCE

TEACHING:
(Rated Excellent or 17+ out of 24)

Economics	**24**
Psychology, Philosophy	**23**
Art & Design, Physics, Leisure/Sport, Biosciences, Nursing, Other Subjects Allied to Medicine	**22**
Modern Languages (French, German, Iberian Studies), History of Art.	**21**
Electronic & Electrical Eng.	**20**

RESEARCH :
*Top grades 5/5** **None**

WHAT IT'S REALLY LIKE	
UNIVERSITY:	
Social Life	★★★
Campus scene	**Unpretentious fun**
Student Union services	**Good**
Politics	**Activity low: fees**
Sport	**Busy**
National team position	**99th**
Sport facilities	**Good**
Arts opportunities	**Drama, music excellent; dance, film, art good**
Student newspaper	**Get Knotted**
Student radio	**GK Radio**
Nightclub	**Legends**
Bars	**LRV, Ember Lounge**
Union ents	**Serious clubnights & live**
Union societies	**23**
Most active society	**Drama**
Parking	**Adequate**
TOWN:	
Entertainment	★★★
Town scene	**Pubs, clubs**
Town/gown relations	**Average**
Risk of violence	**Average**
Cost of living	**Average**
Student concessions	**Good**
Survival + 2 nights out	**£60 pw**
Part-time work campus/town	**Good**

Criminology or Sport & Excercise. Also, BA Social Work.

The Sport & Leisure Department, which is up there employment-wise with the big boys at Brighton and Nottingham Trent.

The Law Society has awarded the University's LPC course an 'Excellent' rating, the highest accolade it can bestow. Staffordshire is one of only five to share this status. See their recent additions to the curriculum: LLB Sports Law/Human Resources Management/Human Rights/Business Law. A Crime Scene House provides simulated scenes for forensic students to develop detection skills. BSc Forensic Science can be studied alone or with Criminology or Psychology.

For niche employment areas, media is also to the fore. The BA degrees come in Journalism, Film, TV, Broadcast Journalism, Music Broadcasting, Sports Journalism, TV & Radio Documentary. While in Media & Entertainment Technology are the BSc degrees in technology in areas such as film, music, computer games design, 3D animation,, simulation, etc, etc.

Art & Design melds media with art – Animation, Media Production, Photography, for example, and BA CGI Animation & Special Effects.

SOCIAL SCENE

Students' Union There are three bars – two at the Stoke campus, **Leek Road Venue** (**LRV** – 1800 capacity) and College Road's newly refurbished **Ember Lounge** (500) and one at Stafford, **Legends**, which goes forth as **Sleepers** during the day.

LRV stages some of the biggest student nights in the Midlands. There are two resident DJs and guest appearances by the famous (DJs and bands). There's also *Comedy Club* on Saturday. It's a busy, well-worked scene. 'We're not on the main gig circuit,' they admit, 'but the DJs and their agents now ring us!' There are also three balls a year, May in March, Summer in June and Graduation in November. May Ball's the biggest.

It isn't all music. There are in fact twenty-three societies at Stoke, and the most active is Drama – there's a good Drama & Theatre Arts degree; at Stafford there are a further ten. The uni newspaper is *GK* (*Get Knotted*) and the student radio station, GK Radio. The paper has received awards from the *Guardian* and the *Daily Telegraph*. Politics are low on the agenda, though they joined the national march on the tuition fees issue.

Sport Academic influence brings good facilities for all and fame for some. They have 41 clubs and came 99th nationally in the team ratings. Hockey is their sport. Cross country and badminton teams are also strong, and they have had their top-ranked swimmers, too.

Facilities include a sports centre, sports halls, squash courts, floodlit synthetic and grass pitches for football or rugby, fitness suites, gym with multi-gym, weights and fitness machines. There's also a

AT A GLANCE	
ACADEMIC FILE:	
Subjects assessed	**27**
Excellent	**48%**
Typical entry requirements	**220 points**
Application acceptance rate	**21%, high**
Students-staff ratio	**18:1**
First/2:1 degree pass rate	**46%**
ACCOMMODATION FILE:	
Guarantee to freshers	**85%**
Style	**Halls**
Catered	**None**
En suite	**25%**
Cost pw (no food/food)	**£53-£75**
Town rent pw	**£45**

dance and aerobics studio at the Sir Stanley Matthews Sports Centre in Leek Road.

Town Contrary to expectation Hanley, not Stoke, is the main man down among the potteries. There are pubs and clubs in both, however, to which you will soon feel like is home. Just outside Hanley is **Festival Park** – multi-screen cinema, Quasar, Water World, Super Bowl, etc. Stoke has a dry ski slope.

Theatres include the **New Victoria** at nearby Newcastle-under-Lyme, the **Rep Theatre** (Stoke) and **Theatre Royal** (Hanley). Sundays and Wednesdays are film nights at Legends in Stafford; the Drama Soc. is forty strong and puts on four plays a year, including panto.

PILLOW TALK

Stoke: 6 on-campus halls of residence, 8 off campus. Student houses: 36-bedroom houses on Leek Road. Student Flats: blocks of flats, two thirds sharing, within two miles of Leek Road. **Stafford:** Stafford Court includes 249 en-suite rooms; an additional 307 rooms will be open by the time you get there and Yarlet House with fifty-one.

GETTING THERE

* By road: Stafford – M6/J14, A513. Stoke – M6 (J15 from south; J16 from north), A500.
* By coach: London, 4:00.
* By rail: Birmingham New Street, 40 mins; Manchester Piccadilly, 1:20; London Euston, 1:45; Nottingham, 2:00; Sheffield, 2:15.

UNIVERSITY OF STIRLING

The University of Stirling
Stirling FK9 4LA

TEL 01786 466813
FAX 01786 463000
EMAIL admission@stir.ac.uk
WEB www.stir.ac.uk

Stirling Students' Association
University of Stirling
Stirling FK9 4LA

TEL 01786 467166
FAX 01786 467190
EMAIL susa-president@stir.ac.uk
WEB www.susaonline.co.uk

VAG VIEW

Stirling is a premier-league university with a reputation for leading the way. It was the first traditional uni to grasp the nettle of modularisation and reap the benefits of doing it in proper semesters – two blocks of fifteen weeks.

CAMPUS

Gateway to the Highlands, the 360-acre campus is set in beautiful surroundings – a loch, Airthrey Castle, even a golf course – well away from big city life.

The student community is small, relaxed and very friendly. Chances are that you will already know from this description whether you are the kind of student that will suit Stirling. It has suited various writers (Iain Banks among them) and many golfers too. Some find it pleasantly secure, others slightly claustrophobic, but the spirit of the place espouses a student-centred ethos.

One told me that he felt that Stirling had given him the kind of individual teaching and personal treatment that he imagined he might have enjoyed as a sixthformer had he gone to a public school. He didn't and many don't – 94% entrants are from the state sector and many represent

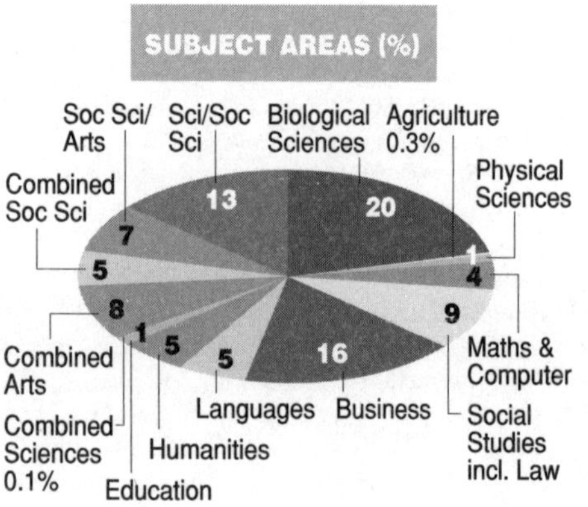

social groups which haven't traditionally gone to university.

FEES, BURSARIES

Fees for English students: £1700 p.a. Check Stirling's web site (www.stir.ac.uk) for bursaries and scholarships.

STUDENT PROFILE

The uni has been ranked first in the UK for widening access to Higher Education. Currently 28% of

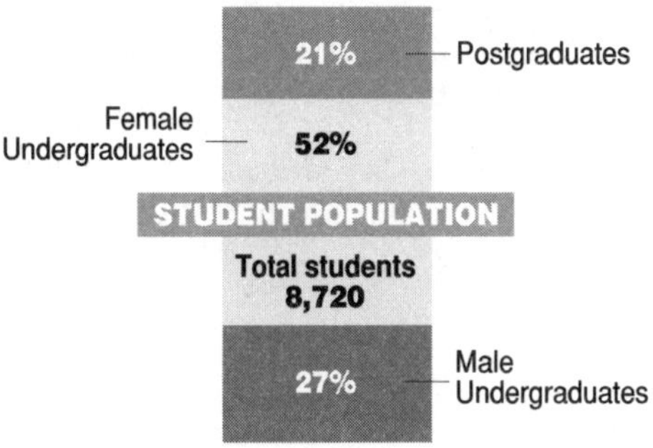

the undergraduate student body are from new-to-uni social groups. There are also many foreign students, mature students, sporty types and stereotypical broke studenty types. Around half are Scottish, and Stirling attracts a lot from Ireland and from Greece for some reason. A nursing and midwifery course accounts for the 35/65 gender balance in favour of girls.

ACADEMIA & JOBS

They were the first to introduce a semester system of modular degree programmes, which has been taken up by many other unis.

Building a degree with subject modules across faculties can make for an invigorating course. A subject, whatever it may be, is given application. And even if the application doesn't draw you into a career in that area, you will have applied your knowledge-base, rehearsed it for real.

Continuous assessment inherent in the semester system (as opposed to the traditional end-of-year system) minimises the stress of 'all or nothing' final exams.

The first semester in the year is fitted in before Christmas. Then follows a 7-week Christmas holiday before the second 15-week semester, which finishes at the end of May.

Students study three courses per semester and for most of these the coursework content is high. Grades are awarded for each course and these determine whether you may study honours, and later what degree you get.

Sensitivity to the particular abilities of a student, where his or her strengths lie, and to the fact that an idea of these emerges in the process of a course is endemic to the modular ideal and seems to flow from sensibilities at the heart of the ethos at Stirling, set as it is in the lap of such beauty

Nevertheless, it is a wholly practical ethos, too. A quarter of graduates come out of the business end of the curriculum, another quarter out of social sciences and biological sciences.

The picture, six months after graduation, is of clerks, sales assistants/managers, personnel and marketing managers, chartered accountants, bank managers, retail managers, general administrators, business analysts, investment advisers and financial administrators.

Social science graduates add a scattering of social workers to the mix, more clerks and sales managers, assistants, etc. Biological scientists supply natural scientists, teaching professionals, and the health provision gives hospital staff nurses (SEN), midwives, care assistants.

One area in which huge sums of money have been spent recently is Sport. Stirling is the home of the Scottish Institute of Sport; there are national tennis and swimming centres; a centre for golf opened in 2004. There are sports bursaries, and sports trainers and coaches make their mark on graduate employment figures.

ACADEMIC EXCELLENCE

TEACHING::	
(Rated Excellent, Highly Satis. or 17+ out of 24)	
Economics, Environmental Science, Theology, Sociology, English, Psychology.	**Excellent**
Business & Mgt Teacher Education, Maths & Stats, Finance & Accounting, Mass Communics, Philosophy, Politics, Social Work, History, Cellular & Molecular Biology, Organismal Biology, French.	**Highly Satis.**
European Languages	**20**
RESEARCH:	
*Top grades 5/5**	
Psychology, Agriculture, Social Work, Accounting, English, French, History, Philosophy, Theology, Media	**Grade 5**

Media is another area in which the uni has

UNIVERSITY/STUDENT PROFILE

University since	**1967**
Situation/style	**Rural campus**
Student population	**8720**
Undergraduates	**6930**
- mature	**13%**
- non EU undergraduates	**2%**
- male/female	**35/65**
- non-traditional student intake	**28%**
- state sector intake	**94%**
- drop-out rate	**8%**
- undergraduate applications	**Down 4%**

been making waves. There's a series of film and media degrees, and some convincing sounding BA Journalism tie-ups, perhaps Politics or Sport being more cutting edge than Religious Studies. Two years ago a news room became part of the teaching resources.

Interesting new development on the nursing front is a return-to-practice scheme after a period of absence – online learning, a dissertation and clinical practice. Stirling's Dementia Services Development Centre has the Iris Murdoch Building for the cognitively impaired.

Stirling is one of only 16 universities in the UK with 5-star sports facilities. This is a small uni, yet they came sixteenth in the national team league tables last year.

Stirling has scored high in the teaching assessments, partly due to their student-centred ethos which touches all faculties. Top of the tree are Economics, Environmental Science, Theology, Sociology, Psychology, English, Business & Management. See, too, the results of the most recent research assessment – ten subjects at Grade 5, in which national and world-class excellence is implicit.

Look at Stirling for social sciences, languages, media, biological sciences, accounting, marketing, management, as well as subjects like religious studies (the combo with politics suddenly looks very modern), psychology (both as social science and as science), tourism and environmental/conservation.

SOCIAL SCENE

Students' Association To sustain life far from the city, SUSA puts on a fairly uninspired show from its base in the **Robbins Centre**, but no-one seems to mind. There are 5 bars: **Studio**, with its breathtaking views, is open from 9.30am for breakfast, and on into the small hours. Although it has its own programme of ents (pub quizzes, NFL Sundays, *Studio Downloaded* – live gigs online), its main function in the evening is as pre-club for **Glow**, the nightclub downstairs, with 3 bars and massive dancefloor. Thursday is *Rock Night*; Friday, *Alter Ego* (indie), Saturday is *Flirt!* (cheese). There isn't a large enough venue to attract many big name groups, but they've had Radio 1's Trevor Nelson recently, and Edith Bowman, and there are live nights and comedy nights too. They won *Student Union of the Year* in the BEDA Scotland Awards (2003).

'Besides SUSA's ents, the halls of residence hold parties each semester, an excellent opportunity to get pissed and finally profess your undying love to the guy/girl across the corridor, whom you've fancied all semester,' writes Suzanne Bush. 'Some academic departments also have parties at the end of the year. But the best ones are those put on by assorted sports clubs every Thursday night in the meat-markets, sorry, clubs in town.'

There are the usual clubs and societies – 'SUDS, the Drama Society, aims to put on at least a couple of productions each semester,' Suzanne continues, 'and there's a ready supply of theatre, cinema and music in the form of the **MacRobert Arts Centre** in the middle of the campus.'

The MacRobert Arts Centre underwent a £6.3-million refurbishment programme in autumn 2002, creating the only professional space for children's theatre in Scotland. In addition to the main theatre, the Centre now houses a full-time dedicated cinema, café bar, crèche, children's room, children's gallery, workshop and rehearsal space.

'The student Musical Society works towards one big production every year. The University Choir brings together students and people from the community and puts on a big concert every semester in Dunblane Cathedral. Also, the university has an orchestra and there's a thriving Live Music Society with student performances on a Sunday night.

'Also, Stirling has a thriving media, a student newspaper, *BRIG*, a campus radio station, Radio Airthrey, offering music, and news programmes, and now Air TV.' Politics is not a big issues until a

WHERE STIRLING GRADUATES END UP

Health & Social Work: 13%; Education: 6%; Wholesale Retail: 12%; Manufacturing: 4%; Financial Activities: 5%; Public Administration, Civil Service & Defence: 7%; Hotel/Restaurant: 8%; Transport & Communications (including Telecommunications): 3%; Agriculture: 0.5%; Personnel: 4%; Computer: 3%; Business & Management: 2%; Accountancy: 3.5%; Media (including Film): 3%; Legal 1.5%; Sport: 2%.

big issue finds its way into this far-off campus, namely Car Parking!! Some time ago the barriers went up and parking permits were required.

Sport There are excellent sports facilities – one of only 16 Universities in the UK with 5-star sports facilities (*Sunday Times*, 2003), and the teams came 16th overall last year. Particular strengths are tennis, swimming and of course golf. They have a particular strength in the BUSA championship for golf. Campus is home to the Scottish Institute for Sport, the Commonwealth Games Council for Scotland, Scottish Swimming, and is now a preferred training site for the Scottish men's rugby team, but Stirling have established a national reputation for its 'sport for all' programmes.

Every week, hundreds of students participate in a range of activities.. The sports hall is the size of 8 badminton courts or 2 basketball courts and can be divided into 2 or 4 activity areas. The Robertson Trust swimming pool within the National Swimming Academy is a 6- lane, 50-metre pool, which can be split into two 25 metre pools by a moveable boom. One of the 25 metre pools has a moveable floor, changing the water depth from 0 metres to 2 metres. There's a conditioning room next to the pool, as well as an Omega timing system and a full range of water polo fittings and equipment. Four indoor tennis courts form the heart of the National Tennis Centre, and there are three squash courts and viewing gallery. The MP Jackson Fitness Centre houses 3 sports science laboratories: athlete assessment laboratory, research laboratory, analytical laboratory, a fitness suite with 50+ pieces of cardiovascular and resistance equipment, and there's a strength and conditioning "super centre" with 5 lifting platforms. By the sports centre there are 3 football pitches, a 6-lane running track with an 8-lane straight with a terracotta blaes surface, and a grass cricket square with artificial wicket. There are also 2 floodlit terracota blaes pitches for hockey, 6-a-side football and training by football and hockey squads. By Airthrey Castle there are 2 rugby pitches, a putting green and a sports pavilion overlooking the 9-hole, par-3 parkland course, which provides breathtaking views of the Ochil Hills and the Wallace Monument. Airthrey Loch forms the beautiful centre piece of the campus, but is also for angling and canoeing: at the northern end there's a practice area for slalom canoeists.

WHAT IT'S REALLY LIKE

UNIVERSITY:	
Social Life	★★★
Campus scene	**Small, friendly, beautiful scene**
Student Union services	**Average**
Politics	**Student issues**
Sport	**Very competitive, 38 clubs**
National team position	**16th**
Sport facilities	**Good**
Arts opportunities	**Excellent**
Student newspaper	**BRIG**
Student radio	**Air 3**
Student TV	**Air TV**
Nightclub	**Glow**
Bars	**Studio, Glow, Cocktail Bar, Sports Bar**
Union ents	**Hip hop, cheese, retro**
Union societies	**37**
Parking	**Expensive permits**
CITY:	
Entertainment	★★
Scene	**Pubs, 3 clubs**
Town/gown relations	**Average**
Risk of violence	**Low**
Cost of living	**Low**
Student concessions	**Some**
Survival + 2 nights out	**£60**
Part-time work campus/town	**Fair**

AT A GLANCE

ACADEMIC FILE:	
Subjects assessed	**20**
Excellent	**95%**
Typical entry requirements	**315 points**
Application acceptance rate	**15%**
Students-staff ratio	**18:1**
First/2:1 degree pass rate	**67%**
ACCOMMODATION FILE:	
Guarantee to freshers	**100%**
Style	**Halls, chalets**
Catered	**None**
En-suite	**10%**
Price range pw	**£56-£71**
Town rent pw	**£55-£65**

PILLOW TALK

All freshers are guaranteed uni accommodation and will normally be allocated a single study bedroom in an on-campus hall. But, if demand is high, you may have to share a twin room, or they'll find you alternative accommodation. In addition to halls, there are 33 on-campus chalet bungalows and flats in Stirling. In halls you may be as many as eighteen to a kitchen, in the uni-owned

Bridgehaugh flats in town you can enjoy en-suite facilities. The Swiss-style chalets are on the less than enticing-sounding Spittal Hill, but in any case they're reckoned to be for fourth years.

There's no catered accommodation but cafés and restaurants are plentiful, just a few minutes' walk away from the Halls. Meals Package and Flexi Meal Cards make a big saving on till prices, and may be purchased at the start of semester.

GETTING THERE

- By road: M9/J11, A9 or A91, A907, A9.
- By coach: London, 9:00; Edinburgh, 2:20.
- By rail: Glasgow/Edinburgh, 55 mins ;Aberdeen, 2:30; London King's Cross, 6:00.

UNIVERSITY OF STRATHCLYDE

The University of Strathclyde
Graham Hills Building
50 George Street
Glasgow G1 1XQ

TEL 0141 552 4400
FAX 0141 552 5860
EMAIL (use web)
WEB www.strath.ac.uk

Strathclyde Students' Association
90 John Street
Glasgow G1 1JH

TEL 0141 567 5000
FAX 0141 567 5050
EMAIL theunion@strath.ac.uk
WEB www.theunion.strath.ac.uk

VAG VIEW

Strathclyde had its beginnings in 1796 with Anderson's Institution, an equal-opportunity, science and technology college. John Anderson had been Professor of Natural Philosophy at Glasgow University and the institution that bore his name was founded under the terms of his will. University status came in 1964 following the merger of the Royal College of Science and the Scottish College of Commerce, which fact alerts us to Strathclyde's second largest faculty after Engineering, the Strathclyde Business School. In 1993, Glasgow's Jordanhill College joined the fold and became Strath's third largest faculty, Education.

CAMPUS

Today Strathclyde University occupies the same site as Anderson's Institution in the heart of Glasgow, though the original buildings have long gone. The concentration of students in the immediate vicinity is extraordinary: Strathclyde and Caledonian universities, the College of Building and Printing, the College of Food & Technology, and the College of Commerce. The Jordanhill campus is in the West End of the city, close to Glasgow University.

FEES, BURSARIES

UK & EU Fees: The level of tuition fees for 2006/07 will be available on their web site (www.stir.ac.uk) in April 2006. For scholarships, see www.strath .ac.uk/scholarship.htm

SUBJECT AREAS (%)

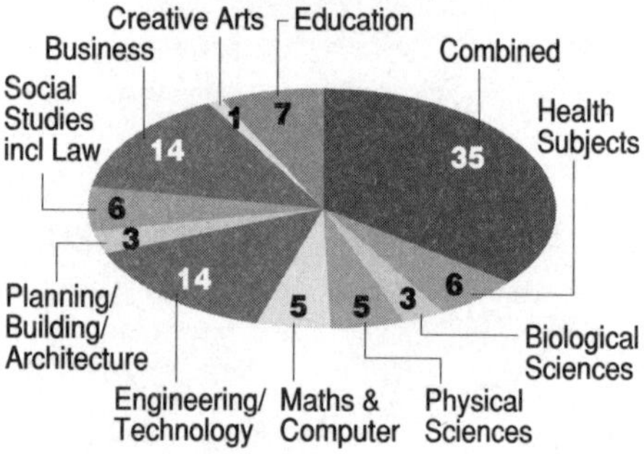

STUDENT PROFILE

Strathclyde is onc of three unis in the city. 'Vibe wise, it has a more relaxed atmosphere in comparison with Glasgow University, which tends to have a more academic outlook,' said a student of Glasgow Uni. Peter Mann, a student at Strathclyde, suggested differences run deeper: 'Caledonian and Strathclyde have a similar kind of population. Glasgow is quite different and generally disliked because it is full of English people. There is not a tremendous amount of mixing.' A student of Caledonian offered this Pythonesque picture of the pecking order: 'Glasgow University looks down on Strathclyde as being John Street Poly, although it's been a university since 1964. And Strathclyde looks down on us as being the old Glasgow Technical College, the lowest of the low.'

There's a 93% state school population and a 30% take from non-traditional uni goers. It's not

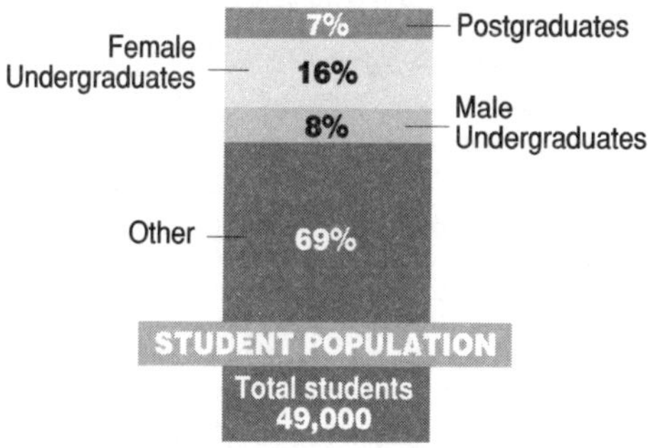

that different from the Cally profile, but Strathclyde carries none of the poly cultural baggage. It was the *Royal* College; Cally was the Poly. Nevertheless, a lot of the students are local. 'There's one guy in SUR [student radio],' said Peter, 'who's from Surrey, and he sticks out like a sore thumb.'

ACADEMIA & JOBS

There is a fine academic reputation. Strathclyde's 92% Excellent and Highly Satisfactory rating in the teaching assessments actually puts it a nose ahead of Glasgow University. The uni came 44th in the last research assessments – with Queens Belfast, Stirling, London Goldsmiths, Kent and Leicester for close company – and the edge which returned them a Grade 5* (that's world class) was neither engineering nor business, the two subjects to which one's mind turns when talking of Strathclyde, but Biomolecular & Medicinal Chemistry. The key thing is the way they teach: audio-visual, video, visual materials, computer-assisted learning programmes are all to the fore. Very close links with industry and commerce ensure a real-world, highly practical emphasis. They have a Learning Resources Base which, among other things, is there to help you in adjusting to study methods, curriculum design etc. Every student is assigned a personal tutor, and there's a built-in early-warning system to prevent any first year getting lost along the way.

The uni's Careers Service has twice received the National Charter Mark for excellence in customer service.

Strath's biggest single graduate employment successes are in the Education Faculty, especially in relation to teaching, social work and speech & language therapy. Key to the social and community work are degrees in such as Community Arts, Community Education, Outdoor Education in the Community, Social Work, Sport in the Community, etc. Also, in Science, the Pharmacy course almost always has 100% employment. Strathclyde's MPharm brings it 8% of the career market. The next largest professional class of graduate jobs goes to accountants – the course is BSc Mathematics, Statistics & Accounting.

Next, in number, are software engineers, and mechanical, process and production engineers, with jobs aplenty in manufacturing, as well as defence, telecommunications, etc – BEng Mechanical, Aero-Mechanical, Electrical & Mechanical, plus a series of MEng Mechanical with Aeronautics, Automotive, Biomedical or Material

UNIVERSITY/STUDENT PROFILE

University since	**1964**
Situation/style	**City campus**
Student population	**49000**
Undergraduates	**11500**
- mature	**16%**
- oon EU undergraduates	**3%**
- male/female	**48/52**
- non-traditional student intake	**30%**
- state sector intake	**93%**
- drop-out rate	**11%**
- undergraduate applications	**Constant**

ACADEMIC EXCELLENCE

TEACHING: *(points out of 24)*	
Physics, Business & Management, Architecture, Electrical & Electronic Engineering, Geography, Mechanical (incl Excellent Manufacturing) Engineering, Pharmacy, Chemistry, Politics.	**Excellent**
Civil Engineering, Computer, Psychol, Hospitality Studies, Maths & Statistics, Teacher Education, History, Law, Sociology, Social Work, Cellular & Molecular Biology, English.	**Highly Satis.**
Chemical Engineering	**19**
Planning & Landscape	**20**
European Languages	**22**
RESEARCH: *Top grades 5/5**	
Subjects Allied to Medicine.	**Grade 5***
Pharmacy,Studies/ Professions Allied to Medicine, Applied Maths, General Eng, Electrical/ Electronic Eng, Mechanical Eng, Law, Politics, Accounting/ Finance, English	**Grade 5**

Engineering orientations, and one combo with Financial Management.

In Mechanical Engineering they lead in the employment table. This is a major focus for Strathclyde, they have an Excellent rating for teaching and an international Grade 5 for research.

The faculty is expanding in a collaboration with Glasgow Uni over Naval Architecture degrees. Oil/mining consultants already benefit from Naval Architecture & Offshore Engineering, which is top rated for teaching and research.

They come second only to Queen's Belfast in the matter of finding employment for electrical engineers into telecommunications, and second to Portsmouth for getting graduates into electrical/electronic manufacturing. Teaching inspection, Excellent. Research Grade 5.

Architecture also shows up as a strong area. Besides the naval architecture degrees, there's the traditional 4-year BSc Architectural Studies (with European Studies); also BEng Architectural Engineering. Teaching inspection, Excellent.

Finally, there's a strong reputation for law – they're commercial & business and European law specialists, and have LLB (based on Scots Law) too.

They are also leaders in forensic science. UCAS list 298 courses, but the Forensic Science Society (www.forensic-science-society.org.uk) take most of their members from Strathclyde and King's College London. Both offer MSc degrees in Forensic Science (KCL's is called Chemistry with Analytical Chemistry). The University of Strathclyde has MSc Forensic & Analytical Chemistry.

A new Centre for Forensic Science – the first of its kind in the UK – will build on the University's international reputation and provide a comprehensive range of educational, research and consultancy services to laboratories, police forces and other agencies.

SOCIAL SCENE

Strathclyde is Glaswegian not only because of the number of Glaswegians who attend, but in the very Glaswegian way students here go about having a good time. 'Their ents are marvelled at by other unions for their ability to bring in droves of students from rival unis, and give them just what they want – an excellent hangover for those on a budget!' reports Rachel Richardson. In fact, it is hard to assimilate the energy that is devoted to exciting pleasure in the students at Strathclyde. Whatever the legal capacity for the big night, it is not uncommon to find between 2,000 and 2,500 students here totally out of their heads. The legendary pleasure zone itself is 10 floors high, yet it is not the skyscraper you expect because in some extraordinary Alice-in-Wonderland fashion they have conspired to fit its ten floors, mezzanine-style, into the space of six or seven, leading this first-time visitor into utter confusion.

> ***Strathclyde is Glaswegian not only because of the number of Glaswegians who attend, but in the very Glaswegian way students here go about having a good time.***

Last summer one of their bars was refurbished and rebranded into a Miller's sponsored bar. It's the ideal venue for small gigs, comedians and DJs, due to its intimate atmosphere. So, now the fun elements of the world-famous 10-floored Union are – Level 2: **Barony Bar** (main bar/club which is home to most of our regular nights); Level 3: **Gameszone** (Scotland's largest pool hall with 26 tables); Level 4: **Darkroom** (second room); Level 5: **Miller's**; Level 6: **The Priory** (relaxed non-smoking café bar); Level 8: **Vertigo** (the larger gig space).

Ents include *12-hour Tuesdays*: 3pm-3am, all drinks 99p (**Barony** & **Darkroom**) and comedy in **Miller's**; *TFI Friday* is hosted by legendary DJ Phil, this night has been running for 9 years and is the most successful student night in Glasgow. Cheap drinks and crazy antics, *TFI* is not for the faint hearted; Wednesday is touted as 'the only university gay night in Glasgow', every Wednesday comes with cocktails, and tunes from DJ Ricci.

WHERE STRATHCLYDE GRADUATES END UP

Health & Social Work: 10%; Education: 13%; Wholesale Retail: 13.5%; Manufacturing: 12%; Financial Activities: 9%; Public Administration, Civil Service & Defence: 5%; Hotel/Restaurant: 4%; Transport & Communications (including Telecommunications): 3%; Construction: 1%; Agriculture: 1%; Mining/Oil Extracting: 2%; Personnel: 2%; Computer: 2%; Business & Management: 2%; Accountancy: 4%; Media (including Film): 0.5%; Legal 1%; Architecture: 3%; Sport: 1%.

Approximate 'graduate track' employed **63%**

WHAT IT'S REALLY LIKE

UNIVERSITY:	
Social Life	★★★★★
Campus scene	**City centre**
Student Union services	**Good**
Politics	**Student issues**
Sport	**38 clubs**
National team position	**35th**
Sport facilities	**Good**
Arts opportunities	**Drama, music, film, art good; dance poor**
Student newspaper	**Strathclyde Telegraph**
Student radio	**SUR**
Nightclub	**Vertigo**
Bars	**Barony, Darkroom, Miller's Lounge, Priory**
Union ents	**Club nights, cheese, live bands**
Union societies	**35-40**
Most active society	**SUPSA, SUDS**
Parking	**Poor/non-existent**
CITY:	
Entertainment	★★★★★
Scene	**Very cool**
Town/gown relations	**Good**
Risk of violence	**Average**
Cost of living	**Average**
Student concessions	**Poor**
Survival + 2 nights out	**£70 pw**
Part-time work campus/town	**Good/excellent**

Recent live acts include El Presidente – Glasgow's hottest new band, Trevor Nelson, Complete Stone Roses (tribute), Colin Murray – a favourite at Strathclyde, Sara Cox (played a 2-hour set to a packed and jumping crowd; Alabama 3 (band behind the Soprano's theme tune), My Latest Novel (supported the Pixies on their recent tour). Up-coming at point of writing is the Smirnoff Tour - Rodney P, Skitz & Nextmen DJs; Xmas Allnighter – Edith Bowman, Rachel Stevens.

Nor is it all booze and sweat at Strath. There are 70 or more clubs and societies. Sport is excellent (see below) and media-wise they have a cracking set-up. 'Three year ago radio station SUR had its first restricted licence,' Peter Mann told me. 'It was funded from our *alumni* fund but we couldn't afford to buy our own equipment at that stage. Nor could we broadcast the following semester due to licensing conflicts with other stations. In that time we have been working to get funding for our own equipment and sorting out webcasting – broadcasting on the Internet. Now we have got the necessaries for the basic studio equipment and an Internet deal with Yahoo., and broadcast full-time. We have more DJ talent than we could possibly use. We get DJs from all over, we don't restrict ourselves to students.

'Then we've got the *Strathclyde Telegraph*. There's a real professionalism around and that shows. There's no TV yet, but there will be. Basically, I started up Fusion last year and then took this sabbatical year to get it off the ground. TV will come later. I did a degree in marketing. I've learned the bits and pieces as I've gone along, electrocuted myself a few times. When I leave here I am going for a job connected with the Internet.'

You'd better believe it.

For drama, they have two theatres – the **Ramshorn** at John Anderson, the **Crawfurd** at Jordanhill; both offer courses in all aspects of theatre and there's plenty of opportunity, too, just to be involved in student productions. The Strathclyde Theatre Group puts on ten major productions a year. The **Collins Gallery**, also on campus, runs year-round exhibitions and workshops, and there's also a concert hall for the many musical productions. Choirs, bands, a symphony orchestra, ensembles, etc go to make up the Music Society, which presents weekly lunchtime recitals by visiting artists as well as by students in the National Trust for Scotland's **Hutchesons' Hall**.

See also *Glasgow City* article, page 195.

SPORT They came 32nd in the national BUSA team league. Successes: Rugby Men won British Unis' Plate; Football Men won British Unis' Vase. Badminton, Volleyball, Rugby, Hockey and Football all won their respective Scottish Leagues.

At John Anderson campus there are indoor facilities for basketball, netball, archery, volley-

AT A GLANCE

ACADEMIC FILE:	
Subjects assessed	**26**
Excellent/Highly Satisfactory	**92%**
Typical entry requirements	**360 points**
Application acceptance rate	**18%**
Students-staff ratio	**17:1**
First/2:1 degree pass rate	**67%**
ACCOMMODATION FILE:	
Availability to freshers	**100%**
Style	**Halls, flats**
Catered	**7%**
En suite	**19%**
Approx price range pw	**£53-£79**
City rent pw	**£50-£80**

ball, tennis, badminton, handball, martial arts, fencing, table tennis, gymnastics, circuit training, yoga, indoor training facilities for track & field, cricket, golf and hockey, a weight training & conditioning room, squash courts and swimming pool. Beyond campus there are grass pitches, artificial floodlit pitches, and a pavilion – team games include hockey, rugby, American football and soccer. Jordanhill has a similar range of indoor and outdoor facilities on campus. Proximity to river, sea and mountains enables a whole range of other sports – from mountaineering to sailing, from rowing to skiing. There are eight bursaries available for low handicap golfers from The Royal and Ancient.

PILLOW TALK

In the city, most uni accommodation is single or shared rooms in self-catering flats, some of it at a student village on JA campus, some of it a walk away. At Jordanhill it's on-campus, catered halls.

GETTING THERE

☛ By road: The John Anderson campus – M74, M8/J15 or A82, M8/J15 or M8/J15. Jordanhill – M74, M8/J19 or A82, M8/J19 or M8/J19.
☛ By rail: Edinburgh, 0:50; Newcastle, 2:30; Aberdeen, 2:45; Birmingham New Street, 5:30; London King's Cross, 6:00.
☛ By air: Glasgow Airport, 15-20 minutes' drive.
☛ By coach: Edinburgh, 1:10; London, 8:20; Birmingham, 6:20; Newcastle, 4:20.

UNIVERSITY OF SUNDERLAND

The University of Sunderland
Student Recruitment & Admissions
Edinburgh Building
Chester Road
Sunderland SR1 3SD

TEL 0191 515 3000
FAX 0191 515 3805
EMAIL student-helpline@sunderland.ac.uk
WEB www.sunderland.ac.uk

Sunderland Students' Union
Wearmouth Hall
Chester Road
Sunderland SR1 3SD

TEL 0191 514 5512
FAX 0191 515 2441
EMAIL su.president@sunderland.ac.uk
WEB www.sunderland.ac.uk

VAG VIEW

Sunderland was an area robbed of its core industries a few decades ago, but has since been reborn and its uni with it. The poly became a university in 1992, the very year that Sunderland became a city. Since then they have been engaged in expansion.

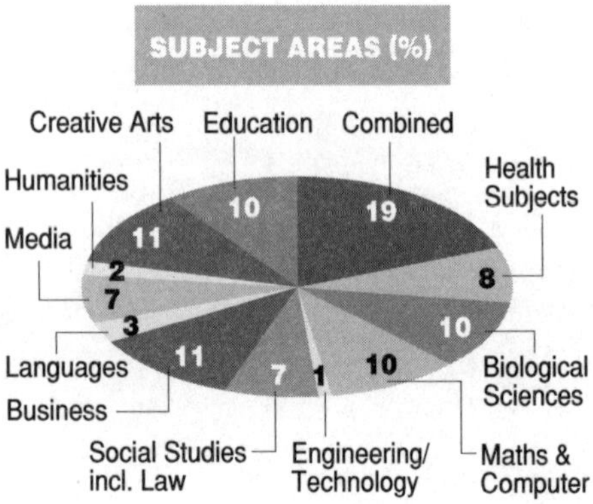

CAMPUS SITES

The uni's Chester Road campus is in easy reach of the town centre and the newer, award-winning St Peter's campus is but a stone's throw out at the mouth of the River Wear. The plan is to get everything over to St Peter's before too long.

Glass was one of the 19th-century industries on which the wealth of Sunderland was created (along with shipbuilding, coal mining and pottery), and in partnership with the National Glass Company, Sunderland's School of Computing levied £6 million from the National Lottery. The school is housed with the Business School at St Peter's, where they also opened a £15-million National Glass Centre. In September 2003 a new £9m Media Centre opened there, part of a centre of excellence for the arts, comprising 4600 square metres of studios, workshops and edit suites, along with facilities for TV & radio production and journalism (note the new MA Journalism). There are also specialist research centres – the Industry Centre, the Ecology Centre, and the Centre for Japanese Studies. Japanese? Well, the mighty Nissan's in town!

The uni's whole strategy is focused on student employability, entrepreneurship and creativity.

Work has begun on the first phase of a £7-million Science Park, which will provide incubator units for fledgling entrepreneurs and accommodation for established knowledge-based businesses at St Peter's Riverside, but it will also offer a first step for businesses set up by Sunderland students.

You can see why the awards were won. St Peter's fits unobtrusively into the landscape, obediently following nature's contours as they fall down to the river. Wearmouth's iron bridge arches splendidly across the water like a young relation of Stephenson's famous iron bridge at nearby Newcastle; cranes complete the backdrop of the area's industrial past, against which the campus is heralded as an expression of the re-born character of the area. The Informatics building and Business School acquiesce in that, and there are clear practical benefits in their design, too. The jutting roofs and walkways (a modern version of Oxbridge cloisters) keep students dry as they criss-cross University Square, to and from the Prospect Building, or stand outside this no-smoking, catering and library resource while pulling on a fag (often in defiance of horizontal rain and a biting North Sea easterly). Rainwater plunges dramatically down huge chrome pipes from roofs topped with strange deckchair-shaped receivers, scanning the northern skies (for light?). Impressive, though the design never quite recovers from the creams and browns that threaten to make St Peter's old before its time.

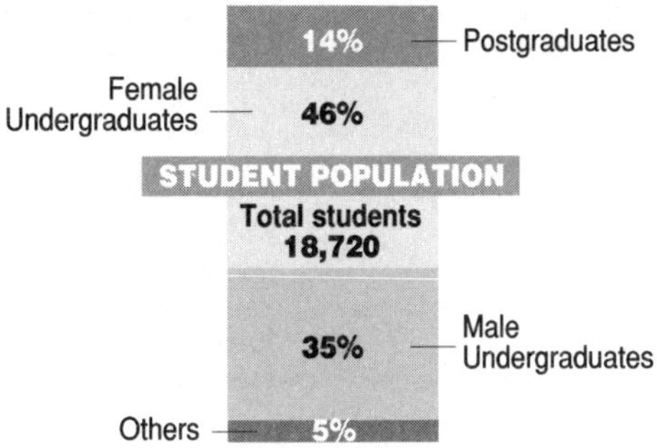

UNIVERSITY/STUDENT PROFILE	
University since	**1892**
Situation/style	**City campus**
Student population	**18720**
Undergraduates	**15145**
- mature	**53%**
- non EU undergraduates	**10%**
- male/female	**43/57**
- non-traditional student intake	**39%, high**
-state school intake	**98%**
- drop-out rate	**13%**
- undergraduate applications	**Up 3%**

ACADEMIC EXCELLENCE	
TEACHING:	
(Rated Excellent or 17+ out of 24)	
Organismal Biosciences, Molecular Biosciences	**24**
Physiology, Nursing	**23**
Media, Pharmacy	**22**
Sociology, Art & Design, History of Art, Music, Education	**21**
Sport, Politics, Psychology	**20**
Electric & Electron Engineering, Mechanical & Manuf Eng	**19**
Iberian Studies	**18**
RESEARCH EXCELLENCE:	
*Top grades 5/5**	**None**

FEES, BURSARIES

UK & EU Fees: £3000 p.a. If in receipt of a HE Maintenance grant there's a bursary of £500. There are also academic achievement scholarships.

STUDENT PROFILE

Sunderland are leaders for widening participation in higher education – attracting young people (32% of undergraduates) from 'low participation' neighbourhoods, and 39% from families new to going to university.

Sunderland is also one of the few campuses on which our senior reporter, who is of a certain age, can pass unnoticed in the SU bar (there's a 53% mature student figure). Besides a large local intake, international students are also attracted in increasing number.

ACADEMIA & JOBS

The university has a strong Disability Support Team, offering a range of advice, including an outstanding learning support programme for dyslexic students.

Education accounts for 17% of graduate jobs, 75% of school-teacher output is into secondary, which is the largest single graduate employment provision. The primary provision is also strong and there's a well-trod path into Further Education lecturing via the media and communications degrees and biological sciences, which scored full marks at the assessments.

Next most popular occupation is in pharmacy, which accounts for around 8% of graduates. There are foundation courses for both Chemical &

WHERE SUNDERLAND GRADUATES END UP

Health & Social Work: 9.5%; Education: 17%; Wholesale Retail: 17%; Manufacturing: 9%; Financial Activities: 9%; Public Administration, Civil Service & Defence: 7%; Hotel/Restaurant: 4%; Transport & Communications (including Telecommunications): 3%; Construction: 1%; Personnel: 3.5%; Computer: 3%; Business & Management: 4%; Media (including Film): 2%; Legal 2%; Publishing: 1.5%; Advertising: 0.5%; Artistic/Literary: 1%; Sport: 2%.

Approximate 'graduate track' employed **58%**

Pharmaceutical Science and Pharmacology. These in addition to the flagship MPharm degree. Teaching inspection, 22.

Computing is another popular and successful employment pathway – AI, Business Computing, Forensic Computing, Intelligent Robotics, Network Computing and a strong Computer Studies presence on the joint honours scheme (a defining factor of the curriculum at Sunderland; most subjects figure). Graduates get jobs as IT consultants and software engineers in particular, as well as programmers and computer operators.

Graphic artists and designers also proliferate and a look into the art and design provision brings us unerringly to another defining aspect, the Glass, Architectural Glass & Ceramics degree. See also, here, the Photography, Video & Digital Imaging degree and those in Animation and Advertising & Design.

Among other notably strong employment niches are sport (note the foundation year available for their BA Sports Sciences, also the BSc version and Sport & Exercise Development), journalism and film/TV production, broadcast, etc, and drama, a difficult employment sector but one where they figure relatively strongly.

Business is always quoted as a big strength here, and around 16% of Sunderland students do graduate with business degrees. Accounts clerks, retail managers, marketing managers, sales consultants are among the most likely jobs in the first six months, however.

There's Business & Administration/Human resource Mgt/Marketing/Enterprise/etc They are commercial and business law specialists and have a LLB with Business Studies.

There's a very strong showing in welfare and community care, and in nursing, where they dropped only one point at the assessments.

SOCIAL SCENE

STUDENTS' UNION The 3 main student haunts are the **Wearmouth Bar** at Chester Road campus, **Manor Quay** nightclub at St Peter's and the **Bonded Warehouse** across the river from St Peter's at Panns Bank.

An early 19th-century marine store and smithy, the **Bonded Warehouse** has a shop and bar downstairs and right across the first floor is this large, beamed bar with snooker table and big screen. Initial custom was 'a slow but steady stream,' then they started a series of comedy nights, which won them a decent audience.

The main nightspot remains **Manor Quay**, however. The club incorporates **Roker Bar** and operates daily as watering hole, food bar, pool and games room. For footie nights *et al* it boasts 'the

WHAT IT'S REALLY LIKE

UNIVERSITY:	
Social Life	★★★★
Campus scene	**Friendly, local**
Student Union services	**Good**
Politics	**Student issues Activity low**
Sport	**32 clubs. Skid Snowbound, Gaelic Footie strong**
National sporting position	**75th**
Sport facilities	**Improving**
Arts opportunities	**Film good; rest 'average'**
Student magazine	**Degrees North**
Student radio	**Utopia fm**
Radio Awards 2005	**3 nominations**
Nightclub	**Manor Quay**
Bars	**Wearmouth, Roker, Bonded Warehouse**
Union ents	**Commercial, Volume, Live**
Union clubs/societies	**51**
Parking	**Adequate**
CITY	
Entertainment	★★★
Scene	**Cheap fun**
Town/gown relations	**Poor**
Risk of violence	**Average**
Cost of living	**Low**
Student concessions	**Average**
Survival + 2 nights out	**£65 pw**
Part-time work campus/town	**Excellent**

biggest screen in Sunderland'. With no residents in the near neighbourhood the 3 am chuck-out time on Mondays, Tuesdays and Thursdays causes no grief. The club is cool, with good size stage, balcony and bar. It's a major town venue and they sort it so that whatever's on at Manor Quay is not duplicated elsewhere.

Tuesday is *Rock Night*; Wednesday, 80's/90's; Friday, *Commercial* (dance and r&b); Saturday, *Volume* indie or *Bands Night*. Recent acts include Dead 60's, Arctic Monkeys, Golden Virgins, The Stranglers, The Subways. There's a Sunday Quiz in **Wearmouth Bar**, and a Karaoke Night on Friday in the **Bonded Warehouse**.

AT A GLANCE

ACADEMIC FILE:	
Subjects assessed	**28**
Excellent	**61%**
Typical entry requirements	**225 points**
Application acceptance rate	**21%**
Students-staff ratio	**17:1**
First/2:1 degree pass rate	**53%**
ACCOMMODATION FILE:	
Guarantee to freshers	**100%**
Style	**Halls, flats, houses**
Catered	**None**
En-suite	**12%**
Approx price range pw	**£38-£60**
City rent pw	**£30-£60**

Besides all this, throughout the year, poets and musicians (roots, jazz, classical) perform on campus. The Royal Shakespeare Company, Northern Play-wrights and Ballet Rambert have done workshops with the drama and dance elements of the Faculty of Arts, Design & Communication. Also on campus is the uni's **Screen on the River**, based in the 400-seater **Tom Cowie Theatre**, a focus for weekend film festivals, and sister cinema to Newcastle's little **Tyneside Cinema**, renowned for its arthouse fare.

There are 19 societies and as many as 32 sports clubs, the most popular being Football, Netball, Rugby and CCSA. The student radio station, nominated 3 times in the national awards in 2005, is Utopia fm, the magazine, *Degrees North*.

SPORT Sports Centre has a 2-storey fitness and cardiovascular suite, a 25-metre swimming pool with canoeing facilities, and a sports hall for badminton, football and basketball. Otherwise it's the city, which 'has a number of fitness clubs and sports centres – the Puma Tennis Centre, Nissan Sports Centre (brilliant football and basketball pitches), and Silksworth Sports Complex, with dry slope ski centre.

TOWN Masses of pubs around Chester Road and city clubs keep students happy. Cost of living is low. Every university wants to play down hassle in town, but Sunderland cannot be classed as the safest of the cities we visit, though uni properties seem to be well protected.

PILLOW TALK

They guarantee all first-years accommodation, whether or not you apply through Clearing. There are self-contained flats, a small number of family houses, and flats in halls. A Domestic Services Manager and a team of domestic staff manage the halls, all of which have 24-hour security. A team of resident tutors is on call during the evenings, throughout the night and at weekends to offer advice and support. 80% of the accommodation is designed and built post 1994. They also manage a range of private properties throughout the city, available to let. Halls are situated on both sides of the river, with the newly built Panns Bank and Scotia Quay being the pride of the university (close to the Bonded Warehouse).

GETTING THERE

☛ By road: A1(M), A690 or A19, A690.
☛ By rail: Newcastle, 0:25; Leeds, 2:15; Edinburgh, 2:30, Manchester, 3:30, London King's Cross, 3:45.
☛ By air: Newcastle International Airport.
☛ By coach: London, 6:20; Bristol, 6:25.

UNIVERSITY OF SURREY

The University of Surrey
Guildford GU2 7XH

TEL 0800 980 3200 (freephone)
FAX 01483 689389
EMAIL information@surrey.ac.uk
WEB www.surrey.ac.uk

Surrey Students' Union
Guildford GU2 7XH

TEL 01483 689223
FAX 01483 534749
EMAIL info@ussu.ac.uk
WEB www.ussu.co.uk

VAG VIEW

Surrey, or UniS as it likes to be called, has roots in Battersea Poly. The rise of Surrey is a triumph of the career orientation of its courses and its teaching. It is many students' first choice.

Since receiving a Royal Charter in 1966, they have gone their own way, done their own thing, and with a great deal of success, making the business of higher education seem almost clinically straightforward. Small surprise, therefore, that they have been making noises about cutting their ties with the clod-hopping State, and going private.

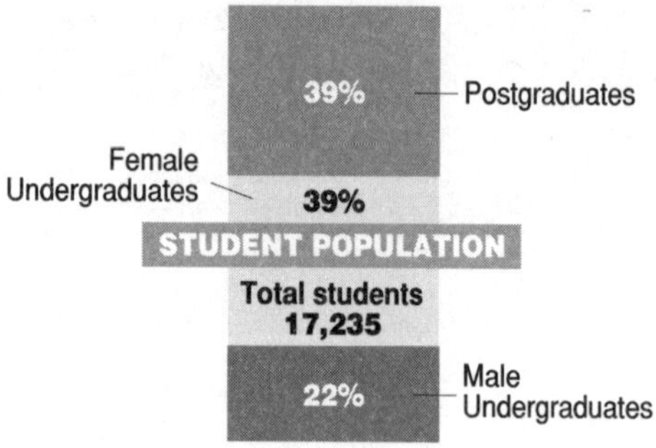

CAMPUS

UniS's self-contained, concrete, in-fill, landscaped campus lies just off the A3 in the ancient city of Guildford, adjacent to the cathedral, 15 minutes walk from the city centre. Writes Madeleine Merchant: 'The campus contains most first-year residences, all the teaching buildings, lecture theatres, library, computer labs, a sports centre, a shop, a health centre, a counselling service, a post office, a NatWest bank, many cafés, restaurants, and bars, the Students' Union building, picnic areas and a lake. It is in an attractive setting with many trees and shrubs, on a hill in the shadow of Guildford Cathedral. Many students complain of being woken up on Sunday mornings by the cathedral bells! A train line runs around a third of the perimeter, and the trains can also be heard in some of the residences.'

Much of the area is covered by CCTV cameras, and it is generally well-lit and perfectly safe, but three years ago, the Student Council debated whether more cameras should be put in for greater safety in off-campus paths nearby, which were deemed not so safe, even if the cameras might overlook some student residences. The Students' Union reported that the university had assumed responsibility of up-keep and maintenance from the council for some of these paths, and improved safety.

UNIVERSITY/STUDENT PROFILE	
University since	**1966**
Situation/style	**Town campus**
Student population	**17235**
Undergraduates	**10450**
- mature	**20%**
- overseas	**7%**
- male/female	**36/64**
- non-traditional student intake	**26%**
- state sector intake	**88%**
- drop-out rate	**6%**
- undergraduate applications	**Constant**

FEES, BURSARIES

UK & EU Fees: £3000 p.a. If in receipt of full HE Maintenance grant there's a bursary of £1000; if in receipt of partial grant, bursaries are on a sliding scale up to £1000, according to household earnings. Scholarships are available for applicants living in certain specified postcodes, applying for certain specified subjects, and for academic achievement.

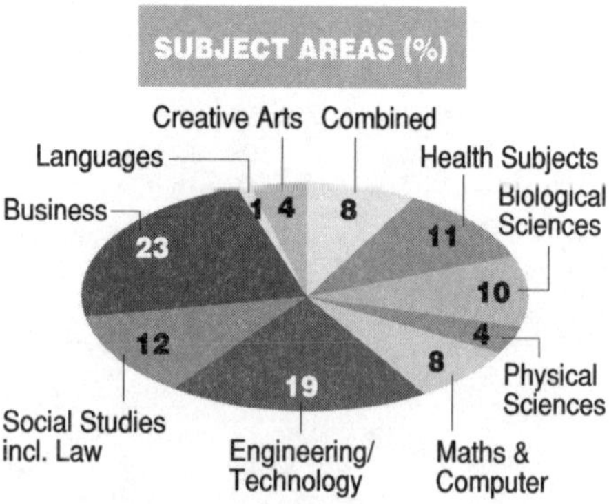

STUDENT PROFILE

'The University of Surrey may be a depressing collection of ugly concrete monstrosities,' writes Alistair Gerard, 'but it's not the buildings that make a university, it's the people, and I wouldn't have chosen to be anywhere else. Campus is a cosmopolitan enclave in the whole middle-class Caucasian experiment that is Guildford. Besides the obvious lean towards science and engineering bods at UniS, around a fifth of undergraduates are from overseas, nearly a quarter are mature students, and the state/independent ratio is well balanced. Students are saved from the male domi-

ACADEMIC EXCELLENCE

TEACHING:
(Rated Excellent or 17+ out of 24)

Business & Management, Music	**Excellent**
Physics, Electronic Eng, Education, Economics	**23**
Psychology, Civil Engineering, Materials Science & Eng	**22**
Organismal Biosciences, Subjects Allied to Medicine, Food Science, Sociology, Molecular Biosciences, Maths	**21**
Dance	**20**
Nursing	**19**
Chemical Eng, Modern Langs	**18**

RESEARCH :
Top grades 5/5/6**

Subjects Allied to Medicine, Electrical & Electronic Eng, Sociology	**Grade 6***
Psychology, Physics, Applied Maths, Statistics, Chemical Eng/Environmental Strategy, European Studies, Russian/Slavonic/East European	**Grade 5**

nance that can affect science unis by the nursing provision and Human Studies. Everyone is happy.'

ACADEMIA & JOBS

Characteristically, Surrey graduates get jobs for which they have been educated – they enter employment not only at graduate level but in occupations directly related to their degrees. This is not typical through the length and breadth of the graduate nation.

'In the third year, most students work for companies in placements, and earn lots of money,' Madeleine reports, 'and from what I've heard, most of these come back in the fourth year with clear ideas about whether they really want to continue working in that field, and many have definite job offers for when they graduate.'

UniS lead the nation in producing computer programmers. See BSc Computer Modelling & Simulation and various alternative applications – Engineering, Communications, Info Technology. All are 4-5 years, depending on whether you take one of these professional years out, after which you are eligible to Associate Membership of the Uni. Look, too, at their BEng Electronics & Computer Eng, and the BSc/MPhys Physics with Computer Modelling.

Most students at Surrey graduate in business and engineering subjects, and the manufacturing industry benefits by taking around a fifth of all those graduating from the uni.

Computer Science, Engineering and Business are the main routes into electrical and electronic manufacturing, with the occasional input from Surrey's sound recording courses. For electronic and aspiring telecommunications engineers, you're talking a world class (Grade 6*) department, with dedicated 4-5-year degrees like B/MEng Telecommunication Systems.

Aaspiring sound recordists and technicians take note, there's also the 4-year BMus Music & Sound Recording (Tonmeister) for the performance spin. Teaching inspection 23 out of 24.

Civil engineers are the next most in demand in the engineering sector. They mix with Computing in the 3/4/5-year B/MEng programmes, or you can of course take the single hons. Again, there's an Associateship of the University in the offing.

Then there's mechanical, process & production, electronic and software engineers, all well serviced with dedicated degrees and interesting combo options relevant to these job sectors.

Note also the B/MEng Space Technology & Planetary Exploration degrees, remembering that both Physics and engineering achieved near full marks in the assessments.

The health provision is next most productive, and is served by the European Institute of Health & Medical Sciences (nursing, midwifery, etc), which scored a world-class Grade 6* for research.

In the business sector the Retail Management degree is singly the most productive at point of employment, and the International Hospitality degrees lead unerringly to careers in the field of hotel management. Throughout the faculty, sales managers, marketing managers and management

WHERE SURREY GRADUATES END UP

Health & Social Work: 6%; Education: 6%; Wholesale Retail: 8%; Manufacturing: 20%; Financial Activities: 7%; Public Administration, Civil Service & Defence: 6%; Hotel/Restaurant: 7%; Transport & Communications (including Telecommunications): 1%; Construction: 2.5%; Personnel: 2.5%; Computer: 4%; Business & Management: 4%; Accountancy: 4%; Media (including Film): 1%; Legal 1.5%; Publishing: 1%; Artistic/Literary: 2%.

Approximate 'graduate track' employed **74%**

WHAT IT'S REALLY LIKE

UNIVERSITY:	
Social Life	★★★★
Campus scene	**Efficient, techy**
Student Union services	**Good**
Politics	**Low interest**
Sport	**45 clubs**
National team position	**60th**
Sport facilities	**Good**
Arts opportunities	**Dance, music good; drama avg, film, art poor**
Student newspaper	**Barefacts**
Student radio	**GU2**
Radio Awards 2005	**1 nomination**
Nightclub	**Rubix**
Bars	**Chancellors + 4**
Union ents	**Cheese, r&b, dance**
Union clubs/societies	**120**
Parking	**Non-existent**
TOWN:	
Entertainment	★★
Scene	**Rich man's clubs/pubs**
Town/gown relations	**OK-good**
Risk of violence	**Low**
Cost of living	**Very high**
Student concessions	**Good**
Survival + 2 nights out	**£70+ pw**
Part-time work campus/town	**Excellent/good**

consultants are produced in quantity.

Graduates of Financial Mathematics and Business Economics degrees find their way, in number, into accountancy, and economists also proliferate.

Again, the biomedical and life sciences provision translates just as successfully into healthy employment figures, especially Surrey's Counselling degrees and their much sought-after BSc Psychology.

> ***'Surrey may be a depressing collection of ugly concrete monstrosities, but it's not the buildings that make a university, it's the people... Students are saved from the male dominance that can affect science unis by the nursing provision and Human Studies. Everyone is happy.'***

SOCIAL SCENE

Students' Union Chancellors bar, one of 5, can be found under Union House and opens as restaurant from 8.30am, transforming itself into a venue in the evening for Cocktail Nights, Chancellors Comedy, Pre *Citrus* and *Flirt* Drinks, Open Mic Night and Live Sky Footy on Saturdays. Nightclub is **Rubix**, with a capacity of 1600. Regular ents are *Flirt!* with Duncan Wilson – 'the cult of chav is with us, homage to world of Burberry, Elizabeth Duke & the Citroen Saxo' – and *Citrus* with Leroy Wilson. Then there are sell-out specials, which go under the name of *UNIFIED*, with such as 'Nicholas from X Factor, Master Stepz, Da Jump Off Ent, to mention a few', across 2 rooms.

Music and dance departments evolve their own series of concerts and the uni choir, orchestra, chamber orchestra and student Drama Society regularly perform. UniS also has a special relationship with Guildford School of Acting, validating its degrees in Acting and Stage Management. See web: www.gsa.drama.ac.uk. Tel: 01483 560 701; e-mail: enquiries@gsa.drama.co.uk.

There is an award-winning student radio station, GU2 (nominated in 2005), newspaper *Barefacts* (award-winning in both 2002 and 2003). There is also a film unit and many other societies in a Student Activities Centre, cultural, religious, political, course/interest-based. Lesbian/Gay is active, but generally, due to student apathy in this direction, political activity is low.

Sport The Campusport Centre is the sports hall. The Varsity Centre is for field, squash and tennis, and pitches. Guildford's Spectrum Leisure Centre, home to ice hockey team, the Guildford Flames, provides facilities for swimming, ice skating and athletics, and the uni provides a bus linking Spectrum with other pick-ups in the city and the uni campus. Uni teams came 60th nationally last year, they have a world-class trampolinist apparently, and the gymnastic team was sent to the world championships in China. Sports bursaries are available.

Writes Madeleine: 'There are many clubs, both competitive – e.g. hockey, waterpolo – and non-competitive: mountain climbing, hiking, etc. Everyone gets Wednesday afternoons free of lectures as these are set aside for BUSA matches. If you aren't interested in sports, the university offers free language courses. As in sport, all levels are catered for.'

Town Writes Alistair. 'London is only 35 minutes away by train. Ergo, Guildford is very expensive. With the introduction of tuition fees, this must now be a consideration. There are sociological implications, too. It's a notoriously blue pocket of middle-class conservatism. Guildford shuts at 11 pm, with the exception of its nightclubs, where prices reflect this. The people who live in Guildford have done their partying; they have moved to a gilt-edged ghetto to live in peace and tranquillity.'

Writes Madeleine: 'There is a mixture of the usual high street shops with student discounts, and the more expensive variety such as French Connection, Gap, House of Fraser etc, two theatres and a large Odeon, two or three nightclubs and many pubs and bars.

'For temporary ways to earn money, Guildford shops and businesses usually have positions available, and the university runs a Job Shop. The union also employs many casual staff. Many student nurses supplement their income by working at the local hospital as "bank" health care assistants, and for agencies.'

PILLOW TALK

All freshers are guaranteed accommodation in the uni's courts of residence flats. None is catered, 30% are en suite, the price per week ranges from £49.00 (duplex) to £85 (en suite). Millennium House is the newest court, the 3-storey building opened in 2001. It has 200 en-suite rooms arranged into flats of six rooms with a shared kitchen. All student rooms have telephones. Calls across campus and modem links to the academic network are free; all 3,000 phones have voice mailboxes. Rent in town is anything from £65.00.

AT A GLANCE

ACADEMIC FILE:	
Assessments	**22**
Excellent	**86%**
Typical entry requirements	**310 points**
Application acceptance rate	**21%, high**
Students-staff ratio	**16:1**
First/2:1 degree pass rate	**59%**
ACCOMMODATION FILE:	
Guarantee to freshers	**100%**
Style	**Flats**
Catered	**None**
En-suite	**1,000 rooms**
Price range pw	**£49-£85**
Town rent pw	**£65+**

PILLOW TALK

The cheapest self-catering flats sting you for around £65 weekly at Digby, rising to £80+ for all-inclusive packages. A limited number of rooms have en-suite facilities and Internet access.

GETTING THERE

☛ Surrey Uni by road: A3, signs to University.
☛ By coach: London, 1:00; Birmingham, 4:30.
☛ By rail: London Waterloo, 30 mins.
☛ By air: Gatwick and Heathrow.

SURREY INSTITUTE OF ART & DESIGN UNIVERSITY COLLEGE

The University College for the Creative Arts
Surrey GU9 7DS
TEL 01252 892609/10/11
FAX 01252 892624
WEB www.ucreative.ac.uk

UNIVERSITY COLLEGE PROFILE

University College since	**1999**
Situation/style	**5 sites in Surrey and Kent**
ACCOMMODATION:	
Availability to freshers	**75%**
Style	**Halls, flats, houses**
Cost pw (no food)	**£43-£85**

The Institute is a youthfully minded, groovy set-up with a fast-track reputation for getting graduates jobs in art and media – fashion, textiles, 3D design, graphics, fine art, interior design, management, film, journalism, photography, digital screen arts, animation. Up until last year threy had two sites, at Farnham and Epsom (Fashion HQ).

Now they have merged with Kent Institute of Art & Design, which does much the same, but with furniture design, silversmithing, interior architecture and modelmaking thrown in, and sites in Maidstone, Rochester and Canterbury, being itself the result of a merger between 3 Kentish art colleges in 1987. There had recently been a multi-million pound spend at Canterbury: fine art studios, art gallery, library, new computer suites and 90-seat lecture theatre.

The new University College for the Creative Arts is bullish in its ambitions. The aim is to acquire university status by August 2007.

UNIVERSITY OF SUSSEX

University of Sussex
Sussex House
Falmer
Brighton BN1 9RH

TEL 01273 678416
FAX 01273 678545
EMAIL ug.admissions@sussex.ac.uk
WEB www.sussex.ac.uk
Sussex Students' Union

Falmer House
Falmer
Brighton BN1 9QF

TEL 01273 678555
FAX 01273 678875
EMAIL info@ussu.ac.uk
WEB www.ussu.co.uk

VAG VIEW

Sussex University first admitted students in October 1961. In its first decade or more, it was the *place to be – home of '60s radicalism, fighter of causes, defender of the student realm. Then all went quiet. Financial problems and a mouldering of relations between the uni and its students meant that 'any student triumphs occurred despite rather than because of the powers that be,' as a student put it.*

Now, they are back on top, and it is a much more exciting place to be.

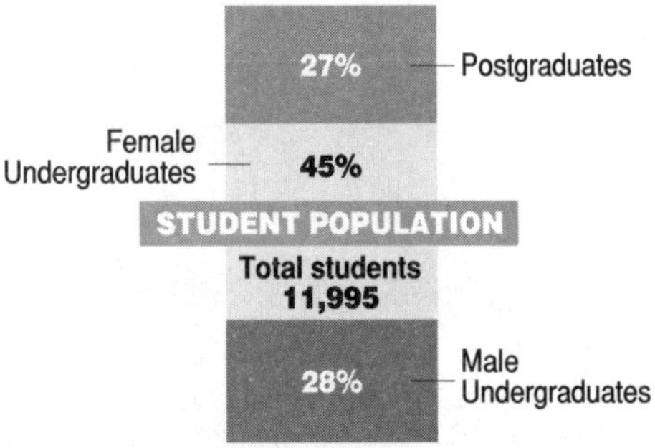

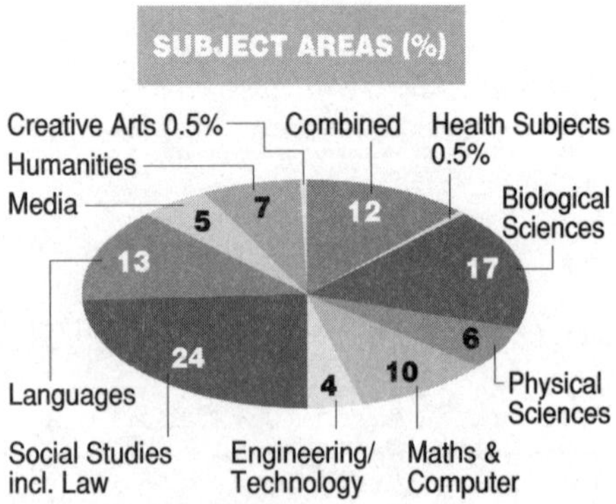

CAMPUS

The Sussex campus, its award-winning design by Sir Basil Spence, is an 18th-century park designated as an area of outstanding beauty, on the South Downs, 5 miles north east of Brighton.

'At times being on campus can feel a bit isolated and claustrophobic,' writes Keren Rosen, 'but it is fifteen minutes to Brighton by bus and you are never more than ten minutes walk from the fields of the South Downs. Escape is always possible.

FEES, BURSARIES

UK & EU Fees: £3000 p.a. If in receipt of full HE Maintenance grant there's a bursary of £1000. Scholarships are available for applicants living in certain postcodes, and for ethnic minorities.

UNIVERSITY/STUDENT PROFILE

University since	**1961**
Situation/style	**Campus**
Student population	**11995**
Undergraduates	**8780**
- mature	**23%**
- non EU undergraduates	**4%**
- male/female	**49/61**
- non-traditional student intake	**18%**
- state sector intake	**85%**
- drop-out rate	**7%**
- undergraduate applications	**Up 4%**

STUDENT PROFILE

'Owing to its strong international links, roughly a third of the student population comes from foreign parts and although the rest tend to come from London and the south of England, in general there is quite a nice mix of backgrounds,' continues Keren. 'There is also a large number of mature students studying at Sussex and although socially it is quite divided they definitely add a different perspective to study.' The ratio of state to independent entrants is roughly 4 to 1. There is likely to be an increase in local students as a deal has been struck whereby Sussex, Brighton and the new University of Chichester guarantee to offer places to applicants from local sixthforms and further education colleges as part of a widening participation policy.

ACADEMIA & JOBS

Sussex don't have the industrial links-ups of Surrey. They are more tied up with what they refer to as 'the knowledge economy' than with industry, so to produce articulate, adaptable adults, capable of finding fulfilment in their own way, not slotting in to someone else's production line. This, they believe, is where the cross-faculty potential inherent in the original academic strategy of this very individual university takes Sussex students. 'Also, we get the feedback from employers that they like the fact that our students are taught in seminars and are used to getting up and giving presentations and are articulate and confident, that they think on their feet, are analytical.'

Two-thirds of Sussex students graduate in social studies, languages, humanities and biological sciences – 20%, 18%, 12% and 17% respectively. More than a third of graduates enter health, education, finance and business management fields. There are strong pockets of jobs in computing, media, publishing, drama and music, and there is something about this liberal, free-thinking campus that favours the generation and development of artistic ideas. They produce writers and Sussex's student media is very active – newspaper *Badger*, magazine *Pulse*, radio station URF, all frequently award winning. Average entry requirements are high, but not unreachable for many.

But at the end of the day, social studies and humanities have less vocational relevance than other areas of study, and it is interesting to see where graduates of these actually do end up.

First, however, it is not true that Sussex has no vocational nous. 'We have an Innovation Centre, where a number of outfits up there were student-started. It is an incubation centre rather than a money-making business park.'

The more obvious vocational academic/job tie-ups produce software engineers, IT Consultants and computer programmers, who come out of computer sciences and engineering. There is a fine reputation for Computer Systems Engineering, AI, Robotics, Cybernetics & Process Automation, etc.

For biosciences they have a similarly fine track record for degrees and jobs. The BSc Psychology (with American Studies, Cognitive Science or Neuroscience) looks particularly attractive, and the new Brighton & Sussex Medical School has lift-off: 5-year BMBS (Bachelor of Medicine, Bachelor of Surgery). Small, personal med school, they are looking for personal qualities, commitment, compassion as well as... Entry GCSE Grade B Maths and English, ABB or 320 points at A level. There was a 10% application acceptance rate in 2004, which is average.

Computing, Psychology and Biological Sciences have international Grade 5 ratings for research, and Electrical & Electronic Engineering and Biosciences scored 21 and 22 points at the teaching

ACADEMIC EXCELLENCE

TEACHING :
(Rated Excellent or 17+ out of 24)

English, Music, Anthropology	**Excellent**
Philosophy, Sociology	**24**
Politics, American Studies, Maths & Statistics	**23**
Linguistics, French, Physics, Biosciences Education	**22**
Electric & Electron Engineering, Economics, Psychology, Media	**21**
History of Art	**20**

RESEARCH:
*Top grades 5/5**

Psychology, Chemistry, Biological Sciences, Physics, Applied Maths, Computer, General Eng, Anthropology, Science/Technology Policy Research, American Studies, English, History of Art/ Architecture/Design, Philosophy, Music	**Grade 5**

WHERE SUSSEX GRADUATES END UP

Health & Social Work: 11%; Education: 12%; Wholesale Retail: 8%; Manufacturing: 9%; Financial Activities: 10%; Public Administration, Civil Service & Defence: 7%; Hotel/Restaurant: 4%; Transport & Communications (including Telecommunications): 4%; Construction: 0.5%; Personnel: 8%; Computer: 5%; Business & Management: 4%; Accountancy: 1%; Media (including Film): 2.5%; Legal 2%; Publishing: 3%; Advertising: 1%; Artistic/Literary: 1%; Sport: 1%.

Approximate 'graduate track' employed **62%**

assessments respectively.

In social studies, humanities and languages we get a less focused picture, although it is precisely in these areas that they have done well in the teaching assessments: Philosophy and Sociology scored full marks, and Politics and American Studies 23 points, Linguistics and French 21. These are the six best results the uni achieved, and their strategy here is to provide subject combinations that are more than the sum of their parts. The curriculum is indeed planned with flair.

There are strong pockets of jobs in computing, media, publishing, drama and music, and there is something about this liberal, free-thinking campus that favours the generation and development of artistic ideas.

Civil Service administration is one significant pathway into employment for Sussex law graduates. In fact, Sussex leads the way countrywide into Civil Service administration through Social, Economic & Political Studies, languages and biological sciences (computer science is important too), and there's a significant flow from these areas of the curriculum into adult education.

Again, with social and biological sciences (including psychology) they have a significant reputation, relative to other unis, in finding graduates jobs in social work and counselling.

But it is also true that a significant number of graduates from these parts of the curriculum are registered as clerks six months after graduation. The same is true of physical sciences, where again they enjoy a strong reputation for teaching and research.

What is interesting is that graduates entering the niche areas of employment at which Sussex excel, such as publishing, radio/TV, journalism come not from departments dedicated to turning out media types – Media Studies and the like – but from across the scholastic board, out of a combination of application encouraged through the cross-faculty curriculum and extra-curricular interest, which is exactly what you want from a university.

Sussex is a small university, but it has more extra-curricular clubs and societies (200) than many. There is a vigorous student culture, and employers like to pick the fruits of that.

STUDENT SCENE

Students' Union The focus is **East Slope Bar**: 'Live music, football, barbeques, but above all a great place to meet friends any night of the week,' says Tom Harle, 'and a great place to watch out for your next bus into town if the weather's not so good. Then there's **Park Village Lounge**: sea, sun, sand, well no, but a huge range of well-priced cocktails, wines and beers and a great place for a quiet evening chill-out. Get a free cocktail if it's your birthday! **Falmer Bar** is the place for a lunch time coffee, or your usual tipple on the way home, a (veggie) burger or nachos to share. Mmeanwhile, **The Hothouse** is packed out every weekend, a great place to hide from over-priced central Brighton clubs.'

Every Friday at the **Hothouse** is *EASY*: hip-hop, r&b, garage, urban, 10pm till 2am, £3 entry. Saturday is *YOOF CLUB*: all the songs you love to hear', also till 2am.

What of student politics in the midst of all this middle-class reverie? I ask. Isn't Sussex all yesterday's '60s-student glory? Apparently not. 'Politics are as important today as they were in the late '60s.'

WHAT IT'S REALLY LIKE

UNIVERSITY:	
Social Life	★★★★
Campus scene	**First-year only holiday camp**
Student Union services	**Average**
Politics	**Aware**
Sport	**Lightweight**
National team position	**48th**
Sport facilities	**Good**
Arts opportunities	**Drama, film excellent; dance, art, music good**
Student newspaper	**Badger**
Student magazine	**Pulse**
Journalism Awards 2005	**Nominated**
Student radio	**URF**
Radio Awards 2005	**Bronze Award**
Nightclub	**The Hot House**
Bars	**Falmer Bar, Grape Vine, East Slope, Park Village**
Union ents	**Cheese**
Union clubs/societies	**200**
Parking	**Poor**
CITY:	
Entertainment	★★★★★
Scene	**Exceptional**
Town/gown relations	**OK**
Risk of violence	**Low**
Cost of living	**High**
Student concessions	**Good**
Survival + 2 nights out	**£80 pw**
Part-time work campus/town	**Average**

AT A GLANCE

ACADEMIC FILE:	
Subjects assessed	**29**
Excellent	**66%**
Typical entry requirements	**330 points**
Application acceptance rate	**16%**
Students-staff ratio	**17:1**
First/2:1 degree pass rate	**70%**
ACCOMMODATION FILE:	
Guarantee to freshers	**95%**
Style	**Halls, houses, flats**
Catered	**None**
En suite	**9%**
Approx price range pw	**£41-£79**
City rent pw	**£65-£90**

Student politics at Sussex is 'doing the right thing', removing Coca-Cola from all Union outlets, presenting a motion of no-confidence in the University Council, campaigning on housing issues for first year students, campaigning about the Falmer (football) stadium project, on widening participation, encouraging a wider social mix among Sussex's privileged student clientele.

Student media is great: *The Pulse* (magazine), *The Badger* (newspaper) and URF, Unversity Radio Falmer. They received 2 nominations (*Pulse* and URF) in the national awards this year and a bronze award for URF's Mara Webster in the Female Presenter of the Year section.

SPORT It's sport-for-all at Sussex, not too keenly competitive – they came 48th in the national team ratings last year. There are two large sports halls, a fitness room with multigym and training facilities, four glass-backed squash courts, sauna, solarium, café and bar. Elsewhere on campus are the pitches, tennis courts, and five more squash courts.

TOWN 'The town centre is small enough to be covered in its entirety on foot, but it manages to squeeze in a huge amount of clubs, pubs, bars and shops to suit every taste,' writes Keren. 'The theatre and art scene has a real emphasis on individuality. As the gay capital of England, Brighton has a laid back, party atmosphere and students and locals live in peaceful harmony. Brightonians do have a tendency to be a little self-consciously cool, verging at times on the pretentious, but there are enough different types of people that it is possible to avoid that world completely if its not your thing.'

It's a great city, lots of free festivals. Right now, Sussex students tend to frequent **Paradox**, the **Event** and **Club Barcelona**.

See *Brighton Student City*, page 79, for more.

PILLOW TALK

The majority of first years get housed on campus, but get in quixk or you'll have to share. This works on a first come, first served basis. Standard of accommodation is pretty high, all self-catering and varies between flats and rooms on corridors.

GETTING THERE

☛ By road: M23, A23, A27.
☛ By coach: London, 1:50.
☛ By rail: London Bridge/Victoria, 1:10; Portsmouth, 1:30; Birmingham New Street, 3:45; Leeds, 4:15; Manchester Piccadilly, 5:00.
☛ By air: Gatwick and Heathrow Airports.

UNIVERSITY OF WALES, SWANSEA

University of Wales, Swansea
Swansea SA2 8PP

TEL 01792 295111
FAX 01792 295110
EMAIL admissions@swansea.ac.uk
WEB www.swansea.ac.uk

Swansea Students' Union
Swansea SA2 8PP

TEL 01792 295466
FAX 01792 206029
EMAIL sugenoff@swan.ac.uk
WEB www.swansea-union.co.uk

VAG VIEW

If Swansea isn't a university that you would immediately consider, despite the evidence of the teaching assessments that the academic provision is excellent, do yourself a favour, go and see it – submit to the evidence of your senses.

'You can come here and never leave it,' a student said to me. 'It's a bit like a black hole.' How else to explain a mere 5% drop-out rate, despite a heavy (28%) student take from new-to-uni social groups? How else to explain why so many students stay on in the area after graduation?

Besides being a place of exquisite beauty,

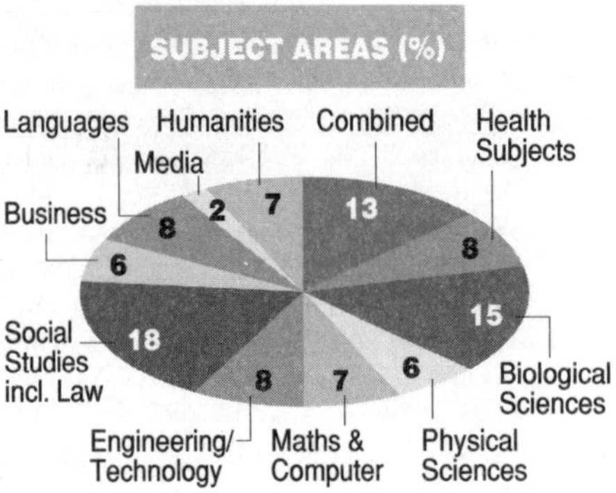

and distinctly laid-back vibes, the uni is also home to the National Assessment and Training Centre for Students with Disabilities. What better agency to sort out this important area of student support?

CAMPUS

The campus is set in a glorious position with wide open Swansea Bay stretched out in front and parkland behind, just a couple of miles west of the town. Further west along the coast you come to the old fishing village of Mumbles (birthplace of Catherine Zeta Jones), its pubs, fish & chip and Indian restaurants a favourite trawl for students, and the Gower Peninsula, described by Dylan Thomas as 'one of the loveliest sea-coast stretches in the whole of Britain.' On a sunny day I didn't disagree, nor do Swansea's surfer dudes. 'It's all so easy, see; everything's in walking distance,' the same student opined. 'Students come to Swansea for that alone.' He was pointing at the surf.

Writes Maxine French: 'The Gower is a stretch of coastline incorporating bays such as Caswell, Port Eynon and Langland, the last a favourite spot for surfers and host recently to the Welsh leg of some mad, never-ending surf competition. During the summer term its almost compulsory to go to Caswell when the Geography Society holds its annual beach party. For those whose lives are not ruled by tide tables, the coast means the Mumbles, renowned for the "Mile", strictly non-athletic, a pub crawl to end all pub crawls, something Dylan Thomas might have liked too.'

He did. In 'Who Do You Wish Was With Us?' he wrote – 'Why don't we live here always? Always and always. Build a bloody house and live like bloody kings!'

UNIVERSITY/STUDENT PROFILE	
University since	**1920**
Situation/style	**Campus-by-the-sea**
Student population	**12205**
Undergraduate	**9716**
- mature	**30%**
- non EU undergraduates	**8%**
- male/female	**39/61**
- non-traditional student intake	**28%**
- state sector intake	**93%**
- drop-out rate	**5%**
- undergraduate applications	**Up 5%**

FEES, BURSARIES

UK & EU Fees: £1200 p.a. in 2006/7; up to £3000 p.a. 2007/8. Students from Wales may benefit from grants up to £1800 from the Welsh Assembly, according to means, from 2007, when candidates may apply for support from the Welsh National Bursary Scheme. Further information is available at www.studentfinancewales.co.uk. Ten sports scholarships of £1000 are available from the uni, and academic scholarships from some departments.

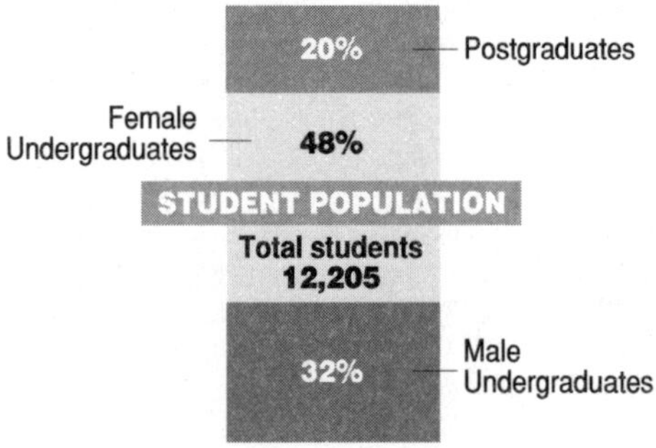

STUDENT PROFILE

Swansea was quoted as one of the government's favoured 'elite access' universities, but now many others have caught up, and their figures of 28% intake from social classes new to the idea of uni, and 18% from 'low partiticpation' neighbourhoods are less than unique. 93% of students come from the state sector, but that is not unusual either. The high mature-student intake is more so, and there's 15% more students in receipt of Disabled Students' Allowance than the sector average. There's also a healthy intake from overseas, and yet a more noticeably Welsh student body than at Cardiff.

Statistics aside, the real point is that Swansea campus, with its healthy population mix, is a very friendly sort of place. People are chatty, the scene a good deal less pressured than in some more cosmopolitan, civic universities. 'There's a fantastic, multi-cultural community feeling at Swansea,' said one student. It does strike one that it would be an

ACADEMIC EXCELLENCE

TEACHING :	
History, Computer Science, Geography, Psychology, Physics, Electrical & Electronic Engineering, Modern Langs (German, Italian, Spanish), Biosciences, Chemical Eng, Materials Eng, Civil Eng, Classics & Ancient History.	**Excellent**
RESEARCH:	
*Top grades 5/5**	
Civil Engineering	**Grade 5***
Physics, Pure Maths, Celtic Studies, German/Dutch/ Scandinavian, Iberian/Latin American, Computer, Social Work	**Grade 5**

easy place to settle, and not simply for the duration of a 3-year degree course.

ACADEMIA & JOBS

Entry requirements are not overly taxing, and there's a good chance of getting in anyway – a 26% application acceptance rate – possibly because Swansea is thought of as a bit off the beaten track. 'Once they are here, people do well,' a student said, adding rather languidly as he nursed a Sunday morning hangover, 'but I guess it comes down to nothing else to do but work.'

Besides the definitive strength of engineering, languages are an important element; both teaching and research assessments show the department as especially strong, and every area of the curriculum benefits from it. New this year are BA Cymraeg gyda Ffrangeg (4 blynedd)/Welsh with French, gyda Almaeneg (German), gyda Sbaeneg (Spanish).

Engineering is indeed an enduring strength. Following the introduction of BEng Aerospace Engineering and BEng Aerospace Communications, this year they have BEng Aerospace Engineering with Power Electronics. Civil engineering is a particularly strong employment sector out of this faculty, and achieved a world-class 5* rating in the research assessment. Employment figures lead us next into the electronic area, well served in the faculty with degrees such as the 3/4-year BEng Electronics with Computer Science or BEng Communications Systems (the extra year in Europe, America, Australia or industry). The uni is highly productive of software engineers and programmers, and there's a fast track into telecommunications and defence from Swansea. Almost as many mechanical and chemical engineers follow in their wake.

Now, a £4.3-million Digital Technium building has opened housing a new Department of Media and Communication Studies – research labs for digital science, incubator units for enterprise, space for partners from the private sector, but linked with the School of Engineering and Department of Computer Science. See degrees like BSc Multimedia Technology, Internet Technology, etc.

There are also BA media and screen studies degrees, and this year BA Screen Studies and a language (French, German, Spanish, Italian, Welsh); also BA Public & Media Relations, Language & Communication, English & Creative Writing. News of the opening of a Richard Burton Centre for Film and Popular Culture follows the handing over of the first of screen legend's diaries to the university by the actor's widow, Sally Burton. The diaries will form part of an archive of her late husband's papers

But look, too, at Swansea's ever sharper and increasingly defining focus on medicine and health sciences. Nursing degrees, Clinical Physiology, Audiology, Midwifery, and BSc Psychology (recognised by the British Psychological Society and the first step to becoming a Chartered Psychologist), all perform well in the employment market. And now, of course, Swansea has launched a MBBCH/Med degree – graduate entry only. The fast-track programme will take students to graduation in 4 years. The Medical School is adjacent to Swansea's Singleton Hospital, but students will enter the University of Wales College of Medicine and the All-Wales Clinical Training Scheme for the final two years of their studies.

WHERE SWANSEA GRADUATES END UP

Health & Social Work: 9%; Education: 10.5%; Wholesale Retail: 10%; Manufacturing: 9%; Financial Activities: 10%; Public Administration, Civil Service & Defence: 12%; Hotel/Restaurant: 4%; Transport & Communications (including Telecommunications): 5%; Construction: 3%; Personnel: 5%; Computer: 2%; Business & Management: 4%; Accountancy: 3%; Media (including Film): 1.5%; Legal 3%; Publishing: 1%; Sport: 2%.

Approximate 'graduate track' employed **66%**

In December 2006, the uni's £50m Institute of Life Science will become home to the School of Medicine's research arm, housing hundreds of interdisciplinary specialists, scientists and researchers.

> ***As Dylan Thomas wrote about this place in 'Who Do You Wish Was With Us?' – 'Why don't we live here always? Always and always. Build a bloody house and live like bloody kings!'***

Aspiring social workers and counsellors should look at the new BScEcon Social Work. They are Grade 5 in research in this area, and supply large numbers of graduates into the sector. There's also a BScEcon joint honours programme, incorporating American Studies, Economic History, Politics, Psychology, Social Policy, etc.

Look, too, at the sporting prowess of this uni. Extra-curricular interest is enormous, and employment stats are good. There is both an HND and BSc Sports Science. See *Sport* below.

Finance is another significant employment area. The record shows some 8% of graduates going into accountancy jobs (3% as chartered accountants). There is also a BSc Actuarial Studies, with the option of an additional year abroad, and a new BSc Actuarial Studies with Accounting. Business admin. degrees yield jobs – some 4% go into this area and a rash of new BA Business Administration/BSc Management/Management Science degrees with a specialization in Accounting is expected this year.

Look, too, at the Economics degrees. There's a foundation course for applicants from outside the EU who want to get on the BSc/MSEs Integrated Management Science/Economics degree (with deferred choice of specialisation).

Education is a major field here – more than 10% of graduates choose it, 5% become instructors in some capacity, there's a well-trod pathway into primary and secondary, and 2% find jobs as educational assistants.

The Law is another good option, with a series of language add-ons and an intercalary year in the US with Law & American Studies.

WHAT IT'S REALLY LIKE

UNIVERSITY:	
Social Life	★★★★
Campus scene	**Laid-back surfers**
Student Union services	**Good**
Politics	**NUS and national issues**
Sport	**70+ clubs**
National team position	**45th**
Sport facilities	**Good**
Arts opportunities	**Drama, dance excellent, music, film, art good**
Student newspaper	**Waterfront**
Student radio	**X-Treme**
Nightclubs/bars	**Divas, Idols, JC's**
Union ents	**Flirt!, Live & Wired; Time & Envy in town**
Union societies	**50+**
Parking	**Adequate**
TOWN:	
Entertainment	★★★
Scene	**Clubs, pubs, sea**
Town/gown relations	**Good**
Risk of violence	**Low**
Cost of living	**Low**
Student concessions	**Good**
Survival + 2 nights out	**£60 pw**
Part-time work campus/town	**Good**

SOCIAL SCENE

STUDENTS' UNION There are 2 bars: **Idols** at Hendrefoelan student village – cosy atmosphere with karaoke every Tuesday, and **JC's**, on campus – great pub with big screen for all sporting events, friendly and popular venue. **Divas** is the union nightclub – extremely popular, with a wide range of nights to cater for all tastes.

Time and Envy in the city centre hand over their club to the Union on Mondays and Wednesdays – Monday is *Student Night*, and Wednesday is *AU Night* (Athletic Union). Besides karaoke at **Idols** every Tuesday, there's a pub quiz at **JC's** each Sunday, and in Divas *Flirt!* on a Friday and *Live and Wired* (basically like an open Mike night) on Sunday.

There are 70+ sports clubs and 50+ societies up and running, RAG and Dance being the most active right now, though politics is a perrennial interest, 'all parties represented, Lib Dem and Socialist and Respect,' they say. And the Tories? main issues this year have been about changes to the university, campaign against the arms trade, and student safety. *Waterfront* is the newspaper; X-treme Radio rules the airwaves.

There's an international Swansea Arts Festival every autumn. **The Glynn Vivian Gallery** in town, **The Swansea Arts Workshop** in the Maritime Quarter (the former docklands) and **The**

Taliesin Arts Centre on campus, deliver year-round exhibitions and events. Taliesin was and is the poetic spirit of Wales, his story among the oldest of Welsh myths. Here is a constantly unfolding programme (for and by students and outsiders) of drama, dance, film and concerts from classical through jazz and rock. The building has a bar and a bookshop. For Swansea-based opera and comedy there's the **Pontardawe Arts Centre**; for comedy, rock, classical and musicals there's the **Penyrheol Theatre**, while **The Grand** delivers Welsh National Opera, Lily Savage, *The Pirates of Penzance*, Paul Merton and the *South Wales Evening Post Fashion Show* in quick succession (classify that!).

SPORT Interest in sport is huge. They are holding the British University games here in spring 2006. Rugby is bigger than huge; Robert Howley and Dafydd James are alumni. Football and netball teams have been Welsh champions. Sports facilities were boosted last year with the opening of the Olympic-size Wales National Pool Swansea and the development of a new athletics track, two outdoor all-weather pitches and an indoor training centre for athletes at the University's sports centre site adjacent to campus. There's a sports centre with hall, squash courts, weight training room, climbing wall and indoor swimming pool (a new Olympic-size pool was recently completed). There are two sets of playing fields, field sport areas, six tennis courts, two netball courts, a rifle range and fishing lake.

There's also sailing, rowing (on the River Tawe), surfing and canoeing, and annual sports scholarships, for which you should apply before you join up.

PILLOW TALK

They have part-catered halls (both en-suite and standard), self-catered halls (en-suite only); self-catered houses and flats, and a small number of shared rooms available at £39.50. All students holding firm offers are guaranteed accommodation provided they accept their place by 1st September.. 'Swansea is small. Wherever you choose to live – in campus halls or in Clyne Halls or two miles away in the student village at Hendrefoelan – you'll find a community of really good friends,' writes Maxine. 'The same is true even in private accommodation at Brynmill, an area close by but considered by many (though probably not by its long-term residents) as a second student village. There is this sense that everyone is linked in some way, friends, friend of a friend and so on. Students here are generally very laid back, and not just the surfers.'

AT A GLANCE

ACADEMIC FILE:	
Subjects assessed	**26**
Excellent	**46%**
Typical entry requirements	**275 points**
Application acceptance rate	**26%, high**
Students-staff ratio	**15:1**
First/2:1 degree pass rate	**57%**
ACCOMMODATION FILE:	
Guarantee to freshers	**98%-100%**
Style	**Halls, houses**
Catered	**25%**
En suite	**18%**
Approx price range pw	**£40-£84**
City rent pw	**£40-£48**

GETTING THERE

- By road: M4/J42B.
- By coach: Cardiff, 1:10.
- By rail: London Paddington, 2:50; Bristol, 2:00; Cardiff, 0:50; Birmingham, 3:15; Manchester, 4:30.
- By air: Cardiff Airport.

UNIVERSITY OF TEESSIDE

The University of Teesside
Middlesbrough
Tees Valley TS1 3BA

TEL 01642 218121
FAX 01642 342067
EMAIL reg@tees.ac.uk
WEB www.tees.ac.uk

Teesside Students' Union
Borough Road
Middlesbrough TS1 3BA

TEL 01642 342234
FAX 01642 342241
EMAIL st.union@utu.org.uk
WEB www.utu.org.uk

VAG VIEW

Teesside (two 'ss') is in Middlesbrough (one 'o'), which must make the 2-syllable soccer chant of 'Boro' strictly incorrect, though I wouldn't argue. They call themselves the Opportunity University, and sit high in the league table of universities that have widened access to higher education.

What this means in their case is that entry requirements are not demanding, may well not include A levels, and that the undergraduate population, many of whom are mature, is largely drawn from the region.

Out-of-towners will cloud these facts with their own preconceptions, just as surely as one's first time view of the town is clouded by the Satanic vision of sulphurous chimneys off the A1. But they would be wrong, for when it comes to 'graduate track' employment, they sat at 19th place nationally last year, ahead of Nottingham, Warwick, Birmingham, Manchester, Edinburgh, etc.

CAMPUS

The campus is located within a few minutes walk of the centre of Middlesbrough, on the south bank of the River Tees, a short hop from the North Yorks Moors and Redcar and Saltburn beaches.

Students using the union building must run a gauntlet of pubs on Southfield Road: **The Dickens' Inn**, licensed till midnight, **The Star & Garter**, offering '£1-a-pint, £2-for-2' (to whom in their cups does that seem like an increasingly good deal?) and **The Fly & Firkin.** The architecture of the union and adjacent, £11-million, 5-storey Learning Resources Centre stuns – these delicately ribbed, green-tinted glass buildings glistening with seductive appeal.

FEES, BURSARIES

UK & EU Fees: £3000 p.a. If in receipt of full HE Maintenance grant there's a bursary of £1300; if in receipt of partial grant, it's £500. All new undergraduate students (home and EU) receive a £500 Welcome grant. There's also a £2000 Elite Athlete bursary scheme, and £1000 p.a. for applicants with 300 points from 3 A' levels, including two grade B.

UNIVERSITY/STUDENT PROFILE

University since	**1970**
Situation/style	**Town campus**
Student population	**20335**
Undergraduates	**17671**
- mature	**43%**
- non EU undergraduates	**4%**
- male/female	**47/53**
- non-traditional student intake	**41%, high**
- state sector intake	**98%**
-drop-out rate	**10%**
- undergraduate applications	**Down 6%**

STUDENT PROFILE

There's a large mature student intake and many come from non-traditional uni heartlands close by. They have a job-seeker's attitude to academia, i.e. serious, and a similar appetite for the hedonistic pleasures that Students' Union and town afford.

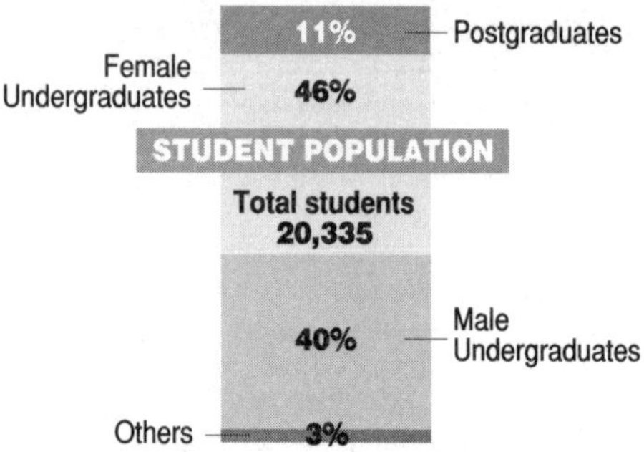

ACADEMIA & JOBS

Teesside's two largest academic schools are Health & Social Care and Computing. Both have increased dramatically in size over the last five years. Together they account for half the student population.

Significantly more than a quarter of Teesside students enter the health sector on graduation – by far the most becoming senior hospital nurses (SRN, RGN), then it's physiotherapists, community & youth workers, non-hospital nurses, occupational therapists, medical radiographers, social workers and midwives.

Teesside dropped only 1 point at the assessments and offer Adult, Child, Learning Disabilities and Mental Health nursing. Note also the various Youth Studies combinations with Sociology, Criminology or Psychology. Most social worker/counsellors come through biological sciences – BSc degrees in Social Work, and BSc Psychology (accredited by the British Psychological Society and the firsat step to becoming a chartered psychologist), which comes on its own or with Counselling or Criminology. They turn out a number of probation officers. See also the new BSc (Hons) Health Psychology, BSc (Hons) Sport and Exercise Psychology.

A significant niche area lies in computer games design. See their 3/4-year dedicated degrees (Animation, Games Art, Games Design, Games Programming, Games Science, Graphics Science). The first subject to be assessed Excellent was Computer Science and this has been a crucial focus of investment. The Innovation Centre incorporates the unique Virtual Reality Centre, with large-scale

ACADEMIC EXCELLENCE

TEACHING:

(Rated Excellent or 17+ out of 24)

Computer Science	**Excellent**
Nursing	**23**
Art & Design Subjects Allied to Medicine	**22**
Electric & Electron Eng, Sport	**21**
Psychology	**20**
Civil Eng, Sociol & Criminology	**19**
Civil Engineering	**18**

RESEARCH :

*Top grades 5/5**

History	**Grade 5**

VR development and viewing facilities, including a purpose-built Hemispherium (immersive VR experience) and VR cinema, as well as labs for the development of VR environments. Look at BScs in Digital Forensics, Digital Music, Digital Music Creation, BA(Hons) Post-Production and Visual Effects, BSc (Hons) Technical Direction in

SUBJECT AREAS (%)

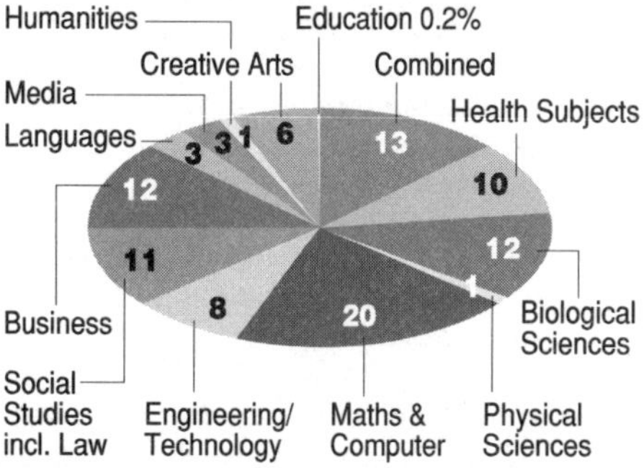

Computer Animation. The uni is part of a plan to create a digital city in Middlesbrough. There'll be new teaching, learning and commercial facilities as well as opportunities for graduate start up-businesses. Opening in 2007, as part of the DigitalCity project, is an £11m Institute of Digital Innovation, which will incorporate business accommodation, commercialisation space, concept testing and shared development facilities for research between business and academia.

Business-wise there's a strong lean towards information management and marketing, with BA e-Business, Business Information Systems, Accounting with Information technology, etc. See also vocational lines such as BA Marketing, and combinations with Retail Mgt, Advertising Mgt, Public Relations.

Their own business start-up scheme - Upgrade2 has assisted over 40 fledgling student companies. Collaboration with local and regional industry is the nub of their strategy in business and industry, which is why the Northern Region Film & Television Archive is housed on campus in a temperature controlled environment, with it's own screening facilities and archive, providing a resource for students of history and media.

Note, too, that they are specialists in European and commercial law. Again, there's a tie-up with Criminology, and a Senior Status LLB for graduates holding a non-Law degree. Links with Cleveland and Durham constabularies underwrite the pioneering BSc in Criminology. See also Crime Scene Science, Applied Science & Forensic Investigation, etc, and Fraud Management. They claim their Crime House Lab, where forensic science students put their investigative skills into practice, is the most elaborate facility of its kind in any UK university, and have just opened a Vehicle Examination Centre for forensic and crime scene science students to practise their skills. See the new BSc Digital Forensics, BSc (Hons) Forensic Investigation and Consumer Law.

A significant graduate population find work as graphic designers, set and interior designers, and there are interesting interior design and advertising specialisms Interior Architecture & Design, Creative Advertising & Promotion, Advertising Management & Public Relations. The Art & Design provision has spawned a useful local project, plans for a new showpiece centre for Art and Design education in collaboration with **Cleveland College of Art and Design**, which has three campuses,

WHERE TEESSIDE GRADUATES END UP

Health & Social Work: 27%; Education: 5%; Wholesale Retail: 13%; Manufacturing: 9%; Financial Activities: 4%; Public Administration, Civil Service & Defence: 11%; Hotel/Restaurant: 5%; Transport & Communications (including Telecommunications): 5%; Construction: 1%; Personnel: 3%; Computer: 5%; Business & Management: 1%; Accountancy: 0.5%; Media (including Film): 1%; Legal 4%; Advertising: 0.5%; Sport: 1.5%.

Approximate 'graduate track' employed **71%**

two in Middlesbrough, one in Hartlepool. Cleveland is hand in glove with Teesside. They are a large art college with 2000 students, about 10% of whom study for Teesside degrees in Design Crafts for the Entertainment Industries, Fine Art, Photography, and Textiles. There's synergy, too, with Cleveland's TV & Film production degree. Web: www.ccad. ac.uk

Teesside are also among the top unis for turning out sports players and officials through their Coaching and Applied Sports Science/Exercise Science degrees. See also the new BA Sport and Leisure Management, BA Sport Management and BSc Sport and Exercise Psychology. See *Sport* below.

SOCIAL SCENE

There's **The Terrace Bar**, and **Club One** is the 1000-capacity nightclub, a huge space with specially treated dancefloor, 8000 watt sound system, DJ control bridge, raised seating areas and no-smoke chill-out room. There's a clubnight every Friday and Saturday, the first being current chart and r&b, and Saturday rotates with indie, retro, school disco and current chart.

On a Friday evening in Club One the buzz is tangible. 'I've lived down south,' said Michelle, 'and I am not being biased, but the scene up here is great, one of the best in the North East.

On a Friday evening in **Club One** the buzz is tangible. 'I've lived down south,' said Michelle, 'and I am not being biased, but the scene up here is great, one of the best in the North East. We've got far too many bars, people are just competing with each other, so it's great for students. We have the **Empire** [renowned for *Sugar Shack* – Jeremy Healy, Boy George, Paul Oakenfold and Sasha and Digweed hit the decks]; it's one of the best known nightclubs in the country, if you look in dance mags. We've got **Tall Trees** in Yarm, which is internationally recognised [a huge club set in fantastic grounds with inimitable nights]. We have our balls there. There are plenty of others, and the **Arena** is nationally known.'

Nor is it all night-time reverie. There are 20 societies and 40 sports clubs. Student media includes a monthly magazine, *Cup of Tees*. Most popular is the International Students Society with about 100 members. Then there are things like the Dilated Pupil Society, the dance music society which is very active now. Drama is doing a series of satirical sketches this Christmas; they do plays regularly. There's a singing society and they're doing a Christmas concert. There's a Cultural Studies society that organises exchange trips and so on, a film sci fi society. Our Law society is very successful in the courtroom battles with high profile universities in the North East, Durham, Newcastle, etc. Art

WHAT IT'S REALLY LIKE

UNIVERSITY:	
Social Life	★★★
Campus scene	**Lively, local scene**
Student Union services	**Good**
Politics	**Activity low: fees, safety, health**
Sport	**Competitive**
National team position	**95th**
Sport facilities	**Poor**
Arts opportunities	**Dance, music excellent, rest OK**
Student magazine	**Cup of Tees**
Student newsletter	**Teesguide**
Nightclub	**Club One**
Bars	**Terrace Bar**
Union ents	**Chart, r&b, Indie, retro, disco**
Union clubs/societies	**60 (40 sport)**
Parking	**Poor**
TOWN:	
Entertainment	★★★★
Scene	**Pubs, big-time clubs**
Town/gown relations	**Average**
Risk of violence	**Average**
Cost of living	**Low**
Student concessions	**Good**
Survival + 2 nights out	**£50-£60 pw**
Part-time work campus/town	**Excellent/good**

AT A GLANCE

ACADEMIC FILE:	
Assessments	**20**
Excellent	**50%**
Typical entry requirements	**185 points**
Application acceptance rate	**26%, high**
Students-staff ratio	**21:1**
First/2:1 degree pass rate	**40%**
ACCOMMODATION FILE:	
Guarantee to freshers	**Most**
Style	**Halls, flats, houses**
Catered	**None**
En-suite	**34%**
Price range pw	**£33-£57**
City rent pw	**£46-$50**

comes via Cleveland College of Art & Design [see above]. They set up the Burlam Road Society.'

Sport In 2004 they opened the £6.5 million Olympia Building with squash courts, floodlit artificial pitch and large sports hall, plus a range of up to the minute teaching facilities and the latest climate simulation facility – designed to test sporting performance in a range of temperatures. But they are languishing 40 places further down the BUSA national team league (at 95th) than they were 2 years ago. No wonder they are offering such generouse sports scholarships.

PILLOW TALK

Campus residences are exclusively for first years. Allocations are made on a first come first served basis. Apply early for any accommodation as there isn't enough to go round. There are houses, halls, flats and managed housing off campus. Five mixed halls of residence all have self-catering facilities; 34% of campus accommodation is en suite.

GETTING THERE

☛ By road: A19, or A1/M, A66.
☛ By rail: Newcastle, 1:15; Leeds, 1:45; Manchester Piccadilly, 2:45; Liverpool Lime Street, 3:45; London King's Cross, 3:30.
☛ By air: Teesside International Airport.
☛ By coach: Birmingham, 3:15; York, 1:15.

THAMES VALLEY UNIVERSITY

Thames Valley University
St Mary's Road
London W5 5RF

TEL 020 8579 5000
FAX 020 8231 1353
EMAIL learning.advice@tvu.ac.uk
WEB www.tvu.ac.uk

Thames Valley Students' Union
St Mary's Road
London W5 5RF

TEL 020 8231 2276
FAX 020 8231 2589
EMAIL matthew.pledger@tvu.ac.uk
WEB www.tvu.ac.uk

VAG VIEW

Formerly West London Poly and incorporating the Ealing School of Art, where Pete Townshend (the Who), Ronnie Wood (the Stones) and Freddie Mercury (Queen)... erm...studied, TVU works with local colleges on access programmes, allowing successful completion of an access course as an alternative to usual entry requirements.

On the face of it, TVU is a model of the government's policy to facilitate access for social groups without a tradition in higher education.

They have had a time of it making that work, after a slamming from the Quality Assurance Agency in 1998, but their 10% drop-out rate today is not the highest in the land by a long way.

Now, there is much optimism following their merger with Reading College and School of Arts & Design, from the new Brentford Campus, home to their enormous Faculty of Health, and perhaps most promising of all, a tie-up with the mighty Imperial College London over a degree in Medicine.

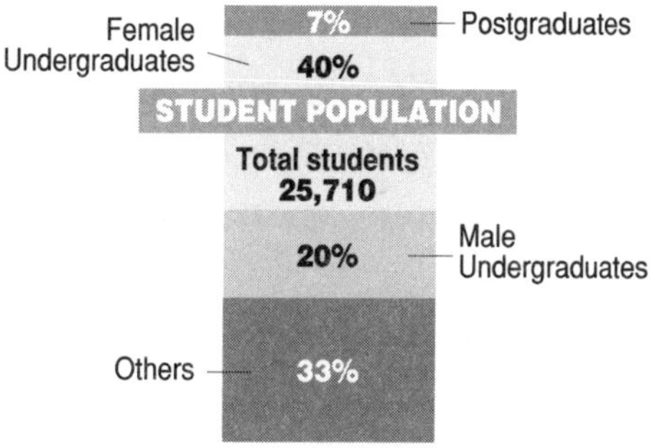

CAMPUS

TVU is based on sites in Ealing (West London, where the Student Union is based) and Slough, and now at Reading and Brentford. Shuttle buses run between the campuses until late each night. There is no university-owned residential campus accommodation at Ealing or Slough, but they will sort you out.

The Reading Campus, Crescent Road, Reading RG1 5RQ (0800 371 434), previously known as Reading College and School of Arts & Design, had been in TVU's sights for some time. After some toing and fro-ing, and a serious blip in negotiations when the college's computer provision failed a re-

SUBJECT AREAS (%)

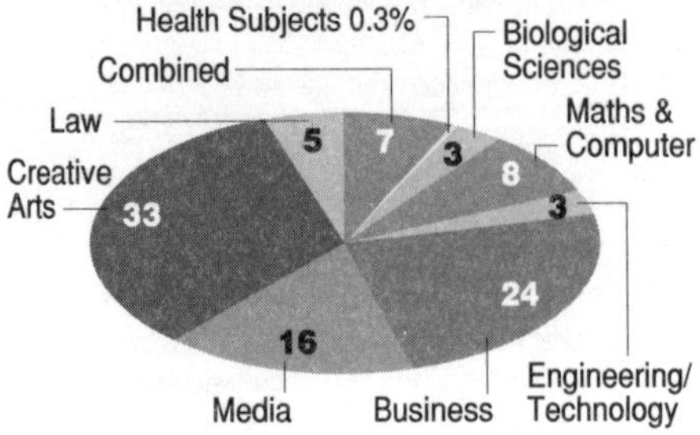

inspection by the Quality Assurance Agency, in January 2004 they merged with the uni and became the Reading campus.

For years TVU had awarded degrees here. The special deals at the college were then HNDs which convert with an extra year into degrees, including engineering, multimedia systems & design, business, fine art, fashion & textiles, design, photography. TVU is now offering business, music (technology and performance), computing, applied law, arts in the community, design, film, graphics, fine art, photography.

There is a Student Union presence, accommodation, an activities centre and football pitch. Nearby there are leisure centres with multi-sports tracks, gymnasiums, dance studios, swimming pools and tennis, squash and badminton courts. See *Reading University* entry for more details about the city.

Brentford Campus is still in the making, off Boston Manor Road. It will be home to TVU's Faculty of Health and Human Sciences – with its many nursing and midwifery students, this is the largest healthcare faculty in the UK. The first phase of the development is completed, and the campus is due to be fully operational by September 2006. It includes 849 study bedrooms, 221 key worker flats and 12,000 sq.m of teaching/office accommodation.

FEES, BURSARIES

UK & EU Fees: £3000 p.a. If in receipt of a Maintenance grant there's a bursary of £1000.

STUDENT PROFILE

'The most positive point to be made about TVU concerns the diversity,' writes student Ian Draysey. 'Students of all ages come from all over the world, and studying there has given me the opportunity to meet people I never would have otherwise. The majority of universities make similar claims, but in this case it's true, honest!'

Today, with most students from the locality, high ethnicity, many from overseas and many mature students, its boast of a diverse mix is valid, but only up to a point – they only take 1% from the independent school sector.

ACADEMIA & JOBS

More than 40% of their students graduate in business and administration, and many find jobs in marketing and market research. There are BA Marketing degrees with Business or Advertising. See also the Public Relations provision. There's also a particular slant towards the catering industry (see their Hospitality Management degrees and International Hotel degrees). See, too, their BA Business Travel & Tourism, Aviation & Business Tourism, Travel & Tourism Mgt, Resort & Event Mgt, which carve out careers.

Advertising is itself a sound niche graduate employment area for TVU. There are well targeted degrees, such as Advertising Specialist and Advertising with options ranging from Design through Radio Broadcasting, Video Production, Photography & Digital Imaging to Marketing. There is indeed a strong (5%) career claim on the media sector. See also BA New Media Journalism.

Smart music producers choose their 3-year Music Technology BA, which gives this uni one of its strongest employment records. Again there is the Specialist degree or one with options.

UNIVERSITY/STUDENT PROFILE

University since	**1992**
Situation/style	**City/suburban campuses**
Student population	**25710**
Undergraduates	**15405**
- mature	**77%, high**
- non EU undergraduates	**6%**
- male/female	**34/66**
- non-traditional student intake	**31%**
- state sector intake	**99%**
- drop-out rate	**28%, high**
- undergraduate applications	**Down 7%**

ACADEMIC EXCELLENCE

TEACHING:
(Rated Excellent or 17+ out of 24)

Sociology, Linguistics, Tourism	**22**
Psychology, Nursing, Health	**20**
Business/Marketing	**19**
Modern Languages	**18**

WHERE THAMES VALLEY GRADUATES END UP

Health & Social Work: 12%; Education: 7%; Wholesale Retail: 18%; Manufacturing: 5%; Financial Activities: 8%; Public Administration, Civil Service & Defence: 7%; Hotel/Restaurant: 6%; Transport & Communications (including Telecommunications): 9%; Construction: 0.5%; Personnel: 3%; Computer: 6%; Business & Management: 1%; Accountancy: 1%; Media (including Film): 5%; Legal 3%; Publishing: 0.5%; Artistic/Literary: 1.5%; Sport: 0.5%.

Statistics also show there's a track record for composers and musicians at TVU. See the BMus (Performance/Composition) and Popular Music Performance degrees.

The big news is that Imperial College London and Thames Valley University (TVU) are working together to provide an opportunity for students who wish to study medicine but may not have had the opportunity to do so. TVU students study the first year of Human Sciences – Pre-medical Option BSc(Hons) – at TVU. Depending on their first semester exam results some may then have the option of transferring to the first year of the College's MBBS course, which is of world renown and of six years' duration. Alternatively, they can continue with their studies at TVU.

Otherwise, TVU's health provision, which will be moving to the new Brentford campus, focuses on Nursing and midwifery and accounts for a hug proportion of jobs for graduates from TVU. There's also Health & Exercise Science, Health Studies, Sports Science & Medicine, a top-up Complementary Approaches to Health degree, and BSc Psychology with Counselling Theory, as well as the single hons accredited by the British Psychological Society, first step to becoming a chartered psychologist. The BSc has an OK assessment, 20.

The law degree recently got a fillip from the LPC Board (a Legal Practice Course is essential to becoming a solicitor) who pronounced it 'Good'.

Finally, there's a strong showing in financial administration. See their Accounting and Finance degrees and foundation year.

AT A GLANCE

ACADEMIC FILE:	
Subjects assessed	**19**
Excellent	**42%**
Typical entryl requirements	**180 points**
Application acceptance rate	**20%**
Students-staff ratio	**25:1**
First/2:1 degree pass rate	**47%**
ACCOMMODATION FILE:	
Availability in college	**None**
Town/city rent pw	**£65-£95**

It is in line with their academic strategy to have help at hand for literacy, numeracy and IT skills.

SOCIAL SCENE

STUDENTS' UNION The Studio opens Monday to Friday, 11 am to 11 pm, the **Coffee Stop**, 8 am - 6 pm, Monday to Thursday, 8 am - 4 pm on Fridays. At the Ealing campus, traditional pool table and jukebox scenario is supplemented by Bhangra music and Hindi films. Ents include live bands, karaoke, DJs and drinking competitions. The uni's degrees in music (including Popular Music Performance) and its association with the London College of Music and Media provide input, and the fledgling Tube Radio, ambitiously aimed not just at students but at the wider community around Ealing, bene-

WHAT IT'S REALLY LIKE

UNIVERSITY:	
Social Life	★★
Campus scene	**London diversity, closed weekends**
Student Union services	**Average-poor**
Politics	**No interest**
Sport	**Local**
National team position	**None**
Sport facilities	**Poor**
Arts opportunities	**Music, film, art**
Student magazine	**Undergrad**
Student newspaper	**The Voice**
Student radio	**Tube**
Nightclub	**The Studio**
Bars	**The Studio Bar**
Union ents	**Some**
Union clubs/societies	**11**
Most popular society	**Tube Radio**
Smoking policy	**None**
Parking	**Adequate**
CITY:	
Entertainment	★★★★★
Scene	**London**
Town/gown relations	**Average**
Risk of violence	**Average**
Cost of living	**Very high**
Student concessions	**Good**
Survival + 2 nights out	**£80 pw**
Part-time work campus/town	**Average/excellent**

fits from LCM's hardware.

The largest venue at TVU is **Artwood's**, with a capacity of 1,200. It has attempted to overcome its school hall demeanour with the installation of a bar to complement its livestock-bothering sound system, and has a good atmosphere when crowded.

Over at the Slough campus, the **Moon and Cucumber** bar, buffet bar, **Hamlyn Hall** and the smokeless **Studio Bar** offer alternative recreational facilities. Slough also houses a gym for those who'd rather build up their muscles than their beer guts.

They say that societies range from the Radio Society to the Asian Society and come under four categories, Cultural (Asian, Chinese), Religious (Christian Union, Islamic), Social (Radio, Music Industry), and Academic (Law, Psychology). Sport at TVU has swung away from the more team-oriented stance of many universities, with activities such as badminton, fencing and aerobics gaining more members than football. There was no team placement in last year's national uni leagues.

GETTING THERE

☛ Ealing: Ealing Broadway Underground (Central and District Lines).

☛ Slough: By road: M4/J6, A4. By rail: London Paddington, 25 mins.

UNIVERSITY OF ULSTER

University of Ulster
University House
Cromore Road
Coleraine
Co. Londonderry BT52 1SA

TEL 028 7034 4221
FAX 028 7032 4908
EMAIL online@ulster.ac.uk
WEB www.ulst.ac.uk

VAG VIEW

Ulster is the largest of the nine universities in Ireland. Spread across four sites (between seven and eighty miles apart) it is an enormous place in terms of students, 80% of whom are local.

The uni came out of a merger in 1984 between Ulster Poly (now the Jordanstown campus) and the New University of Ulster (which was the old university, if you follow). Sites are at Belfast (art college), at Newtownabbey, in the hills above Belfast (the Jordanstown campus), at Coleraine (this is HQ, far northwest of Belfast, near the Giant's Causeway), and in Londonderry (Magee College campus, founded in 1865), yet further west.

To solve communications problems they have formed a wireless microwave network capable of transmitting data of Encyclopedia Britannica *proportions in a second. The Centre for Communications Engineering links them to Queen's Uni and Nortel Networks, and is a feature of their strategy for close working with industry.*

There are plans afoot for massive improvements and expansion.

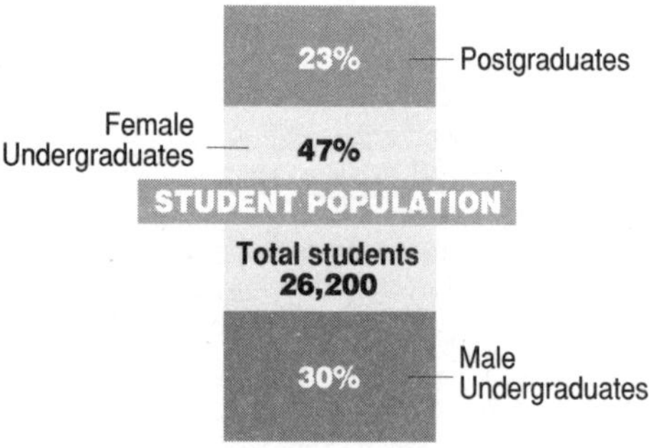

STUDENT PROFILE

There's a high mature undergrad percentage and an unusually high number of part-timers among the predominantly local student body; university strategy ensures that many, too, come from social groups with no great tradition of higher education. Together with all this socio-educational progress comes a high drop-out rate – 13% of non-mature entrants.

CAMPUS

BELFAST York Street, Belfast BT15 1ED. **Location:** close to city centre, part of the city's up and coming Cathedral Quarter, is traditionally considered the home of the School of Art and Design, though other disciplines are increasingly being taught there. **Faculty HQs:** Art & Design (including Interior Design and Textile & Fashion Design). Also American Studies, Architecture, Irish Literature, Chinese, English. **Accommodation:** none, but small number of Belfast students may use Jordanstown. **Ents facilities: Conor Hall** (400-

SUBJECT AREAS (%)

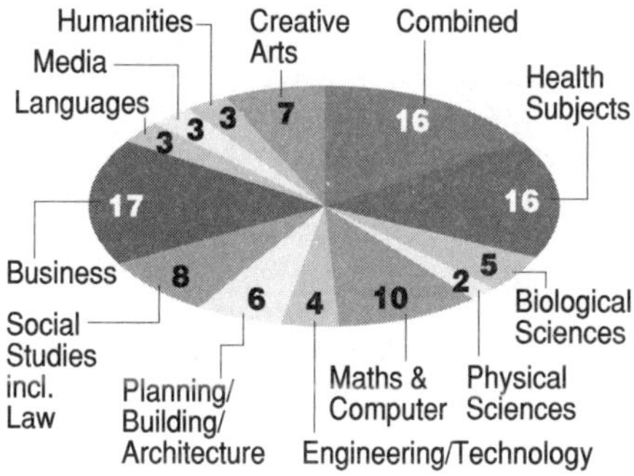

capacity venue). **Sports facilities:** 'What's sport?' said a student when asked. Arts facilities: foyer exhibition area, art shop, artist (writer, artist or musician) in residence. **Arts opportunities:** 'Second to none, vibrant, innovative, love it!' said our student contact. **Media:** monthly magazine, *Ufouria*. See *Belfast Student City*, page 389.

JORDANSTOWN Newtownabbey BT37 OQB. **Location:** seven miles north of Belfast on the shore of Belfast Lough; largest site. **Faculty HQs:** Business & Management (including Government, Law, Marketing), Engineering (including Biomedical Eng), Informatics, Social (economics, accounting, politics, social policy, sociology, counselling) & Health Sciences (nursing, physiotherapy, podiatry, speech & language therapy). Also architecture and construction, languages library management, sport. **Accommodation:** res. blocks, six-bedroom houses, flats & study-bedrooms in halls; self-catering. **Ents facilities: Students' Union Bar** (700 capacity), split level, two stages, tiered seating/standing; regular disco night is Monday. **Sports facilities:** two large sports halls, gym, fitness suite, six squash courts, eight-lane swimming pool and hydrotherapy pool, playing fields, synthetic training pitch, local water sports facility and River Lagan. **Arts facilities:** recital rooms, concert hall. Low key. **Media:** *Naked* is student newspaper.

COLERAINE (address with entry title) **Location:** market town close to north coast, 35 miles from Derry. The original uni, admin HQ and home to the Centre for Molecular Sciences. **Biosciences, health (nursing, optometry), pharmacology, environmental science, dietetics, social sciences (psychology,), humanities (history, geography) languages and Euro studies, media (film, journalism, publishing), business, computer**. **Accommodation:** residential blocks and student houses. Most students prefer to live out in coastal resort towns Portrush and Portstewart. **Ents facilities: Biko Hall** (venue) and recently rebuilt **Uni-Bar**; 550 capacity. Regular disco night is Monday. **Sports facilities:** Biko Hall is sports hall by day, five squash courts, fitness suite, solarium and steam room, playing fields, floodlit football pitch, pavilion, tennis courts, water sports centre on River Bann. **Arts facilities:** the **Octagon** (500-seat recital room), the **Diamond** (1,200-seat concert hall, prestigious **Riverside Theatre**, third largest pro theatre in Ireland, venue for drama, rock and classical concerts, ballet, opera, etc.

MAGEE COLLEGE Northland Road, Londonderry BT48 7JL. **Location:** residential quarter of Derry, Ireland's second largest city. A mixture of historical and new buildings and modern and traditional facil-

UNIVERSITY/STUDENT PROFILE

University since	**1984**
Situation/style	**4 urban/rural campus sites**
Student population	**26200**
Undergraduates	**20160**
- mature	**20%**
- non EU undergraduates	**1%**
- male/female	**39/61**
- non-traditional student intake	**48%, v. high**
- state sector intake	**100%**
drop-out rate	**13%**
- undergraduate applications	**Up 3%**

WHERE ULSTER GRADUATES END UP

Health & Social Work: 20%; Education: 4.5%; Wholesale Retail: 14%; Manufacturing: 8%; Financial Activities: 7%; Public Administration, Civil Service & Defence: 10%; Hotel/Restaurant: 4%; Transport & Communications (including Telecommunications): 2%; Construction: 4%; Agriculture: 0.5%; Personnel: 1.5%; Computer: 5%; Business & Management: 2.5%; Accountancy: 4%; Media (including Film): 0.5%; Legal 1%; Architecture: 2%; Sport: 0.5%.

Approximate 'graduate track' employed **64%**

ACADEMIC EXCELLENCE

TEACHING
(Rated Excellent or 17+ out of 24)

Music, Social Policy & Admin, Environmental Studies. Studies, Land & Property Mgt.	**Excellent**
Business & Management, Celtic Studies	**24**
Tourism, Philosophy, Psychology, Education	**23**
American Studies, Drama, Maths, Nursing, Molecular Biosciences, Subjects Allied to Medicine, Economics, Politics	**22**
Communication & Media, Building, Organismal Biosciences	**21**
Electrical & Electronic Eng, French, General Engineering.	**20**
German, Civil Eng, Art/Design	**19**
Iberian	**18**

RESEARCH :
*Top grades 5/5**

Celtic, Biomedical Science	**Grade 5***
Built Enviro, Law, Art/Design	**Grade 5**

ities, a small and tightly knit student population. New moves bring drama, music, dance and computing to the bedrock business, humanities, social sciences (psychology, law, politics, social policy, community youth work, sociology) & nursing. Languages are also to the fore, and Irish Studies. It is home to the Institute for Legal & Professional Studies. **Accommodation:** three halls of residence and student village (modern houses). **Ents facilities:** two bars, **The Terrapin** (known as 'the wee bar') and **The Bunker** (bar/nightclub, 400 capacity). **Ents:** bands and discos (Thursday); Derry wild with pubs. **Sports facilities:** sports hall, fitness suite and solarium; recent additions include sports pavilion, sand-carpet soccer pitch, synthetic training pitch; sailing at Fahan, rowing and canoeing on the Foyle. **Arts facilities:** the **Great Hall**.

ACADEMIA & JOBS

Here the emphasis is on jobs in the health sector, in retail, in public administration, civil service, etc.

In the former, where there's a good 22-point score in the teaching assessments, most jobs go to nurses (including mental health), to occupational therapists, to ophthalmic opticians – they have between 6% and 10% of the graduate employment market. There's a world-class Grade 5* for research.

Then it's physiotherapists, radiographers (diagnostic and therapeutic), chiropodists (the Podiatry degrees, and speech therapists. The BSc Speech & Language Therapy asks BBB.

Social workers/counsellors spring into the work sector via BSc Social Work. See also BSc Social Psychology. Other Psychology combinations include languages, marketing, international politics and human resource management.

In retail management, for sheer bulk of graduate output, Manchester Met leads, followed by Ulster with their Business Studies programmes and Retail Management, Consumer Studies and Marketing degrees. Note Business & Management scored full marks at the teaching assessments, and there's a sure path to hotel, restaurant manager through their international hospitality management and hotel and tourism management degrees.

For civil service admin and local/regional government admin, Ulster's BSc Economics & Government, Law & Government, Housing Management, Community Development, Social Administration & Policy, Health & Social Care Policy, Social Policy & Governance, etc are clearly relevant, but in fact the majority of their graduates into the sector come on the Health ticket - subjects allied to Medicine: besides the many keenly focused degrees alluded to above, there are courses in Human Nutrition, Food & Nutrition, Dietetics, Clinical Physiology, etc and a Postgrad Diploma/MSc in Health Promotion. See also their Psychology with International Politics out at Magee Campus. Biological Sciences is also a popular route and part of the same Faculty of Life & Health Sciences.

The Faculty of Engineering & Built Environment is also productive through various degrees: Environment Engineering, Architectural Technology/Construction Eng & Management, Building Surveying, Transport & Supply Chain Management and BSc Environmental Health.

Construction engineers/managers also proliferate. BSc Hons Construction Engineering & Management, Architectural Technology & Management, or Building Surveying are the key focus courses, 21 points at assessment, international Grade 5 for research. Property developers, quantity surveyors and estate agents also come out of Ulster in quantity. There's BSc

Property Development & Investment, which puts their employment record out of sight of most of their competitors and they are responsible for 9% of all graduate quantity surveyors, even though the dedicated degree is new. Land & Property Mgt took full marks at the assessments and you won't have to punt as high as the asking grades for their flagship Architectural Technology & Management degree, which helps to make them clear market leaders in engineering design consultancy.

Civil engineers also make a strong showing in

WHAT IT'S REALLY LIKE

UNIVERSITY:	
Social Life	★★★
Campus scenes	**Local, lively, diverse**
Student Union services	**Average**
Politics	**High activity: Irish politics, student funding**
Sport	**Big at Coleraine & Jordanstown**
Sport facilities	**Good**
National team position	**85th**
Arts opportunities	**Art excellent; drama, dance, film, music good**
Student magazine	**Ufouria**
Union ents	**13 pw**
Live venues	**Conor Hall** (Belfast), **Biko Hall** (Coleraine), **The Bunker** (Magee), **Arthur's** (Jordanstown)
Union clubs/societies	**100+**
Most popular society	**Irish Society**
Smoking policy	**Union OK**
Parking	**Adequate**

AT A GLANCE

ACADEMIC FILE:	
Subjects assessed	**42**
Excellent	**67%**
Typical entry requirements	**260 points**
Application acceptance rate	**16%**
Students-staff ratio	**17:1**
First/2:1 class degree pass rate	**63%**
ACCOMMODATION FILE:	
Guarantee to freshers	**100%**
Style	**Halls, flats, houses; not Belfast**
Approx price range pw	**£40-£80**
Approx off-campus rent pw	**£40**

the employment figures.

There's a strong showing in accountancy, too – a dedicated degree and one with Business Studies. Another field where acute powers of analysis are to the fore is in biosciences and Ulster was awarded a world-class Grade 5* for research into Biomedical Science. One result is a niche employment area for bacteriologists and microbiologists. The BSc Environmental degrees may be 3 or 4 years with a Diploma in Industrial Studies or Area Studies (that means a year in Europe or USA). There are also Food & Nutrition and Food Production degrees. There's an Excellent for teaching Environmental Studies and more recently a 22-point tick for Health Sciences.

Many Ulster graduates go into computing as programmers, software engineers/consultants or telecommunications engineers. Besides the BEng Electronics & Software and MEng Software Engineering, there's BSc Computer Science and Computing with orientations like E-Business, Entrepreneurship, Marketing, Psychology or Mathematics.

Check campus location foe course you want to study.

GETTING THERE

☛ An hour by air from London, with at least 24 flights a day each way.

☛ Ulsterbus operates a fast and frequent service across Northern Ireland.

UNIVERSITY COLLEGE, LONDON

University College, London
Gower Street
London WC1E 6BT

TEL 020 7679 3000
FAX 020 7679 3001
EMAIL (via website)
WEB www.ucl.ac.uk/prospective-students

UCL Students' Union
25 Gordon Street
London WC1H 0AH

TEL 020 7387 3611
FAX 020 7383 3937
EMAIL mc.officer@ucl.ac.uk
WEB www.uclu.org

VAG VIEW

The college was the original University of London, the first in England after Oxford and Cambridge, inspired by the first principle of Utilitarianism, 'the greatest happiness of the greatest number'. It was a pioneering move by a group of thinkers, John Stuart Mill among them, for an alternative

SUBJECT AREAS (%)

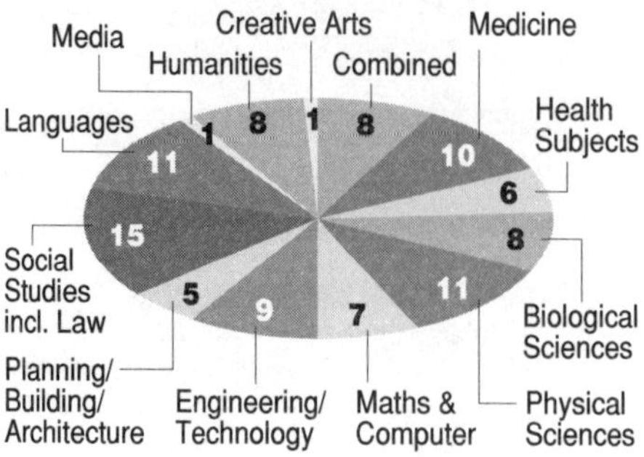

approach to higher education, which, in 1826, meant the privileged education dished out by Oxford and Cambridge.

The idea was to open the doors of education to the rising middle-classes and to free the educational establishment from the doctrinal prejudices of the Anglican Church. Roman Catholics, Jews and Nonconformists were barred from an Oxbridge education in those days. To ensure freedom from dogma, it was decided not to have subjects appertaining to religion taught at UCL.

UCL remains one of our foremost seats of learning, its research record formidable and its Slade School of Fine Art reckoned to be the best in its area. UCL's merger with the School of Slavonic & East European Studies and the foundation of the Wolfson Institute for Biomedical Research would seem to shore up the academic infrastructure yet further.

CAMPUS

The location of UCL's main sites, just to the north of London's West End and hard by the University of London Students' Union building, provides students with amazing resource opportunity. What's more, most halls of residence are within walking distance.

UNIVERSITY/STUDENT PROFILE	
College of London Uni since	**1826**
Situation/style	**Civic**
Student population	**20240**
Undergraduates	**11935**
- mature	**14%**
- non EU undergraduates	**18%**
- male/female	**47/53**
- non-traditional student intake	**17%**
- state sector intake	**59%, v. low**
drop-out rate	**5%**
- undergraduate applications	**Up 5%**

SATELLITE CAMPUSES

Royal Free Hospital Medical School merged with UCL to form the Royal Free & University College Medical School. It is situated in Hampstead, one of the safest, most aesthetically pleasing areas of London.

School of Slavonic & East European Studies – SSEES (pronounced Cease) is an enigmatic institution specialising in the study of Eastern Europe, 'It holds the academically acknowledged best lecturers in their fields,' says Gideon Dewhurst, 'and the largest East European library in Britain. They have new purpose-built premises in Taviton Street.

FEES, BURSARIES

UK & EU Fees: £3000 p.a. If in receipt of full HE Maintenance grant, you will also receive a UCL bursary equal to at least 50% of their grant, according to household earnings. There are bursaries for students studying particular courses. for Chinese national, for students in financial hardship who plans to get involved in the Students' Union. Check all info. at www.ucl.ac. uk/scholarships.

STUDENT PROFILE

The heavy imbalance in favour of public school wallahs is quite ironic in the light of its history. Today, they hardly fill the bill as 'Cockney College', the name given in the 19th century by those who feared the consequences of UCL's open-access stance. Few universities take a smaller percentage of state sector pupils. However, judging by the recent concentration of activity in the areas of special needs and academic counselling, UCL just might be tooling up to make a big change.

ACADEMIA & JOBS

UCL places great importance on its tutorial system. All students are allocated a personal tutor for consultation on academic or personal matters. Further support is offered by departmental and faculty tutors and two advisers specialising in women students. There's also a professional counselling service and a Students' Union Rights & Advice Centre to see you through any problems academic, financial or emotional. Also, a new special educational needs IT suite was opened in December 2001, offering computers and related software and equipment. An IT trainer and a disabilities co-ordinator are at your disposal.

To become a doctor here, you'll need to be

ACADEMIC EXCELLENCE

TEACHING : *(Rated Excellent or 17+ out of 24)*	
History, Law, Anthropology, Architecture, English, Geography, Geological Sciences	**Excellent**
Economics, History of Art, Organismal Biosciences, Subjects Allied to Medicine	**24**
German, Scandinavian Studies, Dentistry, Maths, Physics, Archaeology, Philosophy, Classics, Art & Design	**23**
Linguistics, Dutch, Electrical & Electronic Eng, Psychology, Molecular Biosciences, Anatomy, Library/Info, Politics, Psychology	**22**
Medicine, French	**21**
Italian, Chem & Biochem Eng Pharmacology	**20**
Iberian Studies, Civil Eng	**19**
RESEARCH *Top grades 5/5*/6**	
Hospital-based Clinical - Child Health/Neurology/ Ophthalmology, Pharmacology, Psychology, Chemistry, Chemical Eng, Geography, Law, Anthropology, Economics, English, German, Italian, Classics	**Grade 6***
Linguistics	**Grade 5***
Hospital-based Clinical - Royal Free, Clinical Dentistry, Anatomy, Other Subjects Allied to Medicine, Biochemistry, Biology, Physics, Earth Sciences, Pure Maths, Applied Maths, Statistics, Computer, Civi/ Environmental Eng, Electrical/ Electronic Eng, Mechanical, Aeronautical/Manufacturing Eng, European Studies, French, Dutch, Scandinavian, Archaeol, History, History of Art, Philosophy, Art and Design	**Grade 5**

accepted onto the 4/5-year MB BS. UCL, in partnership with Oxford and Cambridge, now stipulate that all candidates applying to read Medicine sit a written test called the Biomedical Admissions Test (BMAT). The test is being used to assess scientific aptitude, not fitness to practise medicine (which will continue to be assessed in other ways, including interview) and focuses on scientific abilities relevant to the study of medicine.

The approach of the MB BS is lectures, tutorial and lab classes in Phase 1, with a lot of computer-assisted learning and problem-solving exercises. Only in Phase 2 do you go out in small teams of consultants and doctors. Phase 3 offers intensive clinical experience. Entry ABB to include Chemistry + one AS level. Biology must be offered at A or AS. English and Maths at Grade b, GCSE. Teaching inspection, 21. Application acceptance rate was 14% last time, which is better than average. Research Grade 6*: Hospital-based Clinical, Child Health/Neurology/ Ophthalmology, psychology; Grade 5: Hospital-based Clinical.

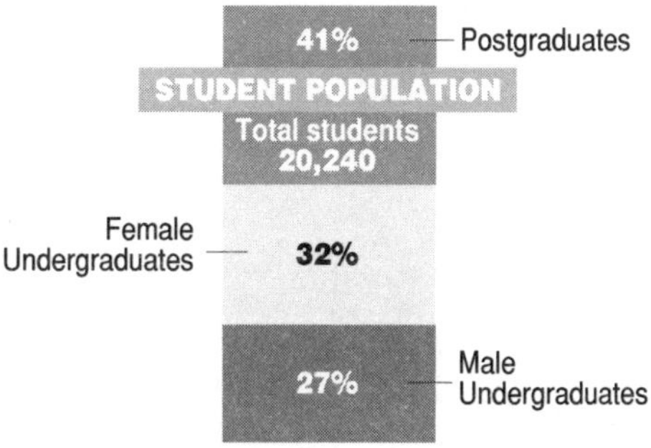

Chiropodists and speech therapists are part of the picture too. Teaching inspection, 23. BSc Speech Science has an international-standard Grade 5 rating for research. and full marks at inspection.

After medicine, languages (21 are offered), and physical and social sciences degrees are popular. With the takeover of the School of Slavonic & Eastern European Studies in 1999, the Language options increased dramatically. This is a premier route into Adult Education for would-be lecturers. On inspection, German and Scandinavian Studies were awarded 23 out of 24, Linguistics and Dutch 22, French 21, Italian 20, Spanish 19. There were both Grade 6* and Grade 5 accolades at the Languages research assessments.

The BA degree in Language and Culture combines study of one foreign language to degree level, plus one or two other languages, with a particular focus in a chosen area of cultural studies – comparative literature, film studies, linguistics, history of art or cultural history – giving students the opportunity to apply their language skills in deepening their knowledge of different cultural fields from a broader and comparative perspective.

UCL have recently teamed up with the famous Scool of Oriental & African Studies (also part of London University) in a Centre of Excellence in Teaching and Learning: Languages of the Wider

World, which 'recognizes, promotes and develops the excellent teaching and learning in less commonly taught languages'.

Physical sciences, humanities and language graduates put UCL among the leaders at point of employment for museum archivists, curators and the like.

Geology, Geophysics, Earth & Space Science are cheek by jowl with History & Philosophy of Science and Information Management, and what about Palaeobiology to set you up in a museum career?

UCL's BSc/MSci degrees in Natural Sciences combine science subjects into a structured and coherent degree, exploiting the increasing overlap of traditional science disciplines such as Biology, Chemistry and Physics which has created new and existing areas of scientific study.

See, too, the Faculty of Social & Historical Sciences, where you'll find Ancient History, Anthropology, Archaeology (Egyptian, General, Mediaeval), History of Art, and what about Archaeology, Classics & Classical Art?

Archaeology is an especially popular degree here. Besides the BA and BSc single hons, there's Mediaeval Archaeology, joint degrees with History of Art and a 4-year Classics & Classical Art. Teaching inspection, 23. Research, Grade 5.

Physics scored 23 points at the assessments and was rated international Grade 5 for research. It's a top flight department. Courses in Astronomy, Astrophysics, Chemical Physics, Theoretical Physics, Earth & Space Science seem to take one a million miles away from investment analysis – and they make their share of physicists and astronomers here – but Maths shares the faculty, and investment advisers and analysts are in fact drawn from here in equal quantity with those from economics.

In the context of Economics, note the single honours BSc degree and BSc Economics & Statistics, etc, as well as BA Economics & Business with East European Studies (in the School of Slavonic & East Euro Studies). They took full marks at the assessments and have a world-class Grade 6* rating for research. It's a launch pad for merchant bankers too, while others again came through maths and the largest group (28%) through Information Science.

As we have seen, they actively encourage you to add an international dimension to your degree programme. A growing number of courses now include a year abroad, and many more can provide an opportunity for students to spend some time abroad, for example as part of a Socrates exchange. A newly established Study Abroad Office advises students on the opportunities open to them, ensures that students going abroad are fully briefed, and also works to expand further UCL's links with overseas organisations.

Academically the college is strong, its reputation world class. Aware that some might be left feeling slightly daunted, there's a surprise new focus on special needs and academic counselling.

UCL is of course renowned for Law – they took a world-class Grade 6* for research, and their drive to promote the internationalisation of study now has German Law sitting alongside English and French Law. UCL in partnership with a consortium of 11 UK universities has agreed that all candidates applying to read Law will be required to sit a written test called the Law National Admissions Test (LNAT). The test is designed to provide an assessment of a candidate's potential for law degree programmes but is not a replacement for A levels.

SOCIAL SCENE

Students' Union UCL obviously lacks the feel of a campus university, but not to its detriment. **Phineas** is the hub. The largest venue is the comfortable **Windeyer**, with a capacity of 550, large dance floor and a variety of catering. Wednesday

WHERE UNIVERSITY COLLEGE GRADUATES END UP

Health & Social Work: 30%; Education: 7%; Wholesale Retail: 7%; Manufacturing: 7%; Financial Activities: 9%; Public Administration, Civil Service & Defence: 6%; Hotel/Restaurant: 2%; Transport & Communications (including Telecommunications): 3%; Construction: 1%; Mining/Oil Extracting: 0.5%; Personnel: 3.5%; Computer: 2%; Business & Management: 4%; Accountancy: 4%; Media (including Film): 3%; Legal 1%; Architecture: 2%; Publishing: 2.5%; Advertising: 0.5%; Artistic/Literary: 0.5%; Sport: 0.5%.

Approximate 'graduate track' employed **76%**

attracts *SportsNite* to the **2econd Floor** bar. Thursday's *2Phat* runs across **Phineas** and **Windeyer**.

The union oversees more than 144 clubs and societies, based, for the most part, in a specially created, open plan area with computers, phones, photocopy and TV/video facilities. The union's many arts societies fill a gap in UCL's academic curriculum. Drama Soc performs to professional level at UCL's **Bloomsbury Theatre** and there's a smaller experimental **Garage Theatre** and a stage in Huntley Street. Student media is active with *Pi Magazine*, the student radio station, Rare fm, and student TV – Bloomsbury Television (BTV). The college has also just signed up the New London Orchestra to boost its musical culture. It will become a kind of orchestra-in-residence at the Bloomsbury Theatre.

Political activity currently focuses on International Student Visas, Keeping Wednesday Afternoons free (for sport), Climate Change.

WHAT IT'S REALLY LIKE

UNIVERSITY:	
Social Life	★★★★★
Campus scene	**Affluent south-east dominates**
Student Union services	**Good**
Politics	**Activity average: ethical, anti-war & internal**
Sport	**54 clubs**
National team position	**46th**
Sport facilities	**Good**
Arts opportunities	**Excellent**
Student magazine	**Pi Magazine**
Student radio	**Rare FM**
Student TV	**BTV**
Nightclub	**Windeyer**
Bars	**Easy J's. Gordons, 2econd Floor, Huntley, Phineas, SSEES**
Union ents	**SportsNite, 2Phat**
Union societies	**90**
Most active society	**Indian Society**
Parking	**None**
CITY:	
Entertainment	★★★★★
Scene	**Wild, expensive**
Town/gown relations	**Average-good**
Risk of violence	**Average**
Cost of living	**High**
Student concessions	**Abundant**
Survival + 2 nights out	**£100 pw**
Part-time work campus/town	**Good/excellent**

AT A GLANCE

ACADEMIC FILE:	
Subjects assessed	**40**
Excellent	**90%**
Typical entry requirements	**385 points**
Application acceptance rate	**13%**
Students-staff ratio	**8:1, the best**
First/2:1 degree pass rate	**74%**
ACCOMMODATION FILE:	
Guarantee to freshers	**100%**
Style	**Halls, houses**
Catered	**23%**
En-suite	**17%**
Price range pw	**£60-£117**
City rent pw	**£100-£180 Zone 1; £75-£85 Zone 2**

SPORT There are 54 active sports clubs, but there's been a massive drop in performance in 2 years from 17th to 46th place in the national BUSA team league. Time to get those Wednesday afternoons off lectures? Facilities include two large grounds (with bars), a gym, fitness centre (with multigyms, squash courts, Dojo, aerobics/dance hall, sunbeds & sauna) and a large sports hall. For those who want to swim, there is access to the University of London Union pool, next door to UCL.

TOWN See *Student City London*, page 292.

PILLOW TALK

Accommodation is guaranteed to freshers if they firmly hold an offer of a place on a degree programme, apply for accommodation by the deadline (currently May 31 of year of entry), and have not previously been a degree student living in London.

There are two types of accommodation on offer: halls of residence (catered/breakfast and evening meal) and student houses (self-catering accommodation, some purpose built, others converted private houses). UCL has a rolling programme of upgrading its accommodation. Newer residences have en-suite facilities and computer points networked to the UCL system. Frances Gardner House is newly built – 215 single en-suite rooms, just 20 mins' walk from campus.

GETTING THERE

☛ UCL: Euston Square (Metropolitan, Circle, Hammersmith & City lines), Warren Street (Victoria, Northern), Euston (Victoria, Northern). Royal Free: Belsize Park Underground (Northern line) or overland railway, Hampstead Heath.

UNIVERSITY OF THE ARTS, LONDON

University of the Arts
65 Davies Street
London W1Y 5DA
TEL 020 7514 6216
FAX 020 7514 8179
EMAIL info@linst.ac.uk
WEB www.arts.ac.uk

UNIVERSITY PROFILE	
Founded	**1986**
Status	**University**
Situation/style	**City sites**
Student population	**26415**
Full-time undergraduates	**10305**
ACCOMMODATION:	
Guarantee to freshers	**No**
Style	**Self-catered halls**
Cost pw (no food)	**£62-£115.50**
City rent pw	**£85-£180**

DEGREE SUBJECT AREAS:
Art, design, fashion, media, printing

Granted University title in 2003 and re-named the following year, this is the old London Institute, the largest arts university of its kind in Europe and one of the biggest arts institutions in the world.

Offering a comprehensive range of courses in art, design, communication and performance, the University of the Arts represents five distinguished colleges with roots that run as deep as 1842.

Described by Newsweek as 'the epicentre of London style', the uni's glittering alumni include Simon Callow CBE, Sir Jimmy Choo, Sir Terence Conran, John Galliano, Anthony Gormley, Jefferson Hack, Maggie Hambling, Howard Hodgkin, Emma Hope, Anish Kapoor, Stella McCartney, Gilbert and George, Chris Ofili, Julia Peyton-Jones and Jane Root.

They have spent £2 million on a high tech system that links these diverse sites.

COLLEGE SITES

CAMBERWELL COLLEGE OF ARTS Peckham Road, London SE5 8UF. Email: enquiries@camb.arts.ac.uk. Web: www.camb.arts.ac.uk. Tel 020 7514 6302. Courses: Art & Design, Book Arts, Communication, Digital Arts and Media, Drawing, Film & Video, Fine Art, Furniture, Graphic Design, Interactive Multimedia, Interior Design, Model Making, New Media, Painting, Photography, Printed Textiles, Product Design, Sculpture, Textile Design, Visual Design & Display.

CENTRAL ST MARTIN'S COLLEGE OF ART & DESIGN Southampton Row, London WC1B 4AP. Email: info@csm.arts.ac.uk. Web: www.csm.arts.ac.uk. Tel 020 7514 7000. Courses range from foundation to PhD. Fashion and Textiles, Media Arts, Fine Art, Graphic Design, Theatre and Performance, 3D Design, Interdisciplinary.

CHELSEA COLLEGE OF ART & DESIGN 16 John Islip Street, London SW1P 4JU. Email: enquiries@chelsea.arts. ac.uk. Web: chelsea.arts.ac.uk. Tel: 020 7514 7751. In 2004, Chelsea moved from its current four sites to a single campus on Millbank by the River Thames, and next to Tate Britain. Courses: Art and Design, Communication, Digital Arts and Media, Drawing, Film and Video, Fine Art, Furniture, Graphic Design, Interactive Multimedia, Interior Design, Knitwear, Model Making, New Media, Painting, Photography, Printmaking, Printed Textiles, Screenprinting, Sculpture, Stitch/embroidery, Textile Design, Visual Design and Display.

LONDON COLLEGE OF FASHION A new centre for all existing London College of Fashion satellite sites is to be developed at Lime Grove, near Shepherds Bush, West London. Some will not have made the move until 2007. Contact University of Arts. Or make enquiries via Email: enquiries@lcf.arts.ac.uk. Web: lcf.arts.ac.uk. Courses: Accessories, Beauty Science and Beauty Therapy, Business and Management, Buying and Merchandising, Culture and Communication, Cosmetic Science, Costume, Curation, Design and Technology, Fashion Design, Footwear, Journalism, Make up and Hair Styling, Marketing, Media, Menswear, Millinery, Photography, Promotion, Styling, Tailoring and Garment Production, Technical Effects, Textiles for Fashion, Womenswear.

LONDON COLLEGE OF COMMUNICATION Elephant & Castle, London SE1 6SB. Email: info@lcp.linst.ac.uk. Web: lcp.linst.ac.uk. Tel: 020 7514 6500. Courses: Animation, Art, Design and Media Management, Book Arts and Crafts, Design, Digital Media, Film and Video, Graphic Design, Interior Design, Journalism, Marketing and Advertising, Media and Cultural Studies, Multimedia, Music Publishing, Photography, Printing, Public Relations, Publishing, Retail Display and Design, Retail Management, Sound Arts, Surface Design, TV and Radio Production, TV, Film and Video, Travel and Tourism, Typography.

UNIVERSITY OF WARWICK

The University of Warwick
Senate House
Coventry CV4 7AL

TEL 02476 523723
FAX 02476 524649
EMAIL ugadmissions@warwick.ac.uk
WEB www.warwick.ac.uk

University of Warwick Students' Union
Gibbet Hill Road
Coventry CV4 7AL

TEL 02476 572777
FAX 02476 572759
EMAIL enquiries@sunion.warwick.ac.uk
WEB www.sunion.warwick.ac.uk

VAG VIEW

Warwick has exploded upon the university scene in the last ten years and there can be few who wouldn't want to have it on their UCAS list. 'I knew from the first time that I visited that it was the place for me,' writes Emma Burhouse. 'As far as I could see, it had the ideal balance of a good reputation, a sound education and excellent social life.'

UNIVERSITY/STUDENT PROFILE

University since	**1964**
Situation/style	**Campus**
Student population	**29150**
Undergraduates	**19960**
- mature	**8%**
- non EU undergraduates	**10%**
- male/female	**43/57**
- non-traditional student intake	**19%**
- state sector intake	**77%, low**
drop-out rate	**4%, low**
- undergraduate applications	**Down 4%**

CAMPUS

Warwick, lovely little market town, big castle... And not a university within ten miles of the place. Don't be fooled, the University of Warwick is not in Warwick, it's in Coventry. The reason it's called Warwick is that it was part-funded by Warwickshire County Council.

'Campus architecture is entirely uninspiring,' reports Simon McGee, 'but the greyness of the endless car parks and square buildings is fortunately balanced by hundreds of acres of surrounding grassland and forest.'

A second campus, ten minutes' walk away, houses the university's Education Institute and Westwood Halls of Residence. The point about Warwick is that like UEA, it is a campus apart from the town, and may seem to some a bit like living in a box.

'If you' re not paying attention, campus can feel a Doctor Seuss cartoon – you are surrounded by pointy concrete and sculptures straight off the set of *Blake Seven*. Some people take to campus life, and others quite frankly don't,' writes Andrew Losowsky.

'If your first priority is the ability to step straight from your lectures into a bustling shopping centre, then Warwick probably isn't for you. Students here have to get a bus in order to clap eyes on old people, babies, dogs. If, however, you enjoy a friendly community, like spending time with lots of students, then maybe you'll fit right in.'

FEES, BURSARIES

UK & EU Fees: £3000 p.a. If in receipt of theHE Maintenance grant there's a bursary of between £300 and £3000, according to household earnings.

STUDENT PROFILE

'You get the usual independent school boys and girls, for whom going to a university is the first time they haven't had to wear a uniform,' and, as Andrew points out, 'an unusually high mix of international students, meaning that, although most of the British students are from a middle-class background, there is still plenty of variety propping up the bar with you. The English – there are few Scots and Welsh – generally have the bland accentless tone of the home counties. Regional individuality may be gently mocked, but is in fact both envied and welcomed. Students on the whole are genuinely friendly here, and if you can't make any friends then you probably don't deserve to.'

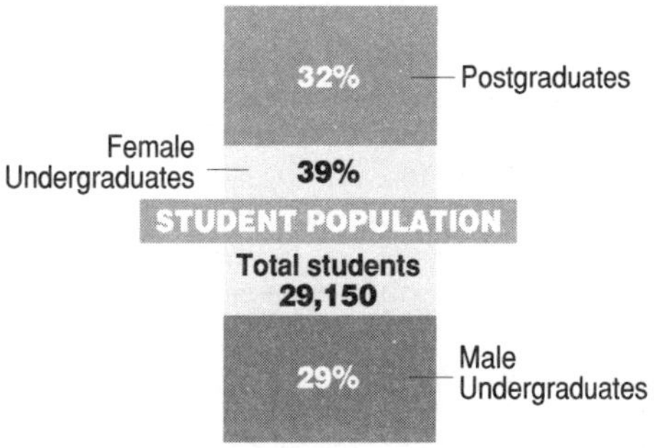

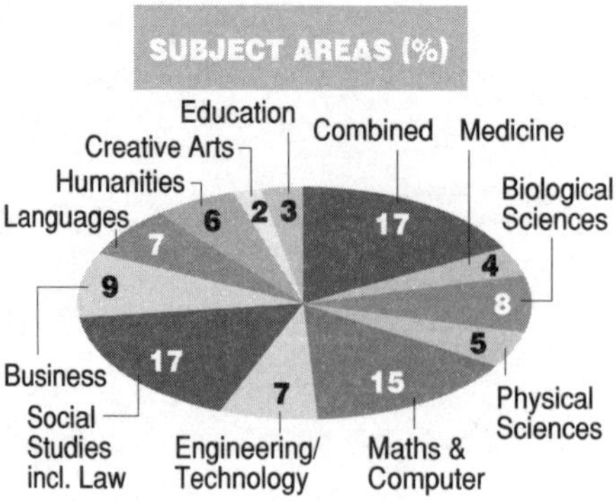

ACADEMIA & JOBS

It is a top-rated uni academically – 92% Excellence ratings or 20+ out of 24; and latterly seven perfect scores – full marks for Politics and International Studies, Philosophy, Economics, Sociology, Theatre Studies, Physics and Warwick's Education Departments (Institute of Education and Continuing Education). There's a fine research record, too – the uni came 6th in the last assessments, only Oxbridge, Imperial, LSE and the Institute of Cancer Research were ahead of them. Small wonder, perhaps, that 75% of graduates attain a first class degree or upper second. Many choose Warwick over Oxbridge and few look at it as second choice. Nottingham may at one time have had the edge with their Faculty of Medicine, but the new Warwick/Leicester graduate medical school opened recently, albeit a graduate not an undergraduate school.

The Leicester Warwick Medical School is a new accelerated 4-year MB ChB for graduates of biological and health sciences.

They are heavily targeted by employers. Over 100 visit campus each autumn to give presentations and skills training sessions; many conduct first interviews with undergraduates on site. There are also five major recruitment fairs here each year.

In the matter of accountancy, there is nothing between Birmingham, Durham and Warwick. Together they are responsible for around 12% of the total number of graduates into the sector. Accounting and Finance, a 3-year BSc, is the dedicated course. Also of interest is Warwick's Mathematics Institute, from which more graduates find their way into Accountancy than at any other university. Various joint courses are available, with, for example, Philosophy, Politics or Economics, all of which scored full marks at the teaching assessments.

It's definitely worth a trawl through their web site, not least because they have a PYDC (Plan Your Degree Course) strategy, which will give serious mathematicians hours of fun.

Education and finance dominate the graduate employment picture. After accountants it's investment analysts. Warwick's programmes stress business skills and enterprise 'working in interdisciplinary terms, just as they would in a corporate setting.' Tax experts and consultants also proliferate, as do actuaries. Three universities are head and shoulders above the rest in equating degree success with employment in actuarial science, namely Heriot-Watt, Warwick and Oxford.

Heriot-Watt and Warwick have dedicated Actuarial Maths degrees (Warwick's is BSc Maths-Operational Research-Statistics-Economics (Actuarial and Financial Mathematics), and together the big three account for more than 20% of jobs in the sector.

Of the 5,000+ graduate teachers that spill onto the scene each year those destined for primary schools generally come through specialist colleges. Warwick is one very important exception, much to be recommended – as usual, they earned full marks in the assessments.

They are European law specialists, too – four years, including a year abroad. There are also Law degrees combined with Business and with Sociology.

They are high up in the employment league, too, for electrical, electronic manufacturing and electronic/telecommunications engineering, and some 5% of software engineers come out of Warwick Uni. – engineers and consultants. There's a BEng/MEng Electronic Eng and Systems Eng, and MEng Computer Science and Computer Systems. There are five BSc Hons - Computational Biology, Computer Systems, Computer Science, single or with Business Studies or Management Sciences. Research Grade 5.

There's also a strong English/creative writing scene – a whole raft of fascinating degrees that combine English with Theatre Studies, languages, American, even Latin, literature. And a useful employment niche in theatre. They have the national teaching centre with the Royal Shakespeare Company – again, full marks for teaching and world-class Grade 6* for research.

STUDENTS' UNION

Students' Union There is one all-purpose venue containing 3 nightclubs: the **Market Place**, the **Cooler** and the **Graduate Club**, plus **Cholo** bar and the **Graduate** pub. The venue can operate as up to 4 different events, if required. Regular clubnights include *Top Banana*, party music; *Score*, Wednesday's after sports entertainment; *Coalition*, hip hop; *Pressure*, drum 'n' bass; *Heat*, international music; *Latin Night*, salsa rhythms; *School Dayz*,

ACADEMIC EXCELLENCE

TEACHING:
(Rated Excellent or 17+ out of 24)

History, Business & Management, Computer Science, English, Law.	**Excellent**
Sociology, Theatre Studies, Politics, Philosophy, Economics, Physics, Education	**24**
Classics, German, Film & TV, Organismal Biosciences, Molecular Biosciences	**23**
Maths	**22**
Italian, French, Engineering, History of Art, Psychology	**21**

RESEARCH:
Top grades 5/5/6**

Applied Maths, Statistics, Drama/Dance/Performing Arts.	**Grade 6***
Economics, Business, English	**Grade 5***
Psychology, Biological Sciences, Chemistry, Physics, Pure Maths, Applied Maths, Computer, General Eng, Law, Politics, Social Work, Sociology, French, German/Dutch/Scandinavian, Italian, Classics, History, History of Art, Philosophy, Media Studies	**Grade 5**

relive the best days of your life; *Vapour*, our very own house night; *Crash*, one of the biggest alternative nights in the Midlands; *Pure*, r&b; *Time Tunnel*, 60s, 70s and 80s music; *Metropolis*, the union gets turned into a major city for the night; and live music. Recent acts include: The Go Team, the Skalatities, Jo O'Meara, Chaka Deamus and thePliers, 911, Grandmaster Flash, Lee 'Scratch' Perry, the Ratpack, The Departure, Bowling for Soup, American Hi-fi, Layo and Bushwaka, etc.

Strong in the student scene are not only ents but clubs & societies – there's an amazing 249 (74-odd sport), which must be a record, and they don't sustain them if interest flags. Encouraging them each year are their own society awards.

Media is especially strong – magazine (*The Word*), newspaper (*The Boar*), student radio (RaW), and WTV, the new student television station. They are always in the national awards. The media website, www.warwickboar.co.uk, won last year and was runner-up this. In 2005, *Boar* had 3 nominations and a runner-up award; RaW had 4 nominations and a silver award.

Strong, too, are arts activities – the **Warwick Arts Centre** is the second largest in the country, has recently been refurbished thanks to a £33 million lottery grant. There is a concert hall, theatre, cinema, and art gallery. Student theatrical societies do well in the Edinburgh Festival and regular get gongs at the NUS Drama Festival. RAG and Community Action (13 projects in Coventry and Leamington Spa) are popular and the non-party political union works hard on ethical, human rights and environmental campaigns, though recently effort has been focused on anti-war and education funding.

SPORT Facilities are excellent – athletics track, games fields, artificial pitch and recently completed, £1-million sports pavilion. The Sports Centre is free for students, and also hosts Bear Rock, a rather vicious looking climbing wall for eager lemmings to try and scale. Teams came 24th last year in the national BUSA league. They have an Olympic trampolinist, but perhaps the general tenor is more accurately given by Ultimate Frisbee being Sports Club of the Year for two years in succession.

TOWN 'Cov has a reputation for being dangerous,' writes Andrew, 'though in fact it's just like any other city. But even cities can be a shock after a year on campus, and few people spend time in Coventry. Which is a shame, as underneath the concrete nightmare is a friendly enough place, if you give it half a chance. Reasons to "brave" Cov practically quadrupled with the recent opening of **Skydome**, a huge multiplex with a sizeable gig venue, nine screen cinema, bars, restaurants and two outstanding clubs. It'll never quite beat the

WHERE WARWICK GRADUATES END UP

Health & Social Work: 4%; Education: 15%; Wholesale Retail: 7%; Manufacturing: 10%; Financial Activities: 14%; Public Administration, Civil Service & Defence: 6%; Hotel/Restaurant: 2%; Transport & Communications (including Telecommunications): 3%; Construction: 1%; Personnel: 5.5%; Computer: 5%; Business & Management: 4%; Accountancy: 12%; Media (including Film): 2%; Legal 2%; Publishing: 1%; Artistic/Literary: 0.5%; Sport: 1%.

Approximate 'graduate track' employed **69%**

WHAT IT'S REALLY LIKE

UNIVERSITY:	
Social Life	★★★★★
Campus scene	**Good mix, non-elitist, vibrant**
Student Union services	**Good-excellent**
Politics	**Activity high, whole spectrum**
Sport	**74 clubs**
National team position	**24th**
Sport facilities	**Good**
Arts opportunities	**Drama, music, film, art excellent; dance good**
National drama awards	**Physical Theatre, Performance, Lighting**
Student magazine	**The Word**
Student newspaper	**The Boar**
Student radio	**RaW**
Student TV	**WTV**
Nightclub	**3: Market Place, Cooler , Graduate Club**
Bars	**Cholo bar, Graduate pub**
Union ents	**Top Banana, Score, etc, etc**
Union clubs/societies	**175**
Most popular society	**Cinema**
Parking	**None**
TOWN/CITY:	
Entertainment	★★★
Scene	**Local homely**
Town/gown relations	**Average**
Risk of violence	**Average**
Cost of living	**Average**
Student concessions	**Average**
Survival + 2 nights out	**£60 pw**
Part-time work campus/town	**Excellent/good**

NEC, but a valiant effort nonetheless, and much closer to home. Most pubs in Cov are of the Rat, Parrot and Firkin ilk, but **The Golden Cross** and **The Hand and Heart** are worth a look for something different.

'As for Leam, it's a haven for trendy bars and homely pubs – don't miss **The Sozzled Sausage**, **Ocean** and **The Jug and Jester**.'

AT A GLANCE

ACADEMIC FILE:	
Subjects assessed	**25**
Excellent	**92%**
Typical entry requirements	**430 points**
Application acceptance rate	**11%, low**
Students-staff ratio	**16:1**
First/2:1 degree pass rate	**79%, high**
ACCOMMODATION FILE:	
Guarantee to freshers	**100%**
Style	**Halls, flats**
Catered	**8%**
En suite	**20%**
Price range pw	**£52-£89**
City rent pw	**£60-£75**

PILLOW TALK

From top quality en-suite halls to basic single rooms in shared accommodation with a lower rent, all study bedrooms have unmetered high-bandwidth connection to ISP services. Everyone gets thrown out in their second year to live in Coventry or Leamington. The university owns plenty of houses, but most people end up going private. Leam is cheap, Cov even more so. If you can't handle a twenty-minute bus ride each day, then Leam is not an option.

GETTING THERE

- By road: M1/J21, M69, A46; or M1/J17, M45, A45, or M40/J15, A46; or M5/J4a, M42/J6, A45.
- By rail: Birmingham New Street, 30 mins; Manchester Piccadilly, 2:30; Nottingham, 1:45; Bristol, 2:30; London Euston, 1:20.
- By air: Birmingham International Airport.
- By coach: London, 1:20; Leeds, 4:00.

UNIVERSITY OF WESTMINSTER

The University of Westminster
309 Regent Street
London W1B 2UW

TEL 020 7911 5000
FAX 020 7911 5858
EMAIL admissions@wmin.ac.uk
WEB www.wmin.ac.uk

Westminster Students' Union
32-38 Wells Street
London W1T 3UW

TEL 020 7911 5000 x 5454
FAX 020 7911 5793
EMAIL gensec@wmin.ac.uk
WEB www.uwsu.com

VAG VIEW

The uni comes out of The Royal Polytechnic Institution, established in 1838 by (among others) Sir George Cayley, the North Yorkshire squire who invented the first man-powered flying machine, inveigling his unwilling butler to fly it solo down Brompton Dale.

On the surface, Westminster might appear to suffer all sorts of drawbacks characteristic of a new university in the metropolis – split sites, low entry requirements/high non-traditional student intake/high drop-out rate. Drop-out rate aside, because of its challenging commitment to an impressive curriculum, Westminster, in point of fact, flies higher than ever Cayley could have dreamt it would.

And right now they are giving their London campuses quite a shake-up, mainly to increase space for ex-curricular student activities.

CAMPUSES

REGENT CAMPUS (address above). **Faculties** on four neighbouring sites: *Regent Street* (Social & Behavioural Sciences, including Psychology, some Business courses), *Little Titchfield Street*, *Euston Centre* and *Wells Street* (Law and Languages). **Academic resources:** Self-Access Language Centre, libraries, IT suites. **Leisure facilities:** Sport and Fitness Centre with cardiovascular and resistance equipment, saunas, solaria and indoor games hall; **Deep End Café** (Regent Street). The gym is on the way out and a bigger social space is in the making.

CAVENDISH CAMPUS 115 New Cavendish Street, London W1M 6UW (use main phone number above). The campus is undergoing a £25-million development, the first phase of which is due for completion this summer. **Courses:** Biosciences, Computing, Health. **Academic resources:** computer suites, science labs, library. **Leisure facilities:** bar and refectory. Soon to be the home of The Hub, see *Social Scene*, below.

MARYLEBONE CAMPUS 35 Marylebone Road, London NW1 5LS (use main tel. above). **Faculties:** Westminster Business School, School of Architecture and the Built Environment. **Academic resources:** library and laboratory. **Leisure facilities:** bar and **Café West**. New venue in the making. See *Social Scene* below.

UNIVERSITY/STUDENT PROFILE	
University since	**1992**
Situation/style	**City sites & campus**
Student population	**26610**
Undergraduates	**18060**
- mature	**43%**
- non EU undergraduates	**9%**
- male/female	**45/55**
- non-traditional student intake	**43%, v. high**
- state sector intake	**96%**
- drop-out rate	**14%, high**
- undergraduate applications	**Constant**

HARROW CAMPUS Watford Road, Northwick Park, Harrow HA1 3TP. Tel: 020 7911 5936; Fax: 020 7911 5943. **Style:** well-designed, self-contained campus, close to horrendous looking hospital. **Faculties:** Harrow Business School, Computer Science, Media, Arts & Design. **Academic resources:** Information Resources Centre, including library, computers (1,000+ campus-wide), AV aids for presentations; also TV, radio, photography and music studios. **Leisure facilities:** venue (**Area 51**), open-air performance court, **The Undercroft Bar**, sports hall, fitness suite and playing fields close by.

FEES, BURSARIES

UK & EU Fees: £3000 p.a. If in receipt of a HE Maintenance grant there's a bursary of £300. Academic scholarships are also available.

STUDENT PROFILE

In its student clientele, Westminster mirrors many other ex-polys. There's a sizeable mature, part-time, local and overseas population – they received a Queen's Award for Enterprise for their success in International Markets, and were the first post-1992 uni to have been so rewarded.

There's also a significant non-degree student

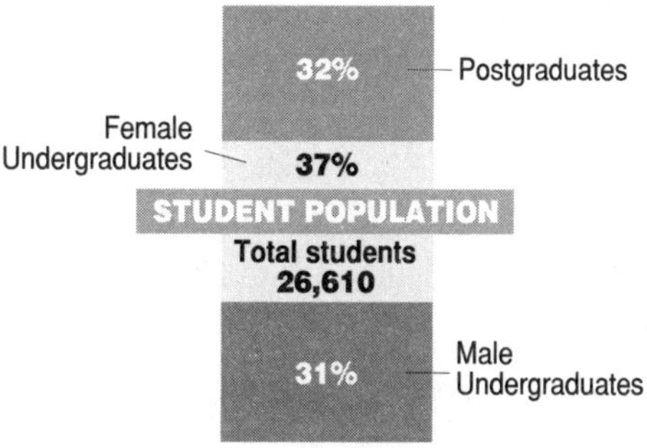

SUBJECT AREAS (%)

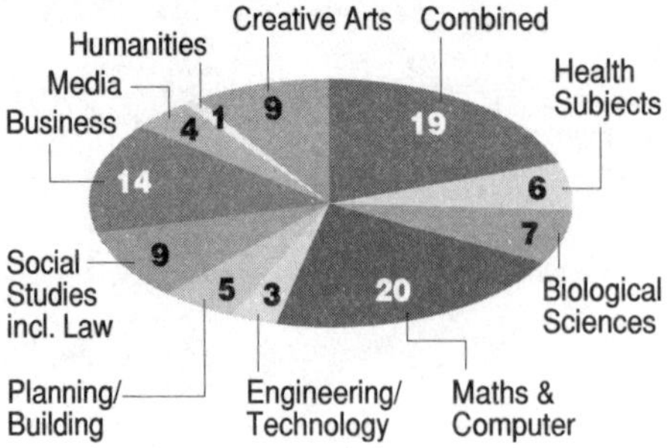

population, and many students are the first in their families to experience university – 40% are from new-to-uni social groups.

ACADEMIA & JOBS

'If you want to study at a traditional university,' writes Calvin Holbrook, 'then don't come to Westminster. The courses here have a mainly hands-on approach that sets students up for the real world. Bookworms need not apply.' This may sound like a put-down, but is certainly not meant as one: 'As a university it's way ahead of its time. If you want to be on the cutting edge, come to Westminster,' Calvin also urges.

In their vocational, modular course planning they have taken advice from the professions and industry, and translated it into a strategy underpinned by an expert language provision. Their School of Professional Language Studies lays claim to one of the widest range of language teaching in the UK – they are particularly strong on Asian Studies: 23 points out of 24 for teaching and an international Grade 5 for research. Russian, Arabic and Chinese also feature.

There's a reputation for finding students work in those most difficult areas of art, design and media. Though it would be wrong to suggest that these jobs come in a flood, relative to most other unis they are areas in which Westminster enjoy success and have some very good courses.

In Art & Design they have graphic design, illustration, photography, animation, mixed media fine art and ceramics. In Communication/Design & Media they cover digital and photographic imaging, film and TV production, journalism, public relations, radio production, music informatics, and commercial music. The latter, for aspiring music industry managers, concerns music production, but also the business side, including the law. Strong industry links, good reputation in business management. You'll be based at the Harrow Campus. They have an international Grade 5 rating for research in media and dropped only one point at the teaching assessments.

The majority of undergraduates read for degrees in business, many of them destined for jobs as accounts and wages clerks – at least in the first instance. Retail is a strength, as is marketing; there are dedicated degrees. See also their human resource business degrees, e-business, commercial law, etc, and the International degrees, making use of their excellent language provision. There are degrees in business at both central London and

ACADEMIC EXCELLENCE

TEACHING : *(Rated Excellent or 17+ out of 24)*	
Tourism, Psychology	**24**
French, Asian Studies, Media, Subjects Allied to Medicine	**23**
Building, International Relations	**22**
Electric/Electron Eng, Anatomy, Art & Design, Biosciences	**21**
Linguistics, German, Civil Eng, Business/Finance, Maths	**20**
Italian	**19**
Russian, Sociology, Iberian	**18**
RESEARCH : Top grades 5/5*	
Law, Asian Studies, Linguistics, Communication, Cultural & Media Studies	**Grade 5**

WHERE WESTMINSTER GRADUATES END UP

Health & Social Work: 9%; Education: 8%; Wholesale Retail: 16%; Manufacturing: 8%; Financial Activities: 9%; Public Administration, Civil Service & Defence: 6%; Hotel/Restaurant: 3.5%; Transport & Communications (including Tele- communications): 3%; Construction: 2%; Personnel: 3%; Computer: 5%; Business & Management: 1.5%; Accountancy: 2%; Media (including Film): 5%; Legal 3%; Architecture: 2%; Publishing: 2%; Advertising: 2%; Artistic/Literary: 3%.

Approximate 'graduate track' employed **55%**

Harrow campuses, so be sure you know where you are destined.

In Law, they are commercial, business and European specialists, but with an interesting range of courses. They are one of a very few unis to receive 24 points (full marks) in the teaching assessments for this.

The computing provision is also strong and directs graduates along the clearest employment pathways. IT consultants, systems analysts, software engineers, analyst/programmers, etc. Westminster's central London Cavendish campus offers BSc degrees in Computing, Computational Mathematics and Software Engineering, each with the possibility of a Foundation or International Foundation (4 years). In Harrow they offer BSc Computer Science (with/without Foundation), Systems Technology, E-Business, Multimedia Computing, AI, etc. There's an international Grade 5 for research.

There's enormous strength in architecture and the building industry. The Architecture degrees are mostly technology, engineering, and there are BA degrees in Interior Design and Urban Design. See, too, the Construction, Surveying and Property degrees, Urban Estate Management. Architects proliferate out of Westminster, as do property/estate managers and developers, town planners and surveyors. Of particular note are their BA Tourism & Planning degrees (and Tourism with Business). They scored full marks at the teaching assessments for these.

Then there is the health provision, with a full-marks assessment score for BSc Psychology with Neuroscience, which comes with accreditation from the British Psychological Society and is the first step to beoming a chartered psychologist. Note there is a foundation course into this, and a sound reputation for employment.

There are nutrition and healt degrees, physiology and pharmacology, sport and exercise, and a whole raft of complementary medicine degrees – they were one of the first to offer these and have made them a success. Traditional Chinese Medicine: Acupuncture, Homeopathy, Nurtritional Therapy, Therapeutic Bodywork – there is a consistently good record of employment in 'human health activities', as well as an impressive 23 points out of 24 in the teaching assessment. The degrees are developed with The London School of Acupuncture & Traditional Chinese Medicine and The London College of Classical Homeopathy.

WHAT IT'S REALLY LIKE

UNIVERSITY:	
Social Life	★★★
Campus scene	**Diverse, non-traditional**
Student Union services	**Average**
Politics	**Interest low**
Sport	**15 clubs**
National sporting position	**None recorded**
Sport facilities	**Improving**
Arts opportunities	**Drama excellent; film, music good; dance, art poor**
Student magazine	**The Smoke**
Radio Station	**Smoke Radio**
TV station	**Smokescreen TV**
Nightclub	**Area 51**
Bars	**Dragon Bar, Undercroft Bar**
Union ents	**R&B and Bhangra, Indie**
Union societies	**20**
Most popular society	**Law Soc, Dram Soc**
Parking	**Adequate**
CITY:	
Entertainment	★★★★★
City scene	**Wild, expensive**
Town/gown relations	**Average-good**
Risk of violence	**Average**
Cost of living	**Very high**
Student concessions	**Good**
Survival + 2 nights out	**£120 pw**
Part-time work campus/town	**Poor/excellent**

You'll be based at the Cavendish Campus in central London. Westminster also award the degrees of The British College of Osteopathic Medicine.

SOCIAL SCENE

There's a hands-on approach that sets students up for the real world. Bookworms need not apply.

'The Uni is about to completely revamp their central London campuses, so it's a pretty exciting time to be a student here,' writes Rob Watson. 'We're opening up a new venue at our Marylebone campus (that's the one opposite Madame Tussards) which is going to be, well, the best student venue in London. It's costing a bomb, it's going to have alcoholic and alcohol-free sections, giant movable plasma screens and little TVs in every table (we don't quite know what they're going to do, but they sound nice...).'

The uni is funding this makeover for the Marylebone site to the tune of £1 million. They are also moving the gym from Regent Street elsewhere and creating a big new social space there too. Meanwhile, at New Cavendish Street, they are creating **The Hub**, a kind of central social space for West End students. They are also working on plans to improve the central London halls.

Out at Harrow, the self-contained campus c,ose to the station, students already have their infamous nightclub, **Area 51**, and a cosy little bar, **The Undercroft**, as well as their typical SU dive-in central, the **Dragon Bar**.

Says Rob: 'We've got a pretty full schedule of events at all these bars and clubs, including club nights and live music nights. We cater for most tastes, with the hugely successful *BLUSH* playing r&b and Bhangra, and *FONO* playing indie. The Freshers and May Balls bring in some of the best performers in the country. This year we had Raghav and the quite brilliant Mitchell Brothers, along with Queens of Noize. But because we cater for so many international and non-drinking students, we also provide activities around London.

'We're battling against student apathy, because many students in our central campuses live at home and don't get involved. We've a huge number of different nationalities and races here, and we have to try and cater for so many different interests, its a big job.'

Some of the best society activity comes out of course disciplines (media, music), and you can't help wondering whether, if they really got this aspect of student life together, they might whittle down the drop-out rate. Clearly, with all these new social spaces in the West End, which will begin to show through in the autumn of 2006, that's what's in the mind of the uni, too.

The student media is excellent. Magazine *The Smoke* was nominated in the 'best magazine' category at the Mirror/NUS awards this year, and the brand new radio station, Smoke Radio, is causing a stir with hardly any financial support from the Uni at all. There is now, too, student television: Smokescreen TV.

SPORT The uni is not known nationally for its sporting prowess; there is no position recorded in the BUSA leagues, although their football and cricket teams are amongst the best in their leagues, and the Ju-Jitsu team win tournaments up and down the country.

AT A GLANCE

ACADEMIC FILE:	
Subjects assessed	**30**
Excellent	**73%**
Typical entry requirements	**240 points**
Application acceptance rate	**21%, high**
Students-staff ratio	**15:1**
First/2:1 degree pass rate	**57%**
ACCOMMODATION FILE:	
Guarantee to freshers	**65%**
Style	**Halls**
Catered	**None**
En-suite	**Harrow Hall**
Price range pw	**£66-£92**
London rent pw	**£100-£180 Zone 1; £75-£85 Zone 2**

PILLOW TALK

There's no accommodation guarantee, except to full-time international students if they apply before the deadline. But they'll bend over backwards to help you find somewhere to lay your weary head. There are halls, rooms or flats in Marylebone Road, Highgate Village and Victoria. The accommodation at Harrow is all en suite.

GETTING THERE

☛ To Regent Campus: Oxford Circus Underground (Bakerloo, Central and Victoria lines).
☛ To Cavendish Campus: Warren Street Underground (Northern and Victoria lines).
☛ To Marylebone Campus: Baker Street Underground (Bakerloo, Metropolitan, Hammersmith & City, Circle, Jubilee lines).
☛ By road to Harrow Campus: A404 accessible via M25, M1 or M40/A40; by Underground – Northwick Park (Metropolitan line).

UNIVERSITY OF WINCHESTER

The University of Winchester
Winchester
Hampshire SO22 4NR

TEL 01962 827234
FAX 01962 827406
EMAIL course.enquiries@winchester.ac.uk
WEB www.winchester.ac.uk
SU WEB www.winchesterstudents.co.uk/

VAG VIEW

Founded as a Diocesan teacher training establishment, and until recently King Alfred's College, a university sector college with a range of Southampton University degrees and a speciality in producing primary school teachers, they are now, since 2005, a university.

They always had ambitions to be something other than what they were, and tried various things to hasten the process. In 1994, for example, they took over, or merged with, The Basingstoke and Winchester School of Nursing and Midwifery and began developing all sorts of multi-disciplinary courses in Health Care. But you'll not find a student nurse or midwife closer than Southampton today. Then, in September 2003, a 'new' Basingstoke campus opened with 'new earn-while-you-learn Foundation Degrees', a feeder site for a future university, the perfect thing to satisfy the widening participation requirement of all universities.

Meanwhile, one or two unusual specialities were emerging, a course in Biopsychology, another in Archaeology (taught by people actively involved on site work), an East Asian Studies course with Business Studies and BA hons combos with Japanese. All but Archaeology disappeared as magically as the nursing provision, but teaching assessments, after years of scoring 18-21 points at best, suddenly returned results of full marks for Archaeology and Education, and 23 out of 24 for bedrock Theology, and 22 points for Business and Sport.

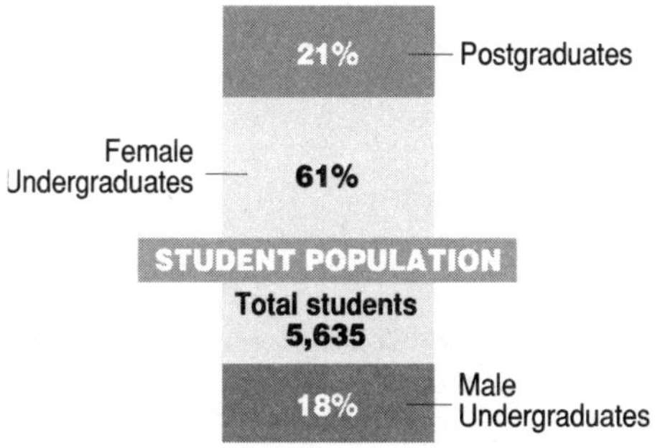

UNIVERSITY/STUDENT PROFILE	
University since	**2005**
Situation/style	**Campus**
Student population	**5635**
Undergraduates	**4430**
- mature	**37%**
- non EU undergraduates	**2%**
- male/female	**22/78**
- non-traditional student intake	**30%**
- state school intake	**97%**
- drop-out rate	**7%**
- undergraduate applications	**Down 7%**

After all, that was the way to go, and, following a swift baptism as University College Winchester, Alfie moved with all speed to achieve university status.

Today, there are three BSc undergraduate courses only, Horticulture, Social Care Studies and Sports Science. The rest are BA (and QTS) or DipHE. There are genuine strengths in arts (particularly performing arts) and in humanities, and a push towards media.

STUDENT PROFILE

There is a high proportion of mature students, and the student body is overwhelmingly female (78%), as you would expect from a uni where many are still studying to be primary school teachers. There are also many part-timers (25% of undergraduates) and locals. There is a kind of innocent cheery fun about the place, modernity, in the shape of such as the Lesbian, Gay and Bisexual Society, managing a pally epiphytic hold on an institution rooted in Christian Fellowship.

Big fish will find it something of a small pond. Indeed, they call their student magazine, *Big Fish Little Pond*. So, perhaps the big fish are already arriving and have wisely begun by taking over the media, and perhaps soon Winchester University will not seem so much like the college of education, which only yesterday it was.

FEES, BURSARIES

UK & EU Fees: £3000 p.a. If in receipt of a full student Maintenance grant there's a bursary of £800 p.a. If in receipt of partial grant, it's £400 p.a. All UK domicile students are eligible to receive the Winchester Scholarship, a package of financial support specially designed to put money in your pocket during your study here at Winchester. This can

ACADEMIC EXCELLENCE

TEACHING :
(Rated Excellent or 17+ out of 24)

Archaeology, Education	**24**
Theology	**23**
Business	**22**
Psychology, Sport	**21**
Asian Studies, Japanese	**20**
Drama, Dance & Cinematics	**19**
American Studies, Media & Film	**18**

RESEARCH:
*Top grades 5/5** **None**

be as much as £1300 over a 4-year course, £900 on a 3-year programme. All 4th-year BA Education undergraduates get a scholarship of £1800, in recognition of the extra costs compared with the three year and PGCE qualified teacher status routes. There are also Winchester Partner Colleges Scholarships, and the King Alfred Scholarship of £2000 (one-off payment) for students under 25 at entry who have been 'looked after' for at least 13 weeks since the age of 14 and who have left care (as defined by the Children (Leaving Care) Act 2000).

CAMPUS

This is a campus uni overlooking the historic cathedral city of Winchester in Hampshire, 15 miles north of Southampton. It has its own theatre and dance studio, Student Union and accommodation.

ACADEMIA

Winchester offers undergraduate courses in American studies, archaeology, English, creative writing, dance, drama, education, film, heritage, history, horticulture, journalism, leisure, management, marketing, media, performing arts, psychology, religious studies, social care, sports, teaching tourism.

There is a feeder site in Basingstoke, where a variety of programmes is offered, including earn-while-you-learn foundation degrees in subject areas taught within the three faculties at the Winchester campus: Community and Performing Arts, Cultural Studies, Education & Social Sciences.

The teaching assessments suggest their strengths lie in Education, Archaeology, Theology, Business, Psychology, Sport, while the research assessments – 21% of the student population is postgraduate – show no national or global strengths, but Grade 4 in History and Theology. Archaeology, Media, Performing Arts and Education all scored Grade 3; Psychology Grade 2.

SUBJECT AREAS (%)

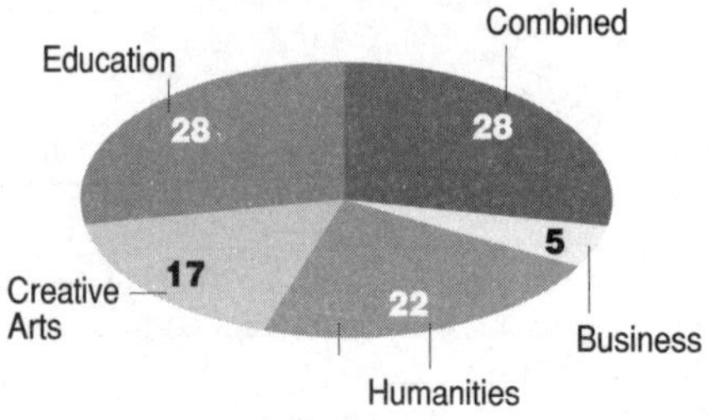

SOCIAL SCENE

Student Union The Union provides three bars - **Bar 22**, **The Lounge** and **C2H** (Close to Home), recently refurbished at a cost of £100,000. Ents include club nights (*Timewarp* or *Club Tropicana*), bar quizzes, comedy evenings, live music, promotions, multi-venue events and theme nights, plus society nights, like *Indie Three Sixty* recently from *BFLP* Magazine. Bigger occasions are the Winton Reunion Weekend (sporty), and the Freshers, Christmas, Summer and Graduation Balls which traditionally play host to top name acts in the **Guildhall**, 'a great venue, with a main hall and lots of smaller rooms with jazz, karaoke, live music and a casino.'

The Stripe Theatre is the performing arts space and film studio on campus, hosting live productions by students and visiting professionals. In town, it's the **Town Arts Centre** and **Theatre Royal** for everything from stand-up comedy to children's theatre, music and dance to plays.

There's a year-round welfare-themed campaign called Play Mates, various societies, from Alternative Music to Ultimate Frisbee, and a media group that is causing something of a stir with *Big Fish Little Pond* magazine and Voice Radio.

Sport They play in BUSA – 5 football teams (1 women's), 2 netball teams, men's rugby and men's basketball – at regional level, against the likes of Plymouth, Bristol, Bath, Bournemouth and Southampton. Other sports teams participate in the Southern England Student Sports Association (SESSA) all over the South East as far as East Anglia, and in SUSC, a collection of local universities. There is currently 1 rugby pitch and 2 football pitches a mile from campus; also a New Club House with bar. A sports hall hosts 5-a-side football, badminton, netball, hockey, volleyball, cricket, and is the home of the Knights and Angels Basketball teams. There are also 2 tennis courts on campus, next to Alwyn Halls, a squash court next to the sports hall, and the uni has recently invest-

WHAT IT'S REALLY LIKE

UNIVERSITY:	
Social Life	★★★
Campus scene	**Emerging**
Student Union services	**Embryonic**
Politics	**Dormant**
Sport	**Regional**
National team position	**Nil points**
Sport facilities	**Poor, but new Club House bar**
Arts opportunities	**Good dance, theatre, media**
Student magazine	**Big Fish Little Pond**
Student radio	**Voice Radio**
Nightclub/bars	**Bar 22, The Lounge, C2H**
Union ents	**Cheese, comedy, studenty**
Union clubs/societies	**Approx. 20**
Parking	**Permit**
CITY:	
Entertainment	★★
Scene	**Quiet, expensive**
Town/gown relations	**Average**
Risk of violence	**Low**
Cost of living	**High**
Student concessions	**Fair**
Survival + 2 nights out	**£80 pw**
Part-time work campus/town	**Excellent**

ed in a new fitness suite – treadmills, bikes, cross trainers, rowing and step machines, and any number of ratchets to stretch, curl, extend and crunch the various parts of you.

CITY There are nightclubs in nearby Eastleigh and Woodmancote, and 15 miles away in Southampton there's **Ocean + Collins** in Vincent Walk, with 1000 capacity, late bar, and a *Big Cheese* Student Night on Thursdays, but Winchester itself is fairly barren. Do not expect the *Brooks Experience* in the Shopping Centre to have anything to do with Jimi Hendrix. Pubs like **The Mash Tun**, the **King's Arms**, the **Forester** have music, and **O'Neills** has a big screen in the High Street, but watch out for squaddies from the nearby barracks. In general, they don't appreciate students, 'unless served on a plate with chips,' writes Stephanie Kirk, who in fact always feels safe here.

'If you have lived in a small town and feel threatened in a large city, Winchester may be the place for you. It is a city, not because of size, but because of its cathedral. It is quiet, picturesque and may prove to be a bit dull for some people.

'Winchester is steeped in history, not only due to King Alfred, but also to King Arthur. Allegedly his famous round table is housed in the city's Great Hall. the cathedral, where our graduation ceremony takes place, is the main focal point, along with winchester boys' school, second only to Eton.'

There is also another side to the city, however. 'I follow Drama, Theatre and Television Studies, and a small group of us worked with a day centre. Most of the people were homeless, or on a very low budget, some are ex-offenders, some drug addicts. None of them wanted anything to do with drama! It took us ten weeks to get a workshop up and running, but the course was so satisfying in the end.'

AT A GLANCE

ACADEMIC FILE:	
Subjects assessed	**15**
Excellent	**73%**
Typical entry requirements	**255 points**
Application acceptance rate	**23%, high**
Students-staff ratio	**22:1**
First/2:1 degree pass rate	**56%**
ACCOMMODATION FILE:	
Guarantee to freshers	**100%**
Style	**Hall, flats**
Approx price range pw	**£70-£82**
City rent pw	**£60**

PILLOW TALK

There are fewer than 1000 study bedrooms available to students, self-catered at West Downs Student Village, catered on the main campus.Some specially adapted rooms are available for disabled students.

GETTING THERE

☛ By road: M3/J10; northwest, A272, B3041; southwest, A3090.

☛ By rail: London, 1:00; Bristol Parkway, 2:15; Birmingham, 3:15; Southampton, 20 mins.

☛ By air: Gatwick, Heathrow, Southampton.

☛ By coach: London, 2:00; Birmingham, 5:30.

UNIVERSITY OF WOLVERHAMPTON

The University of Wolverhampton
Wulfruna Street
Wolverhampton WV1 1SB

TEL 01902 321000
FAX 01902 323744
EMAIL enquiries@wlv.ac.uk
WEB www.wlv.ac.uk

Wolverhampton Students' Union
Wulfruna Street
Wolverhampton WV1 1LY

TEL 01902 322021
FAX 01902 322020
EMAIL president@wlv.ac.uk
WEB www.wolvesunion.org

VAG VIEW

The university was spawned by the Wolverhampton Poly following a merger with three teacher training colleges and West Midlands College of Higher Education. Operating on campus sites in and around Wolverhampton and in Shropshire, they have recruiting associations with dozens of colleges, and were the first to attract entrants via a High Street shop. As many as 25,000 people a year visit the shop and more than 7% sign up.

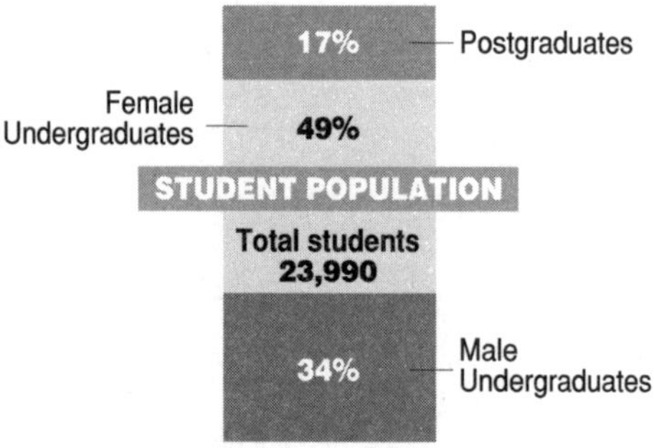

CAMPUSES

City Campus **Location:** a few minutes walk from Wolverhampton rail and bus stations. **Campus scene:** the busy centre of it all. **Courses:** Applied Sciences, Art & Design, Computing, Construction, Engineering, Health Sciences, Languages, Humanities and Social Sciences, including Law.

Compton Park Campus Compton Road West, Wolverhampton WV3 9DY. **Location:** mile or so west of main campus. **Courses:** Business Admin, Info Management, some Human Resourcing, Marketing, some Computing.

Walsall Campus Gorway Road, Walsall WS1 3BD. **Location:** six miles east of town centre. **Campus scene: known as** 'the concrete jungle', but strong community spirit. **Courses:** Education (incl. Sports Studies). New this year 350 study bedrooms, all en-suite. A £7.1 million Sports and Judo Centre includes a full fitness suite, coffee bar and crËche, new tracks and all-weather pitches and the surrounding community will also have access to the facilities.

Shropshire (Telford) Campus Priorslee Hall, Shifnal Road Telford TF2 9NT. **Location:** 12 miles northwest of town. **Campus scene:** the International Students' Association thrives. **Courses:** Business, Computer-aided Product Design.

FEES, BURSARIES

UK & EU Fees: £3000 p.a. If in receipt of full HE Maintenance grant there's a bursary of £300; if in receipt of partial grant, bursaries are on a sliding scale from according to household earnings to ensure bursary plus grant amount to £3000.

STUDENT PROFILE

As many as 49% are from families who have previously not considered uni an option, a quarter from 'lowparticipation' neighbourhoods and a quarter from ethnic minorities. Nearly 40% of its undergraduate intake are mature students, a great number are part-timers, and the SU tells me that there is a high percentage of disabled students, too.

UNIVERSITY/STUDENT PROFILE

University since	**1992**
Situation/style	**City campus, town sites**
Student population	**23990**
Undergraduates	**19925**
- mature	**38%**
- non EU undergraduates	**10%**
- male/female	**41/59**
- non-traditional student intake	**49%, v. high**
- state sector intake	**99%**
drop-out rate	**12%, high**
- undergraduate applications	**Up 2%**

(There are certainly a number of very good special needs degree courses.)

Such cold statistics do little to express the busy and persistently cheerful student scene at Wolverhampton. 'If there is any university with ambition, giving clear signs that it wants to play with academia's big boys, then Wolverhampton surely is the one,' said Mark Wilson. 'It may take a few years, but there is no doubt that it will get there. We are fortunate to have a 21000-strong melting pot of cultures, skills, talents – sectors, like Lesbian, Gay & Bisexual (LGB), mature students or ethnic minorities, get people together and entertain them. It may take time to shake the wally poly stereotype, but the future is looking blinding from where I stand.'

ACADEMIA & JOBS

'The teaching is particularly good for the vocational courses on which we focus,' says Mark. 'Lectures and seminars, but also film screenings, guest speakers, hands-on activities and group work with assessments. The best thing may be that they teach subjects which lead to jobs, engineering, film, computer programming and many more.'

Surprise, then, that the subject that attracted the highest mark – full marks, in fact – ast the teaching assessments was Philosophy, hardly the most likely to find you a job, one might think. But broasdly, Mark is right; this is a university bent on matching degree with job at the end.

They have a newish £4.5-million Learning Centre – 967 study spaces, 130 IT spaces, 200,000 volumes – following the opening of a similar centre in Shropshire.

A close association with industry in this high density industrial area, as well as commerce and the professions, gives confidence, and their employment record is good not only locally. A particular emphasis is on languages – students of all disciplines may study a language and the teaching assessments have been good: Russian scored 22 points out of 24, Spanish 20, French 19, German 17. There's a particular niche in British Sign Language Interpreting, the 3-year degree being pretty much a dead cert for getting a job. A foundation year is available.

SUBJECT AREAS (%)

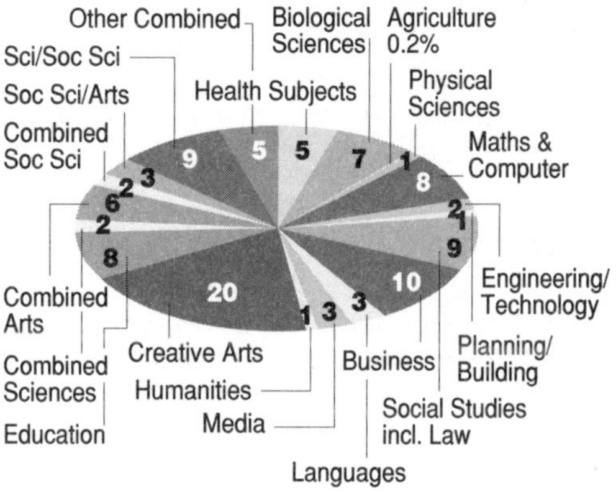

Around a fifth of Wolverhampton students graduate in business subjects. The next most popular degrees may be found in Art & Design, although the employment picture for the latter is less sure in the first six months following graduation. Plenty of work for the graphic designers, artists and photographers, with some others finding jobs in further education as teachers, and in galleries.

The business/finance ticket is more certain. Accountancy, for instance go for the 3 or 4-year sandwich Accounting & Finance, or joint hons with Computing, Law or Marketing. Personnel – look at the Business & Human Resource Management combination. Sales and marketing, look for their dedicated degrees Marketing, Retail Marketing, Entrepreneurship, etc. Or explore the joint honours scheme for tie-ups between Marketing and such as Tourism or Media & Communication. Look also at their series of nine Tourism Management degrees.

There's are strong employment lines at Wolverhampton into the Civil Service through business and through the computer provision. And besides the expected computer engineers, analysts and programmers (4-year sandwich Computer Science/Software Engineering), there's a niche for games design – see the 4-year sandwich Computer Science (Games Development). There's a Virtual Reality Centre in the School of Engineering. Look

WHERE WOLVERHAMPTON GRADUATES END UP

Health & Social Work: 12.5%; Education: 15,5%; Wholesale Retail: 16%; Manufacturing: 6%; Financial Activities: 7.5%; Public Administration, Civil Service & Defence: 7%; Hotel/Restaurant: 4%; Transport & Communications (including Telecommunications): 4%; Construction: 3%; Agriculture: 0.5%; Personnel: 3%; Computer: 6%; Accountancy: 1%; Media (including Film): 1%; Legal 3%; Artistic/Literary: 3%; Sport: 0.5%.

Approximate 'graduate track' employed **54%**

ACADEMIC EXCELLENCE

TEACHING :
(Rated Excellent or 17+ out of 24)

Philosophy	**24**
Education, Molecular & Organismal Biosciences, Politics	**23**
Russian, Subjects Allied to Medicine, Economics, Hospitality Mgt, Sport, Dance	**22**
Linguistics, American Studies, Nursing, Art & Design, Psychology, Theology	**21**
Iberian Studies, Sociology, Building, General Eng, Maths, Civil Engineering, Mathematics	**20**
French, Drama, Dance & Cinematics, Media	**19**

also for up-and-coming courses in Automative Systems Engineering, Computer-Aided Engineering/Product Designs.

Certain, too, are the educational and health provisions. The former produces primary and secondary teachers, educational assistants – there are some good specialisms in the joint hons degree programme, like Special Needs & Inclusion Studies and Deaf Studies – physical education instructors, and further education lecturers.

In health, non-hospital nurses, nurses and midwives proliferate. There's also a Cancer Care top-up. There are also BSc degrees in Complementary Therapies and Health Sciences, and BSc Psychology and BSc Counselling Psychology – 21 out of 24 at the assessments.

Biochemists, biomedical scientists and pharmacists also come out of here in number – this department dropped only one point at the teaching assessments.

The 3% graduates joining the construction industry come out of BA Architecture or BSc Architectural Technology, Building or Quantity Surveying, Civil Engineering, Construction Management, Computer Aided Design (Construction), Interior Architectural Design, Project Management, etc.

Success in the creative arts/design and radio/TV industries directs us to their performance arts and media degrees, to the £2-million, Lottery-funded redevelopment of their **Arena Theatre**, and to the School of Art & Design's **Gallery** space, home to a range of courses, from Animation to Journalism & Editorial Design, from Computer-Aided Design to Sculpture, from Floorcoverings & Interior Textile Design to Painting.

Finally, there's a good reputation for Law. Non-Law graduates may opt for a 2-year full-time or 3-year part-time Senior Status Law Degree, and recently the LPC Board assessed the department 'Good' on a scale of Excellent, Very Good, Good, Satisfactory or Unsatisfactory.

SOCIAL SCENE

STUDENTS' UNION At City Campus, it's **Fat Micks** (dance floor, food, pool tables, widescreen TV, 1200 capacity, licensed till midnight and till 2 am Wednesday and Friday), the **Poly Bar** (a pre-club comedy or light entertainment venue) and now they also have **Zone 34**, replacement for the JL nightclub and host to *Bublicious* Monday DJ) *Double Vision* (long-running night of chart and cheese) on Wednesday and *Quids In* (quid a drink/DJ Spawn), Friday, but also as a centre for student activities.

Wolves has a strategy for developing an on-going programme of these to help students develop the skills they'll need. If you flip onto their web site you'll see the kind of helpful community this union is striving to create, whether it's revision classes, welfare or just plain fun.

WHAT IT'S REALLY LIKE

UNIVERSITY:	
Social Life	★★★
Campus scene	**Local, lively**
Student Union services	**Average**
Politics	**Student issues**
Sport	**20+**
National team position	**91st**
Sport facilities	**Good**
Arts opportunities	**Music, art excellent; drama, dance good; film average**
Student magazine	**Cry Wolf**
Nightclub	**Zone 34**
Bars	**Fat Mick's, Poly Bar, Bertie's, Auntie Rita's**
Union ents	**Chart and cheese**
Union clubs/societies	**50**
Most popular societies	**Qur'an & Sunnah, Christian Union**
Parking	**Poor**
TOWN:	
Entertainment	★★★
Scene	**Pubs, diverse studenty clubs**
Town/gown relations	**OK-ish**
Risk of violence	**Average**
Cost of living	**Low**
Student concessions	**Good**
Survival + 2 nights out	**£50 pw**
Part-time work campus/town	**Good**

At Telford, it's **Auntie Rita's** (capacity 250), licensed to 11 pm – 12 on Wednesday and Friday. **Berties Bar** (capacity 300) is on the third floor of Walsall Campus. Ents are theme nights, quizzes, movie nights, barbecues.

SPORT There are sports hall, squash courts, fitness centre at Wolverhampton; sports hall, playing fields, running track, swimming pool, dance studio, tennis courts at Walsall (see also more to come, above), and at Telford, there's the new sports centre; otherwise it's local facilities, which are good: sports centre, ski slope, windsurfing, etc.

TOWN Wolverhampton can be unnerving, but the SU supplies advice, information, attack alarms. Clubland is good for house, garage, rock, indie, bhangra, jungle techno, acid jazz, folk. Cinemas include **The Light House** (mainstream/foreign); **Wolverhampton Art Gallery** for British and American Pop Art; the uni's own **Arena Theatre** for alternative, touring, student drama and music; the city's **Grand Theatre** for London shows.

AT A GLANCE

ACADEMIC FILE:	
Subjects assessed	**38**
Excellent	**71%**
Typical entry requirements	**200 points**
Application acceptance rate	**24%, high**
Students-staff ratio	**19:1**
First/2:1 degree pass rate	**53%**
ACCOMMODATION FILE:	
Guarantee to freshers	**90%**
Style	**Halls, houses**
Catered	**None**
En suite	**47%**
Approx price range pw	**£50-£70**
Town rent pw	**£45**

GETTING THERE

- By train: London Euston less than two hours;
- By road: M6/J10, M54/J2, M5/J2
- By coach: London, 4:00.

UNIVERSITY OF WORCESTER

The University of Worcester
Henwick Grove
Worcester WR2 6AJ

TEL 01905 855111
01905 855141 (prospectus request)
FAX 01905 855132
WEB www.worc.ac.uk
www.worcsu.com/

SUBJECT AREAS (%)

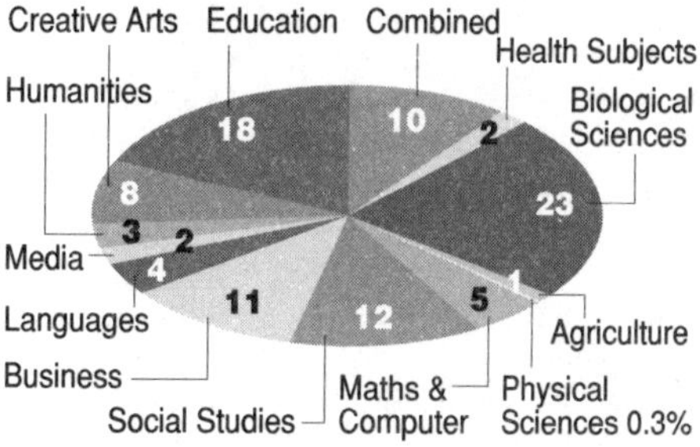

VAG VIEW

Worcester began as a teacher training college in 1946. In the '70s it became a college of higher education. In 1995 it merged with a college of nursing and midwifery, and in 2002 it was granted university college status, platform for their bid for full university status, which was secured last year.

Worcester University is the only Higher Education Institution in Herefordshire and Worcestershire, and has a largely female student body (78%), owing to the primary teacher training and nursing courses. It is not a place for the faint hearted. University of Worcester graduates, Joanne Yapp and Mel Berry, were rival rugby captains this year in the England and Wales Women's Six Nations clash. Sport is another of this uni's major preoccupations.

CAMPUS

Headquarters is a parkland campus within walking distance of the centre of this Cathedral city. On campus there's a new Digital Arts Centre, a Drama Studio, Sports Centre and Students' Union. Now, flush with a £10-million grant from the Government they are creating an additional campus on a 5-acre

UNIVERSITY/STUDENT PROFILE

University College since	**1999**
Situation/style	**City campus**
Total student population	**7555**
Undergraduates	**6160**
- mature	**60%**
- non EU undergraduates	**1%**
- male/female	**22/78**
- non-traditional student intake	**41%**
- state sector intake	**95%**
- drop-out rate	**8%**
- undergraduate applications	**Up 13%**

site in the city, which will include a new library and Learning Centre, teaching and residential accommodation. It is due for completion in 2008.

FEES, BURSARIES

UK & EU Fees: £3000 p.a. If in receipt of full HE Maintenance grant there's a bursary of £500; if in receipt of partial grant, it's £700. Up to 50 academic achievement scholarships of £1000 are available after the first year of study. The uni also works in partnership with Worcestershire County Cricket Club and the Worcester Wolves Basketball Club to award sports scholarships to talented players.

STUDENT PROFILE

Many of the mainly female undergraduates are local and 60% are mature; a fair proportion (41%) are from socio-economic groups new to the idea of going to university, and 15% from 'low-participation neighbourhoods'. They have partnerships with colleges in the region, in order, they say, to widen participation further, though widening into the upper socio-economic and overseas groups might seem to be more of a challenge.

ACADEMIA & JOBS

There's a modular course structure and 6 academic departments: Applied Sciences, Geography & Archaeology; Arts, Humanities & Social Sciences; the Worcester Business School; Education; Health & Social Care; Sport & Exercise Science.

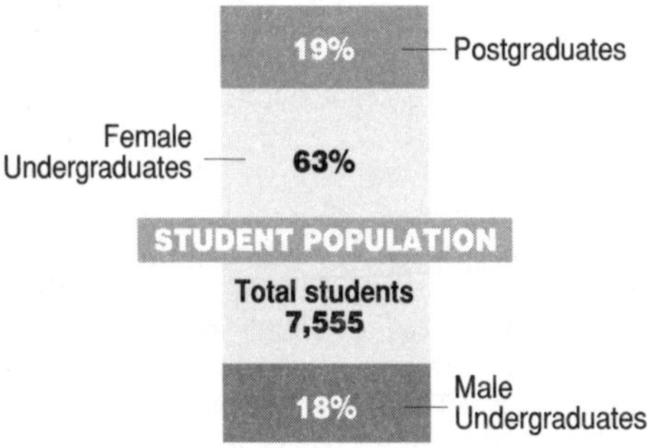

A strong educational, nursing and sporting provision (their teams came 38th in the national BUSA league last year, which is amazing for so small a university), together with degrees in drama and social welfare, make for a strong employment record of great use to the health and welfare of the community they serve.

Teaching inspections results have been fair. Out of 24 points, Education did best with 23; then Sport and Nursing scored 22; Sociology, Art & Design; and Business 21; Biosciences and Psychology, 20 (there is a BSc Psychology accredited by the British Psychological Society, first step to becoming a chartered psychologist); and Health 19. In the 2001 research assessment no subject reached higher than Grade 2 (out of 5).

ACADEMIC EXCELLENCE

TEACHING:
(Rated Excellent or 17+ out of 24)

Education	**23**
Nursing, Sport	**22**
Sociology, Art & Design, Business	**21**
Psychology, Biosciences	**20**
Health Sciences	**19**

Primary school teachers account for almost a quarter of graduates; then there are educational assistants, welfare, community and youth workers, nursery nurses, physical training instructors, police, secondary school teachers, etc. There are also strengths in business, especially personnel, accounting and marketing. There are strong links with firms and organisations in business, creative, education and health.

Among their regional network of partner colleges, the following feed the uni with students on foundation degrees and HNDs: Evesham & Malvern Hills College, Halesowen College, Herefordshire College of Technology, Josiah Mason College, Kidderminster College, Pershore Group of Colleges, Stourbridge College, and Worcester College of Technology. Foundation degrees include Business in the Electronic Age, Commercial Web Development, Food Safety & Quality Management, Learning Support, and Adventure Tourism.

Writes Emma Aves. 'UCW gains greatly from the sense of intimacy which its size brings, you feel truly part of the institution, one that supports you

WHAT IT'S REALLY LIKE

COLLEGE:	
Social Life	★★
Campus scene	**Local, lively, largely female**
Politics	**Controlled**
Sport	**Competitive**
National team position	**38th**
Arts opportunities	**Excellent across the board**
Student magazine	**The Voice**
Nightclub/bar	**The Dive**
Union ents	**Cheese, live + 4 big balls**
Union clubs/societies	**33**
Parking	**Adequate**
CITY:	
Entertainment	★★
Scene	**Cathedral, arts, cricket, rugby, pubs**
Risk of violence	**Low**
Cost of living	**Average**
Student concessions	**Excellent**
Survival + 2 nights out	**£560 pw**
Part-time work campus/town	**Excellent**

AT A GLANCE

ACADEMIC FILE:	
Subjects assessed	**14**
Excellent	**64%**
Typical entry requirements	**180 points**
Application acceptance rate	**26%, high**
Students-staff ratio	**19:1**
First/2:1 degree pass rate	**43%**
ACCOMMODATION FILE:	
Guarantee to freshers	**90%**
Style	**Halls**
Approx price range pw	**£45-£65**
City rent pw	**£45**

throughout your course. The onus is on you to balance your interests and ensure academic requirements are fulfilled, but a personal tutor system is available to all and helps to compensate for the formal nature of lectures.' They also have a Student Advice Bureau and Employment Bureau, and are active in work-related skills training of undergrads.

SOCIAL SCENE

STUDENTS' UNION There are decent ents in the **Dive Bar**, which celebrated its 40th birthday in February 2006 with a party – 2 Bands, DJ, free cake, bar promos. Besides this sort of cheesy fare, they have a Battle of the Bands event and an active Alternative Music Society, which keeps people on their toes into the small hours. Birmingham is 45 mins to an hour away by train, with all its night-time distractions; a return fare without rail card costs £6.40 to £10.70. See *Birmingham Student City*, page 62.

'Activities such as RAG and Student Community Action are enthusiastically attended in order to establish that we are here for more than personal gain,' Emma continues. Indeed, English Student Sophie Nixon runs Kids Club in Dines Green, a local estate, and was recently presented with the Millennium Volunteer of the Year award for the West Midlands. With 15 other student volunteers, Sophie raises drama productions, discos, music lessons, arts & craft sessions, and organises trips out.

There are 33 clubs and societies at Worcester this year, from mountain boarding to the new dance soc. and Loco Show Co., the tried and tested musical theatre society. *The Voice* is the student newspaper, issued twice a semester.

SPORT There is a multi-million pound Sports Centre on campus and huge interest in sport, both through the sports courses and competitively across the board. They have all the traditional sports, and on, right through to Y'ai Chi. Worcester County Cricket Ground overlooks the River Severn – they list a Men's Cricket club only, odd that the women aren't interested. Worcester Rugby offers some of the the best premiership rugby you can see anywhere in England, its ground at Sixways a true Centre of Excellence. The uni's close association with the club – both Men's and Ladies Rugby (always 'ladies' at Worcester, never 'women's'; but never 'gentlemen's', always 'men's') provides exceptional facilities/expertise.

TOWN Pubs and cheesy clubs predominate, but within a 30-mile radius there's Shakespeare country to the east, the Malverns Welsh borders and Wye Valley to the west, the Cotswolds to the southeast, and big city Birmingham an hour to the north.

Royal Worcester (porcelain) is their heritage, but the **Edward Elgar Birthplace Museum** points to another distinguishing mark, England's greatest composer. **The Swan Theatre** (for drama, comedy, dance) and **Huntingdon Hall** (seriously lively venue for jazz, folk, blues and classical), the **Odeon Film Centre**, the **Vue Cinema** complex, the **Worcester Arts Workshop**, and the recently reconstructed **Festival Theatre** at nearby Malvern complete the arts picture.

PILLOW TALK

Accommodation on campus ranges from ancient room-only halls to comfy, modern flats, but there are enough only for 90% of first years and international students.

GETTING THERE

☛ By road: M5/J7.

☛By rail: Birmingham, 60 mins; Cheltenham, 24 mins; Hereford, 40 mins.

UNIVERSITY OF YORK

The University of York
Heslington
York YO1 5DD

TEL 01904 433533
FAX 01904 433538
EMAIL admissions@york.ac.uk
WEB www.york.ac.uk

VAG VIEW

Founded in 1963, York is a small uni with a huge reputation for its teaching. Students are drawn fairly evenly from the Southeast, from the North and elsewhere.

Their academic strengths span a wide disciplinary range within the arts, social sciences and sciences and attract students with high career ambitions. Whilst York offers perhaps fewer vocationally orientated programmes of study than some other universities, its graduates are highly sought after by employers. What's more, it is very popular with its students, who are bright, fun-loving and notably unpretentious.

CAMPUS

It's a purpose-built campus at Heslington, on the south-east edge of the city: 'Very suburban, not at all monumental. It could get on the garden register,' mused Elaine Harwood of English Heritage. Student Gemma Thomas disagrees, 'Overall, the campus is a very pleasant place to live and along with York itself, one of the safest places. Heslington Hall, a gorgeous manor house on the edge of campus, provides an antidote to some of the bleaker aspects. It possesses extensive gardens, part of which, the Quiet Place, a collection of gigantic topiary knobs, is perfect for late-night games of hide-and-seek, or whatever else springs to mind.' The York Quakers, who were among those responsible for raising £70,000 for the Georgian gazebo and garden known as the Quiet Place, will no doubt be pleased it is being put to such imaginative use. Thoughtfully designed as a peaceful student retreat, perhaps it will take over as perennial talking point from the campus ducks, which inhabit the campus-central lake.

Outline planning application for a £500-million extension to Heslington campus has the support of York Council. When it goes ahead, student numbers will increase by 50 per cent.

UNIVERSITY/STUDENT PROFILE	
University since	**1962**
Situation/style	**City campus**
Student population	**9767**
Undergraduates	**7660**
- mature	**20%**
- non EU undergraduates	**7%**
- male/female	**44/56**
- non-traditional student intake	**17%, low**
- state sector intake	**79%, low**
- drop-out rate	**4%, low**
- undergraduate applications	**Constant**

STUDENT PROFILE

'The most important point to consider before choosing York concerns your feelings about ducks,' writes Gemma. 'Do NOT come here if you are anything less than tolerant of them. They are everywhere. On the lake, crossing paths, dive-bombing students wending their way to early morning lectures (or not). After ducks, students form the most numerous campus species. No one type dominates, the balance between state and private sectors a surprise bonus in a university with this much prestige.

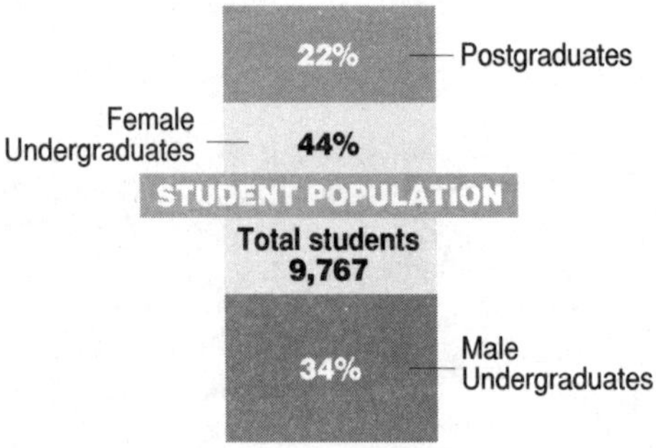

York is a small, friendly, unpretentious university, which makes it incredibly easy to settle in. Also, student welfare is taken very seriously. Nightline, chaplains, a range of counselling services and equal opportunities are promoted heavily.'

ACADEMIA & JOBS

York is known for social sciences, technology, and science. The top 10 subjects at the teaching assessments lost only one point between them.

Computer Science & Engineering is top-rated for teaching and has a world-class Grade 6* reputation for research. There are BSc, BEng, MEng and MMath degrees, regular 3 or 4-year sandwich. Computing is a significant graduate employment area; jobs in electrical and electronic manufacturing are also legion, and for electronic and telecommunications engineers they are leaders.

Social Sciences are also pre-eminent Applied Social Work, Social Policy, Economics, Politics were all top-rated for teaching; Sociology scored 23 points out of 24; and they achieved Grade 5 for research. The £4.2 million Alcuin Research Resource Centre (ARRC) now further enhances its research capacity in this area.

The single most popular employment pathway out of the faculty is accountancy, though accountants also come strongly through mathematics and some through physical sciences. Actuaries also proliferate in these disciplines too. This Economics bias and a Management and Industry axis in physical sciences (also full marks at the teaching assessments) encourage placements in business analysis, finance and investment consultancy, marketing management and management consultancy work.

Jobs also flow in welfare and youth work and care work in the community, from the Applied Social Science – with its Crime, Health, Children & Young People specialities. See also the BA/MA Social Work, and the newer Nursing degree programme: BSc Evidence-based Nursing Practice – Adult, Child, Learning Disability, Mental Health. York is one of a few unis to be awarded Grade 5 for research in Nursing.

In Applied & Natural Science, biosciences (a new BSc Bioarchaeology joins this year) scored full marks at the assessments and Grade 5 for research, and courses such as Chemistry: Biological & Medicinal Chemistry, Chemistry: Management & Industry, Chemistry: Resources & the Environment show the way, and, as in the Social Sciences, illustrate the widely varying ambitions of York's students. Look, too, at BSc Psychology, with its maximum teaching score and world-class reputation for research. Accredited by the British Psychological Society, it's the first step to becoming a chartered psychologist.

The launch of the Hull York Medical School in 2003 has been a great success, as evinced in the low application acceptance rate a year later (8%). They offer a 5-year BMBS (Bachelor of Medicine, Bachelor of Surgery). You may be based at either Hull University campus (see entry) or York; all follow the same curriculum. Hull has a decade's

ACADEMIC EXCELLENCE

TEACHING:	
(Rated Excellent or 17+ out of 24)	
History, Applied Social Work, Architecture (MA), Computing, English, Music, Social Policy	**Excellent**
Electric & Electron Engineering, Archaeology, Economics, Education, Philosophy, Politics, Biosciences, Physics, Psychology	**24**
Sociology	**23**
Management, Languages, Maths	**22**
History of Art, Nursing	**21**
RESEARCH:	
*Top grades 5/5**	
Psychology, Computer, English	**Grade 5***
Community-based Clinical, Nursing, Biological Sciences, Chemistry, Pure Maths, Applied Math, Economics, Politics, Social Policy, Social Work, Sociology, Linguistics, History, Philosophy, Music	**Grade 5**

WHERE YORK GRADUATES END UP

Health & Social Work: 8%; Education: 10%; Wholesale Retail: 9.5%; Manufacturing: 12%; Financial Activities: 11%; Public Administration, Civil Service & Defence: 8.5%; Hotel/Restaurant: 3%; Transport & Communications (including Telecommunications): 3%; Construction: 1%; Personnel: 7%; Computer: 5%; Business & Management: 4%; Accountancy: 4%; Media (including Film): 2%; Legal 1%; Publishing: 1.5%; Artistic/Literary: 0.5%; Sport: 0.5%.

Approximate 'graduate track' employed **66%**

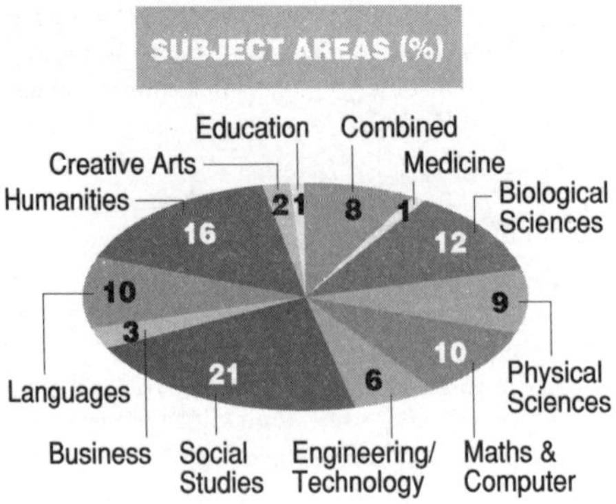

experience in Medicine through its Postgrad Medical School, while York's Biosciences and Health depts are top rated for teaching and research. There is a new Mother and Infant Research Unit (MIRU) at York.

There's an international class Grade 5 rating for research: Community-based clinical subjects, and for medical students, small-group clinical contact from Year 1. Equal emphasis on physical, psychological and social aspects. Entry ABB, including Chemistry at A level and Biology at A or AS. Caring experience and interpersonal skills significant.

Well-trod pathways for humanities and language graduates include education and marketing, museum and gallery work, library and archival work. Here go some of the graduates from the BA Archaeology degrees (full marks in the assessments and a strong employment picture; available too as BSc/Arch), Linguistics (there's an international, Grade 5 for research), Philosophy (again, full marks for teaching), History of Art (21 points), and History – the new £6.5 million, climatically-controlled building housing the Borthwick Institute is the new home for more than seven centuries of North of England history.

Like History Music was top-graded in the assessments and there's a good track record both for musician/composers and music producers. Look at their first class Music Technology Systems B/Meng for the latter. Jazz musicians Jonathan Eato and John Taylor are now part of the department, signalling new initiatives in undergraduate education and a new Master's degree in Improvised Music and Jazz.

Their English/Writing & Performance is another arts niche, a practical, contemporary course pulling directly on the experience of current actors, writers and directors. When the Heslington campus is extended this is one of the areas likely to benefit.

SOCIAL SCENE

Each college has its own Junior Common Room (JCR) Committee, who run about two events per week per college and two or three big events per year. The Students' Union organises up to five large-scale clubnights or other events per 10-week term.

The point about York is the interest and activity levels beyond mere ents. 'Students get involved,' said Helen Woolnough. 'The university has an excellent academic reputation, but its students don't work themselves into the ground twenty-four hours a day and they certainly don't take themselves too seriously.'

Student media: University Radio York (URY), launched by John Peel thirty years ago and now with fm licence, York Television (YTV), and two fortnightly newspapers, *Nouse* (pronounced 'Nooze' after the River Ouse, which flows through York, and of course 'news', which is what it dispenses) and *York Vision*. The performance of these in the 2005 national student awards was staggeringly good. They were simply the best in the country. York took Best Newspaper and Best Radio Station, while the fledgling TV company had three highly recommended judgements (runner-up awards).

Other publications appear occasionally – *Point Shirley*, a literary arts magazine; *PS...*, an arts review; *Havoc*, a miscellany of creative writing; *Matrix*, a women's issue paper; *Christis*, a Christian magazine, and *Mad Alice*, an on-line features magazine.

There is a tradition of political activity and a left-wing slant. Campus-based issues and wider student issues find a place (tuition fees, differential rents, campaign for a venue, security on campus, etc), but national and international issues are also very much on the agenda.

Among some 90 societies there are 8 active drama societies with three venues, the intimate **Drama Barn**, the large and versatile **Wentworth College Audio Visual Studio** and the aforementioned Central Hall, which is huge.

Sport For such a small uni they do well at sport, and recently have leapt up the BUSA league table to 33rd position. The Boat Club goes to Henley Royal Regatta, the Lacrosse team to the world championships, basketball is a bit a speciality and they have the best parachutists in the country apparently. There are forty acres of playing fields – rugby, football, hockey, cricket – floodlit artificial hockey pitch, all-weather (three floodlit) tennis courts, squash courts, a sports centre for archery, badminton (seven courts), basketball, climbing, cricket (five nets), fencing, five-a-side soccer, judo,

WHAT IT'S REALLY LIKE

UNIVERSITY:	
Social Life	★★★★
Campus scene	**Bright, friendly, small and unpretentious**
Student Union services	**Good**
Politics	**Activity high Student issues**
Sport	**50 clubs**
National team position	**33rd**
Sport facilities	**Good**
Arts opportunities	**Drama, film excellent; dance, music, art avg**
National drama awards	**Craft/Imagination**
Student newspapers	**Nouse, York Vision**
National Awards 2005	**Best newspaper**
Student radio station	**URY**
National Awards 2005	**Radio Station of the Year**
Student TV	**YTV**
National Awards 2005	**Highly commended three times**
Nightclub	**College-based only**
Bars	**1 in every college**
Union ents	**Club D, House Trained, Cooker, Dust**
Union clubs/societies	**140**
Most popular societies	**Media, Drama**
Smoking policy	**Bars, halls OK**
Parking	**Non-existent**
CITY:	
Entertainment	★★★
City scene	**Tourist haven**
Town/gown relations	**Good**
Risk of violence	**Low**
Cost of living	**Average**
Student concessions	**Good**
Survival + 2 nights out	**£50 pw**
Part-time work campus/town	**Excellent/good**

karate, netball, sauna, table-tennis, tennis, trampoline, volleyball, a 400-metre, seven-lane athletics track. Rowing and sailing are on the Ouse about a mile from the University, golf at Fulford Golf Club, swimming at the Barbican Centre half a mile from campus. Gliding, hang-gliding, riding and other facilities also found locally.

Town York itself is one of our most beautiful cathedral cities, a magnet for tourists from all over the world owing to the wealth of Viking and Roman remains, as well as its mediaeval resonances in the Minster, in streets like the Shambles (where buildings lean inwards and over you as if out of a fairytale), in street names like Whip-Ma-Whop-Ma-Gate, and in the snickleways which offer those in the know an alternative way to scuttle about. Then there are the waters of the Ouse, lapping over green-field banks or warehouse walls, redolent of the city's merchant past.

It is, however, far from being the clubbing capital of the North. 'From the relaxed atmosphere of the Deramore in Heslington,' notes the union's excellent *Alternative Prospectus* (phone for one), 'to the vibrancy of O'Neill's, ideal as a starting place for a night of fun and frolics in the clubs...' If you are a hardened clubber, take a ride to Leeds.

For theatre, there's the **Arts Centre** and the **Theatre Royal** (good rep), and the **Grand Opera** has a full programme of touring companies and performances, both theatre and music. There's a multi-screen **Warner's** cinema out at Clifton Moor Estate (on the north side of the city), **Odeon** and independent **City Screen** in York, as well as **York Student Cinema** on campus.

PILLOW TALK

All freshers are guaranteed a place in uni accommodation – halls, flats and houses. None is catered – all pay-as-you-eat. Around 36% are en suite.

GETTING THERE

☛ By road: A1237 ring road; Heslington is on the southeast side, 10 miles from A1/M1; 20 from M62.

☛ By coach: London, 4:30; Edinburgh, 5:15.

☛ By rail: Leeds, 20 mins; Sheffield, 1:15; Manchester, 1:30; London King's Cross, 2:00.

☛ By air: Nearest airport is Leeds.

AT A GLANCE

ACADEMIC FILE:	
Subjects assessed	**23**
Excellent	**96%**
Typical entry requirements	**410 points**
Application acceptance rate	**11%**
Students-staff ratio	**14:1**
First/2:1 degree pass rate	**68%**
ACCOMMODATION FILE:	
Guarantee to freshers	**100%**
Style	**Halls, flats, houses**
Catered	**Pay-as-you-eat**
En-suite	**42%**
Approx price range pw	**£58.45-£74.06**
City rent pw	**£50-£60**

YORK ST JOHN UNIVERSITY COLLEGE

York St John University College
Lord Mayor's Walk
York YO31 7EX

TEL 01904 716598
FAX 01904 716940
EMAIL admissions@yorksj.ac.uk
WEB www.yorksj.ac.uk

Founded by the Anglican Church in 1841 as a teacher training college, York St John also offers degrees in performing arts (music, dance, drama), film & TV, social and cultural studies and social sciences, languages, humanities (including Theology and History), and environmental sciences, health sciences (including Occupational Therapy, a professional qualification), Leisure & Tourism Management, and Physical Education (a Sport & Exercise Science degree is relatively new.

In February, 2006, it was granted University College status and now awards its own degrees.

ACADEMIC EXCELLENCE	
TEACHING: (Rated Excellent or 17+ out of 24)	
Occupational Therapy	22
Art, Design & Technology, Business & Management, Theology, Sports	21
Film, TV, Lit & Theatre Studies, Media & Performance Studies, Psychology	20
Linguistics	19

CAMPUS

The college is situated close to York Minster on a very attractive, quadrangle campus, and on one or two other sites in this ancient city.

STUDENT PROFILE

There is a preponderance of females (72% of its 4700 undergraduates) and mature students, and around a quarter of undergraduates are part-timers. Some 96% are recuited through the state sector and 31% come from socio-economic backgrounds not traditionally drawn to university.

ACADEMIA

Between 50% and 70% of the Film, TV, Literature & Theatre Studies degree is in production activity, its success clearly visible in their employment profile. Resources include two theatre studios, two TV studios and eight editing suites. There is a 4-week placement in the second year, an internship with a professional company in the third (as well as professional linking projects) and opportunity for study abroad.

COLLEGE PROFILE	
Founded	**1841**
Status	**Uni College**
Situation/style	**City campus**
Degree undergraduates	**4706**
ACCOMMODATION:	
Guarantee to freshers	**95%**
Style	**Flats**
Catered	**21%**
En-suite	**146**
Approx price range pw	**£50-£89**
City rent pw	**£50-£60**

'Performing arts, the therapies, Counselling Studies, and Linguistics I have heard very good reports about,' said one careers teacher. 'We had someone with straight A grades, could have gone anywhere, but chose Ripon.'

Jobs-wise Education is the strong bias, but hard on its heels comes health & social work, and there is a fine showing in the area of archival/Cultural jobs (galleries, museum, libraries, etc.), and in radio and television. Every undergraduate programme has employment skills integrated into it.

SOCIAL SCENE

There is a bar within the main hub of the Students' Union, and a programme of discos, live music, balls in summer and at Christmas.

They have a weekly newspaper, *The Saint*, 8 societies, the most popular of which is Musical Productions Soc, and 24 sports clubs (there are squash courts and a swimming pool on campus).

With degrees in counselling, welfare is to the fore and the Education & Welfare Committee is one of the strongest in the union.

PILLOW TALK

A new en-suite development 7 minutes from the main campus consists of 25 flats with 146 en-suite single study bedrooms, each flat with a shared kitchen. If you're unable to secure uni accommodation, they promise to help you find an alternative in York.

GETTING THERE

☛ By Road A1 into central York. Otherwise, see York University information.